NATIONAL CENTER FOR EDUCATION STATISTICS

Digest of Education Statistics 1995

Thomas D. Snyder
Project Director

Charlene M. Hoffman
Production Manager

U.S. Department of Education
Office of Educational Research and Improvement   NCES 95-029

U.S. Department of Education
Richard W. Riley
Secretary

Office of Educational Research and Improvement
Sharon P. Robinson
Assistant Secretary

National Center for Education Statistics
Jeanne E. Griffith
Acting Commissioner

National Center for Education Statistics

The purpose of the Center is to collect and report "statistics and information showing the condition and progress of education in the United States and other nations in order to promote and accelerate the improvement of American education."—Section 402(b) of the National Education Statistics Act of 1994 (20 U.S.C. 9001).

October 1995

For sale by the U.S. Government Printing Office
Superintendent of Documents, Mail Stop: SSOP, Washington, DC 20402-9328
ISBN 0-16-048379-4

FOREWORD

This 1995 edition of the *Digest of Education Statistics* is the 31st in a series of publications initiated in 1962. (The *Digest* has been issued annually except for combined editions for the years 1977–78, 1983–84, and 1985–86.) Its primary purpose is to provide a compilation of statistical information covering the broad field of American education from kindergarten through graduate school. The *Digest* includes a selection of data from many sources, both government and private, and draws especially on the results of surveys and activities carried out by the National Center for Education Statistics (NCES). The publication contains information on a variety of subjects in the field of education statistics, including the number of schools and colleges, teachers, enrollments, and graduates, in addition to educational attainment, finances, federal funds for education, employment and income of graduates, libraries, and international education comparisons. Supplemental information on population trends, attitudes on education, education characteristics of the labor force, government finances, and economic trends provides background for evaluating education data.

The *Digest* is divided into seven chapters: "All Levels of Education," "Elementary and Secondary Education," "Postsecondary Education," "Federal Programs for Education and Related Activities," "Outcomes of Education," "International Comparisons of Education," and "Learning Resources and Technology." To qualify for inclusion, material must be nationwide in scope and of current interest and value. The introduction includes a brief overview of current trends in American education, which supplements the tabular materials in chapters 1 through 7. Information on the structure of the statistical tables is contained in the "Guide to Tabular Presentation." The "Guide to Sources" provides a brief synopsis of the surveys used to generate the tabulations for the *Digest*. Also, a "Definitions" section is included to help readers understand terms.

In addition to updating many of the statistics that have appeared in previous years, this edition contains a significant amount of new material, including:

- Detailed trends in expenditures for elementary and secondary schools, table 158;

- Race and ethnicity of college faculty, tables 223 and 224;

- Productivity measures of college faculty, tables 220 and 221;

- Revenues of colleges and universities, by classification of institution, table 322;

- Expenditures of colleges and universities, by classification of institution, table 334;

- Percent of population enrolled in college for OECD countries, table 385; and

- Use of telecommunication technologies in public schools, table 408.

In the past, the *Digest of Education Statistics* has proved to be of interest and value to education researchers and administrators, government officials, the media, the business community, and the general public. We welcome comments and suggestions to improve future editions. We trust that the users of this 31st edition will find it even more valuable than its predecessors.

Jeanne E. Griffith,
Acting Commissioner
National Center for Education Statistics
October 1995

ACKNOWLEDGMENTS

Many people have contributed in one way or another to the development of the *Digest*. Thomas D. Snyder was responsible for the overall development and preparation of this *Digest* which was prepared under the general direction of Jeanne E. Griffith.

Charlene M. Hoffman provided technical assistance in all phases of its preparation and was responsible for Chapter 4, "Federal Programs for Education and Related Activities," and for tables on degrees conferred. Claire Geddes developed the text for chapter introductions and was responsible for materials dealing with higher education enrollment, finance, and faculty characteristics. William Sonnenberg provided statistical computing consultation on all phases of the report. Celestine Davis provided statistical assistance on materials dealing with educational attainment and student assessment. Debra Gerald and William Hussar prepared projections of school enrollment and finance statistics.

A number of individuals outside the Center also expended large amounts of time and effort on the *Digest*. Carla Claycomb, Michelle LaPointe, William Scarbrough, Linda Shafer, and Erica Uhlmann of CSR, Inc., provided research and statistical assistance. Robert Craig and Michelle Brown of Pinkerton Computer Consultants, Inc., provided computer support. In the Office of Information Services, Robert LeGrand and Simone Miranda provided editorial assistance and Phil Carr designed the cover. Jerry Fairbanks of the U.S. Government Printing Office managed the typesetting.

This year's edition of the *Digest* has received extensive reviews by individuals within and outside the Department of Education. We wish to thank them for their time and expert advice. In the Office of Educational Research and Improvement (OERI), W. Vance Grant, Mary Frase, and Shelley Burns reviewed the entire manuscript. Rosemary Clark (U.S. Bureau of the Census) also reviewed the entire document. OERI staff who reviewed portions of the manuscript were: Susan Ahmed, Patricia Q. Brown, Susan Broyles, Robert Burton, Rosa Fernandez, Debra Gerald, Arnold Goldstein, Steven Gorman, Kerry Gruber, Frank Johnson, Frank Morgan, Jeffrey Owings, Peggy Quinn, John Sietsema, and Shi-Chang Wu. Agency reviews were conducted by the Office of Bilingual Education and Minority Languages Affairs, Office for Civil Rights, Office of the Chief Financial Officer, Office of Policy and Planning, Office of Public Affairs, Office of Special Education Programs, Office of Educational Research and Improvement, and Office of Vocational and Adult Education.

Contents

Figures

Tables

1. All Levels of Education

Enrollment, Teachers, and Schools

Enrollment Rates

Educational Attainment

2. Elementary and Secondary Education

Enrollment

Schools and School Districts

High School Seniors, Completions, and Dropouts

Educational Achievement

Student Activities and Behavior

3–A. Postsecondary Education: College and University Education

Enrollment

Institutions

Revenue

Expenditures

Property

3–B. Postsecondary Education: Vocational and Adult Education

Adult Education

4. Federal Programs for Education and Related Activities

5. Outcomes of Education

Educational Characteristics of the Workforce

6. International Comparisons of Education

7. Learning Resources and Technology

Libraries

Computers and Technology

Guide to Sources

Appendix Tables

INTRODUCTION

In the fall of 1995, about 65.1 million persons were enrolled in American schools and colleges (table 1). About 3.8 million were employed as elementary and secondary school teachers and as college faculty. Other professional, administrative, and support staff of educational institutions numbered 4.3 million. Thus about 73 million people were involved, directly or indirectly, in providing or receiving formal education. In a nation with a population of about 263 million, more than 1 out of every 4 persons participated in formal education.

Elementary/Secondary Enrollment

The enrollment rate of 3- and 4-year olds has not changed significantly since the mid 1980s and the enrollment rates for older elementary school age children have not changed in many years (table 6). Thus, changes in elementary school enrollment have been primarily driven by changes in the number of young people in the population. Public school enrollment in kindergarten through grade eight rose from 27.0 million in fall 1985 to an estimated 32.3 million in fall 1995 (table 2). Enrollment in the upper grades declined from 12.4 million in 1985 to 11.3 million in 1990, and then began rising. As a result of these two divergent trends, secondary school enrollment was an estimated 12.7 million in fall 1995, slightly higher than 1985.

Private school enrollment has changed little over the past decade, with about 11 percent of all elementary and secondary students attending private schools. Total private school enrollment at the elementary and secondary level was estimated at 5.7 million in fall 1995.

Projections of the National Center for Education Statistics (NCES) forecast record levels of enrollment by the late 1990s. It is anticipated that by the year 1997, public school enrollments will surpass the previous high set in 1971 and will continue to climb into the next century. Public elementary school enrollment is expected to reach 32.9 million in 1996 and 34.5 million in 2000 (table 3). Between fall 1995 and fall 2000, public elementary enrollment is projected to grow by 7 percent, while public secondary school enrollment is expected to rise by 9 percent.

Higher Education

College enrollment rose to a record level of 14.5 million in fall 1992 and is expected to remain relatively steady through the end of the decade. Despite decreases in the traditional college-age population, recent trends suggest that total enrollment will remain relatively high because of the increased participation of older women students and a high rate of college attendance for recent high school graduates (tables 5 and 6). The number of part-time students has increased more rapidly than full-time students (table 167).

Teachers

An estimated 3.0 million elementary and secondary school teachers will be engaged in classroom instruction in the fall of 1995 (table 4). This number has risen in recent years, up about 17 percent since 1985. The number of public school teachers in 1995 will be about 2.6 million and the number in private schools will be about 0.4 million. About 1.8 million teachers are expected to teach in elementary schools, while about 1.2 million will teach at the secondary level (table 4).

The number of public school teachers has risen at a faster rate than the number of students over the past 10 years, resulting in a decrease in the pupil/teacher ratio. The lower pupil/teacher ratio reflects the trend toward more specialized education programs. In the fall of 1995, there were 17.4 public school pupils per teacher compared with 17.9 public school pupils per teacher 10 years earlier. During the same time period, the pupil/teacher ratio in private schools fell from 16.2 to 15.1 (table 63). Despite the historical trend towards lower pupil/teacher ratios, the changes since the late 1980s have been very small and some of the fluctuations suggest an increase in the pupil/teacher ratio.

The salaries of public school teachers, which lost purchasing power to inflation during the 1970s, rose faster than the inflation rate in the 1980s. The rising salaries reflect an interest by state and local education agencies in boosting teacher salary schedules and, to some extent, an increase in teachers' experience and education levels (tables 68 and 76). The value of teachers' salaries, after adjustment for inflation, rose 10 percent between 1984–85 and 1994–95. Virtually all of this increase occurred during the mid 1980s. Since 1990–91, the average salary for teachers actually fell slightly after adjusting for inflation. The average salary for teachers in 1994–95 was $36,933 (table 76).

Public perception about problems facing the local public schools has shifted in the past several years. Between 1986 and 1990, an increasing number of people believed that drug use was a major problem, but the proportion of people with this opinion dropped to 11 percent in 1994. In contrast, fighting, gangs, and violence, a new category added in 1992, was cited by 18 percent of the population. The lack of financial support is also cited as a major problem by 13 percent of the public (table 22).

Faculty and staff

During the fall of 1992, there were 789,000 instructional faculty and staff members teaching in higher education institutions. Making up this figure were 526,000 full-time, and 263,000 part-time instructors who varied in number of hours and students taught. Full-time instructors generally taught more hours and more students, with 61 percent teaching eight hours or more per week, and two-thirds teaching more than 50 students. About 30 percent of part-time instructors taught eight or more hours per week, and 30 percent taught 50 or more students (tables 220, 221).

Another defining feature of college faculty is that it is disproportionately white males. For full-time faculty, the percentage of white males is 59 percent, and it is slightly less than half, at 49 percent, for part-time faculty (table 222).

Student Performance

Despite some evidence that student achievement has improved, there is still reason for concern. The national assessment measures have not shown a consistent pattern of improvement, especially for upper level skills.

Reading

Overall, the trends in reading achievement are encouraging for many of the country's 13- and 17-year-old students, and some groups of 9-year-olds. However, many of the advancements in performance that had been made in earlier years among black students, as well as among 9-year-olds and 17-year-olds from disadvantaged urban communities, have not continued or have reversed. For example, while 9-year-olds in the bottom quartile of the distribution were more proficient in 1992 than in 1971, their performance has not returned to the higher level that was obtained in 1980. Those in the middle two quartiles showed no difference from the first assessment,

and also showed declines since 1980. For 13-year-olds, overall gains were seen only for students in the top and middle of the distribution, while those in the low end failed to maintain gains they had made between 1971 and 1988. At age 17, middle and lower end students had proficiencies higher in 1992 than in 1971. The average performance for the top performing students returned to the 1971 level, reflecting an increase since 1980 (table 107).

Mathematics

Results from assessments of mathematics proficiency also indicate that students have made some improvements in their skill with basic computations. However, the performance of older students on advanced mathematical operations has shown little or no improvement. The proportion of 9-year-olds who showed beginning skills and understanding rose from 70 percent in 1977–78 to 82 percent in 1989–90. The proportion of 9-year-olds demonstrating skill with numerical operations and beginning problem solving rose from 20 percent to 28 percent during the same time period (table 116).

At ages 9 and 13, significant improvement was observed between 1973 and 1992. For 17-year-old students, performance declined between 1973 and 1982, but an upturn during the past decade has returned performance to the initial level. For all ages, there were significant increases in average proficiency between 1982 and 1992, indicating improvement in the more computational aspects of mathematics (tables 115 and 116). Between 1978 and 1992, there was an increase in the percentage of 17-year-olds reporting they did homework "often" and a decrease in the percentage reporting that they did homework "sometimes." The percentage reporting "never" doing homework remained constant across assessments at approximately 5 percent (table 142).

A 1992 voluntary assessment of the states found that proficiency varied widely among eighth graders in the 44 jurisdictions (41 states, 2 territories, and the District of Columbia) that participated in the program (tables 117 and 119). In 1992, student performance was significantly better than in 1990 in 18 of the jurisdictions participating in both assessments. No state experienced a significant decline in achievement.

Science

Small improvements also were registered in science proficiency between school years ending in 1977 and 1992. The proportion of 9-year-olds who understood simple scientific principles rose from 68 percent in 1977 to 78 percent in 1992. Also, the proportion of 9-year-olds who were able to apply basic scientific information rose. The percentage of 13-

year-olds demonstrating the ability to apply basic scientific information rose from 49 to 61 percent between 1977 and 1992, but no improvement was registered at the higher levels of achievement. No significant changes occurred in the overall achievement of 17-year-olds between 1977 and 1992 with the exception of the ability to analyze scientific procedures and data. For this skill, the percentage of 17-year-old students who demonstrated success increased significantly (table 121).

International Comparisons

On an international assessment of reading literacy, U.S. students scored in the top performing group at ages 9 and 14 (tables 399 and 400). However, in mathematics and science the results of international comparisons are less encouraging. Recent international assessments of mathematics and science have highlighted the relatively low level of achievement of U.S. students, particularly older students, compared with their peers in other countries (tables 391–398). In a 1990 science assessment that was administered to nationally representative groups of 9-year-olds in 10 different countries, U.S. students scored lower than Korean students but about the same as students from Taiwan, Canada, Hungary, Spain, and the former Soviet Union. In a mathematics assessment, U.S. 9-year-olds had averages that were below 5 of the 9 other countries (tables 391 and 392). The U.S. 13-year-olds placed in the middle group of countries with nationally representative science achievement data (table 401). In the mathematics assessment of 13-year-olds, the U.S. students were higher than only 1 of 14 countries (Jordan) and about the same as Slovenia and Spain. The remaining 11 countries all had average test scores that were significantly higher than the U.S. (tables 394 and 397).

Graduates and Degrees

The number of high school graduates in 1994–95 totaled about 2.6 million. Approximately 2.3 million graduated from public schools and less than 0.3 million graduated from private schools. The number of high school graduates has declined from its peak in 1976–77 when 3.2 million people earned their diplomas. Although the number of graduates has been lower in recent years, the ratio of high school graduates to 17-year-olds has remained relatively stable for more than 2 decades, declining slightly in the 1970s and increasing slightly in the 1980s (table 98).

The number of degrees conferred by institutions of higher education is estimated to have been at an all-time high during the 1994–95 school year: 536,000 associate degrees; 1,179,000 bachelor's degrees;

399,000 master's degrees; and 43,000 doctor's degrees (table 236).

The Bureau of the Census has collected annual statistics on the educational attainment of the population in terms of years of school completed. These data indicate that, between 1980 and 1994, the proportion of the adult population 25 years of age and over with 4 years of high school or more rose from 69 percent to 81 percent and the proportion of adults with at least 4 years of college increased from 17 percent to 22 percent. In contrast, the proportion of young adults (25- to 29-year-olds), attaining these levels did not change significantly over this time period (table 8).

Expenditures

Expenditures for public and private education, from preprimary through graduate school, are estimated at $508 billion for 1994–95. The expenditures of elementary and secondary schools are expected to total about $308 billion for 1994–95, while those for institutions of higher education will be about $201 billion. Viewed in another context, the total expenditures for education are expected to amount to about 7.5 percent of the gross domestic product in 1994–95, about the same percentage as in the recent past (table 30).

Summary

The statistical highlights in this section of the report provide a quantitative description of the current American education scene. Clearly, from the large number of participants, the number of years that people spend in school, and the large sums expended by educational institutions, it is evident that the American people have a high regard for education. Yet, data on student proficiency suggest that improvements in recent years have been limited. Wide variations in student proficiency from state to state and mediocre scores of American students in international assessments pose challenges for the future.

NOTE: Readers should be aware of the limitations of statistics. These limitations vary with the exact nature of a particular survey. For example, estimates based on a sample of institutions will differ somewhat from the figures that would have been obtained if a complete census had been taken using the same survey procedures. Although some of the surveys conducted by the National Center for Education Statistics are complete, census-type surveys, all surveys are subject to design, reporting, and processing errors and errors due to nonresponse. More information on survey methodologies can be found in the "Guide to Sources" in the appendix. Price indexes for inflation adjustments can be found in table 38.

CHAPTER 1
All Levels of Education

This chapter provides a broad overview of education in the United States. It brings together material from preprimary, elementary, secondary, and post-secondary education and from the general population to present a composite picture of the American educational system. Tables illustrate the total number of persons enrolled in school, the number of teachers, the number of schools, and total expenditures for education at all levels. This chapter also includes statistics on education-related topics such as education attainment, family characteristics, population, and opinions about schools. Economic indicators and price indexes have been added to assist researchers in preparing comparative analyses.

Figure 1 shows the structure of education in the United States. It presents the three levels of education (elementary, secondary, and postsecondary) and gives the approximate age-range of persons at each level. Pupils ordinarily spend 6 to 8 years in the elementary grades, which may be preceded by 1 or 2 years in nursery school and kindergarten. The elementary school program is followed by a 4- to 6-year program in secondary school. Pupils normally complete the entire program through grade 12 by age 17 or 18.

High school graduates who decide to continue their education may enter a technical or vocational institution, a 2-year college, or a 4-year college or university. A 2-year college normally offers the first 2 years of a standard 4-year college curriculum and a selection of technical-vocational programs. Academic courses completed at a 2-year college are usually transferable for credit at a 4-year college or university. A technical or vocational institution offers post-secondary technical training leading to a specific career.

An associate degree requires at least 2 years of college-level work, and a bachelor's degree normally can be earned in 4 years. At least 1 year beyond the bachelor's is necessary for a master's degree, while a doctor's degree usually requires a minimum of 3 or 4 years beyond the bachelor's.

Professional schools differ widely in admission requirements and in program length. Medical students, for example, generally complete a 4-year program of premedical studies at a college or university before they can enter the 4-year program at a medical school. Law programs normally require 3 years of coursework beyond the bachelor's degree level.

Many of the statistics in this chapter are derived from the statistical activities of the National Center for Education Statistics. In addition, substantial contributions have been drawn from the work of other groups, both government and nongovernment, as shown in the source notes of the appropriate tables. Information on survey methodologies is in the "Guide to Sources" in the appendix and in the publications cited in the source notes.

Enrollment, Teachers, and Schools

Enrollment in elementary and secondary schools grew rapidly during the 1950s and 1960s and peaked in 1971 (table 3). This enrollment rise was caused by what is known as the "baby boom," a dramatic increase in births following World War II. From 1971 to 1984, total elementary and secondary school enrollment decreased every year, reflecting the decline in the school-age population over that period. After these years of decline, enrollment in elementary and secondary schools showed a small increase in the fall of 1985 (table 3).

Public school enrollment in kindergarten through grade eight rose from 27.0 million in fall 1985 to an estimated 32.3 million in fall 1995. Enrollment in the upper grades declined from 12.4 million to 11.3 million in 1990, before showing increases in the early 1990s. The net result of these trends was an overall increase in both the secondary and elementary levels.

The increase from 1985 to 1994 was concentrated in the elementary grades, but this pattern is expected to change. Between fall 1994 and fall 2000, public elementary enrollment is projected to grow by 9 percent, while public secondary school enrollment is expected to rise by 12 percent. The growing numbers of young pupils who have been filling the elementary schools will cause increases at the secondary school level during the mid-1990s. Moreover, by 1997 public school enrollment is projected to surpass the previous high set in 1971 and is expected to continue to increase into the next century.

The proportion of students in private schools and colleges has changed little over the past 10 years. During that time, approximately 11 percent of all elementary and secondary students and about 22 percent of college students attended private schools. In 1995, about 5.7 million students were enrolled in private schools at the elementary and secondary levels and 3.1 million students in institutions of higher education (table 3).

Attendance rates among 3- and 4-year-olds rose from 36 percent in 1984 to 48 percent in 1994, but rates for 5- to 17-year-olds have remained relatively steady over the past 10 years. The proportion of 18- and 19-year-olds attending high school or college rose rapidly from 50 percent in 1984 to 60 percent in 1994 (table 6).

College enrollment fell somewhat to 14.3 million in fall 1993, but estimates indicate that enrollment stabilized in 1994 and 1995. Total college enrollment is expected to remain steady during the mid 1990s, despite decreases in the traditional college-age population (table 2). The stability is partly the result of a larger proportion of 20- to 24-year-olds enrolling in postsecondary education. This proportion rose from 24 percent in 1984 to 31 percent in 1994 (table 6). College enrollment is expected to rise during the late 1990s as increasing numbers of high school students pursue higher education.

Americans have become more educated. In 1994, 81 percent of the population 25 years old and over had completed high school and 22 percent had completed 4 or more years of college. This represents an increase from 1980, when 69 percent had completed high school and 17 percent had 4 years of college (table 8). In 1994, about 6 percent of persons 25 years old or over held a master's degree, 1 percent held a professional degree (e.g., medicine or law), and 1 percent held a doctor's degree (table 9).

An estimated 3.0 million elementary and secondary school teachers were engaged in classroom instruction in the fall of 1995 (table 4). This number has risen about 17 percent since 1985. The number of public school teachers in 1995 was about 2.6 million and the number in private schools was estimated at 0.4 million. About 1.8 million teachers were teaching in elementary schools, while about 1.2 million were employed at the secondary level (table 4).

Expenditures

Education expenditures rose to an estimated high of $508 billion in the 1994–95 school year. Elementary and secondary schools spent about 60 percent of this total, and colleges and universities accounted for the remaining 40 percent. An estimated 7.5 percent of the gross domestic product was spent by elementary and secondary schools and colleges and universities in 1994–95 (table 30).

The proportion of total state and local government funds spent on education declined during the 1980s, at least partly as a result of the drop in elementary and secondary enrollment and the expansion of other governmental services. During the same time period, the proportion of federal funds spent on education rose. Of the 1991 state and local funds spent on education, about 70 percent went to elementary and secondary schools, 25 percent to colleges and universities, and 4 percent to other education programs (table 34).

Figure 1.—The structure of education in the United States

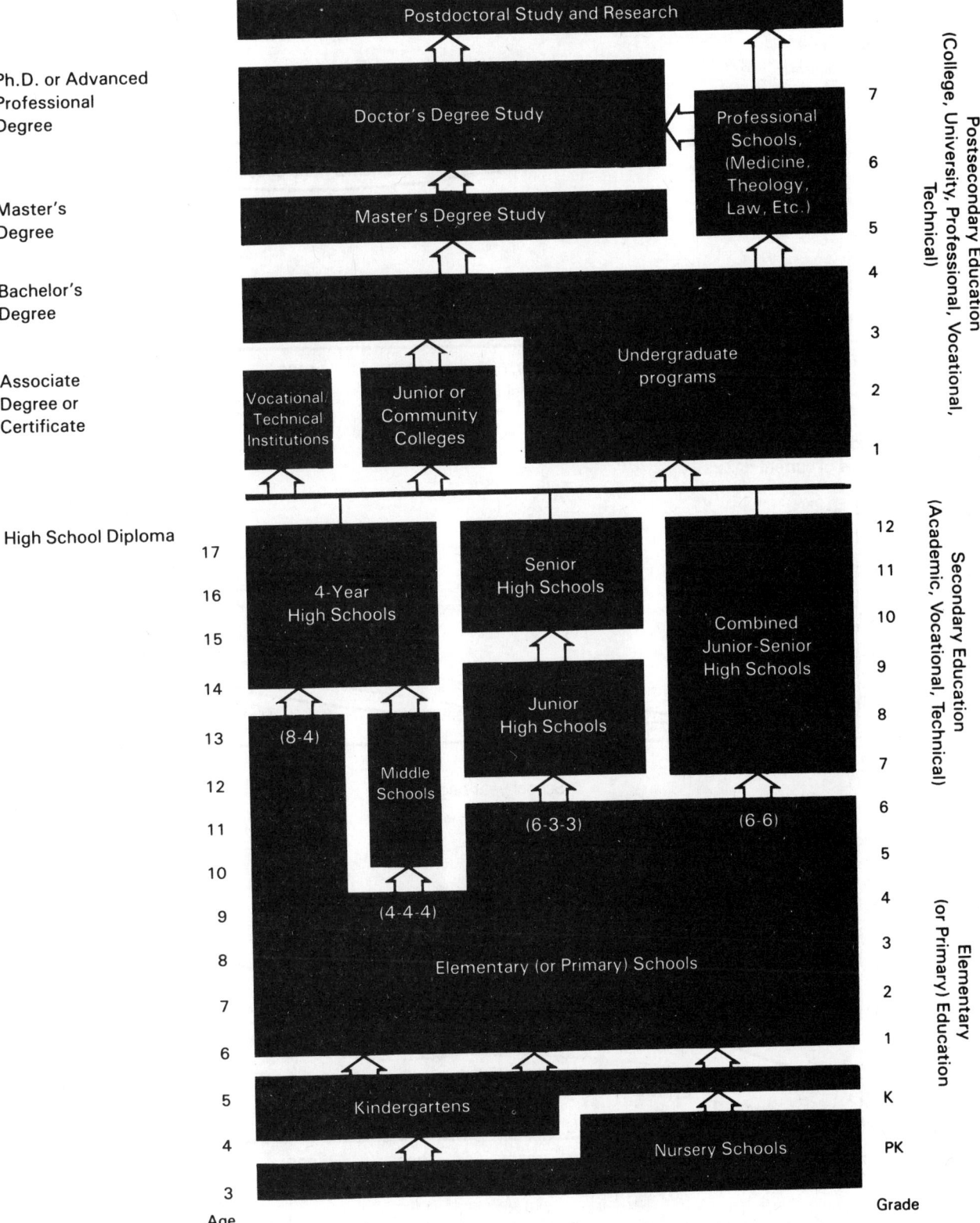

NOTE—Adult education programs, while not separately delineated above, may provide instruction at the elementary, secondary, or higher education level. Chart reflects typical patterns of progression rather than all possible variations.

SOURCE: U.S. Department of Education, National Center for Education Statistics.

Figure 2.-Enrollment and total expenditures in current and constant dollars, by level of education: 1960–61 to 1994–95

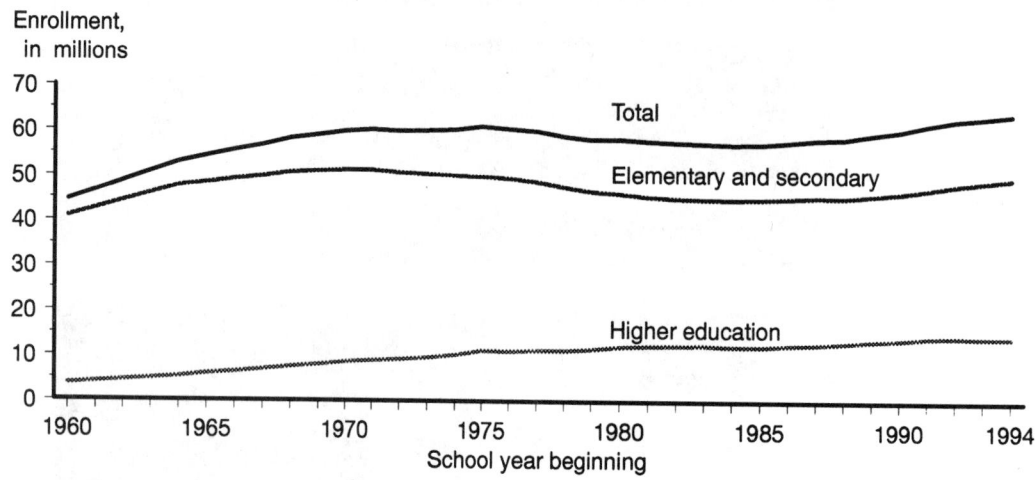

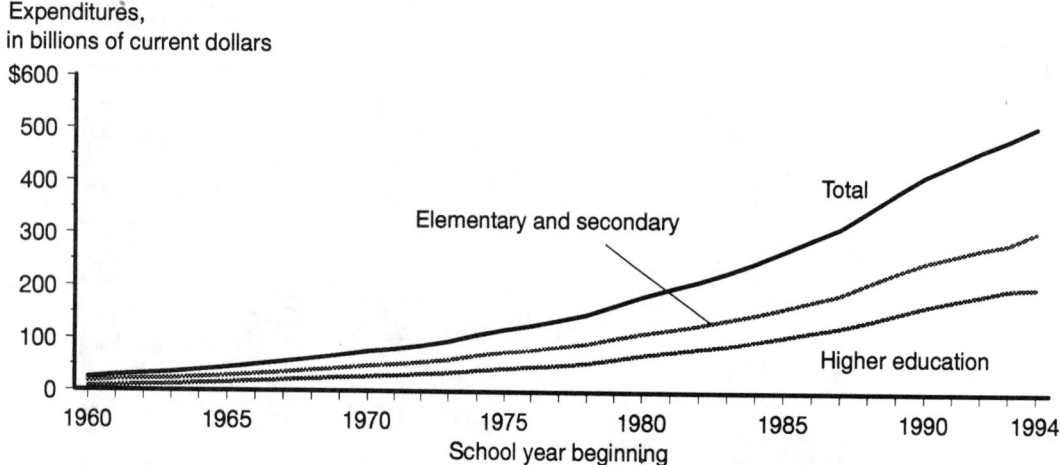

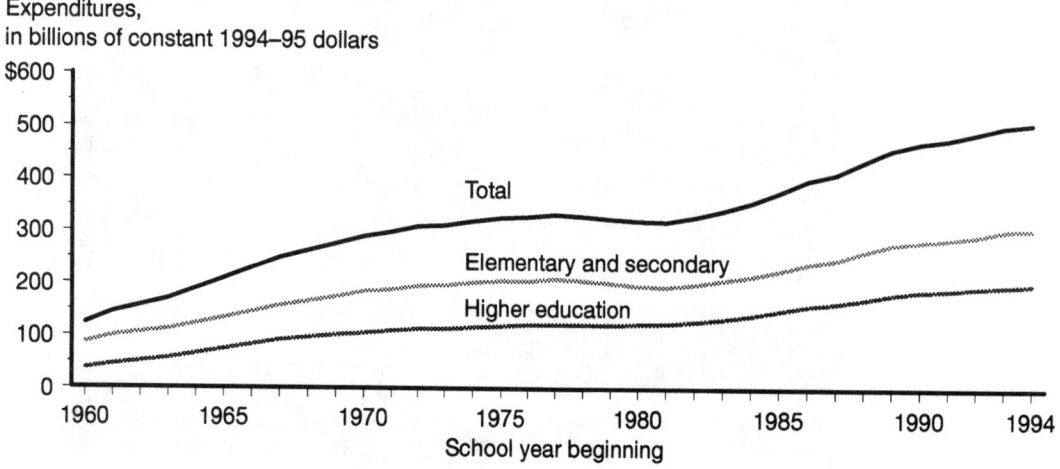

SOURCE: U.S. Department of Education, National Center for Education Statistics, *Statistics of State School Systems; Statistics of Public Elementary and Secondary School Systems; Statistics of Nonpublic Secondary School Systems; Statistics of Nonpublic Elementary and Secondary Schools; Revenues and Expenditures for Public Elementary and Secondary Education; Fall Enrollment in Institutions of Higher Education; Financial Statistics of Institutions of Higher Education;* Common Core of Data surveys; and Integrated Postsecondary Education Data System surveys.

Figure 3.- Years of school completed by persons 25 years and over: 1940 to 1994

Percent of persons

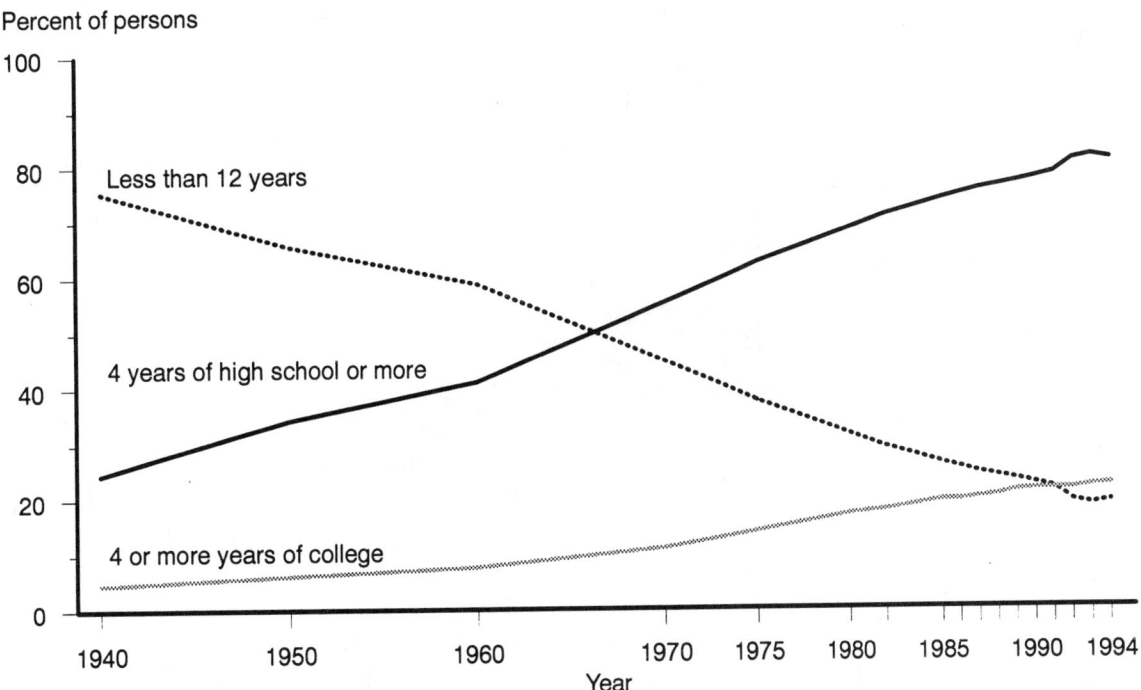

SOURCE: U.S. Department of Commerce, Bureau of the Census, *1960 Census of Population,* Vol. 1, part 1; and *Current Population Reports*, Series P-20; and Current Population Survey, unpublished data.

Figure 4.-Years of school completed by persons 25 to 29 years of age: 1940 to 1994

Percent of persons

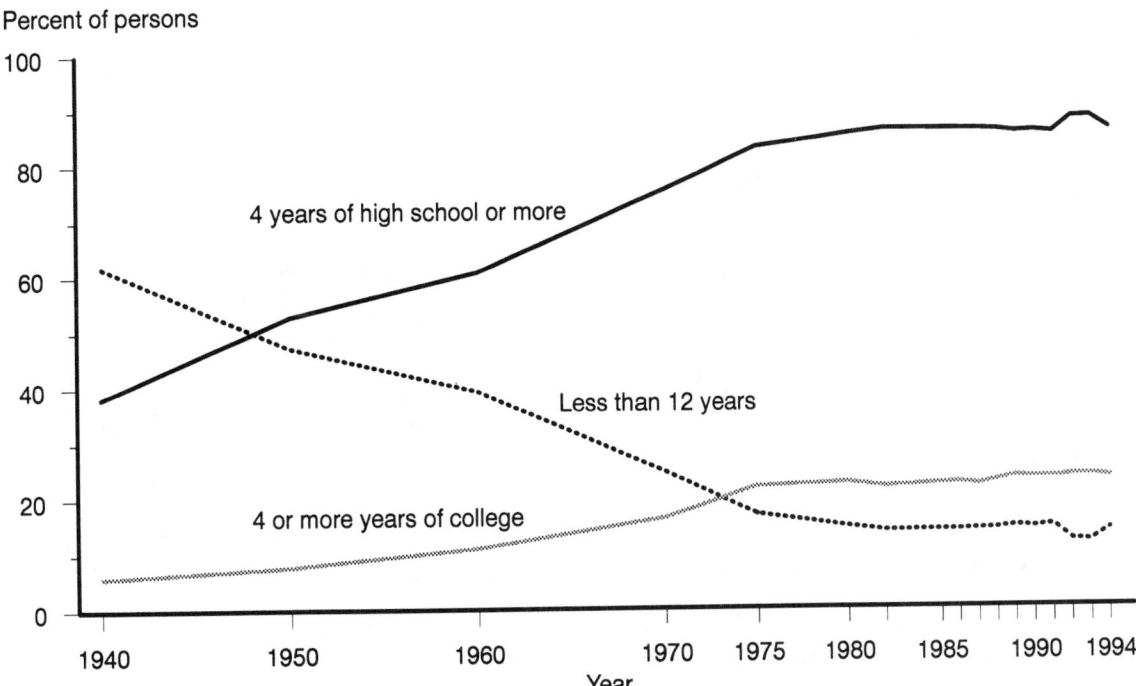

SOURCE: U.S. Department of Commerce, Bureau of the Census, *1960 Census of Population*, Vol. 1, part 1; and *Current Population Reports*, Series P-20; and Current Population Survey, unpublished data.

Figure 5.–Highest degree earned by persons 25 years and older: March 1994

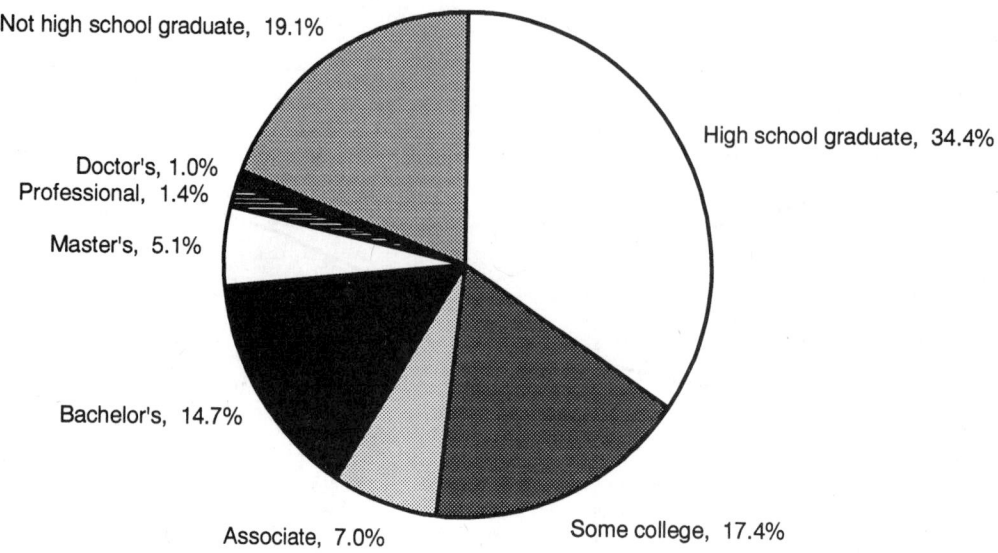

Not high school graduate, 19.1%

High school graduate, 34.4%

Doctor's, 1.0%
Professional, 1.4%

Master's, 5.1%

Bachelor's, 14.7%

Associate, 7.0%

Some college, 17.4%

Total persons age 25 and over = 164.5 million

SOURCE: U.S. Department of Commerce, Bureau of the Census, Current Population Survey, unpublished data.

Figure 6.–Items most frequently cited by the public as a major problem facing the local public schools: 1980 to 1994

Percent citing problem

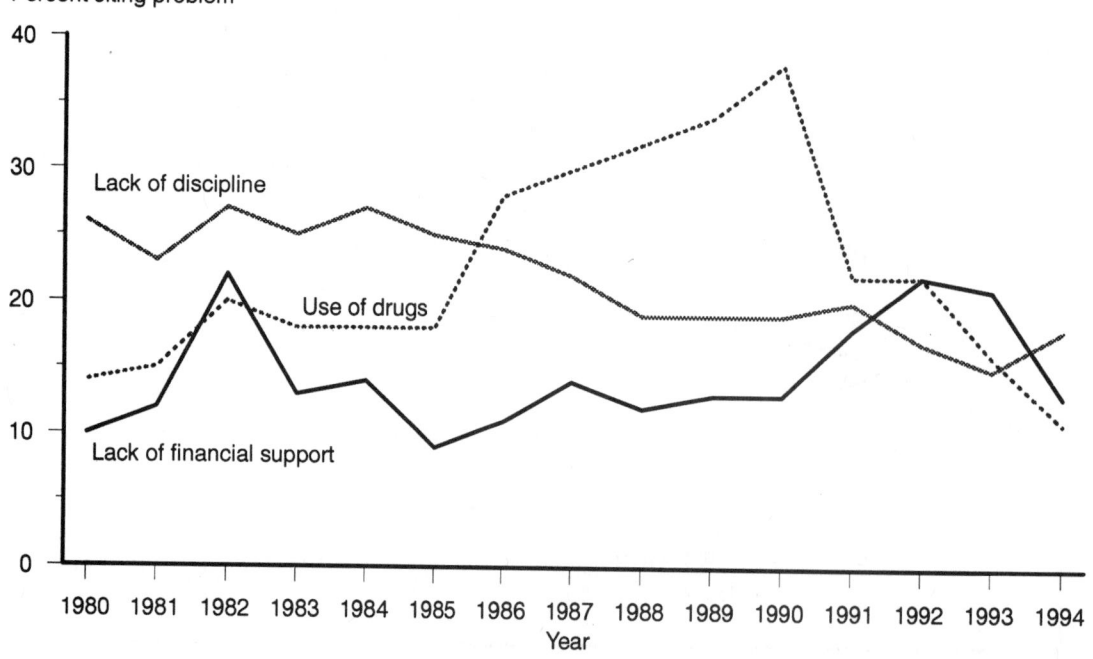

Lack of discipline

Use of drugs

Lack of financial support

Year

SOURCE: "The Annual Gallup Poll of the Public's Attitudes Toward the Public Schools," *Phi Delta Kappan*, various years.

Table 1.—Estimated number of participants in elementary and secondary education and in higher education: Fall 1995

[In millions]

Participants	All levels (elementary, secondary, and higher education)	Elementary and secondary schools			Institutions of higher education		
		Total	Public	Private	Total	Public	Private
1	2	3	4	5	6	7	8
Total	73.3	56.3	50.0	6.3	17.0	13.1	3.9
Enrollment [1]	65.1	50.7	45.0	5.7	14.4	11.3	3.1
Teachers and faculty	3.8	3.0	2.6	0.4	[2]0.8	[2]0.6	[2]0.3
Other professional, administrative, and support staff	4.3	2.6	2.4	0.2	1.7	1.2	0.5

[1] Includes enrollments in local public school systems and in most private schools (religiously affiliated and nonsectarian). Excludes subcollegiate departments of institutions of higher education, residential schools for exceptional children, and federal schools. Elementary and secondary includes most kindergarten and some nursery school enrollment. Excludes preprimary enrollment in schools that do not offer first grade or above. Higher education comprises full-time and part-time students enrolled in degree-credit and nondegree-credit programs in universities, other 4-year colleges, and 2-year colleges.

[2] Includes full-time and part-time faculty with the rank of instructor or above.

NOTE.—The enrollment figures include all students in elementary and secondary schools and colleges and universities. However, the data for teachers and other staff in public and private elementary and secondary schools are reported in terms of full-time equivalents. The staff data for institutions of higher education include all full-time and part-time professional, administrative, and support personnel. Because of rounding, details may not add to totals.

SOURCE: U.S. Department of Education, National Center for Education Statistics, unpublished projections and estimates. (This table was prepared June 1995.)

Table 2.—Enrollment in educational institutions, by level and control of institution: Fall 1980 to fall 2000

[In thousands]

Level of instruction and type of control	Fall 1980	Fall 1985	Fall 1986	Fall 1987	Fall 1988	Fall 1989	Fall 1990	Fall 1991	Fall 1992	Fall 1993[1]	Fall 1994[2]	Projected fall 1995	Projected fall 2000
1	2	3	4	5	6	7	8	9	10	11	12	13	14
All levels	58,305	57,226	57,709	58,254	58,485	59,436	60,267	61,605	62,677	63,253	63,939	65,148	69,924
Public	50,335	48,901	49,467	49,981	50,350	51,121	52,061	53,356	54,200	54,665	55,266	56,348	60,510
Private	7,971	8,325	8,242	8,273	8,135	8,316	8,206	8,248	8,477	8,588	8,673	8,800	9,414
Elementary and secondary education [3]	46,208	44,979	45,205	45,488	45,430	45,898	46,448	47,246	48,190	48,947	49,610	50,709	54,402
Public	40,877	39,422	39,753	40,008	40,189	40,543	41,217	42,047	42,816	43,476	44,034	45,037	48,323
Private	5,331	5,557	[4]5,452	5,479	5,241	5,355	5,232	5,199	5,375	5,471	5,576	5,672	6,079
Grades K-8 [5]	31,639	31,229	31,536	32,165	32,537	33,314	33,973	34,580	35,292	35,795	36,048	36,698	39,152
Public	27,647	27,034	27,420	27,933	28,501	29,152	29,878	30,506	31,081	31,515	31,703	32,293	34,452
Private	3,992	4,195	[4]4,116	4,232	[4]4,036	[4]4,162	4,095	[4]4,074	[4]4,212	[4]4,280	4,345	4,405	4,700
Grades 9–12	14,570	13,750	13,669	13,323	12,893	12,583	12,475	12,666	12,898	13,152	13,563	14,011	15,250
Public	13,231	12,388	12,333	12,076	11,687	11,390	11,338	11,541	11,735	11,961	12,331	12,744	13,871
Private	1,339	1,362	[4]1,336	1,247	[4]1,206	[4]1,193	1,137	[4]1,125	[4]1,163	[4]1,191	1,232	1,267	1,379
Higher education [6]	12,097	12,247	12,504	12,767	13,055	13,539	13,819	14,359	14,486	14,306	14,329	14,439	15,522
Public	9,457	9,479	9,714	9,973	10,161	10,578	10,845	11,310	11,385	11,189	11,232	11,311	12,187
Undergraduate [7]	8,442	8,477	8,661	8,919	9,103	9,488	9,710	10,148	10,216	10,012	10,005	10,089	10,907
First-professional	114	112	112	110	109	113	112	111	111	114	118	117	117
Graduate [8]	901	890	941	945	949	978	1,023	1,050	1,058	1,064	1,109	1,105	1,163
Private	2,640	2,768	2,790	2,793	2,894	2,961	2,974	3,049	3,102	3,117	3,097	3,128	3,335
Undergraduate [7]	2,033	2,120	2,137	2,128	2,213	2,255	2,250	2,291	2,320	2,312	2,296	2,330	2,504
First-professional	163	162	158	158	158	162	162	169	170	179	175	174	177
Graduate [8]	443	486	494	507	522	544	563	589	611	626	626	624	654

[1] Preliminary.

[2] Based on "Early Estimates" surveys for public elementary and secondary schools.

[3] Includes enrollments in local public school systems and in most private schools (religiously affiliated and nonsectarian). Excludes subcollegiate departments of institutions of higher education, residential schools for exceptional children, and federal schools. Excludes preprimary pupils in schools that do not offer first grade or above.

[4] Estimated.

[5] Includes kindergarten and some nursery school pupils.

[6] Includes full-time and part-time students enrolled in degree-credit and nondegree-credit programs in universities and 2-year and 4-year colleges.

[7] Includes unclassified students below the baccalaureate level.

[8] Includes unclassified postbaccalaureate students.

NOTE.—Higher education enrollment projections are based on the middle alternative projections published by the National Center for Education Statistics. Because of rounding, details may not add to totals. Some data have been revised from previously published figures.

SOURCE: U.S. Department of Education, National Center for Education Statistics, Common Core of Data and "Fall Enrollment in Institutions of Higher Education" surveys; Integrated Postsecondary Education Data System (IPEDS), "Fall Enrollment" surveys, and Projections of Education Statistics to 2005. (This table was prepared June 1995.)

Table 3.—Enrollment in educational institutions, by level and by control of institution: 1869–70 to fall 2005

[In thousands]

Year	Total enrollment, all levels	Elementary and secondary, total	Public elementary and secondary schools			Private elementary and secondary schools [1]			Higher education [2]		
			Total	Kindergarten through grade 8	Grades 9 through 12	Total	Kindergarten through grade 8	Grades 9 through 12	Total	Public	Private
1	2	3	4	5	6	7	8	9	10	11	12
1869–70	—	—	6,872	6,792	80	—	—	—	52	—	—
1879–80	—	—	9,868	9,757	110	—	—	—	116	—	—
1889–90	14,491	14,334	12,723	12,520	203	1,611	1,516	95	157	—	—
1899–1900	17,092	16,855	15,503	14,984	519	1,352	1,241	111	238	—	—
1909–10	19,728	19,372	17,814	16,899	915	1,558	1,441	117	355	—	—
1919–20	23,876	23,278	21,578	19,378	2,200	1,699	1,486	214	598	—	—
1929–30	29,430	28,329	25,678	21,279	4,399	2,651	2,310	341	1,101	—	—
1939–40	29,539	28,045	25,434	18,832	6,601	2,611	2,153	458	1,494	797	698
1949–50	31,151	28,492	25,111	19,387	5,725	3,380	2,708	672	2,659	1,355	1,304
Fall 1959	44,497	40,857	35,182	26,911	8,271	5,675	4,640	1,035	3,640	2,181	1,459
Fall 1964	52,996	47,716	41,416	30,025	11,391	[3]6,300	[3]5,000	1,300	5,280	3,468	1,812
Fall 1965	54,394	48,473	42,173	30,563	11,610	6,300	4,900	1,400	5,921	3,970	1,951
Fall 1966	55,629	49,239	43,039	31,145	11,894	[3]6,200	[3]4,800	[3]1,400	6,390	4,349	2,041
Fall 1967	56,803	49,891	43,891	31,641	12,250	[3]6,000	[3]4,600	[3]1,400	6,912	4,816	2,096
Fall 1968	58,257	50,744	44,944	32,226	12,718	5,800	4,400	1,400	7,513	5,431	2,082
Fall 1969	59,055	51,050	45,550	32,513	13,037	[3]5,500	[3]4,200	[3]1,300	8,005	5,897	2,108
Fall 1970	59,838	51,257	45,894	32,558	13,336	5,363	4,052	1,311	8,581	6,428	2,153
Fall 1971	60,220	51,271	46,071	32,318	13,753	[3]5,200	[3]3,900	[3]1,300	8,949	6,804	2,144
Fall 1972	59,941	50,726	45,726	31,879	13,848	[3]5,000	[3]3,700	[3]1,300	9,215	7,071	2,144
Fall 1973	60,047	50,445	45,445	31,401	14,044	[3]5,000	[3]3,700	[3]1,300	9,602	7,420	2,183
Fall 1974	60,297	50,073	45,073	30,971	14,103	[3]5,000	[3]3,700	[3]1,300	10,224	7,989	2,235
Fall 1975	61,004	49,819	44,819	30,515	14,304	[3]5,000	[3]3,700	[3]1,300	11,185	8,835	2,350
Fall 1976	60,490	49,478	44,311	29,997	14,314	5,167	3,825	1,342	11,012	8,653	2,359
Fall 1977	60,003	48,717	43,577	29,375	14,203	5,140	3,797	1,343	11,286	8,847	2,439
Fall 1978	58,897	47,637	42,551	28,463	14,088	5,086	3,732	1,353	11,260	8,786	2,474
Fall 1979	58,221	46,651	41,651	28,034	13,616	[3]5,000	[3]3,700	[3]1,300	11,570	9,037	2,533
Fall 1980	58,305	46,208	40,877	27,647	13,231	5,331	3,992	1,339	12,097	9,457	2,640
Fall 1981	57,916	45,544	40,044	27,280	12,764	[3]5,500	[3]4,100	[3]1,400	12,372	9,647	2,725
Fall 1982	57,591	45,166	39,566	27,161	12,405	[3]5,600	[3]4,200	[3]1,400	12,426	9,696	2,730
Fall 1983	57,432	44,967	39,252	26,981	12,271	5,715	4,315	1,400	12,465	9,683	2,782
Fall 1984	57,150	44,908	39,208	26,905	12,304	[3]5,700	[3]4,300	[3]1,400	12,242	9,477	2,765
Fall 1985	57,226	44,979	39,422	27,034	12,388	5,557	4,195	1,362	12,247	9,479	2,768
Fall 1986	57,709	45,205	39,753	27,420	12,333	[3]5,452	[3]4,116	[3]1,336	12,504	9,714	2,790
Fall 1987	58,254	45,488	40,008	27,933	12,076	5,479	4,232	1,247	12,767	9,973	2,793
Fall 1988	58,485	45,430	40,189	28,501	11,687	5,241	[3]4,036	[3]1,206	13,055	10,161	2,894
Fall 1989	59,436	45,898	40,543	29,152	11,390	5,355	[3]4,162	[3]1,193	13,539	10,578	2,961
Fall 1990	60,267	46,448	41,217	29,878	11,338	5,232	[3]4,095	[3]1,137	13,819	10,845	2,974
Fall 1991	61,605	47,246	42,047	30,506	11,541	5,199	[3]4,074	[3]1,125	14,359	11,310	3,049
Fall 1992	62,677	48,190	42,816	31,081	11,735	5,375	[3]4,212	[3]1,163	14,486	11,385	3,102
Fall 1993[4]	63,253	48,947	43,476	31,515	11,961	5,471	[3]4,280	[3]1,191	14,306	11,189	3,117
Fall 1994[5]	63,939	49,610	44,034	31,703	12,331	5,576	4,345	1,232	14,329	11,232	3,097
Fall 1995[6]	65,148	50,709	45,037	32,293	12,744	5,672	4,405	1,267	14,439	11,311	3,128
Fall 1996[6]	66,371	51,745	45,960	32,863	13,097	5,785	4,483	1,302	14,626	11,476	3,151
Fall 1997[6]	67,776	52,686	46,797	33,420	13,377	5,889	4,559	1,330	15,090	11,850	3,240
Fall 1998[6]	68,559	53,367	47,403	33,825	13,578	5,964	4,614	1,350	15,192	11,931	3,261
Fall 1999[6]	69,289	53,937	47,911	34,133	13,778	6,026	4,656	1,370	15,352	12,055	3,297
Fall 2000[6]	69,924	54,402	48,323	34,452	13,871	6,079	4,700	1,379	15,522	12,187	3,335
Fall 2001[6]	70,472	54,807	48,684	34,681	14,003	6,123	4,731	1,392	15,665	12,296	3,369
Fall 2002[6]	70,951	55,155	48,994	34,856	14,138	6,161	4,755	1,406	15,796	12,396	3,400
Fall 2003[6]	71,261	55,413	49,225	34,963	14,262	6,188	4,770	1,418	15,848	12,435	3,413
Fall 2004[6]	71,657	55,681	49,470	34,931	14,539	6,211	4,765	1,446	15,976	12,529	3,447
Fall 2005[6]	71,948	55,871	49,651	34,703	14,948	6,220	4,734	1,486	16,077	12,607	3,470

[1] Beginning in fall 1980, data include estimates for an expanded universe of private schools. Therefore, these totals may differ from figures shown in other tables, and direct comparisons with earlier years should be avoided.

[2] Data for 1869–70 through 1949–50 include resident degree-credit students enrolled at any time during the academic year. Beginning in 1959, data include all resident and extension students enrolled at the beginning of the fall term.

[3] Estimated.

[4] Preliminary data.

[5] Public elementary and secondary data are based on "Early Estimates" surveys. Other data are projected.

[6] Projected.

—Data not available.

NOTE.—Elementary and secondary enrollment includes pupils in local public school systems and in most private schools (religiously affiliated and nonsectarian), but generally excludes pupils in subcollegiate departments of institutions of higher education, residential schools for exceptional children, and federal schools. Elementary enrollment includes some nursery school pupils. Higher education enrollment includes students in colleges, universities, professional schools, teachers colleges, and 2-year colleges. Higher education enrollment projections are based on the low and middle alternative projections published by the National Center for Education Statistics. Some data have been revised from previously published figures. Because of rounding, details may not add to totals.

SOURCE: U.S. Department of Education, National Center for Education Statistics, *Statistics of State School Systems; Statistics of Public Elementary and Secondary School Systems; Statistics of Nonpublic Elementary and Secondary Schools; Projections of Education Statistics to 2005;* Common Core of Data; "Fall Enrollment in Institutions of Higher Education" surveys; and Integrated Postsecondary Education Data System (IPEDS), "Fall Enrollment" surveys. (This table was prepared June 1995.)

Table 4.—Teachers in elementary and secondary schools, and senior instructional staff in institutions of higher education, by control of institution: Fall 1970 to fall 2005

[In thousands]

Fall	All levels			Elementary and secondary teachers [1]									Higher education senior instructional staff [2]		
	Total	Public	Private	Total			Elementary teachers			Secondary teachers			Total	Public	Private
				Total	Public	Private	Total	Public	Private	Total	Public	Private			
1	2	3	4	5	6	7	8	9	10	11	12	13	14	15	16
1970	2,766	2,373	393	2,292	2,059	233	1,283	1,130	153	1,009	929	80	474	314	160
1975	3,081	2,641	440	2,453	2,198	[3]255	1,353	1,181	[3]172	1,100	1,017	[3]83	628	443	185
1980	3,171	2,679	492	2,485	2,184	301	1,401	1,189	212	1,084	995	89	[3]686	[3]495	[3]191
1981	3,145	2,636	509	2,440	2,127	[3]313	1,404	1,183	[3]221	1,037	945	[3]92	[3]710	[3]506	[3]204
1982	3,168	2,639	529	2,458	2,133	[3]325	1,413	1,182	[3]231	1,045	951	[3]94			
1983	3,200	2,651	549	2,476	2,139	337	1,426	1,186	240	1,050	953	97	724	512	212
1984	3,225	2,673	552	2,508	2,168	[3]340	1,451	1,208	[3]243	1,057	960	[3]97	[3]717	[3]505	[3]212
1985	3,264	2,709	555	2,549	2,206	343	1,483	1,237	246	1,066	969	97	[3]715	[3]503	[3]212
1986	3,314	2,754	560	2,592	2,244	[3]348	1,521	1,271	[3]250	1,071	973	[3]98	[3]722	[3]510	[3]212
1987	3,425	2,832	593	2,632	2,279	353	1,564	1,307	257	1,068	973	95	[4]793	[4]553	[4]240
1988	3,472	2,882	590	2,668	2,323	345	1,604	1,353	251	1,064	970	94	[3]804	[3]559	[3]245
1989	3,503	2,934	569	2,679	2,357	322	1,622	1,387	235	1,057	970	87	[4]824	[4]577	[4]247
1990	3,570	2,972	599	2,753	2,398	355	1,680	1,426	254	1,073	972	101	[3]817	[3]574	[3]244
1991	3,613	3,013	600	2,787	2,432	355	1,713	1,459	254	1,074	973	101	[4]826	[4]581	[4]245
1992	3,655	3,043	613	2,822	2,459	363	1,743	1,483	260	1,079	976	103	834	585	250
1993[3]	3,697	3,080	617	2,871	2,505	366	1,772	1,510	262	1,099	995	104	825	575	251
1994[6]	3,741	3,124	617	2,915	2,547	368	1,754	1,495	259	1,163	1,053	110	826	577	249
1995[6]	3,804	3,176	628	2,971	2,595	376	1,783	1,520	264	1,187	1,075	112	833	581	252
1996[6]	3,864	3,228	635	3,021	2,639	382	1,850	1,576	273	1,234	1,118	117	869	609	261
1997[6]	3,953	3,303	651	3,084	2,694	390	1,883	1,605	278	1,256	1,137	119	875	613	262
1998[6]	4,013	3,354	659	3,138	2,741	397	1,912	1,630	283	1,277	1,156	121	884	619	265
1999[6]	4,073	3,405	668	3,189	2,786	403	1,936	1,650	286	1,292	1,170	122	894	626	268
2000[6]	4,122	3,446	676	3,228	2,820	408	1,953	1,664	289	1,306	1,183	124	—	—	—
2001[6]	—	—	—	3,259	2,847	412	1,964	1,674	290	1,322	1,197	125	—	—	—
2002[6]	—	—	—	3,286	2,871	415	1,972	1,681	291	1,340	1,213	127	—	—	—
2003[6]	—	—	—	3,312	2,894	418	1,979	1,687	292	1,364	1,235	129	—	—	—
2004[6]	—	—	—	3,343	2,921	421	1,984	1,691	293	1,387	1,255	131	—	—	—
2005[6]	—	—	—	3,369	2,945	424							—	—	—

[1] Includes teachers in local public school systems and in most private schools (religiously affiliated and nonsectarian). Excludes subcollegiate departments of institutions of higher education, residential schools for exceptional children, and federal schools. Teachers are reported in terms of full-time equivalents.

[2] Includes full-time and part-time faculty with the rank of instructor or above in colleges, universities, professional schools, teachers colleges, and 2-year colleges. Excludes teaching assistants.

[3] Estimated.

[4] Based on actual survey data. Methodology for this year and later years is not consistent with figures for earlier years.

[5] Preliminary data.

[6] Projected.

—Data not available.

NOTE.—Because of rounding, details may not add to totals. Some data have been revised from previously published figures.

SOURCE: U.S. Department of Education, National Center for Education Statistics, Common Core of Data; *Projections of Education Statistics*, various years; Integrated Postsecondary Education Data System (IPEDS),"Staff" survey; and Equal Employment Opportunity Commission, unpublished data. (This table was prepared June 1995.)

Table 5.—Educational institutions, by level and control of institution: 1978–79 to 1993–94

Level and control of institution	1978–79	1980–81	1982–83	1984–85	1986–87	1987–88	1988–89	1989–90	1990–91	1991–92	1992–93	1993–94
1	2	3	4	5	6	7	8	9	10	11	12	13
All institutions	—	117,707	—	—	121,433	122,111	—	—	119,242	—	—	121,855
Elementary and secondary schools	—	106,746	—	—	109,071	110,055	—	—	109,228	—	—	111,486
Elementary	73,062	72,659	—	—	74,104	76,247	—	—	74,716	—	—	75,591
Secondary	25,259	24,856	—	—	23,844	23,153	—	—	22,873	—	—	22,610
Combined	4,904	5,202	—	—	6,932	8,202	—	—	8,847	—	—	10,678
Other[1]	—	4,029	—	—	4,191	2,453	—	—	2,792	—	—	2,608
Public schools	—	85,982	84,740	84,007	83,455	83,248	83,165	83,425	84,538	84,578	84,501	85,393
Elementary	60,312	59,326	58,051	57,231	58,801	59,311	59,296	59,757	59,015	59,258	59,680	60,052
Secondary	22,834	22,619	22,383	22,320	21,406	20,758	20,550	20,359	20,406	20,120	19,995	20,059
Combined	1,670	1,743	1,605	1,596	1,983	2,179	2,235	2,280	2,325	2,481	2,549	2,674
Other[1]	—	2,294	2,701	2,860	1,265	1,000	1,084	1,029	2,792	2,719	2,277	2,608
Private schools	19,489	20,764	—	—	[2]25,616	26,807	—	—	24,690	25,998	—	26,093
Elementary	12,750	13,333	—	—	[2]15,303	16,936	—	—	15,701	15,716	—	15,539
Secondary	2,425	2,237	—	—	[2]2,438	2,395	—	—	2,467	2,475	—	2,551
Combined	3,234	3,459	—	—	[2]4,949	6,023	—	—	6,522	7,807	—	8,004
Other[1]	1,080	1,735	—	—	[2]2,926	1,453	—	—	(3)	(3)	—	(3)
Postsecondary institutions	—	[4]10,961	—	—	12,362	12,056	11,389	10,606	10,014	9,983	10,601	10,369
Public	—	[4]2,393	—	—	2,363	2,250	2,169	2,120	2,096	2,129	2,146	2,152
Private nonprofit	—	[4]2,359	—	—	3,432	3,254	3,092	2,942	2,808	2,810	2,926	2,890
Proprietary	—	[4]6,209	—	—	6,567	6,552	6,128	5,544	5,110	5,044	5,529	5,327
Noncollegiate institutions	—	[4]7,730	—	—	8,956	8,469	7,824	7,071	6,455	6,382	6,963	6,737
Public	—	[4]896	—	—	830	659	587	557	529	531	522	527
Private nonprofit	—	[4]790	—	—	1,797	1,581	1,434	1,286	1,159	1,148	1,254	1,203
Proprietary	—	[4]6,044	—	—	6,329	6,229	5,803	5,228	4,767	4,703	5,187	5,007
Institutions of higher education[5]	3,134	3,231	3,280	3,331	3,406	3,587	3,565	3,535	3,559	3,601	3,638	3,632
2-year colleges	1,193	1,274	1,296	1,306	1,336	1,452	1,436	1,408	1,418	1,444	1,469	1,442
Public	924	945	933	935	960	992	984	968	972	999	1,024	1,021
Private nonprofit	188	182	363	186	173	186	180	177	167	176	179	181
Proprietary	81	147	(6)	185	203	274	272	263	279	269	266	240
4-year colleges	1,941	1,957	1,984	2,025	2,070	2,135	2,129	2,127	2,141	2,157	2,169	2,190
Public	550	552	560	566	573	599	598	595	595	599	600	604
Private nonprofit	1,376	1,387	1,424	1,430	1,462	1,487	1,478	1,479	1,482	1,486	1,493	1,506
Proprietary	15	18	(6)	29	35	49	53	53	64	72	76	80

[1] Includes special education, alternative, and other schools not classified by grade span. Because of changes in survey definitions, figures for "other" schools are not comparable from year to year.

[2] Data are for 1985–86. Data were collected from a sample survey that differed significantly from earlier surveys. The sample survey was designed to correct an undercount of about 10 percent that was known to have occurred in earlier surveys.

[3] Included in other categories.

[4] Because of changes in survey procedures, figures are not directly comparable with data for later years.

[5] Includes those colleges designated as institutions of higher education by the Higher Education General Information Survey system, even if they have a less than 2–year program. Includes branch campuses. Beginning in 1980, total includes some schools accredited by the Accrediting Commission of Career Schools and Colleges of Technology.

[6] Included under "private nonprofit."

—Data not available.

SOURCE: U.S. Department of Education, National Center for Education Statistics, Common Core of Data and Private School surveys; Higher Education General Information Survey, "Institutional Characteristics of Colleges and Universities;" and Integrated Postsecondary Education Data System, "Institutional Characteristics" surveys. (This table was prepared June 1995.)

Table 6.—Percent of the population 3 to 34 years old enrolled in school,[1] by age: April 1940 to October 1994

Year	Total, 3 to 34 years	3 and 4 years	5 and 6 years	7 to 13 years	14 to 17 years	18 and 19 years	20 to 24 years			25 to 29 years	30 to 34 years
							Total	20 and 21 years	22 to 24 years		
1	2	3	4	5	6	7	8	9	10	11	12
1940[2]	—	—	43.0	95.0	79.3	28.9	6.6	—	—	—	—
1945	—	—	60.4	98.1	78.4	20.7	3.9	—	—	—	—
1947	—	—	58.0	98.5	79.3	24.3	10.2	—	—	3.0	—
1948	—	—	56.0	98.1	81.8	26.9	9.7	—	—	2.6	—
1949	—	—	59.3	98.6	81.6	25.3	9.2	—	—	3.8	—
1950	—	—	58.2	98.7	83.4	29.7	9.2	—	—	3.0	0.9
1951	—	—	54.5	99.1	85.2	26.2	8.6	—	—	2.5	—
1952	—	—	54.7	98.8	85.2	28.8	9.7	—	—	2.6	1.2
1953	—	—	55.7	99.4	85.9	31.2	11.1	—	—	2.9	1.7
1954	—	—	77.3	99.4	87.1	32.4	11.2	—	—	4.1	1.5
1955	—	—	78.1	99.2	86.9	31.5	11.1	—	—	4.2	1.6
1956	—	—	77.6	99.3	88.2	35.4	12.8	—	—	5.1	1.9
1957	—	—	78.6	99.5	89.5	34.9	14.0	—	—	—	—
1958	—	—	80.4	99.5	89.2	37.6	13.4	—	—	—	—
1959	—	—	80.0	99.4	90.2	36.8	12.7	—	—	—	—
1960	—	—	80.7	99.5	90.3	38.4	13.1	—	—	4.9	2.4
1961	—	—	81.7	99.3	91.4	38.0	13.7	—	—	—	—
1962	—	—	82.2	99.3	92.0	41.8	15.6	—	—	—	—
1963	—	—	82.7	99.3	92.9	40.9	17.3	—	—	5.2	2.6
1964	—	—	83.3	99.0	93.1	41.6	16.8	—	—	—	—
1965	55.5	10.6	84.9	99.4	93.2	46.3	19.0	27.6	13.2	6.1	3.2
1966	56.1	12.5	85.8	99.3	93.7	47.2	19.9	29.9	13.2	6.5	2.7
1967	56.6	14.2	87.4	99.3	93.7	47.6	22.0	33.3	13.6	6.6	4.0
1968	56.7	15.7	87.6	99.1	94.2	50.4	21.4	31.2	13.8	7.0	3.9
1969	57.0	16.1	88.4	99.2	94.0	50.2	23.0	34.1	15.4	7.9	4.8
1970	56.4	20.5	89.5	99.2	94.1	47.7	21.5	31.9	14.9	7.5	4.2
1971	56.2	21.2	91.6	99.1	94.5	49.2	21.9	32.2	15.4	8.0	4.9
1972	54.9	24.4	91.9	99.2	93.3	46.3	21.6	31.4	14.8	8.6	4.6
1973	53.5	24.2	92.5	99.2	92.9	42.9	20.8	30.1	14.5	8.5	4.5
1974	53.6	28.8	94.2	99.3	92.9	43.1	21.4	30.2	15.1	9.6	5.7
1975	53.7	31.5	94.7	99.3	93.6	46.9	22.4	31.2	16.2	10.1	6.6
1976	53.1	31.3	95.5	99.2	93.7	46.2	23.3	32.0	17.1	10.0	6.0
1977	52.5	32.0	95.8	99.4	93.6	46.2	22.9	31.8	16.5	10.8	6.9
1978	51.2	34.2	95.3	99.1	93.7	45.4	21.8	29.5	16.3	9.4	6.4
1979	50.3	35.1	95.8	99.2	93.6	45.0	21.7	30.2	15.8	9.6	6.4
1980	49.7	36.7	95.7	99.3	93.4	46.4	22.3	31.0	16.3	9.3	6.4
1981	48.9	36.0	94.0	99.2	94.1	49.0	22.5	31.6	16.5	9.0	6.9
1982	48.6	36.4	95.0	99.2	94.4	47.8	23.5	34.0	16.8	9.6	6.3
1983	48.4	37.5	95.4	99.2	95.0	50.4	22.7	32.5	16.6	9.6	6.4
1984	47.9	36.3	94.5	99.2	94.7	50.1	23.7	33.9	17.3	9.1	6.3
1985	48.3	38.9	96.1	99.2	94.9	51.6	24.0	35.3	16.9	9.2	6.1
1986	48.2	38.9	95.3	99.2	94.9	54.6	23.6	33.0	17.9	8.8	6.0
1987	48.6	38.3	95.1	99.5	95.0	55.6	25.5	38.7	17.5	9.0	5.8
1988	48.7	38.2	96.0	99.7	95.1	55.6	26.1	39.1	18.2	8.3	5.9
1989	49.1	39.1	95.2	99.3	95.7	56.0	27.0	38.5	19.9	9.3	5.7
1990	50.2	44.4	96.5	99.6	95.8	57.2	28.6	39.7	21.0	9.7	5.8
1991	50.7	40.5	95.4	99.6	96.0	59.6	30.2	42.0	22.2	10.2	6.2
1992	51.4	39.7	95.5	99.4	96.7	61.4	31.6	44.0	23.7	9.8	6.1
1993	51.8	40.4	95.4	99.5	96.5	61.6	30.8	42.7	23.6	10.2	5.9
1994	53.1	47.5	96.7	99.3	96.6	59.7	31.1	44.0	23.2	10.4	6.6

[1] Includes enrollment in any type of graded public, parochial, or other private schools. Includes nursery schools, kindergartens, elementary schools, high schools, colleges, universities, and professional schools. Attendance may be on either a full-time or part-time basis and during the day or night. Enrollments in "special" schools, such as trade schools, business colleges, or correspondence schools, are not included.

[2] Data are as of April 1940. Data for all other years are as of October.

—Data not available.

NOTE.—Data are based upon sample surveys of the civilian noninstitutional population.

SOURCE: U.S. Department of Commerce, Bureau of the Census, *Historical Statistics of the United States, Colonial Times to 1970; Current Population Reports*, Series P-20, various years; and Current Population Survey, unpublished data. (This table was prepared April 1995.)

Table 7.—Percent of the population 3 to 34 years old enrolled in school,[1] by race/ethnicity, sex, and age: October 1975 to October 1994

Year and age	Total				Male				Female			
	All races	White, non-Hispanic	Black, non-Hispanic	Hispanic origin	All races	White, non-Hispanic	Black, non-Hispanic	Hispanic origin	All races	White, non-Hispanic	Black, non-Hispanic	Hispanic origin
1	2	3	4	5	6	7	8	9	10	11	12	13
1975												
Total, 3 to 34 years	53.7	53.0	57.7	54.8	56.1	55.2	60.4	58.1	51.5	50.8	55.3	51.7
3 and 4 years	31.5	31.0	34.4	27.3	30.9	31.1	31.4	26.7	32.1	30.9	37.5	27.9
5 and 6 years	94.7	95.1	94.4	92.1	94.4	94.8	94.8	89.7	95.1	95.4	94.0	94.4
7 to 9 years	99.3	99.4	99.3	99.6	99.2	99.2	99.4	99.6	99.5	99.6	99.2	99.5
10 to 13 years	99.3	99.3	99.1	99.2	98.9	99.0	98.9	98.8	99.6	99.6	99.3	99.7
14 and 15 years	98.2	98.5	97.4	95.6	98.4	98.6	97.6	97.4	98.1	98.4	97.2	93.8
16 and 17 years	89.0	89.5	86.8	86.2	90.7	91.2	88.1	88.3	87.2	87.8	85.5	84.0
18 and 19 years	46.9	46.8	46.9	44.0	49.9	49.4	49.6	51.9	44.2	44.2	44.6	37.1
20 and 21 years	31.2	32.1	26.7	27.5	35.3	36.7	28.4	31.3	27.4	27.8	25.3	24.3
22 to 24 years	16.2	16.4	13.9	14.1	20.0	20.8	14.5	15.9	12.6	12.2	13.4	12.5
25 to 29 years	10.1	10.1	9.4	8.3	13.1	13.2	11.6	11.9	7.2	7.2	7.6	5.3
30 to 34 years	6.6	6.6	7.1	5.5	7.7	7.5	8.7	7.2	5.6	5.8	5.9	4.1
1980												
Total, 3 to 34 years	49.7	48.8	54.0	49.8	50.9	50.0	56.2	49.9	48.5	47.7	52.1	49.8
3 and 4 years	36.7	37.4	38.2	28.5	37.8	39.2	36.4	30.1	35.5	35.5	40.0	26.6
5 and 6 years	95.7	95.9	95.5	94.5	95.0	95.4	94.1	94.0	96.4	96.5	97.0	94.9
7 to 9 years	99.1	99.1	99.4	98.4	99.0	99.0	99.5	97.7	99.2	99.2	99.3	99.0
10 to 13 years	99.4	99.4	99.4	99.7	99.4	99.4	99.4	99.4	99.4	99.4	99.3	99.9
14 and 15 years	98.2	98.7	97.9	94.3	98.7	98.9	98.4	96.7	97.7	98.5	97.3	92.1
16 and 17 years	89.0	89.2	90.7	81.8	89.1	89.4	90.7	81.5	88.8	89.0	90.6	82.2
18 and 19 years	46.4	47.0	45.8	37.8	47.0	48.5	42.9	36.9	45.8	45.7	48.3	38.8
20 and 21 years	31.0	33.0	23.3	19.5	32.6	34.8	22.8	21.4	29.5	31.3	23.7	17.6
22 to 24 years	16.3	16.8	13.6	11.7	17.8	18.7	13.4	10.7	14.9	15.0	13.7	12.6
25 to 29 years	9.3	9.4	8.8	6.9	9.8	9.8	10.6	6.8	8.8	9.1	7.5	6.9
30 to 34 years	6.4	6.4	6.9	5.1	5.9	5.6	7.2	6.2	7.0	7.2	6.6	4.1
1985												
Total, 3 to 34 years	48.3	47.8	50.8	47.7	49.2	48.7	52.6	47.5	47.4	46.9	49.2	47.9
3 and 4 years	38.9	40.3	42.8	27.0	36.7	39.1	34.6	26.4	41.2	41.6	50.3	27.7
5 and 6 years	96.1	96.6	95.7	94.5	95.3	95.6	94.5	95.3	97.0	97.6	97.1	93.7
7 to 9 years	99.1	99.4	98.6	98.4	99.0	99.3	98.4	98.9	99.2	99.4	98.9	98.0
10 to 13 years	99.3	99.3	99.5	99.4	99.2	99.2	99.1	99.1	99.4	99.3	99.9	99.7
14 and 15 years	98.1	98.3	98.1	96.1	98.3	98.4	98.5	96.2	97.9	98.1	97.6	96.0
16 and 17 years	91.7	92.5	91.8	84.5	92.4	92.9	92.0	88.9	90.9	92.2	91.6	80.0
18 and 19 years	51.6	53.7	43.5	41.8	52.2	53.4	49.4	38.6	51.0	54.0	37.8	44.7
20 and 21 years	35.3	37.2	27.7	24.0	36.5	38.8	29.9	20.3	34.1	35.7	25.8	27.4
22 to 24 years	16.9	17.5	13.8	11.6	18.8	19.8	13.5	12.6	15.1	15.4	14.0	10.4
25 to 29 years	9.2	9.6	7.4	6.6	9.4	9.7	5.8	8.2	9.1	9.4	8.7	4.9
30 to 34 years	6.1	6.2	5.2	5.7	5.4	5.6	3.9	4.0	6.8	6.9	6.2	7.5
1990												
Total, 3 to 34 years	50.2	49.8	52.2	47.2	50.9	50.4	54.3	46.8	49.5	49.2	50.3	47.7
3 and 4 years	44.4	47.2	41.8	30.7	43.9	47.9	38.1	28.0	44.9	46.6	45.5	33.6
5 and 6 years	96.5	96.7	96.5	94.9	96.5	96.8	96.2	95.8	96.4	96.7	96.9	93.9
7 to 9 years	99.7	99.7	99.8	99.5	99.7	99.7	99.9	99.5	99.6	99.7	99.8	99.4
10 to 13 years	99.6	99.7	99.9	99.1	99.6	99.6	99.9	99.0	99.7	99.7	99.8	99.1
14 and 15 years	99.0	99.0	99.4	99.0	99.1	99.2	99.7	99.1	98.9	98.9	99.1	98.8
16 and 17 years	92.5	93.5	91.7	85.4	92.6	93.4	93.0	85.5	92.4	93.7	90.5	85.3
18 and 19 years	57.2	59.1	55.0	44.0	58.2	59.7	60.4	40.7	56.3	58.5	49.8	47.2
20 and 21 years	39.7	43.1	28.3	27.2	40.3	44.2	31.0	21.7	39.2	42.0	25.8	33.1
22 to 24 years	21.0	21.9	19.7	9.9	22.3	23.7	19.3	11.2	19.9	20.3	20.0	8.4
25 to 29 years	9.7	10.4	6.1	6.3	9.2	10.0	4.7	4.6	10.2	10.7	7.3	8.1
30 to 34 years	5.8	6.2	4.5	3.6	4.8	5.0	2.3	4.0	6.9	7.4	6.3	3.1
1994												
Total, 3 to 34 years	53.1	53.2	56.4	49.0	53.7	53.5	58.4	48.0	52.9	52.9	54.4	50.2
3 and 4 years	47.5	50.1	52.2	30.8	47.6	48.9	57.1	32.6	46.9	51.3	47.1	28.9
5 and 6 years	96.7	96.7	97.1	96.1	97.0	97.1	97.0	96.5	96.4	96.3	97.2	95.7
7 to 9 years	99.3	99.2	99.6	99.2	99.2	99.2	99.6	98.6	99.5	99.3	99.7	99.8
10 to 13 years	99.4	99.3	99.6	99.4	99.4	99.3	99.5	99.3	99.4	99.3	99.7	99.4
14 and 15 years	98.8	99.2	99.2	96.1	98.8	99.4	99.7	94.6	98.7	98.9	98.6	99.4
16 and 17 years	94.3	95.1	95.3	88.3	94.3	95.4	95.2	86.6	94.4	94.8	95.5	90.2
18 and 19 years	59.7	62.6	53.4	51.4	60.4	62.5	53.1	54.2	60.0	62.7	53.7	48.6
20 and 21 years	44.0	50.1	35.3	24.9	42.7	47.6	34.3	23.7	47.0	52.4	36.3	26.4
22 to 24 years	23.2	24.9	22.8	15.1	24.2	25.5	21.4	14.0	23.9	24.3	24.0	16.5
25 to 29 years	10.4	10.8	10.5	8.1	10.5	10.3	10.8	7.1	11.1	11.4	10.3	9.1
30 to 34 years	6.6	6.7	7.3	5.7	5.9	6.0	5.7	4.2	7.5	7.3	8.5	7.3

[1] Includes enrollment in any type of graded public, parochial, or other private schools. Includes nursery schools, kindergartens, elementary schools, high schools, colleges, universities, and professional schools. Attendance may be on either a full-time or part-time basis and during the day or night. Enrollments in "special" schools, such as trade schools, business colleges, or correspondence schools, are not included.

NOTE.—Data are based upon sample surveys of the civilian noninstitutional population.

SOURCE: U.S. Department of Commerce, Bureau of the Census, Current Population Survey, unpublished data. (This table was prepared April 1995.)

Table 8.—Years of school completed by persons age 25 and over and 25 to 29, by race and sex: 1910 to 1994

Age and year	All races — Percent, by years of school completed			All races — Median years of school completed	White [1] — Percent, by years of school completed			White [1] — Median years of school completed	Black and other races [1] — Percent, by years of school completed			Black and other races [1] — Median years of school completed
	Less than 5 years of elementary school	4 years of high school or more	4 or more years of college		Less than 5 years of elementary school	4 years of high school or more	4 or more years of college		Less than 5 years of elementary school	4 years of high school or more	4 or more years of college	
1	2	3	4	5	6	7	8	9	10	11	12	13
Males and females												
25 and over												
1910 [2]	23.8	13.5	2.7	8.1	—	—	—	—	—	—	—	—
1920 [2]	22.0	16.4	3.3	8.2	—	—	—	—	—	—	—	—
1930 [2]	17.5	19.1	3.9	8.4	—	—	—	—	—	—	—	5.7
April 1940	13.7	24.5	4.6	8.6	10.9	26.1	4.9	8.7	41.8	7.7	1.3	6.9
April 1950	11.1	34.3	6.2	9.3	8.9	36.4	6.6	9.7	32.6	13.7	2.2	8.2
April 1960	8.3	41.1	7.7	10.5	6.7	43.2	8.1	10.8	23.5	21.7	3.5	10.1
March 1970	5.3	55.2	11.0	12.2	4.2	57.4	11.6	12.2	14.7	36.1	6.1	11.4
March 1975	4.2	62.5	13.9	12.3	3.3	64.5	14.5	12.4	11.7	46.4	9.2	12.2
March 1980	3.4	68.6	17.0	12.5	2.6	70.5	17.8	12.5	8.8	54.6	11.1	12.3
March 1982	3.0	71.0	17.7	12.6	2.4	72.8	18.5	12.6	7.4	58.1	12.4	12.4
March 1985	2.7	73.9	19.4	12.6	2.2	75.5	20.0	12.7	6.0	63.2	15.4	12.4
March 1986	2.7	74.7	19.4	12.6	2.2	76.2	20.1	12.7	5.5	65.3	15.2	12.4
March 1987	2.4	75.6	19.9	12.7	2.0	77.0	20.5	12.7	5.1	66.7	15.7	12.5
March 1988	2.4	76.2	20.3	12.7	2.0	77.7	20.9	12.7	5.1	66.7	16.4	12.5
March 1989	2.5	76.9	21.1	12.7	2.0	78.4	21.8	12.7	5.6	67.3	16.9	12.5
March 1990	2.4	77.6	21.3	12.7	2.0	79.1	22.0	12.7	5.4	68.7	16.5	12.5
March 1991	2.4	78.4	21.4	12.7	2.0	79.9	22.2	12.8	5.0	69.6	16.7	12.5
March 1992	2.8	80.8	21.4	12.8	1.8	82.2	22.1	12.9	4.1	72.9	17.2	12.6
March 1993	2.1	81.5	21.9	12.9	1.7	82.7	22.6	12.9	4.1	74.7	17.7	12.7
March 1994	1.9	80.9	22.2	—	1.7	82.0	22.9	—	3.3	74.5	18.1	—
25 to 29												
1920 [2]	—	—	—	—	12.9	22.0	4.5	8.5	44.6	6.3	1.2	5.4
April 1940	5.9	38.1	5.9	10.3	3.4	41.2	6.4	10.7	27.0	12.3	1.6	7.1
April 1950	4.6	52.8	7.7	12.1	3.3	56.3	8.2	12.2	16.1	23.6	2.8	8.7
April 1960	2.8	60.7	11.0	12.3	2.2	63.7	11.8	12.3	7.2	38.6	5.4	10.8
March 1970	1.1	75.4	16.4	12.6	0.9	77.8	17.3	12.6	2.2	58.4	10.0	12.2
March 1975	1.0	83.1	21.9	12.8	1.0	84.4	22.8	12.8	0.7	73.8	15.4	12.6
March 1980	0.8	85.4	22.5	12.9	0.8	86.9	23.7	12.9	1.0	77.0	15.2	12.7
March 1982	0.8	86.2	21.7	12.8	0.8	86.9	22.7	12.9	0.7	82.2	15.8	12.8
March 1985	0.7	86.1	22.2	12.9	0.8	86.8	23.2	12.9	0.5	82.4	16.7	12.8
March 1986	0.9	86.1	22.4	12.9	0.9	86.5	23.5	12.9	0.9	84.3	16.3	12.8
March 1987	0.9	86.0	22.0	12.8	0.8	86.3	23.0	12.9	1.1	84.1	16.9	12.8
March 1988	1.0	85.9	22.7	12.8	1.0	86.6	23.5	12.9	1.2	82.0	18.1	12.6
March 1989	1.0	85.5	23.4	12.9	0.9	86.0	24.4	12.9	1.2	83.1	18.1	12.8
March 1990	1.2	85.7	23.2	12.9	1.2	86.3	24.2	12.9	1.1	82.5	18.2	12.8
March 1991	1.0	85.4	23.2	12.9	1.0	85.8	24.6	12.9	0.6	83.1	16.4	12.8
March 1992	0.9	88.1	23.6	13.0	0.9	88.5	25.0	13.0	0.9	85.7	16.9	12.8
March 1993	0.7	88.2	23.7	13.0	0.7	88.5	24.7	13.0	0.5	87.0	18.7	12.9
March 1994	0.8	86.1	23.3	—	0.8	86.5	24.2	—	0.9	84.2	19.1	—
Males												
25 and over												
April 1940	15.1	22.7	5.5	8.6	12.0	24.2	5.9	8.7	46.2	6.9	1.4	5.4
April 1950	12.2	32.6	7.3	9.0	9.8	34.6	7.9	9.3	36.9	12.6	2.1	6.4
April 1960	9.4	39.5	9.7	10.3	7.4	41.6	10.3	10.6	27.7	20.0	3.5	7.9
March 1970	5.9	55.0	14.1	12.2	4.5	57.2	15.0	12.2	17.9	35.4	6.8	9.9
March 1980	3.6	69.2	20.9	12.6	2.7	71.0	22.1	12.6	10.3	55.3	11.9	12.2
March 1990	2.7	77.7	24.4	12.8	2.2	79.1	25.3	12.8	5.9	69.1	18.3	12.6
March 1991	2.7	78.5	24.3	12.8	2.2	79.8	25.4	12.8	6.0	70.1	17.8	12.6
March 1992	2.3	81.0	24.3	12.9	1.9	82.3	25.2	12.9	4.5	73.0	18.8	12.6
March 1993	2.2	81.8	24.8	12.9	1.8	83.0	25.7	13.0	4.7	74.9	19.0	12.7
March 1994	2.1	81.0	25.1	—	1.7	82.1	26.1	—	4.5	74.5	19.0	—
Females												
25 and over												
April 1940	12.4	26.3	3.8	8.7	9.8	28.1	4.0	8.8	37.5	8.4	1.2	6.1
April 1950	10.0	36.0	5.2	9.6	8.1	38.2	5.4	10.0	28.6	14.7	2.4	7.2
April 1960	7.4	42.5	5.8	10.7	6.0	44.7	6.0	11.0	19.7	23.1	3.6	8.5
March 1970	4.7	55.4	8.2	12.1	3.9	57.7	8.6	12.2	11.9	36.6	5.6	10.3
March 1980	3.2	68.1	13.6	12.4	2.5	70.1	14.0	12.5	7.6	54.1	10.4	12.1
March 1990	2.2	77.5	18.4	12.7	1.8	79.0	19.0	12.7	5.0	68.4	15.1	12.5
March 1991	2.1	78.3	18.8	12.7	1.8	79.9	19.3	12.7	4.1	69.1	15.8	12.5
March 1992	2.0	80.6	18.6	12.8	1.7	82.0	19.1	12.8	3.8	72.9	15.9	12.6
March 1993	2.0	81.3	19.2	12.8	1.7	82.5	19.7	12.8	3.5	74.5	16.5	12.7
March 1994	1.7	80.7	19.6	—	1.5	81.9	20.0	—	2.8	74.6	17.4	—

[1] Persons of Hispanic origin are included, as appropriate, in the "white" or in the "black and other races" category.

[2] Estimates based on retrojection, by the Bureau of the Census, of 1940 census data on education by age.

NOTE.—Data for 1975 and subsequent years are for the noninstitutional population.

SOURCE: U.S. Department of Commerce, Bureau of the Census, *U.S. Census of Population, 1960*, Vol. 1, part 1; *Current Population Reports*, Series P-20; Series P-19, No. 4; *1960 Census Monograph*, "Education of the American Population," by John K. Folger and Charles B. Nam; and unpublished data from the Current Population Survey; and U.S. Department of Labor, Bureau of Labor Statistics, Office of Employment and Unemployment Statistics, "Educational Attainment of Workers, March 1991," and unpublished data. (This table was prepared June 1995.)

Table 9.—Highest level of education attained by persons age 18 and over, by age, sex, and race/ethnicity: 1994

[In thousands]

Age, sex, and race	Total population [1]	Elementary level		High school			College					
		Less than 7 years	7 or 8 years	1 to 3 years	4 years	Graduate	Some college	Associate	Bachelor's	Master's	First-professional	Doctorate
1	2	3	4	5	6	7	8	9	10	11	12	13
Total												
18 and over	189,986	7,221	8,102	18,847	2,779	64,320	37,553	12,628	26,168	8,476	2,268	1,626
18 and 19 years old	6,916	77	80	2,129	562	1,991	2,049	22	5	2	—	—
20 to 24 years old	18,559	366	285	1,690	321	5,813	6,950	1,146	1,907	76	1	3
25 years old and over	164,512	6,778	7,737	15,028	1,896	56,515	28,554	11,460	24,256	8,398	2,267	1,623
25 to 29 years old	19,626	488	317	1,690	240	6,674	4,016	1,638	3,785	559	152	68
30 to 34 years old	22,320	499	360	1,837	290	7,809	4,321	1,940	3,842	960	258	205
35 to 39 years old	21,970	574	339	1,471	205	7,516	4,238	2,069	3,911	1,132	329	187
40 to 49 years old	36,119	1,058	807	2,238	257	11,602	6,847	2,971	6,282	2,847	742	468
50 to 59 years old	23,692	899	988	2,280	297	8,721	3,887	1,378	2,993	1,581	340	328
60 to 64 years old	10,005	632	696	1,258	149	3,685	1,430	429	1,020	458	126	121
65 years old and over	30,779	2,628	4,229	4,255	458	10,508	3,814	1,037	2,423	862	320	246
Men												
18 and over	91,222	3,729	3,820	8,761	1,524	29,437	17,867	5,477	13,387	4,378	1,677	1,164
18 and 19 years old	3,462	50	38	1,191	317	936	926	4	—	—	—	—
20 to 24 years old	9,221	217	150	774	212	3,097	3,376	494	876	25	—	—
25 years old and over	78,539	3,462	3,633	6,796	995	25,404	13,565	4,979	12,511	4,353	1,677	1,164
25 to 29 years old	9,765	297	164	902	151	3,387	1,962	707	1,793	268	95	37
30 to 34 years old	11,108	298	187	918	163	4,021	2,003	838	1,876	489	174	141
35 to 39 years old	10,892	278	160	783	109	3,751	1,962	897	2,002	592	231	128
40 to 49 years old	17,793	581	469	1,045	146	5,145	3,383	1,366	3,378	1,408	549	322
50 to 59 years old	11,452	488	507	965	175	3,795	1,848	622	1,655	897	260	240
60 to 64 years old	4,793	313	381	541	65	1,579	664	209	588	243	111	99
65 years old and over	12,736	1,207	1,764	1,642	186	3,726	1,742	340	1,219	456	257	197
Women												
18 and over	98,765	3,492	4,282	10,086	1,255	34,883	19,686	7,151	12,781	4,097	591	462
18 and 19 years old	3,454	27	42	937	245	1,056	1,123	18	5	2	—	—
20 to 24 years old	9,338	149	135	916	109	2,716	3,574	652	1,031	51	1	3
25 years old and over	85,973	3,315	4,104	8,233	902	31,111	14,989	6,481	11,745	4,045	590	458
25 to 29 years old	9,861	192	153	787	89	3,287	2,053	931	1,992	290	56	31
30 to 34 years old	11,212	201	173	919	128	3,788	2,318	1,102	1,965	471	84	64
35 to 39 years old	11,078	296	179	688	95	3,764	2,277	1,172	1,909	539	99	59
40 to 49 years old	18,326	477	338	1,193	111	6,457	3,464	1,604	2,904	1,439	193	146
50 to 59 years old	12,240	411	481	1,315	122	4,926	2,040	755	1,338	685	80	87
60 to 64 years old	5,212	319	315	717	84	2,106	766	220	433	215	15	23
65 years old and over	18,043	1,420	2,465	2,613	272	6,783	2,072	696	1,204	406	63	49
White, non-Hispanic												
18 and over	144,747	2,318	5,819	12,480	1,568	50,407	29,380	10,219	21,873	7,325	1,962	1,397
18 and 19 years old	4,733	16	43	1,292	323	1,463	1,579	15	1	2	—	—
20 to 24 years old	12,726	52	161	923	140	3,931	5,028	891	1,541	56	1	2
25 years old and over	127,288	2,250	5,615	10,264	1,105	45,013	22,773	9,313	20,331	7,267	1,961	1,395
25 to 29 years old	13,608	57	130	916	102	4,629	2,813	1,273	3,055	448	120	63
30 to 34 years old	16,143	77	169	1,093	128	5,693	3,162	1,497	3,179	762	213	170
35 to 39 years old	16,383	84	160	858	122	5,738	3,219	1,626	3,190	949	288	149
40 to 49 years old	27,810	206	433	1,339	125	8,942	5,509	2,481	5,227	2,511	644	392
50 to 59 years old	18,865	289	650	1,570	173	7,236	3,305	1,116	2,555	1,395	276	299
60 to 64 years old	8,208	238	557	938	87	3,244	1,243	369	896	410	123	103
65 years old and over	26,272	1,298	3,516	3,551	368	9,530	3,523	951	2,228	792	296	219
Black, non-Hispanic												
18 and over	21,404	941	887	3,322	633	7,679	4,204	1,255	1,862	492	69	59
18 and 19 years old	1,024	7	10	426	122	263	189	4	4	—	—	—
20 to 24 years old	2,573	16	8	293	93	970	887	125	174	7	—	—
25 years old and over	17,807	918	869	2,604	419	6,447	3,128	1,125	1,684	484	69	59
25 to 29 years old	2,579	22	10	321	56	1,093	555	171	308	32	11	1
30 to 34 years old	2,817	15	40	317	83	1,149	652	227	268	61	2	1
35 to 39 years old	2,648	34	42	315	35	998	549	271	319	66	9	9
40 to 49 years old	3,996	76	141	482	71	1,544	779	248	464	150	23	19
50 to 59 years old	2,337	113	140	421	85	820	313	143	182	100	13	6
60 to 64 years old	945	109	64	228	35	271	109	27	61	32	2	7
65 years old and over	2,483	550	431	520	54	572	171	37	81	44	10	14
Hispanic												
18 and over	17,097	3,551	1,209	2,596	474	4,537	2,666	735	925	241	104	60
18 and 19 years old	897	54	27	354	92	196	173	1	—	—	—	—
20 to 24 years old	2,485	294	107	429	68	753	665	90	71	5	—	1
25 years old and over	13,714	3,203	1,074	1,812	314	3,587	1,828	644	854	236	104	58
25 to 29 years old	2,609	388	166	403	80	763	460	139	174	26	7	3
30 to 34 years old	2,436	385	143	380	69	715	366	133	176	39	18	13
35 to 39 years old	2,021	416	127	249	36	545	308	111	165	45	17	4
40 to 49 years old	2,957	711	200	336	50	784	407	159	190	70	33	17
50 to 59 years old	1,682	456	163	232	27	429	176	61	84	34	15	5
60 to 64 years old	619	250	68	70	27	103	46	18	25	8	1	4
65 years old and over	1,390	598	208	143	25	247	65	22	41	15	13	12

[1] Civilian noninstitutional population.
—Data not applicable or not available.

NOTE.—Data are based on a sample survey of the noninstitutional population. Although cells with fewer than 75,000 people are subject to relatively wide sampling variation, they are included in the table to permit various types of aggregations. Because of rounding, details may not add to totals.

SOURCE: U.S. Department of Commerce, Bureau of the Census, Current Population Survey, unpublished data. (This table was prepared August 1995.)

Table 10.—Number of persons age 18 and over who hold a bachelor's or higher degree, by field of study, sex, race, and age: Spring 1990

[Numbers in thousands]

Field of study	Total	Sex		Race		Age					
		Men	Women	White[1]	Black[1]	18 to 24 years old	25 to 34 years old	35 to 44 years old	45 to 54 years old	55 to 64 years old	65 years old and over
1	2	3	4	5	6	7	8	9	10	11	12
Total population, 18 and over	182,591	87,240	95,350	156,385	20,401	25,145	43,245	37,708	25,489	21,228	29,776
Number of persons with bachelor's or higher degree	33,554	18,145	15,408	30,049	1,908	1,797	9,657	10,215	5,355	3,249	3,281
Percent of population	18.4	20.8	16.2	19.2	9.4	7.1	22.3	27.1	21.0	15.3	11.0
Agriculture and forestry	371	339	32	351	6	9	90	63	77	28	103
Biology	857	506	351	767	34	89	233	305	118	67	43
Business and management	6,189	4,313	1,876	5,531	368	384	2,148	1,697	1,005	500	454
Economics	691	467	224	581	40	76	206	114	127	84	83
Education	5,879	1,633	4,246	5,296	478	220	943	2,125	1,123	702	766
Engineering	3,090	2,821	269	2,635	154	159	1,104	702	466	340	321
English and journalism	1,369	360	1,009	1,306	40	58	367	434	181	124	204
Home economics	385	8	377	350	14	3	75	85	60	76	85
Law	1,004	797	207	948	15	14	260	320	191	123	96
Liberal arts and humanities	3,002	1,174	1,828	2,703	160	164	938	1,021	396	202	282
Mathematics and statistics	699	467	232	648	13	72	171	173	160	84	36
Medicine and dentistry	1,046	752	294	893	36	44	328	309	104	104	157
Nursing, pharmacy, and health technologies	1,913	353	1,560	1,717	83	111	661	602	249	156	134
Physical and earth sciences	856	631	225	781	35	33	239	283	147	82	73
Police science and law enforcement	238	183	55	201	25	9	53	94	37	33	12
Psychology	1,103	458	645	1,001	80	45	356	358	172	113	58
Religion and theology	488	413	75	452	24	14	85	165	72	103	47
Social sciences	1,960	1,034	926	1,769	125	121	527	666	300	178	169
Vocational and technical studies	179	157	22	155	19	12	69	27	37	26	9
Other fields	2,233	1,277	956	1,963	162	159	803	667	329	124	149
Percentage distribution of degree holders, by field											
Total	100.0	100.0	100.0	100.0	100.0	100.0	100.0	100.0	100.0	100.0	100.0
Agriculture and forestry	1.1	1.9	0.2	1.2	0.3	0.5	0.9	0.6	1.4	0.9	3.1
Biology	2.6	2.8	2.3	2.6	1.8	5.0	2.4	3.0	2.2	2.1	1.3
Business and management	18.4	23.8	12.2	18.4	19.3	21.4	22.2	16.6	18.8	15.4	13.8
Economics	2.1	2.6	1.5	1.9	2.1	4.2	2.1	1.1	2.4	2.6	2.5
Education	17.5	9.0	27.6	17.6	25.1	12.2	9.8	20.8	21.0	21.6	23.3
Engineering	9.2	15.5	1.7	8.8	8.1	8.8	11.4	6.9	8.7	10.5	9.8
English and journalism	4.1	2.0	6.5	4.3	2.1	3.2	3.8	4.2	3.4	3.8	6.2
Home economics	1.1	0.0	2.4	1.2	0.7	0.2	0.8	0.8	1.1	2.3	2.6
Law	3.0	4.4	1.3	3.2	0.8	0.8	2.7	3.1	3.6	3.8	2.9
Liberal arts and humanities	8.9	6.5	11.9	9.0	8.4	9.1	9.7	10.0	7.4	6.2	8.6
Mathematics and statistics	2.1	2.6	1.5	2.2	0.7	4.0	1.8	1.7	3.0	2.6	1.1
Medicine and dentistry	3.1	4.1	1.9	3.0	1.9	2.4	3.4	3.0	1.9	3.2	4.8
Nursing, pharmacy, and health technologies	5.7	1.9	10.1	5.7	4.4	6.2	6.8	5.9	4.6	4.8	4.1
Physical and earth sciences	2.6	3.5	1.5	2.6	1.8	1.8	2.5	2.8	2.7	2.5	2.2
Police science and law enforcement	0.7	1.0	0.4	0.7	1.3	0.5	0.5	0.9	0.7	1.0	0.4
Psychology	3.3	2.5	4.2	3.3	4.2	2.5	3.7	3.5	3.2	3.5	1.8
Religion and theology	1.5	2.3	0.5	1.5	1.3	0.8	0.9	1.6	1.3	3.2	1.4
Social sciences	5.8	5.7	6.0	5.9	6.6	6.7	5.5	6.5	5.6	5.5	5.2
Vocational and technical studies	0.5	0.9	0.1	0.5	1.0	0.7	0.7	0.3	0.7	0.8	0.3
Other fields	6.7	7.0	6.2	6.5	8.5	8.8	8.3	6.5	6.1	3.8	4.5

[1] Includes persons of Hispanic origin.

NOTE.—Data are based on a sample survey of the civilian noninstitutional population. Because of rounding, details may not add to totals.

SOURCE: U.S. Department of Commerce, Bureau of the Census, *Current Population Reports*, Series P-70, No. 32, "What's It Worth? Educational Background and Economic Status: Spring 1990." (This table was prepared February 1993.)

Table 11.—Educational attainment of persons 25 years old and over, by state: April 1990

State	Number of persons 25 years old and over	Distribution of population, by highest level of education attained						
		Less than 9th grade	9th to 12th grade, no diploma	High school graduate	Some college, no degree	Associate degree	Bachelor's degree	Graduate or professional degree
1	2	3	4	5	6	7	8	9
United States	158,868,436	10.4	14.4	30.0	18.7	6.2	13.1	7.2
Alabama	2,545,969	13.7	19.4	29.4	16.8	5.0	10.1	5.5
Alaska	323,429	5.1	8.2	28.7	27.6	7.2	15.0	8.0
Arizona	2,301,177	9.0	12.3	26.1	25.4	6.8	13.3	7.0
Arkansas	1,496,150	15.2	18.4	32.7	16.6	3.7	8.9	4.5
California	18,695,499	11.2	12.6	22.3	22.6	7.9	15.3	8.1
Colorado	2,107,072	5.6	10.0	26.5	24.0	6.9	18.0	9.0
Connecticut	2,198,963	8.4	12.4	29.5	15.9	6.6	16.2	11.0
Delaware	428,499	7.2	15.3	32.7	16.9	6.5	13.7	7.7
District of Columbia	409,131	9.6	17.3	21.2	15.6	3.1	16.1	17.2
Florida	8,887,168	9.5	16.1	30.1	19.4	6.6	12.0	6.3
Georgia	4,023,420	12.0	17.1	29.6	17.0	5.0	12.9	6.4
Hawaii	709,820	10.1	9.8	28.7	20.1	8.3	15.8	7.1
Idaho	601,292	7.4	12.9	30.4	24.2	7.5	12.4	5.3
Illinois	7,293,930	10.3	13.5	30.0	19.4	5.8	13.6	7.5
Indiana	3,489,470	8.5	15.8	38.2	16.6	5.3	9.2	6.4
Iowa	1,776,798	9.2	10.7	38.5	17.0	7.7	11.7	5.2
Kansas	1,565,936	7.7	11.0	32.8	21.9	5.4	14.1	7.0
Kentucky	2,333,833	19.0	16.4	31.8	15.2	4.1	8.1	5.5
Louisiana	2,536,994	14.7	17.0	31.7	17.2	3.3	10.5	5.6
Maine	795,613	8.8	12.4	37.1	16.1	6.9	12.7	6.1
Maryland	3,122,665	7.9	13.7	28.1	18.6	5.2	15.6	10.9
Massachusetts	3,962,223	8.0	12.0	29.7	15.8	7.2	16.6	10.6
Michigan	5,842,642	7.8	15.5	32.3	20.4	6.7	10.9	6.4
Minnesota	2,770,562	8.6	9.0	33.0	19.0	8.6	15.6	6.3
Mississippi	1,538,997	15.6	20.1	27.5	16.9	5.2	9.7	5.1
Missouri	3,291,579	11.6	14.5	33.1	18.4	4.5	11.7	6.1
Montana	507,851	8.1	10.9	33.5	22.1	5.6	14.1	5.7
Nebraska	996,049	8.0	10.2	34.7	21.1	7.1	13.1	5.9
Nevada	789,638	6.0	15.2	31.5	25.8	6.2	10.1	5.2
New Hampshire	713,894	6.7	11.2	31.7	18.0	8.1	16.4	7.9
New Jersey	5,166,233	9.4	13.9	31.1	15.5	5.2	16.0	8.8
New Mexico	922,590	11.4	13.5	28.7	20.9	5.0	12.1	8.3
New York	11,818,569	10.2	15.0	29.5	15.7	6.5	13.2	9.9
North Carolina	4,253,494	12.7	17.3	29.0	16.8	6.8	12.0	5.4
North Dakota	396,550	15.0	8.3	28.0	20.5	10.0	13.5	4.5
Ohio	6,924,764	7.9	16.4	36.3	17.0	5.3	11.1	5.9
Oklahoma	1,995,424	9.8	15.6	30.5	21.3	5.0	11.8	6.0
Oregon	1,855,369	6.2	12.3	28.9	25.0	6.9	13.6	7.0
Pennsylvania	7,872,932	9.4	15.9	38.6	12.9	5.2	11.3	6.6
Rhode Island	658,956	11.1	16.9	29.5	15.0	6.3	13.5	7.8
South Carolina	2,167,590	13.6	18.1	29.5	15.8	6.3	11.2	5.4
South Dakota	430,500	13.4	9.5	33.7	18.8	7.4	12.3	4.9
Tennessee	3,139,066	16.0	17.0	30.0	16.9	4.2	10.5	5.4
Texas	10,310,605	13.5	14.4	25.6	21.1	5.2	13.9	6.5
Utah	897,321	3.4	11.5	27.2	27.9	7.8	15.4	6.8
Vermont	357,245	8.7	10.6	34.6	14.7	7.2	15.4	8.9
Virginia	3,974,814	11.2	13.7	26.6	18.5	5.5	15.4	9.1
Washington	3,126,390	5.5	10.7	27.9	25.0	7.9	15.9	7.0
West Virginia	1,171,766	16.8	17.3	36.6	13.2	3.8	7.5	4.8
Wisconsin	3,094,226	9.5	11.9	37.1	16.7	7.1	12.1	5.6
Wyoming	277,769	5.7	11.2	33.2	24.2	6.9	13.1	5.7

SOURCE: U.S. Department of Commerce, Bureau of the Census, Decennial Census, Minority Economic Profiles, unpublished data. (This table was prepared June 1993.)

Table 12.—Educational attainment of persons 25 years old and over, by state and race/ethnicity: April 1990

State	Percent with high school diploma or higher						Percent with bachelor's degree or higher					
	Total	White [1]	Black [1]	Hispanic [2]	Asian/ Pacific Islander [1]	American Indian or Alaskan Native [1]	Total	White [1]	Black [1]	Hispanic [2]	Asian/ Pacific Islander [1]	American Indian or Alaskan Native [1]
1	2	3	4	5	6	7	8	9	10	11	12	13
United States	**75.2**	**77.9**	**63.1**	**49.8**	**77.5**	**65.5**	**20.3**	**21.5**	**11.4**	**9.2**	**36.6**	**9.3**
Alabama	66.9	70.3	54.6	73.8	78.9	64.9	15.7	17.3	9.3	20.1	43.7	11.6
Alaska	86.6	91.1	88.2	80.4	75.4	63.1	23.0	26.8	14.1	14.6	20.5	4.1
Arizona	78.7	82.4	75.1	51.7	80.2	52.1	20.3	22.2	14.3	6.9	37.5	4.6
Arkansas	66.3	68.6	51.5	59.1	66.4	65.4	13.3	14.1	8.4	11.1	24.6	9.8
California	76.2	81.1	75.6	45.0	77.2	71.4	23.4	25.4	14.8	7.1	34.1	11.1
Colorado	84.4	86.1	80.8	58.3	78.3	73.9	27.0	28.3	17.1	8.6	32.1	12.1
Connecticut	79.2	80.9	67.0	53.5	81.9	68.9	27.2	28.5	12.3	12.1	50.8	12.5
Delaware	77.5	80.3	63.2	60.1	86.1	62.0	21.4	23.0	10.6	16.5	55.9	10.2
District of Columbia	73.1	93.1	63.8	52.6	80.2	66.3	33.3	69.0	15.3	24.0	50.9	17.7
Florida	74.4	77.0	56.4	57.2	77.8	68.2	18.3	19.3	9.8	14.2	33.6	11.5
Georgia	70.9	74.9	58.6	66.2	77.5	71.6	19.3	21.8	11.0	20.5	38.6	12.5
Hawaii	80.1	89.3	94.2	73.9	74.7	84.4	22.9	30.2	15.2	10.3	19.4	17.7
Idaho	79.7	80.9	82.8	43.4	80.3	68.1	17.7	18.0	15.8	6.6	27.6	7.2
Illinois	76.2	79.1	65.2	45.0	83.9	71.4	21.0	22.4	11.4	8.0	49.8	13.4
Indiana	75.6	76.5	65.4	62.6	85.8	65.0	15.6	17.6	9.3	10.8	53.1	8.4
Iowa	80.1	80.3	70.1	64.2	76.4	67.6	16.9	16.7	12.8	13.7	47.3	9.7
Kansas	81.3	82.4	71.0	58.1	73.6	75.4	21.1	21.7	11.6	10.1	39.9	8.0
Kentucky	64.6	64.7	61.7	74.0	77.9	59.8	13.6	13.9	7.7	18.9	44.2	8.0
Louisiana	68.3	74.2	53.1	67.6	68.1	49.1	16.1	18.7	9.1	16.6	31.4	5.5
Maine	78.8	78.9	87.6	83.8	74.3	69.9	18.8	18.8	22.3	23.6	44.9	7.7
Maryland	78.4	80.8	70.6	70.3	84.8	73.4	26.5	28.9	16.1	25.2	50.3	19.7
Massachusetts	80.0	81.2	70.0	52.0	74.1	71.1	27.2	27.7	17.0	11.6	54.1	7.6
Michigan	76.8	78.6	64.9	60.9	83.3	67.8	21.8	21.9	17.5	17.2	33.5	7.7
Minnesota	82.4	82.8	76.2	71.1	69.7	68.2	14.7	17.2	8.8	17.1	35.1	8.1
Mississippi	64.3	71.7	47.3	67.7	68.2	57.4	17.8	18.3	11.2	18.0	47.3	11.0
Missouri	73.9	74.9	65.1	71.0	81.5	65.1	19.8	20.3	18.4	10.9	32.1	7.9
Montana	81.0	81.7	80.9	66.4	78.5	68.1	18.9	19.2	12.4	9.4	39.5	8.8
Nebraska	81.8	82.4	73.2	60.0	80.0	69.0	15.3	15.9	9.0	7.0	21.9	8.0
Nevada	78.8	80.9	70.8	53.7	74.1	69.8	24.4	24.2	25.7	25.5	26.1	16.0
New Hampshire	82.2	82.2	86.1	78.2	82.7	65.9	24.9	25.8	13.6	10.8	57.1	14.8
New Jersey	76.7	78.6	67.0	53.9	86.8	66.9	20.4	23.4	14.2	8.7	38.7	5.8
New Mexico	75.1	78.6	74.7	59.6	80.8	58.2	23.1	25.3	12.6	9.3	38.7	13.4
New York	76.7	78.5	64.7	50.4	72.4	65.2	17.4	19.3	9.5	17.9	39.3	7.9
North Carolina	70.0	73.1	58.1	71.0	77.9	51.5	18.1	18.3	17.1	15.9	37.8	8.3
North Dakota	76.7	76.9	95.9	75.2	83.7	64.3	17.0	17.6	9.1	14.2	53.2	8.3
Ohio	75.7	76.9	64.6	63.3	83.5	65.3	17.8	18.7	12.0	10.5	34.7	10.8
Oklahoma	74.6	75.7	70.1	55.9	76.1	68.1	20.6	20.8	9.1	10.1	32.3	8.3
Oregon	81.5	82.3	75.0	53.0	79.4	71.0	17.9	18.5	10.0	11.8	45.2	12.0
Pennsylvania	74.7	75.9	63.5	52.2	77.1	67.8	21.3	21.8	12.7	8.9	30.6	8.3
Rhode Island	72.0	73.0	65.9	46.8	59.6	64.5	16.6	19.8	7.6	19.8	34.4	10.9
South Carolina	68.3	73.6	53.3	71.8	77.4	62.5	17.2	17.6	24.1	13.4	33.1	6.8
South Dakota	77.1	77.8	82.2	71.3	74.3	62.5	16.0	16.7	10.2	21.9	42.6	10.5
Tennessee	67.1	68.2	59.4	71.5	79.3	63.1	20.3	22.6	12.0	7.3	41.3	13.9
Texas	72.1	76.2	66.1	44.6	79.1	70.9	22.3	22.7	15.9	9.1	29.4	6.4
Utah	85.1	86.2	77.0	61.0	80.7	59.3	24.3	24.2	30.5	28.2	52.1	11.1
Vermont	80.8	80.8	82.9	84.7	87.1	66.8	24.5	27.0	11.1	22.4	40.2	14.7
Virginia	75.2	78.3	60.3	70.5	82.1	70.7	22.9	23.3	15.4	11.0	30.2	9.1
Washington	83.8	85.0	81.2	56.7	77.3	72.3	12.3	12.2	10.9	17.6	63.3	6.5
West Virginia	66.0	66.0	64.7	70.3	88.8	57.9	17.7	18.1	8.3	10.0	40.4	5.5
Wisconsin	78.6	79.6	61.3	54.1	71.5	66.8	18.8	19.3	9.5	4.8	28.6	6.2
Wyoming	83.0	83.9	81.2	59.3	77.5	68.2						

[1] Includes persons of Hispanic origin.
[2] Persons of Hispanic origin may be of any race.

SOURCE: U.S. Department of Commerce, Bureau of the Census, Decennial Census, Minority Economic Profiles, unpublished data. (This table was prepared June 1993.)

Table 13.—Years of school completed by persons age 25 and over in the 15 largest states and the 15 largest metropolitan areas: March 1993

State	Percent completing—			Metropolitan area [1]	Percent completing—		
	Less than high school diploma	High school diploma	Bachelor's degree or more		Less than high school diploma	High school diploma	Bachelor's degree or more
1	2	3	4	1	2	3	4
United States [2]	19.8	80.2	21.9				
California	20.3	79.7	25.0	Atlanta, GA	15.9	84.1	31.3
Florida	20.4	79.6	19.8	Boston, MA	13.0	87.0	34.9
Georgia	25.3	74.7	21.1	Chicago, IL	21.4	78.6	25.0
Illinois	20.8	79.2	22.1	Cleveland, OH	14.0	86.0	21.9
Indiana	20.8	79.2	14.1	Dallas, TX	19.1	80.9	27.2
Massachusetts	15.4	84.6	30.0	Detroit, MI	18.3	81.7	22.1
Michigan	18.5	81.5	19.1	Houston, TX	16.7	83.3	30.7
Mississippi	28.3	71.7	17.5	Los Angeles/Anaheim/Riverside, CA	23.4	76.6	23.6
New Jersey	17.9	82.1	27.9	Miami, FL	24.6	75.4	21.2
New York	19.3	80.7	24.2	New York, NY	19.7	80.3	27.7
North Carolina	25.2	74.8	18.5	Philadelphia, PA/NJ	20.4	79.6	23.4
Ohio	17.2	82.8	19.5	Pittsburgh, PA	17.7	82.3	20.5
Pennsylvania	20.2	79.8	18.7	San Francisco, CA	16.0	86.3	33.0
Texas	22.7	77.3	22.1	St. Louis, MO	19.1	80.9	21.2
Virginia	19.3	80.7	25.8	Washington, DC/MD/VA	12.0	88.0	38.2

[1] Metropolitan Statistical Area.
[2] Includes data for all states and the District of Columbia.

SOURCE: U.S. Department of Commerce, Bureau of the Census, *Current Population Reports*, Series P-20, No. 476, *Educational Attainment in the United States: March 1993 and 1992*. (This table was prepared July 1995.)

Table 14.—Estimates of resident population, by age group: July 1, 1960 to July 1, 1994

[In thousands]

Year	Total, all ages	Total, 3 to 34 years	3 and 4 years	5 and 6 years	7 to 13 years	14 to 17 years	18 and 19 years	20 and 21 years	22 to 24 years	25 to 29 years	30 to 34 years
1	2	3	4	5	6	7	8	9	10	11	12
1960	179,979	90,722	8,063	7,811	25,155	11,211	4,886	4,443	6,425	10,823	11,905
1961	182,992	92,597	8,207	7,924	25,293	12,046	5,411	4,635	6,587	10,756	11,738
1962	185,771	94,396	8,190	8,108	25,790	12,751	5,617	4,943	6,710	10,740	11,547
1963	188,483	96,275	8,152	8,251	26,326	13,492	5,461	5,467	6,930	10,848	11,348
1964	191,141	98,281	8,206	8,233	27,011	14,264	5,429	5,685	7,258	11,051	11,144
1965	193,526	100,210	8,190	8,190	27,563	14,146	6,450	5,503	7,902	11,226	11,040
1966	195,576	101,993	8,031	8,251	28,032	14,398	7,183	5,417	8,198	11,521	10,962
1967	197,457	103,635	7,888	8,237	28,392	14,727	6,928	6,289	8,278	11,943	10,953
1968	199,399	105,363	7,645	8,074	28,732	15,170	6,988	6,972	8,082	12,624	11,076
1969	201,385	106,931	7,253	7,930	28,907	15,549	7,119	6,787	8,980	13,119	11,287
1970	203,984	108,653	6,962	7,703	28,969	15,921	7,410	6,850	9,728	13,604	11,505
1971	206,827	110,482	6,805	7,344	28,892	16,326	7,644	7,106	10,596	13,927	11,842
1972	209,284	112,287	6,789	7,051	28,628	16,637	7,854	7,447	10,418	15,142	12,321
1973	211,357	113,954	6,938	6,888	28,159	16,864	8,044	7,658	10,615	15,694	13,094
1974	213,342	115,641	7,117	6,864	27,599	17,033	8,196	7,893	10,864	16,428	13,644
1975	215,465	117,006	6,912	7,014	26,904	17,125	8,418	8,089	11,228	17,183	14,131
1976	217,563	118,073	6,437	7,194	26,321	17,117	8,604	8,240	11,554	18,177	14,428
1977	219,760	118,853	6,190	6,978	25,878	17,042	8,613	8,456	11,856	18,180	15,661
1978	222,095	119,414	6,208	6,499	25,593	16,944	8,617	8,628	12,120	18,585	16,218
1979	224,567	120,126	6,252	6,256	25,174	16,610	8,698	8,653	12,443	19,077	16,961
1980	227,225	121,132	6,366	6,291	24,800	16,143	8,718	8,669	12,716	19,686	17,743
1981	229,466	121,999	6,535	6,315	24,396	15,609	8,582	8,759	12,903	20,169	18,731
1982	231,664	121,823	6,658	6,407	24,121	15,057	8,480	8,768	12,914	20,704	18,714
1983	233,792	122,302	6,877	6,572	23,709	14,740	8,290	8,652	12,981	21,414	19,067
1984	235,825	122,254	7,045	6,694	23,367	14,725	7,932	8,567	12,962	21,459	19,503
1985	237,924	122,512	7,134	6,916	22,976	14,888	7,637	8,370	12,895	21,671	20,025
1986	240,133	122,688	7,187	7,086	22,992	14,824	7,483	8,024	12,720	21,893	20,479
1987	242,289	122,672	7,132	7,178	23,325	14,502	7,502	7,742	12,450	21,857	20,984
1988	244,499	122,713	7,176	7,238	23,791	14,023	7,701	7,606	12,048	21,739	21,391
1989	246,819	122,655	7,315	7,184	24,228	13,536	7,898	7,651	11,607	21,560	21,676
1990	249,402	122,627	7,355	7,240	24,756	13,310	7,693	7,883	11,251	21,232	21,907
1991	252,131	122,580	7,434	7,383	25,113	13,418	7,173	8,013	11,156	20,732	22,158
1992	255,028	122,622	7,591	7,429	25,579	13,653	6,889	7,756	11,295	20,179	22,251
1993	257,783	122,801	7,844	7,518	25,973	13,928	6,899	7,265	11,498	19,625	22,251
1994	260,341	122,931	8,022	7,676	26,188	14,427	6,937	6,972	11,354	19,177	22,177

NOTE.—Some data have been revised from previously published figures. Because of rounding, details may not add to totals.

SOURCE: U.S. Department of Commerce, Bureau of the Census, *Current Population Reports*, Series P-25, Nos. 519, 917, 1000, 1022, 1045, 1057, 1059, 1092, 1095, and

Current Population Reports, PPL-21: U.S. Population Estimates, by Age, Sex, Race, and Hispanic Origin: 1990–1994; and unpublished data. (This table was prepared June 1995.)

Table 15.—Estimates of school-age [1] resident population, by race and sex: July 1, 1960 to July 1, 1994

[In thousands]

Year	Total			White [2]			Black [2]			Other races [2]		
	Total	Male	Female	Total	Male	Female	Total	Male	Female	Total	Male	Female
1	2	3	4	5	6	7	8	9	10	11	12	13
1960	44,176	22,437	21,739	38,366	19,532	18,832	5,366	2,677	2,690	446	228	217
1961	45,263	22,995	22,269	39,220	19,975	19,246	5,575	2,782	2,792	469	238	232
1962	46,648	23,706	22,941	40,352	20,560	19,791	6,025	3,009	3,016	520	264	257
1963	48,070	24,438	23,633	41,524	21,164	20,361	6,272	3,135	3,137	545	275	270
1964	49,509	25,174	24,336	42,692	21,765	20,929				567	285	281
1965	49,900	25,377	24,522	42,891	21,872	21,019	6,440	3,220	3,221	594	300	295
1966	50,681	25,784	24,898	43,469	22,176	21,293	6,619	3,308	3,311	622	314	310
1967	51,357	26,135	25,224	43,969	22,438	21,529	6,768	3,383	3,384	649	325	323
1968	51,974	26,456	25,517	44,422	22,677	21,744	6,903	3,453	3,450	673	338	336
1969	52,386	26,675	25,711	44,697	22,826	21,871	7,016	3,511	3,505			
1970	52,593	26,793	25,801	44,783	22,877	21,906	7,108	3,561	3,547	703	355	349
1971	52,562	26,780	25,782	44,644	22,809	21,834	7,182	3,600	3,583	737	371	365
1972	52,316	26,658	25,658	44,336	22,655	21,681	7,211	3,615	3,596	768	388	380
1973	51,910	26,456	25,455	43,898	22,434	21,464	7,213	3,617	3,596	799	405	394
1974	51,498	26,249	25,249	43,454	22,210	21,244	7,213	3,618	3,596	830	420	409
1975	51,044	26,022	25,022	42,950	21,956	20,994	7,199	3,611	3,588	895	456	440
1976	50,633	25,822	24,811	42,477	21,721	20,755	7,208	3,617	3,591	948	483	465
1977	49,897	25,456	24,441	41,737	21,350	20,386	7,167	3,600	3,568	994	506	487
1978	49,038	25,024	24,013	40,883	20,919	19,964	7,116	3,576	3,540	1,039	530	509
1979	48,041	24,524	23,517	39,910	20,427	19,484	7,037	3,538	3,498	1,094	560	536
1980	47,232	24,135	23,097	39,002	19,982	19,020	6,989	3,520	3,469	1,241	633	608
1981	46,319	23,676	22,643	38,105	19,527	18,578	6,872	3,474	3,398	1,342	675	667
1982	45,585	23,309	22,276	37,365	19,153	18,212	6,826	3,442	3,384	1,394	714	680
1983	45,020	23,031	21,989	36,800	18,873	17,927	6,762	3,412	3,350	1,458	746	712
1984	44,788	22,920	21,868	36,509	18,731	17,778	6,743	3,404	3,339	1,536	785	751
1985	44,782	22,927	21,855	36,393	18,679	17,714	6,729	3,400	3,329	1,660	848	812
1986	44,903	22,996	21,907	36,408	18,701	17,707	6,802	3,438	3,364	1,693	857	836
1987	45,005	23,056	21,949	36,361	18,674	17,687	6,841	3,460	3,381	1,803	922	881
1988	45,051	23,086	21,965	36,279	18,637	17,642	6,881	3,482	3,399	1,891	967	924
1989	44,947	23,036	21,911	36,122	18,550	17,572	6,867	3,475	3,392	1,958	1,011	947
1990	45,306	23,224	22,082	36,320	18,667	17,653	6,916	3,501	3,415	2,070	1,056	1,014
1991	45,917	23,536	22,381	36,759	18,892	17,867	7,012	3,552	3,460	2,143	1,090	1,053
1992	46,662	23,918	22,744	37,288	19,162	18,126	7,147	3,624	3,523	2,226	1,133	1,093
1993	47,419	24,303	23,116	37,802	19,422	18,380	7,297	3,702	3,595	2,319	1,178	1,141
1994	48,291	24,751	23,539	38,406	19,732	18,674	7,474	3,794	3,680	2,411	1,226	1,185

[1] Includes persons 5 to 17 years of age.
[2] Includes persons of Hispanic origin.

NOTE.—Some data have been revised from previously published figures. Because of rounding, details may not add to totals.

SOURCE: U.S. Department of Commerce, Bureau of the Census, Current Population Reports, Series P-25, Nos. 519, 917, 1000, 1022, 1045, 1057, 1092, and Current Population Reports, PPL-21, U.S. Population Estimates, by Age, Sex, Race, and Hispanic Origin: 1990–1994; and unpublished data. (This table was prepared June 1995.)

Table 16.—Estimated total and school-age populations, by state:[1] 1970 to 1994

[In thousands]

State	1970[2] Total, all ages	1970[2] 5- to 17-year-olds	1980[2] Total, all ages	1980[2] 5- to 17-year-olds	1985[3] Total, all ages	1985[3] 5- to 17-year-olds	1990[2] Total, all ages	1990[2] 5- to 17-year-olds	1992[3] Total, all ages	1992[3] 5- to 17-year-olds	1993[3] Total, all ages	1993[3] 5- to 17-year-olds	1994[3] Total, all ages	1994[3] 5- to 17-year-olds
1	2	3	4	5	6	7	8	9	10	11	12	13	14	15
United States	203,302	52,540	226,546	47,407	237,924	44,782	248,710	45,166	255,028	46,662	257,783	47,419	260,341	48,291
Alabama	3,444	934	3,894	866	3,973	798	4,041	774	4,131	767	4,181	771	4,219	778
Alaska	303	88	402	92	532	112	550	117	587	128	598	132	606	136
Arizona	1,775	486	2,718	578	3,184	601	3,665	686	3,835	733	3,945	762	4,075	795
Arkansas	1,923	498	2,286	496	2,327	461	2,351	455	2,395	461	2,426	464	2,453	468
California	19,971	4,999	23,668	4,681	26,441	4,752	29,760	5,337	30,909	5,637	31,217	5,734	31,431	5,844
Colorado	2,210	589	2,890	592	3,209	599	3,294	607	3,463	658	3,564	677	3,656	700
Connecticut	3,032	768	3,108	638	3,201	549	3,287	520	3,279	534	3,278	545	3,275	557
Delaware	548	148	594	125	618	113	666	114	690	120	698	122	706	124
District of Columbia ..	757	164	638	109	635	88	607	80	586	75	579	75	570	76
Florida	6,791	1,609	9,746	1,789	11,351	1,792	12,938	2,011	13,510	2,167	13,726	2,230	13,953	2,300
Georgia	4,588	1,223	5,463	1,231	5,963	1,195	6,478	1,230	6,765	1,275	6,902	1,308	7,055	1,344
Hawaii	770	204	965	198	1,040	194	1,108	196	1,153	202	1,166	205	1,179	209
Idaho	713	200	944	213	994	223	1,007	228	1,066	240	1,100	245	1,133	252
Illinois	11,110	2,859	11,427	2,401	11,400	2,192	11,431	2,095	11,610	2,124	11,686	2,144	11,752	2,168
Indiana	5,195	1,386	5,490	1,200	5,459	1,087	5,544	1,056	5,652	1,050	5,706	1,056	5,752	1,066
Iowa	2,825	743	2,914	604	2,830	543	2,777	525	2,808	533	2,821	536	2,829	541
Kansas	2,249	573	2,364	468	2,427	452	2,478	472	2,518	490	2,535	497	2,554	506
Kentucky	3,221	844	3,661	800	3,695	745	3,685	703	3,753	701	3,794	705	3,827	709
Louisiana	3,645	1,041	4,206	969	4,408	937	4,220	890	4,273	892	4,290	893	4,315	898
Maine	994	260	1,125	243	1,163	222	1,228	223	1,237	225	1,240	226	1,240	228
Maryland	3,924	1,038	4,217	895	4,413	788	4,781	803	4,914	845	4,958	864	5,006	884
Massachusetts	5,689	1,407	5,737	1,153	5,881	989	6,016	940	5,999	955	6,018	978	6,041	1,001
Michigan	8,882	2,450	9,262	2,067	9,076	1,824	9,295	1,754	9,423	1,776	9,460	1,798	9,496	1,824
Minnesota	3,806	1,051	4,076	865	4,184	796	4,375	828	4,474	875	4,524	893	4,567	914
Mississippi	2,217	635	2,521	599	2,588	576	2,573	550	2,613	544	2,640	545	2,669	549
Missouri	4,678	1,183	4,917	1,008	5,000	941	5,117	944	5,193	970	5,235	984	5,278	1,003
Montana	694	197	787	167	822	167	799	163	823	171	841	174	856	179
Nebraska	1,485	389	1,570	324	1,585	305	1,578	309	1,604	317	1,613	321	1,623	326
Nevada	489	127	800	160	951	166	1,202	204	1,331	232	1,382	246	1,457	261
New Hampshire	738	189	921	196	997	182	1,109	194	1,114	201	1,124	206	1,137	212
New Jersey	7,171	1,797	7,365	1,528	7,566	1,340	7,730	1,265	7,813	1,298	7,859	1,326	7,904	1,352
New Mexico	1,017	311	1,303	303	1,438	304	1,515	320	1,581	336	1,616	347	1,654	358
New York	18,241	4,358	17,558	3,552	17,792	3,173	17,990	3,000	18,095	3,055	18,153	3,094	18,169	3,129
North Carolina	5,084	1,323	5,882	1,254	6,254	1,175	6,629	1,147	6,838	1,184	6,952	1,214	7,070	1,246
North Dakota	618	175	653	136	677	133	639	127	635	127	637	128	638	129
Ohio	10,657	2,820	10,798	2,307	10,735	2,090	10,847	2,012	11,005	2,033	11,061	2,048	11,102	2,070
Oklahoma	2,559	640	3,025	622	3,271	635	3,146	609	3,206	627	3,233	633	3,258	643
Oregon	2,092	534	2,633	525	2,673	504	2,842	521	2,975	556	3,035	564	3,086	574
Pennsylvania	11,801	2,925	11,864	2,376	11,771	2,079	11,882	1,996	11,990	2,040	12,030	2,067	12,052	2,099
Rhode Island	950	225	947	186	969	163	1,003	159	1,002	161	1,000	165	997	169
South Carolina	2,591	720	3,122	703	3,303	663	3,487	663	3,595	667	3,630	672	3,664	678
South Dakota	666	187	691	147	698	139	696	144	709	151	716	152	721	154
Tennessee	3,926	1,002	4,591	972	4,715	903	4,877	882	5,021	896	5,094	912	5,175	931
Texas	11,199	3,002	14,229	3,137	16,273	3,318	16,987	3,437	17,667	3,592	18,022	3,660	18,378	3,742
Utah	1,059	312	1,461	350	1,643	418	1,723	457	1,811	472	1,860	482	1,908	491
Vermont	445	118	511	109	530	100	563	102	571	104	576	106	580	108
Virginia	4,651	1,197	5,347	1,114	5,715	1,039	6,187	1,060	6,389	1,099	6,473	1,115	6,552	1,134
Washington	3,413	881	4,132	826	4,400	816	4,867	893	5,146	969	5,259	990	5,343	1,014
West Virginia	1,744	442	1,950	414	1,907	383	1,793	337	1,807	325	1,818	323	1,822	321
Wisconsin	4,418	1,203	4,706	1,011	4,748	908	4,892	927	4,997	970	5,044	981	5,082	997
Wyoming	332	92	470	101	500	108	454	101	464	103	470	103	476	104

[1] Includes Armed Forces residing in each state.
[2] As of April 1.
[3] Estimates as of July 1.

NOTE.—Some data have been revised from previously published figures. Because of rounding, details may not add to totals.

SOURCE: U.S. Department of Commerce, Bureau of the Census, *Current Population Reports*, Series P-25, No. 1095 at the national level, CPH-L-74 (1990 data); and forthcoming state level P-25 Reports. (This table was prepared June 1995.)

Table 17.—Families, by family status and presence of own children under 18: 1970 to 1993

Family status	1970	1980	1986	1987	1988	1989	1990	1991	1992	1993	Change, 1970 to 1980	Change, 1980 to 1993
1	2	3	4	5	6	7	8	9	10	11	12	13
	In thousands										Percent change	
All families	**51,456**	**59,550**	**63,558**	**64,491**	**65,133**	**65,837**	**66,090**	**66,322**	**67,173**	**68,144**	**15.7**	**14.4**
Married-couple family	44,728	49,112	50,933	51,537	51,809	52,100	52,317	52,147	52,457	53,171	9.8	8.3
No own children under 18	19,196	24,151	26,304	26,892	27,209	27,365	27,780	27,750	28,037	28,464	25.8	17.9
With own children under 18	25,532	24,961	24,630	24,645	24,600	24,735	24,537	24,397	24,420	24,707	–2.2	–1.0
One own child under 18	8,163	9,671	9,868	10,032	9,904	9,829	9,583	9,319	9,520	9,466	18.5	–2.1
Two own children under 18	8,045	9,488	9,580	9,606	9,576	9,870	9,784	9,721	9,728	10,007	17.9	5.5
Three or more own children under 18	9,325	5,802	5,182	5,006	5,120	5,035	5,170	5,357	5,173	5,234	–37.8	–9.8
Other family, male householder, no spouse present	1,228	1,733	2,414	2,510	2,715	2,847	2,884	2,907	3,025	3,026	41.1	74.6
No own children under 18	887	1,117	1,479	1,554	1,669	1,779	1,731	1,725	1,742	1,702	25.9	52.4
With own children under 18	341	616	935	955	1,047	1,068	1,153	1,181	1,283	1,324	80.6	114.9
One own child under 18	179	374	600	608	657	619	723	701	768	799	108.9	113.6
Two own children under 18	87	165	260	257	296	326	307	363	391	397	89.7	140.6
Three or more own children under 18	75	77	75	90	94	121	123	117	123	128	2.7	66.2
Other family, female householder, no spouse present	5,500	8,705	10,211	10,445	10,608	10,890	10,890	11,268	11,692	11,947	58.3	37.2
No own children under 18	2,642	3,261	4,106	4,147	4,335	4,371	4,290	4,445	4,648	4,721	23.4	44.8
With own children under 18	2,858	5,445	6,105	6,297	6,273	6,519	6,599	6,823	7,043	7,226	90.5	32.7
One own child under 18	1,008	2,398	2,857	3,079	3,017	3,164	3,225	3,283	3,327	3,425	137.9	42.8
Two own children under 18	810	1,817	2,061	2,072	2,039	2,095	2,173	2,203	2,244	2,400	124.3	32.1
Three or more own children under 18	1,040	1,230	1,186	1,147	1,217	1,260	1,202	1,335	1,472	1,400	18.3	13.8
	Percent of all families										Change in percentage points	
All families	**100.0**	**100.0**	**100.0**	**100.0**	**100.0**	**100.0**	**100.0**	**100.0**	**100.0**	**100.0**	**—**	**—**
Married-couple family	86.9	82.5	80.1	79.9	79.5	79.1	79.2	78.6	78.1	78.0	–4.5	–4.4
No own children under 18	37.3	40.6	41.4	41.7	41.8	41.6	42.0	41.8	41.7	41.8	3.3	1.2
With own children under 18	49.6	41.9	38.8	38.2	37.8	37.6	37.1	36.8	36.4	36.3	–7.7	–5.7
One own child under 18	15.9	16.2	15.5	15.6	15.2	14.9	14.5	14.1	14.2	13.9	0.4	–2.3
Two own children under 18	15.6	15.9	15.1	14.9	14.7	15.0	14.8	14.7	14.5	14.7	0.3	–1.2
Three or more own children under 18	18.1	9.7	8.2	7.8	7.9	7.6	7.8	8.1	7.7	7.7	–8.4	–2.1
Other family, male householder, no spouse present	2.4	2.9	3.8	3.9	4.2	4.3	4.4	4.4	4.5	4.4	0.5	1.5
No own children under 18	1.7	1.9	2.3	2.4	2.6	2.7	2.6	2.6	2.6	2.5	0.2	0.6
With own children under 18	0.7	1.0	1.5	1.5	1.6	1.6	1.7	1.8	1.9	1.9	0.4	0.9
One own child under 18	0.3	0.6	0.9	0.9	1.0	0.9	1.1	1.1	1.1	1.2	0.3	0.5
Two own children under 18	0.2	0.3	0.4	0.4	0.5	0.5	0.5	0.5	0.6	0.6	0.1	0.3
Three or more own children under 18	0.1	0.1	0.1	0.1	0.1	0.2	0.2	0.2	0.2	0.2	(¹)	0.1
Other family, female householder, no spouse present	10.7	14.6	16.1	16.2	16.3	16.5	16.5	17.0	17.4	17.5	3.9	2.9
No own children under 18	5.1	5.5	6.5	6.4	6.7	6.6	6.5	6.7	6.9	6.9	0.3	1.5
With own children under 18	5.6	9.1	9.6	9.8	9.6	9.9	10.0	10.3	10.5	10.6	3.6	1.5
One own child under 18	2.0	4.0	4.5	4.8	4.6	4.8	4.9	5.0	5.0	5.0	2.1	1.0
Two own children under 18	1.6	3.1	3.2	3.2	3.1	3.2	3.3	3.3	3.3	3.5	1.5	0.5
Three or more own children under 18	2.0	2.1	1.9	1.8	1.9	1.9	1.8	2.0	2.2	2.1	(¹)	–0.0

¹ Less than .05 percent.
—Not applicable.

NOTE.—Because of rounding, details may not add to totals.

SOURCE: U.S. Department of Commerce, Bureau of the Census, *Current Population Reports*, Series P-20, *Household and Family Characteristics*, various years; and unpublished data. (This table was prepared May 1995.)

Table 18.—Characteristics of families with own children under 18, by race/ethnicity [1] and family status: 1993

[Numbers in thousands]

Family characteristics	All races				White [2]				Black [2]				Hispanic origin [3]			
	Total	Married-couple families	Other families		Total	Married-couple families	Other families		Total	Married-couple families	Other families		Total	Married-couple families	Other families	
			Male householder, no spouse present	Female householder, no spouse present			Male householder, no spouse present	Female householder, no spouse present			Male householder, no spouse present	Female householder, no spouse present			Male householder, no spouse present	Female householder, no spouse present
1	2	3	4	5	6	7	8	9	10	11	12	13	14	15	16	17
Total families	**68,144**	**53,171**	**3,026**	**11,947**	**57,858**	**47,601**	**2,409**	**7,848**	**7,888**	**3,748**	**460**	**3,680**	**5,318**	**3,674**	**407**	**1,238**
Total families with own children under 18	33,257	24,707	1,324	7,226	27,335	21,686	1,098	4,552	4,560	1,945	182	2,434	3,345	2,355	160	830
Percent of all families	48.8	46.5	43.8	60.5	47.2	45.6	45.6	58.0	57.8	51.9	39.6	66.1	62.9	64.1	39.3	67.0
Percent distribution	100.0	74.3	4.0	21.7	100.0	79.3	4.0	16.7	100.0	42.7	4.0	53.4	100.0	70.4	4.8	24.8
Families with—																
1 child under 18	13,690	9,466	799	3,425	11,168	8,256	661	2,252	1,937	777	116	1,044	1,223	820	91	311
2 children under 18	12,804	10,007	397	2,400	10,869	8,941	334	1,594	1,452	669	46	737	1,155	832	46	278
3 children under 18	4,849	3,817	108	923	3,902	3,303	86	513	750	347	17	386	609	447	18	145
4 children under 18	1,340	1,023	14	303	1,010	856	13	142	261	110	1	150	239	167	4	68
5 children under 18	388	265	6	117	276	231	5	40	97	21	2	74	83	58	1	24
6 or more under 18	186	129	—	57	110	98	—	12	64	20	—	44	36	30	—	6
Total own children under 18	61,184	46,476	1,963	12,746	49,788	40,543	1,627	7,618	8,685	3,744	256	4,685	6,867	4,910	256	1,701
Average number of children under 18 per family with children	1.84	1.88	1.48	1.76	1.82	1.87	1.48	1.67	1.90	1.92	1.41	1.92	2.05	2.08	1.60	2.05
Total families with own children under 6	15,568	11,942	577	3,049	12,686	10,453	464	1,769	2,197	916	94	1,186	1,815	1,307	89	419
Percent of all families	22.8	22.5	19.1	25.5	21.9	22.0	19.3	22.5	27.9	24.4	20.4	32.2	34.1	35.6	21.9	33.8
Percent distribution	100.0	76.7	3.7	19.6	100.0	82.4	3.7	13.9	100.0	41.7	4.3	54.0	100.0	72.0	4.9	23.1
Families with—																
1 child under 6	10,554	8,050	439	2,064	8,659	7,033	357	1,269	1,408	616	69	723	1,202	871	63	268
2 children under 6	4,302	3,425	124	752	3,548	3,035	99	414	583	238	22	323	518	374	21	123
3 children under 6	643	424	13	206	450	360	8	82	167	46	3	118	85	54	5	27
4 or more under 6	69	43	—	27	30	25	—	4	39	16	—	22	10	9	—	1
Total own children under 6	21,019	16,222	722	4,075	17,097	14,194	583	2,320	2,928	1,193	111	1,624	2,565	1,840	126	599
Average number of children under 6 per family with children	1.35	1.36	1.25	1.34	1.35	1.36	1.26	1.31	1.33	1.30	1.18	1.37	1.41	1.41	1.42	1.43
Total families with own children under 3	9,140	7,168	324	1,647	7,470	6,299	252	919	1,281	534	60	686	1,090	798	54	238
Percent of all families	13.4	13.5	10.7	13.8	12.9	13.2	10.5	11.7	16.2	14.2	13.0	18.6	20.5	21.7	13.3	19.2
Percent distribution	100.0	78.4	3.5	18.0	100.0	84.3	3.4	12.3	99.9	41.7	4.7	53.6	100.0	73.2	5.0	21.8
Families with—																
1 child under 3	7,933	6,278	287	1,368	6,558	5,529	225	803	1,032	453	54	525	927	680	44	204
2 or more under 3	1,207	890	37	279	912	770	27	115	249	81	6	162	162	118	10	34
Total own children under 3	10,456	8,213	373	1,871	8,537	7,214	295	1,028	1,444	587	60	796	1,306	957	70	279
Average number of children under 3 per family with children	1.14	1.15	1.15	1.14	1.14	1.15	1.17	1.12	1.13	1.10	—	1.16	1.20	1.20	—	1.17

[1] Race of family is defined as race of head of household.
[2] Includes persons of Hispanic origin.
[3] Persons of Hispanic origin may be of any race.
—Data not available.

NOTE.—Averages and percents only are shown when the base is 75,000 or greater. Even though the standard errors are large, smaller estimated numbers are shown to permit users to combine categories in various ways. Because of rounding, details may not add to totals.

SOURCE: U.S. Department of Commerce, Bureau of the Census, Current Population Reports, Series P-20, no. 477, Household and Family Characteristics: March 1993. (This table was prepared June 1995.)

Table 19.—Household income and poverty rates, by state: 1990 and 1993

| State | Median household income [1] | | Percent of persons below the poverty level | | | | | | | | | | Poverty status of 5- to 17-year-olds, 1993 | | | |
| | | | 1990 [2] | | | | | | | | 1993 | | Number in poverty | | Percent in poverty | |
	1990 [2]	1993	Total	Under 5 years	5 years	6 to 11 years	12 to 17 years	18 to 64 years	65 to 74 years	75 years and over	Total	Standard error	Number (in thousands)	Standard error	Percent	Standard error
1	2	3	4	5	6	7	8	9	10	11	12	13	14	15	16	17
United States	$35,025	$31,241	13.1	20.1	19.7	18.3	16.3	11.0	10.4	16.5	15.1	0.22	10,150	253	20.8	0.20
Alabama	27,498	25,082	18.3	26.1	25.8	24.3	22.3	14.6	19.2	31.1	17.4	1.94	156	34	20.5	1.72
Alaska	48,254	42,931	9.0	13.6	10.6	10.9	9.8	7.9	6.4	10.6	9.1	1.34	11	3	9.5	1.14
Arizona	32,093	30,510	15.7	24.9	24.2	21.8	19.1	14.0	9.3	13.2	15.4	1.81	163	33	23.1	1.76
Arkansas	24,643	23,039	19.1	28.5	26.6	25.2	22.7	15.3	18.0	29.9	20.0	2.04	117	22	25.4	1.84
California	41,716	34,073	12.5	19.0	19.3	18.3	17.1	10.9	6.5	9.5	18.2	0.74	1,623	112	25.7	0.70
Colorado	35,123	34,488	11.7	17.9	16.5	15.3	12.5	10.3	8.5	15.1	9.9	1.59	70	22	11.3	1.40
Connecticut	48,618	39,516	6.8	11.7	11.9	11.2	8.9	5.3	5.6	9.7	8.5	1.65	82	25	14.9	1.75
Delaware	40,641	36,064	8.7	13.3	12.7	11.8	10.8	7.2	8.2	13.5	10.2	1.68	17	5	13.7	1.58
District of Columbia ...	35,807	27,304	16.9	27.0	25.5	25.5	20.4	14.3	15.5	19.7	26.4	2.67	44	8	49.3	2.52
Florida	32,027	28,550	12.7	20.3	20.1	18.8	16.8	11.0	9.0	13.5	17.8	0.94	666	61	26.9	0.91
Georgia	33,819	31,663	14.7	22.1	21.3	20.1	18.1	11.4	16.5	26.7	13.5	1.70	207	48	17.5	1.57
Hawaii	45,248	42,662	8.3	12.6	12.6	11.2	10.8	6.9	6.7	10.4	8.0	1.47	26	8	13.4	1.54
Idaho	29,433	31,010	13.3	19.6	18.9	15.9	13.3	12.0	8.7	15.6	13.1	1.57	38	8	14.2	1.35
Illinois	37,854	32,857	11.9	18.9	18.7	17.0	15.0	10.0	8.9	13.4	13.6	0.94	406	49	18.2	0.88
Indiana	33,558	29,475	10.7	16.8	15.8	14.1	11.8	9.1	8.7	14.0	12.2	1.74	123	37	10.8	1.37
Iowa	30,565	28,663	11.5	17.5	15.4	14.1	11.7	10.3	8.1	15.3	10.3	1.54	61	17	11.1	1.32
Kansas	31,803	29,770	11.5	16.8	16.5	14.1	11.6	10.1	8.5	16.8	13.1	1.69	79	18	16.0	1.53
Kentucky	26,259	24,376	19.0	27.9	26.5	24.6	22.4	16.2	17.5	25.3	20.4	2.09	177	34	25.7	1.89
Louisiana	25,578	26,312	23.6	33.4	33.0	31.1	29.7	19.6	20.5	30.1	26.4	2.37	376	54	39.4	2.18
Maine	32,459	27,438	10.8	15.7	15.9	14.0	11.5	8.9	11.0	18.3	15.4	1.89	47	10	17.7	1.66
Maryland	45,897	39,939	8.3	11.9	11.9	11.5	10.2	6.8	8.8	13.6	9.7	1.61	100	31	13.4	1.53
Massachusetts	43,061	37,064	8.9	14.5	14.8	13.8	11.0	7.3	7.3	12.6	10.7	0.86	159	22	16.4	0.86
Michigan	36,148	32,662	13.1	22.1	20.4	18.1	15.7	11.2	8.7	14.3	15.4	0.97	446	45	24.3	0.96
Minnesota	36,019	33,682	10.2	14.8	14.6	12.5	10.6	8.8	8.4	17.2	11.6	1.71	95	28	12.3	1.46
Mississippi	23,465	22,191	25.2	35.8	35.1	33.5	31.9	20.0	24.0	37.1	24.7	2.12	178	27	31.1	1.90
Missouri	30,720	28,682	13.3	20.4	19.2	17.8	15.1	11.1	11.3	19.7	16.1	1.97	205	45	20.4	1.80
Montana	26,788	26,470	16.1	24.3	23.0	20.3	17.1	14.7	9.9	16.6	14.9	1.77	25	6	14.5	1.45
Nebraska	30,317	31,008	11.1	17.3	15.4	13.4	10.8	9.7	8.6	16.8	10.3	1.48	47	11	13.5	1.38
Nevada	36,138	35,814	10.2	15.1	14.4	12.6	11.9	9.1	8.4	12.3	9.8	1.44	35	9	13.9	1.40
New Hampshire	42,335	37,964	6.4	8.5	8.7	7.3	6.2	5.4	7.7	13.9	9.9	1.76	28	9	13.8	1.69
New Jersey	47,693	40,500	7.6	11.7	12.6	11.7	10.4	6.0	6.8	11.3	10.9	0.84	227	30	16.4	0.83
New Mexico	28,069	26,758	20.6	30.3	30.6	27.6	25.2	17.8	13.7	21.2	17.4	1.86	68	13	18.8	1.59
New York	38,415	31,697	13.0	20.6	21.2	19.6	17.0	11.0	10.0	14.7	16.4	0.76	773	62	24.6	0.73
North Carolina	31,052	28,820	13.0	19.2	18.5	17.2	15.3	10.1	15.7	25.9	14.4	0.92	196	25	17.8	0.84
North Dakota	27,051	28,118	14.4	19.6	18.4	17.2	14.7	13.0	10.8	19.5	11.2	1.55	12	4	9.9	1.22
Ohio	33,452	31,285	12.5	21.1	19.9	17.8	14.6	10.7	8.7	13.8	13.0	0.89	420	47	18.8	0.66
Oklahoma	27,475	26,260	16.7	25.3	24.3	21.7	18.5	14.2	13.5	24.1	19.9	2.00	168	30	23.5	1.77
Oregon	31,755	33,138	12.4	19.7	16.1	14.8	13.3	11.5	8.1	13.1	11.8	1.75	84	23	14.9	1.60
Pennsylvania	33,875	30,995	11.1	17.5	17.0	15.7	13.8	9.5	8.7	13.5	13.2	0.90	390	47	17.8	0.85
Rhode Island	37,501	33,509	9.6	16.3	16.1	13.8	11.0	7.6	8.9	15.6	11.2	1.84	33	9	20.3	1.96
South Carolina	30,597	26,053	15.4	22.8	21.8	21.2	19.1	12.0	17.3	26.5	18.7	1.79	177	30	26.7	1.70
South Dakota	26,223	27,737	15.9	23.6	22.2	20.2	17.3	13.6	11.1	21.3	14.2	1.61	27	5	16.6	1.42
Tennessee	28,908	25,102	15.7	23.9	22.5	20.8	18.5	12.5	17.2	26.7	19.6	1.94	299	49	30.5	1.87
Texas	31,482	28,727	18.1	25.6	25.5	24.2	23.0	15.2	14.9	23.8	17.4	0.97	851	82	22.9	0.90
Utah	34,342	35,786	11.4	15.8	14.4	12.0	10.0	11.0	6.4	12.5	10.7	1.48	75	15	15.1	1.43
Vermont	34,717	31,065	9.9	13.5	13.7	12.5	9.8	8.5	9.7	16.3	10.0	1.70	15	4	14.2	1.65
Virginia	38,838	36,433	10.2	14.5	14.5	13.5	11.9	8.4	11.6	18.5	9.7	1.34	137	35	11.6	1.20
Washington	36,338	35,655	10.9	17.0	16.4	14.3	12.2	9.8	7.0	12.4	12.1	1.63	121	33	12.3	1.36
West Virginia	24,233	22,421	19.7	31.7	30.3	25.9	22.4	17.7	14.1	20.8	22.2	2.17	104	18	31.4	2.02
Wisconsin	34,309	31,766	10.7	17.7	16.4	15.0	11.9	9.2	6.6	12.6	12.6	1.60	155	35	15.0	1.47
Wyoming	31,576	29,442	11.9	18.3	16.2	14.1	11.2	10.5	10.8	14.3	13.3	2.02	12	4	11.4	1.58

[1] In 1993 dollars adjusted by the Consumer Price Index for all urban consumers.
[2] Based on 1989 incomes collected in the 1990 Census. May differ from data derived from the Current Population Survey.

SOURCE: U.S. Department of Commerce, Bureau of the Census, *Decennial Census, Minority Economic Profiles*, unpublished data; and *Current Population Reports*, Series P– 60, no. 185, *Poverty in the United States, 1992; Current Population Reports*, Series P– 60, no. 180, *Money Income of Households, Families, and Persons in the United States: 1991*; and *Current Population Reports*, Series P–60, no. 188, *Income, Poverty, and Valuation of Noncash Benefits: 1993*. (This table was prepared May 1995.)

Table 20.—Poverty status of persons, families, and children under 18, by race/ethnicity: 1959 to 1993

Year and race/ ethnicity	Number below the poverty level, in thousands						Percent below the poverty level					
	All persons	In all families			In families with female householder, no husband present		All persons	In all families			In families with female householder, no husband present	
		Total	House-holder	Related children under 18	Total	Related children under 18		Total	House-holder	Related children under 18	Total	Related children under 18
1	2	3	4	5	6	7	8	9	10	11	12	13
All races												
1959	39,490	34,562	8,320	17,208	7,014	4,145	22.4	20.8	18.5	26.9	49.4	72.2
1960	39,851	34,925	8,243	17,288	7,247	4,095	22.2	20.7	18.1	26.5	48.9	68.4
1965	33,185	28,358	6,721	14,388	7,524	4,562	17.3	15.8	13.9	20.7	46.0	64.2
1970	25,420	20,330	5,260	10,235	7,503	4,689	12.6	10.9	10.1	14.9	38.1	53.0
1971	25,559	20,405	5,303	10,344	7,797	4,850	12.5	10.8	10.0	15.1	38.7	53.1
1972	24,460	19,577	5,075	10,082	8,114	5,094	11.9	10.3	9.3	14.9	38.2	53.1
1973	22,973	18,299	4,828	9,453	8,178	5,171	11.1	9.7	8.8	14.2	37.5	52.1
1974	23,370	18,817	4,922	9,967	8,462	5,361	11.2	9.9	8.8	15.1	36.5	51.5
1975	25,877	20,789	5,450	10,882	8,846	5,597	12.3	10.9	9.7	16.8	37.5	52.7
1976	24,975	19,632	5,311	10,081	9,029	5,583	11.8	10.3	9.4	15.8	37.3	52.0
1977	24,720	19,505	5,311	10,028	9,205	5,658	11.6	10.2	9.3	16.0	36.2	50.3
1978	24,497	19,062	5,280	9,722	9,269	5,687	11.4	10.0	9.1	15.7	35.6	50.6
1979	26,072	19,964	5,461	9,993	9,400	5,635	11.7	10.2	9.2	16.0	34.9	48.6
1980	29,272	22,601	6,217	11,114	10,120	5,866	13.0	11.5	10.3	17.9	36.7	50.8
1981	31,822	24,850	6,851	12,068	11,051	6,305	14.0	12.5	11.2	19.5	38.7	52.3
1982	34,398	27,349	7,512	13,139	11,701	6,696	15.0	13.6	12.2	21.3	40.6	56.0
1983	35,303	27,933	7,647	13,427	12,072	6,747	15.2	13.9	12.3	21.8	40.2	55.4
1984	33,700	26,458	7,277	12,929	11,831	6,772	14.4	13.1	11.6	21.0	38.4	54.0
1985	33,064	25,729	7,223	12,483	11,600	6,716	14.0	12.6	11.4	20.1	37.6	53.6
1986	32,370	24,754	7,023	12,257	11,944	6,943	13.6	12.0	10.9	19.8	38.3	54.4
1987	32,221	24,725	7,005	12,275	12,148	7,074	13.4	12.0	10.7	19.7	38.1	54.7
1988	31,745	24,048	6,876	11,995	11,972	6,742	13.0	11.6	10.4	19.0	37.2	50.6
1989	31,528	24,066	6,784	12,001	11,668	6,808	12.8	11.5	10.3	19.0	35.9	51.1
1990	33,585	25,232	7,098	12,715	12,578	7,363	13.5	12.0	10.7	19.9	37.2	53.4
1991	35,708	27,143	7,712	13,658	13,824	8,065	14.2	12.8	11.5	21.1	39.7	55.5
1992	36,880	27,947	7,960	13,876	13,716	8,032	14.8	13.3	11.7	21.1	39.0	54.3
1993	39,265	29,927	8,393	14,961	14,636	8,503	15.1	13.6	12.3	22.0	38.7	53.7
White [1]												
1960	28,309	24,262	6,115	11,229	4,296	2,357	17.8	16.2	14.9	20.0	39.0	59.9
1965	22,496	18,508	4,824	8,595	4,092	2,321	13.3	11.7	11.1	14.4	35.4	52.9
1970	17,484	13,323	3,708	6,138	3,761	2,247	9.9	8.1	8.0	10.5	28.4	43.1
1975	17,770	13,799	3,838	6,748	4,577	2,813	9.7	8.3	7.7	12.5	29.4	44.2
1980	19,699	14,587	4,195	6,817	4,940	2,813	10.2	8.6	8.0	13.4	28.0	41.6
1985	22,860	17,125	4,983	7,838	5,990	3,372	11.4	9.9	9.1	15.6	29.8	45.2
1987	21,195	15,593	4,567	7,398	5,989	3,474	10.4	8.9	8.1	14.7	29.6	45.8
1988	20,715	15,001	4,471	7,095	5,950	3,385	10.1	8.6	7.9	14.0	29.2	43.0
1989	20,785	15,179	4,409	7,164	5,723	3,320	10.0	8.6	7.8	14.1	28.1	42.8
1990	22,326	15,916	4,622	7,696	6,210	3,597	10.7	9.0	8.1	15.1	29.8	45.9
1991	23,747	17,268	5,022	8,316	6,806	3,941	11.3	9.7	8.8	16.1	31.5	47.1
1992	25,259	18,294	5,160	8,333	6,907	3,783	11.9	10.1	8.9	16.0	30.8	45.3
1993	26,226	18,968	5,452	9,123	7,199	4,102	12.2	10.5	9.4	17.0	31.0	45.6
Black [1]												
1959	9,927	9,112	1,860	5,022	2,416	1,475	55.1	54.9	48.1	65.5	70.6	81.6
1966	8,867	8,090	1,620	4,774	3,160	2,107	41.8	40.9	35.5	50.6	65.3	76.6
1970	7,548	6,683	1,481	3,922	3,656	2,383	33.5	32.2	29.5	41.5	58.7	67.7
1975	7,545	6,533	1,513	3,884	4,168	2,724	31.3	30.1	27.1	41.4	54.3	66.0
1980	8,579	7,190	1,826	3,906	4,984	2,944	32.5	31.1	28.9	42.1	53.4	64.8
1985	8,926	7,504	1,983	4,057	5,342	3,181	31.3	30.5	28.7	43.1	53.2	66.9
1987	9,520	7,848	2,117	4,234	5,789	3,394	32.4	31.2	29.4	44.4	54.1	68.3
1988	9,356	7,650	2,090	4,148	5,601	3,130	31.3	30.0	28.2	42.8	51.9	61.8
1989	9,302	7,704	2,077	4,257	5,530	3,256	30.7	29.7	27.8	43.2	49.4	62.9
1990	9,837	8,160	2,193	4,412	6,005	3,543	31.9	31.0	29.3	44.2	50.6	64.7
1991	10,242	8,504	2,343	4,637	6,557	3,853	32.7	32.0	30.4	45.6	54.8	68.2
1992	10,827	9,134	2,435	4,850	6,799	3,967	33.4	32.9	30.9	46.3	54.0	67.1
1993	10,877	9,242	2,499	5,030	6,955	4,104	33.1	32.9	31.3	45.9	53.0	65.9
Hispanic origin [2]												
1975	2,991	2,755	627	1,619	1,053	694	26.9	26.3	25.1	33.1	57.2	68.4
1980	3,491	3,143	751	1,718	1,319	809	25.7	25.1	23.2	33.0	54.5	65.0
1985	5,236	4,605	1,074	2,512	1,983	1,247	29.0	28.3	25.5	39.6	55.7	72.4
1987	5,422	4,761	1,168	2,606	2,045	1,241	28.0	27.5	25.5	38.9	55.6	70.1
1988	5,357	4,700	1,141	2,576	2,052	1,208	26.7	26.0	23.7	37.3	55.0	65.5
1989	5,430	4,659	1,133	2,496	1,902	1,163	26.2	25.2	23.4	35.5	50.6	65.0
1990	6,006	5,091	1,244	2,750	2,115	1,314	28.1	26.9	25.0	37.7	53.0	68.4
1991	6,339	5,541	1,372	2,977	2,282	1,398	28.7	28.2	26.5	39.8	52.7	68.6
1992	7,592	6,455	1,395	2,946	2,474	1,289	29.6	28.4	26.2	38.8	51.5	65.7
1993	8,126	6,876	1,625	3,666	2,837	1,673	30.6	29.3	27.3	39.9	53.2	66.1

[1] Includes persons of Hispanic origin.
[2] Persons of Hispanic origin may be of any race.

SOURCE: U.S. Department of Commerce, Bureau of the Census, *Current Population Reports*, Series P-60, no. 185, *Poverty in the United States, 1992;* and *Current Population Reports*, Series P-60, no. 188, *Income, Poverty, and Valuation of Noncash Benefits: 1993.* (This table was prepared May 1995.)

Table 21.—Average grade that the public would give the schools in their community and in the nation at large: 1974 to 1994

Year	All adults			No children in school			Public school parents			Private school parents		
	Nation	Local community	Local neighborhood	Nation	Local community	Local neighborhood	Nation	Local community	Local neighborhood	Nation	Local community	Local neighborhood
1	2	3	4	5	6	7	8	9	10	11	12	13
1974	—	2.63	—	—	2.57	—	—	2.80	—	—	2.15	—
1975	—	2.38	—	—	2.31	—	—	2.49	—	—	1.81	—
1976	—	2.38	—	—	2.34	—	—	2.48	—	—	2.22	—
1977	—	2.33	—	—	2.25	—	—	2.59	—	—	2.05	—
1978	—	2.21	—	—	2.11	—	—	2.47	—	—	1.69	—
1979	—	2.21	—	—	2.15	—	—	2.38	—	—	1.88	—
1980	—	2.26	—	—	—	—	—	—	—	—	—	—
1981	1.94	2.20	—	—	2.12	—	—	2.36	—	—	1.88	—
1982	2.01	2.24	—	2.04	2.18	—	2.01	2.35	—	2.02	2.20	—
1983	1.91	2.12	—	1.92	2.10	—	1.92	2.31	—	1.82	1.89	—
1984	2.09	2.36	—	2.11	2.30	—	2.11	2.49	—	2.04	2.17	—
1985	2.14	2.39	—	2.16	2.36	—	2.20	2.44	—	1.93	2.00	—
1986	2.13	2.36	—	—	2.29	—	—	2.55	—	—	2.14	—
1987	2.18	2.44	—	2.20	2.38	—	2.22	2.61	—	2.03	2.01	—
1988	2.08	2.35	—	2.02	2.32	—	2.13	2.48	—	2.00	2.13	—
1989	2.01	2.35	—	1.99	2.27	—	2.06	2.56	—	1.93	2.12	—
1990	1.99	2.29	—	1.98	2.27	—	2.03	2.44	—	1.85	2.09	—
1991	2.00	2.36	—	—	—	—	1.94	2.73	—	1.85	—	—
1992	1.93	2.30	—	1.92	2.40	—	1.97	2.48	—	1.80	2.11	—
1993	1.95	2.41	—	1.97	2.16	—	1.90	2.55	—	1.86	1.90	—
1994	1.95	2.26	2.43	1.95	2.16	2.34	1.90	2.55	2.64	1.86	1.90	2.23

—Data not available.

NOTE.—Average based on a scale where A=4, B=3, C=2, D=1, and F=0.

SOURCE: "The Annual Gallup Poll of the Public's Attitudes Toward the Public Schools," *Phi Delta Kappan,* various years. (This table was prepared April 1995.)

Table 22.—Items most frequently cited by the general public as a major problem facing the local public schools: 1970 to 1994

Problems	Percent																
	1970	1975	1980	1981	1982	1983	1984	1985	1986	1987	1988	1989	1990	1991	1992	1993	1994
1	2	3	4	5	6	7	8	9	10	11	12	13	14	15	16	17	18
Lack of discipline	18	23	26	23	27	25	27	25	24	22	19	19	19	20	17	15	18
Fighting/violence/gangs	—	—	—	—	—	—	—	—	—	—	—	—	—	—	9	13	18
Lack of financial support	17	14	10	12	22	13	14	9	11	14	12	13	13	18	22	21	13
Use of drugs	11	9	14	15	20	18	18	18	28	30	32	34	38	22	22	16	11
Standards/quality of education	—	—	—	—	—	—	—	—	—	—	—	—	—	—	—	—	8
Large schools/overcrowding	—	10	7	5	4	3	4	5	5	8	6	8	7	9	9	8	7
Lack of family structure/ problems of home life	—	—	—	—	—	—	—	—	—	—	—	—	—	—	—	—	5
Crime/vandalism	—	—	—	—	—	—	—	—	—	—	—	—	—	—	—	—	4
Getting good teachers	12	11	6	11	10	8	14	10	6	9	11	7	7	11	5	5	3
Parents' lack of interest	3	2	6	5	5	6	5	3	4	6	7	6	4	7	5	4	3
Poor curriculum/standards	6	5	11	14	11	14	15	11	8	8	11	8	8	10	9	9	3
Pupils' lack of interest/truancy	—	3	5	4	5	5	4	5	3	6	5	3	6	5	3	4	3
Integration/busing	17	15	10	11	6	5	6	4	3	4	4	4	5	5	4	—	3
Lack of respect	—	—	—	1	2	4	1	2	5	7	6	3	3	3	4	3	—
Moral standards	—	—	—	—	—	—	4	2	3	5	4	4	6	4	3	3	—
Low teacher pay	—	—	6	4	7	8	5	4	4	5	3	4	4	2	2	—	—
Teachers' lack of interest	—	—	2	2	3	3	4	3	5	6	5	4	4	2	2	—	—
Drinking/alcoholism	—	—	—	—	—	—	—	—	—	—	—	—	—	—	—	—	—
Lack of proper facilities	11	3	2	2	2	1	2	1	1	2	1	1	2	—	—	—	—

—Data not available.

SOURCE: "The Annual Gallup Poll of the Public's Attitudes Toward the Public Schools," *Phi Delta Kappan,* various years. (This table was prepared April 1995.)

Table 23.—Public opinion of some education programs currently being advanced by the Goals 2000: Educate America Act, 1994

Goals 2000 initiatives	Percent who favor initiatives			
	National totals	No children in school	Public school parents	Nonpublic school parents
1	2	3	4	5
Assistance with high school students' college expenses in return for performing some kind of public service	81	80	83	83
Greater emphasis on, including additional money for, work-study vocational programs for high school students who do not plan to go to college	79	78	82	74
A large increase in funds for early childhood education in those public schools with the highest percentage of children living in poverty	74	74	75	66
More effort to reach agreement on academic achievement goals for children at various stages of school, without specifying how schools should reach these goals	63	62	66	56

SOURCE: *Phi Delta Kappan*, "The Annual Gallup Poll of the Public's Attitudes Toward the Public Schools," September 1994. (This table was prepared April 1995.)

Table 24.—Parental involvement in 8th graders' school-related activities, by selected parental characteristics: 1988

Characteristics of parents	Percent of parents [1] who talk with child regularly about			Percent of parents [1] who report family rules about			Percent of parents [1] who report that they			Percent of parents [1] who have contacted school about child's	
	Current school experiences	High school plans	Plans after high school	Number of hours of television watched on school days	Doing homework	Maintaining certain grade average	Never or seldom help with homework	Belong to a parent-teacher organization	Attend the parent-teacher organization meeting	Academic performance	Academic program
1	2	3	4	5	6	7	8	9	10	11	12
Total	79.4	47.1	38.3	61.7	92.0	72.7	29.4	31.9	36.2	52.5	34.8
Race/ethnicity											
Asian/Pacific Islander	59.8	41.7	36.5	67.1	89.3	74.7	42.8	29.4	41.2	36.0	29.4
Hispanic	67.1	52.7	44.8	68.7	92.3	79.8	44.7	15.5	43.0	48.3	34.5
Black, non-Hispanic	75.0	57.8	51.4	75.3	95.5	82.3	31.4	30.4	47.8	52.1	34.2
White, non-Hispanic	82.3	45.0	35.4	58.5	91.4	70.1	26.8	34.3	33.3	53.7	35.1
American Indian/Alaskan Native	72.5	44.6	39.9	62.9	95.9	75.7	35.5	16.6	35.0	52.5	42.5
Socioeconomic status [2]											
Lower quartile	66.3	43.0	33.5	64.0	92.2	74.2	41.7	12.2	29.2	38.1	24.2
Middle two quartiles	80.7	46.5	38.4	60.8	93.0	74.9	27.5	29.8	35.2	54.1	34.8
Highest quartile	89.0	52.7	42.9	61.6	89.9	66.9	21.9	54.0	44.4	61.9	44.1
Highest education level of parents											
Two-parent families											
Neither completed high school	60.0	40.7	29.6	64.0	92.6	75.2	47.6	10.6	32.7	32.3	21.2
One did not complete high school	72.9	45.7	34.7	61.6	92.6	74.8	33.7	15.4	28.7	42.8	28.6
Both completed high school ..	81.9	46.0	37.7	61.3	93.3	75.5	26.6	30.8	35.8	53.6	35.1
One graduated college [3]	87.2	51.8	42.4	61.1	91.5	69.9	21.8	48.6	42.7	60.9	41.1
Both graduated college	89.5	52.3	40.8	63.0	88.1	61.1	20.5	60.7	46.9	61.5	46.4
Single-parent families (female)											
Did not complete high school	61.0	47.1	34.6	64.3	91.2	73.2	50.3	9.7	25.1	33.9	19.0
Completed high school	77.0	48.1	42.1	62.5	92.7	75.1	33.8	24.6	33.0	53.5	32.7
Graduated college	84.0	51.8	44.8	60.1	87.0	66.3	28.3	46.7	43.9	67.8	45.6
Family composition											
Two-parent family	81.0	47.4	38.0	61.7	92.2	72.6	27.6	34.2	37.3	52.9	35.7
One-parent family	74.2	47.0	40.2	62.1	91.2	73.3	36.2	23.6	32.0	52.0	31.6

[1] The respondent was the parent most knowledgeable about the child's education. The responding parents reported on their own and their spouses' activities.

[2] Socioeconomic status was measured by a composite score on parental education and occupations, and family income.

[3] Includes a small number of cases where one parent was a high school dropout.

NOTE.—Because of rounding, details may not add to totals.

SOURCE: U.S. Department of Education, National Center for Education Statistics, National Education Longitudinal Study of 1988, "Base Year Parent Survey." (This table was prepared July 1990.)

Table 25.—Teachers' opinions about the most important goals for education, by type and control of school: 1990–91

Goal	Percent of teachers indicating item is the most important goal							
	Public school teachers				Private school teachers			
	Total	Elementary schools	Secondary schools	Combined schools	Total	Elementary schools	Secondary schools	Combined schools
1	2	3	4	5	6	7	8	9
Building basic literacy skills	49.9	52.4	45.7	49.1	32.4	34.6	26.6	32.6
Encouraging academic excellence	11.1	8.8	15.5	8.9	13.0	8.9	20.4	14.3
Promoting occupational or vocational skills	1.9	0.7	3.6	4.7	0.2	0.2	0.5	0.2
Promoting good work habits and self-discipline	13.2	11.8	15.7	12.2	8.9	8.6	10.1	8.7
Promoting personal growth	20.4	23.3	15.2	20.4	19.7	21.1	19.3	18.5
Promoting human relations	1.6	1.6	1.7	2.0	1.4	0.7	2.0	1.8
Promoting specific moral values	1.4	1.2	1.6	2.4	3.1	3.1	4.9	2.3
Promoting multicultural awareness or understanding	0.5	0.3	0.9	0.4	—	—	—	—
Fostering religious or spiritual development	—	—	—	—	21.2	22.8	16.1	21.7

—Data not available.

SOURCE: U.S. Department of Education, National Center for Education Statistics, "Schools and Staffing Survey, 1990–91." (This table was prepared May 1993.)

Table 26.—Teachers' perceptions about serious problems in their schools, by type and control of school: 1990–91

Problem area	Percent of teachers indicating item is a serious problem							
	Public school teachers				Private school teachers			
	Total	Elementary schools	Secondary schools	Combined schools	Total	Elementary schools	Secondary schools	Combined schools
1	2	3	4	5	6	7	8	9
Student tardiness	11.2	5.8	20.2	10.3	3.4	1.7	6.1	4.1
Student absenteeism	14.1	6.9	26.5	12.4	2.6	1.0	5.3	3.2
Teacher absenteeism	1.6	1.2	2.2	1.9	0.7	0.4	1.2	0.7
Students cutting class	4.6	1.0	10.6	3.5	0.7	0.1	1.4	1.1
Physical conflicts among students	6.5	6.7	5.8	7.9	1.1	0.7	0.8	1.8
Robbery or theft	3.4	2.6	4.5	3.8	0.8	0.4	2.0	0.7
Vandalism of school property	5.4	4.3	6.7	7.2	0.9	0.6	1.5	0.9
Student pregnancy	6.4	0.8	15.7	8.3	0.3	0.1	1.0	0.3
Student use of alcohol	8.2	1.4	19.5	13.6	2.4	0.1	9.2	1.9
Student drug abuse	4.2	0.8	9.8	7.2	0.5	0.1	1.4	0.6
Student possession of weapons	1.2	0.5	2.3	1.7	0.1	0.1	0.2	0.1
Physical abuse of teachers	0.8	0.7	0.7	1.6	0.2	0.1	0.1	0.4
Verbal abuse of teachers	7.5	6.2	9.3	9.7	1.7	0.7	1.9	2.7
Student disrespect for teachers	13.0	11.3	15.5	13.5	2.9	1.8	3.1	4.1
Students dropping out	6.3	1.2	14.6	8.7	0.2	0.1	0.8	0.2
Student apathy	20.6	12.9	33.2	24.0	4.1	2.1	7.7	4.8
Lack of academic challenge	5.7	3.9	8.3	8.5	1.3	0.7	2.7	1.2
Lack of parental involvement	25.4	21.6	31.2	30.8	4.3	3.1	5.6	4.9
Parental alcoholism/drug abuse	12.0	11.5	12.2	16.7	2.2	1.2	2.9	3.0
Poverty	17.1	18.5	14.1	22.2	2.0	1.6	1.8	2.5
Racial tension	3.8	3.5	4.1	4.9	0.7	0.3	1.1	0.9
Cultural conflict	4.3	4.1	4.5	5.4	0.7	0.4	1.1	0.8

SOURCE: U.S. Department of Education, National Center for Education Statistics, "Schools and Staffing Survey, 1990–91." (This table was prepared May 1993.)

Table 27.—Teachers' perceptions about teaching and school conditions, by type and control of school: 1990–91

Statement	Percent of teachers agreeing or strongly agreeing with statement							
	Public school teachers				Private school teachers			
	Total	Elementary	Secondary	Combined	Total	Elementary	Secondary	Combined
1	2	3	4	5	6	7	8	9
I usually look forward to each working day at this school	91.8	92.7	90.3	91.6	96.2	96.8	94.1	96.2
Staff members in this school generally do not have much school spirit	31.6	26.6	39.5	34.7	16.5	15.5	20.7	15.7
This school's administration knows the problems faced by staff	78.7	80.6	75.9	76.7	84.9	85.9	79.5	86.1
This school's teachers and administration are in close agreement on school discipline policy	72.2	75.5	67.2	71.1	85.2	85.7	78.2	87.7
Level of student misbehavior in this school interferes with my teaching	35.7	35.4	36.2	33.3	19.9	20.6	16.7	20.6
My principal enforces school rules for student conduct and backs me up when I need it	86.8	87.7	85.5	85.8	92.0	91.0	89.2	94.1
Rules for student behavior are consistently enforced by teachers in this school, even for students who are not in their classes	72.0	79.6	59.2	69.7	84.3	88.3	73.7	84.4
Attitudes and habits my students bring to my class greatly reduce their chances for academic success	59.2	56.2	64.3	61.3	29.7	27.1	33.6	30.9
Many of the students I teach are not capable of learning the material I am supposed to teach them	24.8	24.1	25.5	29.6	9.4	8.8	13.0	8.6
My teaching assignments are more difficult than those of other teachers in this school	27.4	23.8	33.1	29.2	20.5	19.0	26.2	19.9
For me, the job of teaching has more advantages than disadvantages	91.8	92.0	91.7	92.0	95.0	95.8	94.1	94.5
If I had the chance to exchange my job as a teacher for another kind of job, I would	31.0	29.6	33.0	32.9	20.3	19.2	22.7	20.4
I plan with the librarian/media specialist for the integration of services into my teaching	34.6	36.3	30.5	44.0	47.5	51.9	30.2	49.8
Library/media materials are adequate to support instructional objectives	38.3	38.8	37.1	42.2	40.7	40.8	37.3	41.9

SOURCE: U.S. Department of Education, National Center for Education Statistics, "Schools and Staffing Survey, 1990–91." (This table was prepared May 1993.)

Table 28.—Public's level of confidence in various institutions: 1994

Institution	Percent of respondents by levels of confidence				
	A great deal	Quite a lot	Some	Very little	Can't say
1	2	3	4	5	6
Small businesses	16.2	36.7	36.8	7.2	3.2
Religious organizations	21.3	28.3	30.9	16.7	2.8
The military	15.8	32.8	34.0	14.1	3.2
Private higher education	14.4	33.9	30.9	12.4	8.4
Youth development and recreation	13.8	33.0	35.6	12.1	5.5
Private elementary or secondary education	13.4	31.9	34.7	13.9	6.2
Public higher education	11.4	33.9	39.2	10.7	4.8
Public elementary or secondary education	11.3	30.7	40.6	14.7	2.7
Federated charitable appeals, e.g., United Way	11.3	26.1	36.1	21.2	5.3
Health organizations	11.2	24.4	43.0	16.6	4.7
Environmental organizations	10.7	22.9	40.3	20.5	5.6
Human services organizations	10.3	22.9	45.0	15.4	6.5
Private and community foundations	8.0	22.5	43.9	16.7	8.9
Recreation for adults	8.6	21.7	43.4	15.0	11.3
Arts, culture, and humanities organizations	8.1	21.2	40.5	18.7	11.6
Work-related organizations	5.5	22.6	48.8	14.6	8.6
Media, e.g., newspapers, TV, radio	6.1	19.8	40.5	32.0	1.6
Public/society benefit, e.g., civil rights, social justice, community improvement organizations	6.0	17.9	45.5	24.4	6.1
Local government	3.8	19.4	45.6	29.0	2.1
Organized labor	6.7	15.9	43.9	29.1	4.4
Major corporations	5.1	17.2	50.6	22.7	4.4
State government	4.4	16.4	46.0	31.2	1.9
Federal government	3.5	15.5	44.2	34.8	1.9
International/foreign, e.g., culture exchange, relief organizations	3.7	14.9	38.3	30.7	12.5
Political organizations, e.g., Republican or Democratic parties	3.9	12.7	40.3	39.7	3.4
Organizations that advocate a particular cause	3.9	12.5	39.5	37.6	6.6
Congress	3.2	12.0	40.9	41.3	2.6

NOTE.—Institutions are listed in rank order as determined by the combined responses of "a great deal" and "quite a lot" of confidence.

SOURCE: Independent Sector, The Gallup Organization, *Giving and Volunteering in the United States, 1994.* (This table was prepared April 1995.)

Table 29.—Percentage of households contributing to education and other charitable organizations and average annual donation, by type of charity: 1989, 1991, and 1993

Type of charity	1989			1991			1993		
	Percentage of total households [1]	Per contributing household	Per total household	Percentage of total households [1]	Per contributing household	Per total household	Percentage of total households [1]	Per contributing household	Per total household
1	2	3	4	5	6	7	8	9	10
Total	**75.1**	**$978**	**$734**	**72.2**	**$899**	**$649**	**73.4**	**$880**	**$646**
Religious	53.2	896	477	51.3	800	410	49.2	817	402
Health	32.4	143	46	32.9	154	51	25.7	139	36
Human services	23.0	263	60	27.5	260	71	26.7	208	56
Youth development	21.6	129	28	22.1	114	25	17.9	106	19
Education	19.1	291	56	21.1	225	47	17.5	424	74
Environment	13.4	88	12	16.3	99	16	11.6	89	10
Arts, culture, and humanities	9.6	193	19	9.4	194	18	8.1	139	11
Public and societal benefit	11.2	120	13	11.2	132	15	11.2	160	18
Private and community foundations	6.4	116	7	6.0	113	7	5.3	144	8
Recreation, adults	6.2	135	8	6.3	164	10	4.6	193	9
International, foreign	4.2	202	8	3.5	198	7	2.8	(2)	(2)
Other	3.0	195	6	2.8	233	7	4.7	81	4

[1] Percents do not add to total because of respondents giving to more than one type of charity.

[2] Sample size too small for reliable data.

NOTE.—Details for total households do not add to total because details only include households which reported a donation amount for the particular type of charity. The percentage of total includes households who reported giving donations, but did not specify amount.

SOURCE: Independent Sector, The Gallup Organization, *Giving and Volunteering in the United States, 1989, 1991, and 1993.* (This table was prepared April 1995.)

Table 30.—Total expenditures of educational institutions related to the gross domestic product, by level of institution: 1959–60 to 1994–95

Year	Gross domestic product (in billions)	School year	Total expenditures for education (amounts in millions of current dollars)					
			All educational institutions		All elementary and secondary schools		All colleges and universities	
			Amount	As a percent of gross domestic product	Amount	As a percent of gross domestic product	Amount	As a percent of gross domestic product
1	2	3	4	5	6	7	8	9
1959	$494.2	1959–60	$23,860	4.8	$16,713	3.4	$7,147	1.4
1961	531.8	1961–62	28,503	5.4	19,673	3.7	8,830	1.7
1963	603.1	1963–64	34,440	5.7	22,825	3.8	11,615	1.9
1965	702.7	1965–66	43,682	6.2	28,048	4.0	15,634	2.2
1967	814.3	1967–68	55,652	6.8	35,077	4.3	20,575	2.5
1969	959.5	1969–70	68,459	7.1	43,183	4.5	25,276	2.6
1970	1,010.7	1970–71	75,741	7.5	48,200	4.8	27,541	2.7
1971	1,097.2	1971–72	80,672	7.4	50,950	4.6	29,722	2.7
1972	1,207.0	1972–73	86,875	7.2	54,952	4.6	31,923	2.6
1973	1,349.6	1973–74	95,396	7.1	60,370	4.5	35,026	2.6
1974	1,458.6	1974–75	108,664	7.4	68,846	4.7	39,818	2.7
1975	1,585.9	1975–76	118,706	7.5	75,101	4.7	43,605	2.7
1976	1,768.4	1976–77	126,417	7.1	79,194	4.5	47,223	2.7
1977	1,974.1	1977–78	137,042	6.9	86,544	4.4	50,498	2.6
1978	2,232.7	1978–79	148,308	6.6	93,012	4.2	55,296	2.5
1979	2,488.6	1979–80	165,627	6.7	103,162	4.1	62,465	2.5
1980	2,708.0	1980–81	182,849	6.8	112,325	4.1	70,524	2.6
1981	3,030.6	1981–82	197,801	6.5	120,486	4.0	77,315	2.6
1982	3,149.6	1982–83	212,081	6.7	128,725	4.1	83,356	2.6
1983	3,405.0	1983–84	228,597	6.7	139,000	4.1	89,597	2.6
1984	3,777.2	1984–85	247,657	6.6	149,400	4.0	98,257	2.6
1985	4,038.7	1985–86	269,485	6.7	161,800	4.0	107,685	2.7
1986	4,268.6	1986–87	291,974	6.8	175,200	4.1	116,774	2.7
1987	4,539.9	1987–88	313,375	6.9	187,999	4.1	125,376	2.8
1988	4,900.4	1988–89	346,883	7.1	209,377	4.3	137,506	2.8
1989	5,250.8	1989–90[1]	381,228	7.3	230,673	4.4	150,555	2.9
1990	5,546.1	1990–91[1]	412,652	7.4	248,930	4.5	163,722	3.0
1991	5,724.8	1991–92[1]	434,102	7.6	261,262	4.6	172,840	3.0
1992	6,020.2	1992–93[2]	458,048	7.6	275,359	4.6	182,689	3.0
1993	6,343.3	1993–94[3]	486,100	7.7	294,600	4.6	191,500	3.0
1994	6,736.9	1994–95[3]	508,300	7.5	307,500	4.6	200,800	3.0

[1] Revised from previously published data.
[2] Preliminary.
[3] Estimated.

NOTE.—Total expenditures for public elementary and secondary schools include current expenditures, interest on school debt, and capital outlay. Data for private elementary and secondary schools are estimated. Total expenditures for colleges and universities include current-fund expenditures and additions to plant value. Excludes expenditures of noncollegiate postsecondary institutions. Because of rounding, details may not add to totals.

SOURCE: U.S. Department of Education, National Center for Education Statistics, *Statistics of State School Systems; Revenues and Expenditures for Public Elementary and Secondary Education; Financial Statistics of Institutions of Higher Education;* Common Core of Data survey; "Financial Statistics of Institutions of Higher Education" survey, Integrated Postsecondary Education Data System (IPEDS) "Finance" survey, and unpublished data; Council of Economic Advisers, *Economic Indicators;* and National Education Association, *Estimates of School Statistics,* various years. (This table was prepared August 1995.)

Table 31.—Total expenditures of educational institutions, by level and control of institution: 1899–1900 to 1994–95

[In millions of current dollars]

School year	Total	Elementary and secondary schools			Colleges and universities		
		Total	Public	Private [1]	Total	Public	Private
1	2	3	4	5	6	7	8
1899–1900	—	—	$215	—	—	—	—
1909–10	—	—	426	—	—	—	—
1919–20	—	—	1,036	—	—	—	—
1929–30	—	—	2,317	—	$632	$292	$341
1939–40	—	—	2,344	—	758	392	367
1949–50	$8,911	$6,249	5,838	$411	2,662	1,430	1,233
1951–52	10,735	7,861	7,344	517	2,874	1,565	1,309
1953–54	13,147	9,733	9,092	641	3,414	1,912	1,502
1955–56	15,907	11,727	10,955	772	4,180	2,348	1,832
1957–58	20,055	14,525	13,569	956	5,530	3,237	2,293
1959–60	23,860	16,713	15,613	1,100	7,147	3,904	3,244
1961–62	28,503	19,673	18,373	1,300	8,830	4,919	3,911
1963–64	34,440	22,825	21,325	1,500	11,615	6,558	5,057
1965–66	43,682	28,048	26,248	1,800	15,634	9,047	6,588
1967–68	55,652	35,077	32,977	2,100	20,575	12,750	7,824
1969–70	68,459	43,183	40,683	2,500	25,276	16,234	9,041
1970–71	75,741	48,200	45,500	2,700	27,541	18,028	9,513
1971–72	80,672	50,950	48,050	2,900	29,722	19,538	10,184
1972–73	86,875	54,952	51,852	3,100	31,923	21,144	10,779
1973–74	95,396	60,370	56,970	3,400	35,026	23,542	11,484
1974–75	108,664	68,846	64,846	4,000	39,818	26,966	12,852
1975–76	118,706	75,101	70,601	4,500	43,605	29,736	13,869
1976–77	126,417	79,194	74,194	5,000	47,223	31,997	15,226
1977–78	137,042	86,544	80,844	5,700	50,498	34,031	16,467
1978–79	148,308	93,012	86,712	6,300	55,296	37,110	18,187
1979–80	165,627	103,162	95,962	7,200	62,465	41,434	21,031
1980–81	182,849	112,325	104,125	8,200	70,524	46,559	23,965
1981–82	197,801	120,486	111,186	9,300	77,315	50,813	26,502
1982–83	212,081	128,725	118,425	10,300	83,356	54,338	29,018
1983–84	228,597	139,000	127,500	11,500	89,597	58,124	31,473
1984–85	247,657	149,400	137,000	12,400	98,257	63,705	34,553
1985–86	269,485	161,800	148,600	13,200	107,685	70,069	37,616
1986–87	291,974	175,200	160,900	14,300	116,774	74,552	42,222
1987–88	313,375	187,999	172,699	15,300	125,376	79,859	45,516
1988–89	346,883	209,377	192,977	16,400	137,506	87,107	50,398
1989–90	381,228	230,673	212,473	18,200	150,555	96,387	54,169
1990–91	412,652	248,930	229,430	19,500	163,722	104,433	59,288
1991–92	434,102	261,262	241,062	20,200	172,840	109,026	63,814
1992–93 [2]	458,048	275,359	253,859	21,500	182,689	115,470	67,220
1993–94 [1]	486,100	294,600	272,000	22,600	191,500	120,900	70,600
1994–95 [1]	508,300	307,500	283,900	23,600	200,800	126,600	74,200

[1] Estimated.
[2] Preliminary.
—Data not available.

NOTE.—Total expenditures for public elementary and secondary schools include current expenditures, interest on school debt, and capital outlay. Data for private elementary and secondary schools are estimated. Total expenditures for colleges and universities include current-fund expenditures and additions to plant value. Excludes expenditures of noncollegiate postsecondary institutions. Some data have been revised from previously published figures. Because of rounding, details may not add to totals.

SOURCE: U.S. Department of Education, National Center for Education Statistics, *Statistics of State School Systems; Revenues and Expenditures for Public Elementary and Secondary Education; Financial Statistics of Institutions of Higher Education;* Common Core of Data survey; "Financial Statistics of Institutions of Higher Education" survey; Integrated Postsecondary Education Data System (IPEDS) "Finance" survey; and National Education Association, *Estimates of School Statistics,* various years. (This table was prepared August 1995.)

Table 32.—Estimated total expenditures of educational institutions, by level, control of institution, and source of funds: 1979–80 to 1992–93

[In billions of current dollars]

Level and control of institution and source of funds	1979–80		1984–85		1989–90		1990–91		1991–92[1]		1992–93[2]	
	Amount	Percent	Amount	Percent	Amount	Percent	Amount	Percent	Amount	Percent	Amount	Percent
1	2	3	4	5	6	7	8	9	10	11	12	13
All levels												
Total public and private	$165.6	100.0	$247.7	100.0	$381.2	100.0	$412.7	100.0	$434.1	100.0	$458.0	100.0
Federal	18.9	11.4	21.3	8.6	31.6	8.3	34.1	8.3	37.2	8.6	40.1	8.8
State	64.3	38.8	96.1	38.8	142.0	37.3	151.6	36.7	155.1	35.7	159.9	34.9
Local	43.3	26.1	63.3	25.6	97.8	25.7	105.5	25.6	111.4	25.7	118.3	25.8
All other	39.1	23.6	66.9	27.0	109.8	28.8	121.5	29.4	130.4	30.0	139.8	30.5
Total public	137.4	100.0	200.7	100.0	308.9	100.0	333.9	100.0	350.1	100.0	369.3	100.0
Federal	14.8	10.8	15.8	7.9	22.9	7.4	24.9	7.5	27.4	7.8	30.1	8.1
State	63.9	46.5	95.5	47.6	140.6	45.5	150.3	45.0	153.5	43.8	158.3	42.9
Local	43.1	31.4	63.1	31.4	97.4	31.5	105.0	31.5	111.0	31.7	117.8	31.9
All other	15.6	11.3	26.3	13.1	47.9	15.5	53.7	16.1	58.2	16.6	63.1	17.1
Total private	28.2	100.0	47.0	100.0	72.4	100.0	78.8	100.0	84.0	100.0	88.7	100.0
Federal	4.1	14.5	5.5	11.7	8.6	11.9	9.2	11.6	9.8	11.6	10.0	11.3
State	0.4	1.6	0.7	1.4	1.4	1.9	1.3	1.7	1.6	1.9	1.6	1.8
Local	0.2	0.6	0.2	0.5	0.4	0.6	0.4	0.5	0.4	0.5	0.4	0.5
All other	23.5	83.4	40.6	86.4	62.0	85.6	67.9	86.1	72.2	86.0	76.7	86.4
Elementary and secondary schools												
Total public and private	103.2	100.0	149.4	100.0	230.7	100.0	248.9	100.0	261.2	100.0	275.3	100.0
Federal	9.4	9.1	9.1	6.1	13.0	5.6	14.2	5.7	15.9	6.1	17.6	6.4
State	44.7	43.3	66.8	44.7	100.5	43.6	108.2	43.5	111.8	42.8	115.8	42.1
Local	41.6	40.3	60.8	40.7	93.9	40.7	101.2	40.6	107.0	40.9	113.5	41.2
All other	7.5	7.3	12.8	8.6	23.3	10.1	25.4	10.2	26.6	10.2	28.3	10.3
Total public	96.0	100.0	137.0	100.0	212.5	100.0	229.4	100.0	241.1	100.0	253.9	100.0
Federal	9.4	9.8	9.1	6.6	13.0	6.1	14.2	6.2	15.9	6.6	17.6	6.9
State	44.7	46.6	66.8	48.7	100.5	47.3	108.2	47.2	111.8	46.4	115.8	45.6
Local	41.6	43.3	60.8	44.3	93.9	44.2	101.2	44.1	107.0	44.4	113.5	44.7
All other	0.3	0.3	0.4	0.3	[3]5.1	[3]2.4	[3]5.9	[3]2.6	[3]6.4	[3]2.7	[3]6.9	[3]2.7
Total private[4]	7.2	100.0	12.4	100.0	18.2	100.0	19.5	100.0	20.2	100.0	21.5	100.0
All other	7.2	100.0	12.4	100.0	18.2	100.0	19.5	100.0	20.2	100.0	21.5	100.0
Institutions of higher education												
Total public and private	62.5	100.0	98.3	100.0	150.6	100.0	163.7	100.0	172.8	100.0	182.7	100.0
Federal	9.5	15.2	12.2	12.4	18.6	12.3	19.9	12.2	21.3	12.3	22.5	12.3
State	19.6	31.4	29.4	29.9	41.6	27.6	43.4	26.5	43.3	25.1	44.0	24.1
Local	1.7	2.7	2.5	2.6	3.9	2.6	4.3	2.6	4.4	2.6	4.7	2.6
All other	31.6	50.6	54.1	55.1	86.5	57.4	96.1	58.7	103.8	60.1	111.4	61.0
Total public	41.4	100.0	63.7	100.0	96.4	100.0	104.4	100.0	109.0	100.0	115.5	100.0
Federal	5.4	13.1	6.7	10.6	9.9	10.3	10.7	10.3	11.5	10.6	12.4	10.8
State	19.2	46.3	28.7	45.1	40.2	41.7	42.1	40.3	41.7	38.3	42.5	36.8
Local	1.5	3.7	2.3	3.6	3.5	3.7	3.9	3.7	4.0	3.7	4.3	3.7
All other	15.3	36.9	25.9	40.7	42.7	44.3	47.7	45.7	51.8	47.5	56.2	48.7
Total private	21.0	100.0	34.6	100.0	54.2	100.0	59.3	100.0	63.8	100.0	67.2	100.0
Federal	4.1	19.4	5.5	15.9	8.6	15.9	9.2	15.4	9.8	15.3	10.0	14.9
State	0.4	2.1	0.7	1.9	1.4	2.6	1.3	2.3	1.6	2.5	1.6	2.3
Local	0.2	0.8	0.2	0.6	0.4	0.7	0.4	0.7	0.4	0.6	0.4	0.6
All other	16.3	77.7	28.2	81.6	43.8	80.8	48.4	81.6	52.1	81.6	55.2	82.1

[1] Revised from previously published data.

[2] Preliminary data.

[3] Revenues from individuals including fees for transportation and books and food service receipts. This expenditure includes only the individual contributions for these categories and excludes contributions from public sources.

[4] Some private elementary and secondary school revenues come from federal, state, and local sources. However, comprehensive data are not available to delineate the sources of revenues for private schools.

NOTE.—Estimated distribution of expenditures by source of funds are obtained from distribution of revenue sources for current funds. Federally-supported student aid that goes to higher education institutions through students' tuition payments is shown under "All other" rather than "federal." Such payments would add substantial amounts and several percentage points to the federal share. Other federal programs, not included in this table because they do not support regular educational institutions, would increase the federal share even further. Typical examples of these payments would be federal support for libraries and museums. Additionally, the federal contribution to education through tax expenditures is not reflected in this table. Because of rounding, details may not add to totals.

SOURCE: U.S. Department of Education, National Center for Education Statistics, Common Core of Data; "Financial Statistics of Institutions of Higher Education" survey; Integrated Postsecondary Education Data System (IPEDS) "Finance" survey, unpublished data. (This table was prepared August 1995.)

Table 33.—Governmental expenditures, by level of government and function: 1970-71 to 1990-91

In millions

Expenditure, by function	All governments[1]							Federal government				State and local governments[2]			
	1970-71	1980-81	1986-87	1987-88	1988-89	1989-90	1990-91	1970-71	1980-81	1989-90	1990-91	1970-71	1980-81	1989-90	1990-91
1	2	3	4	5	6	7	8	9	10	11	12	13	14	15	16
General expenditures[2]	$301,096	$827,877	$1,375,367	$1,461,880	$1,542,620	$1,686,807	$1,804,005	$150,422	$422,301	$1,002,224	$1,059,508	$150,674	$407,449	$834,818	$908,108
Selected federal programs															
National defense and international relations	80,910	174,564	319,993	329,993	346,338	344,069	366,112	80,910	174,564	344,069	366,112	—	—	—	—
Postal service	8,683	20,466	32,243	33,892	36,472	39,065	43,102	8,683	20,466	39,065	43,102	—	—	—	—
Space research and technology	3,334	5,523	7,450	8,866	10,806	12,063	13,514	3,334	5,523	12,063	13,514	—	—	—	—
Education and libraries	64,042	158,012	244,310	260,736	284,963	310,080	334,333	4,629	12,408	40,712	45,256	60,174	147,649	292,250	313,744
Social services and income maintenance															
Public welfare	20,446	74,643	106,407	115,113	126,132	140,734	167,681	2,220	22,395	93,903	119,135	18,226	54,121	110,518	130,402
Hospitals and health	14,835	47,378	72,604	78,789	85,091	92,487	102,817	3,630	11,277	24,647	28,207	11,205	36,101	74,635	81,110
Social insurance administration	2,031	5,075	6,775	7,166	7,352	7,716	8,193	1,086	2,799	7,506	7,995	945	2,276	3,014	3,250
Transportation	23,722	46,578	66,439	70,536	74,289	78,539	84,048	4,062	7,724	23,353	24,768	19,819	39,231	70,628	75,410
Public safety															
Police protection	5,706	16,851	28,778	30,934	32,723	35,921	38,942	478	1,904	5,666	6,725	5,228	14,947	30,577	32,772
Correction	1,979	7,806	17,562	20,154	22,500	26,229	29,297	94	413	1,734	2,122	1,885	7,393	24,635	27,356
Environment and housing															
Natural resources	13,740	43,599	93,006	90,119	64,353	80,915	56,949	10,658	38,896	70,800	46,549	3,082	6,175	12,330	12,575
Housing and community development	4,467	13,894	21,308	25,224	28,230	32,430	33,346	1,913	6,808	29,271	30,199	2,554	7,086	15,479	16,648
Governmental administration															
Financial administration	3,612	10,944	18,698	20,454	22,125	24,200	26,977	1,341	3,714	7,983	10,308	2,271	7,230	16,217	16,995
General control[3]	3,567	11,514	25,438	27,656	30,088	33,346	36,977	540	1,973	6,844	7,900	4,432	12,771	28,619	31,466
Interest on general debt	21,688	97,641	188,046	202,437	220,883	237,691	247,376	16,599	80,510	187,952	195,142	5,089	17,131	49,739	52,234
Other and unallocable	28,334	93,389	127,220	139,812	150,274	191,322	214,115	10,245	30,927	106,656	112,474	15,764	55,338	106,177	114,147

Percentage distribution

Expenditure, by function	All governments							Federal government				State and local governments			
	1970-71	1980-81	1986-87	1987-88	1988-89	1989-90	1990-91	1970-71	1980-81	1989-90	1990-91	1970-71	1980-81	1989-90	1990-91
General expenditures[2]	100.0	100.0	100.0	100.0	100.0	100.0	100.0	100.0	100.0	100.0	100.0	100.0	100.0	100.0	100.0
Selected federal programs															
National defense and international relations	26.9	21.1	23.2	22.6	22.5	20.4	20.3	53.8	41.3	34.3	34.6	—	—	—	—
Postal service	2.9	2.5	2.3	2.3	2.4	2.3	2.4	5.8	4.8	3.9	4.1	—	—	—	—
Space research and technology	1.1	0.7	0.5	0.6	0.7	0.7	0.7	2.2	1.3	1.2	1.3	—	—	—	—
Education and libraries	21.3	19.1	17.8	17.8	18.5	18.4	18.5	3.1	2.9	4.1	4.3	39.9	36.2	35.0	34.5
Social services and income maintenance															
Public welfare	6.8	9.0	7.7	7.9	8.2	8.3	9.3	1.5	5.3	9.4	11.2	12.1	13.3	13.2	14.4
Hospitals and health	4.9	5.7	5.3	5.4	5.5	5.5	5.7	2.4	2.7	2.5	2.7	7.4	8.9	8.9	8.9
Social insurance administration	0.7	0.6	0.5	0.5	0.5	0.5	0.5	0.7	0.7	0.7	0.8	0.6	0.6	0.4	0.4
Transportation	7.9	5.6	4.8	4.8	4.8	4.7	4.7	2.7	1.8	2.3	2.3	13.2	9.6	8.5	8.3
Public safety															
Police protection	1.9	2.0	2.1	2.1	2.1	2.1	2.2	0.3	0.5	0.6	0.6	3.5	3.7	3.7	3.6
Correction	0.7	0.9	1.3	1.4	1.5	1.6	1.6	0.1	0.1	0.2	0.2	1.3	1.8	3.0	3.0
Environment and housing															
Natural resources	4.6	5.3	6.8	6.2	4.2	4.8	3.2	7.1	9.2	7.1	4.4	2.0	1.5	1.5	1.4
Housing and community development	1.5	1.7	1.5	1.7	1.8	1.9	1.8	1.3	1.6	2.9	2.9	1.7	1.7	1.9	1.8
Governmental administration															
Financial administration	1.2	1.3	1.4	1.4	1.4	1.4	1.5	0.9	0.9	0.8	1.0	1.5	1.8	1.9	1.9
General control[3]	1.2	1.4	1.8	1.9	2.0	2.0	2.0	0.4	0.5	0.7	0.7	2.9	3.1	3.4	3.5
Interest on general debt	7.2	11.8	13.7	13.8	14.3	14.1	13.7	11.0	19.1	18.8	18.4	3.4	4.2	6.0	5.8
Other and unallocable	9.4	11.3	9.2	9.6	9.7	11.3	11.9	6.8	7.3	10.6	10.6	10.5	13.6	12.7	12.6

[1] Excludes duplicative intergovernmental transactions.

[2] General expenditures include expenditures through the federal government ($3,466,000 in 1990-91), which are excluded from direct general expenditures.

[3] Includes judicial and legal expenditures and expenditures on general and public buildings and other governmental administration.

—Not applicable.

SOURCE: U.S. Department of Commerce, Bureau of the Census, *Government Finances, 1990-91*, Series GF/91-5. (This table was prepared February 1994.)

Table 34.—Direct general expenditures of state and local governments for all functions and for education, by level and state: 1990–91

[In millions]

State	Total direct general expenditures [1]	Education expenditures							
		Total	Elementary and secondary education			Higher education			Other education [3]
			Total	Current expenditure	Capital outlay [2]	Total	Current expenditure	Capital outlay	
1	2	3	4	5	6	7	8	9	10
United States	$904,642.1	$309,302.4	$217,642.8	$197,455.4	$20,187.3	$78,748.7	$71,684.6	$7,064.1	$12,910.9
Alabama	12,031.0	4,363.7	2,518.0	2,302.9	215.0	1,435.8	1,262.4	173.4	409.9
Alaska	5,572.6	1,302.8	967.1	871.9	95.3	281.2	257.0	24.2	54.5
Arizona	12,831.0	4,608.3	2,983.2	2,448.5	534.8	1,489.0	1,355.7	133.3	136.0
Arkansas	5,787.5	2,320.9	1,469.3	1,355.2	114.1	667.1	604.6	62.5	184.5
California	120,865.2	38,542.4	26,498.5	24,282.2	2,216.3	10,645.7	9,978.8	666.8	1,398.3
Colorado	11,545.9	4,324.0	2,884.6	2,579.8	304.8	1,355.2	1,212.0	143.2	84.1
Connecticut	14,622.0	4,346.3	3,463.7	3,197.6	266.0	697.7	679.6	18.1	184.9
Delaware	2,783.2	1,013.3	574.6	549.4	25.2	364.6	336.7	27.9	74.2
District of Columbia	4,209.8	721.5	620.0	571.5	48.5	101.5	97.8	3.6	—
Florida	45,303.4	14,790.2	11,079.9	9,373.3	1,706.6	3,031.1	2,733.7	297.5	679.2
Georgia	21,282.1	7,191.4	5,309.9	4,703.3	606.5	1,554.9	1,373.4	181.5	326.6
Hawaii	5,218.1	1,269.0	783.2	651.7	131.5	466.7	412.1	54.6	19.2
Idaho	2,963.3	1,148.0	754.9	668.3	86.6	347.6	298.3	49.3	45.4
Illinois	38,017.8	12,711.9	8,772.1	8,077.2	695.0	3,283.7	2,971.7	312.0	656.0
Indiana	16,795.5	6,936.7	4,580.5	4,105.2	475.3	2,075.7	1,813.3	262.4	280.5
Iowa	9,550.2	3,697.6	2,292.2	2,102.9	189.3	1,258.7	1,144.1	114.6	146.8
Kansas	7,984.0	3,080.5	2,005.1	1,874.4	130.7	975.0	901.0	74.0	100.4
Kentucky	10,941.1	3,759.0	2,313.3	2,160.4	152.9	1,127.8	996.0	131.8	317.9
Louisiana	14,247.1	4,463.1	3,038.2	2,860.0	178.2	1,174.8	1,090.8	83.9	250.1
Maine	4,481.1	1,580.6	1,189.2	1,045.4	143.9	331.7	306.8	24.9	59.7
Maryland	18,061.9	6,431.3	4,255.4	3,893.2	362.2	1,927.0	1,747.4	179.6	249.0
Massachusetts	24,610.7	6,351.6	4,840.0	4,566.1	273.9	1,232.6	1,161.6	71.0	279.0
Michigan	33,758.7	12,983.8	8,861.5	8,115.6	745.8	3,789.0	3,431.6	357.3	333.4
Minnesota	18,836.1	6,258.1	4,271.5	3,805.8	465.7	1,706.0	1,576.1	129.8	280.7
Mississippi	6,987.7	2,598.2	1,642.5	1,542.1	100.4	821.2	747.2	74.0	134.5
Missouri	13,740.2	5,336.3	3,928.9	3,459.4	469.6	1,233.8	1,160.2	73.5	173.6
Montana	2,830.4	1,054.4	742.4	659.1	83.4	210.1	198.7	11.5	101.9
Nebraska	5,204.3	2,142.6	1,417.1	1,289.1	128.0	652.3	596.5	55.8	73.2
Nevada	4,802.2	1,531.9	1,178.3	847.4	330.9	321.8	274.1	47.7	31.8
New Hampshire	3,378.8	1,251.6	977.1	883.1	94.0	239.6	238	1.7	34.9
New Jersey	31,765.2	10,538.0	8,391.6	7,966.1	425.5	1,846.4	1,600.7	245.7	300.0
New Mexico	5,199.4	2,041.3	1,286.8	1,142.6	144.1	678.7	622.9	55.8	75.8
New York	98,544.8	27,821.3	21,871.2	20,091.5	1,779.7	4,856.0	4,482.4	373.5	1,094.1
North Carolina	20,448.5	7,949.4	5,235.7	4,641.8	594.0	2,457.1	2,219.4	237.7	256.6
North Dakota	2,248.7	849.2	489.6	469.6	20.0	323.1	291.1	32.0	36.5
Ohio	34,946.0	12,468.0	8,800.5	8,342.7	457.9	3,181.6	2,840.2	341.4	485.8
Oklahoma	9,233.7	3,430.1	2,384.9	2,097.1	287.8	910.6	822.5	88.1	134.7
Oregon	10,610.6	3,896.8	2,626.5	2,521.9	104.5	1,140.4	985.7	154.7	129.9
Pennsylvania	38,190.1	13,446.9	10,240.6	9,196.1	1,044.6	2,127.1	1,925.2	202.0	1,079.1
Rhode Island	3,882.6	1,212.8	844.9	800.2	44.7	278.2	263.2	15.0	89.7
South Carolina	11,171.3	4,236.5	2,852.2	2,530.3	321.9	1,172.8	1,107.3	65.6	211.5
South Dakota	2,073.5	747.4	545.4	517.0	28.4	171.3	156.0	15.3	30.7
Tennessee	13,655.8	4,550.4	2,833.7	2,631.8	201.8	1,445.9	1,224.9	220.9	270.9
Texas	50,233.0	19,914.4	13,930.8	12,720.4	1,210.4	5,533.0	5,080.4	452.7	450.5
Utah	5,337.1	2,254.4	1,368.7	1,238.1	130.6	804.3	717.5	86.9	81.3
Vermont	2,191.2	900.4	591.9	568.4	23.5	251.4	235.6	15.8	57.1
Virginia	20,861.4	7,953.8	5,578.7	4,935.8	642.9	2,062.7	1,893.4	169.2	312.4
Washington	19,119.9	7,114.4	4,876.1	3,953.1	923.0	1,918.6	1,701.8	216.8	319.7
West Virginia	5,160.9	1,975.4	1,359.5	1,264.1	95.4	518.5	488.1	30.3	97.4
Wisconsin	18,195.9	7,051.2	4,740.9	4,454.1	286.8	2,043.3	1,855.2	188.1	267.0
Wyoming	2,329.4	839.3	580.2	530.9	49.3	228.9	213.9	15.0	30.2

[1] Includes state and local government expenditures for education services, social services and income maintenance, transportation, public safety, environment and housing, governmental administration, interest on general debt, and other general expenditures. Includes intergovernmental expenditure to the federal government.

[2] Includes outlays for "other education."

[3] Includes assistance and subsidies to individuals and private institutions for elementary, secondary, and higher education, as well as miscellaneous education expenditures.

—Not applicable.

NOTE.—Current expenditure data in this table differ from figures appearing in other tables because of slightly varying definitions used in the *Governmental Finances* and Common Core of Data surveys. Because of rounding, details may not add to totals.

SOURCE: U.S. Department of Commerce, Bureau of the Census, *Government Finances: 1990–91*, Series GF/91–5. (This table was prepared January 1994.)

Table 35.—Direct general expenditures per capita of state and local governments for all functions and for education, by level and state: 1990–91

State	Total, all direct general expenditures per capita [1]	Education expenditures per capita							
		Total		Elementary and secondary education		Higher education		Other education [2]	
		Amount	As a percent of all functions	Amount	As a percent of all functions	Amount	As a percent of all functions	Amount	As a percent of all functions
1	2	3	4	5	6	7	8	9	10
United States	$3,587.33	$1,226.53	34.2	$863.06	24.1	$312.28	8.7	$51.20	1.4
Alabama	2,942.29	1,067.18	36.3	615.79	20.9	351.14	11.9	100.25	3.4
Alaska	9,776.41	2,285.59	23.4	1,696.74	17.4	493.32	5.0	95.53	1.0
Arizona	3,421.61	1,228.87	35.9	795.53	23.3	397.07	11.6	36.28	1.1
Arkansas	2,439.92	978.47	40.1	619.43	25.4	281.24	11.5	77.79	3.2
California	3,978.45	1,268.68	31.9	872.23	21.9	350.42	8.8	46.03	1.2
Colorado	3,418.99	1,280.41	37.4	854.20	25.0	401.31	11.7	24.90	0.7
Connecticut	4,443.02	1,320.65	29.7	1,052.47	23.7	212.01	4.8	56.18	1.3
Delaware	4,092.90	1,490.19	36.4	845.01	20.6	536.13	13.1	109.06	2.7
District of Columbia	6,935.39	1,188.62	17.1	1,021.45	14.7	167.17	2.4	—	—
Florida	3,412.17	1,113.97	32.6	834.52	24.5	228.30	6.7	51.16	1.5
Georgia	3,213.36	1,085.82	33.8	801.73	24.9	234.78	7.3	49.31	1.5
Hawaii	4,597.48	1,118.06	24.3	690.03	15.0	411.16	8.9	16.87	0.4
Idaho	2,852.09	1,104.90	38.7	726.61	25.5	334.57	11.7	43.72	1.5
Illinois	3,293.58	1,101.26	33.4	759.95	23.1	284.48	8.6	56.83	1.7
Indiana	2,993.85	1,236.50	41.3	816.49	27.3	370.01	12.4	50.00	1.7
Iowa	3,416.89	1,322.94	38.7	820.10	24.0	450.34	13.2	52.51	1.5
Kansas	3,199.99	1,234.66	38.6	803.64	25.1	390.79	12.2	40.23	1.3
Kentucky	2,946.69	1,012.40	34.4	623.03	21.1	303.76	10.3	85.61	2.9
Louisiana	3,350.68	1,049.65	31.3	714.54	21.3	276.29	8.2	58.81	1.8
Maine	3,628.44	1,279.86	35.3	962.95	26.5	268.55	7.4	48.36	1.3
Maryland	3,716.45	1,323.32	35.6	875.59	23.6	396.49	10.7	51.24	1.4
Massachusetts	4,104.51	1,059.31	25.8	807.21	19.7	205.58	5.0	46.53	1.1
Michigan	3,603.62	1,385.97	38.5	945.93	26.2	404.46	11.2	35.59	1.0
Minnesota	4,250.02	1,412.03	33.2	963.78	22.7	384.92	9.1	63.33	1.5
Mississippi	2,695.87	1,002.40	37.2	633.69	23.5	316.82	11.8	51.89	1.9
Missouri	2,663.86	1,034.57	38.8	761.71	28.6	239.19	9.0	33.66	1.3
Montana	3,503.02	1,304.97	37.3	918.86	26.2	260.05	7.4	126.06	3.6
Nebraska	3,266.98	1,345.02	41.2	889.57	27.2	409.48	12.5	45.97	1.4
Nevada	3,740.07	1,193.04	31.9	917.67	24.5	250.63	6.7	24.74	0.7
New Hampshire	3,057.74	1,132.66	37.0	884.26	28.9	216.79	7.1	31.60	1.0
New Jersey	4,093.46	1,357.98	33.2	1,081.39	26.4	237.93	5.8	38.66	0.9
New Mexico	3,358.76	1,318.69	39.3	831.26	24.7	438.44	13.1	48.99	1.5
New York	5,457.12	1,540.66	28.2	1,211.17	22.2	268.91	4.9	60.59	1.1
North Carolina	3,035.26	1,179.96	38.9	777.16	25.6	364.72	12.0	38.08	1.3
North Dakota	3,541.28	1,337.35	37.8	771.06	21.8	508.76	14.4	57.53	1.6
Ohio	3,194.63	1,139.78	35.7	804.51	25.2	290.85	9.1	44.41	1.4
Oklahoma	2,908.26	1,080.35	37.1	751.13	25.8	286.79	9.9	42.42	1.5
Oregon	3,631.26	1,333.60	36.7	898.86	24.8	390.27	10.7	44.47	1.2
Pennsylvania	3,192.89	1,124.23	35.2	856.17	26.8	177.84	5.6	90.22	2.8
Rhode Island	3,867.15	1,207.95	31.2	841.51	21.8	277.13	7.2	89.31	2.3
South Carolina	3,138.01	1,190.03	37.9	801.18	25.5	329.45	10.5	59.40	1.9
South Dakota	2,949.53	1,063.21	36.0	775.83	26.3	243.65	8.3	43.73	1.5
Tennessee	2,757.08	918.72	33.3	572.11	20.8	291.92	10.6	54.70	2.0
Texas	2,895.44	1,147.87	39.6	802.98	27.7	318.92	11.0	25.97	0.9
Utah	3,015.33	1,273.66	42.2	773.28	25.6	454.43	15.1	45.95	1.5
Vermont	3,864.55	1,588.00	41.1	1,043.91	27.0	443.46	11.5	100.64	2.6
Virginia	3,318.70	1,265.32	38.1	887.49	26.7	328.14	9.9	49.70	1.5
Washington	3,810.26	1,417.77	37.2	971.72	25.5	382.34	10.0	63.71	1.7
West Virginia	2,865.60	1,096.81	38.3	754.88	26.3	287.87	10.0	54.05	1.9
Wisconsin	3,672.24	1,423.04	38.8	956.80	26.1	412.37	11.2	53.88	1.5
Wyoming	5,063.84	1,824.46	36.0	1,261.23	24.9	497.57	9.8	65.65	1.3

[1] Includes state and local government expenditures for education services, social services and income maintenance, transportation, public safety, environment and housing, governmental administration, interest on general debt, and other general expenditures. Includes intergovernmental expenditure to the federal government.

[2] Includes assistance and subsidies to individuals and private institutions for elementary, secondary, and higher education, as well as miscellaneous education expenditures.

—Not applicable.

NOTE.—Per capita amounts are based on population figures as of April 1, 1991, and are computed on the basis of amounts rounded to the nearest thousand. Because of rounding, details may not add to totals.

SOURCE: U.S. Department of Commerce, Bureau of the Census, Governments Division, *Government Finances: 1990–91*, Series GF/91–5. (This table was prepared February 1994.)

Table 36.—Gross domestic product, state and local expenditures, personal income, disposable personal income, median family income, and population: 1929 to 1994

Year	Gross domestic product, in billions		State and local expenditures,[1] in millions		Personal income, in billions	Disposable personal income, in billions of 1987 dollars	Disposable personal income per capita		Median family income	Total population in thousands	
	Current dollars	Constant 1987 dollars	All general expenditures	Education expenditures			Current dollars	Constant 1987 dollars		Annual averages of quarterly data[2]	As of July 1[3]
1	2	3	4	5	6	7	8	9	10	11	12
1929	—	—	—	—	—	—	—	—	—	—	121,878
1933	—	—	—	—	—	—	—	—	—	—	125,690
1939	—	—	—	—	—	—	—	—	—	—	131,028
1940	—	—	$9,229	$2,638	—	—	—	—	—	—	132,122
1941	—	—	—	—	—	—	—	—	—	—	133,402
1942	—	—	9,190	2,586	—	—	—	—	—	—	134,860
1943	—	—	—	—	—	—	—	—	—	—	136,739
1944	—	—	8,863	2,793	—	—	—	—	—	—	138,397
1945	—	—	—	—	—	—	—	—	—	—	139,928
1946	—	—	11,028	3,356	—	—	—	—	—	—	141,389
1947	—	—	—	—	—	—	—	—	$3,031	—	144,126
1948	—	—	17,684	5,379	—	—	—	—	3,187	—	146,631
1949	—	—	—	—	—	—	—	—	3,107	—	149,188
1950	—	—	22,787	7,177	—	—	—	—	3,319	—	151,684
1951	—	—	—	—	—	—	—	—	3,709	—	154,287
1952	—	—	26,098	8,318	—	—	—	—	3,890	—	156,954
1953	—	—	27,910	9,390	—	—	—	—	4,242	—	159,565
1954	—	—	30,701	10,557	—	—	—	—	4,167	—	162,391
1955	—	—	33,724	11,907	—	—	—	—	4,418	—	165,275
1956	—	—	36,711	13,220	—	—	—	—	4,780	—	168,221
1957	—	—	40,375	14,134	—	—	—	—	4,966	—	171,274
1958	—	—	44,851	15,919	—	—	—	—	5,087	—	174,882
1959	$494.2	$1,931.3	48,887	17,283	$391.2	$1,284.9	$1,958	$7,256	5,417	177,073	177,830
1960	513.4	1,973.2	51,876	18,719	409.2	1,313.0	1,994	7,264	5,620	180,760	180,671
1961	531.8	2,025.6	56,201	20,574	426.5	1,356.4	2,048	7,382	5,735	183,742	183,691
1962	571.6	2,129.8	60,206	22,216	453.4	1,414.8	2,137	7,583	5,956	186,590	186,538
1963	603.1	2,218.0	63,977	23,729	476.4	1,461.1	2,210	7,718	6,249	189,300	189,242
1964	648.0	2,343.3	69,302	26,286	510.7	1,562.2	2,369	8,140	6,569	191,927	191,889
1965	702.7	2,473.5	74,678	28,563	552.9	1,653.5	2,527	8,508	6,957	194,347	194,303
1966	769.8	2,622.3	82,843	33,287	601.7	1,734.3	2,699	8,822	7,532	196,599	196,560
1967	814.3	2,690.3	93,350	37,919	646.5	1,811.4	2,861	9,114	7,933	198,752	198,712
1968	889.3	2,801.0	102,411	41,158	709.9	1,886.8	3,077	9,399	8,632	200,745	200,706
1969	959.5	2,877.1	116,728	47,238	773.7	1,947.4	3,274	9,606	9,433	202,736	202,677
1970	1,010.7	2,875.8	131,332	52,718	831.0	2,025.3	3,521	9,875	9,867	205,089	205,052
1971	1,097.2	2,965.1	150,674	59,413	893.5	2,099.9	3,779	10,111	10,285	207,692	207,661
1972	1,207.0	3,107.1	168,550	65,814	980.5	2,186.2	4,042	10,414	11,116	209,924	209,896
1973	1,349.6	3,268.6	181,357	69,714	1,098.7	2,334.1	4,521	11,013	12,051	211,939	211,909
1974	1,458.6	3,248.1	198,959	75,833	1,205.7	2,317.0	4,893	10,832	12,902	213,898	213,854
1975	1,585.9	3,221.7	230,721	87,858	1,307.3	2,355.4	5,329	10,906	13,719	215,981	215,973
1976	1,768.4	3,380.8	256,731	97,216	1,446.3	2,440.9	5,796	11,192	14,958	218,086	218,035
1977	1,974.1	3,533.2	274,215	102,780	1,601.3	2,512.6	6,316	11,406	16,009	220,289	220,239
1978	2,232.7	3,703.5	296,983	110,758	1,807.9	2,638.4	7,042	11,851	17,640	222,629	222,585
1979	2,488.6	3,796.8	327,517	119,448	2,033.1	2,710.1	7,787	12,039	19,587	225,106	225,055
1980	2,708.0	3,776.3	369,086	133,211	2,265.4	2,733.6	8,576	12,005	21,023	227,715	227,726
1981	3,030.6	3,843.1	407,449	145,784	2,534.7	2,795.8	9,455	12,156	22,388	229,989	229,966
1982	3,149.6	3,760.3	436,896	154,282	2,690.9	2,820.4	9,989	12,146	23,433	232,201	232,188
1983	3,405.0	3,906.6	466,421	163,876	2,862.5	2,893.6	10,642	12,349	24,674	234,326	234,307
1984	3,777.2	4,148.5	505,008	176,108	3,154.6	3,080.1	11,673	13,029	26,433	236,393	236,348
1985	4,038.7	4,279.8	553,899	192,686	3,379.8	3,162.1	12,339	13,258	27,735	238,510	238,466
1986	4,268.6	4,404.5	605,623	210,819	3,590.4	3,261.9	13,010	13,552	29,458	240,691	240,651
1987	4,539.9	4,539.9	657,134	226,619	3,802.0	3,289.5	13,545	13,545	[4]30,970	242,860	242,804
1988	4,900.4	4,718.6	704,921	242,683	4,075.9	3,404.3	14,477	13,890	[4]32,191	245,093	245,021
1989	5,250.8	4,838.0	762,360	263,898	4,380.3	3,464.9	15,307	14,005	[4]34,213	247,397	247,342
1990	5,546.1	4,897.3	834,818	288,148	4,673.8	3,524.5	16,205	14,101	[4]35,353	249,951	249,911
1991	5,724.8	4,867.6	908,108	309,302	4,860.3	3,538.5	16,766	14,003	[4]35,939	252,688	252,643
1992	6,020.2	4,979.3	972,185	326,770	5,154.3	3,648.1	17,636	14,279	[4]36,812	255,484	255,407
1993	6,343.3	5,134.5	—	—	5,375.1	3,704.1	18,153	14,341	[4]36,959	258,290	258,120
1994	6,738.4	5,344.0	—	—	5,701.7	3,835.7	19,003	14,696	—	260,991	260,651

[1] Data for years prior to 1963 include expenditures for government fiscal years ending during that particular calendar year. Data for 1963 and later years are the aggregations of expenditures for government fiscal years which ended on June 30 of the stated year. General expenditures exclude expenditures of publicly owned utilities and liquor stores, and of insurance-trust activities. Intergovernmental payments between state and local governments are excluded. Payments to the federal government are included.
[2] Population of the United States including Armed Forces overseas; includes Alaska and Hawaii beginning 1960. Quarterly data are averages for the period.
[3] Population of the United States including Armed Forces overseas; includes Alaska and Hawaii beginning 1958. Includes revisions based on the 1990 Census.
[4] Revised methodology.

—Data not available.

NOTE.—Gross domestic product data are adjusted by the GDP implicit price deflator. Personal income data are adjusted by the personal consumption deflator. Some data have been revised from previously published figures.

SOURCE: Executive Office of the President, Economic Report of the President, February 1995, and Economic Indicators, May 1995; and U.S. Department of Commerce, Bureau of the Census, Consumer Income, Series P-60, No. 174; and U.S. Census Bureau, News Release, December 30, 1991. (This table was prepared June 1995.)

Table 37.—Gross domestic product deflator, Consumer Price Index, education price indexes, and federal budget composite deflator: 1919 to 1995

Calendar year			School year						Federal fiscal year	
Year	Gross domestic product deflator	Consumer Price Index [1]	Year	Consumer Price Index [2]	Elementary/ Secondary Price Index	Higher Education Price Index	Research and Development Index	Academic Library Operations Index	Year	Federal budget composite deflator
1	2	3	4	5	6	7	8	9	10	11
1919	—	17.3	1919–20	19.1	—	—	—	—	1919	—
1929	—	17.1	1929–30	17.1	—	—	—	—	1929	—
1934	—	13.4	1934–35	13.6	—	—	—	—	1934	—
1939	—	13.9	1939–40	14.0	—	—	—	—	1939	—
1940	—	14.0	1940–41	14.2	—	—	—	—	1940	0.0978
1941	—	14.7	1941–42	15.6	—	—	—	—	1941	0.1009
1942	—	16.3	1942–43	16.9	—	—	—	—	1942	0.1115
1943	—	17.3	1943–44	17.4	—	—	—	—	1943	0.1199
1944	—	17.6	1944–45	17.8	—	—	—	—	1944	0.1160
1945	—	18.0	1945–46	18.2	—	—	—	—	1945	0.1141
1946	—	19.5	1946–47	21.2	—	—	—	—	1946	0.1193
1947	—	22.3	1947–48	23.3	—	—	—	—	1947	0.1496
1948	—	24.1	1948–49	24.1	—	—	—	—	1948	0.1543
1949	—	23.8	1949–50	23.7	—	—	—	—	1949	0.1582
1950	—	24.1	1950–51	25.1	—	—	—	—	1950	0.1634
1951	—	26.0	1951–52	26.3	—	—	—	—	1951	0.1592
1952	—	26.5	1952–53	26.7	—	—	—	—	1952	0.1627
1953	—	26.7	1953–54	26.9	—	—	—	—	1953	0.1712
1954	—	26.9	1954–55	26.8	—	—	—	—	1954	0.1765
1955	—	26.8	1955–56	26.9	—	—	—	—	1955	0.1801
1956	—	27.2	1956–57	27.7	—	—	—	—	1956	0.1907
1957	—	28.1	1957–58	28.6	—	—	—	—	1957	0.2017
1958	—	28.9	1958–59	29.0	—	—	—	—	1958	0.2124
1959	25.6	29.1	1959–60	29.4	—	25.6	26.7	—	1959	0.2249
1960	26.0	29.6	1960–61	29.8	—	26.5	27.5	—	1960	0.2351
1961	26.3	29.9	1961–62	30.1	—	27.6	28.5	—	1961	0.2407
1962	26.8	30.2	1962–63	30.4	—	28.6	29.5	—	1962	0.2450
1963	27.2	30.6	1963–64	30.8	—	29.8	30.7	—	1963	0.2544
1964	27.7	31.0	1964–65	31.2	—	31.3	32.0	—	1964	0.2596
1965	28.4	31.5	1965–66	31.9	—	32.9	33.8	—	1965	0.2650
1966	29.4	32.4	1966–67	32.9	—	34.9	35.7	—	1966	0.2732
1967	30.3	33.4	1967–68	34.0	—	37.1	38.0	—	1967	0.2812
1968	31.7	34.8	1968–69	35.7	—	39.5	40.3	—	1968	0.2927
1969	33.3	36.7	1969–70	37.8	—	42.1	42.7	—	1969	0.3092
1970	35.1	38.8	1970–71	39.7	—	44.3	45.0	—	1970	0.3282
1971	37.0	40.5	1971–72	41.2	—	46.7	47.1	—	1971	0.3508
1972	38.8	41.8	1972–73	42.8	—	49.9	50.1	—	1972	0.3736
1973	41.3	44.4	1973–74	46.6	—	54.3	54.8	—	1973	0.3961
1974	44.9	49.3	1974–75	51.8	52.7	57.9	59.1	57.8	1974	0.4307
1975	49.2	53.8	1975–76	55.5	57.1	61.7	62.7	61.6	1975	0.4758
1976	52.3	56.9	1976–77	58.7	60.8	65.8	66.8	66.1	1976	0.5098
1977	55.9	60.6	1977–78	62.6	64.6	70.6	71.7	71.8	1977	0.5523
1978	60.3	65.2	1978–79	68.5	70.3	77.5	78.3	78.9	1978	0.5928
1979	65.5	72.6	1979–80	77.6	76.5	85.9	86.6	87.0	1979	0.6441
1980	71.7	82.4	1980–81	86.6	85.7	94.0	94.1	94.6	1980	0.7102
1981	78.9	90.9	1981–82	94.1	93.7	100.0	100.0	100.0	1981	0.7817
1982	83.8	96.5	1982–83	98.2	100.0	104.7	104.6	104.9	1982	0.8369
1983	87.2	99.6	1983–84	101.8	105.6	110.5	110.1	110.4	1983	0.8776
1984	91.0	103.9	1984–85	105.8	112.6	115.6	115.4	116.6	1984	0.9125
1985	94.4	107.6	1985–86	108.8	119.6	120.4	120.4	123.6	1985	0.9452
1986	96.9	109.6	1986–87	111.2	125.7	125.8	125.8	129.7	1986	0.9735
1987	100.0	113.6	1987–88	115.8	132.7	133.1	133.3	138.2	1987	1.0000
1988	103.9	118.3	1988–89	121.2	139.6	140.8	140.3	146.8	1988	1.0361
1989	108.5	124.0	1989–90	127.0	147.6	148.3	147.2	155.9	1989	1.0813
1990	113.3	130.7	1990–91	133.9	156.0	153.1	152.0	162.4	1990	1.1284
1991	117.6	136.2	1991–92	138.2	162.9	158.2	156.3	170.6	1991	1.1783
1992	120.9	140.3	1992–93	142.5	166.8	—	—	—	1992	1.2183
1993	123.5	144.5	1993–94	146.2	—	—	—	—	1993	1.2513
1994	126.1	148.2	1994–95	150.4	—	—	—	—	1994	1.2812
1995	—	—	1995–96	—	—	—	—	—	1995	1.3174

[1] Index for urban wage earners and clerical workers through 1977; 1978 and later figures are for all urban consumers.

[2] Consumer Price Index adjusted to a school-year basis (July through June).

—Data not available.

NOTE.—Some data have been revised from previously published figures.

SOURCE: Council of Economic Advisers, *Economic Indicators*, February 1991 and May 1995, and *Economic Report to the President*, January 1993; U.S. Department of Education, National Institute of Education, *Inflation Measures for Schools and Colleges*; U.S. Department of Labor, Bureau of Labor Statistics, Consumer Price Index; Research Associates of Washington, "Inflation Measures for Schools and Colleges, 1990 Update," and unpublished data; and U.S. Office of Management and Budget, *Budget of the U.S. Government, Fiscal Year 1996*. (This table was prepared June 1995.)

CHAPTER 2
Elementary and Secondary Education

This chapter contains a variety of statistics on public and private elementary and secondary education. Data are presented for enrollments, teachers, schools, student performance, graduates, and expenditures. These data are derived from surveys conducted by the National Center for Education Statistics (NCES) and other public and private organizations.

Enrollments

In fall 1985, public elementary and secondary school enrollments increased for the first time since 1971. Enrollment has continued to rise, resulting in an increase of 10 percent from 1985 to 1993. Elementary and secondary enrollment exhibited different patterns. Between 1985 and 1993, public elementary enrollment rose by 17 percent while secondary enrollment declined by 3 percent (tables 3 and 39).

In contrast to the declining elementary and secondary school enrollments during the 1970s and early 1980s, preprimary education enrollment grew substantially. Between 1970 and 1980, preprimary enrollment of 3- to 5-year-olds rose by 19 percent; between 1980 and 1993, it increased an additional 35 percent. An important feature of the increasing participation of young children in preprimary schools is the increasing proportion in full-day programs. In 1994 about 46 percent of the children attended school all day, compared with 32 percent in 1980 and 17 percent in 1970 (table 45).

Despite drops in total elementary and secondary school enrollment during the late 1970s and early 1980s, increasing numbers and proportions of children were served in programs for the disabled. During the 1976–77 school year, 8 percent of students were served in these programs compared with 12 percent in 1992–93. However, since 1983–84, the increases have been relatively small. Much of the rise since 1976–77 may be attributed to the increasing proportion of children identified as learning disabled, which rose from less than 2 percent of enrollment in 1976–77 to 5 percent of enrollment in 1992–93 (table 51).

Tuition at private schools

The average full tuition (highest tuition charged) for private schools was $3,116 in 1993–94. Schools with religious orientation charged significantly lower tuition than nonsectarian schools. Students at Catholic schools paid $2,178 on average and students at schools with other religious orientations paid $2,915 on average, compared with the average tuition of $6,631 for nonsectarian private schools. Mean tuition paid by private elementary school students was lower than that paid by other schools' students, with Catholic school students paying $1,628. Students at schools with other religious orientations paid $2,606, and students at nonsectarian schools paid $4,693. Mean tuition paid by private secondary school students was substantially higher than that for private elementary school students, averaging $3,643 at Catholic schools, $5,261 at other religiously oriented schools, and $9,525 at nonsectarian schools (table 60).

Teachers and other school staff

During the 1970s and early 1980s, public school enrollment decreased, while the number of teachers rose. The number of public school teachers increased by 7 percent between 1970 and 1985, but school enrollment fell. As a result, the pupil/teacher ratio declined markedly. Between 1970 and 1985, the pupil/teacher ratio for public schools fell from 22.3 to 17.9. After 1985, the number of pupils per teacher continued downward, reaching 17.2 in 1990. Then the pupil/teacher ratio began increasing again, reaching an estimated 17.4 in fall 1995 (table 63).

In 1993–94, 73 percent of public school teachers were women, 48 percent were under 40, and more than 47 percent had a master's degree or above. By comparison, about 75 percent of the 378,000 full-time and part-time private school teachers were women. About 56 percent of the private school teachers were under age 40, and 34 percent had a master's or higher degree (table 66).

Principals tended to be older and have higher level credentials than teachers. Also, they were more likely to be male. About 7 percent of the public school principals were under age 40 and 99 percent had a master's degree or above. About 35 percent of the principals were women (table 86).

In general, public school teachers have higher salaries than private school teachers. In 1993–94, the average base salary for public school teachers was $34,153, compared with $21,968 for private school teachers (table 72). The average salary for public school teachers grew rapidly during the 1980s, reaching $36,933 in 1994–95. After adjustment for inflation, teachers' salaries rose 10 percent between 1984–85 and 1994–95, more than recouping the losses in purchasing power suffered during the 1970s. However, this increase occurred during the 1980s and salary averages for teachers declined slightly during the 1990s (table 76).

The number of nonteaching staff employed by public schools grew at a faster rate than the number of pupils and teachers in the 1970s. During the 1970s, the proportion of the total staff who were teachers declined from 60 percent to 52 percent. In the 1980s, the number of teachers grew at about the same rate as other public school staff. In 1969–70, there were 13.6 pupils per staff member (total staff) compared with 9.1 pupils per staff member in 1993. In 1993–94, the number of pupils per staff member at private schools was 9.3 (tables 59 and 81).

Schools

Over the past decades, the trend to consolidate small schools has brought a steady decline in the total number of public schools in the United States. In 1930, there were more than 247,000 schools, compared with around 85,000 today. But the number of schools has remained relatively stable for the 10 past years, with only a small decline at the secondary level (table 88).

The shift in structure of public school systems toward middle schools (grades 4, 5, or 6 to 6, 7, or 8) is continuing. The number of elementary schools rose by 4 percent to 60,000 between 1983–84 and 1993–94, but middle schools accounted for a disproportionate share of this increase, rising by 39 percent. Meanwhile, the number of junior high schools (grades 7 to 8 and 7 to 9) declined by 33 percent. During this 1983–84 to 1993–94 period, the proportion of elementary schools with traditional 1–6 and 1–8 grade spans dropped, and the proportion with formerly atypical 1–5 spans rose (table 93).

Enrollment has risen faster than the number of schools and the average school size has increased. Elementary schools grew from an average of 401 students in 1983–84 to 468 in 1993–94. During the same time period, the average secondary school size fell from 720 to 695. Schools tend to be smaller in predominantly rural states, such as Nebraska and Montana, and larger in states with large urban populations, such as California and Florida (tables 94, 95, and 96).

Completions and Achievement

Comparisons of the number of public and private high school graduates with the 17-year-old population suggest that the proportion of young people earning regular high school diplomas has not increased over the past 20 years. At its highest point in 1968–69, there were 77 graduates for every 100 persons 17 years of age. This ratio declined during the 1970s, falling to 71 in 1979–80. The ratio has risen slightly in the 1990s, reaching 73 in 1994–95. This indicator is not a graduation rate because many students complete their high school education through alternative programs, such as night schools and the General Educational Development (GED) program. Other measures, such as the dropout rate among 16- to 24-year-olds (which counts GED recipients and special program completers as graduates) suggest some improvements. Between 1968 and 1988, the dropout rate for 16- to 24-year-olds fell from 16.2 percent to 12.9 percent. The dropout rate has continued to fall, reaching 10.5 percent in 1994. The dropout rate statistic is based on the civilian noninstitutional population, which excludes persons in prisons and persons not living in households (tables 98 and 101).

Student achievement is also mixed. Overall improvement was seen in reading proficiency for 13- and 17-year-olds since 1971, with some levelling off in the performance of 17-year-olds since 1984. However, 9-year-olds in 1992 demonstrated about the same reading ability as their counterparts in 1971, despite significant gains that had been made between 1971 and 1980. The increase in reading ability was supported by an overall trend across assessments in other subjects toward higher average proficiencies for 13-year-old students. Significant gaps in performance continue to exist between racial/ethnic subgroups and between male and female students. In the case of racial/ethnic differences, trends toward some narrowing of the gap observed in earlier assessments have stalled since 1988 at all three ages assessed. Gender gaps favoring female students in reading and writing and males in science were essentially the same in 1992 as in 1971 (table 105). In 1992, the first state assessment in reading was administered to fourth grade students and 43 jurisdictions volunteered to participate (table 109).

There have been four national assessments of writing performance conducted during the school years ending in 1984, 1988, 1990, and 1992. The results of trends in average writing achievement from 1984 to 1992 reveal a dramatic shift at grade 8. After declining between 1984 and 1990, average performance increased in 1992 beyond the original 1984 level. There were no significant changes in overall writing performance at grade 11. At grade 4 there was an increase in performance between 1990 and 1992, countering downward fluctuations in the 1980s, so that performance was essentially unchanged between 1984 and 1992 (table 111).

Results from national assessments of mathematics achievement found that at ages 9 and 13, significant improvement was observed between 1973 and 1992. For in-school 17-year-olds, performance declined between 1973 and 1982, but an upturn during the past decade has brought performance back to the 1973 level. For all three ages, there were significant increases in average proficiency between 1982 and 1992, indicating improvement in the more computational aspects of mathematics (table 115).

On a national assessment of educational progress administered to the states on a voluntary basis in both 1990 and 1992, 16 states and 2 territories that participated both years showed significant improvement in eighth grade mathematics performance. Of the 37 jurisdictions participating in both years, none showed a significant decline. (table 117).

The average science proficiency of 9-year-old students has increased significantly since 1970. In contrast, the average proficiency of 13-year-olds showed no significant difference from 1970 and the proficiency of 17-year-olds remained significantly below that achieved by their counterparts in 1969. The average science proficiency of white students at all three age groups remained significantly higher than the average proficiencies of black and Hispanic students. The performance gap between white and black students decreased significantly for 9-year-olds between 1970 and 1992, but the gaps for 13- and 17-year-olds have remained relatively stable since 1970 and 1969, respectively. Since 1977, the performance gap between white and Hispanic students has remained essentially the same for 9- and 17-year-olds, but has decreased significantly for 13-year-olds (table 122).

The Scholastic Assessment Test (SAT, formerly known as the Scholastic Aptitude Test) was not designed as an indicator of student achievement, but rather to help predict how well students will do in college. Between 1983–84 and 1993–94, mathematics SAT scores increased by 8 points, while verbal scores fell by 3 points. However, considerable difference existed among students from different racial/ethnic groups. Between 1983–84 and 1993–94, combined mathematics and verbal scores for white students rose by only 6 points compared with an increase of 25 points for black students and 34 points for Asian American students (table 125).

Over the past 10 years, the average number of science and mathematics courses completed by public high school graduates increased substantially. The mean number of mathematics courses (Carnegie units) completed in high school rose from 2.6 in 1982 to 3.4 in 1992, and the number of science courses rose from 2.2 to 2.9. The average number of courses in vocational-technical areas completed by all high school graduates dropped gradually, from 4.6 units in 1982 to 3.8 units in 1992. As a result of the increased academic course load, the proportion of students completing the recommendations of the National Commission on Excellence (4 units of English, 3 units of social studies, 3 units of science, 3 units of mathematics, and .5 units of computer science) rose from 2.7 percent in 1982 to 29.2 percent in 1992 (tables 132, 133, and 135).

Drugs and violence

Twelfth-grade students at public schools were less likely to feel safe at school and were more likely to report fights between racial/ethnic groups and gangs at school than students at Catholic and other private schools (table 138). The proportion of public and private high school seniors who reported ever using an illicit drug rose from 55 percent in 1975 to 66 percent in 1981. After 1981, the proportion of seniors who had ever used drugs fell. After reaching 41 percent in 1992, the proportion rose again to 46 percent in 1994. Also, the proportion of high school seniors who had ever used cocaine fell from 17 percent in 1985 to 6 percent in 1994. Alcohol remained the most often used drug. The proportion of seniors who had used alcohol within the previous 30 days declined from 72 percent in 1980 to 50 percent in 1994 (table 146).

Resources and Expenditures

The state share of revenues for public elementary and secondary schools grew steadily through most of the 1980s, but in 1987–88 the trend began to reverse. Between 1988–89 and 1992–93, the local share of school funding was about the same as the proportion from state governments. In 1992–93, 45.6 percent of all revenues came from state sources, 47.4 percent came from local sources, and 6.9 percent came from the federal government (table 154).

The expenditure per student in public schools has risen significantly in the past 10 years, especially during the mid 1980s. In 1994–95, the estimated current expenditure per student in average daily attendance was $6,084. After adjustment for inflation, this represents an increase of 23 percent since 1984–85 (table 163).

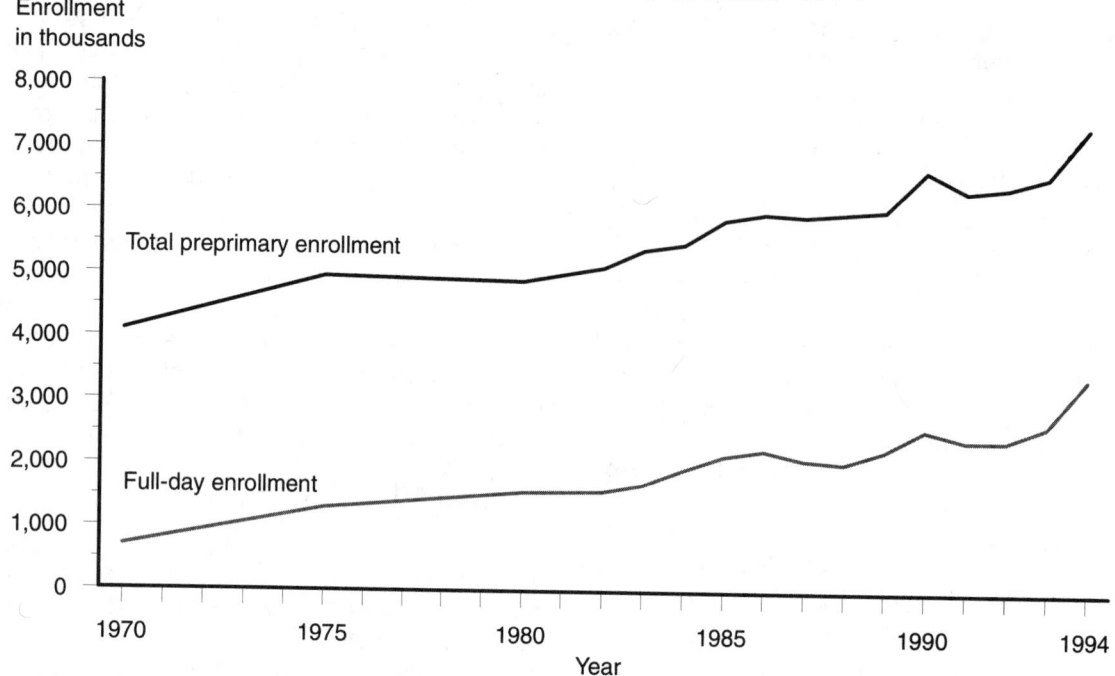

Figure 7.-Preprimary enrollment of 3- to 5-year-olds, by attendance status: October 1970 to October 1994

SOURCE: U.S. Department of Education, National Center for Education Statistics, *Preprimary Enrollment,* various years; and U.S. Department of Commerce, Bureau of the Census, Current Population Survey, unpublished data.

Figure 8.-Enrollment, number of teachers, pupil/teacher ratios, and expenditures in public schools: 1960–61 to 1994–95

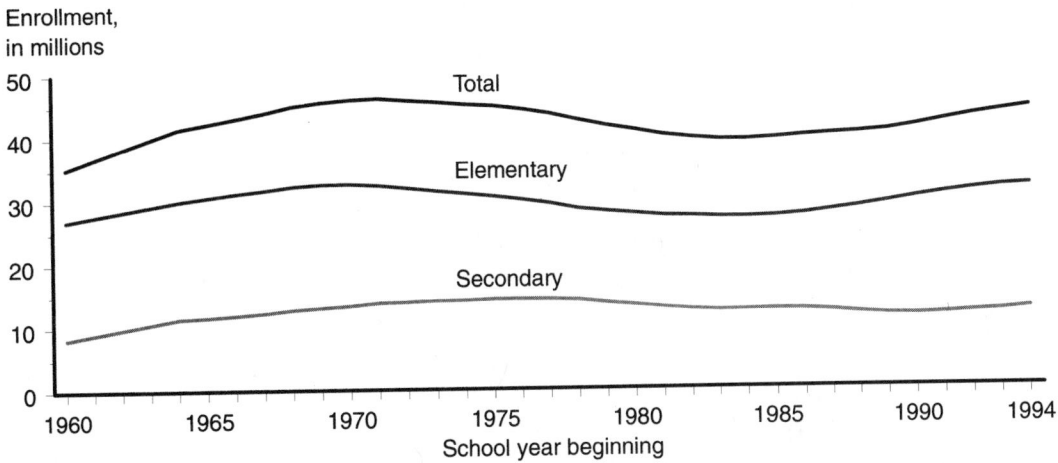

Enrollment, in millions

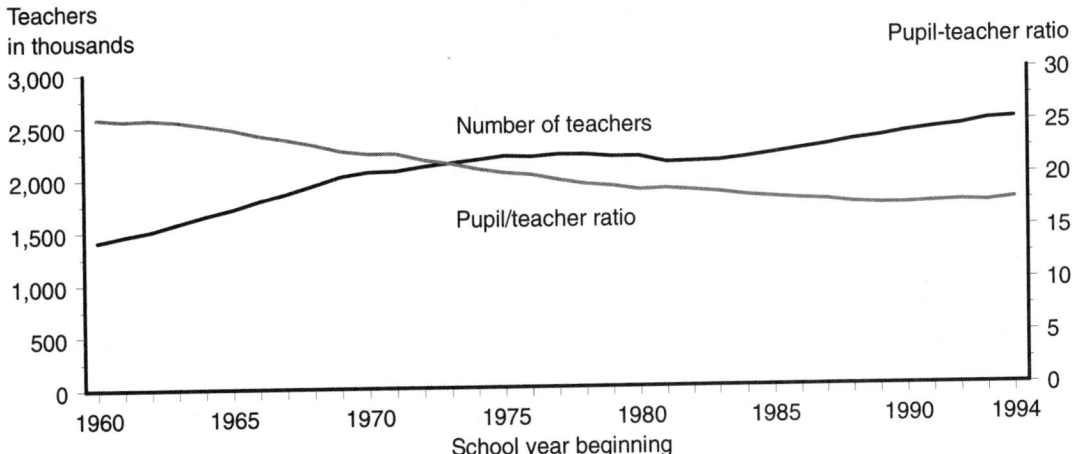

Teachers in thousands / Pupil-teacher ratio

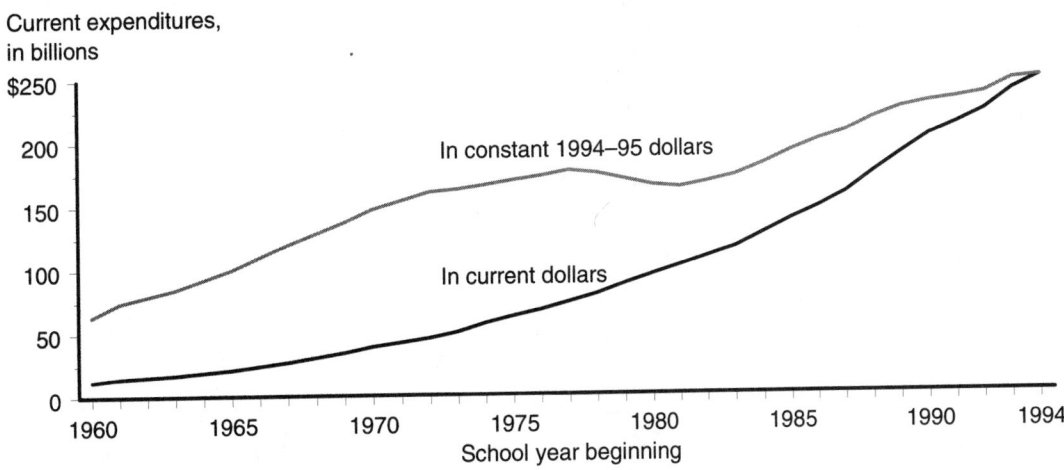

Current expenditures, in billions

SOURCE: U.S. Department of Education, National Center for Education Statistics, *Statistics of State School Systems; Statistics of Public Elementary and Secondary School Systems; Revenues and Expenditures for Public Elementary and Secondary Education;* and Common Core of Data Surveys.

Figure 9.–Percentage change in public elementary and secondary enrollment, by state: Fall 1989 to fall 1994

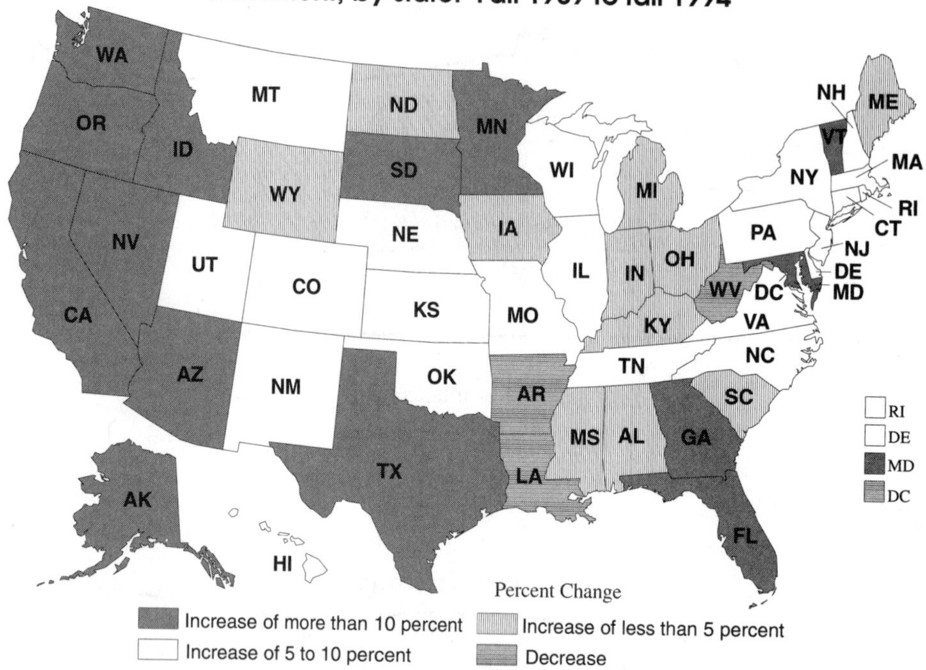

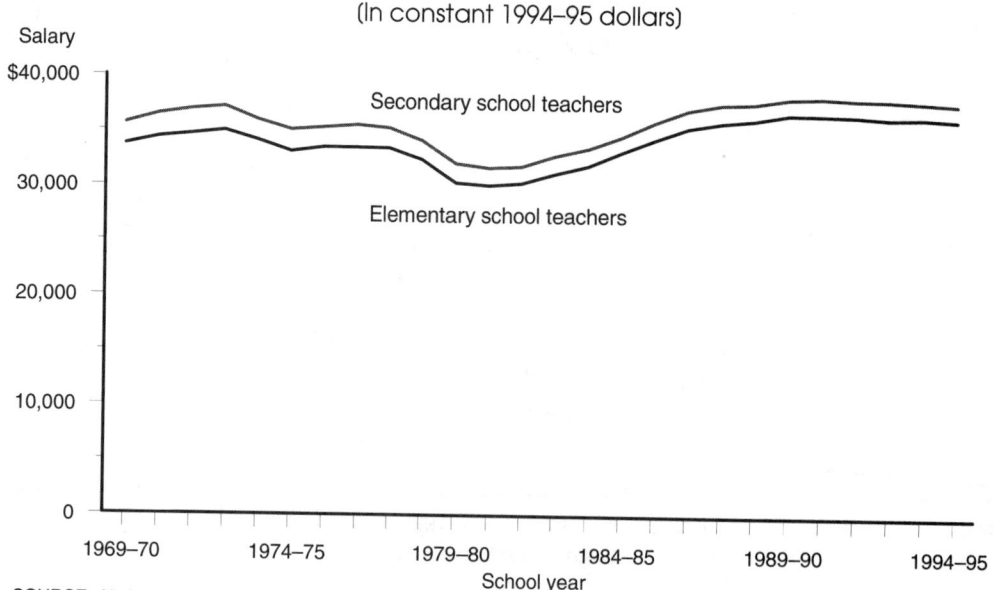

Percent Change

▨ Increase of more than 10 percent   ▦ Increase of less than 5 percent
☐ Increase of 5 to 10 percent   ▨ Decrease

SOURCE: U.S. Department of Education, National Center for Education Statistics, Common Core of Data surveys.

Figure 10.–Average annual salary for public elementary and secondary school teachers: 1969–70 to 1994–95

(In constant 1994–95 dollars)

SOURCE: National Education Association, *Estimates of School Statistics*, latest edition 1994–95. Copyright 1995 by the National Education Association. (All rights reserved.)

Figure 11.-Sources of revenue for public elementary and secondary schools: 1970–71 to 1992–93

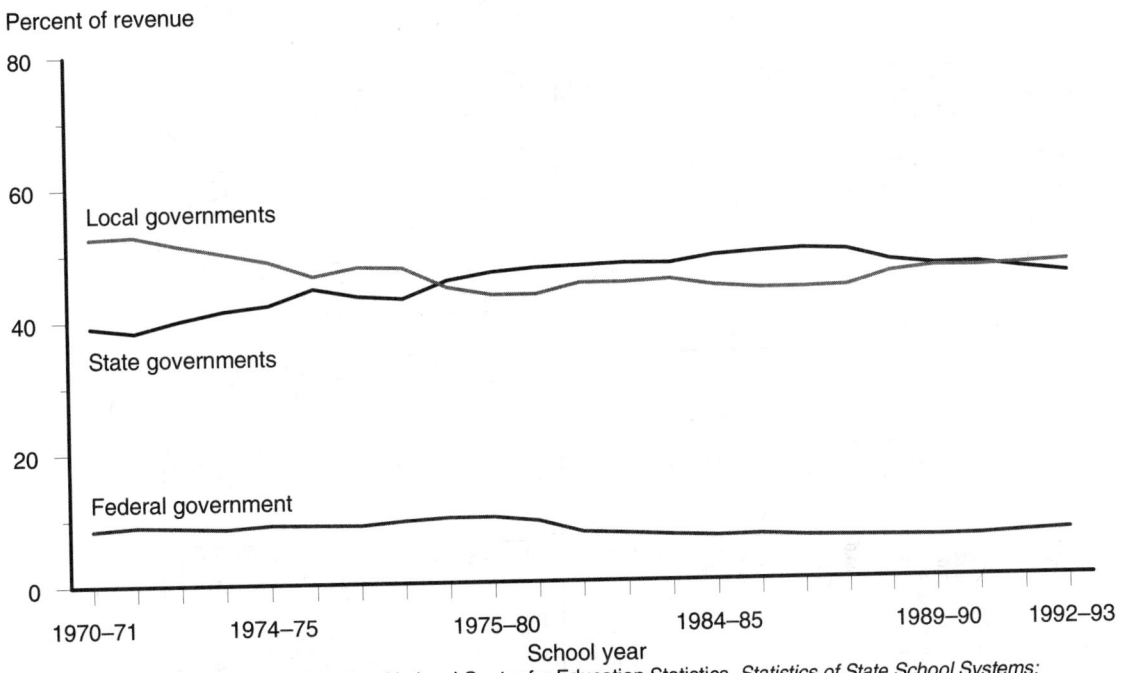

Percent of revenue

SOURCE: U.S Department of Education, National Center for Education Statistics, *Statistics of State School Systems; Revenues and Expenditures for Public Elementary and Secondary Education*; and Common Core of Data surveys.

Figure 12.-Current expenditure per pupil in average daily attendance in public elementary and secondary schools: 1970-71 to 1994–95

Per pupil expenditure

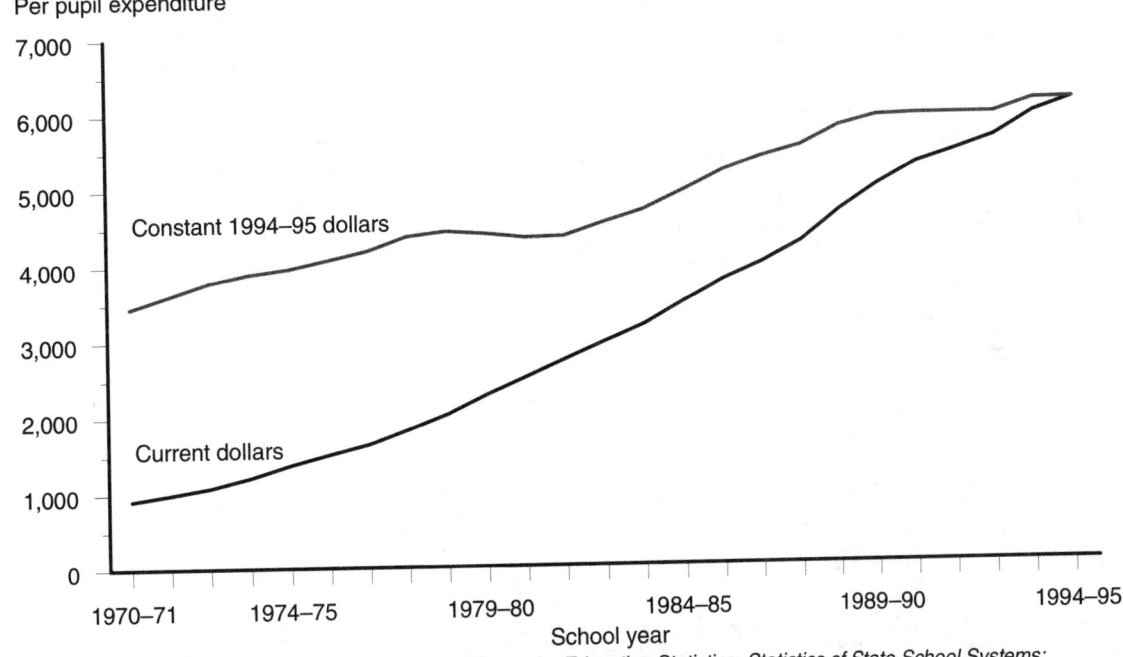

SOURCE: U.S Department of Education, National Center for Education Statistics, *Statistics of State School Systems; Revenues and Expenditures for Public Elementary and Secondary Education*; and Common Core of Data surveys.

Table 38.—Historical summary of public elementary and secondary school statistics: 1869–70 to 1992–93

Item	1869-70	1879-80	1889-90	1899-1900	1909-10	1919-20	1929-30	1939-40	1949-50	1959-60	1969-70	1979-80	1989-90	1990-91	1992-93
1	2	3	4	5	6	7	8	9	10	11	12	13	14	15	16
Population, pupils, and instructional staff															
Total population,[1] in thousands	38,558	50,156	62,622	75,995	90,490	104,514	121,767	130,880	149,199	179,323	201,385	224,567	246,819	249,402	255,028
Population aged 5-17 years,[1] in thousands	11,683	15,066	18,473	21,573	24,011	27,571	31,414	30,151	30,223	43,881	52,386	48,041	44,947	45,306	46,662
Percent of total population 5-17	30.3	30.0	29.5	28.4	26.5	26.4	25.8	23.0	20.3	24.5	26.0	21.4	18.2	18.2	18.3
Total enrollment in elementary and secondary schools, in thousands[2]	[3]7,562	9,867	12,723	15,503	17,814	21,578	25,678	25,434	25,112	36,087	45,550	41,651	40,543	41,217	42,816
Kindergarten and grades 1-8, in thousands	[3]7,481	9,757	12,520	14,984	16,899	19,378	21,279	18,833	19,387	27,602	32,513	28,034	29,152	29,878	31,081
Grades 9-12, in thousands	[3]80	110	203	519	915	2,200	4,399	6,601	5,725	8,485	13,037	13,616	11,390	11,338	11,735
Enrollment as a percent of total population	[3]19.6	19.7	20.3	20.4	19.7	20.6	21.1	19.4	16.8	20.1	22.6	18.5	16.4	16.5	16.8
Enrollment as a percent of 5- to 17-year-olds	[3]64.7	65.5	68.9	71.9	74.2	78.3	81.7	84.4	83.1	82.2	87.0	86.7	90.2	91.0	91.7
Percent of total enrollment in high schools (grades 9-12 and postgraduate)	[3]1.1	1.1	1.6	3.3	5.1	10.2	17.1	26.0	22.8	23.5	28.6	32.7	28.1	27.5	27.4
High school graduates, in thousands	—	—	22	62	111	231	592	1,143	1,063	1,627	2,589	2,748	2,320	2,235	2,233
Average daily attendance, in thousands	4,077	6,144	8,154	10,633	12,827	16,150	21,265	22,042	22,284	32,477	41,934	38,289	37,799	38,427	39,568
Total number of days attended by pupils enrolled, in millions	539	801	1,098	1,535	2,011	2,615	3,673	3,858	3,964	5,782	7,501	[4]6,835	—	—	—
Percent of enrolled pupils attending daily	59.3	62.3	64.1	68.6	72.1	74.8	82.8	86.7	88.7	90.0	90.4	[4]90.1	—	—	—
Average length of school term, in days	132.2	130.3	134.7	144.3	157.5	161.9	172.7	175.0	177.9	178.0	178.9	[4]178.5	—	179.8	—
Average number of days attended per pupil	78.4	81.1	86.3	99.0	113	121.2	143	151.7	157.9	160.2	161.7	[4]160.8	—	—	—
Total instructional staff, in thousands	—	—	—	—	—	678	880	912	963	1,457	2,286	2,406	2,986	3,051	3,140
Supervisors, in thousands	—	—	—	—	—	7	7	7	5	—	—	—	—	—	—
Principals, in thousands	—	—	—	—	—	14	31	32	43	64	91	106	126	127	122
Teachers, librarians, and other nonsupervisory instructional staff,[5] in thousands	201	287	364	423	523	657	843	875	920	1,393	2,195	2,300	2,860	2,924	3,017
Men, in thousands	78	123	126	127	110	93	140	195	196	404	[4]711	[4]782	—	—	—
Women, in thousands	123	164	238	296	413	585	703	681	724	989	[4]1,484	[4]1,518	—	—	—
Percent men	38.7	42.8	34.5	29.9	21.1	14.1	16.6	22.2	21.3	[4]29.0	[4]32.4	[4]34.0	—	—	—
Finance *(Amounts in millions of current dollars)*															
Total revenue receipts	—	—	$143	$220	$433	$970	$2,089	$2,261	$5,437	$14,747	$40,267	$96,881	$208,548	$223,341	$248,496
Federal government	—	—	—	—	—	2	7	40	156	652	3,220	9,504	12,701	13,776	17,267
State governments	—	—	—	—	—	160	354	684	2,166	5,768	16,063	45,349	98,239	105,325	113,397
Local sources, including intermediate	—	—	—	—	—	808	1,728	1,536	3,116	8,327	20,985	42,029	97,608	104,240	117,832
Percent of revenue receipts from:															
Federal government	—	—	—	—	—	0.3	0.4	1.8	2.9	4.4	8.0	9.8	6.1	6.2	6.9
State governments	—	—	—	—	—	16.5	16.9	30.3	39.8	39.1	39.9	46.8	47.1	47.2	45.6
Local sources, including intermediate	—	—	—	—	—	83.2	82.7	68.0	57.3	56.5	52.1	43.4	46.8	46.7	47.4
Total expenditures for public schools	$63	$78	$141	$215	$426	$1,036	$2,317	$2,344	$5,838	$15,613	$40,683	$95,962	[7]212,473	[7]229,430	$253,859
Current expenditures[6]	—	—	114	180	356	861	1,844	1,942	4,687	[7]12,329	[7]34,218	[7]86,984	[7]187,933	[7]202,038	[7]221,353
Capital outlay[8]	—	—	26	35	70	154	371	258	1,014	2,662	4,659	6,506	17,781	19,771	22,669
Interest on school debt	—	—	—	—	—	18	93	131	101	490	1,171	1,874	3,776	4,325	5,439
Other current expenditures[9]	—	—	—	—	—	3	10	13	36	133	636	[10]598	2,983	3,296	4,399
Percent of total expenditures devoted to:															
Current expenditures[6]	—	—	81.3	83.5	83.6	83.1	79.6	82.8	80.3	[7]79.0	[7]84.1	[7]90.6	[7]88.5	[7]88.1	[7]87.2
Capital outlay[8]	—	—	18.7	16.5	16.4	14.8	16.0	11.0	17.4	17.0	11.5	6.8	8.4	8.6	8.9
Interest on school debt	—	—	—	—	—	1.8	4.0	5.6	1.7	3.1	2.9	2.0	1.8	1.9	2.1
Other current expenditures[9]	—	—	—	—	—	0.3	0.4	0.6	0.6	0.8	1.6	[10]0.6	1.4	1.4	1.7

Table 38.—Historical summary of public elementary and secondary school statistics: 1869–70 to 1992–93—Continued

Item	1869–70	1879–80	1889–90	1899–1900	1909–10	1919–20	1929–30	1939–40	1949–50	1959–60	1969–70	1979–80	1989–90	1990–91	1992–93
1	2	3	4	5	6	7	8	9	10	11	12	13	14	15	16
Amounts in current dollars															
Annual salary of instructional staff [11]	$189	$195	$252	$325	$485	$871	$1,420	$1,441	$3,010	$5,174	$9,047	[12]$16,715	[12]$32,638	[12]$34,412	[12]$36,454
Personal income per member of labor force [1]	—	—	—	—	—	—	1,634	1,356	3,400	5,722	9,583	19,370	35,362	37,454	40,588
Total school expenditures per capita of total population	1.59	1.56	2.23	2.83	4.71	9.91	19.03	17.91	39	87	202	427	861	920	995
National income [1] per capita	—	—	—	—	—	—	667	587	1,520	2,287	3,966	9,079	17,217	18,007	18,937
Current expenditure [6,13] per pupil in ADA [14]	15.55	12.71	13.99	16.67	27.85	53.32	86.70	88.09	210	375	816	2,272	4,972	5,258	5,594
Total expenditure [15] per pupil in ADA	—	—	17.23	20.21	33.23	64.16	108.49	105.74	260	471	955	2,491	5,542	5,885	6,305
National income per pupil in ADA [6]	—	—	—	—	—	—	3,845	3,502	10,312	12,627	19,044	53,250	112,423	116,872	122,056
Current expenditure per day [16] per pupil in ADA [6]	0.12	0.10	0.10	0.12	0.18	0.33	0.50	0.50	1.17	2.11	4.56	12.73	—	—	—
Total expenditure per day per pupil in ADA	—	—	0.13	0.14	0.21	0.40	0.63	0.60	1.46	2.65	5.34	13.95	—	—	—
Amounts in constant 1992–93 dollars															
Annual salary of instructional staff [11]	—	—	—	—	—	$6,514	$11,824	$14,696	$18,114	$25,097	$34,134	[12]$30,687	[12]$36,635	[12]$36,624	[12]$36,454
Personal income per member of labor force [1]	—	—	—	—	—	—	13,606	13,829	20,461	27,755	36,158	35,561	39,693	39,862	40,588
Total school expenditures per capita of total population	—	—	—	—	—	74	158	183	236	422	762	785	966	979	995
National income [1] per capita	—	—	—	—	—	—	5,554	5,987	9,147	11,093	14,962	16,668	19,326	19,165	18,937
Current expenditure [6,13] per pupil in ADA [14]	—	—	—	—	—	399	722	898	1,264	1,820	3,079	4,171	5,581	5,596	5,594
Total expenditure [15] per pupil in ADA	—	—	—	—	—	480	903	1,078	1,567	2,285	3,603	4,573	6,221	6,263	6,305
National income per pupil in ADA	—	—	—	—	—	—	32,015	35,715	62,058	61,250	71,854	97,761	126,191	124,385	122,056
Current expenditure per day [16] per pupil in ADA [6]	—	—	—	—	—	2.47	4.16	5.10	7.04	10.23	17.20	23.37	—	—	—
Total expenditure per day per pupil in ADA	—	—	—	—	—	2.81	4.93	5.75	8.26	12.08	18.93	24.06	—	—	—

[1] Data on population and labor force are from the Bureau of the Census, and data on personal income and national income are from the Bureau of Economic Analysis, U.S. Department of Commerce. Population data through 1900 are based on total population from the decennial census. From 1909–10 to 1959–60, population data are total population, including armed forces overseas, as of July 1. Data for later years are for resident population that excludes armed forces overseas.

[2] Data for 1869–70 through 1959–60 are school year enrollment. Data for later years are fall enrollment.

[3] Data for 1870–71.

[4] Estimated by the National Center for Education Statistics.

[5] Prior to 1919–20, data are for the number of different persons employed rather than number of positions.

[6] Prior to 1919–20, includes interest on school debt.

[7] Because of the modification of the scope of "current expenditures for elementary and secondary schools," data for 1959–60 and later years are not entirely comparable with prior years.

[8] Beginning in 1969–70, includes capital outlay by state and local school building authorities.

[9] Includes summer schools, community colleges, and adult education. Beginning in 1959–60, also includes community services, formerly classified with "current expenditures for elementary and secondary schools."

[10] Excludes community colleges and adult education.

[11] Average includes supervisors, principals, teachers, and other nonsupervisory instructional staff.

[12] Estimated by the National Education Association.

[13] Excludes current expenditures not allocable to pupil costs.

[14] "ADA" means average daily attendance in elementary and secondary schools.

[15] The expenditure figure used here is the sum of current expenditures allocable to pupil costs, capital outlay, and interest on school debt.

[16] Per-day rates derived by dividing annual rates by average length of term.

—Data not collected.

NOTE.—Kindergarten enrollment includes a relatively small number of nursery school pupils. Because of rounding, details may not add to totals. Some data have been revised from previously published figures. Beginning in 1959–60, data include Alaska and Hawaii.

SOURCE: U.S. Department of Education, National Center for Education Statistics, *Statistics of State School Systems; Statistics of Public Elementary and Secondary School Systems; Revenues and Expenditures for Public Elementary and Secondary Education, FY 1980;* Common Core of Data surveys; and Council of Economic Advisers, *Economic Indicators.* (This table was prepared June 1995.)

Table 39.—Enrollment in public elementary and secondary schools, by level and state: Fall 1980 to fall 1994

State or other area	Fall 1980 Total	Fall 1981 Total	Fall 1982 Total	Fall 1983 Total	Fall 1984 Total	Fall 1985 Total	Fall 1986 Total	Fall 1987 Total	Fall 1988 Total	Fall 1989 Total	Fall 1990 Total
1	2	3	4	5	6	7	8	9	10	11	12
United States	40,877,481	40,044,093	39,565,610	39,252,308	39,208,252	39,421,961	39,753,172	40,008,213	40,188,690	40,542,707	41,216,683
Alabama	758,721	743,448	724,037	721,901	712,586	730,460	733,735	729,234	724,751	723,743	721,806
Alaska [4]	86,514	90,858	89,413	98,206	104,599	107,345	107,848	106,869	106,481	109,280	113,903
Arizona	513,790	507,199	510,296	506,682	530,062	548,252	534,538	572,421	574,890	607,615	639,853
Arkansas	447,700	437,121	432,565	432,120	432,668	433,410	437,438	437,036	436,387	434,960	436,286
California	4,076,421	4,046,156	4,065,486	4,089,017	4,151,110	4,255,554	4,377,989	4,488,398	4,618,120	4,771,978	4,950,474
Colorado	546,033	544,174	545,209	542,196	545,427	550,642	558,415	560,236	560,081	562,755	574,213
Connecticut [5]	531,459	505,386	486,470	477,585	468,145	462,026	468,847	465,465	460,637	461,560	469,123
Delaware	99,403	95,072	92,646	91,406	91,767	92,901	94,410	95,659	96,678	97,808	99,658
District of Columbia	100,049	94,975	91,105	88,843	87,397	87,092	85,612	86,435	84,792	81,301	80,694
Florida	1,510,225	1,487,721	1,484,734	1,495,543	1,524,107	1,562,283	1,607,320	1,664,774	1,720,930	1,789,925	1,861,592
Georgia	1,068,737	1,056,117	1,053,689	1,050,859	1,062,315	1,079,594	1,096,425	1,110,947	1,107,994	1,126,535	1,151,687
Hawaii	165,068	162,805	162,024	162,241	163,860	164,169	164,640	166,160	167,488	169,493	171,708
Idaho	203,247	204,524	202,973	206,352	208,080	208,669	208,391	212,444	214,615	214,932	220,840
Illinois	1,983,463	1,924,084	1,880,289	1,853,316	1,834,355	1,826,478	1,825,185	1,811,446	1,794,916	1,797,355	1,821,407
Indiana	1,055,589	1,025,172	999,542	984,384	972,659	966,106	966,780	964,129	960,994	954,165	954,525
Iowa	533,857	516,216	504,983	497,287	491,011	485,332	481,286	480,826	478,200	478,486	483,652
Kansas	415,291	409,909	407,074	405,222	405,347	410,229	416,091	421,112	426,596	430,864	437,034
Kentucky	669,798	658,350	651,084	647,414	644,421	643,833	642,778	642,696	637,627	630,688	636,401
Louisiana	777,560	782,053	784,027	800,193	800,941	788,349	795,188	793,093	786,683	783,025	784,757
Maine	222,497	216,293	211,986	209,753	207,537	206,101	211,752	211,817	212,902	213,775	215,149
Maryland	750,665	721,841	699,201	683,491	673,840	671,560	675,747	683,797	688,947	698,806	715,176
Massachusetts	1,021,885	947,037	908,984	878,844	859,391	844,330	833,918	825,320	823,428	825,588	834,314
Michigan	1,797,052	1,724,587	1,674,697	1,635,963	1,609,448	1,602,747	1,597,154	1,589,287	1,582,785	1,576,785	1,584,431
Minnesota	754,318	733,741	715,190	705,236	701,697	705,140	711,134	721,481	726,950	739,553	756,374
Mississippi	477,059	471,615	468,294	467,744	466,058	471,195	498,639	505,550	503,326	502,020	502,417
Missouri	844,648	818,705	802,535	795,453	793,793	795,107	800,606	802,060	806,639	807,934	816,558
Montana	155,193	153,435	152,335	153,646	154,412	153,869	153,327	152,207	152,191	151,265	152,974
Nebraska	280,430	273,340	269,009	266,998	265,599	265,819	267,139	268,100	269,434	270,920	274,081
Nevada	149,481	151,339	151,104	150,442	151,633	154,948	161,239	168,353	176,474	186,834	201,316
New Hampshire	167,232	163,827	160,197	159,030	158,614	160,974	163,717	166,045	169,413	171,696	172,785
New Jersey	1,246,008	1,199,643	1,172,520	1,147,841	1,129,223	1,116,194	1,107,467	1,092,982	1,080,871	1,076,005	1,089,646
New Mexico	271,198	268,091	268,632	269,711	272,478	277,551	281,943	287,229	292,425	296,057	301,881
New York	2,871,724	2,783,017	2,718,678	2,674,818	2,645,811	2,621,378	2,607,719	2,594,070	2,573,715	2,565,841	2,598,337
North Carolina	1,129,376	1,108,960	1,096,815	1,089,606	1,088,724	1,086,165	1,085,248	1,085,976	1,083,156	1,080,744	1,086,871
North Dakota	116,885	117,708	117,078	117,213	118,711	118,570	118,703	119,004	118,809	117,816	117,825
Ohio	1,957,381	1,898,501	1,860,245	1,827,300	1,805,440	1,793,965	1,793,508	1,793,431	1,778,544	1,764,410	1,771,089
Oklahoma	577,807	582,572	593,825	591,389	589,690	592,327	593,183	584,212	580,426	578,580	579,087
Oregon	464,599	457,165	448,184	447,109	446,884	447,527	449,307	455,895	461,752	472,394	472,394
Pennsylvania	1,909,292	1,839,015	1,783,969	1,737,952	1,701,880	1,683,221	1,674,161	1,668,542	1,659,714	1,655,279	1,667,834
Rhode Island	148,956	143,414	139,959	136,412	134,610	133,949	134,690	134,800	133,585	135,729	138,813
South Carolina	619,223	609,158	608,518	604,553	602,718	606,643	611,629	614,921	615,774	616,177	622,112
South Dakota	128,507	125,657	123,897	123,060	123,314	124,291	125,458	126,817	126,910	127,329	129,164
Tennessee	853,569	838,297	828,264	822,057	817,212	813,753	818,073	823,783	821,580	819,660	824,595
Texas	2,900,073	2,935,547	2,985,659	2,989,796	3,040,305	3,131,705	3,209,515	3,236,787	3,283,707	3,328,514	3,382,887
Utah	343,618	355,554	370,183	378,208	390,141	403,305	415,994	423,386	431,119	438,554	446,652
Vermont	95,815	93,183	91,454	90,416	90,089	90,157	92,112	92,755	93,381	94,779	95,762
Virginia	1,010,371	989,548	975,727	966,110	965,222	968,104	975,135	979,417	982,393	985,346	998,601
Washington	757,639	750,188	739,215	736,239	741,177	749,706	761,428	775,755	790,918	810,232	839,709
West Virginia	383,503	377,772	375,115	371,251	362,941	357,923	351,837	344,236	335,912	327,540	322,389
Wisconsin	830,247	804,262	784,830	774,646	767,542	768,234	767,819	772,363	774,857	782,905	797,621
Wyoming	98,305	99,541	101,665	99,254	101,261	102,779	100,955	98,455	97,793	97,172	98,226
Outlying areas											
American Samoa	9,647	9,896	—	10,124	—	—	11,055	11,248	11,764	12,258	12,463
Guam	26,420	25,084	25,676	26,249	—	26,043	25,676	25,936	26,041	26,493	26,391
Northern Marianas	—	—	5,300	—	4,499	4,841	—	—	5,819	6,079	6,101	6,449
Puerto Rico	712,880	721,419	708,794	701,925	692,923	686,914	679,489	672,837	661,693	651,225	644,734
Virgin Islands	25,201	25,525	25,699	26,126	26,122	25,448	24,435	24,020	23,492	21,193	21,750

Table 39.—Enrollment in public elementary and secondary schools, by level and state: Fall 1980 to fall 1994—Continued

State or other areas	Fall 1991			Fall 1992			Fall 1993			Estimated fall 1994 [1]
	Total	Kindergarten through grade 8 [2]	Grades 9 to 12	Total	Kindergarten through grade 8 [2]	Grades 9 to 12	Total	Kindergarten through grade 8 [2]	Grades 9 to 12	Total
1	13	14	15	16	17	18	19	20	21	22
United States	42,046,878	30,505,625	11,541,253	42,815,541	31,080,500	11,735,041	43,476,268	31,515,485	11,960,783	44,034,416
Alabama	722,004	526,473	195,531	730,857	534,471	196,386	734,469	535,818	198,651	[3]733,458
Alaska [4]	118,680	89,124	29,556	122,487	91,640	30,847	125,948	93,601	32,347	[3]122,494
Arizona	656,980	490,242	166,738	673,477	497,917	175,560	709,453	526,412	183,041	791,689
Arkansas	438,518	315,147	123,371	441,490	317,598	123,892	444,271	317,713	126,558	[3]432,317
California	5,107,145	3,720,302	1,386,843	5,249,275	3,845,188	1,404,087	5,328,558	3,904,471	1,424,087	5,340,000
Colorado	593,030	435,621	157,409	612,635	451,321	161,314	625,062	459,930	165,132	[3]640,521
Connecticut [5]	481,050	355,463	125,587	488,476	361,548	126,928	496,298	368,632	127,666	[3]503,216
Delaware	102,196	74,555	27,641	104,321	75,983	28,338	105,547	76,617	28,930	[3]106,813
District of Columbia	80,618	61,019	19,599	80,937	61,133	19,804	80,678	61,434	19,244	[6]80,420
Florida	1,932,131	1,427,613	504,518	1,981,407	1,469,850	511,557	2,040,763	1,515,194	525,569	2,108,978
Georgia	1,177,569	868,130	309,439	1,207,186	891,647	315,539	1,235,304	910,425	324,879	[3]1,270,948
Hawaii	174,747	126,855	47,892	177,448	128,610	48,838	180,430	131,658	48,772	[3]183,164
Idaho	225,680	161,458	64,222	231,668	164,634	67,034	236,774	166,999	69,775	[3]240,448
Illinois	1,848,166	1,327,834	520,332	1,873,567	1,344,549	529,018	1,893,078	1,356,329	536,749	1,919,226
Indiana	956,988	676,481	280,507	960,630	677,249	283,381	965,599	679,006	286,593	972,521
Iowa	491,363	348,231	143,132	494,839	348,648	146,191	498,519	348,006	150,513	[3]498,837
Kansas	445,390	325,126	120,264	451,536	328,244	123,292	457,614	329,708	127,906	[3]460,905
Kentucky	646,024	466,170	179,854	655,041	469,897	185,144	655,265	467,315	187,950	[6]655,489
Louisiana	794,128	590,660	203,468	797,985	590,824	207,161	800,560	587,490	213,070	[3]781,857
Maine	216,400	156,764	59,636	216,453	156,368	60,085	216,995	156,528	60,467	215,517
Maryland	736,238	543,492	192,746	751,850	555,565	196,285	772,638	569,497	203,141	[3]790,935
Massachusetts	846,155	615,990	230,165	859,948	629,649	230,299	877,726	645,518	232,208	897,705
Michigan	1,593,561	1,158,568	434,993	1,603,610	1,164,879	438,731	1,599,377	1,159,968	439,409	1,603,535
Minnesota	773,571	556,735	216,836	793,724	569,298	224,426	810,233	576,980	233,253	826,600
Mississippi	504,127	369,936	134,191	506,668	370,006	136,662	505,907	368,688	137,219	503,301
Missouri	842,965	611,603	231,362	859,357	621,712	237,645	875,639	631,552	244,087	[3]861,542
Montana	155,779	112,780	42,999	160,011	115,315	44,696	163,009	116,668	46,341	[3]164,295
Nebraska	279,552	201,367	78,185	282,414	202,439	79,975	285,097	203,426	81,671	[3]286,405
Nevada	211,810	157,713	54,097	222,974	165,348	57,626	235,800	175,054	60,746	[3]250,747
New Hampshire	177,138	129,698	47,440	181,247	133,182	48,065	185,360	136,211	49,149	[3]186,398
New Jersey	1,109,796	800,696	309,100	1,130,560	817,661	312,899	1,151,307	843,526	307,781	[3]1,174,545
New Mexico	308,667	212,836	95,831	315,668	217,418	98,250	322,292	226,287	96,005	315,730
New York	2,643,993	1,862,215	781,778	2,689,686	1,893,303	796,383	2,733,813	1,920,609	813,204	2,790,700
North Carolina	1,097,598	794,773	302,825	1,114,083	810,576	303,507	1,133,231	828,171	305,060	[3]1,146,639
North Dakota	118,376	84,941	33,435	118,734	84,569	34,165	119,127	84,127	35,000	[3]119,288
Ohio	1,783,767	1,277,403	506,364	1,795,199	1,283,869	511,330	1,807,319	1,290,197	517,122	1,825,410
Oklahoma	588,263	432,334	155,929	597,096	438,796	158,300	604,076	441,094	162,982	[6]611,138
Oregon	498,614	359,348	139,266	510,122	365,416	144,706	516,611	368,141	148,470	[3]521,945
Pennsylvania	1,692,797	1,195,012	497,785	1,717,613	1,215,974	501,639	1,744,082	1,233,113	510,969	1,779,790
Rhode Island	142,144	104,146	37,998	143,798	105,677	38,121	145,676	107,047	38,629	[3]147,490
South Carolina	627,470	456,039	171,431	639,942	466,783	173,159	643,859	467,114	176,745	[3]641,820
South Dakota	131,576	96,423	35,153	134,573	97,882	36,691	142,825	102,281	40,544	143,411
Tennessee	833,651	604,571	229,080	854,329	620,899	233,430	866,991	630,449	236,542	[3]865,729
Texas	3,464,371	2,574,983	889,388	3,541,769	2,634,346	907,423	3,608,262	2,681,053	927,209	3,680,271
Utah	456,430	326,969	129,461	463,870	329,883	133,987	471,365	329,926	141,439	[3]471,557
Vermont	97,137	72,702	24,435	98,558	73,865	24,693	102,755	74,828	27,927	[6]107,131
Virginia	[6]1,016,204	[6]741,005	[6]275,199	1,031,925	757,847	274,078	1,045,471	767,347	278,124	[6]1,059,195
Washington	869,327	632,781	236,546	896,475	651,743	244,732	915,952	660,424	255,528	[3]934,309
West Virginia	320,249	221,545	98,704	318,296	219,037	99,259	314,383	215,784	98,599	[3]309,888
Wisconsin	814,671	579,863	234,808	829,415	588,447	240,968	844,001	595,717	248,284	856,661
Wyoming	102,074	73,890	28,184	100,313	71,798	28,515	100,899	71,402	29,497	[6]101,488
Outlying areas										
American Samoa	13,365	10,050	3,315	13,994	10,582	3,412	14,484	10,974	3,510	[3]14,345
Guam	28,334	20,800	7,534	30,077	22,428	7,649	30,920	23,153	7,767	31,711
Northern Marianas	7,096	5,628	1,468	8,086	6,133	1,953	8,188	6,380	1,808	[6]8,291
Puerto Rico	642,392	474,976	167,416	637,034	469,764	167,270	631,460	464,931	166,529	[3]621,895
Virgin Islands	22,346	16,675	5,671	22,887	16,804	6,083	22,752	16,706	6,046	[3]23,353

[1] Data estimated by state education agencies.

[2] Includes a relatively small number of prekindergarten students.

[3] Actual data.

[4] Beginning in 1983, data include students enrolled in public schools on federal bases and other special arrangements.

[5] Beginning in 1986, data include state vocational/technical schools.

[6] Data estimated by the National Center for Education Statistics.

—Data not available.

NOTE.—Some data have been revised from previously published figures.

SOURCE: U.S. Department of Education, National Center for Education Statistics, Common Core of Data surveys. (This table was prepared May 1995.)

Table 40.—Enrollment in public elementary and secondary schools, by grade and state: Fall 1993

State or other area	Total, all levels	Prekindergarten through grade 8 and elementary unclassified							
		Total	Prekinder-garten [1]	Kindergarten	Grade 1	Grade 2	Grade 3	Grade 4	Grade 5
1	2	3	4	5	6	7	8	9	10
United States	43,476,268	31,515,485	556,918	3,376,636	3,529,072	3,429,290	3,436,917	3,361,095	3,350,464
Alabama	734,469	535,818	8,445	56,598	59,239	55,781	58,612	57,497	58,098
Alaska	125,948	93,601	2,787	10,329	10,663	10,549	10,479	10,156	9,809
Arizona	709,453	526,412	3,164	57,656	60,628	59,285	59,098	57,701	58,110
Arkansas	444,271	317,713	1,248	34,337	34,586	33,737	34,398	34,255	34,834
California	5,328,558	3,904,471	61,281	444,104	444,346	435,329	431,107	420,233	413,420
Colorado	625,062	459,930	7,249	47,598	51,410	51,673	51,222	50,807	51,307
Connecticut	496,298	368,632	6,216	42,338	43,961	41,289	40,244	39,093	37,639
Delaware	105,547	76,617	565	8,153	8,816	8,703	8,455	8,285	8,335
District of Columbia	80,678	61,434	5,216	6,986	7,195	6,728	6,149	5,870	5,435
Florida	2,040,763	1,515,194	34,793	167,140	169,039	168,302	170,860	168,509	166,144
Georgia	1,235,304	910,425	5,534	103,365	103,346	100,224	100,082	99,802	100,493
Hawaii	180,430	131,658	552	15,199	15,158	15,038	14,713	14,813	14,770
Idaho	236,774	166,999	1,389	17,039	17,464	16,872	17,788	18,665	19,015
Illinois	1,893,078	1,356,329	42,359	144,758	147,148	143,397	143,349	138,827	132,833
Indiana	965,599	679,006	3,971	70,226	74,609	71,903	72,471	72,840	74,498
Iowa	498,519	348,006	5,430	36,348	35,131	36,217	36,994	36,370	37,530
Kansas	457,614	329,708	2,432	34,575	36,063	35,896	36,393	35,975	36,525
Kentucky	655,265	467,315	15,732	43,340	46,083	46,151	57,522	48,083	49,333
Louisiana	800,560	587,490	12,857	61,133	63,742	61,535	61,709	60,077	59,614
Maine	216,995	156,528	1,036	17,536	16,995	17,637	17,514	17,237	17,018
Maryland	772,638	569,497	17,984	60,378	64,504	62,421	62,141	61,199	60,377
Massachusetts	877,726	645,518	13,178	76,494	76,002	72,068	71,381	69,111	66,902
Michigan	1,599,377	1,159,968	11,704	132,658	130,499	124,979	124,837	120,049	118,276
Minnesota	810,233	576,980	6,656	62,345	62,208	63,724	64,244	63,194	63,288
Mississippi	505,907	368,688	2,197	37,622	40,553	38,640	38,589	39,236	39,662
Missouri	875,639	631,552	23,597	65,317	67,793	67,635	67,913	66,431	67,614
Montana	163,009	116,668	483	12,021	12,779	12,715	12,894	12,967	12,902
Nebraska	285,097	203,426	3,577	21,374	21,429	21,770	22,097	22,391	22,319
Nevada	235,800	175,054	1,237	19,179	20,487	20,202	19,725	19,305	19,153
New Hampshire	185,360	136,211	1,292	8,194	18,156	16,038	16,237	15,630	15,614
New Jersey	1,151,307	843,526	9,225	90,827	96,030	89,592	87,454	84,767	83,173
New Mexico	322,292	226,287	1,933	23,723	26,035	24,975	24,605	24,182	24,676
New York	2,733,813	1,920,609	31,687	205,238	220,578	209,649	204,260	198,259	196,767
North Carolina	1,133,231	828,171	8,469	93,406	92,701	89,371	90,875	85,989	85,721
North Dakota	119,127	84,127	615	8,752	8,990	8,969	9,223	9,266	9,583
Ohio	1,807,319	1,290,197	17,210	140,778	143,737	140,554	140,822	136,317	138,011
Oklahoma	604,076	441,094	5,456	44,864	53,724	47,482	47,788	48,242	49,154
Oregon	516,611	368,141	837	37,859	40,259	40,704	41,454	41,290	41,885
Pennsylvania	1,744,082	1,233,113	4,181	131,842	145,111	138,527	134,504	131,575	131,962
Rhode Island	145,676	107,047	465	11,348	13,041	11,858	11,659	11,603	11,208
South Carolina	643,859	467,114	7,407	45,490	53,676	51,226	51,457	50,357	50,992
South Dakota	142,825	102,281	612	10,574	10,818	10,908	11,068	11,086	11,084
Tennessee	866,991	630,449	9,976	68,462	70,638	67,305	66,952	65,646	65,662
Texas	3,608,262	2,681,053	120,446	268,646	299,513	288,258	289,284	284,394	284,342
Utah	471,365	329,926	2,690	33,623	33,634	34,245	34,634	35,467	36,281
Vermont	102,755	74,828	2,024	7,766	8,454	8,227	8,284	8,457	8,318
Virginia	1,045,471	767,347	3,186	81,787	84,318	83,296	84,146	81,615	79,683
Washington	915,952	660,424	5,087	68,908	72,729	73,380	73,746	73,824	74,884
West Virginia	314,383	215,784	3,981	20,077	22,623	22,254	22,181	22,349	23,623
Wisconsin	844,001	595,717	17,270	61,136	64,779	64,467	65,336	63,756	64,435
Wyoming	100,899	71,402	—	7,190	7,652	7,605	7,968	8,046	8,153
Outlying areas									
American Samoa	14,484	10,974	1,663	1,056	1,240	1,143	1,093	1,056	987
Guam	30,920	23,153	486	2,866	2,806	2,761	2,585	2,517	2,476
Northern Marianas	8,188	6,380	421	656	809	700	677	633	626
Puerto Rico	631,460	464,931	281	38,305	55,003	50,180	50,072	51,411	51,786
Virgin Islands	22,752	16,706	—	1,624	1,870	1,757	1,745	1,755	1,782

Table 40.—Enrollment in public elementary and secondary schools, by grade and state: Fall 1993—Continued

State or other area	Prekindergarten through grade 8 and elementary unclassified				Grades 9 through 12 and secondary unclassified					
	Grade 6	Grade 7	Grade 8	Elementary unclassified	Total	Grade 9	Grade 10	Grade 11	Grade 12	Secondary unclassified
1	11	12	13	14	15	16	17	18	19	20
United States	3,355,642	3,355,412	3,249,381	514,658	11,960,783	3,487,159	3,050,402	2,751,154	2,423,900	248,168
Alabama	59,400	62,144	60,004	—	198,651	62,141	50,543	46,067	39,900	—
Alaska	9,817	9,852	9,160	—	32,347	9,608	8,514	7,250	6,975	—
Arizona	57,242	55,834	53,500	4,194	183,041	54,878	48,281	41,964	37,614	304
Arkansas	35,107	36,892	36,471	1,848	126,558	36,045	32,711	29,876	27,169	757
California	405,416	398,553	380,223	70,459	1,424,087	406,551	375,992	333,716	277,271	30,557
Colorado	50,619	49,168	47,665	1,212	165,132	47,344	42,536	39,610	34,770	872
Connecticut	37,007	36,127	34,662	10,056	127,666	36,481	32,802	30,393	27,979	11
Delaware	8,302	8,738	8,265	—	28,930	8,930	7,867	6,251	5,882	—
District of Columbia ...	5,211	5,394	4,935	2,315	19,244	5,003	5,403	4,145	3,303	1,390
Florida	163,447	157,906	149,054	—	525,569	164,978	140,271	119,674	100,646	—
Georgia	100,824	99,401	97,354	—	324,879	107,625	82,822	71,728	62,704	—
Hawaii	14,507	13,608	13,245	55	48,772	14,219	12,351	11,957	10,201	44
Idaho	19,444	19,356	19,185	782	69,775	19,537	18,139	16,567	15,044	488
Illinois	134,201	136,363	138,518	54,576	536,749	143,950	131,770	120,785	106,519	33,725
Indiana	76,981	78,353	78,116	5,038	286,593	81,628	72,610	67,005	60,971	4,379
Iowa	37,744	38,861	38,548	8,833	150,513	38,637	36,483	34,893	32,588	7,912
Kansas	36,672	36,913	35,902	2,362	127,906	35,955	32,721	30,761	27,644	825
Kentucky	49,483	51,533	51,306	8,749	187,950	54,502	48,467	43,758	37,629	3,594
Louisiana	60,283	61,553	56,522	28,465	213,070	66,376	51,405	44,676	39,826	10,787
Maine	16,663	16,537	15,844	2,511	60,467	16,630	15,317	14,239	13,446	835
Maryland	60,127	58,407	55,285	6,674	203,141	60,213	50,116	46,082	40,661	6,069
Massachusetts	66,295	64,679	62,412	6,996	232,208	64,643	60,303	55,953	51,309	—
Michigan	118,991	119,423	116,702	41,850	439,409	126,933	110,107	98,594	87,447	16,328
Minnesota	63,677	64,539	63,105	—	233,253	62,353	59,909	56,349	54,642	—
Mississippi	40,203	42,696	39,815	9,475	137,219	41,660	33,709	29,587	26,156	6,107
Missouri	65,680	66,813	66,495	6,264	244,087	71,493	63,147	57,170	50,064	2,213
Montana	13,112	13,285	12,834	676	46,341	12,737	11,935	11,114	10,325	230
Nebraska	22,720	23,138	22,611	—	81,671	22,627	20,770	19,696	18,578	—
Nevada	18,796	18,419	17,825	726	60,746	17,014	16,065	14,899	12,749	19
New Hampshire	15,383	14,997	14,118	552	49,149	14,039	12,499	11,925	10,635	51
New Jersey	82,715	81,942	79,459	58,342	307,781	81,629	73,124	69,108	64,402	19,518
New Mexico	25,403	25,856	24,899	—	96,005	27,115	23,706	20,180	16,767	8,237
New York	195,714	194,988	188,274	75,195	813,204	225,243	200,597	175,038	143,055	69,271
North Carolina	88,232	86,428	86,093	20,886	305,060	94,369	79,553	70,282	60,856	—
North Dakota	9,671	9,729	9,329	—	35,000	9,230	8,971	8,733	8,066	—
Ohio	140,855	145,856	141,534	4,523	517,122	151,241	131,594	122,355	111,932	—
Oklahoma	49,281	47,724	46,153	1,226	162,982	46,597	42,337	38,833	34,744	471
Oregon	41,932	40,605	39,500	1,816	148,470	41,129	38,344	35,518	32,828	651
Pennsylvania	132,960	134,423	130,209	17,819	510,969	143,719	127,919	117,500	107,244	14,587
Rhode Island	11,100	11,136	10,650	2,979	38,629	11,060	10,111	9,205	8,094	159
South Carolina	52,875	53,043	50,591	—	176,745	58,795	45,611	38,390	33,949	—
South Dakota	11,485	11,604	11,427	1,615	40,544	11,276	10,264	9,495	8,936	573
Tennessee	66,547	67,705	64,124	17,432	236,542	71,363	62,534	54,977	47,668	—
Texas	285,414	286,548	274,208	—	927,209	308,461	234,566	205,293	178,889	—
Utah	37,837	37,528	38,031	5,956	141,439	37,270	33,749	34,524	31,692	4,204
Vermont	7,988	7,814	7,496	—	27,927	7,515	6,962	6,673	6,227	550
Virginia	80,889	80,496	78,443	29,488	278,124	80,277	71,469	65,949	60,314	115
Washington	74,094	73,106	70,666	—	255,528	72,322	65,967	61,392	55,847	—
West Virginia	24,649	25,657	25,677	2,713	98,599	26,196	25,214	23,347	21,507	2,335
Wisconsin	64,374	65,495	64,669	—	248,284	69,407	64,586	60,603	53,688	—
Wyoming	8,273	8,247	8,268	—	29,497	8,215	7,659	7,075	6,548	—
Outlying areas										
American Samoa	959	904	873	—	3,510	907	914	821	809	59
Guam	2,338	2,231	2,085	2	7,767	2,964	2,029	1,605	1,154	15
Northern Marianas	612	636	610	—	1,808	480	514	430	384	—
Puerto Rico	51,290	56,314	50,711	9,578	166,529	46,689	44,889	38,516	32,277	4,158
Virgin Islands	1,705	2,130	1,568	770	6,046	1,801	1,343	1,267	1,097	538

[1] Data include imputations for nonrespondents.
—Data not reported or not applicable.

SOURCE: U.S. Department of Education, National Center for Education Statistics, Common Core of Data survey. (This table was prepared March 1995.)

Table 41.—Enrollment in public elementary and secondary schools, by grade and state: Fall 1992

State or other area	Total, all levels	Prekindergarten through grade 8 and elementary unclassified							
		Total	Prekinder-garten[1]	Kindergarten	Grade 1	Grade 2	Grade 3	Grade 4	Grade 5
1	2	3	4	5	6	7	8	9	10
United States	42,815,541	31,080,500	496,814	3,312,777	3,541,708	3,431,291	3,361,362	3,341,737	3,325,427
Alabama	730,857	534,471	7,447	55,460	58,168	56,139	59,481	57,948	58,970
Alaska	122,487	91,640	2,371	10,152	11,030	10,585	10,135	9,748	9,896
Arizona	673,477	497,917	2,544	53,497	58,914	56,814	55,630	55,433	54,630
Arkansas	441,490	317,598	808	33,511	34,929	34,517	34,044	34,632	34,740
California	5,249,275	3,845,188	53,498	431,763	443,955	436,488	424,961	418,418	410,701
Colorado	612,635	451,321	7,410	47,588	51,855	50,686	50,213	50,648	50,165
Connecticut	488,476	361,548	5,731	41,319	43,255	40,774	39,548	38,058	37,138
Delaware	104,321	75,983	463	8,025	9,072	8,523	8,444	8,272	8,311
District of Columbia ...	80,937	61,133	4,818	6,667	7,367	6,606	6,186	5,832	5,524
Florida	1,981,407	1,469,850	31,464	161,701	167,594	169,383	165,858	164,416	160,327
Georgia	1,207,186	891,647	3,303	100,745	101,270	98,952	98,655	99,648	99,130
Hawaii	177,448	128,610	525	14,440	14,761	14,069	14,037	13,754	13,518
Idaho	231,668	164,634	1,231	16,018	16,694	17,354	18,162	18,607	19,055
Illinois	1,873,567	1,344,549	39,682	139,237	148,403	144,406	139,748	133,120	134,215
Indiana	960,630	677,249	3,225	66,065	76,230	72,430	72,869	73,760	75,687
Iowa	494,839	348,648	4,592	36,428	36,630	37,187	36,599	37,692	37,425
Kansas	451,536	328,244	2,391	34,826	36,693	36,014	35,410	36,013	35,666
Kentucky	655,041	469,897	14,564	46,140	48,635	49,824	49,241	49,666	49,984
Louisiana	797,985	590,824	11,439	61,244	66,533	62,791	60,739	61,125	59,945
Maine	216,453	156,368	1,273	17,367	17,914	17,711	17,360	17,154	16,752
Maryland	751,850	555,565	16,081	59,641	62,608	61,983	61,199	60,287	59,139
Massachusetts	859,948	629,649	10,722	75,159	74,381	71,848	69,175	66,822	65,965
Michigan	1,603,610	1,164,879	10,541	135,457	131,010	127,307	121,563	118,963	118,904
Minnesota	793,724	569,298	6,394	61,966	63,609	63,793	62,713	62,606	63,289
Mississippi	506,668	370,006	818	36,423	41,603	39,222	39,189	39,839	40,602
Missouri	859,357	621,712	18,948	65,108	68,905	67,604	65,892	67,098	64,833
Montana	160,011	115,315	554	11,894	13,156	12,679	12,801	12,839	12,937
Nebraska	282,414	202,439	3,134	21,873	21,977	22,112	22,244	22,133	22,286
Nevada	222,974	165,348	1,038	17,839	19,741	19,062	18,731	18,487	18,318
New Hampshire	181,247	133,182	1,005	7,994	18,241	16,262	15,523	15,611	15,238
New Jersey	1,130,560	817,661	9,123	87,427	94,138	87,756	84,855	82,909	82,543
New Mexico	315,668	217,418	2,072	23,723	25,693	24,938	24,319	24,447	23,989
New York	2,689,686	1,893,303	31,290	201,674	217,819	207,369	200,162	197,698	194,157
North Carolina	1,114,083	810,576	6,119	89,809	90,942	88,543	88,051	85,244	85,231
North Dakota	118,734	84,569	640	8,847	9,244	9,294	9,262	9,570	9,638
Ohio	1,795,199	1,283,869	9,900	138,911	146,679	142,053	136,143	137,839	140,200
Oklahoma	597,096	438,796	4,859	45,010	55,354	47,987	48,350	48,793	48,760
Oregon	510,122	365,416	771	37,519	41,015	40,879	40,985	41,443	41,430
Pennsylvania	1,717,613	1,215,974	4,416	129,233	147,186	134,933	130,909	131,248	130,848
Rhode Island	143,798	105,677	498	10,883	13,227	11,654	11,687	11,129	11,086
South Carolina	639,942	466,783	6,523	44,501	54,774	51,456	50,934	51,081	52,262
South Dakota	134,573	97,882	705	10,266	10,642	10,613	10,580	10,645	10,926
Tennessee	854,329	620,899	8,711	64,463	71,432	66,634	65,029	65,195	66,092
Texas	3,541,769	2,634,346	113,197	262,483	300,540	289,289	282,071	282,693	280,989
Utah	463,870	329,883	2,611	32,652	34,113	34,335	35,127	35,956	37,547
Vermont	98,558	73,865	1,780	7,978	8,513	8,309	8,465	8,329	7,993
Virginia	1,031,925	757,847	1,976	82,456	85,065	84,426	81,508	79,821	79,538
Washington	896,475	651,743	5,075	68,562	73,869	73,153	73,524	74,098	73,786
West Virginia	318,296	219,037	2,308	22,081	23,158	22,184	22,298	23,556	24,221
Wisconsin	829,415	588,447	16,227	61,568	65,255	64,424	62,749	63,365	62,708
Wyoming	100,313	71,798	—	7,184	7,917	7,937	8,004	8,049	8,193
Outlying areas									
American Samoa	13,994	10,582	1,462	1,151	1,145	1,089	1,076	981	981
Guam	30,077	22,428	657	2,697	2,737	2,522	2,458	2,392	2,375
Northern Marianas	8,086	6,133	423	677	694	629	593	661	585
Puerto Rico	637,034	469,764	89	37,806	54,606	50,802	50,566	52,944	53,824
Virgin Islands	22,887	16,804	—	1,680	1,846	1,786	1,728	1,878	1,742

Table 41.—Enrollment in public elementary and secondary schools, by grade and state: Fall 1992—Continued

State or other area	Prekindergarten through grade 8 and elementary unclassified				Grades 9 through 12 and secondary unclassified					
	Grade 6	Grade 7	Grade 8	Elementary unclassified	Total	Grade 9	Grade 10	Grade 11	Grade 12	Secondary unclassified
1	11	12	13	14	15	16	17	18	19	20
United States	**3,302,671**	**3,299,060**	**3,129,006**	**538,647**	**11,735,041**	**3,351,831**	**3,027,271**	**2,655,946**	**2,430,536**	**269,457**
Alabama	59,929	62,904	58,025	—	196,386	60,590	50,629	44,000	41,167	—
Alaska	9,542	9,392	8,789	—	30,847	9,187	7,889	7,057	6,714	—
Arizona	53,832	52,793	49,081	4,749	175,560	51,426	46,790	39,584	37,410	350
Arkansas	35,017	37,448	36,011	1,941	123,892	33,518	32,700	29,244	27,651	779
California	399,776	388,439	363,296	73,893	1,404,087	396,482	375,327	329,527	270,675	32,076
Colorado	48,686	47,626	45,025	1,419	161,314	45,363	41,844	38,559	34,533	1,015
Connecticut	36,294	35,526	33,691	10,214	126,928	35,796	32,767	29,988	28,366	11
Delaware	8,342	8,519	8,012	—	28,338	8,519	7,521	6,169	6,129	—
District of Columbia	5,161	5,333	5,000	2,639	19,804	5,068	5,382	4,290	3,433	1,631
Florida	155,932	150,803	142,372	—	511,557	154,379	138,837	117,506	100,835	—
Georgia	99,742	97,828	92,374	—	315,539	102,292	81,135	68,466	63,646	—
Hawaii	13,122	12,231	11,750	6,403	48,838	12,553	11,312	10,966	9,051	4,956
Idaho	18,786	19,035	18,880	812	67,034	18,426	17,654	15,868	14,593	493
Illinois	136,050	140,908	134,317	54,463	529,018	138,154	133,730	117,203	106,475	33,456
Indiana	76,465	78,972	75,477	6,069	283,381	80,394	71,706	63,827	62,234	5,220
Iowa	38,164	38,664	36,892	8,375	146,191	37,151	35,708	32,991	33,057	7,284
Kansas	35,860	35,199	33,288	6,884	123,292	34,006	31,844	28,404	26,706	2,332
Kentucky	50,946	52,560	49,993	8,344	185,144	53,819	48,497	41,441	38,029	3,358
Louisiana	60,543	62,494	55,942	28,029	207,161	62,947	51,863	43,713	38,368	10,270
Maine	16,483	15,977	15,969	2,408	60,085	16,282	15,084	14,041	13,882	796
Maryland	58,196	56,395	52,815	7,221	196,285	56,567	49,977	42,825	40,426	6,490
Massachusetts	64,155	62,981	60,702	7,739	230,299	63,334	59,632	54,908	52,425	—
Michigan	118,147	118,734	114,282	49,971	438,731	122,875	108,508	97,313	90,655	19,380
Minnesota	62,294	62,824	59,810	—	224,426	59,208	57,544	53,861	53,813	—
Mississippi	40,626	42,401	38,132	11,151	136,662	40,580	33,878	28,768	26,328	7,108
Missouri	65,353	67,106	64,546	6,319	237,645	68,595	62,289	54,019	50,534	2,208
Montana	12,895	12,693	12,124	743	44,696	12,252	11,533	10,645	10,019	247
Nebraska	22,742	22,559	21,379	—	79,975	21,718	20,471	18,787	18,999	—
Nevada	17,672	17,426	16,250	784	57,626	15,854	15,523	13,986	12,242	21
New Hampshire	14,874	14,189	13,537	708	48,065	13,477	12,371	11,399	10,752	66
New Jersey	80,979	80,062	77,779	50,090	312,899	81,465	76,142	70,377	67,353	17,562
New Mexico	23,445	23,102	21,690	—	98,250	24,285	21,756	18,037	16,027	18,145
New York	191,720	191,664	184,815	74,935	796,383	218,802	197,530	168,686	142,822	68,543
North Carolina	86,812	85,933	84,291	19,601	303,507	91,379	80,765	67,936	63,427	—
North Dakota	9,539	9,433	9,102	—	34,165	9,017	8,908	8,226	8,014	—
Ohio	141,273	145,143	137,075	8,653	511,330	146,420	131,168	117,657	116,085	—
Oklahoma	47,715	46,537	44,163	1,268	158,300	45,278	42,189	37,011	33,346	476
Oregon	40,254	39,512	39,610	1,998	144,706	39,891	37,891	34,300	31,920	704
Pennsylvania	130,597	131,538	126,293	18,773	501,639	138,987	125,173	113,950	108,244	15,285
Rhode Island	10,952	10,819	10,204	3,538	38,121	10,774	10,102	8,811	8,244	190
South Carolina	52,631	53,059	49,562	—	173,159	55,755	45,819	36,970	34,615	—
South Dakota	10,919	11,000	10,498	1,088	36,691	9,856	9,324	8,887	8,259	365
Tennessee	65,554	66,927	63,358	17,504	233,430	69,086	62,147	52,558	49,639	—
Texas	282,089	279,942	261,053	—	907,423	294,147	233,825	199,245	180,206	—
Utah	37,041	37,849	36,813	5,839	133,987	33,524	35,107	32,676	28,775	3,905
Vermont	7,769	7,502	7,227	—	24,693	6,528	6,217	5,781	5,573	594
Virginia	79,450	79,342	76,775	27,490	274,078	77,033	72,824	63,260	60,854	107
Washington	71,802	70,589	67,285	—	244,732	69,018	64,677	57,051	53,986	—
West Virginia	24,617	26,276	24,791	3,547	99,259	26,714	25,196	22,487	21,844	3,018
Wisconsin	63,723	64,600	60,783	3,045	240,968	65,491	63,079	55,839	55,543	1,016
Wyoming	8,164	8,272	8,078	—	28,515	7,569	7,487	6,846	6,613	—
Outlying areas										
American Samoa	901	910	886	—	3,412	912	862	833	748	57
Guam	2,203	2,324	2,061	2	7,649	2,733	2,160	1,623	1,115	18
Northern Marianas	566	713	437	155	1,953	544	652	446	311	—
Puerto Rico	52,636	57,017	50,913	8,561	167,270	46,610	45,826	38,793	32,344	3,697
Virgin Islands	1,700	2,193	1,549	702	6,083	1,894	1,424	1,155	1,117	493

[1] Data include imputations for nonrespondents.
—Data not reported or not applicable.

SOURCE: U.S. Department of Education, National Center for Education Statistics, Common Core of Data survey. (This table was prepared March 1995.)

Table 42.—Enrollment in public elementary and secondary schools, by grade: Fall 1979 to fall 1993

Grade	Fall 1979	Fall 1980	Fall 1981	Fall 1982	Fall 1983	Fall 1984	Fall 1985	Fall 1986	Fall 1987	Fall 1988	Fall 1989	Fall 1990	Fall 1991	Fall 1992	Fall 1993
1	2	3	4	5	6	7	8	9	10	11	12	13	14	15	16
In thousands															
All grades	**41,651**	**40,877**	**40,044**	**39,566**	**39,252**	**39,208**	**39,422**	**39,753**	**40,008**	**40,189**	**40,543**	**41,217**	**42,047**	**42,816**	**43,476**
Elementary	28,034	27,647	27,280	27,161	26,981	26,905	27,034	27,420	27,933	28,501	29,152	29,878	30,506	31,081	31,515
Kindergarten [1]	2,675	2,689	2,687	2,845	2,859	3,010	3,192	3,310	3,388	3,433	3,486	3,610	3,686	3,810	3,934
lst grade	2,937	2,894	2,951	2,937	3,080	3,113	3,239	3,358	3,407	3,460	3,485	3,499	3,556	3,542	3,529
2nd grade	2,909	2,800	2,782	2,790	2,781	2,904	2,941	3,054	3,173	3,223	3,289	3,327	3,360	3,431	3,429
3rd grade	3,120	2,893	2,806	2,763	2,772	2,765	2,895	2,933	3,046	3,167	3,235	3,297	3,334	3,361	3,437
4th grade	3,148	3,107	2,918	2,798	2,758	2,772	2,771	2,896	2,938	3,051	3,182	3,248	3,315	3,342	3,361
5th grade	3,055	3,130	3,127	2,912	2,798	2,761	2,776	2,775	2,901	2,945	3,067	3,197	3,268	3,325	3,350
6th grade	2,999	3,038	3,180	3,142	2,928	2,831	2,789	2,806	2,811	2,937	2,987	3,110	3,239	3,303	3,356
7th grade	3,128	3,085	3,183	3,288	3,247	3,036	2,938	2,899	2,910	2,905	3,027	3,067	3,181	3,299	3,355
8th grade	3,171	3,086	3,059	3,123	3,222	3,186	2,982	2,870	2,839	2,853	2,853	2,979	3,020	3,129	3,249
Elementary ungraded	894	924	587	563	535	528	511	520	520	527	540	543	545	539	515
Secondary	13,616	13,231	12,764	12,405	12,271	12,304	12,388	12,333	12,076	11,687	11,390	11,338	11,541	11,735	11,961
9th grade	3,526	3,377	3,286	3,248	3,330	3,440	3,439	3,256	3,143	3,106	3,141	3,169	3,313	3,352	3,487
10th grade	3,532	3,368	3,218	3,137	3,103	3,145	3,230	3,215	3,020	2,895	2,868	2,896	2,915	3,027	3,050
11th grade	3,241	3,195	3,039	2,917	2,861	2,819	2,866	2,954	2,936	2,749	2,629	2,612	2,645	2,656	2,751
12th grade	2,969	2,925	2,907	2,787	2,678	2,599	2,550	2,601	2,681	2,650	2,473	2,381	2,392	2,431	2,424
Secondary ungraded	348	366	314	315	299	300	303	308	296	288	279	282	275	269	248
Percent															
All grades	**100.0**	**100.0**	**100.0**	**100.0**	**100.0**	**100.0**	**100.0**	**100.0**	**100.0**	**100.0**	**100.0**	**100.0**	**100.0**	**100.0**	**100.0**
Elementary	67.3	67.6	68.1	68.6	68.7	68.6	68.6	69.0	69.8	70.9	71.9	72.5	72.6	72.6	72.5
Kindergarten [1]	6.4	6.6	6.7	7.2	7.3	7.7	8.1	8.3	8.5	8.5	8.6	8.8	8.8	8.9	9.0
lst grade	7.1	7.1	7.4	7.4	7.8	7.9	8.2	8.4	8.5	8.6	8.6	8.5	8.5	8.3	8.1
2nd grade	7.0	6.8	6.9	7.1	7.1	7.4	7.5	7.7	7.9	8.0	8.1	8.1	8.0	8.0	7.9
3rd grade	7.5	7.1	7.0	7.0	7.1	7.1	7.3	7.4	7.6	7.9	8.0	8.0	7.9	7.9	7.9
4th grade	7.6	7.6	7.3	7.1	7.0	7.1	7.0	7.3	7.3	7.6	7.8	7.9	7.9	7.8	7.7
5th grade	7.3	7.7	7.8	7.4	7.1	7.0	7.0	7.0	7.2	7.3	7.6	7.8	7.8	7.8	7.7
6th grade	7.2	7.4	7.9	7.9	7.5	7.2	7.1	7.1	7.0	7.3	7.4	7.5	7.7	7.7	7.7
7th grade	7.5	7.5	7.9	8.3	8.3	7.7	7.5	7.3	7.3	7.2	7.5	7.4	7.6	7.7	7.7
8th grade	7.6	7.5	7.6	7.9	8.2	8.1	7.6	7.2	7.1	7.1	7.0	7.2	7.2	7.3	7.5
Elementary ungraded	2.1	2.3	1.5	1.4	1.4	1.3	1.3	1.3	1.3	1.3	1.3	1.3	1.3	1.3	1.2
Secondary	32.7	32.4	31.9	31.4	31.3	31.4	31.4	31.0	30.2	29.1	28.1	27.5	27.4	27.4	27.5
9th grade	8.5	8.3	8.2	8.2	8.5	8.8	8.7	8.2	7.9	7.7	7.7	7.7	7.9	7.8	8.0
10th grade	8.5	8.2	8.0	7.9	7.9	8.0	8.2	8.1	7.5	7.2	7.1	7.0	6.9	7.1	7.0
11th grade	7.8	7.8	7.6	7.4	7.3	7.2	7.3	7.4	7.3	6.8	6.5	6.3	6.3	6.2	6.3
12th grade	7.1	7.2	7.3	7.0	6.8	6.6	6.5	6.5	6.7	6.6	6.1	5.8	5.7	5.7	5.6
Secondary ungraded	0.8	0.9	0.8	0.8	0.8	0.8	0.8	0.8	0.7	0.7	0.7	0.7	0.7	0.6	0.6

[1] Includes a relatively small number of prekindergarten pupils. Beginning in fall 1992, includes total prekindergarten pupils.

NOTE.—Some data have been revised from previously published figures. Because of rounding, details may not add to totals.

SOURCE: U.S. Department of Education, National Center for Education Statistics, *Statistics of Public Elementary and Secondary School Systems;* and Common Core of Data surveys. (This table was prepared March 1995.)

Table 43.—Average daily attendance in public elementary and secondary schools, by state: 1969–70 to 1992–93

State or other area	1969–70	1979–80	1980–81	1985–86	1988–89	1989–90	1990–91	1991–92	1992–93
1	2	3	4	5	6	7	8	9	10
United States	41,934,376	38,288,911	37,703,744	36,523,103	37,268,072	37,799,296	38,426,543	38,960,783	39,567,978
Alabama	777,123	711,432	701,925	686,716	684,453	683,833	682,524	681,840	694,078
Alaska	72,489	79,945	83,745	98,535	95,776	98,213	102,585	110,277	110,797
Arizona	391,526	481,905	476,149	494,504	549,219	557,252	573,140	593,413	610,558
Arkansas	414,158	423,610	417,080	408,601	403,106	403,025	408,145	410,902	413,076
California [1]	4,418,423	4,044,736	4,014,917	4,245,090	4,695,920	4,893,341	5,065,647	4,993,009	5,066,708
Colorado	500,388	513,475	508,750	507,876	514,232	519,419	521,899	532,525	568,158
Connecticut	618,881	507,362	501,085	452,058	435,227	439,524	450,808	457,476	468,992
Delaware	120,819	94,058	89,609	84,936	88,397	89,838	91,052	93,909	95,660
District of Columbia	138,600	91,576	85,773	76,241	74,398	71,468	69,092	70,939	71,201
Florida	1,312,693	1,464,461	1,389,487	1,442,921	1,587,882	1,646,583	1,714,394	1,776,539	1,818,011
Georgia	1,019,427	989,433	988,612	1,004,799	1,039,977	1,054,097	1,075,728	1,098,966	1,125,385
Hawaii	168,140	151,563	151,713	151,174	156,114	157,360	160,193	163,212	165,851
Idaho	170,920	189,199	190,144	198,141	201,219	203,987	209,085	213,843	217,933
Illinois	2,084,844	1,770,435	1,765,357	1,604,265	1,560,461	1,587,733	1,618,101	1,630,534	1,685,678
Indiana	1,111,043	983,444	944,424	870,463	882,175	884,568	888,177	895,794	897,799
Iowa	624,403	510,081	501,403	454,341	449,418	450,224	456,614	462,360	467,788
Kansas	470,296	382,019	374,451	371,655	385,364	388,986	397,609	405,083	408,689
Kentucky	647,970	619,868	614,676	577,190	573,221	569,795	569,713	574,226	579,446
Louisiana	776,555	727,601	715,844	732,230	744,142	727,125	720,551	732,485	722,626
Maine	225,146	211,400	207,554	198,358	194,350	195,089	196,229	198,413	200,462
Maryland	785,989	686,336	664,866	592,383	608,699	620,617	637,370	653,203	668,778
Massachusetts	1,056,207	935,960	950,675	745,991	756,285	763,231	770,802	785,840	796,897
Michigan	1,991,235	1,758,427	1,711,139	1,481,068	1,454,871	1,446,996	1,452,700	1,460,795	1,467,900
Minnesota	864,595	748,606	710,836	669,385	690,266	699,001	714,072	727,838	744,567
Mississippi	524,623	454,401	446,515	448,117	477,439	476,048	474,029	473,398	473,262
Missouri	906,132	777,269	756,536	714,230	726,451	729,693	733,680	747,760	759,529
Montana	162,664	144,608	141,641	138,829	138,016	135,406	138,341	141,316	144,718
Nebraska	314,516	270,524	263,797	250,975	253,426	254,754	257,587	262,429	267,975
Nevada	113,421	134,995	138,481	143,941	162,415	173,149	185,755	195,463	204,440
New Hampshire	140,203	154,187	150,316	147,561	152,536	154,915	156,579	160,203	172,376
New Jersey	1,322,124	1,140,111	1,121,272	1,029,797	968,176	997,561	1,016,159	1,036,885	1,053,135
New Mexico	259,997	253,453	240,496	252,892	280,921	290,245	291,215	321,955	304,661
New York	3,099,192	2,530,289	2,475,055	2,276,842	2,234,976	2,244,110	2,278,531	2,319,738	2,347,468
North Carolina	1,104,295	1,072,150	1,055,651	1,014,795	1,004,837	1,012,274	1,012,613	1,023,186	1,035,258
North Dakota	141,961	118,986	111,759	108,947	109,271	109,659	109,691	110,635	111,174
Ohio	2,246,282	1,849,283	1,801,914	1,660,718	1,597,117	1,584,735	1,603,025	1,602,418	1,594,191
Oklahoma	560,993	548,065	542,800	553,370	542,693	543,170	548,387	556,609	560,744
Oregon	436,736	418,593	417,009	401,476	409,717	419,771	431,806	444,272	452,509
Pennsylvania	2,169,225	1,808,630	1,754,782	1,560,746	1,532,806	1,524,839	1,542,077	1,568,279	1,588,514
Rhode Island	163,205	139,195	135,096	122,109	123,321	125,934	129,856	132,278	134,736
South Carolina	600,292	569,612	580,132	558,716	567,133	569,029	573,138	578,236	581,775
South Dakota	158,543	124,934	121,663	118,269	119,400	119,823	121,403	124,171	126,916
Tennessee	836,010	806,696	797,237	762,225	764,354	761,766	767,738	774,596	786,146
Texas	2,432,420	2,608,817	2,647,288	2,923,741	3,033,684	3,075,333	3,085,648	3,175,400	3,237,958
Utah	287,405	312,813	323,048	379,249	403,294	408,917	417,609	426,507	432,781
Vermont	97,772	95,045	90,884	85,875	88,532	87,832	88,901	90,908	93,637
Virginia	995,580	955,105	938,794	904,347	914,445	989,197	1,011,513	1,023,683	1,049,901
Washington	764,735	710,929	704,655	696,372	736,345	755,141	781,371	808,090	833,641
West Virginia	372,278	353,264	351,823	330,145	309,691	301,947	300,067	296,191	294,202
Wisconsin	880,609	770,554	743,505	694,351	700,389	711,466	731,088	748,830	765,184
Wyoming	81,293	89,471	91,381	95,547	91,515	91,277	92,506	93,926	94,109
Outlying areas									
American Samoa	—	—	—	10,816	11,222	11,448	12,272	12,935	14,150
Guam	20,315	—	22,343	23,220	23,203	23,883	25,330	25,330	30,417
Northern Marianas	—	—	—	4,921	6,677	6,809	6,062	6,194	7,334
Puerto Rico	—	656,709	671,661	636,268	608,945	597,436	597,418	558,515	548,067
Virgin Islands	—	—	23,312	23,811	21,159	18,924	19,984	20,498	20,624

[1] Data for California are not strictly comparable with those for other states because California's attendance figures include excused absences.
—Data not available.

SOURCE: U.S. Department of Education, National Center for Education Statistics, *Revenues and Expenditures for Public Elementary and Secondary Education; Statistics of State School Systems;* and Common Core of Data survey. (This table was prepared May 1995.)

Table 44.—Enrollment in public elementary and secondary schools, by race or ethnicity and state: Fall 1986 and fall 1993

State or other area	Percent distribution, fall 1986						Percent distribution, fall 1993					
	Total	White [1]	Black [1]	Hispanic	Asian or Pacific Islander	American Indian/ Alaskan Native	Total	White [1]	Black [1]	Hispanic	Asian or Pacific Islander	American Indian/ Alaskan Native
1	2	3	4	5	6	7	8	9	10	11	12	13
United States	100.0	70.4	16.1	9.9	2.8	0.9	100.0	[2]66.1	[2]16.6	[2]12.7	[2]3.6	[2]1.1
Alabama	100.0	62.0	37.0	0.1	0.4	0.5	100.0	62.4	35.8	0.4	0.6	0.8
Alaska	100.0	65.7	4.3	1.7	3.3	25.1	100.0	65.3	4.9	2.4	4.1	23.3
Arizona	100.0	62.2	4.0	26.4	1.3	6.1	100.0	59.7	4.2	27.6	1.6	6.9
Arkansas	100.0	74.7	24.2	0.4	0.6	0.2	100.0	74.1	24.1	0.9	0.7	0.3
California	100.0	53.7	9.0	27.5	9.1	0.7	100.0	42.3	8.7	37.0	11.2	0.8
Colorado	100.0	78.7	4.5	13.7	2.0	1.0	100.0	74.1	5.4	17.1	2.4	1.0
Connecticut	100.0	77.2	12.1	8.9	1.5	0.2	100.0	73.3	13.0	11.1	2.4	0.2
Delaware	100.0	68.3	27.7	2.5	1.4	0.2	100.0	66.2	28.5	3.4	1.7	0.2
District of Columbia	100.0	4.0	91.1	3.9	0.9	0.1	100.0	4.0	88.5	6.1	1.3	([3])
Florida	100.0	65.4	23.7	9.5	1.2	0.2	100.0	59.6	24.7	13.8	1.7	0.2
Georgia	100.0	60.7	37.9	0.6	0.8	([3])	100.0	59.9	37.0	1.5	1.4	0.2
Hawaii	100.0	23.5	2.3	2.2	71.7	0.3	100.0	23.7	2.6	5.0	68.4	0.3
Idaho	100.0	92.6	0.3	4.9	0.8	1.3	100.0	92.6	0.3	4.9	0.8	1.3
Illinois	100.0	69.8	18.7	9.2	2.3	0.1	100.0	64.8	21.0	11.1	2.9	0.1
Indiana	100.0	88.7	9.0	1.7	0.5	0.1	100.0	85.9	11.1	2.1	0.8	0.2
Iowa	100.0	94.6	3.0	0.9	1.2	0.3	100.0	93.4	3.1	1.6	1.5	0.4
Kansas	100.0	85.6	7.6	4.4	1.9	0.6	100.0	83.4	8.4	5.3	1.8	1.0
Kentucky	100.0	89.2	10.2	0.1	0.5	([3])	100.0	89.3	9.8	0.3	0.5	([3])
Louisiana	100.0	56.5	41.3	0.8	1.1	0.3	100.0	51.7	45.4	1.1	1.3	0.5
Maine	100.0	98.3	0.5	0.2	0.8	0.2	—	—	—	—	—	—
Maryland	100.0	59.7	35.3	1.7	3.1	0.2	100.0	58.9	34.2	2.9	3.7	0.3
Massachusetts	100.0	83.7	7.4	6.0	2.8	0.1	100.0	79.3	8.1	8.8	3.7	0.2
Michigan	100.0	76.4	19.8	1.8	1.2	0.8	100.0	78.1	17.1	2.4	1.4	1.0
Minnesota	100.0	93.9	2.1	0.9	1.7	1.5	100.0	88.8	4.2	1.7	3.5	1.9
Mississippi	100.0	43.9	55.5	0.1	0.4	0.1	100.0	47.9	50.9	0.3	0.5	0.4
Missouri	100.0	83.4	14.9	0.7	0.8	0.2	100.0	82.3	15.7	0.9	0.9	0.2
Montana	100.0	92.7	0.3	0.9	0.5	5.5	100.0	87.8	0.5	1.4	0.8	9.6
Nebraska	100.0	91.4	4.4	2.4	0.8	1.0	100.0	88.3	5.7	3.6	1.2	1.3
Nevada	100.0	77.4	9.6	7.5	3.2	2.3	100.0	70.5	9.2	14.3	4.0	2.0
New Hampshire	100.0	98.0	0.7	0.5	0.8	0.1	100.0	96.9	0.8	1.0	1.0	0.2
New Jersey	100.0	69.1	17.4	10.7	2.7	0.1	100.0	63.4	18.6	12.8	5.1	0.1
New Mexico	100.0	43.1	2.3	45.1	0.8	8.7	100.0	40.5	2.3	46.0	0.9	10.2
New York	100.0	68.4	16.5	12.3	2.7	0.2	100.0	58.3	20.1	16.5	4.7	0.4
North Carolina	100.0	68.4	28.9	0.4	0.6	1.7	100.0	65.7	30.3	1.3	1.1	1.6
North Dakota	100.0	92.4	0.6	1.1	0.8	5.0	100.0	90.3	0.7	0.8	0.7	7.5
Ohio	100.0	83.1	15.0	1.0	0.7	0.1	100.0	82.7	14.9	1.3	1.0	0.1
Oklahoma	100.0	79.0	7.8	1.6	1.0	10.6	100.0	71.6	10.3	3.3	1.2	13.7
Oregon	100.0	89.8	2.2	3.9	2.4	1.7	100.0	86.6	2.4	5.8	3.1	2.0
Pennsylvania	100.0	84.4	12.6	1.8	1.2	0.1	100.0	81.1	13.8	3.3	1.7	0.1
Rhode Island	100.0	87.9	5.6	3.7	2.4	0.3	100.0	81.1	6.8	8.6	3.1	0.4
South Carolina	100.0	54.6	44.5	0.2	0.6	0.1	100.0	57.2	41.4	0.6	0.7	0.2
South Dakota	100.0	90.6	0.5	0.6	0.7	7.6	100.0	84.9	0.7	0.6	0.7	13.0
Tennessee	100.0	76.5	22.6	0.2	0.6	([3])	100.0	75.6	22.9	0.5	0.9	0.1
Texas	100.0	51.0	14.4	32.5	2.0	0.2	100.0	47.7	14.3	35.5	2.2	0.2
Utah	100.0	93.7	0.4	3.0	1.5	1.5	100.0	91.5	0.6	4.5	2.0	1.4
Vermont	100.0	98.4	0.3	0.2	0.6	0.6	100.0	97.5	0.7	0.3	0.9	0.6
Virginia	100.0	72.6	23.7	1.0	2.6	0.1	100.0	67.9	25.8	2.8	3.3	0.2
Washington	100.0	84.5	4.2	3.8	5.1	2.3	100.0	79.9	4.4	6.9	6.2	2.6
West Virginia	100.0	95.9	3.7	0.1	0.3	([3])	100.0	95.3	4.0	0.2	0.4	0.1
Wisconsin	100.0	86.6	8.9	1.9	1.7	1.0	100.0	84.3	9.1	2.9	2.4	1.3
Wyoming	100.0	90.7	0.9	5.9	0.6	1.9	100.0	89.4	1.0	6.2	0.7	2.7
Other areas												
American Samoa	—	—	—	—	—	—	—	—	—	—	—	—
Guam	—	—	—	—	—	—	100.0	9.1	1.9	0.6	88.4	0.1
Northern Marianas	—	—	—	—	—	—	100.0	1.1	([3])	([3])	98.9	([3])
Puerto Rico	—	—	—	—	—	—	100.0	([3])	([3])	100.0	([3])	([3])
Virgin Islands	—	—	—	—	—	—	100.0	1.0	85.4	13.2	0.5	([3])

[1] Excludes persons of Hispanic origin.
[2] Includes estimate for nonresponding state.
[3] Less than 0.05 percent.
—Data not available.

NOTE.—The 1986–87 data were derived from the 1986 Elementary and Secondary School Civil Rights sample survey of public school districts. Because of rounding, details may not add to totals.

SOURCE: U.S. Department of Education, Office for Civil Rights, 1986 State Summaries of Elementary and Secondary School Civil Rights Survey; and National Center for Education Statistics, Common Core of Data survey. (This table was prepared July 1995.)

Table 45.—Enrollment of 3-, 4-, and 5-year-old children in preprimary programs, by level and control of program and by attendance status: October 1965 to October 1994

[In thousands]

Year and age	Total population, 3 to 5 years old	Enrollment by level and control						Enrollment by attendance		
		Total	Percent enrolled	Nursery school		Kindergarten		Full-day	Part-day	Percent full-day
				Public	Private	Public	Private			
1	2	3	4	5	6	7	8	9	10	11
Total, 3 to 5 years old										
1965	12,549	3,407	27.1	127	393	2,291	596	—	—	—
1970	10,949	4,104	37.5	332	762	2,498	511	698	3,405	17.0
1975	10,185	4,955	48.7	570	1,174	2,682	528	1,295	3,659	26.1
1980	9,284	4,878	52.5	628	1,353	2,438	459	1,551	3,327	31.8
1982	9,873	5,105	51.7	729	1,423	2,459	494	1,574	3,531	30.8
1983	10,254	5,384	52.5	809	1,538	2,416	623	1,686	3,700	31.3
1984	10,612	5,480	51.6	742	1,593	2,668	476	1,929	3,550	35.2
1985	10,733	5,865	54.6	846	1,631	2,847	541	2,144	3,722	36.6
1986	10,866	5,971	55.0	829	1,715	2,859	567	2,241	3,730	37.5
1987	10,872	5,931	54.6	819	1,736	2,842	534	2,090	3,841	35.2
1988	10,993	5,978	54.4	851	1,770	2,875	481	2,044	3,935	34.2
1989	11,039	6,026	54.6	930	1,894	2,704	497	2,238	3,789	37.1
1990	11,207	6,659	59.4	1,199	2,180	2,772	509	2,577	4,082	38.7
1991	11,370	6,334	55.7	996	1,828	2,967	543	2,408	3,926	38.0
1992	11,545	6,402	55.5	1,073	1,783	2,995	550	2,410	3,992	37.6
1993	11,954	6,581	55.1	1,205	1,779	3,020	577	2,642	3,939	40.1
1994 [1]	12,328	7,514	61.0	1,848	2,314	2,819	534	3,468	4,046	46.2
3 years old										
1965	4,149	203	4.9	41	153	5	4	—	—	—
1970	3,516	454	12.9	110	322	12	10	142	312	31.3
1975	3,177	683	21.5	179	474	11	18	259	423	37.9
1980	3,143	857	27.3	221	604	16	17	321	536	37.5
1982	3,387	928	27.4	312	578	27	10	280	648	30.2
1983	3,574	1,004	28.1	314	631	21	39	357	648	35.5
1984	3,609	1,004	27.8	295	658	30	22	401	603	39.9
1985	3,594	1,035	28.8	278	679	52	26	350	685	33.8
1986	3,607	1,041	28.9	257	737	26	21	399	642	38.3
1987	3,569	1,022	28.6	264	703	24	31	378	644	37.0
1988	3,719	1,027	27.6	298	678	24	26	369	658	35.9
1989	3,713	1,005	27.1	277	707	3	18	390	615	38.8
1990	3,692	1,205	32.6	347	840	11	7	447	758	37.1
1991	3,811	1,074	28.2	313	702	38	22	388	687	36.1
1992	3,905	1,081	27.7	336	685	26	34	371	711	34.3
1993	4,053	1,097	27.1	369	687	20	20	426	670	38.9
1994 [1]	4,081	1,385	33.9	469	887	19	9	670	715	48.4
4 years old										
1965	4,238	683	16.1	68	213	284	118	—	—	—
1970	3,620	1,007	27.8	176	395	318	117	230	776	22.8
1975	3,499	1,418	40.5	332	644	313	129	411	1,008	29.0
1980	3,072	1,423	46.3	363	701	239	120	467	956	32.8
1982	3,271	1,496	45.7	377	781	225	113	442	1,054	29.5
1983	3,414	1,619	47.4	402	813	231	173	442	1,177	27.3
1984	3,579	1,603	44.8	376	860	257	110	521	1,082	32.5
1985	3,598	1,766	49.1	496	859	276	135	643	1,123	36.4
1986	3,616	1,772	49.0	498	903	257	115	622	1,150	35.1
1987	3,597	1,717	47.7	431	881	280	125	548	1,169	31.9
1988	3,598	1,768	49.1	481	922	261	104	519	1,249	29.4
1989	3,692	1,882	51.0	524	1,055	202	100	592	1,290	31.4
1990	3,723	2,087	56.1	695	1,144	157	91	716	1,371	34.3
1991	3,763	1,994	53.0	584	982	287	140	667	1,326	33.5
1992	3,807	1,982	52.1	602	971	282	126	632	1,350	31.9
1993	4,044	2,178	53.9	719	957	349	154	765	1,413	35.1
1994 [1]	4,202	2,532	60.3	1,020	1,232	198	82	1,095	1,438	43.2
5 years old										
1965	4,162	2,521	60.6	18	27	2,002	474	—	—	—
1970	3,814	2,643	69.3	45	45	2,168	384	326	2,317	12.3
1975	3,509	2,854	81.3	59	57	2,358	381	625	2,228	21.9
1980	3,069	2,598	84.7	44	48	2,183	322	763	1,835	29.4
1982	3,215	2,681	83.4	40	64	2,207	370	852	1,829	31.8
1983	3,266	2,761	84.5	93	94	2,164	410	887	1,875	32.1
1984	3,423	2,872	83.9	72	76	2,381	344	1,007	1,865	35.1
1985	3,542	3,065	86.5	73	94	2,519	379	1,151	1,914	37.6
1986	3,643	3,157	86.7	75	75	2,576	432	1,220	1,937	38.6
1987	3,706	3,192	86.1	124	152	2,538	378	1,163	2,028	36.4
1988	3,676	3,184	86.6	72	170	2,590	351	1,155	2,028	36.3
1989	3,633	3,139	86.4	129	132	2,499	378	1,255	1,883	40.0
1990	3,792	3,367	88.8	157	196	2,604	411	1,414	1,953	42.0
1991	3,796	3,267	86.0	100	143	2,642	382	1,354	1,913	41.4
1992	3,832	3,339	87.1	135	127	2,688	390	1,408	1,931	42.2
1993	3,857	3,306	85.7	116	136	2,651	403	1,451	1,856	43.9
1994 [1]	4,044	3,597	88.9	359	194	2,601	442	1,704	1,893	47.4

[1] Data collected using revised procedures. May not be comparable with figures for earlier years.

—Data not available.

NOTE.—Data are based on sample surveys of the civilian noninstitutional population. Although cells with fewer than 75,000 children are subject to wide sampling variation, they are included in the table to permit various types of aggregations. Enrollment data for 5-year-olds include only those students in preprimary programs. Because of rounding, details may not add to totals.

SOURCE: U.S. Department of Education, National Center for Education Statistics, Preprimary Enrollment, various years; and U.S. Department of Commerce, Bureau of the Census, Current Population Survey, unpublished data. (This table was prepared July 1995.)

Table 46.—Child care, nursery school, and kindergarten experiences prior to first grade, by educational attainment of parents: 1991

Educational experiences	Total	Parents' highest level of educational attainment [1]					
		Less than high school	High school or equivalency	Vocational/ technical or some college	College graduate	Graduate or professional school	No parent in household
1	2	3	4	5	6	7	8
Use of nonparental home-based child care prior to starting first grade							
Number of 1st and 2nd grade children, in thousands	7,547	791	2,393	2,288	1,051	947	78
Percent using child care by relatives	28	28	34	34	20	17	24
In own home [2]	10	12	11	12	8	8	6
In other home	18	16	23	22	12	9	18
Percent using child care by nonrelatives	27	11	22	31	32	37	12
In own home [2]	6	3	4	5	8	11	4
In other home	21	8	18	26	24	26	8
Attendance at day care centers, nursery schools, prekindergarten, and Head Start on a regular basis prior to starting first grade							
Total	100	100	100	100	100	100	100
Percent attending day care center, not nursery school ..	15	8	15	17	16	12	18
Percent attending nursery school, not day care center	34	27	32	31	40	48	29
Percent attending day care center and nursery school ..	22	11	18	27	23	23	19
Percent not attending day care center or nursery school	29	53	34	25	21	16	34
Attendance at kindergarten programs							
Total	100	100	100	100	100	100	100
Percent attending kindergarten	98	95	98	99	99	98	99
Public kindergartens	84	92	90	83	79	73	85
Full-day	33	45	38	31	23	23	46
Part-day	51	47	52	52	56	50	39
Private kindergartens	14	3	8	16	20	25	14
Full-day	7	1	4	8	11	14	8
Part-day	7	2	4	8	9	11	6
Percent not attending kindergarten	2	4	2	1	1	2	1

[1] Highest level of schooling completed by either parent or guardian in the household or the only parent or guardian in the household.
[2] Includes those in own home as well as those in both own and other home.

SOURCE: U.S. Department of Education, National Center for Education Statistics, "Experiences in Child Care and Early Childhood Progams of First and Second Graders." (This table was prepared April 1992.)

Table 47.—Percent of preschool children attending center-based programs, by child and family characteristics: 1991

Child and family characteristics	Number of preschool eligible children (in thousands) [1]	Percent attending any center-based program [2]	Type of center-based program [2]		
			Day care center, not nursery school	Nursery school, not day care center	Both
1	2	3	4	5	6
Total	**8,442**	**53**	**14**	**35**	**4**
Child's age [3]					
3-year-olds	3,749	42	15	24	4
4-year-olds	3,636	60	13	43	5
5-year-olds	1,044	64	11	46	6
6-year-olds and older	14	—	—	—	—
Child's race/ethnicity					
White, non-Hispanic	5,880	54	13	36	5
Black, non-Hispanic	1,241	58	21	35	3
Hispanic	1,002	39	10	27	3
Other	319	53	10	36	6
Household income					
$10,000 or less	1,495	45	11	31	3
$10,001 to $20,000	1,439	44	13	28	4
$20,001 to $30,000	1,717	45	13	28	3
$30,001 to $40,000	1,325	53	14	34	6
$40,001 to $50,000	936	60	18	38	4
$50,001 to $75,000	975	68	15	47	7
More than $75,000	556	80	15	57	9
Parent's highest education [4]					
Less than high school	789	30	7	23	1
High school graduate or equivalent ...	2,744	57	12	29	3
Vocational/technical or some college ...	2,554	56	16	34	5
College graduate	1,281	65	16	44	5
Graduate or professional school ...	1,020	73	15	51	8
Mother's employment status					
Working 35 hours per week or more ...	2,795	60	25	28	7
Working less than 35 hours per week ...	1,908	58	12	40	6
Looking for work	518	43	9	32	2
Not in labor force	3,014	45	5	39	2

[1] Number of children 3 to 6 years of age not enrolled in kindergarten or higher level programs.

[2] Includes children enrolled in nursery school, prekindergarten, and Head Start.

[3] Calculated as of January 1, 1991.

[4] Highest level of schooling completed by either parent or guardian in the household or the only parent or guardian in the household.

—Estimate suppressed because there were fewer than 30 respondents.

SOURCE: U.S. Department of Education, National Center for Education Statistics, National Household Education Survey, Spring 1991. (This table was prepared April 1994.)

Table 48.—Percent of public school kindergarten teachers indicating the importance of various factors for kindergarten readiness: Spring 1993

Kindergarten readiness factors	Not at all important	Not very important	Somewhat important	Very important	Essential	Percent rating readiness factor as "Very important" or "Essential," by percentage of school's students eligible for free or reduced-price lunches		
						Less than 20 percent	20 to 49 percent	50 percent or more
1	2	3	4	5	6	7	8	9
Is physically healthy, rested, well nourished	0	(1)	4	24	72	97	95	95
Finishes tasks	3	11	47	31	9	43	40	37
Can count to 20 or more	33	34	26	5	3	8	6	9
Takes turns and shares	2	8	34	37	19	64	55	52
Has good problem-solving skills	8	23	44	20	5	29	23	23
Is enthusiastic and curious in approaching new activities	1	3	19	43	33	83	76	73
Is able to use pencils or paint brushes ...	15	27	38	16	5	23	21	19
Is not disruptive of the class	2	8	30	36	24	61	58	61
Knows the English language	13	12	33	24	17	40	45	39
Is sensitive to other children's feelings ...	1	6	35	41	17	61	58	56
Sits still and pays attention	3	12	43	30	12	46	37	43
Knows the letters of the alphabet	27	30	33	6	4	7	9	13
Can follow directions	2	7	31	41	19	61	61	58
Identifies primary colors and basic shapes ...	13	24	40	17	7	22	21	27
Communicates needs, wants, and thoughts verbally in child's primary language	1	1	15	41	43	85	84	83

[1] Less than 0.5 percent.

SOURCE: U.S. Department of Education, National Center for Education Statistics, Kindergarten Teacher Survey on Student Readiness. (This table was prepared April 1994.)

Table 49.—Participation of public kindergarten children in selected activities 5 days a week, by length and size of class and teacher preparation: Spring 1993

Activity	Total	Percent of kindergarten classes participating in activity every day						
		Length of kindergarten class		Size of kindergarten class			Teacher majored in early childhood education	
		Full-day	Half-day	Less than 20	20 to 25	More than 25	Yes	No
1	2	3	4	5	6	7	8	9
Listening to stories read aloud	90	91	90	87	92	91	91	89
Running, climbing, jumping, and other gross motor activities	58	72	48	55	57	64	60	56
Free play	66	72	62	64	67	67	67	66
Choosing from a set of specific options (like building blocks, objects, or books)	69	72	67	69	71	65	72	66
Using objects for math or science	49	61	41	48	51	48	53	45
Dramatic play, arts and crafts, music (creative activities)	64	66	63	62	65	66	68	60
Using worksheets for literary skills	14	25	13	21	18	17	19	18
Using worksheets for math or science	18	20	9	17	12	15	16	12

SOURCE: U.S. Department of Education, National Center for Education Statistics, Kindergarten Teacher Survey on Student Readiness. (This table was prepared April 1994.)

Table 50.—Public school pupils transported at public expense and current expenditures for transportation: 1929–30 to 1992–93

School year	Average daily attendance, all students	Pupils transported at public expense		Expenditures for transportation (in current dollars)		Expenditures for transportation (in constant 1992–93 dollars)	
		Number	Percent of total	Total [1] (in thousands)	Average per pupil transported	Total [1] (in thousands)	Average per pupil transported
1	2	3	4	5	6	7	8
1929–30	21,265,000	1,902,826	8.9	$54,823	$29	$456,485	$240
1931–32	22,245,000	2,419,173	10.9	58,078	24	574,153	237
1933–34	22,458,000	2,794,724	12.4	53,908	19	580,217	208
1935–36	22,299,000	3,250,658	14.6	62,653	19	649,805	200
1937–38	22,298,000	3,769,242	16.9	75,637	20	752,542	200
1939–40	22,042,000	4,144,161	18.8	83,283	20	849,367	205
1941–42	21,031,000	4,503,081	21.4	92,922	21	849,391	189
1943–44	19,603,000	4,512,412	23.0	107,754	24	881,357	195
1945–46	19,849,000	5,056,966	25.5	129,756	26	1,013,785	200
1947–48	20,910,000	5,854,041	28.0	176,265	30	1,078,205	184
1949–50	22,284,000	6,947,384	31.2	214,504	31	1,290,891	186
1951–52	23,257,000	7,697,130	33.1	268,827	35	1,457,770	189
1953–54	25,643,871	8,411,719	32.8	307,437	37	1,629,386	194
1955–56	27,740,149	9,695,819	35.0	353,972	37	1,876,645	194
1957–58	29,722,275	10,861,689	36.5	416,491	38	2,078,590	191
1959–60	32,477,440	12,225,142	37.6	486,338	40	2,359,028	193
1961–62	34,682,340	13,222,667	38.1	576,361	44	2,732,911	207
1963–64	37,405,058	14,475,778	38.7	673,845	47	3,113,928	215
1965–66	39,154,497	15,536,567	39.7	787,358	51	3,516,930	226
1967–68	40,827,965	17,130,873	42.0	981,006	57	4,111,323	240
1969–70	41,934,376	18,198,577	43.4	1,218,557	67	4,597,613	253
1971–72	42,254,272	19,474,355	46.1	1,507,830	77	5,222,442	268
1973–74	41,438,054	21,347,039	51.5	1,858,141	87	5,680,033	266
1975–76	41,269,720	21,772,483	52.8	2,377,313	109	6,109,606	281
1977–78	40,079,590	[2]21,800,000	54.4	2,731,041	125	6,214,641	[2]285
1979–80	38,288,911	21,713,515	56.7	3,833,145	177	7,037,201	324
1980–81	37,703,744	[2]22,272,000	59.1	[2]4,408,000	198	[2]7,253,000	[2]326
1981–82	37,094,652	[2]22,246,000	60.0	[2]4,793,000	215	[2]7,259,000	[2]326
1982–83	36,635,868	[2]22,199,000	60.6	[2]5,000,000	225	[2]7,261,000	[2]327
1983–84	36,362,978	[2]22,031,000	60.6	[2]5,284,000	240	[2]7,399,000	[2]336
1984–85	36,404,261	[2]22,320,000	61.3	[2]5,722,000	256	[2]7,711,000	[2]345
1985–86	36,523,103	[2]22,041,000	60.3	[2]6,123,000	278	[2]8,020,000	[2]364
1986–87	36,863,867	[2]22,397,000	60.8	[2]6,551,000	292	[2]8,394,000	[2]375
1987–88	37,050,707	[2]22,158,000	59.8	[2]6,888,000	311	[2]8,475,000	[2]382
1988–89	37,268,072	[2]22,635,000	60.7	[2]7,550,000	334	[2]8,879,000	[2]392
1989–90	37,799,296	[2]22,459,000	59.4	8,036,749	358	9,020,970	[2]402
1990–91	38,426,543	[2]22,000,000	57.3	8,678,954	394	9,236,826	[2]420
1991–92	38,960,783	[2]23,165,000	59.5	8,789,770	379	9,064,323	[2]391
1992–93	39,567,978	[2]23,439,000	59.2	9,241,795	394	9,241,795	[2]394

[1] Excludes capital outlay for years through 1979–80, and 1989–90 to 1992–93. From 1980–81 to 1988–89 total transportation figures include capital outlay.

[2] Estimate based on data appearing in January issues of School Bus Fleet.

NOTE.—Constant dollars are adjusted for inflation using the Consumer Price Index computed on a school year basis. Some data have been revised from previously published figures.

SOURCE: U.S. Department of Education, National Center for Education Statistics, Statistics of State School Systems; Revenues and Expenditures for Public Elementary and Secondary Education, and unpublished data; and Bobbit Publishing Co., School Bus Fleet, January issues. (This table was prepared June 1995.)

Table 51.—Children 0 to 21 years old served in federally supported programs for the disabled, by type of disability: 1976–77 to 1992–93

Type of disability	1976–77	1980–81	1981–82	1982–83	1983–84	1984–85	1985–86	1986–87	1987–88	1988–89	1989–90	1990–91	1991–92	1992–93
1	2	3	4	5	6	7	8	9	10	11	12	13	14	15
Number served,[1] in thousands														
All disabilities	3,692	4,142	4,198	4,255	4,298	4,315	4,317	4,374	4,447	4,544	4,641	4,762	4,949	5,125
Specific learning disabilities	796	1,462	1,622	1,741	1,806	1,832	1,862	1,914	1,928	1,987	2,050	2,130	2,234	2,354
Speech or language impairments	1,302	1,168	1,135	1,131	1,128	1,126	1,125	1,136	953	967	973	985	997	996
Mental retardation	959	829	786	757	727	694	660	643	582	564	548	534	538	519
Serious emotional disturbance	283	346	339	352	361	372	375	383	373	376	381	390	399	401
Hearing impairments	87	79	75	73	72	69	66	65	56	56	57	58	60	60
Orthopedic impairments	87	58	58	57	56	56	57	57	47	47	48	49	51	52
Other health impairments	141	98	79	50	53	68	57	52	45	43	52	55	58	65
Visual impairments	38	31	29	28	29	28	27	26	22	23	22	23	24	23
Multiple disabilities	—	68	71	63	65	69	86	97	77	85	86	96	97	102
Deaf-blindness	—	3	2	2	2	2	2	2	1	2	2	1	1	1
Autism and other	—	—	—	—	—	—	—	—	—	—	—	—	5	19
Preschool disabled[2]	(3)	(3)	(3)	(3)	(3)	(3)	(3)	(3)	363	394	422	441	484	531
Percentage distribution of children served														
All disabilities	100.0	100.0	100.0	100.0	100.0	100.0	100.0	100.0	100.0	100.0	100.0	100.0	100.0	100.0
Specific learning disabilities	21.6	35.3	38.6	40.9	42.0	42.4	43.1	43.8	43.4	43.6	44.2	44.7	45.1	45.9
Speech or language impairments	35.3	28.2	27.0	26.6	26.2	26.1	26.1	26.0	21.4	21.1	21.0	20.7	20.2	19.4
Mental retardation	26.0	20.0	18.7	17.8	16.9	16.1	15.3	14.7	13.1	12.7	11.8	11.2	10.9	10.1
Serious emotional disturbance	7.7	8.4	8.1	8.3	8.4	8.6	8.7	8.8	8.4	8.3	8.2	8.2	8.1	7.8
Hearing impairments	2.4	1.9	1.8	1.7	1.7	1.6	1.5	1.5	1.3	1.3	1.2	1.2	1.2	1.2
Orthopedic impairments	2.4	1.4	1.4	1.3	1.3	1.3	1.3	1.3	1.1	1.1	1.0	1.0	1.0	1.0
Other health impairments	3.8	2.4	1.9	1.2	1.2	1.6	1.3	1.2	1.0	1.0	1.1	1.2	1.2	1.3
Visual impairments	1.0	0.7	0.7	0.7	0.7	0.7	0.6	0.6	0.5	0.5	0.5	0.5	0.5	0.5
Multiple disabilities	—	1.6	1.7	1.5	1.5	1.6	2.0	2.2	1.7	1.8	1.9	2.0	2.0	2.0
Deaf-blindness	—	0.1	(4)	(4)	0.1	(4)	(4)	(4)	(4)	(4)	(4)	(4)	(4)	(4)
Autism and other	—	—	—	—	—	—	—	—	—	—	—	—	0.1	0.4
Preschool disabled[2]	(3)	(3)	(3)	(3)	(3)	(3)	(3)	(3)	8.2	8.7	9.1	9.3	9.8	10.4
Number served as a percent of total enrollment[5]														
All disabilities	8.33	10.13	10.47	10.75	10.95	11.00	10.95	11.00	11.11	11.30	11.44	11.55	11.77	11.97
Specific learning disabilities	1.80	3.58	4.05	4.40	4.60	4.67	4.72	4.81	4.82	4.94	5.06	5.17	5.31	5.50
Speech or language impairments	2.94	2.86	2.83	2.86	2.87	2.87	2.85	2.86	2.38	2.41	2.40	2.39	2.37	2.33
Mental retardation	2.16	2.03	1.96	1.91	1.85	1.77	1.68	1.62	1.45	1.40	1.35	1.30	1.28	1.21
Serious emotional disturbance	0.64	0.85	0.85	0.89	0.92	0.95	0.95	0.96	0.93	0.94	0.94	0.95	0.95	0.94
Hearing impairments	0.20	0.19	0.19	0.18	0.18	0.18	0.17	0.16	0.14	0.14	0.14	0.14	0.14	0.14
Orthopedic impairments	0.20	0.14	0.14	0.14	0.14	0.14	0.14	0.14	0.12	0.12	0.12	0.12	0.12	0.12
Other health impairments	0.32	0.24	0.20	0.13	0.13	0.17	0.14	0.13	0.11	0.11	0.13	0.13	0.14	0.15
Visual impairments	0.09	0.08	0.07	0.07	0.07	0.07	0.07	0.07	0.05	0.06	0.06	0.06	0.06	0.05
Multiple disabilities	—	0.17	0.18	0.16	0.17	0.17	0.22	0.24	0.19	0.21	0.21	0.23	0.23	0.24
Deaf-blindness	—	0.01	(6)	0.01	0.01	(6)	0.01	(6)	(6)	(6)	(6)	(6)	(6)	(6)
Autism and other	—	—	—	—	—	—	—	—	—	—	—	—	0.01	0.04
Preschool disabled[2]	(3)	(3)	(3)	(3)	(3)	(3)	(3)	(3)	0.91	0.98	1.04	1.07	1.15	1.24

[1] Includes students served under Chapter I and Individuals with Disabilities Education Act (IDEA), formerly the Education of the Handicapped Act.

[2] Includes preschool children 3–5 years and 0–5 years served under Chapter I and IDEA, respectively.

[3] Prior to 1987–88, these students were included in the counts by handicapping condition. Beginning in 1987–88, states were no longer required to report preschool handicapped students (0–5 years) by handicapping condition.

[4] Less than .05.

[5] Based on the enrollment in public schools, kindergarten through 12th grade, including a relatively small number of prekindergarten students.

[6] Less than .005.

—Data not available.

NOTE.—Counts are based on reports from the 50 states and District of Columbia only (i.e., figures from U.S. territories are not included). Increases since 1987–88 are due in part to new legislation enacted fall 1986, which mandates public school special education services for all handicapped children ages 3 through 5. Some data have been revised from previously published figures. Because of rounding, details may not add to totals.

SOURCE: U.S. Department of Education, Office of Special Education and Rehabilitative Services, *Annual Report to Congress on the Implementation of The Individuals with Disabilities Education Act*, various years, and unpublished tabulations; and National Center for Education Statistics, Common Core of Data survey. (This table was prepared June 1995.)

Table 52.—Percentage distribution of disabled persons 3 to 21 years old receiving education services for the disabled, by age group and educational environment: 1991–92

Type of disability	All environments	Regular class	Resource room	Separate class	Public separate school facility	Private separate school facility	Public residential facility	Private residential facility	Homebound/hospital environment
1	2	3	4	5	6	7	8	9	10
All persons, 3 to 21 years old	**100.0**	**35.7**	**34.4**	**24.0**	**2.7**	**1.8**	**0.6**	**0.2**	**0.5**
3 to 5 years old	100.0	45.7	11.3	29.5	4.9	7.2	0.3	0.1	1.2
6 to 21 years old	100.0	34.9	36.3	23.5	2.5	1.4	0.6	0.3	0.5
Mental retardation	100.0	5.0	25.4	59.2	7.7	1.1	0.9	0.3	0.3
Speech or language impairments	100.0	85.5	9.1	3.9	0.2	1.2	(1)	(1)	0.1
Visual impairments	100.0	39.6	21.2	19.6	3.1	5.5	9.5	1.1	0.4
Serious emotional disturbance	100.0	15.8	27.8	36.9	7.8	6.2	2.4	1.5	1.6
Orthopedic impairments	100.0	32.4	21.0	34.4	5.6	1.6	0.3	0.6	4.1
Other health impairments	100.0	35.3	27.6	21.5	2.1	1.2	0.2	0.4	11.9
Specific learning disabilities	100.0	24.6	54.2	20.1	0.6	0.3	0.1	(1)	0.1
Deaf-blindness	100.0	6.0	6.1	36.5	17.0	4.5	25.2	2.9	1.8
Multiple disabilities	100.0	6.2	18.1	47.1	16.0	6.6	2.4	1.3	2.2
Hearing impairments	100.0	27.1	20.5	31.3	5.8	3.7	10.8	0.8	0.1

[1] Less than 0.05 percent.

NOTE.—This table reflects a compilation of data reported by the states. There are some reporting variations, e.g., estimated or incomplete data and nonstandard definitions, from state to state. Data include Puerto Rico. Data for 3- to 5-year-old children are no longer collected by type of disability. Because of rounding, details may not add to totals.

SOURCE: U.S. Department of Education, Office of Special Education and Rehabilitative Services, *Sixteenth Annual Report to Congress on the Implementation of The Individuals with Disabilities Education Act, 1993.* (This table was prepared May 1995.)

Table 53.—Number of children served under Individuals with Disabilities Education Act and Chapter 1 of the Education Consolidation and Improvement Act, State Operated Programs, by age group and state: 1990–91 and 1991–92

State	Birth to age 21		Ages 0 to 5		Percent change, birth to 21, 1990–91 to 1991–92	State	Birth to age 21		Ages 0 to 5		Percent change, birth to 21, 1990–91 to 1991–92
	1990–91	1991–92	1990–91	1991–92			1990–91	1991–92	1990–91	1991–92	
1	2	3	4	5	6	1	2	3	4	5	6
United States	**4,761,742**	**4,948,601**	**440,661**	**483,824**	**3.9**						
Alabama	94,945	96,975	7,498	8,344	2.1	Missouri	101,955	105,521	4,889	6,491	3.5
Alaska	14,745	16,106	1,813	2,089	9.2	Montana	17,204	18,038	1,934	2,071	4.8
Arizona	57,235	61,076	4,936	5,784	6.7	Nebraska	32,761	35,975	2,961	3,356	9.8
Arkansas	47,835	49,018	5,274	5,648	2.5	Nevada	18,440	20,530	1,742	2,364	11.3
California	469,282	494,058	40,489	44,351	5.3	New Hampshire	19,658	21,047	2,077	2,153	7.1
Colorado	57,102	60,357	4,894	5,444	5.7	New Jersey	181,319	184,621	17,190	17,445	1.8
Connecticut	64,562	66,192	6,142	6,471	2.5	New Mexico	36,037	38,207	2,247	2,652	6.0
Delaware	14,294	14,435	1,579	1,677	1.0	New York	307,458	324,677	26,353	31,511	5.6
District of Columbia	6,290	7,104	411	588	12.9	North Carolina	123,126	127,867	10,700	11,984	3.9
Florida	236,013	253,606	16,387	18,289	7.5	North Dakota	12,504	12,679	1,374	1,377	1.4
Georgia	101,997	107,660	7,333	8,378	5.6	Ohio	205,440	210,268	12,487	13,629	2.4
Hawaii	13,169	14,163	1,273	1,577	7.5	Oklahoma	65,653	68,576	5,359	5,983	4.5
Idaho	22,017	22,755	3,129	3,209	3.4	Oregon	55,149	56,702	3,581	3,943	2.8
Illinois	239,185	245,931	26,122	27,353	2.8	Pennsylvania	219,428	214,035	23,156	22,236	−2.5
Indiana	114,643	118,924	8,937	9,874	3.7	Rhode Island	21,076	21,588	2,112	2,263	2.4
Iowa	60,695	61,510	6,329	6,391	1.3	South Carolina	77,765	79,872	8,346	9,199	2.7
Kansas	45,212	47,063	4,308	4,952	4.1	South Dakota	14,987	15,284	2,366	2,463	2.0
Kentucky	79,421	81,681	11,008	12,989	2.8	Tennessee	104,898	111,315	7,536	10,926	6.1
Louisiana	73,663	78,760	7,541	8,600	6.9	Texas	350,636	367,860	30,955	33,082	4.9
Maine	27,987	27,891	2,895	2,497	−0.3	Utah	47,747	50,009	4,565	5,043	4.7
Maryland	91,940	92,520	10,409	10,615	0.6	Vermont	12,263	11,101	1,200	1,130	−9.5
Massachusetts	154,616	156,633	17,014	18,293	1.3	Virginia	113,971	122,647	11,791	13,359	7.6
Michigan	166,927	172,238	14,963	18,370	3.2	Washington	85,395	91,286	11,409	12,462	6.9
Minnesota	80,896	83,028	10,529	11,205	2.6	West Virginia	43,135	44,338	3,630	4,372	2.8
Mississippi	60,934	61,197	5,704	4,731	0.4	Wisconsin	86,930	91,742	12,213	12,885	5.5
						Wyoming	11,202	11,935	1,571	1,726	6.5

NOTE.—Individuals with Disabilities Education Act (IDEA), formerly known as the Education of the Handicapped Act, now extends the right to a free and appropriate education to 3- to 5-year-old disabled children.

SOURCE: U.S. Department of Education, Office of Special Education and Rehabilitative Services, *Annual Report to Congress on the Implementation of The Individuals with Disabilities Education Act,* various years; and unpublished tabulations. (This table was prepared August 1994.)

Table 54.—State legislation on gifted and talented programs and number and percent of students receiving services in public elementary and secondary schools, by state: 1989–90

State	State-mandated gifted and talented programs	Discretionary state-supported gifted and talented programs	Gifted and talented students receiving services	Gifted and talented students as a percent of enrollment [1]	State	State-mandated gifted and talented programs	Discretionary state-supported gifted and talented programs	Gifted and talented students receiving services	Gifted and talented students as a percent of enrollment [1]
1	2	3	4	5	1	2	3	4	5
Alabama	X		17,827	2.5	Montana		X	—	—
Alaska	X		4,577	4.2	Nebraska		X	[2] 25,000	9.2
Arizona			—	—	Nevada		X	6,389	3.4
Arkansas	X		31,519	7.2	New Hampshire			—	—
California		X	223,712	4.7	New Jersey		X	122,626	11.4
Colorado		X	—	—	New Mexico			—	—
Connecticut		[3] X	—	—	New York		X	[2] 150,000	5.8
Delaware		X	5,025	5.1	North Carolina	X	X	67,119	6.2
Florida	X		61,458	3.4	North Dakota			1,151	1.0
Georgia	X		49,384	4.4	Ohio		X	65,486	3.7
Hawaii	X		8,863	5.2	Oklahoma	X		43,297	7.5
Idaho			—	—	Oregon	X	X	—	—
Illinois	X	X	[2] 141,537	7.9	Pennsylvania	X		80,386	4.9
Indiana		X	[2] 45,000	4.7	Rhode Island		X	[2] 5,674	4.2
Iowa	X	X	[2] 18,970	4.0	South Carolina	X		46,961	7.6
Kansas	X		13,096	3.0	South Dakota	X	X	4,825	3.8
Kentucky	X		[2] 31,825	5.0	Tennessee	X		15,600	1.9
Louisiana	X		[2] 19,000	2.4	Texas	X		206,583	6.2
Maine	X	X	[2] 15,785	—	Utah	X	X	—	—
Maryland		X	[2] 60,000	8.6	Vermont			—	—
Massachusetts			—	—	Virginia	X	X	101,579	10.3
Michigan		X	[2] 182,414	11.6	Washington		X	—	—
Minnesota		X	39,725	5.4	West Virginia	X		11,989	3.7
Mississippi	X	X	18,279	3.6	Wisconsin	X		—	—
Missouri		X	[2] 36,200	4.5	Wyoming		X	—	—

[1] Percent based on enrollment figures collected by the National Center for Education Statistics.

[2] Estimated by reporting state.

[3] Legislation only mandates that gifted and talented students enrolled in public schools be identified.

X=Indicates that legislation has been passed.

—Data not available.

NOTE.—The District of Columbia was not included in the survey.

SOURCE: Council of State Directors of Programs for the Gifted, *The 1990 State of the States Gifted and Talented Education Report.* (This table was prepared May 1992.)

Table 55.—Enrollment in grades 9 to 12 in public and private schools compared with population 14 to 17 years of age: 1889–90 to fall 1993

[Numbers in thousands]

Year	Enrollment, grades 9 to 12[1]			Population 14 to 17 years of age[3]	Enrollment as a percent of population 14 to 17 years of age[4]
	All schools	Public schools	Private schools[2]		
1	2	3	4	5	6
1889–90	298	203	95	5,355	5.6
1899–1900	630	519	111	6,152	10.2
1909–10	1,032	915	117	7,220	14.3
1919–20	2,414	2,200	214	7,736	31.2
1929–30	4,741	4,399	[5]341	9,341	50.7
1939–40	7,059	6,601	[6]458	9,720	72.6
1949–50	6,397	5,725	672	8,405	76.1
1951–52	6,538	5,882	656	8,516	76.8
1953–54	7,038	6,290	747	8,861	79.4
1955–56	7,696	6,873	823	9,207	83.6
1957–58	8,790	7,860	931	10,139	86.7
Fall 1959	9,306	8,271	1,035	11,155	83.4
Fall 1961	10,489	9,369	1,120	12,046	87.1
Fall 1963	12,170	10,883	1,287	13,492	90.2
Fall 1965	13,010	11,610	1,400	14,146	92.0
Fall 1966	13,294	11,894	1,400	14,398	92.3
Fall 1967	13,650	12,250	1,400	14,727	92.7
Fall 1968	14,118	12,718	1,400	15,170	93.1
Fall 1969	14,337	13,037	1,300	15,549	92.2
Fall 1970	14,647	13,336	1,311	15,921	92.0
Fall 1971	15,053	13,753	[7]1,300	16,326	92.2
Fall 1972	15,148	13,848	[7]1,300	16,637	91.0
Fall 1973	15,344	14,044	[7]1,300	16,864	91.0
Fall 1974	15,403	14,103	[7]1,300	17,033	90.4
Fall 1975	15,604	14,304	[7]1,300	17,125	91.1
Fall 1976	15,656	14,314	1,342	17,117	91.5
Fall 1977	15,546	14,203	1,343	17,042	91.2
Fall 1978	15,441	14,088	1,353	16,944	91.1
Fall 1979	14,916	13,616	[7]1,300	16,610	89.8
Fall 1980	14,570	13,231	1,339	16,143	90.3
Fall 1981	14,164	12,764	[7]1,400	15,609	90.7
Fall 1982	13,805	12,405	[7]1,400	15,057	91.7
Fall 1983	13,671	12,271	[7]1,400	14,740	92.7
Fall 1984	13,704	12,304	[7]1,400	14,725	93.1
Fall 1985	13,750	12,388	1,362	14,888	92.4
Fall 1986	13,669	12,333	[7]1,336	14,824	92.2
Fall 1987	13,323	12,076	1,247	14,502	91.9
Fall 1988	12,893	11,687	[7]1,206	14,023	91.9
Fall 1989	12,583	11,390	[7]1,193	13,536	93.0
Fall 1990	12,475	11,338	1,137	13,313	93.7
Fall 1991	12,666	11,541	[7]1,125	13,424	94.4
Fall 1992	12,898	11,735	[7]1,163	13,661	94.4
Fall 1993	13,152	11,961	[7]1,191	13,802	95.3

[1] Includes a relatively small number of secondary ungraded and postgraduate students.

[2] Data for most years are partly estimated.

[3] Data for 1890 through 1950 and for 1960 are from the decennial censuses of population. The other figures are Bureau of the Census estimates as of July 1 preceding the opening of the school year.

[4] Gross enrollment ratio based on school enrollment of all ages in grades 9 to 12 divided by the 14- to 17-year-old population. Differs from enrollment rates in other tables which are based on the enrollment of persons in the given age group only.

[5] Data are for 1927–28.

[6] Data are for 1940–41.

[7] Estimated.

NOTE.—Includes enrollment in public schools that are a part of state and local school systems and also in most private schools, both religiously affiliated and nonsectarian. Excludes enrollment in subcollegiate departments of institutions of higher education, residential schools for exceptional children, and federal schools. Because of rounding, details may not add to totals. Some data have been revised from previously published figures.

SOURCE: U.S. Department of Education, National Center for Education Statistics, *Statistics of State School Systems; Statistics of Public Elementary and Secondary School Systems; Statistics of Nonpublic Elementary and Secondary Schools;* Common Core of Data survey; and *Projections of Education Statistics to 2005.* (This table was prepared June 1995.)

Table 56.—Enrollment in foreign language courses compared with enrollment in grades 9 to 12 of public secondary schools: Fall 1948 to fall 1990

[In thousands]

Language	Fall 1948	Fall 1960	Fall 1965	Fall 1968	Fall 1970	Fall 1974	Fall 1976	Fall 1978	Fall 1982	Fall 1985	Fall 1990	Percent change in enrollment 1976 to 1985	1985 to 1990
1	2	3	4	5	6	7	8	9	10	11	12	13	14
Total enrollment, grades 9 to 12	[1]5,602	8,589	11,610	12,718	13,336	14,103	14,314	14,088	12,405	12,388	11,338	−13.5	−8.5
All foreign languages[2]													
Number enrolled	1,170	2,522	3,659	3,890	3,779	3,295	3,174	3,200	2,910	4,029	4,257	26.9	5.7
Percent of all students	20.9	29.4	31.5	30.6	28.3	23.3	22.2	22.7	23.3	32.2	37.5	—	—
Modern foreign languages													
Number enrolled	741	1,867	3,068	3,518	3,514	3,127	3,023	3,048	2,740	3,852	4,093	27.4	6.3
Percent of all students	13.2	21.7	26.4	27.7	26.4	22.1	21.1	21.6	21.9	31.1	36.1	—	—
Spanish													
Number enrolled	443	933	1,427	1,698	1,811	1,678	1,717	1,631	1,563	2,334	2,611	35.9	11.9
Percent of all students	7.9	10.9	12.3	13.4	13.6	11.9	12.0	11.6	12.5	18.8	23.0	—	—
French													
Number enrolled	254	744	1,251	1,328	1,231	978	888	856	858	1,134	1,089	27.7	−3.9
Percent of all students	4.5	8.7	10.8	10.4	9.2	6.9	6.2	6.1	6.9	9.2	9.6	—	—
German													
Number enrolled	43	151	328	423	411	393	353	331	267	312	295	−11.5	−5.3
Percent of all students	0.8	1.8	2.8	3.3	3.1	2.8	2.5	2.3	2.1	2.5	2.6	—	—
Russian													
Number enrolled	—	10	27	24	20	15	11	9	6	6	16	−46.7	174.9
Percent of all students	—	0.1	0.2	0.2	0.2	0.1	0.1	0.1	([3])	([3])	0.1	—	—
Italian													
Number enrolled	—	20	25	27	27	40	46	46	44	47	40	3.1	−14.0
Percent of all students	—	0.2	0.2	0.2	0.2	0.3	0.3	0.3	0.4	0.4	0.4	—	—
Other modern foreign languages[4]													
Number enrolled	1	9	9	18	15	23	9	176	3	18	40	—	—
Percent of all students	([3])	0.1	0.1	0.1	0.1	0.2	0.1	1.2	([3])	0.1	0.4	—	—
Latin													
Number enrolled	429	655	591	372	265	167	150	152	170	177	164	17.6	−7.4
Percent of all students	7.7	7.6	5.1	2.9	2.0	1.2	1.1	1.1	1.4	1.4	1.4	—	—

[1] Estimated.
[2] Includes enrollment in ancient Greek (not shown separately). Fewer than 1,000 students were enrolled in this language in each of the years shown.
[3] Less than 0.05 percent.
[4] Includes students enrolled in unspecified modern foreign languages. In 1978, a relatively large number of students were not identified by field of study.
—Data not reported, not available, or not applicable.

NOTE.—Because of rounding, details may not add to totals.

SOURCE: U.S. Department of Education, National Center for Education Statistics, Common Core of Data survey; and American Council on the Teaching of Foreign Languages, *Foreign Language Enrollments in Public Secondary Schools, Fall 1989 and Fall 1990*. (This table was prepared April 1992.)

Table 57.—Student participation in school programs and services, by control, level of school, and type of community: 1993–94

Control, level, and community type	Total students		Percent of students participating in program or service							
	Number	Percent distribution	Bilingual education	English as a second language	Remedial reading	Remedial mathematics	Programs for the handicapped	Programs for the gifted and talented	Diagnostic and prescriptive	Extended day
1	2	3	4	5	6	7	8	9	10	11
Public total	41,621,660	100.0	3.07	3.97	10.88	6.90	6.88	6.43	0.27	2.50
School level [1]										
Elementary	26,886,026	64.6	3.98	4.75	13.46	7.77	6.76	6.25	0.31	3.58
Secondary	13,757,801	33.1	1.39	2.58	5.63	5.03	6.54	6.90	0.20	0.48
Combined	977,833	2.3	1.80	1.88	13.70	9.39	14.84	4.72	0.44	1.31
Community type										
Central city	13,496,625	32.4	5.72	6.45	12.39	7.89	7.04	6.32	0.23	3.56
Urban fringe/large town	12,953,165	31.1	2.09	4.07	8.88	5.72	6.34	7.33	0.23	2.72
Rural/small town	15,171,870	36.5	1.55	1.67	11.24	7.03	7.19	5.75	0.35	1.37
Private total	4,970,646	100.0	0.81	0.58	6.35	4.16	2.98	4.93	0.89	9.20
School level [1]										
Elementary	2,803,359	56.4	0.77	0.45	7.22	4.33	0.93	3.34	0.94	12.48
Secondary	811,087	16.3	0.19	0.62	4.24	3.06	3.43	8.56	0.47	0.23
Combined	1,356,199	27.3	1.25	0.83	5.82	4.46	6.95	6.05	1.03	7.76
Community type										
Central city	2,567,358	51.7	0.74	0.67	7.20	4.58	2.54	5.66	0.72	10.53
Urban fringe/large town	1,563,761	31.5	1.05	0.58	5.93	4.30	3.93	4.77	0.85	9.42
Rural/small town	839,526	16.9	0.55	0.28	4.55	2.57	2.54	3.01	1.48	4.70

[1] Elementary schools have grade 6 or lower or a low grade of ungraded and no grade higher than 8. Secondary schools have no grade lower than 7. Combined schools have grades lower than 7 and higher than 8.

NOTE.—Students may participate in more than one program or service. Includes only kindergarten pupils who attend schools that offer first grade or above. Excludes prekindergarten students. Totals differ from data appearing in other tables because of varying survey processing procedures and time period coverages.

SOURCE: U.S. Department of Education, National Center for Education Statistics, "Schools and Staffing Survey, 1993–94." (This table was prepared August 1995.)

Table 58.—Private elementary and secondary enrollment and schools, by selected characteristics: 1993–94

Selected characteristics	Kindergarten through 12th grade enrollment [1]				Schools			
	Total	Catholic	Other religious	Non-sectarian	Total	Catholic	Other religious	Non-sectarian
1	2	3	4	5	6	7	8	9
Total	4,970,646	2,516,130	1,686,064	768,451	26,093	8,351	12,180	5,563
School enrollment								
Less than 150	890,343	168,200	509,028	213,115	14,155	1,572	8,499	4,084
150 to 299	1,482,210	853,139	467,749	161,322	6,820	3,815	2,232	773
300 to 499	1,243,578	719,037	359,278	165,263	3,272	1,885	973	414
500 to 749	736,057	432,557	196,751	106,749	1,228	729	327	172
750 or more	618,457	343,197	153,257	122,003	619	350	149	120
Percent minority students								
Less than 5%	1,855,365	876,589	774,050	204,726	10,750	3,152	6,137	1,461
5%, but less than 20%	1,620,369	761,747	502,822	355,800	7,482	2,376	3,070	2,036
20%, but less than 50%	704,432	375,825	189,615	138,992	3,785	1,095	1,395	1,295
50% or more	790,479	501,969	219,577	68,933	4,076	1,727	1,578	771
Community type								
Central city	2,567,358	1,397,446	820,133	349,779	10,921	4,090	4,518	2,313
Urban fringe/large town	1,563,762	813,576	485,541	264,645	7,980	2,641	3,204	2,135
Rural/small town	839,525	305,108	380,391	154,027	7,192	1,620	4,458	1,114

[1] Includes only kindergarten pupils who attend schools that offer first grade.

NOTE.—Data are based upon a sample survey and may not be strictly comparable with data reported elsewhere. Includes only schools that offer first grade or above. Excludes prekindergarten students. Because of rounding, details may not add to totals.

SOURCE: U.S. Department of Education, National Center for Education Statistics, "Schools and Staffing Survey, 1993–94." (This table was prepared August 1995.)

Table 59.—Private elementary and secondary staff and student-staff ratios, by level and orientation of school: 1993–94

Orientation and type of staff	Full-time equivalent staff				Students per full-time equivalent staff member			
	Total	Elementary [1]	Secondary [2]	Combined [3]	Total	Elementary [1]	Secondary [2]	Combined [3]
1	2	3	4	5	6	7	8	9
Total	**534,636**	**240,894**	**104,213**	**189,529**	**9.3**	**11.6**	**7.8**	**7.2**
Principals	23,589	13,180	2,459	7,950	210.7	212.7	329.8	170.6
Assistant principals	8,361	3,094	2,113	3,154	594.5	906.1	383.9	430.0
Other managers	7,801	1,510	3,483	2,808	637.2	1,856.5	232.9	483.0
Instruction coordinators	6,063	1,837	1,293	2,933	819.8	1,526.1	627.3	462.4
Teachers	330,838	155,220	60,644	114,974	15.0	18.1	13.4	11.8
Teacher aides	33,905	16,516	2,566	14,823	146.6	169.7	316.1	91.5
Guidance counselors	8,640	1,713	3,758	3,169	575.3	1,636.5	215.8	428.0
Librarians/media specialists	8,946	4,320	1,950	2,676	555.6	648.9	415.9	506.8
Library/media center aides	3,768	1,942	588	1,238	1,319.2	1,443.5	1,379.4	1,095.5
Student support staff [4]	11,003	2,207	2,684	6,112	451.8	1,270.2	302.2	221.9
Secretaries/clerical staff	37,634	15,170	9,061	13,403	132.1	184.8	89.5	101.2
Other employees [5]	54,092	24,187	13,615	16,290	91.9	115.9	59.6	83.3
Catholic								
Total	206,094	135,831	59,239	11,024	12.2	13.6	10.0	6.9
Principals	8,186	6,702	1,177	307	307.4	275.8	503.0	247.1
Assistant principals	2,854	1,210	1,475	169	881.6	1,527.5	401.4	448.9
Other managers	3,139	717	2,168	254	801.6	2,577.8	273.1	298.7
Instruction coordinators	1,138	619	477	42	2,211.0	2,985.9	1,241.1	1,806.2
Teachers	132,240	88,524	37,132	6,584	19.0	20.9	15.9	11.5
Teacher aides	9,078	8,144	176	758	277.2	226.9	3,363.7	100.1
Guidance counselors	3,843	1,144	2,341	358	654.7	1,615.6	252.9	211.9
Librarians/media specialists	4,291	2,836	1,230	225	586.4	651.7	481.3	337.2
Library/media center aides	1,969	1,489	363	117	1,277.9	1,241.3	1,630.9	648.4
Student support staff [4]	2,287	1,418	568	301	1,100.2	1,303.4	1,042.3	252.0
Secretaries/clerical staff	13,731	8,139	4,841	751	183.2	227.1	122.3	101.0
Other employees [5]	23,338	14,889	7,291	1,158	107.8	124.1	81.2	65.5
Other religious orientation								
Total	184,521	72,798	16,970	94,753	9.1	9.9	7.3	8.9
Principals	9,917	4,535	573	4,809	170.0	158.4	217.2	175.4
Assistant principals	3,184	1,102	278	1,804	529.5	651.7	447.7	467.5
Other managers	1,932	584	340	1,008	872.7	1,229.7	366.0	836.8
Instruction coordinators	2,298	775	153	1,370	733.7	926.7	813.4	615.7
Teachers	120,253	46,973	10,366	62,914	14.0	15.3	12.0	13.4
Teacher aides	10,021	4,827	171	5,023	168.3	148.8	727.8	167.9
Guidance counselors	2,001	473	403	1,125	842.6	1,518.3	308.8	749.7
Librarians/media specialists	2,596	977	349	1,270	649.5	735.1	356.6	664.1
Library/media center aides	990	330	112	548	1,703.1	2,176.3	1,111.1	1,539.1
Student support staff [4]	1,318	489	231	598	1,279.3	1,468.7	538.7	1,410.4
Secretaries/clerical staff	13,551	5,033	1,637	6,881	124.4	142.7	76.0	122.6
Other employees [5]	16,460	6,700	2,357	7,403	102.4	107.2	52.8	113.9
Non-sectarian								
Total	144,025	32,267	28,005	83,753	5.3	7.3	3.4	5.2
Principals	5,486	1,943	709	2,834	140.1	121.9	133.5	154.2
Assistant principals	2,323	782	360	1,181	330.8	303.0	262.9	369.9
Other managers	2,730	209	975	1,546	281.5	1,133.6	97.1	282.6
Instruction coordinators	2,627	443	663	1,521	292.5	534.8	142.7	287.2
Teachers	78,345	19,723	13,146	45,476	9.8	12.0	7.2	9.6
Teacher aides	14,806	3,545	2,219	9,042	51.9	66.8	42.6	48.3
Guidance counselors	2,796	96	1,014	1,686	274.8	2,468.0	93.3	259.1
Librarians/media specialists	2,059	507	371	1,181	373.2	467.3	255.1	369.9
Library/media center aides	809	123	113	573	949.9	1,926.3	837.4	762.5
Student support staff [4]	7,398	300	1,885	5,213	103.9	789.8	50.2	83.8
Secretaries/clerical staff	10,352	1,998	2,583	5,771	74.2	118.6	36.6	75.7
Other employees [5]	14,294	2,598	3,967	7,729	53.8	91.2	23.9	56.5

[1] Includes schools beginning with grade 6 or below and with no grade higher than 8.
[2] Schools have no grade lower than 7.
[3] Schools have grades lower than 7 and higher than 8.
[4] Includes student support services professional staff, such as school psychologists, social workers, occupational therapists, speech therapists, and nurses.
[5] Includes cafeteria workers and maintenance staff.

NOTE.—Data are based upon a sample survey and may not be strictly comparable with data reported elsewhere. Includes only schools that offer first grade or above.

SOURCE: U.S. Department of Education, National Center for Education Statistics, "Schools and Staffing Survey, 1993–94." (This table was prepared August 1995.)

Table 60.—Private elementary and secondary enrollment and schools, by amount of tuition, level, and orientation of school: 1993–94

Orientation and tuition	Kindergarten through 12th grade enrollment [1]				Schools				Average tuition paid by students			
	Total	Elementary	Secondary	Combined	Total	Elementary	Secondary	Combined	Total	Elementary	Secondary	Combined
1	2	3	4	5	6	7	8	9	10	11	12	13
Total	**4,970,646**	**2,803,359**	**811,087**	**1,356,199**	**26,093**	**15,538**	**2,551**	**8,004**	**$3,116**	**$2,138**	**$4,578**	**$4,266**
Catholic	2,516,130	1,848,257	592,011	75,862	8,351	6,924	1,161	266	2,178	1,628	3,643	4,153
Less then $1,000	393,901	378,724	(2)	(2)	1,786	1,706	(2)	(2)	—	—	—	—
$1,000 to $2,499	1,368,046	1,274,601	81,955	(2)	4,834	4,542	235	(2)	—	—	—	—
$2,500 to $4,999	675,708	188,123	452,901	(2)	1,533	642	782	(2)	—	—	—	—
$5,000 or more	71,929	(2)	(2)	(2)	(2)	(2)	(2)	(2)	—	—	—	—
Other religious	1,686,064	718,170	124,447	843,448	12,180	6,328	612	5,240	2,915	2,606	5,261	2,831
Less then $1,000	113,382	66,259	(2)	45,878	2,435	1,386	(2)	1,044	—	—	—	—
$1,000 to $2,499	839,447	387,917	(2)	435,788	6,759	3,645	(2)	3,012	—	—	—	—
$2,500 to $4,999	513,773	187,164	62,993	263,615	2,198	970	316	913	—	—	—	—
$5,000 or more	203,014	68,255	38,655	96,104	738	303	172	263	—	—	—	—
Non-sectarian	768,451	236,932	94,629	436,890	5,563	2,287	778	2,498	6,631	4,693	9,525	7,056
Less then $1,000	49,128	(2)	(2)	(2)	912	(2)	(2)	(2)	—	—	—	—
$1,000 to $2,499	121,869	(2)	(2)	(2)	666	(2)	(2)	(2)	—	—	—	—
$2,500 to $4,999	200,857	119,326	(2)	74,395	1,810	1,301	(2)	465	—	—	—	—
$5,000 or more	396,244	82,596	74,283	239,364	2,166	456	408	1,302	—	—	—	—

[1] Only includes kindergarten students who attend schools that offer first grade or above.
[2] Too few sample cases (fewer than 30 schools) for reliable estimates.
—Data not applicable.

NOTE.—Data are based upon a sample survey and may not be strictly comparable with data reported elsewhere. Elementary schools have grade 6 or lower and no grade higher than 8. Secondary schools have no grade lower than 7. Combined schools have grades lower than 7 and higher than 8. Excludes prekindergarten students. Because of rounding and missing values in cells with too few sample cases, details may not add to totals.

SOURCE: U.S. Department of Education, National Center for Education Statistics, "Schools and Staffing Survey, 1993–94." (This table was prepared August 1995.)

Table 61.—Summary statistics on Catholic elementary and secondary schools, by level: 1919–20 to 1993–94

School year	Number of schools			Enrollment			Instructional staff		
	Total	Elementary	Secondary	Total	Elementary	Secondary	Total	Elementary	Secondary
1	2	3	4	5	6	7	8	9	10
1919–20	8,103	6,551	1,552	1,925,521	1,795,673	129,848	[1] 49,516	[1] 41,592	[1] 7,924
1929–30	10,046	7,923	2,123	2,464,467	2,222,598	241,869	[1] 72,552	[1] 58,245	[1] 14,307
1939–40	10,049	7,944	2,105	2,396,305	2,035,182	361,123	[1] 81,057	[1] 60,081	[1] 20,976
1949–50	10,778	8,589	2,189	3,066,387	2,560,815	505,572	[1] 94,295	[1] 66,525	[1] 27,770
Fall 1960	12,893	10,501	2,392	5,253,791	4,373,422	880,369	[1] 151,902	[1] 108,169	[1] 43,733
1969–70	11,771	9,695	2,076	4,658,098	3,607,168	1,050,930	[2] 195,400	[2] 133,200	[2] 62,200
1970–71	11,350	9,370	1,980	4,363,566	3,355,478	1,008,088	166,208	112,750	53,458
1974–75	10,127	8,437	1,690	3,504,000	2,602,000	902,000	150,179	100,011	50,168
1975–76	9,993	8,340	1,653	3,415,000	2,525,000	890,000	149,276	99,319	49,957
1979–80	9,640	8,100	1,540	3,139,000	2,293,000	846,000	147,294	97,724	49,570
1980–81	9,559	8,043	1,516	3,106,000	2,269,000	837,000	145,777	96,739	49,038
1981–82	9,494	7,996	1,498	3,094,000	2,266,000	828,000	146,172	96,847	49,325
1982–83	9,432	7,950	1,482	3,007,189	2,211,412	795,777	146,460	97,337	49,123
1983–84	9,401	7,937	1,464	2,969,000	2,179,000	790,000	146,913	98,591	48,322
1984–85	9,325	7,876	1,449	2,903,000	2,119,000	784,000	149,888	99,820	50,068
1985–86	9,220	7,790	1,430	2,821,000	2,061,000	760,000	146,594	96,741	49,853
1986–87	9,102	7,693	1,409	2,726,000	1,998,000	728,000	141,930	93,554	48,376
1987–88	8,992	7,601	1,391	2,623,000	1,942,000	681,000	139,887	93,199	46,688
1988–89	8,867	7,505	1,362	2,551,000	1,912,000	639,000	137,700	93,154	44,546
1989–90	8,719	7,395	1,324	2,499,000	1,894,000	606,000	136,900	94,197	42,703
1990–91	8,587	7,291	1,296	2,475,439	1,883,906	591,533	131,198	91,039	40,159
1991–92	8,508	7,239	1,269	2,442,924	1,856,302	586,622	153,334	109,084	44,250
1992–93	8,423	7,174	1,249	2,444,842	1,860,937	583,905	154,816	109,825	44,991
1993–94	8,345	7,114	1,231	2,444,609	1,859,947	584,662	157,201	112,199	45,002

[1] Includes part-time teachers.
[2] Includes estimates for the nonreporting schools.

NOTE.—Data reported by the National Catholic Educational Association and data reported by the National Center for Education Statistics are not directly comparable because survey procedures and definitions differ. Excludes prekindergarten enrollment.

SOURCE: National Catholic Educational Association, *A Statistical Report on Catholic Elementary and Secondary Schools for the Years 1967–68 to 1969–70*, as compiled from the *Official Catholic Directory* (Copyright © 1970 by the National Catholic Educational Association); *Catholic Schools in America* (1978 edition, Copyright © 1978 by the Franklin Press); and *United States Catholic Elementary and Secondary Schools, 1989–90, 1990–91, 1991–92, 1992–93, and 1993–94* (Copyright © 1990, 1991, 1992, 1993, and 1994 by the National Catholic Educational Association. All rights reserved.) (This table was prepared August 1994.)

Table 62.-Private elementary and secondary schools, enrollment, teachers, and high school graduates, by state: [1]
Fall 1993

State	Number of schools		Enrollment		Teachers		High school graduates, 1992–93	
	Total	Standard error	Total	Standard error	Total	Standard error	Total	Standard error
1	2	3	4	5	6	7	8	9
United States [2]	26,093	205	4,836,442	12,875	338,162	1,319	247,278	697
Alabama	410	79	72,630	4,724	5,424	456	4,174	348
Alaska	66	—	5,884	0	476	—	213	—
Arizona	263	—	41,957	—	2,796	—	2,415	—
Arkansas	179	30	29,011	3,995	2,023	335	1,023	—
California	3,145	65	569,062	1,987	35,170	248	24,436	65
Colorado	391	68	53,732	7,798	4,115	632	1,826	283
Connecticut	360	22	70,198	1,875	6,345	125	6,291	46
Delaware	90	—	22,308	—	1,780	—	1,446	—
District of Columbia	80	—	15,854	—	1,544	—	1,054	—
Florida	1,262	83	233,743	3,789	16,842	424	9,820	54
Georgia	580	81	97,726	3,586	8,283	300	5,630	127
Hawaii	121	—	30,537	—	2,144	—	1,886	—
Idaho	78	—	8,019	—	552	—	341	—
Illinois	1,347	12	293,038	794	17,550	70	14,724	98
Indiana	619	—	91,986	—	6,139	—	4,061	—
Iowa	290	30	50,602	211	3,291	34	2,495	—
Kansas	206	—	37,045	—	2,382	—	1,668	—
Kentucky	296	—	58,058	—	3,815	—	2,949	—
Louisiana	458	19	145,512	4,036	9,286	301	7,844	—
Maine	140	—	16,999	—	1,535	—	1,914	—
Maryland	522	—	112,481	—	8,646	—	5,648	—
Massachusetts	648	29	126,744	1,362	11,329	168	10,281	—
Michigan	1,075	—	187,741	—	11,322	—	8,925	—
Minnesota	542	—	86,051	—	5,595	—	3,453	—
Mississippi	221	30	58,655	1,564	3,995	150	3,901	180
Missouri	719	69	117,466	616	7,973	85	5,839	212
Montana	82	—	9,111	—	684	—	355	—
Nebraska	223	—	39,564	—	2,575	—	1,904	—
Nevada	58	—	10,723	—	654	—	646	—
New Hampshire	130	—	18,386	—	1,742	—	1,730	—
New Jersey	878	—	195,921	—	14,281	—	11,025	—
New Mexico	166	—	20,007	—	1,569	—	1,029	—
New York	1,985	59	473,119	4,776	34,771	482	26,625	125
North Carolina	463	18	69,000	1,803	5,746	147	2,983	—
North Dakota	59	—	7,577	—	529	—	332	—
Ohio	1,016	58	246,805	3,480	14,872	306	12,398	172
Oklahoma	190	62	25,837	3,584	2,250	450	1,536	288
Oregon	250	—	34,092	—	2,254	—	1,700	—
Pennsylvania	1,846	54	342,298	4,260	21,880	235	18,532	304
Rhode Island	112	—	23,153	—	1,835	—	1,408	—
South Carolina	297	21	51,600	1,819	3,989	155	2,383	—
South Dakota	96	—	9,575	—	707	—	254	—
Tennessee	496	54	84,538	2,909	6,684	162	4,970	—
Texas	1,353	98	211,337	7,591	16,726	708	8,447	469
Utah	66	—	9,793	—	749	—	590	—
Vermont	85	—	9,107	—	945	—	1,120	—
Virginia	515	55	84,438	4,584	7,391	621	4,580	—
Washington	486	53	70,205	1,858	4,798	348	2,644	—
West Virginia	145	—	13,539	—	1,085	—	672	—
Wisconsin	954	—	141,762	—	8,927	—	5,129	—
Wyoming	35	—	1,919	—	167	—	31	—

[1] Includes special education, vocational/technical education, and alternative schools. Excludes prekindergarten enrollment.

[2] The National Center for Education Statistics employed an area frame sample to account for noninclusion of schools at the national level. However, caution should be exercised in interpreting state by state characteristics since the samples were not designed to produce such numbers.

—Insufficient data to compute a standard error.

NOTE.—Tabulation includes only schools that offer first grade or above.

SOURCE: U.S. Department of Education, National Center for Education Statistics, "Private School Survey, 1993–94." (This table was prepared August, 1995.)

Table 63.—Public and private elementary and secondary teachers and pupil-teacher ratios, by level: Fall 1955 to fall 1995

Year	Public and private elementary and secondary			Public elementary and secondary			Private elementary and secondary		
	Kindergarten to grade 12	Elementary	Secondary	Kindergarten to grade 12	Elementary	Secondary	Kindergarten to grade 12	Elementary	Secondary
1	2	3	4	5	6	7	8	9	10
Number of teachers, in thousands									
1955	1,286	827	459	1,141	733	408	[1]145	[1]94	[1]51
1960	1,600	991	609	1,408	858	550	[1]192	[1]133	[1]59
1961	1,643	992	651	1,461	869	592	182	123	59
1962	1,708	1,021	686	1,508	886	621	[1]200	135	59
1963	1,790	1,050	739	1,578	908	669	[1]212	135	[1]65
1964	1,865	1,086	779	1,648	940	708	[1]217	142	[1]70
1965	1,933	1,112	822	1,710	965	746	223	147	76
1966	2,012	1,153	859	1,789	1,006	783	[1]223	[1]147	[1]76
1967	2,079	1,188	891	1,855	1,040	815	[1]224	[1]148	[1]76
1968	2,161	1,223	938	1,936	1,076	860	225	147	78
1969	2,245	1,260	986	2,016	1,109	908	[1]229	[1]151	[1]78
1970	2,292	1,283	1,009	2,059	1,130	929	233	153	80
1971	2,293	1,263	1,030	2,063	1,111	952	[1]230	[1]152	[1]78
1972	2,337	1,296	1,041	2,106	1,142	964	[1]231	[1]154	[1]77
1973	2,372	1,308	1,064	2,136	1,151	985	[1]236	[1]157	[1]79
1974	2,410	1,330	1,079	2,165	1,166	998	[1]245	[1]164	[1]81
1975	2,453	1,353	1,100	2,198	1,181	1,017	[1]255	[1]172	[1]83
1976	2,457	1,351	1,106	2,189	1,168	1,021	268	183	85
1977	2,488	1,375	1,113	2,209	1,185	1,024	279	190	89
1978	2,479	1,376	1,103	2,207	1,191	1,016	272	185	87
1979	2,461	1,379	1,082	2,185	1,191	994	[1]276	[1]188	[1]88
1980	2,485	1,401	1,084	2,184	1,189	995	301	212	89
1981	2,440	1,404	1,037	2,127	1,183	945	[1]313	[1]221	[1]92
1982	2,458	1,413	1,045	2,133	1,182	951	[1]325	[1]231	[1]94
1983	2,476	1,426	1,050	2,139	1,186	953	337	240	97
1984	2,508	1,451	1,057	2,168	1,208	960	[1]340	[1]243	[1]97
1985	2,549	1,483	1,066	2,206	1,237	969	343	246	97
1986	2,592	1,521	1,071	2,244	1,271	973	[1]348	[1]250	[1]98
1987	2,632	1,564	1,068	2,279	1,307	973	353	257	95
1988	2,668	1,604	1,064	2,323	1,353	970	345	251	94
1989	2,679	1,622	1,057	2,357	1,387	970	322	235	87
1990	2,753	1,680	1,073	2,398	1,426	972	355	254	101
1991	2,787	1,713	1,074	2,432	1,459	973	355	254	101
1992	2,822	1,743	1,079	2,459	1,483	976	[1]363	[1]260	[1]103
1993[2]	2,871	1,772	1,099	2,505	1,510	995	366	262	104
1994[2]	2,915	1,754	1,163	2,547	1,495	1,053	368	259	110
1995[3]	2,971	1,784	1,187	2,595	1,520	1,075	375	264	112
Pupil-teacher ratios									
1955	27.4	31.4	20.3	26.9	30.2	20.9	[1]31.7	[1]40.4	[1]15.7
1960	26.4	29.4	21.4	25.8	28.4	21.7	[1]30.7	[1]36.1	[1]18.6
1961	26.4	29.6	21.5	25.6	28.3	21.7	32.5	39.0	19.0
1962	26.3	29.5	21.4	25.7	28.5	21.7	[1]30.5	[1]36.3	[1]18.5
1963	26.0	29.3	21.2	25.5	28.4	21.5	[1]29.7	[1]35.2	[1]18.6
1964	25.6	28.7	21.2	25.1	27.9	21.5	[1]29.0	[1]34.2	[1]18.3
1965	25.1	28.4	20.6	24.7	27.6	20.8	28.3	33.3	18.4
1966	24.5	27.7	20.2	24.1	26.9	20.3	[1]27.8	[1]32.7	[1]18.4
1967	24.0	26.9	20.1	23.7	26.3	20.3	[1]26.8	[1]31.1	[1]18.4
1968	23.5	26.0	20.2	23.2	25.4	20.4	25.8	29.9	17.9
1969	22.7	25.1	19.7	22.6	24.7	20.0	[1]24.0	[1]27.8	[1]16.7
1970	22.4	24.6	19.5	22.3	24.3	19.8	23.0	26.5	16.4
1971	22.4	25.0	19.1	22.3	24.9	19.3	[1]22.6	[1]25.7	[1]16.7
1972	21.7	23.9	18.9	21.7	23.9	19.1	[1]21.6	[1]24.0	[1]16.9
1973	21.3	23.0	19.1	21.3	23.0	19.3	[1]21.2	[1]23.6	[1]16.5
1974	20.8	22.6	18.5	20.8	22.6	18.7	[1]20.4	[1]22.6	[1]16.0
1975	20.3	21.7	18.6	20.4	21.7	18.8	[1]19.6	[1]21.5	[1]15.7
1976	20.1	21.7	18.3	20.2	21.8	18.5	19.3	20.9	15.8
1977	19.6	20.9	17.9	19.7	21.1	18.2	18.4	20.0	15.1
1978	19.2	20.9	17.1	19.3	21.0	17.3	18.7	20.2	15.6
1979	19.0	20.5	17.0	19.1	20.6	17.2	[1]18.1	[1]19.7	[1]14.8
1980	18.6	20.1	16.6	18.7	20.4	16.8	17.7	18.8	15.0
1981	18.7	20.0	16.8	18.8	20.3	16.9	[1]17.6	[1]18.6	[1]15.2
1982	18.4	19.8	16.4	18.6	20.2	16.6	[1]17.2	[1]18.2	[1]14.9
1983	18.2	19.6	16.2	18.4	19.9	16.4	17.0	18.0	14.4
1984	17.9	19.3	16.0	18.1	19.7	16.1	[1]16.8	[1]17.7	[1]14.4
1985	17.6	19.1	15.6	17.9	19.5	15.8	16.2	17.1	14.0
1986	17.4	18.8	15.5	17.7	19.3	15.7	[1]15.7	[1]16.5	[1]13.6
1987	17.3	18.8	15.0	17.6	19.3	15.2	15.5	16.4	13.1
1988	17.0	18.6	14.7	17.3	19.0	14.9	15.2	16.1	12.8
1989	17.1	18.8	14.5	17.2	19.0	14.6	16.6	17.7	13.7
1990	16.9	18.5	14.3	17.2	19.0	14.6	14.7	16.1	11.3
1991	17.0	18.6	14.3	17.3	19.0	14.7	14.6	16.0	11.1
1992	17.1	18.5	14.7	17.4	18.9	15.1	[1]14.8	[1]16.2	[1]11.3
1993[2]	17.0	18.4	14.8	17.4	18.8	15.2	14.9	16.3	11.5
1994[2]	17.0	18.7	14.5	17.3	19.0	14.9	15.2	16.8	11.2
1995[3]	17.1	18.7	14.6	17.4	19.1	14.9	15.1	16.7	11.3

[1] Estimated.
[2] Preliminary data.
[3] Projected.

small number of nursery school teachers and students. Some data have been revised from previously published figures. Because of rounding, details may not add to totals.

NOTE.—Data for teachers are expressed in full-time equivalents. Distribution of unclassified teachers by level is estimated. Distribution of elementary and secondary school teachers by level is determined by reporting units. Kindergarten includes a relatively

SOURCE: U.S. Department of Education, National Center for Education Statistics, *Statistics of Public Elementary and Secondary Day Schools*; Common Core of Data surveys; and *Projections of Education Statistics to 2005*. (This table was prepared June 1995.)

Table 64.—Public elementary and secondary teachers, by level and state: Fall 1989 to fall 1994

[In full-time equivalents]

State or other area	Number of teachers, fall 1989	Number of teachers, fall 1990	Number of teachers, fall 1991	Number of teachers, fall 1992 [1]				Number of teachers, fall 1993				Estimated number of teachers, 1994
				Total	Elementary	Secondary	Unclassified	Total	Elementary	Secondary	Unclassified	
1	2	3	4	5	6	7	8	9	10	11	12	13
United States	2,356,702	2,398,169	2,432,243	2,458,598	1,361,002	889,952	207,644	2,505,074	1,397,802	894,550	212,722	2,547,267
Alabama	39,928	36,266	40,480	41,917	23,391	18,526	—	43,002	23,929	19,073	—	[2]41,792
Alaska	6,492	6,710	7,118	7,282	5,146	2,136	—	7,193	4,702	2,491	—	7,307
Arizona	32,134	32,987	33,978	36,076	26,251	9,825	—	37,493	27,188	10,305	—	37,606
Arkansas	25,585	25,984	25,785	26,016	13,682	12,251	83	26,014	13,706	12,208	100	[2]28,789
California	212,687	217,228	224,000	218,253	140,258	55,121	22,874	221,779	142,436	56,384	22,959	221,500
Colorado	31,954	32,342	33,093	33,419	17,285	16,134	—	33,661	17,439	16,222	—	34,687
Connecticut	34,618	34,785	34,383	34,193	17,060	12,552	4,581	34,526	20,132	9,345	5,049	34,500
Delaware	5,982	5,961	6,095	6,252	3,210	3,042	—	6,380	3,259	3,121	—	[2]6,417
District of Columbia	6,055	5,950	6,346	6,064	3,340	2,305	419	6,056	3,353	2,259	444	[3]6,061
Florida	104,127	108,088	109,939	107,590	47,266	39,826	20,498	110,653	48,139	40,876	21,638	116,785
Georgia	61,487	63,058	63,816	66,942	46,065	20,877	—	75,602	54,863	20,739	—	77,675
Hawaii	8,866	9,083	9,451	10,083	5,073	3,752	1,258	10,111	5,739	4,328	44	10,205
Idaho	10,715	11,254	11,626	11,827	6,145	5,493	189	12,007	6,185	5,642	180	12,300
Illinois	106,183	108,775	110,153	111,461	65,107	28,952	17,402	110,874	65,188	28,207	17,479	112,991
Indiana	54,370	54,806	54,509	54,552	27,731	23,673	3,148	55,107	27,649	24,948	2,510	55,500
Iowa	30,423	31,045	31,395	31,403	18,107	12,195	1,101	31,616	18,321	12,188	1,107	[2]31,888
Kansas	28,727	29,140	29,324	29,753	14,698	12,199	2,856	30,283	14,712	12,561	3,010	[2]30,459
Kentucky	35,731	36,777	37,571	37,868	26,485	11,383	—	37,324	26,178	11,146	—	[3]37,485
Louisiana	44,608	45,401	46,170	46,904	26,322	11,010	9,572	46,913	26,556	10,377	9,980	[2]47,231
Maine	15,206	15,513	15,416	15,375	10,428	4,947	—	15,344	10,440	4,904	—	15,300
Maryland	41,646	42,562	43,616	44,495	23,698	20,797	—	44,171	25,027	19,144	—	45,000
Massachusetts	59,040	54,003	55,963	57,225	20,905	28,625	7,695	58,766	21,480	29,367	7,919	62,733
Michigan	80,150	80,008	82,967	82,301	32,761	39,492	10,048	80,267	34,136	36,419	26	80,476
Minnesota	43,101	43,574	44,903	45,050	23,273	21,777	—	46,956	23,981	22,949	26	47,371
Mississippi	27,591	28,062	28,111	27,829	16,729	10,381	719	28,376	18,592	9,184	600	28,342
Missouri	51,362	52,359	52,643	52,984	28,180	24,804	—	54,543	28,729	25,814	—	[2]56,339
Montana	9,627	9,613	9,883	10,135	6,731	3,404	—	9,950	6,914	3,036	—	9,980
Nebraska	18,464	18,764	19,069	19,323	10,968	8,337	18	19,552	11,180	8,372	—	[2]19,723
Nevada	9,175	10,373	11,409	11,953	6,465	4,234	1,254	12,579	6,563	4,648	1,368	[2]13,238
New Hampshire	10,572	10,637	11,464	11,654	8,096	3,558	—	11,972	8,059	3,913	—	11,691
New Jersey	79,597	79,886	80,515	83,057	45,999	26,373	10,685	84,564	46,855	26,509	11,200	86,237
New Mexico	16,150	16,703	17,498	17,912	10,353	4,473	3,086	18,404	10,570	4,564	3,270	18,272
New York	174,610	176,390	171,914	176,375	88,304	62,774	25,297	179,413	90,022	63,453	25,938	184,500
North Carolina	63,160	64,283	65,326	66,630	38,471	23,916	4,243	69,421	40,237	24,935	4,249	69,970
North Dakota	7,809	7,591	7,733	7,794	5,242	2,552	—	7,755	5,211	2,544	—	[2]7,996
Ohio	101,417	103,088	103,372	106,233	70,953	35,150	130	107,444	71,186	36,103	155	103,929
Oklahoma	35,631	37,221	37,650	38,433	18,582	15,835	4,016	39,031	18,735	16,180	4,116	[3]39,644
Oregon	25,630	26,174	26,745	26,634	15,156	9,392	2,086	26,488	14,386	8,716	3,386	[2]26,207
Pennsylvania	105,415	100,275	100,475	100,912	45,421	43,691	11,800	101,301	45,974	43,358	11,969	102,350
Rhode Island	9,369	9,522	9,709	10,069	4,577	4,165	1,327	9,823	4,404	4,103	1,316	9,222
South Carolina	36,337	36,963	37,115	37,295	25,404	11,891	—	38,620	26,252	12,368	—	38,955
South Dakota	8,191	8,511	8,868	8,767	5,570	2,371	826	9,557	5,897	2,589	1,071	9,477
Tennessee	42,824	43,051	43,062	43,566	30,249	11,659	1,658	46,066	32,072	12,398	1,596	48,921
Texas	199,397	219,298	219,192	219,385	111,778	81,100	26,507	224,830	113,630	82,139	29,061	228,895
Utah	17,611	17,884	18,305	19,191	9,726	7,133	2,332	19,053	8,918	7,780	2,355	21,788
Vermont	6,852	7,257	7,031	7,521	3,063	2,820	1,638	8,102	3,371	3,140	1,591	[3]8,480
Virginia	62,138	63,638	64,537	68,181	41,185	26,996	—	70,220	42,205	28,015	—	[3]71,424
Washington	40,279	41,764	42,931	44,295	23,948	16,820	3,527	45,524	24,232	17,533	3,759	[2]46,335
West Virginia	21,653	21,476	20,997	20,961	9,923	7,495	3,543	21,029	10,070	7,394	3,565	[2]20,868
Wisconsin	49,329	49,302	52,028	53,387	33,358	18,801	1,228	52,822	35,585	17,237	—	55,825
Wyoming	6,697	6,784	6,564	5,821	2,884	2,937	—	6,537	3,215	3,322	—	[3]6,601
Outlying areas												
American Samoa	659	662	671	725	454	195	76	656	455	182	19	784
Guam	1,622	1,543	1,499	1,628	921	689	18	1,644	794	845	5	985
Northern Marianas	358	416	430	425	228	171	26	431	265	166	0	[3]438
Puerto Rico	33,427	34,260	37,291	38,381	21,146	14,070	3,165	39,816	21,935	14,596	3,285	40,215
Virgin Islands	1,595	1,575	1,581	1,595	779	692	124	1,570	773	722	75	1,550

[1] Data have been revised from previously published figures.
[2] Actual fall data.
[3] Estimated by the National Center for Education Statistics.
—Data not available, not reported, or not applicable.

NOTE.—Distribution of elementary and secondary teachers determined by reporting units. Teachers reported in full-time equivalents.

SOURCE: U.S. Department of Education, National Center for Education Statistics, Common Core of Data surveys. (This table was prepared May 1995.)

Table 65.—Teachers, enrollment, and pupil-teacher ratios in public elementary and secondary schools, by state: Fall 1988 to fall 1993

State or other area	Pupil-teacher ratio, fall 1988	Pupil-teacher ratio, fall 1989	Pupil-teacher ratio, fall 1990	Fall 1991			Fall 1992			Fall 1993		
				Teachers	Enrollment	Pupil-teacher ratio	Teachers	Enrollment	Pupil-teacher ratio	Teachers	Enrollment	Pupil-teacher ratio
1	2	3	4	5	6	7	8	9	10	11	12	13
United States	**17.3**	**17.2**	**17.2**	**2,432,243**	**42,046,878**	**17.3**	**2,458,598**	**42,815,541**	**17.4**	**2,505,074**	**43,476,268**	**17.4**
Alabama	18.7	18.1	19.9	40,480	722,004	17.8	41,917	730,857	17.4	43,002	734,469	17.1
Alaska	17.0	16.8	17.0	7,118	118,680	16.7	7,282	122,487	16.8	7,193	125,948	17.5
Arizona	18.2	18.9	19.4	33,978	656,980	19.3	36,076	673,477	18.7	37,493	709,453	18.9
Arkansas	15.7	17.0	16.8	25,785	438,518	17.0	26,016	441,490	17.0	26,014	444,271	17.1
California	22.7	22.4	22.8	224,000	5,107,145	22.8	218,253	5,249,275	24.1	221,779	5,328,558	24.0
Colorado	17.8	17.6	17.8	33,093	593,030	17.9	33,419	612,635	18.3	33,661	625,062	18.6
Connecticut	13.0	13.3	13.5	34,383	481,050	14.0	34,193	488,476	14.3	34,526	496,298	14.4
Delaware	16.4	16.4	16.7	6,095	102,196	16.8	6,252	104,321	16.7	6,380	105,547	16.5
District of Columbia	14.3	13.4	13.6	6,346	80,618	12.7	6,064	80,937	13.3	6,056	80,678	13.3
Florida	17.1	17.2	17.2	109,939	1,932,131	17.6	107,590	1,981,407	18.4	110,653	2,040,763	18.4
Georgia	18.5	18.3	18.3	63,816	1,177,569	18.5	66,942	1,207,186	18.0	75,602	1,235,304	16.3
Hawaii	19.2	19.1	18.9	9,451	174,747	18.5	10,083	177,448	17.6	10,111	180,430	17.8
Idaho	20.6	20.1	19.6	11,626	225,680	19.4	11,827	231,668	19.6	12,007	236,774	19.7
Illinois	17.1	16.9	16.7	110,153	1,848,166	16.8	111,461	1,873,567	16.8	110,874	1,893,078	17.1
Indiana	17.8	17.5	17.4	54,509	956,988	17.6	54,552	960,630	17.6	55,107	965,599	17.5
Iowa	15.8	15.7	15.6	31,395	491,363	15.7	31,403	494,839	15.8	31,616	498,519	15.8
Kansas	15.2	15.0	15.0	29,324	445,390	15.2	29,753	451,536	15.2	30,283	457,614	15.1
Kentucky	17.8	17.7	17.3	37,571	646,024	17.2	37,868	655,041	17.3	37,324	655,265	17.6
Louisiana	18.2	17.6	17.3	46,170	794,128	17.2	46,904	797,985	17.0	46,913	800,560	16.6
Maine	14.6	14.1	13.9	15,416	216,400	14.0	15,375	216,453	14.1	15,344	216,995	14.1
Maryland	16.8	16.8	16.8	43,616	736,238	16.9	44,495	751,850	16.9	44,171	772,638	17.5
Massachusetts	13.7	14.0	15.4	55,963	846,155	15.1	57,225	859,948	15.0	58,766	877,726	14.9
Michigan	19.8	19.7	19.8	82,967	1,593,561	19.2	82,301	1,603,610	19.5	80,267	1,599,377	19.9
Minnesota	17.0	17.2	17.4	44,903	773,571	17.2	45,050	793,724	17.6	46,956	810,233	17.3
Mississippi	18.4	18.2	17.9	28,111	504,127	17.9	27,829	506,668	18.2	28,376	505,907	17.8
Missouri	15.9	15.7	15.6	52,643	842,965	16.0	52,984	859,357	16.2	54,543	875,639	16.1
Montana	15.8	15.7	15.9	9,883	155,779	15.8	10,135	160,011	15.8	9,950	163,009	16.4
Nebraska	15.0	14.7	14.6	19,069	279,552	14.7	19,323	282,414	14.6	19,552	285,097	14.6
Nevada	20.3	20.4	19.4	11,409	211,810	18.6	11,953	222,974	18.7	12,579	235,800	18.7
New Hampshire	16.2	16.2	16.2	11,464	177,138	15.5	11,654	181,247	15.6	11,972	185,360	15.5
New Jersey	13.6	13.5	13.6	80,515	1,109,796	13.8	83,057	1,130,560	13.6	84,564	1,151,307	13.6
New Mexico	18.5	18.3	18.1	17,498	308,667	17.6	17,912	315,668	17.6	18,404	322,292	17.5
New York	14.9	14.7	14.7	171,914	2,643,993	15.4	176,375	2,689,686	15.2	179,413	2,733,813	15.2
North Carolina	17.5	17.1	16.9	65,326	1,097,598	16.8	66,630	1,114,083	16.7	69,421	1,133,231	16.3
North Dakota	15.4	15.1	15.5	7,733	118,376	15.3	7,794	118,734	15.2	7,755	119,127	15.4
Ohio	17.6	17.4	17.2	103,372	1,783,767	17.3	106,233	1,795,199	16.9	107,444	1,807,319	16.8
Oklahoma	16.5	16.2	15.6	37,650	588,263	15.6	38,433	597,096	15.5	39,031	604,076	15.5
Oregon	18.4	18.4	18.0	26,745	498,614	18.6	26,634	510,122	19.2	26,488	516,611	19.5
Pennsylvania	15.9	15.7	16.6	100,475	1,692,797	16.8	100,912	1,717,613	17.0	101,301	1,744,082	17.2
Rhode Island	14.5	14.5	14.6	9,709	142,144	14.6	10,069	143,798	14.3	9,823	145,676	14.8
South Carolina	17.2	17.0	16.8	37,115	627,470	16.9	37,295	639,942	17.2	38,620	643,859	16.7
South Dakota	15.4	15.5	15.2	8,868	131,576	14.8	8,767	134,573	15.3	9,557	142,825	14.9
Tennessee	19.3	19.1	19.2	43,062	833,651	19.4	43,566	854,329	19.6	46,066	866,991	18.8
Texas	16.7	16.7	15.4	219,192	3,464,371	15.8	219,385	3,541,769	16.1	224,830	3,608,262	16.0
Utah	24.5	24.9	25.0	18,305	456,430	24.9	19,191	463,870	24.2	19,053	471,365	24.7
Vermont	13.6	13.8	13.2	7,031	97,137	13.8	7,521	98,558	13.1	8,102	102,755	12.7
Virginia	16.1	15.9	15.7	64,537	1,016,204	15.7	68,181	1,031,925	15.1	70,220	1,045,471	14.9
Washington	20.4	20.1	20.1	42,931	869,327	20.2	44,295	896,475	20.2	45,524	915,952	20.1
West Virginia	15.1	15.1	15.0	20,997	320,249	15.3	20,961	318,296	15.2	21,029	314,383	14.9
Wisconsin	16.0	15.9	16.2	52,028	814,671	15.7	53,387	829,415	15.5	52,822	844,001	16.0
Wyoming	14.6	14.5	14.5	6,564	102,074	15.6	5,821	100,313	17.2	6,537	100,899	15.4
Outlying areas												
American Samoa	17.5	18.6	18.8	671	13,365	19.9	725	13,994	19.3	656	14,484	22.1
Guam	18.6	16.3	17.1	1,499	28,334	18.9	1,628	30,077	18.5	1,644	30,920	18.8
Northern Marianas	18.2	17.0	15.5	430	7,096	16.5	425	8,086	19.0	431	8,188	19.0
Puerto Rico	19.8	19.5	18.8	37,291	642,392	17.2	38,381	637,034	16.6	39,816	631,460	15.9
Virgin Islands	14.7	13.3	13.8	1,581	22,346	14.1	1,595	22,887	14.3	1,570	22,752	14.5

NOTE.—Some data have been revised from previously published figures. Teachers reported in full-time equivalents.

SOURCE: U.S. Department of Education, National Center for Education Statistics, Common Core of Data surveys. (This table was prepared March 1995.)

Table 66.—Teachers in public and private elementary and secondary schools, by selected characteristics: 1993–94

Selected characteristics	Total [1]	Percent of teachers, by highest degree earned						Percent of teachers, by years of full-time teaching experience			
		No degree	Associate	Bachelor's	Master's	Education specialist	Doctor's	Less than 3	3 to 9	10 to 20	Over 20
1	2	3	4	5	6	7	8	9	10	11	12
Public schools											
Total	**2,561,294**	**0.6**	**0.2**	**52.0**	**42.0**	**4.6**	**0.7**	**9.7**	**25.5**	**35.0**	**29.8**
Men	694,098	1.3	0.4	46.2	45.7	5.1	1.3	8.9	21.6	29.9	39.6
Women	1,867,195	0.3	0.1	54.1	40.6	4.4	0.5	10.0	26.9	37.0	26.1
Race/ethnicity											
White, non-Hispanic	2,216,605	0.5	0.1	51.8	42.5	4.4	0.7	9.4	25.5	35.2	30.0
Black, non-Hispanic	188,371	0.5	0.2	48.4	44.6	5.4	0.9	8.5	20.9	35.6	35.3
Hispanic	108,744	0.9	0.5	62.8	29.8	4.6	1.4	16.7	32.1	34.1	17.1
Asian or Pacific Islander	27,510	0.9	0.4	49.3	34.7	13.1	1.7	14.9	29.7	29.2	26.2
American Indian or Alaskan Native	20,064	0.8	0.3	54.9	39.1	4.3	0.6	11.4	27.7	34.6	26.6
Age											
Less than 30	479,413	0.6	0.1	76.3	21.5	1.5	0.1	33.9	61.8	4.3	(2)
30 to 39	761,670	0.4	0.2	52.8	42.0	4.0	0.5	7.0	28.5	62.3	2.2
40 to 49	980,923	0.5	0.2	43.1	49.6	5.8	0.8	3.0	12.2	33.5	51.3
50 or more	339,265	1.1	0.2	41.4	48.8	6.7	1.9	1.0	5.8	21.8	71.5
Level											
Elementary	1,500,106	0.2	0.0	54.6	40.5	4.2	0.5	9.9	26.6	35.7	27.8
Secondary	813,348	1.2	0.4	46.7	45.5	5.1	1.1	9.0	22.8	34.3	33.9
Combined	68,235	0.9	0.3	54.7	37.8	5.6	0.8	12.6	27.2	35.4	24.8
Private schools											
Total	**378,365**	**5.2**	**1.5**	**59.0**	**29.8**	**2.9**	**1.7**	**20.9**	**33.9**	**29.6**	**15.6**
Men	93,130	4.4	0.9	47.3	40.6	2.6	4.3	21.7	28.2	28.7	21.4
Women	285,235	5.4	1.7	62.8	26.3	3.0	0.8	20.6	35.8	29.9	13.7
Race/ethnicity											
White, non-Hispanic	347,811	4.8	1.3	59.4	30.2	2.6	1.6	20.4	33.6	30.0	16.0
Black, non-Hispanic	11,664	8.3	3.7	55.8	26.4	4.8	1.0	26.9	34.9	27.9	10.3
Hispanic	12,221	11.1	4.9	57.4	19.9	4.4	2.3	25.5	41.8	21.6	11.1
Asian or Pacific Islander	5,167	6.8	0.9	46.1	36.8	5.7	3.6	26.1	34.6	26.6	12.7
American Indian or Alaskan Native	1,502	3.4	6.0	49.4	16.1	25.1	0.0	29.4	42.8	17.9	9.9
Age											
Less than 30	102,157	7.2	1.3	74.5	14.9	1.7	0.5	42.9	54.3	2.7	(2)
30 to 39	108,748	5.0	1.6	57.7	31.0	3.1	1.6	19.1	35.3	44.6	1.0
40 to 49	115,812	3.6	1.9	53.1	35.9	3.4	2.2	9.5	25.2	42.1	23.2
50 or more	51,648	5.0	1.0	44.0	43.3	3.7	3.0	6.6	10.2	22.9	60.3
Level											
Elementary	171,754	4.9	1.8	67.0	23.0	2.6	0.7	22.5	35.2	28.4	13.9
Secondary	61,787	1.2	0.6	46.5	45.6	3.0	3.2	19.0	28.2	30.2	22.6
Combined	106,106	7.9	1.9	54.4	30.4	3.4	2.1	20.2	35.9	30.4	13.5

[1] Data are based upon a sample survey and may not be strictly comparable with data reported elsewhere.

[2] Less than .05 percent.

NOTE.—Excludes prekindergarten teachers. Details may not add to totals because of survey item nonresponse and rounding.

SOURCE: U.S. Department of Education, National Center for Education Statistics, "Schools and Staffing Survey, 1993–94." (This table was prepared August 1995.)

Table 67.—Highest degree earned and number of years teaching experience for teachers in public elementary and secondary schools, by state: 1993–94

State	Total [1]	Percent of teachers, by highest degree [2]				Percent of teachers, by years of full-time teaching experience			
		Bachelor's	Master's	Education specialist	Doctor's	Less than 3	3 to 9	10 to 20	Over 20
1	2	3	4	5	6	7	8	9	10
United States	**2,561,294**	**52.0**	**42.0**	**4.6**	**0.7**	**9.7**	**25.5**	**35.0**	**29.8**
Alabama	44,791	38.5	52.6	7.8	0.7	11.1	22.0	42.2	24.7
Alaska	8,152	59.0	35.3	4.2	(3)	8.0	29.3	42.7	20.0
Arizona	37,600	51.4	43.3	4.0	0.7	13.1	29.1	38.1	19.8
Arkansas	30,621	64.9	32.5	1.8	0.5	9.2	27.3	40.2	23.3
California	209,032	58.6	32.6	6.8	1.0	9.8	27.8	31.8	30.7
Colorado	35,723	46.5	49.4	2.5	0.5	9.4	26.1	38.7	25.7
Connecticut	35,465	19.6	62.4	15.7	1.4	6.4	19.8	35.5	38.3
Delaware	7,027	46.0	48.3	5.1	—	7.7	24.1	36.2	32.0
District of Columbia	5,185	41.2	54.4	2.4	2.0	10.8	14.7	30.6	43.9
Florida	106,535	57.2	37.0	3.3	1.4	8.7	29.4	37.8	24.0
Georgia	74,907	48.9	42.5	7.7	(3)	13.3	28.3	35.6	22.8
Hawaii	11,137	47.8	21.7	27.5	1.0	16.2	28.1	22.0	33.7
Idaho	12,166	74.4	21.7	2.6	0.6	12.4	33.3	33.7	20.6
Illinois	111,511	49.7	46.1	3.4	0.5	9.0	25.1	30.8	35.1
Indiana	57,732	21.4	72.9	4.9	—	5.6	24.7	37.1	32.6
Iowa	35,861	67.3	31.3	1.2	(3)	10.1	23.3	32.1	34.5
Kansas	31,164	53.5	42.8	2.3	1.1	12.3	28.2	35.2	24.3
Kentucky	41,571	23.4	56.8	18.7	0.8	9.5	26.8	32.9	30.8
Louisiana	48,948	60.5	31.2	6.9	0.5	9.7	29.8	35.1	25.5
Maine	15,658	68.4	28.4	1.6	(3)	7.0	28.7	37.4	26.9
Maryland	43,862	43.3	49.6	6.2	0.6	11.7	23.6	32.4	32.4
Massachusetts	58,416	38.8	54.8	3.9	0.9	8.4	17.1	33.6	41.0
Michigan	83,288	46.6	48.1	4.7	0.6	7.4	21.5	29.4	41.9
Minnesota	44,150	63.4	33.6	2.6	(3)	13.0	20.0	33.0	34.0
Mississippi	29,851	56.3	37.5	4.3	(3)	10.5	22.8	39.8	26.9
Missouri.	62,454	54.3	42.4	2.2	0.6	10.6	26.9	37.2	25.3
Montana	12,851	71.3	26.0	1.8	0.5	11.1	27.5	39.0	22.5
Nebraska	20,411	61.5	36.0	1.9	(3)	10.1	24.4	39.0	26.5
Nevada	12,822	50.5	42.8	5.7	0.6	12.0	33.2	35.0	19.8
New Hampshire	12,299	60.2	35.9	2.6	0.7	10.6	26.8	38.2	24.4
New Jersey	83,935	56.2	37.4	4.8	1.0	5.8	21.1	34.6	38.5
New Mexico	19,265	53.2	43.6	2.2	(3)	12.5	32.5	33.9	21.1
New York	178,701	25.0	68.1	5.3	1.5	10.3	23.9	29.7	36.1
North Carolina	72,305	61.8	35.0	1.2	0.5	9.7	26.6	38.8	25.0
North Dakota	8,404	79.3	18.0	1.6	—	12.1	27.2	37.7	23.0
Ohio	111,518	53.2	41.8	3.1	(3)	6.8	23.2	38.6	31.4
Oklahoma	42,220	56.9	39.5	3.2	(3)	10.4	27.0	41.2	21.5
Oregon	25,706	51.5	43.1	4.0	0.8	7.4	27.0	39.6	26.0
Pennsylvania	114,571	46.7	45.6	6.9	(3)	6.9	18.3	33.0	41.8
Rhode Island	9,217	40.1	53.3	5.7	1.0	7.2	21.9	28.6	42.3
South Carolina	39,623	48.8	43.4	5.6	0.7	10.5	25.1	42.3	22.1
South Dakota	10,579	75.1	23.2	1.5	—	10.4	28.6	37.3	23.8
Tennessee	47,662	51.2	42.0	4.8	1.2	12.4	22.9	35.5	29.2
Texas	223,800	69.7	26.8	1.8	0.9	12.1	30.1	37.5	20.4
Utah	19,884	70.6	23.5	4.2	(3)	12.7	32.8	36.1	18.3
Vermont	7,327	49.4	47.5	2.1	—	12.3	25.3	34.4	28.0
Virginia	64,937	64.4	31.3	2.4	0.5	10.5	26.0	37.5	26.1
Washington	48,452	56.3	37.5	3.6	1.0	10.8	30.1	32.2	26.9
West Virginia	21,473	41.7	53.1	4.3	—	4.4	21.6	42.7	31.4
Wisconsin	62,958	59.3	38.1	1.7	0.6	9.1	24.7	29.5	36.7
Wyoming	7,567	71.3	26.5	1.4	(3)	9.4	22.6	41.6	26.5

[1] Data are based on a head count of all teachers rather than on the number of full-time equivalent teachers appearing in other tables.

[2] Teachers with less than a bachelor's degree are not shown.

[3] Less than 0.5 percent.

—Data not available.

NOTE.—Excludes prekindergarten teachers. Details may not add to totals due to rounding or item nonresponse. Cell entries may be underestimates due to item nonresponse.

SOURCE: U.S. Department of Education, National Center for Education Statistics, "Schools and Staffing Survey, 1993–94." (This table was prepared June 1995.)

Table 68.—Selected characteristics of public school teachers: Spring 1961 to spring 1991

Item	1961	1966	1971	1976	1981	1986	1991
1	2	3	4	5	6	7	8
Number of teachers, in thousands	**1,408**	**1,710**	**2,055**	**2,196**	**2,185**	**2,206**	**2,398**
Sex (percent)							
Men	31.3	31.1	34.3	32.9	33.1	31.2	27.9
Women	68.7	68.9	65.7	67.1	66.9	68.8	72.1
Median age (years)							
All teachers	41	36	35	33	37	41	42
Men	34	33	33	33	38	42	43
Women	46	40	37	33	36	41	42
Race (percent)							
White	—	—	88.3	90.8	91.6	89.6	86.8
Black	—	—	8.1	8.0	7.8	6.9	8.0
Other	—	—	3.6	1.2	0.7	3.4	5.2
Marital status (percent)							
Single	22.3	22.0	19.5	20.1	18.5	12.9	11.7
Married	68.0	69.1	71.9	71.3	73.0	75.7	75.7
Widowed, divorced, or separated	9.7	9.0	8.6	8.6	8.5	11.4	12.6
Highest degree held (percent) [1]							
Less than bachelor's	14.6	7.0	2.9	0.9	0.4	0.3	0.6
Bachelor's	61.9	69.6	69.6	61.6	50.1	48.3	46.3
Master's or specialist degree	23.1	23.2	27.1	37.1	49.3	50.7	52.6
Doctor's	0.4	0.1	0.4	0.4	0.3	0.7	0.5
College credits earned in last 3 years							
Percent who earned credits	—	—	60.7	63.2	56.1	53.1	50.3
Mean number of credits earned [2]	—	—	14	—	9	4	4
Median years of teaching experience	11	8	8	8	12	15	15
Teaching for first year (percent)	8.0	9.1	9.1	5.5	2.4	3.1	3.0
Average number of pupils per class							
Elementary teachers, not departmentalized	29	28	27	25	25	24	24
Elementary teachers, departmentalized	—	—	25	23	22	—	—
Secondary teachers	28	26	27	25	23	25	26
Mean number of students taught per day by secondary teachers	138	132	134	126	118	94	93
Average number of hours in required school day	7.4	7.3	7.3	7.3	7.3	7.3	7.2
Average number of hours per week spent on all teaching duties							
All teachers	47	47	47	46	46	49	47
Elementary teachers	49	47	46	44	44	47	44
Secondary teachers	46	48	48	48	48	51	50
Average number of days of classroom teaching in school year	—	181	181	180	180	180	180
Average number of nonteaching days in school year	—	5	4	5	6	5	5
Average annual salary as classroom teacher	[3] $5,264	$6,253	$9,261	$12,005	$17,209	$24,504	$31,790
Total income, including spouse's (if married)	—	—	$15,021	$19,957	$29,831	$43,413	$55,491
Willingness to teach again (percent)							
Certainly would	49.9	52.6	44.9	37.5	21.8	22.7	28.6
Probably would	26.9	25.4	29.5	26.1	24.6	26.3	30.5
Chances about even	12.5	12.9	13.0	17.5	17.6	19.8	18.5
Probably would not	7.9	7.1	8.9	13.4	24.0	22.0	17.0
Certainly would not	2.8	2.0	3.7	5.6	12.0	9.3	5.4

[1] Figures for curriculum specialist or professional diploma based on six years of college study are not included.

[2] Measured in semester hours.

[3] Includes extra pay for extra duties.

—Data not available.

NOTE.—Data are based upon sample surveys of public school teachers. Data differ from figures appearing in other tables because of varying processing procedures and time period coverages. Because of rounding, percents may not add to 100.0.

Table 69.—Public secondary school teachers, by subject taught: Spring 1966 to spring 1991

[Percentage distribution]

Teaching field in which largest portion of time was spent	1966	1971	1976	1981	1986	1991
1	2	3	4	5	6	7
Total secondary school teachers, in thousands	746	927	1,016	995	970	1,012
All fields	100.0	100.0	100.0	100.0	100.0	100.0
Agriculture	1.6	0.6	0.6	1.1	0.6	0.3
Art	2.0	3.7	2.4	3.1	1.5	2.6
Business education	7.0	5.9	4.6	6.2	6.5	3.5
English	18.1	20.4	19.9	23.8	21.8	25.0
Foreign language	6.4	4.8	4.2	2.8	3.7	3.8
Health and physical education	6.9	8.3	7.9	6.5	5.6	7.5
Home economics	5.9	5.1	2.8	3.6	2.6	3.1
Industrial arts	5.1	4.1	3.9	5.2	2.2	2.1
Mathematics	13.9	14.4	18.2	15.3	19.2	14.5
Music	4.7	3.8	3.0	3.7	4.8	4.2
Science	10.8	10.6	13.1	12.1	11.0	13.3
Social studies	15.3	14.0	12.4	11.2	13.6	11.0
Special education	0.4	1.1	3.0	2.1	3.5	5.2
Other	1.9	3.1	4.0	3.3	3.4	3.9

NOTE.—Because of rounding, percents may not add to 100.0. Data are based upon sample surveys of public school teachers.

SOURCE: National Education Association, *Status of the American Public School Teacher, 1990–91.* (Copyright © 1992 by the National Education Association. All rights reserved.) (This table was prepared January 1993.)

Table 70.—Percent of vocational and nonvocational public school teachers of grades 9 to 12, by selected demographic and educational characteristics: 1990–91

Characteristics of teachers	Total	Teacher type		Characteristics of teachers	Total	Teacher type	
		Nonvocational	Vocational			Nonvocational	Vocational
1	2	3	4	1	2	3	4
Total	100.0	100.0	100.0				
Sex				Major field of study			
Male	48.6	48.0	51.7	Mathematics and sciences	10.4	12.3	1.0
Female	51.4	52.0	48.3	Social sciences	8.7	10.0	1.9
				Letters and humanities	12.4	14.6	1.5
Race/ethnicity				Education			
White	89.1	89.4	87.8	General	45.3	52.2	9.5
Black	6.6	6.1	8.7	Special education	4.0	4.7	0.1
Hispanic	2.8	3.0	2.0	Vocational education	13.9	2.8	71.7
Asian	0.8	0.8	0.7	Occupationally specific	3.8	2.3	11.6
American Indian or Alaskan Native	0.7	0.7	0.9	Other	1.4	1.1	2.7
Age				Age at which first began to teach full-time or part-time			
Under 30 years	11.0	11.5	8.4	25 or under	69.8	71.3	62.6
30 to 39 years	26.9	27.3	24.8	26 to 35	22.9	22.4	25.4
40 to 49 years	41.1	41.4	39.6	36 to 45	6.0	5.2	9.9
50 years and over	21.0	19.7	27.2	46 to 55	1.1	1.0	1.9
				Over 55	0.1	0.1	0.3
Highest college degree							
Less than a bachelor's degree	1.7	0.3	8.3				
Bachelor's degree	45.4	45.3	45.5				
Master's degree	46.4	47.4	41.4				
Education specialist [1]	5.3	5.5	4.5				
Doctorate or first professional	1.3	1.5	0.3				

[1] Education specialist degrees or certificates are generally awarded for one year's work beyond the master's level.

SOURCE: U.S. Department of Education, National Center for Education Statistics, "Schools and Staffing Survey, 1990–91." (This table was prepared July 1994.)

Table 71.—Mobility of public and private elementary and secondary teachers, by selected school and teacher characteristics: 1988–89 and 1991–92

Characteristic	Percentage distribution of public school teachers						Percentage distribution of private school teachers					
	1987–88 to 1988–89			1990–91 to 1991–92			1987–88 to 1988–89			1990–91 to 1991–92		
	Remained teaching in the same school	Remained in teaching but changed schools	Left teaching	Remained teaching in the same school	Remained in teaching but changed schools	Left teaching	Remained teaching in the same school	Remained in teaching but changed schools	Left teaching	Remained teaching in the same school	Remained in teaching but changed schools	Left teaching
1	2	3	4	5	6	7	8	9	10	11	12	13
Total	**86.5**	**7.9**	**5.6**	**87.6**	**7.3**	**5.1**	**77.8**	**9.5**	**12.7**	**81.1**	**6.6**	**12.3**
Sex												
Male	87.7	7.3	5.1	89.1	6.4	4.5	83.7	6.1	10.2	81.6	6.3	12.1
Female	86.1	8.1	5.8	87.1	7.6	5.3	76.2	10.4	13.4	81.0	6.6	12.3
Race/ethnicity												
White, non-Hispanic	86.5	7.8	5.7	87.6	7.3	5.1	78.7	9.2	12.1	81.3	6.7	12.0
Total minority	87.0	8.6	4.4	87.5	7.1	5.3	64.4	14.2	21.4	79.3	5.3	15.4
Black, non-Hispanic	86.2	8.8	5.1	85.5	8.3	6.1	29.6	35.7	34.7	78.4	2.4	19.3
Hispanic	88.9	8.2	2.9	89.6	6.0	4.4	68.6	10.2	21.3	77.4	9.0	13.6
Age												
Less than 25	78.7	17.0	4.3	73.8	17.2	9.1	63.2	17.9	19.0	62.4	13.8	23.8
25 to 29	75.0	16.1	9.0	76.6	14.3	9.0	64.8	17.5	17.6	70.4	11.8	17.8
30 to 39	85.2	9.0	5.8	85.9	9.9	4.2	78.5	9.1	12.4	78.7	7.5	13.7
40 to 49	91.2	6.4	2.4	92.5	5.5	2.0	82.0	7.5	10.5	87.2	5.2	7.7
50 to 59	90.4	3.9	5.7	89.3	4.0	6.7	82.3	6.4	11.3	87.0	3.3	9.6
60 to 64	72.0	4.5	23.4	71.0	2.2	26.8	79.8	3.3	16.9	81.1	1.1	17.8
65 and over	83.3	0.0	16.7	48.9	10.3	40.9	88.2	3.9	7.9	73.4	5.9	20.7
Full-time teaching experience												
Less than 1 year	76.9	11.5	11.6	51.5	31.3	17.2	67.0	5.6	27.4	67.0	4.6	28.4
1 to 3 years	77.4	14.3	8.3	79.7	13.1	7.2	70.6	13.5	15.9	73.5	9.8	16.7
1 year	77.3	14.2	8.5	79.0	12.6	8.4	64.1	17.0	18.8	71.2	10.0	18.8
2 years	78.8	13.6	7.6	78.7	14.1	7.1	73.5	12.0	14.6	75.0	9.2	15.8
3 years	76.0	15.2	8.8	81.6	12.4	5.9	74.0	11.7	14.3	75.1	10.2	14.7
4 to 9 years	82.9	11.1	6.0	84.8	9.9	5.3	75.7	11.6	12.8	79.2	8.1	12.7
10 to 19 years	89.3	6.7	4.0	91.0	6.5	2.4	81.1	7.5	11.4	88.6	5.3	6.2
20 to 24 years	93.6	4.1	2.2	93.3	3.3	3.4	85.5	7.1	7.4	92.3	3.0	4.7
25 years or more	84.9	4.1	11.0	85.9	3.1	11.0	88.3	4.3	7.4	83.0	2.4	14.6
Level taught												
Elementary	85.0	9.5	5.5	87.1	8.1	4.8	76.7	10.8	12.5	81.9	6.7	11.3
Secondary	88.1	6.2	5.6	88.2	6.4	5.5	78.9	8.2	12.9	80.3	6.4	13.3
School size												
Less than 150	85.6	9.8	4.5	86.6	8.1	5.3	64.4	16.2	19.4	72.6	10.3	17.0
150 to 299	84.6	9.9	5.4	88.0	7.7	4.3	79.6	8.4	12.1	79.4	6.8	13.8
300 to 499	86.9	7.5	5.6	85.8	8.5	5.7	80.3	9.5	10.2	86.4	5.9	7.7
500 to 749	86.8	7.5	5.7	87.7	7.6	4.7	84.9	5.9	9.2	85.5	4.7	9.8
750 or more	87.7	7.4	4.9	88.6	6.1	5.4	82.2	4.9	12.8	91.0	2.3	6.7
Percent minority enrollment												
Less than 5%	88.0	6.9	5.1	89.6	5.7	4.6	77.6	9.2	13.2	81.2	7.3	11.5
5 to 19%	86.6	7.6	5.8	88.1	6.4	5.5	82.2	7.4	10.3	82.0	5.8	12.2
20 to 49%	87.3	7.6	5.2	85.6	8.6	5.9	71.8	9.3	18.9	82.4	5.3	12.2
50% or more	85.0	9.7	5.3	86.2	8.9	4.9	69.6	16.8	13.6	76.7	10.2	13.1
Community type												
Central city	—	—	—	88.8	6.4	4.8	—	—	—	80.6	6.3	13.1
Urban fringe/small town	—	—	—	87.0	7.4	5.6	—	—	—	84.0	6.5	9.4
Rural/small town	—	—	—	86.0	8.7	5.3	—	—	—	78.5	7.7	13.8

—Data not available or not applicable.

NOTE.—Details may not add to 100 percent due to rounding.

SOURCES: U.S. Department of Education, National Center for Education Statistics, *Characteristics of Stayers, Movers, and Leavers: Results from the Teacher Followup Survey: 1991–92.* (This table was prepared May 1994.)

Table 72.—Average salaries for full-time teachers in public and private elementary and secondary schools, by selected characteristics: 1993–94

Selected characteristics	Total earned income	Base salary	Number of full-time teachers	School year supplemental contract		Supplemental contract during summer		Number of teachers with nonschool employment		
				Number of teachers	Supplemental salary	Number of teachers	Supplemental salary	Teaching or tutor	Education related	Not education related
1	2	3	4	5	6	7	8	9	10	11
	Public schools									
Total	$35,924	$34,153	2,340,182	815,827	$2,075	401,505	$2,070	118,369	80,014	237,177
Men	39,591	36,182	642,803	348,855	2,922	147,294	2,530	37,293	39,150	124,487
Women	34,536	33,384	1,697,380	466,972	1,442	254,210	1,803	81,076	40,863	112,689
Race/ethnicity										
White, non-Hispanic	36,000	34,221	2,011,889	722,694	2,067	328,487	2,015	99,783	68,991	208,306
Black, non-Hispanic	35,548	33,889	181,896	48,968	2,325	40,819	2,221	10,734	5,490	16,336
Hispanic	34,837	32,996	102,965	31,653	1,930	24,122	2,477	5,817	3,644	7,337
Asian or Pacific Islander	37,701	36,134	25,383	6,391	1,873	5,381	2,285	1,298	910	2,327
American Indian or Alaskan Native	34,945	32,994	18,050	6,121	2,068	2,696	2,310	737	979	2,871
Age										
Less than 30	27,974	25,966	440,029	193,398	1,930	91,979	1,880	20,334	15,319	45,970
30 to 39	33,448	31,737	684,515	242,075	2,146	120,762	1,891	33,174	24,735	66,564
40 to 49	39,586	37,803	901,801	301,456	2,115	150,854	2,273	48,720	30,658	96,996
50 or more	41,951	40,414	313,838	78,898	2,064	37,910	2,290	16,141	9,303	27,647
Level										
Elementary	34,611	33,517	1,193,249	254,890	1,503	170,052	1,801	47,820	27,084	90,749
Secondary	37,291	34,815	1,146,933	560,937	2,335	231,453	2,267	70,549	52,930	146,427
	Private schools									
Total	$23,395	$21,968	301,440	64,064	$1,894	62,810	$2,122	20,202	11,424	33,880
Men	28,948	26,120	71,854	27,419	2,408	21,317	2,584	3,993	4,969	14,126
Women	21,657	20,669	229,586	36,645	1,509	41,493	1,885	16,209	6,456	19,754
Race/ethnicity										
White, non-Hispanic	23,415	22,000	277,853	59,475	1,903	55,913	2,109	18,426	10,677	31,505
Black, non-Hispanic	22,532	20,796	8,927	1,350	2,451	3,024	2,173	(1)	(1)	(1)
Hispanic	22,013	20,672	9,786	2,013	1,209	2,269	2,298	(1)	(1)	(1)
Asian or Pacific Islander	27,611	25,861	3,786	997	2,054	1,185	2,643	(1)	(1)	(1)
American Indian or Alaskan Native	23,130	21,625	1,088	(1)	(1)	(1)	(1)	(1)	(1)	(1)
Age										
Less than 30	19,776	18,052	86,939	22,069	1,719	23,361	1,959	6,532	3,967	13,391
30 to 39	23,700	22,193	82,809	19,182	1,922	18,856	2,165	5,466	3,708	9,895
40 to 49	25,225	23,999	91,749	17,251	2,047	16,365	2,274	5,925	3,098	7,892
50 or more	26,437	25,362	39,943	5,562	2,013	4,228	2,248	2,279	(1)	2,702
Level										
Elementary	20,962	19,977	179,373	23,015	1,514	33,301	1,846	11,805	5,645	18,074
Secondary	26,970	24,896	122,068	41,048	2,106	29,509	2,435	8,397	5,780	15,805

[1] Too few sample cases (fewer than 30) for a reliable estimate.

NOTE.—Details may not add to totals because of rounding or missing values in cells with too few cases, or survey item nonresponse.

SOURCE: U.S. Department of Education, National Center for Education Statistics, "Schools and Staffing Survey, 1993–94." (This table was prepared August 1995.)

Table 73.—New public school teachers' expectations and ideals before and after their first year of teaching: 1990 and 1991

Item	Percent of teachers							
	Agree strongly		Somewhat agree		Somewhat disagree		Disagree strongly	
	Before 1st year	After 1st year	Before 1st year	After 1st year	Before 1st year	After 1st year	Before 1st year	After 1st year
1	2	3	4	5	6	7	8	9
Attitudes about teachers and students								
All children can learn	93	88	6	10	(1)	1	(1)	(1)
I can really make a difference in the lives of my children	83	68	16	30	1	1	(1)	(1)
If I do my job well, my students will benefit regardless of how the rest of the school functions	42	43	47	46	10	9	1	2
Many children come to school with so many problems that it's very difficult for them to be good students	28	47	47	42	18	8	6	3
Even the best teachers will find it difficult to really teach more than two-thirds of their students	8	14	38	44	39	30	15	11
Attitudes about teacher preparation								
My training has prepared me to teach students from a variety of ethnic backgrounds	42	30	39	40	15	21	5	9
All teachers should take a national standardized test to demonstrate their qualifications	31	24	35	34	19	23	15	19
I wish I had more practical training to be a teacher before I begin teaching in my own classroom	26	28	32	33	23	25	18	14

[1] Less than 0.5 percent.

SOURCE: Metropolitan Life/Louis Harris Associates, Inc., *The American Teacher, 1991,* copyrighted. (This table was prepared April 1992.)

Table 74.—New public school teachers' experiences working with students, school personnel, and parents: 1991 and 1992

Item	Percent who found the first two years of teaching					Percent rating 2-year experience as very satisfying					
	Total	Very satisfying	Somewhat satisfying	Somewhat unsatisfying	Very unsatisfying	School level			Presence of lower income students		
						Elementary	Junior/middle	High	All/many	Some	Few/none
1	2	3	4	5	6	7	8	9	10	11	12
Your students	100	70	27	2	1	78	60	60	70	66	75
Other teachers in your school	100	58	37	5	(1)	62	58	47	56	54	68
Your principal	100	48	37	9	4	53	49	38	45	45	61
Administrators other than your principal	100	32	47	14	3	34	33	28	32	29	40
Parents	100	25	48	18	7	34	16	11	18	25	43

[1] Less than 0.5%.

NOTE.—Because of rounding, details may not add to totals.

SOURCE: Metropolitan Life/Louis Harris Associates, Inc., *The American Teacher, 1992,* copyrighted. (This table was prepared May 1993.)

Table 75.—New public school teachers'[1] reasons for leaving or thinking about leaving the teaching profession: 1992

Major factors for leaving the teaching profession	Total	School level			School location			Presence of lower income students		
		Elementary	Junior/middle	High	Inner city/urban	Suburban/small town	Rural	All/many	Some	Few/none
1	2	3	4	5	6	7	8	9	10	11
Percent of teachers very likely or fairly likely to leave	**19**	**17**	**18**	**27**	**24**	**18**	**14**	**21**	**19**	**14**
Reasons for leaving or thinking about leaving the teaching profession (percent of teachers)										
Lack of support or help for students from their parents	40	32	41	51	40	38	46	50	36	23
Need to earn more money	29	30	22	32	27	28	39	31	26	38
Lack of support from school administration	29	26	35	27	35	27	27	39	27	10
Social problems faced by students make teaching too difficult	25	23	18	33	35	21	22	32	22	13
Don't feel prepared to teach students with different ethnic and cultural backgrounds	5	3	6	6	8	4	5	5	6	3
Teaching became boring and less satisfying	5	4	4	6	8	3	7	6	6	(2)

[1] Includes teachers with not more than 2 years of experience.
[2] Less than 0.5%.

SOURCE: Metropolitan Life/Louis Harris Associates, Inc., *The American Teacher, 1992,* copyrighted. (This table was prepared May 1993.)

Table 76.—Estimated average annual salary of teachers in public elementary and secondary schools: 1959–60 to 1994–95

School year	Current dollars			Constant 1994–95 dollars [1]		
	All teachers	Elementary teachers	Secondary teachers	All teachers	Elementary teachers	Secondary teachers
1	2	3	4	5	6	7
1959–60	$4,995	$4,815	$5,276	$25,569	$24,647	$27,007
1961–62	5,515	5,340	5,775	27,597	26,721	28,898
1963–64	5,995	5,805	6,266	29,236	28,309	30,558
1965–66	6,485	6,279	6,761	30,569	29,598	31,870
1967–68	7,423	7,208	7,692	32,830	31,879	34,020
1969–70	8,626	8,412	8,891	34,346	33,494	35,401
1970–71	9,268	9,021	9,568	35,091	34,156	36,227
1971–72	9,705	9,424	10,031	35,473	34,446	36,664
1972–73	10,174	9,893	10,507	35,747	34,760	36,917
1973–74	10,770	10,507	11,077	34,743	33,895	35,733
1974–75	11,641	11,334	12,000	33,806	32,915	34,849
1975–76	12,600	12,280	12,937	34,173	33,305	35,087
1976–77	13,354	12,989	13,776	34,222	33,286	35,303
1977–78	14,198	13,845	14,602	34,095	33,248	35,066
1978–79	15,032	14,681	15,450	33,006	32,236	33,924
1979–80	15,970	15,569	16,459	30,941	30,164	31,888
1980–81	17,644	17,230	18,142	30,635	29,917	31,500
1981–82	19,274	18,853	19,805	30,805	30,132	31,653
1982–83	20,695	20,227	21,291	31,714	30,996	32,627
1983–84	21,935	21,487	22,554	32,414	31,752	33,329
1984–85	23,600	23,200	24,187	33,561	32,992	34,396
1985–86	25,199	24,718	25,846	34,830	34,165	35,725
1986–87	26,569	26,057	27,244	35,926	35,234	36,839
1987–88	28,034	27,519	28,798	36,399	35,730	37,391
1988–89	29,564	29,022	30,218	36,691	36,018	37,503
1989–90	31,367	30,832	32,049	37,156	36,522	37,964
1990–91	33,085	32,491	33,897	37,159	36,492	38,071
1991–92	34,063	33,479	34,824	37,070	36,434	37,898
1992–93	35,029	34,337	35,880	36,966	36,236	37,865
1993–94	35,819	35,298	36,671	36,846	36,310	37,722
1994–95	36,933	36,356	37,763	36,933	36,356	37,763

[1] Based on the Consumer Price Index, prepared by the Bureau of Labor Statistics, U.S. Department of Labor.

NOTE.—Some data have been revised from previously published figures.

SOURCE: National Education Association, *Estimates of School Statistics;* and unpublished data. (Latest edition 1994–95. Copyright © 1995 by the National Education Association. All rights reserved.) (This table was prepared April 1995.)

Table 77.—Estimated average annual salary of teachers in public elementary and secondary schools, by state: 1969–70 to 1994–95

State	Current dollars							Constant 1994–95 dollars [1]						Percent change, 1979–80 to 1994–95 in constant dollars
	1969–70	1979–80	1989–90	1991–92	1992–93	1993–94	1994–95	1969–70	1979–80	1989–90	1991–92	1992–93	1993–94	
1	2	3	4	5	6	7	8	9	10	11	12	13	14	15
United States	$8,626	$15,970	$31,367	$34,063	$35,029	[2]$35,819	[2]$36,933	$34,346	$30,941	$37,156	$37,070	$36,966	$36,846	19.4
Alabama	6,818	13,060	24,828	26,971	26,953	28,705	31,144	27,147	25,303	29,410	29,352	28,444	29,528	23.1
Alaska	10,560	27,210	43,153	44,661	46,701	47,512	47,951	42,047	52,717	51,117	48,603	49,284	48,874	-9.0
Arizona	8,711	15,054	29,402	31,176	31,352	31,800	[2]32,090	34,684	29,166	34,828	33,928	33,086	32,711	10.0
Arkansas	6,307	12,299	22,352	27,070	27,433	28,098	28,409	25,112	23,828	26,477	29,460	28,950	28,903	19.2
California	10,315	18,020	37,998	39,922	40,035	40,264	[2]40,667	41,071	34,912	45,010	43,446	42,249	41,418	16.5
Colorado	7,761	16,205	30,758	33,072	33,541	33,826	34,571	30,902	31,396	36,434	35,991	35,396	34,796	10.1
Connecticut	9,262	16,229	40,461	46,971	48,343	49,769	51,300	36,878	31,442	47,928	51,117	51,017	51,196	63.2
Delaware	9,015	16,148	33,377	34,548	36,217	37,469	39,076	35,895	31,286	39,537	37,598	38,220	38,543	24.9
District of Columbia	10,285	22,190	38,402	38,798	38,702	42,543	42,959	40,952	42,991	45,489	42,223	40,843	43,762	-0.1
Florida	8,412	14,149	28,803	31,070	31,172	31,944	32,588	33,494	27,413	34,119	33,813	32,896	32,860	18.9
Georgia	7,276	13,853	28,006	29,372	30,223	30,712	32,828	28,971	26,839	33,174	31,965	31,895	31,592	22.3
Hawaii	9,453	19,920	32,047	34,528	36,470	36,564	38,518	37,639	38,593	37,961	37,576	38,487	37,612	-0.2
Idaho	6,890	13,611	23,861	26,334	27,011	27,756	29,783	27,434	26,370	28,265	28,659	28,505	28,552	12.9
Illinois	9,569	17,601	32,794	36,461	38,632	39,387	41,041	38,101	34,101	38,846	39,680	40,769	40,516	20.4
Indiana	8,833	15,599	30,902	34,006	35,066	35,712	[2]36,516	35,170	30,222	36,605	37,008	37,005	36,736	20.8
Iowa	8,355	15,203	26,747	29,202	30,130	30,760	31,511	33,267	29,455	31,683	31,780	31,796	31,642	7.0
Kansas	7,612	13,690	28,744	30,731	32,863	33,919	34,936	30,309	26,523	34,049	33,444	34,681	34,891	31.7
Kentucky	6,953	14,520	26,292	30,870	31,115	31,625	32,257	27,685	28,131	31,144	33,595	32,836	32,531	14.7
Louisiana	7,028	13,760	24,300	25,963	26,102	26,285	26,574	27,983	26,659	28,785	28,255	27,546	27,038	-0.3
Maine	7,572	13,071	26,881	30,097	30,250	30,996	31,856	30,149	25,324	31,842	32,754	31,923	31,884	25.8
Maryland	9,383	17,558	36,319	38,728	38,753	39,453	40,636	37,360	34,017	43,022	42,147	40,896	40,584	19.5
Massachusetts	8,764	17,253	34,712	37,845	38,774	40,852	[2]42,078	34,895	33,426	41,118	41,186	40,919	42,023	25.9
Michigan	9,826	19,663	37,072	41,490	43,901	45,186	[2]47,412	39,124	38,096	43,914	45,152	46,329	46,481	24.5
Minnesota	8,658	15,912	32,190	34,451	35,093	36,146	37,412	34,473	30,828	38,131	37,492	37,034	37,182	21.4
Mississippi	5,798	11,850	24,292	24,367	24,367	25,153	26,910	23,086	22,958	28,775	26,518	25,715	25,874	17.2
Missouri	7,799	13,682	27,094	28,895	29,382	30,310	31,217	31,053	26,508	32,094	31,446	31,007	31,179	17.8
Montana	7,606	14,537	25,081	27,590	27,617	28,200	28,785	30,285	28,164	29,710	30,025	29,144	29,008	2.2
Nebraska	7,375	13,516	25,522	27,231	28,768	29,564	30,822	29,365	26,186	30,232	29,635	30,359	30,411	17.7
Nevada	9,215	16,295	30,590	33,857	34,119	33,955	34,836	36,691	31,570	36,235	36,846	36,006	34,928	10.3
New Hampshire	7,771	13,017	28,986	33,170	33,931	34,121	[2]34,974	30,942	25,219	34,335	36,098	35,808	35,099	38.7
New Jersey	9,130	17,161	35,676	41,027	42,680	44,693	46,801	36,353	33,248	42,260	44,649	45,041	45,974	40.8
New Mexico	7,796	14,887	24,756	26,239	26,532	27,922	28,865	31,041	28,842	29,325	28,555	27,999	28,722	0.1
New York	10,336	19,812	38,925	43,335	44,999	45,772	47,250	41,155	38,384	46,109	47,160	47,488	47,084	23.1
North Carolina	7,494	14,117	27,883	28,791	29,315	29,728	31,079	29,839	27,351	33,029	31,332	30,936	30,580	13.6
North Dakota	6,696	13,263	23,016	24,495	25,211	25,506	26,327	26,661	25,696	27,264	26,657	26,605	26,237	2.5
Ohio	8,300	15,269	31,218	32,932	34,519	35,678	36,685	33,048	29,583	36,979	35,839	36,428	36,701	24.0
Oklahoma	6,882	13,107	23,070	25,339	25,918	27,009	27,971	27,402	25,394	27,328	27,576	27,352	27,783	10.1
Oregon	8,818	16,266	30,840	34,100	35,880	37,590	38,700	35,110	31,514	36,531	37,110	37,865	38,667	22.8
Pennsylvania	8,858	16,515	33,338	38,715	41,215	42,411	44,489	35,270	31,997	39,490	42,132	43,495	43,627	39.0
Rhode Island	8,776	18,002	36,057	36,417	37,933	39,261	40,729	34,943	34,877	42,711	39,632	40,031	40,386	16.8
South Carolina	6,927	13,063	27,217	28,068	29,224	29,566	30,341	27,581	25,309	32,240	30,546	30,840	30,413	19.9
South Dakota	6,403	12,348	21,300	23,291	24,289	25,259	[2]26,017	25,495	23,923	25,231	25,347	25,632	25,983	8.8
Tennessee	7,050	13,972	27,052	28,621	28,960	30,514	31,270	28,071	27,070	32,044	31,147	30,562	31,389	15.5
Texas	7,255	14,132	27,496	29,041	29,935	30,519	31,310	28,887	27,380	32,570	31,605	31,591	31,394	14.4
Utah	7,644	14,909	23,686	26,339	27,239	27,706	28,676	30,436	28,885	28,057	28,664	28,746	28,500	-0.7
Vermont	7,968	12,484	29,012	33,646	34,824	34,517	[2]36,311	31,726	24,187	34,366	36,616	36,750	35,506	50.1
Virginia	8,070	14,060	30,938	31,764	33,212	33,009	33,753	32,132	27,240	36,648	34,568	35,049	33,955	23.9
Washington	9,225	18,820	30,457	34,823	35,759	35,863	36,120	36,731	36,462	36,078	37,897	37,737	36,891	-0.9
West Virginia	7,650	13,710	22,842	27,366	30,301	30,549	31,923	30,460	26,562	27,057	29,782	31,977	31,425	20.2
Wisconsin	8,963	16,006	31,921	35,227	35,926	35,990	[2]37,349	35,688	31,010	37,812	38,337	37,913	37,022	20.4
Wyoming	8,232	16,012	28,141	30,425	30,080	30,952	31,300	32,777	31,022	33,334	33,111	31,744	31,839	0.9

[1] Based on the Consumer Price Index prepared by the Bureau of Labor Statistics, U.S. Department of Labor. Price index does not account for different rates of change in the cost of living among states.

[2] Estimated by the National Education Association.

NOTE.—Some data have been revised from previously published data.

SOURCE: National Education Association, *Estimates of School Statistics;* and unpublished data. (Latest edition 1994–95. Copyright © 1995 by the National Education Association. All rights reserved.) (This table was prepared April 1995.)

Table 78.—Minimum and average teacher salaries, by state: 1990–91, 1992–93, and 1993–94

State	1990–91				1992–93				1993–94			Percent change, 1990–91 to 1993–94 (constant dollars)[1]	
	Minimum (beginning) salary	Average salary	Minimum (beginning) salary (in 1993–94 dollars)[1]	Average salary (in 1993–94 dollars)[1]	Minimum (beginning) salary	Average salary	Minimum (beginning) salary (in 1993–94 dollars)[1]	Average salary (in 1993–94 dollars)[1]	Minimum (beginning) salary	Average salary	Minimum (beginning) salary as a percent of average salary	Minimum salary	Average salary
1	2	3	4	5	6	7	8	9	10	11	12	13	14
United States	$21,542	$32,880	$23,521	$35,900	$22,505	$35,104	$23,088	$36,013	$23,258	$35,813	64.9	-1.1	-0.2
Alabama	22,114	26,846	24,145	29,312	[2]21,250	27,490	21,800	28,202	[3]22,500	28,659	78.5	-6.8	-2.2
Alaska	[2]29,950	43,406	32,701	47,393	31,055	46,799	31,859	48,011	[2]31,800	[3]47,902	66.4	-2.8	1.1
Arizona	[2]21,375	30,773	23,338	33,599	[2]22,150	31,352	22,724	32,164	21,825	31,825	68.6	-6.5	-5.3
Arkansas	[4]17,458	[3]23,735	19,061	25,915	[2]20,250	28,013	20,775	28,739	[3]19,694	[3]28,312	69.6	3.3	9.2
California	[2]24,570	[2]39,118	26,827	42,711	[3]23,980	39,922	24,601	40,956	[2]25,500	[2]40,636	62.8	-4.9	-4.9
Colorado	19,786	31,819	21,603	34,742	19,776	33,541	20,288	34,410	20,091	33,826	59.4	-7.0	-2.6
Connecticut	25,312	43,398	27,637	47,384	27,622	48,918	28,338	50,185	28,052	50,389	55.7	1.5	6.3
Delaware	21,112	35,246	23,051	38,483	22,377	36,217	22,957	37,155	22,795	37,469	60.8	-1.1	-2.6
District of Columbia	23,327	[2]39,362	25,470	42,977	23,305	40,228	23,909	41,270	25,825	43,014	60.0	1.4	0.1
Florida	21,368	30,555	23,331	33,361	21,607	31,172	22,167	31,979	23,171	31,944	72.5	-0.7	-4.2
Georgia	20,471	[3]28,950	22,351	31,609	21,010	28,758	21,554	29,503	21,885	[5]29,214	74.9	-2.1	-7.6
Hawaii	23,792	33,548	25,977	36,629	25,100	36,472	25,750	37,417	25,100	36,564	68.6	-3.4	-0.2
Idaho	15,685	25,510	17,126	27,853	[2]17,164	27,011	17,609	27,711	[3]18,700	27,756	67.4	9.2	-0.3
Illinois	[3]21,954	[3]34,642	23,970	37,824	[3]25,177	38,701	25,829	39,704	[7]25,171	[7]39,416	63.9	5.0	4.2
Indiana	[3]20,247	[3]32,931	22,107	35,956	21,503	35,068	22,060	35,976	22,021	[3]35,741	61.6	-0.4	-0.6
Iowa	19,404	27,949	21,186	30,516	[2]20,500	30,124	21,031	30,904	20,709	30,760	67.3	-2.3	0.8
Kansas	[6]18,954	[6]28,188	20,695	30,777	[6]20,445	30,713	20,975	31,509	[3]22,624	[6]31,700	71.4	9.3	3.0
Kentucky	19,311	29,115	21,085	31,789	20,638	31,115	21,173	31,921	[2]21,257	31,639	67.2	0.8	-0.5
Louisiana	17,486	26,170	19,092	28,574	[3]17,686	26,074	18,144	26,749	18,195	26,243	69.3	-4.7	-8.2
Maine	18,878	28,531	20,612	31,152	19,350	30,250	19,851	31,034	19,840	30,996	64.0	-3.7	-0.5
Maryland	23,548	[3]38,312	25,711	41,831	24,508	38,753	25,143	39,757	24,703	39,475	62.6	-3.9	-5.6
Massachusetts	[2]21,800	36,090	23,802	39,405	[2]23,375	39,245	23,981	40,262	[2]23,000	38,960	59.0	-3.4	-1.1
Michigan	[2]22,400	[2]37,800	24,457	41,272	[2]23,856	42,256	24,474	43,351	24,400	[2]45,218	54.0	-0.2	9.6
Minnesota	[3]21,029	33,128	22,960	36,171	[2]22,050	35,093	22,621	36,002	[5]23,408	[3]36,146	64.8	1.9	-0.1
Mississippi	[2]18,950	[2]24,609	20,691	26,869	17,960	24,367	18,425	24,998	18,833	25,153	74.9	-9.0	-6.4
Missouri	[2]20,293	[2]27,636	22,157	30,174	20,745	29,421	21,282	30,183	21,078	30,324	69.5	-4.9	0.5
Montana	[2]18,400	26,696	20,090	29,148	[2]18,775	27,617	19,261	28,332	[2]18,750	28,200	66.5	-6.7	-3.3
Nebraska	18,344	26,592	20,029	29,034	20,237	28,768	20,761	29,513	20,804	29,564	70.4	3.9	1.8
Nevada	[8]24,358	[8]35,269	26,595	38,508	[8]23,664	37,360	24,277	38,328	[8]24,155	[8]37,181	65.0	-9.2	-3.4
New Hampshire	[2]20,635	31,273	22,530	34,145	[2]22,750	33,931	23,339	34,810	[2]22,400	34,121	65.6	-0.6	-0.1
New Jersey	24,500	38,411	26,750	41,939	27,655	43,355	28,371	44,478	29,346	45,582	64.4	9.7	8.7
New Mexico	19,124	[3]25,800	20,880	28,170	19,675	26,463	20,185	27,149	22,057	27,922	79.0	5.6	-0.9
New York	[9]26,375	[9]42,080	28,797	45,945	[9]26,639	44,999	27,329	46,165	[9]26,903	[9]45,772	58.8	-6.6	-0.4
North Carolina	19,810	29,165	21,630	31,844	19,820	29,108	20,333	29,862	20,002	29,727	67.3	-7.5	-6.6
North Dakota	16,274	23,574	17,769	25,739	17,267	25,211	17,714	25,864	17,453	25,506	68.4	-1.8	-0.9
Ohio	18,452	31,964	20,147	34,900	[3]19,082	34,100	19,576	34,983	19,553	35,912	54.4	-2.9	2.9
Oklahoma	[6]18,575	[6]24,378	20,281	26,617	20,582	26,355	21,115	27,038	22,181	27,612	80.3	9.4	3.7
Oregon	[8]20,357	[8]32,295	22,227	35,261	22,551	35,883	23,156	36,813	[8]23,186	[8]37,589	61.7	4.3	6.6
Pennsylvania	[2]23,250	[3]36,057	25,385	39,369	[2]26,575	41,515	27,263	42,590	28,231	42,411	66.6	11.2	7.7
Rhode Island	20,887	[2]38,220	22,805	41,730	[2]22,350	40,548	22,929	41,598	23,365	39,261	59.5	2.5	-5.9
South Carolina	[3]19,757	[3]28,174	21,572	30,762	[3]20,381	29,151	20,909	29,906	20,533	[3]29,414	69.8	-4.8	-4.4
South Dakota	16,676	22,363	18,208	24,417	18,471	24,291	18,949	24,920	18,935	25,259	75.0	4.0	3.4
Tennessee	20,150	28,248	22,001	30,843	[2]20,982	29,313	21,526	30,072	19,625	30,514	64.3	-10.8	-1.1
Texas	[2]20,150	[2]28,100	22,001	30,681	21,411	30,974	21,966	31,776	21,806	[10]30,519	71.5	-0.9	-0.5
Utah	17,234	[3]25,415	18,817	27,749	18,229	26,997	18,701	27,696	18,787	[3]28,056	67.0	-0.2	1.1
Vermont	[2]18,509	[2]29,714	20,209	32,443	[2]21,900	35,328	22,467	36,243	22,982	34,517	66.6	13.7	6.4
Virginia	[3]22,206	[3]32,692	24,246	35,695	22,856	32,896	23,448	33,748	23,273	33,472	69.5	-4.0	-6.2
Washington	[3]20,612	[3]32,975	22,505	36,004	21,428	35,870	21,983	36,799	[5]23,183	35,860	64.6	3.0	-0.4
West Virginia	18,728	25,966	20,448	28,351	21,278	30,301	21,829	31,086	21,450	30,549	70.2	4.9	7.8
Wisconsin	20,689	33,077	22,589	36,115	22,889	36,477	23,482	37,422	23,677	36,644	64.6	4.8	1.5
Wyoming	19,238	28,996	21,005	31,659	[3]19,966	30,317	20,483	31,102	[2]20,416	30,954	66.0	-2.8	-2.2

[1] Based on the Consumer Price Index prepared by the Bureau of Labor Statistics, U.S. Department of Labor. Price index does not account for different rates of change in the cost of living among states.
[2] Estimated by the American Federation of Teachers. See NOTE.
[3] Preliminary or state estimate.
[4] Excludes state-paid health insurance.
[5] Reflects the redefinition of classroom teacher.
[6] Estimated to exclude fringe benefits.
[7] Preliminary or state estimate. Includes pay for extra duties.
[8] Includes 6 percent pension pick-up in Oregon and 9.5 percent in Nevada.

[9] Median salary.

[10] Including incentive pay or career ladder stipends and revision of classroom teacher definition.

NOTE.—Data in this table reflect results of surveys conducted by the American Federation of Teachers. Because of differing survey and estimation methods, these data are not entirely comparable with figures appearing in other tables.

SOURCE: American Federation of Teachers, *Survey and Analysis of Salary Trends, 1991, 1993 and 1994.* (This table was prepared June 1995.)

Table 79.—Average annual salary of instructional staff[1] in public elementary and secondary schools, by state: 1939–40 to 1994–95

State or other area	Current dollars									Constant 1994–95 dollars[2]				
	1939–40	1949–50	1959–60	1969–70	1979–80	1989–90	1992–93	1993–94	1994–95	1969–70	1979–80	1989–90	1992–93	1993–94
1	2	3	4	5	6	7	8	9	10	11	12	13	14	15
United States	$1,441	$3,010	$5,174	$9,047	$16,715	$32,638	$36,454	$37,383	$38,415	$36,022	$32,384	$38,661	$38,470	$38,455
Alabama	744	2,111	4,002	6,954	13,338	26,200	28,183	30,015	32,597	27,689	25,841	31,035	29,742	30,875
Alaska	—	—	6,859	10,993	27,697	[3]43,161	[3]46,897	[3]47,679	[3]48,929	43,771	53,661	51,126	49,491	49,046
Arizona	1,544	3,556	5,590	8,975	16,180	33,592	38,221	[3]39,794	[3]41,325	35,736	31,348	39,791	40,335	40,935
Arkansas	584	1,801	3,295	6,461	12,704	22,296	28,494	29,189	29,677	25,726	24,613	26,411	30,070	30,026
California	2,351	—	[3]6,600	10,950	18,626	[3]39,309	[3]41,890	42,116	[3]42,538	43,599	36,086	46,563	44,207	43,323
Colorado	1,393	2,821	4,997	8,105	16,840	31,832	34,617	34,975	35,712	32,272	32,626	37,707	36,532	35,977
Connecticut	1,861	3,558	6,008	9,597	16,989	41,888	49,939	51,418	53,020	38,212	32,915	49,618	52,701	52,892
Delaware	1,684	3,273	[3]5,800	9,387	16,845	34,620	37,691	39,031	40,668	37,376	32,636	41,009	39,776	40,150
District of Columbia	2,350	3,920	6,280	10,700	23,027	43,637	39,933	39,257	42,088	42,604	44,613	51,690	42,142	40,382
Florida	1,012	2,958	5,080	8,785	14,875	30,275	32,474	33,350	[3]33,617	34,979	28,819	35,862	34,270	34,306
Georgia	770	1,963	[4]3,904	7,520	14,547	29,541	31,738	32,283	34,507	29,942	28,184	34,993	33,493	33,208
Hawaii	—	—	5,390	9,600	20,436	32,956	37,586	37,671	37,319	38,224	39,593	39,038	39,665	38,751
Idaho	1,057	2,481	4,216	7,081	14,110	24,758	28,168	28,928	31,063	28,194	27,337	29,327	29,726	29,757
Illinois	1,700	3,458	[5]5,814	9,789	18,271	33,912	39,901	40,737	42,448	38,977	35,399	40,170	42,108	41,905
Indiana	1,433	3,401	5,542	9,239	16,256	31,905	36,107	36,743	[3]37,569	36,787	31,495	37,793	38,104	37,796
Iowa	1,017	2,420	[3]4,030	8,779	15,776	27,619	31,183	31,830	32,622	34,955	30,565	32,716	32,908	32,742
Kansas	1,014	2,628	[3]4,450	7,811	14,513	30,154	34,269	35,640	36,709	31,101	28,118	35,719	36,164	36,662
Kentucky	826	1,936	3,327	7,325	15,350	27,482	32,349	33,561	34,232	29,166	29,739	32,554	34,138	34,523
Louisiana	1,006	2,983	4,978	7,264	14,020	25,036	29,159	30,560	27,629	28,923	27,163	29,656	32,967	31,436
Maine	894	2,115	3,694	8,059	13,743	27,831	31,826	32,049	33,182	32,088	26,626	32,967	33,586	32,968
Maryland	1,642	3,594	5,557	9,885	18,308	37,520	40,034	40,878	42,300	39,359	35,470	44,444	42,248	42,050
Massachusetts	2,037	3,338	[6]5,545	9,347	18,900	40,175	45,456	47,893	[3]48,543	37,217	36,617	47,589	47,970	49,266
Michigan	1,576	3,420	5,654	10,125	20,682	[3]37,286	43,901	[3]46,392	[3]48,507	40,315	40,070	44,167	46,329	47,722
Minnesota	1,276	3,013	5,275	9,250	16,654	33,340	36,222	37,309	38,615	36,831	32,266	39,493	38,225	38,378
Mississippi	559	1,416	3,314	5,959	12,274	25,079	25,223	26,070	27,870	23,727	23,780	29,707	26,618	26,817
Missouri	1,159	2,581	4,536	8,064	14,543	28,166	30,598	31,521	32,466	32,108	28,176	33,364	32,290	32,424
Montana	1,184	2,962	[3]4,425	7,875	15,080	29,526	28,755	29,040	30,052	31,356	29,216	34,975	30,345	29,872
Nebraska	829	2,292	3,876	7,633	14,236	27,024	30,508	31,595	[3]32,803	30,392	27,581	32,011	32,195	32,501
Nevada	1,557	3,209	5,693	9,615	17,290	31,970	35,764	35,603	36,553	38,284	33,498	37,870	37,742	36,623
New Hampshire	1,258	2,712	4,455	8,016	13,508	[3]29,798	[3]36,456	38,599	[3]39,564	31,917	26,171	35,297	38,472	39,705
New Jersey	2,093	3,511	5,871	9,650	18,851	37,485	44,862	46,979	49,196	38,423	36,522	44,403	47,343	48,326
New Mexico	1,144	3,215	5,382	10,021	15,406	25,790	27,381	28,611	28,866	39,900	29,848	30,549	28,895	29,431
New York	2,604	3,706	6,537	11,240	20,400	40,000	45,900	46,900	48,300	44,754	39,523	47,382	48,439	48,244
North Carolina	946	2,688	4,178	7,762	14,445	28,952	30,515	30,968	32,360	30,906	27,986	34,295	34,295	31,856
North Dakota	745	2,324	3,695	6,840	13,684	23,788	26,058	25,692	26,515	27,235	26,512	28,178	27,499	26,428
Ohio	1,587	3,088	5,124	8,594	16,100	32,467	35,674	36,853	37,867	34,219	31,193	38,459	37,647	37,909
Oklahoma	1,014	2,736	4,659	7,257	13,500	23,944	26,872	27,981	28,928	28,895	26,155	28,363	28,358	28,783
Oregon	1,333	3,323	5,535	9,200	16,996	32,100	37,200	38,920	40,100	36,631	32,928	38,024	39,258	40,036
Pennsylvania	1,640	3,006	5,308	8,899	17,060	34,110	42,129	43,300	45,422	35,433	33,052	40,405	44,459	44,541
Rhode Island	1,809	3,294	[7]5,499	9,030	18,425	36,704	38,640	39,992	41,464	35,955	35,697	43,478	40,777	41,138
South Carolina	743	1,891	3,450	7,069	13,670	28,453	30,599	30,970	31,512	28,147	26,485	33,704	32,291	31,858
South Dakota	807	2,064	3,725	7,200	13,010	22,120	24,289	24,977	[3]25,726	28,686	25,206	26,202	25,632	25,693
Tennessee	862	2,302	3,929	7,187	14,193	27,949	30,063	31,685	32,452	28,616	27,498	33,107	31,726	32,593
Texas	1,079	3,122	4,708	7,598	14,729	28,549	30,452	31,046	31,444	30,253	28,536	33,818	32,136	31,936
Utah	1,394	3,103	5,096	8,049	17,403	24,591	28,222	28,669	29,672	32,049	33,717	29,129	29,783	29,491
Vermont	981	2,348	4,466	8,225	13,300	29,012	33,216	35,691	[3]36,681	32,749	25,768	34,366	35,053	36,714
Virginia	899	2,328	4,312	8,364	14,655	31,656	33,056	33,826	34,587	33,303	28,393	37,498	34,884	34,796
Washington	1,706	3,487	[7]5,643	9,792	19,735	31,828	37,402	37,490	[3]37,752	38,989	38,235	37,702	39,471	38,565
West Virginia	1,170	2,425	3,952	7,954	14,395	23,842	31,428	31,656	33,051	31,670	27,889	28,242	33,166	32,563
Wisconsin	1,379	3,007	[8]4,870	9,150	16,335	32,445	36,676	36,040	[3]37,534	36,432	31,648	38,433	38,705	37,073
Wyoming	1,169	2,798	4,937	8,496	16,830	29,047	31,227	31,832	32,300	33,828	32,607	34,408	32,954	32,744
Outlying areas														
American Samoa	—	—	852	5,130	—	—	—	—	—	20,426	—	—	—	—
Guam	—	—	4,107	7,800	—	—	—	—	—	31,057	—	—	—	—
Puerto Rico	—	—	[9]2,360	—	—	—	—	—	—	—	—	—	—	—
Virgin Islands	—	—	3,407	—	—	—	—	—	—	—	—	—	—	—

[1] Includes supervisors, principals, classroom teachers, and other instructional staff.
[2] Based on the Consumer Price Index prepared by the Bureau of Labor Statistics, U.S. Department of Labor. Price index does not account for different rates of change in the cost of living among states.
[3] Estimated.
[4] Excludes kindergarten teachers.
[5] Includes administrators.
[6] Includes clerical assistants to instructional personnel.
[7] Includes attendance personnel.
[8] Excludes vocational schools not operated as part of the regular public school system.

[9] Median salary.
—Data not available.

NOTE.—Some data have been revised from previously published data.

SOURCE: U.S. Department of Education, National Center for Education Statistics, *Statistics of State School Systems;* National Education Association, *Estimates of School Statistics;* (Latest edition 1994–95. Copyright © 1995 by the National Education Association. All rights reserved.) and unpublished data. (This table was prepared April 1995.)

Table 80.—Estimated average annual salary of instructional staff [1] in public elementary and secondary schools and average annual earnings of full-time employees in all industries: 1929–30 to 1994–95

| School year | Current dollars | | Constant 1994–95 dollars [2] | | |
	Average salary of instructional staff	Earnings per full-time employee working for wages or salary [3]	Average salary of instructional staff	Earnings per full-time employee working for wages or salary [3]	Ratio of instructional staff salary to salary for all full-time employees
1	2	3	4	5	6
1929–30	$1,420	$1,386	$12,478	$12,179	1.02
1931–32	1,417	1,198	14,783	12,498	1.18
1933–34	1,227	1,070	13,937	12,153	1.15
1935–36	1,283	1,160	14,043	12,696	1.11
1937–38	1,374	1,224	14,427	12,852	1.12
1939–40	1,441	1,282	15,509	13,798	1.12
1941–42	1,507	1,576	14,537	15,203	0.96
1943–44	1,728	2,030	14,916	17,522	0.85
1945–46	1,995	2,272	16,449	18,733	0.88
1947–48	2,639	2,692	17,035	17,378	0.98
1949–50	3,010	2,930	19,116	18,608	1.03
1951–52	3,450	3,322	19,743	19,011	1.04
1953–54	3,825	3,628	21,393	20,292	1.05
1955–56	4,156	3,924	23,252	21,954	1.06
1957–58	4,702	4,276	24,764	22,521	1.10
1959–60	5,174	4,632	26,485	23,711	1.12
1961–62	5,700	4,928	28,522	24,659	1.16
1963–64	6,240	5,373	30,431	26,203	1.16
1965–66	6,935	5,838	32,690	27,519	1.19
1967–68	7,630	6,444	33,745	28,500	1.18
1969–70	9,047	7,334	36,022	29,202	1.23
1970–71	9,698	7,815	36,719	29,589	1.24
1971–72	10,213	8,334	37,330	30,462	1.23
1972–73	10,634	8,858	37,363	31,123	1.20
1973–74	11,254	9,647	36,304	31,120	1.17
1974–75	12,167	10,420	35,334	30,260	1.17
1975–76	13,124	11,218	35,594	30,424	1.17
1976–77	13,840	11,991	35,467	30,729	1.15
1977–78	14,698	12,829	35,296	30,807	1.15
1978–79	15,764	13,851	34,614	30,413	1.14
1979–80	16,715	15,095	32,384	29,244	1.11
1980–81	18,404	16,495	31,955	28,640	1.12
1981–82	20,327	17,818	32,488	28,478	1.14
1982–83	21,641	18,883	33,163	28,936	1.15
1983–84	23,005	19,749	33,995	29,184	1.16
1984–85	24,666	20,626	35,077	29,332	1.20
1985–86	26,362	21,518	36,438	29,742	1.23
1986–87	27,706	22,432	37,464	30,332	1.24
1987–88	29,219	23,467	37,938	30,469	1.25
1988–89	30,850	24,502	38,287	30,408	1.26
1989–90	32,638	25,555	38,661	30,271	1.28
1990–91	34,412	26,668	38,650	29,952	1.29
1991–92	35,550	27,829	38,688	30,286	1.28
1992–93	36,454	28,937	38,470	30,537	1.26
1993–94	37,383	—	38,455	—	—
1994–95	38,415	—	38,415	—	—

[1] Includes supervisors, principals, classroom teachers, and other instructional staff.
[2] Based on the Consumer Price Index prepared by the Bureau of Labor Statistics, U.S. Department of Labor.
[3] Calendar-year data from the U.S. Department of Commerce have been converted to a school-year basis by averaging the two appropriate calendar years in each case.
—Data not available.

NOTE.—Some data have been revised from previously published figures.

SOURCE: U.S. Department of Education, National Center for Education Statistics, *Statistics of State School Systems*, and unpublished data; National Education Association, *Estimates of School Statistics, 1994–95*, (Copyright © 1995 by the National Education Association. All rights reserved.); and unpublished data; and U.S. Department of Commerce, *Survey of Current Business*, July and August issues. (This table was prepared May 1995.)

Table 81.—Staff employed in public elementary and secondary school systems, by functional area: 1949–50 to fall 1993

[In full-time equivalents]

Numbers

School year (1)	Total (2)	Admin. Total (3)	Intermediate district staff (4)	School district superintendents (5)	Assistants to superintendents (6)	Instruction coordinators (7)	Instr. Total (8)	Principals & asst. principals (9)	Teachers (10)	Instructional aides (11)	Librarians (12)	Guidance counselors (13)	Psychological personnel (14)	Other instructional staff (15)	Support Total (16)	Secretarial & clerical (17)	Transportation staff (18)	Food service (19)	Plant operation & maintenance (20)	Health (21)	Recreational & other staff (22)
1949–50	1,300,031	33,642	5,843	18,025	[1]	9,774	963,110	43,137	913,671	[2]	[2]	[2]	[2]	6,302	303,280	31,824	81,626	68,814	105,874	9,412	5,730
1959–60	2,089,283	42,423	9,901	13,361	5,386	13,775	1,457,329	63,554	1,353,372	[2]	17,363	14,643	2,121	6,277	589,531	75,930	113,111	161,925	192,655	16,104	29,807
1969–70	3,360,763	65,282	7,113	13,014	13,618	31,537	2,285,568	90,593	2,016,244	57,418	42,689	48,763	6,168	23,693	1,009,913	164,476	175,351	270,338	273,395	26,562	99,791
Fall 1980	4,168,286	78,784	—	13,269	44,961	20,554	2,859,573	124,536	2,184,216	325,755	48,018	63,973	14,033	116,517	1,229,929	223,647	[4]	[4]	[4]	[4]	1,006,282
Fall 1984	4,062,271	[3]65,222	—	—	—	—	[3]2,691,787	129,297	2,167,950	288,967	47,024	63,310	[5]	[5]	[3]1,305,262	[5]	[5]	[5]	[5]	[5]	[5]
Fall 1985	4,159,624	[3]67,404	—	—	—	—	[3]2,756,232	129,285	2,205,987	306,860	47,442	66,646	[5]	[5]	[3]1,335,988	[5]	[5]	[5]	[5]	[5]	[5]
Fall 1986	4,232,805	[3]74,541	—	—	—	—	2,822,059	131,564	2,243,579	330,398	47,938	68,580	[5]	[5]	1,336,205	[5]	[5]	[5]	[5]	[5]	[5]
Fall 1987	4,311,941	[3]74,191	—	—	—	—	2,859,626	125,927	2,279,241	335,991	48,185	70,282	[5]	[5]	1,378,124	[5]	[5]	[5]	[5]	[5]	[5]
Fall 1988	4,319,356	[3]69,334	—	—	—	—	2,930,547	126,609	2,323,213	356,682	48,980	75,063	[5]	[5]	1,319,475	[5]	[5]	[5]	[5]	[5]	[5]
Fall 1989	4,431,033	[3]70,302	—	—	—	—	2,985,851	125,594	2,356,702	374,172	49,769	79,614	[5]	[5]	1,374,880	[5]	[5]	[5]	[5]	[5]	[5]
Fall 1990	4,494,076	[3]75,868	—	—	—	—	3,051,404	127,417	2,398,169	395,959	49,909	79,950	[5]	[5]	1,366,804	[5]	[5]	[5]	[5]	[5]	[5]
Fall 1991	4,559,359	[3]76,084	—	—	—	—	3,103,939	129,304	2,432,243	410,538	49,917	81,937	[5]	[5]	1,379,336	[5]	[5]	[5]	[5]	[5]	[5]
Fall 1992	4,702,568	[6]76,400	[7]	[7]	45,713	30,687	[6]3,139,695	122,402	2,458,598	427,322	50,324	81,049	[5]	[5]	[6]1,486,473	[5]	[5]	[5]	[5]	[5]	[5]
Fall 1993	4,803,121	[6]79,763	[7]	[7]	46,515	33,248	[6]3,210,395	121,268	2,505,074	450,598	50,501	82,954	[5]	[5]	[6]1,512,963	[5]	[5]	[5]	[5]	[5]	[5]

Percentage distribution

School year (1)	Total (2)	Admin. Total (3)	(4)	(5)	(6)	(7)	Instr. Total (8)	(9)	(10)	(11)	(12)	(13)	(14)	(15)	Support Total (16)	(17)	(18)	(19)	(20)	(21)	(22)
1949–50	100.0	2.6	0.4	1.4	[1]	0.8	74.1	3.3	70.3	[2]	[2]	[2]	[2]	0.5	23.3	2.4	6.3	5.3	8.1	0.7	0.4
1959–60	100.0	2.0	0.5	0.6	0.3	0.7	69.8	3.0	64.8	[2]	0.8	0.7	0.1	0.3	28.2	3.6	5.4	7.8	9.2	0.8	1.4
1969–70	100.0	1.9	0.2	0.4	0.4	0.9	68.0	2.7	60.0	1.7	1.3	1.5	0.2	0.7	30.1	4.9	5.2	8.0	8.1	0.8	3.0
Fall 1980	100.0	1.9	—	0.3	1.1	0.5	68.6	3.0	52.4	7.8	1.2	1.5	0.3	2.8	29.5	5.4	[4]	[4]	[4]	[4]	24.1
Fall 1984	100.0	[3]1.6	—	—	—	—	[3]66.3	3.1	53.4	7.1	1.2	1.6	[5]	[5]	[3]32.1	[5]	[5]	[5]	[5]	[5]	[5]
Fall 1985	100.0	[3]1.6	—	—	—	—	[3]66.3	3.1	53.0	7.4	1.1	1.6	[5]	[5]	[3]32.1	[5]	[5]	[5]	[5]	[5]	[5]
Fall 1986	100.0	1.8	—	—	—	—	66.7	3.1	53.0	7.8	1.1	1.6	[5]	[5]	31.6	[5]	[5]	[5]	[5]	[5]	[5]
Fall 1987	100.0	1.7	—	—	—	—	66.3	2.9	52.9	8.3	1.1	1.6	[5]	[5]	32.0	[5]	[5]	[5]	[5]	[5]	[5]
Fall 1988	100.0	1.6	—	—	—	—	67.8	2.9	53.8	8.4	1.1	1.7	[5]	[5]	30.5	[5]	[5]	[5]	[5]	[5]	[5]
Fall 1989	100.0	1.6	—	—	—	—	67.4	2.8	53.2	8.8	1.1	1.8	[5]	[5]	31.0	[5]	[5]	[5]	[5]	[5]	[5]
Fall 1990	100.0	1.7	—	—	—	—	67.9	2.8	53.4	9.0	1.1	1.8	[5]	[5]	30.4	[5]	[5]	[5]	[5]	[5]	[5]
Fall 1991	100.0	1.7	—	—	—	—	68.1	2.8	53.3	9.1	1.1	1.8	[5]	[5]	30.3	[5]	[5]	[5]	[5]	[5]	[5]
Fall 1992	100.0	[6]1.6	[7]	[7]	1.0	0.7	[6]66.8	2.6	52.3	9.1	1.1	1.7	[5]	[5]	[6]31.6	[5]	[5]	[5]	[5]	[5]	[5]
Fall 1993	100.0	[6]1.7	[7]	[7]	1.0	0.7	[6]66.8	2.5	52.2	9.4	1.1	1.7	[5]	[5]	[6]31.5	[5]	[5]	[5]	[5]	[5]	[5]

Pupils per staff member

School year (1)	Total (2)	Admin. Total (3)	(4)	(5)	(6)	(7)	Instr. Total (8)	(9)	(10)	(11)	(12)	(13)	(14)	(15)	Support Total (16)	(17)	(18)	(19)	(20)	(21)	(22)
1949–50	19.3	746.4	4,297.7	1,393.1	[1]	2,569.2	26.1	582.1	27.5	[2]	[2]	[2]	[2]	3,984.7	82.8	789.1	307.6	364.9	237.2	2,668.0	4,382.4
1959–60	16.8	829.3	3,553.4	2,633.2	6,532.2	2,554.1	24.1	553.6	26.0	[2]	2,026.3	2,402.7	16,589.1	5,605.1	59.7	463.4	311.0	217.3	182.6	2,184.7	1,180.3
1969–70	13.6	697.7	6,403.8	3,500.1	3,344.9	1,444.3	19.9	502.8	22.6	793.3	1,067.0	934.1	7,384.9	1,922.5	45.1	276.9	259.8	168.5	166.6	1,714.9	456.5
Fall 1980	9.8	518.9	—	3,080.7	909.2	1,988.8	14.3	381.8	18.7	125.5	851.3	639.0	2,913.0	350.8	33.2	182.8	[4]	[4]	[4]	[4]	40.6
Fall 1984	9.7	[3]601.2	—	—	—	—	[3]14.6	314.8	18.1	135.7	833.8	619.3	[5]	[5]	[3]30.0	[5]	[5]	[5]	[5]	[5]	[5]
Fall 1985	9.5	[3]584.9	—	—	—	—	[3]14.1	304.9	17.9	128.5	831.0	591.5	[5]	[5]	[3]29.5	[5]	[5]	[5]	[5]	[5]	[5]
Fall 1986	9.4	533.3	—	—	—	—	14.0	302.2	17.7	120.3	829.3	579.7	[5]	[5]	29.8	[5]	[5]	[5]	[5]	[5]	[5]
Fall 1987	9.3	539.3	—	—	—	—	13.7	317.7	17.6	119.1	830.3	569.3	[5]	[5]	29.0	[5]	[5]	[5]	[5]	[5]	[5]
Fall 1988	9.3	579.6	—	—	—	—	13.6	317.4	17.3	112.7	820.5	535.4	[5]	[5]	30.5	[5]	[5]	[5]	[5]	[5]	[5]
Fall 1989	9.1	576.7	—	—	—	—	13.5	322.8	17.2	108.4	814.6	509.2	[5]	[5]	29.5	[5]	[5]	[5]	[5]	[5]	[5]
Fall 1990	9.2	543.3	—	—	—	—	13.5	323.5	17.2	104.1	825.8	515.5	[5]	[5]	30.2	[5]	[5]	[5]	[5]	[5]	[5]
Fall 1991	9.2	552.6	—	—	—	—	13.5	325.2	17.3	102.4	842.3	513.2	[5]	[5]	30.5	[5]	[5]	[5]	[5]	[5]	[5]
Fall 1992	9.1	[6]560.4	[7]	[7]	936.6	1,395.2	[6]13.6	349.8	17.4	100.2	850.8	528.3	[5]	[5]	[6]28.8	[5]	[5]	[5]	[5]	[5]	[5]
Fall 1993	9.1	[6]545.1	[7]	[7]	934.7	1,307.6	[6]13.5	358.5	17.4	96.5	860.9	524.1	[5]	[5]	[6]28.7	[5]	[5]	[5]	[5]	[5]	[5]

[1] Data included in column 5.
[2] Data included in column 10.
[3] Data not comparable with figures for years prior to 1984.
[4] Data included in column 22.
[5] Data included in column 16.
[6] Because of classification revisions, data are not directly comparable with figures for prior years.
[7] Data included in column 6.

—Data not available.

NOTE.—Some data have been revised from previously published figures. Because of variations in data collection instruments, some categories are only roughly comparable over time. Because of rounding, details may not add to totals.

SOURCE: U.S. Department of Education, National Center for Education Statistics, *Statistics of State School Systems*, Common Core of Data survey, and unpublished estimates. (This table was prepared March 1995.)

Table 82.—Staff employed in public school systems, by type of assignment and state: Fall 1993

[In full-time equivalents]

State or other area	Total	School district staff			School staff							Student support staff	Other support services staff
		Officials and administrators	Administrative support staff	Instruction coordinators	Principals and assistant principals	School and library support staff	Teachers	Instructional aides	Guidance counselors	Librarians			
1	2	3	4	5	6	7	8	9	10	11	12	13
United States [1]	4,803,121	46,515	145,827	33,248	121,268	229,566	2,505,074	450,598	82,954	50,501	123,924	1,013,645
Alabama [2]	80,922	251	1,084	393	2,133	2,339	43,002	3,897	1,607	1,194	488	24,534
Alaska	15,731	166	524	427	415	1,084	7,193	2,146	226	156	382	3,012
Arizona	74,679	407	683	180	1,633	5,846	37,493	9,519	972	773	7,022	10,151
Arkansas	50,502	656	1,012	784	1,420	1,608	26,014	2,501	1,203	948	1,297	13,059
California [2]	431,085	2,036	20,337	4,248	10,195	27,635	221,779	55,984	4,976	928	9,434	73,533
Colorado	62,922	775	2,059	577	1,812	4,298	33,661	4,995	1,024	704	1,421	11,596
Connecticut	62,014	906	1,586	416	1,536	3,151	34,526	6,178	1,108	654	2,864	9,089
Delaware	11,640	93	374	61	398	463	6,380	846	203	116	455	2,251
District of Columbia	10,591	420	298	168	379	450	6,056	366	261	173	68	1,952
Florida	226,911	1,676	11,659	801	5,760	11,584	110,653	22,238	4,584	2,513	6,517	48,926
Georgia [3,4]	151,326	950	3,667	1,000	3,436	6,377	75,602	20,056	2,118	2,053	4,060	32,007
Hawaii	18,292	142	334	226	467	699	10,111	2,203	531	286	450	2,843
Idaho	19,983	116	433	185	593	774	12,007	1,709	387	168	348	3,263
Illinois	199,221	1,623	5,219	1,507	4,408	9,230	110,874	17,609	2,756	1,973	5,172	38,850
Indiana	113,892	870	417	1,293	2,741	7,736	55,107	13,633	1,651	1,047	1,590	27,807
Iowa	60,267	759	788	372	1,737	4,424	31,616	4,945	1,305	652	2,133	11,536
Kansas	55,783	473	2,142	166	1,630	2,412	30,283	4,178	1,054	973	1,784	10,688
Kentucky	81,279	1,141	1,630	626	1,804	3,194	37,324	9,322	1,271	1,187	2,911	20,869
Louisiana	93,193	1,469	1,836	496	1,843	2,921	46,913	9,431	1,027	1,217	3,258	22,782
Maine	28,865	444	669	118	843	1,247	15,344	3,452	597	241	991	4,919
Maryland	82,753	627	488	669	2,528	3,692	44,171	7,277	1,724	1,078	1,993	18,506
Massachusetts	104,196	968	5,395	957	2,075	2,748	58,766	10,611	1,886	567	1,667	18,556
Michigan	169,283	1,922	2,713	915	4,677	6,933	80,267	12,629	2,826	1,500	8,150	46,751
Minnesota	74,859	1,278	1,730	487	1,594	3,318	46,956	6,089	901	984	2,859	8,663
Mississippi	59,853	833	1,334	399	1,478	2,245	28,376	8,886	814	640	1,856	12,992
Missouri	114,763	810	4,460	1,990	2,389	7,705	54,543	6,047	2,333	1,261	1,482	31,743
Montana [4,5]	18,950	174	515	139	480	877	9,950	1,725	395	339	481	3,875
Nebraska [4]	37,033	607	770	212	933	1,371	19,552	3,325	702	558	949	8,054
Nevada	22,418	309	529	87	610	1,327	12,579	1,257	443	239	358	4,680
New Hampshire	22,010	329	442	148	566	852	11,972	2,902	576	254	384	3,585
New Jersey	160,202	1,728	6,923	1,378	4,508	8,212	84,564	12,806	3,135	1,800	8,556	26,592
New Mexico	36,694	441	910	468	837	2,251	18,404	4,066	557	243	851	7,666
New York	353,603	2,825	24,421	2,176	6,930	8,802	179,413	26,272	5,688	2,983	8,563	85,530
North Carolina	133,060	1,319	2,998	767	3,909	5,179	69,421	20,721	2,726	2,151	2,533	21,336
North Dakota	13,780	268	328	58	386	461	7,755	1,290	235	179	336	2,484
Ohio	201,828	5,443	8,991	383	4,868	14,114	107,444	9,804	3,754	1,776	1,310	43,941
Oklahoma	72,494	622	1,350	435	1,974	4,200	39,031	6,172	1,270	860	400	16,180
Oregon	50,392	716	1,372	338	1,576	3,380	26,488	5,236	1,300	665	1,370	7,951
Pennsylvania	190,884	1,267	5,926	1,576	3,866	9,898	101,301	12,676	3,523	2,170	9,666	39,015
Rhode Island	15,442	158	487	78	366	701	9,823	1,320	279	82	333	1,815
South Carolina [4]	68,902	263	2,369	503	2,166	3,821	38,620	7,121	1,476	1,085	628	10,850
South Dakota	17,066	326	726	14	621	320	9,557	1,801	371	208	545	2,577
Tennessee [4]	91,690	870	2,619	659	4,267	4,460	46,066	8,981	1,310	1,280	2,539	18,639
Texas	433,102	2,564	2,260	1,257	10,722	16,921	224,830	38,816	7,676	4,143	3,306	120,607
Utah	35,301	105	650	411	875	1,998	19,053	4,309	513	267	426	6,694
Vermont [6]	16,046	325	182	309	495	773	8,102	2,378	333	199	513	2,437
Virginia	129,394	1,794	1,742	1,077	3,389	5,451	70,220	11,209	3,039	1,945	3,015	26,513
Washington	87,966	1,029	2,448	636	2,426	4,551	45,524	7,940	1,663	1,255	2,365	18,129
West Virginia	38,486	268	1,862	334	1,120	408	21,029	2,858	584	360	844	8,819
Wisconsin	88,640	835	1,662	314	3,138	4,389	52,822	7,565	1,788	1,339	2,662	12,126
Wyoming	12,933	119	474	30	316	736	6,537	1,301	273	135	339	2,673
Outlying areas												
American Samoa	1,339	25	48	32	56	81	656	11	18	6	40	366
Guam	3,839	14	97	20	57	166	1,644	471	77	50	108	1,135
Northern Marianas	1,101	9	51	8	29	42	431	233	18	4	167	109
Puerto Rico	68,005	297	89	672	1,298	4,090	39,816	—	909	857	2,058	17,919
Virgin Islands	3,328	36	375	0	83	88	1,570	353	75	44	325	379

[1] Includes imputations for undercounts in designated states.
[2] Includes imputation for prekindergarten teachers.
[3] Includes imputation for instruction coordinators.
[4] Includes imputation for support staff.
[5] Includes imputation for instruction aides.
[6] All staff, except teachers, estimated by the National Center for Education Statistics.

—Data not available or not applicable.

SOURCE: U.S. Department of Education, National Center for Education Statistics, Common Core of Data survey; and unpublished estimates. (This table was prepared March 1995.)

Table 83.—Staff employed in public school systems, by type of assignment and state: Fall 1992

[In full-time equivalents]

State or other area	Total	School district staff			School staff						Student support staff	Other support services staff
		Officials and administrators	Administrative support staff	Instruction coordinators	Principals and assistant principals	School and library support staff	Teachers	Instructional aides	Guidance counselors	Librarians		
1	2	3	4	5	6	7	8	9	10	11	12	13
United States [1]	4,702,568	45,713	140,115	30,687	122,402	225,410	2,458,598	427,322	81,049	50,324	114,948	1,006,001
Alabama [2]	78,838	260	1,073	383	2,035	2,313	41,917	3,636	1,505	1,154	469	24,093
Alaska	14,792	502	609	318	422	916	7,282	1,775	228	158	284	2,298
Arizona	71,591	404	684	199	1,564	5,639	36,076	8,741	915	783	6,652	9,934
Arkansas	48,879	555	568	195	1,416	1,686	26,016	3,436	1,190	948	390	12,479
California [2]	427,297	2,121	20,344	4,131	10,059	27,054	218,253	55,098	4,992	955	9,161	75,129
Colorado	62,785	824	2,186	613	1,857	4,170	33,419	4,662	1,063	732	1,411	11,848
Connecticut	63,648	827	1,742	421	1,492	3,474	34,193	6,592	1,093	623	3,275	9,916
Delaware	11,390	89	369	61	386	465	6,252	828	189	118	448	2,185
District of Columbia	10,567	425	302	141	365	600	6,064	344	260	170	76	1,820
Florida	217,356	1,599	7,478	834	5,795	13,437	107,590	20,858	4,464	2,529	3,213	49,559
Georgia [3]	141,530	648	4,723	0	4,991	6,188	66,942	17,871	1,941	1,923	3,510	32,793
Hawaii	17,731	71	444	372	499	414	10,083	1,165	540	300	567	3,276
Idaho	19,571	114	431	197	592	731	11,827	1,578	374	170	355	3,202
Illinois	199,380	1,660	5,196	2,358	4,383	9,321	111,461	16,289	2,852	2,030	5,000	38,831
Indiana	111,919	884	436	1,268	2,777	7,615	54,552	13,265	1,564	1,005	1,449	27,104
Iowa	60,208	786	813	368	1,737	4,380	31,403	4,548	1,284	663	2,055	12,171
Kansas	54,185	476	2,168	140	1,596	2,200	29,753	3,716	1,017	962	1,701	10,456
Kentucky	79,191	1,013	2,159	434	1,787	2,978	37,868	8,381	1,205	1,155	2,118	20,093
Louisiana	92,180	1,465	1,808	0	2,328	2,832	46,904	8,792	928	1,198	3,127	22,798
Maine	28,937	460	650	120	853	1,269	15,375	3,548	604	253	972	4,832
Maryland	80,861	305	1,213	556	2,533	3,704	44,495	6,354	1,695	1,086	1,396	17,524
Massachusetts	101,278	963	5,385	940	2,085	2,757	57,225	9,814	1,872	574	1,604	18,059
Michigan	173,863	1,879	2,538	1,690	5,094	6,104	82,301	13,461	2,998	1,557	7,073	49,168
Minnesota	79,215	1,281	2,360	405	1,620	4,241	45,050	7,798	894	989	3,132	11,445
Mississippi	57,876	615	1,268	314	1,373	2,144	27,829	8,416	793	626	1,128	13,370
Missouri [3]	109,417	842	4,193	1,048	2,354	7,287	52,984	5,696	2,200	1,226	1,258	30,330
Montana [3,4]	19,124	296	500	128	498	857	10,135	1,614	394	336	578	3,788
Nebraska [3]	35,644	570	707	299	925	1,285	19,323	3,172	678	547	902	7,236
Nevada [3]	21,452	198	533	116	590	1,066	11,953	1,325	421	220	504	4,526
New Hampshire	21,239	321	457	148	566	863	11,654	2,545	584	253	379	3,469
New Jersey	151,460	1,659	5,853	1,279	4,566	8,110	83,057	10,423	3,073	1,810	8,306	23,324
New Mexico	34,803	385	829	422	812	2,149	17,912	3,328	608	253	830	7,275
New York	343,900	2,825	24,067	1,905	6,797	8,654	176,375	23,356	5,598	2,986	8,289	83,048
North Carolina [3]	128,428	1,322	2,898	744	3,848	4,223	66,630	20,127	2,526	2,135	2,433	21,541
North Dakota	13,797	275	341	67	387	464	7,794	1,227	223	177	319	2,523
Ohio	200,793	5,561	9,222	312	4,864	13,224	106,233	9,241	3,757	1,807	1,317	45,255
Oklahoma	71,621	630	1,208	428	1,799	4,260	38,433	6,022	1,251	840	363	16,387
Oregon	51,681	751	1,430	485	1,595	3,902	26,634	4,847	1,312	740	1,515	8,470
Pennsylvania	191,370	1,274	4,546	1,824	4,034	9,979	100,912	12,534	3,557	2,201	9,886	40,623
Rhode Island	15,833	158	420	76	374	750	10,069	1,316	307	93	367	1,903
South Carolina	67,106	274	2,280	568	2,166	3,721	37,295	6,727	1,427	1,062	564	11,022
South Dakota	15,548	310	686	15	506	262	8,767	1,605	328	194	304	2,571
Tennessee	84,088	839	2,188	627	4,132	4,156	43,566	7,807	1,105	1,280	2,225	16,163
Texas	420,243	2,602	2,150	1,458	10,558	15,855	219,385	36,734	7,404	4,108	3,189	116,800
Utah	34,838	130	521	219	850	1,933	19,191	4,097	421	223	592	6,661
Vermont	14,970	296	169	275	480	725	7,521	2,165	316	193	444	2,386
Virginia	126,619	1,798	1,728	1,104	3,322	5,417	68,181	10,702	2,966	1,928	2,977	26,496
Washington	81,398	1,039	2,504	0	2,394	4,445	44,295	7,552	1,572	1,233	1,797	14,567
West Virginia	38,487	258	1,835	347	1,143	429	20,961	2,872	561	365	826	8,890
Wisconsin	92,139	758	1,713	335	2,867	4,257	53,387	8,105	1,744	1,322	3,897	13,754
Wyoming	11,502	116	190	0	336	505	5,821	1,217	256	131	322	2,608
Outlying areas												
American Samoa	1,350	18	47	42	56	87	725	40	41	6	22	266
Guam	3,517	16	128	23	68	170	1,628	104	68	34	50	1,228
Northern Marianas	1,096	11	27	11	29	52	425	219	17	5	170	130
Puerto Rico	67,643	344	32	1,351	1,213	3,982	38,381	—	897	867	2,141	18,435
Virgin Islands	3,353	36	375	—	83	88	1,595	353	75	44	325	379

[1] Includes imputations for undercounts in designated states.
[2] Includes imputation for prekindergarten teachers.
[3] Includes imputation for support staff.
[4] Includes imputation for instruction aides.
—Data not available or not applicable.

SOURCE: U.S. Department of Education, National Center for Education Statistics, Common Core of Data survey; and unpublished estimates. (This table was prepared March 1995.)

Table 84.—Staff and teachers in public elementary and secondary schools, by state: Fall 1987 to fall 1993

| State or other area | Teachers as a percent of staff | | | | Fall 1991 | | | Fall 1992 [1] | | | Fall 1993 | | |
	Fall 1987	Fall 1988	Fall 1989	Fall 1990	Staff	Teachers	Teachers as a percent of staff	Staff	Teachers	Teachers as a percent of staff	Staff	Teachers	Teachers as a percent of staff
1	2	3	4	5	6	7	8	9	10	11	12	13	14
United States	[2]52.9	[2]53.8	[2]53.2	[2]53.4	[2]4,559,359	2,432,243	[2]53.3	[2]4,702,568	[2]2,458,598	[2]52.3	[2]4,803,121	[2]2,505,074	[2]52.2
Alabama	53.4	53.2	50.0	48.7	81,950	40,480	49.4	[3]78,838	[3]41,917	[3]53.2	[3]80,922	[3]43,002	[3]53.1
Alaska	[4]83.9	46.5	48.3	50.3	13,992	7,118	50.9	14,792	7,282	49.2	15,731	7,193	45.7
Arizona	52.0	52.7	52.7	52.0	65,505	33,978	51.9	71,591	36,076	50.4	74,679	37,493	50.2
Arkansas	53.6	54.7	51.8	52.2	51,652	25,785	49.9	48,879	26,016	53.2	50,502	26,014	51.5
California	49.9	50.2	50.7	51.7	429,387	224,000	52.2	[3]427,297	[3]218,253	[3]51.1	[3]431,085	[3]221,779	[3]51.4
Colorado	52.6	52.5	52.7	52.6	62,592	33,093	52.9	62,785	33,419	53.2	62,922	33,661	53.5
Connecticut	[5]87.2	[5]86.9	55.5	56.3	60,500	34,383	56.8	63,648	34,193	53.7	62,014	34,526	55.7
Delaware	55.2	54.8	54.8	55.2	10,987	6,095	55.5	11,390	6,252	54.9	11,640	6,380	54.8
District of Columbia	56.0	58.4	57.0	58.3	11,143	6,346	57.0	10,567	6,064	57.4	10,591	6,056	57.2
Florida	51.9	50.8	50.5	49.8	219,733	109,939	50.0	217,356	107,590	49.5	226,911	110,653	48.8
Georgia	52.2	49.7	48.8	48.9	132,921	63,816	48.0	[3]141,530	66,942	[3]47.3	[3]151,326	75,602	[3]50.0
Hawaii	42.6	42.1	60.2	59.9	15,559	9,451	60.7	17,731	10,083	56.9	18,292	10,111	55.3
Idaho	63.3	63.0	62.4	62.3	18,621	11,626	62.4	19,571	11,827	60.4	19,983	12,007	60.1
Illinois	56.4	56.4	56.6	56.7	196,930	110,153	55.9	199,380	111,461	55.9	199,221	110,874	55.7
Indiana	51.0	51.2	50.9	50.7	108,746	54,509	50.1	111,919	54,552	48.7	113,892	55,107	48.4
Iowa	54.5	53.9	53.4	53.0	60,305	31,395	52.1	60,208	31,403	52.2	60,267	31,616	52.5
Kansas	57.4	57.6	57.3	56.8	51,637	29,324	56.8	54,185	29,753	54.9	55,783	30,283	54.3
Kentucky	50.9	49.9	50.1	49.5	77,165	37,571	48.7	79,191	37,868	47.8	81,279	37,324	45.9
Louisiana	48.3	48.9	49.9	49.8	[4]66,339	46,170	[4]69.6	92,180	46,904	50.9	93,193	46,913	50.3
Maine	58.2	57.3	57.8	57.3	27,082	15,416	56.9	28,937	15,375	53.1	28,865	15,344	53.2
Maryland	54.4	54.4	54.4	53.9	79,925	43,616	54.6	80,861	44,495	55.0	82,753	44,171	53.4
Massachusetts	57.5	56.5	56.7	57.2	98,974	55,963	56.5	101,278	57,225	56.5	104,196	58,766	56.4
Michigan	47.0	47.1	46.9	46.4	178,111	82,967	46.6	173,863	82,301	47.3	169,283	80,267	47.4
Minnesota	56.9	56.3	56.5	56.2	78,273	44,903	57.4	79,215	45,050	56.9	74,859	46,956	62.7
Mississippi	[4]63.3	[4]63.1	49.0	48.3	59,200	28,111	47.5	57,876	27,829	48.1	59,853	28,376	47.4
Missouri	51.3	51.8	50.6	50.6	100,735	52,643	52.3	[3]109,417	52,984	[3]48.4	114,763	54,543	47.5
Montana	[4]77.4	[4]77.5	[4]76.8	[4]76.4	[4]13,078	9,883	[4]75.6	[3]19,124	10,135	[3]53.0	[3]18,950	9,950	[3]52.5
Nebraska	55.7	55.8	55.4	53.4	34,676	19,069	55.0	[3]35,644	19,323	[3]54.2	[3]37,033	19,552	[3]52.8
Nevada	[4]85.7	[4]85.8	[4]89.0	[4]89.4	[4]13,145	11,409	[4]86.8	[3]21,452	11,953	[3]55.7	22,418	12,579	56.1
New Hampshire	55.6	54.4	51.4	51.8	20,480	11,464	56.0	21,239	11,654	54.9	22,010	11,972	54.4
New Jersey	55.5	55.3	54.3	54.2	148,491	80,515	54.2	151,460	83,057	54.8	160,202	84,564	52.8
New Mexico	51.7	52.3	50.2	50.3	34,509	17,498	50.7	34,803	17,912	51.5	36,694	18,404	50.2
New York	52.0	55.3	50.6	50.9	338,335	171,914	50.8	343,900	176,375	51.3	353,603	179,413	50.7
North Carolina	52.3	52.0	51.6	51.2	126,332	65,326	51.7	[3]128,428	66,630	[3]51.9	133,060	69,421	52.2
North Dakota	56.4	56.1	55.3	54.5	13,594	7,733	56.9	13,797	7,794	56.5	13,780	7,755	56.3
Ohio	54.2	54.1	54.0	54.0	194,727	103,372	53.1	200,793	106,233	52.9	201,828	107,444	53.2
Oklahoma	54.1	54.8	54.2	54.2	69,725	37,650	54.0	71,621	38,433	53.7	72,494	39,031	53.8
Oregon	52.8	53.1	53.1	53.2	50,479	26,745	53.0	51,681	26,634	51.5	50,392	26,488	52.6
Pennsylvania	55.7	55.4	55.4	52.5	190,607	100,475	52.7	191,370	100,912	52.7	190,884	101,301	53.1
Rhode Island	61.3	62.3	61.7	60.2	15,452	9,709	62.8	15,833	10,069	63.6	15,442	9,823	63.6
South Carolina	57.1	58.0	57.4	56.0	66,597	37,115	55.7	67,106	37,295	55.6	[3]68,902	38,620	[3]56.1
South Dakota	57.5	59.4	58.0	56.3	14,753	8,868	60.1	15,548	8,767	56.4	17,066	9,557	56.0
Tennessee	50.5	50.5	49.8	49.4	84,518	43,062	51.0	84,088	43,566	51.8	[3]91,690	46,066	[3]50.2
Texas	49.6	60.1	59.9	66.0	337,473	219,192	65.0	420,243	219,385	52.2	433,102	224,830	51.9
Utah	57.1	57.2	56.2	55.2	33,297	18,305	55.0	34,838	19,191	55.1	35,301	19,053	54.0
Vermont	54.0	57.3	57.3	53.6	13,923	7,031	50.5	14,970	7,521	50.2	[3]16,046	8,102	[3]50.5
Virginia	52.4	51.9	51.7	49.0	[5]130,621	64,537	[5]49.4	126,619	68,181	53.8	129,394	70,220	54.3
Washington	56.1	55.7	55.5	55.1	78,039	42,931	55.0	81,398	44,295	54.4	87,966	45,524	51.8
West Virginia	54.8	54.8	54.9	54.9	38,550	20,997	54.5	38,487	20,961	54.5	38,486	21,029	54.6
Wisconsin	59.4	59.0	59.0	58.1	88,249	52,028	59.0	92,139	53,387	57.9	88,640	52,822	59.6
Wyoming	50.8	50.4	49.9	53.1	13,134	6,564	50.0	11,502	5,821	50.6	12,933	6,537	50.5
Outlying areas													
American Samoa	54.4	53.7	53.1	52.6	1,277	671	52.5	1,350	725	53.7	1,339	656	49.0
Guam	48.8	50.5	54.3	52.6	2,965	1,499	50.6	3,517	1,628	46.3	3,839	1,644	42.8
Northern Marianas ..	59.6	51.9	52.0	51.1	906	430	47.5	1,096	425	38.8	1,101	431	39.1
Puerto Rico	78.2	53.5	53.5	55.4	67,948	37,291	54.9	67,643	38,381	56.7	68,005	39,816	58.5
Virgin Islands	48.9	48.1	48.0	48.0	3,290	1,581	48.1	3,353	1,595	47.6	3,328	1,570	47.2

[1] Some data have been revised from previously published figures.
[2] U.S. totals include imputations for underreporting and nonreporting states.
[3] Includes imputations for underreporting.
[4] Support staff underreported.
[5] Data estimated by the National Center for Education Statistics.

SOURCE: U.S. Department of Education, National Center for Education Statistics, Common Core of Data survey; and unpublished estimates. (This table was prepared April 1995.)

Table 85.—Staff, enrollment, and pupil-staff ratios in public elementary and secondary schools, by state: Fall 1986 to fall 1993

State or other area	Pupil-staff ratio					Fall 1991			Fall 1992 [1]			Fall 1993		
	Fall 1986	Fall 1987	Fall 1988	Fall 1989	Fall 1990	Staff	Enrollment	Pupil-staff ratio	Staff	Enrollment	Pupil-staff ratio	Staff	Enrollment	Pupil-staff ratio
1	2	3	4	5	6	7	8	9	10	11	12	13	14	15
United States	[2]9.4	[2]9.3	[2]9.3	[2]9.1	[2]9.2	[2]4,559,359	42,046,878	[2]9.2	[2]4,702,568	42,815,541	[2]9.1	[2]4,803,121	43,476,268	[2]9.1
Alabama	10.3	10.3	9.9	9.1	9.7	81,950	722,004	8.8	[3]78,838	730,857	[3]9.3	[3]80,922	734,469	[3]9.1
Alaska	11.0	[4]14.7	7.9	8.1	8.5	13,992	118,680	8.5	14,792	122,487	8.3	15,731	125,948	8.0
Arizona	9.5	9.7	9.6	10.0	10.1	65,505	656,980	10.0	71,591	673,477	9.4	74,679	709,453	9.5
Arkansas	9.4	9.2	8.6	8.8	8.8	51,652	438,518	8.5	48,879	441,490	9.0	50,502	444,271	8.8
California	11.4	11.4	11.4	11.4	11.8	429,387	5,107,145	11.9	[3]427,297	5,249,275	[3]12.3	[3]431,085	5,328,558	[3]12.4
Colorado	9.5	9.5	9.4	9.3	9.3	62,592	593,030	9.5	62,785	612,635	9.8	62,922	625,062	9.9
Connecticut	[5]11.9	[5]11.6	[5]11.3	7.4	7.6	60,500	481,050	8.0	63,648	488,476	7.7	62,014	496,298	8.0
Delaware	8.9	8.9	9.0	9.0	9.2	10,987	102,196	9.3	11,390	104,321	9.2	11,640	105,547	9.1
District of Columbia	7.2	7.8	8.3	7.7	7.9	11,143	80,618	7.2	10,567	80,937	7.7	10,591	80,678	7.6
Florida	9.0	9.0	8.7	8.7	8.6	219,733	1,932,131	8.8	217,356	1,981,407	9.1	226,911	2,040,763	9.0
Georgia	9.8	9.3	9.2	8.9	8.9	132,921	1,177,569	8.9	[3]141,530	1,207,186	[3]8.5	[3]151,326	1,235,304	[3]8.2
Hawaii	10.4	9.2	8.1	11.5	11.3	15,559	174,747	11.2	17,731	177,448	10.0	18,292	180,430	9.9
Idaho	13.0	13.1	13.0	12.5	12.2	18,621	225,680	12.1	19,571	231,668	11.8	19,983	236,774	11.8
Illinois	9.8	9.7	9.6	9.6	9.5	196,930	1,848,166	9.4	199,380	1,873,567	9.4	199,221	1,893,078	9.5
Indiana	9.3	9.2	9.1	8.9	8.8	108,746	956,988	8.8	111,919	960,630	8.6	113,892	965,599	8.5
Iowa	8.5	8.5	8.5	8.4	8.3	60,305	491,363	8.1	60,208	494,839	8.2	60,267	498,519	8.3
Kansas	8.8	8.9	8.7	8.6	8.5	51,637	445,390	8.6	54,185	451,536	8.3	55,783	457,614	8.2
Kentucky	9.5	9.3	8.9	8.8	8.6	77,165	646,024	8.4	79,191	655,041	8.3	81,279	655,265	8.1
Louisiana	9.0	8.9	8.9	8.8	8.6	[4]66,339	794,128	[4]12.0	92,180	797,985	8.7	93,193	800,560	8.6
Maine	9.2	8.7	8.4	8.1	8.0	27,082	216,400	8.0	28,937	216,453	7.5	28,865	216,995	7.5
Maryland	9.3	9.3	9.2	9.1	9.1	79,925	736,238	9.2	80,861	751,850	9.3	82,753	772,638	9.3
Massachusetts	8.2	8.0	7.7	7.9	8.8	98,974	846,155	8.5	101,278	859,948	8.5	104,196	877,726	8.4
Michigan	9.3	9.3	9.3	9.2	9.2	178,111	1,593,561	8.9	173,863	1,603,610	9.2	169,283	1,599,377	9.4
Minnesota	10.2	9.7	9.6	9.7	9.8	78,273	773,571	9.9	79,215	793,724	10.0	74,859	810,233	10.8
Mississippi	[4]12.3	[4]11.9	[4]11.6	8.9	8.6	59,200	504,127	8.5	57,876	506,668	8.8	59,853	505,907	8.5
Missouri	8.7	8.3	8.2	8.0	7.9	100,735	842,965	8.4	[3]109,417	859,357	[3]7.9	114,763	875,639	7.6
Montana	[4]12.2	[4]12.2	[4]12.3	[4]12.1	[4]12.2	[4]13,078	155,779	[4]11.9	[3]19,124	160,011	[3]8.4	[3]18,950	163,009	[3]8.6
Nebraska	8.5	8.4	8.3	8.1	7.8	34,676	279,552	8.1	[3]35,644	282,414	[3]7.9	[3]37,033	285,097	[3]7.7
Nevada	[4]17.5	[4]17.3	[4]17.4	[4]18.1	[4]17.3	[4]13,145	211,938	[4]16.1	[3]21,452	222,974	[3]10.4	22,418	235,800	10.5
New Hampshire	8.9	8.9	8.8	8.4	8.4	20,480	177,138	8.6	21,239	181,247	8.5	22,010	185,360	8.4
New Jersey	7.9	7.7	7.5	7.3	7.4	148,491	1,109,796	7.5	151,460	1,130,560	7.5	160,202	1,151,307	7.2
New Mexico	9.9	9.8	9.7	9.2	9.1	34,509	308,667	8.9	34,803	315,668	9.1	36,694	322,292	8.8
New York	8.2	7.9	8.2	7.4	7.5	338,335	2,643,993	7.8	343,900	2,689,686	7.8	353,603	2,733,813	7.7
North Carolina	9.8	9.5	9.1	8.8	8.7	126,332	1,097,598	8.7	[3]128,428	1,114,083	[3]8.7	133,060	1,133,231	8.5
North Dakota	8.7	8.8	8.6	8.3	8.5	13,594	118,376	8.7	13,797	118,734	8.6	13,780	119,127	8.6
Ohio	9.8	9.7	9.5	9.4	9.3	194,727	1,783,767	9.2	200,793	1,795,199	8.9	201,828	1,807,319	9.0
Oklahoma	9.1	9.2	9.1	8.8	8.4	69,725	588,263	8.4	71,621	597,090	8.3	72,494	604,076	8.3
Oregon	9.6	9.7	9.8	9.8	9.6	50,479	498,614	9.9	51,681	510,122	9.9	50,392	516,611	10.3
Pennsylvania	9.1	9.0	8.8	8.7	8.7	190,607	1,692,797	8.9	191,370	1,717,613	9.0	190,884	1,744,082	9.1
Rhode Island	9.4	9.3	9.0	8.9	8.8	15,452	142,144	9.2	15,833	143,798	9.1	15,442	145,676	9.4
South Carolina	9.9	9.8	9.9	9.7	9.4	66,597	627,470	9.4	67,106	639,942	9.5	[3]68,902	643,859	[3]9.3
South Dakota	9.0	8.9	9.1	9.0	8.5	14,753	131,576	8.9	15,548	134,573	8.7	17,066	142,825	8.4
Tennessee	10.1	9.9	9.7	9.5	9.5	84,518	833,651	9.9	84,088	854,329	10.2	[3]91,690	866,991	[3]9.5
Texas	8.6	8.6	10.0	10.0	10.2	337,473	3,464,371	10.3	420,243	3,541,769	8.4	433,102	3,608,262	8.3
Utah	14.0	14.1	14.0	14.0	13.8	33,297	456,430	13.7	34,838	463,870	13.3	35,301	471,365	13.4
Vermont	—	7.5	7.8	7.9	7.1	13,923	97,137	7.0	14,970	98,558	6.6	[3]16,046	102,755	[3]6.4
Virginia	9.0	8.6	8.4	8.2	7.7	[6]130,621	1,016,204	[6]7.8	126,619	1,031,925	8.1	129,394	1,045,471	8.1
Washington	11.5	11.3	11.4	11.2	11.1	78,039	869,327	11.1	81,398	896,475	11.0	87,966	915,952	10.4
West Virginia	8.4	8.3	8.3	8.3	8.2	38,550	320,249	8.3	38,487	318,296	8.3	38,486	314,383	8.2
Wisconsin	9.7	9.6	9.4	9.4	9.4	88,249	814,671	9.2	92,139	829,415	9.0	88,640	844,001	9.5
Wyoming	7.0	7.4	7.4	7.2	7.7	13,134	102,074	7.8	11,502	100,313	8.7	12,933	100,899	7.8
Outlying areas														
American Samoa	9.5	9.3	9.4	9.9	9.9	1,277	13,365	10.5	1,350	13,994	10.4	1,339	14,484	10.8
Guam	8.6	9.0	9.4	8.9	9.0	2,965	28,334	9.6	3,517	30,077	8.6	3,839	30,920	8.1
Northern Marianas	—	11.4	9.5	8.9	7.9	906	7,096	7.8	1,096	8,086	7.4	1,101	8,188	7.4
Puerto Rico	16.6	15.9	10.6	10.4	10.4	67,948	642,392	9.5	67,643	637,034	9.4	68,005	631,460	9.3
Virgin Islands	7.5	7.4	7.1	6.4	6.6	3,290	22,346	6.8	3,353	22,887	6.8	3,328	22,752	6.8

[1] Some data have been revised from previously published figures.
[2] U.S. totals include imputations for underreporting and nonreporting states.
[3] Includes imputations for underreporting.
[4] Support staff underreported.
[5] Support staff not reported.
[6] Estimated by the National Center for Education Statistics.

—Data not available.

SOURCE: U.S. Department of Education, National Center for Education Statistics, Common Core of Data survey; and unpublished estimates. (This table was prepared April 1995.)

Table 86.—Principals in public and private elementary and secondary schools, by selected characteristics: 1993–94

Selected characteristics	Total [1]	Percent of principals, by highest degree earned [2]				Average years of experience		Average annual salary of principals, by length of school year			
		Bachelor's	Master's	Education specialist	Doctor's and first-professional	As a principal	Other	Total	10 months or less	11 months	12 months
1	2	3	4	5	6	7	8	9	10	11	12
					Public schools						
Total	79,618	1.4	63.4	25.8	9.3	8.7	19.8	$54,858	$50,103	$53,117	$58,399
Men	52,114	1.1	65.1	24.7	9.1	10.3	20.6	54,922	49,545	52,946	58,492
Women	27,505	2.0	60.2	27.9	9.8	5.6	18.2	54,736	50,908	53,439	58,195
Race/ethnicity											
White, non-Hispanic .	67,081	1.5	62.8	26.5	9.2	9.0	19.5	54,466	48,797	52,893	58,311
Black, non-Hispanic .	8,018	0.0	64.4	23.7	11.9	7.1	21.4	57,669	58,346	54,061	58,836
Hispanic	3,269	2.7	74.5	17.3	5.5	6.3	21.2	55,862	50,035	54,898	59,597
Asian or Pacific Islander	620	6.7	50.9	25.4	17.0	5.6	22.0	59,447	56,916	64,890	59,115
American Indian or Alaskan Native	631	1.1	65.8	24.8	8.2	8.2	20.5	51,117	46,401	49,121	55,337
Age											
Under 40	5,936	4.5	71.2	18.9	5.3	2.8	16.0	46,542	41,817	46,877	49,779
40 to 44	14,571	1.6	65.4	26.2	6.7	5.0	19.0	52,038	48,033	49,581	55,443
45 to 49	25,427	0.9	59.8	30.0	9.3	7.1	20.7	55,423	50,663	53,705	58,872
50 to 54	18,868	1.0	63.9	24.9	10.3	10.3	21.1	56,559	52,464	54,279	59,643
55 or over	14,817	1.4	63.8	22.4	12.4	15.1	19.1	57,826	52,414	56,355	62,148
Type of school											
Elementary	53,688	1.5	64.2	25.7	8.6	8.9	17.9	54,160	50,306	52,929	57,617
Secondary	23,187	1.1	62.0	25.9	11.0	8.2	24.1	56,711	49,231	53,779	60,186
Combined	2,743	2.6	60.2	27.9	9.4	7.5	21.4	52,843	50,729	51,878	54,075
					Private schools						
Total	25,015	27.8	55.3	8.8	6.3	8.8	13.1	29,714	20,347	31,661	32,288
Men	11,606	25.8	55.3	7.5	10.3	9.0	14.3	32,039	18,767	41,098	34,205
Women	13,410	29.4	55.3	9.8	3.1	8.6	12.0	27,701	21,429	27,292	30,265
Race/ethnicity											
White, non-Hispanic .	23,133	27.5	56.0	8.7	6.3	8.7	13.2	29,725	19,634	31,470	32,510
Black, non-Hispanic .	1,060	28.1	46.2	11.6	4.9	8.3	9.1	28,836	(3)	30,563	(3)
Hispanic	524	34.5	44.0	9.2	12.1	10.1	17.2	31,101	21,557	34,697	(3)
Age											
Under 40	4,794	44.4	42.7	9.6	1.6	3.5	9.7	24,427	16,320	33,527	27,349
40 to 44	4,403	36.5	46.3	8.6	5.4	5.3	12.9	29,373	18,207	29,892	32,088
45 to 49	5,144	23.1	61.4	8.4	5.7	8.3	13.7	32,691	22,875	31,782	36,009
50 to 54	4,120	15.8	62.0	8.1	11.5	9.6	15.3	35,096	26,303	35,067	36,550
55 or over	6,553	21.7	60.9	9.0	7.4	14.8	13.8	28,090	21,630	29,823	30,078
Type of school											
Elementary	13,355	27.6	57.2	8.4	5.0	9.4	11.4	27,151	22,721	29,583	28,215
Secondary	4,890	21.1	56.5	11.4	10.0	8.1	17.4	37,300	21,086	34,918	40,131
Combined	6,770	33.4	50.3	7.6	6.2	8.0	13.3	29,290	14,876	39,671	32,765

[1] Total differs from data appearing in other tables because of varying survey processing procedures and time period coverages.

[2] Percentages for those with less than a bachelor's degree are not shown.

[3] Too few cases for reliable estimate.

NOTE.—Details may not add to 100 percent because of rounding and survey item nonresponse.

SOURCE: U.S. Department of Education, National Center for Education Statistics, "Schools and Staffing Survey, 1993–94." (This table was prepared July 1995.)

Table 87.—Public elementary and secondary students, schools, pupil-teacher ratios, and finances, by type of locale: 1993

Characteristic	Total [1]	Large central city [2]	Mid-size central city [3]	Urban fringe of large city [4]	Urban fringe of mid-size city [5]	Large town [6]	Small town [7]	Rural [8]	Unknown [9]
1	2	3	4	5	6	7	8	9	10
Schools, enrollment, and teachers, 1993–94									
Enrollment, in thousands	44,082	6,197	8,124	7,453	4,970	1,303	5,679	9,682	673
Schools	87,110	8,677	13,562	12,279	8,321	2,553	12,224	27,415	2,079
Average school size [10]	512	724	610	630	615	526	486	314	324
Pupil-teacher ratio [11]	17.8	19.0	17.9	18.6	18.3	17.7	17.2	16.7	20.5
Enrollment (percent distribution)	100.0	14.1	18.4	16.9	11.3	3.0	12.9	22.0	1.5
Schools (percent distribution)	100.0	10.0	15.6	14.1	9.6	2.9	14.0	31.5	2.4
Revenues and expenditures, 1992–93 (in millions)									
Total revenue	$223,291	$36,428	$39,787	$41,589	$26,467	$6,398	$27,672	$44,644	$304
Federal	15,426	3,649	3,096	1,628	1,353	427	1,795	3,429	49
Impact aid	549	36	96	37	82	26	81	192	0
Bilingual education	20	6	4	1	2	1	2	4	0
Indian education	34	1	3	1	0	1	5	22	0
Children with disabilites	1,603	404	372	255	159	47	142	218	6
Eisenhower science awards	34	9	7	4	3	1	3	7	0
Drug Free schools	102	18	25	12	11	3	9	22	1
Chapter 2 (block grants)	246	64	56	30	26	8	19	42	1
Vocational education	327	83	76	36	33	9	28	51	11
Chapter 1	3,458	1,159	760	273	315	100	252	595	4
Other and unclassified	9,052	1,869	1,697	980	722	231	1,252	2,277	25
State	103,301	17,190	19,174	15,073	12,363	3,017	13,046	23,365	74
State school lunch programs	233	64	46	30	42	5	15	31	0
Local	104,563	15,589	17,517	24,889	12,751	2,955	12,830	17,851	182
Property tax [12]	18,743	5,272	2,859	4,524	1,647	751	1,533	2,157	0
Parent government contribution [12]	56,325	7,906	11,383	15,216	7,870	1,405	5,509	6,900	136
Lunch sales	2,936	302	625	639	406	98	310	552	4
Transportation	42	8	9	13	3	1	4	3	0
Other and unclassified	26,517	2,102	2,640	4,497	2,825	699	5,474	8,238	41
Total revenue (percent distribution)	100.0	100.0	100.0	100.0	100.0	100.0	100.0	100.0	100.0
Federal	6.9	10.0	7.8	3.9	5.1	6.7	6.5	7.7	16.0
State	46.3	47.2	48.2	36.2	46.7	47.2	47.1	52.3	24.2
Local	46.8	42.8	44.0	59.8	48.2	46.2	46.4	40.0	59.8
Total expenditures	215,242	34,972	38,424	40,357	25,442	6,204	26,666	42,733	444
Current expenditures	203,273	33,551	36,212	38,109	24,013	5,804	25,095	40,067	422
Instruction	100,706	20,226	20,671	20,263	12,726	3,043	9,140	14,431	206
Operation and maintenance	16,554	3,292	3,492	3,414	2,042	499	1,453	2,316	47
Food service	6,816	1,438	1,524	1,026	802	209	596	1,213	8
Other	79,197	8,594	10,525	13,406	8,443	2,054	13,906	22,107	161
Other current	1,266	171	280	247	217	65	133	148	5
Capital outlay	6,411	675	1,188	1,138	750	219	850	1,576	15
Interest on debt	4,292	575	744	862	461	116	589	942	3
Current expenditures (percent distribution)	100.0	100.0	100.0	100.0	100.0	100.0	100.0	100.0	100.0
Instruction	49.5	60.3	57.1	53.2	53.0	52.4	36.4	36.0	48.8
Operation and maintenance	8.1	9.8	9.6	9.0	8.5	8.6	5.8	5.8	11.0
Food service	3.4	4.3	4.2	2.7	3.3	3.6	2.4	3.0	2.0
Other	39.0	25.6	29.1	35.2	35.2	35.4	55.4	55.2	38.2
Current expenditure per student	4,901	5,560	4,652	5,477	5,053	4,484	4,612	4,358	19,612
Instruction expenditure per student	2,428	3,352	2,656	2,912	2,678	2,350	1,680	1,570	9,563

[1] Includes data for districts not identified by locale.
[2] Central city of metropolitan statistical area (MSA) with population of 400,000 or more or a population density of 6,000 or more persons per square mile.
[3] Central city of an MSA but not designated as a large central city.
[4] Place within the MSA of a large central city.
[5] Place within the MSA of a mid-size central city.
[6] Place not within an MSA but with population of 25,000 or more and defined as urban.
[7] Place not within an MSA with a population of at least 2,500 but less than 25,000.
[8] Place with a population of less than 2,500.
[9] Urbanicity code was not determined.
[10] Average for schools reporting enrollment.
[11] Ratio for schools reporting both FTE teachers and fall enrollment data.

[12] Property tax and parent government contributions are determined on the basis of independence or dependence of the local school system and are mutually exclusive.

NOTE.—Locale classification procedures not comparable with previous years. Enrollments by locale were used to distribute revenue and expenditure amounts by locale classification.

SOURCE: U.S. Department of Education, National Center for Education Statistics, Common Core of Data survey; and U.S. Department of Commerce, Bureau of the Census, *Survey of Local Government Finances*, unpublished data. (This table was prepared July 1995.)

Table 88.—Public school districts and public and private elementary and secondary schools: 1929–30 to 1993–94

School year	Public school districts [1]	Public schools [2]					Private schools [2,3]		
		Total, all schools [4]	Total, regular schools [5]	Elementary schools		Secondary schools	Total [4]	Elementary schools	Secondary schools
				Total	One-teacher				
1	2	3	4	5	6	7	8	9	10
1929–30	—	—	—	238,306	149,282	23,930	—	9,275	3,258
1937–38	119,001	—	—	221,660	121,178	25,467	—	9,992	3,327
1939–40	117,108	—	—	—	113,600	—	—	11,306	3,568
1945–46	101,382	—	—	160,227	86,563	24,314	—	9,863	3,294
1947–48	94,926	—	—	146,760	75,096	25,484	—	10,071	3,292
1949–50	83,718	—	—	128,225	59,652	24,542	—	10,375	3,331
1951–52	71,094	—	—	123,763	50,742	23,746	—	10,666	3,322
1953–54	63,057	—	—	110,875	42,865	25,637	—	11,739	3,913
1955–56	54,859	—	—	104,427	34,964	26,046	—	12,372	3,887
1957–58	47,594	—	—	95,446	25,341	25,507	—	13,065	3,994
1959–60	40,520	—	—	91,853	20,213	25,784	—	13,574	4,061
1961–62	35,676	—	—	81,910	13,333	25,350	—	14,762	4,129
1963–64	31,705	—	—	77,584	9,895	26,431	—	—	4,451
1965–66	26,983	—	—	73,216	6,491	26,597	17,849	15,340	4,606
1967–68	22,010	—	94,197	70,879	4,146	27,011	—	—	—
1970–71	17,995	—	89,372	65,800	1,815	25,352	—	14,372	3,770
1973–74	16,730	—	88,655	65,070	1,365	25,906	—	—	—
1975–76	16,376	88,597	87,034	63,242	1,166	25,330	—	—	—
1976–77	16,271	—	86,501	62,644	1,111	25,378	19,910	16,385	5,904
1978–79	16,014	—	84,816	61,982	1,056	24,504	19,489	16,097	5,766
1980–81	15,912	85,982	83,688	61,069	921	24,362	20,764	16,792	5,678
1982–83	15,824	84,740	82,039	59,656	798	23,988	—	—	—
1983–84	15,747	84,178	81,418	59,082	838	23,947	[6] 27,694	[6] 20,872	[6] 7,862
1984–85	—	84,007	81,147	58,827	825	23,916	—	—	—
1985–86	—	—	—	—	—	—	[6] 25,616	[6] 20,252	[6] 7,387
1986–87	[7] 15,713	83,455	82,190	60,784	763	23,389	—	—	—
1987–88	[7] 15,577	83,248	82,248	61,490	729	22,937	[6] 26,807	[6] 22,959	[6] 8,418
1988–89	[7] 15,376	83,165	82,081	61,531	583	22,785	—	—	—
1989–90	[7] 15,367	83,425	82,396	62,037	630	22,639	—	—	—
1990–91	[7] 15,358	84,538	81,746	61,340	617	22,731	[6] 24,690	[6] 22,223	[6] 8,989
1991–92	[7] 15,173	84,578	81,859	61,739	569	22,601	[6] 25,998	[6] 23,523	[6] 9,282
1992–93	[7] 15,025	84,501	82,224	62,229	430	22,544	—	—	—
1993–94	[7] 14,881	85,393	82,785	62,726	442	22,733	[6] 26,093	[6] 23,543	[6] 10,555

[1] Includes operating and nonoperating districts.

[2] Schools with both elementary and secondary programs are included under elementary schools and also under secondary schools.

[3] Data for most years are partly estimated.

[4] Includes regular schools and special schools not classified by grade span.

[5] Includes elementary, secondary, and combined elementary/secondary schools.

[6] These data are from sample surveys and should not be compared directly with the data for earlier years.

[7] Because of expanded survey coverage, data are not directly comparable with figures for earlier years.

—Data not available.

SOURCE: U.S. Department of Education, National Center for Education Statistics, *Statistics of State School Systems; Statistics of Public Elementary and Secondary School Systems; Statistics of Nonpublic Elementary and Secondary Schools; Private Schools in American Education;* and Common Core of Data surveys. (This table was prepared June 1995.)

Table 89.—Public school districts and enrollment, by size of district: 1988–89 to 1993–94

Enrollment size of district	1988–89	1989–90	1990–91	1991–92			1992–93			1993–94		
	Number of districts	Number of districts	Number of districts	Number of districts	Percent of districts	Percent of students	Number of districts	Percent of districts	Percent of students	Number of districts	Percent of districts	Percent of students
1	2	3	4	5	6	7	8	9	10	11	12	13
Total	15,376	15,367	15,358	15,173	100.0	100.0	15,025	100.0	100.0	14,881	100.0	100.0
25,000 or more	177	179	190	195	1.3	29.1	202	1.3	29.6	206	1.3	29.9
10,000 to 24,999	473	479	489	502	3.3	18.0	510	3.4	18.0	525	3.4	18.2
5,000 to 9,999	924	913	937	941	6.2	15.7	955	6.4	15.6	973	6.4	15.6
2,500 to 4,999	1,907	1,937	1,940	1,981	13.1	16.6	2,002	13.3	16.5	2,008	13.3	16.3
1,000 to 2,499	3,529	3,547	3,542	3,525	23.2	13.8	3,530	23.5	13.6	3,570	23.5	13.5
600 to 999	1,813	1,801	1,799	1,793	11.8	3.4	1,798	12.0	3.3	1,785	12.0	3.2
300 to 599	2,266	2,283	2,275	2,222	14.6	2.3	2,200	14.6	2.3	2,162	14.6	2.2
1 to 299	3,984	3,910	3,816	3,648	24.0	1.2	3,465	23.1	1.1	3,294	23.1	1.0
Size not reported [1]	303	318	370	366	2.4	—	363	2.4	—	358	2.4	—

[1] Includes school districts reporting enrollment of 0.

—Data not reported.

NOTE.—Because of rounding, details may not add to totals.

SOURCE: U.S. Department of Education, National Center for Education Statistics, Common Core of Data surveys. (This table was prepared July 1995.)

Table 90.—Number and percentage of public elementary and secondary education agencies, by state and type of agency: 1993–94

State or other area	Total agencies	Regular school districts, including supervisory union components		Regional education service agencies and supervisory union administrative centers		State-operated agencies		Federally operated and other agencies	
		Number	Percent	Number	Percent	Number	Percent	Number	Percent
1	2	3	4	5	6	7	8	9	10
United States	**16,360**	**14,881**	**91.0**	**1,165**	**7.1**	**198**	**1.2**	**116**	**0.7**
Alabama	131	127	96.9	0	0.0	1	0.8	3	2.3
Alaska	56	56	100.0	0	0.0	0	0.0	0	0.0
Arizona	242	228	94.2	4	1.7	1	0.4	9	3.7
Arkansas	336	315	93.8	17	5.1	4	1.2	0	0.0
California	1,063	1,002	94.3	58	5.5	3	0.3	0	0.0
Colorado	192	176	91.7	16	8.3	0	0.0	0	0.0
Connecticut	179	166	92.7	6	3.4	4	2.2	3	1.7
Delaware	22	19	86.4	0	0.0	3	13.6	0	0.0
District of Columbia	1	1	100.0	0	0.0	0	0.0	0	0.0
Florida	74	67	90.5	0	0.0	1	1.4	6	8.1
Georgia	184	181	98.4	0	0.0	0	0.0	3	1.6
Hawaii	1	1	100.0	0	0.0	0	0.0	0	0.0
Idaho	114	113	99.1	0	0.0	1	0.9	0	0.0
Illinois	1,049	922	87.9	91	8.7	5	0.5	31	3.0
Indiana	326	294	90.2	28	8.6	3	0.9	1	0.3
Iowa	428	397	92.8	15	3.5	15	3.5	1	0.2
Kansas	304	304	100.0	0	0.0	0	0.0	0	0.0
Kentucky	255	176	69.0	0	0.0	77	30.2	2	0.8
Louisiana	71	66	93.0	0	0.0	4	5.6	1	1.4
Maine	325	282	86.8	42	12.9	1	0.3	0	0.0
Maryland	24	24	100.0	0	0.0	0	0.0	0	0.0
Massachusetts	438	351	80.1	86	19.6	1	0.2	0	0.0
Michigan	619	558	90.1	57	9.2	4	0.6	0	0.0
Minnesota	477	405	84.9	68	14.3	4	0.8	0	0.0
Mississippi	164	149	90.9	4	2.4	10	6.1	1	0.6
Missouri	543	541	99.6	1	0.2	1	0.2	0	0.0
Montana	577	495	85.8	79	13.7	3	0.5	0	0.0
Nebraska	814	695	85.4	112	13.8	7	0.9	0	0.0
Nevada	18	17	94.4	0	0.0	1	5.6	0	0.0
New Hampshire	246	178	72.4	68	27.6	0	0.0	0	0.0
New Jersey	620	608	98.1	12	1.9	0	0.0	0	0.0
New Mexico	96	88	91.7	0	0.0	8	8.3	0	0.0
New York	752	714	94.9	38	5.1	0	0.0	0	0.0
North Carolina	125	121	96.8	0	0.0	2	1.6	2	1.6
North Dakota	306	260	85.0	38	12.4	3	1.0	5	1.6
Ohio	790	661	83.7	102	12.9	3	0.4	24	3.0
Oklahoma	554	554	100.0	0	0.0	0	0.0	0	0.0
Oregon	291	280	96.2	7	2.4	3	1.0	1	0.3
Pennsylvania	612	501	81.9	100	16.3	11	1.8	0	0.0
Rhode Island	37	36	97.3	0	0.0	1	2.7	0	0.0
South Carolina	108	95	88.0	11	10.2	0	0.0	2	1.9
South Dakota	219	178	81.3	17	7.8	5	2.3	19	8.7
Tennessee	140	140	100.0	0	0.0	0	0.0	0	0.0
Texas	1,046	1,046	100.0	0	0.0	0	0.0	0	0.0
Utah	47	40	85.1	5	10.6	2	4.3	0	0.0
Vermont	345	285	82.6	60	17.4	0	0.0	0	0.0
Virginia	161	141	87.6	18	11.2	0	0.0	2	1.2
Washington	296	296	100.0	0	0.0	0	0.0	0	0.0
West Virginia	57	55	96.5	0	0.0	2	3.5	0	0.0
Wisconsin	427	427	100.0	0	0.0	0	0.0	0	0.0
Wyoming	58	49	84.5	5	8.6	4	6.9	0	0.0
Outlying areas									
American Samoa	1	1	100.0	0	0.0	0	0.0	0	0.0
Guam	1	1	100.0	0	0.0	0	0.0	0	0.0
Northern Marianas	1	1	100.0	0	0.0	0	0.0	0	0.0
Puerto Rico	1	1	100.0	0	0.0	0	0.0	0	0.0
Virgin Islands	1	1	100.0	0	0.0	0	0.0	0	0.0

SOURCE: U.S. Department of Education, National Center for Education Statistics, Common Core of Data survey. (This table was prepared June 1995.)

Table 91.—Selected statistics for public school districts enrolling more than 20,000 pupils, by state: 1993–94

Name of district, by state	State	Enrollment, fall 1993	Classroom teachers,[1] fall 1993	Pupils per teacher, fall 1993	Percent minority pupils, fall 1993	Number of schools, 1993–94	Number of 1992–93 graduates[2]	Revenue receipts: Total	Revenue receipts: Federal	Revenue receipts: State	Revenue receipts: Local	Total expenditures	Current expenditures: Total	Current expenditures: Instruction	Capital outlay	Interest on school debt	Current expenditure per pupil 1992–93[4]
1	2	3	4	5	6	7	8	9	10	11	12	13	14	15	16	17	18
Districts with more than 20,000 students	—	14,536,579	—	—	—	20,477	655,424	$81,083,789	$7,047,765	$38,550,426	$35,485,598	$76,682,319	$72,746,705	$43,456,091	$2,432,391	$1,503,223	$5,096
Birmingham City	Ala.	42,847	2,463	17.4	91.1	90	1,753	169,344	25,212	100,973	43,159	155,250	152,689	85,628	2,041	520	3,591
Huntsville City	Ala.	25,075	1,532	16.4	40.8	42	1,343	125,194	9,920	60,333	54,941	104,661	100,527	57,992	4,073	61	4,033
Jefferson County	Ala.	40,733	2,368	17.2	15.0	58	2,256	149,848	11,811	97,679	40,358	136,410	132,801	81,812	3,047	562	3,271
Mobile County	Ala.	66,580	3,451	19.3	49.5	88	3,310	233,691	33,446	145,750	54,495	192,442	185,878	115,524	5,481	1,083	2,779
Montgomery County	Ala.	35,244	1,992	17.7	64.7	53	1,723	125,268	18,286	80,642	26,340	109,705	107,668	65,828	1,963	74	3,045
Anchorage	Alaska	47,340	2,142	22.1	29.0	82	2,239	354,841	38,368	241,644	74,829	294,134	286,982	146,234	7,115	37	6,203
Mesa Unified	Ariz.	67,639			29.0	71	3,265	291,052	13,964	146,264	130,824	258,780	240,676	151,152	10,078	8,026	3,665
Paradise Valley	Ariz.	30,042	1,480	20.3	10.5	33	1,528	134,579	3,567	56,440	74,572	125,253	109,811	69,192	4,380	11,062	3,808
Peoria Unified	Ariz.	24,752	1,172	21.1	21.5	25	1,175	99,742	3,134	53,069	43,539	91,223	81,112	50,545	3,382	6,729	3,514
Phoenix Union High	Ariz.	20,168	1,168	17.3	68.1	15	2,776	151,520	12,239	10,597	128,684	137,527	122,781	65,195	6,114	8,632	6,527
Scottsdale	Ariz.	22,096	1,140	19.4	11.3	26	1,284	102,132	2,758	21,219	78,155	95,756	85,256	48,988	2,621	7,879	4,048
Tucson Unified	Ariz.	60,529			51.8	110	2,672	264,112	23,151	128,754	112,207	260,504	233,553	132,373	10,213	16,738	4,035
Washington	Ariz.	24,016	1,283	18.7	20.0	32		93,510	6,122	51,341	36,047	91,291	87,482	57,518	2,695	1,114	3,702
Little Rock	Ark.	25,543	1,623	15.7	66.9	48	1,590	130,581	9,934	51,815	68,832	134,142	126,398	73,943	3,155	4,589	4,881
Pulaski County Special	Ark.	20,426	1,217	16.8	30.7	36	1,196	92,319	6,700	55,754	29,865	89,279	84,166	51,749	3,124	1,989	3,880
ABC Unified	Calif.	21,243	826	25.7	76.4	30	1,403	100,405	5,596	75,261	19,548	103,138	101,180	61,101	1,849	109	4,752
Anaheim Union High	Calif.	23,466	846	27.7	60.6	20	2,717	114,083	7,603	70,113	36,367	115,980	113,341	66,450	2,639	0	4,898
Bakersfield City Elementary	Calif.	26,386	1,069	24.7	71.4	36		130,728	13,375	99,572	17,781	112,574	107,388	65,647	2,780	2,406	4,077
Capistrano Unified	Calif.	31,262	1,240	25.2	21.8	32	1,562	166,755	3,513	76,601	86,641	134,330	131,118	80,746	2,858	354	4,364
Chino Unified	Calif.	26,607	1,094	24.3	45.8	28	1,124	125,160	3,332	82,034	39,794	123,191	114,154	70,485	8,360	677	4,419
Clovis Unified	Calif.	27,416	1,113	24.6	32.8	29	1,388	161,119	49,724	80,464	30,931	159,877	148,071	79,596	7,289	4,517	5,686
Compton Unified	Calif.	28,482	1,001	28.5	99.6	38	606	134,466	18,505	99,831	16,130	139,924	135,622	75,305	4,302	0	4,736
Corona-Norco Unified	Calif.	25,655	987	26.0	49.6	33	1,282	107,534	4,923	71,522	31,089	101,760	96,484	58,631	5,276	853	3,846
East Side Union High	Calif.	22,032	968	22.8	79.7	14	4,363	116,643	7,286	68,799	40,558	115,057	112,143	66,374	2,061	153	4,974
Elk Grove Unified	Calif.	22,038	1,308	24.5	51.8	36	1,543	186,807	7,501	126,770	52,536	152,187	145,061	75,853	6,973	0	4,753
Fairfield-Suisun Joint	Calif.	20,756	843	24.6	50.9	27	965	78,355	4,092	65,315	17,948	78,819	77,571	49,961	1,248	1,286	3,737
Fontana Unified	Calif.	29,764	1,111	26.8	68.9	32	1,270	139,197	8,418	113,374	17,405	136,388	129,896	70,897	5,206	800	4,419
Fremont Unified	Calif.	28,928	1,162	24.9	43.3	40	1,559	133,459	4,724	81,438	47,297	119,357	117,096	78,564	1,461	20	4,112
Fresno Unified	Calif.	76,349	3,158	24.2	73.0	86	2,981	361,702	39,346	252,721	69,635	383,254	375,562	218,984	7,672	20	4,953
Garden Grove Unified	Calif.	41,664	1,608	25.9	71.7	63	2,359	177,929	16,827	106,898	54,204	180,239	178,314	110,645	1,905	20	4,332
Glendale Unified	Calif.	28,742	1,083	26.5	41.0	29	1,649	124,470	11,147	79,909	33,414	115,163	113,084	74,152	2,079	0	3,990
Grossmont Union High	Calif.	20,010	810	24.7	28.0	13	3,424	107,429	4,412	57,187	45,830	108,341	104,915	54,911	3,426	0	5,343
Hacienda La Puente Unified	Calif.	21,831	821	26.6	85.9	35	1,291	135,670	11,603	98,162	25,905	128,824	126,141	60,896	2,655	28	5,736
Hayward Unified	Calif.	20,115	803	25.0	69.4	33	853	94,661	7,742	63,945	22,974	84,089	83,091	48,614	998	0	4,064
Irvine Unified	Calif.	21,519	898	24.0	32.5	30	1,606	107,083	5,444	39,890	61,749	103,554	96,952	62,135	5,432	1,170	4,549
Kern High	Calif.	22,646	844	26.8	49.1	20	3,990	179,308	8,441	76,691	94,176	104,692	118,433	58,366	2,255	4	5,363
Lodi Unified	Calif.	25,155	1,041	24.2	49.6	36	1,089	113,152	7,921	80,754	24,477	104,647	100,783	62,330	3,603	261	4,005
Long Beach Unified	Calif.	76,783	3,018	25.4	77.5	80	3,430	394,557	47,670	271,662	75,225	369,390	361,647	212,602	7,743	0	4,795
Los Angeles Unified	Calif.	639,129	24,933	25.6	87.9	640	25,439	3,451,551	348,942	2,462,366	640,243	3,700,377	3,650,772	2,168,098	49,605	261	5,706
Montebello Unified	Calif.	32,321	1,093	29.6	95.5	30	1,691	149,019	14,527	110,597	23,895	147,845	146,441	84,922	1,404	0	4,470
Moreno Valley Unified	Calif.	31,621	1,263	25.0	53.6	33	1,346	147,372	7,166	118,507	21,699	131,804	126,331	74,087	5,319	154	4,030
Mt. Diablo Unified	Calif.	34,110	1,471	23.2	28.8	54	1,741	148,368	6,574	79,841	61,953	140,405	139,153	83,971	1,232	20	4,143
Oakland Unified	Calif.	51,748	2,187	23.7	93.1	89	1,837	279,738	30,421	198,286	51,031	278,611	269,832	159,616	7,748	1,031	5,267
Ontario-Montclair Elementary	Calif.	26,387	861	26.3	76.9	31		92,074	8,228	70,130	13,716	88,966	87,528	55,786	1,438	0	3,912
Orange Unified	Calif.	22,649	1,016	26.0	46.3	38	1,494	113,093	5,518	42,930	64,645	112,958	111,177	66,181	1,722	59	4,221
Pasadena Unified	Calif.	22,032	899	24.5	82.9	31	1,020	116,940	10,220	69,130	37,590	116,029	115,098	69,218	931	0	5,131
Placentia-Yorba Linda Unified	Calif.	22,482	887	25.3	35.5	29	1,276	101,971	3,373	53,276	45,322	99,388	96,227	59,411	3,027	134	4,272
Pomona Unified	Calif.	29,880	1,133	26.4	88.1	35	971	140,867	17,352	102,961	20,554	148,322	144,233	77,375	3,109	980	4,892
Poway Unified	Calif.	28,106	1,113	25.3	25.9	28	1,517	129,465	3,022	69,534	56,909	118,617	110,620	65,996	7,475	522	4,083
Rialto Unified	Calif.	31,621	874	25.7	75.3	21	937	104,707	5,168	84,396	15,143	89,316	82,929	49,200	6,328	59	3,822
Richmond Unified	Calif.	31,329	1,264	24.8	74.4	56	1,477	151,743	16,315	91,236	44,192	141,348	138,586	80,223	2,762	20	4,429
Riverside Unified	Calif.	33,655	1,320	25.5	51.1	39	1,596	148,118	10,439	97,748	39,931	146,555	143,748	85,664	2,771	36	4,338
Sacramento City Unified	Calif.	49,997	1,972	25.4	69.0	75	2,028	230,375	26,220	159,612	44,543	238,089	232,363	135,071	5,726	0	4,600
Saddleback Valley Unified	Calif.	27,720	1,152	24.1	24.2	34	1,652	125,877	2,891	53,508	69,478	123,130	118,925	75,617	3,702	503	4,392
San Bernardino City Unified	Calif.	43,933	1,783	24.6	70.5	57	1,478	205,371	17,515	158,905	28,951	193,233	190,268	111,652	2,965	503	4,366
San Diego City Unified	Calif.	127,258	5,170	24.6	67.8	156	6,106	666,031	57,406	297,671	310,954	656,641	645,010	370,985	11,535	96	5,155
San Francisco Unified	Calif.	61,631	2,851	21.6	86.2	108	3,635	325,128	28,846	156,815	139,467	304,357	300,316	173,417	4,041	0	4,853
San Jose Unified	Calif.	30,905	1,351	22.9	65.0	48	1,654	164,547	12,877	81,928	69,742	158,591	153,174	91,033	5,107	310	5,028

Table 91.—Selected statistics for public school districts enrolling more than 20,000 pupils, by state: 1993–94—Continued

Name of district, by state	State	Enrollment, fall 1993	Classroom teachers,[1] fall 1993	Pupils per teacher, fall 1993	Percent minority pupils, fall 1993	Number of schools, 1993–94	Number of 1992–93 graduates[2]	Revenue and expenditures,[3] 1992–93 (in thousands of dollars)									Current expenditure per pupil 1992–93[4]
								Revenue receipts				Total expenditures	Current expenditures				
								Total	Federal	State	Local		Total	Instruction	Capital outlay	Interest on school debt	
1	2	3	4	5	6	7	8	9	10	11	12	13	14	15	16	17	18
San Juan Unified	Calif.	47,650	1,853	25.7	19.5	87	2,656	226,354	13,291	151,415	61,648	207,757	202,917	124,823	4,840	0	4,237
Santa Ana Unified	Calif.	48,407	1,693	28.6	95.1	46	1,842	218,339	19,870	131,085	67,384	204,427	190,916	123,144	13,145	366	3,975
Stockton City Unified	Calif.	34,337	1,488	23.1	81.3	41	1,065	171,743	20,409	118,121	33,213	183,854	177,401	96,589	6,351	102	5,229
Sweetwater Union High	Calif.	28,769	1,209	23.8	79.8	19	3,579	144,721	9,574	107,236	27,911	144,850	140,638	77,632	4,212	0	4,894
Torrance Unified	Calif.	21,233	826	25.7	47.6	30	1,333	91,807	3,042	55,452	33,313	86,916	84,579	48,962	2,308	29	4,093
Visalia Unified	Calif.	23,369	921	25.4	48.5	31	1,070	102,675	6,885	76,316	19,474	102,596	101,961	61,918	635	0	4,505
Vista Unified	Calif.	21,947	862	25.5	44.7	23	919	108,455	4,914	67,997	35,544	94,001	89,011	52,863	4,982	8	4,286
Adams-Arapahoe	Colo.	27,430	1,472	18.6	36.3	44	1,211	139,920	6,798	84,701	48,421	142,447	132,103	78,569	3,468	6,876	4,838
Boulder Valley	Colo.	24,085	1,353	17.8	15.3	48	1,324	138,130	4,569	19,745	113,816	129,736	122,906	71,977	3,103	3,727	5,211
Cherry Creek	Colo.	33,343	1,834	18.2	14.6	42	1,904	204,919	2,778	56,104	146,037	189,043	170,321	105,066	5,941	12,781	5,329
Colorado Springs	Colo.	31,799	1,522	20.9	25.6	57	1,609	145,947	7,644	71,956	66,347	131,628	129,704	80,212	1,924	0	4,050
Denver	Colo.	62,673	3,584	17.5	69.3	111	2,596	386,894	29,203	78,667	279,024	365,284	316,834	184,114	35,414	13,036	5,034
Jefferson County	Colo.	82,760	3,834	21.6	12.3	129	4,365	433,024	11,007	211,012	211,005	424,421	393,333	231,924	10,698	20,390	4,837
Northglenn-Thornton	Colo.	22,791	1,170	19.5	21.8	38	1,147	122,520	4,873	70,202	47,445	116,870	100,900	60,015	8,125	7,845	4,553
Poudre School District	Colo.	20,485	1,011	20.3	13.4	43	1,118	108,127	3,876	42,230	62,021	99,043	94,890	57,157	3,235	918	4,747
Bridgeport City	Conn.	20,495	1,322	15.5	87.6	38	693	157,774	18,250	99,511	40,013	146,579	141,162	93,508	2,890	2,527	6,899
Hartford	Conn.	25,292	1,791	14.1	93.8	33	846	237,164	21,289	134,766	81,109	228,146	223,760	146,254	2,167	2,219	8,817
D.C. Public Schools	D.C.	80,678	4,530	17.8	96.0	173	3,136	731,548	84,327	0	647,221	695,075	678,385	328,497	16,690	0	8,382
Alachua County	Fla.	28,426	1,594	17.8	40.3	40	1,248	150,948	14,787	88,388	47,773	140,786	126,844	66,488	6,572	7,370	4,552
Bay County	Fla.	23,873	1,442	16.6	19.0	32	1,148	117,486	11,375	71,783	34,328	113,435	110,349	64,632	3,013	73	4,750
Brevard County	Fla.	62,556	3,561	17.6	19.3	78	2,943	318,226	20,323	168,119	129,784	281,624	268,365	159,391	7,480	5,779	4,396
Broward County	Fla.	189,862	9,546	19.9	47.5	184	8,246	1,051,501	73,511	517,651	460,339	1,026,532	930,983	490,008	59,307	36,242	5,228
Clay County	Fla.	23,142	1,288	18.0	11.5	25	1,260	108,087	6,288	71,612	30,187	95,910	91,782	52,801	3,894	234	4,016
Collier County	Fla.	23,924	1,382	17.3	33.4	33	1,001	157,906	13,814	27,421	116,671	145,550	129,278	73,287	6,563	9,709	5,671
Dade County	Fla.	308,465	15,271	20.2	83.9	314	14,555	1,850,267	238,119	950,032	662,116	1,802,305	1,728,572	959,030	40,468	33,265	5,698
Duval County	Fla.	119,785	5,943	20.2	42.9	154	4,606	615,275	54,402	359,187	201,686	521,804	495,827	274,603	17,222	8,755	4,214
Escambia County	Fla.	44,641	2,624	17.0	37.5	70	2,081	242,649	31,540	153,072	58,037	230,725	217,240	118,968	8,808	4,677	4,905
Hillsborough County	Fla.	135,104	8,010	16.9	40.0	170	5,972	749,832	90,795	409,583	249,454	694,197	658,549	353,904	27,589	8,059	4,981
Lake County	Fla.	22,669	1,226	18.5	23.0	40	1,042	114,426	9,810	63,091	41,525	107,215	97,937	51,503	7,225	2,053	4,410
Lee County	Fla.	47,390	2,479	19.1	25.6	70	2,297	277,007	24,457	71,352	181,198	257,601	231,578	118,829	16,095	9,928	5,026
Leon County	Fla.	29,836	1,699	17.6	39.7	45	1,349	167,248	13,658	93,572	60,018	154,344	140,773	72,079	7,786	5,785	4,820
Manatee County	Fla.	29,685	1,640	18.1	27.3	55	1,167	159,238	12,140	68,823	78,275	137,029	131,982	74,102	4,401	646	4,626
Marion County	Fla.	32,702	1,830	17.9	27.4	44	1,431	164,818	14,088	97,734	52,996	151,609	140,848	79,454	6,367	4,394	4,471
Okaloosa County	Fla.	28,856	1,594	18.1	19.1	36	1,656	131,729	11,287	83,213	37,229	119,140	115,904	64,859	1,476	1,760	4,113
Orange County	Fla.	113,638	6,372	17.8	44.4	146	4,951	619,585	43,197	272,254	304,134	565,690	529,060	268,885	19,113	17,517	4,804
Osceola County	Fla.	23,122	1,151	20.1	34.4	28	1,059	108,776	5,397	54,567	48,812	100,637	92,146	49,903	5,209	3,282	4,221
Palm Beach County	Fla.	122,145	6,804	18.0	42.6	125	5,247	769,160	50,052	217,650	501,458	660,077	624,015	370,160	13,192	22,870	5,358
Pasco County	Fla.	38,265	2,079	18.4	10.4	43	1,777	193,985	14,180	103,977	75,828	185,290	167,699	89,604	9,138	8,453	4,591
Pinellas County	Fla.	100,135	5,499	18.2	22.9	142	4,905	570,656	39,848	259,292	271,516	478,893	465,690	262,216	12,422	781	4,750
Polk County	Fla.	69,718	3,826	18.2	29.9	104	3,073	330,689	30,438	199,796	100,455	329,346	310,158	170,851	15,315	3,873	4,580
Saint Lucie County	Fla.	25,250	1,217	20.7	37.9	31	845	136,110	13,566	55,184	67,360	124,877	111,033	60,304	8,765	5,079	4,659
Sarasota County	Fla.	30,205	1,672	18.1	15.9	38	1,591	200,372	12,944	44,735	142,693	182,723	163,906	85,986	9,940	8,877	5,592
Seminole County	Fla.	52,688	2,620	20.1	25.5	51	2,542	255,427	12,436	134,450	108,541	219,439	205,406	121,331	8,629	5,404	3,982
Volusia County	Fla.	53,972	3,031	17.8	23.0	67	2,490	279,882	17,748	137,783	124,351	259,894	231,487	129,438	10,400	18,007	4,403
Atlanta	Ga.	59,244	3,616	16.4	93.1	112	2,555	455,638	52,069	121,427	282,142	386,779	382,392	224,974	4,387	0	6,401
Bibb County	Ga.	25,158	1,519	16.6	64.5	39	1,075	109,891	13,603	62,819	33,469	108,792	103,818	65,302	2,696	2,278	4,133
Chatham County	Ga.	35,358	2,229	15.9	62.1	44	1,434	203,415	18,613	98,302	86,500	179,777	164,041	106,268	11,365	4,371	4,726
Clayton County	Ga.	37,961	2,202	17.2	45.8	42	1,766	178,168	10,845	84,382	82,941	163,268	157,775	94,264	2,903	2,590	4,308
Cobb County	Ga.	77,563	4,761	16.3	19.0	86	4,089	348,015	11,399	157,143	179,473	348,410	324,655	208,719	9,794	13,961	4,344
DeKalb County	Ga.	81,468	5,114	15.9	77.2	106	4,227	435,543	19,952	170,136	245,455	436,983	420,605	281,687	12,846	3,532	5,316
Fulton County	Ga.	50,190	3,060	16.4	48.0	53	2,283	307,257	12,310	84,853	210,094	255,766	239,663	138,942	7,357	8,746	5,057
Gwinnett County	Ga.	76,482	4,334	17.6	15.7	66	3,738	349,315	9,262	161,830	178,223	343,434	313,761	206,471	17,407	12,266	4,348
Muscogee County	Ga.	31,984	2,004	16.0	58.1	51	1,630	228,395	16,736	95,974	115,685	154,756	149,827	90,192	3,458	1,471	4,671
Richmond County	Ga.	35,422	2,064	17.2	64.7	56	1,565	161,407	17,271	88,714	55,422	146,006	140,906	87,515	3,356	1,744	4,049
Hawaii Public Schools	Hawaii	180,529	—	—	76.3	241	9,309	1,065,809	79,517	962,375	23,917	1,016,323	980,659	580,597	35,664	0	5,526
Boise City ISD	Idaho	26,099	1,362	19.2	—	45	1,367	107,794	5,630	51,503	50,661	94,768	90,594	57,858	1,895	2,279	3,607
City of Chicago	Ill.	409,499	21,722	18.9	88.6	609	15,445	2,427,068	360,275	831,124	1,235,669	2,333,374	2,284,616	1,387,464	47,422	1,336	5,551
Elgin Unified	Ill.	29,653	1,465	20.2	34.1	50	1,405	128,700	6,020	41,396	81,284	141,370	134,365	86,871	1,744	5,261	4,656
Rockford	Ill.	27,688	1,623	17.1	33.9	50	1,360	127,630	9,149	47,170	71,311	140,271	135,057	79,343	1,282	3,932	4,814

Table 91.—Selected statistics for public school districts enrolling more than 20,000 pupils, by state: 1993-94—Continued

Name of district, by state	State	Enrollment, fall 1993	Classroom teachers,[1] fall 1993	Pupils per teacher, fall 1993	Percent minority pupils, fall 1993	Number of schools, 1993-94	Number of 1992-93 graduates[2]	Revenue receipts — Total	Federal	State	Local	Total expenditures	Current expenditures — Total	Instruction	Capital outlay	Interest on school debt	Current expenditure per pupil 1992-93[4]
1	2	3	4	5	6	7	8	9	10	11	12	13	14	15	16	17	18
Evansville-Vanderburgh Schools	Ind.	23,826	1,401	17.0	15.1	38	1,345	130,977	8,821	62,214	59,942	119,041	116,390	72,108	1,936	715	4,926
Fort Wayne Community Schools	Ind.	31,726	1,729	18.3	27.9	53	1,784	169,759	12,472	83,811	73,476	161,773	156,710	94,760	4,152	911	4,906
Gary Community Schools	Ind.	24,150	1,245	19.4	98.7	43	1,269	140,312	15,759	86,029	38,524	134,781	128,888	75,103	3,424	2,469	5,321
Indianapolis Public Schools	Ind.	46,656	2,661	17.5	56.1	92	1,612	335,857	32,241	188,706	114,910	282,748	273,290	151,705	7,793	1,665	5,852
South Bend Community Schools	Ind.	21,469	1,249	17.2	38.3	36	1,231	123,938	5,927	69,012	48,999	107,149	102,274	61,058	3,992	883	4,779
Des Moines Independent Community	Iowa	31,652	2,622	12.1	21.6	65	1,522	177,770	13,223	89,352	75,195	170,385	166,953	108,736	2,616	816	5,334
Kansas City Unified	Kans.	22,096	1,250	17.7	64.5	48	769	122,365	11,635	72,149	38,581	122,341	119,131	66,904	3,201	9	5,415
Shawnee Mission Unified	Kans.	31,827	2,046	15.6	8.8	57	1,986	153,784	3,600	47,565	102,619	177,252	149,744	91,270	25,355	2,153	4,749
Wichita Unified	Kans.	47,132	2,818	16.7	36.7	104	2,171	250,000	13,750	92,152	144,098	258,266	252,934	149,209	5,280	52	5,290
Fayette County	Ky.	33,087	2,042	16.2	25.0	57	1,611	146,427	9,306	65,654	71,467	141,274	134,882	76,629	2,903	3,489	4,119
Jefferson County	Ky.	93,529	5,381	17.4	32.3	150	4,805	470,432	55,779	210,937	203,716	422,239	406,824	248,003	8,764	6,651	4,354
Caddo Parish	La.	51,255	2,955	17.3	60.3	76	2,237	215,528	22,395	117,671	75,462	208,213	200,882	118,756	4,124	3,207	3,878
Calcasieu Parish	La.	34,373	2,094	16.4	31.3	58	1,575	145,001	12,020	74,322	58,659	139,699	130,939	78,683	4,182	4,578	3,855
East Baton Rouge Parish	La.	63,179	3,844	16.4	60.7	103	2,680	276,319	26,832	153,971	95,516	273,383	270,580	161,029	2,803	20,517	4,286
Jefferson Parish	La.	57,210	3,370	17.0	50.2	82	2,254	274,785	26,635	129,562	118,588	272,875	249,426	155,870	2,932	3,088	4,353
Lafayette Parish	La.	31,108	1,743	17.8	34.5	40	1,463	123,086	11,816	67,385	43,885	117,613	111,509	69,782	3,016	9,135	3,629
Orleans Parish	La.	85,983	4,590	18.7	93.7	121	2,849	376,431	65,740	184,482	126,209	387,001	366,556	232,380	11,310	4,887	4,341
Rapides Parish	La.	24,488	1,603	15.3	42.5	53	1,178	114,785	14,528	62,136	38,121	110,300	103,102	59,800	2,311	4,020	4,144
Saint Tammany Parish	La.	30,487	1,861	16.4	16.5	44	1,300	125,415	7,254	67,606	50,555	123,548	116,401	71,222	3,127	1,607	3,971
Terrebonne Parish	La.	22,033	1,193	18.5	34.3	43	908	73,161	8,864	45,363	18,934	72,623	70,351	42,852	665		3,242
Anne Arundel County	Md.	69,020	3,884	17.8	20.1	113	3,864	416,890	18,186	162,785	235,919	352,719	344,926	203,014	3,772	4,021	5,116
Baltimore City	Md.	113,354	6,191	18.3	84.2	178	3,315	665,348	85,031	377,347	202,970	558,703	533,834	331,332	20,620	4,249	4,824
Baltimore County	Md.	96,402	5,688	16.9	26.1	156	5,392	595,527	18,181	199,097	378,249	523,315	509,472	303,645	10,892	2,951	5,462
Carroll County	Md.	23,730	1,306	16.7	3.6	36	1,455	139,229	4,309	64,806	70,114	112,951	109,786	64,984	1,747	1,418	4,739
Charles County	Md.	20,101	1,201	16.7	27.3	32	1,117	120,918	5,393	54,715	60,810	103,149	101,570	55,748	1,579	0	5,196
Frederick County	Md.	30,451	1,817	16.8	10.1	49	1,745	189,441	5,890	76,643	106,908	146,252	139,785	82,570	4,104	2,363	4,771
Harford County	Md.	34,775	2,010	16.7	15.5	47	1,758	193,855	8,356	98,471	87,028	158,368	154,045	93,600	3,717	606	4,558
Howard County	Md.	34,416	2,060	16.7	23.3	55	2,073	263,318	4,093	73,910	185,315	204,628	191,592	110,770	8,261	4,775	5,813
Montgomery County	Md.	113,429	6,551	17.3	42.0	178	6,587	925,026	29,124	187,550	708,352	771,737	732,016	449,220	20,712	19,009	6,652
Prince George's County	Md.	115,918	6,356	18.2	78.2	175	6,240	717,115	42,833	317,520	356,762	616,216	611,422	333,285	4,377	417	5,405
Boston City	Mass.	63,738	—	—	80.7	117	2,840	489,025	49,588	117,680	321,757	455,828	441,600	276,723	3,145	11,083	7,076
Springfield City	Mass.	24,113	—	—	67.6	43	1,018	156,671	13,335	107,307	36,029	110,300	106,797	57,962	745	2,758	4,434
Worcester Public Schools	Mass.	21,924	—	—	40.2	49	757	133,703	14,339	59,684	59,680	117,660	115,273	75,764	584	1,803	5,386
Detroit Public Schools	Mich.	173,295	7,799	22.2	93.4	262	6,751	1,049,094	131,372	631,911	285,811	1,020,988	990,486	536,289	9,145	21,357	5,748
Flint City	Mich.	26,206	1,153	22.7	71.3	43	1,097	174,392	17,209	80,408	76,775	172,618	170,605	73,990	2,013	0	6,410
Grand Rapids Public Schools	Mich.	27,092	1,144	23.7	71.8	75	0	184,484	21,939	49,775	112,770	172,153	162,043	73,131	4,280	5,830	6,019
Lansing City	Mich.	20,503	939	21.8	48.3	42	819	133,744	7,405	41,915	84,424	139,663	134,240	69,615	3,645	1,778	6,438
Utica Community	Mich.	23,350	1,080	21.6	3.9	37	1,667	134,347	2,228	2,630	129,489	132,126	124,327	74,487	3,256	4,543	5,080
Anoka Junction	Minn.	37,777	1,988	19.0	5.9	47	2,140	206,268	5,250	115,757	85,261	216,093	199,679	115,489	12,664	3,750	5,467
Minneapolis Special	Minn.	44,533	2,844	15.7	59.0	138	1,664	320,995	26,030	93,693	201,272	317,073	291,832	174,756	18,699	6,542	6,887
Osseo ISD 279	Minn.	20,998	1,155	18.2	12.6	30	1,051	120,249	2,590	60,699	56,960	121,773	112,638	68,923	3,442	5,693	5,453
Rosemount	Minn.	24,152	1,289	18.7	6.8	27	1,229	117,339	1,967	64,518	50,854	114,594	98,766	63,867	6,759	9,069	4,283
Saint Paul Independent	Minn.	39,239	2,225	17.6	49.4	128	1,566	261,606	23,809	121,737	116,060	252,978	235,038	145,427	13,388	4,552	6,173
Jackson Municipal Schools	Miss.	33,444	—	—	83.8	59	1,439	138,230	16,886	55,187	66,157	132,281	125,182	73,961	2,094	5,005	3,739
Kansas City	Mo.	36,599	2,891	12.7	75.5	83	1,168	338,080	22,087	169,752	146,241	311,388	297,768	135,625	13,401	219	8,316
Parkway	Mo.	22,690	1,259	18.0	25.0	27	1,592	117,815	1,885	27,950	87,980	129,280	125,819	79,713	1,176	2,285	5,552
Saint Louis City	Mo.	41,213	3,105	13.3	80.7	110	1,175	312,624	38,620	148,080	125,924	286,982	274,002	143,693	5,096	7,884	6,706
Springfield	Mo.	24,632	1,372	18.0	6.3	56	1,377	87,626	6,705	31,136	49,785	97,046	92,708	58,028	1,569	2,769	3,813
Lincoln	Neb.	30,017	2,019	14.9	10.9	48	1,668	176,098	9,463	46,435	120,200	162,662	157,821	109,171	3,702	1,139	5,307
Omaha City	Neb.	43,609	2,660	16.4	36.6	82	2,367	238,993	19,427	82,383	137,183	240,481	214,572	133,176	20,946	4,963	4,972
Clark County	Nev.	145,327	7,189	20.2	34.9	193	5,891	448,790	33,473	226,864	188,453	671,517	616,436	363,986	17,080	38,001	4,526
Washoe County	Nev.	43,715	2,289	19.1	23.2	75	1,910	117,869	7,959	52,383	57,527	183,108	174,926	112,429	3,435	4,747	4,159
Jersey City	N.J.	30,697	1,995	15.4	89.5	37	1,133	291,098	27,366	178,019	85,713	258,297	244,200	144,683	7,543	6,554	8,543
Newark	N.J.	46,835	3,428	13.7	90.7	80	1,659	543,953	55,407	401,372	87,174	473,202	455,176	261,353	12,313	5,713	9,501
Paterson City	N.J.	22,617	1,643	13.8	92.4	35	715	232,012	20,957	170,968	40,087	193,284	188,403	114,831	4,881	0	8,522
Albuquerque	N.M.	92,697	5,433	17.1	52.8	130	4,403	379,960	29,355	313,125	37,480	354,514	354,227	202,533	287	0	3,864

Table 91.—Selected statistics for public school districts enrolling more than 20,000 pupils, by state: 1993–94—Continued

Columns 9–17 fall under the heading *Revenue and expenditures,[3] 1992–93 (in thousands of dollars)*, with columns 9–12 under *Revenue receipts* and columns 14–17 under *Current expenditures*.

1	2	3	4	5	6	7	8	9	10	11	12	13	14	15	16	17	18
Name of district, by state	State	Enrollment, fall 1993	Classroom teachers,[1] fall 1993	Pupils per teacher, fall 1993	Percent minority pupils, fall 1993	Number of schools, 1993–94	Number of 1992–93 graduates[2]	Revenue receipts Total	Federal	State	Local	Total expenditures	Current expenditures Total	Instruction	Capital out-lay	Interest on school debt	Current expenditure per pupil 1992–93[4]
Las Cruces	N.M.	21,857	1,139	19.2	63.0	33	1,040	86,658	8,628	67,099	10,931	78,082	75,415	40,467	447	2,220	3,582
Buffalo City	N.Y.	48,128	3,153	15.3	62.8	74	2,062	374,384	41,937	253,937	78,510	360,014	352,950	223,137	4,695	2,369	7,308
New York City	N.Y.	1,005,521	55,353	18.2	82.5	1,064	34,765	7,484,189	776,099	3,036,036	3,672,054	7,589,571	7,301,451	5,020,100	74,070	214,050	7,420
Rochester City	N.Y.	35,568	2,461	14.5	76.9	55	842	328,171	28,930	165,054	134,187	314,870	304,705	184,143	8,339	1,826	8,688
Syracuse City	N.Y.	23,337	1,469	15.9	46.4	34	835	194,133	15,905	116,676	61,552	185,635	177,785	109,694	2,960	4,890	7,636
Yonkers City	N.Y.	21,271	1,333	16.0	70.3	33	685	204,176	14,663	63,897	125,616	201,963	194,556	120,826	3,360	4,047	9,610
Buncombe County	N.C.	23,384	1,384	16.9	7.1	35	1,311	112,218	6,568	72,822	32,828	105,563	100,703	62,652	1,625	3,235	4,402
Charlotte-Mecklenburg	N.C.	82,842	4,851	17.1	45.0	121	4,104	414,483	26,265	236,416	151,802	405,667	383,828	227,917	9,795	12,044	4,779
Cumberland County	N.C.	49,247	2,896	17.0	50.2	69	2,614	196,363	24,324	132,388	39,651	196,277	191,760	120,954	4,517	0	4,002
Durham County	N.C.	27,545	1,954	14.1	56.4	44	1,389	155,292	8,617	82,344	64,331	142,059	130,583	78,342	3,998	7,478	4,783
Forsyth County-Winston Salem	N.C.	38,609	2,783	13.9	39.4	57	2,103	194,051	11,422	113,651	68,978	191,294	185,045	115,505	2,940	3,309	4,863
Gaston County	N.C.	28,858	1,770	16.3	19.8	54	1,566	122,775	8,369	84,051	30,355	116,220	112,970	74,137	2,632	618	3,875
Guilford County	N.C.	54,451	3,519	15.5	40.3	92	3,110	134,701	6,006	76,304	52,391	127,496	122,344	73,312	3,743	1,409	4,709
New Hanover County Schools	N.C.	20,363	1,266	16.1	31.2	30	1,194	96,174	7,401	58,160	30,613	85,950	83,402	51,515	1,822	726	4,251
Robeson County	N.C.	23,414	1,389	16.9	76.5	41	1,205	102,531	18,423	68,389	15,719	98,947	96,625	60,388	1,874	448	4,174
Wake County	N.C.	73,263	4,769	15.4	31.0	94	3,740	458,342	15,630	195,076	247,636	327,487	313,059	190,617	3,455	10,973	4,465
Akron City	Ohio	33,495	1,997	16.8	44.4	63	1,767	193,668	15,383	79,549	98,736	176,967	175,257	101,806	1,631	79	5,200
Cincinnati City	Ohio	52,381	3,058	17.1	65.9	83	1,848	481,547	29,701	130,458	321,388	339,785	331,983	202,000	3,390	4,412	6,444
Cleveland City	Ohio	73,633	4,205	17.5	77.6	129	2,254	696,062	64,556	230,558	400,948	498,553	479,861	268,904	6,987	11,725	6,765
Columbus City	Ohio	63,877	4,096	15.6	53.9	144	2,331	432,326	38,604	145,545	248,177	414,247	398,718	213,814	7,385	8,144	6,182
Dayton City	Ohio	28,886	1,775	16.3	64.8	50	838	191,895	24,870	80,921	86,104	172,229	169,752	98,368	2,451	26	5,773
Toledo City	Ohio	39,238	2,287	17.2	47.0	61	1,640	244,221	22,521	113,742	107,958	245,861	240,584	125,453	4,831	446	6,079
Oklahoma City	Okla.	38,052	2,238	17.0	60.0	81	1,271	160,501	18,655	87,853	53,993	156,294	154,242	86,265	1,920	132	4,132
Tulsa	Okla.	41,341	2,458	16.8	43.0	80	1,697	175,902	14,914	86,245	74,743	181,497	168,572	91,044	11,215	1,710	4,057
Beaverton	Oreg.	27,488	1,250	22.0	15.7	40	1,615	143,485	3,728	29,842	109,915	152,021	138,281	84,802	13,171	569	5,091
Portland	Oreg.	54,073	2,810	19.2	30.4	101	2,813	374,192	26,812	113,461	233,919	376,211	363,060	204,134	3,426	9,725	6,604
Salem-Keizer	Oreg.	30,930	1,411	21.9	13.1	48	1,617	164,134	8,714	79,490	75,930	168,448	152,088	94,196	14,302	2,058	5,060
Philadelphia	Penn.	207,667	10,489	19.8	78.3	259	8,590	1,388,395	204,151	654,546	529,698	1,340,118	1,303,730	793,034	6,402	29,986	6,470
Pittsburgh City	Penn.	40,107	2,443	16.4	55.1	83	2,253	365,632	31,867	127,011	206,754	348,402	339,839	187,068	2,405	6,158	8,402
Providence City	R.I.	22,832	—	—	70.6	36	879	140,245	13,774	64,440	62,031	130,375	127,444	85,693	696	2,235	5,785
Aiken County	S.C.	24,802	1,359	18.3	34.6	35	1,382	104,527	8,257	55,523	40,747	97,786	94,085	57,498	2,136	1,565	3,790
Berkeley County	S.C.	28,181	1,503	18.7	34.8	37	1,475	112,039	13,265	64,095	34,679	106,953	102,475	56,200	2,517	1,961	3,611
Charleston County	S.C.	44,883	2,672	16.8	58.9	72	1,870	199,660	22,898	87,506	89,256	191,534	180,909	111,549	4,518	6,107	4,036
Greenville County	S.C.	53,280	3,192	16.7	28.0	92	2,817	233,155	15,315	106,410	111,430	223,937	213,535	127,600	5,258	5,144	4,055
Horry County	S.C.	24,746	1,551	16.0	31.0	36	1,441	122,805	11,870	39,134	71,801	116,022	108,991	65,745	1,284	5,747	4,383
Richland	S.C.	27,014	1,786	15.1	75.9	51	1,336	144,319	14,828	53,650	75,841	135,193	130,252	72,617	2,475	2,466	4,816
Chattanooga City	Tenn.	20,284	1,188	17.1	62.2	37	1,003	93,467	12,253	36,705	44,509	89,707	84,779	54,405	3,485	1,443	4,186
Hamilton County	Tenn.	23,891	1,371	17.4	5.3	40	1,252	87,689	4,974	40,691	42,024	87,660	84,371	57,208	1,523	1,766	3,495
Knox County	Tenn.	51,742	2,979	17.4	14.3	86	2,822	222,555	20,674	89,217	112,664	203,033	197,401	125,152	3,474	2,158	3,827
Memphis City	Tenn.	105,978	5,387	19.7	82.4	162	5,239	444,620	65,070	185,997	193,553	432,227	420,155	277,060	10,371	1,701	3,945
Nashville-Davidson County	Tenn.	72,483	4,439	16.3	44.0	119	2,926	312,339	24,414	114,123	173,802	304,214	292,085	194,065	4,971	3,714	4,199
Shelby County	Tenn.	41,994	2,174	19.3	19.5	41	2,183	133,577	6,019	67,450	60,108	130,670	122,787	84,689	4,169	2,528	2,976
Sumner County	Tenn.	20,424	1,105	18.5	7.7	33	1,285	70,191	3,856	36,032	30,303	67,029	63,693	43,003	808		3,122
Aldine ISD	Texas	43,539	2,687	16.2	75.3	43	1,530	224,028	15,614	120,889	87,525	185,032	154,041	94,098	26,671	4,320	3,608
Alief ISD	Texas	33,315	1,996	16.7	73.2	29	1,246	178,707	8,356	77,303	93,048	151,100	118,296	72,493	23,736	9,068	3,669
Amarillo ISD	Texas	28,864	1,740	16.6	37.5	49	1,211	134,123	11,760	68,406	53,957	108,947	102,421	61,474	3,232	3,294	3,586
Arlington ISD	Texas	48,667	2,737	17.8	33.9	57	2,258	196,290	9,978	41,308	145,004	197,290	150,813	94,773	33,372	13,105	3,140
Austin ISD	Texas	71,664	4,468	16.0	59.0	102	2,884	407,138	30,524	117,946	258,668	334,088	300,014	166,633	15,938	18,136	4,297
Beaumont ISD	Texas	20,258	1,263	16.0	70.2	34	714	113,458	12,235	36,457	64,766	90,126	87,551	48,466	2,323	252	4,295
Brownsville ISD	Texas	39,402	2,476	15.9	97.2	40	1,628	249,307	38,420	189,129	21,758	183,298	161,348	100,835	19,779	2,171	4,140
Clear Creek ISD	Texas	24,496	1,397	17.5	19.1	27	1,182	112,792	2,468	13,839	96,485	118,743	91,458	58,252	5,161	5,161	3,858
Conroe ISD	Texas	26,140	1,729	15.1	19.1	33	1,151	135,740	5,495	64,070	66,175	128,025	100,863		20,566	6,596	3,967
Corpus Christi	Texas	42,374	2,564	16.5	74.1	62	1,729	224,888	20,749	126,822	77,317	196,474	172,606	106,379	16,946	6,922	4,113
Cypress-Fairbanks ISD	Texas	48,252	2,925	16.5	29.8	47	2,072	227,156	4,901	72,802	149,453	234,706	204,288	103,387	16,794	13,624	4,408
Dallas ISD	Texas	142,652	8,530	16.7	86.3	196	4,707	757,844	99,140	119,296	539,408	619,032	580,915	338,310	22,025	16,092	4,158
Ector County ISD	Texas	28,188	1,645	17.1	52.5	41	1,071	134,951	12,231	55,199	67,521	105,834	101,060	56,965	3,491	1,283	3,593
El Paso ISD	Texas	64,141	3,877	16.5	80.2	79	3,027	336,098	41,227	202,108	92,763	303,798	262,653	158,697	33,770	7,375	4,088

Table 91.—Selected statistics for public school districts enrolling more than 20,000 pupils, by state: 1993-94—Continued

Name of district, by state	State	Enrollment, fall 1993	Classroom teachers, fall 1993	Pupils per teacher, fall 1993	Percent minority pupils, fall 1993	Number of schools, 1993-94	Number of 1992-93 graduates [2]	Revenue and expenditures,[3] 1992-93 (in thousands of dollars)									Current expenditure per pupil 1992-93 [4]
								Revenue receipts				Total expenditures	Current expenditures		Capital out-lay	Interest on school debt	
								Total	Federal	State	Local		Total	Instruction			
1	2	3	4	5	6	7	8	9	10	11	12	13	14	15	16	17	18
Fort Bend ISD	Texas	41,981	2,331	18.0	54.5	39	1,802	185,998	6,623	85,972	93,393	208,669	177,028	93,121	21,668	9,973	4,359
Fort Worth ISD	Texas	72,114	4,063	17.7	69.6	129	2,466	397,554	41,537	185,459	170,558	322,362	302,970	170,664	11,237	8,155	4,263
Garland ISD	Texas	41,134	2,283	18.0	35.7	58	1,851	182,869	8,703	82,993	91,173	159,576	136,828	81,222	13,417	9,331	3,384
Houston ISD	Texas	200,445	11,410	17.6	87.6	256	6,773	1,096,666	120,455	345,368	630,843	946,762	797,767	455,490	130,478	18,517	4,029
Humble ISD	Texas	21,306	1,309	16.3	17.4	24	1,142	104,802	3,149	44,887	56,766	118,687	77,371	45,520	34,876	6,440	3,726
Irving ISD	Texas	25,435	1,439	17.7	47.8	31	978	117,934	7,323	19,263	91,348	129,667	99,894	56,053	21,299	8,474	4,018
Katy ISD	Texas	22,537	1,276	17.7	19.0	24	1,102	104,225	2,919	30,793	70,513	101,261	83,168	49,195	10,667	7,426	3,840
Killeen ISD	Texas	26,793	1,547	17.3	56.2	37	841	122,227	19,461	85,579	17,187	105,444	87,394	51,153	15,846	2,204	3,554
Klein ISD	Texas	28,057	1,742	16.1	28.5	27	1,649	139,581	4,360	69,112	66,109	136,296	109,034	64,856	22,076	5,186	3,932
Laredo ISD	Texas	23,871	1,382	17.3	98.1	28	1,150	140,224	20,956	105,917	13,351	99,374	90,338	50,244	7,737	1,299	3,771
Lewisville ISD	Texas	24,804	1,525	16.3	15.1	32	1,095	107,157	3,674	39,073	64,410	109,767	78,919	48,655	22,479	8,369	3,412
Lubbock ISD	Texas	30,571	2,069	14.8	53.5	58	1,391	170,119	15,560	59,426	95,133	150,406	132,972	77,198	12,308	5,126	4,304
McAllen ISD	Texas	21,691	1,411	15.4	88.3	30	1,087	148,321	13,296	103,987	31,038	99,908	93,067	55,582	4,125	2,716	4,299
Mesquite ISD	Texas	28,185	1,484	19.0	23.6	36	1,183	123,919	5,485	64,615	53,819	99,754	89,143	52,065	1,289	9,322	3,264
Midland ISD	Texas	22,799	1,291	17.7	45.0	35	938	102,713	5,475	38,849	58,389	93,725	78,613	46,664	12,605	2,507	3,537
North East ISD	Texas	43,122	2,641	16.3	41.5	49	2,529	219,290	11,380	78,004	129,906	172,809	163,749	99,236	6,964	2,096	3,873
Northside ISD	Texas	54,992	3,515	15.6	58.2	76	3,010	286,594	11,686	149,071	119,837	239,061	204,247	127,090	20,253	14,561	3,785
Pasadena ISD	Texas	39,265	2,230	17.6	55.7	50	1,586	195,436	13,075	104,123	78,238	173,100	151,679	89,046	17,526	3,895	3,861
Plano ISD	Texas	34,956	2,120	16.5	18.6	44	2,068	180,226	4,417	18,507	157,302	179,357	141,553	87,572	26,038	11,766	4,277
Richardson ISD	Texas	33,495	2,050	16.3	35.2	50	1,992	168,928	5,932	20,380	142,616	152,342	137,451	82,382	8,686	6,205	4,141
Round Rock ISD	Texas	22,887	1,554	14.7	23.2	31	1,162	117,135	4,019	53,599	59,517	106,944	89,304	53,711	11,433	6,207	4,098
San Antonio ISD	Texas	59,544	3,646	16.3	94.1	107	2,063	381,675	56,897	234,935	89,843	302,533	291,702	172,586	8,638	2,193	4,873
Spring Branch ISD	Texas	27,663	1,784	15.5	55.8	36	395	166,326	12,157	22,710	131,459	148,905	135,282	71,075	7,212	6,411	4,937
Ysleta ISD	Texas	49,388	1,298	38.0	86.8	63	2,674	271,494	28,847	189,690	52,957	215,173	196,029	116,256	14,074	5,070	3,978
Alpine	Utah	41,601	1,594	26.1	4.1	47	2,220	133,434	7,606	86,204	39,624	129,152	120,708	71,237	4,568	3,876	2,994
Davis County	Utah	57,933	2,311	25.1	4.8	69	3,319	185,724	12,988	122,459	50,277	181,655	163,938	104,016	9,935	7,782	2,870
Granite	Utah	79,746	3,247	24.6	10.7	100	4,032	249,749	17,646	154,427	77,676	237,874	227,576	147,732	7,029	3,269	2,841
Jordan	Utah	70,256	2,808	25.0	5.4	69	3,749	237,583	10,758	139,246	87,579	221,297	210,427	125,947	8,839	2,031	3,057
Salt Lake City	Utah	26,077	1,157	22.5	28.2	40	1,057	116,239	12,284	37,031	66,924	111,315	102,083	56,970	9,232	0	3,930
Weber County	Utah	26,987	1,093	24.7	5.6	36	1,659	88,373	6,000	56,681	25,692	85,141	79,003	52,471	3,018	3,120	2,961
Chesapeake City	Va.	33,182	—	—	35.4	41	1,695	141,238	9,585	63,583	68,070	153,914	147,519	92,050	4,416	1,979	4,663
Chesterfield County	Va.	47,919	—	—	19.9	53	2,704	208,700	6,787	86,079	115,834	213,219	198,682	123,453	3,143	11,394	4,228
Fairfax County	Va.	135,413	—	—	32.1	198	8,814	854,601	26,262	109,565	718,774	868,404	830,487	467,767	12,664	25,253	6,224
Hampton City	Va.	22,991	—	—	54.0	34	1,272	99,362	9,687	45,341	44,334	105,255	103,145	65,737	1,951	159	4,521
Henrico County	Va.	34,952	—	—	33.4	54	2,106	172,516	6,708	53,334	112,474	180,567	170,942	104,272	4,495	5,130	4,985
Newport News City	Va.	31,894	—	—	54.5	37	1,465	140,532	13,436	64,680	62,416	149,798	144,881	89,210	2,068	2,849	4,808
Norfolk City	Va.	36,450	—	—	66.2	56	1,282	198,500	26,932	77,972	93,596	199,630	193,067	109,461	4,548	2,015	5,209
Prince William County	Va.	44,881	—	—	27.2	61	2,590	241,384	10,105	84,068	147,211	252,032	239,513	140,849	5,025	7,494	5,338
Richmond City	Va.	27,465	—	—	90.8	59	952	208,128	21,361	51,062	135,705	200,727	192,820	107,078	4,507	3,400	7,035
Virginia Beach City	Va.	74,880	—	—	28.8	80	3,680	312,751	25,861	140,694	146,196	339,620	313,479	202,478	17,993	8,148	4,234
Edmonds	Wash.	20,415	988	20.7	17.0	37	—	115,018	4,596	81,856	28,566	115,774	103,305	60,629	8,391	4,078	5,120
Kent	Wash.	23,817	1,153	20.7	18.0	36	—	129,703	4,805	87,889	37,009	126,416	111,992	67,450	7,694	6,730	4,827
Lake Washington	Wash.	23,380	1,097	21.3	13.0	40	—	150,199	3,350	100,461	46,388	136,358	118,155	72,478	8,101	10,102	4,934
Seattle	Wash.	45,159	2,303	19.6	58.0	108	—	309,544	31,506	180,016	98,022	303,017	285,342	156,684	17,610	65	6,416
Spokane	Wash.	31,128	1,601	19.4	12.2	65	—	167,918	11,511	122,798	33,609	168,417	160,978	98,156	3,674	3,765	5,156
Tacoma	Wash.	31,083	1,752	17.7	36.6	69	—	209,615	21,242	132,716	55,657	196,869	184,037	110,099	11,447	1,385	5,897
Kanawha County	W.Va.	33,644	2,080	16.2	10.1	88	2,203	174,558	13,209	102,162	59,187	169,106	166,125	95,828	2,981	0	4,883
Madison Metropolitan	Wis.	24,452	1,710	14.3	25.4	51	1,363	181,782	4,887	31,679	145,216	179,773	173,526	110,849	2,782	3,465	7,151
Milwaukee City	Wis.	95,259	4,936	19.3	73.0	150	3,036	730,107	61,978	366,716	301,413	655,441	648,147	397,020	7,294	0	6,873
Racine Unified	Wis.	22,260	1,379	16.1	34.3	37	1,087	137,804	6,190	66,487	65,127	139,518	135,687	86,988	1,268	2,563	5,961

[1] Data exclude teachers reported as working in school district offices rather than in schools.

[2] Includes all categories of high school completers such as GEDs.

[3] Expenditures by local school districts only. Excludes expenditures by local school districts by state education agencies for local school districts.

[4] Current expenditure per pupil based on fall enrollment collected by the Bureau of the Census, not the enrollment figure shown in column 3.

ISD=Independent school district.

—Data not available or not applicable.

NOTE.—Data on finances and per pupil expenditures prepared by the Bureau of the Census.

SOURCE: U.S. Department of Education, National Center for Education Statistics, Common Core of Data survey; and U.S. Department of Commerce, "Survey of Local Government Finances." (This table was prepared July 1995.)

Table 92.—Enrollment of the 130 largest public school districts: Fall 1993

Name of school district	State	Rank order [1]	Enrollment, fall 1993	Name of school district	State	Rank order [1]	Enrollment, fall 1993
1	2	3	4	1	2	3	4
New York City	N.Y.	1	1,005,521	Cincinnati City	Ohio	66	52,381
Los Angeles Unified	Calif.	2	639,129	Oakland Unified	Calif.	67	51,748
City of Chicago	Ill.	3	409,499	Knox County	Tenn.	68	51,742
Dade County	Fla.	4	308,465	Caddo Parish	La.	69	51,255
Philadelphia	Penn.	5	207,667	Fulton County	Ga.	70	50,190
Houston ISD	Texas	6	200,445	Sacramento City Unified	Calif.	71	49,997
Broward County	Fla.	7	189,862	Ysleta ISD	Texas	72	49,388
Hawaii Public Schools	Hawaii	8	180,529	Cumberland County	N.C.	73	49,247
Detroit Public Schools	Mich.	9	173,295	Arlington ISD	Texas	74	48,667
Clark County	Nev.	10	145,327	Santa Ana Unified	Calif.	75	48,407
Dallas ISD	Texas	11	142,652	Cypress-Fairbanks ISD	Texas	76	48,252
Fairfax County	Va.	12	135,413	Buffalo City	N.Y.	77	48,128
Hillsborough County	Fla.	13	135,104	Chesterfield County	Va.	78	47,919
San Diego City Unified	Calif.	14	127,258	San Juan Unified	Calif.	79	47,650
Palm Beach County	Fla.	15	122,145	Lee County	Fla.	80	47,390
Duval County	Fla.	16	119,785	Anchorage	Alaska	81	47,340
Prince George's County	Md.	17	115,918	Wichita Unified	Kans.	82	47,132
Orange County	Fla.	18	113,638	Newark	N.J.	83	46,835
Montgomery County	Md.	19	113,429	Indianapolis Public Schools	Ind.	84	46,656
Baltimore City	Md.	20	113,354	Seattle	Wash.	85	45,159
Memphis City	Tenn.	21	105,978	Charleston County	S.C.	86	44,883
Pinellas County	Fla.	22	100,135	Prince William County	Va.	87	44,881
Baltimore County	Md.	23	96,402	Escambia County	Fla.	88	44,641
Milwaukee City	Wis.	24	95,259	Minneapolis Special	Minn.	89	44,533
Jefferson County	Ky.	25	93,529	San Bernardino City Unified	Calif.	90	43,933
Albuquerque	N.M.	26	92,697	Washoe County	Nev.	91	43,715
Orleans Parish	La.	27	85,983	Omaha City	Neb.	92	43,609
Charlotte-Mecklenburg	N.C.	28	82,842	Aldine ISD	Texas	93	43,539
Jefferson County	Colo.	29	82,760	North East ISD	Texas	94	43,122
DeKalb County	Ga.	30	81,468	Birmingham City	Ala.	95	42,847
D.C. Public Schools	D.C.	31	80,678	Corpus Christi	Texas	96	42,374
Granite	Utah	32	79,746	Shelby County	Tenn.	97	41,994
Cobb County	Ga.	33	77,563	Fort Bend ISD	Texas	98	41,981
Long Beach Unified	Calif.	34	76,783	Garden Grove Unified	Calif.	99	41,664
Gwinnett County	Ga.	35	76,482	Alpine	Utah	100	41,601
Fresno Unified	Calif.	36	76,349	Tulsa	Okla.	101	41,341
Virginia Beach City	Va.	37	74,880	Saint Louis City	Mo.	102	41,213
Cleveland City	Ohio	38	73,633	Garland ISD	Texas	103	41,134
Wake County	N.C.	39	73,263	Jefferson County	Ala.	104	40,733
Nashville-Davidson County	Tenn.	40	72,483	Pittsburgh City	Penn.	105	40,107
Fort Worth ISD	Texas	41	72,114	Brownsville ISD	Texas	106	39,402
Austin ISD	Texas	42	71,664	Pasadena ISD	Texas	107	39,265
Jordan	Utah	43	70,256	Saint Paul Independent	Minn.	108	39,239
Polk County	Fla.	44	69,718	Toledo City	Ohio	109	39,238
Anne Arundel County	Md.	45	69,020	Forsyth County-Winston Salem	N.C.	110	38,609
Mesa Unified	Ariz.	46	67,639	Pasco County	Fla.	111	38,265
Mobile County	Ala.	47	66,580	Oklahoma City	Okla.	112	38,052
El Paso ISD	Texas	48	64,141	Clayton County	Ga.	113	37,961
Columbus City	Ohio	49	63,877	Anoka Junction	Minn.	114	37,777
Boston City	Mass.	50	63,738	Kansas City	Mo.	115	36,599
East Baton Rouge Parish	La.	51	63,179	Norfolk City	Va.	116	36,450
Denver	Colo.	52	62,673	Rochester City	N.Y.	117	35,568
Brevard County	Fla.	53	62,556	Richmond County	Ga.	118	35,422
San Francisco Unified	Calif.	54	61,631	Chatham County	Ga.	119	35,358
Tucson Unified	Ariz.	55	60,529	Montgomery County	Ala.	120	35,244
San Antonio ISD	Texas	56	59,544	Plano ISD	Texas	121	34,956
Atlanta	Ga.	57	59,244	Henrico County	Va.	122	34,952
Davis County	Utah	58	57,933	Harford County	Md.	123	34,775
Jefferson Parish	La.	59	57,270	Howard County	Md.	124	34,416
Northside ISD	Texas	60	54,992	Calcasieu Parish	La.	125	34,373
Guilford County	N.C.	61	54,451	Stockton City Unified	Calif.	126	34,337
Portland	Oreg.	62	54,073	Mt. Diablo Unified	Calif.	127	34,110
Volusia County	Fla.	63	53,972	Riverside Unified	Calif.	128	33,655
Greenville County	S.C.	64	53,280	Kanawha County	W.Va.	129	33,644
Seminole County	Fla.	65	52,688	Akron City	Ohio	130	33,495

[1] Public school districts ranked by size of enrollment in fall 1993.
ISD=Independent School District.

SOURCE: U.S. Department of Education, National Center for Education Statistics, Common Core of Data survey. (This table was prepared August 1995.)

Table 93.—Public elementary and secondary schools, by type of school: 1967–68 to 1993–94

Year	Total, all public schools	Regular schools											Other schools [7]
		Total [1]	Elementary schools				Secondary schools					Combined elementary/ secondary schools [6]	
			Total [2]	Middle schools [3]	One-teacher schools	Other elementary schools	Total [4]	Junior high [5]	3-year or 4-year high schools	5-year or 6-year high schools	Other high schools		
1	2	3	4	5	6	7	8	9	10	11	12	13	14
1967–68	—	94,197	67,186	—	4,146	63,040	23,318	7,437	10,751	4,650	480	3,693	—
1970–71	—	89,372	64,020	2,080	1,815	60,125	23,572	7,750	11,265	3,887	670	1,780	—
1972–73	—	88,864	62,942	2,308	1,475	59,159	23,919	7,878	11,550	3,962	529	2,003	—
1974–75	—	87,456	61,759	3,224	1,247	57,288	23,837	7,690	11,480	4,122	545	1,860	—
1975–76	88,597	87,034	61,704	3,916	1,166	56,622	23,792	7,521	11,572	4,113	586	1,538	1,563
1976–77	—	86,501	61,123	4,180	1,111	55,832	23,857	7,434	11,658	4,130	635	1,521	—
1978–79	—	84,816	60,312	5,879	1,056	53,377	22,834	6,282	11,410	4,429	713	1,670	—
1980–81	85,982	83,688	59,326	6,003	921	52,402	22,619	5,890	10,758	4,193	1,778	1,743	2,294
1982–83	84,740	82,039	58,051	6,875	798	50,378	22,383	5,948	11,678	4,067	690	1,605	2,701
1983–84	84,178	81,418	57,471	6,885	838	49,748	22,336	5,936	11,670	4,046	684	1,611	2,760
1984–85	84,007	81,147	57,231	6,893	825	49,513	22,320	5,916	11,671	4,021	712	1,596	2,860
1986–87	83,455	82,190	58,801	7,452	763	50,586	21,406	5,142	11,453	4,197	614	1,983	[8] 1,265
1987–88	83,248	82,248	59,311	7,641	729	50,941	20,758	4,900	11,279	4,048	531	2,179	[8] 1,000
1988–89	83,165	82,081	59,296	7,957	583	50,756	20,550	4,687	11,350	3,994	519	2,235	[8] 1,084
1989–90	83,425	82,396	59,757	8,272	630	50,855	20,359	4,512	11,492	3,812	543	2,280	[8] 1,029
1990–91	84,538	81,746	59,015	8,545	617	49,853	20,406	4,561	11,537	3,723	585	2,325	2,792
1991–92	84,578	81,859	59,258	8,829	569	49,860	20,120	4,298	11,528	3,699	595	2,481	2,719
1992–93	84,501	82,224	59,680	9,154	430	50,096	19,995	4,115	11,651	3,613	616	2,549	2,719
1993–94	85,393	82,785	60,052	9,573	442	50,037	20,059	3,970	11,858	3,595	636	2,674	2,608

[1] Excludes special education, alternative, and other schools not classified by grade span.
[2] Includes schools beginning with grade 6 or below and with no grade higher than 8.
[3] Includes schools with grade spans beginning with 4, 5, or 6 and ending with grade 6, 7, or 8.
[4] Includes schools with no grade lower than 7.
[5] Includes schools with grades 7 and 8 or grades 7 through 9.
[6] Includes schools beginning with grade 6 or lower and ending with grade 9 or above.

[7] Includes special education, alternative, and other schools not classified by grade span.
[8] Because of revision in data collection procedures, figures not comparable to data for other years.
—Data not available.

SOURCE: U.S. Department of Education, National Center for Education Statistics, *Statistics of State School Systems;* and Common Core of Data surveys. (This table was prepared June 1995.)

Table 94.—Public elementary and secondary schools, by type and size of school: 1993–94

Enrollment size of school	Number of schools, by type					Enrollment, by type of school [1]				
	Total [2]	Elementary [3]	Secondary [4]	Combined elementary/ secondary [5]	Other [2]	Total [2]	Elementary [3]	Secondary [4]	Combined elementary/ secondary [5]	Other [2]
1	2	3	4	5	6	7	8	9	10	11
Total	**85,393**	**60,052**	**20,059**	**2,674**	**2,608**	**43,278,061**	**28,095,832**	**13,932,581**	**1,117,571**	**132,077**
Percent [6]	100.00	100.00	100.00	100.00	100.00	100.00	100.00	100.00	100.00	100.00
Under 100	8.67	5.85	12.50	28.65	55.38	0.82	0.62	0.92	3.03	14.75
100 to 199	9.92	9.32	10.80	13.76	19.86	2.87	3.02	2.28	4.79	17.89
200 to 299	11.51	12.50	8.74	10.21	10.77	5.61	6.77	3.13	6.04	16.63
300 to 399	13.65	15.94	7.84	8.04	5.98	9.21	11.91	3.94	6.72	13.23
400 to 499	13.53	16.07	7.23	7.14	2.63	11.75	15.44	4.67	7.71	7.42
500 to 599	11.71	13.63	7.02	7.03	1.56	12.40	15.96	5.55	9.23	5.26
600 to 699	8.77	9.79	6.43	5.80	1.20	10.96	13.52	6.00	8.98	4.89
700 to 799	6.09	6.42	5.58	4.26	0.36	8.79	10.24	6.03	7.64	1.72
800 to 999	7.17	6.59	9.35	5.91	0.84	12.32	12.47	12.07	12.56	4.59
1,000 to 1,499	6.08	3.52	13.91	6.25	1.08	14.03	8.70	24.54	17.91	8.05
1,500 to 1,999	1.83	0.32	6.41	1.80	0.12	6.04	1.15	15.84	7.28	1.41
2,000 to 2,999	0.93	0.03	3.64	0.93	0.12	4.21	0.17	12.29	5.28	1.81
3,000 or more	0.14	0.00	0.54	0.22	0	0.99	0.04	2.75	2.83	0
Average enrollment [6] ...	518	468	695	418	146	518	468	695	418	158

[1] These enrollment data should be regarded as approximations only. Totals differ from those reported in other tables because this table represents data reported by schools rather than by states or school districts. Excludes data for schools not reporting enrollment.
[2] Includes special education, alternative, and other schools not classified by grade span.
[3] Includes schools beginning with grade 6 or below and with no grade higher than 8.

[4] Includes schools with no grade lower than 7.
[5] Includes schools beginning with grade 6 or below and ending with grade 9 or above.
[6] Data are for schools reporting their enrollment size.

NOTE.—Because of rounding, details may not add to totals.

SOURCE: U.S. Department of Education, National Center for Education Statistics, Common Core of Data survey. (This table was prepared June 1995.)

Table 95.—Public elementary and secondary schools, by type and state: 1989–90 to 1993–94

State or other area	Total, all schools,[1] 1989–90	Total, all schools,[1] 1990–91	Total, all schools,[1] 1991–92	Total, all schools,[1] 1992–93	Number of schools, 1993–94			Combined elementary/secondary schools[4]				Other[5]
					Total[1]	Elementary schools[2]	Secondary schools[3]	Total	Prekindergarten, kindergarten, or first grade to grade 12	Other schools ending with grade 12	Other combined schools	
1	2	3	4	5	6	7	8	9	10	11	12	13
United States	83,425	84,538	84,578	84,501	85,393	60,052	20,059	2,674	1,514	591	569	2,608
Alabama	1,292	1,297	1,291	1,294	1,294	849	289	156	124	9	23	0
Alaska	495	498	495	494	496	190	89	204	151	4	49	13
Arizona	1,026	1,049	1,091	1,118	1,133	829	261	13	7	4	2	30
Arkansas	1,097	1,098	1,098	1,090	1,070	646	416	8	6	0	2	0
California	7,433	7,913	7,927	7,665	7,734	5,588	1,882	173	111	43	19	91
Colorado	1,337	1,344	1,397	1,399	1,419	1,005	341	15	2	7	6	58
Connecticut	983	985	988	993	1,000	764	204	16	9	5	2	16
Delaware	170	173	175	176	177	118	41	18	14	2	2	0
District of Columbia	184	181	180	181	173	117	39	6	2	0	4	11
Florida	2,505	2,516	2,517	2,594	2,615	1,824	415	317	178	73	66	59
Georgia	1,732	1,734	1,728	1,724	1,755	1,364	319	72	15	41	16	0
Hawaii	234	235	238	238	241	184	47	10	7	1	2	0
Idaho	574	582	597	605	603	378	202	15	9	1	5	8
Illinois	4,225	4,239	4,238	4,185	4,195	3,095	890	27	22	5	0	183
Indiana	1,923	1,915	1,908	1,902	1,912	1,397	423	35	15	9	11	57
Iowa	1,607	1,588	1,577	1,560	1,556	1,075	451	22	6	16	0	8
Kansas	1,459	1,477	1,472	1,483	1,482	1,042	430	7	2	2	3	3
Kentucky	1,385	1,400	1,400	1,395	1,372	991	319	23	2	11	10	39
Louisiana	1,536	1,533	1,518	1,453	1,459	983	313	113	89	13	11	50
Maine	748	747	743	742	706	555	133	14	9	3	2	4
Maryland	1,217	1,220	1,228	1,263	1,271	1,016	211	18	9	4	5	26
Massachusetts	1,817	1,842	1,764	1,772	1,791	1,416	332	30	20	8	2	13
Michigan	3,314	3,313	3,360	3,340	3,356	2,304	688	67	33	19	15	297
Minnesota	1,564	1,590	1,635	1,622	2,083	1,126	624	84	20	31	33	249
Mississippi	954	972	973	978	1,009	565	230	79	66	10	3	135
Missouri	2,151	2,199	2,205	2,188	2,217	1,413	587	29	4	16	9	188
Montana	758	900	898	899	900	541	358	1	0	1	0	0
Nebraska	1,524	1,506	1,495	1,454	1,427	1,018	363	25	13	7	5	21
Nevada	331	354	375	383	407	303	90	8	3	5	0	6
New Hampshire	444	439	449	450	461	357	103	1	0	0	1	0
New Jersey	2,264	2,272	2,284	2,292	2,287	1,778	388	4	1	2	1	117
New Mexico	658	681	686	700	709	521	170	9	5	3	1	9
New York	3,996	4,010	4,009	4,032	4,082	2,926	911	153	91	40	22	92
North Carolina	1,952	1,955	1,950	1,948	1,958	1,504	400	32	18	5	9	22
North Dakota	679	663	651	642	640	369	223	9	4	2	3	39
Ohio	3,715	3,731	3,805	3,821	3,818	2,667	879	125	49	22	54	147
Oklahoma	1,859	1,880	1,817	1,829	1,820	1,200	613	1	0	0	1	6
Oregon	1,190	1,199	1,196	1,217	1,219	893	273	40	31	7	2	13
Pennsylvania	3,276	3,260	3,252	3,197	3,193	2,364	711	29	9	9	11	89
Rhode Island	294	309	314	313	311	242	61	3	2	0	1	5
South Carolina	1,103	1,097	1,102	1,104	1,094	788	248	11	5	4	2	47
South Dakota	799	802	673	733	777	455	299	0	0	0	0	23
Tennessee	1,535	1,543	1,519	1,514	1,523	1,108	323	52	38	5	9	40
Texas	5,937	5,991	6,052	6,184	6,324	4,408	1,510	406	227	88	91	0
Utah	718	714	712	714	718	469	215	14	5	5	4	20
Vermont	336	397	395	399	400	302	55	18	15	3	0	25
Virginia	1,779	1,811	1,810	1,816	1,828	1,352	344	15	4	6	5	117
Washington	1,858	1,936	1,956	2,017	2,030	1,256	505	99	43	27	29	170
West Virginia	1,035	1,015	987	949	907	633	196	24	9	0	15	54
Wisconsin	2,019	2,018	2,029	2,030	2,032	1,481	527	24	10	13	1	0
Wyoming	404	415	419	410	409	283	118	0	0	0	0	8
Outlying areas												
American Samoa	30	30	27	30	31	24	6	0	0	0	0	1
Guam	37	35	35	35	35	29	5	0	0	0	0	1
Northern Marianas	26	26	24	24	25	21	4	0	0	0	0	0
Puerto Rico	1,661	1,619	1,590	1,593	1,584	1,012	330	200	4	4	192	42
Virgin Islands	34	33	33	33	32	23	8	1	0	0	1	0

[1] Includes special education, alternative, and other schools not classified by grade span.
[2] Includes schools beginning with grade 6 or below and with no grade higher than 8.
[3] Includes schools with no grade lower than 7.
[4] Includes schools beginning with grade 6 or below and ending with grade 9 or above.
[5] Includes special education, alternative, and other schools not classified by grade span.

SOURCE: U.S. Department of Education, National Center for Education Statistics, Common Core of Data survey. (This table was prepared June 1995.)

Table 96.—Public elementary schools, by grade span and average school size, by state: 1993–94

State or other area	Total	Schools, by grade span						Average number of students per school[1]
		Prekindergarten, kindergarten, or 1st grade to grades 3 or 4	Prekindergarten, kindergarten, or 1st grade to grade 5	Prekindergarten, kindergarten, or 1st grade to grade 6	Prekindergarten, kindergarten, or 1st grade to grade 8	Grades 4, 5, or 6 to 6, 7, or 8	Other grade spans	
1	2	3	4	5	6	7	8	9
United States	**60,052**	**4,870**	**18,444**	**17,217**	**4,566**	**9,573**	**5,382**	**468**
Alabama	849	79	230	206	80	171	83	487
Alaska	190	5	26	108	19	15	17	357
Arizona	829	52	126	339	147	106	59	562
Arkansas	646	79	53	375	10	75	54	395
California	5,588	187	1,507	2,533	531	636	194	610
Colorado	1,005	30	454	254	11	187	69	424
Connecticut	764	80	275	165	43	133	68	449
Delaware	118	42	12	10	0	29	25	563
District of Columbia	117	7	3	95	4	5	3	432
Florida	1,824	29	1,118	231	27	336	83	761
Georgia	1,364	43	676	137	31	269	208	620
Hawaii	184	1	33	123	7	16	4	611
Idaho	378	34	80	163	21	46	34	370
Illinois	3,095	338	547	664	711	450	385	406
Indiana	1,397	58	540	469	41	214	75	437
Iowa	1,075	137	298	305	22	202	111	287
Kansas	1,042	71	300	276	142	157	96	289
Kentucky	991	51	395	231	123	169	22	425
Louisiana	983	118	283	209	64	202	107	513
Maine	555	85	91	86	113	91	89	257
Maryland	1,016	23	546	196	12	182	57	537
Massachusetts	1,416	211	438	287	71	232	177	422
Michigan	2,304	194	871	557	61	399	222	434
Minnesota	1,126	141	200	500	27	130	128	437
Mississippi	565	72	88	150	54	109	92	514
Missouri	1,413	87	378	476	124	215	133	381
Montana	541	34	71	242	77	48	69	186
Nebraska	1,018	61	96	508	163	58	132	166
Nevada	303	9	117	92	22	41	22	540
New Hampshire	357	59	68	88	47	63	32	357
New Jersey	1,778	260	424	319	267	304	204	436
New Mexico	521	23	188	158	4	92	56	409
New York	2,926	258	892	869	71	492	344	597
North Carolina	1,504	91	623	250	121	317	102	515
North Dakota	369	16	21	247	46	16	23	190
Ohio	2,667	328	721	838	91	440	249	423
Oklahoma	1,200	55	322	235	301	192	95	340
Oregon	893	51	304	265	99	134	40	369
Pennsylvania	2,364	296	840	637	61	385	145	469
Rhode Island	242	40	43	90	4	27	38	385
South Carolina	788	87	312	105	19	187	78	547
South Dakota	455	32	100	140	75	76	32	204
Tennessee	1,108	100	287	270	224	161	66	498
Texas	4,408	434	1,599	785	101	933	556	551
Utah	469	10	101	313	3	35	7	559
Vermont	302	31	20	118	60	23	50	213
Virginia	1,352	86	639	201	4	252	170	522
Washington	1,256	61	385	504	50	165	91	450
West Virginia	633	65	150	282	35	75	26	293
Wisconsin	1,481	107	486	390	120	241	137	371
Wyoming	283	22	67	126	5	40	23	215
Outlying areas								
American Samoa	24	0	1	0	20	1	2	457
Guam	29	0	21	0	0	6	2	798
Northern Marianas	21	0	0	10	0	0	11	244
Puerto Rico	1,012	103	37	753	4	40	75	294
Virgin Islands	23	0	0	23	0	0	0	549

[1] Average for schools reporting enrollment data.

NOTE.—Includes schools beginning with grade 6 or below and with no grade higher than 8. Excludes schools not reported by level, such as special education schools for the disabled.

SOURCE: U.S. Department of Education, National Center for Education Statistics, Common Core of Data survey. (This table was prepared June 1995.)

Table 97.—Public secondary schools, by grade span and average school size, by state: 1993–94

| State or other area | Total | Schools, by grade span | | | | | | | Average number of students per school [1] |
| | | Grades 7 to 8 and 7 to 9 | Grades 7 to 12 | Grades 8 to 12 | Grades 9 to 12 | Grades 10 to 12 | Other spans ending with grade 12 | Other grade spans | |
1	2	3	4	5	6	7	8	9	10
United States	20,059	3,970	3,175	420	10,902	956	102	534	695
Alabama	289	33	71	12	151	11	1	10	709
Alaska	89	16	27	2	40	0	1	3	445
Arizona	261	83	7	3	155	10	1	2	929
Arkansas	416	77	215	3	45	61	0	15	435
California	1,882	451	91	35	1,114	132	10	49	939
Colorado	341	57	63	2	192	18	3	6	573
Connecticut	204	37	7	3	148	3	1	5	700
Delaware	41	9	2	2	28	0	0	0	900
District of Columbia	39	19	0	0	18	1	1	0	659
Florida	415	31	41	15	254	23	10	41	1,154
Georgia	319	27	14	31	239	4	0	4	1,062
Hawaii	47	12	9	3	21	0	0	2	1,332
Idaho	202	51	38	7	78	19	0	9	467
Illinois	890	231	28	8	598	8	3	14	678
Indiana	423	72	115	1	223	8	1	3	792
Iowa	451	76	114	1	242	17	1	0	400
Kansas	430	67	62	2	279	13	3	4	357
Kentucky	319	43	43	2	206	6	1	18	668
Louisiana	313	63	50	10	176	8	1	5	766
Maine	133	26	11	1	90	4	0	1	492
Maryland	211	30	6	2	164	1	2	6	1,043
Massachusetts	332	49	50	15	210	6	0	2	775
Michigan	688	111	110	18	414	17	0	18	714
Minnesota	624	91	233	20	175	67	8	30	477
Mississippi	230	49	41	9	107	13	3	8	667
Missouri	587	79	218	13	239	19	2	17	518
Montana	358	183	1	0	171	2	0	1	175
Nebraska	363	43	225	0	81	12	0	2	316
Nevada	90	15	18	2	50	1	0	4	780
New Hampshire	103	26	0	0	75	2	0	0	558
New Jersey	388	72	41	11	248	8	2	6	899
New Mexico	170	38	28	2	86	9	0	7	629
New York	911	148	196	16	472	25	1	53	959
North Carolina	400	69	20	3	270	27	1	10	858
North Dakota	223	17	159	5	29	9	2	2	222
Ohio	879	182	146	31	484	19	2	15	699
Oklahoma	613	134	0	0	362	91	5	21	317
Oregon	273	63	22	9	166	9	0	4	657
Pennsylvania	711	111	183	15	335	50	6	11	836
Rhode Island	61	20	5	1	30	5	0	0	831
South Carolina	248	40	23	6	158	7	1	13	823
South Dakota	299	112	0	0	180	5	2	0	164
Tennessee	323	68	38	6	194	17	0	0	867
Texas	1,510	284	180	22	893	34	19	78	720
Utah	215	77	29	4	51	46	2	6	943
Vermont	55	6	23	1	25	0	0	0	568
Virginia	344	48	17	44	214	11	0	10	957
Washington	505	122	64	14	248	40	5	12	638
West Virginia	196	60	31	1	74	27	0	3	600
Wisconsin	527	100	57	6	338	22	1	3	540
Wyoming	118	42	3	1	62	9	0	1	337
Outlying areas									
American Samoa	6	0	0	0	6	0	0	0	575
Guam	5	0	0	0	5	0	0	0	1,550
Northern Marianas	4	1	2	0	1	0	0	0	764
Puerto Rico	330	155	28	2	5	124	1	15	683
Virgin Islands	8	5	0	0	2	1	0	0	1,215

[1] Average for schools reporting enrollment data.

NOTE.—Includes schools with no grade lower than 7. Excludes schools not reported by level, such as special education schools for the disabled.

SOURCE: U.S. Department of Education, National Center for Education Statistics, Common Core of Data survey. (This table was prepared June 1995.)

Table 98.—High school graduates compared with population 17 years of age: 1869–70 to 1994–95

[Numbers in thousands]

School year	Population 17 years old [1]	High school graduates					Graduates as a percent of 17-year-old population
		Total [2]	Sex		Control		
			Male	Female	Public [3]	Private [4]	
1	2	3	4	5	6	7	8
1869–70	815	16	7	9	—	—	2.0
1879–80	946	24	11	13	—	—	2.5
1889–90	1,259	44	19	25	22	22	3.5
1899–1900	1,489	95	38	57	62	33	6.4
1909–10	1,786	156	64	93	111	45	8.8
1919–20	1,855	311	124	188	231	80	16.8
1929–30	2,296	667	300	367	592	75	29.0
1939–40	2,403	1,221	579	643	1,143	78	50.8
1947–48	2,261	1,190	563	627	1,073	117	52.6
1949–50	2,034	1,200	571	629	1,063	136	59.0
1951–52	2,086	1,197	569	627	1,056	141	57.4
1953–54	2,135	1,276	613	664	1,129	147	59.8
1955–56	2,242	1,415	680	735	1,252	163	63.1
1956–57	2,272	1,434	690	744	1,270	164	63.1
1957–58	2,325	1,506	725	781	1,332	174	64.8
1958–59	2,458	1,627	784	843	1,435	192	66.2
1959–60	2,672	1,858	895	963	1,627	231	69.5
1960–61	2,892	1,964	955	1,009	1,725	239	67.9
1961–62	2,768	1,918	938	980	1,678	240	69.3
1962–63	2,740	1,943	956	987	1,710	233	70.9
1963–64	2,978	2,283	1,120	1,163	2,008	275	76.7
1964–65	3,684	2,658	1,311	1,347	2,360	298	72.1
1965–66	3,489	2,665	1,323	1,342	2,367	298	76.4
1966–67	3,500	2,672	1,328	1,344	2,374	298	76.3
1967–68	3,532	2,695	1,338	1,357	2,395	300	76.3
1968–69	3,659	2,822	1,399	1,423	2,522	300	77.1
1969–70	3,757	2,889	1,430	1,459	2,589	300	76.9
1970–71	3,872	2,938	1,454	1,484	2,638	300	75.9
1971–72	3,973	3,002	1,487	1,515	2,700	302	75.6
1972–73	4,049	3,035	1,500	1,535	2,729	306	75.0
1973–74	4,132	3,073	1,512	1,561	2,763	310	74.4
1974–75	4,256	3,133	1,542	1,591	2,823	310	73.6
1975–76	4,272	3,148	1,552	1,596	2,837	311	73.7
1976–77	4,272	3,152	1,548	1,604	2,837	315	73.8
1977–78	4,286	3,127	1,531	1,596	2,825	302	73.0
1978–79	4,327	3,101	1,517	1,584	2,801	300	71.7
1979–80	4,262	3,043	1,491	1,552	2,748	295	71.4
1980–81	4,212	3,020	1,483	1,537	2,725	295	71.7
1981–82	4,134	2,995	1,471	1,524	2,705	290	72.4
1982–83	3,962	2,888	1,437	1,451	2,598	290	72.9
1983–84	3,784	2,767	—	—	2,495	272	73.1
1984–85	3,699	2,677	—	—	2,414	263	72.4
1985–86	3,670	2,643	—	—	2,383	260	72.0
1986–87	3,754	2,694	—	—	2,429	265	71.8
1987–88	3,849	2,773	—	—	2,500	273	72.1
1988–89	3,842	2,727	—	—	2,459	268	71.0
1989–90	3,574	2,588	—	—	2,320	268	72.4
1990–91	3,417	2,503	—	—	2,235	268	73.2
1991–92	3,381	2,482	—	—	2,226	256	73.4
1992–93	3,430	2,490	—	—	2,233	257	72.6
1993–94 [5]	3,466	2,479	—	—	2,225	254	71.5
1994–95 [5]	3,477	2,553	—	—	2,300	253	73.4

[1] Derived from Current Population Reports, Series P-25. 17-year-old population adjusted to reflect October 17-year-old population.

[2] Includes graduates of public and private schools.

[3] Data for 1929–30 and preceding years are from Statistics of Public High Schools and exclude graduates of high schools which failed to report to the Office of Education.

[4] For most years, private school data have been estimated based on periodic private school surveys. For years through 1957–58, private includes data for subcollegiate departments of institutions of higher education and residential schools for exceptional children.

[5] Public high school graduates based on state estimates.

—Data not available.

NOTE.—Includes graduates of regular day school programs. Excludes graduates of other programs, when separately reported, and recipients of high school equivalency certificates. Some data have been revised from previously published figures. Because of rounding, details may not add to totals.

SOURCE: U.S. Department of Education, National Center for Education Statistics, Statistics of Public High Schools; Biennial Survey of Education in the United States; Statistics of State School Systems; Statistics of Nonpublic Elementary and Secondary Schools; Common Core of Data surveys; and U.S. Department of Commerce, Bureau of the Census, Current Population Reports, Series P-25. (This table was prepared May 1995.)

Table 99.—Public high school graduates, by state: 1969–70 to 1994–95

State	1969–70	1979–80	1980–81	1985–86	1989–90	1990–91	1991–92	1992–93	Estimated 1993–94	Estimated 1994–95	Percent change, 1989–90 to 1994–95
1	2	3	4	5	6	7	8	9	10	11	12
United States	2,588,639	2,747,678	2,725,285	2,382,616	[1]2,320,337	2,234,893	2,226,016	2,233,241	[1]2,224,846	[1]2,299,695	-0.9
Alabama	45,286	45,190	44,894	39,620	40,485	39,042	38,680	36,007	[2]34,449	37,091	-8.4
Alaska	3,297	5,223	5,343	5,464	5,386	5,458	5,535	5,535	[2]5,762	5,945	10.4
Arizona	22,040	28,633	28,416	27,533	32,103	31,282	31,264	31,747	[2]30,055	31,191	-2.8
Arkansas	26,068	29,052	29,577	26,227	26,475	25,668	25,845	25,655	[2]24,788	[3]25,778	-2.6
California	260,908	249,217	242,172	229,026	236,291	234,164	244,594	249,320	258,000	262,000	10.9
Colorado	30,312	36,804	35,897	32,621	32,967	31,293	31,059	31,839	[2]32,325	33,088	0.4
Connecticut	34,755	37,683	38,369	33,571	27,878	27,290	27,079	26,799	[2]26,799	26,800	-3.9
Delaware	6,985	7,582	7,349	5,791	5,550	5,223	5,325	5,492	[2]5,230	5,215	-6.0
District of Columbia [4]	4,980	4,959	4,848	3,875	3,626	3,369	3,385	3,136	[3]2,929	[3]3,120	-14.0
Florida	70,478	87,324	88,755	83,029	88,934	87,419	93,674	89,428	88,018	90,311	1.5
Georgia	56,859	61,621	62,963	59,082	56,605	60,088	57,742	57,602	[2]58,315	57,778	2.1
Hawaii	10,407	11,493	11,472	9,958	10,325	8,974	9,160	8,854	[2]9,870	9,949	-3.6
Idaho	12,296	13,187	12,679	12,059	11,971	11,961	12,734	12,974	13,281	13,900	16.1
Illinois	126,864	135,579	136,795	114,319	108,119	103,329	102,742	103,628	[2]102,126	105,829	-2.1
Indiana	69,984	73,143	73,381	59,817	60,012	57,892	56,630	57,559	55,138	58,969	-1.7
Iowa	44,063	43,445	42,635	34,279	31,796	28,593	29,224	30,677	30,247	31,671	-0.4
Kansas	33,394	30,890	29,397	25,587	25,367	24,414	24,129	24,720	[2]25,129	26,090	2.9
Kentucky	37,473	41,203	41,714	37,288	38,005	35,835	33,896	36,361	[3]34,077	[3]36,431	-4.1
Louisiana	43,641	46,297	46,199	39,965	36,053	33,489	32,247	33,682	[2]34,510	[3]36,020	-0.1
Maine	14,003	15,445	15,554	13,006	13,839	13,151	13,177	12,103	[2]12,351	12,996	-6.1
Maryland	46,462	54,270	54,050	46,700	41,566	39,014	39,720	39,523	[2]39,134	41,411	-0.4
Massachusetts	63,865	73,802	74,831	60,360	[5]55,941	50,216	50,317	48,321	47,358	48,259	-13.7
Michigan	121,000	124,316	124,372	101,042	93,807	88,234	87,756	85,302	83,600	88,500	-5.7
Minnesota	60,480	64,908	64,166	51,988	49,087	46,474	46,228	48,002	48,578	50,900	3.7
Mississippi	29,653	27,586	28,083	25,134	25,182	23,665	22,912	23,597	23,370	23,117	-8.2
Missouri	55,315	62,265	60,359	49,204	48,957	46,928	46,556	46,864	46,542	46,932	-4.1
Montana	11,520	12,135	11,634	9,761	9,370	9,013	9,046	9,389	9,600	9,970	6.4
Nebraska	21,280	22,410	21,411	17,845	17,664	16,500	17,057	17,569	[2]17,147	19,871	12.5
Nevada	5,449	8,473	9,069	8,784	9,477	9,370	8,811	9,042	[2]9,495	9,971	5.2
New Hampshire	8,516	11,722	11,552	10,648	10,766	10,059	10,329	10,065	9,404	9,274	-13.9
New Jersey	86,498	94,564	93,168	78,781	69,824	67,003	66,669	67,134	[2]66,125	65,838	-5.7
New Mexico	16,060	18,424	17,915	15,468	14,884	15,157	14,824	15,172	14,892	15,146	1.8
New York	190,000	204,064	198,465	162,165	143,318	133,562	134,573	132,963	133,200	135,500	-5.5
North Carolina	68,886	70,862	69,395	65,865	64,782	62,792	61,157	60,460	[2]57,495	59,705	-7.8
North Dakota	11,150	9,928	9,924	7,610	7,690	7,573	7,438	7,310	7,310	7,522	-2.2
Ohio	142,248	144,169	143,503	119,561	114,513	107,484	104,522	109,200	107,700	110,070	-3.9
Oklahoma	36,293	39,305	38,875	34,452	35,606	33,007	32,670	30,542	[3]28,949	[3]31,299	-12.1
Oregon	32,236	29,939	28,729	26,286	25,473	24,597	25,305	26,301	[2]26,524	27,500	8.0
Pennsylvania	151,014	146,458	144,645	122,871	110,527	104,770	103,881	103,715	103,060	107,230	-3.0
Rhode Island	10,146	10,864	10,719	8,908	7,825	7,744	7,859	7,640	[2]7,458	7,770	-0.7
South Carolina	34,940	38,697	38,347	34,500	32,483	32,999	30,698	31,297	32,400	33,900	4.4
South Dakota	11,757	10,689	10,385	7,870	7,650	7,127	7,261	7,952	[2]8,591	8,578	12.1
Tennessee	49,000	49,845	50,648	43,263	46,094	44,847	45,138	44,166	[2]44,166	45,388	-1.5
Texas	139,046	171,449	171,665	161,150	172,480	174,306	162,270	160,546	160,087	162,385	-5.9
Utah	18,395	20,035	19,886	19,774	21,196	22,219	23,513	24,197	[2]27,706	29,177	37.7
Vermont	6,095	6,733	6,424	5,794	6,127	5,212	5,231	5,215	[3]5,094	[3]5,676	-7.4
Virginia	58,562	66,621	67,126	63,113	60,605	58,441	57,338	56,948	[3]54,054	[3]58,526	-3.4
Washington	50,425	50,402	50,046	45,805	45,941	42,514	44,381	45,262	47,883	49,559	7.9
West Virginia	26,139	23,369	23,580	21,870	21,854	21,064	20,054	20,228	[2]20,336	20,800	-4.8
Wisconsin	66,753	69,332	67,743	58,340	52,038	49,340	48,563	50,027	[2]48,371	53,495	2.8
Wyoming	5,363	6,072	6,161	5,587	5,823	5,728	5,818	6,174	[3]5,818	[3]6,254	7.4
Outlying areas											
American Samoa	[6]367	—	—	608	703	597	680	712	[2]739	[3]782	11.2
Guam	972	—	—	840	1,033	1,014	1,018	912	985	1,073	3.9
Northern Marianas	—	—	—	—	227	273	264	245	[3]232	[3]252	11.0
Puerto Rico	24,917	—	—	31,597	29,049	29,329	29,396	29,064	[2]27,730	27,253	-6.2
Virgin Islands	[6]432	—	—	1,044	1,260	981	916	927	[2]886	900	-28.6

[1] National total includes estimates for nonreporting states.

[2] Actual count.

[3] Data estimated by the National Center for Education Statistics.

[4] Beginning in 1985–86, graduates from adult programs are excluded.

[5] Data from *Projections of Education Statistics to 2002* published by the National Center for Education Statistics (NCES).

[6] Data are for 1970–71.

—Data not reported.

NOTE.—Data include graduates of regular day school programs, but exclude graduates of other programs and persons receiving high school equivalency certificates. They also exclude graduates of subcollegiate departments of institutions of higher education, federal schools for American Indians and on federal installations, and residential schools for disabled children. Some data have been revised from previously published figures. All 1993–94 and 1994–95 data are state estimates unless otherwise indicated.

SOURCE: U.S. Department of Education, National Center for Education Statistics, Common Core of Data surveys. (This table was prepared May 1995.)

Table 100.—General Educational Development (GED) credentials issued, and number and age of test takers: United States and outlying areas, 1971 to 1994

Year	Number of credentials issued, in thousands [1]	Number completing test battery, in thousands [2]	Number of test takers, in thousands [3]	Percentage distribution of test takers, by age				
				19 years old or less	20- to 24-year-olds	25- to 29-year-olds	30- to 34-year-olds	35 years old or over
1	2	3	4	5	6	7	8	9
1971	227	—	377	—	—	—	—	—
1972	245	—	419	—	—	—	—	—
1973	249	—	423	—	—	—	—	—
1974	295	412	540	35	27	13	9	17
1975	342	507	652	33	26	14	9	18
1976	337	507	656	31	28	14	10	17
1977	331	488	680	40	24	13	9	14
1978	381	467	641	31	27	13	10	19
1979	435	583	744	35	27	13	8	16
1980	488	708	779	37	27	13	8	15
1981	500	701	770	37	27	13	8	15
1982	494	692	756	37	28	13	8	15
1983	477	678	740	34	29	14	9	15
1984	437	613	676	32	28	15	9	16
1985	427	622	685	33	26	15	10	16
1986	439	648	713	33	26	15	10	16
1987	458	662	729	33	24	15	10	18
1988	421	617	701	36	23	14	10	17
1989	364	554	645	36	24	13	10	16
1990	419	628	727	35	25	14	10	17
1991	471	672	770	33	27	14	10	17
1992	465	653	754	32	28	13	11	16
1993	476	652	757	33	27	14	11	16
1994	498	682	788	35	26	13	10	16

[1] Number of people receiving high school equivalency credentials based on the GED tests.

[2] Number of people completing the entire GED battery of five tests.

[3] Number of people taking the GED tests (one or more subtests).

—Data not available.

NOTE.—Because of rounding, percentages may not add to 100.

SOURCE: American Council on Education, General Educational Development Testing Service. (This table was prepared June 1995.)

Table 101.—Percent of high school dropouts among persons 16 to 24 years old, [1] by sex and race/ethnicity: October 1967 to October 1994

Year	Total				Men				Women			
	All races	White, non-Hispanic	Black, non-Hispanic	Hispanic origin	All races	White, non-Hispanic	Black, non-Hispanic	Hispanic origin	All races	White, non-Hispanic	Black, non-Hispanic	Hispanic origin
1	2	3	4	5	6	7	8	9	10	11	12	13
1967 [2]	17.0	15.4	28.6	—	16.5	14.7	30.6	—	17.3	16.1	26.9	—
1968 [2]	16.2	14.7	27.4	—	15.8	14.4	27.1	—	16.5	15.0	27.6	—
1969 [2]	15.2	13.6	26.7	—	14.3	12.6	26.9	—	16.0	14.6	26.7	—
1970 [2]	15.0	13.2	27.9	—	14.2	12.2	29.4	—	15.7	14.1	26.6	—
1971 [2]	14.7	13.4	23.7	—	14.2	12.6	25.5	—	15.2	14.2	22.1	—
1972	14.6	12.3	21.3	34.3	14.1	11.7	22.3	33.7	15.1	12.8	20.5	34.9
1973	14.1	11.6	22.2	33.5	13.7	11.5	21.5	30.4	14.5	11.8	22.8	36.4
1974	14.3	11.9	21.2	33.0	14.2	12.0	20.1	33.8	14.4	11.8	22.1	32.2
1975	13.9	11.4	22.9	29.2	13.3	11.0	23.0	26.7	14.5	11.8	22.9	31.6
1976	14.1	12.0	20.5	31.4	14.1	12.1	21.2	30.3	14.2	11.8	19.9	32.3
1977	14.1	11.9	19.8	33.0	14.5	12.6	19.5	31.6	13.8	11.2	20.0	34.3
1978	14.2	11.9	20.2	33.3	14.6	12.2	22.5	33.6	13.9	11.6	18.3	33.1
1979	14.6	12.0	21.1	33.8	15.0	12.6	22.4	33.0	14.2	11.5	20.0	34.5
1980	14.1	11.4	19.1	35.2	15.1	12.3	20.8	37.2	13.1	10.5	17.7	33.2
1981	13.9	11.4	18.4	33.2	15.1	12.5	19.9	36.0	12.8	10.2	17.1	30.4
1982	13.9	11.4	18.4	31.7	14.5	12.1	21.2	30.5	13.3	10.9	15.9	32.8
1983	13.7	11.2	18.0	31.6	14.9	12.2	19.9	34.3	12.5	10.1	16.2	29.1
1984	13.1	11.0	15.5	29.8	14.0	12.0	16.8	30.6	12.3	10.1	14.3	29.0
1985	12.6	10.4	15.2	27.6	13.4	11.1	16.1	29.9	11.8	9.8	14.3	25.2
1986	12.2	9.7	14.2	30.1	13.1	10.3	15.0	32.8	11.4	9.1	13.5	27.2
1987	12.7	10.4	14.1	28.6	13.2	10.8	15.0	29.1	12.1	10.0	13.3	28.1
1988	12.9	9.6	14.5	35.8	13.5	10.4	15.0	36.0	12.2	8.9	14.1	35.4
1989	12.6	9.4	13.9	33.0	13.6	10.3	14.9	34.4	11.7	8.5	13.0	31.6
1990	12.1	9.0	13.2	32.4	12.3	9.3	11.9	34.3	11.8	8.7	14.4	30.3
1991	12.5	8.9	13.6	35.3	13.0	8.9	13.5	39.2	11.9	8.9	13.7	31.1
1992 [3]	11.0	7.7	13.7	29.4	11.3	8.0	12.5	32.1	10.7	7.5	14.8	26.6
1993 [3]	11.0	7.9	13.6	27.5	11.2	8.2	12.6	28.1	10.9	7.7	14.4	26.9
1994 [3]	10.5	7.7	12.6	30.0	12.3	8.0	14.1	31.6	8.1	7.5	11.3	28.1

[1] "Status" dropouts.

[2] White and black include persons of Hispanic origin.

[3] Because of changes in data collection procedures, data may not be comparable with figures for earlier years.

—Data not available.

NOTE.—"Status" dropouts are persons who are not enrolled in school and who are not high school graduates. People who have received GED credentials are counted as graduates. Data are based upon sample surveys of the civilian noninstitutional population.

SOURCE: U.S. Department of Commerce, Bureau of the Census, Current Population Survey, unpublished tabulations; and U.S. Department of Education, National Center for Education Statistics, Dropout Rates in the United States. (This table was prepared May 1995.)

Table 102.—Percent of high school dropouts among persons 14 to 34 years old,[1] by age, sex, and race/ethnicity: October 1970 to October 1994

Year, race/ethnicity, and sex	Total, 14 to 34 years	14 and 15 years	16 and 17 years	18 and 19 years	20 and 21 years	22 to 24 years	25 to 29 years	30 to 34 years
1	2	3	4	5	6	7	8	9
October 1970								
All races	17.0	1.8	8.0	16.2	16.6	18.7	22.5	26.5
Male	16.2	1.7	7.1	16.0	16.1	17.9	21.4	26.2
Female	17.7	1.9	8.9	16.3	16.9	19.4	23.6	26.8
White[2]	15.2	1.7	7.3	14.1	14.6	16.3	19.9	24.6
Male	14.4	1.7	6.3	13.3	14.1	15.3	19.0	24.2
Female	16.0	1.8	8.4	14.8	15.1	17.2	20.7	24.9
Black[2]	30.0	2.4	12.8	31.2	29.6	37.8	44.4	43.5
Male	30.4	2.0	13.3	36.4	29.6	39.5	43.1	45.9
Female	29.5	2.8	12.4	26.6	29.6	36.4	45.6	41.5
October 1980								
All races	13.0	1.7	8.9	15.7	16.0	15.2	13.9	14.6
Male	13.2	1.3	8.9	16.9	17.8	16.4	13.8	14.0
Female	12.8	2.2	8.8	14.7	14.3	14.0	14.0	15.2
White, non-Hispanic	10.2	1.2	8.6	12.7	12.1	11.8	10.4	11.0
Male	10.5	1.0	8.5	13.6	13.5	13.2	10.6	10.7
Female	9.9	1.4	8.6	11.9	10.9	10.4	10.3	11.3
Black, non-Hispanic	18.6	2.0	7.0	21.0	24.6	23.6	22.4	23.1
Male	18.9	1.6	7.2	22.2	30.8	24.6	22.2	21.9
Female	18.4	2.5	6.8	19.8	19.6	22.8	22.6	24.0
Hispanic origin	35.2	5.7	16.5	39.0	41.6	40.6	40.9	45.4
Male	35.6	3.3	18.1	43.1	41.4	42.9	40.1	43.9
Female	34.8	7.9	15.0	34.6	41.9	38.6	41.7	47.0
October 1990								
All races	11.9	0.9	6.3	14.2	12.8	13.8	13.9	12.9
Male	12.2	0.8	6.6	14.6	13.2	14.0	14.5	13.3
Female	11.6	1.0	6.1	13.8	12.4	13.6	13.4	12.5
White, non-Hispanic	8.3	0.8	5.4	11.1	9.4	9.5	9.2	8.7
Male	8.8	0.7	5.9	11.4	9.6	9.8	9.8	9.4
Female	7.8	1.0	5.0	10.8	9.1	9.1	8.5	8.0
Black, non-Hispanic	14.4	0.7	6.9	16.6	15.6	13.6	19.3	16.7
Male	13.4	0.3	6.3	15.5	12.4	13.2	18.9	16.4
Female	15.1	1.0	7.5	17.6	18.6	13.9	19.6	16.9
Hispanic origin	34.3	1.1	12.9	34.2	31.6	42.8	41.7	42.4
Male	34.8	0.9	13.1	39.4	37.9	41.4	42.6	41.4
Female	33.8	1.3	12.5	29.4	25.0	44.4	40.7	43.5
October 1993[3]								
All races	10.6	1.1	4.8	11.8	13.4	12.9	12.1	11.8
Male	11.1	1.0	4.0	12.1	13.9	13.5	13.2	12.7
Female	10.1	1.2	5.7	11.5	12.9	12.3	11.1	10.8
White, non-Hispanic	7.3	0.9	3.9	9.5	9.8	8.4	8.2	7.5
Male	7.8	0.7	3.1	10.1	9.7	9.4	8.7	8.5
Female	6.8	1.1	4.7	8.7	9.9	7.4	7.6	6.6
Black, non-Hispanic	12.5	1.2	4.5	12.8	19.0	17.0	13.3	14.8
Male	12.1	1.0	3.5	10.5	22.8	14.7	15.0	13.7
Female	12.9	1.4	5.5	15.2	15.8	19.1	11.9	15.7
Hispanic origin	30.7	2.4	9.9	28.3	29.0	37.8	38.5	38.9
Male	32.0	3.1	8.4	32.2	28.9	39.8	40.8	39.3
Female	29.3	1.8	11.8	25.0	29.0	35.8	35.8	38.5
October 1994[3]								
All races	11.2	1.2	5.0	13.4	13.9	12.9	12.8	13.0
Male	10.3	1.3	4.7	12.4	12.6	12.0	11.7	11.8
Female	12.2	1.2	5.2	14.3	15.3	13.8	14.0	14.3
White, non-Hispanic	7.5	0.8	4.1	9.9	9.0	8.0	8.3	8.6
Male	8.2	0.6	4.0	10.5	9.7	8.1	9.5	9.8
Female	6.8	1.1	4.2	9.3	8.4	7.9	7.1	7.4
Black, non-Hispanic	12.3	0.8	4.3	19.8	15.6	12.4	15.0	14.5
Male	13.5	0.3	4.7	23.6	17.4	12.8	17.0	15.9
Female	11.3	1.4	3.9	16.2	13.9	12.1	13.5	13.3
Hispanic origin	31.6	3.9	11.1	25.6	36.7	38.8	37.2	39.2
Male	30.2	2.4	9.0	25.2	34.6	37.5	36.5	38.1
Female	32.8	5.4	13.0	26.0	38.3	39.9	37.8	40.2

[1] "Status" dropouts.
[2] Includes persons of Hispanic origin.
[3] Because of changes in data collection procedures, data may not be comparable with figures for earlier years.

NOTE.—"Status" dropouts are persons who are not enrolled in school and who are not high school graduates. People who have received GED credentials are counted as graduates. Data are based upon sample surveys of the civilian noninstitutional population.

SOURCE: U.S. Department of Commerce, Bureau of the Census, Current Population Survey, unpublished data. (This table was prepared May 1995.)

Table 103.—Students with disabilities exiting the educational system, by age, type of disability, and basis of exit: United States and outlying areas, 1991–92

Student characteristics	Total exiting the system		Graduated with diploma		Graduated through certificate		Reached maximum age [1]		Dropped out [2]		Other reasons for exit [3]	
	Number	Percent	Number	Percent	Number	Percent	Number	Percent	Number	Percent	Number	Percent
1	2	3	4	5	6	7	8	9	10	11	12	13
Age group												
14 to 21 (and over)	229,368	100.0	100,742	43.9	30,839	13.4	4,337	1.9	51,489	22.4	41,961	18.3
14	11,403	100.0	138	1.2	223	2.0	8	0.1	3,460	30.3	7,574	66.4
15	12,934	100.0	171	1.3	158	1.2	16	0.1	4,768	36.9	7,821	60.5
16	20,634	100.0	505	2.4	217	1.1	44	0.2	11,479	55.6	8,389	40.7
17	36,665	100.0	14,356	39.2	1,929	5.3	70	0.2	12,678	34.6	7,632	20.8
18	69,081	100.0	45,063	65.2	7,263	10.5	115	0.2	11,060	16.0	5,580	8.1
19	45,079	100.0	29,325	65.1	7,593	16.8	68	0.2	5,461	12.1	2,632	5.8
20	18,131	100.0	7,444	41.1	7,190	39.7	588	3.2	1,777	9.8	1,132	6.2
21	10,991	100.0	2,816	25.6	5,107	46.5	1,866	17.0	649	5.9	553	5.0
Over 21	4,450	100.0	924	20.8	1,159	26.0	1,562	35.1	157	3.5	648	14.6
Type of disability												
All disabilities, 14 to 21 and over	229,368	100.0	100,742	43.9	30,839	13.4	4,337	1.9	51,489	22.4	41,961	18.3
Specific learning disabilities ..	132,497	100.0	65,851	49.7	14,318	10.8	662	0.5	28,257	21.3	23,409	17.7
Mental retardation	38,993	100.0	14,088	36.1	10,797	27.7	2,359	6.0	7,650	19.6	4,099	10.5
Serious emotional disturbance	34,001	100.0	9,557	28.1	2,217	6.5	338	1.0	11,894	35.0	9,995	29.4
Speech or language impairments	8,108	100.0	3,562	43.9	596	7.4	87	1.1	1,633	20.1	2,230	27.5
Multiple disabilities	4,028	100.0	1,560	38.7	977	24.3	529	13.1	546	13.6	416	10.3
Other health impairments	3,642	100.0	1,771	48.6	614	16.9	67	1.8	606	16.6	584	16.0
Hearing impairments	3,403	100.0	1,900	55.8	587	17.2	69	2.0	444	13.0	403	11.8
Orthopedic impairments	2,749	100.0	1,379	50.2	439	16.0	123	4.5	252	9.2	556	20.2
Visual impairments	1,449	100.0	879	60.7	172	11.9	55	3.8	166	11.5	177	12.2
Autism	291	100.0	82	28.2	75	25.8	29	10.0	27	9.3	78	26.8
Deaf-blindness	143	100.0	72	50.3	42	29.4	15	10.5	6	4.2	8	5.6
Traumatic brain injury	64	100.0	41	64.1	5	7.8	4	6.3	8	12.5	6	9.4

[1] Upper age limits for service eligibility vary by state.

[2] These figures reflect an estimate of those who were actually known to have dropped out and do not include youth who simply stopped coming to school or whose status was unknown.

[3] Includes students who died or no longer received special education services, but whose exit reason is unknown.

NOTE.—It can be assumed that a substantial proportion of the "Other" category includes students who are no longer in school and have neither graduated nor reached the maximum age. Therefore, the overall dropout figure probably exceeds 23 percent.

SOURCE: U.S. Department of Education, Office of Special Education and Rehabilitative Services, Sixteenth Annual Report to Congress on the Implementation of The Individuals with Disabilities Education Act, 1994. (This table was prepared May 1995.)

Table 104.—Employment status, wages earned, and living arrangements of special education students out of high school more than 1 year: 1987 [1]

Type of disability	Percent of youth working for pay		Average hourly wage earned	Percent earning		Percent living	
	Full-time	Part-time		Less than $3.00	More than $5.00	Independently [2]	With parents
1	2	3	4	5	6	7	8
All conditions	**29.2**	**17.2**	**$4.35**	**11.9**	**21.0**	**17.3**	**68.9**
Learning disabled	37.9	19.3	4.63	7.6	25.0	22.0	66.6
Speech impaired	28.8	21.2	4.09	13.9	26.5	13.2	73.0
Mentally retarded	19.8	11.6	3.68	24.7	11.5	9.2	75.7
Emotionally disturbed	18.5	21.5	3.94	16.3	12.4	15.1	65.9
Hard of hearing	22.9	22.6	4.08	6.5	26.2	16.6	77.8
Deaf	23.6	14.7	4.08	3.4	6.6	20.2	71.6
Orthopedically impaired	1.3	12.6	(3)	(3)	(3)	11.8	76.8
Other health impaired	13.9	14.9	(3)	(3)	(3)	15.8	70.8
Visually impaired	10.0	14.3	3.12	29.3	10.6	26.0	64.4
Multiple disabilities	1.3	4.4	(3)	(3)	(3)	3.1	50.2
Deaf-blind	0.0	9.5	(3)	(3)	(3)	(3)	(3)

[1] Data based on students who completed, reached maximum age for services, or dropped out of high school during the 1985–86 school year.

[2] Living independently includes living alone, with a spouse or roommate, in military housing, or in a college dormitory.

[3] Too few cases to report.

SOURCE: U.S. Department of Education, Office of Special Education and Rehabilitative Services, The Eleventh Annual Report to Congress on the Implementation of the Education of the Handicapped Act, 1989. (This table was prepared December 1988.)

Table 105.—Average student proficiency in reading, by age and selected characteristics of students: 1971 to 1992

Selected characteristics of students	9-year-olds						13-year-olds						17-year-olds[1]					
	1971	1980	1984	1988	1990	1992	1971	1980	1984	1988	1990	1992	1971	1980	1984	1988	1990	1992
1	2	3	4	5	6	7	8	9	10	11	12	13	14	15	16	17	18	19
Total	207.6	215.0	210.9	211.8	209.2	210.5	255.2	258.5	257.1	257.5	256.8	259.8	285.2	285.5	288.8	290.1	290.2	289.7
Sex																		
Male	201.2	210.0	207.5	207.5	204.0	205.9	249.6	254.3	252.6	251.8	250.5	254.2	278.9	281.8	283.8	286.0	284.0	284.2
Female	213.9	220.1	214.2	216.3	214.5	215.4	260.8	262.6	261.7	263.0	263.1	265.3	291.3	289.2	293.9	293.8	296.5	295.7
Race/ethnicity																		
White	214.0	221.3	218.2	217.7	217.0	217.9	260.9	264.4	262.6	261.3	262.3	266.4	291.4	292.8	295.2	294.7	296.6	297.4
Black	170.1	189.3	185.7	188.5	181.8	184.5	222.4	232.8	236.3	242.9	241.5	237.6	238.7	243.1	264.3	274.4	267.3	260.6
Hispanic	(2)	190.2	187.2	193.7	189.4	191.7	(2)	237.2	239.6	240.1	237.8	239.2	(2)	261.4	268.1	270.8	274.8	271.2
Parental education																		
Not high school graduate	188.6	194.3	195.1	192.5	192.6	194.9	238.4	238.5	240.0	246.5	240.8	239.2	261.3	262.1	269.4	267.4	269.7	270.8
Graduated high school	207.8	213.0	208.9	210.8	209.1	207.4	255.5	253.5	253.4	252.7	251.4	252.1	283.0	277.5	281.2	282.0	282.9	280.5
Post high school	223.9	226.0	222.9	220.0	217.7	219.5	270.2	270.9	267.6	265.3	266.9	269.9	302.2	298.9	301.2	299.5	299.9	298.6
Control of school																		
Public	—	213.5	209.4	210.2	207.5	208.6	—	256.9	255.2	256.1	255.0	257.2	—	284.4	287.7	288.7	288.6	287.8
Private	—	227.0	222.8	223.4	228.3	224.7	—	270.6	271.2	268.3	269.7	276.3	—	298.4	303.0	299.6	311.0	309.6
Type of community																		
Advantaged urban	229.8	232.5	230.8	222.4	227.1	233.6	272.9	276.8	274.5	266.3	270.0	280.8	305.9	300.8	302.2	301.0	299.9	302.6
Disadvantaged urban	179.2	187.6	191.5	192.0	186.1	183.5	234.3	241.6	238.9	239.0	241.0	230.9	259.7	258.1	265.7	275.0	273.3	266.7
Extreme rural	200.2	211.8	201.2	213.7	209.4	206.5	247.4	254.8	254.9	262.4	251.2	257.2	276.8	279.0	282.7	286.6	289.9	285.3
Other	207.8	214.5	211.3	211.3	209.8	211.6	255.4	257.9	257.1	257.3	257.5	261.2	285.2	286.6	289.6	288.3	290.9	292.6
Region																		
Northeast	213.0	221.1	215.7	215.2	217.4	217.6	261.1	260.0	260.4	258.6	258.9	264.6	291.3	285.9	292.2	294.8	295.7	297.3
Southeast	193.9	210.3	204.3	207.2	197.4	199.3	244.7	252.6	256.4	257.6	255.5	253.8	270.5	280.1	284.7	285.5	285.1	278.4
Central	214.9	216.7	215.3	218.2	212.7	215.8	260.1	264.5	258.8	255.9	257.4	263.5	290.7	287.4	290.0	291.2	293.5	293.8
West	205.0	212.8	207.8	207.9	209.6	209.3	253.6	256.4	253.8	257.5	255.6	257.5	283.7	287.3	288.4	289.0	286.8	290.4

1 All participants of this age were in school.

2 Test scores of Hispanics were not tabulated separately.

— Data not available.

NOTE.—These test scores are from the National Assessment of Educational Progress (NAEP). The NAEP scores have been evaluated at certain performance levels. A score of 300 implies an ability to find, understand, summarize, and explain relatively complicated literary and informational material. A score of 250 implies an ability to search for specific information, interrelate ideas, and make generalizations about literature, science, and social studies materials.

A score of 200 implies an ability to understand, combine ideas, and make inferences based on short uncomplicated passages about specific or sequentially related information. A score of 150 implies an ability to follow brief written directions and carry out simple, discrete reading tasks. Scale ranges from 0 to 500.

SOURCE: U.S. Department of Education, National Center for Education Statistics, National Assessment of Educational Progress, The Reading Report Card, 1971–88 and NAEP 1992 Trends in Academic Progress, by Educational Testing Service. (This table was prepared April 1994.)

Table 106.—Student proficiency in reading, by percentile and age: 1971 to 1992

Percentile	9-year-olds						13-year-olds						17-year-olds[1]					
	1971	1980	1984	1988	1990	1992	1971	1980	1984	1988	1990	1992	1971	1980	1984	1988	1990	1992
1	2	3	4	5	6	7	8	9	10	11	12	13	14	15	16	17	18	19
Average	207.6	215.0	210.9	211.8	209.2	210.5	255.2	258.5	257.1	257.5	256.8	259.8	285.2	285.5	288.8	290.1	290.2	289.7
Standard deviation	42.1	37.9	41.1	41.2	44.7	40.3	35.7	34.9	35.5	34.7	36.0	39.4	45.8	41.8	40.3	37.1	41.3	43.0
Percentiles																		
5th	134.8	148.5	140.5	141.9	134.8	140.7	192.8	199.1	196.7	199.5	195.7	190.9	206.1	213.0	219.9	226.1	220.0	214.3
10th	151.6	165.1	156.7	156.6	150.1	156.0	207.8	212.8	210.2	212.9	209.8	207.9	225.3	230.6	236.0	241.5	236.9	232.7
25th	180.0	191.1	183.7	184.3	178.7	183.1	232.3	235.3	233.9	234.2	233.2	234.7	255.5	258.7	262.5	265.7	263.5	262.6
50th	209.3	217.2	212.6	212.6	210.3	213.6	257.0	259.6	258.2	257.9	257.3	261.6	287.7	287.5	290.3	291.1	291.1	293.0
75th	236.7	241.3	239.6	240.1	240.3	239.3	279.9	282.8	281.6	281.4	281.5	287.0	316.7	314.6	316.8	316.0	318.6	319.4
90th	260.5	261.7	262.8	263.0	265.7	259.9	299.6	302.3	301.7	301.6	302.0	309.2	341.7	337.5	339.6	336.9	342.7	342.7
95th	274.1	273.3	276.5	277.5	280.4	272.1	310.8	313.9	313.7	313.3	314.4	321.9	356.5	350.9	352.6	348.5	356.0	355.8

1 All participants of this age were in school.

NOTE.—These test scores are from the National Assessment of Educational Progress (NAEP). The NAEP scores have been evaluated at certain performance levels. A score of 300 implies an ability to find, understand, summarize, and explain relatively complicated literary and informational material. A score of 250 implies an ability to search for specific information, interrelate ideas, and make generalizations about literature, science, and social studies materials. A score of 200 implies an ability to understand, combine ideas, and make inferences based on short uncomplicated passages about specific or sequentially related information. A score of 150 implies an ability to follow brief written directions and carry out simple, discrete reading tasks. Scale ranges from 0 to 500.

SOURCE: U.S. Department of Education, National Center for Education Statistics, National Assessment of Educational Progress, The Reading Report Card, 1971–88, and NAEP 1992 Trends in Academic Progress, by Educational Testing Service. (This table was prepared April 1994.)

Table 107.—Student proficiency in reading, by age, amount of time spent on homework, reading habits, and reading materials in the home: 1971, 1984, and 1992

Time spent on homework, reading habits, and reading materials in the home	Average proficiency score						Percent					
	9-year-olds		13-year-olds		17-year-olds [1]		9-year-olds		13-year-olds		17-year-olds [1]	
	1984	1992	1984	1992	1984	1992	1984	1992	1984	1992	1984	1992
1	2	3	4	5	6	7	8	9	10	11	12	13
Materials read a few times a year or more												
Poems	211	211	260	264	290	294	70	70	68	74	76	84
Plays	211	208	260	262	290	293	56	54	59	64	63	71
Biographies	213	212	261	263	292	294	45	47	62	72	59	69
Science books	212	211	259	261	289	293	84	88	90	92	70	80
Books about other places	211	211	259	262	289	294	79	81	83	80	81	84
Frequency of reading for fun												
Daily	214	215	264	269	297	304	53	56	35	37	31	27
Weekly	212	212	254	260	290	291	28	28	35	32	34	33
Monthly	204	204	255	257	290	287	7	6	14	13	17	18
Yearly	197	197	252	250	280	282	3	3	7	8	10	12
Never	198	189	239	246	269	268	9	7	8	10	9	11
Time spent on homework each day												
None	212	211	254	253	276	274	36	32	23	21	22	22
Didn't do assignment	198	193	247	251	287	286	4	4	4	4	11	12
Less than 1 hour	218	215	261	260	290	291	42	47	36	36	26	29
1 to 2 hours	216	211	266	269	296	298	13	12	29	29	27	25
More than 2 hours	201	195	264	267	303	308	6	5	9	10	13	12
	1971	1992	1971	1992	1971	1992	1971	1992	1971	1992	1971	1992
Reading materials in the home [2]												
0 to 2	186	197	227	241	246	269	28	37	17	22	11	18
3	208	214	249	256	274	286	33	33	25	31	22	27
4	223	224	267	271	296	299	39	30	58	48	67	55

[1] Excludes persons not enrolled in school.
[2] The 4 items in the scale were: newspaper subscription, magazine subscription, more than 25 books in the home, and encyclopedia in the home.

NOTE.—These test scores are from the National Assessment of Educational Progress (NAEP). The NAEP scores have been evaluated at certain performance levels. A score of 300 implies an ability to find, understand, summarize, and explain relatively complicated literary and informational material. A score of 250 implies an ability to search for specific information, interrelate ideas, and make generalizations about literature, science, and social studies materials. A score of 200 implies an ability to understand, combine ideas, and make inferences based on short uncomplicated passages about specific or sequentially related information. A score of 150 implies an ability to follow brief written directions and carry out simple, discrete reading tasks. Scale ranges from 0 to 500.

SOURCE: U.S. Department of Education, National Center for Education Statistics, National Assessment of Educational Progress, *The Reading Report Card, 1971–88,* and *NAEP 1992 Trends in Academic Progress,* by Educational Testing Service. (This table was prepared April 1994.)

Table 108.—Percent of students at or above selected reading proficiency levels,[1] by sex, race/ethnicity, and age: 1971 to 1992

Sex, race/ethnicity, and level	9-year-olds[2]							13-year-olds[2]							17-year-olds[2]						
	1971	1975	1980	1984	1988	1990	1992	1971	1975	1980	1984	1988	1990	1992	1971	1975	1980	1984	1988	1990	1992
1	2	3	4	5	6	7	8	9	10	11	12	13	14	15	16	17	18	19	20	21	22
Total																					
Level 150[3]	90.6	93.1	94.6	92.3	92.7	90.1	92.3	99.8	99.7	99.9	99.8	99.9	99.8	99.5	99.6	99.7	99.9	100.0	100.0	99.9	99.8
Level 200[4]	58.7	62.1	67.7	61.5	62.6	58.9	62.0	93.0	93.2	94.8	93.9	94.9	93.8	92.7	96.0	96.4	97.2	98.3	98.9	98.1	97.1
Level 250[5]	15.6	14.6	17.7	17.2	17.5	18.4	16.2	57.8	58.6	60.7	59.0	58.7	58.7	61.6	78.6	80.1	80.7	83.1	85.7	84.1	82.5
Level 300[6]	0.9	0.6	0.6	1.0	1.4	1.7	0.7	9.8	10.2	11.3	11.0	10.9	11.0	15.3	39.0	38.7	37.8	40.3	40.9	41.4	43.2
Level 350[7]	0.0	0.0	0.0	0.0	0.0	0.0	0.0	0.1	0.2	0.2	0.3	0.2	0.4	0.6	6.8	6.2	5.3	5.7	4.6	7.0	6.8
Male																					
Level 150[3]	87.9	91.0	92.9	90.4	90.4	87.9	90.2	99.6	99.6	99.8	99.7	99.7	99.7	99.2	99.4	99.5	99.8	99.9	100.0	99.8	99.7
Level 200[4]	52.7	56.2	62.7	58.0	58.4	53.8	56.9	90.7	90.9	93.4	92.2	92.8	91.4	90.4	94.7	95.3	96.3	97.6	98.5	97.0	96.3
Level 250[5]	12.0	11.5	14.6	15.9	15.8	16.1	14.2	51.6	51.7	55.9	54.0	52.3	52.4	55.5	74.4	75.6	77.9	79.6	82.9	79.7	78.4
Level 300[6]	0.6	0.3	0.4	0.8	1.1	1.4	0.5	7.3	7.0	9.1	9.0	8.6	7.6	12.8	33.9	33.7	35.0	35.4	37.1	36.1	38.4
Level 350[7]	0.0	0.0	0.0	0.0	0.0	0.0	0.0	0.1	0.1	0.2	0.2	0.1	0.2	0.4	5.2	5.1	4.5	4.8	3.5	5.6	5.3
Female																					
Level 150[3]	93.2	95.3	96.4	94.2	94.9	92.4	94.4	99.9	99.9	99.9	99.9	100.0	99.9	99.8	99.8	99.8	99.9	99.9	100.0	99.9	99.9
Level 200[4]	64.6	68.1	72.7	65.2	66.9	64.2	67.3	95.2	95.5	96.1	95.8	96.9	96.3	95.0	97.3	97.5	98.1	99.0	99.3	99.2	97.9
Level 250[5]	19.2	17.7	20.7	18.4	19.1	20.8	18.2	64.0	65.5	65.4	64.0	65.0	65.0	67.5	82.6	84.3	83.6	86.8	88.2	88.6	86.8
Level 300[6]	1.3	0.9	0.8	1.1	1.6	2.0	0.8	12.3	13.5	13.6	13.2	13.2	14.5	17.7	44.0	43.6	40.7	45.0	44.4	46.8	48.5
Level 350[7]	0.0	0.0	0.0	0.0	0.0	0.1	0.0	0.2	0.3	0.3	0.4	0.4	0.5	0.8	8.4	7.3	6.0	6.7	5.5	8.5	8.4
White[8]																					
Level 150[3]	94.0	96.0	97.1	95.4	95.1	93.5	95.8	99.9	99.9	100.0	99.9	100.0	99.9	99.8	99.9	99.9	100.0	100.0	100.0	100.0	99.9
Level 200[4]	65.0	69.0	74.2	68.6	68.4	66.0	69.3	96.2	96.4	97.1	96.2	96.0	96.0	95.9	97.9	98.6	99.1	99.0	99.3	98.8	98.6
Level 250[5]	18.0	17.4	21.0	20.9	20.3	22.6	19.6	64.2	65.5	67.8	65.1	63.7	64.8	68.5	83.7	86.2	86.2	88.0	88.7	88.3	88.0
Level 300[6]	1.1	0.7	0.8	0.8	1.6	0.5	0.0	11.3	12.1	13.6	13.1	12.4	13.3	18.1	43.2	43.9	43.3	46.3	45.4	47.5	50.1
Level 350[7]	0.0	0.0	0.0	0.0	0.0	0.0	0.0	0.2	0.3	0.3	0.4	0.3	0.5	0.8	7.7	7.2	6.2	6.9	5.5	8.7	8.3
Black[8]																					
Level 150[3]	69.7	80.7	84.9	81.3	83.2	76.9	79.6	98.4	98.6	99.3	99.4	99.8	99.4	98.7	97.6	97.7	99.0	99.9	100.0	99.6	99.1
Level 200[4]	22.0	31.6	41.3	36.6	39.4	33.9	36.6	74.2	76.9	84.1	85.5	91.3	87.7	82.0	81.9	82.0	85.6	95.7	98.0	95.7	91.6
Level 250[5]	1.6	2.0	4.1	4.5	5.6	5.2	4.6	21.1	24.8	30.1	34.6	40.2	41.7	38.4	40.1	43.0	44.0	65.7	75.8	69.1	61.4
Level 300[6]	0.0	0.0	0.0	0.1	0.2	0.2	0.3	0.8	1.5	1.8	2.8	4.6	4.6	5.7	7.7	8.1	7.1	16.2	24.9	19.7	16.9
Level 350[7]	0.0	0.0	0.0	0.0	0.0	0.0	0.0	0.0	0.0	0.0	0.0	0.1	0.1	0.1	0.4	0.4	0.2	0.9	1.4	1.5	1.6
Hispanic																					
Level 150[3]	—	80.8	84.5	82.0	85.9	83.7	83.4	—	99.6	99.7	99.5	99.2	99.1	98.1	—	99.3	99.8	99.8	99.9	99.7	99.8
Level 200[4]	—	34.6	41.6	39.6	45.9	40.9	43.1	—	81.3	86.8	86.7	87.4	85.8	83.4	—	88.7	93.3	95.6	96.3	95.9	93.4
Level 250[5]	—	2.6	5.0	4.3	8.6	5.8	7.2	—	32.0	35.4	39.0	38.0	37.2	40.9	—	52.9	62.2	68.3	71.5	75.2	69.2
Level 300[6]	—	0.0	0.0	0.1	0.4	0.5	0.0	—	2.2	2.3	4.1	4.4	3.9	6.0	—	12.6	16.5	21.2	23.3	27.1	27.3
Level 350[7]	—	0.0	0.0	0.0	0.0	0.0	0.0	—	0.0	0.0	0.1	0.0	0.1	0.0	—	1.2	1.3	2.0	1.3	2.4	2.3

[1] As measured by the National Assessment of Educational Progress (NAEP).
[2] All participants of this age were in school.
[3] Able to follow brief written directions and carry out simple, discrete reading tasks.
[4] Able to understand, combine ideas, and make inferences based on short uncomplicated passages about specific or sequentially related information.
[5] Able to search for specific information, interrelate ideas, and make generalizations about literature, science, and social studies materials.
[6] Able to find, understand, summarize, and explain relatively complicated literary and informational material.
[7] Able to understand the links between ideas even when those links are not explicitly stated and to make appropriate generalizations even when the texts lack clear introductions or explanations.
[8] Data for 1971 include persons of Hispanic origin.
—Data not available.

SOURCE: U.S. Department of Education, National Center for Education Statistics, National Assessment of Educational Progress, *The Reading Report Card, 1971–88* and *NAEP 1992 Trends in Academic Progress*, by Educational Testing Service. (This table was prepared April 1994.)

Table 109.—Average proficiency in reading for 4th graders in public schools,[1] by selected characteristics, region, and state: 1994

Region and state	Average	Race/ethnicity						Sex		Parental education[2]			
		White	Black	His-panic	Asian	Pacific Islander	Amer-ican Indian	Male	Female	Did not finish high school	Grad-uated high school	Some edu-cation after high school	Grad-uated college
1	2	3	4	5	6	7	8	9	10	11	12	13	14
United States	**213**	**223**	**187**	**190**	**231**	**217**	**201**	**208**	**219**	**189**	**208**	**222**	**223**
Region													
Northeast	213	225	185	192	(3)	(3)	(3)	209	217	(3)	203	223	222
Southeast	209	220	190	186	(3)	(3)	(3)	203	215	188	208	223	217
Central	219	225	184	200	(3)	(3)	(3)	213	226	(3)	216	222	227
West	213	223	188	187	4 227	(3)	(3)	208	218	189	203	222	224
State													
Alabama	209	221	189	180	(3)	(3)	(3)	204	214	198	202	218	218
Arizona	207	220	185	190	(3)	(3)	183	202	212	190	202	220	219
Arkansas	210	219	185	193	(3)	(3)	(3)	205	214	198	204	222	216
California	198	212	184	176	212	4 214	(3)	195	201	167	193	208	208
Colorado	214	223	192	194	(3)	(3)	205	210	219	193	214	221	223
Connecticut	223	235	191	192	(3)	(3)	(3)	219	227	206	210	234	232
Delaware 4	207	216	190	192	(3)	(3)	(3)	201	213	186	203	218	215
Florida	206	219	185	190	(3)	(3)	(3)	200	211	188	196	220	213
Georgia	208	223	187	187	(3)	(3)	(3)	203	213	189	200	220	218
Hawaii	202	220	192	186	218	192	(3)	195	209	191	196	215	208
Indiana	221	225	194	202	(3)	(3)	(3)	217	224	200	217	230	230
Iowa	224	226	4 187	205	(3)	(3)	(3)	219	228	212	220	232	230
Kentucky	213	216	192	198	(3)	(3)	(3)	208	218	196	213	223	219
Louisiana	198	214	182	177	(3)	(3)	(3)	195	201	189	197	210	201
Maine 4	229	230	(3)	219	(3)	(3)	(3)	226	232	215	226	237	236
Maryland	211	224	187	199	233	(3)	(3)	206	215	196	204	216	218
Massachusetts	224	231	200	196	4 203	(3)	(3)	222	226	208	213	230	233
Minnesota	219	223	174	203	(3)	(3)	197	215	223	(3)	213	221	229
Mississippi	203	221	188	183	(3)	(3)	(3)	197	208	193	200	214	208
Missouri	218	224	194	201	(3)	(3)	213	214	222	200	217	228	226
Montana	223	227	—	209	—	—	204	219	228	212	220	228	231
Nebraska 4	221	225	192	206	(3)	(3)	203	217	225	(3)	216	233	231
New Hampshire 4	224	225	(3)	214	(3)	(3)	(3)	219	230	208	221	236	231
New Jersey 4	220	231	194	201	238	(3)	(3)	217	223	194	210	226	230
New Mexico	206	219	197	198	(3)	(3)	187	202	209	189	201	221	216
New York 4	213	227	192	195	230	(3)	(3)	209	217	197	209	224	221
North Carolina	215	226	195	190	(3)	(3)	202	210	221	197	205	227	224
North Dakota	226	228	(3)	213	(3)	(3)	4 198	222	230	(3)	217	233	234
Pennsylvania	216	225	182	189	(3)	(3)	(3)	212	220	189	211	222	225
Rhode Island	221	226	198	196	204	(3)	(3)	216	225	205	218	230	229
South Carolina	205	220	186	184	(3)	(3)	(3)	201	209	190	194	217	214
Tennessee	214	221	189	197	(3)	(3)	(3)	209	218	201	214	226	219
Texas	213	227	192	199	(3)	(3)	(3)	211	215	196	209	225	223
Utah	218	222	(3)	201	(3)	(3)	196	214	223	(3)	213	226	227
Virginia	214	225	194	207	(3)	(3)	(3)	209	220	197	208	221	222
Washington	214	218	199	191	221	209	208	210	218	198	210	217	224
West Virginia	214	216	203	193	(3)	(3)	(3)	209	219	197	214	227	222
Wisconsin	225	229	198	204	(3)	(3)	(3)	222	228	213	224	228	222
Wyoming	222	225	(3)	210	(3)	(3)	4 211	219	225	204	216	230	228
Department of Defense Overseas Schools	219	225	206	213	223	216	211	214	223	(3)	210	226	224
Guam	183	193	172	173	181	184	(3)	174	191	166	177	191	186

[1] As measured by the National Assessment of Educational Progress (NAEP). Forty-one states and Guam participated in the test, but the sample size in two states was insufficient to permit a reliable estimate.

[2] Parents' highest level of education. Data not shown for students who did not know parents' level of education.

[3] Sample size is insufficient to permit a reliable estimate

[4] Did not satisfy one or more of the guidelines for school sample participation rates. Data are subject to appreciable nonresponse bias.

—Data not available.

NOTE.—These test scores are from the National Assessment of Educational Progress (NAEP). The NAEP scores have been evaluated at certain performance levels. A score of 300 implies an ability to find, understand, summarize, and explain relatively complicated literary and informational material. A score of 250 implies an ability to search for specific information, interrelate ideas, and make generalizations about literature, science, and social studies materials. A score of 200 implies an ability to understand, combine ideas, and make inferences based on short uncomplicated passages about specific or sequentially related information. A score of 150 implies an ability to follow brief written directions and carry out simple, discrete reading tasks. Scale ranges from 0 to 500. Excludes states not participating in the survey.

SOURCE: U.S. Department of Education, National Center for Education Statistics, National Assessment of Educational Progress, *1994 NAEP Reading: A First Look*, prepared by Educational Testing Service. (This table was prepared May 1995.)

Table 110.—Average proficiency in reading for 4th graders in public schools,[1] by reading and television watching habits, region, and state: 1992

Region and state	Frequency of reading for fun				Amount of television watched each day				
	Almost every day	Once or twice a week	Once or twice a month	Never or hardly ever	Six or more hours	Four to five hours	Three hours	Two hours	One hour or less
1	2	3	4	5	6	7	8	9	10
United States	**223**	**218**	**209**	**199**	**198**	**216**	**223**	**223**	**220**
Region									
Northeast	231	220	211	200	201	221	232	227	229
Southeast	216	214	208	201	198	214	218	217	217
Central	227	220	211	204	199	215	226	228	224
West	219	218	206	191	197	215	218	221	214
State									
Alabama	212	210	205	197	198	209	216	215	210
Arizona	217	211	203	199	201	210	214	217	210
Arkansas	217	213	206	199	200	217	220	217	212
California	212	200	196	190	184	205	208	208	210
Colorado	225	216	215	202	203	218	220	223	220
Connecticut	230	220	219	207	204	219	226	232	233
Delaware[2]	220	215	210	197	198	216	216	225	218
District of Columbia	192	190	184	178	184	190	190	193	193
Florida	214	212	206	195	196	210	214	220	212
Georgia	219	215	206	198	200	216	220	220	215
Hawaii	210	203	202	192	193	208	210	208	205
Idaho	226	220	217	205	206	219	223	225	224
Indiana	229	222	221	206	210	223	227	228	225
Iowa	233	225	218	210	212	224	231	234	229
Kentucky	219	215	214	201	203	218	219	217	213
Louisiana	208	206	206	194	195	207	210	209	209
Maine[2]	234	227	224	213	215	226	233	230	232
Maryland	221	211	207	194	194	213	220	223	220
Massachusetts	234	225	223	211	211	226	230	234	234
Michigan	224	216	209	207	198	217	222	225	225
Minnesota	230	221	212	204	204	220	228	229	227
Mississippi	202	202	200	192	192	202	208	209	195
Missouri	227	222	220	205	208	222	227	229	222
Nebraska[2]	228	223	221	203	204	224	228	227	222
New Hampshire[2]	236	228	224	210	216	229	228	233	235
New Jersey[2]	232	225	220	203	205	225	229	233	235
New Mexico	218	212	214	194	196	212	217	220	211
New York[2]	221	216	214	201	202	214	224	223	221
North Carolina	219	212	207	198	197	214	218	222	217
North Dakota	234	226	222	212	211	226	231	231	229
Ohio	226	217	214	204	204	220	225	224	222
Oklahoma	225	225	221	207	211	224	227	227	220
Pennsylvania	227	221	221	206	202	221	228	230	227
Rhode Island	223	217	216	197	203	217	222	223	223
South Carolina	216	211	210	196	198	212	215	222	215
Tennessee	219	213	208	201	199	218	219	218	214
Texas	218	215	212	202	200	213	220	222	218
Utah	228	222	214	207	209	220	225	224	224
Virginia	228	223	216	204	205	223	228	232	230
West Virginia	224	218	212	201	204	218	223	223	219
Wisconsin	233	222	217	206	211	225	228	230	227
Wyoming	230	224	217	207	210	223	227	229	227
Outlying areas									
Guam	187	186	175	174	176	190	193	184	178

[1] As measured by the National Assessment of Educational Progress (NAEP). Forty-one states, the District of Columbia, and Guam participated in the test.

[2] Did not satisfy one or more of the guidelines for school sample participation rates. Data are subject to appreciable nonresponse bias.

NOTE.—These test scores are from the National Assessment of Educational Progress (NAEP). The NAEP scores have been evaluated at certain performance levels. A score of 300 implies an ability to find, understand, summarize, and explain complicated literary and informational material. A score of 250 implies an ability to search for specific information, interrelate ideas, and make generalizations about literature, science, and social studies materials. A score of 200 implies an ability to understand, combine ideas, and make inferences based on short uncomplicated passages about specific or sequentially related information. A score of 150 implies an ability to follow brief written directions and carry out simple, discrete reading tasks. Scale ranges from 0 to 500.

SOURCE: U.S. Department of Education, National Center for Education Statistics, National Assessment of Educational Progress, *NAEP 1992 Reading Report Card for the Nation and the States,* prepared by Educational Testing Service. (This table was prepared January 1994.)

Table 111.—Average writing performance of 4th, 8th, and 11th graders, by selected characteristics of students: 1984 to 1992

Selected characteristics of students	4th graders				8th graders				11th graders			
	1984	1988	1990	1992	1984	1988	1990	1992	1984	1988	1990	1992
1	2	3	4	5	6	7	8	9	10	11	12	13
All students	**203.8**	**205.7**	**201.7**	**207.1**	**266.7**	**263.7**	**256.6**	**274.4**	**289.7**	**291.3**	**287.1**	**287.3**
Sex												
Male	200.5	199.0	195.0	198.3	257.5	253.7	245.6	263.6	281.1	282.2	276.4	279.4
Female	207.6	212.6	208.7	216.1	276.2	273.5	267.9	285.0	298.6	299.3	298.2	296.4
Race/ethnicity												
White	210.7	214.9	211.0	216.7	271.7	269.1	262.1	279.2	296.8	296.2	292.8	294.1
Black	181.6	173.3	171.4	175.0	247.1	246.0	239.0	258.1	270.3	275.2	268.2	263.2
Hispanic	188.5	190.3	184.1	189.4	246.9	250.4	245.7	265.0	259.1	273.8	276.9	273.6
Parental education												
Not high school graduate	178.7	194.2	185.7	191.2	257.7	254.3	245.6	257.9	273.6	275.8	268.0	271.0
Graduated high school	191.8	199.4	196.6	202.2	260.8	257.6	252.5	267.9	283.5	284.6	278.2	278.4
Post high school	208.0	211.4	213.9	201.4	271.4	275.1	266.9	279.6	297.6	296.1	292.2	292.3
Graduated college	218.1	212.4	209.0	213.7	277.8	270.5	264.9	284.3	299.9	299.0	297.5	295.7
Control of school												
Public	201.9	204.2	200.4	205.2	264.4	262.1	253.6	272.4	287.8	289.9	285.5	286.5
Private	215.4	216.0	216.2	221.6	281.8	275.5	276.7	287.6	305.4	299.7	305.8	295.4
Type of community												
Advantaged urban	221.2	218.4	216.8	235.9	285.7	270.9	279.4	293.5	305.8	295.2	295.2	296.6
Disadvantaged urban	199.2	174.8	175.2	183.9	249.2	245.8	244.5	251.7	267.1	256.1	273.4	270.4
Extreme rural	188.2	202.3	201.9	203.2	259.6	268.3	252.3	267.3	286.8	291.9	285.6	288.5
Other	202.8	207.4	203.2	206.9	266.1	263.7	255.0	275.1	290.0	290.9	287.9	288.9
Region												
Northeast	212.4	204.0	211.1	216.1	273.3	265.1	261.4	284.7	290.9	295.0	295.4	290.2
Southeast	203.5	200.1	192.3	193.0	266.9	268.2	251.8	266.3	287.3	289.4	280.0	277.8
Central	200.8	211.9	203.0	213.9	263.8	258.1	259.1	277.2	291.3	291.8	288.8	291.4
West	200.8	207.3	201.2	205.7	263.5	264.0	255.0	271.3	288.8	289.2	284.8	289.4

NOTE.—These test scores are from the National Assessment of Educational Progress (NAEP). The writing scale score ranges from 0 to 500 and is defined as the average of a respondent's estimated scores on specific writing tasks. The average response method is used to estimate average writing achievement for each participant as if each had performed all 11 writing tasks.

SOURCE: U.S. Department of Education, National Center for Education Statistics, National Assessment of Educational Progress, The Writing Report Card, 1984-88 and NAEP 1992 Trends in Academic Progress, by Educational Testing Service. (This table was prepared April 1994.)

Table 112.—Student values and attitudes toward writing, by grade level: 1984, 1990, and 1992

Statements about writing	Percent of students reporting the statement is true more than half the time								
	Grade 4			Grade 8			Grade 11		
	1984	1990	1992	1984	1990	1992	1984	1990	1992
1	2	3	4	5	6	7	8	9	10
Writing helps me think more clearly	—	—	—	44	46	42	52	47	50
Writing helps me tell others what I think	—	—	—	52	56	52	55	58	57
Writing helps tell others how I feel	—	—	—	50	56	52	55	60	60
Writing helps me understand my own feelings	—	—	—	40	47	44	47	50	49
People who write well have a better chance of getting good jobs	—	—	—	47	53	51	54	58	59
People who write well are more influential	—	—	—	49	55	52	54	60	60
I like to write	55	57	54	39	42	43	40	39	43
I am a good writer	59	62	63	41	44	44	38	44	49
People like what I write	52	56	55	38	39	44	35	42	46
I write on my own outside of school	47	42	46	36	35	37	31	28	33
I don't like to write things that will be graded	37	33	32	31	36	37	27	30	30
If I didn't have to write for school, I wouldn't write anything	33	27	28	17	19	18	15	16	17

—Data not available.

SOURCE: U.S. Department of Education, National Center for Education Statistics, *NAEP 1992 Trends in Academic Progress*, by Educational Testing Service. (This table was prepared April 1994.)

Table 113.—Student writing in school, by type of writing assignment: 1984, 1988, and 1990

Type of writing assignment	Percent of students reporting at least one paper written for English class last week								
	9-year-olds			13-year-olds			17-year-olds [1]		
	1984	1988	1990	1984	1988	1990	1984	1988	1990
1	2	3	4	5	6	7	8	9	10
Essay, composition, or theme	19.3	25.1	24.0	40.9	48.4	45.0	59.6	63.6	64.0
Book report	36.1	40.5	38.0	35.4	34.8	34.0	30.4	30.7	28.0
Other report	28.3	32.0	31.0	26.5	29.4	30.0	37.7	38.4	39.0
Letter	38.5	38.7	42.0	20.8	25.3	24.0	15.9	19.6	18.0
Story	37.2	43.3	43.0	41.6	48.9	49.0	39.7	39.7	39.0
Poem	25.7	29.7	27.0	14.7	14.7	17.0	18.3	20.9	25.0
Play	13.9	15.2	14.0	10.4	12.2	12.0	12.6	11.3	14.0

[1] Excludes persons of this age not enrolled in school.

SOURCE: U.S. Department of Education, National Center for Education Statistics, National Assessment of Educational Progress, *The Writing Report Card, 1984–88*; and *Trends in Academic Progress*, prepared by Educational Testing Service. (This table was prepared January 1992.)

Table 114.—Average student proficiency in geography, U.S. history, and literature, by student characteristics: 1986 and 1988

| Characteristic | Percentage distribution of 12th graders in 1988 | Geography scores of 12th graders in 1988 | History scores in 1988 | | | Literature scores of 11th graders in 1986 | Characteristic | Percentage distribution of 12th graders in 1988 | Geography scores of 12th graders in 1988 | History scores in 1988 | | | Literature scores of 11th graders in 1986 |
| | | | 4th graders | 8th graders | 12th graders | | | | | 4th graders | 8th graders | 12th graders | |
1	2	3	4	5	6	7	1	2	3	4	5	6	7
United States	**100**	**293.1**	**220.6**	**263.9**	**295.0**	**285.0**	**Hours spent on homework each day**						
Sex							None assigned	8	277.0	223.6	253.4	280.7	—
Male	48	301.2	222.9	266.2	298.5	282.8	Did not do it	9	289.0	209.0	247.2	291.6	—
Female	52	285.7	218.2	261.6	291.8	287.3	½ hour or less	21	295.0	221.6	264.2	295.4	—
							1 hour	34	294.0	223.2	265.7	295.6	—
Race							2 hours	17	295.0	—	267.9	299.4	—
White	76	301.1	227.5	270.4	301.1	289.9	More than 2 hours	10	299.0	—	267.2	302.4	—
Black	14	258.4	199.5	246.0	274.4	267.5							
Hispanic	7	271.8	202.7	244.3	273.9	264.8	**Parents' level of education**						
							Not high school diploma	8	267.0	202.7	244.9	274.2	266.2
Region							Graduated high school	24	283.5	214.1	256.1	285.3	273.4
Northeast	26	295.0	222.6	270.1	296.9	293.0	Some college	23	294.2	228.0	269.1	296.8	288.3
Southeast	23	283.3	215.5	258.0	289.2	282.6	Graduated college	43	305.3	231.4	274.9	306.0	297.6
Central	25	298.2	223.8	265.3	297.9	284.3							
West	26	295.3	220.7	262.8	295.5	280.4	**Reading materials in the home**						
							0 to 2 types	13	273.0	207.7	246.6	275.0	—
Size and type of community							0 to 3 types	—	—	—	—	—	265.4
Rural	[1]5	—	220.0	266.8	296.2	273.7	3 types	24	287.0	220.2	261.3	289.3	—
Urban disadvantaged	[1]5	—	198.2	246.2	273.8	265.2	4 types	63	300.0	231.1	272.0	302.0	279.3
Urban advantaged	[1]14	—	236.9	275.9	307.8	301.4	5 types	—	—	—	—	—	291.7
School program							**Parents living at home**						
Academic	59	304.0	—	—	307.1	298.7	Both	78	297.0	223.1	268.1	298.9	290.3
General	32	278.0	—	—	279.8	271.7	One parent	17	285.0	212.2	255.1	289.7	282.1
Vocational/technical	9	276.0	—	—	275.1	265.9	Neither	5	274.0	202.0	248.3	273.2	271.6
Hours of TV viewing each day							**Mothers working outside the home**						
0 to 2 hours	51	300.0	222.6	269.6	299.0	—	Full-time	55	293.0	—	265.3	296.3	288.1
3 to 5 hours	44	289.0	225.5	265.0	293.3	—	Part-time	17	299.0	—	267.4	299.9	292.5
6 or more hours	6	266.0	210.8	251.1	276.7	—	Not at all	25	295.0	—	264.2	295.3	286.2

[1] Data are for 11th graders in 1986.
—Data not available.

NOTE.—These test scores are from the National Assessment of Educational Progress (NAEP). As with the NAEP reading scale, these scales range from 0 to 500. However, the distribution of scores varies by subject. Therefore, direct score comparisons among the subjects should be avoided.

SOURCE: U.S. Department of Education, National Center for Education Statistics, National Assessment of Educational Progress, *Literature and U.S. History, The U.S. History Report Card,* and *The Geography Learning of High-School Seniors,* prepared by Educational Testing Service. (This table was prepared October 1990.)

Table 115.—Average mathematics proficiency, by age and by selected characteristics of students: 1978 to 1992

Selected characteristics of students	9-year-olds					13-year-olds					17-year-olds [1]				
	1978	1982	1986	1990	1992	1978	1982	1986	1990	1992	1978	1982	1986	1990	1992
1	2	3	4	5	6	7	8	9	10	11	12	13	14	15	16
All students	**218.6**	**219.0**	**221.7**	**229.6**	**229.6**	**264.1**	**268.6**	**269.0**	**270.4**	**273.1**	**300.4**	**298.5**	**302.0**	**304.6**	**306.7**
Sex															
Male	217.4	217.1	221.7	229.1	230.8	263.6	269.2	270.0	271.2	274.1	303.8	301.5	304.7	306.3	308.9
Female	219.9	220.8	221.7	230.2	228.4	264.7	268.0	267.9	269.6	272.0	297.1	295.6	299.4	302.9	304.5
Race/ethnicity															
White	224.1	224.0	226.9	235.2	235.1	271.6	274.4	273.6	276.3	278.9	305.9	303.7	307.5	309.5	311.9
Black	192.4	194.9	201.6	208.4	208.0	229.6	240.4	249.2	249.1	250.2	268.4	271.8	278.6	288.5	285.8
Hispanic	202.9	204.0	205.4	213.8	211.9	238.0	252.4	254.3	254.6	259.3	276.3	276.7	283.1	283.5	292.2
Television watched per day															
0 to 2 hours	—	218.0	222.0	231.0	231.0	—	273.0	276.0	277.0	280.0	305.0	303.0	310.0	312.0	314.0
3 to 5 hours	—	227.0	229.0	234.0	233.0	—	269.0	271.0	271.0	273.0	296.0	294.0	299.0	300.0	300.0
6 or more hours	—	214.0	213.0	221.0	219.0	—	256.0	255.0	258.0	255.0	279.0	280.0	282.0	287.0	285.0
Reading materials in the home [2]															
0 to 2 items	201.0	203.0	208.0	196.0	—	239.0	250.0	255.0	240.0	—	277.0	281.0	281.0	271.0	—
3 items	221.0	221.0	224.0	211.0	—	260.0	267.0	266.0	255.0	—	296.0	295.0	297.0	286.0	—
4 items	231.0	231.0	234.0	226.0	—	275.0	279.0	276.0	266.0	—	308.0	306.0	309.0	299.0	—

[1] All participants of this age group were in school.

[2] The 4 items in the scale were: newspaper subscription; magazine subscription; more than 25 books in the home; and encyclopedia in the home.

—Data not available.

NOTE.—These test scores are from the National Assessment of Educational Progress (NAEP). Performers at the 150 level know some basic addition and subtraction facts, and most can add two-digit numbers without regrouping. They recognize simple situations in which addition and subtraction apply. Performers at the 200 level have considerable understanding of two-digit numbers and know some basic multiplication and division facts. Performers at the 250 level have an initial understanding of the four basic operations. They can also compare information from graphs and charts, and are developing an ability to analyze simple logical relations. Performers at the 300 level can compute decimals, simple fractions, and percents. They can identify geometric figures, measure lengths and angles, and calculate areas of rectangles. They are developing the skills to operate with signed numbers, exponents, and square roots. Performers at the 350 level can apply a range of reasoning skills to solve multi-step problems. They can solve routine problems involving fractions and percents, recognize properties of basic geometric figures, and work with exponents and square roots. Scale ranges from 0 to 500.

SOURCE: U.S. Department of Education, National Center for Education Statistics, National Assessment of Educational Progress, *Trends in Academic Progress* and *NAEP 1992 Trends in Academic Progress*, prepared by Educational Testing Service. (This table was prepared April 1994.)

Table 116.—Percent of students at or above selected mathematics proficiency levels, [1] by race/ethnicity and age: 1978 to 1992

Race/ethnicity and year	9-year-olds [2]				13-year-olds [3]				17-year-olds [3]			
	Simple arithmetic facts	Beginning skills and understanding	Numerical operations and beginning problem solving	Moderately complex procedures and reasoning	Beginning skills and understanding	Numerical operations and beginning problem solving	Moderately complex procedures and reasoning	Multi-step problem solving and algebra	Beginning skills and understanding	Numerical operations and beginning problem solving	Moderately complex procedures and reasoning	Multi-step problem solving and algebra
1	2	3	4	5	6	7	8	9	10	11	12	13
All students												
1978	97	70	20	1	95	65	18	1	100	92	52	7
1982	97	71	19	1	98	71	17	0	100	93	48	6
1986	98	74	21	1	99	73	16	0	100	96	52	6
1990	99	82	28	1	98	75	17	0	100	96	56	7
1992	99	81	28	1	99	78	19	0	100	97	59	7
White [4]												
1978	98	76	23	1	98	73	21	1	100	96	58	8
1982	98	77	22	1	99	78	21	1	100	96	55	6
1986	99	80	25	1	99	79	19	0	100	98	59	8
1990	100	87	33	2	99	82	21	0	100	98	63	8
1992	100	87	32	1	100	85	23	0	100	98	66	9
Black [4]												
1978	88	42	4	0	80	29	2	0	99	71	17	0
1982	90	46	4	0	90	38	3	0	100	76	17	1
1986	94	53	6	0	95	49	4	0	100	86	21	0
1990	97	60	9	0	95	49	4	0	100	92	33	2
1992	97	60	10	0	95	51	4	0	100	90	30	1
Hispanic												
1978	93	54	9	0	86	36	4	0	99	78	23	1
1982	94	56	8	0	96	52	6	0	100	81	22	1
1986	96	58	7	0	97	56	6	0	99	89	27	1
1990	98	68	11	0	97	57	6	0	100	86	30	2
1992	97	65	12	0	98	63	7	0	100	94	39	1

[1] As measured by the National Assessment of Educational Progress (NAEP).

[2] Virtually no students were able to perform multi-step problems and algebra.

[3] Virtually all students knew simple arithmetic facts. Data are only for students enrolled in school.

[4] Excludes persons of Hispanic origin.

SOURCE: U.S. Department of Education, National Center for Education Statistics, National Assessment of Educational Progress, *NAEP 1992 Trends in Academic Progress*, prepared by Educational Testing Service. (This table was prepared May 1994.)

Table 117.—Average proficiency in mathematics content areas for 8th graders in public schools, by region and state: 1990 and 1992

Region and state	All areas		Numbers and operations		Measurement		Geometry		Data analysis, statistics, and probability		Algebra and functions		1992 percent of students at or above		
	1990	1992	1990	1992	1990	1992	1990	1992	1990	1992	1990	1992	Level 200 [1]	Level 250 [2]	Level 300 [3]
1	2	3	4	5	6	7	8	9	10	11	12	13	14	15	16
United States	262	266	266	270	258	264	259	262	262	267	260	266	96	67	18
Region															
Northeast	270	267	272	271	267	265	268	263	273	269	268	266	96	65	21
Southeast	254	258	260	263	248	253	251	253	253	258	256	259	95	58	12
Central	265	273	270	277	262	272	261	269	265	274	262	272	98	75	22
West	261	267	263	270	257	266	260	263	261	267	259	266	96	68	19
State															
Alabama	253	251	259	258	248	245	249	245	251	250	252	253	93	51	9
Arizona	260	[4]265	265	269	257	264	256	260	259	265	258	264	97	68	14
Arkansas	256	255	262	262	254	251	253	250	255	254	253	255	94	58	9
California	256	260	260	263	252	258	256	259	255	258	256	258	93	61	15
Colorado	267	[4]272	269	273	265	273	266	269	270	274	266	270	98	75	20
Connecticut	270	[4]273	274	277	268	275	266	268	271	274	268	270	97	74	24
Delaware	261	262	265	267	259	258	256	257	262	262	259	263	96	64	14
District of Columbia	231	[4]234	239	243	222	221	229	231	223	229	235	237	82	32	4
Florida	255	259	260	264	252	254	251	255	255	259	255	260	94	61	14
Georgia	259	259	263	265	253	253	257	253	260	259	257	259	95	60	12
Hawaii	251	[4]257	257	261	249	254	252	257	243	249	249	256	93	57	13
Idaho	271	[4]274	275	277	269	276	269	271	273	274	270	274	99	80	20
Indiana	267	269	271	272	265	269	264	266	269	273	265	267	98	72	19
Iowa	278	283	282	285	276	287	274	278	280	285	275	280	100	86	29
Kentucky	257	[4]261	261	266	254	259	253	256	258	262	257	260	96	64	13
Louisiana	246	249	253	256	241	242	243	244	243	248	246	249	92	50	7
Maine	—	278	—	280	—	282	—	274	—	282	—	274	99	83	24
Maryland	261	264	264	269	256	261	257	259	261	266	262	264	95	64	19
Massachusetts	—	272	—	276	—	270	—	267	—	274	—	271	98	74	22
Michigan	264	267	269	270	261	266	261	261	265	268	264	267	96	69	18
Minnesota	275	[4]282	279	282	272	285	272	278	279	284	274	281	99	83	29
Mississippi	—	246	—	256	—	236	—	239	—	243	—	245	90	45	6
Missouri	—	270	—	272	—	271	—	266	—	272	—	270	98	74	18
Nebraska	276	277	279	279	273	278	273	274	278	278	273	275	98	81	25
New Hampshire	273	[4]278	275	280	272	280	271	273	275	281	272	274	99	82	23
New Jersey	270	271	274	276	267	268	266	265	270	271	268	272	97	73	22
New Mexico	256	[4]259	259	263	254	257	257	256	253	258	257	257	96	61	10
New York	261	266	264	270	255	262	260	261	263	268	260	265	94	68	19
North Carolina	250	[4]258	256	261	242	253	249	254	248	258	251	259	95	59	11
North Dakota	281	283	286	286	279	285	278	277	285	286	275	279	100	87	28
Ohio	264	267	269	272	259	266	260	262	266	270	262	267	97	70	17
Oklahoma	263	[4]267	268	271	258	266	260	262	264	269	262	267	97	72	16
Pennsylvania	266	271	270	274	264	271	263	265	268	273	265	270	98	73	20
Rhode Island	260	[4]265	264	269	257	263	256	259	259	266	261	266	97	68	15
South Carolina	—	260	—	265	—	257	—	256	—	258	—	259	96	60	14
Tennessee	—	258	—	264	—	253	—	252	—	259	—	257	95	59	11
Texas	258	[4]264	262	267	254	260	258	262	257	263	256	266	96	64	17
Utah	—	274	—	276	—	275	—	269	—	275	—	272	99	78	21
Virginia	264	267	268	272	260	265	261	261	264	268	265	267	97	68	18
West Virginia	256	258	260	263	253	256	254	254	256	260	254	257	97	60	9
Wisconsin	274	277	278	280	273	279	272	272	277	280	271	275	98	80	26
Wyoming	272	[4]274	275	276	270	278	270	272	273	275	270	271	99	79	19
Outlying areas															
Guam	232	[4]234	240	240	229	228	236	239	214	221	230	235	80	34	5
Virgin Islands	219	[4]222	229	231	216	211	223	222	196	214	219	221	76	18	1

[1] Indicates ability to perform simple additive reasoning and problem solving.

[2] Indicates ability to perform simple multiplicative reasoning and 2–step problem solving.

[3] Indicates ability to perform reasoning and problem solving involving fractions, decimals, percents, elementary geometry, and simple algebra.

[4] Statistically significant increases from 1990 to 1992.

— Did not participate in 1990 Trial State Assessment.

NOTE.—These test scores are from the National Assessment of Educational Progress (NAEP). Forty-one states, the District of Columbia, and two outlying areas participated in the 1992 Trial State Assessment of 8th graders. Seven of these states did not participate in the 1990 assessment. Scale ranges from 0 to 500.

SOURCE: U.S. Department of Education, National Center for Education Statistics, National Assessment of Educational Progress, *NAEP 1992 Mathematics Report Card for the Nation and the States,* prepared by Educational Testing Service. (This table was prepared April 1993.)

Table 118.—Average proficiency in mathematics content areas for 4th graders in public schools, by region and state: 1992

Region and state	Average proficiency in content areas							Parental education[1]				Percent of students at or above	
	All areas	Numbers and operations	Meas-ure-ment	Ge-ome-try	Data analysis, statistics, and probability	Algebra and functions	Esti-ma-tion	Did not finish high school	Grad-uated high school	Some edu-cation after high school	Grad-uated col-lege	Level 200[2]	Level 250[3]
1	2	3	4	5	6	7	8	9	10	11	12	13	14
United States	217	214	222	220	218	216	206	203	212	223	225	71	16
Region													
Northeast	223	220	227	224	223	222	205	—	215	229	231	75	22
Southeast	209	205	214	212	210	206	195	198	203	217	215	61	10
Central	222	219	228	224	223	220	212	—	218	228	229	77	19
West	217	214	221	222	217	215	213	202	216	218	224	70	15
State													
Alabama	207	204	213	209	209	204	198	202	203	216	211	58	9
Arizona	214	210	219	219	214	213	205	202	210	225	220	68	12
Arkansas	209	205	215	212	211	206	197	198	208	215	213	62	9
California	207	204	210	213	206	208	202	189	200	217	216	60	11
Colorado	220	216	225	227	220	217	212	200	212	228	228	75	17
Connecticut	226	223	230	230	225	225	217	205	218	225	235	79	23
Delaware	217	214	220	219	219	215	203	196	213	219	225	69	15
District of Columbia	191	189	193	198	189	191	171	186	187	198	196	37	5
Florida	212	208	219	215	214	211	200	199	204	221	219	66	12
Georgia	214	211	219	216	218	213	199	202	205	223	221	67	14
Hawaii	213	211	216	218	212	210	199	199	203	219	218	65	14
Idaho	220	216	227	226	219	217	211	200	215	228	227	77	14
Indiana	220	216	226	223	222	218	210	209	216	230	226	75	14
Iowa	229	227	234	229	230	226	221	211	223	235	236	84	24
Kentucky	214	211	218	215	215	212	205	203	210	222	223	67	12
Louisiana	203	199	208	206	204	201	188	194	198	214	207	54	7
Maine	231	227	236	236	231	228	220	215	225	240	240	86	26
Maryland	216	214	220	219	217	215	200	201	206	226	224	67	17
Massachusetts	226	224	229	229	225	222	217	195	219	230	234	80	22
Michigan	219	215	225	222	218	216	209	201	212	224	227	73	17
Minnesota	227	225	233	230	227	225	223	—	220	230	236	81	24
Mississippi	200	198	206	202	199	195	188	193	197	209	205	50	6
Missouri	221	217	226	224	223	220	211	210	216	227	228	76	17
Nebraska	224	221	230	229	225	220	216	—	222	230	230	78	20
New Hampshire	229	225	234	233	229	227	222	211	222	232	236	84	23
New Jersey	226	225	230	226	225	224	213	210	219	230	234	80	23
New Mexico	212	207	216	219	214	210	203	202	207	223	221	65	10
New York	217	215	221	218	221	215	204	210	211	225	227	71	16
North Carolina	211	208	216	215	214	210	198	201	204	220	219	64	12
North Dakota	228	224	235	229	229	225	222	—	224	234	233	85	21
Ohio	217	214	223	221	218	216	210	205	215	221	227	71	15
Oklahoma	219	216	224	220	221	217	211	209	215	225	225	76	13
Pennsylvania	223	221	229	223	223	221	212	211	220	236	230	77	20
Rhode Island	214	212	218	216	213	212	206	200	207	220	224	68	12
South Carolina	211	208	218	215	211	207	195	204	204	219	220	63	12
Tennessee	209	207	213	211	211	209	200	201	205	213	217	63	9
Texas	217	214	220	220	218	216	199	211	213	225	224	71	14
Utah	223	219	229	227	221	221	213	205	216	228	230	79	18
Virginia	220	217	224	222	223	217	206	203	210	219	230	73	18
West Virginia	214	210	223	217	214	211	204	201	210	222	223	68	11
Wisconsin	228	225	234	228	229	225	219	219	225	237	234	83	23
Wyoming	224	221	230	228	224	222	216	215	221	232	229	82	17
Outlying area													
Guam	191	188	192	201	189	192	173	183	186	206	191	40	4

[1] Parents' highest level of education.
[2] Indicates ability to perform simple additive reasoning and problem solving.
[3] Indicates ability to perform simple multiplicative reasoning and 2–step problem solving.
—Sample size insufficient to permit reliable estimate. There were fewer than 62 students.

NOTE.—These test scores are from the National Assessment of Educational Progress (NAEP). Forty-one states, the District of Columbia, and Guam participated in the 1992 Trial State Assessment of 4th graders. Scale ranges from 0 to 500.

SOURCE: U.S. Department of Education, National Center for Education Statistics, National Assessment of Educational Progress, *NAEP 1992 Mathematics Report Card for the Nation and the States,* prepared by Educational Testing Service. (This table was prepared April 1993.)

Table 119.—Selected characteristics of 8th grade students in public schools, by region and state: 1992 [1]

Region and state	Math units required for graduation	Year of revision of state guides with NCTM standards [2]	Length of school year 1989	Length of school year 1992	Passing test in math required for graduation in 1993	Percent of students with 4 or more hours of math instruction each week	Percent of students reporting — Spending 30 minutes or more on math homework each day	Spending 1 or 2 hours on all homework each day	Spending more than 2 hours on all homework each day	Positive attitudes towards math [3]	Both parents living at home	Watching 6 or more hours of television each day
1	2	3	4	5	6	7	8	9	10	11	12	13
United States	—	—	—	—	—	32	64	59	8	59	75	13
Region												
Northeast	—	—	—	—	—	35	59	62	8	56	75	14
Southeast	—	—	—	—	—	37	65	56	7	59	71	17
Central	—	—	—	—	—	24	63	65	6	63	79	11
West	—	—	—	—	—	30	68	56	10	56	75	12
State												
Alabama	2	1989	175	175	Yes	60	65	59	7	62	72	20
Alaska	2	Devel.,1994	—	180	No	—	—	—	—	—	72	20
Arizona	2	1992	175	175	No	34	65	56	5	54	76	9
Arkansas	3	1993	178	178	No	42	61	56	7	60	75	20
California	2	1991	180	180	No	43	67	63	10	56	74	10
Colorado	(4)	1994	180	(5)	No	27	65	61	7	58	77	7
Connecticut	3	Devel.,1995	180	180	No	21	61	70	9	59	79	11
Delaware	2	Devel.,1994	180	180	No	30	57	62	5	63	73	17
District of Columbia	3	1993	190	180	No	52	63	63	10	73	45	31
Florida	3	Devel.,1994	180	180	Yes	40	62	57	7	61	71	15
Georgia	3	1992	180	180	Yes	56	65	59	7	66	71	18
Hawaii	3	Devel.,1994	183	180	Yes	34	68	55	11	54	75	22
Idaho	2	1994	180	180	No	28	63	57	5	56	83	7
Illinois	2	Devel.,1994	180	180	No	—	—	—	—	—	—	—
Indiana	2	1991	180	180	No	32	62	60	6	61	78	9
Iowa	(4)	1987	180	180	No	20	61	63	4	63	83	7
Kansas	2	1991	—	180	No	—	—	—	—	—	—	—
Kentucky	3	1993	175	175	No	47	61	54	6	57	78	13
Louisiana	3	Devel.,1994	180	180	Yes	54	62	61	10	63	71	20
Maine	2	Devel.,1994	—	175	No	12	66	70	8	61	81	8
Maryland	3	1985	180	180	Yes	45	60	65	7	61	73	17
Massachusetts	(4)	1994	—	180	No	28	67	70	9	57	77	8
Michigan	3	Devel.,1994	180	180	Yes	39	67	61	7	60	75	13
Minnesota	1	Devel.,1994	175	175	No	41	64	59	5	57	85	5
Mississippi	2	1993	—	180	Yes	60	68	60	8	67	70	21
Missouri	2	1990	—	174	No	44	66	60	6	60	77	12
Montana	2	Devel.,1995	180	180	No	—	—	—	—	—	—	—
Nebraska	(4)	Devel.,1994	(5)	(5)	No	25	69	61	5	60	81	8
Nevada	2	1993	—	180	Yes	—	—	—	—	—	—	—
New Hampshire	2	1993	180	180	No	38	62	68	9	58	81	7
New Jersey	3	1993	180	180	Yes	28	62	68	10	62	78	13
New Mexico	3	1992	180	180	Yes	26	65	56	7	56	75	11
New York	2	Devel.,1994	180	180	Yes	20	54	66	9	62	75	15
North Carolina	2	1992	180	180	Yes	52	64	64	7	65	73	16
North Dakota	2	1993	180	180	No	44	70	63	6	55	85	5
Ohio	2	1990	182	182	Yes	26	62	62	6	62	74	12
Oklahoma	2	1993	175	175	No	37	69	59	7	58	78	11
Oregon	2	Devel.,1994	175	(5)	No	—	—	—	—	—	—	—
Pennsylvania	3	none	180	180	No	24	58	63	4	59	79	9
Rhode Island	2	Devel.,1994	180	180	No	43	62	67	7	56	78	9
South Carolina	3	1993	—	180	Yes	59	61	61	7	70	73	17
South Dakota	2	Devel.,1995	—	175	No	—	—	—	—	—	—	—
Tennessee	2	1991	—	180	Yes	60	67	62	6	58	73	14
Texas	3	1991	175	175	Yes	38	67	57	8	61	75	12
Utah	2	1993	—	180	No	28	62	56	5	55	85	5
Vermont	(6)	Devel.,1994	—	175	No	—	—	—	—	—	—	—
Virginia	2	1988	180	180	Yes	38	65	63	7	63	77	15
Washington	2	Devel.,1994	—	180	No	—	—	—	—	—	—	—
West Virginia	2	1992	180	180	Yes	40	57	55	5	58	78	13
Wisconsin	2	Devel.,1995	180	180	No	32	59	61	5	59	80	8
Wyoming	(4)	1990	175	175	No	24	60	55	5	58	81	8
Outlying areas												
Guam	—	—	—	—	—	28	68	47	12	50	79	20
Virgin Islands	—	—	—	180	—	31	61	47	11	75	56	32

[1] Data are for 1992 unless otherwise specified.
[2] Standards recommended by the National Council of Teachers of Mathematics.
[3] Percent of students agreeing or strongly agreeing with positive statements about mathematics.
[4] Local board determines.
[5] No statewide policy.
[6] 5 units of math and science combined.

—Data not available or not applicable.

SOURCE: U.S. Department of Education, National Center for Education Statistics, National Assessment of Educational Progress, *The State of Mathematics Achievement*, by Educational Testing Service; and Council of Chief State School Officers, *State Education Indicators*. (This table was prepared June 1994.)

Table 120.— Mathematics proficiency of 17-year-olds, by highest mathematics course taken, sex, and race/ethnicity: 1978, 1990, and 1992

Year, sex, and race/ethnicity	Percent of students	Average proficiency by highest mathematics course taken						Percent of students at or above			
		All areas	Prealgebra or general mathematics	Algebra I	Geometry	Algebra II	Precalculus or calculus	200 [1]	250 [2]	300 [3]	350 [4]
1	2	3	4	5	6	7	8	9	10	11	12
1978											
Total	100.0	300.4	267	286	307	321	334	99.8	92.0	51.5	7.3
Male	48.7	303.8	269	289	310	325	337	99.9	93.0	55.1	9.5
Female	51.3	297.1	264	284	304	318	329	99.7	91.0	48.2	5.2
White	83.1	305.9	272	291	310	325	338	100.0	95.6	57.6	8.5
Black	11.8	268.4	247	264	281	292	297	98.8	70.7	16.8	0.5
Hispanic	4.0	276.3	256	273	294	303	306	99.3	78.3	23.4	1.4
Other [5]	1.1	312.9	—	—	—	—	—	100.0	94.5	64.7	15.4
1990											
Total	100.0	304.6	273	288	299	319	344	100.0	96.0	56.1	7.2
Male	48.6	306.3	274	291	302	323	347	99.9	95.8	57.6	8.8
Female	51.4	302.9	271	285	296	316	341	100.0	96.2	54.7	5.6
White	73.3	309.5	277	292	304	323	347	100.0	97.6	63.2	8.3
Black	15.6	288.5	264	278	285	302	329	99.9	92.4	32.8	2.0
Hispanic	6.9	283.5	259	278	286	306	323	99.6	85.8	30.1	1.9
Other [5]	4.2	312.5	—	—	—	—	—	100.0	97.9	61.6	15.9
1992											
Total	100.0	306.7	271	289	302	320	343	100.0	96.6	59.1	7.2
Male	50.7	308.9	275	291	306	323	344	100.0	96.9	60.5	9.1
Female	49.3	304.5	267	287	297	317	341	100.0	96.3	57.7	5.2
White	74.7	311.9	276	293	306	323	347	100.0	98.3	66.4	8.7
Black	14.8	285.8	256	279	283	301	313	100.0	89.6	29.8	0.9
Hispanic	7.4	292.2	269	285	297	312	320	100.0	94.1	39.2	1.2
Other [5]	3.1	317.1	—	—	—	—	—	100.0	96.5	69.8	16.9

[1] Indicates ability to perform simple additive reasoning and problem solving.
[2] Indicates ability to perform simple multiplicative reasoning and 2–step problem solving.
[3] Indicates ability to perform reasoning and problem solving involving fractions, decimals, percents, elementary geometry, and simple algebra.
[4] Indicates ability to perform reasoning and problem solving involving geometry, algebra, and beginning statistics and probability.
[5] Includes Asian/Pacific Islanders and American Indians/Alaskan Natives.
—Data not available.

NOTE.—These test scores are from the National Assessment of Educational Progress (NAEP). Scale ranges from 0 to 500.

SOURCE: U.S. Department of Education, National Center for Education Statistics, National Assessment of Educational Progress, *Trends in Academic Progress* and *NAEP 1992 Trends in Academic Progress,* prepared by Educational Testing Service. (This table was prepared May 1994.)

Table 121.—Percent of students at or above selected science proficiency levels,[1] by race/ethnicity and age: 1977 to 1992

Sex, race/ ethnicity, and year	9-year-olds [2]				13-year-olds [3]				17-year-olds [3]			
	Know everyday science facts	Understand simple scientific principles	Apply general scientific information	Analyze scientific procedures and data	Understand simple scientific principles	Apply general scientific information	Analyze scientific procedures and data	Integrate specialized scientific information	Understand simple scientific principles	Apply general scientific information	Analyze scientific procedures and data	Integrate specialized scientific information
1	2	3	4	5	6	7	8	9	10	11	12	13
Total												
1977	93.5	68.0	25.7	3.2	86.0	48.8	11.1	0.7	97.1	81.6	41.7	8.5
1982	95.2	70.7	24.3	2.3	89.8	50.9	9.6	0.4	95.7	76.6	37.3	7.1
1986	96.2	72.0	27.5	3.0	91.6	52.5	9.1	0.2	97.1	80.7	41.3	7.9
1990	97.0	76.4	31.1	3.1	92.3	56.5	11.2	0.4	96.7	81.2	43.3	9.2
1992	97.4	78.0	32.8	3.4	93.1	61.3	12.0	0.2	97.8	83.3	46.6	10.1
Male												
1977	94.3	69.5	27.4	3.7	87.2	52.3	13.1	0.9	97.8	85.2	48.8	11.8
1982	95.0	69.7	25.6	2.5	91.9	56.2	12.6	0.5	96.8	81.2	45.2	10.4
1986	96.8	74.1	29.9	3.8	92.9	57.3	11.9	0.3	97.4	82.4	48.8	11.4
1990	96.8	76.3	33.1	4.2	92.7	59.8	14.0	0.6	96.8	82.5	48.2	13.0
1992	97.7	80.4	37.2	4.6	93.1	62.9	14.2	0.3	98.0	85.0	50.9	13.6
Female												
1977	92.8	66.5	24.0	2.6	84.7	45.4	9.0	0.4	96.4	78.0	34.8	5.3
1982	95.5	71.8	23.0	2.1	87.9	46.0	6.9	0.2	94.6	72.2	29.9	3.9
1986	95.6	70.0	25.1	2.2	90.3	47.7	6.3	0.1	96.9	79.1	34.1	4.5
1990	97.1	76.4	29.1	2.0	92.0	53.3	8.5	0.2	96.6	79.9	38.7	5.5
1992	97.1	75.7	28.6	2.2	93.1	59.6	9.9	0.2	97.5	81.6	42.0	6.6
White [4]												
1977	97.7	76.8	30.8	3.9	92.2	56.5	13.4	0.8	99.2	88.2	47.5	10.0
1982	98.3	78.4	29.4	2.9	94.4	58.3	11.5	0.4	98.6	84.9	43.9	8.6
1986	98.2	78.9	32.7	3.8	96.1	61.0	11.3	0.3	98.8	87.8	48.7	9.6
1990	99.2	84.4	37.5	3.9	96.9	66.5	14.2	0.5	99.0	89.6	51.2	11.4
1992	99.2	85.5	39.4	4.3	97.9	71.1	15.0	0.3	99.3	90.5	55.4	12.8
Black [4]												
1977	72.4	27.2	3.5	0.2	57.3	14.9	1.2	0.0	83.6	40.5	7.7	0.4
1982	82.1	38.9	3.9	0.1	68.6	17.1	0.8	0.0	79.7	35.0	6.5	0.2
1986	88.6	46.2	8.3	0.3	73.6	19.6	1.1	0.0	90.9	52.2	12.5	0.9
1990	88.0	46.4	8.5	0.1	77.6	24.3	1.5	0.1	88.3	51.4	15.7	1.5
1992	90.7	51.3	9.2	0.3	73.8	26.2	1.8	0.0	92.1	55.7	14.1	0.8
Hispanic												
1977	84.6	42.0	8.8	0.3	62.2	18.1	1.8	0.0	93.1	61.5	18.5	1.8
1982	85.1	40.2	4.2	0.0	75.5	24.1	2.4	0.0	86.9	48.0	11.1	1.4
1986	89.6	50.1	10.7	0.2	76.7	24.9	1.5	0.0	93.3	60.0	14.8	1.1
1990	93.6	56.3	11.6	0.4	80.2	30.0	3.3	0.1	91.9	59.9	21.1	2.1
1992	92.4	55.5	11.7	0.4	86.2	36.5	3.3	0.0	94.6	68.3	23.0	2.5

[1] As measured by the National Assessment of Educational Progress (NAEP).
[2] Virtually no students were able to integrate specialized scientific information.
[3] Virtually all students knew everyday science facts. Data exclude persons not enrolled in school.
[4] Excludes persons of Hispanic origin.

SOURCE: U.S. Department of Education, National Assessment of Educational Progress, *Trends in Academic Progress* and *NAEP 1992 Trends in Academic Progress,* prepared by Educational Testing Service. (This table was prepared May 1994.)

Table 122.—Average science proficiency, by age and by selected characteristics of students: 1977 to 1992

Selected characteristics of students	9-year-olds					13-year-olds					17-year-olds [1]				
	1977	1982	1986	1990	1992	1977	1982	1986	1990	1992	1977	1982	1986	1990	1992
1	2	3	4	5	6	7	8	9	10	11	12	13	14	15	16
All students	**219.9**	**220.8**	**224.3**	**228.7**	**230.6**	**247.4**	**250.1**	**251.4**	**255.2**	**258.0**	**289.5**	**283.3**	**288.5**	**290.4**	**294.1**
Sex															
Male	222.1	221.0	227.3	230.3	234.7	251.1	255.6	256.1	258.5	260.1	297.0	291.9	294.9	295.6	299.1
Female	217.6	220.7	221.3	227.1	226.7	243.7	245.0	246.9	251.8	256.0	282.2	275.2	282.3	285.4	289.0
Race/ethnicity															
White, non-Hispanic	229.6	229.0	231.9	237.5	239.1	256.1	257.3	259.2	264.1	267.1	297.7	293.1	297.5	300.9	304.2
Black, non-Hispanic	174.8	187.0	196.2	196.4	200.3	208.1	217.1	221.6	225.7	224.4	240.2	234.7	252.8	253.0	256.2
Hispanic	191.9	189.0	199.4	206.2	204.7	213.4	225.5	226.1	231.6	237.5	262.3	248.7	259.3	261.5	270.2
Parental education															
Not high school graduate	198.5	198.2	203.6	209.8	217.2	223.5	225.3	229.4	232.9	233.8	265.3	258.5	257.5	261.4	262.0
Graduated high school	223.0	218.0	219.6	225.8	222.0	245.3	243.1	244.8	247.3	246.4	284.4	275.2	277.0	276.3	280.2
Some college	237.2	229.1	235.8	237.6	236.6	260.3	258.8	257.8	262.8	265.9	295.6	290.1	295.1	296.5	295.9
Graduated college	232.3	230.5	235.2	236.2	238.9	266.4	263.5	264.4	267.5	269.2	309.3	300.2	303.8	305.5	308.3
Type of school															
Public	218.0	219.7	222.6	227.7	229.1	245.2	248.5	250.9	253.6	257.2	288.2	282.3	287.1	289.0	292.2
Private	234.6	231.5	233.0	236.8	240.2	267.7	263.7	263.1	269.0	264.5	308.4	292.0	321.3	307.8	311.7
Type of community															
Advantaged urban	242.0	243.2	243.1	241.2	252.3	267.9	276.3	267.2	268.3	274.6	304.2	304.5	302.0	304.9	298.4
Disadvantaged urban	180.5	192.2	191.6	208.5	201.6	215.7	222.3	222.7	226.6	224.5	256.3	249.6	241.1	254.0	262.7
Extreme rural	224.5	212.4	224.0	233.0	227.6	244.8	244.9	257.5	249.3	262.3	289.0	283.3	296.2	293.9	295.3
Other	220.2	221.5	222.7	228.6	231.0	247.0	250.8	251.9	258.7	259.7	290.8	284.4	289.8	292.5	298.7
Region															
Northeast	224.4	221.8	228.2	231.1	234.4	255.2	254.1	257.6	256.8	256.8	296.3	284.4	292.2	292.6	300.1
Southeast	205.1	213.9	218.8	219.9	222.8	235.1	238.7	244.7	251.3	254.2	276.4	276.3	283.5	283.6	283.0
Central	225.2	226.3	227.9	234.2	237.5	253.8	253.8	249.4	260.4	262.5	294.0	289.3	294.4	299.6	304.2
West	220.9	219.9	222.1	229.5	227.4	243.0	252.4	252.3	252.6	258.0	286.5	280.9	283.2	285.8	290.4

[1] Excludes persons not enrolled in school.

NOTE.—These test scores are from the National Assessment of Educational Progress (NAEP). Performers at the 150 level know some general scientific facts of the type that could be learned from everyday experiences. Performers at the 200 level are developing some understanding of simple scientific principles, particularly in the life sciences. Performers at the 250 level can interpret data from simple tables and make inferences about the outcomes of experimental procedures. They exhibit knowledge and understanding of the life sciences and also demonstrate some knowledge of basic information from the physical sciences. Performers at the 300 level can evaluate the appropriateness of the design of an experiment and have the skill to apply their scientific knowledge in interpreting information from text and graphs. These students also exhibit a growing understanding of principles from the physical sciences. Performers at the 350 level can infer relationships and draw conclusions using detailed scientific knowledge from the physical sciences, particularly chemistry. They also can apply basic principles of genetics and interpret the societal implications of research in this field. Scale ranges from 0 to 500.

SOURCE: U.S. Department of Education, National Center for Education Statistics, National Assessment of Educational Progress, NAEP 1992 Trends in Academic Progress, prepared by Educational Testing Service. (This table was prepared May 1994.)

Table 123.—Twelfth graders' achievement on history, mathematics, reading, and science tests: 1992

Achievement test	Total	Sex		Race/ethnicity					Socioeconomic status [1]			Control of school		
		Male	Female	White	Black	Hispanic	Asian	American Indian	Low	Middle	High	Public	Catholic	Other private
1	2	3	4	5	6	7	8	9	10	11	12	13	14	15
	Twelfth graders' achievement, standardized score [2]													
History	51.2	51.9	50.5	52.5	45.9	47.4	52.1	44.5	45.8	50.5	55.9	50.8	55.1	54.9
Mathematics	51.4	51.8	51.0	52.9	44.8	47.3	54.3	45.2	45.5	50.6	56.7	50.9	55.1	56.1
Reading	51.0	49.9	52.2	52.4	45.5	47.2	51.4	45.2	45.9	50.4	55.5	50.6	54.7	55.0
Science	51.1	52.4	49.7	52.9	43.3	46.5	51.8	44.8	45.4	50.5	55.9	50.7	53.9	55.0
	Distribution of twelfth graders' achievement, by score quartile [3]													
History	100.0	100.0	100.0	100.0	100.0	100.0	100.0	100.0	100.0	100.0	100.0	100.0	100.0	100.0
Lower quartile	20.2	19.6	20.9	15.5	39.6	32.4	16.8	41.1	37.6	20.5	7.9	21.4	7.1	13.8
Lower middle quartile	24.6	21.5	27.9	23.4	28.1	28.9	25.6	32.5	30.9	26.9	16.5	25.2	21.0	17.2
Upper middle quartile	26.9	26.3	27.4	28.4	21.5	23.5	25.5	13.6	21.1	27.7	29.2	26.8	31.2	22.1
Upper quartile	28.3	32.5	23.8	32.7	10.8	15.3	32.2	12.7	10.3	24.8	46.5	26.6	40.7	46.9
Mathematics	100.0	100.0	100.0	100.0	100.0	100.0	100.0	100.0	100.0	100.0	100.0	100.0	100.0	100.0
Lower quartile	19.7	20.1	19.2	14.8	41.2	31.6	11.9	42.8	37.0	20.4	7.6	20.9	8.2	7.6
Lower middle quartile	24.2	22.4	26.0	22.5	30.0	30.6	21.1	29.8	32.4	26.3	15.2	24.9	17.0	17.3
Upper middle quartile	27.6	26.9	28.4	29.5	20.3	22.9	28.4	18.5	22.4	29.3	28.4	27.2	34.3	28.5
Upper quartile	28.5	30.6	26.3	33.2	8.5	14.9	38.7	8.9	8.3	23.9	50.0	27.0	40.5	46.6
Reading	100.0	100.0	100.0	100.0	100.0	100.0	100.0	100.0	100.0	100.0	100.0	100.0	100.0	100.0
Lower quartile	21.1	25.6	16.4	16.6	38.2	31.6	23.2	41.2	36.3	21.6	9.8	22.3	8.1	14.0
Lower middle quartile	24.6	24.5	24.7	22.6	31.3	32.9	20.0	31.1	32.4	26.8	15.8	25.5	18.1	13.6
Upper middle quartile	26.4	25.0	27.9	28.3	20.7	21.2	24.9	15.5	20.8	27.4	28.6	25.8	36.3	25.2
Upper quartile	27.8	24.9	30.9	32.5	9.8	14.3	31.9	12.2	10.5	24.3	45.9	26.4	37.5	47.2
Science	100.0	100.0	100.0	100.0	100.0	100.0	100.0	100.0	100.0	100.0	100.0	100.0	100.0	100.0
Lower quartile	20.9	18.2	23.6	14.0	52.6	34.3	17.7	37.6	39.0	20.9	8.4	21.9	11.7	10.5
Lower middle quartile	24.5	21.1	28.1	23.0	25.2	33.8	25.2	35.8	31.9	26.8	16.0	25.0	22.0	17.4
Upper middle quartile	26.3	27.1	25.5	29.0	16.0	18.9	26.5	20.9	19.8	28.3	27.4	26.3	27.3	26.1
Upper quartile	28.3	33.6	22.7	33.9	6.2	13.1	30.5	5.7	9.3	24.1	48.3	26.8	39.0	46.0

[1] Socioeconomic status was measured by a composite score on parental education and occupations, and family income. The "Low" SES group is the lowest quartile; the "Middle" SES group is the middle two quartiles; and the "High" SES group is the upper quartile.

[2] In the full data file, the standardized scores have a mean of 50 and a standard deviation of 10. Because dropouts and students who were retained in grades between 8 and 11 were excluded from this tabulation, the scores are slightly higher.

[3] In the full data file, twenty-five percent of all students fall into each one of the quartile groupings. Because dropouts and students who were retained in grades between 8 and 11 were excluded from this tabulation, the scores are slightly higher.

NOTE.—Because of rounding, details may not add to totals.

SOURCE: U.S. Department of Education, National Center for Education Statistics, "National Education Longitudinal Study of 1988, Second Followup" survey. (This table was prepared July 1995.)

Table 124.—Scholastic Aptitude Test score averages for college-bound high school seniors, by sex: 1966–67 to 1993–94

School year	Verbal score			Mathematical score		
	Total	Male	Female	Total	Male	Female
1	2	3	4	5	6	7
1966–67	466	463	468	492	514	467
1967–68	466	464	466	492	512	470
1968–69	463	459	466	493	513	470
1969–70	460	459	461	488	509	465
1970–71	455	454	457	488	507	466
1971–72	453	454	452	484	505	461
1972–73	445	446	443	481	502	460
1973–74	444	447	442	480	501	459
1974–75	434	437	431	472	495	449
1975–76	431	433	430	472	497	446
1976–77	429	431	427	470	497	445
1977–78	429	433	425	468	494	444
1978–79	427	431	423	467	493	443
1979–80	424	428	420	466	491	443
1980–81	424	430	418	466	492	443
1981–82	426	431	421	467	493	443
1982–83	425	430	420	468	493	445
1983–84	426	433	420	471	495	449
1984–85	431	437	425	475	499	452
1985–86	431	437	426	475	501	451
1986–87	430	435	425	476	500	453
1987–88	428	435	422	476	498	455
1988–89	427	434	421	476	500	454
1989–90	424	429	419	476	499	455
1990–91	422	426	418	474	497	453
1991–92	423	428	419	476	499	456
1992–93	424	428	420	478	502	457
1993–94	423	425	421	479	501	460

NOTE.—Possible scores on each part of the SAT range from 200 to 800. Data for the years 1966–67 through 1970–71 are estimates derived from the test scores of all participants.

SOURCE: College Entrance Examination Board, *National Report on College-Bound Seniors*, various years. (Copyright © 1994 by the College Entrance Examination Board. All rights reserved.) (This table was prepared March 1995.)

Table 125.—Scholastic Aptitude Test score averages, by race/ethnicity: 1975–76 to 1993–94

Racial/ethnic background	1975–76	1977–78	1978–79	1979–80	1980–81	1981–82	1982–83	1983–84	1984–85	1986–87	1987–88	1988–89	1989–90	1990–91	1991–92	1992–93	1993–94
1	2	3	4	5	6	7	8	9	10	11	12	13	14	15	16	17	18
SAT-Verbal																	
All students	431	429	427	424	424	426	425	426	431	430	428	427	424	422	423	424	423
White	451	446	444	442	442	444	443	445	449	447	445	446	442	441	442	444	443
Black	332	332	330	330	332	341	339	342	346	351	353	351	352	351	352	353	352
Mexican-American	371	370	370	372	373	377	375	376	382	379	382	381	380	377	372	374	372
Puerto Rican	364	349	345	350	353	360	358	358	368	360	355	360	359	361	366	367	367
Asian-American	414	401	396	396	397	398	395	398	404	405	408	409	410	411	413	415	416
American Indian	388	387	386	390	391	388	388	390	392	393	393	384	388	393	395	400	396
Other	410	399	393	394	388	392	386	388	391	405	410	414	410	411	417	422	425
SAT-Mathematical																	
All students	472	468	467	466	466	467	468	471	475	476	476	476	476	474	476	478	479
White	493	485	483	482	483	483	484	487	490	489	490	491	491	489	491	494	495
Black	354	354	358	360	362	366	369	373	376	377	384	386	385	385	385	388	388
Mexican-American	410	402	410	413	415	416	417	420	426	424	428	430	429	427	425	428	427
Puerto Rican	401	388	388	394	398	403	403	405	409	400	402	406	405	406	406	409	411
Asian-American	518	510	511	509	513	513	514	519	518	521	522	525	528	530	532	535	535
American Indian	420	419	421	426	425	424	425	427	428	432	435	428	437	437	442	447	441
Other	458	450	447	449	447	449	446	450	448	455	460	467	467	466	473	477	480

NOTE.—Possible scores on each part of the SAT range from 200 to 800. No racial/ethnic group data are available prior to 1975–76. No data are available for 1985–86 due to changes in the Student Descriptive Questionnaire completed when students registered for the test.

SOURCE: College Entrance Examination Board, *National Report on College Bound Seniors*, various years. (Copyright © 1994 by the College Entrance Examination Board. All rights reserved.) (This table was prepared March 1995.)

Table 126.—Distribution of Scholastic Aptitude Test scores, by sex of student: 1975–76 to 1993–94

Year	Number of test takers	Percent of students with specified scores											
		200 or higher	250 or higher	300 or higher	350 or higher	400 or higher	450 or higher	500 or higher	550 or higher	600 or higher	650 or higher	700 or higher	750 or higher
1	2	3	4	5	6	7	8	9	10	11	12	13	14

						Verbal							
Total													
1975–76	999,809	100.00	96.26	89.26	77.47	60.27	43.01	28.11	15.58	8.20	3.55	1.23	0.25
1980–81	994,046	100.00	95.46	87.32	75.34	58.44	40.64	25.76	13.87	7.00	3.01	1.03	0.21
1985–86	1,000,748	100.00	95.81	88.92	77.55	61.77	43.17	28.03	15.75	7.87	3.25	0.99	0.14
1986–87	1,080,426	100.00	96.08	88.57	76.62	60.18	43.02	27.85	15.44	8.14	3.42	1.07	0.13
1987–88	1,134,364	100.00	95.81	88.62	76.44	60.53	42.38	26.91	14.94	7.32	3.22	0.92	0.09
1988–89	1,088,223	100.00	95.72	88.21	75.39	59.55	42.17	26.77	14.85	7.76	3.16	0.87	0.10
1989–90	1,025,523	100.00	95.20	87.44	74.97	58.70	40.67	25.11	14.41	7.43	3.13	1.00	0.12
1990–91	1,032,685	100.00	94.89	86.96	74.38	57.58	40.38	25.22	14.08	7.25	3.15	1.03	0.13
1991–92	1,034,131	100.00	94.70	86.95	74.29	58.68	40.96	25.42	14.02	7.28	3.18	0.98	0.13
1992–93	1,044,465	100.00	94.85	87.20	74.71	58.70	40.85	25.77	14.87	7.77	3.37	1.00	0.12
1993–94	1,050,386	100.00	94.76	86.97	74.58	57.72	40.26	25.95	14.76	7.58	3.32	1.11	0.14
Male													
1975–76	494,626	100.00	96.39	89.54	77.90	60.90	43.65	28.69	16.04	8.49	3.69	1.29	0.26
1980–81	478,448	100.00	95.97	88.50	77.16	60.73	42.89	27.53	15.03	7.67	3.30	1.13	0.23
1985–86	481,477	100.00	96.19	89.87	79.10	63.74	45.17	29.77	17.02	8.71	3.68	1.11	0.15
1986–87	520,326	100.00	96.23	89.12	77.72	61.79	44.91	29.71	16.93	9.22	4.02	1.26	0.15
1987–88	544,065	100.00	96.14	89.54	78.21	62.92	45.04	29.25	16.70	8.44	3.82	1.13	0.11
1988–89	521,229	100.00	96.00	89.06	77.04	61.86	44.81	29.15	16.63	8.93	3.75	1.07	0.12
1989–90	490,420	100.00	95.40	88.00	76.04	60.19	42.62	27.05	15.91	8.40	3.60	1.15	0.14
1990–91	493,252	100.00	95.08	87.45	75.29	58.94	41.99	26.71	15.18	7.98	3.51	1.16	0.14
1991–92	491,748	100.00	94.89	87.46	75.34	60.23	42.68	26.98	15.16	8.00	3.55	1.10	0.15
1992–93	495,086	100.00	94.98	87.55	75.35	59.75	42.21	27.18	16.01	8.60	3.83	1.18	0.15
1993–94	493,063	100.00	94.67	86.93	74.71	58.21	41.15	26.90	15.54	8.10	3.61	1.23	0.15
Female													
1975–76	505,183	100.00	96.14	88.97	77.05	59.65	42.38	27.55	15.13	7.92	3.42	1.17	0.24
1980–81	515,598	100.00	94.99	86.23	73.66	56.32	38.56	24.11	12.80	6.39	2.73	0.94	0.18
1985–86	519,271	100.00	95.46	88.04	76.11	59.95	41.31	26.42	14.57	7.09	2.85	0.88	0.12
1986–87	560,100	100.00	95.93	88.07	75.60	58.67	41.26	26.13	14.05	7.14	2.87	0.90	0.11
1987–88	590,299	100.00	95.50	87.76	74.82	58.33	39.93	24.76	13.32	6.29	2.66	0.74	0.06
1988–89	566,994	100.00	95.45	87.42	73.88	57.42	39.75	24.58	13.21	6.68	2.61	0.69	0.08
1989–90	535,103	100.00	95.01	86.93	73.98	57.34	38.88	23.34	13.04	6.53	2.70	0.86	0.10
1990–91	539,433	100.00	94.71	86.52	73.55	56.33	38.90	23.85	13.08	6.58	2.81	0.92	0.12
1991–92	542,383	100.00	94.53	86.49	73.34	57.28	39.40	24.00	12.98	6.62	2.84	0.87	0.12
1992–93	549,379	100.00	94.74	86.88	74.13	57.76	39.62	24.50	13.84	7.01	2.95	0.83	0.09
1993–94	557,323	100.00	94.84	87.01	74.47	57.28	39.49	25.10	14.06	7.12	3.06	1.00	0.12
						Mathematical							
Total													
1975–76	999,776	100.00	98.78	93.65	83.55	70.87	57.16	41.82	26.94	16.34	8.49	3.75	1.16
1980–81	993,672	100.00	98.85	92.99	82.77	70.48	55.57	40.59	25.98	14.45	7.08	2.71	0.66
1985–86	1,000,747	100.00	98.91	93.63	84.64	71.98	57.41	42.32	29.29	17.95	9.56	4.08	1.01
1986–87	1,080,426	100.00	98.91	93.30	84.22	71.61	57.40	42.37	29.67	18.32	9.94	3.86	1.02
1987–88	1,134,364	100.00	99.08	93.93	84.62	72.17	57.43	43.03	29.55	17.60	9.26	3.78	0.91
1988–89	1,088,223	100.00	99.08	94.04	84.57	71.97	57.94	42.81	29.33	18.01	10.07	4.27	1.11
1989–90	1,025,523	100.00	98.89	93.77	84.21	71.57	57.71	43.20	29.59	18.41	10.14	4.23	1.18
1990–91	1,032,685	100.00	98.83	93.63	83.49	70.80	56.63	42.68	29.27	17.85	9.70	4.51	1.32
1991–92	1,034,131	100.00	98.70	93.65	84.25	71.81	57.96	43.36	28.83	18.12	10.10	4.60	1.37
1992–93	1,044,465	100.00	98.49	93.34	84.28	72.33	58.55	44.39	29.78	18.80	10.63	5.11	1.62
1993–94	1,050,386	100.00	98.51	93.75	84.49	72.99	59.13	44.48	30.21	18.90	10.56	4.85	1.42
Male													
1975–76	494,619	100.00	99.13	95.37	87.63	77.29	65.30	50.65	34.93	22.71	12.70	6.02	1.99
1980–81	478,301	100.00	99.20	94.98	87.17	77.17	63.99	49.45	33.92	20.38	10.75	4.46	1.17
1985–86	481,477	100.00	99.24	95.38	88.49	78.26	65.53	51.16	37.47	24.49	14.00	6.44	1.73
1986–87	520,326	100.00	99.16	94.91	87.75	77.36	64.90	50.74	37.66	24.82	14.47	6.15	1.75
1987–88	544,065	100.00	99.31	95.37	87.91	77.48	64.40	50.71	36.91	23.63	13.43	5.96	1.57
1988–89	521,229	100.00	99.30	95.45	88.00	77.62	65.19	50.91	37.13	24.43	14.62	6.70	1.89
1989–90	490,420	100.00	99.16	95.17	87.70	77.13	64.71	50.81	36.85	24.40	14.41	6.53	2.00
1990–91	493,252	100.00	99.08	94.91	86.79	76.22	63.65	50.40	36.59	23.82	13.93	6.96	2.23
1991–92	491,748	100.00	98.99	95.05	87.50	77.03	64.73	50.88	36.01	24.05	14.28	6.96	2.24
1992–93	495,086	100.00	98.83	94.73	87.55	77.69	65.50	52.10	37.18	25.00	15.09	7.77	2.69
1993–94	493,063	100.00	98.86	94.97	87.55	77.92	65.65	51.91	37.27	24.78	14.75	7.28	2.29
Female													
1975–76	505,157	100.00	98.45	91.96	79.56	64.59	49.20	33.17	19.12	10.11	4.37	1.53	0.34
1980–81	515,371	100.00	98.53	91.14	78.69	64.27	47.76	32.37	18.60	8.94	3.66	1.09	0.19
1985–86	519,270	100.00	98.61	92.01	81.07	66.16	49.87	34.12	21.70	11.88	5.45	1.89	0.34
1986–87	560,100	100.00	98.67	91.80	80.93	66.26	50.44	34.59	22.25	12.29	5.74	1.73	0.33
1987–88	590,299	100.00	98.87	92.60	81.58	67.28	51.00	35.94	22.78	12.05	5.42	1.77	0.30
1988–89	566,994	100.00	98.87	92.75	81.42	66.77	51.27	35.37	22.15	12.11	5.90	2.03	0.39
1989–90	535,103	100.00	98.65	92.50	81.01	66.47	51.30	36.22	22.94	12.92	6.22	2.12	0.44
1990–91	539,433	100.00	98.60	92.45	80.48	65.85	50.22	35.62	22.57	12.40	5.83	2.26	0.49
1991–92	542,383	100.00	98.45	92.37	81.31	67.07	51.82	36.54	22.32	12.74	6.30	2.45	0.57
1992–93	549,379	100.00	98.18	92.09	81.34	67.50	52.28	37.45	23.11	13.21	6.61	2.72	0.65
1993–94	557,323	100.00	98.25	92.72	81.79	68.64	53.36	37.92	23.96	13.69	6.86	2.69	0.65

NOTE.—Possible scores on each part of the SAT range from 200 to 800. In some years, mathematics and verbal test results were not available for every student.

SOURCE: College Entrance Examination Board, *National Report on College-Bound Seniors*, various years. (Copyright © 1994 by the College Entrance Examination Board. All rights reserved.) (This table was prepared April 1995.)

Table 127.—Scholastic Aptitude Test score averages, by intended area of study:[1] 1977–78 to 1993–94

Test and year	Intended area of study[2]									
	Arts and humanities	Biological sciences and related areas	Business, commerce, and communications	Computer and information sciences	Education	Engineering	Mathematics	Physical sciences	Social sciences and related areas	Miscellaneous[3]
1	2	3	4	5	6	7	8	9	10	11
Verbal										
1977–78	439	436	409	420	396	448	464	499	448	422
1978–79	436	435	408	419	392	445	459	498	446	420
1979–80	434	433	406	417	389	444	455	495	448	419
1980–81	434	433	406	416	391	446	456	498	446	420
1981–82	436	434	409	417	394	449	455	496	450	424
1982–83	438	432	409	413	394	448	453	496	451	421
1983–84	440	434	410	411	398	453	457	501	451	423
1984–85	445	439	414	413	404	453	459	506	454	429
1986–87	447	438	415	403	408	456	475	507	452	410
1987–88	444	434	414	400	407	453	468	500	447	409
1988–89	445	433	414	396	406	452	473	504	447	410
1989–90	441	430	410	392	406	449	473	503	441	408
1990–91	440	428	407	390	406	446	469	497	437	410
1991–92	442	428	407	394	407	447	467	497	435	414
1992–93	444	427	407	400	409	448	468	497	435	415
1993–94	441	427	407	406	407	446	471	496	435	414
Change, 1982–83 to 1993–94	3	−5	−2	−7	13	−2	18	0	−16	−7
Mathematical										
1977–78	454	474	448	499	422	540	585	566	464	461
1978–79	452	472	448	498	420	536	580	561	463	458
1979–80	452	472	446	496	418	535	577	560	463	459
1980–81	453	472	446	492	418	534	572	558	463	459
1981–82	452	470	446	489	419	537	569	558	464	461
1982–83	454	470	445	484	418	539	572	560	466	460
1983–84	456	475	449	483	425	543	578	564	467	463
1984–85	462	480	455	488	432	545	578	569	471	469
1986–87	469	482	459	476	437	554	602	576	472	453
1987–88	471	482	462	470	442	547	596	568	472	455
1988–89	473	481	465	472	440	551	606	577	473	459
1989–90	475	481	465	468	442	550	609	577	471	460
1990–91	473	478	462	467	441	548	605	572	466	463
1991–92	475	479	463	472	443	550	606	573	465	472
1992–93	478	480	465	479	446	553	607	574	464	481
1993–94	480	482	468	488	447	553	611	574	467	472
Change, 1982–83 to 1993–94	26	12	23	4	29	14	39	14	1	12

[1] Students indicated their first and second choices of fields of study. Only their first choices are reported here.

[2] Based on classifications reported by College Entrance Examination Board.

[3] Includes "trade and vocational," "other," and "undecided" through 1984–85. Data for 1985–86 to 1993–94 exclude "other."

NOTE.—Possible scores on each part of the SAT range from 200 to 800. No data are available for 1985–86 due to changes in the Student Descriptive Questionnaire completed when students registered for the test.

SOURCE: College Entrance Examination Board, *National Report on College-Bound Seniors*, various years. (Copyright © 1994 by the College Entrance Examination Board. All rights reserved.) (This table was prepared April 1995.)

Table 128.—Scholastic Aptitude Test score averages, by class rank:[1] 1976–77 to 1993–94

Year	Top tenth		Second tenth		Second fifth		Third fifth		Fourth fifth		Lowest fifth	
	Verbal	Mathematics	Verbal	Mathematics	Verbal	Mathematics	Verbal	Mathematics	Verbal	Mathematics	Verbal	Mathematics
1	2	3	4	5	6	7	8	9	10	11	12	13
1976–77	518	574	452	499	415	453	372	401	347	374	339	364
1977–78	515	570	450	494	414	451	372	400	349	374	339	364
1978–79	514	568	448	494	413	451	371	400	347	372	337	364
1979–80	510	568	446	494	411	451	370	401	346	373	339	366
1980–81	511	567	447	496	412	453	371	402	348	374	339	368
1981–82	511	568	449	497	415	454	374	404	349	375	343	368
1982–83	508	570	447	498	414	455	374	403	351	375	343	369
1983–84	511	575	450	503	417	459	377	406	353	377	341	365
1984–85	516	577	455	508	421	463	381	411	357	380	346	369
1986–87	518	585	456	511	418	461	380	409	358	380	353	374
1987–88	515	585	454	511	417	463	379	411	358	382	352	373
1988–89	515	585	453	512	416	463	376	410	354	381	346	373
1989–90	512	585	449	512	412	463	373	410	351	381	342	370
1990–91	512	584	448	511	411	462	372	409	350	379	340	368
1991–92	512	585	448	511	412	464	373	411	350	379	338	363
1992–93	513	586	449	513	412	466	373	413	350	380	336	363
1993–94	512	586	447	514	410	467	373	415	349	382	332	363

[1] Self-reported class rank.

NOTE.—Possible scores on each part of the SAT range from 200 to 800.

SOURCE: College Entrance Examination Board, *National Report on College-Bound Seniors*, various years. (Copyright © 1994 by the College Entrance Examination Board. All rights reserved.) (This table was prepared April 1995.)

Table 129.—Scholastic Aptitude Test score averages, by state: 1974–75 to 1993–94

State	1974–75 Verbal	1974–75 Mathematical	1980–81 Verbal	1980–81 Mathematical	1985–86 Verbal	1985–86 Mathematical	1990–91 Verbal	1990–91 Mathematical	1991–92 Verbal	1991–92 Mathematical	1992–93 Verbal	1992–93 Mathematical	1993–94 Verbal	1993–94 Mathematical	Percent of graduates taking SAT, 1993–94[1]
1	2	3	4	5	6	7	8	9	10	11	12	13	14	15	16
United States	434	472	424	466	431	475	422	474	423	476	424	478	423	479	42
Alabama	426	457	457	488	476	514	476	515	476	520	480	526	482	529	8
Alaska	461	481	449	486	445	479	439	481	433	475	438	477	434	477	49
Arizona	496	525	476	514	466	509	442	490	440	493	444	497	443	496	26
Arkansas	482	510	477	510	482	519	482	523	474	516	478	519	477	518	6
California	435	473	426	475	423	481	415	482	416	484	415	484	413	482	46
Colorado	479	515	467	513	466	514	453	506	453	507	454	509	456	513	28
Connecticut	442	471	430	463	440	474	429	468	430	470	430	474	426	472	80
Delaware	439	476	429	470	442	475	428	464	432	463	429	465	428	464	68
District of Columbia	—	—	—	—	413	439	405	435	405	437	405	441	406	443	53
Florida	441	474	424	463	426	469	416	466	416	468	416	466	413	466	49
Georgia	397	427	390	426	402	440	400	444	398	444	399	445	398	446	65
Hawaii	414	478	390	464	403	477	405	478	401	477	401	478	401	480	58
Idaho	493	524	486	523	475	512	463	505	460	503	465	507	461	508	16
Illinois	460	510	459	508	466	519	471	535	473	537	475	541	478	546	14
Indiana	418	463	406	451	415	459	408	457	409	459	409	460	410	466	60
Iowa	523	568	515	566	519	576	515	578	512	584	520	583	506	574	5
Kansas	503	540	502	542	498	544	493	546	487	546	494	548	494	550	10
Kentucky	470	507	474	509	483	519	473	520	470	518	476	522	474	523	11
Louisiana	456	491	461	494	474	507	476	518	471	520	481	527	481	530	9
Maine	437	471	426	465	434	466	421	458	422	460	422	463	420	463	68
Maryland	436	471	423	461	436	475	429	475	431	476	431	478	429	479	64
Massachusetts	434	469	422	462	436	473	426	470	428	474	427	476	426	475	79
Michigan	451	498	456	508	462	514	461	519	464	523	469	528	472	537	11
Minnesota	506	552	486	539	482	540	480	543	492	561	489	556	495	562	9
Mississippi	477	503	473	502	485	516	477	520	478	526	481	521	485	528	4
Missouri	465	500	462	504	476	519	476	526	475	529	481	532	485	537	10
Montana	500	547	485	539	485	541	464	518	465	523	459	516	463	523	21
Nebraska	459	507	489	537	493	549	481	543	478	540	479	544	482	543	9
Nevada	465	497	445	487	445	485	435	484	434	488	432	488	429	484	30
New Hampshire	449	485	439	479	450	485	440	481	440	483	442	487	438	486	69
New Jersey	424	454	414	450	424	465	417	469	420	471	419	473	418	475	71
New Mexico	486	516	474	510	489	527	474	522	475	521	478	525	475	528	12
New York	441	484	427	471	427	471	413	468	416	466	416	471	416	472	76
North Carolina	399	428	391	427	399	436	400	444	405	450	406	453	405	455	60
North Dakota	510	554	494	544	508	556	502	571	501	567	518	583	497	559	5
Ohio	456	499	457	500	460	503	450	496	450	501	454	505	456	510	24
Oklahoma	480	514	485	526	487	521	476	521	480	527	482	530	482	537	9
Oregon	440	468	431	469	444	486	439	483	439	486	441	492	436	491	53
Pennsylvania	430	470	421	459	429	465	417	459	418	459	418	460	417	462	70
Rhode Island	432	469	415	452	432	466	421	459	421	460	419	464	420	462	68
South Carolina	382	412	374	406	395	431	395	437	394	437	396	442	395	443	60
South Dakota	523	561	519	561	531	567	496	551	490	550	502	558	483	548	5
Tennessee	477	511	475	514	486	521	487	528	484	529	486	531	488	535	12
Texas	431	467	415	455	419	458	411	463	410	466	413	472	412	474	48
Utah	516	553	511	548	506	541	494	537	496	545	500	549	509	558	4
Vermont	439	476	427	467	442	474	424	466	429	468	426	467	427	472	68
Virginia	431	463	424	461	435	473	424	466	425	468	425	469	424	469	65
Washington	489	522	472	517	461	502	433	480	432	484	435	486	434	488	49
West Virginia	462	502	458	495	462	502	441	485	440	484	439	485	439	482	17
Wisconsin	492	544	477	533	478	536	481	542	481	548	485	551	487	557	9
Wyoming	506	548	478	528	484	534	466	514	462	516	463	507	459	521	12

[1] Based on the number of high school graduates in 1994 as projected by the Western Interstate Commission for Higher Education and the number of 1994 seniors who took the SAT.

—Data not available.

NOTE.—Possible scores on each part of the SAT range from 200 to 800. Rankings of states based on SAT scores alone are invalid because of the varying proportions of students in each state taking the tests.

SOURCE: College Entrance Examination Board, News Release, "College Board Reports SAT Scores Up Again This Year for All Students and Most Ethnic Subgroups." "SAT Math Scores for Class of 1994 Continue Upward Trend while Verbal Scores Plateau near 1980 Levels." (Copyright © 1994 by the College Entrance Examination Board. All rights reserved.) (This table was prepared April 1995.)

Table 130.—American College Testing (ACT) score [1] averages, by sex: 1967 to 1994

Type of test and sex	1967	1970	1975	1980	1982	1983	1984	1985	1986	1987	1988	1989	1990[1]	1991[1]	1992[1]	1993[1]	1994[1]
1	2	3	4	5	6	7	8	9	10	11	12	13	14	15	16	17	18
Participants: [2] Total (in thousands) ..	788	714	822	836	805	835	849	739	730	777	842	855	817	796	832	876	892
								Test scores [3]									
Composite, total	19.9	18.6	18.5	18.5	18.4	18.3	18.5	18.6	18.8	18.7	18.8	18.6	20.6	20.6	20.6	20.7	20.8
Male	20.3	19.5	19.3	19.3	19.2	19.1	19.3	19.4	19.6	19.5	19.6	19.3	21.0	20.9	20.9	21.0	20.9
Female	19.4	17.8	17.9	17.8	17.8	17.6	17.9	17.9	18.1	18.1	18.1	18.0	20.3	20.4	20.5	20.5	20.7
English, total	18.5	17.7	17.9	17.8	17.9	17.8	18.1	18.1	18.5	18.4	18.5	18.4	20.5	20.3	20.2	20.3	20.3
Male	17.6	17.1	17.3	17.3	17.3	17.3	17.5	17.6	17.9	17.9	18.0	17.8	20.1	19.8	19.8	19.8	19.8
Female	19.4	18.3	18.3	18.2	18.4	18.2	18.6	18.6	18.9	18.9	19.0	18.9	20.9	20.7	20.6	20.6	20.7
Math, total	20.0	17.6	17.4	17.3	17.2	16.9	17.3	17.2	17.3	17.2	17.2	17.1	19.9	20.0	20.0	20.1	20.2
Male	21.1	19.3	18.9	18.9	18.6	18.4	18.6	18.6	18.8	18.6	18.4	18.3	20.7	20.6	20.7	20.8	20.8
Female	18.8	16.2	16.2	16.0	16.0	15.7	16.1	16.0	16.0	16.1	16.1	16.1	19.3	19.4	19.5	19.6	19.6
Social studies, total [4]	19.7	17.4	17.2	17.2	17.3	17.1	17.3	17.4	17.6	17.5	17.4	17.2	—	21.2	21.1	21.2	21.2
Male	20.3	18.7	18.3	18.3	18.1	18.0	18.1	18.3	18.6	18.4	18.4	18.1	—	21.3	21.1	21.2	21.1
Female	19.0	16.4	16.4	16.4	16.6	16.4	16.5	16.6	16.9	16.7	16.6	16.4	—	21.1	21.1	21.2	21.4
Natural science, total [5] ..	20.8	21.1	21.1	21.0	20.8	20.9	21.0	21.2	21.4	21.4	21.4	21.2	—	20.7	20.7	20.8	20.9
Male	21.6	22.4	22.4	22.3	22.2	22.4	22.4	22.6	22.7	22.8	22.8	22.6	—	21.3	21.4	21.5	21.6
Female	20.0	20.0	20.0	20.0	19.7	19.6	19.9	20.0	20.2	20.1	20.2	20.0	—	20.1	20.1	20.3	20.4
								Percent									
Obtaining composite scores of— 26 or above [6]	14	14	13	13	13	13	13	14	14	14	14	14	12	11	12	12	13
15 or below [7]	21	33	33	33	34	35	33	32	31	31	31	32	35	35	35	35	34
Planned major field of study Business [8]	18	21	20	19	19	18	19	21	22	23	23	22	20	18	15	13	12
Engineering [9]	8	6	8	10	11	10	9	9	9	8	9	9	9	10	10	9	9
Social science [10]	10	9	6	6	6	6	7	7	8	9	10	11	10	10	10	9	9
Education [11]	16	12	9	7	6	6	6	6	7	8	8	8	8	10	5	8	8

[1] 1990 and later data are not comparable with previous years because a new version of the ACT was introduced. Estimated average composite scores for the new version for prior years were: 1989, 20.6; 1988, 1987, and 1986, 20.8; and 1982, 20.3.

[2] Beginning in 1985, data are for seniors who graduated in year shown and had taken the ACT in their junior or senior years.

[3] Minimum score, 1; maximum score, 36.

[4] Beginning in 1990, the test was changed to "reading".

[5] Beginning in 1990, the test was changed to "science reasoning".

[6] Beginning in 1990, scores were 27 or above.

[7] As of 1990, scores were 18 or below.

[8] Includes political and persuasive (e.g., sales) fields through 1975; thereafter, business and commerce.

[9] In 1993 and 1994, includes engineering and engineering related technologies.

[10] Includes religion through 1975.

[11] Includes education and teacher education.

—Not available.

SOURCE: The American College Testing program, *High School Profile Report*, annual. (This table prepared April 1995.)

Table 131.—Percent of high school seniors reporting they are in general, college preparatory, and vocational programs, by student characteristics: 1982 and 1992

Student characteristics	General [1]		College preparatory or academic		Vocational	
	1982	1992	1982	1992	1982	1992
1	2	3	4	5	6	7
All seniors	35.2	45.3	37.9	43.0	26.9	11.7
Males	38.1	46.3	36.8	41.8	25.1	11.9
Females	32.4	44.2	38.9	44.2	28.7	11.6
Race/ethnicity						
White	34.8	43.3	40.6	45.7	24.6	11.0
Black	35.1	48.9	33.3	35.6	31.6	15.4
Hispanic	37.4	56.4	24.9	30.6	37.7	13.1
Asian	27.5	40.3	55.9	50.9	16.6	8.8
American Indian	55.3	60.8	19.1	22.6	25.6	16.7
Test performance quartile						
Lowest test quartile	42.0	61.5	12.3	15.2	45.6	23.3
Second test quartile	44.6	53.9	20.5	30.0	34.9	16.1
Third test quartile	37.9	39.7	37.6	50.0	24.5	10.4
Highest test quartile	18.9	25.4	73.1	72.0	8.0	2.6
Socioeconomic status [2]						
Low quartile	40.3	55.6	20.5	23.2	39.2	21.2
Middle 2 quartiles	36.2	46.0	36.4	40.9	27.4	13.1
High quartile	27.4	36.2	60.1	60.8	12.5	3.0
Control of school						
Public	36.7	47.1	34.5	40.0	28.8	12.9
Catholic	21.9	24.4	67.4	73.5	10.7	2.2
Other private	22.1	33.1	67.6	65.9	10.3	1.0
Location of school						
Urban	32.2	43.3	37.4	45.5	30.4	11.2
Suburban	33.6	45.5	41.4	44.6	25.0	9.8
Rural/nonmetropolitan area	39.6	46.5	32.6	38.6	27.9	14.9

[1] Includes special education, "other," and "don't know."

[2] Socioeconomic status was measured by a composite score on parental education and occupations, and family income. The "Low" SES group is the lowest quartile; the "Middle" SES group is the middle two quartiles; and the "High" SES group is the upper quartile.

SOURCE: U.S. Department of Education, National Center for Education Statistics, "High School and Beyond," First Followup survey; and "National Education Longitudinal Study of 1988," Second Followup Student survey. (This table was prepared April 1995.)

Table 132.—Average number of Carnegie units earned by public high school graduates in various subject fields, by student characteristics: 1982 to 1992

Student characteristics	Total	English	History/social studies	Mathematics Total	Less than algebra	Algebra or higher	Science Total	General science	Biology	Chemistry	Physics	Foreign languages	Arts	Vocational education[1]	Personal use[2]	Computer science[3]
1	2	3	4	5	6	7	8	9	10	11	12	13	14	15	16	17
1982 graduates	21.44	3.87	3.16	2.55	0.92	1.62	2.16	0.74	0.93	0.34	0.16	0.96	1.45	4.64	2.64	0.08
Male	21.28	3.84	3.16	2.63	1.01	1.63	2.22	0.78	0.89	0.35	0.21	0.78	1.28	4.62	2.76	0.09
Female	21.58	3.89	3.17	2.46	0.85	1.62	2.11	0.70	0.96	0.33	0.12	1.14	1.62	4.66	2.53	0.07
Race/ethnicity																
White	21.51	3.84	3.19	2.59	0.80	1.79	2.24	0.73	0.96	0.37	0.19	1.02	1.51	4.53	2.59	0.09
Black	21.13	4.06	3.09	2.53	1.39	1.14	2.04	0.81	0.89	0.25	0.09	0.70	1.25	4.82	2.64	0.08
Hispanic	21.19	3.88	3.02	2.26	1.24	1.03	1.79	0.77	0.79	0.16	0.07	0.76	1.30	5.26	2.92	0.04
Asian	22.18	3.82	3.19	3.14	0.74	2.41	2.59	0.51	1.09	0.60	0.39	1.89	1.32	3.12	3.10	0.14
American Indian	21.32	3.92	3.22	2.09	1.14	0.95	1.96	0.72	0.78	0.35	0.11	0.45	1.67	5.09	2.93	0.04
Academic track																
Academic[4]	21.80	4.04	3.34	2.97	0.82	2.15	2.58	0.73	1.10	0.51	0.25	1.43	1.87	2.87	2.69	0.08
Vocational[5]	20.37	3.41	2.67	1.68	1.06	0.63	1.33	0.70	0.56	0.04	0.03	0.18	0.57	8.08	2.45	0.07
Both[6]	22.80	3.99	3.34	2.54	1.04	1.49	2.10	0.83	0.90	0.26	0.11	0.68	1.40	6.29	2.46	0.10
Neither[7]	19.11	3.48	2.72	1.72	1.08	0.64	1.40	0.72	0.62	0.04	0.02	0.21	0.80	5.79	2.99	0.07
1987 graduates	22.77	4.01	3.31	3.02	0.98	2.04	2.51	0.76	1.08	0.47	0.20	1.36	1.42	4.43	2.70	0.31
Male	22.65	3.98	3.30	3.07	1.04	2.03	2.54	0.78	1.04	0.47	0.25	1.16	1.24	4.52	2.84	0.33
Female	22.89	4.03	3.33	2.97	0.93	2.05	2.49	0.73	1.13	0.47	0.16	1.55	1.60	4.36	2.56	0.29
Race/ethnicity																
White	22.91	4.01	3.29	3.03	0.86	2.17	2.58	0.74	1.11	0.50	0.22	1.35	1.49	4.52	2.64	0.33
Black	22.14	4.09	3.32	2.96	1.45	1.51	2.32	0.90	1.00	0.31	0.11	1.09	1.19	4.47	2.71	0.23
Hispanic	22.54	3.97	3.20	2.87	1.45	1.42	2.21	0.77	1.05	0.29	0.10	1.50	1.32	4.27	3.20	0.21
Asian	23.88	3.85	3.50	3.72	0.77	2.95	3.02	0.65	1.11	0.81	0.45	2.49	1.18	2.92	3.21	0.39
American Indian	23.18	4.20	3.19	3.06	1.51	1.56	2.44	0.81	1.22	0.32	0.09	0.75	1.69	4.70	3.13	0.22
Academic track																
Academic[4]	23.08	4.14	3.51	3.34	0.83	2.51	2.85	0.73	1.20	0.64	0.29	1.80	1.75	2.96	2.75	0.31
Vocational[5]	21.11	3.54	2.60	1.96	1.30	0.66	1.50	0.76	0.68	0.05	0.01	0.21	0.43	8.35	2.52	0.25
Both[6]	23.48	4.01	3.28	2.86	1.15	1.71	2.26	0.83	1.04	0.28	0.11	0.92	1.14	6.54	2.49	0.39
Neither[7]	19.30	3.37	2.56	2.00	1.47	0.53	1.52	0.76	0.70	0.05	0.01	0.24	0.73	5.56	3.32	0.15
1990 graduates	23.50	4.09	3.50	3.20	0.99	2.21	2.75	0.84	1.14	0.54	0.23	1.60	1.55	4.10	2.72	0.35
Male	23.34	4.05	3.47	3.22	1.06	2.16	2.78	0.87	1.11	0.53	0.28	1.39	1.31	4.23	2.88	0.36
Female	23.65	4.13	3.52	3.18	0.93	2.25	2.72	0.82	1.17	0.54	0.19	1.78	1.76	3.98	2.57	0.34
Race/ethnicity																
White	23.53	4.08	3.48	3.18	0.89	2.29	2.80	0.83	1.15	0.56	0.25	1.59	1.61	4.13	2.66	0.35
Black	23.30	4.23	3.49	3.23	1.32	1.92	2.67	0.96	1.11	0.44	0.16	1.23	1.34	4.36	2.74	0.39
Hispanic	23.77	4.05	3.44	3.21	1.41	1.81	2.49	0.83	1.10	0.42	0.14	1.97	1.48	4.00	3.13	0.32
Asian	24.06	4.02	3.70	3.64	0.83	2.81	2.97	0.68	1.12	0.74	0.42	2.52	1.30	2.89	3.02	0.34
American Indian	22.63	4.01	3.36	3.17	1.25	1.93	2.48	0.83	1.09	0.42	0.15	1.15	1.11	4.43	2.91	0.37
Academic track																
Academic[4]	23.57	4.17	3.63	3.40	0.84	2.56	2.98	0.82	1.21	0.66	0.30	1.94	1.80	2.84	2.81	0.33
Vocational[5]	22.07	3.52	2.63	2.02	1.52	0.50	1.64	0.88	0.71	0.04	0.01	0.17	0.43	9.17	2.48	0.23
Both[6]	23.95	4.02	3.35	2.98	1.30	1.67	2.41	0.92	1.06	0.31	0.11	0.99	1.10	6.64	2.48	0.44
Neither[7]	20.21	3.49	2.71	1.97	1.56	0.41	1.58	0.82	0.71	0.03	0.02	0.26	0.57	6.58	3.05	0.23
1992 graduates	23.76	4.18	3.58	3.39	0.98	2.41	2.87	0.84	1.19	0.58	0.26	1.67	1.62	3.76	2.69	0.35
Male	23.58	4.13	3.55	3.38	1.06	2.32	2.88	0.88	1.14	0.56	0.30	1.44	1.42	3.91	2.87	0.34
Female	23.95	4.23	3.61	3.40	0.88	2.52	2.90	0.80	1.25	0.61	0.24	1.92	1.81	3.57	2.51	0.38
Race/ethnicity																
White	23.83	4.17	3.61	3.38	0.87	2.51	2.93	0.83	1.21	0.61	0.28	1.70	1.68	3.73	2.63	0.34
Black	23.21	4.20	3.59	3.37	1.35	2.02	2.74	0.94	1.15	0.47	0.18	1.28	1.45	3.92	2.66	0.38
Hispanic	23.62	4.26	3.38	3.36	1.24	2.12	2.60	0.81	1.16	0.47	0.16	1.76	1.44	3.79	3.03	0.41
Asian	24.45	4.14	3.51	3.65	0.74	2.91	3.22	0.73	1.20	0.79	0.50	2.43	1.38	3.18	2.93	0.43
American Indian	23.38	4.09	3.63	3.16	1.55	1.61	2.55	1.03	0.99	0.35	0.18	0.92	1.53	4.53	2.97	0.25
Academic track																
Academic[4]	23.84	4.25	3.69	3.56	0.87	2.69	3.05	0.81	1.24	0.69	0.31	1.97	1.85	2.72	2.75	0.33
Vocational[5]	21.44	3.57	2.69	2.11	1.62	0.49	1.70	0.91	0.75	0.03	0.01	0.10	0.40	8.38	2.49	0.22
Both[6]	24.28	4.11	3.40	3.11	1.23	1.88	2.57	0.95	1.11	0.36	0.15	1.01	1.10	6.48	2.50	0.48
Neither[7]	19.19	3.08	2.59	2.17	1.42	0.75	1.76	0.93	0.78	0.04	0.01	0.14	0.66	5.92	2.87	0.19

[1] Includes nonoccupational vocational education, vocational general introduction, agriculture, business, marketing, health, occupational home economics, trade and industry, and technical courses.

[2] Includes personal and social courses, religion and theology, and courses not included in the other subject fields.

[3] Computer courses are included in mathematics and vocational categories.

[4] Includes students who complete at least 12 Carnegie units in academic courses, but less than 3 Carnegie units in any specific labor market preparation field.

[5] Includes students who complete at least 3 Carnegie units in a specific labor market preparation field, but less than 12 Carnegie units in academic courses.

[6] Includes students who complete at least 12 Carnegie units in academic courses and at least 3 Carnegie units in a specific labor market preparation field.

[7] Includes students who complete less than 12 Carnegie units in academic courses and less than 3 Carnegie units in a specific labor market preparation field.

NOTE.—The Carnegie unit is a standard of measurement that represents one credit for the completion of a 1-year course.

SOURCE: U.S. Department of Education, National Center for Education Statistics, "High School and Beyond," First Followup survey; "1990 High School Transcript Study" and the "National Education Longitudinal Study of 1988," Second Followup survey. (This table was prepared August 1994.)

Table 133.—Average number of Carnegie units earned by public school graduates in vocational education courses, by student characteristics: 1982 to 1992

Student characteristics	Total	General labor market preparation	Consumer and homemaking education	Specific labor market preparation								
				Total	Agriculture	Business	Marketing	Health	Occupational home economics	Trade and industrial	Technical/communications	Other
1	2	3	4	5	6	7	8	9	10	11	12	13
1982 graduates	4.64	1.06	0.68	2.89	0.21	1.03	0.16	0.05	0.17	1.06	0.11	0.10
Male	4.62	1.02	0.31	3.29	0.35	0.48	0.14	0.02	0.05	1.98	0.14	0.13
Female	4.66	1.10	1.03	2.53	0.08	1.54	0.18	0.08	0.29	0.20	0.09	0.07
Race/ethnicity												
White	4.53	1.04	0.63	2.87	0.23	1.06	0.15	0.04	0.17	1.01	0.12	0.09
Black	4.82	1.08	0.92	2.82	0.10	0.97	0.22	0.12	0.23	0.97	0.11	0.10
Hispanic	5.26	1.18	0.87	3.21	0.24	0.98	0.15	0.06	0.20	1.37	0.07	0.14
Asian	3.12	0.98	0.28	1.86	0.05	0.57	0.04	0.03	0.05	0.87	0.16	0.09
American Indian	5.09	1.25	0.53	3.32	0.26	0.72	0.13	0.07	0.10	1.85	0.05	0.14
Academic track												
Academic [1]	2.87	0.93	0.59	1.36	0.06	0.58	0.07	0.03	0.07	0.37	0.11	0.07
Vocational [2]	8.08	1.18	0.66	6.24	0.62	1.81	0.32	0.08	0.41	2.78	0.11	0.11
Both [3]	6.29	0.94	0.51	4.84	0.32	1.75	0.29	0.11	0.26	1.94	0.12	0.05
Neither [4]	5.79	1.76	1.47	2.56	0.16	0.99	0.19	0.05	0.19	0.52	0.10	0.36
1987 graduates	4.43	0.93	0.60	2.90	0.19	0.97	0.16	0.07	0.19	0.96	0.24	0.12
Male	4.52	0.90	0.33	3.29	0.32	0.57	0.13	0.02	0.08	1.74	0.29	0.14
Female	4.36	0.95	0.86	2.55	0.07	1.35	0.19	0.12	0.29	0.23	0.18	0.12
Race/ethnicity												
White	4.52	0.94	0.60	2.99	0.24	0.98	0.15	0.07	0.18	1.01	0.26	0.10
Black	4.47	0.98	0.73	2.77	0.09	0.99	0.17	0.12	0.26	0.75	0.16	0.23
Hispanic	4.27	0.97	0.60	2.70	0.06	0.98	0.16	0.08	0.17	0.97	0.13	0.15
Asian	2.92	0.69	0.34	1.88	0.01	0.65	0.16	0.11	0.08	0.44	0.31	0.12
American Indian	4.70	0.87	0.64	3.19	0.19	1.09	0.08	0.09	0.09	1.30	0.21	0.14
Academic track												
Academic [1]	2.96	0.84	0.57	1.54	0.05	0.61	0.08	0.04	0.07	0.35	0.25	0.09
Vocational [2]	8.35	1.09	0.67	6.59	0.66	1.61	0.35	0.19	0.57	2.88	0.20	0.13
Both [3]	6.54	0.98	0.52	5.04	0.40	1.74	0.30	0.13	0.33	1.85	0.24	0.05
Neither [4]	5.56	1.42	1.24	2.90	0.14	0.78	0.23	0.06	0.27	0.64	0.11	0.67
1990 graduates	4.10	0.83	0.57	2.70	0.20	0.90	0.16	0.04	0.17	0.87	0.22	0.14
Male	4.23	0.78	0.33	3.12	0.31	0.58	0.14	0.02	0.06	1.58	0.27	0.16
Female	3.98	0.87	0.79	2.32	0.09	1.19	0.18	0.06	0.27	0.22	0.18	0.13
Race/ethnicity												
White	4.13	0.80	0.55	2.78	0.24	0.88	0.16	0.04	0.15	0.94	0.22	0.15
Black	4.36	0.96	0.79	2.62	0.06	1.08	0.18	0.04	0.27	0.64	0.23	0.12
Hispanic	4.00	0.85	0.54	2.61	0.15	0.96	0.19	0.02	0.27	0.75	0.17	0.10
Asian	2.89	0.73	0.32	1.85	0.04	0.66	0.05	0.01	0.05	0.73	0.26	0.05
American Indian	4.43	0.84	0.72	2.87	0.36	0.96	0.15	—	0.08	0.95	0.16	0.21
Academic track												
Academic [1]	2.84	0.77	0.56	1.51	0.06	0.61	0.08	0.02	0.07	0.34	0.23	0.10
Vocational [2]	9.17	1.12	0.65	7.40	0.96	1.44	0.33	0.11	0.51	3.54	0.14	0.37
Both [3]	6.64	0.83	0.52	5.30	0.46	1.71	0.38	0.10	0.40	1.93	0.22	0.10
Neither [4]	6.58	2.01	1.31	3.25	0.25	0.84	0.18	0.08	0.19	0.70	0.14	0.87
1992 graduates	3.76	0.69	0.54	2.53	0.19	0.85	0.13	0.06	0.18	0.79	0.22	0.11
Male	3.91	0.69	0.36	2.86	0.30	0.59	0.13	0.02	0.07	1.36	0.26	0.13
Female	3.57	0.68	0.70	2.19	0.08	1.10	0.13	0.10	0.28	0.23	0.19	0.09
Race/ethnicity												
White	3.73	0.67	0.53	2.52	0.22	0.84	0.13	0.05	0.15	0.80	0.22	0.11
Black	3.92	0.74	0.68	2.52	0.12	0.93	0.14	0.08	0.35	0.61	0.20	0.09
Hispanic	3.79	0.74	0.46	2.59	0.09	0.92	0.13	0.09	0.21	0.71	0.26	0.18
Asian	3.18	0.56	0.36	2.25	0.03	0.85	0.07	0.07	0.06	0.88	0.26	0.03
American Indian	4.53	0.66	0.50	3.37	0.20	0.75	0.10	0.06	0.35	1.73	0.12	0.06
Academic track												
Academic [1]	2.72	0.63	0.54	1.55	0.07	0.63	0.08	0.03	0.09	0.33	0.21	0.10
Vocational [2]	8.38	1.00	0.61	6.78	1.01	1.17	0.25	0.15	0.65	3.14	0.19	0.21
Both [3]	6.48	0.70	0.47	5.30	0.45	1.61	0.30	0.13	0.43	2.04	0.16	0.08
Neither [4]	5.92	2.22	1.18	2.53	0.51	0.50	0.10	0.07	0.11	0.59	0.16	0.48

[1] Includes students who complete at least 12 Carnegie units in academic courses, but less than 3 Carnegie units in any specific labor market preparation field.

[2] Includes students who complete at least 3 Carnegie units in a specific labor market preparation field, but less than 12 Carnegie units in academic courses.

[3] Includes students who complete at least 12 Carnegie units in academic courses and at least 3 Carnegie units in a specific labor market preparation field.

[4] Includes students who complete less than 12 Carnegie units in academic courses and less than 3 Carnegie units in a specific labor market preparation field.

NOTE.—The Carnegie unit is a standard of measurement that represents one credit for the completion of a 1-year course.

SOURCE: U.S. Department of Education, National Center for Education Statistics, "High School and Beyond," First Followup survey; "1990 High School Transcript Study" and the "National Education Longitudinal Study of 1988," Second Followup survey. (This table was prepared August 1994.)

Table 134.—Percent of 17-year-old students taking science courses for 1 year or more, by selected student characteristics: 1982, 1986, 1990, and 1992

Selected characteristics of students	Biology	General science	Chemistry	Physical science	Earth and space science	Life science	Physics
1	2	3	4	5	6	7	8
1982							
All students	76	61	31	33	27	27	11
Male	74	63	31	33	30	29	14
Female	78	59	30	33	25	26	9
White, non-Hispanic	78	61	33	32	28	27	11
Black, non-Hispanic	66	66	19	34	28	27	12
Hispanic	62	58	13	35	20	31	9
1986							
All students	83	78	37	41	38	40	10
Male	87	84	42	43	41	45	14
Female	88	82	39	40	34	34	8
White, non-Hispanic	89	84	42	41	38	40	10
Black, non-Hispanic	84	83	29	45	44	40	18
Hispanic	84	82	24	37	23	41	13
1990							
All students	85	78	42	41	35	30	13
Male	87	84	45	42	35	32	16
Female	91	81	45	40	34	28	13
White, non-Hispanic	90	84	46	39	34	28	13
Black, non-Hispanic	87	76	46	47	35	35	15
Hispanic	79	82	31	55	38	44	17
1992							
All students	89	81	46	—	—	—	12
Male	91	86	47	—	—	—	15
Female	93	83	51	—	—	—	12
White, non-Hispanic	93	86	52	—	—	—	13
Black, non-Hispanic	92	78	36	—	—	—	14
Hispanic	87	79	36	—	—	—	13

—Data not available.

SOURCE: U.S. Department of Education, National Center for Education Statistics, National Assessment of Educational Progress, *NAEP 1992 Trends in Academic Progress*, prepared by Educational Testing Service. (This table was prepared March 1994.)

Table 135.—Percent of high school graduates earning minimum credits in selected combinations of academic courses, by sex and race/ethnicity: 1982 to 1992

Year of graduation and course combinations taken [1]	All students	Sex		Race/ethnicity			
		Male	Female	White	Black	Hispanic	Asian
1	2	3	4	5	6	7	8
1982 graduates							
4 Eng., 3 S.S., 3 Sci., 3 Math, .5 Comp., & 2 F.L. [2]	1.9	2.0	1.7	2.2	0.7	0.5	6.0
4 Eng., 3 S.S., 3 Sci., 3 Math, & .5 Comp. [3]	2.7	3.3	2.1	3.1	1.0	0.9	7.1
4 Eng., 3 S.S., 3 Sci., 3 Math, & 2 F.L.	8.8	8.5	9.2	10.1	5.2	3.5	17.0
4 Eng., 3 S.S., 3 Sci., 3 Math	13.4	14.3	12.6	14.9	10.1	6.3	21.0
4 Eng., 3 S.S., 2 Sci., 2 Math	29.2	29.1	29.3	30.2	28.1	23.5	34.5
1987 graduates							
4 Eng., 3 S.S., 3 Sci., 3 Math, & .5 Comp., & 2 F.L. [2]	12.0	13.3	10.9	12.7	8.3	5.5	24.3
4 Eng., 3 S.S., 3 Sci., 3 Math, & & .5 Comp. [3]	16.3	18.4	14.4	17.2	11.7	8.6	28.1
4 Eng., 3 S.S., 3 Sci., 3 Math, & & 2 F.L.	20.9	20.9	20.9	21.8	16.1	11.8	41.9
4 Eng., 3 S.S., 3 Sci., 3 Math	28.6	30.1	27.2	29.7	24.3	17.9	48.3
4 Eng., 3 S.S., 2 Sci., 2 Math	54.6	54.6	54.7	53.5	57.2	55.1	71.8
1990 graduates							
4 Eng., 3 S.S., 3 Sci., 3 Math, & .5 Comp., & 2 F.L. [2]	17.3	17.7	16.9	18.1	14.4	15.7	23.8
4 Eng., 3 S.S., 3 Sci., 3 Math, & .5 Comp. [3]	22.7	23.9	21.6	22.7	25.1	20.3	27.8
4 Eng., 3 S.S., 3 Sci., 3 Math, & 2 F.L.	30.6	29.8	31.4	32.6	23.4	24.8	44.1
4 Eng., 3 S.S., 3 Sci., 3 Math	39.9	40.7	39.2	40.6	41.3	32.7	51.2
4 Eng., 3 S.S., 2 Sci., 2 Math	66.8	66.2	67.3	65.4	71.8	70.4	75.5
1992 graduates							
4 Eng., 3 S.S., 3 Sci., 3 Math, & .5 Comp., & 2 F.L. [2]	23.2	20.9	25.4	23.6	21.5	19.9	29.3
4 Eng., 3 S.S., 3 Sci., 3 Math, & .5 Comp. [3]	29.2	28.0	30.4	29.5	27.0	28.6	32.2
4 Eng., 3 S.S., 3 Sci., 3 Math, $ 2 F.L.	36.9	33.9	39.8	38.8	31.9	25.0	46.0
4 Eng., 3 S.S., 3 Sci., 3 Math	46.8	46.5	47.1	48.5	43.2	35.9	50.8
4 Eng., 3 S.S., 2 Sci., 2 Math	72.8	72.0	73.6	72.1	77.0	73.0	76.1

[1] Eng. = English; S.S. = social studies; Sci. = science; Comp. = computer science; and F.L. = foreign language.

[2] The National Commission on Excellence in Education recommended that all college-bound high school students take these courses as a minimum.

[3] The National Commission on Excellence in Education recommended that all high school students take these courses as a minimum.

SOURCE: U.S. Department of Education, National Center for Education Statistics, "1990 High School Transcript Study," and "National Education Longitudinal Study," Second Followup survey. (This table was prepared March 1994.)

Table 136.—Reasons given by twelfth graders for taking current mathematics and science classes, by selected student and school characteristics: 1992

Class subject and opinion	All 12th graders	Sex		Race/ethnicity					Socioeconomic status quartile [1]				Control of school attended		
		Male	Female	White	Black	His-panic	Asian	Amer-ican In-dian	Lowest	Second	Third	Highest	Public	Catholic	Other private
1	2	3	4	5	6	7	8	9	10	11	12	13	14	15	16
Mathematics class															
I am interested in mathematics	74.5	77.4	71.3	72.9	74.6	80.4	81.9	87.7	78.0	74.6	73.1	74.2	73.8	78.4	81.7
I do well in mathematics	77.1	80.2	73.7	76.4	76.1	79.7	83.6	76.8	79.5	77.8	76.3	76.1	76.7	78.4	82.1
I need it for college or trade school	87.2	86.6	87.8	86.5	89.8	86.5	90.8	90.5	83.3	85.4	88.9	88.6	87.1	87.9	87.5
I need it for a job after high school	64.7	65.9	63.4	62.5	69.7	70.9	66.3	83.9	71.2	68.5	65.5	57.8	65.9	58.1	51.9
I need it for advanced placement	53.6	53.3	54.0	49.6	58.4	62.5	72.6	56.9	59.8	46.7	52.2	55.7	54.1	47.2	53.9
Advised to take class by:															
Teacher	65.9	63.3	68.8	63.6	74.8	71.1	66.7	70.6	69.2	65.1	66.3	64.7	65.7	66.2	70.0
Guidance counselor	64.8	62.9	66.8	60.7	77.8	76.2	64.2	83.0	76.4	67.5	62.6	58.6	65.8	55.1	59.6
Parent	71.6	69.1	74.2	70.5	74.6	74.4	73.3	79.8	66.3	67.2	70.3	76.6	71.8	68.4	71.4
Friend	42.2	41.4	43.2	39.8	52.5	43.7	50.8	56.2	46.1	43.2	41.7	40.7	42.5	40.6	39.1
Sibling	30.9	29.5	32.5	26.3	37.2	43.1	46.2	51.5	40.4	29.7	27.7	29.4	31.8	21.9	28.9
Science class															
I am interested in science	78.8	82.7	74.4	78.5	77.4	78.9	83.6	74.9	74.5	76.7	76.9	82.7	77.9	81.1	89.9
I do well in science	80.6	83.9	77.0	80.1	76.7	86.1	84.2	86.6	78.1	80.1	77.1	84.0	80.1	79.8	90.2
I need it for college or trade school	83.3	81.7	85.0	82.4	86.4	83.5	88.4	88.8	78.5	81.9	84.6	84.8	83.3	85.3	80.7
I need it for a job after high school	47.0	47.9	45.9	44.5	53.2	57.6	51.3	55.9	53.4	47.6	50.4	41.6	47.8	45.7	35.7
I need it for advanced placement	50.2	49.7	50.9	47.1	51.6	59.0	66.8	59.6	48.9	47.9	46.8	53.9	49.2	53.5	60.3
Advised to take class by:															
Teacher	58.9	56.2	61.9	57.6	61.7	63.7	61.0	67.2	61.3	57.7	58.3	59.0	57.8	60.3	74.1
Guidance counselor	59.4	57.8	61.2	56.2	71.4	70.9	59.7	57.9	74.0	59.5	59.9	55.5	67.0	44.1	67.3
Parent	66.3	63.4	69.4	65.7	69.1	70.5	64.1	73.8	61.9	59.9	66.4	70.6	67.0	58.7	67.4
Friend	43.5	43.4	43.6	42.9	40.9	44.6	49.7	62.9	45.6	41.6	41.0	45.0	43.6	36.6	52.5
Sibling	28.7	26.8	31.0	25.3	35.0	35.5	44.3	57.6	36.1	25.2	25.2	29.6	29.4	21.0	30.5

[1] Socioeconomic status was measured by a composite score on parental education and occupations, and family income.

SOURCE: U.S. Department of Education, National Center for Education Statistics, "National Education Longitudinal Study of 1988," Second Followup survey. (This table was prepared February 1994.)

Table 137.—Expected occupations of 8th, 10th, and 12th graders at age 30, by selected student and school characteristics: 1988, 1990, and 1992

[Percentage distribution]

Expected occupation at age 30	8th graders in 1988	10th graders in 1990	12th graders in 1992														
			Total	Sex		Race/ethnicity						Socioeconomic status [1]			Control of school attended		
				Male	Female	White	Black	His-panic	Asian	Amer-ican In-dian	Low	Middle	High	Public	Catholic	Other private
1	2	3	4	5	6	7	8	9	10	11	12	13	14	15	16	17
Total	100.0	100.0	100.0	100.0	100.0	100.0	100.0	100.0	100.0	100.0	100.0	100.0	100.0	100.0	100.0	100.0
Craftsperson or operator	4.2	5.6	3.5	6.6	0.5	3.7	3.4	2.7	2.4	2.7	6.8	3.9	0.7	3.9	0.9	0.3
Farmer or farm manager	1.0	1.1	0.9	1.4	0.3	1.0	0.6	0.7	0.1	(2)	1.4	1.0	0.5	0.9	0.6	0.6
Housewife/homemaker	2.3	2.0	1.0	0.1	2.0	1.2	0.4	0.7	0.8	(2)	0.9	1.1	1.2	1.1	0.7	1.5
Laborer or farm worker	0.6	0.8	0.7	1.3	0.1	0.7	0.3	0.6	1.2	1.9	1.2	0.8	0.2	0.7	0.4	0.8
Military, police, or security officer	9.6	5.7	6.6	11.2	2.0	6.4	7.7	7.4	5.1	10.0	9.3	7.4	3.6	7.0	3.3	1.7
Professional, business, or managerial	34.5	45.7	50.8	45.9	55.7	50.0	55.1	47.1	61.3	43.3	38.7	48.1	63.0	49.4	66.3	59.2
Teacher	(3)	4.1	7.5	4.1	10.8	8.4	3.7	6.7	3.4	4.8	6.2	7.6	8.2	7.3	8.1	11.1
Business owner	6.2	5.3	6.0	7.8	4.3	5.6	6.8	7.7	7.0	6.4	6.7	6.4	4.9	6.3	3.8	3.3
Technical	6.2	4.7	5.4	7.5	3.4	5.0	5.5	7.5	6.0	8.2	7.1	5.9	3.5	5.7	2.4	3.6
Salesperson, clerical, or office worker	2.8	4.9	4.8	3.1	6.5	4.6	5.3	6.4	4.1	5.2	8.0	4.7	3.1	4.9	2.6	5.8
Service worker	4.9	1.8	2.4	0.5	4.2	2.3	3.1	2.5	0.6	5.8	4.6	2.3	0.9	2.5	1.5	0.8
Other employment	17.0	7.7	10.2	10.3	10.2	10.8	8.0	9.6	8.0	10.6	8.8	10.8	10.2	10.3	9.6	11.3
Don't know or no plans	10.5	10.5	0.2	0.2	0.2	0.2	0.2	0.5	0.2	1.0	0.4	0.2	0.1	0.2	(2)	0.1

[1] Socioeconomic status was measured by a composite score on parental education and occupations, and family income. The "Low" SES group is the lowest quartile; the "Middle" SES group is the middle two quartiles; and the "High" SES group is the upper quartile.

[2] Less than .05 percent.

[3] Included under "Professional, business, or managerial."

SOURCE: U.S. Department of Education, National Center for Education Statistics, "National Education Longitudinal Study of 1988," First and Second Followup surveys. (This table was prepared March 1994.)

Table 138.—Eighth, tenth, and twelfth graders' attitudes about school climate, by student and school characteristics: 1988, 1990, and 1992

Statements about school climate	Eighth graders in 1988	Tenth graders in 1990	Percent who strongly agree or agree with statement														
			Twelfth graders in 1992														
			Total	Sex		Race/ethnicity					Socioeconomic status quartile [1]				Control of school attended		
				Male	Female	White	Black	Hispanic	Asian	American Indian	Lowest	Second	Third	Highest	Public	Catholic	Other private
1	2	3	4	5	6	7	8	9	10	11	12	13	14	15	16	17	18
There is real school spirit	68.6	70.4	71.4	72.9	69.8	72.1	67.4	71.0	70.7	62.0	73.4	71.3	72.0	69.5	70.4	82.2	76.0
Discipline is fair	69.1	70.2	68.0	67.0	69.0	68.0	58.6	74.7	75.6	73.0	66.3	66.2	68.1	69.7	67.3	69.9	77.0
Teaching is good	80.2	81.9	85.4	84.8	86.0	85.1	84.1	88.5	85.5	88.3	85.6	84.2	84.3	87.2	84.7	90.4	93.7
Teachers are interested in students	75.2	76.0	81.6	81.5	81.8	81.9	78.4	83.7	80.1	83.0	80.3	80.5	80.1	84.8	80.4	91.1	95.4
I don't feel safe at this school	11.8	8.0	10.4	10.8	10.1	8.6	16.1	14.7	15.8	13.0	13.1	11.2	10.5	7.5	11.1	4.9	3.5
Disruptions by other students interfere with my learning	39.6	39.9	33.1	31.6	34.7	30.8	38.1	39.8	41.4	40.5	37.0	35.9	34.6	26.3	34.2	25.4	21.8
Fights often occur between different racial/ethnic groups	—	—	22.7	22.2	23.2	20.9	22.2	31.9	30.5	29.9	25.1	23.9	23.5	18.6	24.5	8.3	3.0
There are many gangs in school	—	—	16.3	16.4	16.2	12.5	17.5	36.4	27.2	23.2	21.9	15.8	16.7	12.1	17.7	4.5	1.5
Students are graded fairly	—	—	78.3	78.6	78.0	79.5	71.6	77.6	77.3	74.7	74.8	76.3	78.3	82.4	77.3	84.1	91.8
There is a lot of cheating on tests and assignments	—	—	58.8	56.0	61.7	59.7	57.1	53.8	63.5	59.8	55.8	59.1	61.8	58.6	60.2	56.9	32.6
Some teachers ignore cheating when they see it	—	—	30.9	29.3	32.6	32.7	25.4	26.0	30.7	24.8	26.9	31.4	32.7	31.9	31.9	26.5	16.9

[1] Socioeconomic status was measured by a composite score on parental education and occupations, and family income.

SOURCE: U.S. Department of Education, National Center for Education Statistics, "National Education Longitudinal Study of 1988," Base Year and First and Second Followup surveys. (This table was prepared February 1994.)

Table 139.—Home activities of 3- to 8-year-olds, by grade of student: 1991

Home activities	Total	Not enrolled in school	Grade of student enrollment					
			Nursery school [1]	Kindergarten [2]	First grade	Second grade	Third grade or higher	Ungraded
1	2	3	4	5	6	7	8	9
Number of children	22,294	4,853	3,571	4,023	3,993	3,554	2,270	29
	Percent of children who are read to							
Total	100	100	100	100	100	100	100	—
Never or several times per year	7	4	2	4	5	11	24	—
Several times per month or per week	58	54	51	56	62	67	62	—
Every day	35	42	47	40	33	22	14	—
	Percent of children who were read to in the previous week							
Total	100	100	100	100	100	100	100	—
Never	12	7	5	5	10	20	35	—
One or two times	27	24	20	24	30	36	34	—
Three or more times	61	69	76	71	60	44	31	—
	Average hours of television watched daily and percentage of families with television-related rules							
Average hours of TV daily [3]	2.5	3.1	2.6	2.5	2.2	2.2	2.3	—
Percentage with TV-related rules [4]								
What shows child may watch	85	82	87	85	86	87	86	—
How early or late child may watch	89	80	87	90	94	94	93	—
Hours child may watch overall	56	50	55	56	59	60	61	—
Hours child may watch on weekdays	60	47	55	61	66	67	68	—

[1] Includes children enrolled in nursery school, prekindergarten, and Head Start.
[2] Includes children enrolled in kindergarten and in transitional grades between kindergarten and first grade, such as transitional kindergarten or prefirst grade.
[3] Includes hours watching television shows and video tapes.
[4] Includes children whose parents reported viewing hours.
—Unweighted number of cases is less than 30.

SOURCE: U.S. Department of Education, National Center for Education Statistics, Home Activities of 3- to 8-year-olds. (This table was prepared April 1992.)

Table 140.—Participation of 10th and 12th graders in extracurricular activities, by selected student characteristics: 1990 and 1992

Extracurricular activities	Total 1990 10th graders	1992 12th graders													
		Total	Sex		Race/ethnicity					Socioeconomic status [1]			Control of school attended		
			Male	Female	White	Black	Hispanic	Asian	American Indian	Low	Middle	High	Public	Catholic	Other private
1	2	3	4	5	6	7	8	9	10	11	12	13	14	15	16
Athletics															
Interscholastic team sport	—	30.4	41.2	19.7	30.8	32.3	25.8	28.3	30.4	25.3	30.1	34.4	29.6	31.2	48.9
Interscholastic individual sport	—	20.3	26.8	13.9	20.9	21.2	14.9	21.6	20.7	13.6	18.7	27.7	20.0	24.6	21.8
Intramural team sport	—	22.7	31.8	13.8	22.3	25.8	20.8	24.9	27.9	20.4	22.9	24.1	22.0	29.7	29.6
Intramural individual sport	—	13.3	16.7	10.0	12.5	16.7	14.0	14.7	18.2	10.8	12.5	15.9	13.5	13.3	10.7
Performing arts															
Cheerleading	5.9	7.6	2.0	13.0	7.4	10.6	6.7	5.1	11.9	6.5	7.9	7.8	7.6	8.3	5.9
School band or orchestra	20.9	19.8	15.1	24.5	19.6	24.4	16.9	17.7	16.8	17.6	19.6	22.0	19.8	12.0	31.3
School play or musical	11.0	15.4	14.1	16.7	16.1	15.9	10.6	13.7	14.0	11.4	14.8	19.4	15.0	14.2	26.2
School government/clubs															
Student government	7.3	15.4	13.1	17.7	15.4	16.7	14.7	14.6	14.3	11.0	14.7	19.8	15.0	14.5	27.9
Academic honor society	7.7	18.5	14.4	22.7	19.6	14.0	12.5	27.2	13.6	9.6	15.9	29.5	17.7	28.0	22.9
School yearbook/newspaper	8.8	18.8	14.0	23.5	19.7	14.3	16.8	18.9	21.2	14.3	16.9	25.1	17.0	28.0	46.7
School service clubs	11.5	13.9	10.3	17.4	13.6	13.6	14.4	19.3	11.6	8.4	12.5	19.6	13.6	17.3	15.4
School academic clubs	30.7	25.1	22.9	27.4	25.8	20.7	22.6	32.3	17.7	18.8	24.1	31.1	25.1	26.4	24.5
School hobby clubs	7.3	7.7	8.1	7.4	7.4	6.6	9.1	11.3	10.8	6.7	7.0	9.3	7.4	9.8	11.0
School FTA, FHA, and FFA	11.7	17.7	14.7	20.7	17.6	22.5	16.4	8.8	22.1	24.8	19.7	9.9	19.4	2.4	2.9

[1] Socioeconomic status was measured by a composite score on parental education and occupations, and family income. The "Low" SES group is the lowest quartile; the "Middle" SES group is the middle two quartiles; and the "High" SES group is the upper quartile.

SOURCE: U.S. Department of Education, National Center for Education Statistics, "National Education Longitudinal Study of 1988," First and Second Followup surveys. (This table was prepared March 1994.)

Table 141.—Percent of high school seniors who plan to go to college after graduation, by student characteristics: 1982 and 1992

Student characteristics	No college		Right after high school		After a year		After more than a year		Don't know	
	1982	1992	1982	1992	1982	1992	1982	1992	1982	1992
1	2	3	4	5	6	7	8	9	10	11
All seniors	18.3	4.0	58.3	76.6	7.1	10.7	3.9	4.1	12.3	4.6
Male	22.8	5.7	53.4	73.0	6.6	10.2	4.0	5.6	13.1	5.5
Female	14.0	2.3	63.0	80.1	7.6	11.1	3.8	2.7	11.6	3.8
Race/ethnicity.										
White	18.2	3.9	60.2	76.6	7.0	10.6	3.4	4.4	11.3	4.5
Black	14.6	5.4	57.5	75.2	8.2	11.2	5.7	3.2	14.1	5.2
Hispanic	24.1	3.5	45.6	75.4	7.5	11.6	5.8	3.6	17.0	5.9
Asian	5.6	2.6	81.7	83.4	5.6	8.6	2.1	2.4	5.1	3.1
American Indian	22.2	5.8	48.5	65.7	9.0	15.5	3.3	5.3	17.1	7.7
Test performance quartile.										
Lowest test quartile	32.3	11.4	32.8	59.3	9.1	15.1	4.5	3.4	21.3	10.9
Second test quartile	26.5	3.9	45.2	71.2	7.8	14.3	4.8	4.4	15.8	6.3
Third test quartile	15.6	2.0	61.9	81.2	7.9	9.9	3.8	4.1	10.8	2.8
Highest test quartile	3.8	0.6	85.4	90.9	4.7	4.8	2.4	2.6	3.8	1.2
Socioeconomic status [1].										
Low quartile	29.1	8.1	38.3	60.3	7.6	16.5	5.8	5.8	19.2	9.4
Middle 2 quartiles	18.3	4.1	56.6	74.6	8.1	11.8	4.1	4.7	12.9	4.8
High quartile	6.6	1.1	82.8	91.1	5.0	4.6	1.5	1.7	4.1	1.5
Control of school.										
Public	19.4	4.4	56.0	74.8	7.3	11.4	4.1	4.5	13.1	4.9
Catholic	8.2	0.5	80.0	93.0	5.1	4.3	1.4	0.7	5.4	1.6
Other private	9.9	0.7	77.3	92.0	6.4	3.0	2.5	0.6	3.9	3.7
Location of school.										
Urban	16.6	3.0	59.3	79.5	8.2	10.1	4.0	3.0	11.8	4.4
Suburban	15.5	3.3	62.3	78.6	6.8	9.7	4.1	4.4	11.3	4.0
Rural/nonmetropolitan area	24.0	5.9	51.4	71.2	6.9	12.3	3.6	4.9	14.2	5.8

[1] Socioeconomic status was measured by a composite score on parental education and occupations, and family income. The "Low" SES group is the lowest quartile; the "Middle" SES group is the middle two quartiles; and the "High" SES group is the upper quartile.

SOURCE: U.S. Department of Education, National Center for Education Statistics, "High School and Beyond," First Followup survey; and "National Education Longitudinal Study of 1988," Second Followup Student survey. (This table was prepared April 1995.)

Table 142.—Percent of high school seniors who say they engage in various activities, by student characteristics: 1982 and 1992

Activity	Total	Sex		Race/ethnicity					Socioeconomic status [1]			Control of school attended		
		Male	Female	White	Black	Hispanic	Asian	American Indian	Low	Middle	High	Public	Catholic	Other private
1	2	3	4	5	6	7	8	9	10	11	12	13	14	15
Percent of 12th graders, 1982														
At least once a week														
Talking with friends	92.7	92.5	93.0	94.2	89.1	88.9	86.7	91.3	88.6	93.7	95.6	92.3	96.4	97.2
Reading for pleasure	50.4	43.4	57.1	51.0	53.9	43.1	56.4	50.3	45.2	50.1	56.8	50.1	51.4	56.2
Going on dates	61.3	60.6	62.0	63.9	51.9	58.1	40.3	54.5	55.8	63.4	62.8	61.4	60.7	60.7
Driving or riding around	62.4	65.9	59.1	65.2	48.9	60.7	42.4	62.3	56.2	65.0	65.1	62.6	64.6	55.0
Thinking or daydreaming	68.5	61.8	74.8	71.1	64.6	58.0	62.4	53.9	63.3	67.5	75.9	67.7	75.2	76.5
Talking with parents	83.9	79.9	87.6	85.6	80.1	78.0	79.8	76.0	78.5	84.7	87.8	83.4	87.7	87.9
Reading front page of newspaper	69.1	70.8	67.5	69.7	71.9	63.3	73.5	61.8	61.5	69.1	77.0	68.5	75.7	72.0
Five or more hours on weekdays														
Watches television	11.5	11.9	11.2	9.4	22.2	13.8	8.1	20.9	16.5	11.5	6.4	12.1	8.0	3.9
Percent of 12th graders, 1992														
At least once a week														
Use personal computer	23.7	28.1	19.3	23.9	23.6	20.9	27.0	23.8	18.9	23.3	27.7	23.4	25.2	28.0
Work on hobbies	40.9	44.4	37.4	42.0	34.8	39.9	37.8	49.8	36.3	41.1	43.5	40.6	43.4	43.2
Attend religious activities	31.0	28.1	33.8	31.4	33.7	26.9	30.4	14.6	22.2	29.4	39.9	29.4	38.8	54.9
Attend youth groups	22.4	24.6	20.1	22.5	23.3	18.5	26.4	22.1	16.6	21.3	28.1	21.8	22.9	33.3
Perform community service	11.3	10.7	11.9	11.1	12.1	10.9	14.0	9.2	7.7	9.5	16.7	9.7	22.3	31.2
Driving or riding around	73.3	74.3	72.3	75.7	67.8	66.2	66.7	71.0	69.6	75.3	72.4	73.4	77.8	63.0
Do things with friends	88.1	88.2	88.0	90.7	79.8	82.4	85.9	77.2	80.8	88.1	93.2	87.5	94.5	91.9
Do things with parent	66.7	61.2	72.1	68.2	62.0	63.8	63.4	61.2	59.6	66.3	71.7	66.0	73.6	72.8
Talk with other adult	47.7	45.4	49.9	48.8	44.3	46.2	43.0	44.0	47.6	49.0	45.0	47.3	46.4	58.8
Take music, art, or dance class	10.1	7.9	12.2	9.9	9.7	9.8	14.0	10.6	7.1	8.8	14.0	9.7	13.4	12.4
Take sports lessons	7.3	9.7	5.0	7.0	7.4	8.2	9.4	11.6	5.6	6.6	9.5	7.1	11.1	7.8
Play ball or other sport	26.3	38.8	14.0	27.1	22.9	23.6	28.7	29.4	20.7	24.5	33.1	25.6	34.0	31.4
More than an hour a day														
Reading for pleasure	55.4	53.1	57.7	56.3	51.0	53.5	54.4	59.3	51.6	55.0	58.6	55.0	56.0	62.9
Plays video games	13.0	19.2	6.8	11.7	19.9	13.0	13.5	21.1	16.9	13.7	9.4	13.3	10.4	8.9
Five or more hours on weekdays														
Watches television	8.4	8.5	8.4	6.4	21.3	9.3	6.4	12.7	12.0	9.4	4.1	8.7	7.9	4.1

[1] Socioeconomic status was measured by a composite score on parental education and occupations, and family income. The "Low" SES group is the lowest quartile; the "Middle" SES group is the middle two quartiles; and the "High" SES group is the upper quartile.

SOURCE: U.S. Department of Education, National Center for Education Statistics, "National Education Longitudinal Study of 1988," Second Followup survey, and "High School and Beyond," First Followup survey. (This table was prepared March 1994.)

Table 143.—Percent of high school seniors who participate in selected school-sponsored extracurricular activities, by student characteristics: 1982 and 1992

Student characteristics	Academic clubs, 1992	Athletics		Cheerleading and drill team		Hobby clubs		Music		Vocational clubs	
		1982	1992	1982	1992	1982	1992	1982	1992	1982	1992
1	2	3	4	5	6	7	8	9	10	11	12
All seniors	25.1	50.0	40.0	13.5	7.6	19.5	7.7	27.6	19.8	23.5	17.7
Male	22.9	58.9	51.4	4.3	2.0	22.9	8.1	19.2	15.1	20.4	14.7
Female	27.4	41.4	28.5	22.1	13.0	16.4	7.4	35.6	24.5	26.4	20.7
Race/ethnicity											
White	25.8	49.8	41.1	13.1	7.4	18.7	7.4	26.7	19.6	21.9	17.6
Black	20.7	51.8	38.9	16.9	10.6	18.5	6.6	34.7	24.4	31.0	22.5
Hispanic	22.6	49.9	32.9	14.1	6.7	23.6	9.1	26.8	16.9	27.5	16.4
Asian	32.3	43.7	42.3	6.3	5.1	26.1	11.3	20.6	17.7	7.0	8.8
American Indian	17.7	52.8	42.5	11.5	11.9	30.3	10.8	26.5	16.8	30.0	22.1
Test performance quartile											
Lowest test quartile	18.1	44.2	39.6	14.3	8.5	19.9	8.9	28.0	17.9	33.2	25.0
Second test quartile	20.1	44.9	40.2	12.8	7.2	21.3	6.3	25.3	17.7	30.3	22.3
Third test quartile	26.3	51.3	43.8	13.9	7.9	18.3	7.2	26.6	20.7	23.0	17.9
Highest test quartile	37.1	58.7	48.8	12.9	7.9	17.8	9.1	31.6	23.2	11.4	11.4
Socioeconomic status [1]											
Low quartile	18.8	40.4	30.4	11.0	6.5	18.4	6.7	23.6	17.6	30.8	24.8
Middle 2 quartiles	24.1	51.0	38.8	14.3	7.9	20.2	7.0	28.5	19.6	24.8	19.7
High quartile	31.1	58.6	49.3	14.4	7.8	19.2	9.3	30.4	22.0	13.6	9.9
Control of school											
Public	25.1	48.8	38.6	13.5	7.6	19.4	7.4	27.8	19.8	25.3	19.4
Catholic	26.4	56.6	51.3	14.8	8.3	20.8	9.8	23.6	12.0	5.8	2.4
Other private	24.5	66.9	58.5	11.6	5.9	22.2	11.0	30.6	31.3	12.6	2.9
Location of school											
Urban	24.7	45.9	37.3	11.8	7.7	20.3	8.9	28.3	18.2	20.0	12.1
Suburban	24.8	50.3	41.2	11.3	6.8	19.6	7.4	25.9	18.4	18.9	13.7
Rural/nonmetropolitan area	26.0	52.3	41.1	18.1	8.4	18.9	7.0	29.8	23.1	32.9	28.0

[1] Socioeconomic status was measured by a composite score on parental education and occupations, and family income.

SOURCE: U.S. Department of Education, National Center for Education Statistics, "High School and Beyond," First Followup survey, 1980 Sophomore Cohort; and "National Education Longitudinal Study of 1988," Second Followup survey. (This table was prepared April 1995.)

Table 144.—Percent of high school students who reported experience with drugs and violence on school property, by race/ethnicity, grade, and sex: 1993

Type of violence	Race/ethnicity			Grade			
	White	Black	His-panic	9	10	11	12
1	2	3	4	5	6	7	8
Felt too unsafe to go to school [1]							
Total	3.0	7.1	10.1	6.1	5.2	3.3	3.0
Male	2.9	7.0	10.4	5.8	5.1	3.2	3.3
Female	3.1	7.3	9.8	6.4	5.4	3.5	2.7
Carried a weapon on school property [1,2]							
Total	10.9	15.0	13.3	12.6	11.5	11.9	10.8
Male	17.7	18.2	20.2	19.1	17.0	18.2	17.2
Female	3.4	11.9	6.6	5.6	5.6	5.0	4.1
Threatened or injured with a weapon on school property [3]							
Total	6.3	11.2	8.6	9.4	7.3	7.3	5.5
Male	8.1	12.6	10.7	10.6	9.1	9.5	7.6
Female	4.4	9.8	6.4	8.1	5.4	4.8	3.3
In a physical fight on school property [3]							
Total	15.0	22.0	17.9	23.1	17.2	13.8	11.4
Male	22.5	28.6	24.1	33.2	25.0	20.0	16.5
Female	6.8	15.5	11.7	12.7	8.8	7.0	6.1
Property stolen or deliberately damaged on school property [3]							
Total	32.0	35.5	32.2	37.2	32.8	32.3	28.9
Male	35.9	39.2	36.7	41.3	37.5	36.4	33.2
Female	27.7	31.8	27.6	33.0	27.6	27.9	24.2

Type of drug-related behavior	Race/ethnicity			Grade			
	White	Black	His-panic	9	10	11	12
1	2	3	4	5	6	7	8
Cigarette use on school property [1]							
Total	14.6	5.9	11.1	11.3	12.3	13.9	15.0
Male	14.7	7.3	10.6	11.4	12.8	12.9	16.5
Female	14.5	4.5	11.6	11.3	11.8	14.9	13.3
Smokeless tobacco use on school property [4]							
Total	8.7	1.4	2.3	5.6	6.3	7.3	7.7
Male	16.0	2.8	4.4	10.8	11.3	12.9	14.5
Female	0.9	0.1	0.2	0.2	1.0	1.1	0.7
Alcohol use on school property [1]							
Total	4.6	6.9	6.8	5.2	4.7	5.2	5.5
Male	5.5	8.7	7.3	5.5	4.8	6.3	7.5
Female	3.6	5.1	6.2	4.8	4.7	3.9	3.5
Marijuana use on school property [1]							
Total	5.0	7.3	7.5	4.4	6.5	6.5	5.1
Male	7.1	10.1	10.0	5.9	9.2	8.7	7.3
Female	2.8	4.5	4.9	2.8	3.6	4.0	2.7
Offered, sold, or given an illegal drug on school property [3]							
Total	24.1	17.5	34.1	21.8	23.7	27.5	23.0
Male	28.8	20.3	41.5	24.6	27.9	32.9	28.2
Female	18.9	14.8	26.8	18.4	19.2	21.7	17.5

[1] On one or more of the 30 days preceding the survey.
[2] Such as a gun, knife, or club.
[3] One or more times during the 12 months preceding the survey.
[4] Used chewing tobacco or snuff during the 30 days preceding the survey.

SOURCE: U.S. Department of Health and Human Services, Centers for Disease Control and Prevention, National Center for Chronic Disease, Prevention and Health Promotion, Division of Adolescent and School Health, *The Youth Risk Behavior Surveillance System: 1993.* (This table was prepared June 1995.)

Table 145.—Percent of 12- to 17-year-olds reporting drug use during the past 30 days and the past year: 1972 to 1993

Type of drug and frequency of use	1972	1974	1976	1977	1979	1982	1985	1988	1990	1991	1992	1993
1	2	3	4	5	6	7	8	9	10	11	12	13
Percent reporting drug use during past 30 days												
Any illicit use	—	—	—	—	17.6	12.7	14.9	9.2	8.1	6.8	6.1	6.6
Marijuana	7.0	12.0	12.3	16.6	16.7	11.5	11.9	6.4	5.2	4.3	4.0	4.9
Hallucinogens	1.4	1.3	0.9	1.6	2.2	1.4	1.2	0.8	0.9	0.8	0.6	0.5
Cocaine	0.6	1.0	1.0	0.8	1.4	1.6	1.4	1.1	0.6	0.4	0.3	0.4
Heroin	—	—	—	—	—	—	0.1	0.1	0.0	0.1	0.1	0.0
Nonmedical use of:												
Stimulants	—	1.0	1.2	1.3	1.2	2.6	1.6	1.2	1.0	0.5	0.2	0.5
Sedatives	—	1.0	—	0.8	1.1	1.3	1.0	0.6	0.9	0.5	0.4	0.2
Tranquilizers	—	1.0	1.1	0.7	0.6	0.9	0.6	0.2	0.5	0.4	0.2	0.2
Analgesics	—	—	—	—	0.6	0.7	1.7	0.9	1.4	1.1	0.8	0.7
Alcohol	—	34.0	32.4	31.2	37.2	30.2	31.0	25.2	24.5	20.3	15.7	18.0
Cigarettes	—	25.0	23.4	22.3	12.1	14.7	15.3	11.8	11.6	10.8	9.6	9.6
Percent reporting drug use during past year												
Any illicit use	—	—	—	—	26.0	22.0	23.3	16.8	15.9	14.8	11.7	13.6
Marijuana	—	18.5	18.4	22.3	24.1	20.6	19.4	12.6	11.3	10.1	8.1	10.1
Hallucinogens	3.6	4.3	2.8	3.1	4.7	3.6	2.6	2.8	2.4	2.1	1.9	2.1
Cocaine	1.5	2.7	2.3	2.6	4.2	4.1	3.9	2.9	2.2	1.5	1.1	0.8
Heroin	—	—	—	0.6	—	—	0.3	0.4	0.6	0.2	0.1	0.1
Nonmedical use of:												
Stimulants	—	3.0	2.2	3.7	2.9	5.6	4.1	2.8	3.0	1.9	1.3	1.6
Sedatives	—	2.0	1.2	2.0	2.2	3.7	2.8	1.7	2.2	1.3	1.0	0.8
Tranquilizers	—	2.0	1.8	2.9	2.7	3.3	3.4	1.5	1.5	1.3	1.0	0.7
Analgesics	—	—	—	—	2.2	3.7	4.0	3.0	4.8	3.3	2.4	2.2
Alcohol	—	51.0	49.3	47.5	53.6	52.4	51.6	44.5	41.0	40.3	32.6	35.2
Cigarettes	—	—	—	—	—	24.8	25.5	22.8	22.2	20.1	18.2	19.1

—Data not available.

SOURCE: U.S. Department of Health and Human Services, Substance Abuse and Mental Health Services Administration, *Preliminary Estimates from the 1993 National Household Survey on Drug Abuse.* (This table was prepared August 1994.)

Table 146.—Percent of high school seniors reporting drug use, by type of drug and frequency of use: 1975 to 1994

Type of drug and frequency of use	Class of 1975	Class of 1979	Class of 1980	Class of 1981	Class of 1982	Class of 1983	Class of 1984	Class of 1985	Class of 1986	Class of 1987	Class of 1988	Class of 1989	Class of 1990	Class of 1991	Class of 1992	Class of 1993	Class of 1994
1	2	3	4	5	6	7	8	9	10	11	12	13	14	15	16	17	18
Percent reporting having ever used drugs																	
Alcohol [1]	90.4	93.0	93.2	92.6	92.8	92.6	92.6	92.2	91.3	92.2	92.0	90.7	89.5	88.0	87.5	80.0	80.4
Any illicit drug abuse	55.2	65.1	65.4	65.6	64.4	62.9	61.6	60.6	57.6	56.6	53.9	50.9	47.9	44.1	40.7	42.9	45.6
Marijuana only	19.0	27.7	26.7	22.8	23.3	22.5	21.3	20.9	19.9	20.8	21.4	19.5	18.5	17.2	15.6	16.2	18.0
Any illicit drug other than marijuana [2]	36.2	37.4	38.7	42.8	41.1	40.4	40.3	39.7	37.7	35.8	32.5	31.4	29.4	26.9	25.1	26.7	27.6
Use of selected drugs																	
Cocaine	9.0	15.4	15.7	16.5	16.0	16.2	16.1	17.3	16.9	15.2	12.1	10.3	9.4	7.8	6.1	6.1	5.9
Heroin	2.2	1.1	1.1	1.1	1.2	1.2	1.3	1.2	1.1	1.2	1.1	1.3	1.3	0.9	1.2	1.1	1.2
LSD	11.3	9.5	9.3	9.8	9.6	8.9	8.0	7.5	7.2	8.4	7.7	8.3	8.7	8.8	8.6	10.3	10.5
Marijuana/hashish	47.3	60.4	60.3	59.5	58.7	57.0	54.9	54.2	50.9	50.2	47.2	43.7	40.7	36.7	32.6	35.3	38.2
PCP	—	12.8	9.6	7.8	6.0	5.6	5.0	4.9	4.8	3.0	2.9	3.9	2.8	2.9	2.4	2.9	2.8
Percent reporting use of drugs in the past 12 months																	
Alcohol [1]	84.8	88.1	87.9	87.0	86.8	87.3	86.0	85.6	84.5	85.7	85.3	82.7	80.6	77.7	76.8	72.7	73.0
Any illicit drug abuse	45.0	54.2	53.1	52.1	49.4	47.4	45.8	46.3	44.3	41.7	38.5	35.4	32.5	29.4	27.1	31.0	35.8
Marijuana only	18.8	26.0	22.7	18.1	19.3	19.0	17.8	18.9	18.4	17.6	17.4	15.4	14.6	13.2	12.2	13.9	17.8
Any illicit drug other than marijuana [2]	26.2	28.2	30.4	34.0	30.1	28.4	28.0	27.4	25.9	24.1	21.1	20.0	17.9	16.2	14.9	17.1	18.0
Use of selected drugs																	
Cocaine	5.6	12.0	12.3	12.4	11.5	11.4	11.6	13.1	12.7	10.3	7.9	6.5	5.3	3.5	3.1	3.3	3.6
Heroin	1.0	0.5	0.5	0.5	0.6	0.6	0.5	0.6	0.5	0.5	0.5	0.6	0.5	0.4	0.6	0.5	0.6
LSD	7.2	6.6	6.5	6.5	6.1	5.4	4.7	4.4	4.5	5.2	4.8	4.9	5.4	5.2	5.6	6.8	6.9
Marijuana/hashish	40.0	50.8	48.8	46.1	44.3	42.3	40.0	40.6	38.8	36.3	33.1	29.6	27.0	23.9	21.9	26.0	30.7
PCP	—	7.0	4.4	3.2	2.2	2.6	2.3	2.9	2.4	1.3	1.2	2.4	1.2	1.4	1.4	1.4	1.6
Percent reporting use of drugs in the past 30 days																	
Alcohol [1]	68.2	71.8	72.0	70.7	69.7	69.4	67.2	65.9	65.3	66.4	63.9	60.0	57.1	54.0	51.3	48.6	50.1
Any illicit drug abuse	30.7	38.9	37.2	36.9	32.5	30.5	29.2	29.7	27.1	24.7	21.3	19.7	17.2	16.4	14.4	18.3	21.9
Marijuana only	15.3	22.2	18.8	15.2	15.5	15.1	14.1	14.8	13.9	13.1	11.3	10.6	9.2	9.3	8.1	10.4	13.1
Any illicit drug other than marijuana [2]	15.4	16.8	18.4	21.7	17.0	15.4	15.1	14.9	13.2	11.6	10.0	9.1	8.0	7.1	6.3	7.9	8.8
Use of selected drugs																	
Cocaine	1.9	5.7	5.2	5.8	5.0	4.9	5.8	6.7	6.2	4.3	3.4	2.8	1.9	1.4	1.3	1.3	1.5
Heroin	0.4	0.2	0.2	0.2	0.2	0.2	0.3	0.3	0.2	0.2	0.2	0.3	0.2	0.2	0.3	0.2	0.3
LSD	2.3	2.4	2.3	2.5	2.4	1.9	1.5	1.6	1.7	1.8	1.8	1.8	1.9	1.9	2.0	2.4	2.6
Marijuana/hashish	27.1	36.5	33.7	31.6	28.5	27.0	25.2	25.7	23.4	21.0	18.0	16.7	14.0	13.8	11.9	15.5	19.0
PCP	—	2.4	1.4	1.4	1.0	1.3	1.0	1.6	1.3	0.6	0.3	1.4	0.4	0.5	0.6	1.0	0.7

[1] Survey question changed in 1993; data are not comparable to figures for earlier years.

[2] Other illicit drugs include any use of hallucinogens, cocaine, and heroin, or any use of other opiates, stimulants, sedatives, or tranquilizers not under a doctor's orders.

—Data not available.

NOTE.—A revised questionnaire was used in 1982 and later years to reduce the inappropriate reporting of nonprescription stimulants. This slightly reduced the positive responses for some types of drug abuse.

SOURCE: U.S. Department of Health and Human Services, Alcohol, Drug Abuse, and Mental Health Administration, *Drug Use Among American High School Students and Other Young Adults, National Trends Through 1988;* and press releases dated January 1992, April 1993, and January 1994; and University of Michigan, Institute for Social Research, *Monitoring the Future,* unpublished data. (This table was prepared June 1995.)

Table 147.—Percent of teachers and students who feel that school violence is a major problem, by type of violent action: 1993

Teacher and student characteristics	Verbal insults	Threats to students	Threats to teachers	Pushing, shoving, grabbing, or slapping	Kicking, biting, or hitting with a fist	Threatening with a knife or gun	Using knives or firing guns	Stealing
1	2	3	4	5	6	7	8	9
All teachers	**16**	**12**	**4**	**28**	**13**	**3**	**2**	**19**
Location								
Urban	36	22	8	39	20	5	4	28
Suburban or rural	22	9	2	24	10	2	2	15
School level								
Elementary	18	8	2	24	12	1	1	10
Secondary	30	14	5	29	13	3	3	23
Quality of education in teachers' school[1]								
Excellent	—	6	2	17	5	1	1	10
Good	—	17	5	35	16	4	3	25
Fair or poor	—	29	13	64	46	9	9	47
Income level of students in teacher's school[1]								
All or many lower income students	—	20	6	38	20	4	3	28
Some lower income students	—	8	3	23	9	2	1	13
Few or no lower income students	—	6	2	17	5	1	2	11
Number of minority students in teacher's school[1]								
All or many minority students	—	22	8	40	23	5	4	30
Some minority students	—	11	4	24	10	3	2	19
Few or no minority students	—	5	1	20	5	(2)	1	9
Student opinions								
All students	**34**	**23**	**15**	**33**	**27**	**20**	**19**	**38**
Location								
Urban	40	28	19	39	31	23	24	38
Suburban or rural	31	21	13	29	26	17	16	38

[1] As reported by teachers in this survey.
[2] less than 0.5 percent.

SOURCE: Metropolitan Life/Louis Harris Associates, Inc. "The American Teacher: 1993". (This table was prepared May 1995.)

Table 148.—Ages for compulsory school attendance and compulsory provision of services for special education students, by state: 1992–93 and March 1994

State	Compulsory attendance (March 1994)	Compulsory provision of services for special education (1992–93)[1]	State	Compulsory attendance (March 1994)	Compulsory provision of services for special education (1992–93)[1]
1	2	3	1	2	3
Alabama	7 to 16	3 to 20	Missouri	7 to 16	3 to 20
Alaska	[2]7 to 16	3 to 21	Montana	[3]7 to 16	3 to 18
Arizona	[4]6 to 16	3 to 21	Nebraska	7 to 16	Birth to 20
Arkansas	5 to 17	3 to 20	Nevada	7 to 17	3 to 21
California	6 to 18	3 to 21	New Hampshire	6 to 16	3 to 20
Colorado	7 to 16	3 to 20	New Jersey	6 to 16	3 to 21
Connecticut	7 to 16	3 to 21	New Mexico	5 to 16	3 to 21
Delaware	5 to 16	3 to 20	New York	[5]6 to 16	[6]3 to 21
District of Columbia	7 to 17	[6]3 to 21	North Carolina	7 to 16	3 to 20
Florida	6 to 16	3 to 18	North Dakota	7 to 16	3 to 20
Georgia	7 to 16	3 to 21	Ohio	6 to 18	3 to 21
Hawaii	6 to 18	3 to 20	Oklahoma	5 to 18	3 to 21
Idaho	7 to 16	3 to 20	Oregon	7 to 18	3 to 20
Illinois	7 to 16	3 to 20	Pennsylvania	8 to 17	3 to 21
Indiana	[7]7 to 16	3 to 17	Rhode Island	6 to 16	3 to 20
Iowa	6 to 16	Birth to 20	South Carolina	[8]5 to 17	3 to 20
Kansas	7 to 16	3 to 21	South Dakota	[3]6 to 16	3 to 20
Kentucky	[9]6 to 16	3 to 20	Tennessee	7 to 17	3 to 21
Louisiana	7 to 17	3 to 21	Texas	6 to 17	3 to 21
Maine	7 to 17	3 to 19	Utah	6 to 18	[6]3 to 21
Maryland	5 to 16	Birth to 20	Vermont	7 to 16	3 to 21
Massachusetts	6 to 16	3 to 21	Virginia	5 to 18	2 to 21
Michigan	6 to 16	Birth to 25	Washington	[10]8 to 18	3 to 21
Minnesota	[11]7 to 16	Birth to 20	West Virginia	6 to 16	3 to 22
Mississippi	6 to 16	3 to 20	Wisconsin	[12]6 to 18	3 to 20
			Wyoming	7 to 16	3 to 20

[1] Lower age limit for eligibility has been updated for 1992–93, upper age limit is for 1989–90.
[2] Ages 7 to 16 or high school graduation.
[3] May leave after completion of eighth grade.
[4] Ages 6 to 16 or tenth grade completion.
[5] Ages 6 to 17 for New York City and Buffalo.
[6] State has established two points in the program year by which children must be 3 years of age to be eligible for services.
[7] Effective 1992–93, students between 16 and 18 are required to submit to an exit interview and have written parental approval before leaving high school.
[8] Permits parental waiver of kindergarten at age 5.
[9] Must have parental signature for leaving school between ages of 16 and 18.

[10] Or can exit if age 15 and has completed grade 8, has a useful occupation, has met graduation requirements or has certificate of education competency.
[11] Will change to 7 to 18 in the year 2000.
[12] Ages 6 to 18 or high school graduation.

NOTE.—The Education of the Handicapped Act (EHA) Amendments of 1986 make it mandatory for all states receiving EHA funds to serve all 3- to 18-year-old handicapped children.

SOURCE: U.S. Department of Education, Office of Special Education and Rehabilitative Services, Section 619 Profile, Fourth Edition, June 1993; Education Commission of the States, "Compulsory School Age Requirements, March 1994," and unpublished revisions. (This table was prepared August 1994.)

Table 149.—Tenth and twelfth graders' attendance patterns, by selected student and school characteristics: 1990 and 1992

Attendance pattern	All students	Sex		Race/ethnicity					Socioeconomic status [1]			Control of school attended		
		Male	Female	White	Black	Hispanic	Asian	American Indian	Low	Middle	High	Public	Catholic	Other private
1	2	3	4	5	6	7	8	9	10	11	12	13	14	15
Percent of 10th graders in 1990														
Number of days missed first half of current school year														
None	14.3	17.1	11.6	13.0	21.2	12.5	23.1	12.0	13.1	15.0	14.9	14.0	18.3	15.1
1 or 2 days	23.2	24.9	21.5	22.8	27.2	20.6	28.6	12.5	20.0	23.0	26.6	22.6	26.4	33.6
3 or 4 days	27.7	27.1	28.3	28.8	24.5	25.0	23.9	33.7	25.3	27.6	29.5	27.9	26.6	27.7
5 or more days	34.8	30.9	38.7	35.4	27.1	41.9	24.4	41.9	41.6	34.3	29.0	35.4	28.8	23.5
Number of times late first half of current school year														
None	25.2	25.4	24.9	27.8	17.8	17.8	22.0	18.6	23.9	25.7	26.6	25.3	27.7	17.9
1 or 2 days	38.2	38.1	38.3	38.0	41.1	36.7	39.7	31.3	37.4	38.6	38.2	37.8	39.8	44.6
3 or more days	36.7	36.6	36.8	34.2	41.1	45.5	38.3	50.1	38.7	35.7	35.2	36.9	32.4	37.5
Cut classes														
Never or almost never	84.8	83.5	86.2	85.8	86.5	75.8	87.1	81.4	82.3	84.5	89.0	84.0	95.2	90.9
At least sometimes	15.2	16.5	13.8	14.2	13.5	24.2	12.9	18.6	17.7	15.5	11.0	16.0	4.8	9.1
Percent of 12th graders in 1992														
Number of days missed first half of current school year														
None	8.7	10.5	6.9	7.4	15.8	6.9	15.6	11.3	8.7	8.6	8.8	8.6	10.2	9.1
1 or 2 days	30.3	30.8	29.9	29.9	31.0	31.6	34.3	22.4	27.5	30.8	31.7	30.2	31.2	32.7
3 to 6 days	35.0	35.0	35.1	36.2	31.2	34.4	27.4	37.8	34.0	34.0	37.7	34.8	37.5	37.8
7 or more days	25.9	23.7	28.2	26.5	22.1	27.1	22.7	28.6	29.8	26.6	21.8	26.4	21.1	20.5
Number of times late first half of current school year														
None	19.0	17.7	20.3	20.6	14.0	14.7	16.2	19.1	19.7	19.0	18.7	19.2	19.5	12.3
1 or 2 days	33.5	32.4	34.5	34.4	32.1	28.7	33.8	25.3	32.8	34.2	33.1	33.0	36.4	37.6
3 or more days	47.6	49.9	45.2	45.0	53.9	56.6	50.0	55.6	47.5	46.8	48.2	47.8	44.1	50.1
Cut classes														
Never or almost never	75.6	72.8	78.4	76.5	77.7	67.9	72.7	73.7	76.2	75.6	75.4	74.3	87.1	86.3
At least sometimes	24.4	27.2	21.6	23.5	22.3	32.1	27.3	26.3	23.8	24.4	24.6	25.7	12.9	13.7

[1] Socioeconomic status was measured by a composite score on parental education and occupations, and family income. The "Low" SES group is the lowest quartile; the "Middle" SES group is the middle two quartiles; and the "High" SES group is the upper quartile.

SOURCE: U.S. Department of Education, National Center for Education Statistics, "National Education Longitudinal Study of 1988," First and Second Followup surveys. (This table was prepared March 1994.)

Table 150.—Tenth graders who agree or strongly agree with statements on why they go to school: 1990

Reason for going to school	Percent of 10th graders													
	All 10th graders	Sex		Race/ethnicity					Socioeconomic status [1]			Control of school attended		
		Male	Female	White	Black	Hispanic	Asian	American Indian	Low	Middle	High	Public	Catholic	Other private
1	2	3	4	5	6	7	8	9	10	11	12	13	14	15
Think subjects are interesting	71.0	70.1	71.9	68.8	79.1	74.5	77.3	81.2	72.8	68.7	74.9	70.7	75.5	71.4
Get a feeling of satisfaction	76.9	74.2	79.6	74.8	85.8	81.3	79.6	81.6	78.2	75.3	79.1	76.3	81.7	81.3
Nothing else to do	30.3	33.4	27.3	30.1	29.0	31.1	32.4	31.3	33.2	30.8	26.5	30.8	24.2	28.4
Need education to get a job	96.6	95.3	97.8	96.5	96.7	96.8	97.1	93.4	95.4	96.5	97.7	96.4	97.8	98.2
To meet friends	82.7	83.0	82.4	85.5	66.1	80.1	84.9	80.8	76.8	82.5	87.4	82.8	83.5	78.6
Play on a team or belong to a club	53.6	58.4	49.0	55.3	49.3	45.3	56.3	46.2	40.4	54.3	64.1	53.1	59.1	58.8
Teachers care and expect student to succeed	74.0	72.6	75.4	72.4	81.6	76.0	74.6	79.4	75.2	72.8	75.5	73.2	80.6	79.6

[1] Socioeconomic status was measured by a composite score on parental education and occupations, and family income. The "Low" SES group is the lowest quartile; the "Middle" SES group is the middle two quartiles; and the "High" SES group is the upper quartile.

SOURCE: U.S. Department of Education, National Center for Education Statistics, "National Education Longitudinal Study of 1988," First Followup survey. (This table was prepared February 1993.)

Table 151.—State requirements for high school graduation, in Carnegie units: 1980 and 1993

State	1980 All courses	1993 All courses	English/ language arts	Social studies	Mathematics	Science	Physical education/ health	Electives	Other courses	First graduating class to which these requirements apply	Notes
1	2	3	4	5	6	7	8	9	10	11	12
Alabama Standard	20	22	4	3	2	2	1.5	9.5		1989	Must become computer literate through related coursework. Minimum competency test is required for graduation.
Advanced	—	22	4	4	3	3	1.5	4	2 foreign languages, .5 home/personal management		
Alaska	19	21	4	3	2	2	1	9			Minimum competency test is required for graduation.
Arizona	16	20	4	2.5	2	2	—	9	.5 free enterprise	1991	
Arkansas	16	20	4	3	3	2	1	6.5	.5 fine arts	1988	Social studies options: 2 or 3 units social studies and 1 practical arts.
California Standard	(1)	13	3	3	2	2	2	—	1 fine arts or foreign language	—	The state board has published "Model Graduation Requirements" to be used as a guide by local districts. These include specifics in core subjects plus computer studies and foreign language. Test and cut-off standards for early exit, with parental approval. Minimum competency test is required for graduation.
Advanced	—	16	3	3	3	2	2	—	2 in same foreign language, 1 fine arts	—	
Colorado	—	(2)	(2)	(2)	(2)	(2)	(2)	(2)		—	State has constitutional prohibition against state requirements. School accreditation requirements total 30 units covering language arts, social studies, math, foreign language, fine/vocational/practical arts, health/safety, and physical education.
Connecticut	(2)	20	4	3	3	2	1	6	1 arts or vocational education	1988	
Delaware	18	19	4	3	2	2	1.5	6.5		1987	Minimum competency test is required for graduation.
District of Columbia	18	23.5	4	3.5	3	3	1.5	3.5	2 foreign languages; 1 career/vocational; .5 fine arts; .5 music	1996	Electives must include life skills seminar or passage of a test. D.C. requires 100 hours of community service without credit.
Florida Standard	(2)	24	4	3	3	3	0.5	9	.5 practical/exploratory vocational education; .5 performing arts or speech and debate; .5 life management skills	1989	2 of science units must include labs. Students must have 1.5 GPA to graduate. Junior and senior students may receive dual credits for college coursework. Vocational students may substitute certain vocational courses to satisfy up to 2 required credits in each of the areas of English, math, and science. Minimum competency test is required for graduation.
Academic scholars	—	26	4	3	4	4	1	7	2 of same foreign language; 1 fine arts	—	
Georgia Standard	20	21	4	3	3	3	1	6	1 computer technology and/or fine arts and/or vocational education and/or ROTC	1997	Students who completed 4 units of vocational education receive a state seal of endorsement from the State Board of Education. Algebra is required. Minimum competency is required for graduation.
Advanced	—	21	4	3	3	3	1	4	2 foreign languages; 1 fine arts, vocational education, computer technology, or ROTC	1988	
Hawaii	20	22	4	4	3	3	1.5	6	.5 guidance	1997	

Table 151.—State requirements for high school graduation, in Carnegie units: 1980 and 1993—Continued

State	1980 All courses	1993 All courses	English/ language arts	Social studies	Mathe- matics	Science	Physical education/ health	Electives	Other courses	First graduating class to which these requirements apply	Notes
1	2	3	4	5	6	7	8	9	10	11	12
Idaho	18	21	4	2	2	2	1.5	6	.5 each: reading, speech, and consumer education; 2 humanities	1989	Practical arts may substitute for 1 unit of humanities. State requires a C average, demonstrated competency in core curriculum on a junior class competency test, or adherence to local district's achievement plan for graduation. State level minimum competency test is an option for the local districts. If passed, students receive special proficiency endorsement on their diploma.
Illinois	16	16	3	2	2	1	4.5	2.25	.25 consumer education; 1 art, foreign language, music, or vocational education	1988	1 year of math may be computer technology. 1 year of social studies must be U.S. history or half U.S. history and half American government. Beginning 1985–86, the school boards were allowed to excuse 11–12th grades from physical education to: 1)participate in interscholastic athletics or 2)enroll in academic class required for college admission or to graduate from high school. 9–12th grade pupils may elect to take a consumer education proficiency test; if passed, they are excused from requirement.
Indiana Standard	16	19.5	4	2	2	2	1.5	8		1989	State does not use standard Carnegie units.
Academic honors	—	24	4	3	4	4	1	4 or	3 or 4 in foreign language (3 in 1 or 2 years each in 2)	1990	
Iowa	—	—	—	—	—	—	1	—		1989	Legislative requirements in effect for many years. Local districts determine remaining requirements. State allows junior and senior students to receive dual credits for college coursework.
Kansas	17	21	4	3	2	2	1	9		1989	
Kentucky Standard	18	20	4	2	3	2	1	7	1 additional math, science, social studies, or vocational education	1987	
Commonwealth	—	22	5	2	—	—	1	1	1 foreign language in advance placement and 6 units in math and science	1986	
Louisiana Standard	20	23	4	3	3	3	2	7.5	.5 computer literacy	1989	Students with ACT score of 29 or above, 3.5 GPA with no semester grade lower than a B, no unexcused absences, and no suspensions receive a Scholar Program seal on their diploma. Algebra is required. Minimum competency test is required for graduation.
Scholar program	—	23	4	3	3	3	2	7.5	.5 computer literacy	1987	
Regents' scholar	—	24	4	3.5	3	3	2	4.5	3 foreign languages, 1 fine arts	1983	American history is required. All students must pass computer proficiency standards. 1 of the science units must include a lab.
Maine	(3)	16	4	2	2	2	1.5	3.5	1 fine arts	1989	
Maryland	20	21	4	3	3	2	1	5	1 fine arts; 1 industrial arts/technology education, home economics, vocational education, or computer studies; and 1 community service	1997	After grade 11, 4 credits must be earned. Students can earn statewide certificate of merit with fulfillment of additional requirements. Special education certificates are available for students unable to meet requirements but who complete a special education program. Minimum competency test, writing test, and passage of quiz on citizenship are required for graduation.
Massachusetts	—	—	—	1	—	—	4	—	—	—	American history is required. Local boards determine additional requirements.

Table 151.—State requirements for high school graduation, in Carnegie units: 1980 and 1993—Continued

State	1980 All courses	1993 All courses	English/language arts	Social studies	Mathematics	Science	Physical education/health	Electives	Other courses	First graduating class to which these requirements apply	Notes
Michigan Standard[4]	—	—	4	3	3	2	1	—	2 foreign languages, fine or performing arts, or vocational education; .5 computer education	—	
College preparatory[4]	—	—	4	3	3	2	1	—	At least 2 years foreign language		
Minnesota	15	20	4	3	3	2	1	9.5		1982	Junior and senior students may receive dual credits for college coursework.
Mississippi	16	18	4	2	1	2	1.5	8		1989	At least 1 science unit must include a lab. Minimum competency test is required for graduation.
Missouri Standard	20	22	3	2	2	2	1	10	1 practical arts; 1 fine arts	1988	
College preparatory	20	24	4	3	2	3	1	8	1 practical arts; 1 fine arts	1988	College preparation diploma became available to qualifying graduates. For college preparation, specific core subjects must be taken.
Montana	16	20	4	2	2	2	1	7	1 fine arts; 1 vocational education; 1 practical arts	1992	
Nebraska	—	—	—	—	—	—	—	—		1991	200 credit hours are required for graduation, with at least 80 percent in core curriculum courses.
Nevada	19	22.5	4	2	2	2	2.5	8.5	1 arts/humanities; .5 computer literacy	1992	Computer literacy may be waived by demonstration of competency. Minimum competency test is required for graduation.
New Hampshire	16	19.75	4	2.5	2	2	1.25	4	.5 arts; .5 computer science; 3 units from 2 of the following: arts, foreign language, practical arts, or vocational education	1989	Minimum competency test for high school graduation is an option of the local districts.
New Jersey	—	21.5	4	3	3	2	4	4	1 fine, practical, or performing arts; .5 career exploration	1990	92 credit hours are required for graduation. State does not use standard Carnegie units. Minimum competency test is required for graduation.
New Mexico	20	23	4	3	3	2	1	9	1 communication skills	1990	State board requires student computer literacy prior to graduation. Languages other than English can satisfy communication skills requirement, emphasizing writing and speaking. Students preparing for college have an advanced curriculum. State level minimum competency test is an option of the local districts; passing students receive a special proficiency endorsement on their diploma.
New York Local diploma	16	18.5	4	4	2	2	.5	(5)	1 art and/or music; .5 health; 2 noncredit units of physical education beyond the total	1989	3-5 units from a sequence of specific courses must be chosen by the Regents' diploma students. Minimum competency test is required for graduation.
Regents' diploma	18	18.5	4	4	2	2	.5	(5)		1989	For a Regents' diploma, comprehensive exams are required in most subjects.
North Carolina Standard	16	20	4	2	2	2	1	9		1987	1 science class must include a lab. Minimum competency test is required for graduation.
Scholars program	—	22	4	3	3	3	1	4	2 foreign languages; 2 additional: English, math, social science, or foreign language	1994	
North Dakota	17	17	4	3	2	2	1	5	Social studies must include 1 unit of world history, and 1 unit of U.S. history, each with a strong geography component	1994	1 unit of higher level foreign language may be substituted for the 4th unit of English; 1 unit math may be business math. Although 17 units are required, the local education agencies are urged to require a minimum of 20 units.
Ohio	17	18	3	2	2	1	1	9		1988	Minimum competency test is required for graduation.

Table 151.—State requirements for high school graduation, in Carnegie units: 1980 and 1993—Continued

State	1980 All courses	1993 All courses	English/language arts	Social studies	Mathematics	Science	Physical education/health	Electives	Other courses	First graduating class to which these requirements apply	Notes
1	2	3	4	5	6	7	8	9	10	11	12
Oklahoma											
Standard	18	20	4	2	2	2	—	10		1987	
College preparatory	10.5	15	4	2	3	2	—	—	4 from: math, history, computer science, economics, English, geography, government, foreign language, sociology, science, speech, and psychology	1988	If foreign language is elected, 2 years in the same language is required. Total hour requirement is less, but more rigorous and restrictive for college preparatory path.
Oregon	21	22	3	3.5	2	2	2	8	.5 career development; 1 applied arts, fine arts, or foreign language	1988	Minimum competency test is required for graduation. 3.5 GPA students receive an honors seal on their diploma.
Pennsylvania	13	21	4	3	3	3	1	5	2 arts/humanities	1989	Computer science can be an option instead of arts and humanities. State has prescribed learning objectives and curriculum guidelines for 12 goals of quality education.
Rhode Island											
Standard	16	16	4	2	2	2	—	6	2 foreign languages; .5 arts; .5 computer literacy	1989	
College preparatory	16	18	4	2	3	2	—	4		1989	
South Carolina											
Standard	18	20	4	3	3	2	1	7		1987	If approved, 1 unit of computer science can count for a math requirement. 1 unit of science and 6 or more in a specific occupational service area can fulfill the science requirement. Junior and senior students may receive dual credits for college coursework. Minimum competency test is required for graduation.
Academic achievement honors	—	22	4	3	3	2	1	7	2 foreign languages	1986	
South Dakota	16	20	4	3	2	3	—	7	.5 computer studies; .5 fine arts	1989	Requirements include 3 science courses and 7 electives.
Tennessee											
Standard	18	20	4	1	2	2	1.5	9	.5 economics	1989	Economics requirement may include: 1 semester in economics, out-of-school experiences through Junior Achievement, or marketing education. Minimum competency test is required for graduation.
Honors, general education	—	20.5	4	3	3	3	1.5	2	2 in same foreign language; 2 fine visual or performing arts	1988	
Honors, vocational education	—	20.5	4	3	3	3	1.5	2	4 in same vocational education program	1989	
Texas											
Standard	18	21	4	2.5	3	2	1.5/.5	7	.5 economics/free enterprise	1988	1.5 units of physical education and .5 of health are required for either program. Minimum competency test is required for graduation. Junior and senior students can receive dual credits for college coursework.
College preparatory	18	22	4	2.5	3	3	1.5/.5	3	.5 economics/free enterprise; 2 foreign languages; 1 computer science; 1 fine arts	1988	
Utah	15	24	3	3	2	2	2	9.5	1.5 arts; 1 vocational education; optional .5 computer science	1988	State board makes specific course recommendations for college entry, vocational, etc.

Table 151.—State requirements for high school graduation, in Carnegie units: 1980 and 1993—Continued

State	1980 All courses	1993 All courses	English/ language arts	Social studies	Mathematics	Science	Physical education/ health	Electives	Other courses	First graduating class to which these requirements apply	Notes
1	2	3	4	5	6	7	8	9	10	11	12
Vermont	—	14.5	4	3	0 to 5	0 to 5	1.5	—	1 arts; 5 units in math and science	1989	To allow more flexibility to both vocational education students and smaller or more rural districts, the previous math and science requirement of 3 units in each was modified to a combination of 5 units which may be 2 of one and 3 of the other.
Virginia Standard	18	21	4	3	2	2	2	6	1 additional math or science; 1 fine or practical arts	1989	An appropriate vocational education class or ROTC may satisfy math or science. B average or better earns a state seal on the diploma. Junior and senior students can receive dual credits for college coursework. Minimum competency test is required for graduation.
Advanced studies	18	23	4	3	3	3	2	4	3 foreign languages; 1 fine or practical arts	1989	
Washington	—	19	3	2.5	2	2	2	5.5	1 occupational education; 1 fine/ visual or performing arts	1991	State has approved, but not implemented, an advanced studies certificate.
West Virginia	18	21	4	3	2	2	2	7	1 applied arts, fine or performing arts, or foreign language	1989	
Wisconsin	(2)	13	4	3	2	2	2	—		1989	Electives and passage of a minimum competency test as a requirement for graduation are options of local districts. State recommends that districts require a total of 22 units.
Wyoming	18	18	(2)	1	(2)	(2)	(2)	(2)	Local board determines remaining requirements	—	Accreditation standards indicate 4 units of English/ language arts, 3 social studies courses, 2 math courses, and 2 science courses.

[1] State permits local board to set minimum academic standards.
[2] Local boards determine requirements.
[3] State requires four credits in English/language arts. Local boards determine remaining requirements.
[4] Legislative requirements in effect for many years. Local boards determine additional requirements. The state board, in January 1984, published graduation requirement guidelines which local districts are urged to incorporate. Included in the recommendations are a minimum of 15.5 units, which includes an option of 2 units picked from a foreign language/fine or performing arts/vocational education and .5 computer education. Recommendations include modified academic course work for students who are college bound.

[5] Electives vary for the local (regular) and the Regents' (college-bound) diploma.
—Data not available or not applicable.

NOTE.—Local school districts frequently have other graduation requirements in addition to state requirements.

SOURCE: Education Commission of the States, *Clearinghouse Notes,* "Minimum High School Graduation Requirements: Standard Diplomas," 1980 and August 1993. (This table was prepared August 1994.)

Table 152.—States using minimum-competency testing, by government level setting standards, grade levels assessed, and expected uses of standards: November 1992

States using minimum-competency testing	Government level setting standards [1]	Grade levels assessed [1]	Expected uses					First graduating class assessed [1]	Still using competency tests in 1992
			Grade promotion [1]	High school graduation [1]	Early exit [1]	Remediation [1]	Other [1]		
1	2	3	4	5	6	7	8	9	10
Alabama	State	3,6,9,11		X		X	X	1985	Yes
Arizona	State/local	8,12	(2)	X				1976	
Arkansas	State	3,4,6,8				X			Yes
California	State/local	4–11,16 yr. old+	X	X	X	X		1979	Yes
Colorado	Local	9,12	(3)						
Connecticut [4]	State	4,6,8				X	X	1981	
Delaware	State	1–8,11		X			X	1983	
Florida	State/local	3,5,8,11	X	X	X		X	1985	Yes
Georgia	State	K,1,3,6,8,10	(5)	X		X	X	1983	Yes
Hawaii [6]	State	3,9–12		X		X	X		
Idaho	State	8–12				X	X	1982	
Illinois	Local	Local option					X		
Indiana	Local	3,6,8,10				X	(3)		
Kansas [7]	State	2,4,6,8,10				X			
Kentucky [8]		K–12	X	X		X			Yes
Louisiana [9]	State	2,3,4,5	X			X		1982	Yes
Maryland	State	7,9		X		X	X		Yes
Massachusetts	Local	Local option				X			
Michigan	State	4,7,10				X	(3)		
Mississippi	State	3,5,8,11		X			X	[10] 1987	Yes
Missouri	State	8+					X		Yes
Nebraska	Local	5+		X		X	X	1982	Yes
Nevada	State	3,6,9,11	(2)	(2)		X	(2)	1985	Yes
New Hampshire [11]	State	4,8,12		X		X	X	1985	Yes
New Jersey	State	9–12					X	1981	Yes
New Mexico	State	Local option, 10–12		X		X		1979	Yes
New York	State	3,5,6,8–12		X			X	1980	Yes
North Carolina [12]	State	3,6,8,10					(2)	1990	
Ohio	Local	Local option [13]					X		
Oklahoma [14]	None	3,6,9,12		X				1978	
Oregon	Local	Local option				X			
Pennsylvania	State	3,5,8				X		1990	Yes
South Carolina [15]	State	1,2,3,6,8,11	X	X		X	X	1982	Yes
Tennessee [16]	State/local	3,6,8,9–12	X	X		X		1987	Yes
Texas [17]	State	1,3,5,7,9,11,12		X		X	X	1988	
Utah	Local	Local option				X	X	1981	
Vermont	State	1–8	(18)			X	X	1981	
Virginia	State/local	K–6,10–12		X			X		
Wisconsin	Local	1–4,5–8,9–10	(3)	(3)		X			
Wyoming	Local	Local option				X			

[1] Based on information from November 1985.

[2] Legislation in 1983 called for development of a minimum course of study and criteria for high school graduation standards and for grade-to-grade promotion. Local school districts were to implement standards.

[3] Local option.

[4] A new program of state testing for grade 4 began in 1985 and expanded to grades 6 and 8 in 1986. The 9th grade state proficiency test, begun in 1980, was administered for the final time in 1986.

[5] Beginning in fall 1985, 3rd grade students had to demonstrate acceptable performance on criterion-referenced tests in mathematics and reading before promotion to the 4th grade. Beginning in 1988–89 school year, students must pass school readiness test to be eligible for first grade.

[6] Students have three options: paper-and-pencil test; performance test; or course. First time taken (grade 9) must be paper-and-pencil test.

[7] The Kansas Minimum Competency Assessment (MCA) was re-established by 1984 legislative action (SB 473). The MCA was in effect for 5 school years, 1984–85 through 1988–89.

[8] Legislation in 1984 required the state superintendent to recommend process of using test results for promotion and graduation to the 1986 legislature.

[9] Grade 8 was added beginning with 1986–87 school year.

[10] Although first class assessed graduated in 1987, the first class required to pass for graduation was the class of 1989.

[11] Students are tested in elementary, middle, and high school. Some local districts test at grades other than 4, 8, and 12.

[12] Grades 3, 6, and 8 are given an annual standardized achievement test. Local school districts use the results as a diagnostic tool.

[13] Locally based tests in the areas of English composition, mathematics, and reading are required at least once in grades 1–4. Tests in grades 5–8 and 9–11 will be implemented no later than 1989–90.

[14] Test was given in Oklahoma during the 1978–79 school year. There has been no followup to the program. However, a plan for statewide testing was submitted for legislative action in January 1985.

[15] The South Carolina Education Improvement Act of 1984 specified that the 11th grade test being used to gather baseline data be replaced in 1985–86 school year with an exit examination in the 10th grade. All students graduating in 1990 and after must pass the examination.

[16] Local districts use the state-designated tests at grades 3, 6, and 8 for remediation and to advise on grade retention. The Tennessee high school test, first taken at grade 9, is required for graduation.

[17] Texas HB 72 (1984) mandated the new testing program. New requirements became effective in 1985–86 school year.

[18] Vermont Basic Competency Program requires students to master the basics before they complete 8th grade.

NOTE.—Some states have dates for assessing the first high school graduating class but do not expect to use the results to determine whether students will graduate.

SOURCE: Education Commission of the States, *Clearinghouse Notes*, "State Activity—Minimum Competency Testing, as of November 1985"; and "Student Minimal Competency Testing." (This table was prepared March 1993.)

Table 153.—States requiring testing for initial certification of teachers, by authorization, year enacted, year effective, and test used: 1987 and 1990

State	1987				Assessment for certification 1990			
	Authority [1]	Enacted	Effective	Test used [2]	Basic skills	Professional skills	Content knowledge	In-class observation
1	2	3	4	5	6	7	8	9
Alabama	St. Bd.	1980	1981	State				
Alaska	—	—	—	—				
Arizona	Leg.	1980	1980	State	X	X		
Arkansas	Leg.	1979	1983	NTE		X	X	
California	Leg.	1981	1982	State	X		X	
Colorado	Leg.	1981	1983	California Achievement	X			X
Connecticut	St. Bd.	1982	1985	State	X		X	X
Delaware	St. Bd.	1982	1983	P.P.S.T.	X			
District of Columbia	—	—	—	—	X		X	
Florida	Leg.	1978	1980	State		X	X	X
Georgia	St. Bd.	1975	1980	State			X	X
Hawaii	St. Bd.	1986	1986	NTE	X	X	X	
Idaho	Leg.	1987	1988	NTE		X	X	
Illinois	Leg.	1985	1988	State		X	X	
Indiana	Leg.	1984	1985	NTE	X	X	X	
Iowa	—	—	—	—	X	X	X	X
Kansas	Leg.	1984	1986	To be determined	X	X		
Kentucky	Leg.	1984	1985	NTE				X
Louisiana	Leg.	1977	1978	NTE	X	X	X	
Maine	Leg.	1984	1988	NTE	X	X	X	X
Maryland	St. Bd.	1986	1986	NTE	X	X	X	
Massachusetts	Leg.	1985	(3)	To be determined	(4)			
Michigan	Leg.	1986	1991	To be determined 5				
Minnesota	—	—	—	—	X			
Mississippi	Leg.	1975	1977	NTE		X	X	X
Missouri	Leg.	1985	1988	To be determined			X	
Montana	B.P.E.	1985	1986	NTE	X	X		
Nebraska	Leg.	1984	1989	To be determined 5	X			
Nevada	St. Bd.	1984	(3)	To be determined	X	X	X	
New Hampshire	St. Bd.	1984	1985	NTE	X			
New Jersey	St. Bd.	1984	1985	NTE			X	
New Mexico	St. Bd.	1981	1983	NTE	X	X		X
New York	St. Bd.	1980	1984	NTE	X	X		
North Carolina	St. Bd.	1964	1964	NTE				X
North Dakota	—	—	—	—				
Ohio [6]	St. Bd.	1986	1987	NTE		X	X	
Oklahoma	Leg.	1980	1982	State				X
Oregon	O.T.S.P.C.	1984	1985	C.B.E.S.T.	X	X	X	X
Pennsylvania	St. Bd.	1985	1987	State	X	X	X	
Rhode Island	St. Bd.	1985	1986	NTE	X	X		X
South Carolina	Leg.	1979	1982	NTE and State		X		X
South Dakota	St. Bd.	1985	1986	NTE				
Tennessee	St. Bd.	1980	1981	NTE				X
Texas	Leg.	1981	1986	State		X	X	
Utah	—	—	—	—			X	
Vermont	—	—	—	—				
Virginia	Leg.	1979	1980	NTE	X	X	X	X
Washington	St. Bd.	1984	(3)	To be determined 7				X
West Virginia [8]	St. Bd.	1982	1985	State	X		X	X
Wisconsin	S.P.I.	1986	1990	To be determined	X			
Wyoming	—	—	—	—				

[1] St. Bd. = State Board of Education; Leg. = Legislature; B.P.E. = Board of Public Education; O.T.S.P.C. = Oregon Teacher Standards and Practice Commission; S.P.I. = Superintendent of Public Instruction.

[2] NTE = National Teacher Examination; State = State developed test; C.B.E.S.T. = California Basic Education Skills Test; P.P.S.T. = Preprofessional Skills Test.

[3] Effective year is yet to be determined.

[4] Test required for foreign language, bilingual, and English as a Second Language.

[5] For basic skills and subject-matter competencies.

[6] Test requirements set by local school districts.

[7] State and undetermined tests will be used.

[8] Required for individuals entering West Virginia-approved education programs as of fall 1985.

—Data not available or not applicable.

SOURCE: Education Commission of the States, Clearinghouse Notes, "States Requiring Testing for Initial Certification of Teachers, April 1987;" "State Education Leader, Winter 1989;" and "State Education Indicators, 1990." (This table was prepared March 1992.)

Table 154.—Revenues for public elementary and secondary schools, by source of funds: 1919–20 to 1992–93

School year	In thousands				Percentage distribution			
	Total	Federal	State	Local (including intermediate) [1]	Total	Federal	State	Local (including intermediate) [1]
1	2	3	4	5	6	7	8	9
1919–20	$970,121	$2,475	$160,085	$807,561	100.0	0.3	16.5	83.2
1929–30	2,088,557	7,334	353,670	1,727,553	100.0	0.4	16.9	82.7
1939–40	2,260,527	39,810	684,354	1,536,363	100.0	1.8	30.3	68.0
1941–42	2,416,580	34,305	759,993	1,622,281	100.0	1.4	31.4	67.1
1943–44	2,604,322	35,886	859,183	1,709,253	100.0	1.4	33.0	65.6
1945–46	3,059,845	41,378	1,062,057	1,956,409	100.0	1.4	34.7	63.9
1947–48	4,311,534	120,270	1,676,362	2,514,902	100.0	2.8	38.9	58.3
1949–50	5,437,044	155,848	2,165,689	3,115,507	100.0	2.9	39.8	57.3
1951–52	6,423,816	227,711	2,478,596	3,717,507	100.0	3.5	38.6	57.9
1953–54	7,866,852	355,237	2,944,103	4,567,512	100.0	4.5	37.4	58.1
1955–56	9,686,677	441,442	3,828,886	5,416,350	100.0	4.6	39.5	55.9
1957–58	12,181,513	486,484	4,800,368	6,894,661	100.0	4.0	39.4	56.6
1959–60	14,746,618	651,639	5,768,047	8,326,932	100.0	4.4	39.1	56.5
1961–62	17,527,707	760,975	6,789,190	9,977,542	100.0	4.3	38.7	56.9
1963–64	20,544,182	896,956	8,078,014	11,569,213	100.0	4.4	39.3	56.3
1965–66	25,356,858	1,996,954	9,920,219	13,439,686	100.0	7.9	39.1	53.0
1967–68	31,903,064	2,806,469	12,275,536	16,821,063	100.0	8.8	38.5	52.7
1969–70	40,266,923	3,219,557	16,062,776	20,984,589	100.0	8.0	39.9	52.1
1970–71	44,511,292	3,753,461	17,409,086	23,348,745	100.0	8.4	39.1	52.5
1971–72	50,003,645	4,467,969	19,133,256	26,402,420	100.0	8.9	38.3	52.8
1972–73	52,117,930	4,525,000	20,843,520	26,749,412	100.0	8.7	40.0	51.3
1973–74	58,230,892	4,930,351	24,113,409	29,187,132	100.0	8.5	41.4	50.1
1974–75	64,445,239	5,811,595	27,211,116	31,422,528	100.0	9.0	42.2	48.8
1975–76	71,206,073	6,318,345	31,776,101	33,111,627	100.0	8.9	44.6	46.5
1976–77	75,322,532	6,629,498	32,688,903	36,004,134	100.0	8.8	43.4	47.8
1977–78	81,443,160	7,694,194	35,013,266	38,735,700	100.0	9.4	43.0	47.6
1978–79	87,994,143	8,600,116	40,132,136	39,261,891	100.0	9.8	45.6	44.6
1979–80	96,881,165	9,503,537	45,348,814	42,028,813	100.0	9.8	46.8	43.4
1980–81	105,949,087	9,768,262	50,182,659	45,998,166	100.0	9.2	47.4	43.4
1981–82	110,191,257	8,186,466	52,436,435	49,568,356	100.0	7.4	47.6	45.0
1982–83	117,497,502	8,339,990	56,282,157	52,875,354	100.0	7.1	47.9	45.0
1983–84	126,055,419	8,576,547	60,232,981	57,245,892	100.0	6.8	47.8	45.4
1984–85	137,294,678	9,105,569	67,168,684	61,020,425	100.0	6.6	48.9	44.4
1985–86	149,127,779	9,975,622	73,619,575	65,532,582	100.0	6.7	49.4	43.9
1986–87	158,523,693	10,146,013	78,830,437	69,547,243	100.0	6.4	49.7	43.9
1987–88	169,561,974	10,716,687	84,004,415	74,840,873	100.0	6.3	49.5	44.1
1988–89	192,016,374	11,902,001	91,768,911	88,345,462	100.0	6.2	47.8	46.0
1989–90	208,547,573	12,700,784	98,238,633	97,608,157	100.0	6.1	47.1	46.8
1990–91	223,340,537	13,776,066	105,324,533	104,239,939	100.0	6.2	47.2	46.7
1991–92 [2]	234,588,732	15,493,330	108,783,449	110,311,953	100.0	6.6	46.4	47.0
1992–93	248,496,276	17,267,351	113,396,992	117,831,933	100.0	6.9	45.6	47.4

[1] Includes a relatively small amount from nongovernmental sources (gifts and tuition and transportation fees from patrons). These sources accounted for 2.7 percent of total revenues in 1992–93.

[2] Revised from previously published figures.

NOTE.—Beginning in 1980–81, revenues for state education agencies are excluded. Beginning in 1988–89, data reflect new survey collection procedures and may not be entirely comparable with figures for earlier years. Because of rounding, details may not add to totals.

SOURCE: U.S. Department of Education, National Center for Education Statistics, *Statistics of State School Systems; Revenues and Expenditures for Public Elementary and Secondary Education;* and Common Core of Data surveys. (This table was prepared May 1995.)

Table 155.—Revenues for public elementary and secondary schools, by source and state: 1992–93

[Amounts in thousands of dollars]

State or other area	Total	Federal		State		Local and intermediate		Private [1]	
		Amount	Percent of total	Amount	Percent of total	Amount	Percent of total	Amount	Percent of total
1	2	3	4	5	6	7	8	9	10
United States	**$248,496,276**	**$17,267,351**	**6.9**	**$113,396,992**	**45.6**	**$111,125,147**	**44.7**	**$6,706,786**	**2.7**
Alabama	2,982,753	347,381	11.6	1,732,506	58.1	661,483	22.2	241,384	8.1
Alaska	1,182,527	173,239	14.6	767,809	64.9	215,825	18.3	25,654	2.2
Arizona	3,402,888	299,926	8.8	1,411,844	41.5	1,614,522	47.4	76,596	2.3
Arkansas	1,933,846	184,934	9.6	1,104,347	57.1	552,744	28.6	91,822	4.7
California	28,039,018	2,256,461	8.0	17,439,021	62.2	8,014,478	28.6	329,058	1.2
Colorado	3,337,266	164,527	4.9	1,403,076	42.0	1,657,801	49.7	111,862	3.4
Connecticut	3,971,766	137,383	3.5	1,544,471	38.9	2,180,356	54.9	109,555	2.8
Delaware	631,885	43,448	6.9	417,965	66.1	160,103	25.3	10,369	1.6
District of Columbia	722,230	74,961	10.4	—	—	643,603	89.1	3,666	0.5
Florida	11,369,988	947,311	8.3	5,511,186	48.5	4,449,712	39.1	461,779	4.1
Georgia	5,997,559	463,476	7.7	3,019,826	50.4	2,391,963	39.9	122,294	2.0
Hawaii	1,067,810	81,518	7.6	962,375	90.1	6,628	0.6	17,288	1.6
Idaho	896,846	75,605	8.4	548,181	61.1	255,240	28.5	17,821	2.0
Illinois	10,575,035	747,825	7.1	3,013,710	28.5	6,559,514	62.0	253,986	2.4
Indiana	5,625,542	293,928	5.2	2,933,242	52.1	2,223,837	39.5	174,534	3.1
Iowa	2,694,532	144,390	5.4	1,299,696	48.2	1,091,553	40.5	158,893	5.9
Kansas	2,373,507	129,930	5.5	1,178,800	49.7	998,030	42.0	66,747	2.8
Kentucky	3,071,172	309,365	10.1	2,058,542	67.0	679,447	22.1	23,819	0.8
Louisiana	3,490,001	410,067	11.7	1,876,960	53.8	1,113,956	31.9	89,018	2.6
Maine	1,337,730	82,713	6.2	678,159	50.7	562,223	42.0	14,636	1.1
Maryland	4,923,313	264,767	5.4	1,940,701	39.4	2,564,887	52.1	152,958	3.1
Massachusetts	5,881,335	331,561	5.6	1,925,405	32.7	3,506,202	59.6	118,167	2.0
Michigan	10,766,136	664,798	6.2	3,295,411	30.6	6,606,216	61.4	199,711	1.9
Minnesota	4,698,237	225,048	4.8	2,261,916	48.1	2,030,657	43.2	180,617	3.8
Mississippi	1,773,823	303,590	17.1	951,723	53.7	451,147	25.4	67,362	3.8
Missouri	4,260,954	274,161	6.4	1,632,185	38.3	2,178,370	51.1	176,238	4.1
Montana	845,249	77,552	9.2	454,922	53.8	279,191	33.0	33,585	4.0
Nebraska	1,597,612	100,340	6.3	529,662	33.2	868,644	54.4	98,966	6.2
Nevada	1,176,376	54,833	4.7	402,727	34.2	676,163	57.5	42,654	3.6
New Hampshire	1,062,532	32,794	3.1	84,340	7.9	920,676	86.6	24,723	2.3
New Jersey	10,994,535	461,806	4.2	4,553,681	41.4	5,727,146	52.1	251,901	2.3
New Mexico	1,429,383	179,606	12.6	1,052,830	73.7	161,003	11.3	35,944	2.5
New York	22,574,304	1,352,381	6.0	8,848,907	39.2	12,032,177	53.3	340,840	1.5
North Carolina	5,356,917	433,593	8.1	3,388,467	63.3	1,321,306	24.7	213,551	4.0
North Dakota	551,527	65,639	11.9	237,908	43.1	218,531	39.6	29,449	5.3
Ohio	10,993,728	634,495	5.8	4,178,051	38.0	5,751,140	52.3	430,043	3.9
Oklahoma	2,770,975	197,037	7.1	1,663,413	60.0	782,957	28.3	127,568	4.6
Oregon	3,135,734	196,684	6.3	1,183,893	37.8	1,664,634	53.1	90,523	2.9
Pennsylvania	12,060,334	736,599	6.1	4,826,383	40.0	6,252,064	51.8	245,287	2.0
Rhode Island	968,667	57,892	6.0	392,841	40.6	510,745	52.7	7,189	0.7
South Carolina	3,061,004	286,136	9.3	1,439,690	47.0	1,199,057	39.2	136,122	4.4
South Dakota	603,085	69,969	11.6	164,040	27.2	350,490	58.1	18,587	3.1
Tennessee	3,394,425	351,089	10.3	1,546,611	45.6	1,255,944	37.0	240,782	7.1
Texas	17,446,887	1,305,976	7.5	6,983,217	40.0	8,654,014	49.6	503,680	2.9
Utah	1,657,433	117,788	7.1	961,278	58.0	521,167	31.4	57,201	3.5
Vermont	637,740	35,072	5.5	198,114	31.1	392,648	61.6	11,906	1.9
Virginia	5,867,838	365,225	6.2	1,886,029	32.1	3,451,606	58.8	164,978	2.8
Washington	5,499,862	307,058	5.6	3,920,527	71.3	1,107,991	20.1	164,286	3.0
West Virginia	1,841,575	142,379	7.7	1,234,018	67.0	438,001	23.8	27,176	1.5
Wisconsin	5,346,988	237,669	4.4	2,047,701	38.3	2,957,776	55.3	103,843	1.9
Wyoming	613,864	35,428	5.8	308,687	50.3	259,578	42.3	10,171	1.7
Outlying areas									
American Samoa	35,031	24,957	71.2	9,810	28.0	77	0.2	187	0.5
Guam	210,480	20,160	9.6	—	—	186,977	88.8	3,344	1.6
Northern Marianas	41,015	11,576	28.2	29,285	71.4	116	0.3	38	0.1
Puerto Rico	1,433,524	485,326	33.9	946,249	66.0	358	(2)	1,590	0.1
Virgin Islands	143,438	27,912	19.5	—	—	115,459	80.5	68	(2)

[1] Includes revenues from gifts, and tuition and fees from patrons.
[2] Less than .05 percent.
—Data not available or not applicable.

NOTE.—Excludes revenues for state education agencies. Because of rounding, details may not add to totals.

SOURCE: U.S. Department of Education, National Center for Education Statistics, Common Core of Data survey. (This table was prepared December 1994.)

Table 156.—Revenues for public elementary and secondary schools, by source and state: 1991–92

[Amounts in thousands of dollars]

State or other area	Total	Federal		State		Local and intermediate		Private [1]	
		Amount	Percent of total	Amount	Percent of total	Amount	Percent of total	Amount	Percent of total
1	2	3	4	5	6	7	8	9	10
United States	**$234,588,732**	**$15,493,330**	**6.6**	**$108,783,449**	**46.4**	**$104,087,332**	**44.4**	**$6,224,621**	**2.7**
Alabama	2,823,340	322,576	11.4	1,659,018	58.8	611,248	21.6	230,497	8.2
Alaska	1,120,970	128,612	11.5	762,663	68.0	205,165	18.3	24,530	2.2
Arizona	3,226,760	284,615	8.8	1,366,934	42.4	1,510,219	46.8	64,992	2.0
Arkansas	1,828,439	197,915	10.8	1,095,488	59.9	478,138	26.2	56,899	3.1
California	26,868,216	2,027,474	7.5	17,696,851	65.9	6,830,548	25.4	313,344	1.2
Colorado	3,058,633	152,090	5.0	1,307,982	42.8	1,510,328	49.4	88,233	2.9
Connecticut	3,891,100	126,225	3.2	1,583,668	40.7	2,063,543	53.0	117,664	3.0
Delaware	607,998	46,144	7.6	400,819	65.9	150,409	24.7	10,627	1.7
District of Columbia	711,172	66,508	9.4	—	—	641,350	90.2	3,314	0.5
Florida	10,810,522	788,420	7.3	5,227,256	48.4	4,350,167	40.2	444,679	4.1
Georgia	5,332,428	409,741	7.7	2,545,306	47.7	2,255,693	42.3	121,687	2.3
Hawaii	1,000,848	75,310	7.5	903,444	90.3	4,893	0.5	17,201	1.7
Idaho	861,955	69,859	8.1	532,475	61.8	242,120	28.1	17,501	2.0
Illinois	9,959,661	680,351	6.8	2,881,367	28.9	6,177,317	62.0	220,627	2.2
Indiana	5,127,888	272,355	5.3	2,710,144	52.9	1,975,429	38.5	169,960	3.3
Iowa	2,486,610	132,718	5.3	1,176,197	47.3	1,025,899	41.3	151,796	6.1
Kansas	2,264,365	123,564	5.5	959,173	42.4	1,112,810	49.1	68,817	3.0
Kentucky	2,939,351	296,573	10.1	1,969,899	67.0	651,896	22.2	20,984	0.7
Louisiana	3,377,061	363,958	10.8	1,848,734	54.7	1,068,290	31.6	96,079	2.8
Maine	1,246,798	73,876	5.9	621,026	49.8	548,461	44.0	3,435	0.3
Maryland	4,692,155	238,573	5.1	1,792,755	38.2	2,511,988	53.5	148,839	3.2
Massachusetts	5,621,629	296,702	5.3	1,728,360	30.7	3,483,002	62.0	113,565	2.0
Michigan	9,659,095	599,076	6.2	2,566,851	26.6	6,289,097	65.1	204,071	2.1
Minnesota	4,512,902	200,853	4.5	2,327,594	51.6	1,817,120	40.3	167,335	3.7
Mississippi	1,701,274	289,302	17.0	910,068	53.5	436,000	25.6	65,904	3.9
Missouri	4,053,529	258,032	6.4	1,538,752	38.0	2,088,076	51.5	168,668	4.2
Montana	821,111	72,483	8.8	343,293	41.8	373,016	45.4	32,318	3.9
Nebraska	1,506,050	93,705	6.2	517,098	34.3	761,716	50.6	133,530	8.9
Nevada	1,122,853	46,957	4.2	434,762	38.7	601,857	53.6	39,277	3.5
New Hampshire	1,015,187	31,098	3.1	86,597	8.5	871,238	85.8	26,253	2.6
New Jersey	10,523,004	436,024	4.1	4,438,939	42.2	5,451,200	51.8	196,841	1.9
New Mexico	1,368,013	169,616	12.4	1,009,593	73.8	154,408	11.3	34,395	2.5
New York	21,573,865	1,210,481	5.6	8,696,709	40.3	11,447,389	53.1	219,286	1.0
North Carolina	5,149,448	364,253	7.1	3,274,259	63.6	1,299,512	25.2	211,424	4.1
North Dakota	539,184	59,909	11.1	241,401	44.8	207,434	38.5	30,439	5.6
Ohio	9,736,287	571,416	5.9	3,974,682	40.8	4,797,389	49.3	392,800	4.0
Oklahoma	2,541,023	117,060	4.6	1,580,811	62.2	749,822	29.5	93,330	3.7
Oregon	2,869,231	183,784	6.4	877,897	30.6	1,722,487	60.0	85,063	3.0
Pennsylvania	11,561,337	664,767	5.7	4,788,825	41.4	5,874,822	50.8	232,923	2.0
Rhode Island	896,056	53,653	6.0	344,820	38.5	486,720	54.3	10,863	1.2
South Carolina	2,914,730	262,740	9.0	1,409,019	48.3	1,119,150	38.4	123,822	4.2
South Dakota	559,944	61,986	11.1	151,173	27.0	327,868	58.6	18,918	3.4
Tennessee	3,093,743	324,252	10.5	1,305,270	42.2	1,225,443	39.6	238,778	7.7
Texas	16,891,646	1,120,400	6.6	7,326,385	43.4	7,975,106	47.2	469,755	2.8
Utah	1,527,561	106,069	6.9	874,332	57.2	493,354	32.3	53,807	3.5
Vermont	645,751	32,761	5.1	204,369	31.6	395,643	61.3	12,978	2.0
Virginia	5,560,446	322,156	5.8	1,729,400	31.1	3,340,445	60.1	168,445	3.0
Washington	5,086,074	288,382	5.7	3,644,053	71.6	998,771	19.6	154,867	3.0
West Virginia	1,706,418	129,763	7.6	1,144,434	67.1	406,703	23.8	25,517	1.5
Wisconsin	4,966,200	216,430	4.4	1,958,288	39.4	2,693,730	54.2	97,752	2.0
Wyoming	628,872	31,762	5.1	314,216	50.0	272,903	43.4	9,990	1.6
Outlying areas									
American Samoa	34,234	22,648	66.2	11,423	33.4	—	—	163	0.5
Guam	164,582	16,958	10.3	—	—	145,142	88.2	2,482	1.5
Northern Marianas	41,046	9,314	22.7	31,391	76.5	340	0.8	0	(2)
Puerto Rico	1,371,616	443,759	32.4	927,114	67.6	327	(2)	416	(2)
Virgin Islands	158,004	41,429	26.2	—	—	116,505	73.7	69	(2)

[1] Includes revenues from gifts, and tuition and fees from patrons.
[2] Less than .05 percent.
—Data not available or not applicable.

NOTE.—Excludes revenues for state education agencies. Because of rounding, details may not add to totals. Some data have been revised from previously published figures.

SOURCE: U.S. Department of Education, National Center for Education Statistics, Common Core of Data survey. (This table was prepared May 1995.)

Table 157.—Summary of expenditures for public elementary and secondary education, by purpose: 1919–20 to 1992–93

Purpose of expenditures	1919–20	1929–30	1939–40	1949–50	1959–60	1969–70	1979–80	1989–90 [1]	1991–92 [1]	1992–93
1	2	3	4	5	6	7	8	9	10	11
	Amounts in thousands of dollars									
Total expenditures, all schools ...	**$1,036,151**	**$2,316,790**	**$2,344,049**	**$5,837,643**	**$15,613,255**	**$40,683,429**	**$95,961,561**	**$212,473,108**	**$241,062,373**	**$243,859,297**
Current expenditures, all schools	864,396	1,853,377	1,955,166	4,722,887	12,461,955	34,853,578	87,581,727	190,915,446	215,613,632	215,751,579
Public elementary and secondary schools	861,120	1,843,552	1,941,799	4,687,274	12,329,389	34,217,773	86,984,142	187,932,903	211,221,254	211,352,533
Administration	36,752	78,680	91,571	220,050	528,408	1,606,646	4,263,757	—	—	—
Instruction	632,556	1,317,727	1,403,285	3,112,340	8,350,738	23,270,158	53,257,937	—	—	—
Plant operation	115,707	216,072	194,365	427,587	1,085,036	2,537,257	[2] 9,744,785	—	—	—
Plant maintenance	30,432	78,810	73,321	214,164	422,586	974,941	([2])	—	—	—
Fixed charges	9,286	50,270	50,116	261,469	909,323	3,266,920	11,793,934	—	—	—
Other school services [3]	36,387	101,993	129,141	451,663	1,033,297	2,561,856	7,923,729	—	—	—
Other current expenditures										
Summer schools	([4])	([4])	([4])	([4])	13,263	106,481	24,753	2,982,543	4,392,378	4,399,046
Adult education[4]	3,277	9,825	13,367	35,614	26,858	128,778	—	([5])	([5])	([5])
Community colleges	([4])	([4])	([4])	([4])	34,492	138,813	—	([5])	([5])	([5])
Community services	([3])	([3])	([3])	([3])	57,953	261,731	572,832	([5])	([5])	([5])
Capital outlay [6]	153,543	370,878	257,974	1,014,176	2,661,786	4,659,072	6,506,167	17,781,342	20,282,891	22,668,507
Interest on school debt	18,212	92,536	130,909	100,578	489,514	1,170,782	1,873,666	3,776,321	5,165,850	5,439,211
	Percentage distribution									
Total expenditures, all schools	**100.0**	**100.0**	**100.0**	**100.0**	**100.0**	**100.0**	**100.0**	**100.0**	**100.0**	**100.0**
Current expenditures, all schools	83.4	80.0	83.4	80.9	79.8	85.7	91.2	89.9	89.4	88.5
Public elementary and secondary schools	83.1	79.6	82.8	80.3	79.0	84.1	90.6	88.5	87.6	86.7
Administration	3.5	3.4	3.9	3.8	3.4	3.9	4.4	—	—	—
Instruction	61.0	56.9	59.9	53.3	53.5	57.2	55.5	—	—	—
Plant operation	11.2	9.3	8.3	7.3	6.9	6.2	[2] 10.2	—	—	—
Plant maintenance	2.9	3.4	3.1	3.7	2.7	2.4	([2])	—	—	—
Fixed charges	0.9	2.2	2.1	4.5	5.8	8.0	12.3	—	—	—
Other school services [3]	3.5	4.4	5.5	7.7	6.6	6.3	8.3	—	—	—
Other current expenditures										
Summer schools	([4])	([4])	([4])	([4])	0.1	0.3	([7])	1.4	1.8	1.8
Adult education[4]	0.3	0.4	0.6	0.6	0.2	0.3	—	([5])	([5])	([5])
Community colleges	([4])	([4])	([4])	([4])	0.2	0.3	—	([5])	([5])	([5])
Community services	([3])	([3])	([3])	([3])	0.4	0.6	0.6	([5])	([5])	([5])
Capital outlay [6]	14.8	16.0	11.0	17.4	17.0	11.5	6.8	8.4	8.4	9.3
Interest on school debt	1.8	4.0	5.6	1.7	3.1	2.9	2.0	1.8	2.1	2.2

[1] Revised from previously published data.

[2] Plant operation also includes plant maintenance.

[3] Prior to 1959–60, items included under "other school services" were listed under "auxiliary services," a more comprehensive classification that also included community services.

[4] Prior to 1959–60, data shown for adult education represent combined expenditures for adult education, summer schools, and community colleges.

[5] Included under summer schools.

[6] Prior to 1969–70, excludes capital outlay by state and local schoolhousing authorities.

[7] Less than 0.05 percent.

—Data not available.

NOTE.—Beginning in 1959–60, includes Alaska and Hawaii. Beginning in 1980–81, state administration expenditures were excluded from both "total" and "current" expenditures. Beginning in 1988–89, extensive changes were made in the data collection procedures. Because of rounding, details may not add to totals.

SOURCE: U.S. Department of Education, National Center for Education Statistics, *Statistics of State School Systems;* and Common Core of Data surveys. (This table was prepared July 1995.)

Table 158.—Total expenditures for public elementary and secondary education, by function and subfunction: 1989–90 to 1992–93

Items	Expenditures (in thousands)				Percentage distribution			
	1989–90	1990–91	1991–92	1992–93	1989–90	1990–91	1991–92	1992–93
1	2	3	4	5	6	7	8	9
Total expenditures	$212,473,108	$229,429,715	$241,062,373	$253,859,297	—	—	—	—
Current expenditures	187,932,903	202,037,752	211,221,254	221,352,533	100.00	100.00	100.00	100.00
Salaries	[1]123,371,072	[1]132,729,751	138,220,586	144,289,751	65.65	65.70	65.44	65.19
Employee benefits	[1]31,376,416	[1]33,934,301	36,031,004	39,378,782	16.70	16.80	17.06	17.79
Purchased services	[1]15,443,358	[1]16,376,134	17,844,459	18,087,929	8.22	8.11	8.45	8.17
Tuition	[1]1,012,623	[1]1,192,505	939,291	969,687	0.54	0.59	0.44	0.44
Supplies	[1]14,007,262	[1]14,829,909	14,995,849	16,403,678	7.45	7.34	7.10	7.41
Other	[1]2,722,172	[1]2,975,152	3,190,064	2,222,706	1.45	1.47	1.51	1.00
Instruction	113,550,405	122,223,362	128,418,502	135,067,681	60.42	60.50	60.80	61.02
Salaries	84,350,068	90,742,284	94,973,704	99,108,741	44.88	44.91	44.96	44.77
Employee benefits	20,702,032	22,347,524	23,675,941	26,139,941	11.02	11.06	11.21	11.81
Purchased services	2,558,153	2,722,639	3,343,852	3,359,530	1.36	1.35	1.58	1.52
Tuition	1,012,623	1,192,505	939,291	969,687	0.54	0.59	0.44	0.44
Supplies	4,275,002	4,584,754	4,702,106	5,060,358	2.27	2.27	2.23	2.29
Other	652,526	633,656	783,608	429,423	0.35	0.31	0.37	0.19
Students [2]	8,265,657	8,926,010	9,226,186	9,767,799	4.40	4.42	4.37	4.41
Salaries	6,073,265	6,565,965	6,787,605	7,136,306	3.23	3.25	3.21	3.22
Employee benefits	1,528,864	1,660,082	1,750,887	1,908,890	0.81	0.82	0.83	0.86
Purchased services	431,976	455,996	444,443	489,718	0.23	0.23	0.21	0.22
Supplies	173,526	191,482	181,565	195,504	0.09	0.09	0.09	0.09
Other	58,025	52,485	61,686	37,381	0.03	0.03	0.03	0.02
Instructional services [3]	7,806,238	8,467,142	8,829,364	9,248,020	4.15	4.19	4.18	4.18
Salaries	5,123,186	5,560,129	5,805,242	6,015,806	2.73	2.75	2.75	2.72
Employee benefits	1,266,016	1,408,217	1,463,142	1,605,102	0.67	0.70	0.69	0.73
Purchased services	547,862	622,487	687,650	742,995	0.29	0.31	0.33	0.34
Supplies	759,207	776,863	774,059	821,105	0.40	0.38	0.37	0.37
Other	109,965	99,445	99,271	63,012	0.06	0.05	0.05	0.03
General administration	5,455,371	5,791,253	6,045,783	5,859,527	2.90	2.87	2.86	2.65
Salaries	2,486,406	2,603,562	2,687,020	2,784,492	1.32	1.29	1.27	1.26
Employee benefits	770,967	777,381	815,037	852,280	0.41	0.38	0.39	0.39
Purchased services	1,393,617	1,482,427	1,547,143	1,591,496	0.74	0.73	0.73	0.72
Supplies	166,495	172,898	158,845	211,534	0.09	0.09	0.08	0.10
Other	637,886	754,985	837,737	419,725	0.34	0.37	0.40	0.19
School administration	10,891,620	11,695,344	12,274,916	12,794,748	5.80	5.79	5.81	5.78
Salaries	8,310,370	8,935,903	9,290,692	9,594,725	4.42	4.42	4.40	4.33
Employee benefits	2,089,463	2,257,783	2,409,835	2,631,212	1.11	1.12	1.14	1.19
Purchased services	241,248	247,750	278,807	300,012	0.13	0.12	0.13	0.14
Supplies	188,393	189,711	196,804	207,165	0.10	0.09	0.09	0.09
Other	62,146	64,197	98,778	61,633	0.03	0.03	0.05	0.03
Operation and maintenance	20,261,415	21,290,655	21,917,957	22,781,833	10.78	10.54	10.38	10.29
Salaries	8,395,005	8,849,559	9,139,268	9,384,126	4.47	4.38	4.33	4.24
Employee benefits	2,423,326	2,633,075	2,787,333	2,927,308	1.29	1.30	1.32	1.32
Purchased services	5,554,610	5,721,125	5,857,816	6,014,322	2.96	2.83	2.77	2.72
Supplies	3,579,084	3,761,738	3,820,651	4,262,220	1.90	1.86	1.81	1.93
Other	309,391	325,157	312,888	193,857	0.16	0.16	0.15	0.09
Transportation	8,030,990	8,678,954	8,789,770	9,241,795	4.27	4.30	4.16	4.18
Salaries	3,045,942	3,285,127	3,267,418	3,409,715	1.62	1.63	1.55	1.54
Employee benefits	808,635	892,985	965,750	1,045,043	0.43	0.44	0.46	0.47
Purchased services	3,094,099	3,345,232	3,564,856	3,764,150	1.65	1.66	1.69	1.70
Supplies	897,799	961,447	817,908	877,073	0.48	0.48	0.39	0.40
Other	184,516	194,163	173,838	145,814	0.10	0.10	0.08	0.07
Other student services	4,989,078	5,587,837	6,094,512	6,542,220	2.65	2.77	2.89	2.96
Salaries	2,533,744	2,900,394	2,890,670	3,203,556	1.35	1.44	1.37	1.45
Employee benefits	868,792	980,859	1,152,949	1,193,949	0.46	0.49	0.55	0.54
Purchased services	786,814	798,922	1,154,831	1,226,120	0.42	0.40	0.55	0.55
Supplies	295,241	294,527	308,445	331,727	0.16	0.15	0.15	0.15
Other	504,488	613,135	587,617	586,868	0.27	0.30	0.28	0.27
Food services	8,116,277	8,430,490	8,826,600	9,248,708	4.32	4.17	4.18	4.18
Salaries	(1)	(1)	3,122,197	3,355,578	—	—	1.48	1.52
Employee benefits	(1)	(1)	960,079	1,015,157	—	—	0.45	0.46
Purchased services	(1)	(1)	715,611	476,920	—	—	0.34	0.22
Supplies	(1)	(1)	3,853,699	4,214,077	—	—	1.82	1.90
Other	(1)	(1)	175,014	186,976	—	—	0.08	0.08
Enterprise operations [4]	565,852	946,705	797,663	800,203	0.30	0.47	0.38	0.36
Salaries	(1)	(1)	256,767	296,706	—	—	0.12	0.13
Employee benefits	(1)	(1)	50,050	59,897	—	—	0.02	0.03
Purchased services	(1)	(1)	249,450	122,667	—	—	0.12	0.06
Supplies	(1)	(1)	181,768	222,916	—	—	0.09	0.10
Other	(1)	(1)	59,628	98,017	—	—	0.03	0.04
Other current expenditures	2,982,543	3,295,717	4,392,378	4,399,046	—	—	—	—
Community services	872,531	964,370	1,176,422	1,345,069	—	—	—	—
Non-public school programs	493,252	527,609	652,403	645,623	—	—	—	—
Adult education	1,229,456	1,365,523	1,498,962	1,487,700	—	—	—	—
Community colleges	11,555	5,356	5,136	5,454	—	—	—	—
Other	375,750	432,858	1,059,455	915,200	—	—	—	—
Capital outlay [5]	17,781,342	19,771,478	20,282,891	22,668,507	—	—	—	—
Interest on school debt	3,776,321	4,324,768	5,165,850	5,439,211	—	—	—	—

[1] Includes estimated data for subfunctions of Food services and Enterprises operations.

[2] Includes expenditures for health, attendance, and speech pathology services.

[3] Includes expenditures for curriculum development, staff training, libraries, and media and computer centers.

[4] Includes expenditures for operations funded by sales of products or services (e.g., school bookstore or computer time).

[5] Includes expenditures for property, and for buildings and alterations completed by school district staff or contractors.

—Data not available or not applicable.

NOTE.—Excludes expenditures for state education agencies. Because of rounding, details may not add to totals.

SOURCE: U.S. Department of Education, National Center for Education Statistics, Common Core of Data survey. (This table was prepared March 1995.)

Table 159.—Current expenditures for public elementary and secondary education, by state: 1959–60 to 1994–95

[In thousands of dollars]

State or other area	1959–60	1969–70	1979–80	1980–81	1983–84	1984–85	1985–86	1986–87
1	2	3	4	5	6	7	8	9
United States	**$12,329,389**	**$34,217,773**	**$86,984,142**	**$94,321,093**	**$115,392,342**	**$126,337,491**	**$137,164,965**	**$146,364,922**
Alabama	171,130	422,730	1,146,713	1,393,137	1,396,804	1,590,856	1,761,154	1,775,997
Alaska	20,641	81,374	377,947	476,368	692,418	754,967	818,219	769,015
Arizona	104,054	281,941	949,753	1,075,362	1,326,552	1,436,844	1,649,832	1,836,908
Arkansas	83,896	235,083	666,949	709,394	903,510	1,005,347	1,085,943	1,118,904
California	[4] 1,481,908	3,831,595	9,172,158	9,936,642	12,143,642	13,477,768	15,040,898	16,512,668
Colorado	136,760	369,218	1,243,049	1,369,883	1,697,085	1,868,058	2,018,579	2,129,964
Connecticut	185,336	588,710	1,227,892	1,440,881	1,818,683	2,117,798	2,144,094	2,414,708
Delaware	33,425	108,747	269,108	270,439	323,760	353,191	391,558	418,116
District of Columbia	45,617	141,138	298,448	295,155	371,113	387,918	406,910	441,135
Florida	276,506	961,273	2,766,468	3,336,657	4,071,134	4,589,068	5,092,668	5,650,083
Georgia	208,096	599,371	1,608,028	1,688,714	2,301,496	2,629,681	2,979,980	3,254,786
Hawaii	42,499	141,324	351,889	395,038	500,554	521,692	575,456	576,749
Idaho	42,719	103,107	313,927	352,912	417,426	467,532	492,092	513,011
Illinois	663,849	1,896,067	4,579,355	4,773,179	5,332,566	5,662,354	6,066,390	6,463,564
Indiana	318,073	809,105	1,851,292	1,898,194	2,434,738	2,696,072	2,851,080	3,106,616
Iowa	197,768	527,086	1,186,659	1,337,504	1,532,171	1,599,674	1,644,359	1,708,440
Kansas	153,346	362,593	830,133	958,281	1,209,537	1,315,469	1,423,225	1,486,814
Kentucky	132,068	353,265	1,054,459	1,096,472	1,354,120	1,384,722	1,434,962	1,583,158
Louisiana	230,402	503,217	1,303,902	1,767,692	1,950,869	2,191,478	2,333,748	2,260,393
Maine	51,465	155,907	385,492	401,355	540,351	599,189	688,673	760,446
Maryland	209,606	721,794	1,783,056	1,937,159	2,322,690	2,446,771	2,634,209	2,845,404
Massachusetts	324,408	907,341	2,638,734	2,794,762	2,898,355	3,139,486	3,403,505	3,744,131
Michigan	605,048	1,799,945	4,642,847	5,196,249	5,386,329	5,735,303	6,184,767	6,427,556
Minnesota	267,376	781,243	1,786,768	1,900,322	2,253,402	2,461,571	2,637,722	2,818,390
Mississippi	100,020	262,760	756,018	716,878	982,605	1,023,720	1,058,301	1,112,535
Missouri	242,447	642,030	1,504,988	1,643,258	1,965,436	2,106,539	2,277,576	2,515,846
Montana	54,079	127,176	358,118	380,092	502,290	538,245	567,901	583,861
Nebraska	87,692	231,612	581,615	629,017	813,214	870,019	911,983	948,149
Nevada	23,770	87,273	281,901	287,752	374,201	397,254	495,147	513,014
New Hampshire	33,185	101,370	295,400	340,518	431,288	473,151	522,604	589,850
New Jersey	459,413	1,343,564	3,638,533	3,648,914	4,666,185	4,697,534	5,735,895	6,099,473
New Mexico	73,396	183,736	515,451	560,213	721,641	784,442	808,036	865,789
New York	1,383,706	4,111,839	8,760,500	9,259,948	11,879,638	12,681,301	13,686,039	14,724,687
North Carolina	238,059	676,193	1,880,862	2,112,417	2,353,506	2,674,774	2,991,747	3,193,337
North Dakota	46,254	97,895	228,483	254,197	337,961	365,341	379,470	374,941
Ohio	632,932	1,639,805	3,836,576	4,149,858	5,051,057	5,504,161	5,856,999	6,114,426
Oklahoma	151,181	339,105	1,055,844	1,193,373	1,581,443	1,575,467	1,740,981	1,707,396
Oregon	154,691	403,844	1,126,812	1,292,624	1,475,990	1,560,242	1,662,372	1,747,125
Pennsylvania	732,486	1,912,644	4,584,320	4,955,115	5,843,492	6,660,369	6,750,520	7,176,886
Rhode Island	48,686	145,443	362,046	395,389	486,328	525,824	569,935	608,318
South Carolina	116,939	367,689	997,984	1,006,088	1,314,792	1,556,552	1,708,603	1,814,160
South Dakota	47,899	109,375	238,332	242,215	314,627	338,800	360,832	368,266
Tennessee	175,152	473,226	1,319,303	1,429,938	1,627,147	1,836,012	1,990,889	2,167,026
Texas	605,577	1,518,181	4,997,689	5,310,181	7,642,784	8,996,476	9,642,812	10,152,521
Utah	69,755	179,981	518,251	587,648	730,904	813,817	906,484	932,740
Vermont	24,132	78,921	189,811	224,901	290,206	313,026	346,164	378,264
Virginia	207,399	704,677	1,881,519	2,045,412	2,584,005	2,845,540	3,183,707	3,444,952
Washington	239,069	699,984	1,825,782	1,791,477	2,373,841	2,565,957	2,702,652	2,808,636
West Virginia	108,673	249,404	678,386	754,889	988,532	1,090,514	1,164,882	1,229,069
Wisconsin	254,626	777,288	1,908,523	2,035,879	2,455,671	2,655,729	2,893,797	3,086,878
Wyoming	32,175	69,584	226,067	271,153	424,251	453,874	488,616	489,825
Outlying areas								
American Samoa	308	—	—	—	—	13,348	14,997	19,497
Guam	3,020	16,652	—	—	54,251	58,815	78,545	78,278
Northern Marianas	—	—	—	—	5,534	9,394	12,556	15,714
Puerto Rico	54,375	—	—	713,000	822,589	856,743	842,827	872,050
Virgin Islands	1,662	—	—	—	70,411	—	76,751	97,585

Table 159.—Current expenditures for public elementary and secondary education, by state: 1959–60 to 1994–95—Continued

[In thousands of dollars]

State or other area	1987–88	1988–89	1989–90	1990–91	1991–92 [1]	1992–93	Estimated 1993–94 [2]	Estimated 1994–95 [2]
1	10	11	12	13	14	15	16	17
United States	**$157,097,951**	**$173,098,906**	**$187,932,903**	**$202,037,752**	**$211,221,254**	**$221,352,533**	[3] **$237,182,329**	[3] **$247,584,221**
Alabama	1,873,390	2,188,020	2,275,233	2,475,216	2,465,523	2,610,514	2,744,664	3,033,517
Alaska	756,577	739,020	828,051	854,499	931,869	967,765	1,097,693	1,141,601
Arizona	2,002,395	2,143,148	2,258,653	2,469,543	2,599,587	2,753,510	2,910,700	2,968,900
Arkansas	1,211,156	1,319,370	1,404,621	1,510,092	1,656,201	1,703,604	1,372,457	1,428,108
California	17,402,063	19,417,178	21,485,782	22,748,218	23,696,863	24,219,792	27,658,107	28,284,179
Colorado	2,172,563	2,324,625	2,451,831	2,642,850	2,754,087	2,919,916	3,069,000	3,267,129
Connecticut	2,748,567	2,984,542	3,404,429	3,540,411	3,667,337	3,737,765	3,713,000	3,797,000
Delaware	440,631	479,327	520,953	543,933	572,180	599,893	[5] 656,824	703,998
District of Columbia	489,357	584,035	632,458	647,901	677,429	670,654	[6] 705,345	[6] 710,835
Florida	6,288,977	7,245,515	8,228,531	9,045,710	9,314,079	9,661,012	10,364,990	10,935,064
Georgia	3,549,038	4,006,069	4,505,964	4,804,225	4,856,583	5,273,143	5,495,475	5,839,532
Hawaii	608,264	643,319	700,012	827,579	884,591	946,074	917,883	924,980
Idaho	532,274	570,013	627,794	708,045	760,440	804,231	876,788	999,675
Illinois	6,923,298	7,655,153	8,125,493	8,932,538	9,244,655	9,942,737	11,999,465	12,479,444
Indiana	3,330,525	3,779,468	4,024,098	4,379,142	4,544,829	4,797,946	5,086,000	5,391,000
Iowa	1,859,173	1,925,623	2,004,742	2,136,561	2,356,196	2,459,141	2,539,555	2,620,059
Kansas	1,568,041	1,712,260	1,848,302	1,938,012	2,028,440	2,224,080	2,339,560	2,409,747
Kentucky	1,741,799	1,918,741	2,134,011	2,480,363	2,709,623	2,823,993	[6] 2,980,621	[6] 3,014,498
Louisiana	2,289,241	2,468,307	2,802,793	3,023,690	3,189,111	3,199,842	[6] 3,387,055	[6] 3,344,378
Maine	839,860	921,931	1,048,195	1,070,965	1,121,360	1,217,418	1,247,610	1,298,388
Maryland	3,128,165	3,505,018	3,845,123	4,240,862	4,362,679	4,556,233	4,716,127	4,942,501
Massachusetts	4,098,062	4,516,604	4,760,390	4,906,828	5,035,973	5,281,067	[6] 5,687,260	[6] 5,880,815
Michigan	6,913,261	7,492,267	8,025,621	8,545,805	9,156,501	9,532,994	9,824,703	10,080,145
Minnesota	2,981,209	3,282,296	3,474,398	3,740,820	3,936,695	4,135,284	4,292,000	4,522,750
Mississippi	1,221,560	1,365,846	1,472,710	1,510,552	1,536,295	1,600,752	1,709,551	1,795,029
Missouri	2,747,234	3,096,666	3,288,738	3,487,786	3,611,613	3,710,426	[5] 3,658,649	3,878,740
Montana	590,226	592,454	641,345	719,963	751,710	785,159	[5] 824,418	836,400
Nebraska	995,235	1,105,009	1,233,622	1,297,643	1,381,290	1,430,039	1,510,121	1,600,729
Nevada	555,272	628,657	712,898	864,379	962,800	1,035,623	1,087,500	1,172,639
New Hampshire	677,507	733,240	821,671	890,116	927,625	972,963	1,107,568	1,191,196
New Jersey	6,621,860	7,309,147	8,119,069	8,897,612	9,664,774	9,915,429	10,317,823	10,730,536
New Mexico	916,305	975,552	1,020,148	1,134,156	1,212,189	1,240,310	1,572,210	1,906,562
New York	16,073,392	17,127,596	18,090,978	19,514,583	19,781,384	20,898,267	21,818,000	22,930,000
North Carolina	3,424,194	3,892,971	4,288,474	4,605,384	4,661,685	4,930,704	5,152,422	5,368,824
North Dakota	385,427	431,814	459,391	460,581	491,293	508,648	518,231	528,595
Ohio	6,446,903	7,484,434	7,994,379	8,407,428	9,124,731	9,572,879	[5] 9,484,035	10,334,011
Oklahoma	1,692,283	1,833,743	1,905,332	2,107,513	2,269,776	2,442,320	[6] 2,607,022	[6] 2,666,562
Oregon	1,944,657	2,123,241	2,297,944	2,453,934	2,626,803	2,849,009	2,890,000	2,996,000
Pennsylvania	7,679,986	8,579,546	9,496,788	10,087,322	10,371,796	10,944,392	11,710,499	12,530,234
Rhode Island	663,800	747,852	801,908	823,655	865,898	934,815	[5] 980,331	1,009,741
South Carolina	1,932,502	2,118,732	2,322,432	2,494,254	2,564,949	2,690,009	2,690,009	2,754,569
South Dakota	389,436	428,014	447,068	481,304	518,156	553,005	582,349	619,620
Tennessee	2,352,183	2,668,341	2,790,808	2,903,209	2,859,755	3,139,223	[6] 3,361,292	[6] 3,393,388
Texas	10,791,854	11,761,447	12,764,500	13,695,327	14,709,628	15,121,655	17,416,150	18,011,390
Utah	974,666	1,043,759	1,130,135	1,235,916	1,296,723	1,376,319	[5] 1,528,385	1,617,774
Vermont	456,992	485,226	546,901	599,018	606,410	625,064	[6] 687,591	[6] 724,771
Virginia	3,793,475	4,151,050	4,561,874	4,958,213	4,995,270	5,228,196	5,588,694	[6] 5,724,452
Washington	3,005,980	3,209,992	3,550,672	3,906,471	4,259,021	4,679,873	5,126,302	5,347,702
West Virginia	1,231,966	1,202,486	1,316,637	1,473,640	1,503,977	1,626,005	1,815,385	1,824,462
Wisconsin	3,318,247	3,688,311	3,929,920	4,292,434	4,597,004	4,954,900	5,173,401	5,480,701
Wyoming	466,921	491,930	509,084	521,549	545,870	547,938	581,509	[6] 591,351
Outlying areas								
American Samoa	20,186	22,314	21,838	24,946	26,972	23,636	29,397	29,436
Guam	76,359	94,368	106,033	116,406	132,494	155,920	150,035	155,569
Northern Marianas	19,694	16,118	20,476	26,822	32,498	32,007	[6] 41,437	[6] 42,423
Puerto Rico	935,392	1,030,387	1,045,407	1,142,863	1,207,235	1,244,716	[5] 1,500,440	1,601,209
Virgin Islands	89,217	111,750	128,065	119,950	121,660	120,510	130,379	145,052

[1] Data revised from previously published figures.

[2] Data estimated by state education agencies.

[3] U.S. total includes National Center for Education Statistics estimates for nonreporting states.

[4] Includes an estimated $144,942,000 for summer schools, adult education, and community colleges.

[5] Actual count.

[6] Estimated by the National Center for Education Statistics.

NOTE.—Beginning in 1980–81, expenditures for state administration are excluded. Because of rounding, details may not add to totals.

SOURCE: U.S. Department of Education, National Center for Education Statistics, Statistics of State School Systems; and Common Core of Data surveys. (This table was prepared May 1995.)

Table 160.—Total expenditures for public elementary and secondary education, by function and state: 1992–93

[In thousands]

State or other area	Total expenditures							
	Total	Current expenditures						
		Current expenditures for public schools	Instruction	Student services				
				Total	Students [2]	Instructional [3]	General administration	School administration
1	2	3	4	5	6	7	8	9
United States	$253,859,297	$221,352,533	$135,067,681	$76,235,942	$9,767,799	$9,248,020	$5,859,527	$12,794,748
Alabama	2,915,655	2,610,514	1,623,693	773,464	87,366	86,788	63,036	150,602
Alaska	1,097,909	967,765	495,869	441,461	97,054	50,492	59,142	58,432
Arizona	3,632,089	2,753,510	1,608,841	989,933	114,098	95,118	116,648	150,196
Arkansas	1,898,548	1,703,604	1,069,660	519,528	67,793	67,347	52,762	97,409
California	26,990,569	24,219,792	14,515,129	8,693,446	1,246,422	1,059,248	147,393	1,866,020
Colorado	3,543,846	2,919,916	1,791,024	1,022,879	121,356	101,198	100,691	193,386
Connecticut	3,995,740	3,737,765	2,368,773	1,220,892	207,398	111,435	77,976	204,851
Delaware	669,882	599,893	375,684	202,360	27,924	8,643	7,773	34,812
District of Columbia ...	727,604	670,654	339,266	302,282	58,319	30,681	30,872	34,057
Florida	11,694,573	9,661,012	5,609,755	3,566,770	428,607	528,175	130,282	664,988
Georgia	6,108,216	5,273,143	3,324,731	1,630,162	182,533	251,044	83,256	321,170
Hawaii	1,087,683	946,074	580,597	304,362	54,159	40,745	8,119	54,350
Idaho	903,040	804,231	504,461	260,672	37,051	24,502	22,950	47,873
Illinois	10,976,188	9,942,737	5,886,997	3,695,575	534,742	356,710	290,981	515,804
Indiana	5,613,875	4,797,946	2,984,096	1,598,786	197,079	136,164	88,408	264,241
Iowa	2,692,069	2,459,141	1,529,933	820,898	76,892	187,886	86,256	122,337
Kansas	2,468,279	2,224,080	1,304,668	816,085	109,169	86,060	86,501	141,011
Kentucky	3,060,263	2,823,993	1,713,290	968,533	100,677	89,808	105,104	180,563
Louisiana	3,497,352	3,199,842	1,906,733	1,007,563	112,580	121,832	81,771	174,447
Maine	1,316,834	1,217,418	806,903	366,084	34,002	32,765	23,541	67,884
Maryland	4,948,849	4,556,233	2,822,084	1,522,110	171,052	204,029	24,597	330,513
Massachusetts	5,472,560	5,281,067	3,239,997	1,868,806	225,205	161,142	348,585	227,194
Michigan	11,273,173	9,532,994	5,535,516	3,722,486	622,004	420,455	212,200	604,814
Minnesota	5,057,306	4,135,284	2,646,040	1,323,114	125,533	193,236	101,170	196,051
Mississippi	1,771,848	1,600,752	997,074	472,867	53,349	58,424	55,473	84,704
Missouri	4,289,248	3,710,426	2,253,749	1,292,890	144,207	140,200	120,647	219,033
Montana	860,640	785,159	487,327	265,132	32,541	25,378	28,631	42,077
Nebraska	1,586,049	1,430,039	885,855	422,808	52,843	46,547	55,328	74,481
Nevada	1,294,227	1,035,623	612,677	388,280	45,650	32,403	17,753	74,922
New Hampshire	1,043,940	972,963	634,198	306,599	52,259	29,112	36,539	54,530
New Jersey	10,710,608	9,915,429	5,847,981	3,800,586	165,462	751,793	562,957	469,431
New Mexico	1,429,889	1,240,310	727,371	451,556	65,160	105,523	49,054	40,666
New York	23,709,998	20,898,267	14,035,286	6,254,766	812,349	446,333	526,690	878,872
North Carolina	5,782,158	4,930,704	3,037,814	1,509,934	226,610	184,281	100,909	321,316
North Dakota	562,212	508,648	312,211	155,299	14,170	10,346	28,062	23,624
Ohio	10,960,801	9,572,879	5,471,610	3,747,551	434,703	440,171	247,006	568,841
Oklahoma	2,632,696	2,442,320	1,440,157	787,220	105,478	73,492	103,492	143,072
Oregon	3,121,655	2,849,009	1,701,141	1,053,453	136,031	148,805	61,951	183,725
Pennsylvania	12,435,568	10,944,392	6,956,917	3,577,579	498,476	342,764	300,886	518,519
Rhode Island	968,852	934,815	626,154	287,742	51,909	31,741	21,538	44,888
South Carolina	3,052,790	2,690,009	1,594,927	857,238	112,147	147,015	48,326	171,864
South Dakota	619,106	553,005	339,207	182,691	21,840	18,640	17,541	31,775
Tennessee	3,505,660	3,139,223	1,907,725	1,071,617	116,865	150,078	46,919	211,165
Texas	19,684,207	15,121,655	8,890,632	5,248,579	687,962	741,977	654,200	868,640
Utah	1,650,709	1,376,319	910,053	380,212	35,647	51,494	15,596	79,651
Vermont	675,999	625,064	406,682	199,569	36,049	19,190	18,452	40,899
Virginia	5,958,623	5,228,196	3,121,272	1,837,789	253,424	278,275	70,548	319,930
Washington	5,848,789	4,679,873	2,800,395	1,665,971	284,730	232,036	125,951	236,376
West Virginia	1,844,445	1,626,005	1,007,685	523,330	50,505	45,094	38,997	98,899
Wisconsin	5,606,762	4,954,900	3,143,002	1,662,810	205,869	234,106	144,330	255,899
Wyoming	609,717	547,938	334,840	193,622	32,544	17,298	11,738	33,947
Outlying areas								
American Samoa	27,503	23,636	10,792	8,916	2,554	1,386	467	1,610
Guam	180,738	155,920	69,877	76,036	19,263	4,684	6,322	8,571
Northern Marianas	35,996	32,007	28,814	0	0	0	0	0
Puerto Rico	1,269,885	1,244,716	895,535	202,923	39,094	0	92,015	5,837
Virgin Islands	139,591	120,510	68,564	45,905	6,140	7,744	9,253	6,858

Table 160.—Total expenditures for public elementary and secondary education, by function and state: 1992–93—Continued

[In thousands]

State or other area	Total expenditures							
	Current expenditures					Other current expenditures [1]	Capital outlay	Interest on school debt
	Student services			Food services	Enterprise operations [4]			
	Operation and maintenance	Student transportation	Other support services					
1	10	11	12	13	14	15	16	17
United States	$22,781,833	$9,241,795	$6,542,220	$9,248,708	$800,203	$4,399,046	$22,668,507	$5,439,211
Alabama	227,077	106,954	51,641	213,357	0	42,606	207,608	54,926
Alaska	141,442	32,691	2,208	26,281	4,154	5,978	81,731	42,435
Arizona	314,320	106,892	92,661	125,821	28,916	18,537	691,713	168,329
Arkansas	144,126	65,082	25,009	101,398	13,018	9,145	144,028	41,770
California	2,551,495	709,647	1,113,221	1,008,592	2,625	463,528	2,238,315	68,933
Colorado	273,658	90,639	141,950	102,912	3,102	9,397	372,398	242,134
Connecticut	374,489	165,839	78,903	70,062	78,037	118,441	50,865	88,670
Delaware	56,674	36,582	29,951	21,849	0	14,618	49,529	5,842
District of Columbia ...	114,036	13,510	20,806	27,469	1,638	5,645	40,212	11,093
Florida	1,124,811	385,346	304,562	484,487	0	344,125	1,430,981	258,454
Georgia	467,771	197,853	126,536	312,901	5,349	153,162	597,124	84,787
Hawaii	103,341	20,243	23,404	61,115	0	34,614	82,431	24,564
Idaho	79,020	38,753	10,524	39,097	0	1,222	81,511	16,076
Illinois	1,088,552	455,744	453,043	360,165	0	90,978	692,343	250,130
Indiana	539,048	264,354	109,493	215,063	0	37,128	483,802	295,000
Iowa	219,193	84,155	44,179	100,980	7,330	6,333	196,176	30,419
Kansas	261,228	92,880	39,236	103,327	0	2,974	205,927	35,298
Kentucky	288,307	168,348	35,726	142,170	0	5,600	172,078	58,591
Louisiana	282,204	184,084	50,645	243,342	42,203	20,752	173,158	103,600
Maine	123,801	61,240	22,851	44,368	63	13,126	54,515	31,775
Maryland	463,925	234,935	93,059	143,179	68,861	21,205	327,484	43,926
Massachusetts	559,329	224,114	123,238	157,011	15,253	43,596	59,431	88,466
Michigan	1,071,120	422,081	369,811	274,991	0	436,190	933,898	370,092
Minnesota	345,918	223,099	138,108	166,129	0	175,651	622,251	124,120
Mississippi	133,013	64,764	23,140	130,177	634	10,968	130,628	29,501
Missouri	360,106	230,153	78,543	163,786	0	61,384	400,361	117,078
Montana	84,533	35,544	16,427	32,283	417	2,535	61,811	11,135
Nebraska	128,978	42,492	22,139	54,372	67,004	1,601	133,084	21,325
Nevada	109,902	40,236	67,413	34,667	0	7,297	195,957	55,350
New Hampshire	85,231	43,493	5,435	32,166	0	3,076	42,168	25,733
New Jersey	1,165,546	483,412	201,986	266,862	0	138,364	552,607	104,208
New Mexico	121,201	67,891	2,061	60,478	905	4,020	159,550	26,009
New York	1,955,478	1,135,189	499,855	608,215	0	775,817	1,609,676	426,238
North Carolina	421,859	171,475	83,485	318,264	64,692	27,121	495,852	328,481
North Dakota	45,117	23,469	10,511	23,820	17,318	3,048	42,782	7,734
Ohio	921,414	263,753	871,664	350,579	3,139	635,061	600,822	152,038
Oklahoma	225,144	86,775	49,767	136,038	78,905	3,663	169,870	16,842
Oregon	279,163	109,660	134,117	93,264	1,152	8,465	217,462	46,719
Pennsylvania	1,140,962	499,729	276,243	404,262	5,634	263,227	971,889	256,060
Rhode Island	83,909	42,727	11,031	20,919	0	5,807	13,027	15,203
South Carolina	242,373	79,885	55,628	157,634	80,210	46,498	229,028	87,255
South Dakota	56,727	23,174	12,994	29,835	1,273	1,270	55,483	9,348
Tennessee	327,424	138,251	80,915	159,881	0	25,091	248,711	92,636
Texas	1,738,440	447,197	110,161	919,133	63,311	68,034	3,921,245	573,273
Utah	133,967	40,020	23,836	82,207	3,848	41,872	197,818	34,701
Vermont	51,815	23,257	9,906	16,938	1,874	4,448	38,204	8,283
Virginia	583,456	232,667	99,489	196,231	72,904	95,924	506,710	127,793
Washington	486,465	191,578	108,835	147,298	66,209	18,650	952,017	198,249
West Virginia	164,401	103,030	22,404	94,767	223	25,464	179,865	13,111
Wisconsin	460,073	214,069	148,465	149,088	0	44,220	504,295	103,347
Wyoming	60,249	22,840	15,006	19,476	0	1,573	48,076	12,130
Outlying areas								
American Samoa	1,408	602	888	3,929	0	1,538	2,329	0
Guam	20,048	11,234	5,915	10,007	0	943	23,875	0
Northern Marianas	0	0	0	3,193	0	168	3,821	0
Puerto Rico	35,179	30,240	559	146,258	0	15,029	10,140	0
Virgin Islands	6,994	3,147	5,769	6,010	30	1,550	17,531	0

[1] Includes expenditures for adult education, community colleges, private school programs funded by local and state education agencies, and community services.
[2] Includes expenditures for health, attendance, and speech pathology services.
[3] Includes expenditures for curriculum development, staff training, libraries, and media and computer centers.
[4] Includes expenditures for operations funded by sales of products or services (e.g., school bookstore or computer time).

NOTE.—Excludes expenditures for state education agencies. Because of rounding, details may not add to totals.

SOURCE: U.S. Department of Education, National Center for Education Statistics, Common Core of Data survey. (This table was prepared April 1995.)

Table 161.—Total expenditures for public elementary and secondary education, by function and state: 1991–92

[In thousands]

State or other area	Total expenditures							
		Current expenditures						
	Total	Current expenditures for public schools	Instruction	Student services				
				Total	Students[2]	Instructional[3]	General administration	School administration
1	2	3	4	5	6	7	8	9
United States	$241,062,373	$211,221,254	$128,418,502	$73,178,489	$9,226,186	$8,829,364	$6,045,783	$12,274,916
Alabama	2,709,113	2,465,523	1,530,671	729,057	79,863	80,108	66,221	142,297
Alaska	1,061,618	931,869	477,181	426,462	89,206	49,023	61,074	56,710
Arizona	3,403,843	2,599,587	1,530,371	940,306	106,703	91,313	111,140	144,953
Arkansas	1,853,918	1,656,201	997,925	511,278	66,654	64,927	51,992	95,257
California	26,489,786	23,696,863	14,043,571	8,679,298	1,257,224	1,084,876	161,129	1,854,153
Colorado	3,243,602	2,754,087	1,680,544	975,589	117,876	99,126	97,128	181,039
Connecticut	3,906,492	3,667,337	2,318,953	1,194,739	187,507	107,553	94,951	196,368
Delaware	624,424	572,180	357,975	191,857	25,096	8,844	7,605	33,066
District of Columbia ...	744,995	677,429	329,160	316,678	57,020	28,932	29,206	33,642
Florida	11,549,469	9,314,079	5,443,663	3,407,022	414,233	526,126	131,304	650,462
Georgia	5,622,712	4,856,583	3,038,173	1,537,209	163,825	234,623	77,606	302,791
Hawaii	1,069,758	884,591	536,115	290,261	49,289	39,081	8,509	50,188
Idaho	887,414	760,440	477,575	245,659	35,374	23,627	22,040	45,201
Illinois	10,297,081	9,244,655	5,527,540	3,393,834	507,832	339,920	279,768	491,876
Indiana	5,326,248	4,544,829	2,820,296	1,520,217	182,201	131,192	83,697	252,084
Iowa	2,612,279	2,356,196	1,450,954	798,839	71,821	180,426	80,470	120,723
Kansas	2,235,883	2,028,440	1,198,174	734,374	94,531	73,417	80,376	130,690
Kentucky	2,916,682	2,709,623	1,659,238	917,761	90,750	87,606	97,579	172,716
Louisiana	3,685,384	3,189,111	1,907,970	992,773	111,139	111,884	77,090	176,136
Maine	1,260,497	1,121,360	749,202	343,844	31,333	30,106	23,080	63,512
Maryland	4,733,645	4,362,679	2,640,368	1,508,358	159,428	186,573	23,860	320,725
Massachusetts	5,239,454	5,035,973	3,021,391	1,844,304	216,834	148,493	335,005	226,314
Michigan	10,619,388	9,156,501	5,289,436	3,600,806	585,756	415,055	207,118	574,896
Minnesota	4,764,683	3,936,695	2,499,154	1,282,172	120,340	195,467	95,722	186,453
Mississippi	1,704,886	1,536,295	959,580	448,809	51,193	51,308	57,837	82,400
Missouri	4,234,128	3,611,613	2,190,803	1,263,593	140,690	141,866	116,854	214,457
Montana	829,713	751,710	468,290	250,980	28,525	23,360	27,979	40,640
Nebraska	1,551,596	1,381,290	833,269	398,649	48,979	43,728	51,259	68,844
Nevada	1,279,069	962,800	573,131	359,346	41,496	31,881	17,349	69,238
New Hampshire	1,024,639	927,625	587,947	309,488	48,019	26,424	35,035	51,774
New Jersey	10,111,348	9,664,774	5,500,065	3,812,718	174,093	678,251	859,478	440,553
New Mexico	1,385,897	1,212,189	706,900	445,940	62,377	102,562	48,401	41,304
New York	22,621,184	19,781,384	13,235,322	5,962,065	805,959	426,406	489,988	852,893
North Carolina	5,571,534	4,661,685	2,874,483	1,423,437	205,141	180,569	97,534	305,399
North Dakota	536,006	491,293	298,310	153,975	13,579	15,711	24,230	23,655
Ohio	10,561,175	9,124,731	5,199,164	3,602,791	409,589	425,923	225,634	546,420
Oklahoma	2,495,569	2,269,776	1,356,636	747,320	95,060	67,944	99,399	135,042
Oregon	2,846,443	2,626,803	1,560,133	976,240	123,679	131,375	57,561	172,267
Pennsylvania	11,069,811	10,371,796	6,563,590	3,419,578	470,702	327,344	280,753	489,279
Rhode Island	897,659	865,898	576,979	269,102	45,677	28,819	20,272	42,090
South Carolina	2,958,676	2,564,949	1,513,667	822,642	102,673	142,571	50,192	164,313
South Dakota	598,471	518,156	317,164	170,314	18,975	16,746	17,101	30,370
Tennessee	3,309,850	2,859,755	1,819,528	944,310	89,114	142,574	41,043	183,111
Texas	17,973,294	14,709,628	8,844,120	4,946,500	619,995	664,514	720,885	793,213
Utah	1,526,785	1,296,723	851,578	365,324	33,704	48,810	14,853	76,669
Vermont	656,031	606,410	392,739	195,371	32,783	18,253	20,828	38,169
Virginia	5,651,487	4,995,270	2,974,172	1,754,756	243,624	268,862	64,815	300,747
Washington	5,314,540	4,259,021	2,544,864	1,514,031	243,303	208,679	122,866	245,538
West Virginia	1,707,485	1,503,977	909,827	496,366	44,062	43,262	35,602	92,494
Wisconsin	5,164,963	4,597,004	2,900,182	1,556,215	188,109	216,523	132,424	237,900
Wyoming	621,768	545,870	340,459	185,929	23,251	16,798	11,941	33,883
Outlying areas								
American Samoa	32,005	26,972	11,381	10,310	3,199	2,073	419	1,621
Guam	146,451	132,494	61,571	62,183	17,752	3,012	2,345	8,077
Northern Marianas	35,588	32,498	29,491	0	0	0	0	0
Puerto Rico	1,227,075	1,207,235	861,439	187,726	19,357	0	89,882	6,156
Virgin Islands	136,751	121,660	68,547	46,273	6,068	7,977	9,071	7,069

Table 161.—Total expenditures for public elementary and secondary education, by function and state: 1991–92—Continued

[In thousands]

State or other area	Total expenditures							
	Current expenditures					Other current expenditures [1]	Capital outlay	Interest on school debt
	Student services			Food services	Enterprise operations [4]			
	Operation and maintenance	Student transportation	Other support services					
1	10	11	12	13	14	15	16	17
United States	$21,917,957	$8,789,770	$6,094,512	$8,826,600	$797,663	$4,392,378	$20,282,891	$5,165,850
Alabama	210,231	102,075	48,262	205,794	0	36,539	161,998	45,054
Alaska	137,924	30,619	1,906	25,335	2,892	5,834	74,987	48,928
Arizona	304,322	98,014	83,861	118,298	10,612	16,929	620,332	166,996
Arkansas	144,664	62,894	24,890	89,925	57,074	8,680	149,114	39,923
California	2,567,624	745,018	1,009,274	971,605	2,389	455,972	2,270,678	66,274
Colorado	270,373	87,677	122,369	95,521	2,432	7,362	368,775	113,378
Connecticut	358,871	161,015	88,474	73,910	79,736	113,310	45,892	79,953
Delaware	53,761	35,755	27,730	22,348	0	14,053	32,554	5,638
District of Columbia ...	128,666	12,657	26,557	30,190	1,401	6,040	49,586	11,940
Florida	1,030,789	359,368	294,740	463,394	0	326,618	1,670,581	238,191
Georgia	448,185	185,510	124,670	279,361	1,840	137,788	548,583	79,758
Hawaii	98,103	21,819	23,273	58,214	0	32,437	127,328	25,403
Idaho	73,308	36,956	9,153	37,206	0	1,048	111,069	14,857
Illinois	1,076,122	443,627	254,690	323,281	0	83,408	749,323	219,696
Indiana	521,958	248,007	101,077	204,316	0	33,318	463,757	284,343
Iowa	226,570	81,906	36,921	95,895	10,507	4,911	221,977	29,196
Kansas	234,852	85,543	34,964	95,892	0	2,591	166,419	38,433
Kentucky	278,475	158,834	31,801	132,625	0	5,433	143,478	58,148
Louisiana	280,561	180,359	55,604	243,941	44,427	18,070	136,361	341,841
Maine	115,625	57,596	22,593	28,314	0	13,088	95,084	30,964
Maryland	484,923	245,187	87,661	148,288	65,664	21,030	305,481	44,455
Massachusetts	569,041	219,596	129,021	156,150	14,127	42,457	87,460	73,564
Michigan	1,053,384	412,241	352,355	266,259	0	402,869	824,002	236,016
Minnesota	335,963	215,788	132,438	155,370	0	154,633	578,076	95,279
Mississippi	121,389	62,220	22,462	127,906	0	7,849	131,335	29,406
Missouri	351,103	218,717	79,907	157,216	0	56,096	475,331	91,088
Montana	81,851	33,020	15,604	32,333	106	2,263	64,170	11,570
Nebraska	123,934	39,804	22,101	50,349	99,023	1,299	150,365	18,642
Nevada	104,401	37,897	57,083	30,323	0	5,607	249,570	61,092
New Hampshire	81,613	42,337	24,286	30,190	0	3,114	63,550	30,350
New Jersey	1,005,605	472,145	182,594	351,991	0	119,327	251,128	76,119
New Mexico	120,898	64,576	5,822	57,324	2,026	3,900	150,846	18,962
New York	1,871,766	1,001,153	513,901	583,997	0	749,338	1,704,794	385,668
North Carolina	393,627	162,685	78,481	296,022	67,743	24,199	545,898	339,752
North Dakota	45,373	22,826	8,600	21,644	17,363	3,722	34,406	6,585
Ohio	893,086	244,691	857,447	318,653	4,122	616,487	585,230	234,727
Oklahoma	218,310	81,550	50,014	132,392	33,428	2,851	206,855	16,087
Oregon	270,530	98,241	122,588	86,356	4,075	8,815	169,219	41,606
Pennsylvania	1,096,688	490,267	264,545	385,693	2,935	284,172	145,234	268,609
Rhode Island	79,606	41,722	10,917	19,816	0	4,853	13,629	13,279
South Carolina	232,133	73,437	57,323	149,431	79,208	43,099	268,986	81,643
South Dakota	52,906	21,945	12,271	29,778	899	1,170	72,341	6,804
Tennessee	290,579	125,273	72,616	95,916	0	201,887	232,861	15,346
Texas	1,652,044	414,656	81,194	866,966	52,041	69,018	2,603,297	591,350
Utah	130,567	37,946	22,774	76,581	3,240	62,526	133,777	33,759
Vermont	51,551	22,931	10,854	16,606	1,694	3,767	40,292	5,563
Virginia	545,889	223,439	107,380	191,224	75,119	87,801	447,247	121,169
Washington	444,950	141,741	106,953	138,708	61,418	18,741	867,224	169,554
West Virginia	161,505	99,568	19,873	97,662	122	22,190	166,213	15,105
Wisconsin	431,254	203,819	146,187	140,607	0	42,478	445,380	80,101
Wyoming	60,501	23,100	16,454	19,483	0	1,394	60,818	13,686
Outlying areas								
American Samoa	1,334	621	1,043	5,281	0	1,911	3,122	0
Guam	16,390	9,755	4,852	8,741	0	746	13,210	0
Northern Marianas	0	0	0	3,006	0	106	2,985	0
Puerto Rico	41,518	30,320	493	158,071	0	11,539	8,301	0
Virgin Islands	6,857	3,325	5,908	6,798	42	1,876	13,215	0

[1] Includes expenditures for adult education, community colleges, private school programs funded by local and state education agencies, and community services.

[2] Includes expenditures for health, attendance, and speech pathology services.

[3] Includes expenditures for curriculum development, staff training, libraries, and media and computer centers.

[4] Includes expenditures for operations funded by sales of products or services (e.g., school bookstore or computer time).

NOTE.—Excludes expenditures for state education agencies. Because of rounding, details may not add to totals. Some data have been revised from previously published figures.

SOURCE: U.S. Department of Education, National Center for Education Statistics, Common Core of Data survey. (This table was prepared May 1995.)

Table 162.—Expenditures for instruction in public elementary and secondary schools, by subfunction and state: 1991–92 and 1992–93

[In thousands of dollars]

State or other area	1991–92						1992–93 [1]					
	Total	Salaries	Employee benefits	Purchased services [2]	Supplies	Tuition and other	Total	Salaries	Employee benefits	Purchased services [2]	Supplies	Tuition and other
1	2	3	4	5	6	7	8	9	10	11	12	13
United States	$128,418,502	$94,973,704	$23,675,941	$3,343,852	$4,702,106	$1,722,899	$135,067,681	$99,108,741	$26,139,941	$3,359,530	$5,060,358	$1,399,111
Alabama	1,530,671	1,186,319	256,446	2,505	72,406	12,995	1,623,693	1,220,956	299,686	5,253	81,135	16,663
Alaska	477,181	338,355	77,000	19,365	22,138	20,324	495,869	353,602	80,329	19,469	21,389	21,080
Arizona	1,530,371	1,265,784	204,278	10,171	28,537	21,600	1,608,841	1,328,278	216,456	13,101	29,130	21,875
Arkansas	997,925	779,234	166,375	14,377	30,255	7,685	1,069,660	831,953	180,185	16,610	32,636	8,275
California	14,043,571	10,220,066	2,751,264	354,571	495,794	221,770	14,515,129	10,314,041	3,127,651	367,576	453,964	251,897
Colorado	1,680,544	1,301,574	257,148	51,236	65,576	5,009	1,791,024	1,386,469	276,573	55,063	66,802	6,117
Connecticut	2,318,953	1,810,954	400,308	35,256	58,966	13,470	2,368,773	1,847,591	408,141	36,677	61,827	14,536
Delaware	357,975	250,525	83,949	5,379	14,134	3,989	375,684	266,206	86,933	5,778	14,588	2,179
District of Columbia	329,160	244,369	63,214	4,188	3,270	14,118	339,266	245,876	72,417	5,415	2,534	13,024
Florida	5,443,663	3,673,334	1,196,867	344,183	168,194	61,085	5,609,755	3,749,838	1,249,289	361,158	188,728	60,742
Georgia	3,038,173	2,289,070	595,997	21,769	127,232	4,105	3,324,731	2,439,241	733,272	26,215	122,002	4,001
Hawaii	536,115	403,433	90,594	17,077	23,652	1,360	580,597	434,573	97,597	18,778	28,332	1,317
Idaho	477,575	350,301	93,438	8,956	24,575	306	504,461	368,810	102,409	8,612	24,199	431
Illinois	5,527,540	4,328,102	774,030	92,589	218,071	114,748	5,886,997	4,610,529	841,002	100,960	216,235	118,272
Indiana	2,820,296	2,121,762	567,225	28,816	95,955	6,537	2,984,096	2,224,815	620,270	32,815	99,938	6,258
Iowa	1,450,954	1,049,306	232,453	69,700	92,298	7,198	1,529,933	1,093,206	255,436	72,230	99,755	9,307
Kansas	1,198,174	945,658	176,788	10,344	60,077	5,307	1,304,668	1,025,667	194,625	9,999	67,798	6,578
Kentucky	1,659,238	1,339,088	249,530	99	70,488	33	1,713,290	1,378,010	272,907	77	62,284	12
Louisiana	1,907,970	1,400,813	418,442	10,509	73,575	4,631	1,906,733	1,428,493	384,409	11,134	78,137	4,561
Maine	749,202	524,487	136,423	19,049	26,940	42,302	806,903	535,747	181,558	20,846	26,217	42,535
Maryland	2,640,368	1,860,211	590,017	46,030	67,130	76,980	2,822,084	1,926,293	678,806	67,309	78,095	71,581
Massachusetts	3,021,393	2,209,557	300,650	255,982	83,353	171,849	3,239,997	2,348,009	360,063	267,342	90,522	174,061
Michigan	5,289,436	3,788,523	1,225,082	65,196	191,334	19,301	5,535,516	4,001,460	1,247,306	70,841	196,417	19,491
Minnesota	2,499,154	1,859,365	477,783	55,626	90,111	16,269	2,646,040	1,962,920	506,526	65,704	93,979	16,910
Mississippi	959,580	763,669	139,963	12,324	38,949	4,674	997,074	768,952	139,823	18,913	64,694	4,691
Missouri	2,190,803	1,680,164	296,006	39,415	169,301	5,917	2,253,749	1,725,911	298,765	42,718	179,470	6,885
Montana	468,290	340,895	83,842	10,696	29,043	3,713	487,327	351,786	91,149	10,588	29,921	3,884
Nebraska	833,269	616,114	146,081	14,962	35,004	21,109	885,855	652,268	157,670	20,111	34,670	21,137
Nevada	573,131	430,826	115,778	3,057	22,355	1,114	612,677	463,075	122,885	3,342	22,181	1,194
New Hampshire	587,947	430,418	82,204	14,991	18,689	41,644	634,198	450,309	107,139	13,621	20,261	42,868
New Jersey	5,500,065	4,143,069	758,450	50,736	148,048	399,761	5,847,981	4,320,192	1,211,474	57,051	206,598	52,666
New Mexico	706,900	528,430	120,907	6,320	45,938	5,304	727,371	539,987	139,341	5,708	38,193	4,141
New York	13,235,322	9,863,756	2,724,832	333,825	309,991	2,917	14,035,286	10,333,111	3,058,003	312,409	329,471	2,292
North Carolina	2,874,483	2,197,618	511,824	36,323	126,520	2,188	3,037,814	2,281,597	565,384	46,057	142,129	2,646
North Dakota	298,310	219,410	53,226	8,475	15,689	1,510	312,211	229,288	56,720	8,496	15,745	1,962
Ohio	5,199,164	3,822,364	1,007,834	93,375	205,407	70,184	5,471,610	3,994,653	1,101,414	87,034	215,889	72,620
Oklahoma	1,356,636	1,046,831	233,555	13,948	60,010	2,292	1,440,157	1,113,925	253,374	15,875	55,578	1,405
Oregon	1,560,133	1,022,157	395,396	46,286	89,021	7,274	1,701,141	1,115,174	426,688	56,660	93,322	9,296
Pennsylvania	6,563,590	4,224,835	1,500,129	548,674	200,916	89,036	6,956,917	4,594,521	1,617,909	467,682	202,715	74,090
Rhode Island	576,979	412,927	116,601	14,600	14,193	18,658	626,154	438,409	137,202	16,267	13,398	20,877
South Carolina	1,513,667	1,164,160	269,298	14,696	63,798	1,716	1,594,927	1,215,329	294,545	19,625	63,436	1,992
South Dakota	317,164	231,454	48,734	8,134	19,594	9,248	339,207	246,661	52,636	9,626	21,197	9,088
Tennessee	1,819,528	1,368,786	244,446	150,514	50,981	4,801	1,907,725	1,465,548	208,748	56,660	72,350	6,251
Texas	8,844,120	7,083,493	1,089,776	187,693	418,224	64,934	8,890,632	7,055,521	1,114,660	119,715	566,819	33,917
Utah	851,578	593,388	208,462	10,995	36,947	1,786	910,053	624,019	215,723	15,134	40,748	14,428
Vermont	392,739	274,292	67,479	22,135	12,964	15,868	406,682	285,739	75,086	15,670	12,653	17,534
Virginia	2,974,172	2,220,005	591,338	31,258	104,331	27,240	3,121,272	2,352,245	595,672	39,849	105,942	27,564
Washington	2,544,864	1,822,901	544,177	63,905	96,863	17,016	2,800,395	2,005,997	591,742	76,485	105,406	20,765
West Virginia	909,827	645,963	217,710	7,323	37,365	1,467	1,007,685	713,453	247,803	8,278	36,601	1,550
Wisconsin	2,990,182	2,040,800	657,784	43,244	110,877	47,478	3,143,002	2,208,288	720,016	47,589	116,900	50,209
Wyoming	340,459	244,790	64,705	12,869	17,015	1,079	334,840	240,201	64,524	11,238	17,425	1,453
Outlying areas												
American Samoa	11,381	8,761	1,360	283	791	185	10,792	8,654	1,342	202	444	150
Guam	61,571	51,411	8,145	714	1,244	57	69,877	58,419	10,119	606	483	251
Northern Marianas	29,491	19,436	4,496	2,519	3,021	19	28,814	19,775	4,501	2,094	2,381	63
Puerto Rico	861,439	715,789	101,810	9,249	5,792	28,799	895,535	743,954	108,074	8,861	6,761	27,886
Virgin Islands	68,547	55,340	10,868	453	635	1,250	68,564	55,151	10,791	516	596	1,510

[1] Preliminary data.

[2] Includes purchased professional services of teachers or others who provide instruction to students and travel for instructional staff.

NOTE.—Excludes expenditures for state education agencies. Because of rounding, details may not add to totals. Some 1991–92 data have been revised from previously published figures.

SOURCE: U.S. Department of Education, National Center for Education Statistics, Common Core of Data surveys. (This table was prepared May 1995.)

**Table 163.—Total and current expenditure per pupil in public elementary and secondary schools:
1919–20 to 1994–95**

School year	Expenditure per pupil in average daily attendance				Expenditure per pupil in fall enrollment [1]			
	Unadjusted dollars		Constant 1994–95 [2] dollars		Unadjusted dollars		Constant 1994–95 dollars [2]	
	Total expenditure	Current expenditure	Total expenditure	Current expenditure	Total expenditure	Current expenditure	Total expenditure	Current expenditure
1	2	3	4	5	6	7	8	9
1919–20	$64	$53	$505	$421	$48	$40	$378	$315
1929–30	108	87	953	762	90	72	789	631
1931–32	97	81	1,011	846	82	69	856	716
1933–34	76	67	866	766	65	57	736	651
1935–36	88	74	963	813	74	63	814	688
1937–38	100	84	1,047	881	86	72	899	756
1939–40	106	88	1,138	948	92	76	986	822
1941–42	110	98	1,061	948	94	84	909	812
1943–44	125	117	1,076	1,010	105	99	907	851
1945–46	146	136	1,203	1,125	124	116	1,025	958
1947–48	205	181	1,322	1,171	179	158	1,155	1,023
1949–50	260	210	1,654	1,336	231	187	1,467	1,185
1951–52	314	246	1,800	1,408	275	215	1,576	1,233
1953–54	351	265	1,963	1,481	312	236	1,746	1,317
1955–56	387	294	2,165	1,646	354	269	1,979	1,505
1957–58	447	341	2,357	1,797	408	311	2,149	1,639
1959–60	471	375	2,411	1,920	440	350	2,252	1,794
1961–62	517	419	2,588	2,097	485	393	2,428	1,967
1963–64	559	460	2,725	2,245	520	428	2,536	2,089
1965–66	654	538	3,082	2,535	607	499	2,861	2,353
1967–68	786	658	3,478	2,911	732	612	3,236	2,708
1969–70	955	816	3,803	3,249	878	750	3,495	2,987
1970–71	1,049	911	3,973	3,450	970	842	3,672	3,188
1971–72	1,128	990	4,122	3,617	1,034	907	3,780	3,317
1972–73	1,211	1,077	4,253	3,784	1,116	993	3,922	3,489
1973–74	1,364	1,207	4,400	3,894	1,244	1,101	4,013	3,552
1974–75	1,545	1,365	4,486	3,963	1,424	1,258	4,135	3,652
1975–76	1,697	1,504	4,603	4,078	1,564	1,385	4,241	3,757
1976–77	1,816	1,638	4,654	4,196	1,673	1,509	4,288	3,866
1977–78	2,002	1,823	4,809	4,377	1,842	1,677	4,423	4,026
1978–79	2,210	2,020	4,852	4,436	2,029	1,855	4,456	4,074
1979–80	2,491	2,272	4,825	4,401	2,290	2,089	4,437	4,047
1980–81	[3] 2,742	2,502	[3] 4,762	4,344	[3] 2,529	2,307	[3] 4,392	4,006
1981–82	[3] 2,973	2,726	[3] 4,752	4,356	[3] 2,754	2,525	[3] 4,402	4,035
1982–83	[3] 3,203	2,955	[3] 4,909	4,529	[3] 2,966	2,736	[3] 4,545	4,193
1983–84	[3] 3,471	3,173	[3] 5,130	4,689	[3] 3,216	2,940	[3] 4,752	4,344
1984–85	[3] 3,722	3,470	[3] 5,293	4,935	[3] 3,456	3,222	[3] 4,914	4,582
1985–86	[3] 4,020	3,756	[3] 5,556	5,191	[3] 3,724	3,479	[3] 5,148	4,809
1986–87	[3] 4,308	3,970	[3] 5,825	5,369	[3] 3,995	3,682	[3] 5,402	4,979
1987–88	[3] 4,654	4,240	[3] 6,043	5,505	[3] 4,310	3,927	[3] 5,596	5,098
1988–89	5,109	4,645	6,341	5,764	4,738	4,307	5,880	5,345
1989–90	5,542	4,972	6,565	5,889	5,167	4,635	6,121	5,491
1990–91	5,885	5,258	6,610	5,905	5,486	4,902	6,162	5,505
1991–92	6,075	5,421	6,611	5,900	5,629	5,023	6,126	5,467
1992–93	6,305	5,594	6,653	5,904	5,826	5,170	6,149	5,456
1993–94 [3]	6,653	5,903	6,843	6,072	6,148	5,455	6,324	5,612
1994–95 [3]	6,857	6,084	6,857	6,084	6,336	5,623	6,336	5,623

[1] Data for 1919–20 to 1953–54 are based on school-year enrollment.
[2] Based on the Consumer Price Index, prepared by the Bureau of Labor Statistics, U.S. Department of Labor, adjusted to a school-year basis.
[3] Estimated.

NOTE.—Beginning in 1980–81, state administration expenditures are excluded from both "total" and "current" expenditures. Beginning in 1988–89, extensive changes were made in the data collection procedures. Some data have been revised from previously published figures.

SOURCE: U.S. Department of Education, National Center for Education Statistics, *Statistics of State School Systems; Revenues and Expenditures for Public Elementary and Secondary Education;* and Common Core of Data surveys. (This table was prepared May 1995.)

Table 164.—Current expenditure per pupil in average daily attendance in public elementary and secondary schools, by state: 1959–60 to 1992–93

State or other area	Unadjusted dollars												
	1959–60	1969–70	1979–80	1980–81	1983–84	1985–86	1986–87	1987–88	1988–89	1989–90	1990–91	1991–92	1992–93
1	2	3	4	5	6	7	8	9	10	11	12	13	14
United States	$375	$816	$2,272	$2,502	$3,173	$3,756	$3,970	$4,240	$4,645	$4,972	$5,258	$5,421	$5,594
Alabama	241	544	1,612	1,985	2,055	2,565	2,573	2,718	3,197	3,327	3,627	3,616	3,761
Alaska	546	1,123	4,728	5,688	8,627	8,304	8,010	7,971	7,716	8,431	8,330	8,450	8,735
Arizona	404	720	1,971	2,258	2,751	3,336	3,544	3,744	3,902	4,053	4,309	4,381	4,510
Arkansas	225	568	1,574	1,701	2,235	2,658	2,733	2,989	3,273	3,485	3,700	4,031	4,124
California	2 424	867	2,268	2,475	2,963	3,543	3,728	3,840	4,135	4,391	4,491	4,746	4,780
Colorado	396	738	2,421	2,693	3,373	3,975	4,147	4,220	4,521	4,720	5,064	5,172	5,139
Connecticut	436	951	2,420	2,876	4,023	4,743	5,435	6,230	6,857	7,746	7,853	8,016	7,970
Delaware	456	900	2,861	3,018	3,849	4,610	4,825	5,017	5,422	5,799	5,974	6,093	6,271
District of Columbia	431	1,018	3,259	3,441	4,766	5,337	5,742	6,132	7,850	8,850	9,377	9,549	9,419
Florida	318	732	1,889	2,401	2,932	3,529	3,794	4,092	4,563	4,997	5,276	5,243	5,314
Georgia	253	588	1,625	1,708	2,352	2,966	3,181	3,434	3,852	4,275	4,466	4,419	4,686
Hawaii	325	841	2,322	2,604	3,334	3,807	3,787	3,919	4,121	4,448	5,166	5,420	5,704
Idaho	290	603	1,659	1,856	2,146	2,484	2,585	2,667	2,833	3,078	3,386	3,556	3,690
Illinois	438	909	2,587	2,704	3,298	3,781	4,106	4,369	4,906	5,118	5,520	5,670	5,898
Indiana	369	728	1,882	2,010	2,725	3,275	3,556	3,794	4,284	4,549	4,930	5,074	5,344
Iowa	368	844	2,326	2,668	3,274	3,619	3,770	4,124	4,285	4,453	4,679	5,096	5,257
Kansas	348	771	2,173	2,559	3,284	3,829	3,933	4,076	4,443	4,752	4,874	5,007	5,442
Kentucky	233	545	1,701	1,784	2,311	2,486	2,733	3,011	3,347	3,745	4,354	4,719	4,874
Louisiana	372	648	1,792	2,469	2,694	3,187	3,069	3,138	3,317	3,855	4,196	4,354	4,428
Maine	283	692	1,824	1,934	2,700	3,472	3,850	4,258	4,744	5,373	5,458	5,652	6,073
Maryland	393	918	2,598	2,914	3,858	4,447	4,777	5,201	5,758	6,196	6,654	6,679	6,813
Massachusetts	409	859	2,819	2,940	3,595	4,562	5,145	5,471	5,972	6,237	6,366	6,408	6,627
Michigan	415	904	2,640	3,037	3,556	4,176	4,353	4,692	5,150	5,546	5,883	6,268	6,494
Minnesota	425	904	2,387	2,673	3,395	3,941	4,180	4,386	4,755	4,971	5,239	5,409	5,554
Mississippi	206	501	1,664	1,605	2,244	2,362	2,350	2,548	2,861	3,094	3,187	3,245	3,382
Missouri	344	709	1,936	2,172	2,748	3,189	3,472	3,786	4,263	4,507	4,754	4,830	4,885
Montana	411	782	2,476	2,683	3,604	4,091	4,194	4,246	4,293	4,736	5,204	5,319	5,425
Nebraska	337	736	2,150	2,384	3,221	3,634	3,756	3,943	4,360	4,842	5,038	5,263	5,336
Nevada	430	769	2,088	2,078	2,690	3,440	3,440	3,623	3,871	4,117	4,653	4,926	5,066
New Hampshire	347	723	1,916	2,265	2,980	3,542	3,933	4,457	4,807	5,304	5,685	5,790	5,644
New Jersey	388	1,016	3,191	3,254	4,496	5,570	5,953	6,564	7,549	8,139	8,756	9,321	9,415
New Mexico	363	707	2,034	2,329	2,928	3,195	3,558	3,691	3,473	3,515	3,895	3,765	4,071
New York	562	1,327	3,462	3,741	5,117	6,011	6,497	7,151	7,663	8,062	8,565	8,527	8,902
North Carolina	237	612	1,754	2,001	2,303	2,948	3,129	3,368	3,874	4,236	4,548	4,556	4,763
North Dakota	367	690	1,920	2,275	3,028	3,483	3,437	3,519	3,952	4,189	4,199	4,441	4,575
Ohio	365	730	2,075	2,303	2,982	3,527	3,673	3,998	4,686	5,045	5,245	5,694	6,005
Oklahoma	311	604	1,926	2,199	2,859	3,146	3,099	3,093	3,379	3,508	3,843	4,078	4,355
Oregon	448	925	2,692	3,100	3,677	4,141	4,337	4,789	5,182	5,474	5,683	5,913	6,296
Pennsylvania	409	882	2,535	2,824	3,648	4,325	4,616	4,989	5,597	6,228	6,541	6,613	6,890
Rhode Island	413	891	2,601	2,927	3,938	4,667	4,985	5,329	6,064	6,368	6,343	6,546	6,938
South Carolina	220	613	1,752	1,734	2,183	3,058	3,214	3,408	3,736	4,081	4,352	4,436	4,624
South Dakota	347	690	1,908	1,991	2,685	3,051	3,097	3,249	3,585	3,731	3,965	4,173	4,357
Tennessee	238	566	1,635	1,794	2,101	2,612	2,827	3,068	3,491	3,664	3,782	3,692	3,993
Texas	332	624	1,916	2,006	2,784	3,298	3,409	3,608	3,877	4,151	4,438	4,632	4,670
Utah	322	626	1,657	1,819	2,053	2,390	2,415	2,454	2,588	2,764	2,960	3,040	3,180
Vermont	344	807	1,997	2,475	3,359	4,031	4,399	5,207	5,481	6,227	6,738	6,671	6,675
Virginia	274	708	1,970	2,179	2,870	3,520	3,780	4,149	4,539	4,612	4,902	4,880	4,980
Washington	420	915	2,568	2,542	3,465	3,881	3,964	4,164	4,359	4,702	5,000	5,270	5,614
West Virginia	258	670	1,920	2,146	2,879	3,528	3,784	3,858	3,883	4,360	4,911	5,078	5,527
Wisconsin	413	883	2,477	2,738	3,513	4,168	4,523	4,747	5,266	5,524	5,871	6,139	6,475
Wyoming	450	856	2,527	2,967	4,523	5,114	5,201	5,051	5,375	5,577	5,638	5,812	5,822
Outlying areas													
American Samoa	—	—	—	—	—	1,387	1,846	1,908	1,988	1,908	2,033	2,085	1,670
Guam	236	820	—	—	2,301	3,383	3,344	3,295	4,067	4,440	4,596	5,231	5,126
Northern Marianas	—	—	—	—	1,142	2,552	3,099	3,366	2,414	3,007	4,425	5,247	4,364
Puerto Rico	106	—	—	—	1,247	1,325	1,384	1,504	1,692	1,750	1,913	2,162	2,271
Virgin Islands	271	—	—	—	2,710	3,223	4,277	4,036	5,281	6,767	6,002	5,935	5,843

Table 164.—Current expenditure per pupil in average daily attendance in public elementary and secondary schools, by state: 1959–60 to 1992–93—Continued

State or other area	Constant 1992–93 dollars [1]												
	1959–60	1969–70	1979–80	1980–81	1983–84	1984–85	1985–86	1986–87	1987–88	1988–89	1989–90	1990–91	1991–92
1	15	16	17	18	19	20	21	22	23	24	25	26	27
United States	$1,820	$3,079	$4,171	$4,117	$4,444	$4,919	$5,087	$5,217	$5,462	$5,581	$5,596	$5,591	$5,594
Alabama	1,170	2,052	2,959	3,266	2,877	3,359	3,297	3,344	3,759	3,735	3,860	3,729	3,761
Alaska	2,650	4,235	8,679	9,359	12,080	10,876	10,264	9,807	9,074	9,464	8,865	8,714	8,735
Arizona	1,958	2,717	3,618	3,716	3,852	4,370	4,541	4,607	4,589	4,550	4,586	4,518	4,510
Arkansas	1,092	2,142	2,890	2,798	3,129	3,481	3,502	3,678	3,849	3,912	3,938	4,157	4,124
California	2,057	3,272	4,163	4,072	4,149	4,641	4,776	4,725	4,863	4,929	4,779	4,894	4,780
Colorado	1,922	2,784	4,444	4,430	4,723	5,206	5,314	5,192	5,316	5,298	5,389	5,333	5,139
Connecticut	2,115	3,589	4,443	4,731	5,633	6,212	6,964	7,666	8,065	8,694	8,358	8,267	7,970
Delaware	2,211	3,396	5,253	4,966	5,390	6,038	6,182	6,173	6,377	6,509	6,358	6,283	6,271
District of Columbia	2,091	3,842	5,983	5,662	6,674	6,990	7,358	7,545	9,232	9,933	9,980	9,848	9,419
Florida	1,541	2,763	3,468	3,951	4,105	4,623	4,862	5,035	5,366	5,609	5,615	5,407	5,314
Georgia	1,229	2,218	2,984	2,810	3,293	3,884	4,076	4,225	4,530	4,798	4,753	4,557	4,686
Hawaii	1,574	3,171	4,262	4,284	4,669	4,986	4,853	4,821	4,846	4,993	5,498	5,589	5,704
Idaho	1,405	2,276	3,046	3,054	3,005	3,253	3,312	3,282	3,331	3,455	3,604	3,667	3,690
Illinois	2,127	3,431	4,749	4,449	4,619	4,953	5,261	5,375	5,769	5,744	5,875	5,847	5,898
Indiana	1,788	2,747	3,456	3,307	3,816	4,290	4,556	4,667	5,038	5,106	5,247	5,232	5,344
Iowa	1,784	3,185	4,271	4,389	4,585	4,740	4,831	5,073	5,039	4,998	4,980	5,255	5,257
Kansas	1,687	2,909	3,989	4,211	4,598	5,016	5,039	5,015	5,225	5,333	5,187	5,164	5,442
Kentucky	1,131	2,057	3,123	2,935	3,237	3,256	3,502	3,704	3,937	4,204	4,634	4,866	4,874
Louisiana	1,804	2,445	3,290	4,063	3,772	4,174	3,933	3,861	3,901	4,327	4,466	4,490	4,428
Maine	1,371	2,613	3,348	3,182	3,780	4,547	4,933	5,239	5,579	6,031	5,809	5,828	6,073
Maryland	1,905	3,465	4,770	4,794	5,402	5,824	6,121	6,399	6,772	6,954	7,081	6,888	6,813
Massachusetts	1,983	3,241	5,176	4,837	5,034	5,976	6,593	6,731	7,023	7,001	6,775	6,609	6,627
Michigan	2,013	3,411	4,847	4,996	4,980	5,469	5,578	5,772	6,056	6,226	6,261	6,464	6,494
Minnesota	2,063	3,409	4,382	4,399	4,754	5,161	5,356	5,396	5,592	5,579	5,575	5,578	5,554
Mississippi	999	1,890	3,054	2,642	3,143	3,093	3,011	3,135	3,364	3,472	3,391	3,347	3,382
Missouri	1,668	2,673	3,555	3,574	3,848	4,177	4,448	4,658	5,013	5,059	5,059	4,981	4,885
Montana	1,993	2,950	4,547	4,415	5,046	5,358	5,374	5,224	5,048	5,317	5,539	5,486	5,425
Nebraska	1,635	2,778	3,947	3,923	4,510	4,759	4,812	4,851	5,128	5,435	5,362	5,428	5,336
Nevada	2,088	2,903	3,834	3,419	3,767	4,506	4,408	4,458	4,552	4,621	4,952	5,080	5,066
New Hampshire	1,684	2,728	3,517	3,727	4,173	4,639	5,040	5,484	5,653	5,954	6,050	5,971	5,644
New Jersey	1,880	3,834	5,859	5,354	6,296	7,295	7,628	8,076	8,878	9,136	9,319	9,612	9,415
New Mexico	1,759	2,668	3,734	3,833	4,100	4,185	4,559	4,542	4,084	3,945	4,145	3,883	4,071
New York	2,724	5,006	6,356	6,156	7,165	7,873	8,325	8,799	9,012	9,049	9,115	8,794	8,902
North Carolina	1,151	2,310	3,221	3,292	3,224	3,861	4,009	4,144	4,556	4,755	4,840	4,698	4,763
North Dakota	1,779	2,602	3,525	3,742	4,239	4,562	4,405	4,330	4,647	4,702	4,469	4,579	4,575
Ohio	1,771	2,754	3,809	3,789	4,176	4,619	4,706	4,919	5,511	5,662	5,582	5,872	6,005
Oklahoma	1,510	2,281	3,537	3,617	4,003	4,121	3,971	3,805	3,974	3,937	4,090	4,205	4,355
Oregon	2,175	3,489	4,942	5,100	5,149	5,423	5,557	5,892	6,094	6,145	6,048	6,097	6,296
Pennsylvania	1,986	3,327	4,653	4,646	5,108	5,665	5,915	6,138	6,583	6,991	6,962	6,820	6,890
Rhode Island	2,005	3,362	4,775	4,815	5,514	6,113	6,388	6,557	7,132	7,148	6,751	6,751	6,938
South Carolina	1,067	2,311	3,217	2,853	3,057	4,005	4,118	4,193	4,393	4,581	4,632	4,574	4,624
South Dakota	1,682	2,603	3,502	3,276	3,759	3,996	3,969	3,997	4,216	4,188	4,219	4,303	4,357
Tennessee	1,155	2,136	3,002	2,951	2,942	3,421	3,622	3,775	4,105	4,112	4,025	3,807	3,993
Texas	1,612	2,355	3,517	3,300	3,898	4,320	4,369	4,439	4,559	4,659	4,724	4,777	4,670
Utah	1,564	2,363	3,042	2,993	2,874	3,131	3,094	3,094	3,019	3,044	3,102	3,150	3,180
Vermont	1,668	3,046	3,666	4,071	4,703	5,280	5,637	6,407	6,446	6,989	7,171	6,879	6,675
Virginia	1,330	2,671	3,617	3,585	4,019	4,611	4,844	5,104	5,338	5,176	5,217	5,032	4,980
Washington	2,039	3,454	4,715	4,183	4,852	5,083	5,079	5,123	5,127	5,278	5,321	5,435	5,614
West Virginia	1,254	2,528	3,526	3,530	4,032	4,621	4,849	4,747	4,566	4,894	5,227	5,236	5,527
Wisconsin	2,003	3,330	4,547	4,505	4,919	5,459	5,795	5,841	6,193	6,200	6,249	6,331	6,475
Wyoming	2,185	3,230	4,639	4,882	6,333	6,698	6,664	6,215	6,322	6,260	6,000	5,993	5,822
Outlying areas													
American Samoa	—	—	—	—	—	1,816	2,366	2,348	2,338	2,141	2,163	2,150	1,670
Guam	1,147	3,093	—	—	3,222	4,430	4,285	4,054	4,783	4,983	4,891	5,394	5,126
Northern Marianas	—	—	—	—	1,599	3,342	3,971	4,141	—	3,376	4,709	5,410	4,364
Puerto Rico	515	—	—	—	1,746	1,735	1,774	1,851	1,990	1,964	2,036	2,229	2,271
Virgin Islands	1,313	—	—	—	3,795	4,222	5,481	4,966	6,211	7,596	6,388	6,121	5,843

[1] Based on the Consumer Price Index, prepared by the Bureau of Labor Statistics, U.S. Department of Labor, adjusted to a school-year basis. These data do not reflect differences in inflation rates from state to state.

[2] Estimated by the National Center for Education Statistics.

—Data not available or not applicable.

NOTE.—Beginning in 1980–81, state administration expenditures are excluded from both "total" and "current" expenditures. Beginning in 1988–89, extensive changes were made in the data collection procedures. Some data have been revised from previously published figures.

SOURCE: U.S. Department of Education, National Center for Education Statistics, *Statistics of State School Systems;* and Common Core of Data surveys. (This table was prepared May 1995.)

CHAPTER 3
Postsecondary Education

Postsecondary education in this country is diverse; American colleges and universities offer a wide range of programs. For example, a community college may offer vocational training or the first 2 years of training at the college level. A university typically offers a full undergraduate course of study leading to a bachelor's degree as well as first-professional and graduate programs leading to advanced degrees. Vocational and technical institutions offer training programs which are designed to prepare students for specific careers. Other types of educational opportunities for adults include community groups, churches, libraries, and businesses.

In recent decades, postsecondary education has become more accessible to all segments of the population. The growth of community colleges and low-cost institutions means that the student's cost to attend can be held to a minimum. Federal student financial aid and other aid programs also have attracted many students who otherwise would have found it difficult to finance a college education.

This chapter provides an overview of the latest statistics on postsecondary education, which includes academic, vocational and continuing professional education programs after high school. To maintain comparability over time, most of the data in the *Digest* are for higher education institutions, which include 2- and 4-year colleges and universities and exclude vocational and professional education programs. This chapter highlights historical data that enable the reader to observe long-range trends in American higher education.

Other chapters provide related information on postsecondary education. Data on price indexes and on the number of degrees held by the general population are in chapter 1. Chapter 4 contains tabulations on federal funding for postsecondary education. Information on employment outcomes for college graduates is in chapter 5. Chapter 7 contains data on college libraries and use of computers by young adults. Further information on survey methodologies is in the "Guide to Sources" in the appendix and in the publications cited in the source notes.

Enrollment

Higher education enrollment increased by 30 percent between 1973 and 1983. Since then, enroll-ments have risen more slowly. Between 1983 and 1993, enrollment increased about 15 percent, from 12.5 million to 14.3 million. Much of this growth was in part-time and female enrollment. Between 1983 and 1993, the number of men enrolled rose 7 percent, while the number of women increased by 22 percent (table 167). In addition to the enrollment in 2-year colleges, 4-year colleges, and universities, 1.0 million students attended postsecondary less-than-2-year institutions (table 165). The number of older students has been growing more rapidly than the number of younger students. Between 1980 and 1990, the enrollment of students under age 25 increased by 3 percent. During the same period, enrollment of persons 25 and over rose by 34 percent. From 1990 to 2000, NCES projects a rise of 12 percent in enrollments of persons over 25 and an increase of 13 percent in the number under 25 (table 169).

Enrollment trends have differed at the undergraduate, graduate, and first-professional levels. Undergraduate enrollment increased rapidly during the 1970s, but dipped between 1983 and 1985. Since 1985, undergraduate enrollment has shown an increase every year except 1993, rising 16 percent between 1985 and 1993. Graduate enrollment had been steady at about 1.3 million in the late 1970s and early 1980s, but rose about 23 percent between 1985 and 1993. After rising very rapidly during the 1970s, enrollment in first-professional programs stabilized in the 1980s. There was a 7 percent increase in first-professional enrollment between 1990 and 1993 (tables 181, 182, and 183).

Since 1984, the number of women in graduate schools has exceeded the number of men. Between 1983 and 1993, the number of male full-time graduate students increased by 24 percent, compared with 58 percent for full-time women. Among part-time graduate students, men increased by 7 percent compared with 29 percent for women (table 182).

The proportion of American college students who are minorities has been rising. In 1976, 15.7 percent were minorities, compared with 23.4 percent in 1993. Much of the change can be attributed to rising numbers of Hispanic and Asian students. The proportion of students who were black has fluctuated over the past 15 years, before rising to 10.2 percent in 1993.

These percentages exclude foreign students enrolled in U.S. colleges and universities (table 201).

Despite the sizable numbers of small colleges, most students attend the larger colleges and universities. In fall 1993, 37 percent of higher education campuses had fewer than 1,000 students; however, these campuses enrolled only 4 percent of college students. While 12 percent of the campuses enrolled over 10,000 students each, they accounted for 51 percent of total college enrollment (table 208).

Faculty, staff, and salaries

The student/staff ratio at colleges and universities dropped from 5.4 in 1976 to 4.9 in 1991. During the same time period, the student/faculty ratio dropped from 16.6 to 16.4. The proportion of administrative staff and other nonteaching professional staff rose from 15 percent in 1976 to 22 percent in 1991, while the proportion of nonprofessional staff declined from 42 percent to 37 percent (table 214).

Approximately 2.5 million people were employed in colleges and universities in the fall of 1991, including 1.6 million professional and .9 million nonprofessional staff. About 40 percent of the staff were faculty or teaching assistants, 22 percent were other nonteaching professionals, 16 percent were clerical or secretarial, and the remaining 21 percent were technical, paraprofessional, skilled crafts, service, and maintenance staff (table 215).

Colleges differ widely in their practices of employing part-time and full-time staff. In fall 1991, 53 percent of the employees at public 2-year colleges were employed full-time compared with 75 percent at public and private 4-year colleges. A higher proportion of the faculty at public 4-year colleges were employed full-time (79 percent) than at private 4-year colleges (64 percent) or public 2-year colleges (43 percent) (table 216).

Full-time and part-time faculty and instructional staff also differ by the number and types of students that they teach. Sixty-seven percent of full-time faculty teach 50 students or more, while only 30 percent of part-time faculty teach that many students. Of the full-time faculty teaching undergraduate students, 61 percent teach three or more classes. Eighteen percent of part-time faculty teach 3 or more undergraduate classes (tables 220, 221).

The actual amount of time that full-time faculty spent teaching was a little over 54 percent in 1992. For the remaining faculty time, research and scholarship accounted for 18 percent of the time; professional growth, 5 percent; administration, 13 percent; outside consulting, 3 percent; service and non-teaching activities, 7 percent. Full-time faculty taught a range of hours per week. Fifteen percent taught less than four hours a week, 39 percent taught 4 to 9.9 hours, and the remaining 46 percent taught 10 or more hours per week teaching (table 220).

About 13 percent of full-time faculty in colleges and universities were minorities in 1992–93. Five percent of the faculty were Asian/Pacific Islanders; 5 percent, black; 3 percent, Hispanic; and .5 percent, American Indian (table 223). The majority of college faculty in fall 1992 were white and male. Fifty-nine percent of full-time faculty fell in this category, while 28 percent were white and female. The situation was the same for part-time faculty, though there were fewer men and more women. White males comprised 49 percent of part-time faculty, and white females accounted for just over 40 percent (table 222).

College faculty generally suffered losses in the purchasing power of their salaries from 1972–73 to 1980–81, when average salaries fell 17 percent after adjustment for inflation. During the 1980s, average salaries rose and recouped most of the losses. Since 1989–90, faculty salaries have been relatively stable. Average salaries for men in 1993–94 ($49,579) were considerably higher than the average for women ($40,058) and have increased at a slightly faster rate since 1980–81 (table 226).

The proportion of faculty with tenure has remained relatively stable in recent years. About 64 percent of full-time faculty had tenure in 1993–94, but a large difference existed between the proportion of men and women with tenure. Seventy-one percent of men compared with 50 percent of women had tenure in 1993–94. About 67 percent of the faculty at public institutions had tenure, compared with 57 percent of faculty at private institutions (table 232).

Despite tenure, the age distribution of full-time faculty falls more heavily in the lower age brackets. Faculty under the age of thirty compose one percent of the total, but 36 percent are ages 30 to 44, and 37 percent are 45 to 54 years old. Thirteen percent are 55 to 59; 9 percent, 60 to 64; and 4 percent, 65 or older (table 224).

Degrees

During the 1994–95 academic year, 10,246 institutions offered postsecondary education. This included 2,215 4-year colleges, 1,473 2-year colleges, and 6,558 vocational and technical institutions (tables 233 and 350).

More people are completing college. Between 1982–83 and 1992–93, the number of associate, bachelor's, master's, and doctor's degrees rose. Associate degrees increased 14 percent, bachelor's degrees increased 20 percent, master's degrees increased 27 percent, and doctor's degrees increased 29 percent during this period. The number of first-professional degrees was about the same in 1992–93 as it was in 1982–83, though it declined in the mid 1980s before increasing in the early 1990s (table 236).

The total number of bachelor's degrees increased slowly during the early 1980s and more rapidly towards the end of that decade, especially for women. Between 1982–83 and 1992–93, the number of bachelor's degrees awarded to men increased by 11 percent, while those awarded to women rose by 29 percent (table 236).

Of the 1,165,000 bachelor's degrees conferred in 1992–93, the largest numbers of degrees were conferred in the fields of business management and administrative services (257,000), social sciences (136,000), and education (108,000). At the master's degree level, the largest fields were education (96,000) and business management and administrative services (90,000). The largest fields at the doctor's degree level were education (7,000), engineering and engineering technology (6,000), biological sciences (4,000), and physical sciences (4,000) (tables 243, 244, and 245).

The pattern of bachelor's degrees by field of study has shifted significantly in recent years. Declines are significant in male majority fields such as engineering and computer and information sciences. Engineering and engineering technologies fell 1 percent between 1982–83 and 1987–88, and then posted a decline of 12 percent between 1987–88 and 1992–93. Computer and information sciences grew rapidly during the 1970s and early 1980s, but dropped 30 percent between 1987–88 and 1992–93, back to 1982–83 levels.

In contrast, some fields that had been growing slowly, such as social sciences and psychology, began to increase rapidly. For example, the number of bachelor's degrees conferred in social sciences and history increased by 5 percent between 1982–83 and 1987–88, but rose 35 percent between 1987–88 and 1992–93. Psychology increased 12 percent during the first 5-year period and rose by 48 percent between 1987–88 and 1992–93. In 1987–88, the number of degrees conferred in education rose for the first time since 1972–73. The number of education degrees rose a total of 18 percent between 1987–88 and 1992–93. To some extent, these shifts during the 1987–88 and 1992–93 period highlight the increasing female majority on college campuses by reflecting significant increases in degrees in some predominantly female fields and decreases in many predominantly male fields (tables 243, 272, 274, 275, 276, 285, and 287).

Only about half of the students who enrolled full-time in a 4-year college in 1980 graduated with a bachelor's degree by 1986, according to the High School and Beyond survey. About 55 percent of the students who enrolled in private 4-year colleges earned a bachelor's or higher degree by 1986 compared with 46 percent in public 4-year colleges (table 303).

Finances

For the 1994–95 academic year, annual undergraduate charges for tuition, room, and board were estimated to be $5,962 at public colleges and $16,222 at private colleges. Between 1984–85 and 1994–95, charges at public colleges have risen by 23 percent, and charges at private colleges have increased by 39 percent, after adjustment for inflation (tables 37 and 306).

Trend data show increases in the expenditures per student at institutions of higher education through the late 1980s and relatively small fluctuations thereafter. After adjustment for inflation at colleges and universities, current-fund expenditures per student rose about 17 percent between 1981–82 and 1986–87, but increased 3 percent between 1986–87 and 1992–93 (table 328).

Scholarships and fellowships have been rising more rapidly than most other types of college expenditures in recent years. At public universities, between 1982–83 and 1992–93, inflation adjusted scholarships and fellowships expenditures per full-time-equivalent student rose 85 percent compared with 13 percent for instruction expenditures per student. At private universities during the same period, the per student scholarships and fellowships costs rose 100 percent, and the instruction costs rose by 41 percent (tables 335 and 338). Another rapidly rising expenditure for public colleges during the decade was research, which rose by 48 percent per student at public 4-year colleges (table 336).

Figure 13.-Enrollment, degrees conferred, and expenditures in institutions of higher education: 1960–61 to 1994–95

Enrollment, in millions

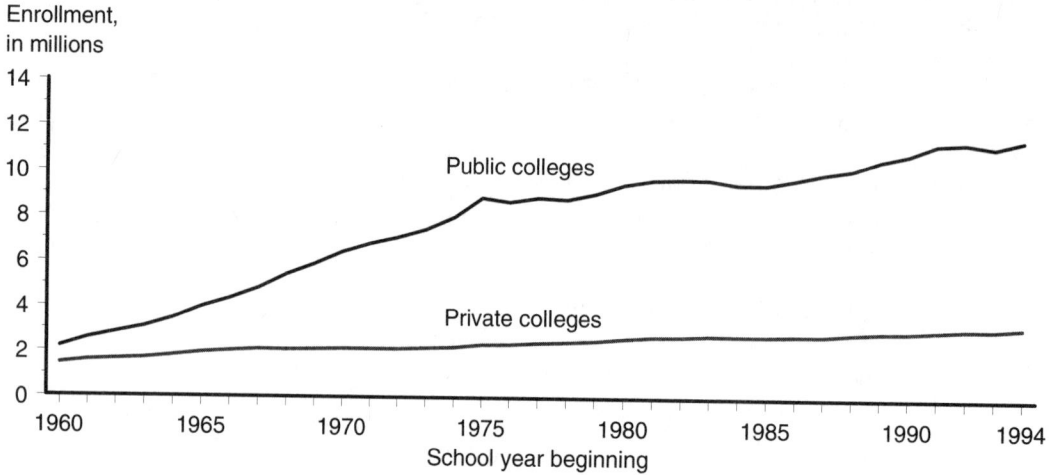

School year beginning

Degrees, in millions

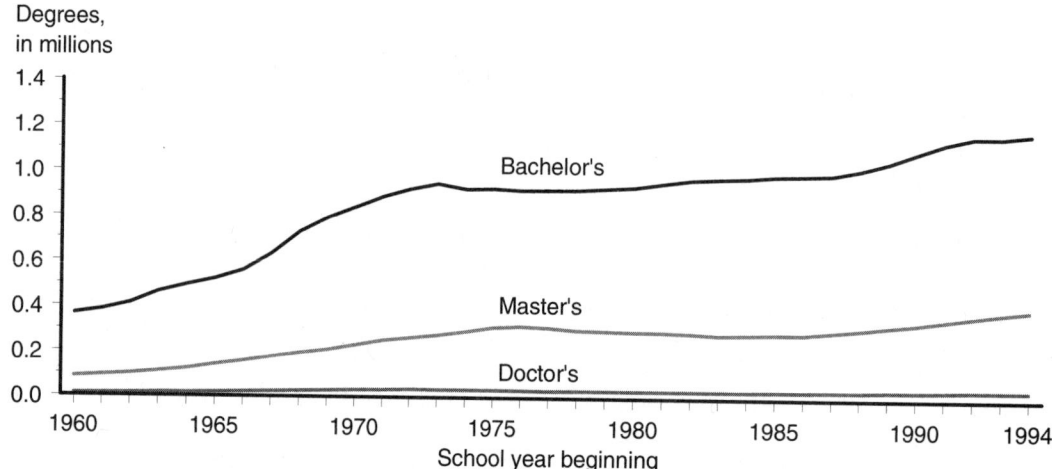

School year beginning

Expenditures, in billions of constant 1994-95 dollars

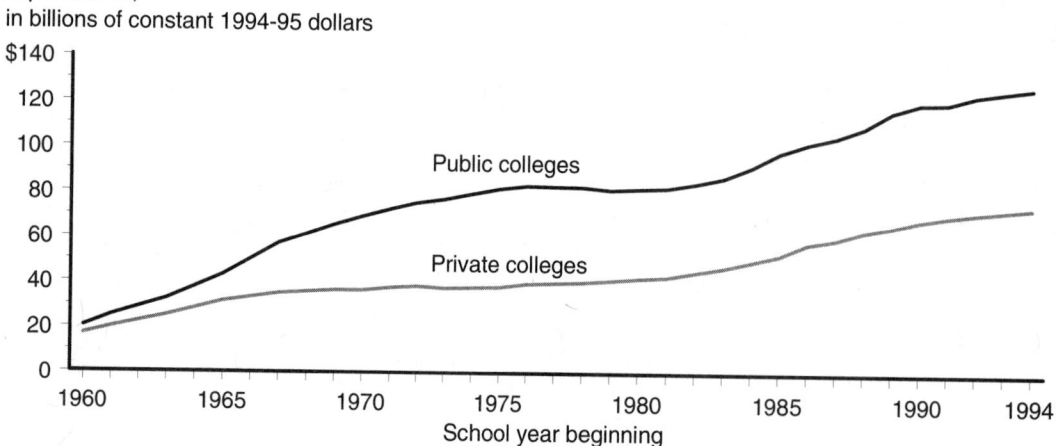

School year beginning

NOTE: Enrollment, degree, and finance data for 1993–94 and 1994–95 are estimated.

SOURCE: U.S. Department of Education, National Center for Education Statistics, HEGIS, "Fall Enrollment in Institutions of Higher Education," "Degrees and Other Formal Awards Conferred," and "Financial Statistics of Institutions of Higher Education" surveys; and Integrated Postsecondary Education Data System (IPEDS), "Fall Enrollment," "Completions," and "Finance" surveys.

Figure 14.–Percentage change in total enrollment of institutions of higher education, by state: Fall 1989 to fall 1993

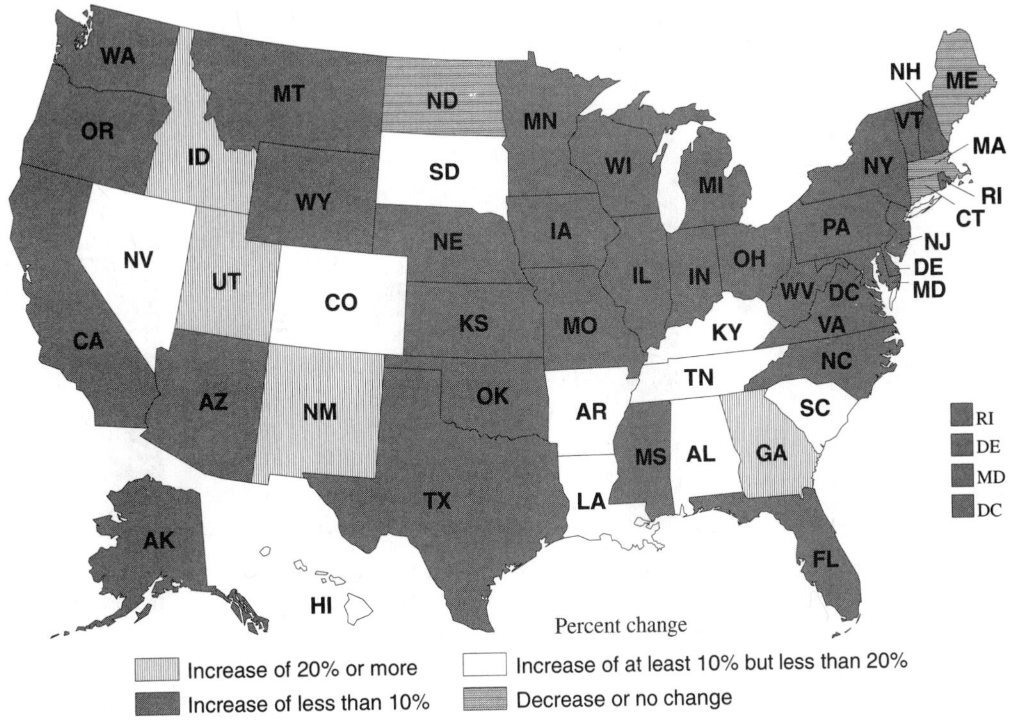

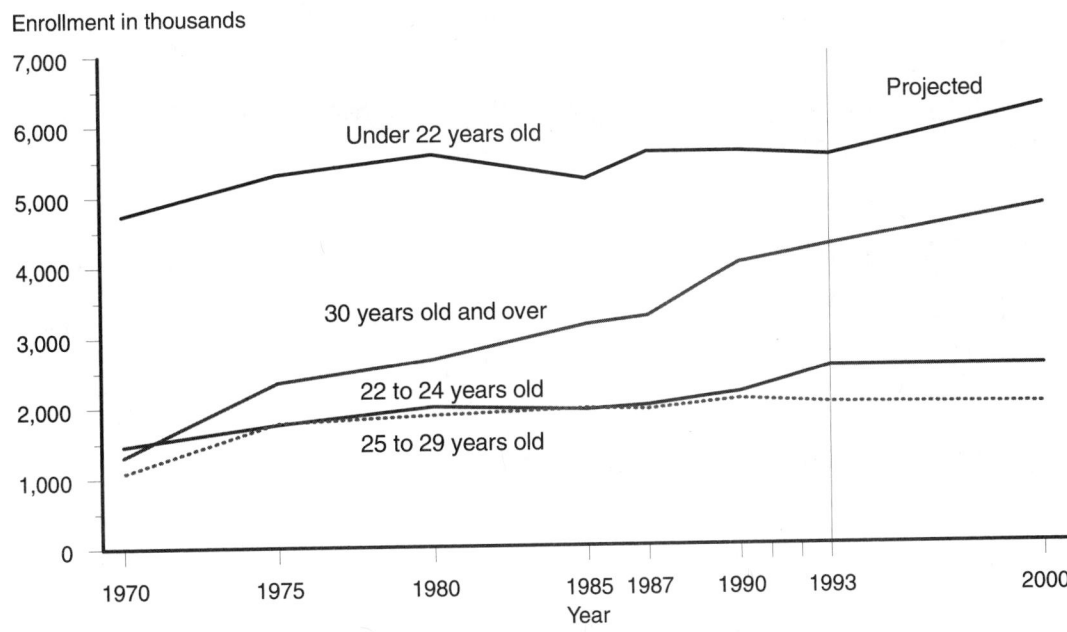

Percent change

Increase of 20% or more		Increase of at least 10% but less than 20%
Increase of less than 10%		Decrease or no change

SOURCE: U.S. Department of Education, National Center for Education Statistics, Integrated Postsecondary Education Data System (IPEDS), "Fall Enrollment" surveys.

Figure 15.–Enrollment in institutions of higher education, by age: Fall 1970 to fall 2000

Enrollment in thousands

SOURCE: U.S. Department of Education, National Center for Education Statistics, "Fall Enrollment in Institutions of Higher Education" surveys; Integrated Postsecondary Education Data System (IPEDS), "Fall Enrollment" surveys; *Projections of Education Statistics to 2005*; and U.S. Department of Commerce, Bureau of the Census, *Current Population Reports*, Series P-20, "Social and Economic Characteristics of Students," various years.

Figure 16.-Full-time–equivalent students per staff member in public and private institutions of higher education: 1976, 1989, and 1991

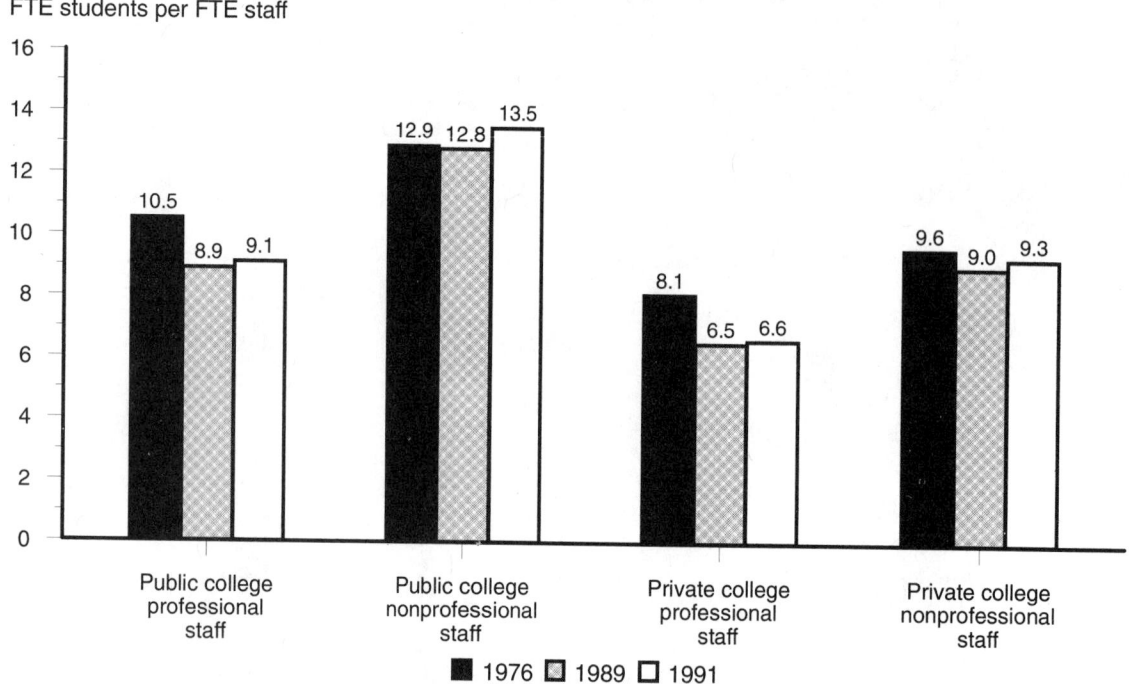

SOURCE: U.S. Department of Education, National Center for Education Statistics, Higher Education General Information Survey (HEGIS), "Staff, 1976" survey, and Integrated Postsecondary Education Data System (IPEDS), "Staff" surveys.

Figure 17.-Trends in bachelor's degrees conferred in selected fields of study: 1982-83, 1987-88, and 1992-93

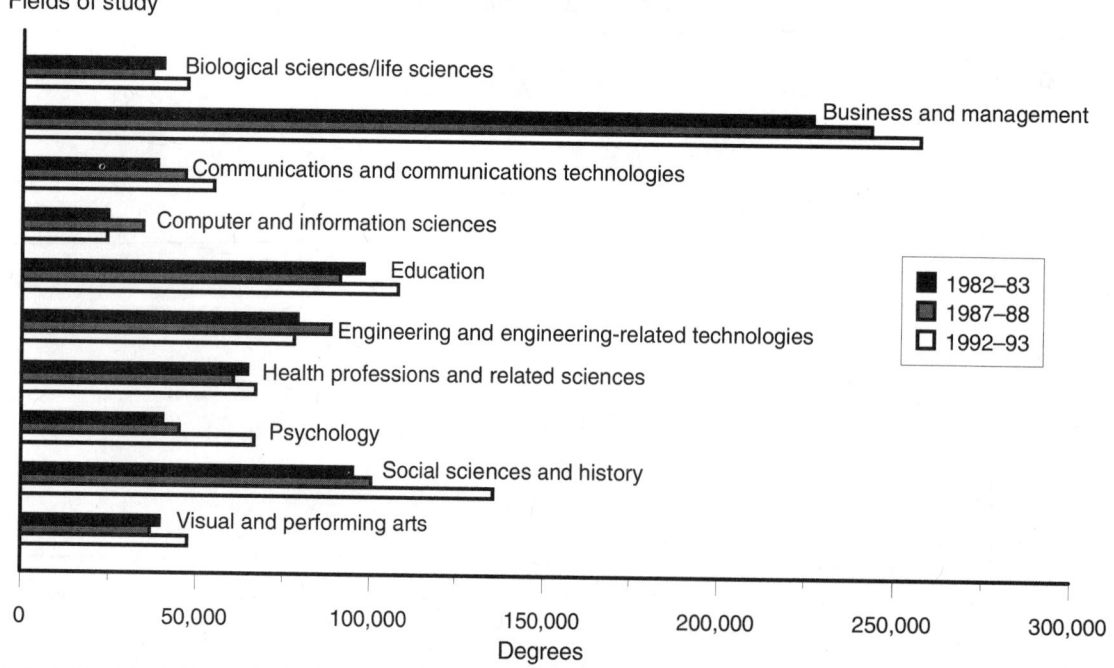

SOURCE: U.S. Department of Education, National Center for Education Statistics, Higher Education General Information Survey (HEGIS), "Degrees and Other Formal Awards Conferred" surveys, and Integrated Postsecondary Education Data System (IPEDS), "Completions" surveys.

Figure 18.-Sources of current-fund revenue for public institutions of higher education: 1992–93

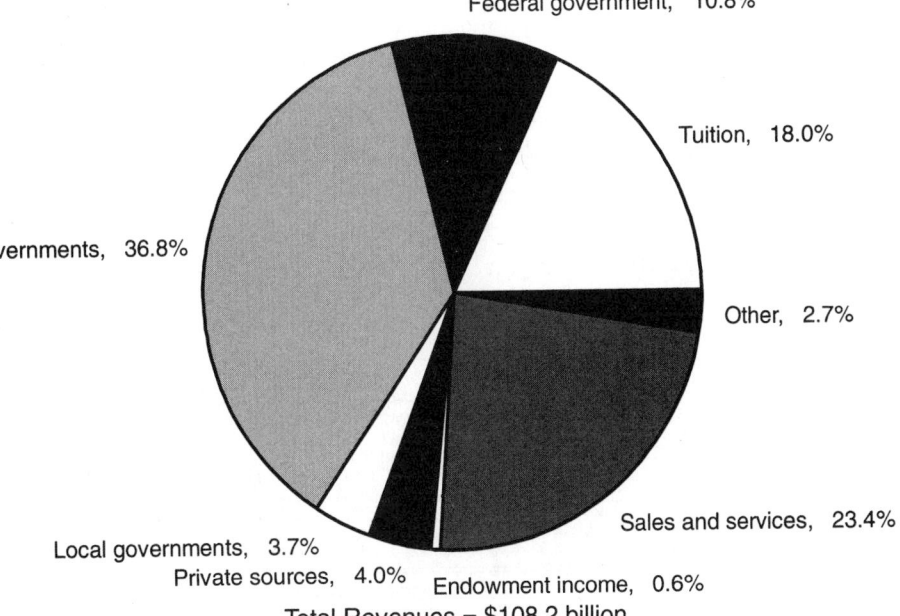

Federal government,   10.8%

Tuition,   18.0%

State governments,   36.8%

Other,   2.7%

Local governments,   3.7%

Private sources,   4.0%

Endowment income,   0.6%

Sales and services,   23.4%

Total Revenues = $108.2 billion

SOURCE: U.S. Department of Education, National Center for Education Statistics, Integrated Postsecondary Education Data System (IPEDS), "Finance, FY93" survey.

Figure 19.-Sources of current-fund revenue for private institutions of higher education: 1992–93

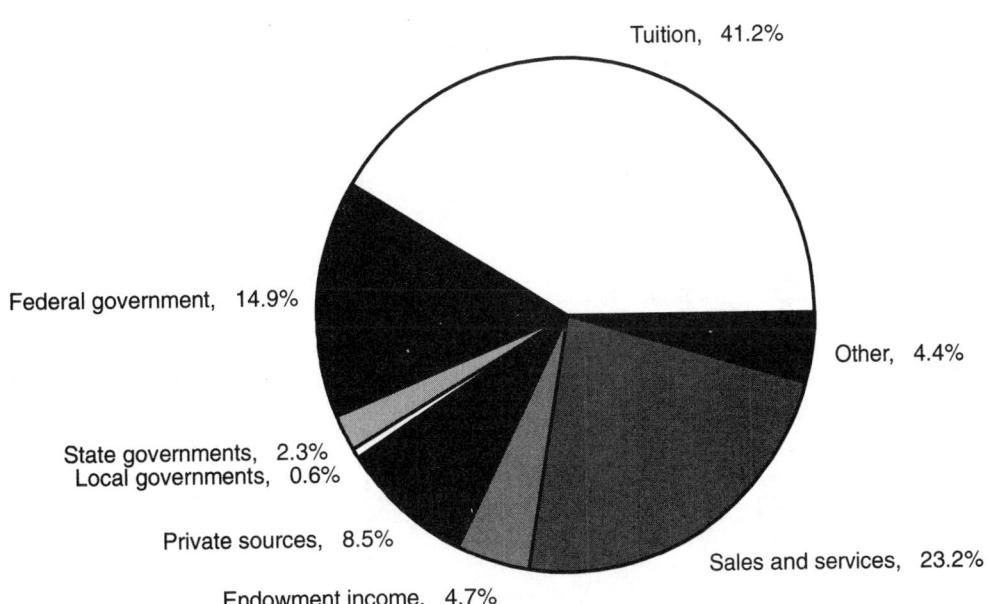

Tuition,   41.2%

Federal government,   14.9%

Other,   4.4%

State governments,   2.3%
Local governments,   0.6%

Private sources,   8.5%

Endowment income,   4.7%

Sales and services,   23.2%

Total Revenues = $62.7 billion

SOURCE: U.S. Department of Education, National Center for Education Statistics, Integrated Postsecondary Education Data System (IPEDS), "Finance, FY93" survey.

Table 165.—Enrollment and staff in, and degrees conferred by, institutions of higher education and noncollegiate postsecondary institutions: 1992–93 and fall 1993

Level of institutional accreditation, type of degree, and sex of student	All post-secondary	Institutions of higher education					Noncollegiate postsecondary institutions				
		Total	Public	Private			Total	Public	Private		
				Total	Nonprofit	Propri-etary			Total	Nonprofit	Propri-etary
1	2	3	4	5	6	7	8	9	10	11	12
Enrollment, fall 1993											
Total	15,333,371	14,305,658	11,189,088	3,116,570	2,889,752	226,818	1,027,713	341,367	686,346	168,207	518,139
4-year institutions	8,739,791	8,739,791	5,851,760	2,888,031	2,803,395	84,636	—	—	—	—	—
Men	4,082,257	4,082,257	2,739,819	1,342,438	1,292,763	49,675	—	—	—	—	—
Women	4,657,534	4,657,534	3,111,941	1,545,593	1,510,632	34,961	—	—	—	—	—
2-year institutions	5,565,867	5,565,867	5,337,328	228,539	86,357	142,182	—	—	—	—	—
Men	2,345,459	2,345,459	2,244,692	100,767	33,834	66,933	—	—	—	—	—
Women	3,220,408	3,220,408	3,092,636	127,772	52,523	75,249	—	—	—	—	—
Less than 2 year [1]	1,027,713	—	—	—	—	—	1,027,713	341,367	686,346	168,207	518,139
Men	396,693	—	—	—	—	—	396,693	161,344	235,349	88,134	147,215
Women	631,020	—	—	—	—	—	631,020	180,023	450,997	80,073	370,924
Staff, fall 1991											
Total	2,662,085	2,545,235	1,783,328	761,907	742,924	18,983	116,850	29,054	87,796	24,966	62,830
Professional staff	1,693,416	1,595,460	1,133,264	462,196	447,795	14,401	97,956	23,154	74,802	19,497	55,305
Administrative	162,647	144,755	84,446	60,309	58,023	2,286	17,892	1,815	16,077	3,604	12,473
Faculty	893,843	826,252	580,908	245,344	236,066	9,278	67,591	18,450	49,141	13,567	35,574
Faculty assistants	197,946	197,751	173,560	24,191	24,054	137	195	0	195	111	84
Other professionals	438,980	426,702	294,350	132,352	129,652	2,700	12,278	2,889	9,389	2,215	7,174
Nonprofessional staff	968,669	949,775	650,064	299,711	295,129	4,582	18,894	5,900	12,994	5,469	7,525
Student/staff ratio	5.7	5.6	6.3	4.0	3.8	12.1	7.9	9.8	7.3	6.1	7.8
Degrees conferred, 1992–93											
Less than 1 year awards and 1- to 4-year awards	1,086,426	217,781	157,931	59,850	13,446	46,404	868,645	208,365	660,280	72,669	587,611
4-year institutions	19,794	19,794	9,408	10,386	8,651	1,735	—	—	—	—	—
Men	9,136	9,136	4,941	4,195	3,379	816	—	—	—	—	—
Women	10,658	10,658	4,467	6,191	5,272	919	—	—	—	—	—
2-year institutions	197,987	197,987	148,523	49,464	4,795	44,669	—	—	—	—	—
Men	86,673	86,673	65,322	21,351	2,277	19,074	—	—	—	—	—
Women	111,314	111,314	83,201	28,113	2,518	25,595	—	—	—	—	—
Less than 2 year	868,645	—	—	—	—	—	868,645	208,365	660,280	72,669	587,611
Men	312,613	—	—	—	—	—	312,613	105,282	207,331	32,686	174,645
Women	556,032	—	—	—	—	—	556,032	103,083	452,949	39,983	412,966
Associate [2]	533,503	514,756	430,321	84,435	47,713	36,722	18,747	2,297	16,450	1,864	14,586
4-year	77,995	76,327	38,549	37,778	29,716	8,062	1,668	—	1,668	929	739
Men	33,874	33,063	15,805	17,258	11,914	5,344	811	—	811	506	305
Women	44,121	43,264	22,744	20,520	17,802	2,718	857	—	857	423	434
2-year	455,496	438,429	391,772	46,657	17,997	28,660	17,067	2,286	14,781	935	13,846
Men	185,985	178,901	157,234	21,667	8,030	13,637	7,084	1,117	5,967	244	5,723
Women	269,511	259,528	234,538	24,990	9,967	15,023	9,983	1,169	8,814	691	8,123
Less than 2 year	12	—	—	—	—	—	12	11	1	—	1
Men	11	—	—	—	—	—	11	11	—	—	—
Women	1	—	—	—	—	—	1	—	1	—	1
Bachelor's [2]	1,174,347	1,165,178	785,112	380,066	373,346	6,720	9,169	9	9,160	7,232	1,928
Men	537,316	532,881	358,798	174,083	169,909	4,174	4,435	1	4,434	3,496	938
Women	637,031	632,297	426,314	205,983	203,437	2,546	4,734	8	4,726	3,736	990
Master's [2]	372,320	369,585	213,843	155,742	154,115	1,627	2,735	23	2,712	1,491	1,221
Men	170,820	169,258	94,045	75,213	74,234	979	1,562	9	1,553	892	661
Women	201,500	200,327	119,798	80,529	79,881	648	1,173	14	1,159	599	560
Doctor's [2]	42,808	42,132	27,392	14,740	14,571	169	676	—	676	313	363
Men	26,498	26,073	17,010	9,063	8,980	83	425	—	425	232	193
Women	16,310	16,059	10,382	5,677	5,591	86	251	—	251	81	170
First-professional [2]	77,777	75,387	29,628	45,759	45,275	484	2,390	52	2,338	1,617	721
Men	46,757	45,153	17,126	28,027	27,755	272	1,604	21	1,583	1,093	490
Women	31,020	30,234	12,502	17,732	17,520	212	786	31	755	524	231

[1] Includes institutions that offer non-accredited associate, bachelor's or advanced degree programs.

[2] Includes noncollegiate institutions that offer non-accredited degree programs.

—Not applicable.

NOTE.—Enrollment data are preliminary.

SOURCE: U.S. Department of Education, National Center for Education Statistics, Integrated Postsecondary Education Data System (IPEDS), "Fall Enrollment," "Staff," and "Completions" surveys. (This table was prepared May 1995.)

Table 166.—Historical summary of faculty, students, degrees, and finances in institutions of higher education: 1869–70 to 1992–93

Item	1869-70	1879-80	1889-90	1899-1900	1909-10	1919-20	1929-30	1939-40	1949-50	1959-60	1969-70	1979-80	1989-90	1991-92	1992-93
1	2	3	4	5	6	7	8	9	10	11	12	13	14	15	16
Total institutions[1]	563	811	998	977	951	1,041	1,409	1,708	1,851	2,008	2,525	3,152	3,535	3,601	3,638
Total faculty[2]	[3]5,553	[3]11,522	[3]15,809	23,868	36,480	48,615	82,386	146,929	246,722	380,554	[4]450,000	[4]675,000	[5]824,220	[5]826,252	[3]835,000
Men	[3]4,887	[3]7,328	[3]12,704	19,151	29,132	35,807	60,017	106,328	186,189	296,773	[4]346,000	[4]479,000	[5]577,298	[5]525,599	[3]531,000
Women	[3]666	[3]4,194	[3]3,105	4,717	7,348	12,808	22,369	40,601	60,533	83,781	[4]104,000	[4]196,000	[5]246,922	[5]300,653	[3]304,000
Total fall enrollment[6]	[3]52,286	[3]115,817	[3]156,756	237,592	[3]355,213	597,880	1,100,737	1,494,203	2,659,021	3,639,847	8,004,660	11,569,899	13,538,560	14,358,953	14,486,315
Men	[3]41,160	[3]77,972	[3]100,453	152,254	[3]214,648	314,938	619,935	893,250	1,853,068	2,332,617	4,746,201	5,682,877	6,190,015	6,501,844	6,523,516
Women	[3]11,126	[3]37,845	[3]56,303	85,338	[3]140,565	282,942	480,802	600,953	805,953	1,307,230	3,258,459	5,887,022	7,348,545	7,857,109	7,962,799
Earned degrees conferred															
Associate, total	—	—	—	—	—	—	—	—	—	—	206,023	400,910	455,102	504,231	[7]514,756
Men	—	—	—	—	—	—	—	—	—	—	117,432	183,737	191,195	207,481	[7]211,964
Women	—	—	—	—	—	—	—	—	—	—	88,591	217,173	263,907	296,750	[7]302,792
Bachelor's[8], total	9,371	12,896	15,539	27,410	37,199	48,622	122,484	186,500	432,058	392,440	792,656	929,417	1,051,344	1,136,553	[7]1,165,178
Men	7,993	10,411	12,857	22,173	28,762	31,980	73,615	109,546	328,841	254,063	451,380	473,611	491,696	520,811	[7]532,881
Women	1,378	2,485	2,682	5,237	8,437	16,642	48,869	76,954	103,217	138,377	341,276	455,806	559,648	615,742	[7]632,297
Master's[9], total	0	879	1,015	1,583	2,113	4,279	14,969	26,731	58,183	74,435	208,291	298,081	324,301	352,838	[7]369,585
Men	0	868	821	1,280	1,555	2,985	8,925	16,508	41,220	50,898	125,624	150,749	153,653	161,842	[7]169,258
Women	0	11	194	303	558	1,294	6,044	10,223	16,963	23,537	82,667	147,332	170,648	190,996	[7]200,327
First-professional[8], total	(8)	(8)	(8)	(8)	(8)	(8)	(8)	(8)	(8)	(8)	34,578	70,131	70,988	74,146	[7]75,387
Men	(8)	(8)	(8)	(8)	(8)	(8)	(8)	(8)	(8)	(8)	32,794	52,716	43,961	45,071	[7]45,153
Women	(8)	(8)	(8)	(8)	(8)	(8)	(8)	(8)	(8)	(8)	1,784	17,415	27,027	29,075	[7]30,234
Doctor's, total	1	54	149	382	443	615	2,299	3,290	6,420	9,829	29,866	32,615	38,371	40,659	[7]42,132
Men	1	51	147	359	399	522	1,946	2,861	5,804	8,801	25,890	22,943	24,401	25,557	[7]26,073
Women	0	3	2	23	44	93	353	429	616	1,028	3,976	9,672	13,970	15,102	[7]16,059
Finances, in thousands															
Current-fund revenue															
Educational and general income	—	—	$21,464	$35,084	$76,883	$199,922	$554,511	$715,211	$2,374,645	$5,785,537	$21,515,242	$58,519,982	$139,635,477	$161,395,896	[7]$170,880,503
Current-fund expenditures															
Educational and general expenditures	—	—	95,426	253,599	67,917	172,929	483,065	571,288	1,833,845	4,688,352	16,486,177	56,913,588	134,655,571	156,189,161	[7]165,241,040
—	—	—	—	—	—	—	507,142	674,688	2,245,661	5,601,376	21,043,113	44,542,843	105,585,076	121,567,156	[7]128,977,968
Value of physical property	—	—	95,426	253,599	457,594	747,333	2,065,049	[10]2,753,780	4,799,964	13,548,548	42,093,580	83,733,387	164,635,000	181,995,647	190,441,253
Market value of endowment funds	—	—	[11]78,788	[11]194,998	[11]323,661	[11]569,071	[11]1,372,068	[11]1,686,283	[11]2,601,223	[11]5,322,080	11,206,632	20,743,045	67,978,726	79,117,709	88,881,171

[1] Prior to 1979-80, excludes branch campuses.

[2] Total number of different individuals (not reduced to full-time equivalent). Beginning in 1959-60, data are for the first term of the academic year. Beginning in 1969-70, data include only instructional faculty with the rank of instructor or above.

[3] Estimated.

[4] Estimated number of senior instructional staff. Excludes graduate assistants.

[5] Because of revised survey procedures, data may not be directly comparable with figures prior to 1989-90.

[6] Data for 1869-70 to 1949-50 are for resident degree-credit students who enrolled at any time during the academic year.

[7] Preliminary data.

[8] From 1869-70 to 1959-60, first-professional degrees included under bachelor's degrees.

[9] Figures for years prior to 1969-70 are not precisely comparable with later data.

[10] Includes unexpended plant funds.

[11] Book value. Includes other nonexpendable funds.

— Data not available.

NOTE.—Some data have been revised from previously published figures.

SOURCE: U.S. Department of Education, National Center for Education Statistics, *Biennial Survey of Education in the United States; Education Directory, Colleges and Universities; Faculty and Other Professional Staff in Institutions of Higher Education; Fall Enrollment in Institutions of Higher Education; Earned Degrees Conferred; Financial Statistics of Institutions of Higher Education;* and "Fall Enrollment in Institutions of Higher Education," "Degrees and Other Formal Awards Conferred," and "Financial Statistics of Institutions of Higher Education" surveys; and Integrated Postsecondary Education Data System (IPEDS), "Fall Enrollment," "Completions," and "Finance" surveys. (This table was prepared April 1995.)

Table 167.—Total fall enrollment in institutions of higher education, by attendance status, sex of student, and control of institution: 1947 to 1993

Year	Total enrollment	Attendance status		Sex of student		Control of institution			
		Full-time	Part-time	Men	Women	Public	Private		
							Total	Nonprofit	Proprietary
1	2	3	4	5	6	7	8	9	10
1947[1]	2,338,226	—	—	1,659,249	678,977	1,152,377	1,185,849	—	—
1948[1]	2,403,396	—	—	1,709,367	694,029	1,185,588	1,217,808	—	—
1949[1]	2,444,900	—	—	1,721,572	723,328	1,207,151	1,237,749	—	—
1950[1]	2,281,298	—	—	1,560,392	720,906	1,139,699	1,141,599	—	—
1951[1]	2,101,962	—	—	1,390,740	711,222	1,037,938	1,064,024	—	—
1952[1]	2,134,242	—	—	1,380,357	753,885	1,101,240	1,033,002	—	—
1953[1]	2,231,054	—	—	1,422,598	808,456	1,185,876	1,045,178	—	—
1954[1]	2,446,693	—	—	1,563,382	883,311	1,353,531	1,093,162	—	—
1955[1]	2,653,034	—	—	1,733,184	919,850	1,476,282	1,176,752	—	—
1956[1]	2,918,212	—	—	1,911,458	1,006,754	1,656,402	1,261,810	—	—
1957	3,323,783	—	—	2,170,765	1,153,018	1,972,673	1,351,110	—	—
1959	3,639,847	2,421,016	[2]1,218,831	2,332,617	1,307,230	2,180,982	1,458,865	—	—
1961	4,145,065	2,785,133	[2]1,359,932	2,585,821	1,559,244	2,561,447	1,583,618	—	—
1963	4,779,609	3,183,833	[2]1,595,776	2,961,540	1,818,069	3,081,279	1,698,330	—	—
1964	5,280,020	3,573,238	[2]1,706,782	3,248,713	2,031,307	3,467,708	1,812,312	—	—
1965	5,920,864	4,095,728	[2]1,825,136	3,630,020	2,290,844	3,969,596	1,951,268	—	—
1966	6,389,872	4,438,606	[2]1,951,266	3,856,216	2,533,656	4,348,917	2,040,955	—	—
1967	6,911,748	4,793,128	[2]2,118,620	4,132,800	2,778,948	4,816,028	2,095,720	—	—
1968	7,513,091	5,210,155	2,302,936	4,477,649	3,035,442	5,430,652	2,082,439	—	—
1969	8,004,660	5,498,883	2,505,777	4,746,201	3,258,459	5,896,868	2,107,792	—	—
1970	8,580,887	5,816,290	2,764,597	5,043,642	3,537,245	6,428,134	2,152,753	—	—
1971	8,948,644	6,077,232	2,871,412	5,207,004	3,741,640	6,804,309	2,144,335	—	—
1972	9,214,820	6,072,389	3,142,471	5,238,757	3,976,103	7,070,635	2,144,185	—	—
1973	9,602,123	6,189,493	3,412,630	5,371,052	4,231,071	7,419,516	2,182,607	—	—
1974	10,223,729	6,370,273	3,853,456	5,622,429	4,601,300	7,988,500	2,235,229	—	—
1975	11,184,859	6,841,334	4,343,525	6,148,997	5,035,862	8,834,508	2,350,351	—	—
1976	11,012,137	6,717,058	4,295,079	5,810,828	5,201,309	8,653,477	2,358,660	2,314,298	44,362
1977	11,285,787	6,792,925	4,492,862	5,789,016	5,496,771	8,846,993	2,438,794	2,386,652	52,142
1978	11,260,092	6,667,657	4,592,435	5,640,998	5,619,094	8,785,893	2,474,199	2,408,331	65,868
1979	11,569,899	6,794,039	4,775,860	5,682,877	5,887,022	9,036,822	2,533,077	2,461,773	71,304
1980	12,096,895	7,097,958	4,998,937	5,874,374	6,222,521	9,457,394	2,639,501	2,527,787	[3]111,714
1981	12,371,672	7,181,250	5,190,422	5,975,056	6,396,616	9,647,032	2,724,640	2,572,405	[3]152,235
1982	12,425,780	7,220,618	5,205,162	6,031,384	6,394,396	9,696,087	2,729,693	2,552,739	[3]176,954
1983	12,464,661	7,261,050	5,203,611	6,023,725	6,440,936	9,682,734	2,781,927	2,589,187	192,740
1984	12,241,940	7,098,388	5,143,552	5,863,574	6,378,366	9,477,370	2,764,570	2,574,419	190,151
1985	12,247,055	7,075,221	5,171,834	5,818,450	6,428,605	9,479,273	2,767,782	2,571,791	195,991
1986	12,503,511	7,119,550	5,383,961	5,884,515	6,618,996	9,713,893	2,789,618	2,572,479	[4]217,139
1987	12,766,642	7,231,085	5,535,557	5,932,056	6,834,586	9,973,254	2,793,388	2,602,350	[4]191,038
1988	13,055,337	7,436,768	5,618,569	6,001,896	7,053,441	10,161,388	2,893,949	2,673,567	220,382
1989	13,538,560	7,660,950	5,877,610	6,190,015	7,348,545	10,577,963	2,960,597	2,731,174	229,423
1990	13,818,637	7,820,985	5,997,652	6,283,909	7,534,728	10,844,717	2,973,920	2,760,227	213,693
1991	14,358,953	8,115,329	6,243,624	6,501,844	7,857,109	11,309,563	3,049,390	2,819,041	230,349
1992[5]	14,486,315	8,161,118	6,325,197	6,523,516	7,962,799	11,384,567	3,101,748	2,871,479	230,269
1993[6]	14,305,658	8,127,740	6,177,918	6,427,716	7,877,942	11,189,088	3,116,570	2,889,752	226,818

[1] Degree-credit enrollment only.
[2] Includes part-time resident students and all extension students.
[3] Large increases are due to the addition of schools accredited by the Accrediting Commission of Career Schools and Colleges of Technology.
[4] Because of imputation techniques, data are not consistent with figures for other years.
[5] Revised from previously published data.

[6] Preliminary data.
—Data not available.

SOURCE: U.S. Department of Education, National Center for Education Statistics, "Fall Enrollment in Colleges and Universities;" and Integrated Postsecondary Education Data System (IPEDS), "Fall Enrollment" surveys. (This table was prepared February 1995.)

Table 168.—Total fall enrollment in institutions of higher education, by control and type of institution: 1963 to 1993

Year	All institutions					Public institutions					Private institutions				
	Total	4-year			2-year	Total	4-year			2-year	Total	4-year			2-year
		Total	University	Other 4-year			Total	University	Other 4-year			Total	University	Other 4-year	
1	2	3	4	5	6	7	8	9	10	11	12	13	14	15	16
1963[1]	4,779,609	3,929,248	—	—	850,361	3,081,279	2,341,468	—	—	739,811	1,698,330	1,587,780	—	—	110,550
1964[1]	5,280,020	4,291,094	—	—	988,926	3,467,708	2,592,929	—	—	874,779	1,812,312	1,698,165	—	—	114,147
1965[1]	5,920,864	4,747,912	—	—	1,172,952	3,969,596	2,928,332	—	—	1,041,264	1,951,268	1,819,580	—	—	131,688
1966[1]	6,389,872	5,063,902	—	—	1,325,970	4,348,917	3,159,748	—	—	1,189,169	2,040,955	1,904,154	—	—	136,801
1967[1]	6,911,748	5,398,986	—	—	1,512,762	4,816,028	3,443,975	—	—	1,372,053	2,095,720	1,955,011	—	—	140,709
1968[1]	7,513,091	5,720,795	—	—	1,792,296	5,430,652	3,784,178	—	—	1,646,474	2,082,439	1,936,617	—	—	145,822
1969	8,004,660	5,937,127	—	—	2,067,533	5,896,868	3,962,522	—	—	1,934,346	2,107,792	1,974,605	—	—	133,187
1970	8,580,887	6,261,502	—	—	2,319,385	6,428,134	4,232,722	—	—	2,195,412	2,152,753	2,028,780	—	—	123,973
1971	8,948,644	6,369,355	—	—	2,579,289	6,804,309	4,346,990	—	—	2,457,319	2,144,335	2,022,365	—	—	121,970
1972	9,214,820	6,458,634	—	—	2,756,186	7,070,635	4,429,696	—	—	2,640,939	2,144,185	2,028,938	—	—	115,247
1973	9,602,123	6,590,023	—	—	3,012,100	7,419,516	4,529,895	—	—	2,889,621	2,182,607	2,060,128	—	—	122,479
1974	10,223,729	6,819,735	—	—	3,403,994	7,988,500	4,703,018	—	—	3,285,482	2,235,229	2,116,717	—	—	118,512
1975	11,184,859	7,214,740	2,838,266	4,376,474	3,970,119	8,834,508	4,998,142	2,124,221	2,873,921	3,836,366	2,350,351	2,216,598	714,045	1,502,553	133,753
1976	11,012,137	7,128,816	2,780,289	4,348,527	3,883,321	8,653,477	4,901,691	2,079,929	2,821,762	3,751,786	2,358,660	2,227,125	700,360	1,526,765	131,535
1977	11,285,787	7,242,845	2,793,418	4,449,427	4,042,942	8,846,993	4,945,224	2,070,032	2,875,192	3,901,769	2,438,794	2,297,621	723,386	1,574,235	141,173
1978	11,260,092	7,231,625	2,780,729	4,451,222	4,028,467	8,785,893	4,912,203	2,062,295	2,849,908	3,873,690	2,474,199	2,319,422	718,434	1,601,314	154,777
1979	11,569,899	7,353,233	2,839,582	4,513,651	4,216,666	9,036,822	4,980,012	2,099,525	2,880,487	4,056,810	2,533,077	2,373,221	740,057	1,633,164	159,856
1980	12,096,895	7,570,608	2,902,014	4,668,594	4,526,287	9,457,394	5,128,612	2,154,283	2,974,329	4,328,782	2,639,501	2,441,996	747,731	1,694,265	[2]197,505
1981	12,371,672	7,655,461	2,901,344	4,754,117	4,716,211	9,647,032	5,166,324	2,152,474	3,013,850	4,480,708	2,724,640	2,489,137	748,870	1,740,267	[2]235,503
1982	12,425,780	7,654,074	2,883,735	4,770,339	4,771,706	9,696,087	5,176,434	2,152,547	3,023,887	4,519,653	2,729,693	2,477,640	731,188	1,746,452	252,053
1983	12,464,661	7,741,195	2,888,813	4,852,382	4,723,466	9,682,734	5,223,404	2,154,790	3,068,614	4,459,330	2,781,927	2,517,791	734,023	1,783,768	264,136
1984	12,241,940	7,711,167	2,870,329	4,840,838	4,530,773	9,477,370	5,198,273	2,138,621	3,059,652	4,279,097	2,764,570	2,512,894	731,708	1,781,186	251,676
1985	12,247,055	7,715,978	2,870,692	4,845,286	4,531,077	9,479,273	5,209,540	2,141,112	3,068,428	4,269,733	2,767,782	2,506,438	729,580	1,776,858	261,344
1986	12,503,511	7,823,963	2,897,207	4,926,756	4,679,548	9,713,893	5,300,202	2,160,646	3,139,556	4,413,691	2,789,618	2,523,761	736,561	1,787,200	[3]265,857
1987	12,766,642	7,990,420	2,929,327	5,061,093	4,776,222	9,973,254	5,432,200	2,188,008	3,244,192	4,541,054	2,793,388	2,558,220	741,319	1,816,901	[3]235,168
1988	13,055,337	8,180,182	2,978,593	5,201,589	4,875,155	10,161,388	5,545,901	2,229,868	3,316,033	4,615,487	2,893,949	2,634,281	748,725	1,885,556	259,668
1989	13,538,560	8,387,671	3,019,115	5,368,556	5,150,889	10,577,963	5,694,303	2,266,056	3,428,247	4,883,660	2,960,597	2,693,368	753,059	1,940,309	267,229
1990	13,818,637	8,578,554	3,044,670	5,533,884	5,240,083	10,844,717	5,848,242	2,290,464	3,557,778	4,996,475	2,973,920	2,730,312	754,206	1,976,106	243,608
1991	14,358,953	8,707,053	3,065,429	5,641,624	5,651,900	11,309,563	5,904,748	2,301,222	3,603,526	5,404,815	3,049,390	2,802,305	764,207	2,038,098	247,085
1992[4]	14,486,315	8,763,925	3,050,345	5,713,580	5,722,390	11,384,567	5,900,012	2,283,834	3,616,178	5,484,555	3,101,748	2,863,913	766,511	2,097,402	237,835
1993[5]	14,305,658	8,739,791	3,022,728	5,717,063	5,565,867	11,189,088	5,851,760	2,259,692	3,592,068	5,337,328	3,116,570	2,888,031	763,036	2,124,995	228,539

—Data not available.

[1] Data for 2-year branch campuses of 4-year institutions are included with the 4-year institutions.
[2] Large increases are due to the addition of schools accredited by the Accrediting Commission of Career Schools and Colleges of Technology.
[3] Because of imputation techniques, data are not consistent with figures for other years.
[4] Revised from previously published data.
[5] Preliminary data.

SOURCE: U.S. Department of Education, National Center for Education Statistics, "Fall Enrollment in Colleges and Universities," and Integrated Postsecondary Education Data System (IPEDS), "Fall Enrollment" surveys. (This table was prepared March 1995.)

Table 169.—Total fall enrollment in institutions of higher education, by attendance status, sex, and age: Fall 1970 to fall 2000

[In thousands]

Sex and age	1970			1975			1980			1985			1987			1990			1993			2000 (projected)		
	Total	Full-time	Part-time	Total	Full-time	Part-time	Total	Full-time	Part-time	Total	Full-time	Part-time	Total	Full-time	Part-time	Total	Full-time	Part-time	Total	Full-time	Part-time	Total	Full-time	Part-time
1	2	3	4	5	6	7	8	9	10	11	12	13	14	15	16	17	18	19	20	21	22	23	24	25
Men and women, total	8,581	5,815	2,766	11,185	6,841	4,344	12,097	7,098	4,999	12,247	7,075	5,172	12,767	7,231	5,536	13,819	7,821	5,998	14,306	8,128	6,178	15,522	8,624	6,898
14 to 17 years old	259	242	17	278	242	36	247	216	31	235	203	32	237	142	95	167	141	26	175	159	16	246	227	19
18 and 19 years old	2,600	2,406	194	2,786	2,510	276	2,901	2,580	320	2,600	2,322	278	2,847	2,488	359	2,800	2,479	321	2,640	2,330	310	3,123	2,726	396
20 and 21 years old	1,880	1,647	233	2,243	1,854	390	2,423	2,060	364	2,383	1,975	408	2,504	2,024	480	2,619	2,121	498	2,708	2,219	488	2,849	2,304	545
22 to 24 years old	1,457	881	576	1,754	1,008	746	1,989	1,174	815	1,933	1,227	705	1,989	1,223	766	2,166	1,387	779	2,524	1,639	885	2,526	1,597	929
25 to 29 years old	1,074	407	668	1,774	692	1,082	1,871	610	1,261	1,953	695	1,258	1,930	693	1,237	2,063	802	1,261	2,008	755	1,253	1,979	688	1,291
30 to 34 years old	487	100	388	967	279	687	1,243	264	979	1,261	310	951	1,266	293	972	1,360	403	957	1,472	413	1,059	1,445	373	1,072
35 years old and over	823	134	689	1,383	256	1,127	1,422	193	1,229	1,885	345	1,540	1,993	367	1,626	2,644	487	2,157	2,779	613	2,167	3,356	708	2,648
Men, total	5,044	3,505	1,540	6,149	3,926	2,222	5,874	3,689	2,185	5,818	3,608	2,211	5,932	3,611	2,321	6,284	3,808	2,476	6,428	3,891	2,537	6,948	4,150	2,798
14 to 17 years old	130	124	5	126	109	17	99	84	15	121	102	19	114	69	46	82	70	12	83	72	10	126	114	12
18 and 19 years old	1,349	1,265	84	1,397	1,269	128	1,375	1,229	146	1,230	1,108	122	1,363	1,190	173	1,351	1,198	153	1,224	1,086	138	1,467	1,287	180
20 and 21 years old	1,095	990	105	1,245	1,053	192	1,259	1,104	154	1,216	1,027	189	1,258	1,029	229	1,304	1,055	250	1,294	1,084	209	1,347	1,118	229
22 to 24 years old	964	650	314	1,047	686	362	1,064	687	377	1,048	730	318	1,003	669	334	1,107	757	350	1,260	868	392	1,283	883	400
25 to 29 years old	783	327	456	1,122	474	649	993	379	615	991	395	596	964	371	593	976	413	563	950	386	564	945	342	603
30 to 34 years old	308	72	236	557	184	373	576	129	447	574	149	424	541	146	395	564	162	402	661	177	484	664	159	505
35 years old and over	415	75	340	654	152	502	507	77	430	639	97	542	690	138	552	901	154	747	955	216	739	1,118	247	870
Women, total	3,537	2,311	1,225	5,036	2,915	2,120	6,223	3,409	2,814	6,429	3,468	2,961	6,835	3,620	3,214	7,535	4,013	3,521	7,878	4,237	3,641	8,574	4,474	4,100
14 to 17 years old	129	117	12	152	133	19	148	132	17	113	101	12	123	73	50	85	71	13	93	87	6	119	113	7
18 and 19 years old	1,250	1,140	110	1,389	1,241	147	1,526	1,352	174	1,370	1,214	156	1,484	1,298	186	1,450	1,281	168	1,416	1,244	172	1,656	1,439	217
20 and 21 years old	786	657	128	998	800	198	1,165	955	209	1,166	948	218	1,246	995	251	1,315	1,067	248	1,414	1,135	279	1,502	1,186	316
22 to 24 years old	493	231	262	706	322	384	925	487	438	885	497	388	986	554	432	1,059	630	429	1,263	770	493	1,243	713	530
25 to 29 years old	291	80	212	652	218	433	878	232	646	962	299	662	966	323	643	1,087	389	699	1,058	369	689	1,034	347	687
30 to 34 years old	179	28	151	410	95	315	667	135	531	687	161	527	725	147	578	796	242	555	811	236	575	781	214	567
35 years old and over	409	59	349	729	105	625	914	115	799	1,246	248	998	1,303	229	1,074	1,743	333	1,410	1,824	397	1,427	2,239	461	1,778

NOTE.—Distribution by age is based on samples of the civilian noninstitutional population. Because of rounding, details may not add to totals.

SOURCE: U.S. Department of Education, National Center for Education Statistics, "Fall Enrollment in Institutions of Higher Education" surveys; Integrated Postsecondary Education Data System (IPEDS), "Fall Enrollment" surveys; Projections of Education Statistics to 2005; and U.S. Department of Commerce, Bureau of the Census, Current Population Reports, Social and Economic Characteristics of Students, various years. (This table was prepared June 1995.)

Table 170.—Total fall enrollment in institutions of higher education, by level, sex, age, and attendance status of student: Fall 1993

Attendance status and age of student	All levels			Undergraduate			First-professional			Graduate		
	Total	Men	Women	Total	Men	Women	Total	Men	Women	Total	Men	Women
1	2	3	4	5	6	7	8	9	10	11	12	13
All students	14,305,658	6,427,716	7,877,942	12,323,959	5,483,682	6,840,277	292,431	172,788	119,643	1,689,268	771,246	918,022
Under 18	245,920	98,896	147,024	245,286	98,647	146,639	56	27	29	578	222	356
18 and 19	2,722,131	1,237,569	1,484,562	2,720,798	1,237,102	1,483,696	156	84	72	1,177	383	794
20 and 21	2,607,019	1,228,707	1,378,312	2,589,995	1,221,262	1,368,733	6,782	3,167	3,615	10,242	4,278	5,964
22 to 24	2,492,269	1,252,571	1,239,698	2,124,328	1,077,790	1,046,538	107,913	60,625	47,288	260,028	114,156	145,872
25 to 29	2,025,972	980,118	1,045,854	1,446,230	674,123	772,107	99,848	62,727	37,121	479,894	243,268	236,626
30 to 34	1,338,069	579,400	758,669	1,008,988	401,347	607,641	33,117	21,020	12,097	295,964	157,033	138,931
35 to 39	1,019,588	388,960	630,628	787,287	280,941	506,346	17,890	10,650	7,240	214,411	97,369	117,042
40 to 49	1,181,248	399,544	781,704	872,239	287,473	584,766	14,724	7,749	6,975	294,285	104,322	189,963
50 to 64	339,497	113,834	225,663	260,447	87,359	173,088	3,638	1,702	1,936	75,412	24,773	50,639
65 and over	78,375	30,997	47,378	72,877	28,554	44,323	258	146	112	5,240	2,297	2,943
Age unknown	255,570	117,120	138,450	195,484	89,084	106,400	8,049	4,891	3,158	52,037	23,145	28,892
Full-time	8,127,740	3,890,603	4,237,137	7,179,482	3,381,997	3,797,485	259,764	153,873	105,891	688,494	354,733	333,761
Under 18	111,151	44,204	66,947	110,937	44,117	66,820	45	20	25	169	67	102
18 and 19	2,324,860	1,057,170	1,267,690	2,323,726	1,056,782	1,266,944	153	82	71	981	306	675
20 and 21	2,070,480	983,843	1,086,637	2,055,691	977,319	1,078,372	6,707	3,128	3,579	8,082	3,396	4,686
22 to 24	1,583,062	840,071	742,991	1,304,599	700,230	604,369	104,670	58,865	45,805	173,793	80,976	92,817
25 to 29	884,787	472,116	412,671	564,648	285,851	278,797	89,976	56,723	33,253	230,163	129,542	100,621
30 to 34	433,467	200,114	233,353	295,838	117,483	178,355	26,414	16,825	9,589	111,215	65,806	45,409
35 to 39	276,170	111,100	165,070	199,982	71,005	128,977	13,077	7,772	5,305	63,111	32,323	30,788
40 to 49	268,390	103,182	165,208	190,408	69,746	120,662	9,685	5,201	4,484	68,297	28,235	40,062
50 to 64	57,723	21,942	35,781	40,268	15,138	25,130	2,121	1,033	1,088	15,334	5,771	9,563
65 and over	9,359	4,356	5,003	8,271	3,806	4,465	170	105	65	918	445	473
Age unknown	108,291	52,505	55,786	85,114	40,520	44,594	6,746	4,119	2,627	16,431	7,866	8,565
Part-time	6,177,918	2,537,113	3,640,805	5,144,477	2,101,685	3,042,792	32,667	18,915	13,752	1,000,774	416,513	584,261
Under 18	134,769	54,692	80,077	134,349	54,530	79,819	11	7	4	409	155	254
18 and 19	397,271	180,399	216,872	397,072	180,320	216,752	3	2	1	196	77	119
20 and 21	536,539	244,864	291,675	534,304	243,943	290,361	75	39	36	2,160	882	1,278
22 to 24	909,207	412,500	496,707	819,729	377,560	442,169	3,243	1,760	1,483	86,235	33,180	53,055
25 to 29	1,141,185	508,002	633,183	881,582	388,272	493,310	9,872	6,004	3,868	249,731	113,726	136,005
30 to 34	904,602	379,286	525,316	713,150	283,864	429,286	6,703	4,195	2,508	184,749	91,227	93,522
35 to 39	743,418	277,860	465,558	587,305	209,936	377,369	4,813	2,878	1,935	151,300	65,046	86,254
40 to 49	912,858	296,362	616,496	681,831	217,727	464,104	5,039	2,548	2,491	225,988	76,087	149,901
50 to 64	281,774	91,892	189,882	220,179	72,221	147,958	1,517	669	848	60,078	19,002	41,076
65 and over	69,016	26,641	42,375	64,606	24,748	39,858	88	41	47	4,322	1,852	2,470
Age unknown	147,279	64,615	82,664	110,370	48,564	61,806	1,303	772	531	35,606	15,279	20,327
Percentage distribution												
All students	100.0	100.0	100.0	100.0	100.0	100.0	100.0	100.0	100.0	100.0	100.0	100.0
Under 18	1.7	1.5	1.9	2.0	1.8	2.1	(¹)	(¹)	(¹)	(¹)	(¹)	(¹)
18 and 19	19.0	19.3	18.8	22.1	22.6	21.7	0.1	(¹)	0.1	0.1	(¹)	0.1
20 and 21	18.2	19.1	17.5	21.0	22.3	20.0	2.3	1.8	3.0	0.6	0.6	0.6
22 to 24	17.4	19.5	15.7	17.2	19.7	15.3	36.9	35.1	39.5	15.4	14.8	15.9
25 to 29	14.2	15.2	13.3	11.7	12.3	11.3	34.1	36.3	31.0	28.4	31.5	25.8
30 to 34	9.4	9.0	9.6	8.2	7.3	8.9	11.3	12.2	10.1	17.5	20.4	15.1
35 to 39	7.1	6.1	8.0	6.4	5.1	7.4	6.1	6.2	6.1	12.7	12.6	12.7
40 to 49	8.3	6.2	9.9	7.1	5.2	8.5	5.0	4.5	5.8	17.4	13.5	20.7
50 to 64	2.4	1.8	2.9	2.1	1.6	2.5	1.2	1.0	1.6	4.5	3.2	5.5
65 and over	0.5	0.5	0.6	0.6	0.5	0.6	0.1	0.1	0.1	0.3	0.3	0.3
Age unknown	1.8	1.8	1.8	1.6	1.6	1.6	2.8	2.8	2.6	3.1	3.0	3.1
Full-time	100.0	100.0	100.0	100.0	100.0	100.0	100.0	100.0	100.0	100.0	100.0	100.0
Under 18	1.4	1.1	1.6	1.5	1.3	1.8	(¹)	(¹)	(¹)	(¹)	(¹)	0.2
18 and 19	28.6	27.2	29.9	32.4	31.2	33.4	0.1	0.1	0.1	0.1	0.1	0.2
20 and 21	25.5	25.3	25.6	28.6	28.9	28.4	2.6	2.0	3.4	1.2	1.0	1.4
22 to 24	19.5	21.6	17.5	18.2	20.7	15.9	40.3	38.3	43.3	25.2	22.8	27.8
25 to 29	10.9	12.1	9.7	7.9	8.5	7.3	34.6	36.9	31.4	33.4	36.5	30.1
30 to 34	5.3	5.1	5.5	4.1	3.5	4.7	10.2	10.9	9.1	16.2	18.6	13.6
35 to 39	3.4	2.9	3.9	2.8	2.1	3.4	5.0	5.1	5.0	9.2	9.1	9.2
40 to 49	3.3	2.7	3.9	2.7	2.1	3.2	3.7	3.4	4.2	9.9	8.0	12.0
50 to 64	0.7	0.6	0.8	0.6	0.4	0.7	0.8	0.7	1.0	2.2	1.6	2.9
65 and over	0.1	0.1	0.1	0.1	0.1	0.1	0.1	0.1	0.1	0.1	0.1	0.1
Age unknown	1.3	1.3	1.3	1.2	1.2	1.2	2.6	2.7	2.5	2.4	2.2	2.6
Part-time	100.0	100.0	100.0	100.0	100.0	100.0	100.0	100.0	100.0	100.0	100.0	100.0
Under 18	2.2	2.2	2.2	2.6	2.6	2.6	(¹)	(¹)	(¹)	(¹)	(¹)	(¹)
18 and 19	6.4	7.1	6.0	7.7	8.6	7.1	(¹)	(¹)	(¹)	(¹)	(¹)	0.2
20 and 21	8.7	9.7	8.0	10.4	11.6	9.5	0.2	0.2	0.3	0.2	0.2	0.2
22 to 24	14.7	16.3	13.6	15.9	18.0	14.5	9.9	9.3	10.8	8.6	8.0	9.1
25 to 29	18.5	20.0	17.4	17.1	18.5	16.2	30.2	31.7	28.1	25.0	27.3	23.3
30 to 34	14.6	14.9	14.4	13.9	13.5	14.1	20.5	22.2	18.2	18.5	21.9	16.0
35 to 39	12.0	11.0	12.8	11.4	10.0	12.4	14.7	15.2	14.1	15.1	15.6	14.8
40 to 49	14.8	11.7	16.9	13.3	10.4	15.3	15.4	13.5	18.1	22.6	18.3	25.7
50 to 64	4.6	3.6	5.2	4.3	3.4	4.9	4.6	3.5	6.2	6.0	4.6	7.0
65 and over	1.1	1.1	1.2	1.3	1.2	1.3	0.3	0.2	0.3	0.4	0.4	0.4
Age unknown	2.4	2.5	2.3	2.1	2.3	2.0	4.0	4.1	3.9	3.6	3.7	3.5

¹ Less than .05 percent.

NOTE.—Because of rounding, details may not add to 100.0 percent.

SOURCE: U.S. Department of Education, National Center for Education Statistics, Integrated Postsecondary Education Data System, "Fall Enrollment, 1993" survey. (This table was prepared April 1995.)

Table 171.—Total fall enrollment in institutions of higher education, by type and control of institution, and age and attendance status of student: 1993

Attendance status and age of student	All institutions			Public institutions			Private institutions		
	Total	4-year	2-year	Total	4-year	2-year	Total	4-year	2-year
1	2	3	4	5	6	7	8	9	10
All students	14,305,658	8,739,791	5,565,867	11,189,088	5,851,760	5,337,328	3,116,570	2,888,031	228,539
Under 18	245,920	112,217	133,703	196,178	66,397	129,781	49,742	45,820	3,922
18 and 19	2,722,131	1,703,521	1,018,610	2,109,469	1,140,149	969,320	612,662	563,372	49,290
20 and 21	2,607,019	1,789,498	817,521	2,023,501	1,239,368	784,133	583,518	550,130	33,388
22 to 24	2,492,269	1,707,290	784,979	2,024,090	1,270,865	753,225	468,179	436,425	31,754
25 to 29	2,025,972	1,233,292	792,680	1,582,751	821,872	760,879	443,221	411,420	31,801
30 to 34	1,338,069	706,440	631,629	1,064,932	456,191	608,741	273,137	250,249	22,888
35 to 39	1,019,588	519,311	500,277	819,190	335,086	484,104	200,398	184,225	16,173
40 to 49	1,181,248	612,919	568,329	942,905	389,907	552,998	238,343	223,012	15,331
50 to 64	339,497	151,039	188,458	276,864	92,736	184,128	62,633	58,303	4,330
65 and over	78,375	22,079	56,296	69,019	13,865	55,154	9,356	8,214	1,142
Age unknown	255,570	182,185	73,385	80,189	25,324	54,865	175,381	156,861	18,520
Full-time	8,127,740	6,084,421	2,043,319	5,962,562	4,074,055	1,888,507	2,165,178	2,010,366	154,812
Under 18	111,151	75,070	36,081	75,580	42,712	32,868	35,571	32,358	3,213
18 and 19	2,324,860	1,625,439	699,421	1,729,060	1,075,406	653,654	595,800	550,033	45,767
20 and 21	2,070,480	1,644,331	426,149	1,520,282	1,120,894	399,388	550,198	523,437	26,761
22 to 24	1,583,062	1,303,527	279,535	1,217,718	959,668	258,050	365,344	343,859	21,485
25 to 29	884,787	672,135	212,652	636,950	442,260	194,690	247,837	229,875	17,962
30 to 34	433,467	291,480	141,987	318,994	188,274	130,720	114,473	103,206	11,267
35 to 39	276,170	177,314	98,856	203,559	111,990	91,569	72,611	65,324	7,287
40 to 49	268,390	172,244	96,146	193,412	103,577	89,835	74,978	68,667	6,311
50 to 64	57,723	35,556	22,167	37,945	17,883	20,062	19,778	17,673	2,105
65 and over	9,359	5,355	4,004	4,544	1,477	3,067	4,815	3,878	937
Age unknown	108,291	81,970	26,321	24,518	9,914	14,604	83,773	72,056	11,717
Part-time	6,177,918	2,655,370	3,522,548	5,226,526	1,777,705	3,448,821	951,392	877,665	73,727
Under 18	134,769	37,147	97,622	120,598	23,685	96,913	14,171	13,462	709
18 and 19	397,271	78,082	319,189	380,409	64,743	315,666	16,862	13,339	3,523
20 and 21	536,539	145,167	391,372	503,219	118,474	384,745	33,320	26,693	6,627
22 to 24	909,207	403,763	505,444	806,372	311,197	495,175	102,835	92,566	10,269
25 to 29	1,141,185	561,157	580,028	945,801	379,612	566,189	195,384	181,545	13,839
30 to 34	904,602	414,960	489,642	745,938	267,917	478,021	158,664	147,043	11,621
35 to 39	743,418	341,997	401,421	615,631	223,096	392,535	127,787	118,901	8,886
40 to 49	912,858	440,675	472,183	749,493	286,330	463,163	163,365	154,345	9,020
50 to 64	281,774	115,483	166,291	238,919	74,853	164,066	42,855	40,630	2,225
65 and over	69,016	16,724	52,292	64,475	12,388	52,087	4,541	4,336	205
Age unknown	147,279	100,215	47,064	55,671	15,410	40,261	91,608	84,805	6,803
	Percentage distribution								
All students	100.0	100.0	100.0	100.0	100.0	100.0	100.0	100.0	100.0
Under 18	1.7	1.3	2.4	1.8	1.1	2.4	1.6	1.6	1.7
18 and 19	19.0	19.5	18.3	18.9	19.5	18.2	19.7	19.5	21.6
20 and 21	18.2	20.5	14.7	18.1	21.2	14.7	18.7	19.0	14.6
22 to 24	17.4	19.5	14.1	18.1	21.7	14.1	15.0	15.1	13.9
25 to 29	14.2	14.1	14.2	14.1	14.0	14.3	14.2	14.2	13.9
30 to 34	9.4	8.1	11.3	9.5	7.8	11.4	8.8	8.7	10.0
35 to 39	7.1	5.9	9.0	7.3	5.7	9.1	6.4	6.4	10.0
40 to 49	8.3	7.0	10.2	8.4	6.7	10.4	7.6	7.7	7.1
50 to 64	2.4	1.7	3.4	2.5	1.6	3.4	2.0	2.0	6.7
65 and over	0.5	0.3	1.0	0.6	0.2	1.0	0.3	0.3	1.9
Age unknown	1.8	2.1	1.3	0.7	0.4	1.0	5.6	5.4	0.5
									8.1
Full-time	100.0	100.0	100.0	100.0	100.0	100.0	100.0	100.0	100.0
Under 18	1.4	1.2	1.8	1.3	1.0	1.7	1.6	1.6	2.1
18 and 19	28.6	26.7	34.2	29.0	26.4	34.6	27.5	27.4	29.6
20 and 21	25.5	27.0	20.9	25.5	27.5	21.1	25.4	26.0	17.3
22 to 24	19.5	21.4	13.7	20.4	23.6	13.7	16.9	17.1	13.9
25 to 29	10.9	11.0	10.4	10.7	10.9	10.3	11.4	11.4	11.6
30 to 34	5.3	4.8	6.9	5.3	4.6	6.9	5.3	5.1	7.3
35 to 39	3.4	2.9	4.8	3.4	2.7	4.8	3.4	3.2	4.7
40 to 49	3.3	2.8	4.7	3.2	2.5	4.8	3.5	3.4	4.1
50 to 64	0.7	0.6	1.1	0.6	0.4	1.1	0.9	0.9	1.4
65 and over	0.1	0.1	0.2	0.1	0.0	0.2	0.2	0.2	0.2
Age unknown	1.3	1.3	1.3	0.4	0.2	0.8	3.9	3.6	7.6
Part-time	100.0	100.0	100.0	100.0	100.0	100.0	100.0	100.0	100.0
Under 18	2.2	1.4	2.8	2.3	1.3	2.8	1.5	1.5	1.0
18 and 19	6.4	2.9	9.1	7.3	3.6	9.2	1.8	1.5	4.8
20 and 21	8.7	5.5	11.1	9.6	6.7	11.2	3.5	3.0	9.0
22 to 24	14.7	15.2	14.3	15.4	17.5	14.4	10.8	10.5	13.9
25 to 29	18.5	21.1	16.5	18.1	21.4	16.4	20.5	20.7	18.8
30 to 34	14.6	15.6	13.9	14.3	15.1	13.9	16.7	16.8	15.8
35 to 39	12.0	12.9	11.4	11.8	12.5	11.4	13.4	13.5	12.1
40 to 49	14.8	16.6	13.4	14.3	16.1	13.4	17.2	17.6	12.2
50 to 64	4.6	4.3	4.7	4.6	4.2	4.8	4.5	4.6	3.0
65 and over	1.1	0.6	1.5	1.2	0.7	1.5	0.5	0.5	0.3
Age unknown	2.4	3.8	1.3	1.1	0.9	1.2	9.6	9.7	9.2

NOTE.—Because of rounding, details may not add to 100.0 percent.

SOURCE: U.S. Department of Education, National Center for Education Statistics, Integrated Postsecondary Education Data System, "Fall Enrollment, 1993" survey. (This table was prepared April 1995.)

Table 172.—Total fall enrollment in institutions of higher education, by level of enrollment, sex, attendance status, and type and control of institution: 1992 and 1993

Attendance status, and type and control of institution	Total			Undergraduate			First-professional			Graduate		
	Total	Men	Women	Total	Men	Women	Total	Men	Women	Total	Men	Women
1	2	3	4	5	6	7	8	9	10	11	12	13
1992[1]												
Total	14,486,315	6,523,516	7,962,799	12,536,656	5,582,463	6,954,193	280,922	168,620	112,302	1,668,737	772,433	896,304
Full-time	8,161,118	3,926,441	4,234,677	7,243,442	3,424,275	3,819,167	252,138	151,025	101,113	665,538	351,141	314,397
Part-time	6,325,197	2,597,075	3,728,122	5,293,214	2,158,188	3,135,026	28,784	17,595	11,189	1,003,199	421,292	581,907
Total 4-year	8,763,925	4,110,240	4,653,685	6,814,307	3,169,197	3,645,110	280,922	168,620	112,302	1,668,696	772,423	896,273
Full-time	6,081,112	2,974,625	3,106,487	5,163,437	2,472,459	2,690,978	252,138	151,025	101,113	665,537	351,141	314,396
Part-time	2,682,813	1,135,615	1,547,198	1,650,870	696,738	954,132	28,784	17,595	11,189	1,003,159	421,282	581,877
Total 2-year	5,722,390	2,413,276	3,309,114	5,722,349	2,413,266	3,309,083	—	—	—	41	10	31
Full-time	2,080,006	951,816	1,128,190	2,080,005	951,816	1,128,189	—	—	—	1	—	1
Part-time	3,642,384	1,461,460	2,180,924	3,642,344	1,461,450	2,180,894	—	—	—	40	10	30
Public, total	11,384,567	5,074,396	6,310,171	10,216,297	4,536,925	5,679,372	110,689	63,511	47,178	1,057,581	473,960	583,621
Full-time	6,010,875	2,883,119	3,127,756	5,484,363	2,601,606	2,882,757	105,895	60,842	45,053	420,617	220,671	199,946
Part-time	5,373,692	2,191,277	3,182,415	4,731,934	1,935,319	2,796,615	4,794	2,669	2,125	636,964	253,289	383,675
Public 4-year	5,900,012	2,765,229	3,134,783	4,731,783	2,227,768	2,504,015	110,689	63,511	47,178	1,057,540	473,950	583,590
Full-time	4,095,310	2,005,043	2,090,267	3,568,799	1,723,530	1,845,269	105,895	60,842	45,053	420,616	220,671	199,945
Part-time	1,804,702	760,186	1,044,516	1,162,984	504,238	658,746	4,794	2,669	2,125	636,924	253,279	383,645
Public 2-year	5,484,555	2,309,167	3,175,388	5,484,514	2,309,157	3,175,357	—	—	—	41	10	31
Full-time	1,915,565	878,076	1,037,489	1,915,564	878,076	1,037,488	—	—	—	1	—	1
Part-time	3,568,990	1,431,091	2,137,899	3,568,950	1,431,081	2,137,869	—	—	—	40	10	30
Private, total	3,101,748	1,449,120	1,652,628	2,320,359	1,045,538	1,274,821	170,233	105,109	65,124	611,156	298,473	312,683
Full-time	2,150,243	1,043,322	1,106,921	1,759,079	822,669	936,410	146,243	90,183	56,060	244,921	130,470	114,451
Part-time	951,505	405,798	545,707	561,280	222,869	338,411	23,990	14,926	9,064	366,235	168,003	198,232
Private 4-year	2,863,913	1,345,011	1,518,902	2,082,524	941,429	1,141,095	170,233	105,109	65,124	611,156	298,473	312,683
Full-time	1,985,802	969,582	1,016,220	1,594,638	748,929	845,709	146,243	90,183	56,060	244,921	130,470	114,451
Part-time	878,111	375,429	502,682	487,886	192,500	295,386	23,990	14,926	9,064	366,235	168,003	198,232
Private 2-year	237,835	104,109	133,726	237,835	104,109	133,726	—	—	—	—	—	—
Full-time	164,441	73,740	90,701	164,441	73,740	90,701	—	—	—	—	—	—
Part-time	73,394	30,369	43,025	73,394	30,369	43,025	—	—	—	—	—	—
1993[2]												
Total	14,305,658	6,427,716	7,877,942	12,323,959	5,483,682	6,840,277	292,431	172,788	119,643	1,689,268	771,246	918,022
Full-time	8,127,740	3,890,603	4,237,137	7,179,482	3,381,997	3,797,485	259,764	153,873	105,891	688,494	354,733	333,761
Part-time	6,177,918	2,537,113	3,640,805	5,144,477	2,101,685	3,042,792	32,667	18,915	13,752	1,000,774	416,513	584,261
Total 4-year	8,739,791	4,082,257	4,657,534	6,758,398	3,138,286	3,620,112	292,431	172,788	119,643	1,688,962	771,183	917,779
Full-time	6,084,421	2,962,387	3,122,034	5,136,163	2,453,781	2,682,382	259,764	153,873	105,891	688,494	354,733	333,761
Part-time	2,655,370	1,119,870	1,535,500	1,622,235	684,505	937,730	32,667	18,915	13,752	1,000,468	416,450	584,018
Total 2-year	5,565,867	2,345,459	3,220,408	5,565,561	2,345,396	3,220,165	—	—	—	306	63	243
Full-time	2,043,319	928,216	1,115,103	2,043,319	928,216	1,115,103	—	—	—	—	—	—
Part-time	3,522,548	1,417,243	2,105,305	3,522,242	1,417,180	2,105,062	—	—	—	306	63	243
Public, total	11,189,088	4,984,511	6,204,577	10,011,787	4,447,266	5,564,521	113,654	63,973	49,681	1,063,647	473,272	590,375
Full-time	5,962,562	2,848,010	3,114,552	5,425,772	2,565,659	2,860,113	108,088	61,023	47,065	428,702	221,328	207,374
Part-time	5,226,526	2,136,501	3,090,025	4,586,015	1,881,607	2,704,408	5,566	2,950	2,616	634,945	251,944	383,001
Public 4-year	5,851,760	2,739,819	3,111,941	4,674,765	2,202,637	2,472,128	113,654	63,973	49,681	1,063,341	473,209	590,132
Full-time	4,074,055	1,989,410	2,084,645	3,537,265	1,707,059	1,830,206	108,088	61,023	47,065	428,702	221,328	207,374
Part-time	1,777,705	750,409	1,027,296	1,137,500	495,578	641,922	5,566	2,950	2,616	634,639	251,881	382,758
Public 2-year	5,337,328	2,244,692	3,092,636	5,337,022	2,244,629	3,092,393	—	—	—	306	63	243
Full-time	1,888,507	858,600	1,029,907	1,888,507	858,600	1,029,907	—	—	—	—	—	—
Part-time	3,448,821	1,386,092	2,062,729	3,448,515	1,386,029	2,062,486	—	—	—	306	63	243
Private, total	3,116,570	1,443,205	1,673,365	2,312,172	1,036,416	1,275,756	178,777	108,815	69,962	625,621	297,974	327,647
Full-time	2,165,178	1,042,593	1,122,585	1,753,710	816,338	937,372	151,676	92,850	58,826	259,792	133,405	126,387
Part-time	951,392	400,612	550,780	558,462	220,078	338,384	27,101	15,965	11,136	365,829	164,569	201,260
Private 4-year	2,888,031	1,342,438	1,545,593	2,083,633	935,649	1,147,984	178,777	108,815	69,962	625,621	297,974	327,647
Full-time	2,010,366	972,977	1,037,389	1,598,898	746,722	852,176	151,676	92,850	58,826	259,792	133,405	126,387
Part-time	877,665	369,461	508,204	484,735	188,927	295,808	27,101	15,965	11,136	365,829	164,569	201,260
Private 2-year	228,539	100,767	127,772	228,539	100,767	127,772	—	—	—	—	—	—
Full-time	154,812	69,616	85,196	154,812	69,616	85,196	—	—	—	—	—	—
Part-time	73,727	31,151	42,576	73,727	31,151	42,576	—	—	—	—	—	—

[1] Revised from previously published data.
[2] Preliminary data.
—Not applicable.

SOURCE: U.S. Department of Education, National Center for Education Statistics, Integrated Postsecondary Education Data System (IPEDS), "Fall Enrollment" surveys. (This table was prepared January 1995.)

Table 173.—Total fall enrollment in institutions of higher education, by type and control of institution, attendance status, and sex of student: 1970 to 1993

Type and control of institution, sex and attendance status of student	1970	1975	1980	1985	1987	1988	1989	1990	1991	1992[1]	1993[2]
1	2	3	4	5	6	7	8	9	10	11	12
Total	8,580,887	11,184,859	12,096,895	12,247,055	12,766,642	13,055,337	13,538,560	13,818,637	14,358,953	14,486,315	14,305,658
Full-time	5,816,290	6,841,334	7,097,958	7,075,221	7,231,085	7,436,768	7,660,950	7,820,985	8,115,329	8,161,118	8,127,740
Men	3,504,095	3,926,753	3,689,244	3,607,720	3,610,888	3,661,779	3,740,243	3,807,752	3,929,375	3,926,441	3,890,603
Women	2,312,195	2,914,581	3,408,714	3,467,501	3,620,197	3,774,989	3,920,707	4,013,233	4,185,954	4,234,677	4,237,137
Part-time	2,764,597	4,343,525	4,998,937	5,171,834	5,535,557	5,618,569	5,877,610	5,997,652	6,243,624	6,325,197	6,177,918
Men	1,539,547	2,222,244	2,185,130	2,210,730	2,321,168	2,340,117	2,449,772	2,476,157	2,572,469	2,597,075	2,537,113
Women	1,225,050	2,121,281	2,813,807	2,961,104	3,214,389	3,278,452	3,427,838	3,521,495	3,671,155	3,728,122	3,640,805
4-year, total	6,261,502	7,214,740	7,570,608	7,715,978	7,990,420	8,180,182	8,387,671	8,578,554	8,707,053	8,763,925	8,739,791
Full-time	4,587,379	5,080,256	5,344,163	5,384,614	5,522,416	5,693,176	5,805,249	5,937,023	6,040,799	6,081,112	6,084,421
Men	2,732,796	2,891,192	2,809,528	2,781,412	2,790,721	2,843,186	2,870,555	2,926,360	2,967,978	2,974,625	2,962,387
Women	1,854,583	2,189,064	2,534,635	2,603,202	2,731,695	2,849,990	2,934,694	3,010,663	3,072,821	3,106,487	3,122,034
Part-time	1,674,123	2,134,484	2,226,445	2,331,364	2,468,004	2,487,006	2,582,422	2,641,531	2,666,254	2,682,813	2,655,370
Men	936,189	1,092,461	1,017,813	1,034,804	1,068,512	1,069,021	1,102,660	1,124,780	1,131,956	1,135,615	1,119,870
Women	737,934	1,042,023	1,208,632	1,296,560	1,399,492	1,417,985	1,479,762	1,516,751	1,534,298	1,547,198	1,535,500
Public 4-year	4,232,722	4,998,142	5,128,612	5,209,540	5,432,200	5,545,901	5,694,303	5,848,242	5,904,748	5,900,012	5,851,760
Full-time	3,086,491	3,469,821	3,592,193	3,623,341	3,736,150	3,842,375	3,934,437	4,033,654	4,088,970	4,095,310	4,074,055
Men	1,813,584	1,947,823	1,873,397	1,863,689	1,882,064	1,910,326	1,937,888	1,982,369	2,005,941	2,005,043	1,989,410
Women	1,272,907	1,521,998	1,718,796	1,759,652	1,854,086	1,932,049	1,996,549	2,051,285	2,083,029	2,090,267	2,084,645
Part-time	1,146,231	1,528,321	1,536,419	1,586,199	1,696,050	1,703,526	1,759,866	1,814,588	1,815,778	1,804,702	1,777,705
Men	609,422	760,469	685,051	693,115	722,562	721,832	743,137	764,248	764,969	760,186	750,409
Women	536,809	767,852	851,368	893,084	973,488	981,694	1,016,729	1,050,340	1,050,809	1,044,516	1,027,296
Private 4-year	2,028,780	2,216,598	2,441,996	2,506,438	2,558,220	2,634,281	2,693,368	2,730,312	2,802,305	2,863,913	2,888,031
Full-time	1,500,888	1,610,435	1,751,970	1,761,273	1,786,266	1,850,801	1,870,812	1,903,369	1,951,829	1,985,802	2,010,366
Men	919,212	943,369	936,131	917,723	908,657	932,860	932,667	943,991	962,037	969,582	972,977
Women	581,676	667,066	815,839	843,550	877,609	917,941	938,145	959,378	989,792	1,016,220	1,037,389
Part-time	527,892	606,163	690,026	745,165	771,954	783,480	822,556	826,943	850,476	878,111	877,665
Men	326,767	331,992	332,762	341,689	345,950	347,189	359,523	360,532	366,987	375,429	369,461
Women	201,125	274,171	357,264	403,476	426,004	436,291	463,033	466,411	483,489	502,682	508,204
2-year, total	2,319,385	3,970,119	4,526,287	4,531,077	4,776,222	4,875,155	5,150,889	5,240,083	5,651,900	5,722,390	5,565,867
Full-time	1,228,911	1,761,078	1,753,795	1,690,607	1,708,669	1,743,592	1,855,701	1,883,962	2,074,530	2,080,006	2,043,319
Men	771,299	1,035,561	879,716	826,308	820,167	818,593	869,688	881,392	961,397	951,816	928,216
Women	457,612	725,517	874,079	864,299	888,502	924,999	986,013	1,002,570	1,113,133	1,128,190	1,115,103
Part-time	1,090,474	2,209,041	2,772,492	2,840,470	3,067,553	3,131,563	3,295,188	3,356,121	3,577,370	3,642,384	3,522,548
Men	603,358	1,129,783	1,167,317	1,175,926	1,252,656	1,271,096	1,347,112	1,351,377	1,440,513	1,461,460	1,417,243
Women	487,116	1,079,258	1,605,175	1,664,544	1,814,897	1,860,467	1,948,076	2,004,744	2,136,857	2,180,924	2,105,305
Public 2-year	2,195,412	3,836,366	4,328,782	4,269,733	4,541,054	4,615,487	4,883,660	4,996,475	5,404,815	5,484,555	5,337,328
Full-time	1,129,165	1,662,621	1,595,493	1,496,905	1,530,912	1,567,973	1,674,249	1,716,843	1,885,607	1,915,565	1,888,507
Men	720,440	988,701	811,871	742,673	744,110	745,912	793,251	810,664	881,576	878,076	858,600
Women	408,725	673,920	783,622	754,232	786,802	822,061	880,998	906,179	1,004,031	1,037,489	1,029,907
Part-time	1,066,247	2,173,745	2,733,289	2,772,828	3,010,142	3,047,514	3,209,411	3,279,632	3,519,208	3,568,990	3,448,821
Men	589,439	1,107,680	1,152,268	1,138,011	1,224,730	1,230,888	1,302,074	1,317,730	1,413,870	1,431,091	1,386,092
Women	476,808	1,066,065	1,581,021	1,634,817	1,785,412	1,816,626	1,907,337	1,961,902	2,105,338	2,137,899	2,062,729
Private 2-year	123,973	133,753	[3] 197,505	261,344	[4] 235,168	259,668	267,229	243,608	247,085	237,835	228,539
Full-time	99,746	98,457	[3] 158,302	193,702	[4] 177,757	175,619	181,452	167,119	188,923	164,441	154,812
Men	50,859	46,860	[3] 67,845	83,635	[4] 76,057	72,681	76,437	70,728	79,821	73,740	69,616
Women	48,887	51,597	[3] 90,457	110,067	[4] 101,700	102,938	105,015	96,391	109,102	90,701	85,196
Part-time	24,227	35,296	[3] 39,203	67,642	[4] 57,411	84,049	85,777	76,489	58,162	73,394	73,727
Men	13,919	22,103	[3] 15,049	37,915	[4] 27,926	40,208	45,038	33,647	26,643	73,394[sic]	73,727[sic]
Women	10,308	13,193	[3] 24,154	29,727	[4] 29,485	43,841	40,739	42,842	31,519	43,025	42,576

[1] Data revised from previously published figures.
[2] Preliminary data.
[3] Large increase is due to the addition of schools accredited by the Accrediting Commission of Career Schools and Colleges of Technology.
[4] Because of imputation techniques, data are not consistent with figures for other years.

SOURCE: U.S. Department of Education, National Center for Education Statistics, *Fall Enrollment in Colleges and Universities,* and Integrated Postsecondary Education Data Systems (IPEDS), "Fall Enrollment" surveys. (This table was prepared February 1995.)

Table 174.—Fall enrollment and number of institutions of higher education, by affiliation [1] of institution: 1980 to 1993

Affiliation	Enrollment			Fall 1993 [3]					Number of institutions [2]	
	Total, fall 1980	Total, fall 1990	Total, fall 1992	Total	Full-time Men	Full-time Women	Part-time Men	Part-time Women	Fall 1980	Fall 1993
1	2	3	4	5	6	7	8	9	10	11
All institutions	12,096,895	13,818,637	14,486,315	14,305,658	3,890,603	4,237,137	2,537,113	3,640,805	3,226	3,550
Public institutions	9,457,394	10,844,717	11,384,567	11,189,088	2,848,010	3,114,552	2,136,501	3,090,025	1,493	1,594
Private institutions	2,639,501	2,973,920	3,101,748	3,116,570	1,042,593	1,122,585	400,612	550,780	1,733	1,956
Independent nonprofit	1,521,614	1,471,446	1,506,699	1,497,743	517,738	517,273	203,528	259,204	795	709
Proprietary	111,714	213,693	230,269	226,818	81,584	77,118	35,024	33,092	164	313
Religiously affiliated	1,006,173	1,288,781	1,364,780	1,392,009	443,271	528,194	162,060	258,484	774	934
Advent Christian Church	143	—	—	—	—	—	—	—	1	—
African Methodist Episcopal Zion Church	1,091	88	—	—	—	—	—	—	3	—
African Methodist Episcopal	4,541	3,220	3,149	3,643	1,415	1,851	146	231	6	6
American Baptist	6,131	10,800	10,859	11,767	2,765	3,546	1,828	3,628	11	12
American Evangelical Lutheran Church	—	—	783	819	415	264	59	81	—	1
American Lutheran and Lutheran Church in America	3,092	—	1,618	1,324	357	538	203	226	3	1
American Lutheran	21,608	—	9,500	10,138	3,655	4,361	497	1,625	13	9
American Lutheran	7,814	8,307	8,181	9,045	4,013	3,830	647	555	10	12
Assemblies of God Church	38,231	99,314	103,746	102,041	35,504	41,690	11,390	13,457	33	64
Baptist	3,925	958	1,453	1,463	577	590	182	114	3	3
Brethren Church	1,301	2,239	2,251	2,330	913	1,363	20	34	1	1
Brethren in Christ Church	1,705	2,519	2,653	3,139	1,279	1,463	164	233	3	4
Christian and Missionary Alliance Church	14,913	30,397	33,988	31,360	6,322	9,430	6,886	8,722	12	15
Christian Church (Disciples of Christ)	1,342	2,263	2,967	3,016	1,297	1,190	332	197	7	10
Christian Churches and Churches of Christ	2,486	2,174	1,965	2,240	866	1,143	103	128	4	3
Christian Methodist Episcopal	—	—	—	—	—	—	—	—	—	—
Christian Reformed Church	5,408	4,488	3,947	3,956	1,748	1,928	135	145	3	2
Church of Christ (Scientist)	2,773	2,557	5,353	4,043	1,713	1,761	340	229	6	5
Church of God of Prophecy	—	249	225	0	—	—	—	—	—	—
Church of God	6,082	5,627	5,954	6,441	2,572	2,760	543	566	9	8
Church of New Jerusalem	170	—	—	—	—	—	—	—	1	—
Church of the Brethren	8,482	4,463	3,000	2,852	999	1,450	172	231	6	3
Church of the Nazarene	11,716	10,779	13,707	13,852	5,148	6,295	1,002	1,407	10	10
Churches of Christ	9,343	14,331	20,171	22,157	7,809	8,105	2,999	3,244	9	16
Cumberland Presbyterian	594	746	653	734	314	215	78	127	2	2
Evangelical Congregational Church	80	88	94	98	15	4	60	19	1	1
Evangelical Convent Church of America	1,401	1,035	1,331	1,417	476	521	162	258	1	1
Evangelical Free Church of America	833	2,355	3,458	3,743	1,387	1,119	858	379	1	4
Evangelical Lutheran Church	743	49,210	32,682	36,755	13,786	17,674	1,912	3,383	3	26
Free Methodist	5,543	5,902	8,321	8,269	2,786	3,759	670	1,054	5	5
Free Will Baptist Church	1,132	1,177	1,091	1,197	379	342	266	210	4	2
Friends United Meeting	1,109	—	—	—	—	—	—	—	1	—
Friends	5,157	5,844	6,311	6,529	2,446	3,130	389	564	5	6
General Conference Mennonite Church	820	1,243	1,341	841	373	387	31	50	2	1
Greek Orthodox	204	148	173	171	131	35	3	2	1	1
Interdenominational	1,254	11,103	5,363	5,244	2,547	2,062	371	264	4	9
Jewish	5,738	15,628	16,991	19,942	13,407	5,276	798	461	24	71
Latter-Day Saints	39,172	42,274	41,025	40,725	17,960	18,977	1,798	1,990	4	3
Lutheran Church—Missouri Synod	11,727	13,827	9,894	9,925	3,708	4,394	660	1,163	15	8

Table 174.—Fall enrollment and number of institutions of higher education, by affiliation[1] of institution: 1980 to 1993—Continued

Affiliation	Enrollment								Number of institutions[2]	
	Total, fall 1980	Total, fall 1990	Total, fall 1992	Fall 1993[3]					Fall 1980	Fall 1993
				Total	Full-time		Part-time			
					Men	Women	Men	Women		
1	2	3	4	5	6	7	8	9	10	11
Lutheran Church in America	23,877	5,796	7,246	7,416	2,423	3,139	689	1,165	20	4
Mennonite Brethren Church	1,344	1,864	2,089	2,115	567	674	282	592	3	3
Mennonite Church	4,008	2,859	2,794	3,486	1,336	1,623	211	316	6	6
Missionary Church Inc.	487	699	984	1,158	312	421	155	270	1	1
Moravian Church	2,434	2,511	2,589	2,727	622	1,174	361	570	2	2
Multiple Protestant Denominations	5,526	211	194	189	35	51	36	67	8	1
North American Baptist	155	—	141	173	70	42	41	20	1	1
Pentecostal Holiness Church	767	566	904	916	341	337	101	137	3	3
Presbyterian U.S. and United Presbyterian	47,144	76,625	70,276	72,123	27,458	31,608	5,235	7,822	57	64
Presbyterian Church in America	—	1,877	3,601	3,643	1,637	1,637	214	155	—	3
Protestant Episcopal	5,396	4,559	4,665	4,640	1,947	2,347	140	206	12	11
Protestant, other	4,072	38,136	66,806	62,238	22,864	24,950	6,777	7,647	11	68
Reformed Church in America	2,713	5,525	5,416	5,345	2,202	2,785	157	201	4	4
Reformed Episcopal Church	67	—	—	—	—	—	—	—	1	—
Reformed Presbyterian Church	2,014	1,556	1,651	1,693	686	659	197	151	4	2
Reorganized Latter-Day Saints Church	4,274	4,793	9,317	9,922	2,527	1,742	2,255	3,398	2	2
Roman Catholic	422,842	530,742	572,801	585,722	151,621	199,532	82,278	152,291	229	251
Russian Orthodox	47	—	34	30	27	0	3	0	1	1
Seventh-Day Adventists	19,168	15,771	16,723	16,572	6,163	6,947	1,258	2,204	11	11
Southern Baptist	85,281	49,493	40,764	43,148	14,146	15,151	6,348	7,503	54	30
Undenominational	—	1,714	10,239	10,760	3,375	4,108	1,778	1,499	—	9
Unitarian Universalist	87	82	87	93	28	53	4	8	2	2
United Brethren Church	545	601	608	565	239	242	55	29	1	1
United Church of Christ	14,169	19,219	22,500	23,282	6,789	9,921	2,414	4,158	16	19
United Methodist	127,099	148,851	139,329	142,031	48,923	58,752	13,596	20,760	91	88
Wesleyan Church	3,583	5,311	5,705	6,846	2,655	3,343	331	517	5	3
Wisconsin Evangelical Lutheran Synod	808	931	771	1,078	477	551	17	33	1	3
Other religiously affiliated	462	13,136	12,348	12,882	4,719	4,952	1,423	1,788	1	16

[1] Religious affiliation as reported by institutions of higher education.
[2] Because data are derived from the "Fall Enrollment" survey, counts of institutions may differ from counts on other tables.
[3] Preliminary data.
—Data not applicable or not reported.

SOURCE: U.S. Department of Education, National Center for Education Statistics, "Fall Enrollment in Institutions of Higher Education" surveys; and Integrated Postsecondary Education Data System (IPEDS), "Fall Enrollment" surveys. (This table was prepared June 1995).

Table 175.—Total first-time freshmen fall enrollment in institutions of higher education, by sex of student, attendance status, and type and control of institution: Fall 1955 to fall 1993

[In thousands]

Year	Total, all freshmen	Men			Women			Type of institution, by control			
								4-year		2-year	
		Total	Full-time	Part-time	Total	Full-time	Part-time	Public	Private	Public	Private
1	2	3	4	5	6	7	8	9	10	11	12
1955[1]	670	416	—	—	254	—	—	[2]283	[2]247	[2]117	[2]23
1956[1]	718	443	—	—	275	—	—	[2]293	[2]262	[2]137	[2]25
1957[1]	724	442	—	—	282	—	—	[2]294	[2]263	[2]141	[2]27
1958[1]	775	465	—	—	310	—	—	[2]328	[2]272	[2]146	[2]29
1959[1]	822	488	—	—	334	—	—	[2]348	[2]292	[2]153	[2]28
1960[1]	923	540	—	—	384	—	—	[2]396	[2]313	[2]182	[2]32
1961[1]	1,018	592	—	—	426	—	—	[2]438	[2]336	[2]210	[2]34
1962[1]	1,031	598	—	—	432	—	—	[2]445	[2]325	[2]225	[2]36
1963[1]	1,046	604	—	—	442	—	—	—	—	—	—
1964[1]	1,225	702	—	—	523	—	—	[2]539	[2]363	[2]275	[2]47
1965[1]	1,442	829	—	—	613	—	—	[2]642	[2]399	[2]348	[2]53
1966	1,554	890	—	—	665	—	—	[2]626	[2]383	[2]478	[2]67
1967	1,641	931	761	170	710	574	136	[2]645	[2]368	[2]561	[2]67
1968	1,893	1,082	847	235	810	624	187	[2]725	[2]378	[2]718	[2]72
1969	1,967	1,118	876	242	849	649	200	[2]737	[2]393	[2]776	[2]61
1970	2,063	1,152	896	256	911	691	221	[2]754	[2]397	[2]854	[2]58
1971	2,119	1,171	896	275	949	710	238	[2]738	[2]386	[2]937	[2]58
1972	2,153	1,158	858	299	995	716	279	680	381	1,037	55
1973	2,226	1,182	867	315	1,044	740	304	699	379	1,089	59
1974	2,366	1,244	896	348	1,122	777	345	746	386	1,176	58
1975	2,515	1,328	942	386	1,187	821	366	772	395	1,284	64
1976	2,347	1,170	855	316	1,177	808	369	717	414	1,153	63
1977	2,394	1,156	840	316	1,239	841	398	737	405	1,186	67
1978	2,390	1,142	817	324	1,248	834	414	737	407	1,174	73
1979	2,503	1,180	840	340	1,323	866	457	760	415	1,254	74
1980	2,588	1,219	862	357	1,369	887	481	765	418	1,314	91
1981	2,595	1,218	852	366	1,378	886	492	754	419	1,318	104
1982	2,505	1,199	837	362	1,306	851	455	731	404	1,254	116
1983	2,444	1,159	825	334	1,285	853	431	728	404	1,190	122
1984	2,357	1,112	786	326	1,245	827	418	714	403	1,130	110
1985	2,292	1,076	775	301	1,216	827	389	717	399	1,060	116
1986	2,219	1,047	769	278	1,173	821	352	720	392	991	[3]117
1987	2,246	1,047	779	267	1,200	847	352	758	405	980	104
1988	2,379	1,100	807	293	1,279	892	387	783	426	1,049	121
1989	2,341	1,095	791	303	1,246	865	381	762	414	1,049	[3]116
1990	2,257	1,045	771	274	1,211	846	366	727	400	1,041	[4]88
1991	2,278	1,068	798	270	1,209	855	355	718	393	1,070	[4]97
1992[5]	2,186	1,014	761	253	1,172	844	328	703	407	989	[4]87
1993[6]	2,161	1,008	762	245	1,153	846	307	702	411	973	[4]74

[1] Excludes first-time freshmen in occupational programs not creditable towards a bachelor's degree.

[2] Data for 2-year branches of 4-year college systems are aggregated with the 4-year institutions.

[3] Because of imputation techniques, data are not consistent with figures for other years.

[4] Data not comparable with pre-1990 figures because of a change in reporting procedures.

[5] Revised.

[6] Preliminary data.

—Data not available.

NOTE.—Alaska and Hawaii are included in all years. Because of rounding, details may not add to totals.

SOURCE: U.S. Department of Education, National Center for Education Statistics, *Fall Enrollment in Higher Education*, various years; "Fall Enrollment in Colleges and Universities" survey; and Integrated Postsecondary Education Data System (IPEDS), "Fall Enrollment" surveys. (This table was prepared April 1995.)

Table 176.—Total first-time freshmen fall enrollment in institutions of higher education, by attendance status, sex, control of institution, and state: Fall 1991 to fall 1993

State or other area	Fall 1991	Fall 1992	Fall 1993 [1]								
			Total	Full-time			Part-time			Public in-stitutions	Private institu-tions
				Total	Men	Women	Total	Men	Women		
1	2	3	4	5	6	7	8	9	10	11	12
United States	2,277,920	2,186,090	2,160,709	1,608,273	762,239	846,034	552,436	245,407	307,029	1,675,818	484,891
Alabama	42,271	42,604	41,812	33,707	15,014	18,693	8,105	3,432	4,673	36,678	5,134
Alaska	2,378	2,584	2,700	2,220	1,001	1,219	480	175	305	2,334	366
Arizona	57,927	31,358	36,671	21,233	10,513	10,720	15,438	6,920	8,518	33,880	2,791
Arkansas	18,214	18,680	17,406	15,333	6,990	8,343	2,073	903	1,170	14,445	2,961
California	293,739	252,762	250,810	129,056	61,883	67,173	121,754	58,469	63,285	224,646	26,164
Colorado	32,089	33,359	31,353	22,774	11,629	11,145	8,579	4,070	4,509	27,411	3,942
Connecticut	22,222	22,490	21,489	16,287	7,801	8,486	5,202	1,955	3,247	13,403	8,086
Delaware	7,955	7,227	7,361	5,938	2,621	3,317	1,423	566	857	6,493	868
District of Columbia	7,655	8,427	8,954	7,217	3,023	4,194	1,737	587	1,150	1,297	7,657
Florida	73,751	72,311	71,351	51,154	24,358	26,796	20,197	9,014	11,183	55,423	15,928
Georgia	55,090	56,389	59,784	46,816	20,613	26,203	12,968	5,619	7,349	46,215	13,569
Hawaii	8,525	9,461	9,752	6,514	2,964	3,550	3,238	1,565	1,673	7,442	2,310
Idaho	10,408	10,960	11,069	9,690	4,705	4,985	1,379	564	815	7,040	4,029
Illinois	120,988	116,824	112,542	72,622	35,437	37,185	39,920	17,613	22,307	89,235	23,307
Indiana	50,761	50,147	49,111	40,944	19,989	20,955	8,167	3,159	5,008	35,176	13,935
Iowa	32,644	37,659	35,922	29,116	14,108	15,008	6,806	2,614	4,192	27,427	8,495
Kansas	26,182	25,453	25,304	18,442	9,375	9,067	6,862	3,003	3,859	22,710	2,594
Kentucky	31,713	29,736	31,334	27,183	11,933	15,250	4,151	1,690	2,461	23,415	7,919
Louisiana	30,323	31,810	30,160	26,368	11,528	14,840	3,792	1,621	2,171	25,602	4,558
Maine	9,088	8,765	8,751	7,796	3,798	3,998	955	327	628	5,612	3,139
Maryland	31,912	32,133	31,675	21,868	10,264	11,604	9,807	3,783	6,024	27,103	4,572
Massachusetts	63,966	64,751	68,316	56,452	25,798	30,654	11,864	4,633	7,231	34,876	33,440
Michigan	83,483	88,518	87,025	59,308	27,181	32,127	27,717	12,025	15,692	70,991	16,034
Minnesota	43,702	50,869	43,794	34,121	16,779	17,342	9,673	3,840	5,833	34,370	9,424
Mississippi	27,648	25,960	26,223	22,464	10,338	12,126	3,759	1,429	2,330	24,263	1,960
Missouri	39,441	39,886	40,868	33,164	15,340	17,824	7,704	3,311	4,393	27,332	13,536
Montana	6,146	6,413	6,950	6,130	3,094	3,036	820	356	464	5,891	1,059
Nebraska	15,842	17,362	15,943	12,970	6,268	6,702	2,973	1,296	1,677	12,542	3,401
Nevada	5,968	4,620	5,367	3,230	1,628	1,602	2,137	983	1,154	5,229	138
New Hampshire	11,484	11,316	11,659	9,687	4,480	5,207	1,972	750	1,222	6,010	5,649
New Jersey	43,950	44,932	44,971	36,416	17,242	19,174	8,555	3,509	5,046	36,427	8,544
New Mexico	12,708	11,818	13,358	8,398	4,134	4,264	4,960	2,077	2,883	12,581	777
New York	157,449	159,302	157,349	139,977	65,544	74,433	17,372	7,334	10,038	95,093	62,256
North Carolina	54,851	55,075	52,857	45,966	20,951	25,015	6,891	3,266	3,625	38,811	14,046
North Dakota	7,923	8,813	8,322	7,554	4,037	3,517	768	343	425	7,529	793
Ohio	94,645	92,902	90,190	72,936	33,979	38,957	17,254	7,971	9,283	66,033	24,157
Oklahoma	30,115	30,296	30,252	20,441	9,997	10,444	9,811	4,169	5,642	27,132	3,120
Oregon	23,088	22,930	23,293	17,211	8,516	8,695	6,082	2,838	3,244	19,487	3,806
Pennsylvania	111,285	113,567	100,372	83,451	40,218	43,233	16,921	6,689	10,232	58,944	41,428
Rhode Island	12,717	12,813	13,106	11,436	5,806	5,630	1,670	649	1,021	5,289	7,817
South Carolina	33,471	30,185	30,070	24,552	11,118	13,434	5,518	2,452	3,066	23,893	6,177
South Dakota	6,288	6,513	6,691	6,088	2,839	3,249	603	218	385	5,437	1,254
Tennessee	36,882	35,721	35,341	30,393	14,049	16,344	4,948	1,990	2,958	24,628	10,713
Texas	129,666	127,584	129,921	92,229	45,006	47,223	37,692	16,924	20,768	113,106	16,815
Utah	26,125	23,536	24,465	18,347	8,452	9,895	6,118	3,052	3,066	18,687	5,778
Vermont	6,242	6,274	6,347	5,339	2,659	2,680	1,008	268	740	3,545	2,802
Virginia	45,006	45,011	43,820	37,456	17,087	20,369	6,364	3,106	3,258	33,068	10,752
Washington	70,043	68,649	70,476	40,388	19,932	20,456	30,088	14,439	15,649	65,035	5,441
West Virginia	17,447	17,029	15,727	13,716	6,587	7,129	2,011	729	1,282	13,210	2,517
Wisconsin	50,511	47,271	47,351	35,064	16,691	18,373	12,287	5,445	6,842	38,613	8,738
Wyoming	5,675	4,686	4,858	3,730	1,936	1,794	1,128	479	649	4,663	195
U.S. Service Schools	38,316	10,349	10,116	7,381	5,006	2,375	2,735	1,188	1,547	10,116	—
Outlying areas	35,320	35,409	41,759	36,872	15,136	21,736	4,887	2,455	2,432	15,977	25,782
American Samoa	979	989	967	711	367	344	256	142	114	967	—
Federated States of Micronesia	158	409	235	226	116	110	9	2	7	235	—
Guam	726	709	1,490	1,053	435	618	437	209	228	1,490	—
Marshall Islands	139	139	166	156	85	71	10	5	5	166	—
Northern Marianas	262	173	455	81	35	46	374	230	144	455	—
Palau	10	24	24	19	7	12	5	2	3	24	—
Puerto Rico	32,480	32,664	38,057	34,305	13,985	20,320	3,752	1,854	1,898	12,275	25,782
Virgin Islands	705	302	365	321	106	215	44	11	33	365	—

[1] Preliminary data.

—Data not available or not applicable.

SOURCE: U.S. Department of Education, National Center for Education Statistics, Integrated Postsecondary Education Data System, "Fall Enrollment" surveys. (This table was prepared March 1995.)

Table 177.—College enrollment rates of high school graduates, by race/ethnicity: 1960 to 1994

[Numbers in thousands]

Year	High school graduates [1]				Enrolled in college [2]						Hispanic [4]		
	Total	White [3]	Black [3,4]	His-panic [4]	Total		White [3]		Black [3,4]		Number	Percent	
					Number	Percent	Number	Percent	Number	Percent		Annual	3-year moving average
1	2	3	4	5	6	7	8	9	10	11	12	13	14
1960	1,679	1,565	—	—	758	45.1	717	45.8	—	—	—	—	—
1961	1,763	1,612	—	—	847	48.0	798	49.5	—	—	—	—	—
1962	1,838	1,660	—	—	900	49.0	840	50.6	—	—	—	—	—
1963	1,741	1,615	—	—	784	45.0	736	45.6	—	—	—	—	—
1964	2,145	1,964	—	—	1,037	48.3	967	49.2	—	—	—	—	—
1965	2,659	2,417	—	—	1,354	50.9	1,249	51.7	—	—	—	—	—
1966	2,612	2,403	—	—	1,309	50.1	1,243	51.7	—	—	—	—	—
1967	2,525	2,267	—	—	1,311	51.9	1,202	53.0	—	—	—	—	—
1968	2,606	2,303	—	—	1,444	55.4	1,304	56.6	—	—	—	—	—
1969	2,842	2,538	—	—	1,516	53.3	1,402	55.2	—	—	—	—	—
1970	2,757	2,461	—	—	1,427	51.8	1,280	52.0	—	—	—	—	—
1971	2,872	2,596	—	—	1,535	53.4	1,402	54.0	—	—	—	—	—
1972	2,961	2,614	—	—	1,457	49.2	1,292	49.4	—	—	—	—	—
1973	3,059	2,707	—	—	1,425	46.6	1,302	48.1	—	—	—	—	—
1974	3,101	2,736	—	—	1,474	47.5	1,288	47.1	—	—	—	—	—
1975	3,186	2,825	—	—	1,615	50.7	1,446	51.2	—	—	—	52.6	—
1976	2,987	2,640	320	152	1,458	48.8	1,291	48.9	134	41.9	80	52.6	—
1977	3,140	2,768	335	156	1,590	50.6	1,403	50.7	166	49.6	80	51.3	48.9
1978	3,161	2,750	352	133	1,584	50.1	1,378	50.1	161	45.7	57	42.9	46.3
1979	3,160	2,776	324	154	1,559	49.3	1,376	49.6	147	45.4	69	44.8	46.8
1980	3,089	2,682	361	129	1,524	49.3	1,339	49.9	151	41.8	68	52.7	49.9
1981	3,053	2,626	359	146	1,646	53.9	1,434	54.6	154	42.9	76	52.1	49.3
1982	3,100	2,644	384	174	1,568	50.6	1,376	52.0	140	36.5	75	43.1	49.8
1983	2,964	2,496	392	138	1,562	52.7	1,372	55.0	151	38.5	75	54.3	47.3
1984	3,012	2,514	438	185	1,662	55.2	1,455	57.9	176	40.2	82	44.3	49.9
1985	2,666	2,241	333	141	1,539	57.7	1,332	59.4	141	42.3	72	51.1	46.6
1986	2,786	2,307	386	169	1,499	53.8	1,292	56.0	141	36.5	75	44.4	43.0
1987	2,647	2,207	337	176	1,503	56.8	1,249	56.6	175	51.9	59	33.5	45.0
1988	2,673	2,187	382	179	1,575	58.9	1,328	60.7	172	45.0	102	57.0	48.6
1989	2,454	2,051	337	168	1,463	59.6	1,238	60.4	178	52.8	93	55.4	53.2
1990	2,355	1,921	341	112	1,410	59.9	1,182	61.5	158	46.3	53	47.3	53.3
1991	2,276	1,867	320	154	1,420	62.4	1,207	64.6	146	45.6	88	57.1	53.1
1992	2,398	1,900	353	199	1,479	61.7	1,204	63.4	169	47.9	109	54.8	58.1
1993	2,338	1,910	302	200	1,464	62.6	1,200	62.8	168	55.6	125	62.5	55.4
1994	2,517	2,065	318	178	1,559	61.9	1,313	63.6	162	50.9	87	48.9	—

[1] Individuals age 16 to 24 who graduated from high school during the preceding 12 months.

[2] Enrollment in college as of October of each year for individuals age 16 to 24 who graduated from high school during the preceding 12 months.

[3] Includes persons of Hispanic origin.

[4] Due to the small sample size, data are subject to relatively large sampling errors.

—Data not available.

NOTE.—Data are based upon sample surveys of the civilian population. High school graduate data in this table differ from figures appearing in other tables because of varying survey procedures and coverage. High school graduates include GED recipients.

SOURCE: American College Testing Program, unpublished tabulations, 1987, derived from statistics collected by the U.S. Bureau of the Census; and U.S. Department of Labor, *College Enrollment of 1993 High School Graduates*, and unpublished data. (This table was prepared June 1995.)

Table 178.—College enrollment rates of high school graduates, by sex: 1960 to 1994

[Numbers in thousands]

Year	Total high school graduates[1]			Enrolled in college[2]					
	Total	Males	Females	Total		Males		Females	
				Number	Percent	Number	Percent	Number	Percent
1	2	3	4	5	6	7	8	9	10
1960	1,679	756	923	758	45.1	408	54.0	350	37.9
1961	1,763	790	973	847	48.0	445	56.3	402	41.3
1962	1,838	872	966	900	49.0	480	55.0	420	43.5
1963	1,741	794	947	784	45.0	415	52.3	369	39.0
1964	2,145	997	1,148	1,037	48.3	570	57.2	467	40.7
1965	2,659	1,254	1,405	1,354	50.9	718	57.3	636	45.3
1966	2,612	1,207	1,405	1,309	50.1	709	58.7	600	42.7
1967	2,525	1,142	1,383	1,311	51.9	658	57.6	653	47.2
1968	2,606	1,184	1,422	1,444	55.4	748	63.2	696	48.9
1969	2,842	1,352	1,490	1,516	53.3	812	60.1	704	47.2
1970	2,757	1,343	1,414	1,427	51.8	741	55.2	686	48.5
1971	2,872	1,369	1,503	1,535	53.4	788	57.6	747	49.7
1972	2,961	1,420	1,541	1,457	49.2	749	52.7	708	45.9
1973	3,059	1,458	1,601	1,425	46.6	730	50.1	695	43.4
1974	3,101	1,491	1,610	1,474	47.5	736	49.4	738	45.8
1975	3,186	1,513	1,673	1,615	50.7	796	52.6	819	49.0
1976	2,987	1,450	1,537	1,458	48.8	685	47.2	773	50.3
1977	3,140	1,482	1,658	1,590	50.6	773	52.2	817	49.3
1978	3,161	1,485	1,676	1,584	50.1	758	51.0	826	49.3
1979	3,160	1,474	1,686	1,559	49.3	743	50.4	816	48.4
1980	3,089	1,500	1,589	1,524	49.3	701	46.7	823	51.8
1981	3,053	1,490	1,563	1,646	53.9	816	54.8	830	53.1
1982	3,100	1,508	1,592	1,568	50.6	739	49.0	829	52.1
1983	2,964	1,390	1,574	1,562	52.7	721	51.9	841	53.4
1984	3,012	1,429	1,583	1,662	55.2	800	56.0	862	54.5
1985	2,666	1,286	1,380	1,539	57.7	754	58.6	785	56.9
1986	2,786	1,331	1,455	1,499	53.8	744	55.9	755	51.9
1987	2,647	1,278	1,369	1,503	56.8	746	58.4	757	55.3
1988	2,673	1,334	1,339	1,575	58.9	761	57.0	814	60.8
1989	2,454	1,208	1,245	1,463	59.6	696	57.6	767	61.6
1990	2,355	1,169	1,185	1,410	59.9	676	57.8	735	62.0
1991	2,276	1,139	1,137	1,420	62.4	656	57.6	763	67.1
1992	2,398	1,216	1,182	1,479	61.7	725	59.6	754	63.8
1993	2,338	1,118	1,219	1,464	62.6	668	59.7	797	65.4
1994	2,517	1,244	1,273	1,559	61.9	754	60.6	805	63.2

[1] Individuals age 16 to 24 who graduated from high school during the preceding 12 months.

[2] Enrollment in college as of October of each year for individuals age 16 to 24 who graduated from high school during the preceding 12 months.

NOTE.—Data are based upon sample surveys of the civilian population. High school graduate data in this table differ from figures appearing in other tables because of varying survey procedures and coverage. High school graduates include GED recipients.

SOURCE: American College Testing Program, unpublished tabulations, 1987, derived from statistics collected by the U.S. Bureau of the Census; and U.S. Department of Labor, *College Enrollment of 1993 High School Graduates,* and unpublished data. (This table was prepared June 1995.)

Table 179.—Graduation, college preparation, and college application rates of high school students, by selected school characteristics: 1993–94

Selected school characteristics	Public schools			Private schools		
	Number of schools with 12th graders	1993 graduation rate of fall 1992 12th graders	Average college application rate of 12th graders	Number of schools with 12th graders	1993 graduation rate of fall 1992 12th graders	Average college application rate of 12th graders
1	2	3	4	5	6	7
Total	**17,838**	**92.6**	**57.4**	**7,875**	**98.2**	**87.5**
Percent minority students						
Less than 5%	6,843	94.1	56.4	2,926	98.9	84.8
5% to 19%	3,784	93.7	60.2	2,735	98.5	90.0
20% to 49%	3,850	92.1	58.5	1,439	97.7	90.2
50% or more	3,360	90.1	54.2	775	96.5	79.9
Community type						
Central city	3,698	90.0	55.2	3,202	98.4	89.1
Suburban/large town	3,527	92.5	62.0	2,306	97.8	87.2
Small town/rural	10,613	94.8	55.1	2,368	98.6	82.5

NOTE.—Data are based upon a sample survey and may not be strictly comparable with data reported elsewhere. Only includes schools with students enrolled in 12th grade. Because of rounding, details may not add to totals.

SOURCE: U.S. Department of Education, National Center for Education Statistics, "Schools and Staffing Survey, 1993–94." (This table was prepared August 1995.)

Table 180.—Enrollment rates of 18- to 24-year-olds in institutions of higher education, by race/ethnicity: 1967 to 1994

Year	Total		White, non-Hispanic		Black, non-Hispanic		Hispanic origin	
	Enrollment as a percent of 18- to 24-year-olds	Enrollment as a percent of high school graduates	Enrollment as a percent of 18- to 24-year-olds	Enrollment as a percent of high school graduates	Enrollment as a percent of 18- to 24-year-olds	Enrollment as a percent of high school graduates	Enrollment as a percent of 18- to 24-year-olds	Enrollment as a percent of high school graduates
1	2	3	4	5	6	7	8	9
1967[1]	25.5	33.7	26.9	34.5	13.0	23.3	—	—
1968[1]	26.0	34.2	27.5	34.9	14.5	25.2	—	—
1969[1]	27.3	35.0	28.7	35.6	16.0	27.2	—	—
1970[1]	25.7	32.7	27.1	33.2	15.5	26.0	—	—
1971[1]	26.2	33.2	27.2	33.5	18.2	29.2	—	—
1972	25.5	31.1	27.2	31.9	18.3	25.2	13.4	24.1
1973	24.0	28.9	25.5	29.5	15.9	22.5	16.1	27.6
1974	24.6	29.8	25.8	29.9	17.6	24.6	18.0	30.7
1975	26.3	31.4	27.4	31.3	20.4	30.1	20.4	33.0
1976	26.7	32.3	27.6	32.1	22.5	32.1	20.0	34.7
1977	26.1	31.4	27.2	31.3	21.1	29.1	17.2	30.5
1978	25.3	30.0	26.5	30.1	20.1	27.9	15.2	25.9
1979	25.0	29.9	26.3	30.2	19.8	27.5	16.7	27.8
1980	25.7	30.5	27.3	31.0	19.4	26.0	16.1	27.6
1981	26.2	31.3	27.7	31.6	19.9	26.6	16.6	28.5
1982	26.6	31.6	28.1	32.0	19.9	26.5	16.8	27.6
1983	26.2	31.3	28.0	31.8	19.2	25.3	17.3	29.9
1984	27.1	31.8	28.9	32.6	20.3	25.6	17.9	28.8
1985	27.8	32.5	30.0	33.9	19.6	24.5	16.9	25.0
1986	27.9	32.7	29.7	33.3	21.9	26.9	17.6	28.3
1987	29.7	35.4	31.9	36.6	23.0	28.2	17.7	26.6
1988	30.2	36.0	33.1	37.4	21.1	26.8	17.1	29.1
1989	30.9	36.5	34.2	38.3	23.4	28.5	16.0	26.6
1990	32.1	37.7	35.2	39.2	25.3	30.4	16.2	26.8
1991	33.3	39.3	36.8	41.0	23.4	28.2	17.8	31.4
1992	34.4	42.0	37.3	42.8	25.2	33.9	21.3	37.5
1993	34.0	41.6	36.8	42.6	24.5	32.8	21.7	36.1
1994	34.6	42.3	38.1	43.7	27.7	35.6	18.8	33.1

[1] Data for white and black enrollment include persons of Hispanic origin.
—Data not available.

NOTE.—Data are based upon sample surveys of the civilian noninstitutional population. Percents based on 18- to 24-year-old high school graduates for 1992, 1993, and 1994, use a slightly different definition of graduation and may not be directly comparable with figures for other years. All college students are counted as high school graduates.

SOURCE: U.S. Department of Commerce, Bureau of the Census, Current Population Survey, unpublished data. (This table was prepared May 1995.)

Table 181.—Total undergraduate fall enrollment[1] in institutions of higher education, by sex of student, attendance status, and control of institution: 1969 to 1993

[In thousands]

Year	Total	Full-time	Part-time	Men	Women	Men		Women		Men		Women	
						Full-time	Part-time	Full-time	Part-time	Public	Private	Public	Private
1	2	3	4	5	6	7	8	9	10	11	12	13	14
1969	6,884	4,991	1,893	4,008	2,876	2,952	1,056	2,039	837	2,997	1,011	2,162	714
1970	7,376	5,280	2,096	4,254	3,122	3,097	1,157	2,183	939	3,241	1,013	2,387	735
1971	7,743	5,512	2,231	4,418	3,325	3,201	1,217	2,311	1,014	3,427	991	2,580	745
1972	7,941	5,488	2,453	4,429	3,512	3,121	1,308	2,367	1,145	3,467	962	2,756	756
1973	8,261	5,580	2,681	4,538	3,723	3,135	1,403	2,445	1,278	3,579	959	2,943	780
1974	8,798	5,726	3,072	4,765	4,033	3,191	1,574	2,535	1,498	3,799	966	3,232	801
1975	9,679	6,169	3,510	5,257	4,422	3,459	1,798	2,710	1,712	4,245	1,012	3,581	841
1976	9,429	6,030	3,399	4,902	4,527	3,242	1,660	2,788	1,739	3,949	953	3,668	859
1977	9,717	6,094	3,623	4,897	4,820	3,188	1,709	2,906	1,914	3,937	960	3,906	914
1978	9,691	5,967	3,724	4,766	4,925	3,072	1,694	2,895	2,030	3,812	954	3,974	951
1979	9,998	6,080	3,919	4,821	5,178	3,087	1,734	2,993	2,185	3,865	956	4,181	995
1980	10,475	6,362	4,113	5,000	5,475	3,227	1,773	3,135	2,340	4,014	985	4,427	1,048
1981	10,755	6,449	4,306	5,109	5,646	3,261	1,848	3,188	2,458	4,090	1,018	4,558	1,088
1982	10,825	6,484	4,341	5,170	5,655	3,299	1,871	3,184	2,470	4,140	1,031	4,573	1,081
1983	10,846	6,514	4,332	5,158	5,688	3,304	1,854	3,210	2,478	4,117	1,042	4,580	1,107
1984	10,618	6,348	4,270	5,007	5,611	3,195	1,812	3,153	2,459	3,990	1,017	4,504	1,107
1985	10,597	6,320	4,277	4,962	5,635	3,156	1,806	3,163	2,471	3,953	1,010	4,525	1,110
1986	10,798	6,352	4,446	5,018	5,780	3,146	1,871	3,206	2,575	4,002	1,015	4,658	1,122
1987	11,046	6,463	4,584	5,068	5,978	3,164	1,905	3,299	2,679	4,076	992	4,842	1,136
1988	11,317	6,642	4,674	5,138	6,179	3,206	1,931	3,436	2,743	4,113	1,024	4,990	1,189
1989	11,743	6,841	4,902	5,311	6,432	3,279	2,032	3,562	2,869	4,272	1,039	5,216	1,216
1990	11,959	6,976	4,983	5,380	6,579	3,337	2,043	3,639	2,940	4,353	1,027	5,357	1,223
1991	12,439	7,221	5,218	5,571	6,868	3,436	2,135	3,786	3,082	4,531	1,040	5,617	1,251
1992[2]	12,537	7,243	5,293	5,582	6,954	3,424	2,158	3,819	3,135	4,537	1,046	5,679	1,275
1993[3]	12,324	7,179	5,144	5,484	6,840	3,382	2,102	3,797	3,043	4,447	1,036	5,565	1,276

[1] Includes unclassified undergraduate students.
[2] Revised from previously published data.
[3] Preliminary data.

NOTE.—Because of rounding, details may not add to totals.

SOURCE: U.S. Department of Education, National Center for Education Statistics, "Fall Enrollment in Colleges and Universities;" and Integrated Postsecondary Education Data System, "Fall Enrollment" survey. (This table was prepared February 1995.)

Table 182.—Total graduate fall enrollment[1] in institutions of higher education, by attendance status, sex of student, and control of institution: 1969 to 1993

[In thousands]

Year	Total	Full-time	Part-time	Men	Women	Men Full-time	Men Part-time	Women Full-time	Women Part-time	Men Public	Men Private	Women Public	Women Private
1	2	3	4	5	6	7	8	9	10	11	12	13	14
1969	955	363	593	590	366	252	338	111	255	393	197	273	93
1970	1,031	379	651	630	400	264	366	115	285	423	207	301	99
1971	1,012	388	621	615	394	269	346	119	275	415	200	296	100
1972	1,066	394	671	626	439	268	358	126	313	427	199	330	109
1973	1,123	410	715	648	477	273	375	137	340	442	206	358	119
1974	1,190	427	762	663	526	276	387	151	375	454	209	398	128
1975	1,263	453	810	700	563	290	410	163	400	481	219	425	138
1976	1,333	463	870	714	619	287	427	176	443	477	237	454	165
1977	1,319	473	845	700	617	289	411	184	434	458	243	443	174
1978	1,312	468	844	682	630	280	402	188	442	441	241	453	177
1979	1,309	476	833	669	640	280	389	196	444	427	242	457	182
1980	1,343	485	860	675	670	281	394	204	466	426	247	474	195
1981	1,343	484	859	674	669	277	397	207	462	419	255	468	201
1982	1,322	485	838	670	653	280	390	205	447	417	253	453	200
1983	1,340	497	843	677	663	286	391	211	452	418	259	454	209
1984[2]	1,345	501	844	672	673	286	386	215	459	411	261	459	215
1985	1,376	509	867	677	700	289	388	220	479	414	263	477	223
1986	1,435	522	913	693	742	294	399	228	514	433	260	508	234
1987	1,452	527	925	693	759	294	400	233	525	429	264	516	243
1988	1,472	553	919	697	774	304	393	249	526	429	268	520	254
1989	1,522	572	949	710	811	309	401	263	548	437	273	541	271
1990	1,586	599	987	737	849	321	416	278	571	456	281	567	282
1991	1,639	642	997	761	878	341	419	300	578	471	290	580	299
1992[2]	1,669	666	1,003	772	896	351	421	314	582	474	298	584	313
1993[3]	1,689	688	1,001	771	918	355	417	334	584	473	298	590	328

[1] Includes unclassified postbaccalaureate students.
[2] Revised from previously published data.
[3] Preliminary data.

NOTE.—Because of rounding, details may not add to totals.

SOURCE: U.S. Department of Education, National Center for Education Statistics, "Fall Enrollment in Colleges and Universities;" and Integrated Postsecondary Education Data System (IPEDS), "Fall Enrollment" survey. (This table was prepared February 1995.)

Table 183.—Total first-professional fall enrollment in institutions of higher education, by attendance status, sex of student, and control of institution: 1969 to 1993

Year	Total	Full-time	Part-time	Men	Women	Men Full-time	Men Part-time	Women Full-time	Women Part-time	Men Public	Men Private	Women Public	Women Private
1	2	3	4	5	6	7	8	9	10	11	12	13	14
1969	164,737	143,081	21,656	148,926	15,811	131,368	17,558	11,713	4,098	64,241	84,685	8,354	7,457
1970	173,411	157,384	16,027	158,649	14,762	144,270	14,379	13,114	1,648	68,956	89,693	6,501	8,261
1971	192,668	176,224	16,444	174,058	18,610	159,386	14,672	16,838	1,772	98,233	75,825	9,430	9,180
1972	206,659	190,039	16,620	183,443	23,216	168,990	14,453	21,049	2,167	79,723	103,720	10,842	12,374
1973	218,990	201,663	17,327	186,297	32,693	171,731	14,566	29,932	2,761	81,811	104,486	16,138	16,555
1974	235,452	216,329	19,123	194,079	41,373	178,926	15,153	37,403	3,970	84,271	109,808	20,085	21,288
1975	242,267	219,886	22,381	192,100	50,167	177,117	14,983	42,769	7,398	79,240	112,860	23,557	26,610
1976	244,292	220,124	24,168	189,810	54,482	171,967	17,843	48,157	6,325	77,873	111,937	23,468	31,014
1977	251,357	226,318	25,039	191,451	59,906	173,165	18,286	53,153	6,753	78,189	113,262	24,901	35,005
1978	256,904	232,540	24,364	192,221	64,683	174,906	17,315	57,634	7,049	77,748	114,473	26,839	37,844
1979	263,404	238,949	24,455	193,363	70,041	176,394	16,969	62,555	7,486	77,122	116,241	29,026	41,015
1980	277,767	251,359	26,408	199,344	78,423	181,448	17,896	69,911	8,512	81,022	118,322	33,415	45,008
1981	274,595	248,328	26,267	192,936	81,659	175,414	17,522	72,914	8,745	77,562	115,374	34,177	47,482
1982	278,425	252,108	26,317	191,200	87,225	173,941	17,259	78,167	9,058	76,273	114,927	37,183	50,042
1983	278,529	249,636	28,893	188,096	90,433	169,071	19,025	80,565	9,868	74,938	113,158	38,484	51,949
1984	278,598	249,708	28,890	184,949	93,649	166,286	18,663	83,422	10,227	73,722	111,227	40,186	53,463
1985	274,200	246,619	27,581	179,792	94,408	162,368	17,424	84,251	10,157	71,373	108,419	40,435	53,973
1986	270,401	245,647	24,754	173,851	96,550	158,557	15,294	87,090	9,460	70,326	103,525	41,699	54,851
1987	268,332	241,807	26,525	170,129	98,203	153,668	16,461	88,139	10,064	68,089	102,040	41,947	56,256
1988	267,109	241,228	25,881	166,912	100,197	151,045	15,867	90,183	10,014	66,196	100,716	42,743	57,454
1989	274,451	247,812	26,639	168,773	105,678	152,511	16,262	95,301	10,377	67,548	101,225	45,090	60,588
1990	273,366	245,854	27,512	166,798	106,568	149,805	16,993	96,049	10,519	66,071	100,727	45,674	60,894
1991	280,531	252,012	28,519	169,875	110,656	152,356	17,519	99,656	11,000	64,821	105,054	46,661	63,995
1992[1]	280,922	252,138	28,784	168,620	112,302	151,025	17,595	101,113	11,189	63,511	105,109	47,178	65,124
1993[2]	292,431	259,764	32,667	172,788	119,643	153,873	18,915	105,891	13,752	63,973	108,815	49,681	69,962

[1] Revised from previously published data.
[2] Preliminary data.

SOURCE: U.S. Department of Education, National Center for Education Statistics, "Fall Enrollment in Colleges and Universities;" and Integrated Postsecondary Education Data System (IPEDS), "Fall Enrollment" survey. (This table was prepared February 1995.)

Table 184.—Total fall enrollment in institutions of higher education, by state: 1970 to 1993

State or other area	Fall 1970	Fall 1975	Fall 1980	Fall 1985	Fall 1989	Fall 1990	Fall 1991	Fall 1992 [1]	1993 [2]	Percent change, 1989 to 1993
1	2	3	4	5	6	7	8	9	10	11
United States	8,580,887	11,184,859	12,096,895	12,247,055	13,538,560	13,818,637	14,358,953	14,486,315	14,305,658	5.7
Alabama	103,936	164,700	164,306	179,343	208,562	218,589	224,331	230,537	233,525	12.0
Alaska	9,471	13,998	21,296	27,479	28,627	29,833	30,793	30,902	30,638	7.0
Arizona	109,619	173,542	202,716	216,854	252,625	264,148	272,971	274,671	272,300	7.8
Arkansas	52,039	65,547	77,607	77,958	88,572	90,425	94,340	97,578	99,262	12.1
California	1,257,245	1,787,932	1,790,993	1,650,439	1,802,884	1,808,740	2,024,274	1,978,003	1,836,349	1.9
Colorado	123,395	149,814	162,916	161,314	201,114	227,131	235,108	241,352	239,805	19.2
Connecticut	124,700	148,491	159,632	159,348	169,438	168,604	165,824	165,874	162,300	−4.2
Delaware	25,260	32,389	32,939	31,883	40,562	42,004	42,988	42,763	43,528	7.3
District of Columbia	77,158	84,190	86,675	78,868	79,800	80,156	77,964	81,909	81,916	2.7
Florida	235,525	344,267	411,891	451,392	578,123	588,086	611,781	618,285	623,403	7.8
Georgia	126,511	173,585	184,159	196,826	242,289	251,786	277,023	293,606	302,844	25.0
Hawaii	36,562	46,671	47,181	49,937	54,188	56,436	57,302	61,162	62,871	16.0
Idaho	34,567	39,075	43,018	42,668	48,969	51,881	55,397	57,798	58,768	20.0
Illinois	452,146	584,089	644,245	678,689	709,952	729,246	753,297	748,805	734,089	3.4
Indiana	192,668	213,820	247,253	250,567	275,821	284,832	290,301	296,912	294,685	6.8
Iowa	108,902	121,678	140,449	152,897	169,901	170,515	171,024	172,805	172,797	1.7
Kansas	102,485	120,833	136,605	141,359	158,497	163,733	167,699	169,419	170,135	7.3
Kentucky	98,591	125,253	143,066	141,724	166,014	177,852	187,958	188,322	187,332	12.8
Louisiana	120,728	153,213	160,058	177,176	180,202	186,840	197,438	204,379	201,987	12.1
Maine	34,134	40,443	43,264	52,201	58,230	57,186	57,178	57,977	56,294	−3.3
Maryland	149,607	205,570	225,526	231,649	254,533	259,700	267,931	268,399	268,005	5.3
Massachusetts	303,809	384,485	418,415	421,175	426,476	417,833	419,381	422,976	420,127	−1.5
Michigan	392,726	496,405	520,131	507,293	560,320	569,803	568,491	559,729	568,210	1.4
Minnesota	160,788	184,756	206,691	221,162	253,097	253,789	255,054	272,920	268,118	5.9
Mississippi	73,967	99,962	102,364	101,180	116,370	122,883	125,350	123,754	122,408	5.2
Missouri	183,930	223,115	234,421	241,146	278,505	289,899	297,154	296,617	297,062	6.7
Montana	30,062	30,843	35,177	35,958	37,660	35,876	37,821	39,644	39,557	5.0
Nebraska	66,915	74,705	89,488	97,769	108,844	112,831	113,648	122,603	115,523	6.1
Nevada	13,669	30,187	40,455	43,656	56,471	61,728	62,664	63,877	63,947	13.2
New Hampshire	29,400	41,030	46,794	52,283	59,081	59,510	63,718	63,924	64,043	8.4
New Jersey	216,121	297,114	321,610	297,658	314,091	324,286	334,641	343,232	343,029	9.2
New Mexico	44,461	51,944	58,283	68,295	81,350	85,500	93,507	99,276	101,460	24.7
New York	806,479	1,005,063	992,237	1,000,098	1,029,518	1,048,286	1,056,487	1,064,822	1,063,779	3.3
North Carolina	171,925	251,786	287,537	327,288	345,502	352,138	371,968	383,453	371,280	7.5
North Dakota	31,495	29,743	34,069	37,939	40,404	37,878	38,739	40,470	40,316	−0.2
Ohio	376,267	436,052	489,145	514,745	550,720	557,690	569,326	573,183	562,402	2.1
Oklahoma	110,155	146,613	160,295	169,173	175,855	173,221	183,536	187,846	183,342	4.3
Oregon	122,177	145,281	157,458	137,967	161,822	165,741	167,107	165,834	165,834	2.5
Pennsylvania	411,044	470,536	507,716	533,198	610,479	604,060	620,036	626,904	621,228	1.8
Rhode Island	45,898	64,479	66,869	69,927	76,503	78,273	79,112	79,165	77,407	1.2
South Carolina	69,518	133,023	132,476	131,902	145,730	159,302	164,907	171,443	174,302	19.6
South Dakota	30,639	30,260	32,761	32,772	32,666	34,208	36,332	37,596	38,166	16.8
Tennessee	135,103	181,435	204,581	194,845	218,866	226,238	238,042	242,970	244,936	11.9
Texas	442,225	624,390	701,391	769,692	879,335	901,437	917,443	938,526	942,178	7.1
Utah	81,687	87,323	93,987	103,994	114,815	121,303	130,419	133,083	138,139	20.3
Vermont	22,209	29,095	30,628	31,416	35,946	36,398	37,436	37,377	36,415	1.3
Virginia	151,915	244,671	280,504	292,416	344,284	353,442	356,325	354,172	348,535	1.2
Washington	183,544	227,168	303,603	231,553	255,760	263,384	274,760	275,556	279,845	9.4
West Virginia	63,153	78,619	81,973	76,659	82,455	84,790	88,602	90,252	88,852	7.8
Wisconsin	202,058	240,701	269,086	275,069	291,966	299,774	308,986	307,902	309,036	5.8
Wyoming	15,220	18,078	21,147	24,204	29,159	31,326	32,118	31,548	30,702	5.3
U.S. Service Schools	17,079	36,897	49,808	54,052	55,607	48,087	52,921	52,622	52,647	−5.3
Outlying areas	67,237	104,270	137,749	164,890	162,955	164,618	168,771	169,759	172,989	6.2
American Samoa	—	689	976	758	1,011	1,219	1,267	1,295	1,264	25.0
Federated States of Micronesia	—	—	—	—	838	975	837	1,028	1,148	37.0
Guam	2,719	3,800	3,217	4,601	4,350	4,741	5,016	4,845	5,843	34.3
Marshall Islands	—	—	—	—	—	—	—	374	386	
Northern Marianas	—	—	—	318	419	661	847	796	1,261	201.0
Palau	—	—	—	—	1,037	491	355	445	436	−58.0
Puerto Rico	63,073	97,517	131,184	155,917	152,603	154,065	157,733	158,120	159,709	4.7
Trust Territory of the Pacific	—	185	224	724	—	—	—	—	—	
Virgin Islands	1,445	2,079	2,148	2,572	2,697	2,466	2,716	2,856	2,942	9.1

[1] Revised.
[2] Preliminary data.
—Data not reported or not applicable.

SOURCE: U.S. Department of Education, National Center for Education Statistics, "Fall Enrollment in Colleges and Universities;" and Integrated Postsecondary Education Data System (IPEDS), "Fall Enrollment" survey. (This table was prepared February 1995.)

Table 185.—Total fall enrollment in public institutions of higher education, by state: 1970 to 1993

State or other area	Fall 1970	Fall 1975	Fall 1980	Fall 1985	Fall 1989	Fall 1990	Fall 1991	Fall 1992[1]	Fall 1993[2]	Percent change, 1989 to 1993
1	2	3	4	5	6	7	8	9	10	11
United States	**6,428,134**	**8,834,508**	**9,457,394**	**9,479,273**	**10,577,963**	**10,844,717**	**11,309,563**	**11,384,567**	**11,189,088**	**5.8**
Alabama	87,884	145,698	143,674	158,688	187,575	195,939	202,311	206,287	210,094	12.0
Alaska	8,563	13,218	20,561	26,510	26,274	27,792	29,019	29,037	28,708	9.3
Arizona	107,315	168,666	194,034	202,036	239,314	248,213	253,631	255,907	246,754	3.1
Arkansas	43,599	56,127	66,068	66,123	76,416	78,645	82,152	85,829	87,942	15.1
California	1,123,529	1,617,558	1,599,838	1,444,207	1,590,568	1,594,710	1,804,654	1,748,649	1,604,158	0.9
Colorado	108,562	136,370	145,598	142,031	175,850	200,653	206,645	212,427	209,932	19.4
Connecticut	73,391	93,567	97,788	98,616	109,697	109,556	107,321	107,786	105,446	−3.9
Delaware	21,151	27,082	28,325	27,933	33,037	34,252	35,311	35,313	35,771	8.3
District of Columbia	12,194	15,159	13,900	12,747	12,439	12,595	12,033	12,285	10,959	−11.9
Florida	189,450	287,745	334,349	362,241	485,280	489,081	506,342	511,226	518,480	6.8
Georgia	101,900	142,593	140,158	148,956	186,776	196,413	218,924	233,078	239,755	28.4
Hawaii	32,963	43,278	43,269	43,246	43,644	45,728	45,682	49,605	50,618	16.0
Idaho	27,072	31,298	34,491	33,666	38,447	41,315	44,149	46,607	47,524	23.6
Illinois	315,634	444,458	491,274	520,224	536,643	551,333	571,249	566,614	549,745	2.4
Indiana	136,739	159,453	189,224	193,833	216,433	223,953	228,378	234,624	231,259	6.9
Iowa	68,390	83,572	97,454	109,765	116,889	117,834	120,360	122,841	122,267	4.6
Kansas	88,215	107,761	121,987	127,220	145,134	149,117	152,349	153,399	154,016	6.1
Kentucky	77,240	105,265	114,884	110,836	137,297	147,095	155,773	157,838	156,160	13.7
Louisiana	101,127	132,054	136,703	153,173	151,733	158,290	168,822	177,373	173,950	14.6
Maine	25,405	31,092	31,878	33,188	40,511	41,500	40,928	40,846	39,819	−1.7
Maryland	118,988	176,544	195,051	198,992	216,769	220,783	228,638	227,987	226,666	4.6
Massachusetts	116,127	173,564	183,765	185,602	187,772	186,035	180,559	183,119	181,461	−3.4
Michigan	339,625	436,655	454,147	434,270	479,714	487,359	486,301	473,322	483,145	0.7
Minnesota	130,567	148,630	162,379	173,984	198,610	199,211	199,753	212,158	207,131	4.3
Mississippi	64,968	89,919	90,661	90,704	103,035	109,038	111,386	109,911	109,373	6.2
Missouri	132,540	158,196	165,179	168,829	192,322	200,093	203,125	198,610	197,821	2.9
Montana	27,287	27,798	31,178	32,032	33,197	31,865	33,453	33,765	34,326	3.4
Nebraska	51,454	61,240	73,509	81,202	91,337	94,614	94,692	103,196	95,782	4.9
Nevada	13,576	30,010	40,280	43,368	56,184	61,242	61,985	63,192	63,229	12.5
New Hampshire	15,979	24,205	24,119	26,669	33,370	32,163	34,518	35,255	35,571	6.6
New Jersey	145,373	227,764	247,028	237,297	253,544	261,601	270,728	278,385	278,361	9.8
New Mexico	40,795	47,605	55,077	66,059	79,359	83,403	89,853	94,901	98,093	23.6
New York	449,437	613,842	563,251	563,251	600,978	616,884	605,898	606,308	604,989	0.7
North Carolina	123,761	201,288	228,154	267,044	277,062	285,405	305,473	315,518	303,556	9.6
North Dakota	30,192	27,954	31,709	34,802	37,555	34,690	35,218	36,783	36,644	−2.4
Ohio	281,099	336,931	381,765	379,164	412,073	427,613	436,292	437,027	429,756	4.3
Oklahoma	91,438	124,372	137,188	146,827	151,410	151,073	160,166	164,728	160,901	6.3
Oregon	108,483	129,785	140,102	119,612	141,311	144,427	144,451	144,902	143,352	1.4
Pennsylvania	232,982	287,436	292,499	300,523	335,101	343,478	354,435	359,856	351,747	5.0
Rhode Island	25,527	32,311	35,052	35,389	40,604	42,350	42,503	43,264	40,833	0.6
South Carolina	47,101	107,690	107,683	105,854	118,639	131,134	137,012	145,580	148,933	25.5
South Dakota	23,936	21,925	24,328	23,339	25,075	26,596	28,888	30,346	31,427	25.3
Tennessee	98,897	139,526	156,835	147,951	167,056	175,049	186,441	192,302	194,225	16.3
Texas	365,522	542,212	613,552	677,192	782,495	802,314	816,554	832,458	834,696	6.7
Utah	49,588	56,536	59,598	69,426	79,623	86,108	94,802	96,958	100,271	25.9
Vermont	12,536	17,145	17,984	18,844	20,925	20,910	21,485	21,397	21,001	0.4
Virginia	123,279	215,253	246,500	250,754	287,624	291,286	298,107	297,522	293,810	2.2
Washington	162,718	202,531	276,028	201,532	221,362	227,632	238,345	238,763	241,813	9.2
West Virginia	51,363	68,117	71,228	66,531	72,478	74,108	78,215	79,284	77,500	6.9
Wisconsin	170,374	210,535	235,179	238,735	247,262	253,529	260,082	256,890	256,669	3.8
Wyoming	15,220	18,078	21,121	24,204	28,553	30,623	31,251	30,687	30,002	5.1
U.S. Service Schools	17,079	36,897	49,808	54,052	55,607	48,087	52,921	52,622	52,647	−5.3
Outlying areas	46,680	59,923	60,692	65,411	67,056	66,244	66,074	66,702	69,115	3.1
American Samoa	—	689	976	758	1,011	1,219	1,267	1,295	1,264	25.0
Federated States of Micronesia	—	—	—	—	838	975	837	1,028	1,148	37.0
Guam	2,719	3,800	3,217	4,601	4,350	4,741	5,016	4,845	5,843	34.3
Marshall Islands	—	—	—	—	—	—	—	374	386	—
Northern Marianas	—	—	—	318	419	661	847	796	1,261	201.0
Palau	—	—	—	—	1,037	491	355	445	436	−58.0
Puerto Rico	42,516	53,170	54,127	56,438	56,704	55,691	55,036	55,063	55,835	1.5
Trust Territory of the Pacific	—	185	224	724	—	—	—	—	—	—
Virgin Islands	1,445	2,079	2,148	2,572	2,697	2,466	2,716	2,856	2,942	9.1

[1] Revised.
[2] Preliminary data.
—Data not reported or not applicable.

SOURCE: U.S. Department of Education, National Center for Education Statistics, "Fall Enrollment in Colleges and Universities;" and Integrated Postsecondary Education Data System (IPEDS), "Fall Enrollment" survey. (This table was prepared February 1995).

Table 186.—Total fall enrollment in private institutions of higher education, by state: 1970 to 1993

State or other area	Fall 1970	Fall 1975	Fall 1980	Fall 1985	Fall 1989	Fall 1990	Fall 1991	Fall 1992 [1]	1993 [2]	Percent change, 1989 to 1993
1	2	3	4	5	6	7	8	9	10	11
United States	2,152,753	2,350,351	2,639,501	2,767,782	2,960,597	2,973,920	3,049,390	3,101,748	3,116,570	5.3
Alabama	16,052	19,002	20,632	20,655	20,987	22,650	22,020	24,250	23,431	11.6
Alaska	908	780	735	969	2,353	2,041	1,774	1,865	1,930	–18.0
Arizona	2,304	4,876	8,682	14,818	13,311	15,935	19,340	18,764	25,546	91.9
Arkansas	8,440	9,420	11,539	11,835	12,156	11,780	12,188	11,749	11,320	–6.9
California	133,716	170,374	191,155	206,232	212,316	214,030	219,620	229,354	232,191	9.4
Colorado	14,833	13,444	17,318	19,283	25,264	26,478	28,463	28,925	29,873	18.2
Connecticut	51,309	54,924	61,844	60,732	59,741	59,048	58,503	58,088	56,854	–4.8
Delaware	4,109	5,307	4,614	3,950	7,525	7,752	7,677	7,450	7,757	3.1
District of Columbia	64,964	69,031	72,775	66,121	67,361	67,561	65,931	69,624	70,957	5.3
Florida	46,075	56,522	77,542	89,151	92,843	99,005	105,439	107,059	104,923	13.0
Georgia	24,611	30,992	44,001	47,870	55,513	55,373	58,099	60,528	63,089	13.6
Hawaii	3,599	3,393	3,912	6,691	10,544	10,708	11,620	11,557	12,253	16.2
Idaho	7,495	7,777	8,527	9,002	10,522	10,566	11,248	11,191	11,244	6.9
Illinois	136,512	139,631	152,971	158,465	173,309	177,913	182,048	182,191	184,344	6.4
Indiana	55,929	54,367	58,029	56,734	59,388	60,879	61,923	62,288	63,426	6.8
Iowa	40,512	38,106	42,995	43,132	53,012	52,681	50,664	49,964	50,530	–4.7
Kansas	14,270	13,072	14,618	14,139	13,363	14,616	15,350	16,020	16,119	20.6
Kentucky	21,351	19,988	28,182	30,888	28,717	30,757	32,185	30,484	31,172	8.5
Louisiana	19,601	21,159	23,355	24,003	28,469	28,550	28,616	27,006	28,037	–1.5
Maine	8,729	9,351	11,386	19,013	17,719	15,686	16,250	17,131	16,475	–7.0
Maryland	30,619	29,026	30,475	32,657	37,764	38,917	39,293	40,412	41,339	9.5
Massachusetts	187,682	210,921	234,650	235,573	238,704	231,798	238,822	239,857	238,666	–0.0
Michigan	53,101	59,750	65,984	73,023	80,606	82,444	82,190	86,407	85,065	5.5
Minnesota	30,221	36,126	44,312	47,178	54,487	54,578	55,301	60,762	60,987	11.9
Mississippi	8,999	10,043	11,703	10,476	13,335	13,845	13,964	13,843	13,035	–2.2
Missouri	51,390	64,919	69,242	72,317	86,183	89,806	94,029	98,007	99,241	15.2
Montana	2,775	3,045	3,999	3,926	4,463	4,011	4,368	5,879	5,231	17.2
Nebraska	15,461	13,465	15,979	16,567	17,507	18,217	18,956	19,407	19,741	12.8
Nevada	93	177	175	288	287	486	679	685	718	150.2
New Hampshire	13,421	16,825	22,675	25,614	25,711	27,347	29,200	28,669	28,472	10.7
New Jersey	70,748	69,350	74,582	60,361	60,547	62,685	63,913	64,847	64,668	6.8
New Mexico	3,666	4,339	3,206	2,236	1,991	2,097	3,654	4,375	3,367	69.1
New York	357,042	391,221	428,986	436,847	428,540	431,402	450,589	458,514	458,790	7.1
North Carolina	48,164	50,498	59,383	60,244	68,440	66,733	66,495	67,935	67,724	–1.0
North Dakota	1,303	1,789	2,360	3,137	2,849	3,188	3,521	3,687	3,672	28.9
Ohio	95,168	99,121	107,380	135,581	138,647	130,077	133,034	136,156	132,646	–4.3
Oklahoma	18,717	22,241	23,107	22,346	24,445	22,148	23,370	23,118	22,441	–8.2
Oregon	13,694	15,496	17,356	18,355	20,511	21,314	22,656	22,513	22,482	9.6
Pennsylvania	178,062	183,100	215,217	232,675	275,378	260,582	265,601	267,048	269,481	–2.1
Rhode Island	20,371	32,168	31,817	34,538	35,899	35,923	36,609	35,901	36,574	1.9
South Carolina	22,417	25,333	24,793	26,048	27,091	28,168	27,895	25,863	25,369	–6.4
South Dakota	6,703	8,335	8,433	9,433	7,591	7,612	7,444	7,250	6,739	–11.2
Tennessee	36,206	41,909	47,746	46,894	51,810	51,189	51,601	50,668	50,711	–2.1
Texas	76,703	82,178	87,839	92,500	96,840	99,123	100,889	106,068	107,482	11.0
Utah	32,099	30,787	34,389	34,568	35,192	35,195	35,617	36,125	37,868	7.6
Vermont	9,673	11,950	12,644	12,572	15,021	15,488	15,951	15,980	15,414	2.6
Virginia	28,636	29,418	34,004	41,662	56,660	62,156	58,218	56,650	54,725	–3.4
Washington	20,826	24,637	27,575	30,021	34,398	35,752	36,415	36,793	38,032	10.6
West Virginia	11,790	10,502	10,745	10,128	9,977	10,682	10,387	10,968	11,352	13.8
Wisconsin	31,684	30,166	33,907	36,334	44,704	46,245	48,904	51,012	52,367	17.1
Wyoming	—	—	26	—	606	703	867	861	700	15.5
Outlying areas	20,557	44,347	77,057	99,479	95,899	98,374	102,697	103,057	103,874	8.3
American Samoa	—	—	—	—	—	—	—	—	—	—
Federated States of Micronesia	—	—	—	—	—	—	—	—	—	—
Guam	—	—	—	—	—	—	—	—	—	—
Marshall Islands	—	—	—	—	—	—	—	—	—	—
Northern Marianas	—	—	—	—	—	—	—	—	—	—
Palau	—	—	—	—	—	—	—	—	—	—
Puerto Rico	20,557	44,347	77,057	99,479	95,899	98,374	102,697	103,057	103,874	8.3
Trust Territory of the Pacific	—	—	—	—	—	—	—	—	—	—
Virgin Islands	—	—	—	—	—	—	—	—	—	—

[1] Revised.
[2] Preliminary data.
—Data not reported or not applicable.

SOURCE: U.S. Department of Education, National Center for Education Statistics, "Fall Enrollment in Colleges and Universities;" and Integrated Postsecondary Education Data System (IPEDS), "Fall Enrollment" survey. (This table was prepared February 1995.)

Table 187.—Total fall enrollment in all institutions of higher education, by attendance status, sex, and state: 1992 and 1993

State or other area	Fall 1992 [1]					Fall 1993 [2]				
	Total	Full-time		Part-time		Total	Full-time		Part-time	
		Men	Women	Men	Women		Men	Women	Men	Women
1	2	3	4	5	6	7	8	9	10	11
United States	14,486,315	3,926,441	4,234,677	2,597,075	3,728,122	14,305,658	3,890,603	4,237,137	2,537,113	3,640,805
Alabama	230,537	71,666	83,196	32,058	43,617	233,525	71,148	82,841	33,714	45,822
Alaska	30,902	5,531	6,565	7,111	11,695	30,638	5,566	6,651	6,784	11,637
Arizona	274,671	63,213	60,132	62,855	88,471	272,300	64,181	64,053	59,430	84,636
Arkansas	97,578	31,252	37,429	10,599	18,298	99,262	31,427	37,720	11,376	18,739
California	1,978,003	419,555	443,155	482,314	632,979	1,836,349	406,101	435,586	432,747	561,915
Colorado	241,352	63,317	63,134	49,079	65,822	239,805	63,284	63,610	48,383	64,528
Connecticut	165,874	40,451	42,559	32,810	50,054	162,300	39,634	42,464	31,570	48,632
Delaware	42,763	11,369	14,185	7,037	10,172	43,528	11,497	14,338	7,258	10,435
District of Columbia	81,909	23,601	26,717	14,735	16,856	81,916	23,544	26,983	14,146	17,243
Florida	618,285	143,053	155,554	132,008	187,670	623,403	141,429	155,591	135,506	190,877
Georgia	293,606	90,549	103,684	40,013	59,360	302,844	92,115	107,003	41,417	62,309
Hawaii	61,162	15,724	17,990	12,055	15,393	62,871	15,898	18,564	12,539	15,870
Idaho	57,798	18,729	19,951	7,523	11,595	58,768	19,469	20,463	7,674	11,162
Illinois	748,805	183,974	191,403	152,580	220,848	734,089	181,736	191,806	146,735	213,812
Indiana	296,912	95,523	98,494	42,033	60,862	294,685	94,283	97,858	41,745	60,799
Iowa	172,805	61,125	61,686	18,740	31,254	172,797	60,629	61,612	18,549	32,007
Kansas	169,419	48,325	49,050	27,664	44,380	170,135	48,178	49,373	27,220	45,364
Kentucky	188,322	54,610	66,549	23,733	43,430	187,332	54,597	66,751	23,505	42,479
Louisiana	204,379	65,673	78,248	22,256	38,202	201,987	64,588	77,444	22,422	37,533
Maine	57,977	15,660	16,726	8,563	17,028	56,294	15,523	17,008	8,097	15,666
Maryland	268,399	58,455	65,793	57,001	87,150	268,005	57,985	65,487	56,519	88,014
Massachusetts	422,976	126,454	139,903	62,297	94,322	420,127	124,561	138,201	63,123	94,242
Michigan	559,729	136,771	151,238	112,414	159,306	568,210	136,177	150,788	117,085	164,160
Minnesota	272,920	77,948	81,676	45,302	67,994	268,118	75,511	80,410	44,827	67,370
Mississippi	123,754	43,153	50,681	11,253	18,667	122,408	42,717	50,496	10,916	18,279
Missouri	296,617	82,861	85,658	51,588	76,510	297,062	81,671	87,341	51,166	76,884
Montana	39,644	14,699	15,010	3,825	6,110	39,557	14,922	15,290	3,813	5,532
Nebraska	122,603	33,827	34,961	22,007	31,808	115,523	31,939	34,103	20,687	28,794
Nevada	63,877	10,321	10,825	18,136	24,595	63,947	9,734	10,460	18,437	25,316
New Hampshire	63,924	19,026	21,374	9,121	14,403	64,043	18,880	21,145	9,229	14,789
New Jersey	343,232	83,080	89,583	69,089	101,480	343,029	83,378	90,846	67,955	100,850
New Mexico	99,276	23,504	25,879	20,031	29,862	101,460	24,215	27,078	19,887	30,280
New York	1,064,822	314,586	357,176	151,549	241,511	1,063,779	317,224	362,414	147,374	236,767
North Carolina	383,453	107,997	128,505	59,787	87,164	371,280	107,253	128,415	54,978	80,634
North Dakota	40,470	16,560	15,158	3,842	4,910	40,316	16,722	15,417	3,550	4,627
Ohio	573,183	169,313	184,095	94,053	125,722	562,402	164,434	182,990	91,593	123,385
Oklahoma	187,846	55,222	61,602	29,969	41,053	183,342	52,795	56,202	30,484	43,861
Oregon	167,415	47,476	46,692	31,504	41,743	165,834	46,585	46,506	31,818	40,925
Pennsylvania	626,904	194,518	198,805	91,701	141,880	621,228	190,522	198,637	92,270	139,799
Rhode Island	79,165	23,727	25,371	11,824	18,243	77,407	23,936	24,740	11,007	17,724
South Carolina	171,443	51,199	59,191	22,474	38,579	174,302	49,955	58,119	24,544	41,684
South Dakota	37,596	12,538	13,587	4,153	7,318	38,166	13,243	14,545	3,742	6,636
Tennessee	242,970	73,920	82,669	35,506	50,875	244,936	73,381	82,828	36,459	52,268
Texas	938,526	252,047	259,075	182,412	244,992	942,178	251,344	259,172	185,881	245,781
Utah	133,083	46,597	44,012	20,970	21,504	138,139	47,405	46,397	21,967	22,370
Vermont	37,377	12,208	12,891	3,823	8,455	36,415	11,834	12,477	3,787	8,317
Virginia	354,172	92,319	106,929	64,208	90,716	348,535	91,543	105,504	62,481	89,007
Washington	275,556	75,411	83,025	47,346	69,774	279,845	78,096	86,050	47,007	68,692
West Virginia	90,252	30,102	30,827	10,141	19,182	88,852	29,701	30,733	9,733	18,685
Wisconsin	307,902	87,628	98,007	50,031	72,236	309,036	88,106	98,766	49,879	72,285
Wyoming	31,548	8,317	8,977	5,355	8,899	30,702	8,715	8,724	4,688	8,575
U.S. Service Schools	52,622	21,757	9,095	8,597	13,173	52,647	21,292	9,137	9,410	12,808
Outlying areas	169,759	51,030	79,587	15,211	23,931	172,989	51,176	78,522	17,829	25,462
American Samoa	1,295	448	446	233	168	1,264	438	439	227	160
Federated States of Micronesia	1,028	279	240	257	252	1,148	279	260	288	321
Guam	4,845	855	1,261	1,362	1,367	5,843	1,051	1,626	1,546	1,620
Marshall Islands	374	134	123	43	74	386	222	146	10	8
Northern Marianas	796	149	165	161	321	1,261	147	198	433	483
Palau	445	224	126	28	67	436	221	126	26	63
Puerto Rico	158,120	48,647	76,408	12,678	20,387	159,709	48,467	74,841	14,879	21,522
Virgin Islands	2,856	294	818	449	1,295	2,942	351	886	420	1,285

[1] Revised from previously published data.

[2] Preliminary data.

SOURCE: U.S. Department of Education, National Center for Education Statistics, Integrated Postsecondary Education Data System (IPEDS), "Fall Enrollment" survey. (This table was prepared February 1995.)

Table 188.—Total fall enrollment in public institutions of higher education, by attendance status, sex, and state: 1992 and 1993

State or other area	Fall 1992 [1]					Fall 1993 [2]				
	Total	Full-time		Part-time		Total	Full-time		Part-time	
		Men	Women	Men	Women		Men	Women	Men	Women
1	2	3	4	5	6	7	8	9	10	11
United States	11,384,567	2,883,119	3,127,756	2,191,277	3,182,415	11,189,088	2,848,010	3,114,552	2,136,501	3,090,025
Alabama	206,287	62,757	71,913	30,502	41,115	210,094	62,613	72,000	32,005	43,476
Alaska	29,037	5,169	5,935	6,852	11,081	28,708	5,282	6,133	6,484	10,809
Arizona	255,907	53,924	53,768	61,574	86,641	246,754	53,172	53,337	57,886	82,359
Arkansas	85,829	26,383	31,823	10,098	17,525	87,942	26,779	32,315	10,854	17,994
California	1,748,649	339,356	362,878	448,200	598,215	1,604,158	324,690	352,169	400,062	527,237
Colorado	212,427	54,341	54,627	43,003	60,456	209,932	53,942	54,658	42,375	58,957
Connecticut	107,786	23,013	25,041	22,842	36,890	105,446	22,376	24,620	22,313	36,137
Delaware	35,313	9,785	12,330	5,533	7,665	35,771	9,924	12,497	5,608	7,742
District of Columbia	12,285	2,026	2,129	3,607	4,523	10,959	1,928	2,163	2,912	3,956
Florida	511,226	104,797	120,371	114,699	171,359	518,480	104,745	121,237	118,013	174,485
Georgia	233,078	67,441	77,311	34,868	53,458	239,755	67,997	79,748	36,051	55,959
Hawaii	49,605	11,908	14,255	9,723	13,719	50,618	12,346	14,736	9,706	13,830
Idaho	46,607	14,613	14,273	7,064	10,657	47,524	14,916	14,720	7,349	10,539
Illinois	566,614	125,056	131,144	124,634	185,780	549,745	122,920	130,253	119,228	177,344
Indiana	234,624	69,515	74,466	38,140	52,503	231,259	68,190	72,858	37,895	52,316
Iowa	122,841	43,437	42,032	14,389	22,983	122,267	43,007	41,796	14,245	23,219
Kansas	153,399	42,921	42,946	25,933	41,599	154,016	42,670	43,110	25,695	42,541
Kentucky	157,838	43,785	53,732	21,380	38,941	156,160	43,561	53,741	21,143	37,715
Louisiana	177,373	56,338	67,165	19,256	34,614	173,950	55,168	66,119	18,931	33,732
Maine	40,846	11,352	10,641	7,225	11,628	39,819	11,112	10,570	6,862	11,275
Maryland	227,987	48,184	54,253	49,436	76,114	226,666	47,709	53,821	48,933	76,203
Massachusetts	183,119	46,761	52,469	32,774	51,115	181,461	45,369	51,706	33,337	51,049
Michigan	473,322	115,249	121,931	98,178	137,964	483,145	114,628	122,296	102,934	143,287
Minnesota	212,158	57,990	57,971	38,899	57,298	207,131	56,178	56,801	38,221	55,931
Mississippi	109,911	38,758	44,882	9,967	16,304	109,373	38,628	44,850	9,756	16,139
Missouri	198,610	52,822	58,223	33,256	54,309	197,821	52,284	57,610	33,396	54,531
Montana	33,765	13,379	12,900	2,932	4,554	34,326	13,583	13,218	3,156	4,369
Nebraska	103,196	27,328	27,242	20,362	28,264	95,782	25,186	26,070	19,111	25,415
Nevada	63,192	10,052	10,549	18,078	24,513	63,229	9,492	10,204	18,362	25,171
New Hampshire	35,255	10,539	11,701	5,140	7,875	35,571	10,485	11,710	5,285	8,091
New Jersey	278,385	63,613	71,087	57,967	85,718	278,361	63,949	72,117	57,214	85,081
New Mexico	94,901	22,073	24,422	19,354	29,052	98,093	23,047	25,848	19,589	29,609
New York	606,308	163,453	194,074	93,872	154,909	604,989	165,661	197,828	91,197	150,303
North Carolina	315,518	80,842	98,717	55,520	80,439	303,556	80,772	98,924	50,387	73,473
North Dakota	36,783	15,227	13,370	3,663	4,523	36,644	15,396	13,586	3,389	4,273
Ohio	437,027	124,410	138,480	71,479	102,658	429,756	121,237	137,989	70,349	100,181
Oklahoma	164,728	45,835	52,889	27,509	38,495	160,901	43,734	47,496	28,190	41,481
Oregon	144,902	39,055	37,698	29,272	38,877	143,352	38,227	37,309	29,747	38,069
Pennsylvania	359,856	110,185	114,093	52,195	83,383	351,747	107,370	112,558	51,541	80,278
Rhode Island	43,264	9,081	12,260	7,916	14,007	40,833	8,758	11,366	7,324	13,385
South Carolina	145,580	41,674	47,447	20,670	35,789	148,933	40,317	46,554	22,871	39,191
South Dakota	30,346	10,775	10,550	3,401	5,620	31,427	11,449	11,705	3,054	5,219
Tennessee	192,302	52,941	61,080	32,495	45,786	194,225	52,269	61,038	33,502	47,416
Texas	832,458	211,023	220,096	169,687	231,652	834,696	209,912	219,895	172,992	231,897
Utah	96,958	30,715	28,314	18,857	19,072	100,271	30,967	29,554	19,864	19,886
Vermont	21,397	6,611	6,629	2,547	5,610	21,001	6,434	6,589	2,528	5,450
Virginia	297,522	75,023	83,164	57,353	81,982	293,810	74,443	82,672	56,022	80,673
Washington	238,763	63,799	69,043	42,480	63,441	241,813	65,719	71,245	42,459	62,390
West Virginia	79,284	26,291	26,187	9,281	17,525	77,500	25,883	25,741	8,878	16,998
Wisconsin	256,890	71,758	79,549	43,375	62,208	256,669	72,273	79,617	43,198	61,581
Wyoming	30,687	7,999	8,611	5,243	8,834	30,002	8,021	8,718	4,688	8,575
U.S. Service Schools	52,622	21,757	9,095	8,597	13,173	52,647	21,292	9,137	9,410	12,808
Outlying areas	66,702	19,052	30,563	6,295	10,792	69,115	19,946	31,182	7,010	10,977
American Samoa	1,295	448	446	233	168	1,264	438	439	227	160
Federated States of Micronesia	1,028	279	240	257	252	1,148	279	260	288	321
Guam	4,845	855	1,261	1,362	1,367	5,843	1,051	1,626	1,546	1,620
Marshall Islands	374	134	123	43	74	386	222	146	10	8
Northern Marianas	796	149	165	161	321	1,261	147	198	433	483
Palau	445	224	126	28	67	436	221	126	26	63
Puerto Rico	55,063	16,669	27,384	3,762	7,248	55,835	17,237	27,501	4,060	7,037
Virgin Islands	2,856	294	818	449	1,295	2,942	351	886	420	1,285

[1] Revised.
[2] Preliminary data.

SOURCE: U.S. Department of Education, National Center for Education Statistics, Integrated Postsecondary Education Data System (IPEDS), "Fall Enrollment" surveys. (This table was prepared February 1995.)

Table 189.—Total fall enrollment in private institutions of higher education, by attendance status, sex, and state: 1992 and 1993

State or other area	Fall 1992 [1]					Fall 1993 [2]				
	Total	Full-time		Part-time		Total	Full-time		Part-time	
		Men	Women	Men	Women		Men	Women	Men	Women
1	2	3	4	5	6	7	8	9	10	11
United States	3,101,748	1,043,322	1,106,921	405,798	545,707	3,116,570	1,042,593	1,122,585	400,612	550,780
Alabama	24,250	8,909	11,283	1,556	2,502	23,431	8,535	10,841	1,709	2,346
Alaska	1,865	362	630	259	614	1,930	284	518	300	828
Arizona	18,764	9,289	6,364	1,281	1,830	25,546	11,009	10,716	1,544	2,277
Arkansas	11,749	4,869	5,606	501	773	11,320	4,648	5,405	522	745
California	229,354	80,199	80,277	34,114	34,764	232,191	81,411	83,417	32,685	34,678
Colorado	28,925	8,976	8,507	6,076	5,366	29,873	9,342	8,952	6,008	5,571
Connecticut	58,088	17,438	17,518	9,968	13,164	56,854	17,258	17,844	9,257	12,495
Delaware	7,450	1,584	1,855	1,504	2,507	7,757	1,573	1,841	1,650	2,693
District of Columbia	69,624	21,575	24,588	11,128	12,333	70,957	21,616	24,820	11,234	13,287
Florida	107,059	38,256	35,183	17,309	16,311	104,923	36,684	34,354	17,493	16,392
Georgia	60,528	23,108	26,373	5,145	5,902	63,089	24,118	27,255	5,366	6,350
Hawaii	11,557	3,816	3,735	2,332	1,674	12,253	3,552	3,828	2,833	2,040
Idaho	11,191	4,116	5,678	459	938	11,244	4,553	5,743	325	623
Illinois	182,191	58,918	60,259	27,946	35,068	184,344	58,816	61,553	27,507	36,468
Indiana	62,288	26,008	24,028	3,893	8,359	63,426	26,093	25,000	3,850	8,483
Iowa	49,964	17,688	19,654	4,351	8,271	50,530	17,622	19,816	4,304	8,788
Kansas	16,020	5,404	6,104	1,731	2,781	16,119	5,508	6,263	1,525	2,823
Kentucky	30,484	10,825	12,817	2,353	4,489	31,172	11,036	13,010	2,362	4,764
Louisiana	27,006	9,335	11,083	3,000	3,588	28,037	9,420	11,325	3,491	3,801
Maine	17,131	4,308	6,085	1,338	5,400	16,475	4,411	6,438	1,235	4,391
Maryland	40,412	10,271	11,540	7,565	11,036	41,339	10,276	11,666	7,586	11,811
Massachusetts	239,857	79,693	87,434	29,523	43,207	238,666	79,192	86,495	29,786	43,193
Michigan	86,407	21,522	29,307	14,236	21,342	85,065	21,549	28,492	14,151	20,873
Minnesota	60,762	19,958	23,705	6,403	10,696	60,987	19,333	23,609	6,606	11,439
Mississippi	13,843	4,395	5,799	1,286	2,363	13,035	4,089	5,646	1,160	2,140
Missouri	98,007	30,039	27,435	18,332	22,201	99,241	29,387	29,731	17,770	22,353
Montana	5,879	1,320	2,110	893	1,556	5,231	1,339	2,072	657	1,163
Nebraska	19,407	6,499	7,719	1,645	3,544	19,741	6,753	8,033	1,576	3,379
Nevada	685	269	276	58	82	718	242	256	75	145
New Hampshire	28,669	8,487	9,673	3,981	6,528	28,472	8,395	9,435	3,944	6,698
New Jersey	64,847	19,467	18,496	11,122	15,762	64,668	19,429	18,729	10,741	15,769
New Mexico	4,375	1,431	1,457	677	810	3,367	1,168	1,230	298	671
New York	458,514	151,133	163,102	57,677	86,602	458,790	151,563	164,586	56,177	86,464
North Carolina	67,935	27,155	29,788	4,267	6,725	67,724	26,481	29,491	4,591	7,161
North Dakota	3,687	1,333	1,788	179	387	3,672	1,326	1,831	161	354
Ohio	136,156	44,903	45,615	22,574	23,064	132,646	43,197	45,001	21,244	23,204
Oklahoma	23,118	9,387	8,713	2,460	2,558	22,441	9,061	8,706	2,294	2,380
Oregon	22,513	8,421	8,994	2,232	2,866	22,482	8,358	9,197	2,071	2,856
Pennsylvania	267,048	84,333	84,712	39,506	58,497	269,481	83,152	86,079	40,729	59,521
Rhode Island	35,901	14,646	13,111	3,908	4,236	36,574	15,178	13,374	3,683	4,339
South Carolina	25,863	9,525	11,744	1,804	2,790	25,369	9,638	11,565	1,673	2,493
South Dakota	7,250	1,763	3,037	752	1,698	6,739	1,794	2,840	688	1,417
Tennessee	50,668	20,979	21,589	3,011	5,089	50,711	21,112	21,790	2,957	4,852
Texas	106,068	41,024	38,979	12,725	13,340	107,482	41,432	39,277	12,889	13,884
Utah	36,125	15,882	15,698	2,113	2,432	37,868	16,438	16,843	2,103	2,484
Vermont	15,980	5,597	6,262	1,276	2,845	15,414	5,400	5,888	1,259	2,867
Virginia	56,650	17,296	23,765	6,855	8,734	54,725	17,100	22,832	6,459	8,334
Washington	36,793	11,612	13,982	4,866	6,333	38,032	12,377	14,805	4,548	6,302
West Virginia	10,968	3,811	4,640	860	1,657	11,352	3,818	4,992	855	1,687
Wisconsin	51,012	15,870	18,458	6,656	10,028	52,367	15,833	19,149	6,681	10,704
Wyoming	861	318	366	112	65	700	694	6	—	—
Outlying areas	103,057	31,978	49,024	8,916	13,139	103,874	31,230	47,340	10,819	14,485
American Samoa	—	—	—	—	—	—	—	—	—	—
Federated States of Micronesia	—	—	—	—	—	—	—	—	—	—
Guam	—	—	—	—	—	—	—	—	—	—
Marshall Islands	—	—	—	—	—	—	—	—	—	—
Northern Marianas	—	—	—	—	—	—	—	—	—	—
Palau	—	—	—	—	—	—	—	—	—	—
Puerto Rico	103,057	31,978	49,024	8,916	13,139	103,874	31,230	47,340	10,819	14,485
Virgin Islands	—	—	—	—	—	—	—	—	—	—

[1] Revised.
[2] Preliminary data.
—Data not reported or not applicable.

SOURCE: U.S. Department of Education, National Center for Education Statistics, Integrated Postsecondary Education Data System (IPEDS), "Fall Enrollment" surveys. (This table was prepared February 1995).

Table 190.—Total fall enrollment in institutions of higher education, by control, type of institution, and state: 1992 and 1993

State or other area	Fall 1992[1]				Fall 1993[2]			
	Public 4-year	Public 2-year	Private 4-year	Private 2-year	Public 4-year	Public 2-year	Private 4-year	Private 2-year
1	2	3	4	5	6	7	8	9
United States	5,900,012	5,484,555	2,863,913	237,835	5,851,760	5,337,328	2,888,031	228,539
Alabama	127,517	78,770	20,900	3,350	128,350	81,744	21,399	2,032
Alaska	28,451	586	1,506	359	28,108	600	1,682	248
Arizona	97,231	158,676	17,759	1,005	95,346	151,408	24,469	1,077
Arkansas	66,623	19,206	10,203	1,546	65,966	21,976	10,288	1,032
California	515,109	1,233,540	215,513	13,841	490,479	1,113,679	217,520	14,671
Colorado	131,870	80,557	24,817	4,108	132,113	77,819	25,981	3,892
Connecticut	62,147	45,639	56,399	1,689	59,904	45,542	55,223	1,631
Delaware	24,072	11,241	7,450	—	25,036	10,735	7,757	—
District of Columbia	12,285	—	69,624	—	10,959	—	70,957	—
Florida	184,736	326,490	100,989	6,070	191,457	327,023	100,368	4,555
Georgia	154,213	78,865	52,262	8,266	155,834	83,921	56,569	6,520
Hawaii	23,281	26,324	11,557	—	23,911	26,707	12,253	—
Idaho	39,738	6,869	2,937	8,254	40,434	7,090	2,574	8,670
Illinois	199,909	366,705	175,254	6,937	197,377	352,368	177,790	6,554
Indiana	193,911	40,713	58,846	3,442	191,356	39,903	59,837	3,589
Iowa	67,145	55,696	47,831	2,133	66,115	56,152	48,372	2,158
Kansas	89,046	64,353	15,018	1,002	89,296	64,720	15,161	958
Kentucky	109,888	47,950	25,962	4,522	107,945	48,215	26,221	4,951
Louisiana	149,550	27,823	26,325	681	146,158	27,792	27,435	602
Maine	33,521	7,325	15,528	1,603	32,395	7,424	14,767	1,708
Maryland	112,831	115,156	39,426	986	112,298	114,368	40,287	1,052
Massachusetts	104,625	78,494	224,689	15,168	101,732	79,729	223,667	14,999
Michigan	256,001	217,321	83,320	3,087	263,279	219,866	82,364	2,701
Minnesota	126,484	85,674	55,245	5,517	121,591	85,540	56,355	4,632
Mississippi	58,437	51,474	11,448	2,395	57,665	51,708	11,816	1,219
Missouri	122,585	76,025	93,025	4,982	119,116	78,705	93,515	5,726
Montana	29,684	4,081	3,460	2,419	30,396	3,930	4,375	856
Nebraska	60,400	42,796	18,880	527	59,515	36,267	19,149	592
Nevada	30,588	32,604	660	25	30,536	32,693	693	25
New Hampshire	25,998	9,257	24,809	3,860	26,137	9,434	24,496	3,976
New Jersey	139,672	138,713	60,614	4,233	138,391	139,970	60,506	4,162
New Mexico	51,333	43,568	3,538	837	52,238	45,855	2,801	566
New York	343,889	262,419	427,990	30,524	341,772	263,217	428,607	30,183
North Carolina	156,593	158,925	64,728	3,207	155,661	147,895	64,906	2,818
North Dakota	28,671	8,112	3,449	238	28,521	8,123	3,404	268
Ohio	283,820	153,207	115,229	20,927	274,583	155,173	116,587	16,059
Oklahoma	97,516	67,212	19,852	3,266	96,417	64,484	20,193	2,248
Oregon	64,854	80,048	22,208	305	63,113	80,239	22,296	186
Pennsylvania	239,753	120,103	223,267	43,781	234,187	117,560	221,793	47,688
Rhode Island	25,278	17,986	35,901	—	24,434	16,399	34,462	2,112
South Carolina	87,083	58,497	23,530	2,333	88,293	60,640	23,465	1,904
South Dakota	30,191	155	7,065	185	31,216	211	6,528	211
Tennessee	115,098	77,204	46,669	3,999	115,774	78,451	47,498	3,213
Texas	421,906	410,552	101,159	4,909	422,811	411,885	102,486	4,996
Utah	62,361	34,597	35,011	1,114	74,011	26,260	36,669	1,199
Vermont	15,866	5,531	15,803	177	15,532	5,469	15,240	174
Virginia	163,418	134,104	52,583	4,067	162,567	131,243	50,424	4,301
Washington	83,016	155,747	34,348	2,445	84,695	157,118	35,957	2,075
West Virginia	71,973	7,311	10,096	872	70,340	7,160	10,395	957
Wisconsin	149,473	107,417	49,231	1,781	145,188	111,481	50,474	1,893
Wyoming	12,044	18,643	—	861	12,012	17,990	—	700
U.S. Service Schools	18,328	34,294	—	—	19,200	33,447	—	—
Outlying areas	56,126	10,576	91,336	11,721	56,824	12,291	90,886	12,988
American Samoa	—	1,295	—	—	—	1,264	—	—
Federated States of Micronesia	—	1,028	—	—	—	1,148	—	—
Guam	3,156	1,689	—	—	3,697	2,146	—	—
Marshall Islands	—	374	—	—	—	386	—	—
Northern Marianas	—	796	—	—	—	1,261	—	—
Palau	—	445	—	—	—	436	—	—
Puerto Rico	50,114	4,949	91,336	11,721	50,185	5,650	90,886	12,988
Virgin Islands	2,856	—	—	—	2,942	—	—	—

[1] Revised.
[2] Preliminary data.
—Data not reported or not applicable.

SOURCE: U.S. Department of Education, National Center for Education Statistics, Integrated Postsecondary Education Data System (IPEDS), "Fall Enrollment" surveys. (This table was prepared February 1995.)

Table 191.—Total fall enrollment in institutions of higher education, by level of enrollment and state: 1991 to 1993

State or other area	Fall 1991			Fall 1992[1]				Fall 1993[2]			
	Under-graduate	First-profes-sional	Graduate	Total	Under-graduate	First-profes-sional	Graduate	Total	Under-graduate	First-profes-sional	Graduate
1	2	3	4	5	6	7	8	9	10	11	12
United States	12,439,287	280,531	1,639,135	14,486,315	12,536,656	280,922	1,668,737	14,305,658	12,323,959	292,431	1,689,268
Alabama	200,342	3,065	20,924	230,537	206,607	3,389	20,541	233,525	208,019	3,520	21,986
Alaska	29,450	—	1,343	30,902	29,349	—	1,553	30,638	29,047	—	1,591
Arizona	242,478	1,518	28,975	274,671	244,028	1,564	29,079	272,300	239,657	2,720	29,923
Arkansas	85,742	1,613	6,985	97,578	88,536	1,712	7,330	99,262	90,123	1,705	7,434
California	1,808,267	32,564	183,443	1,978,003	1,765,630	31,291	181,082	1,836,349	1,628,210	35,331	172,808
Colorado	196,759	3,066	35,283	241,352	202,777	3,137	35,438	239,805	200,368	3,183	36,254
Connecticut	130,809	3,263	31,752	165,874	131,462	3,202	31,210	162,300	128,063	3,309	30,928
Delaware	37,398	2,130	3,460	42,763	37,538	1,370	3,855	43,528	37,913	1,403	4,212
District of Columbia	46,235	8,493	23,236	81,909	48,815	8,450	24,644	81,916	47,701	8,732	25,483
Florida	547,717	8,225	55,839	618,285	552,553	8,684	57,048	623,403	554,662	8,693	60,048
Georgia	237,260	7,925	31,838	293,606	251,697	8,974	32,935	302,844	259,718	8,970	34,156
Hawaii	49,599	439	7,264	61,162	53,012	450	7,700	62,871	54,512	516	7,843
Idaho	47,912	556	6,929	57,798	50,003	580	7,215	58,768	51,651	509	6,608
Illinois	641,614	17,042	94,641	748,805	638,139	16,712	93,954	734,089	621,576	16,817	95,696
Indiana	253,051	5,414	31,836	296,912	258,714	5,458	32,740	294,685	255,747	5,470	33,468
Iowa	146,801	6,224	17,999	172,805	150,046	6,313	16,446	172,797	149,762	6,580	16,455
Kansas	146,387	2,150	19,162	169,419	147,725	2,160	19,534	170,135	148,164	2,129	19,842
Kentucky	164,420	4,555	18,983	188,322	164,790	4,995	18,537	187,332	163,460	4,946	18,926
Louisiana	169,207	5,943	22,288	204,379	173,861	5,919	24,599	201,987	171,195	6,071	24,721
Maine	51,430	634	5,114	57,977	52,059	630	5,288	56,294	50,391	663	5,240
Maryland	226,154	3,838	37,939	268,399	224,927	3,849	39,623	268,005	223,272	3,900	40,833
Massachusetts	332,752	13,133	73,496	422,976	334,873	13,132	74,971	420,127	329,593	13,421	77,113
Michigan	497,367	9,824	61,300	559,729	489,014	9,708	61,007	568,210	490,372	11,361	66,477
Minnesota	223,446	6,835	24,773	272,920	237,535	6,896	28,489	268,118	231,090	7,082	29,946
Mississippi	112,737	2,121	10,492	123,754	111,510	1,800	10,444	122,408	109,959	1,779	10,670
Missouri	252,568	8,265	36,321	296,617	252,028	8,397	36,192	297,062	251,661	10,050	35,351
Montana	34,120	227	3,474	39,644	36,198	222	3,224	39,557	35,945	223	3,389
Nebraska	98,398	2,979	12,271	122,603	107,851	2,844	11,908	115,523	101,048	3,159	11,316
Nevada	56,754	196	5,714	63,877	57,512	205	6,160	63,947	57,227	202	6,518
New Hampshire	54,685	690	8,343	63,924	54,534	304	9,086	64,043	54,884	484	8,675
New Jersey	285,281	6,321	43,039	343,232	293,190	6,394	43,648	343,029	293,162	6,512	43,355
New Mexico	82,656	630	10,221	99,276	85,622	630	13,024	101,460	88,301	649	12,510
New York	860,227	26,833	169,427	1,064,822	865,839	27,006	171,977	1,063,779	865,052	27,393	171,334
North Carolina	335,109	6,177	30,682	383,453	345,470	6,088	31,895	371,280	331,937	6,196	33,147
North Dakota	35,844	503	2,392	40,470	37,307	505	2,658	40,316	37,226	497	2,593
Ohio	491,277	12,274	65,775	573,183	495,892	12,260	65,031	562,402	484,422	12,304	65,676
Oklahoma	158,210	3,434	21,892	187,846	161,499	3,575	22,772	183,342	157,413	3,349	22,580
Oregon	147,139	3,738	16,230	167,415	146,778	3,770	16,867	165,834	146,370	4,013	15,451
Pennsylvania	526,549	14,852	78,635	626,904	530,713	15,177	81,014	621,228	524,312	15,190	81,726
Rhode Island	69,165	316	9,631	79,165	69,364	312	9,489	77,407	67,598	324	9,485
South Carolina	143,494	2,549	18,864	171,443	148,044	2,425	20,974	174,302	149,183	2,470	22,649
South Dakota	32,079	484	3,769	37,596	32,788	502	4,306	38,166	33,573	516	4,077
Tennessee	209,991	5,276	22,775	242,970	213,672	5,548	23,750	244,936	214,249	5,451	25,236
Texas	804,194	16,823	96,426	938,526	820,888	16,969	100,669	942,178	822,359	17,017	102,802
Utah	119,343	1,228	9,848	133,083	122,208	1,263	9,612	138,139	125,984	1,247	10,908
Vermont	32,276	852	4,308	37,377	32,113	881	4,383	36,415	31,228	885	4,302
Virginia	305,280	6,421	44,624	354,172	302,927	6,308	44,937	348,535	296,858	6,396	45,281
Washington	250,598	3,240	20,922	275,556	251,058	3,244	21,254	279,845	254,630	3,285	21,930
West Virginia	76,059	1,318	11,225	90,252	76,817	1,359	12,076	88,852	75,138	1,413	12,301
Wisconsin	274,389	3,445	31,152	307,902	273,254	3,471	31,177	309,036	274,280	3,509	31,247
Wyoming	28,909	219	2,990	31,548	28,791	222	2,535	30,702	27,713	224	2,765
U.S. Service Schools	49,359	671	2,891	52,622	49,099	666	2,857	52,647	47,981	663	4,003
Outlying areas	156,050	2,906	9,815	169,759	156,078	2,774	10,907	172,989	158,854	3,256	10,879
American Samoa	1,267	—	—	1,295	1,295	—	—	1,264	1,264	—	—
Federated States of Micronesia	837	—	—	1,028	1,028	—	—	1,148	1,148	—	—
Guam	4,782	—	234	4,845	4,581	—	264	5,843	5,522	—	321
Marshall Islands	—	—	—	374	374	—	—	386	386	—	—
Northern Marianas	847	—	—	796	796	—	—	1,261	1,261	—	—
Palau	355	—	—	445	445	—	—	436	436	—	—
Puerto Rico	145,498	2,906	9,329	158,120	144,975	2,774	10,371	159,709	146,164	3,256	10,289
Virgin Islands	2,464	—	252	2,856	2,584	—	272	2,942	2,673	—	269

[1] Revised.
[2] Preliminary data.
—Data not reported or not applicable.

SOURCE: U.S. Department of Education, National Center for Education Statistics, Integrated Postsecondary Education Data System (IPEDS), "Fall Enrollment" survey. (This table was prepared February 1995.)

Table 192.—Total fall enrollment in institutions of higher education, by control, level of enrollment, and state: 1993 [1]

State or other area	Public					Private				
	Undergraduate			First-pro-fessional	Graduate	Undergraduate			First-pro-fessional	Graduate
	Total	4-year	2-year			Total	4-year	2-year		
1	2	3	4	5	6	7	8	9	10	11
United States	10,011,787	4,674,765	5,337,022	113,654	1,063,647	2,312,172	2,083,633	228,539	178,777	625,621
Alabama	187,261	105,517	81,744	2,247	20,586	20,758	18,726	2,032	1,273	1,400
Alaska	27,351	26,751	600	—	1,357	1,696	1,448	248	—	234
Arizona	222,075	70,667	151,408	1,556	23,123	17,582	16,505	1,077	1,164	6,800
Arkansas	78,986	57,010	21,976	1,705	7,251	11,137	10,105	1,032	—	183
California	1,498,921	385,242	1,113,679	7,888	97,349	129,289	114,618	14,671	27,443	75,459
Colorado	180,466	102,647	77,819	1,739	27,727	19,902	16,010	3,892	1,444	8,527
Connecticut	89,799	44,257	45,542	1,144	14,503	38,264	36,633	1,631	2,165	16,425
Delaware	32,438	21,703	10,735	—	3,333	5,475	5,475	—	1,403	879
District of Columbia	10,020	10,020	—	—	939	37,681	37,681	—	8,732	24,544
Florida	476,985	149,962	327,023	3,231	38,264	77,677	73,122	4,555	5,462	21,784
Georgia	210,177	126,256	83,921	2,997	26,581	49,541	43,021	6,520	5,973	7,575
Hawaii	43,707	17,000	26,707	459	6,452	10,805	10,805	—	57	1,391
Idaho	40,988	33,898	7,090	509	6,027	10,663	1,993	8,670	—	581
Illinois	499,601	147,233	352,368	4,279	45,865	121,975	115,421	6,554	12,538	49,831
Indiana	200,110	160,207	39,903	3,462	27,687	55,637	52,048	3,589	2,008	5,781
Iowa	106,567	50,415	56,152	2,678	13,022	43,195	41,037	2,158	3,902	3,433
Kansas	133,249	68,529	64,720	2,045	18,722	14,915	13,957	958	84	1,120
Kentucky	136,974	88,759	48,215	2,851	16,335	26,486	21,535	4,951	2,095	2,591
Louisiana	151,259	123,467	27,792	2,660	20,031	19,936	19,334	602	3,411	4,690
Maine	35,883	28,459	7,424	270	3,666	14,508	12,800	1,708	393	1,574
Maryland	199,277	84,909	114,368	3,080	24,309	23,995	22,943	1,052	820	16,524
Massachusetts	164,351	84,622	79,729	415	16,695	165,242	150,243	14,999	13,006	60,418
Michigan	416,853	196,987	219,866	7,302	58,990	73,519	70,818	2,701	4,059	7,487
Minnesota	187,982	102,442	85,540	2,548	16,601	43,108	38,476	4,632	4,534	13,345
Mississippi	99,137	47,429	51,708	1,196	9,040	10,822	9,603	1,219	583	1,630
Missouri	178,119	99,414	78,705	2,455	17,247	73,542	67,816	5,726	7,595	18,104
Montana	30,840	26,910	3,930	223	3,263	5,105	4,249	856	—	126
Nebraska	84,103	47,836	36,267	1,426	10,253	16,945	16,353	592	1,733	1,063
Nevada	56,633	23,940	32,693	202	6,394	594	569	25	—	124
New Hampshire	32,339	22,905	9,434	—	3,232	22,545	18,569	3,976	484	5,443
New Jersey	247,862	107,892	139,970	3,416	27,083	45,300	41,138	4,162	3,096	16,272
New Mexico	85,323	39,468	45,855	649	12,121	2,978	2,412	566	—	389
New York	539,634	276,417	263,217	4,746	60,609	325,418	295,235	30,183	22,647	110,725
North Carolina	274,413	126,518	147,895	2,580	26,563	57,524	54,706	2,818	3,616	6,584
North Dakota	33,689	25,566	8,123	497	2,458	3,537	3,269	268	—	135
Ohio	375,756	220,889	154,867	7,594	46,406	108,666	92,607	16,059	4,710	19,270
Oklahoma	139,847	75,363	64,484	1,899	19,155	17,566	15,318	2,248	1,450	3,425
Oregon	129,352	49,113	80,239	1,594	12,406	17,018	16,832	186	2,419	3,045
Pennsylvania	309,249	191,689	117,560	4,454	38,044	215,063	167,375	47,688	10,736	43,682
Rhode Island	35,337	18,938	16,399	13	5,483	32,261	30,149	2,112	311	4,002
South Carolina	125,911	65,271	60,640	1,846	21,176	23,272	21,368	1,904	624	1,473
South Dakota	27,192	26,981	211	420	3,815	6,381	6,170	211	96	262
Tennessee	172,087	93,636	78,451	2,633	19,505	42,162	38,949	3,213	2,818	5,731
Texas	742,236	330,351	411,885	9,760	82,700	80,123	75,127	4,996	7,257	20,102
Utah	92,357	66,097	26,260	779	7,135	33,627	32,428	1,199	468	3,773
Vermont	18,976	13,507	5,469	375	1,650	12,252	12,078	174	510	2,652
Virginia	251,723	120,480	131,243	4,191	37,896	45,135	40,834	4,301	2,205	7,385
Washington	227,411	70,293	157,118	1,584	12,818	27,219	25,144	2,075	1,701	9,112
West Virginia	64,131	56,971	7,160	1,413	11,956	11,007	10,050	957	—	345
Wisconsin	231,856	120,375	111,481	1,757	23,056	42,424	40,531	1,893	1,752	8,191
Wyoming	27,013	9,023	17,990	224	2,765	700	—	700	—	—
U.S. Service Schools	47,981	14,534	33,447	663	4,003	—	—	—	—	—
Outlying areas	62,550	50,259	12,291	1,527	5,038	96,304	83,316	12,988	1,729	5,841
American Samoa	1,264	—	1,264	—	—	—	—	—	—	—
Federated States of Micronesia	1,148	—	1,148	—	—	—	—	—	—	—
Guam	5,522	3,376	2,146	—	321	—	—	—	—	—
Marshall Islands	386	—	386	—	—	—	—	—	—	—
Northern Marianas	1,261	—	1,261	—	—	—	—	—	—	—
Palau	436	—	436	—	—	—	—	—	—	—
Puerto Rico	49,860	44,210	5,650	1,527	4,448	96,304	83,316	12,988	1,729	5,841
Virgin Islands	2,673	2,673	—	—	269	—	—	—	—	—

[1] Preliminary data.
—Data not reported or not applicable.

SOURCE: U.S. Department of Education, National Center for Education Statistics, Integrated Postsecondary Education Data System (IPEDS), "Fall Enrollment, 1993" survey. (This table was prepared February 1995.)

Table 193.—Total fall enrollment in institutions of higher education, by control, level of enrollment, and state: 1992[1]

State or other area	Public Undergraduate Total	4-year	2-year	First-pro- fessional	Graduate	Private Undergraduate Total	4-year	2-year	First-pro- fessional	Graduate
1	2	3	4	5	6	7	8	9	10	11
United States	10,216,297	4,731,783	5,484,514	110,689	1,057,581	2,320,359	2,082,524	237,835	170,233	611,156
Alabama	184,878	106,108	78,770	2,216	19,193	21,729	18,379	3,350	1,173	1,348
Alaska	27,731	27,145	586	—	1,306	1,618	1,259	359	—	247
Arizona	230,977	72,301	158,676	1,564	23,366	13,051	12,046	1,005	—	5,713
Arkansas	76,979	57,773	19,206	1,712	7,138	11,557	10,011	1,546	—	192
California	1,636,556	403,016	1,233,540	6,705	105,388	129,074	115,233	13,841	24,586	75,694
Colorado	182,995	102,438	80,557	1,691	27,741	19,782	15,674	4,108	1,446	7,697
Connecticut	92,129	46,490	45,639	1,123	14,534	39,333	37,644	1,689	2,079	16,676
Delaware	32,227	20,986	11,241	—	3,086	5,311	5,311	—	1,370	769
District of Columbia	11,182	11,182	—	—	1,103	37,633	37,633	—	8,450	23,541
Florida	471,242	144,752	326,490	3,252	36,732	81,311	75,241	6,070	5,432	20,316
Georgia	203,783	124,918	78,865	3,442	25,853	47,914	39,648	8,266	5,532	7,082
Hawaii	42,799	16,475	26,324	450	6,356	10,213	10,213	—	—	1,344
Idaho	39,740	32,871	6,869	580	6,287	10,263	2,009	8,254	—	928
Illinois	515,960	149,255	366,705	4,284	46,370	122,179	115,242	6,937	12,428	47,584
Indiana	204,253	163,540	40,713	3,407	26,964	54,461	51,019	3,442	2,051	5,776
Iowa	107,344	51,648	55,696	2,622	12,875	42,702	40,569	2,133	3,691	3,571
Kansas	132,831	68,478	64,353	2,084	18,484	14,894	13,892	1,002	76	1,050
Kentucky	138,579	90,629	47,950	2,956	16,303	26,211	21,689	4,522	2,039	2,234
Louisiana	154,512	126,689	27,823	2,669	20,192	19,349	18,668	681	3,250	4,407
Maine	36,897	29,572	7,325	267	3,682	15,162	13,559	1,603	363	1,606
Maryland	201,039	85,883	115,156	3,000	23,948	23,888	22,902	986	849	15,675
Massachusetts	165,809	87,315	78,494	423	16,887	169,064	153,896	15,168	12,709	58,084
Michigan	413,530	196,209	217,321	5,651	54,141	75,484	72,397	3,087	4,057	6,866
Minnesota	193,420	107,746	85,674	2,374	16,364	44,115	38,598	5,517	4,522	12,125
Mississippi	99,843	48,369	51,474	1,201	8,867	11,667	9,272	2,395	599	1,577
Missouri	178,974	102,949	76,025	2,432	17,204	73,054	68,072	4,982	5,965	18,988
Montana	30,410	26,329	4,081	222	3,133	5,788	3,369	2,419	—	91
Nebraska	91,003	48,207	42,796	1,384	10,809	16,848	16,321	527	1,460	1,099
Nevada	56,827	24,223	32,604	205	6,160	685	660	25	—	—
New Hampshire	31,966	22,709	9,257	—	3,289	22,568	18,708	3,860	304	5,797
New Jersey	247,899	109,186	138,713	3,407	27,079	45,291	41,058	4,233	2,987	16,569
New Mexico	82,550	38,982	43,568	630	11,721	3,072	2,235	837	—	1,303
New York	541,181	278,762	262,419	4,749	60,378	324,658	294,134	30,524	22,257	111,599
North Carolina	287,368	128,443	158,925	2,537	25,613	58,102	54,895	3,207	3,551	6,282
North Dakota	33,771	25,659	8,112	505	2,507	3,536	3,298	238	—	151
Ohio	382,697	229,531	153,166	7,608	46,722	113,195	92,268	20,927	4,652	18,309
Oklahoma	143,190	75,978	67,212	2,113	19,425	18,309	15,043	3,266	1,462	3,347
Oregon	130,019	49,971	80,048	1,144	13,739	16,759	16,454	305	2,626	3,128
Pennsylvania	317,393	197,290	120,103	4,431	38,032	213,320	169,539	43,781	10,746	42,982
Rhode Island	37,561	19,575	17,986	13	5,690	31,803	31,803	—	299	3,799
South Carolina	124,385	65,888	58,497	1,822	19,373	23,659	21,326	2,333	603	1,601
South Dakota	25,866	25,711	155	422	4,058	6,922	6,737	185	80	248
Tennessee	171,299	94,095	77,204	2,572	18,431	42,373	38,374	3,999	2,976	5,319
Texas	740,792	330,240	410,552	9,886	81,780	80,096	75,187	4,909	7,083	18,889
Utah	89,345	54,748	34,597	782	6,831	32,863	31,749	1,114	481	2,781
Vermont	19,362	13,831	5,531	377	1,658	12,751	12,574	177	504	2,725
Virginia	256,057	121,953	134,104	4,171	37,294	46,870	42,803	4,067	2,137	7,643
Washington	224,396	68,649	155,747	1,603	12,764	26,662	24,217	2,445	1,641	8,490
West Virginia	66,231	58,920	7,311	1,359	11,694	10,586	9,714	872	—	382
Wisconsin	231,491	124,074	107,417	1,754	23,645	41,763	39,982	1,781	1,717	7,532
Wyoming	27,930	9,287	18,643	222	2,535	861	—	861	—	—
U.S. Service Schools	49,099	14,805	34,294	666	2,857	—	—	—	—	—
Outlying areas	60,300	49,724	10,576	1,124	5,278	95,778	84,057	11,721	1,650	5,629
American Samoa	1,295	—	1,295	—	—	—	—	—	—	—
Federated States of Micronesia	1,028	—	1,028	—	—	—	—	—	—	—
Guam	4,581	2,892	1,689	—	264	—	—	—	—	—
Marshall Islands	374	—	374	—	—	—	—	—	—	—
Northern Marianas	796	—	796	—	—	—	—	—	—	—
Palau	445	—	445	—	—	—	—	—	—	—
Puerto Rico	49,197	44,248	4,949	1,124	4,742	95,778	84,057	11,721	1,650	5,629
Virgin Islands	2,584	2,584	—	—	272	—	—	—	—	—

—Data not reported or not applicable.
[1] Revised from previously published data.

SOURCE: U.S. Department of Education, National Center for Education Statistics, Integrated Postsecondary Education Data System (IPEDS), "Fall Enrollment, 1992" survey. (This table was prepared February 1995.)

Table 194.—Full-time-equivalent fall enrollment in institutions of higher education, by control and type of institution: 1969 to 1993

Year	All institutions			Public institutions			Private institutions		
	Total	4-year	2-year	Total	4-year	2-year	Total	4-year	2-year
1	2	3	4	5	6	7	8	9	10
1969	6,334,139	4,899,526	1,434,612	4,577,985	3,259,676	1,318,309	1,756,153	1,639,850	116,303
1970	6,737,817	5,145,410	1,592,404	4,953,149	3,468,572	1,484,577	1,784,665	1,676,838	107,827
1971	7,148,575	5,357,708	1,790,867	5,344,356	3,660,624	1,683,732	1,804,219	1,697,084	107,135
1972	7,253,712	5,406,792	1,846,921	5,452,851	3,706,238	1,746,613	1,800,862	1,700,554	100,308
1973	7,453,467	5,439,226	2,014,241	5,629,568	3,721,035	1,908,533	1,823,899	1,718,191	105,708
1974	7,805,454	5,606,248	2,199,206	5,944,799	3,847,542	2,097,257	1,860,655	1,758,706	101,949
1975	8,479,688	5,900,403	2,579,285	6,522,310	4,056,500	2,465,810	1,957,378	1,843,903	113,475
1976	8,312,502	5,848,001	2,464,501	6,349,903	3,998,450	2,351,453	1,962,599	1,849,551	113,048
1977	8,415,339	5,935,076	2,480,263	6,396,476	4,039,071	2,357,405	2,018,863	1,896,005	122,858
1978	8,348,482	5,932,357	2,416,125	6,279,199	3,996,126	2,283,073	2,069,283	1,936,231	133,052
1979	8,487,317	6,016,072	2,471,245	6,392,617	4,059,304	2,333,313	2,094,700	1,956,768	137,932
1980	8,819,013	6,161,372	2,657,641	6,642,294	4,158,267	2,484,027	2,176,719	2,003,105	[1]173,614
1981	9,014,521	6,249,847	2,764,674	6,781,300	4,208,506	2,572,794	2,233,221	2,041,341	[1]191,880
1982	9,091,648	6,248,923	2,842,725	6,850,589	4,220,648	2,629,941	2,241,059	2,028,275	212,784
1983	9,166,398	6,325,222	2,841,176	6,881,479	4,265,807	2,615,672	2,284,919	2,059,415	225,504
1984	8,951,695	6,292,711	2,658,984	6,684,664	4,237,895	2,446,769	2,267,031	2,054,816	212,215
1985	8,943,433	6,294,339	2,649,094	6,667,781	4,239,622	2,428,159	2,275,652	2,054,717	220,935
1986	9,064,165	6,360,325	2,703,842	6,778,045	4,295,494	2,482,551	2,286,122	2,064,831	[2]221,291
1987	9,229,736	6,486,504	2,743,230	6,937,690	4,395,728	2,541,961	2,292,045	2,090,776	201,269
1988	9,464,271	6,664,146	2,800,125	7,096,905	4,505,774	2,591,131	2,367,366	2,158,372	208,994
1989	9,780,881	6,813,602	2,967,279	7,371,590	4,619,828	2,751,762	2,409,291	2,193,774	215,517
1990	9,983,436	6,968,008	3,015,428	7,557,982	4,740,049	2,817,933	2,425,454	2,227,959	197,495
1991	10,360,606	7,081,454	3,279,152	7,862,845	4,795,704	3,067,141	2,497,761	2,285,750	212,011
1992[3]	10,435,759	7,128,362	3,307,397	7,911,701	4,797,884	3,113,817	2,524,058	2,330,478	193,580
1993[4]	10,351,817	7,121,323	3,230,494	7,812,394	4,765,983	3,046,411	2,539,423	2,355,340	184,083

[1] Large increases are due to the addition of schools accredited by the Accrediting Commission of Career Schools and Colleges of Technology in 1980 and 1981.

[2] Because of imputation techniques, data are not consistent with figures for other years.

[3] Revised from previously published data.

[4] Preliminary data.

NOTE.—Because of a revision in data compilation procedures, figures for 1986 and later years are not directly comparable with data for earlier years.

SOURCE: U.S. Department of Education, National Center for Education Statistics, "Fall Enrollment in Colleges and Universities;" and Integrated Postsecondary Education Data System (IPEDS), "Fall Enrollment" surveys. (This table was prepared January 1995.)

Table 195.—Full-time-equivalent fall enrollment in institutions of higher education, by control, type of institution, and state: 1991 to 1993

State or other area	Public 4-year			Public 2-year			Private 4-year			Private 2-year		
	1991	1992[1]	1993[2]	1991	1992[1]	1993[2]	1991	1992[1]	1993[2]	1991	1992[1]	1993[2]
1	2	3	4	5	6	7	8	9	10	11	12	13
United States	4,795,704	4,797,884	4,765,983	3,067,141	3,113,817	3,046,411	2,285,750	2,330,478	2,355,340	212,011	193,580	184,083
Alabama	105,558	105,069	105,089	53,198	55,679	56,950	16,989	18,830	19,224	2,774	2,950	1,750
Alaska	18,006	18,039	18,072	—	235	253	924	974	1,004	342	359	238
Arizona	78,313	79,429	78,324	78,410	79,433	76,627	15,834	15,853	22,320	1,454	1,005	1,077
Arkansas	53,812	56,106	55,685	12,187	12,376	14,074	9,303	9,446	9,599	2,078	1,526	951
California	442,688	433,625	417,202	646,591	626,990	577,405	169,340	175,364	178,651	10,838	12,568	13,271
Colorado	103,912	104,438	104,399	38,048	41,449	40,444	17,139	17,934	18,942	5,090	4,011	3,867
Connecticut	47,380	46,388	45,083	22,224	23,073	22,805	43,604	42,727	42,414	1,038	1,212	1,163
Delaware	20,089	20,281	20,946	6,782	6,629	6,349	5,402	5,072	5,182	—	—	—
District of Columbia	7,220	7,405	6,839	—	—	—	52,991	55,456	56,151	—	—	—
Florida	140,863	142,906	147,729	181,328	182,004	180,327	78,365	80,717	79,769	6,697	5,815	4,454
Georgia	122,182	125,076	126,594	44,323	52,110	54,825	44,497	46,568	50,329	7,316	7,298	5,685
Hawaii	18,435	18,660	19,311	13,541	15,729	16,025	9,201	9,116	9,287	—	—	—
Idaho	29,544	30,993	31,449	4,382	4,630	5,007	2,168	2,279	2,141	8,154	8,056	8,522
Illinois	165,495	165,247	163,884	198,713	197,756	191,411	134,676	137,704	139,625	8,580	6,182	5,819
Indiana	150,534	153,190	151,282	23,434	25,216	23,954	51,745	52,037	53,004	3,169	2,829	2,953
Iowa	59,456	58,773	58,156	37,395	39,895	39,833	40,187	40,369	40,644	2,006	1,913	1,930
Kansas	73,573	73,356	73,783	35,306	36,435	36,132	12,006	12,411	12,663	776	868	819
Kentucky	88,921	89,506	88,286	28,558	30,134	30,565	22,545	22,079	22,256	4,858	4,280	4,618
Louisiana	121,435	126,708	123,798	12,759	16,916	17,155	22,854	22,376	23,050	1,990	680	602
Maine	25,381	24,626	24,035	4,403	4,594	4,593	11,160	11,657	11,545	1,354	1,373	1,506
Maryland	86,728	86,358	85,869	59,956	60,510	59,917	27,675	28,175	28,575	742	836	870
Massachusetts	81,987	81,357	79,000	46,403	48,116	48,436	186,478	185,982	184,779	8,928	9,735	9,592
Michigan	208,975	206,325	209,703	117,260	114,237	114,289	60,390	62,785	62,076	2,225	2,279	1,971
Minnesota	97,675	94,668	91,811	44,375	56,709	55,659	43,906	45,596	46,201	3,479	4,804	3,833
Mississippi	53,693	52,038	51,147	40,851	40,955	41,568	8,941	9,589	9,928	2,644	2,044	1,107
Missouri	102,422	99,726	97,160	42,940	42,758	44,231	67,790	69,008	69,802	2,810	4,367	5,150
Montana	25,680	26,088	26,678	2,808	3,039	2,992	2,570	2,807	3,556	908	1,591	571
Nebraska	48,504	48,846	48,511	18,044	23,029	18,634	15,382	15,823	16,285	403	428	443
Nevada	21,699	21,696	21,318	13,188	13,998	13,807	273	575	559	302	25	25
New Hampshire	21,279	21,630	21,763	5,150	5,368	5,316	19,824	19,216	18,876	2,711	3,048	3,108
New Jersey	103,519	104,568	103,462	77,385	81,494	83,472	44,703	45,071	45,114	3,271	3,439	3,435
New Mexico	39,219	40,008	41,227	22,190	23,693	25,099	2,271	2,705	2,214	539	762	566
New York	267,929	268,332	268,270	177,556	179,438	182,769	333,933	342,511	344,043	30,038	28,056	27,827
North Carolina	128,412	131,736	131,718	91,592	95,541	91,489	55,736	58,312	58,064	4,212	2,947	2,538
North Dakota	24,287	25,105	25,257	6,281	6,567	6,592	2,945	3,107	3,094	222	234	264
Ohio	239,094	234,763	228,303	85,100	91,025	92,358	93,186	94,134	95,266	12,186	14,318	10,381
Oklahoma	79,792	78,795	77,877	47,257	43,586	38,250	17,741	17,292	17,652	3,502	2,776	1,948
Oregon	54,724	53,812	52,787	44,921	46,742	46,522	19,179	19,172	19,345	280	299	182
Pennsylvania	201,401	204,341	200,053	68,138	68,492	67,024	176,509	179,575	179,371	41,486	27,916	29,184
Rhode Island	19,518	19,476	18,836	9,449	9,693	8,696	31,383	30,937	29,658	—	—	2,025
South Carolina	71,835	72,719	71,698	35,302	36,394	37,219	22,511	20,969	21,103	2,405	2,117	1,748
South Dakota	23,642	24,707	26,215	137	141	171	5,774	5,651	5,336	127	116	128
Tennessee	92,917	94,401	94,910	46,088	47,696	47,353	42,335	42,201	43,144	4,424	3,586	2,846
Texas	338,908	338,888	339,313	224,211	234,411	233,900	80,862	85,507	86,388	4,780	4,802	4,875
Utah	48,233	49,252	58,244	21,382	23,857	17,260	31,945	32,383	33,985	940	969	1,085
Vermont	14,034	13,646	13,415	2,413	2,530	2,479	13,449	13,295	12,729	132	163	161
Virginia	137,445	137,313	136,339	69,749	69,624	68,650	44,847	43,721	42,023	3,408	3,430	3,698
Washington	73,712	75,079	76,501	93,604	94,077	96,449	27,176	27,593	29,432	2,109	2,372	1,988
West Virginia	57,150	57,750	56,628	4,942	4,947	4,840	6,762	8,575	8,860	2,078	861	944
Wisconsin	129,432	126,240	123,700	61,238	62,623	65,297	38,344	39,242	40,082	1,339	1,581	1,665
Wyoming	10,545	10,180	9,976	11,355	11,298	11,364	—	—	—	867	754	700
U.S. Service Schools	18,517	18,220	18,348	34,294	19,946	19,575	—	—	—	—	—	—
Outlying areas	48,527	48,186	48,931	7,507	7,950	9,021	79,912	78,952	77,146	9,268	10,745	11,393
American Samoa	—	—	—	997	1,029	1,007	—	—	—	—	—	—
Federated States of Micronesia	—	—	—	597	690	743	—	—	—	—	—	—
Guam	2,386	2,418	2,908	864	689	912	—	—	—	—	—	—
Marshall Islands	—	—	—	—	296	374	—	—	—	—	—	—
Northern Marianas	—	—	—	488	476	653	—	—	—	—	—	—
Palau	—	—	—	309	382	377	—	—	—	—	—	—
Puerto Rico	44,502	43,962	44,107	4,252	4,388	4,955	79,912	78,952	77,146	9,268	10,745	11,393
Virgin Islands	1,639	1,806	1,916	—	—	—	—	—	—	—	—	—

[1] Revised from previously published data.
[2] Preliminary data.
—Data not reported or not applicable.

SOURCE: U.S. Department of Education, National Center for Education Statistics, Integrated Postsecondary Education Data System (IPEDS), "Fall Enrollment" surveys. (This table was prepared February 1995.)

Table 196.—Full-time-equivalent fall enrollment in institutions of higher education, by control and state: 1980 to 1993

State or other area	Total 1980	Total 1985	Total 1990	Total 1992[1]	Total 1993[2]	Public 1990	Public 1992[1]	Public 1993[2]	Private 1990	Private 1992[1]	Private 1993[2]
1	2	3	4	5	6	7	8	9	10	11	12
United States	8,819,013	8,943,433	9,983,436	10,435,759	10,351,817	7,557,982	7,911,701	7,812,394	2,425,454	2,524,058	2,539,423
Alabama	138,910	149,895	174,610	182,528	183,013	154,343	160,748	162,039	20,267	21,780	20,974
Alaska	10,073	14,098	18,496	19,607	19,567	17,087	18,274	18,325	1,409	1,333	1,242
Arizona	127,114	134,954	167,617	175,720	178,348	153,500	158,862	154,951	14,117	16,858	23,397
Arkansas	64,307	63,230	74,449	79,454	80,309	63,472	68,482	69,759	10,977	10,972	10,550
California	1,099,559	1,062,439	1,156,288	1,248,547	1,186,529	979,663	1,060,615	994,607	176,625	187,932	191,922
Colorado	123,589	121,804	159,032	167,832	167,652	138,350	145,887	144,843	20,682	21,945	22,809
Connecticut	112,612	107,803	115,791	113,400	111,465	70,870	69,461	67,888	44,921	43,939	43,577
Delaware	26,284	25,750	31,612	31,982	32,477	26,059	26,910	27,295	5,553	5,072	5,182
District of Columbia	62,126	59,198	61,845	62,861	62,990	7,590	7,405	6,839	54,255	55,456	56,151
Florida	290,647	308,315	383,385	411,442	412,279	302,579	324,910	328,056	80,806	86,532	84,223
Georgia	152,369	161,952	198,549	231,052	237,433	149,115	177,186	181,419	49,434	53,866	56,014
Hawaii	35,859	36,986	41,097	43,505	44,623	32,496	34,389	35,336	8,601	9,116	9,287
Idaho	33,938	32,649	41,275	45,958	47,119	31,408	35,623	36,456	9,867	10,335	10,663
Illinois	432,365	450,504	493,364	506,889	500,739	353,247	363,003	355,295	140,117	143,886	145,444
Indiana	193,445	195,630	222,835	233,272	231,193	168,984	178,406	175,236	53,851	54,866	55,957
Iowa	120,083	128,492	138,565	140,950	140,563	95,772	98,668	97,989	42,793	42,282	42,574
Kansas	101,147	100,807	118,969	123,070	123,397	106,570	109,791	109,915	12,399	13,279	13,482
Kentucky	113,709	110,539	137,651	145,999	145,725	111,858	119,640	118,851	25,793	26,359	26,874
Louisiana	132,780	148,983	154,132	166,680	164,605	129,357	143,624	140,953	24,775	23,056	23,652
Maine	34,471	37,993	42,021	42,250	41,679	29,876	29,220	28,628	12,145	13,030	13,051
Maryland	149,202	148,091	169,972	175,879	175,231	141,950	146,868	145,786	28,022	29,011	29,445
Massachusetts	315,937	321,022	320,299	325,190	321,807	130,962	129,473	127,436	189,337	195,717	194,371
Michigan	366,058	354,690	389,814	385,626	388,039	326,952	320,562	323,992	62,862	65,064	64,047
Minnesota	162,559	170,958	190,608	201,777	197,504	143,424	151,377	147,470	47,184	50,400	50,034
Mississippi	85,621	86,846	103,957	104,626	103,750	92,269	92,993	92,715	11,688	11,633	11,035
Missouri	180,156	178,090	210,104	215,859	216,343	142,953	142,484	141,391	67,151	73,375	74,952
Montana	29,428	29,992	29,905	33,525	33,797	26,835	29,127	29,670	3,070	4,398	4,127
Nebraska	68,505	70,778	80,989	88,126	83,873	65,739	71,875	67,145	15,250	16,251	16,728
Nevada	22,467	23,093	33,814	36,294	35,709	33,392	35,694	35,125	422	600	584
New Hampshire	39,456	41,733	45,762	49,262	49,063	24,948	26,998	27,079	20,814	22,264	21,984
New Jersey	218,838	201,270	221,468	234,572	235,483	174,324	186,062	186,934	47,144	48,510	48,549
New Mexico	43,722	47,169	59,517	67,168	69,106	57,870	63,701	66,326	1,647	3,467	2,780
New York	760,305	763,596	798,696	818,337	822,909	446,379	447,770	451,039	352,317	370,567	371,870
North Carolina	235,266	249,901	269,025	288,536	283,809	208,321	227,277	223,207	60,704	61,259	60,602
North Dakota	30,188	32,456	33,118	35,013	35,207	30,276	31,672	31,849	2,842	3,341	3,358
Ohio	369,342	383,898	420,499	434,240	426,308	317,837	325,788	320,661	102,662	108,452	105,647
Oklahoma	115,701	126,691	128,203	142,449	135,727	108,933	122,381	116,127	19,270	20,068	19,600
Oregon	110,649	102,247	120,176	120,025	118,836	101,424	100,554	99,309	18,752	19,471	19,527
Pennsylvania	404,192	422,349	464,179	480,324	475,632	261,305	272,833	267,077	202,874	207,491	208,555
Rhode Island	50,628	53,016	60,168	60,106	59,215	28,804	29,169	27,532	31,364	30,937	31,683
South Carolina	109,346	109,303	127,225	132,199	131,768	101,918	109,113	108,917	25,307	23,086	22,851
South Dakota	27,873	26,988	28,256	30,615	31,850	22,128	24,848	26,386	6,128	5,767	5,464
Tennessee	161,058	152,967	175,961	187,884	188,253	130,184	142,097	142,263	45,777	45,787	45,990
Texas	527,724	566,736	637,742	663,608	664,476	553,436	573,299	573,213	84,306	90,309	91,263
Utah	78,199	84,095	94,012	106,461	110,574	63,495	73,109	75,504	30,517	33,352	35,070
Vermont	25,572	25,649	29,072	29,634	28,784	16,048	16,176	15,894	13,024	13,458	12,890
Virginia	199,549	204,928	251,708	254,088	250,710	202,285	206,937	204,989	49,423	47,151	45,721
Washington	194,440	171,668	189,521	199,121	204,370	160,889	169,156	172,950	28,632	29,965	31,420
West Virginia	60,394	58,438	68,235	72,133	71,272	59,229	62,697	61,468	9,006	9,436	9,804
Wisconsin	206,790	211,749	229,975	229,686	230,744	192,107	188,863	188,997	37,868	40,823	41,747
Wyoming	14,725	17,037	21,888	22,232	22,040	21,185	21,478	21,340	703	754	700
U.S. Service Schools	49,736	53,968	47,985	38,166	37,923	47,985	38,166	37,923	—	—	—
Outlying areas	117,637	145,530	140,954	145,833	146,491	55,908	56,136	57,952	85,046	89,697	88,539
American Samoa	824	497	952	1,029	1,007	952	1,029	1,007	—	—	—
Federated States of Micronesia	—	—	549	690	743	549	690	743	—	—	—
Guam	2,115	3,049	2,956	3,107	3,820	2,956	3,107	3,820	—	—	—
Marshall Islands	—	—	—	296	374	—	296	374	—	—	—
Northern Marianas	—	183	376	476	653	376	476	653	—	—	—
Palau	—	—	423	382	377	423	382	377	—	—	—
Puerto Rico	113,285	139,627	134,193	138,047	137,601	49,147	48,350	49,062	85,046	89,697	88,539
Trust Territory of the Pacific	195	680	—	—	—	—	—	—	—	—	—
Virgin Islands	1,218	1,494	1,505	1,806	1,916	1,505	1,806	1,916	—	—	—

[1] Revised from previously published data.
[2] Preliminary data.
—Data not reported or not applicable.

SOURCE: U.S. Department of Education, National Center for Education Statistics, Integrated Postsecondary Education Data System (IPEDS), "Fall Enrollment" surveys. (This table was prepared February 1995.)

Table 197.—Residence and migration of all new undergraduate students [1] in institutions of higher education, by state: Fall 1992

State or other area	Students enrolled in institutions located in the state [2]	Student residents of state — Attending college in any state [3]	Student residents of state — Attending college in home state [4]	Ratio of students remaining to — Students enrolled (col.4 ÷ col.2)	Ratio of students remaining to — Student residents (col.4 ÷ col.3)	Migration of students — Out of (col.3–col.4)	Migration of students — Into (col.2–col.4)	Migration of students — Net (col.8–col.7)
1	2	3	4	5	6	7	8	9
United States	**2,066,058**	**2,028,759**	**1,718,436**	**0.83**	**0.85**	**310,323**	**347,622**	**[5] 37,299**
Alabama	42,234	36,912	34,298	0.81	0.93	2,614	7,936	5,322
Alaska	2,480	3,474	2,127	0.86	0.61	1,347	353	–994
Arizona	30,438	27,236	24,996	0.82	0.92	2,240	5,442	3,202
Arkansas	18,364	17,751	15,341	0.84	0.86	2,410	3,023	613
California	213,910	211,656	196,614	0.92	0.93	15,042	17,296	2,254
Colorado	34,082	30,340	25,586	0.75	0.84	4,754	8,496	3,742
Connecticut	22,769	27,631	16,374	0.72	0.59	11,257	6,395	–4,862
Delaware	7,227	5,832	4,334	0.60	0.74	1,498	2,893	1,395
District of Columbia	8,427	2,573	1,211	0.14	0.47	1,362	7,216	5,854
Florida	70,565	67,769	57,423	0.81	0.85	10,346	13,142	2,796
Georgia	52,148	51,377	43,780	0.84	0.85	7,597	8,368	771
Hawaii	9,445	9,644	7,874	0.83	0.82	1,770	1,571	–199
Idaho	10,960	9,339	7,395	0.67	0.79	1,944	3,565	1,621
Illinois	114,044	122,220	105,034	0.92	0.86	17,186	9,010	–8,176
Indiana	49,304	43,916	38,478	0.78	0.88	5,438	10,826	5,388
Iowa	36,538	32,517	28,825	0.79	0.89	3,692	7,713	4,021
Kansas	25,453	23,111	20,742	0.81	0.90	2,369	4,711	2,342
Kentucky	29,114	27,271	24,356	0.84	0.89	2,915	4,758	1,843
Louisiana	31,810	30,176	26,831	0.84	0.89	3,345	4,979	1,634
Maine	8,765	10,059	6,532	0.75	0.65	3,527	2,233	–1,294
Maryland	33,288	36,314	26,124	0.78	0.72	10,190	7,164	–3,026
Massachusetts	59,460	51,008	37,880	0.64	0.74	13,128	21,580	8,452
Michigan	87,772	88,771	81,831	0.93	0.92	6,940	5,941	–999
Minnesota	41,718	42,336	34,113	0.82	0.81	8,223	7,605	–618
Mississippi	24,848	23,178	21,230	0.85	0.92	1,948	3,618	1,670
Missouri	38,821	36,375	30,828	0.79	0.85	5,547	7,993	2,446
Montana	6,413	6,636	4,873	0.76	0.73	1,763	1,540	–223
Nebraska	16,156	16,193	13,569	0.84	0.84	2,624	2,587	–37
Nevada	4,521	5,126	3,650	0.81	0.71	1,476	871	–605
New Hampshire	11,297	9,308	5,863	0.52	0.63	3,445	5,434	1,989
New Jersey	44,611	64,431	41,016	0.92	0.64	23,415	3,595	–19,820
New Mexico	11,419	11,734	9,722	0.85	0.83	2,012	1,697	–315
New York	153,852	157,069	132,243	0.86	0.84	24,826	21,609	–3,217
North Carolina	55,013	45,935	42,947	0.78	0.93	2,988	12,066	9,078
North Dakota	8,684	7,100	5,812	0.67	0.82	1,288	2,872	1,584
Ohio	91,169	89,456	78,698	0.86	0.88	10,758	12,471	1,713
Oklahoma	30,050	29,706	26,979	0.90	0.91	2,727	3,071	344
Oregon	22,733	21,353	18,193	0.80	0.85	3,160	4,540	1,380
Pennsylvania	100,964	94,435	79,950	0.79	0.85	14,485	21,014	6,529
Rhode Island	12,813	8,046	5,743	0.45	0.71	2,303	7,070	4,767
South Carolina	20,906	19,733	16,808	0.80	0.85	2,925	4,098	1,173
South Dakota	6,398	5,998	4,529	0.71	0.76	1,469	1,869	400
Tennessee	34,622	32,909	28,040	0.81	0.85	4,869	6,582	1,713
Texas	124,246	123,208	114,300	0.92	0.93	8,908	9,946	1,038
Utah	23,536	18,931	17,726	0.75	0.94	1,205	5,810	4,605
Vermont	6,274	4,478	2,707	0.43	0.60	1,771	3,567	1,796
Virginia	44,683	40,877	32,505	0.73	0.80	8,372	12,178	3,806
Washington	64,913	62,565	57,843	0.89	0.92	4,722	7,070	2,348
West Virginia	16,941	15,003	12,745	0.75	0.85	2,258	4,196	1,938
Wisconsin	46,043	44,993	38,734	0.84	0.86	6,259	7,309	1,050
Wyoming	3,817	4,258	3,084	0.81	0.72	1,174	733	–441
State unknown [6]	—	20,492	—	—	—	20,492	—	–20,492
Outlying areas	30,461	32,257	29,734	0.98	0.92	2,523	727	–1,796
American Samoa	—	166	—	—	—	166	—	–166
Guam	709	607	489	0.69	0.81	118	220	102
Northern Marianas	173	184	173	1.00	0.94	11	—	–11
Palau	572	327	157	0.27	0.48	170	415	245
Puerto Rico	29,007	30,062	28,915	1.00	0.96	1,147	92	–1,055
Virgin Islands	—	911	—	—	—	911	—	–911
Foreign countries	—	35,503	—	—	—	35,503	—	–35,503

[1] Students who are enrolled at the reporting institution for the first time.
[2] All of the new students reported by the institutions in that state; i.e., all in-migrants and "remaining" students.
[3] All students living in a particular state when admitted to an institution in any state. Students may be enrolled in any state.
[4] Students who attend institutions in their home state.
[5] Includes students coming to U.S. colleges from foreign countries and the outlying areas.
[6] Students are reported in "state unknown" when an institution is unable to determine the student's home state.

—Data not available or not applicable.

NOTE.—Data for U.S. Service Schools are included in state totals.

SOURCE: U.S. Department of Education, National Center for Education Statistics, Integrated Postsecondary Education Data System (IPEDS), "Residence of First-Time Students" survey, 1992. (This table was prepared May 1994.)

Table 198.—Residence and migration of all freshmen students [1] graduating from high school in the past 12 months, by state: Fall 1992

State or other area	Students enrolled in institutions located in the state [2]	Student residents of state — Attending college in any state [3]	Student residents of state — Attending college in home state [4]	Ratio of students remaining to— Students enrolled (col.4 ÷ col.2)	Ratio of students remaining to— Student residents (col.4 ÷ col.3)	Migration of students — Out of (col.3– col.4)	Migration of students — Into (col.2– col.4)	Migration of students — Net (col.8– col.7)
1	2	3	4	5	6	7	8	9
United States	**1,354,837**	**1,332,410**	**1,078,273**	**0.80**	**0.81**	**254,137**	**276,564**	**[5] 22,427**
Alabama	28,564	23,768	21,672	0.76	0.91	2,096	6,892	4,796
Alaska	1,422	2,243	1,158	0.81	0.52	1,085	264	–821
Arizona	17,128	15,037	13,193	0.77	0.88	1,844	3,935	2,091
Arkansas	12,904	12,242	10,423	0.81	0.85	1,819	2,481	662
California	136,588	136,870	124,362	0.91	0.91	12,508	12,226	–282
Colorado	18,692	16,747	12,643	0.68	0.75	4,104	6,049	1,945
Connecticut	15,151	19,768	9,550	0.63	0.48	10,218	5,601	–4,617
Delaware	5,189	3,814	2,525	0.49	0.66	1,289	2,664	1,375
District of Columbia	5,794	1,502	393	0.07	0.26	1,109	5,401	4,292
Florida	46,538	46,598	37,812	0.81	0.81	8,786	8,726	–60
Georgia	34,276	34,323	27,604	0.81	0.80	6,719	6,672	–47
Hawaii	5,635	6,428	4,871	0.86	0.76	1,557	764	–793
Idaho	8,016	6,374	4,932	0.62	0.77	1,442	3,084	1,642
Illinois	65,150	72,460	58,049	0.89	0.80	14,411	7,101	–7,310
Indiana	36,896	30,654	27,060	0.73	0.88	3,594	9,836	6,242
Iowa	23,245	20,152	16,997	0.73	0.84	3,155	6,248	3,093
Kansas	16,318	14,750	12,806	0.78	0.87	1,944	3,512	1,568
Kentucky	5,721	6,201	3,966	0.69	0.64	2,235	1,755	–480
Louisiana	23,537	21,907	19,141	0.81	0.87	2,766	4,396	1,630
Maine	6,327	7,179	4,258	0.67	0.59	2,921	2,069	–852
Maryland	22,457	25,559	16,641	0.74	0.65	8,918	5,816	–3,102
Massachusetts	43,745	36,245	24,391	0.56	0.67	11,854	19,354	7,500
Michigan	56,372	57,014	51,450	0.91	0.90	5,564	4,922	–642
Minnesota	25,722	26,845	19,888	0.77	0.74	6,957	5,834	–1,123
Mississippi	17,633	16,208	14,574	0.83	0.90	1,634	3,059	1,425
Missouri	27,243	25,780	21,252	0.78	0.82	4,528	5,991	1,463
Montana	4,560	4,793	3,312	0.73	0.69	1,481	1,248	–233
Nebraska	12,427	12,383	10,211	0.82	0.82	2,172	2,216	44
Nevada	2,353	2,980	1,760	0.75	0.59	1,220	593	–627
New Hampshire	8,656	6,865	3,865	0.45	0.56	3,000	4,791	1,791
New Jersey	29,591	48,053	26,723	0.90	0.56	21,330	2,868	–18,462
New Mexico	7,535	7,839	6,221	0.83	0.79	1,618	1,314	–304
New York	105,105	108,998	87,233	0.83	0.80	21,765	17,872	–3,893
North Carolina	40,438	31,811	29,394	0.73	0.92	2,417	11,044	8,627
North Dakota	6,797	5,307	4,259	0.63	0.80	1,048	2,538	1,490
Ohio	59,194	58,829	50,203	0.85	0.85	8,626	8,991	365
Oklahoma	16,976	16,992	14,819	0.87	0.87	2,173	2,157	–16
Oregon	15,064	14,509	11,723	0.78	0.81	2,786	3,341	555
Pennsylvania	74,657	68,143	55,822	0.75	0.82	12,321	18,835	6,514
Rhode Island	10,422	6,000	3,980	0.38	0.66	2,020	6,442	4,422
South Carolina	15,324	14,333	11,790	0.77	0.82	2,543	3,534	991
South Dakota	4,321	4,017	2,804	0.65	0.70	1,213	1,517	304
Tennessee	24,873	22,838	19,179	0.77	0.84	3,659	5,694	2,035
Texas	80,501	81,097	73,511	0.91	0.91	7,586	6,990	–596
Utah	15,535	12,378	11,388	0.73	0.92	990	4,147	3,157
Vermont	4,926	3,364	1,785	0.36	0.53	1,579	3,141	1,562
Virginia	35,377	31,650	24,673	0.70	0.78	6,977	10,704	3,727
Washington	27,026	27,520	23,667	0.88	0.86	3,853	3,359	–494
West Virginia	12,241	10,127	8,604	0.70	0.85	1,523	3,637	2,114
Wisconsin	32,183	33,078	27,875	0.87	0.84	5,203	4,308	–895
Wyoming	2,492	2,752	1,861	0.75	0.68	891	631	260
State unknown [6]	—	9,086	—	—	—	9,086	—	9,086
Outlying areas	26,042	27,272	25,662	0.99	0.94	1,610	380	–1,230
American Samoa	—	138	—	—	—	138	—	–138
Guam	607	516	419	0.69	0.81	97	188	91
Northern Marianas	173	181	173	1.00	0.96	8	—	–8
Palau	260	270	150	0.58	0.56	120	110	–10
Puerto Rico	25,002	25,837	24,920	1.00	0.96	917	82	–835
Virgin Islands	—	330	—	—	—	330	—	–330
Foreign countries	—	21,197	—	—	—	21,197	—	–21,197

—Data not available or not applicable.

[1] Students who are enrolled at the reporting institution for the first time.

[2] All of the new students reported by the institutions in that state; i.e., all in-migrants and "remaining" students.

[3] All students living in a particular state when first admitted to an institution in any state. Students may be enrolled in any state.

[4] Students who attend institutions in their home state.

[5] Includes students coming to U.S. colleges from foreign countries and the outlying areas.

[6] Students are reported in "state unknown" when an institution is unable to determine the student's home state.

NOTE.—Data for U.S. Service Schools are included in state totals.

SOURCE: U.S. Department of Education, National Center for Education Statistics, Integrated Postsecondary Education Data System (IPEDS), "Residence of First-Time Students" survey, 1992. (This table was prepared May 1994.)

Table 199.—Residence and migration of all freshmen students [1] in 4-year colleges graduating from high school in the past 12 months, by state: Fall 1992

State or other area	Students enrolled in institutions located in the state [2]	Student residents of state		Ratio of students remaining to—		Migration of students		
		Attending college in any state [3]	Attending college in home state [4]	Students enrolled (col.4 ÷ col.2)	Student residents (col.4 ÷ col.3)	Out of (col.3– col.4)	Into (col.2– col.4)	Net (col.8– col.7)
1	2	3	4	5	6	7	8	9
United States	**900,018**	**880,261**	**648,221**	**0.72**	**0.74**	**232,040**	**251,797**	**[5] 19,757**
Alabama	17,582	13,079	11,238	0.64	0.86	1,841	6,344	4,503
Alaska	1,422	2,130	1,158	0.81	0.54	972	264	−708
Arizona	9,466	7,710	6,093	0.64	0.79	1,617	3,373	1,756
Arkansas	11,241	10,217	8,934	0.79	0.87	1,283	2,307	1,024
California	54,131	56,455	44,890	0.83	0.80	11,565	9,241	−2,324
Colorado	15,388	13,479	9,778	0.64	0.73	3,701	5,610	1,909
Connecticut	11,906	16,184	6,458	0.54	0.40	9,726	5,448	−4,278
Delaware	4,230	2,874	1,633	0.39	0.57	1,241	2,597	1,356
District of Columbia	5,794	1,456	393	0.07	0.27	1,063	5,401	4,338
Florida	23,280	24,714	16,408	0.70	0.66	8,306	6,872	−1,434
Georgia	23,238	23,288	17,110	0.74	0.73	6,178	6,128	−50
Hawaii	2,800	3,490	2,060	0.74	0.59	1,430	740	−690
Idaho	4,206	4,432	3,208	0.76	0.72	1,224	998	−226
Illinois	34,201	40,928	27,341	0.80	0.67	13,587	6,860	−6,727
Indiana	31,871	25,537	22,419	0.70	0.88	3,118	9,452	6,334
Iowa	14,898	12,222	9,310	0.62	0.76	2,912	5,588	2,676
Kansas	10,682	9,842	8,038	0.75	0.82	1,804	2,644	840
Kentucky	4,768	4,991	3,121	0.65	0.63	1,870	1,647	−223
Louisiana	20,305	18,317	15,923	0.78	0.87	2,394	4,382	1,988
Maine	5,375	6,062	3,353	0.62	0.55	2,709	2,022	−687
Maryland	13,436	16,628	8,013	0.60	0.48	8,615	5,423	−3,192
Massachusetts	35,495	28,655	17,242	0.49	0.60	11,413	18,253	6,840
Michigan	36,309	36,904	31,702	0.87	0.86	5,202	4,607	−595
Minnesota	18,095	19,511	12,962	0.72	0.66	6,549	5,133	−1,416
Mississippi	7,696	6,595	5,102	0.66	0.77	1,493	2,594	1,101
Missouri	21,418	20,014	15,920	0.74	0.80	4,094	5,498	1,404
Montana	4,128	4,042	2,915	0.71	0.72	1,127	1,213	86
Nebraska	9,766	9,708	7,769	0.80	0.80	1,939	1,997	58
Nevada	1,662	2,045	1,106	0.67	0.54	939	556	−383
New Hampshire	6,766	5,140	2,339	0.35	0.46	2,801	4,427	1,626
New Jersey	16,890	34,934	14,229	0.84	0.41	20,705	2,661	−18,044
New Mexico	4,613	4,968	3,636	0.79	0.73	1,332	977	−355
New York	71,357	75,353	54,428	0.76	0.72	20,925	16,929	−3,996
North Carolina	32,175	23,776	21,581	0.67	0.91	2,195	10,594	8,399
North Dakota	5,088	3,840	2,928	0.58	0.76	912	2,160	1,248
Ohio	46,481	46,331	38,363	0.83	0.83	7,968	8,118	150
Oklahoma	9,844	9,740	7,956	0.81	0.82	1,784	1,888	104
Oregon	8,314	7,930	5,451	0.66	0.69	2,479	2,863	384
Pennsylvania	58,986	52,546	41,022	0.70	0.78	11,524	17,964	6,440
Rhode Island	8,934	4,422	2,590	0.29	0.59	1,832	6,344	4,512
South Carolina	12,057	10,970	8,602	0.71	0.78	2,368	3,455	1,087
South Dakota	4,314	3,835	2,798	0.65	0.73	1,037	1,516	479
Tennessee	17,286	15,138	11,810	0.68	0.78	3,328	5,476	2,148
Texas	51,591	53,210	46,084	0.89	0.87	7,126	5,507	−1,619
Utah	9,837	6,717	6,249	0.64	0.93	468	3,588	3,120
Vermont	4,671	3,040	1,643	0.35	0.54	1,397	3,028	1,631
Virginia	29,066	25,158	18,585	0.64	0.74	6,573	10,481	3,908
Washington	12,419	12,922	9,658	0.78	0.75	3,264	2,761	−503
West Virginia	10,953	8,923	7,646	0.70	0.86	1,277	3,307	2,030
Wisconsin	22,417	23,011	18,286	0.82	0.79	4,725	4,131	−594
Wyoming	1,170	1,489	740	0.63	0.50	749	430	−319
State unknown [6]	—	5,359	—	—	—	5,359	—	−5,359
Outlying areas	20,963	22,210	20,721	0.99	0.93	1,489	242	−1,247
American Samoa	—	135	—	—	—	135	—	−135
Guam	594	498	410	0.69	0.82	88	184	96
Northern Marianas	—	8	—	—	—	8	—	−8
Palau	—	91	—	—	—	91	—	−91
Puerto Rico	20,369	21,165	20,311	1.00	0.96	854	58	−796
Virgin Islands	—	313	—	—	—	313	—	−313
Foreign countries	—	18,510	—	—	—	18,510	—	−18,510

[1] Students who are enrolled at the reporting institution for the first time.

[2] All of the new students reported by the institutions in that state; i.e., all in-migrants and "remaining" students.

[3] All students living in a particular state when first admitted to an institution in any state. Students may be enrolled in any state.

[4] Students who attend institutions in their home state.

[5] Includes students coming to U.S. colleges from foreign countries and the outlying areas.

[6] Students are reported in "state unknown" when an institution is unable to determine the student's home state.

—Data not available or not applicable.

NOTE.—Data for U.S. Service Schools are included in state totals.

SOURCE: U.S. Department of Education, National Center for Education Statistics, Integrated Postsecondary Education Data System (IPEDS), "Residence of First-Time Students" survey, 1992. (This table was prepared May 1994.)

Table 200.—Total fall enrollment in institutions of higher education, by type and control of institution and race/ethnicity of student: 1976 to 1993

Type and control of institution and race/ethnicity of student	Number, in thousands								Percentage distribution by type and control[1]						
	1976	1980	1984	1988	1990	1991	1992[2]	1993[3]	1976	1980	1988	1990	1991	1992[2]	1993[3]
1	2	3	4	5	6	7	8	9	10	11	12	13	14	15	16
All students															
Total	10,985.6	12,086.8	12,233.0	13,043.1	13,818.6	14,359.0	14,486.3	14,305.7	100.0	100.0	100.0	100.0	100.0	100.0	100.0
White, non-Hispanic	9,076.1	9,833.0	9,814.7	10,283.2	10,722.5	10,989.8	10,874.8	10,603.7	84.3	83.5	81.1	79.9	78.8	77.5	76.6
Total minority	1,690.8	1,948.8	2,083.8	2,398.8	2,704.7	2,952.8	3,163.8	3,245.1	15.7	16.5	18.9	20.1	21.2	22.5	23.4
Black, non-Hispanic	1,033.0	1,106.8	1,075.8	1,129.6	1,247.0	1,335.4	1,392.7	1,410.3	9.6	9.4	8.9	9.3	9.6	9.9	10.2
Hispanic	383.8	471.7	534.9	680.0	782.4	866.6	954.9	989.0	3.6	4.0	5.4	5.8	6.2	6.8	7.1
Asian or Pacific Islander	197.9	286.4	389.5	496.7	572.4	637.2	696.9	724.1	1.8	2.4	3.9	4.3	4.6	5.0	5.2
American Indian/Alaskan Native	76.1	83.9	83.6	92.5	102.8	113.7	119.3	121.7	0.7	0.7	0.7	0.8	0.8	0.8	0.9
Nonresident alien	218.7	305.0	334.6	361.2	391.5	416.4	447.7	456.8	—	—	—	—	—	—	—
4-year															
Total	7,106.5	7,565.4	7,706.1	8,175.0	8,578.6	8,707.1	8,763.9	8,739.8	100.0	100.0	100.0	100.0	100.0	100.0	100.0
White, non-Hispanic	5,999.0	6,274.5	6,300.4	6,581.6	6,768.1	6,791.0	6,743.6	6,643.2	86.6	85.7	83.6	82.0	81.2	80.2	79.3
Total minority	931.0	1,049.9	1,123.6	1,291.8	1,486.1	1,573.3	1,663.3	1,731.0	13.4	14.3	16.4	18.0	18.8	19.8	20.7
Black, non-Hispanic	603.7	634.3	617.0	656.3	722.8	757.8	791.0	811.3	8.7	8.7	8.3	8.8	9.1	9.4	9.7
Hispanic	173.6	216.6	246.1	296.0	358.2	382.9	409.9	432.1	2.5	3.0	3.8	4.3	4.6	4.9	5.2
Asian or Pacific Islander	118.7	162.1	222.4	297.4	357.2	381.5	407.4	429.1	1.7	2.2	3.8	4.3	4.6	4.8	5.1
American Indian/Alaskan Native	35.0	36.9	38.1	42.1	47.9	51.1	54.9	58.5	0.5	0.5	0.5	0.6	0.6	0.7	0.7
Nonresident alien	176.5	240.9	282.1	301.5	324.3	342.8	357.0	365.6	—	—	—	—	—	—	—
Public	4,892.9	5,127.6	5,196.0	5,544.0	5,848.2	5,904.7	5,900.0	5,851.8	69.1	68.0	68.1	68.5	68.1	67.7	67.3
White, non-Hispanic	4,120.2	4,243.0	4,229.9	4,454.8	4,605.6	4,597.4	4,532.0	4,432.9	59.5	57.9	56.6	55.8	55.0	53.9	52.9
Total minority	666.7	740.8	795.9	907.7	1,046.2	1,101.7	1,155.4	1,202.1	9.6	10.1	11.5	12.7	13.2	13.7	14.4
Black, non-Hispanic	421.8	438.2	426.7	448.5	495.1	516.2	535.4	548.2	6.1	6.0	5.7	6.0	6.2	6.4	6.5
Hispanic	129.3	156.4	178.8	215.8	262.5	278.7	295.1	311.5	1.9	2.1	2.7	3.2	3.3	3.5	3.7
Asian or Pacific Islander	87.5	117.2	160.3	210.2	250.6	266.2	281.8	296.6	1.3	1.6	2.7	3.0	3.2	3.4	3.5
American Indian/Alaskan Native	28.2	29.0	30.1	33.3	38.0	40.6	43.0	45.9	0.4	0.4	0.4	0.5	0.5	0.5	0.5
Nonresident alien	106.0	143.8	170.1	181.4	196.4	205.6	212.6	216.7	—	—	—	—	—	—	—
Private	2,213.6	2,437.8	2,510.2	2,631.0	2,730.3	2,802.3	2,863.9	2,888.0	30.9	32.0	31.9	31.5	31.9	32.3	32.7
White, non-Hispanic	1,878.8	2,031.5	2,070.5	2,126.8	2,162.5	2,193.5	2,211.6	2,210.3	27.1	27.7	27.0	26.2	26.2	26.3	26.4
Total minority	264.3	309.2	327.7	384.1	439.8	471.5	507.9	528.8	3.8	4.2	4.9	5.3	5.6	6.0	6.3
Black, non-Hispanic	182.0	196.1	190.4	207.8	227.7	241.5	255.7	263.1	2.6	2.7	2.6	2.8	2.9	3.0	3.1
Hispanic	44.3	60.2	67.3	80.2	95.7	104.2	114.8	120.6	0.6	0.8	1.0	1.2	1.2	1.4	1.4
Asian or Pacific Islander	31.2	44.9	62.1	87.2	106.6	115.3	125.6	132.5	0.5	0.6	1.1	1.3	1.4	1.5	1.6
American Indian/Alaskan Native	6.8	7.9	7.9	8.8	9.9	10.6	11.8	12.6	0.1	0.1	0.1	0.1	0.1	0.1	0.2
Nonresident alien	70.5	97.1	112.0	120.1	127.9	137.2	144.4	148.9	—	—	—	—	—	—	—
2-year															
Total	3,879.1	4,521.4	4,526.9	4,868.1	5,240.1	5,651.9	5,722.4	5,565.9	100.0	100.0	100.0	100.0	100.0	100.0	100.0
White, non-Hispanic	3,077.1	3,558.5	3,514.3	3,701.5	3,954.3	4,198.8	4,131.2	3,960.6	80.2	79.8	77.0	76.4	75.3	73.4	72.3
Total minority	759.8	898.9	960.1	1,106.9	1,218.6	1,379.6	1,500.6	1,514.1	19.8	20.2	23.0	23.6	24.7	26.6	27.7
Black, non-Hispanic	429.3	472.5	458.7	473.3	524.3	577.6	601.6	599.0	11.2	10.6	9.8	10.1	10.4	10.7	10.9
Hispanic	210.2	255.1	288.8	383.9	424.2	483.7	545.0	556.8	5.5	5.7	8.0	8.2	8.7	9.7	10.2
Asian or Pacific Islander	79.2	124.3	167.1	199.3	215.2	255.7	289.5	295.0	2.1	2.8	4.1	4.2	4.6	5.1	5.4
American Indian/Alaskan Native	41.2	47.0	45.5	50.4	54.9	62.6	64.4	63.2	1.1	1.1	1.0	1.1	1.1	1.1	1.2
Nonresident alien	42.2	64.1	52.5	59.6	67.1	73.5	90.6	91.2	—	—	—	—	—	—	—
Public	3,748.1	4,328.8	4,260.4	4,612.4	4,996.5	5,404.8	5,484.6	5,337.3	96.7	95.8	94.7	95.4	95.6	95.8	95.9
White, non-Hispanic	2,974.3	3,413.1	3,312.5	3,509.0	3,779.8	4,024.8	3,961.2	3,793.7	77.5	76.6	73.0	73.1	72.2	70.3	69.3
Total minority	734.5	855.4	899.0	1,047.0	1,153.0	1,310.3	1,436.4	1,456.0	19.1	19.2	21.8	22.3	23.5	25.5	26.6
Black, non-Hispanic	409.5	437.9	417.3	432.6	481.4	537.2	565.0	566.1	10.7	9.8	9.0	9.3	9.6	10.0	10.3
Hispanic	207.5	249.8	277.3	371.1	408.9	463.4	527.1	539.8	5.4	5.6	7.7	7.9	8.3	9.4	9.9
Asian or Pacific Islander	78.2	122.5	162.4	195.5	210.3	250.1	284.0	289.7	2.0	2.7	4.1	4.1	4.5	5.0	5.3
American Indian/Alaskan Native	39.3	45.2	42.0	47.8	52.4	59.6	60.3	60.5	1.0	1.0	1.0	1.0	1.1	1.1	1.1
Nonresident alien	39.2	60.3	48.9	56.4	63.6	69.7	86.9	87.6	—	—	—	—	—	—	—
Private	131.0	192.6	266.4	255.7	243.6	247.1	237.8	228.5	3.3	4.2	5.3	4.6	4.4	4.2	4.1
White, non-Hispanic	102.8	145.4	201.8	192.6	174.5	174.0	170.0	166.9	2.7	3.3	4.0	3.4	3.1	3.0	3.0
Total minority	25.3	43.5	61.2	60.0	65.6	69.3	64.1	58.1	0.7	1.0	1.2	1.3	1.2	1.1	1.1
Black, non-Hispanic	19.8	34.6	41.4	40.7	42.9	40.4	36.6	32.9	0.5	0.8	0.8	0.8	0.7	0.7	0.6
Hispanic	2.6	5.3	11.6	12.9	15.3	20.3	17.9	17.1	0.1	0.1	0.3	0.3	0.4	0.3	0.3
Asian or Pacific Islander	0.9	1.8	4.7	3.8	4.9	5.6	5.5	5.4	(4)	(4)	0.1	0.1	0.1	0.1	0.1
American Indian/Alaskan Native	1.8	1.8	3.5	2.7	2.5	3.0	4.1	2.7	(4)	(4)	(4)	(4)	(4)	0.1	(4)
Nonresident alien	3.0	3.7	3.5	3.2	3.5	3.8	3.7	3.6	—	—	—	—	—	—	—

[1] Distribution for U.S. citizens only.
[2] Revised from previously published data.
[3] Preliminary data.
[4] Less than 0.05 percent.
—Not applicable.

NOTE.—Because of underreporting and nonreporting of racial/ethnic data, some figures are slightly lower than corresponding data in other tables. Because of rounding, details may not add to totals.

SOURCE: U.S. Department of Education, National Center for Education Statistics, "Fall Enrollment in Colleges and Universities;" and Integrated Postsecondary Education Data System (IPEDS), "Fall Enrollment" surveys. (This table was prepared March 1995.)

Table 201.—Total fall enrollment in institutions of higher education, by level of study, sex, and race/ethnicity of student: 1976 to 1993

Level of study, sex, and race/ethnicity of student	Number, in thousands								Percent distribution by level of study [1]						
	1976	1980	1984	1988	1990	1991	1992 [2]	1993 [3]	1976	1980	1988	1990	1991	1992 [2]	1993 [3]
1	2	3	4	5	6	7	8	9	10	11	12	13	14	15	16
All students															
Total	10,985.6	12,086.8	12,233.0	13,043.1	13,818.6	14,359.0	14,486.3	14,305.7	100.0	100.0	100.0	100.0	100.0	100.0	100.0
White, non-Hispanic	9,076.1	9,833.0	9,814.7	10,283.2	10,722.5	10,989.8	10,874.8	10,603.7	84.3	83.5	81.1	79.9	78.8	77.5	76.6
Total minority	1,690.8	1,948.8	2,083.8	2,398.8	2,704.7	2,952.8	3,163.8	3,245.1	15.7	16.5	18.9	20.1	21.2	22.5	23.4
Black, non-Hispanic	1,033.0	1,106.8	1,075.8	1,129.6	1,247.0	1,335.4	1,392.7	1,410.3	9.6	9.4	8.9	9.3	9.6	9.9	10.2
Hispanic	383.8	471.7	534.9	680.0	782.4	866.6	954.9	989.0	3.6	4.0	5.4	5.8	6.2	6.8	7.1
Asian or Pacific Islander	197.9	286.4	389.5	496.7	572.4	637.2	696.9	724.1	1.8	2.4	3.9	4.3	4.6	5.0	5.2
American Indian/Alaskan Native	76.1	83.9	83.6	92.5	102.8	113.7	119.3	121.7	0.7	0.7	0.7	0.8	0.8	0.8	0.9
Nonresident alien	218.7	305.0	334.6	361.2	391.5	416.4	447.7	456.8	—	—	—	—	—	—	—
Men	5,794.4	5,868.1	5,858.3	5,998.2	6,283.9	6,501.8	6,523.5	6,427.7	52.4	48.0	45.4	45.0	44.8	44.5	44.4
White, non-Hispanic	4,813.7	4,772.9	4,689.9	4,711.6	4,861.0	4,962.2	4,884.3	4,756.0	44.7	40.5	37.2	36.2	35.6	35.4	34.3
Total minority	826.6	884.4	937.9	1,051.3	1,176.6	1,280.3	1,366.1	1,398.5	7.7	7.5	8.3	8.8	9.2	9.7	10.1
Black, non-Hispanic	469.9	463.7	436.8	442.7	484.7	517.0	536.8	542.9	4.4	3.9	3.5	3.6	3.7	3.8	3.9
Hispanic	209.7	231.6	253.8	310.3	353.9	390.5	427.7	441.4	1.9	2.0	2.4	2.6	2.8	3.0	3.2
Asian or Pacific Islander	108.4	151.3	210.0	259.2	294.9	325.1	351.4	363.0	1.0	1.3	2.0	2.2	2.3	2.5	2.6
American Indian/Alaskan Native	38.5	37.8	37.4	39.1	43.1	47.6	50.2	51.1	0.4	0.3	0.3	0.3	0.3	0.4	0.4
Nonresident alien	154.1	210.8	230.4	235.3	246.3	259.4	273.1	273.2	—	—	—	—	—	—	—
Women	5,191.2	6,218.7	6,374.7	7,044.9	7,534.7	7,857.1	7,962.8	7,877.9	47.6	52.0	54.6	55.0	55.2	55.5	55.6
White, non-Hispanic	4,262.4	5,060.1	5,124.7	5,571.6	5,861.5	6,027.6	5,990.5	5,847.7	39.6	42.9	43.9	43.7	43.2	42.7	42.2
Total minority	864.2	1,064.4	1,145.8	1,347.4	1,528.1	1,672.5	1,797.7	1,846.6	8.0	9.0	10.6	11.4	12.0	12.8	13.3
Black, non-Hispanic	563.1	643.0	639.0	686.9	762.3	818.4	855.9	867.4	5.2	5.5	5.4	5.7	5.9	6.1	6.3
Hispanic	174.1	240.1	281.2	369.6	428.5	476.0	527.2	547.6	1.6	2.0	2.9	3.2	3.4	3.8	4.0
Asian or Pacific Islander	89.4	135.2	179.5	237.5	277.5	312.0	345.5	361.1	0.8	1.1	1.9	2.1	2.2	2.5	2.6
American Indian/Alaskan Native	37.6	46.1	46.1	53.4	59.7	66.1	69.1	70.5	0.3	0.4	0.4	0.4	0.5	0.5	0.5
Nonresident alien	64.6	94.2	104.1	125.9	145.2	157.0	174.6	183.6	—	—	—	—	—	—	—
Undergraduate															
Total	9,419.0	10,469.1	10,610.8	11,304.2	11,959.1	12,439.3	12,536.7	12,324.0	100.0	100.0	100.0	100.0	100.0	100.0	100.0
White, non-Hispanic	7,740.5	8,480.7	8,484.0	8,906.7	9,272.6	9,507.7	9,386.8	9,102.9	83.4	82.7	80.2	79.0	77.9	76.4	75.5
Total minority	1,535.3	1,778.5	1,911.0	2,192.4	2,467.7	2,697.9	2,892.0	2,952.9	16.6	17.3	19.8	21.0	22.1	23.6	24.5
Black, non-Hispanic	943.4	1,018.0	994.9	1,038.8	1,147.2	1,229.3	1,280.5	1,288.4	10.2	9.9	9.4	9.8	10.1	10.4	10.7
Hispanic	352.9	433.1	495.2	631.2	724.6	804.2	887.7	918.0	3.8	4.2	5.7	6.2	6.6	7.2	7.6
Asian or Pacific Islander	169.3	248.7	343.0	436.6	500.5	558.7	612.9	633.9	1.8	2.4	3.9	4.3	4.6	5.0	5.3
American Indian/Alaskan Native	69.7	77.9	77.8	85.9	95.5	105.8	110.9	112.7	0.8	0.8	0.8	0.8	0.9	0.9	0.9
Nonresident alien	143.2	209.9	215.8	205.0	218.7	233.6	257.9	268.1	—	—	—	—	—	—	—
Men	4,896.8	4,997.4	5,002.4	5,133.7	5,379.8	5,571.0	5,582.5	5,483.7	51.8	47.3	45.1	44.7	44.6	44.3	44.3
White, non-Hispanic	4,052.2	4,054.9	4,005.1	4,053.8	4,184.4	4,273.0	4,195.1	4,067.6	43.7	39.5	36.5	35.6	35.0	34.2	33.7
Total minority	748.2	802.7	855.0	956.0	1,069.3	1,165.2	1,244.1	1,269.5	8.1	7.8	8.6	9.1	9.5	10.1	10.5
Black, non-Hispanic	430.7	428.2	404.8	408.2	448.0	478.1	495.5	499.0	4.6	4.2	3.7	3.8	3.9	4.0	4.1
Hispanic	191.7	211.2	233.9	287.2	326.9	361.4	397.0	409.2	2.1	2.1	2.6	2.8	3.0	3.2	3.4
Asian or Pacific Islander	91.1	128.5	181.7	224.4	254.5	281.5	305.0	314.1	1.0	1.3	2.0	2.2	2.3	2.5	2.6
American Indian/Alaskan Native	34.8	34.8	34.6	36.2	39.9	44.2	46.6	47.2	0.4	0.3	0.3	0.3	0.4	0.4	0.4
Nonresident alien	96.4	139.8	142.3	124.0	126.1	132.8	143.3	146.5	—	—	—	—	—	—	—
Women	4,522.1	5,471.7	5,608.4	6,170.4	6,579.3	6,868.3	6,954.2	6,840.3	48.2	52.7	54.9	55.3	55.4	55.7	55.7
White, non-Hispanic	3,688.3	4,425.8	4,478.9	4,852.9	5,088.2	5,234.8	5,191.7	5,035.3	39.8	43.1	43.7	43.3	42.9	42.3	41.8
Total minority	787.0	975.8	1,056.0	1,236.5	1,398.5	1,532.7	1,647.9	1,683.4	8.5	9.5	11.1	11.9	12.6	13.4	14.0
Black, non-Hispanic	512.7	590.6	590.2	630.6	699.2	751.1	785.0	789.4	5.5	5.8	5.7	6.0	6.2	6.4	6.5
Hispanic	161.2	221.8	261.3	344.0	397.6	442.7	490.7	508.7	1.7	2.2	3.1	3.4	3.6	4.0	4.2
Asian or Pacific Islander	78.2	120.2	161.4	212.2	246.0	277.2	307.9	319.8	0.8	1.2	1.9	2.1	2.3	2.5	2.7
American Indian/Alaskan Native	34.9	43.1	43.2	49.7	55.5	61.6	64.3	65.5	0.4	0.4	0.4	0.5	0.5	0.5	0.5
Nonresident alien	46.8	70.1	73.5	81.1	92.6	100.8	114.6	121.6	—	—	—	—	—	—	—
Graduate															
Total	1,322.5	1,340.9	1,343.7	1,471.9	1,586.2	1,639.1	1,668.7	1,689.3	100.0	100.0	100.0	100.0	100.0	100.0	100.0
White, non-Hispanic	1,115.6	1,104.7	1087.3	1153.2	1228.4	1258.0	1,267.4	1,274.9	89.2	88.5	87.3	86.6	86.0	85.3	84.6
Total minority	134.5	144.0	141.1	167.2	190.5	204.1	217.8	232.5	10.8	11.5	12.7	13.4	14.0	14.7	15.4
Black, non-Hispanic	78.5	75.1	67.4	76.5	83.9	88.9	94.0	101.7	6.3	6.0	5.8	5.9	6.1	6.3	6.7
Hispanic	26.4	32.1	31.7	39.5	47.2	50.9	55.2	58.2	2.1	2.6	3.0	3.3	3.5	3.7	3.9
Asian or Pacific Islander	24.5	31.6	37.1	45.7	53.2	57.6	61.5	65.2	2.0	2.5	3.5	3.8	3.9	4.1	4.3
American Indian/Alaskan Native	5.1	5.2	4.8	5.6	6.2	6.6	7.0	7.3	0.4	0.4	0.4	0.4	0.5	0.5	0.5
Nonresident alien	72.4	92.2	115.3	151.4	167.3	177.0	183.6	181.8	—	—	—	—	—	—	—
Men	707.9	672.2	671.0	697.8	737.4	761.0	772.4	771.2	52.2	48.3	44.7	43.8	43.7	43.6	43.1
White, non-Hispanic	589.1	538.5	521.3	516.5	538.8	550.7	553.7	551.2	47.1	43.1	39.1	38.0	37.7	37.3	36.6
Total minority	63.7	65.0	64.2	73.3	82.1	87.8	93.3	98.1	5.1	5.2	5.6	5.8	6.0	6.3	6.5
Black, non-Hispanic	32.0	28.2	24.9	27.4	29.3	31.0	33.0	35.1	2.6	2.3	2.1	2.1	2.1	2.2	2.3
Hispanic	14.6	15.7	14.7	17.4	20.6	22.4	23.6	24.9	1.2	1.3	1.3	1.5	1.5	1.6	1.7
Asian or Pacific Islander	14.4	18.6	22.4	26.2	29.7	31.8	33.8	35.0	1.2	1.5	2.0	2.1	2.2	2.3	2.3
American Indian/Alaskan Native	2.7	2.5	2.2	2.3	2.6	2.7	2.9	3.0	0.2	0.2	0.2	0.2	0.2	0.2	0.2
Nonresident alien	55.1	68.7	85.6	108.0	116.4	122.4	125.4	121.9	—	—	—	—	—	—	—
Women	614.6	668.7	672.6	774.1	848.8	878.2	896.3	918.0	47.8	51.7	55.3	56.2	56.3	56.4	56.9
White, non-Hispanic	526.5	566.2	566.0	636.8	689.5	707.3	713.7	723.7	42.1	45.3	48.2	48.6	48.4	48.1	48.0
Total minority	70.8	79.0	76.9	93.9	108.3	116.3	124.5	134.4	5.7	6.3	7.1	7.6	8.0	8.4	8.9
Black, non-Hispanic	46.5	46.9	42.5	49.1	54.6	57.9	60.9	66.6	3.7	3.8	3.7	3.8	4.0	4.1	4.4
Hispanic	11.8	16.4	17.1	22.0	26.6	28.6	31.6	33.3	0.9	1.3	1.7	1.9	2.0	2.1	2.2
Asian or Pacific Islander	10.1	13.0	14.7	19.5	23.6	25.9	27.8	30.2	0.8	1.0	1.5	1.7	1.8	1.9	2.0
American Indian/Alaskan Native	2.4	2.7	2.6	3.3	3.6	3.9	4.1	4.3	0.2	0.2	0.2	0.3	0.3	0.3	0.3
Nonresident alien	17.3	23.5	29.7	43.4	50.9	54.6	58.2	59.9	—	—	—	—	—	—	—

Table 201.—Total fall enrollment in institutions of higher education, by level of study, sex, and race/ethnicity of student: 1976 to 1993—Continued

Level of study, sex, and race/ethnicity of student	Number, in thousands								Percent distribution by level of study [1]						
	1976	1980	1984	1988	1990	1991	1992 [2]	1993 [3]	1976	1980	1988	1990	1991	1992 [2]	1993 [3]
1	2	3	4	5	6	7	8	9	10	11	12	13	14	15	16
First-professional									100.0	100.0	100.0	100.0	100.0	100.0	100.0
Total	244.1	276.8	278.5	267.1	273.4	280.5	280.9	292.4	91.3	90.4	85.1	82.6	81.5	80.3	79.1
White, non-Hispanic	220.0	247.7	243.4	223.2	221.5	224.0	220.6	225.9	8.7	9.6	14.9	17.4	18.5	19.7	20.9
Total minority	21.1	26.3	31.7	39.1	46.5	50.8	54.1	59.6	4.6	4.7	5.5	5.9	6.3	6.6	7.1
Black, non-Hispanic	11.2	12.8	13.4	14.3	15.9	17.2	18.2	20.2	1.9	2.4	3.6	4.0	4.2	4.4	4.5
Hispanic	4.5	6.5	8.0	9.3	10.7	11.4	12.0	12.8	1.7	2.2	5.5	7.0	7.6	8.2	8.8
Asian or Pacific Islander	4.1	6.1	9.3	14.4	18.7	20.8	22.5	25.0	0.5	0.3	0.4	0.4	0.5	0.5	0.6
American Indian/Alaskan Native	1.3	0.8	1.0	1.1	1.1	1.3	1.5	1.7	—	—	—	—	—	—	—
Nonresident alien	3.1	2.9	3.4	4.7	5.4	5.8	6.2	6.9							
Men	189.6	198.5	184.9	166.7	166.8	169.9	168.6	172.8	77.6	71.6	62.3	60.8	60.3	59.8	58.8
White, non-Hispanic	172.4	179.5	163.6	141.3	137.8	138.6	135.5	137.2	71.5	65.5	53.8	51.4	50.4	49.3	48.0
Total minority	14.7	16.7	18.8	22.1	25.3	27.2	28.8	30.9	6.1	6.1	8.4	9.4	9.9	10.5	10.8
Black, non-Hispanic	7.2	7.4	7.1	7.1	7.4	7.9	8.2	8.8	3.0	2.7	2.7	2.8	2.9	3.0	3.1
Hispanic	3.5	4.6	5.2	5.7	6.4	6.7	7.0	7.2	1.5	1.7	2.2	2.4	2.6	2.6	2.5
Asian or Pacific Islander	2.9	4.1	5.9	8.6	10.8	11.9	12.7	13.9	1.2	1.5	3.3	4.0	4.3	4.6	4.9
American Indian/Alaskan Native	1.0	0.5	0.6	0.6	0.6	0.7	0.8	0.9	0.4	0.2	0.2	0.2	0.3	0.3	0.3
Nonresident alien	2.5	2.3	2.5	3.4	3.8	4.1	4.4	4.8	—	—	—	—	—	—	—
Women	54.5	78.4	93.6	100.4	106.6	110.7	112.3	119.6	22.4	28.4	37.7	39.2	39.7	40.2	41.2
White, non-Hispanic	47.6	68.1	79.8	82.0	83.7	85.4	85.1	88.8	19.7	24.9	31.2	31.2	31.1	31.0	31.1
Total minority	6.4	9.6	12.9	17.1	21.3	23.5	25.3	28.8	2.6	3.5	6.5	7.9	8.6	9.2	10.1
Black, non-Hispanic	3.9	5.5	6.3	7.2	8.5	9.3	10.0	11.4	1.6	2.0	2.7	3.2	3.4	3.6	4.0
Hispanic	1.0	1.9	2.8	3.6	4.3	4.7	4.9	5.5	0.4	0.7	1.4	1.6	1.7	1.8	1.9
Asian or Pacific Islander	1.1	2.0	3.5	5.8	7.9	8.9	9.8	11.1	0.5	0.7	2.2	3.0	3.2	3.6	3.9
American Indian/Alaskan Native	0.2	0.3	0.4	0.5	0.5	0.6	0.7	0.7	0.1	0.1	0.2	0.2	0.2	0.2	0.3
Nonresident alien	0.5	0.6	0.9	1.4	1.6	1.7	1.8	2.1	—	—	—	—	—	—	—

[1] Distribution for U.S. citizens only.
[2] Revised from previously published data.
[3] Preliminary data.
—Not applicable.

NOTE.—Because of underreporting and nonreporting of racial/ethnic data, some figures are slightly lower than corresponding data in other tables. Because of rounding, details may not add to totals.

SOURCE: U.S. Department of Education, National Center for Education Statistics, "Fall Enrollment in Colleges and Universities;" and Integrated Postsecondary Education Data System (IPEDS), "Fall Enrollment" survey. (This table was prepared March 1995.)

Table 202.—Total number of institutions and fall enrollment in institutions of higher education, by percentage minority enrollment: 1993 [1]

Percent minority	Total enrollment	Public institutions					Private institutions				
		Total	4-year institutions			2-year	Total	4-year institutions			2-year
			Total	University	Other 4-year			Total	University	Other 4-year	
1	2	3	4	5	6	7	8	9	10	11	12
All institutions											
Number of institutions	3,546	1,593	599	94	505	994	1,953	1,551	62	1,489	402
Total enrollment	14,305,658	11,189,088	5,851,760	2,259,692	3,592,068	5,337,328	3,116,570	2,888,031	763,036	2,124,995	228,539
U.S. citizens	13,848,811	10,884,714	5,635,019	2,134,958	3,500,061	5,249,695	2,964,097	2,739,149	696,460	2,042,689	224,948
Minority	3,245,065	2,658,131	1,202,132	346,148	855,984	1,455,999	586,934	528,842	149,104	379,738	58,092
80 percent or more minority enrollment											
Number of institutions	171	79	35	0	35	44	92	66	1	65	26
Total enrollment	556,274	460,850	205,857	0	205,857	254,993	95,424	79,128	10,538	68,590	16,296
U.S. citizens	539,019	446,680	199,324	0	199,324	247,356	92,339	76,219	9,707	66,512	16,120
Minority	488,007	399,644	182,273	0	182,273	217,371	88,363	74,052	9,535	64,517	14,311
60 to 79 percent minority enrollment											
Number of institutions	108	66	21	1	20	45	42	19	0	19	23
Total enrollment	569,698	527,789	171,100	20,061	151,039	356,689	41,909	32,075	0	32,075	9,834
U.S. citizens	544,707	504,666	162,243	18,152	144,091	342,423	40,041	30,809	0	30,809	9,232
Minority	379,473	352,988	114,920	13,233	101,687	238,068	26,485	20,316	0	20,316	6,169
40 to 59 percent minority enrollment											
Number of institutions	229	118	30	2	28	88	111	61	1	60	50
Total enrollment	1,221,442	1,074,626	425,175	64,787	360,388	649,451	146,816	125,998	27,658	98,340	20,818
U.S. citizens	1,169,217	1,034,677	408,713	61,004	347,709	625,964	134,540	114,058	23,388	90,670	20,482
Minority	564,055	500,983	196,088	32,680	163,408	304,895	63,072	53,099	9,571	43,528	9,973
20 to 39 percent minority enrollment											
Number of institutions	693	337	97	16	81	240	356	271	27	244	85
Total enrollment	3,522,345	2,723,626	1,176,854	453,736	723,118	1,546,772	798,719	755,810	338,353	417,457	42,909
U.S. citizens	3,389,026	2,648,489	1,128,007	426,170	701,837	1,520,482	740,537	698,306	302,230	396,076	42,231
Minority	927,261	729,818	303,409	114,758	188,651	426,409	197,443	184,957	77,253	107,704	12,486
Less than 20 percent minority enrollment											
Number of institutions	2,345	993	416	75	341	577	1,352	1,134	33	1,101	218
Total enrollment	8,435,899	6,402,197	3,872,774	1,721,108	2,151,666	2,529,423	2,033,702	1,895,020	386,487	1,508,533	138,682
U.S. citizens	8,206,842	6,250,202	3,736,732	1,629,632	2,107,100	2,513,470	1,956,640	1,819,757	361,135	1,458,622	136,883
Minority	886,269	674,698	405,442	185,477	219,965	269,256	211,571	196,418	52,745	143,673	15,153

[1] Preliminary data. Minority includes black, Hispanic, Asian or Pacific Islander, and American Indian/Alaskan Native students.

SOURCE: U.S. Department of Education, National Center for Education Statistics, Integrated Postsecondary Education Data System (IPEDS), "Fall Enrollment" survey. (This table was prepared June 1995.)

Table 203.—Total fall enrollment in institutions of higher education, by race/ethnicity of student and by state: 1993 [1] and 1992

State or other area	1993										1992
	Total	White, non-Hispanic	Minority enrollment, by race/ethnicity					Nonresident alien	Percent minority [2]	Percent minority [3]	
			Total	Black, non-Hispanic	Hispanic	Asian/ Pacific Islander	American Indian/ Alaskan Native				
1	2	3	4	5	6	7	8	9	10	11
United States	14,305,658	10,603,746	3,245,065	1,410,300	988,960	724,124	121,681	456,847	23.4	22.5
Alabama	233,525	171,999	56,833	52,113	1,548	2,094	1,078	4,693	24.8	23.7
Alaska	30,638	24,421	5,594	1,306	791	832	2,665	623	18.6	18.3
Arizona	272,300	202,042	63,059	9,294	35,718	7,625	10,422	7,199	23.8	22.2
Arkansas	99,262	80,285	16,647	14,204	652	1,012	779	2,330	17.2	16.8
California	1,836,349	980,194	768,881	133,532	322,898	292,064	20,387	87,274	44.0	40.5
Colorado	239,805	195,676	38,430	7,820	20,622	7,135	2,853	5,699	16.4	15.8
Connecticut	162,300	133,346	23,802	11,419	6,939	5,032	412	5,152	15.1	14.2
Delaware	43,528	35,424	7,213	5,456	661	948	148	891	16.9	16.0
District of Columbia	81,916	41,065	32,076	24,850	2,886	4,144	196	8,775	43.9	43.7
Florida	623,403	433,723	171,878	75,424	77,292	16,572	2,590	17,802	28.4	27.5
Georgia	302,844	213,261	82,574	70,987	4,269	6,534	784	7,009	27.9	26.4
Hawaii	62,871	17,290	40,117	1,613	1,443	36,776	285	5,464	69.9	69.6
Idaho	58,768	53,752	3,475	390	1,468	883	734	1,541	6.1	5.5
Illinois	734,089	529,185	186,761	91,130	55,721	37,525	2,385	18,143	26.1	25.6
Indiana	294,685	257,136	29,144	17,539	5,752	4,774	1,079	8,405	10.2	9.8
Iowa	172,797	153,417	11,262	4,979	2,435	3,303	545	8,118	6.8	6.2
Kansas	170,135	145,565	18,047	7,902	4,314	3,434	2,397	6,523	11.0	10.7
Kentucky	187,332	168,389	15,919	12,454	1,073	1,797	595	3,024	8.6	8.2
Louisiana	201,987	137,023	59,315	50,074	4,526	3,644	1,071	5,649	30.2	29.7
Maine	56,294	53,838	1,832	464	255	595	518	624	3.3	4.4
Maryland	268,005	185,191	73,937	53,538	5,503	13,954	942	8,877	28.5	27.3
Massachusetts	420,127	335,563	60,368	21,344	15,810	21,601	1,613	24,196	15.2	14.4
Michigan	568,210	462,897	89,727	60,662	10,920	13,672	4,473	15,586	16.2	15.3
Minnesota	268,118	241,946	19,696	6,016	3,275	8,002	2,403	6,476	7.5	6.8
Mississippi	122,408	83,462	36,810	34,959	523	905	423	2,136	30.6	29.8
Missouri	297,062	249,403	36,937	25,682	4,212	5,704	1,339	10,722	12.9	12.6
Montana	39,557	33,956	4,416	153	394	314	3,555	1,185	11.5	12.9
Nebraska	115,523	104,954	7,847	3,322	2,105	1,566	854	2,722	7.0	7.2
Nevada	63,947	50,859	11,184	3,125	3,873	3,207	979	1,904	18.0	18.7
New Hampshire	64,043	60,003	3,103	939	854	1,022	288	937	4.9	5.4
New Jersey	343,029	245,151	84,266	38,146	26,955	18,203	962	13,612	25.6	24.8
New Mexico	101,460	58,836	40,704	2,489	30,069	1,397	6,749	1,920	40.9	39.8
New York	1,063,779	739,565	284,699	131,868	91,251	58,107	3,473	39,515	27.8	26.9
North Carolina	371,280	281,031	84,678	71,137	3,853	6,299	3,389	5,571	23.2	22.6
North Dakota	40,316	35,616	2,876	263	229	282	2,102	1,824	7.5	7.3
Ohio	562,402	476,871	69,559	49,922	7,743	10,055	1,839	15,972	12.7	12.1
Oklahoma	183,342	142,680	32,919	13,002	3,592	3,563	12,762	7,743	18.7	17.7
Oregon	165,834	140,855	18,532	2,711	4,943	8,539	2,339	6,447	11.6	10.6
Pennsylvania	621,228	528,595	75,624	46,315	9,671	18,335	1,303	17,009	12.5	12.5
Rhode Island	77,407	66,784	8,249	3,057	2,441	2,492	259	2,374	11.0	10.2
South Carolina	174,302	130,396	40,716	36,933	1,297	1,990	496	3,190	23.8	23.7
South Dakota	38,166	34,723	2,516	312	191	331	1,682	927	6.8	7.5
Tennessee	244,936	198,786	41,679	35,843	2,124	3,061	651	4,471	17.3	17.1
Texas	942,178	609,184	305,876	89,307	175,973	36,505	4,091	27,118	33.4	32.4
Utah	138,139	123,496	8,725	988	3,513	2,784	1,440	5,918	6.6	5.9
Vermont	36,415	34,226	1,386	355	417	471	143	803	3.9	4.0
Virginia	348,535	265,467	76,503	53,682	6,483	15,228	1,110	6,565	22.4	21.3
Washington	279,845	230,388	43,062	9,902	8,487	20,020	4,653	6,395	15.7	14.8
West Virginia	88,852	82,063	4,897	3,433	433	870	161	1,892	5.6	5.4
Wisconsin	309,036	275,022	27,464	12,853	5,818	6,472	2,321	6,550	9.1	8.7
Wyoming	30,702	28,115	2,023	277	1,056	240	450	564	6.7	7.3
U.S. Service Schools	52,647	40,631	11,228	4,815	3,689	2,210	514	788	21.7	21.2
Outlying areas	172,989	1,011	171,053	2,453	159,673	8,909	18	925	99.4	99.5
American Samoa	1,264	0	1,264	0	0	1,264	0	0	100.0	100.0
Federated States of Micronesia	1,148	0	1,148	0	0	1,148	0	0	100.0	100.0
Guam	5,843	574	4,786	48	57	4,671	10	483	89.3	89.5
Marshall Islands	386	1	385	0	0	385	0	0	99.7	100.0
Northern Marianas	1,261	84	981	2	2	976	1	196	92.1	89.5
Palau	436	0	436	0	0	436	0	0	100.0	100.0
Puerto Rico	159,709	122	159,496	4	159,486	5	1	91	99.9	100.0
Virgin Islands	2,942	230	2,557	2,399	128	24	6	155	91.7	91.3

[1] Preliminary data.

[2] Percent minority based on U.S. citizen enrollment (total enrollment less enrollment of nonresident aliens).

[3] Revised from previously published data.

NOTE.—Because of adjustments to underreported and nonreported racial/ethnic data, figures are slightly different from corresponding data in other tables.

SOURCE: U.S. Department of Education, National Center for Education Statistics, Integrated Postsecondary Education Data System (IPEDS), "Fall Enrollment" surveys. (This table was prepared March 1995.)

Table 204.—Percent of students enrolled in postsecondary institutions, by disability status and selected student characteristics: 1992–93

Selected student characteristics	Undergraduate			Graduate and first-professional [1]		
	All students	Disabled students [2]	Nondisabled students	All students	Disabled students [2]	Nondisabled students
1	2	3	4	5	6	7
Total	**100.0**	**6.3**	**93.7**	**100.0**	**4.0**	**96.0**
Sex	100.0	100.0	100.0	100.0	100.0	100.0
Male	44.5	53.0	44.3	46.4	51.0	45.6
Female	55.5	47.0	55.8	53.6	49.0	54.4
Race/ethnicity	100.0	100.0	100.0	100.0	100.0	100.0
White, non-Hispanic	76.8	80.8	74.8	81.4	85.3	79.2
Black, non-Hispanic	10.3	9.3	10.3	6.4	4.4	6.1
Hispanic	8.0	6.3	9.1	4.0	5.1	4.7
Asian American	4.0	1.7	4.9	7.5	3.8	9.2
American Indian	1.0	1.9	1.0	0.8	1.3	0.9
Age	100.0	100.0	100.0	100.0	100.0	100.0
15 to 23	55.1	37.8	55.7	11.4	6.7	11.9
24 to 29	17.1	15.2	16.6	34.7	20.4	34.4
30 or older	27.8	47.0	27.7	53.9	72.9	53.7
Veteran status	100.0	100.0	100.0	100.0	100.0	100.0
Veteran	7.5	17.5	6.8	6.1	16.4	5.7
Not a veteran	92.5	82.6	93.2	93.9	83.6	94.3
Dependency status	100.0	100.0	100.0	100.0	100.0	100.0
Dependent	47.9	33.0	48.8	8.6	4.9	8.9
Independent	20.5	23.0	17.2	46.6	31.1	36.9
Independent with dependents	31.6	44.0	34.0	44.9	64.0	54.2
Housing status	100.0	100.0	100.0	100.0	100.0	100.0
School-owned	12.8	7.4	13.2	5.9	6.1	6.0
Off-campus, not with parents	58.8	69.7	57.2	84.2	84.1	84.3
With parents	25.9	20.1	27.0	7.5	5.2	7.4
With relatives	2.2	2.7	2.4	2.3	4.3	2.3
Other	0.2	0.2	0.2	0.1	0.3	0.1
Attendance status	100.0	100.0	100.0	100.0	100.0	100.0
Full-time	32.8	25.9	32.6	25.4	20.0	26.1
Part-time	67.2	74.1	67.5	74.6	80.0	73.9
Field of study	100.0	100.0	100.0	100.0	100.0	100.0
Business	22.8	21.9	22.8	16.0	11.5	15.7
Computer science	4.6	6.2	4.7	3.0	2.6	3.0
Education	10.3	9.4	11.0	25.7	33.3	26.1
Engineering	6.9	6.9	6.8	6.5	6.0	6.5
Health	13.5	12.4	14.0	11.5	7.4	11.6
Humanities	11.3	11.9	10.6	8.5	8.8	8.2
Life sciences	5.4	4.8	5.7	5.1	6.6	5.5
Mathematics	0.9	0.6	1.0	1.4	2.4	1.4
Physical sciences	1.1	1.2	1.2	2.6	2.6	2.7
Social sciences	8.0	7.2	7.8	9.1	9.2	9.0
Vocational	5.3	6.4	5.1	0.8	0.8	0.8
Other technical/professional	10.0	11.1	9.3	9.8	8.9	9.5

[1] Includes chiropractic medicine, medicine, dentistry, optometry, osteopathic medicine, pharmacy, podiatry, and veterinary medicine.

[2] Disabled students are those who reported that they had one or more of the following conditions: a specific learning disability, a visual handicap, hard of hearing, deafness, a speech disability, an orthopedic handicap, or a health impairment.

NOTE.—Because of rounding and survey item nonresponse, details may not add to totals.

SOURCE: U.S. Department of Education, National Center for Education Statistics, "The 1992–93 National Postsecondary Student Aid Study." (This table was prepared July 1995.)

Table 205.—Enrollment of persons 14 to 34 years of age[1] in institutions of higher education, by race/ethnicity, sex, and year of college: October 1965 to October 1994

Characteristic	1965	1970	1975	1980	1984[2]	1985	1986	1987	1988	1989	1990	1991	1992	1993	1994
1	2	3	4	5	6	7	8	9	10	11	12	13	14	15	16
						Numbers in thousands									
All students	**5,675**	**7,413**	**9,697**	**10,181**	**10,858**	**10,863**	**10,605**	**10,919**	**10,937**	**11,068**	**11,303**	**11,589**	**11,671**	**11,409**	**12,298**
White, non-Hispanic[3]															
Total	5,317	6,759	8,141	8,453	8,764	8,781	8,284	8,519	8,616	8,786	8,892	8,916	8,883	8,592	9,076
Men	3,326	4,066	4,566	4,225	4,487	4,361	4,158	4,221	4,155	4,220	4,298	4,323	4,207	4,168	4,313
Women	1,991	2,693	3,576	4,228	4,277	4,420	4,126	4,299	4,461	4,565	4,594	4,594	4,676	4,424	4,764
Black, non-Hispanic[3]															
Total	274	522	927	996	1,124	1,036	1,126	1,162	1,096	1,116	1,167	1,190	1,205	1,227	1,478
Men	126	253	433	431	538	458	484	505	423	425	508	523	467	515	650
Women	148	269	494	565	586	578	642	657	674	690	659	667	738	713	828
Hispanic origin															
Total	—	—	411	443	524	579	677	667	654	640	617	721	816	867	982
Men	—	—	219	222	232	280	331	369	313	311	297	310	349	391	443
Women	—	—	192	221	292	299	346	298	341	330	321	411	468	475	539
Year of college															
First	1,861	2,212	2,886	2,958	3,023	2,956	2,965	2,915	3,131	2,983	3,109	2,995	3,274	3,139	3,357
Second	1,256	1,739	2,376	2,411	2,454	2,585	2,564	2,745	2,598	2,680	2,798	2,959	3,002	2,964	3,075
Third	896	1,248	1,491	1,716	1,981	1,931	1,803	2,011	1,979	2,017	1,958	2,009	2,136	2,080	2,244
Fourth	803	1,074	1,354	1,403	1,599	1,642	1,640	1,556	1,631	1,676	1,817	1,877	1,681	1,692	1,902
Fifth or higher	859	1,140	1,590	1,692	1,802	1,749	1,633	1,690	1,598	1,711	1,620	1,749	1,578	1,535	1,719
						Percentage distribution									
All students	**100.0**	**100.0**	**100.0**	**100.0**	**100.0**	**100.0**	**100.0**	**100.0**	**100.0**	**100.0**	**100.0**	**100.0**	**100.0**	**100.0**	**100.0**
White, non-Hispanic[3]															
Total	93.7	91.2	84.0	83.0	80.7	80.8	78.1	78.0	78.8	79.4	78.7	76.9	76.1	75.3	73.8
Men	58.6	54.8	47.1	41.5	41.3	40.1	39.2	38.7	38.0	38.1	38.0	37.3	36.0	36.5	35.1
Women	35.1	36.3	36.9	41.5	39.4	40.7	38.9	39.4	40.8	41.2	40.6	39.6	40.1	38.8	38.7
Black, non-Hispanic[3]															
Total	4.8	7.0	9.6	9.8	10.4	9.5	10.6	10.6	10.0	10.1	10.3	10.3	10.3	10.8	12.0
Men	2.2	3.4	4.5	4.2	5.0	4.2	4.6	4.6	3.9	3.8	4.5	4.5	4.0	4.5	5.3
Women	2.6	3.6	5.1	5.5	5.4	5.3	6.1	6.0	6.2	6.2	5.8	5.8	6.3	6.2	6.7
Hispanic origin															
Total	—	—	4.2	4.4	4.8	5.3	6.4	6.1	6.0	5.8	5.5	6.2	7.0	7.6	8.0
Men	—	—	2.3	2.2	2.1	2.6	3.1	3.4	2.9	2.8	2.6	2.7	3.0	3.4	3.6
Women	—	—	2.0	2.2	2.7	2.8	3.3	2.7	3.1	3.0	2.8	3.5	4.0	4.2	4.4
Year of college															
First	32.8	29.8	29.8	29.1	27.8	27.2	28.0	26.7	28.6	27.0	27.5	25.8	28.1	27.5	27.3
Second	22.1	23.5	24.5	23.7	22.6	23.8	24.2	25.1	23.8	24.2	24.8	25.5	25.7	26.0	25.0
Third	15.8	16.8	15.4	16.9	18.2	17.8	17.0	18.4	18.1	18.2	17.3	17.3	18.3	18.2	18.3
Fourth	14.1	14.5	14.0	13.8	14.7	15.1	15.5	14.3	14.9	15.1	16.1	16.2	14.4	14.8	15.5
Fifth or higher	15.1	15.4	16.4	16.6	16.6	16.1	15.4	15.5	14.6	15.5	14.3	15.1	13.5	13.5	14.0

[1] Totals differ from those shown in other tables. This table presents data collected in sample surveys of households rather than surveys of institutions. Excludes persons age 35 and over.
[2] Data for 1984 to 1993 are controlled to 1980 census base.
[3] Data for 1965 and 1970 include persons of Hispanic origin.
—Data not available.

NOTE.—Data are based upon sample surveys of the civilian noninstitutional population. Because of rounding, details may not add to totals.

SOURCE: U.S. Department of Commerce, Bureau of the Census, *Current Population Reports*, Series P–20, No. 403, and unpublished data. (This table was prepared May 1995.)

Table 206.—Enrollment in postsecondary education, by major field of study, age, and level of student: 1992–93

Field of study	All students Total, in thousands	Percentage distribution, by age — Under 25	25 to 34	Over 35	Undergraduate 2-year institutions Total, in thousands	Percentage distribution, by age — Under 25	25 to 34	Over 35	4-year institutions Total, in thousands	Percentage distribution, by age — Under 25	25 to 34	Over 35	Graduate and first-professional Total, in thousands	Percentage distribution, by age — Under 25	25 to 34	Over 35
1	2	3	4	5	6	7	8	9	10	11	12	13	14	15	16	17
Total	**21,096**	**54.1**	**25.0**	**20.9**	**9,881**	**48.5**	**26.9**	**24.6**	**8,558**	**71.7**	**16.7**	**11.7**	**2,657**	**18.6**	**45.0**	**36.4**
Agriculture	299	58.2	23.6	18.2	141	47.0	29.7	23.3	125	82.6	8.4	9.0	32	12.4	56.2	31.4
Architecture	118	62.2	25.4	12.3	40	52.7	28.7	18.6	62	78.2	14.5	7.3	15	21.4	62.0	16.6
Business and management	4,082	51.8	27.1	21.0	1,945	46.8	27.5	25.6	1,766	65.0	20.5	14.6	372	15.3	56.9	27.9
Accounting	897	49.8	28.5	21.7	450	40.1	31.7	28.2	401	63.9	22.5	13.6	47	21.9	48.5	29.6
Business	2,125	51.8	27.5	20.8	870	48.1	26.4	25.5	988	64.9	20.2	14.9	267	15.1	57.8	27.1
Secretary/bookkeeping	973	51.2	26.6	22.2	582	47.8	27.4	24.8	333	64.2	19.7	16.1	58	10.7	59.2	30.1
Marketing	87	80.3	10.8	8.8	43	78.6	8.8	12.7	44	82.0	12.9	5.1	(¹)	(¹)	(¹)	(¹)
Communications/journalism	516	70.6	18.3	11.1	174	60.4	22.5	17.2	296	84.3	11.9	3.8	47	21.3	43.5	35.2
Computer science	927	41.7	30.8	27.5	583	37.1	29.0	34.0	296	59.6	27.4	13.1	47	15.4	56.3	28.3
Cosmetology	271	59.8	24.5	15.7	271	59.8	24.5	15.7	(¹)	(¹)	(¹)	(¹)	(¹)	(¹)	(¹)	(¹)
Consumer/personal services	10	68.9	7.0	24.2	10	68.9	7.0	24.2	(¹)	(¹)	(¹)	(¹)	(¹)	(¹)	(¹)	(¹)
Education	2,325	47.2	24.3	28.6	690	49.0	26.4	24.6	1,005	69.0	16.8	14.2	631	10.4	33.9	55.7
Engineering	1,229	60.9	27.5	11.6	501	49.5	31.7	18.8	564	80.5	15.0	4.6	164	28.6	57.5	13.9
Foreign languages	130	53.2	15.8	31.0	40	29.7	6.6	63.7	72	74.9	13.9	11.2	18	18.7	43.9	37.4
Health	2,809	47.3	30.6	22.2	1,735	44.1	32.4	23.5	766	62.0	20.5	17.4	307	28.2	45.0	26.8
Medical doctor	147	51.1	41.9	7.0	38	51.9	36.0	12.1	27	76.5	17.7	5.9	81	42.1	52.9	5.0
Nursing	1,286	38.8	33.9	27.3	872	35.6	37.6	26.7	355	51.7	23.9	24.4	59	8.1	38.9	53.1
Other	1,375	54.7	26.2	19.0	825	52.7	26.8	20.6	384	70.1	17.9	12.0	167	30.9	41.2	27.9
Home economics	165	58.4	17.4	24.3	90	54.4	19.9	25.7	60	76.8	12.7	10.5	15	9.3	20.3	70.4
Law	293	45.2	33.5	21.2	133	46.8	24.6	28.7	45	53.8	26.2	20.1	115	40.1	46.8	13.2
Letters	301	57.3	24.0	18.6	104	37.0	36.4	26.6	157	80.4	10.3	9.3	40	19.9	45.7	34.4
Liberal arts	636	55.8	23.5	20.6	435	56.6	22.1	21.4	177	59.0	25.3	15.6	24	18.6	37.1	44.3
Library science	15	6.0	25.6	68.5	(¹)	(¹)	(¹)	(¹)	(¹)	(¹)	(¹)	(¹)	15	6.0	25.6	68.5
Life sciences	630	74.2	17.3	8.5	149	66.6	20.0	13.5	401	86.8	9.1	4.1	81	26.0	52.7	21.2
Mathematics	190	54.9	23.9	21.1	66	49.3	21.1	29.6	89	73.0	17.3	9.7	36	19.9	45.9	34.2
Philosophy and theology	144	36.3	27.0	36.7	16	61.3	26.1	12.6	59	63.4	14.4	22.2	69	7.2	38.1	54.7
Physical sciences	254	57.5	30.4	12.1	54	49.7	33.3	17.0	133	78.8	15.5	5.7	67	21.5	57.5	21.0
Protective services	465	65.6	22.9	11.5	285	60.1	26.9	13.0	171	76.6	15.2	8.2	9	30.3	44.3	25.4
Psychology	444	64.8	19.5	15.7	116	58.5	19.4	22.2	279	74.6	15.8	9.6	49	23.9	40.5	35.6
Social work/public administration	234	40.0	27.1	32.9	65	36.6	31.2	32.3	99	58.0	16.6	25.4	70	17.7	38.0	44.3
Social sciences	974	70.0	18.1	11.9	181	60.8	18.8	20.4	677	80.6	12.4	7.0	116	22.4	49.9	27.7
Visual and performing arts	788	59.6	17.3	23.2	318	48.3	18.6	33.1	388	77.2	11.8	11.0	81	19.2	38.0	42.8
Other and not reported	2,847	53.6	22.9	23.4	1,741	48.7	24.6	26.8	901	72.4	15.3	12.3	205	13.5	42.4	44.0

¹Too few sample cases for a reliable estimate.

NOTE.—Because of different survey editing and processing procedures, enrollment data in this table may differ from those appearing in other tables. Because of rounding, details may not add to totals. Includes students who enrolled at any time during the 1992–93 academic year.

SOURCE: U.S. Department of Education, National Center for Education Statistics, "The 1992–93 National Postsecondary Student Aid Study," unpublished data. (This table was prepared July 1995.)

Table 207.—Graduate enrollment in science and engineering programs in institutions of higher education, by field of study: United States and outlying areas, fall 1981 to fall 1992

Field of engineering or science	1981	1982	1983	1984[1]	1985[1]	1986[1]	1987[1]	1988	1989	1990	1991	1992	Percent change, 1985 to 1992
1	2	3	4	5	6	7	8	9	10	11	12	13	14
Total, all fields	378,104	384,872	392,376	396,449	405,596	416,577	422,585	425,932	436,071	454,065	472,950	495,937	22.3
Engineering, total	80,479	84,581	91,111	92,780	96,214	102,135	104,104	103,137	104,150	107,728	113,300	118,047	22.7
Aerospace	1,883	1,941	2,305	2,340	2,538	2,804	3,015	3,223	3,454	3,866	4,052	4,036	59.0
Agricultural	802	875	969	954	941	1,054	1,063	1,039	1,031	936	978	989	5.1
Biomedical	1,057	1,116	1,244	1,345	1,373	1,549	1,689	1,755	1,919	2,130	2,233	2,479	80.6
Chemical	6,496	7,189	7,563	7,373	7,150	7,012	7,111	6,618	6,460	6,735	7,127	7,415	3.7
Civil	14,515	14,510	14,921	15,203	14,916	14,987	14,718	14,822	14,919	15,553	17,356	19,385	30.0
Electrical	20,193	22,017	25,116	26,198	28,203	29,969	31,399	32,035	33,257	33,722	34,973	36,272	28.6
Engineering science	1,965	2,130	2,261	2,153	2,098	2,362	2,343	2,386	2,077	2,020	2,154	2,218	5.7
Industrial	10,026	9,870	9,373	9,535	10,805	11,843	12,416	11,638	11,328	11,505	12,832	13,735	27.1
Mechanical	10,618	11,467	12,911	13,855	14,157	15,713	16,366	16,186	16,212	16,788	17,647	18,768	32.6
Metallurgical/materials	3,125	3,124	3,447	3,657	3,943	4,208	4,366	4,335	4,589	4,946	5,164	5,470	38.7
Mining	462	449	524	502	489	512	513	489	418	437	489	479	−2.0
Nuclear	1,283	1,301	1,203	1,234	1,220	1,265	1,279	1,303	1,323	1,278	1,282	1,286	5.4
Petroleum	521	586	737	744	782	747	818	742	665	670	705	737	−5.8
Other engineering	7,533	8,006	8,537	7,687	7,599	8,110	7,008	6,566	6,498	7,142	6,308	4,778	−37.1
All sciences, total	297,625	300,291	301,265	303,669	309,382	314,442	318,481	322,795	331,921	346,337	359,650	377,890	22.1
Physical sciences, total	27,382	28,199	29,456	30,056	30,981	32,248	32,730	32,962	33,619	34,135	34,799	35,496	14.6
Astronomy	597	632	618	639	671	689	722	731	789	810	829	869	29.5
Chemistry	16,347	17,015	17,796	17,752	18,300	18,737	18,819	18,572	18,812	19,101	19,388	19,904	8.8
Physics	10,150	10,306	10,806	11,331	11,672	12,439	12,807	13,308	13,657	13,868	14,140	14,264	22.2
Other physical sciences	288	246	236	334	338	383	382	351	361	356	442	459	35.8
Earth, atmospheric, and ocean sciences	14,422	15,174	15,590	15,655	15,591	15,210	14,522	14,067	13,830	14,195	14,720	15,609	0.1
Atmospheric sciences	882	889	896	907	964	961	952	940	912	929	968	1,089	13.0
Geosciences	8,808	9,621	10,321	10,370	10,294	9,819	8,998	8,463	8,052	7,694	7,583	7,759	−24.6
Oceanography	2,082	2,091	2,063	2,102	2,081	2,128	2,127	2,033	2,207	2,333	2,386	2,530	21.6
Other environmental sciences	2,650	2,573	2,310	2,276	2,252	2,302	2,445	2,631	2,659	3,239	3,783	4,231	87.9
Mathematical sciences, total	15,915	17,199	17,380	17,459	17,591	17,967	18,524	19,103	19,308	19,801	19,978	20,375	15.8
Mathematics and applied mathematics	—	—	—	—	15,465	15,633	16,031	16,516	16,784	17,123	17,232	17,426	12.7
Statistics	—	—	—	—	2,126	2,334	2,493	2,587	2,524	2,678	2,746	2,949	38.7
Computer sciences, total	16,437	19,812	23,616	25,810	29,602	31,175	31,901	32,053	32,320	34,349	34,788	36,936	24.8
Life sciences, total	103,124	102,789	102,228	103,767	103,976	106,025	106,498	108,707	112,572	117,134	122,574	129,830	24.9
Agricultural sciences, total	12,100	12,314	12,396	12,181	11,364	11,281	10,942	10,940	10,979	11,125	11,315	11,609	2.2
Biological sciences, total	46,979	46,310	45,771	45,892	46,201	46,873	46,901	47,682	48,970	50,090	51,875	54,437	17.8
Anatomy	1,072	1,074	1,037	1,029	993	973	1,016	1,056	1,078	996	1,051	1,031	3.8
Biochemistry	4,061	4,124	4,205	4,462	4,656	4,875	4,813	4,921	5,082	5,053	5,207	5,386	15.7
Biology	14,203	13,397	13,051	12,890	12,710	12,678	12,331	12,393	12,761	13,035	13,299	13,897	9.3
Biometry/epidemiology	1,182	1,166	1,156	1,004	1,360	1,434	1,556	1,682	1,722	1,871	2,032	2,369	74.2
Biophysics	463	440	450	433	441	547	591	592	655	642	697	751	70.3
Botany	3,498	3,644	3,299	3,251	3,188	3,149	3,005	2,936	2,844	2,720	2,675	2,690	−15.6
Cell biology	1,018	1,143	1,182	1,256	1,429	1,716	1,964	2,078	2,234	2,555	2,809	3,093	116.4
Ecology	1,101	1,051	1,007	1,088	1,028	1,022	963	999	1,084	1,136	1,180	1,301	26.6
Entomology/parasitology	1,664	1,540	1,475	1,438	1,342	1,306	1,244	1,240	1,181	1,173	1,171	1,193	−11.1
Genetics	937	990	1,035	1,059	1,120	1,262	1,314	1,289	1,365	1,408	1,520	1,643	46.7
Microbiology	4,070	4,130	4,262	4,326	4,446	4,372	4,452	4,773	4,827	4,872	4,936	5,008	12.6
Nutrition	4,355	4,359	4,351	4,277	4,314	4,321	4,288	4,228	4,259	4,268	4,251	4,245	−1.6
Pathology	1,444	1,460	1,449	1,454	1,321	1,362	1,397	1,357	1,393	1,386	1,492	1,517	14.8
Pharmacology	2,024	2,084	2,069	2,050	2,107	2,078	2,072	2,124	2,267	2,352	2,432	2,545	20.8
Physiology	2,144	2,058	1,994	2,160	2,211	2,220	2,213	2,220	2,206	2,236	2,332	2,319	4.9
Zoology	2,625	2,503	2,430	2,303	2,135	2,083	2,113	2,034	2,088	2,109	2,196	2,203	3.2
Other biosciences	1,118	1,147	1,319	1,412	1,400	1,475	1,569	1,760	1,924	2,278	2,595	3,246	131.9
Health fields, total	44,045	44,165	44,061	45,694	46,411	47,871	48,655	50,085	52,623	55,919	59,384	63,784	37.4
Medical fields	9,027	8,758	8,565	8,714	9,280	9,227	9,730	10,110	10,243	10,962	11,564	12,470	34.4
Anesthesiology	—	—	—	—	75	102	107	201	277	310	443	594	692.0
Cardiology	—	—	—	—	3	3	0	0	0	0	0	8	166.7
Oncology/cancer research	—	—	—	—	66	69	81	89	104	113	156	200	203.0
Endocrinology	—	—	—	—	53	57	63	70	82	74	66	74	39.6
Gastroenterology	—	—	—	—	1	5	0	0	0	1	4	0	−100.0
Hematology	—	—	—	—	4	9	7	6	4	4	4	5	25.0
Neurology	191	204	261	317	346	391	503	612	744	843	997	1,117	222.8
Obstetrics and gynecology	—	—	—	—	7	4	8	9	7	5	10	3	−57.1
Ophthalmology	—	—	—	—	17	18	19	33	37	31	23	20	17.6
Otorhinolaryngology	—	—	—	—	5	6	8	6	9	4	3	0	−100.0
Pediatrics	—	—	—	—	185	163	219	227	136	140	153	154	−16.8
Preventive medicine and community health	7,226	6,816	6,679	6,841	7,279	7,222	7,556	7,678	7,687	8,246	8,371	8,737	20.0
Psychiatry	—	—	—	—	101	125	122	106	67	71	46	96	−5.0
Pulmonary disease	—	—	—	—	4	3	3	4	2	0	0	0	−100.0
Radiology	—	—	—	—	239	215	183	208	192	196	233	252	5.4
Surgery	—	—	—	—	56	62	67	75	81	81	84	82	46.4
Other clinical medicine	1,610	1,738	1,625	1,556	839	783	784	786	814	843	973	1,128	34.4
Other health fields	35,018	35,407	35,496	36,980	37,131	38,644	38,925	39,975	42,380	44,957	47,820	51,314	38.2
Dentistry	942	836	776	854	833	947	1,062	1,083	1,004	956	1,016	1,067	28.1
Nursing	15,703	16,254	16,945	17,987	17,977	18,424	18,479	18,910	19,733	21,245	22,116	23,333	29.8
Pharmaceutical sciences	2,549	2,519	2,641	2,519	2,553	2,682	2,607	2,613	2,834	2,938	3,011	2,846	11.5
Speech pathology/audiology	8,596	8,592	8,592	7,836	7,986	7,957	7,497	7,668	8,088	8,510	9,121	10,017	25.4
Veterinary sciences	481	471	466	557	637	630	731	752	801	900	894	942	47.9
Other health related	6,747	6,735	6,832	7,318	7,145	8,004	8,949	8,949	9,920	10,408	11,662	13,109	83.5
Psychology, total	40,691	40,082	40,912	40,937	41,173	41,417	42,750	44,127	46,003	48,678	51,791	53,820	30.7
Psychology, general[2]	—	—	—	—	41	54	193	15,479	17,126	18,524	21,230	23,117	56,282.9
Clinical psychology[2]	—	—	—	—	40,605	40,769	41,938	20,842	19,726	20,383	19,855	18,738	−53.9
Other psychology[2]	—	—	—	—	527	594	619	7,806	9,151	9,771	10,706	11,965	2,170.4

Table 207.—Graduate enrollment in science and engineering programs in institutions of higher education, by field of study: United States and outlying areas, fall 1981 to fall 1992—Continued

Field of engineering or science	1981	1982	1983	1984 [1]	1985 [1]	1986 [1]	1987 [1]	1988	1989	1990	1991	1992	Percent change, 1985 to 1992
1	2	3	4	5	6	7	8	9	10	11	12	13	14
Social sciences, total	79,654	77,036	72,083	69,985	70,468	70,400	71,556	71,776	74,269	78,045	81,000	85,824	21.8
Agricultural economics	2,262	2,267	2,295	2,279	2,268	2,248	2,203	2,259	2,276	2,273	2,364	2,513	10.8
Anthropology	6,118	5,948	5,644	5,590	5,631	6,805	5,835	5,945	6,128	6,494	6,729	7,129	26.6
Economics (except agricultural)	13,344	13,735	13,064	12,507	12,430	12,103	12,020	12,036	12,143	12,306	12,728	13,266	6.7
Geography	3,187	3,166	3,060	3,035	2,936	3,055	3,223	3,208	3,479	3,530	3,760	4,097	39.5
History and philosophy of science	248	256	253	274	272	266	294	288	304	331	337	360	32.4
Linguistics	3,139	2,803	3,022	3,160	3,055	3,109	3,282	3,243	3,285	3,404	3,425	3,288	7.6
Political science	30,791	29,887	28,050	25,921	27,012	27,251	27,601	27,859	29,291	30,595	31,887	33,770	25.0
Sociology	7,816	7,246	6,920	6,740	6,586	5,532	6,986	7,087	7,393	7,784	8,292	8,861	34.5
Sociology/anthropology	1,110	1,133	1,200	1,075	1,034	1,021	982	991	1,022	1,212	1,032	1,123	8.6
Other social sciences	11,639	10,595	8,575	9,404	9,244	9,010	9,130	8,860	8,947	10,116	10,446	11,417	23.5

—Data not available.

[1] Includes estimates for master's degree granting institutions which were surveyed on a sample basis from 1985 through 1987.

[2] Large percentage change due to change in reporting practices.

NOTE.—Some data have been revised from previously published figures. Because of rounding, details may not add to totals

SOURCE: National Science Foundation, Division of Science Resources Studies, *Academic Science/Engineering: Graduate Enrollment and Support, Fall 1992.* (This table was prepared April 1994.)

Table 208.—Institutions of higher education and branches, by type, control, and size of enrollment: Fall 1992 and fall 1993 [1]

Control of institution branch and size of total enrollment	All institutions		Universities		All other 4-year institutions		2-year institutions	
	Number [2]	Enrollment	Number [2]	Enrollment	Number [2]	Enrollment	Number [2]	Enrollment
1	2	3	4	5	6	7	8	9
Fall 1992 [3]								
Total	3,568	14,486,315	156	3,050,345	1,993	5,713,580	1,419	5,722,390
Under 200	385	41,617	0	0	259	27,181	126	14,436
200 to 499	457	157,332	0	0	253	87,315	204	70,017
500 to 999	491	359,210	0	0	317	233,825	174	125,385
1,000 to 2,499	850	1,400,340	0	0	550	877,704	300	522,636
2,500 to 4,999	535	1,866,093	5	20,872	277	958,888	253	886,333
5,000 to 9,999	435	3,101,208	28	222,041	200	1,385,554	207	1,493,613
10,000 to 19,999	283	3,914,772	54	768,929	115	1,582,765	114	1,563,078
20,000 to 29,999	98	2,383,636	45	1,127,111	19	465,249	34	791,276
30,000 or more	34	1,262,107	24	911,392	3	95,099	7	255,616
Fall 1993 [1]								
Total	3,546	14,305,658	156	3,022,728	1,994	5,717,063	1,396	5,565,867
Under 200	363	39,145	0	0	252	26,224	111	12,921
200 to 499	457	155,431	0	0	241	83,526	216	71,905
500 to 999	482	354,224	0	0	326	240,474	156	113,750
1,000 to 2,499	849	1,402,827	0	0	564	912,092	285	490,735
2,500 to 4,999	538	1,862,075	5	20,965	270	931,534	263	909,576
5,000 to 9,999	449	3,177,683	27	212,373	205	1,421,668	217	1,543,642
10,000 to 19,999	283	3,887,575	55	772,721	113	1,532,665	115	1,582,189
20,000 to 29,999	95	2,302,829	45	1,117,177	22	534,112	28	651,540
30,000 or more	30	1,123,869	24	899,492	1	34,768	5	189,609
Public institutions	1,593	11,189,088	94	2,259,692	505	3,592,068	994	5,337,328
Under 200	7	898	0	0	2	159	5	739
200 to 499	40	14,297	0	0	9	3,636	31	10,661
500 to 999	113	88,362	0	0	26	20,950	87	67,412
1,000 to 2,499	335	583,335	0	0	84	142,487	251	440,848
2,500 to 4,999	372	1,302,366	0	0	113	407,043	259	895,323
5,000 to 9,999	364	2,597,982	5	45,195	145	1,030,228	214	1,522,559
10,000 to 19,999	245	3,395,058	27	394,184	103	1,418,685	115	1,582,189
20,000 to 29,999	89	2,147,936	40	985,836	22	534,112	27	627,988
30,000 or more	28	1,058,854	22	834,477	1	34,768	5	189,609
Private institutions	1,953	3,116,570	62	763,036	1,489	2,124,995	402	228,539
Under 200	356	38,247	0	0	250	26,065	106	12,182
200 to 499	417	141,134	0	0	232	79,890	185	61,244
500 to 999	369	265,862	0	0	300	219,524	69	46,338
1,000 to 2,499	514	819,492	0	0	480	769,605	34	49,887
2,500 to 4,999	166	559,709	5	20,965	157	524,491	4	14,253
5,000 to 9,999	85	579,701	22	167,178	60	391,440	3	21,083
10,000 to 19,999	38	492,517	28	378,537	10	113,980	0	0
20,000 to 29,999	6	154,893	5	131,341	0	0	1	23,552
30,000 or more	2	65,015	2	65,015	0	0	0	0

[1] These preliminary data represent the institution branches and enrollments reported in the "Fall Enrollment" survey.

[2] Some institutions do not report separate enrollment data for each branch campus. For this reason, counts of institutions in this table are somewhat lower than figures appearing in other tables.

[3] Data revised from previously published figures.

SOURCE: U.S. Department of Education, National Center for Education Statistics, Integrated Postsecondary Education Data System (IPEDS), "Fall Enrollment" surveys. (This table was prepared February 1995.)

Table 209.—Enrollment of the 120 largest college and university campuses: [1] Fall 1993

Institution	State	Rank	Control [2]	Type [3]	Total enroll-ment, fall 1993	Institution	State	Rank	Control [2]	Type [3]	Total enroll-ment, fall 1994
1	2	3	4	5	6	1	2	3	4	5	6
University of Minnesota, Twin Cities	Minn.	1	1	1	51,880	Cuyahoga Community College District	Ohio	61	1	2	25,913
Ohio State University, Main Campus	Ohio	2	1	1	50,623	University of North Texas	Tex.	62	1	1	25,759
University of Texas at Austin	Tex.	3	1	1	48,555	Broward Community College	Fla.	63	1	2	25,714
Miami-Dade Community College	Fla.	4	1	2	48,232	San Francisco State University	Calif.	64	1	1	25,713
Texas A&M University	Tex.	5	1	1	42,524	University of New Mexico, Main Campus	N.Mex.	65	1	1	25,663
Arizona State University	Ariz.	6	1	1	41,250	SUNY at Buffalo	N.Y.	66	1	1	25,635
University of Wisconsin, Madison	Wisc.	7	1	1	39,999	University of Illinois at Chicago	Ill.	67	1	1	25,445
Michigan State University	Mich.	8	1	1	39,743	Iowa State University	Iowa	68	1	1	25,413
Houston Community College System	Tex.	9	1	2	39,321	Eastern Michigan University	Mich.	69	1	1	24,600
University of Illinois, Urbana Campus	Ill.	10	1	1	38,912	Austin Community College	Tex.	70	1	2	24,564
Pennsylvania State U., Main Campus	Pa.	11	1	1	37,658	University of Nebraska, Lincoln	Nebr.	71	1	1	24,491
Northern Virginia Community College	Va.	12	1	2	37,477	University of North Carolina, Chapel Hill	N.C.	72	1	1	24,334
University of Florida	Fla.	13	1	1	37,324	Florida International University	Fla.	73	1	1	24,321
Purdue University, Main Campus	Ind.	14	1	1	37,094	University of Massachusetts at Amherst	Mass.	74	1	1	24,234
University of Michigan, Ann Arbor	Mich.	15	1	1	36,845	University of Toledo	Ohio	75	1	1	24,188
Indiana University, Bloomington	Ind.	16	1	1	35,551	Milwaukee Area Technical College	Wisc.	76	1	2	24,072
University of Arizona	Ariz.	17	1	1	35,279	Texas Tech University	Tex.	77	1	1	24,007
University of South Florida	Fla.	18	1	1	34,768	Central Michigan University	Mich.	78	1	1	23,998
University of California, Los Angeles	Calif.	19	1	1	34,446	Southern Illinois University, Carbondale	Ill.	79	1	1	23,881
Wayne State University	Mich.	20	1	1	34,280	University of Wisconsin, Milwaukee	Wisc.	80	1	1	23,806
University of Washington	Wash.	21	1	1	34,000	University of Texas, Arlington	Tex.	81	1	1	23,763
Rutgers University, New Brunswick	N.J.	22	1	1	33,568	University of Central Florida	Fla.	82	1	1	23,692
Community College of the Air Force	Ala.	23	1	2	33,447	University of Kentucky	Ky.	83	1	1	23,670
New York University	N.Y.	24	2	1	33,309	Georgia State University	Ga.	84	1	1	23,605
U. of Maryland, College Park Campus	Md.	25	1	1	32,441	International Correspondence Schools	Pa.	85	2	2	23,552
University of Houston-University Park	Tex.	26	1	1	32,124	California State University, Sacramento	Calif.	86	1	1	23,316
Brigham Young University	Utah	27	2	1	31,706	University of Connecticut	Conn.	87	1	1	23,182
College of Du Page	Ill.	28	1	2	31,132	Northern Illinois University	Ill.	88	1	1	23,177
University of California, Berkeley	Calif.	29	1	1	30,341	West Virginia University	W.Va.	89	1	1	23,080
Temple University	Pa.	30	1	1	30,040	El Camino College	Calif.	90	1	2	22,953
University of Georgia	Ga.	31	1	1	28,753	Saint Petersburg Junior College	Fla.	91	1	2	22,799
University of Cincinnati, Main Campus	Ohio	32	1	1	28,662	De Anza College	Calif.	92	1	2	22,701
Boston University	Mass.	33	2	1	28,653	Kent State University, Main Campus	Ohio	93	1	1	22,700
Florida State University	Fla.	34	1	1	28,575	Valencia Community College	Fla.	94	1	2	22,593
University of Colorado at Boulder	Colo.	35	1	1	28,352	California State University, Fullerton	Calif.	95	1	1	22,565
Pima Community College	Ariz.	36	1	2	28,268	Portland Community College	Oreg.	96	1	2	22,527
Oakland Community College	Mich.	37	1	2	28,232	University of California, Davis	Calif.	97	1	1	22,476
San Diego State University	Calif.	38	1	1	28,131	University of Pennsylvania	Pa.	98	2	1	22,469
North Carolina State University, Raleigh	N.C.	39	1	1	27,810	Mount San Antonio College	Calif.	99	1	2	22,438
University of Iowa	Iowa	40	1	1	27,688	Pasadena City College	Calif.	100	1	2	22,248
University of Southern California	Calif.	41	2	1	27,658	University of Missouri, Columbia	Mo.	101	1	1	22,225
Indiana U. - Purdue U. at Indianapolis	Ind.	42	1	1	27,552	Nassau Community College	N.Y.	102	1	2	22,215
University of Pittsburgh, Main Campus	Pa.	43	1	1	27,528	Orange Coast College	Calif.	103	1	2	21,928
Macomb Community College	Mich.	44	1	2	27,391	Virginia Commonwealth University	Va.	104	1	1	21,854
Colorado State University	Colo.	45	1	1	27,384	Santa Monica College	Calif.	105	1	2	21,768
Tarrant County Junior College District	Tex.	46	1	2	27,353	University of Delaware	Del.	106	1	1	21,735
California State University, Northridge	Calif.	47	1	1	27,282	University of Oklahoma, Norman Campus	Okla.	107	1	1	21,696
University of Utah	Utah	48	1	1	27,113	Ball State University	Ind.	108	1	1	21,626
California State University, Long Beach	Calif.	49	1	1	27,073	Hillsborough Community College	Fla.	109	1	2	21,497
San Jose State University	Calif.	50	1	1	27,057	University of Virginia, Main Campus	Va.	110	1	1	21,394
University of South Carolina, Columbia	S.C.	51	1	1	26,710	Auburn University, Main Campus	Ala.	111	1	1	21,363
City College of San Francisco	Calif.	52	1	1	26,630	George Mason University	Va.	112	1	1	21,300
Western Michigan University	Mich.	53	1	1	26,555	Florida Community College, Jacksonville	Fla.	113	1	2	21,228
Northeastern University	Mass.	54	2	1	26,554	University of Louisville	Ky.	114	1	1	21,172
University of Tennessee, Knoxville	Tenn.	55	1	1	26,397	Rancho Santiago College	Calif.	115	1	2	20,920
University of Kansas, Main Campus	Kans.	56	1	1	26,127	Southwest Texas State University	Tex.	116	1	1	20,879
La. St. U. & A&M & Hebert Laws Center	La.	57	1	1	26,085	Community College of Allegheny County	Pa.	117	1	2	20,721
University of Akron, Main Campus	Ohio	58	1	1	26,032	Illinois State University	Ill.	118	1	1	20,610
Virginia Polytechnic Inst. and State Univ.	Va.	59	1	1	26,030	Santa Rosa Junior College	Calif.	119	1	2	20,428
Harvard University	Mass.	60	2	1	26,007	American River College	Calif.	120	1	2	20,377

[1] College and university campuses ranked by fall 1993 preliminary data.

[2] Publicly controlled institutions are identified by a "1," privately controlled, by a "2."

[3] The types of institutions are identified as follows: "1" for 4-year institutions and "2" for 2-year institutions.

NOTE.—Excludes nonreporting institutions and also institutions that reported enrollment data with other branch campuses.

SOURCE: U.S. Department of Education, National Center for Education Statistics, Integrated Postsecondary Education Data System (IPEDS), "Fall Enrollment, 1993" survey. (This table was prepared June 1995.)

Table 210.—Selected statistics for college and university campuses enrolling more than 14,600 students in 1993

Institution	State	Control [1]	Type [2]	Total enrollment, fall 1986	Total enrollment, fall 1991	Total enrollment, fall 1992	Total enrollment, fall 1993	Enrollment, by sex, fall 1993		Enrollment, by attendance status, fall 1993	
								Men	Women	Full-time	Part-time
1	2	3	4	5	6	7	8	9	10	11	12
United States, all institutions	—	—	—	12,503,511	14,358,953	14,486,315	14,305,658	6,427,716	7,877,942	8,127,740	6,177,918
Colleges with enrollment over 14,600	—	—	—	4,764,824	5,336,900	5,297,135	5,197,910	2,454,205	2,743,705	3,024,764	2,173,146
Auburn University, Main Campus	Ala.	1	1	19,363	21,836	21,551	21,363	11,826	9,537	18,152	3,211
University of Alabama	Ala.	1	1	16,210	19,793	19,233	19,480	9,666	9,814	16,105	3,375
University of Alabama at Birmingham	Ala.	1	1	13,538	15,922	15,735	15,913	7,238	8,675	9,761	6,152
University of Alaska, Anchorage	Alaska	1	1	4,318	18,383	17,257	17,275	6,918	10,357	6,392	10,883
Arizona State University	Ariz.	1	1	42,014	42,615	43,628	41,250	20,990	20,260	27,927	13,323
Glendale Community College	Ariz.	1	2	15,299	18,221	18,618	17,520	7,775	9,745	5,375	12,145
Mesa Community College	Ariz.	1	2	18,233	19,089	20,911	19,508	9,108	10,400	6,232	13,276
Northern Arizona University	Ariz.	1	1	13,154	17,689	18,485	18,817	7,898	10,919	12,546	6,271
Pima Community College	Ariz.	1	2	22,959	29,088	30,175	28,268	12,748	15,520	7,443	20,825
University of Arizona	Ariz.	1	1	31,563	35,210	35,118	35,279	18,071	17,208	27,205	8,074
American River College	Calif.	1	2	19,264	22,584	21,416	20,377	8,864	11,513	4,618	15,759
Calif Polytechnic State U., San Luis Obispo	Calif.	1	1	15,867	17,572	16,373	15,449	8,900	6,549	13,609	1,840
California State Polytechnic U., Pomona	Calif.	1	1	17,671	18,772	18,294	17,050	9,899	7,151	11,694	5,356
California State University, Chico	Calif.	1	1	14,854	15,669	15,164	14,706	7,242	7,464	12,748	1,958
California State University, Fresno	Calif.	1	1	17,748	19,820	18,902	17,956	8,221	9,735	14,039	3,917
California State University, Fullerton	Calif.	1	1	24,271	25,484	24,402	22,565	9,826	12,739	13,358	9,207
California State University, Long Beach	Calif.	1	1	33,580	32,335	30,067	27,073	12,429	14,644	16,830	10,243
California State University, Los Angeles	Calif.	1	1	20,764	20,801	19,399	17,788	7,428	10,360	10,109	7,679
California State University, Northridge	Calif.	1	1	29,873	30,441	29,088	27,282	11,710	15,572	16,825	10,457
California State University, Sacramento	Calif.	1	1	23,670	25,862	24,466	23,316	10,391	12,925	15,953	7,363
Cerritos College	Calif.	1	2	18,276	23,699	21,471	19,653	8,617	11,036	4,892	14,761
City College of San Francisco	Calif.	1	2	23,176	31,190	29,708	26,630	12,181	14,449	7,338	19,292
De Anza College	Calif.	1	2	24,347	27,844	24,779	22,701	10,651	12,050	7,080	15,621
Diablo Valley College	Calif.	1	2	18,990	23,272	21,020	18,888	8,699	10,189	6,390	12,498
El Camino College	Calif.	1	2	25,755	27,605	24,469	22,953	10,444	12,509	6,010	16,943
Fresno City College	Calif.	1	2	14,651	18,712	18,431	16,554	7,748	8,806	4,671	11,883
Fullerton College	Calif.	1	2	16,702	20,793	20,432	18,387	8,990	9,397	5,454	12,933
Grossmont College	Calif.	1	2	15,290	16,894	16,332	14,789	6,361	8,428	5,098	9,691
Long Beach City College	Calif.	1	2	20,720	30,785	19,861	18,745	8,672	10,073	4,456	14,289
Los Angeles City College	Calif.	1	2	14,855	15,637	17,017	15,378	7,195	8,183	4,878	10,500
Los Angeles Pierce College	Calif.	1	2	18,516	19,296	18,697	15,702	7,027	8,675	4,460	11,242
Los Angeles Valley College	Calif.	1	2	18,178	17,755	19,033	16,684	7,454	9,230	3,672	13,012
Mount San Antonio College	Calif.	1	2	20,290	23,211	23,073	22,438	10,499	11,939	6,864	15,574
Orange Coast College	Calif.	1	2	22,554	23,303	23,822	21,928	10,913	11,015	6,899	15,029
Palomar College	Calif.	1	2	14,836	18,465	18,884	18,983	8,604	10,379	5,166	13,817
Pasadena City College	Calif.	1	2	20,067	21,392	22,024	22,248	10,061	12,187	6,247	16,001
Rancho Santiago College	Calif.	1	2	21,512	24,670	25,660	20,920	11,079	9,841	4,901	16,019
Riverside Community College	Calif.	1	2	14,420	20,788	21,902	20,293	8,491	11,802	5,214	15,079
Sacramento City College	Calif.	1	2	13,300	17,959	16,968	16,052	6,879	9,173	5,062	10,990
Saddleback College	Calif.	1	2	15,052	17,584	17,990	16,649	6,938	9,711	4,160	12,489
San Diego Mesa College	Calif.	1	2	17,984	28,022	21,446	20,217	9,435	10,782	4,816	15,401
San Diego State University	Calif.	1	1	35,004	33,406	30,887	28,131	13,138	14,993	19,136	8,995
San Francisco State University	Calif.	1	1	25,866	27,913	26,528	25,713	10,685	15,028	16,200	9,513
San Joaquin Delta College	Calif.	1	2	14,735	16,991	16,210	15,806	6,973	8,833	5,221	10,585
San Jose State University	Calif.	1	1	26,504	30,061	29,625	27,057	13,029	14,028	16,567	10,490
Santa Monica College	Calif.	1	2	17,747	23,009	23,405	21,768	9,563	12,205	6,351	15,417
Santa Rosa Junior College	Calif.	1	2	20,475	25,061	23,390	20,428	8,664	11,764	6,263	14,165
Southwestern College	Calif.	1	2	11,867	14,739	16,282	15,384	7,119	8,265	4,810	10,574
Stanford University	Calif.	2	1	14,037	15,150	15,674	15,980	9,717	6,263	12,634	3,346
University of California, Berkeley	Calif.	1	1	31,461	30,796	30,616	30,341	16,486	13,855	27,146	3,195
University of California, Davis	Calif.	1	1	19,804	24,011	22,880	22,476	11,361	11,115	20,286	2,190
University of California, Irvine	Calif.	1	1	14,523	16,897	17,181	16,815	8,462	8,353	15,731	1,084
University of California, Los Angeles	Calif.	1	1	34,417	36,613	35,403	34,446	17,931	16,515	32,254	2,192
University of California, San Diego	Calif.	1	1	15,914	17,876	18,239	17,851	9,568	8,283	17,025	826
University of California, Santa Barbara	Calif.	1	1	17,999	18,483	18,651	18,581	9,289	9,292	17,537	1,044
University of Southern California	Calif.	2	1	30,831	28,624	28,586	27,658	15,433	12,225	20,627	7,031
Colorado State University	Colo.	1	1	18,844	27,080	27,306	27,384	13,457	13,927	19,370	8,014
Metropolitan State College of Denver	Colo.	1	1	15,011	17,863	17,617	17,721	8,327	9,394	9,544	8,177
University of Colorado at Boulder	Colo.	1	1	23,580	28,836	28,524	28,352	15,178	13,174	21,415	6,937
University of Connecticut	Conn.	1	1	23,657	24,844	24,131	23,182	11,525	11,657	16,415	6,767
University of Delaware	Del.	1	1	18,631	20,863	21,136	21,735	9,753	11,982	15,804	5,931
George Washington University	D.C.	2	1	18,707	19,202	18,600	18,992	9,786	9,206	10,254	8,738
Broward Community College	Fla.	1	2	18,373	24,766	25,348	25,714	10,263	15,451	7,568	18,146
Florida Atlantic University	Fla.	1	1	10,729	13,864	14,673	15,769	6,791	8,978	6,823	8,946
Florida Community College, Jacksonville	Fla.	1	2	15,072	21,023	21,459	21,228	8,874	12,354	5,270	15,958
Florida International University	Fla.	1	1	16,744	23,841	23,093	24,321	10,395	13,926	11,673	12,648
Florida State University	Fla.	1	1	22,990	28,521	28,424	28,575	13,160	15,415	22,816	5,759
Hillsborough Community College	Fla.	1	2	13,269	20,328	21,275	21,497	9,055	12,442	4,765	16,732
Miami-Dade Community College	Fla.	1	2	39,980	51,457	51,768	48,232	20,020	28,212	16,791	31,441
Palm Beach Community College	Fla.	1	2	12,742	17,147	18,193	18,586	7,300	11,286	4,836	13,750
Saint Petersburg Junior College	Fla.	1	2	16,116	21,297	22,297	22,799	8,868	13,931	7,076	15,723
University of Central Florida	Fla.	1	1	16,833	21,424	21,873	23,692	11,423	12,269	13,170	10,522
University of Florida	Fla.	1	1	35,172	36,227	36,447	37,324	20,269	17,055	31,273	6,051
University of South Florida	Fla.	1	1	29,439	33,257	34,145	34,768	15,009	19,759	17,455	17,313
Valencia Community College	Fla.	1	2	12,574	20,843	22,081	22,593	9,756	12,837	7,128	15,465

Table 210.—Selected statistics for college and university campuses enrolling more than 14,600 students in 1993—Continued

Enrollment, by level, fall 1993		Earned degrees conferred, 1992–93					Financial statistics, 1992–93, in thousands			Full-time-equivalent enrollment, fall 1992	Full-time-equivalent enrollment, fall 1993
Undergraduate	Postbaccalaureate	Associate	Bachelor's	Master's	Doctor's	First professional	Current-fund revenues	Current-fund expenditures	Educational and general expenditures		
13	14	15	16	17	18	19	20	21	22	23	24
12,323,959	1,981,699	514,756	1,165,178	369,585	42,132	75,387	$170,880,503	$165,241,040	$128,977,968	10,435,759	10,351,817
4,275,498	922,412	110,624	502,205	173,142	28,159	26,681	³71,035,876	³68,564,305	³52,894,266	3,866,508	3,811,942
17,985	3,378	—	4,104	730	123	92	314,869	304,138	265,179	19,638	19,386
15,379	4,101	—	3,062	892	134	169	253,960	237,575	193,891	17,304	17,393
11,658	4,255	—	1,604	842	108	243	899,433	859,733	378,885	11,961	12,183
16,746	529	567	676	151	—	—	102,212	102,200	94,863	10,718	10,769
30,178	11,072	—	6,243	1,778	270	154	434,224	417,103	366,159	34,520	33,067
17,520	—	543	—	—	—	—	35,542	34,422	31,359	10,011	9,454
19,508	—	872	—	—	—	—	43,768	41,235	37,475	11,210	10,691
13,931	4,886	—	2,592	982	47	—	162,146	150,006	132,362	14,917	14,927
28,268	—	1,107	—	—	—	—	65,789	66,031	65,202	15,244	14,438
26,558	8,721	—	4,844	1,262	373	282	693,848	679,395	565,551	29,994	30,331
20,377	—	635	—	—	—	—	—	—	—	10,368	9,911
14,315	1,134	—	3,319	312	—	—	149,190	149,176	137,085	15,063	14,333
15,204	1,846	—	2,719	324	—	—	133,361	127,198	121,372	14,683	13,800
13,165	1,541	—	3,026	297	—	—	123,209	120,294	114,936	13,845	13,513
14,692	3,264	—	3,137	525	—	—	141,579	140,029	132,589	16,277	15,551
18,828	3,737	—	4,289	802	—	—	137,084	130,526	121,773	18,236	16,968
21,426	5,647	—	4,607	978	—	—	181,303	181,010	169,103	22,646	20,810
13,509	4,279	—	2,718	877	—	—	134,146	125,508	119,178	14,132	13,082
21,679	5,603	—	4,216	828	—	—	184,995	171,911	163,514	22,009	20,893
18,738	4,578	—	4,291	909	—	—	160,233	156,276	148,623	19,492	18,826
19,653	—	978	—	—	—	—	51,784	51,857	47,750	10,522	9,850
26,630	—	1,160	—	—	—	—	135,617	132,033	126,527	15,188	13,818
22,701	—	1,289	—	—	—	—	—	—	—	13,087	12,327
18,888	—	820	—	—	—	—	52,320	47,843	43,177	11,475	10,588
22,953	—	1,187	—	—	—	—	62,154	65,215	58,878	12,108	11,701
16,554	—	1,097	—	—	—	—	53,406	50,318	44,351	10,157	8,662
18,387	—	409	—	—	—	—	—	—	—	10,836	9,798
14,789	—	846	—	—	—	—	—	—	—	8,965	8,353
18,745	—	813	—	—	—	—	56,313	56,888	56,330	9,450	9,255
15,378	—	385	—	—	—	—	44,527	45,178	45,178	8,993	8,405
15,702	—	655	—	—	—	—	45,081	44,567	44,567	9,849	8,236
16,684	—	445	—	—	—	—	41,861	41,924	41,924	9,236	8,042
22,438	—	1,042	—	—	—	—	62,734	59,606	59,158	12,314	12,095
21,928	—	841	—	—	—	—	76,342	74,033	66,222	13,152	11,947
18,983	—	752	—	—	—	—	58,591	59,290	54,393	9,424	9,807
22,248	—	766	—	—	—	—	66,687	60,409	60,409	9,952	11,621
20,920	—	575	—	—	—	—	71,871	66,598	62,206	11,893	10,281
20,293	—	990	—	—	—	—	51,830	51,551	44,945	11,062	10,279
16,052	—	810	—	—	—	—	—	—	—	8,993	8,753
16,649	—	622	—	—	—	—	81,822	84,878	82,718	8,357	8,355
20,217	—	301	—	—	—	—	51,753	36,717	31,978	10,604	9,989
22,299	5,832	—	5,392	1,435	19	—	216,067	213,766	200,759	24,282	22,627
19,101	6,612	—	3,879	1,283	6	—	174,343	169,061	158,788	20,102	19,890
15,806	—	630	—	—	—	—	52,320	50,654	46,146	8,909	8,776
21,254	5,803	—	4,364	1,437	—	—	194,333	194,140	182,946	22,421	20,652
21,768	—	1,186	—	—	—	—	72,997	68,011	56,286	12,060	11,529
20,428	—	730	—	—	—	—	63,618	57,744	55,492	11,891	11,021
15,384	—	588	—	—	—	—	42,944	42,282	37,580	8,643	8,362
7,007	8,973	—	1,730	1,846	581	263	1,623,009	1,541,641	1,004,348	13,794	13,940
21,577	8,764	—	5,829	1,670	810	374	832,569	840,426	781,878	28,863	28,388
17,220	5,256	—	4,355	608	306	372	1,071,460	1,012,669	605,737	21,618	21,157
13,404	3,411	—	3,223	512	155	84	633,272	618,334	402,226	16,518	16,159
22,892	11,554	—	5,992	2,199	657	590	1,685,826	1,667,160	1,090,878	33,778	33,100
14,360	3,491	—	3,375	408	280	69	1,005,151	973,289	623,891	17,725	17,353
16,331	2,250	—	4,155	410	205	—	320,395	318,349	271,093	18,001	17,944
14,688	12,970	—	3,194	2,589	415	637	924,404	914,426	684,566	23,293	23,337
20,444	6,940	—	3,482	719	197	116	342,109	335,813	288,578	22,444	22,435
17,721	—	—	2,022	—	—	—	63,840	63,582	63,582	12,911	12,843
21,725	6,627	—	4,409	1,114	299	166	433,983	405,996	349,872	24,309	24,038
15,492	7,690	—	3,239	1,114	216	176	357,796	352,381	300,654	19,566	19,019
18,652	3,083	13	3,093	583	144	—	352,858	324,325	278,685	17,753	18,139
6,941	12,051	34	1,619	2,204	167	578	675,349	660,730	298,676	13,296	13,664
25,714	—	1,895	—	—	—	—	68,993	67,624	61,210	13,792	13,663
12,449	3,320	8	2,029	479	36	—	120,827	121,193	107,074	9,797	10,328
21,228	—	1,571	—	—	—	—	78,927	80,255	78,581	10,842	10,630
19,518	4,803	—	3,620	950	25	—	159,485	156,224	141,295	15,773	16,638
22,148	6,427	608	5,533	1,340	262	165	344,227	337,722	284,756	24,776	25,036
21,497	—	2,024	—	—	—	—	46,595	46,727	42,668	29,938	27,351
48,232	—	4,984	—	—	—	—	199,997	200,029	188,421	9,519	9,454
18,586	—	1,561	—	—	—	—	43,169	43,614	40,258	12,330	12,357
22,799	—	2,513	—	—	—	—	54,827	53,121	52,880	15,740	17,276
19,482	4,210	190	4,165	783	33	—	157,511	151,934	138,859	32,837	33,603
27,756	9,568	1,306	5,439	1,598	372	686	805,126	807,289	740,140	24,062	24,177
25,732	9,036	267	5,143	1,400	108	96	387,235	378,699	339,724	12,158	12,322
22,593	—	2,430	—	—	—	—	56,295	55,384	50,126		

Table 210.—Selected statistics for college and university campuses enrolling more than 14,600 students in 1993—Continued

Institution	State	Con-trol[1]	Type[2]	Total enrollment, fall 1986	Total enrollment, fall 1991	Total enrollment, fall 1992	Total enrollment, fall 1993	Enrollment, by sex, fall 1993		Enrollment, by attendance status, fall 1993	
								Men	Women	Full-time	Part-time
1	2	3	4	5	6	7	8	9	10	11	12
DeKalb College	Ga.	1	2	8,786	15,282	15,532	16,349	6,494	9,855	5,674	10,675
Georgia State University	Ga.	1	1	21,835	23,966	24,050	23,605	9,919	13,686	11,132	12,473
University of Georgia	Ga.	1	1	25,698	28,691	28,493	28,753	13,578	15,175	24,377	4,376
University of Hawaii at Manoa	Hi.	1	1	18,918	19,308	19,799	20,061	9,187	10,874	14,126	5,935
Boise State University	Iowa	1	1	10,933	14,136	14,526	14,886	6,378	8,508	8,056	6,830
Belleville Area College	Ill.	1	2	11,382	14,984	15,440	14,624	6,265	8,359	3,948	10,676
City Colleges of Chicago-Harry S Truman College	Ill.	1	2	15,493	16,553	14,547	15,566	7,246	8,320	4,399	11,167
College of Du Page	Ill.	1	2	23,155	30,897	31,621	31,132	13,345	17,787	8,675	22,457
De Paul University	Ill.	2	1	13,132	16,404	16,489	16,479	7,572	8,907	9,107	7,372
Illinois State University	Ill.	1	1	21,924	22,510	21,761	20,610	9,080	11,530	16,865	3,745
Northern Illinois University	Ill.	1	1	24,680	24,895	24,052	23,177	10,549	12,628	17,024	6,153
Northwestern University	Ill.	2	1	16,226	17,099	17,285	17,551	9,192	8,359	13,943	3,608
Southern Illinois University, Carbondale	Ill.	1	1	23,446	24,863	24,761	23,881	13,899	9,982	18,265	5,616
Triton College	Ill.	1	2	17,871	16,767	16,804	15,308	6,804	8,504	3,739	11,569
University of Illinois at Chicago	Ill.	1	1	25,318	24,659	24,610	25,445	12,213	13,232	19,005	6,440
University of Illinois, Urbana Campus	Ill.	1	1	39,263	38,755	38,396	38,912	21,680	17,232	33,727	5,185
William Rainey Harper College	Ill.	1	2	15,954	17,562	17,610	16,212	6,730	9,482	4,786	11,426
Ball State University	Ind.	1	1	18,531	21,211	21,235	21,626	9,945	11,681	17,515	4,111
Indiana University, Bloomington	Ind.	1	1	32,417	35,487	36,071	35,551	16,822	18,729	29,811	5,740
Indiana U. - Purdue U. at Indianapolis	Ind.	1	1	23,468	27,786	28,342	27,552	11,675	15,877	12,173	15,379
Purdue University, Main Campus	Ind.	1	1	32,984	38,068	37,746	37,094	21,572	15,522	30,846	6,248
Iowa State University	Iowa	1	1	27,073	25,773	25,695	25,413	14,917	10,496	21,693	3,720
University of Iowa	Iowa	1	1	30,670	28,648	28,145	27,688	13,713	13,975	20,891	6,797
Johnson County Community College	Kans.	1	2	8,937	15,225	15,494	15,353	6,715	8,638	4,923	10,430
Kansas State U. of Agr. and App. Sci.	Kans.	1	1	17,687	20,712	20,451	20,050	10,587	9,463	16,316	3,734
University of Kansas, Main Campus	Kans.	1	1	25,822	26,655	26,457	26,127	13,012	13,115	20,442	5,685
Eastern Kentucky University	Ky.	1	1	12,674	16,463	16,811	16,343	6,766	9,577	11,997	4,346
University of Kentucky	Ky.	1	1	20,692	23,541	23,699	23,670	11,706	11,964	18,371	5,299
University of Louisville	Ky.	1	1	20,143	22,933	21,987	21,172	9,937	11,235	12,625	8,547
Western Kentucky University	Ky.	1	1	12,203	15,675	15,653	15,271	6,205	9,066	10,767	4,504
Delgado Community College	La.	1	2	7,317	14,424	15,112	14,932	5,713	9,219	6,175	8,757
La. St. U. & A&M & Hebert Laws Center	La.	1	1	28,421	26,936	27,358	26,085	13,123	12,962	20,331	5,754
University of New Orleans	La.	1	1	16,083	16,084	16,308	15,570	6,948	8,622	9,119	6,451
University of Southwestern Louisiana	La.	1	1	15,510	16,180	16,648	16,573	7,414	9,159	12,351	4,222
Johns Hopkins University	Md.	2	1	11,606	13,672	14,506	15,074	8,117	6,957	6,988	8,086
Towson State University	Md.	1	1	15,421	15,398	15,230	14,696	5,714	8,982	9,600	5,096
U. of Maryland, College Park Campus	Md.	1	1	38,639	34,621	32,916	32,441	16,957	15,484	23,555	8,886
Boston University	Mass.	2	1	27,055	28,086	28,375	28,653	13,686	14,967	22,168	6,485
Harvard University	Mass.	2	1	23,730	24,894	25,012	26,007	13,713	12,294	18,587	7,420
Northeastern University	Mass.	2	1	34,093	28,887	27,586	26,554	14,242	12,312	14,070	12,484
University of Massachusetts at Amherst	Mass.	1	1	27,797	24,784	24,185	24,234	12,321	11,913	18,705	5,529
Central Michigan University	Mich.	1	1	17,993	17,812	17,268	23,998	10,841	13,157	14,462	9,536
Eastern Michigan University	Mich.	1	1	21,338	23,958	24,096	24,600	10,008	14,592	13,855	10,745
Henry Ford Community College	Mich.	1	2	14,595	15,509	13,743	14,890	7,278	7,612	3,583	11,307
Lansing Community College	Mich.	1	2	20,405	21,779	21,204	18,419	7,991	10,428	4,618	13,801
Macomb Community College	Mich.	1	2	31,318	31,804	26,498	27,391	13,184	14,207	6,411	20,980
Michigan State University	Mich.	1	1	44,088	42,790	39,138	39,743	19,364	20,379	31,921	7,822
Oakland Community College	Mich.	1	2	26,670	28,852	26,088	28,232	11,669	16,563	5,863	22,369
University of Michigan, Ann Arbor	Mich.	1	1	34,972	35,343	35,476	36,845	20,206	16,639	33,113	3,732
Wayne State University	Mich.	1	1	28,764	33,914	34,945	34,280	15,499	18,781	15,634	18,646
Western Michigan University	Mich.	1	1	21,747	27,901	27,281	26,555	12,313	14,242	16,943	9,612
Saint Cloud State University	Minn.	1	1	14,220	16,321	16,042	15,118	7,161	7,957	11,806	3,312
University of Minnesota, Twin Cities	Minn.	1	1	63,994	56,350	54,671	51,880	25,528	26,352	22,548	29,332
Southwest Missouri State University	Mo.	1	1	15,233	19,504	19,002	18,160	8,266	9,894	13,493	4,667
University of Missouri, Columbia	Mo.	1	1	22,727	24,726	23,418	22,225	11,214	11,011	18,126	4,099
University of Missouri, Saint Louis	Mo.	1	1	12,328	15,611	14,918	15,411	6,355	9,056	6,079	9,332
University of Nebraska, Lincoln	Nebr.	1	1	23,899	24,620	24,573	24,491	13,105	11,386	19,110	5,381
University of Nebraska, Omaha	Nebr.	1	1	13,907	15,979	16,221	15,897	7,323	8,574	8,488	7,409
Community College of Southern Nevada	Nev.	1	2	11,069	15,015	17,745	17,118	7,360	9,758	1,904	15,214
University of Nevada, Las Vegas	Nev.	1	1	12,847	19,145	18,694	18,534	8,557	9,977	8,467	10,067
Camden County College	N.J.	1	2	8,126	14,350	15,714	15,585	6,268	9,317	5,588	9,997
Rutgers University, New Brunswick	N.J.	1	1	33,969	33,376	33,577	33,568	15,652	17,916	24,115	9,453
Albuquerque Technical Vocational Institute	N.Mex.	1	2	13,117	12,755	13,771	14,841	6,230	8,611	4,173	10,668
New Mexico State University, Main Campus	N.Mex.	1	1	13,718	15,344	15,500	15,788	7,972	7,816	11,268	4,520
University of New Mexico, Main Campus	N.Mex.	1	1	24,124	24,092	25,279	25,663	11,580	14,083	15,387	10,276
Columbia University, New York	N.Y.	2	1	17,574	18,878	19,290	19,023	9,979	9,044	15,107	3,916
CUNY, Bernard Baruch College	N.Y.	1	1	16,126	15,355	15,346	15,064	6,601	8,463	8,883	6,181
CUNY, Borough of Manhattan Community College	N.Y.	1	2	12,580	14,869	15,677	16,702	5,672	11,030	9,531	7,171
CUNY, Brooklyn College	N.Y.	1	1	14,625	15,634	15,467	15,580	6,084	9,496	8,049	7,531
CUNY, City College	N.Y.	1	1	12,782	14,696	14,783	14,832	7,891	6,941	8,481	6,351
CUNY, Hunter College	N.Y.	1	1	19,581	18,853	18,390	18,657	4,973	13,684	8,921	9,736
CUNY, Kingsborough Community College	N.Y.	1	2	12,005	14,509	14,331	14,994	5,510	9,484	7,266	7,728
Fordham University	N.Y.	2	1	12,256	13,329	14,534	14,663	6,123	8,540	7,342	7,321
Nassau Community College	N.Y.	1	2	19,363	21,550	22,367	22,215	9,988	12,227	11,188	11,027
New York University	N.Y.	2	1	31,665	33,441	33,695	33,309	14,757	18,552	20,902	12,407
Queens College	N.Y.	1	1	16,134	18,254	17,930	17,753	6,672	11,081	9,134	8,619
Regents College-University of the State of N.Y.	N.Y.	1	1	17,201	12,668	14,463	15,628	6,524	9,104	—	15,628
Saint John's University of New York	N.Y.	2	1	19,211	19,037	18,813	18,188	8,576	9,612	13,276	4,912
SUNY at Albany	N.Y.	1	1	16,112	18,805	19,001	16,759	8,062	8,697	12,282	4,477
SUNY at Buffalo	N.Y.	1	1	23,977	26,012	25,357	25,635	14,094	11,541	18,711	6,924
SUNY at Stony Brook	N.Y.	1	1	14,527	17,696	17,125	17,205	8,359	8,846	13,111	4,094
Syracuse University, Main Campus	N.Y.	2	1	21,120	20,906	20,496	19,353	9,258	10,095	14,112	5,241

Table 210.—Selected statistics for college and university campuses enrolling more than 14,600 students in 1993—Continued

Enrollment, by level, fall 1993		Earned degrees conferred, 1992–93					Financial statistics, 1992–93, in thousands			Full-time-equivalent enrollment, fall 1992	Full-time-equivalent enrollment, fall 1993
Undergraduate	Postbaccalaureate	Associate	Bachelor's	Master's	Doctor's	First professional	Current-fund revenues	Current-fund expenditures	Educational and general expenditures		
13	14	15	16	17	18	19	20	21	22	23	24
16,349	—	814			—	—	47,690	46,636	43,080	8,820	9,260
16,740	6,865	8	2,515	1,623	119	151	166,336	163,866	162,105	16,060	16,055
22,301	6,452	3	4,777	1,181	352	306	535,326	527,200	482,379	25,880	26,076
13,439	6,622	—	2,527	1,088	147	115	419,692	424,718	378,690	16,093	16,375
12,988	1,898	274	1,149	189	—	—	96,285	93,513	72,912	10,674	10,738
14,624	—	1,159	—	—	—	—	33,863	34,876	30,733	7,876	7,534
15,566	—	431	—	—	—	—	38,375	39,852	39,852	7,513	8,150
31,132	—	1,808	—	—	—	—	77,786	71,879	67,000	16,305	16,218
9,788	6,691	—	1,633	1,456	18	286	148,209	142,399	127,674	11,954	12,022
17,524	3,086	—	4,062	565	42	—	176,948	178,150	143,556	19,307	18,296
16,805	6,372	—	3,559	1,331	122	89	211,735	213,311	164,340	20,147	19,334
9,689	7,862	—	1,966	2,139	363	429	646,814	622,845	589,223	15,181	15,350
19,460	4,421	538	5,009	789	185	151	300,085	294,309	262,613	21,926	20,402
15,308	—	794	—	—	—	—	46,008	46,533	42,694	8,564	7,625
16,444	9,001	—	2,533	1,356	247	526	812,745	792,093	517,861	20,366	21,483
27,759	11,153	—	5,779	2,389	705	271	801,575	789,977	694,642	34,756	35,708
16,212	—	1,250	—	—	—	—	61,861	64,660	57,452	9,086	8,624
18,930	2,696	223	3,578	718	59	—	226,690	213,890	185,732	18,748	19,106
27,480	8,071	58	5,536	1,664	348	270	639,894	570,678	435,568	32,387	32,011
20,392	7,160	552	1,976	493	30	560	780,002	715,031	365,955	18,868	18,250
30,278	6,816	693	5,898	1,197	504	88	640,395	605,673	526,832	33,901	33,277
20,391	5,022	—	3,948	785	322	71	511,471	497,139	395,523	23,176	23,111
18,441	9,247	—	3,565	1,425	331	517	978,317	968,578	496,653	23,894	23,486
15,353	—	747	—	—	—	—	61,543	54,985	49,967	8,442	8,426
16,435	3,615	108	3,111	694	155	95	245,833	244,366	224,506	18,049	17,748
18,960	7,167	—	3,519	1,122	193	188	306,272	298,247	251,602	22,851	22,569
14,483	1,860	262	1,704	385	—	—	114,253	112,564	96,678	13,953	13,693
17,527	6,143	—	2,780	945	192	329	690,467	650,190	441,933	20,331	20,408
16,042	5,130	176	1,977	782	54	305	309,780	303,875	269,406	16,542	15,976
13,204	2,067	325	1,818	518	—	—	104,315	100,130	88,624	12,872	12,518
14,932	—	784	—	—	—	—	39,762	39,278	36,094	9,134	9,116
20,026	6,059	—	3,204	887	188	289	416,451	412,659	343,349	23,787	22,574
11,801	3,769	—	1,352	450	38	—	95,910	94,545	83,794	12,160	11,605
14,986	1,587	64	1,582	313	28	—	102,080	107,213	85,757	14,073	14,013
5,134	9,940	7	996	2,202	318	130	1,313,332	1,309,429	868,884	9,815	10,104
12,831	1,865	—	2,744	360	—	—	111,684	110,247	81,088	12,099	11,593
23,331	9,110	—	5,238	1,486	490	—	558,069	535,298	432,158	27,424	26,937
18,084	10,569	6	3,430	2,570	271	676	732,370	710,023	606,160	24,331	24,692
10,704	15,303	11	1,806	2,719	540	714	1,305,057	1,326,215	1,204,874	20,883	21,477
21,381	5,173	331	3,029	1,334	59	172	281,824	272,308	255,314	19,699	18,976
18,375	5,859	138	3,956	819	370	—	443,882	427,889	350,407	20,804	20,787
15,866	8,132	—	3,067	2,250	6	—	166,766	158,433	127,823	15,000	18,030
19,353	5,247	—	2,841	1,057	—	—	160,859	157,446	132,964	17,593	18,006
14,890	—	1,308	—	—	—	—	46,183	46,407	43,006	6,889	7,381
18,419	—	1,901	—	—	—	—	74,486	67,461	66,236	11,319	9,253
27,391	—	2,642	—	—	—	—	76,395	68,383	62,831	13,258	13,458
30,760	8,983	—	7,275	1,631	401	313	838,838	803,828	668,618	34,394	34,927
28,232	—	1,820	—	—	—	—	80,542	79,728	74,346	12,424	13,376
23,384	13,461	—	5,408	2,780	654	687	2,067,791	1,797,408	995,857	33,306	34,519
20,233	14,047	—	2,927	2,312	299	441	417,781	396,596	385,624	23,166	22,874
20,017	6,538	—	4,165	1,345	54	—	240,296	222,653	172,057	21,266	20,600
13,699	1,419	92	2,633	294	—	—	95,550	90,339	77,109	13,871	13,096
38,338	13,542	7	5,474	2,220	627	590	1,441,786	1,394,496	999,285	35,105	34,089
16,505	1,655	7	2,459	327	—	—	114,417	109,264	90,927	16,101	15,322
16,365	5,860	—	3,803	1,154	260	287	631,960	575,637	366,779	20,757	19,678
12,662	2,749	—	1,683	470	19	40	79,948	76,322	70,450	9,101	9,783
19,625	4,866	9	3,008	696	221	142	367,685	361,418	289,426	21,322	21,191
13,309	2,588	—	1,397	533	—	—	87,235	86,458	78,644	11,461	11,392
17,118	—	523	—	—	—	—	29,675	28,863	28,408	7,499	7,014
15,085	3,449	—	1,815	472	7	—	140,261	129,749	125,797	12,905	12,408
15,585	—	939	—	—	—	—	40,637	39,399	37,318	8,905	8,946
25,113	8,455	—	5,207	1,333	376	13	—	—	—	27,796	27,698
14,841	—	530	—	—	—	—	48,201	44,160	41,174	7,130	7,756
13,154	2,634	252	1,775	667	62	—	232,550	228,666	195,531	12,772	13,049
17,519	8,144	—	—	—	—	—	607,778	570,144	332,938	19,080	19,326
6,928	12,095	—	1,335	4,244	687	545	1,034,607	1,010,243	969,799	16,490	16,633
12,575	2,489	—	1,915	675	—	—	102,089	102,285	102,066	11,515	11,300
16,702	—	1,480	—	—	—	—	67,046	67,569	66,867	11,022	11,940
11,054	4,526	—	1,361	747	—	—	105,308	104,853	104,629	10,971	10,912
11,747	3,085	—	1,236	950	—	—	126,564	126,328	125,841	10,784	10,931
14,087	4,570	—	1,648	1,172	—	—	129,963	130,797	129,148	12,291	12,692
14,994	—	1,583	—	—	—	—	63,054	63,862	63,270	9,313	9,862
5,910	8,753	—	1,361	1,498	117	428	162,215	161,100	144,607	9,851	10,225
22,215	—	2,954	—	—	—	—	106,609	106,609	106,609	14,797	14,892
15,225	18,084	353	3,036	4,324	404	764	1,331,580	1,295,897	841,771	25,941	25,706
14,461	3,292	—	1,821	832	—	—	122,722	123,521	120,250	12,624	12,487
15,628	—	1,819	2,579	—	—	—	9,780	9,635	9,635	5,716	6,176
12,952	5,236	587	2,707	882	33	419	181,052	166,870	159,903	15,717	15,228
11,416	5,343	—	2,667	1,364	152	—	229,210	221,385	192,647	15,221	13,954
17,087	8,548	49	3,225	1,524	320	493	408,740	422,225	391,154	20,908	21,349
11,095	6,110	—	2,298	1,174	283	127	638,386	655,021	355,634	14,503	14,649
12,307	7,046	12	3,036	1,698	190	271	389,054	378,537	310,722	17,179	16,141

Table 210.—Selected statistics for college and university campuses enrolling more than 14,600 students in 1993—Continued

Institution	State	Control[1]	Type[2]	Total enrollment, fall 1986	Total enrollment, fall 1991	Total enrollment, fall 1992	Total enrollment, fall 1993	Enrollment, by sex, fall 1993		Enrollment, by attendance status, fall 1993	
								Men	Women	Full-time	Part-time
1	2	3	4	5	6	7	8	9	10	11	12
Central Piedmont Community College	N.C.	1	2	17,544	24,872	26,428	16,575	7,142	9,433	4,358	12,217
East Carolina University	N.C.	1	1	15,284	17,926	19,264	18,186	7,803	10,383	14,521	3,665
North Carolina State Universitiy, Raleigh	N.C.	1	1	24,887	27,791	27,766	27,810	16,888	10,922	18,448	9,362
University of North Carolina, Chapel Hill	N.C.	1	1	22,826	23,833	23,977	24,334	10,304	14,030	19,540	4,794
University of North Carolina, Charlotte	N.C.	1	1	12,109	15,584	15,781	15,942	7,762	8,180	10,616	5,326
Bowling Green State U., Main Campus	Ohio	1	1	17,799	18,685	18,173	17,767	7,603	10,164	15,135	2,632
Cleveland State University	Ohio	1	1	17,951	18,607	17,813	16,881	8,258	8,623	9,288	7,593
Columbus State Community College	Ohio	1	2	7,751	15,204	16,507	17,042	7,185	9,857	6,313	10,729
Cuyahoga Community College District	Ohio	1	2	23,318	23,427	24,832	25,913	9,214	16,699	8,429	17,484
Kent State University, Main Campus	Ohio	1	1	20,846	24,525	24,098	22,700	9,552	13,148	16,600	6,100
Miami University, Oxford Campus	Ohio	1	1	15,988	16,318	16,098	16,281	7,408	8,873	14,640	1,641
Ohio State University, Main Campus	Ohio	1	1	53,873	54,311	52,179	50,623	26,279	24,344	39,205	11,418
Ohio University, Main Campus	Ohio	1	1	16,021	18,688	18,862	19,086	9,210	9,876	17,330	1,756
Sinclair Community College	Ohio	1	2	16,094	17,456	18,922	18,751	7,186	11,565	6,241	12,510
University of Akron, Main Campus	Ohio	1	1	25,944	28,230	27,063	26,032	12,544	13,488	14,638	11,394
University of Cincinnati, Main Campus	Ohio	1	1	30,213	30,051	28,779	28,662	14,908	13,754	19,531	9,131
University of Toledo	Ohio	1	1	21,176	24,947	24,539	24,188	11,876	12,312	17,017	7,171
Wright State University, Main Campus	Ohio	1	1	16,075	16,789	16,749	16,460	7,546	8,914	10,952	5,508
Oklahoma State University, Main Campus	Okla.	1	1	21,676	19,770	19,602	19,153	10,538	8,615	14,663	4,490
Tulsa Junior College	Okla.	1	2	15,292	18,650	19,583	19,098	7,507	11,591	4,911	14,187
University of Central Oklahoma	Okla.	1	1	13,806	14,699	15,167	15,043	6,207	8,836	8,523	6,520
University of Oklahoma, Norman Campus	Okla.	1	1	22,313	21,250	21,724	21,696	11,706	9,990	14,966	6,730
Portland Community College	Oreg.	1	2	19,494	23,078	22,803	22,527	10,445	12,082	6,880	15,647
Portland State University	Oreg.	1	1	15,640	15,986	17,357	16,243	7,402	8,841	7,648	8,595
University of Oregon	Oreg.	1	1	17,142	18,631	17,285	16,877	8,273	8,604	14,229	2,648
Community College of Allegheny County	Pa.	1	2	17,251	21,431	21,743	20,721	8,494	12,227	8,210	12,511
Community College of Philadelphia	Pa.	1	2	14,860	17,547	19,476	19,786	6,765	13,021	5,782	14,004
International Correspondence Schools	Pa.	2	2	—	20,722	18,728	23,552	9,892	13,660	—	23,552
Pennsylvania State U., Main Campus	Pa.	1	1	35,261	38,989	38,446	37,658	21,176	16,482	33,153	4,505
Temple University	Pa.	1	1	30,615	30,750	30,229	30,040	14,536	15,504	19,301	10,739
University of Pennsylvania	Pa.	2	1	21,742	22,229	22,418	22,469	11,901	10,568	18,269	4,200
University of Pittsburgh, Main Campus	Pa.	1	1	28,449	27,973	27,852	27,528	13,790	13,738	19,359	8,169
Community College of Rhode Island	R.I.	1	2	13,096	17,330	17,986	16,399	6,133	10,266	4,803	11,596
University of Rhode Island	R.I.	1	1	14,367	15,387	15,449	14,925	6,843	8,082	10,091	4,834
Clemson University	S.C.	1	1	13,062	17,295	17,666	16,609	9,252	7,357	13,757	2,852
University of South Carolina, Columbia	S.C.	1	1	22,965	26,131	26,471	26,710	11,728	14,982	16,922	9,788
Memphis State University	Tenn.	1	1	20,043	20,449	20,578	20,373	9,166	11,207	12,820	7,553
Middle Tennessee State University	Tenn.	1	1	11,408	15,673	16,787	17,383	8,100	9,283	12,767	4,616
University of Tennessee, Knoxville	Tenn.	1	1	25,842	26,266	26,579	26,397	13,490	12,907	19,713	6,684
Austin Community College	Tex.	1	2	18,340	23,049	25,186	24,564	11,233	13,331	6,356	18,208
El Paso Community College	Tex.	1	2	13,827	16,953	18,479	18,843	7,353	11,490	8,509	10,334
Houston Community College System	Tex.	1	2	26,002	38,005	37,410	39,321	17,544	21,777	9,812	29,509
North Harris-Montgomery Comm. College District	Tex.	1	2	11,311	17,192	17,537	17,587	6,983	10,604	6,272	11,315
San Antonio College	Tex.	1	2	20,790	19,093	20,051	18,944	8,259	10,685	6,992	11,952
Southwest Texas State University	Tex.	1	1	19,778	21,575	21,302	20,879	9,772	11,107	14,671	6,208
Tarrant County Junior College District	Tex.	1	2	24,091	28,338	28,516	27,353	11,840	15,513	8,080	19,273
Texas A&M University	Tex.	1	1	36,617	40,997	41,710	42,524	24,547	17,977	37,777	4,747
Texas Tech. University	Tex.	1	1	23,479	24,757	24,154	24,007	13,043	10,964	19,554	4,453
University of Texas, Arlington	Tex.	1	1	23,247	25,135	24,729	23,763	12,495	11,268	12,960	10,803
University of Texas, Austin	Tex.	1	1	46,140	49,961	49,253	48,555	26,068	22,487	41,730	6,825
University of Texas, El Paso	Tex.	1	1	13,753	16,798	17,223	17,006	8,090	8,916	10,374	6,632
University of Texas, San Antonio	Tex.	1	1	12,413	15,759	16,767	17,097	7,991	9,106	10,003	7,094
University of Houston, University Park	Tex.	1	1	28,164	33,607	33,022	32,124	16,169	15,955	18,730	13,394
University of North Texas	Tex.	1	1	21,269	27,020	26,433	25,759	12,396	13,363	16,705	9,054
Brigham Young University	Utah	2	1	30,226	32,019	32,289	31,706	15,999	15,707	28,349	3,357
Salt Lake Community College	Utah	1	2	8,815	15,970	17,024	17,437	8,755	8,682	6,908	10,529
University of Utah	Utah	1	1	24,726	26,706	26,795	27,113	14,692	12,421	17,495	9,618
Utah State University	Utah	1	1	13,029	16,288	16,513	17,556	8,941	8,615	11,074	6,482
George Mason University	Va.	1	1	17,652	20,693	20,829	21,300	9,818	11,482	11,227	10,073
Northern Virginia Community College	Va.	1	2	33,682	37,338	38,343	37,477	17,186	20,291	9,227	28,250
Old Dominion University	Va.	1	1	15,463	16,686	16,507	15,974	7,829	8,145	9,616	6,358
Tidewater Community College	Va.	1	2	15,531	18,136	16,944	17,511	7,671	9,840	4,618	12,893
University of Virginia, Main Campus	Va.	1	1	21,615	21,341	21,535	21,394	9,998	11,396	17,034	4,360
Virginia Commonwealth University	Va.	1	1	19,641	21,608	21,939	21,854	8,913	12,941	13,347	8,507
Virginia Polytechnic Inst. and State Univ.	Va.	1	1	24,637	26,257	26,003	26,030	15,419	10,611	22,480	3,550
University of Washington	Wash.	1	1	33,674	34,269	34,597	34,000	17,132	16,868	27,708	6,292
Washington State University	Wash.	1	1	16,193	17,838	17,871	18,822	9,998	8,824	16,479	2,343
West Virginia University	W.Va.	1	1	17,174	22,460	22,712	23,080	11,479	11,601	17,793	5,287
Milwaukee Area Technical College	Wisc.	1	2	20,032	23,156	23,170	24,072	10,273	13,799	5,860	18,212
University of Wisconsin, Madison	Wisc.	1	1	44,584	43,030	41,824	39,999	20,466	19,533	33,851	6,148
University of Wisconsin, Milwaukee	Wisc.	1	1	25,930	26,040	24,991	23,806	10,957	12,849	13,150	10,656
Wisc. Area Vocational Technical Adult Ed.	Wisc.	1	2	20,032	17,861	17,451	15,588	6,578	9,010	9,890	5,698
Community College of the Air Force	Ala.	1	2	34,617	34,294	34,294	33,447	13,895	19,552	12,563	20,884

Table 210.—Selected statistics for college and university campuses enrolling more than 14,600 students in 1993—Continued

Enrollment, by level, fall 1993		Earned degrees conferred, 1992–93					Financial statistics, 1992–93, in thousands			Full-time-equivalent enrollment, fall 1992	Full-time-equivalent enrollment, fall 1993
Undergraduate	Postbacca-laureate	Associate	Bachelor's	Master's	Doctor's	First professional	Current-fund revenues	Current-fund expenditures	Educational and general expenditures		
13	14	15	16	17	18	19	20	21	22	23	24
16,575	—	819	—	—	—	—	47,935	47,924	42,719	11,826	8,461
14,858	3,328	—	2,561	671	5	74	281,718	262,677	228,812	16,504	15,918
21,986	5,824	108	3,897	806	283	74	515,030	500,655	437,330	22,126	22,065
15,709	8,625	—	3,502	1,452	388	443	800,719	782,773	679,864	20,978	21,325
13,354	2,588	—	2,328	503	—	—	124,040	119,842	93,881	12,599	12,679
14,902	2,865	6	3,245	686	78	—	187,950	190,921	146,735	16,439	16,138
11,710	5,171	—	1,695	994	26	267	130,896	130,595	121,617	12,791	12,253
17,042	—	1,278	—	—	—	—	48,708	42,829	38,904	9,620	9,917
25,913	—	1,423	—	—	—	—	117,464	103,563	96,342	13,507	14,302
17,811	4,889	—	3,130	968	139	—	211,601	205,417	159,795	19,833	18,934
14,413	1,868	232	3,482	546	54	—	199,425	192,652	143,399	15,164	15,268
37,044	13,579	287	7,815	2,371	685	710	1,330,851	1,238,144	797,101	45,361	43,594
16,171	2,915	149	3,497	880	89	80	227,563	221,176	180,741	17,841	18,020
18,751	—	1,191	—	—	—	—	65,620	57,098	51,613	10,488	10,443
21,782	4,250	681	2,684	814	110	155	188,512	181,789	159,439	20,108	19,153
21,280	7,382	658	3,136	1,086	226	280	775,510	716,756	391,921	22,856	23,091
20,798	3,390	686	2,369	602	63	221	180,555	166,746	153,089	20,037	19,840
12,610	3,850	—	1,797	882	36	76	158,250	157,082	145,010	13,072	13,074
14,406	4,747	—	2,695	713	225	64	284,107	269,410	218,337	16,682	16,356
19,098	—	1,280	—	—	—	—	48,065	45,340	40,093	13,184	9,676
11,605	3,438	—	1,987	575	—	—	59,999	59,061	50,340	10,995	11,057
14,707	6,989	—	2,417	1,131	137	213	258,557	252,806	203,356	17,616	17,501
22,527	—	1,273	—	—	—	—	90,030	82,542	76,465	12,315	12,136
11,186	5,057	—	1,804	800	39	—	109,721	106,630	94,217	11,468	10,967
13,274	3,603	—	2,925	775	237	162	230,662	222,054	179,269	15,455	15,255
20,721	—	1,882	—	—	—	—	90,089	87,341	82,447	13,040	12,412
19,786	—	996	—	—	—	—	64,715	63,478	62,833	10,358	10,486
23,552	—	—	—	—	—	—	42,537	33,801	33,801	7,669	9,645
30,963	6,695	80	8,307	1,180	495	—	775,400	722,722	624,587	35,606	34,868
19,392	10,648	18	3,579	1,363	282	641	776,930	716,366	386,253	23,698	23,437
11,448	11,021	28	2,668	2,236	506	585	1,555,181	1,457,972	760,781	19,821	19,909
17,607	9,921	—	3,253	1,978	333	412	662,636	612,614	570,874	22,578	22,495
16,399	—	1,507	—	—	—	—	55,562	55,759	51,913	9,694	8,698
11,350	3,575	17	2,128	585	98	5	205,721	210,392	177,578	12,319	11,943
12,513	4,096	—	2,776	1,039	84	—	312,581	308,062	250,134	15,754	14,821
16,255	10,455	14	3,219	1,919	281	327	327,469	317,860	282,485	21,207	20,620
15,485	4,888	—	2,091	825	104	112	158,547	155,225	135,014	15,616	15,756
15,426	1,957	8	2,032	327	47	—	95,731	91,995	81,854	14,201	14,558
18,986	7,411	—	3,548	1,329	249	198	454,299	435,890	368,745	22,640	22,267
24,564	—	620	—	—	—	—	63,358	62,213	61,582	12,667	12,472
18,843	—	688	—	—	—	—	62,816	60,467	60,055	12,018	11,980
39,321	—	1,020	—	—	—	—	121,800	111,347	111,347	18,218	19,723
17,587	—	636	—	—	—	—	41,190	47,081	45,284	9,789	10,072
18,944	—	759	—	—	—	—	62,332	59,625	59,061	11,623	11,006
18,083	2,796	30	2,967	524	—	—	141,452	135,213	102,115	17,658	17,096
27,353	—	1,524	—	—	—	—	75,326	74,812	68,450	15,049	14,553
34,441	8,083	—	6,579	1,293	496	166	763,302	777,254	685,003	38,920	39,612
19,565	4,442	—	3,365	715	125	199	243,298	218,739	179,039	21,492	21,285
19,408	4,355	—	2,918	1,136	77	—	148,142	145,189	121,376	17,925	17,221
35,206	13,349	—	7,861	2,600	686	560	821,914	810,176	702,542	45,177	44,419
14,368	2,638	—	1,468	377	5	—	109,096	108,512	86,181	13,135	12,975
14,832	2,265	—	1,792	423	—	—	85,215	81,077	71,304	12,379	12,797
24,692	7,432	—	3,414	1,487	204	458	292,376	283,025	249,886	24,514	24,018
19,181	6,578	—	3,365	1,275	204	—	193,209	178,993	148,601	20,809	20,196
28,775	2,931	29	5,590	1,051	74	151	437,616	429,170	288,909	30,313	29,663
17,437	—	1,049	—	—	—	—	62,597	58,722	51,549	10,158	10,444
22,268	4,845	—	3,137	917	211	237	732,215	702,414	440,254	21,376	21,325
14,668	2,888	52	1,823	654	91	—	222,578	213,073	190,567	12,843	13,604
13,350	7,950	—	2,756	1,280	70	221	172,531	166,308	130,991	14,878	15,081
37,477	—	2,261	—	—	—	—	75,824	75,843	75,322	18,976	18,716
10,847	5,127	—	2,167	810	74	—	130,348	122,018	101,612	12,665	12,021
17,511	—	1,185	—	—	—	—	36,212	36,970	36,677	8,660	8,949
12,446	8,948	—	2,949	1,481	315	511	833,352	794,447	404,241	18,651	18,661
15,327	6,527	17	2,480	1,173	102	249	698,496	661,322	279,737	16,902	16,640
19,127	6,903	38	3,904	1,266	369	76	467,132	466,007	394,475	23,624	23,791
24,938	9,062	—	5,794	1,955	416	338	1,238,242	1,212,002	913,787	30,636	30,188
15,789	3,033	—	3,279	525	163	86	377,553	366,300	315,708	16,495	17,383
15,577	7,503	—	2,989	1,124	97	216	330,780	322,954	285,004	19,798	19,753
24,072	—	1,504	—	—	—	—	106,005	106,854	98,269	11,622	11,977
27,908	12,091	—	6,217	2,141	676	514	1,354,844	1,317,396	990,337	37,622	36,252
19,004	4,802	—	2,678	1,130	95	—	219,718	217,874	199,151	17,759	17,316
15,588	—	1,115	—	—	—	—	60,094	60,428	56,335	11,082	11,804
33,447	—	10,000	—	—	—	—	—	—	—	19,949	19,578

[1] Publicly controlled institutions are identified by a "1;" and privately controlled, by a "2."

[2] The types of institutions are identified as follows: "1" 4-year institutions; "2" 2-year institutions.

[3] Excludes data for nonreporting institutions.

—Data not available or not applicable.

SOURCE: U.S. Department of Education, National Center for Education Statistics, "Fall Enrollment in Institutions of Higher Education" survey; and Integrated Postsecondary Education Data System (IPEDS), "Completions," "Finance," and "Fall Enrollment" surveys. (This table was prepared June 1995.)

Table 211.—Selected statistics on historically black colleges and universities: [1] 1980, 1988, and 1993

Item	Total	Public		Private	
		4-year	2-year	4-year	2-year
1	2	3	4	5	6
Number of institutions, fall 1993	**103**	**40**	**10**	**49**	**4**
Total enrollment, fall 1980	233,557	155,085	13,132	62,924	2,416
Men	106,387	70,236	6,758	28,352	1,041
Men, black	81,818	53,654	2,781	24,412	971
Women	127,170	84,849	6,374	34,572	1,375
Women, black	109,171	70,582	4,644	32,589	1,356
Total enrollment, fall 1988	239,755	158,606	15,066	64,644	1,439
Men	100,561	66,097	6,772	27,219	473
Men, black	78,268	50,545	3,192	24,081	450
Women	139,194	92,509	8,294	37,425	966
Women, black	115,883	73,893	5,894	35,145	951
Total enrollment, fall 1993	282,856	189,032	19,165	73,398	1,261
Men	116,397	77,823	8,091	30,028	455
Men, black	93,110	61,508	3,720	27,474	408
Women	166,459	111,209	11,074	43,370	806
Women, black	138,088	89,359	6,857	41,090	782
Full-time enrollment, fall 1993	217,462	139,072	11,017	66,440	933
Men	91,611	59,619	4,464	27,150	378
Women	125,851	79,453	6,553	39,290	555
Part-time enrollment, fall 1993	65,394	49,960	8,148	6,958	328
Men	24,786	18,204	3,627	2,878	77
Women	40,608	31,756	4,521	4,080	251
Earned degrees conferred, 1992–93					
Associate	2,805	1,267	1,281	104	153
Men	1,047	437	510	50	50
Men, black	482	188	205	41	48
Women	1,758	830	771	54	103
Women, black	974	289	532	50	103
Bachelor's	26,140	16,867	—	9,273	—
Men	9,764	6,318	—	3,446	—
Men, black	7,924	4,836	—	3,088	—
Women	16,376	10,549	—	5,827	—
Women, black	14,096	8,605	—	5,491	—
Master's	4,612	3,708	—	904	—
Men	1,617	1,300	—	317	—
Men, black	821	652	—	169	—
Women	2,995	2,408	—	587	—
Women, black	1,945	1,501	—	444	—
Doctor's	219	65	—	154	—
Men	94	16	—	78	—
Men, black	44	7	—	37	—
Women	125	49	—	76	—
Women, black	84	27	—	57	—
First-professional	966	404	—	562	—
Men	500	215	—	285	—
Men, black	295	80	—	215	—
Women	466	189	—	277	—
Women, black	332	113	—	219	—
Financial statistics, 1992–93, in thousands of dollars					
Current-fund revenues	$3,258,171	$1,689,795	$87,936	$1,468,329	$12,110
Tuition and fees	796,725	351,387	15,457	425,079	4,802
Federal government [2]	658,749	240,780	14,706	400,625	2,639
State governments [2]	786,358	710,717	41,634	33,297	710
Local governments [2]	93,509	82,060	10,346	1,103	0
Private gifts, grants, and contracts	168,781	28,552	413	137,952	1,864
Endowment income	30,045	2,436	26	27,500	82
Sales and services	664,603	240,911	3,912	417,852	1,928
Other sources	59,401	32,952	1,442	24,922	85
Current-fund expenditures	3,184,303	1,651,220	86,639	1,433,065	13,379
Educational and general expenditures	2,612,086	1,435,870	82,520	1,081,273	12,423
Auxiliary enterprises	322,274	215,351	4,119	101,849	956
Hospitals	249,309	0	0	249,309	0
Independent operations	633	0	0	633	0

[1] Historically black colleges and universities are accredited institutions of higher education established prior to 1964 with the principal mission of educating black Americans. Federal regulations, 20 U.S. Code, Section 1061 (2), allow for certain exceptions to the founding date. Most institutions are in the southern and border states and were established prior to 1954.

[2] Includes appropriations, grants, contracts, and independent operations.

—Not applicable.

SOURCE: U.S. Department of Education, National Center for Education Statistics, "Fall Enrollment in Institutions of Higher Education;" and Integrated Postsecondary Education Data System (IPEDS), "Fall Enrollment," "Completions," and "Finance" surveys. (This table was prepared May 1995.)

Table 212.—Fall enrollment, degrees conferred, and expenditures in historically black colleges and universities, by institution: 1993

Institution	Type and control [1]	Enrollment, 1993		Degrees conferred, 1992–93					Expenditures, 1992–93 (In thousands)	
		Total	Black	Associate	Bachelor's	Master's	Doctor's	First-professional	Current-fund expenditures	Educational and general expenditures
1	2	3	4	5	6	7	8	9	10	11
Total	—	282,856	231,198	2,805	26,140	4,612	219	966	$3,184,303	$2,612,086
** Alabama A&M University, AL	1	5,593	4,384	2	433	301	1	—	46,831	45,761
Alabama State University, AL	1	5,608	5,474	1	311	100	—	—	41,393	34,646
Bishop State Community College, AL [2]	2	4,650	2,444	314	—	—	—	—	18,172	16,852
C. A. Fredd State Technical College, AL	2	241	209	3	—	—	—	—	2,486	2,465
Carver State Technical College, AL [3]	2	—	—	—	—	—	—	—	—	—
Concordia College, AL	4	387	372	37	—	—	—	—	3,664	3,390
J.F. Drake Technical College, AL	2	825	393	52	—	—	—	—	3,757	3,625
Lawson State Community College, AL	2	2,307	2,212	126	—	—	—	—	9,042	8,615
Miles College, AL	3	868	866	—	92	—	—	—	6,203	5,615
Oakwood College, AL	3	1,451	1,312	9	170	—	—	—	17,848	13,795
Selma University, AL	3	360	358	10	13	—	—	—	4,572	4,274
Stillman College, AL	3	953	933	—	135	—	—	—	11,553	9,931
Talladega College, AL	3	1,027	965	—	118	—	—	—	11,629	9,974
Trenholm State Technical College, AL	2	945	719	54	—	—	—	—	5,479	5,270
** Tuskegee University, AL	3	3,371	3,115	—	506	48	—	44	70,656	64,514
Arkansas Baptist College, AR	3	315	314	—	20	—	—	—	1,921	1,831
Philander Smith College, AR	3	915	774	—	68	—	—	—	5,625	5,013
Shorter College, AR	4	209	173	12	—	—	—	—	936	848
** University of Arkansas, Pine Bluff, AR	1	4,075	3,329	3	310	1	—	—	28,601	25,799
** Delaware State College, DE	1	3,301	2,066	—	280	76	—	—	36,143	31,886
Howard University, DC	3	10,538	9,268	—	1,514	334	98	272	541,334	310,479
** University of the District of Columbia, DC	1	10,608	8,793	205	522	139	—	—	98,826	97,586
Bethune-Cookman College, FL	3	2,210	2,119	—	287	—	—	—	27,861	23,618
Edward Waters College, FL	3	786	744	—	53	—	—	—	6,501	6,041
** Florida A&M University, FL	1	9,876	8,770	22	1,056	157	9	2	103,308	93,557
Florida Memorial College, FL	3	1,579	1,242	—	214	—	—	—	14,211	12,853
Albany State College, GA	1	3,257	2,857	—	271	59	—	—	23,798	19,312
Clark Atlanta University, GA	3	5,128	4,933	—	427	280	39	—	78,898	75,365
** Fort Valley State College, GA	1	2,743	2,522	4	218	70	—	—	27,209	23,746
Interdenominational Theological Center, GA .	3	374	353	—	—	3	3	77	6,177	6,105
Morehouse College, GA	3	3,005	2,941	—	520	—	—	—	40,957	35,239
Morehouse School of Medicine, GA	3	161	135	—	—	—	—	33	36,634	36,634
Morris Brown College, GA	3	2,126	2,024	—	89	—	—	—	30,067	25,726
Paine College, GA	3	723	707	—	59	—	—	—	8,959	7,770
Savannah State College, GA	1	3,197	2,901	2	253	6	—	—	23,594	19,385
Spelman College, GA	3	2,065	2,010	—	412	—	—	—	32,371	26,366
** Kentucky State University, KY	1	2,485	1,185	81	180	24	—	—	31,227	28,119
Dillard University, LA	3	1,585	1,578	—	223	—	—	—	18,354	16,353
Grambling State University, LA	1	7,833	7,492	60	807	143	3	—	53,948	43,247
** Southern University and A&M College, Baton Rouge, LA	1	9,502	8,791	25	812	152	—	92	78,196	67,473
Southern University, New Orleans, LA	1	4,277	3,980	35	356	58	—	—	19,780	18,981
Southern University, Shreveport-Bossier City Campus, LA	2	1,083	998	81	—	—	—	—	6,640	6,348
Xavier University of Louisiana, LA	3	3,391	3,059	—	494	136	—	7	37,942	35,251
Bowie State University, MD	1	4,946	3,424	—	378	339	—	—	30,202	26,702
Coppin State College, MD	1	3,265	2,970	—	258	75	—	—	22,235	20,277
Morgan State University, MD	1	5,729	5,348	—	515	89	5	—	60,095	52,042
** University of Maryland, Eastern Shore, MD ...	1	2,637	1,826	—	234	58	2	—	32,322	27,720
Lewis College of Business, MI	4	262	262	11	—	—	—	—	2,022	2,003
** Alcorn State University, MS	1	2,712	2,513	24	349	45	—	—	32,170	26,507
Coahoma Community College, MS	2	964	944	109	—	—	—	—	7,338	6,745
Hinds Community College, Utica Campus, MS	2	638	625	89	—	—	—	—	—	—
Jackson State University, MS	1	6,346	5,970	—	682	142	10	—	60,271	51,059
Mary Holmes College, MS	4	403	383	93	—	—	—	—	6,756	6,183
Mississippi Valley State University, MS	1	2,330	2,320	—	240	2	—	—	20,332	17,135
Rust College, MS	3	1,180	1,103	8	124	—	—	—	12,208	10,455
Tougaloo College, MS	3	1,153	1,151	—	98	—	—	—	12,282	11,248
Harris-Stowe State College, MO	1	1,898	1,365	—	88	—	—	—	8,865	8,865
** Lincoln University, MO	1	3,623	994	94	282	92	—	—	26,523	24,401
Barber-Scotia College, NC	3	732	729	—	168	—	—	—	7,640	6,990
Bennett College, NC	3	664	646	—	94	—	—	—	10,518	9,647
Elizabeth City State University, NC	1	2,130	1,555	—	275	—	—	—	26,464	21,822
Fayetteville State University, NC	1	4,032	2,523	12	378	95	—	—	33,481	27,875
Johnson C. Smith University, NC	3	1,391	1,380	—	172	—	—	—	18,416	16,050
Livingstone College, NC	3	704	701	—	75	1	—	7	9,866	8,909

Table 212.—Fall enrollment, degrees conferred, and expenditures in historically black colleges and universities, by institution: 1993—Continued

Institution	Type and control [1]	Enrollment, 1993		Degrees conferred, 1992–93					Expenditures, 1992–93 (In thousands)	
		Total	Black	Associate	Bachelor's	Master's	Doctor's	First-professional	Current-fund expenditures	Educational and general expenditures
1	2	3	4	5	6	7	8	9	10	11
** North Carolina Agricultural and Technical State University, NC	1	8,013	6,851	—	863	224	—	—	85,432	73,809
North Carolina Central University, NC	1	5,645	4,739	—	602	206	—	95	49,708	41,808
St. Augustine's College, NC	3	1,745	1,603	—	224	—	—	—	24,677	20,669
Shaw University, NC	3	2,504	2,370	16	290	—	—	—	22,653	21,048
Winston-Salem State University, NC	1	2,909	2,202	—	448	—	—	—	27,825	22,795
Central State University, OH	1	3,068	2,767	—	280	—	—	—	39,217	32,408
Wilberforce University, OH	3	984	956	—	118	—	—	—	11,615	9,768
** Langston University, OK	1	3,439	1,783	—	518	9	—	—	21,982	18,508
Cheyney University of Pennsylvania, PA	1	1,519	1,429	—	149	78	—	—	21,380	18,655
Lincoln University, PA	1	1,445	1,326	—	188	62	—	—	23,955	21,928
Allen University, SC	3	290	289	—	21	—	—	—	4,461	4,099
Benedict College, SC	3	1,266	1,229	—	209	—	—	—	15,146	13,703
Claflin College, SC	3	972	947	—	207	—	—	—	9,896	8,401
Clinton Junior College, SC [4]	4	—	—	—	—	—	—	—	—	—
Denmark Technical College, SC	2	780	733	50	—	—	—	—	5,915	5,023
Morris College, SC	3	938	935	—	130	—	—	—	9,183	7,905
** South Carolina State College, SC	1	4,779	4,507	—	568	75	11	—	48,067	38,171
Voorhees College, SC	3	724	713	—	56	—	—	—	6,831	5,571
Fisk University, TN	3	856	846	—	162	10	—	—	12,194	10,522
Knoxville College, TN	3	846	837	20	83	—	—	—	11,477	9,963
Lane College, TN	3	649	647	—	69	—	—	—	6,543	5,501
Le Moyne-Owen College, TN	3	1,321	1,319	—	143	—	—	—	9,756	8,534
Meharry Medical College, TN	3	697	577	—	—	6	7	89	79,885	47,771
** Tennessee State University, TN	1	7,851	4,894	190	534	141	24	—	64,225	59,465
Huston-Tillotson College, TX	3	539	422	—	67	—	—	—	7,234	6,395
Jarvis Christian College, TX	3	497	491	—	64	—	—	—	9,140	8,279
Paul Quinn College, TX	3	670	650	—	85	—	—	—	6,420	6,115
** Prairie View A&M University, TX	1	5,848	5,080	—	632	220	—	—	64,569	52,143
St. Philip's College, TX	2	6,732	1,300	403	—	—	—	—	27,810	27,578
Southwestern Christian College, TX	3	182	148	41	3	—	—	—	2,615	2,286
Texas College, TX	3	452	424	—	40	—	—	—	5,398	4,729
Texas Southern University, TX	1	10,641	8,895	—	404	204	—	215	67,573	61,934
Wiley College, TX	3	541	514	—	37	—	—	—	5,956	5,411
Hampton University, VA	3	5,759	5,062	—	861	86	—	—	65,372	56,648
Norfolk State University, VA	1	8,652	7,139	54	772	156	—	—	61,509	48,164
St. Paul's College, VA	3	672	614	—	108	—	—	—	9,253	8,236
** Virginia State University, VA	1	3,996	3,569	—	451	88	—	—	44,773	33,911
Virginia Union University, VA	3	1,539	1,511	—	151	—	7	33	16,157	13,674
Bluefield State College, WV	1	2,601	211	244	352	—	—	—	12,090	11,072
West Virginia State College, WV	1	4,756	611	163	475	—	—	—	22,587	19,117
** University of the Virgin Islands, St Thomas Campus, VI	1	1,867	1,512	46	143	22	—	—	30,520	28,078

[1] 1=public 4-year; 2=public 2-year; 3=private 4-year; and 4=private 2-year.
[2] Carver State Technical College and Southwest State Technical College merged with Bishop State Community College in 1993.
[3] Carver State Technical College merged with Bishop State Community College in 1993.
[4] Lost accreditation.
—Data not reported or not applicable.

** Land-grant institution.

SOURCE: U.S. Department of Education, National Center for Education Statistics, Integrated Postsecondary Education Data System (IPEDS), "Fall Enrollment, 1993," "Completions, 1992–93," and "Finance, 1992–93" surveys. (This table was prepared May 1995.)

Table 213.—Fall enrollment in historically black colleges and universities, by type and control of institution: 1976 to 1993

Year	Total enrollment	Type of institution		Public institutions			Private institutions		
		4-year	2-year	Total	4-year	2-year	Total	4-year	2-year
1	2	3	4	5	6	7	8	9	10
1976	222,613	206,676	15,937	156,836	143,528	13,308	65,777	63,148	2,629
1977	226,062	209,898	16,164	158,823	145,450	13,373	67,239	64,448	2,791
1978	227,797	211,651	16,146	163,237	150,168	13,069	64,560	61,483	3,077
1979	230,124	214,147	15,977	166,315	153,139	13,176	63,809	61,008	2,801
1980	233,557	218,009	15,548	168,217	155,085	13,132	65,340	62,924	2,416
1981	232,460	217,152	15,308	166,991	154,269	12,722	65,469	62,883	2,586
1982	228,371	212,017	16,354	165,871	151,472	14,399	62,500	60,545	1,955
1983	234,446	217,909	16,537	170,051	155,665	14,386	64,395	62,244	2,151
1984	227,519	212,844	14,675	164,116	151,289	12,827	63,403	61,555	1,848
1985	225,801	210,648	15,153	163,677	150,002	13,675	62,124	60,646	1,478
1986	223,275	207,231	16,044	162,048	147,631	14,417	61,227	59,600	1,627
1987	227,994	211,654	16,340	165,486	150,560	14,926	62,508	61,094	1,414
1988	239,755	223,250	16,505	173,672	158,606	15,066	66,083	64,644	1,439
1989	249,096	232,890	16,206	181,151	166,481	14,670	67,945	66,409	1,536
1990	257,152	240,497	16,655	187,046	171,969	15,077	70,106	68,528	1,578
1991	269,280	252,038	17,242	197,847	182,204	15,643	71,433	69,834	1,599
1992	279,541	261,089	18,452	204,966	188,143	16,823	74,575	72,946	1,629
1993	282,856	262,430	20,426	208,197	189,032	19,165	74,659	73,398	1,261

SOURCE: U.S. Department of Education, National Center for Education Statistics, Higher Education General Information Survey (HEGIS), "Fall Enrollment in Colleges and Universities;" and Integrated Postsecondary Education Data System (IPEDS), "Fall Enrollment" survey. (This table was prepared February 1995.)

Table 214.—Employees in institutions of higher education, by primary occupation, employment status, and control of institution: Fall 1976, fall 1989, and fall 1991

Primary occupation and control of institution	Fall 1976					Fall 1989				Fall 1991			
	Total staff			Full-time equivalent staff		Total staff		Full-time equivalent staff		Total staff		Full-time equivalent staff	
	Number	Per-cent	Full-time	Total	FTE students per FTE staff	Number	Per-cent	Total	FTE students per FTE staff	Number	Per-cent	Total	FTE students per FTE staff
1	2	3	4	5	6	7	8	9	10	11	12	13	14
Total, all institutions	1,863,790	100.0	1,339,911	1,541,339	5.4	2,473,116	100.0	2,044,031	4.8	2,545,235	100.0	2,094,628	4.9
Professional staff	1,073,119	57.6	709,400	845,456	9.8	1,531,071	61.9	1,198,556	8.2	1,595,460	62.7	1,244,588	8.3
Executive/administrative/managerial	101,263	5.4	97,003	98,972	84.0	144,670	5.8	141,323	69.2	144,755	5.7	141,718	73.1
Faculty (instruction and research)	633,210	34.0	434,071	500,533	16.6	824,220	33.3	624,375	15.7	826,252	32.5	632,565	16.4
Instruction and research assistants	160,086	8.6	28,007	82,684	100.5	163,298	6.6	67,364	145.2	197,751	7.8	81,467	127.2
Non-faculty professionals	178,560	9.6	150,319	163,267	50.9	398,883	16.1	365,493	26.8	426,702	16.8	388,838	26.6
Nonprofessional staff	790,671	42.4	630,511	695,883	11.9	942,045	38.1	845,475	11.6	949,775	37.3	850,040	12.2
Public, total	1,329,122	100.0	946,354	1,092,558	5.8	1,720,769	100.0	1,407,724	5.2	1,783,328	100.0	1,449,398	5.4
Professional staff	769,836	57.9	502,325	601,942	10.5	1,078,737	62.7	830,110	8.9	1,133,264	63.5	868,112	9.1
Executive/administrative/managerial	60,733	4.6	58,649	59,579	106.6	83,632	4.9	81,882	90.0	84,446	4.7	82,835	94.9
Faculty (instruction and research)	448,733	33.8	313,367	357,761	17.7	577,298	33.5	436,409	16.9	580,908	32.6	446,113	17.6
Instruction and research assistants	127,925	9.6	19,076	63,420	100.1	140,898	8.2	57,400	128.4	173,560	9.7	70,707	111.2
Non-faculty professionals	132,445	10.0	111,233	121,182	52.4	276,909	16.1	254,419	29.0	294,350	16.5	268,458	29.3
Nonprofessional staff	559,286	42.1	444,029	490,616	12.9	642,032	37.3	577,614	12.8	650,064	36.5	581,286	13.5
Private, total	534,668	100.0	393,557	448,781	4.4	752,347	100.0	636,307	3.8	761,907	100.0	645,231	3.9
Professional staff	303,283	56.7	207,075	243,514	8.1	452,334	60.1	368,446	6.5	462,196	60.7	376,476	6.6
Executive/administrative/managerial	40,530	7.6	38,354	39,393	49.8	61,038	8.1	59,441	40.5	60,309	7.9	58,883	42.4
Faculty (instruction and research)	184,477	34.5	120,704	142,772	13.7	246,922	32.8	187,967	12.8	245,344	32.2	186,452	13.4
Instruction and research assistants	32,161	6.0	8,931	19,264	101.9	22,400	3.0	9,964	241.8	24,191	3.2	10,760	232.1
Non-faculty professionals	46,115	8.6	39,086	42,085	46.6	121,974	16.2	111,074	21.7	132,352	17.4	120,380	20.7
Nonprofessional staff	231,385	43.3	186,482	205,267	9.6	300,013	39.9	267,861	9.0	299,711	39.3	268,755	9.3

NOTE.—Because of rounding, details may not add to totals.

SOURCE: U.S. Department of Education, National Center for Education Statistics, Higher Education General Information Survey (HEGIS), "Staff, 1976" survey; and Integrated Postsecondary Education Data System (IPEDS), "Staff" survey. (This table was prepared April 1994.)

Table 215.—Employees in institutions of higher education, by primary occupation, sex, employment status, and by type and control of institution: Fall 1991

Primary occupation and type and control of institution	Full-time and part-time					Full-time				Part-time		
	Total		Men	Women		Total		Men	Women	Total	Men	Women
	Number	Percent		Number	Percent women	Number	Percent full-time					
1	2	3	4	5	6	7	8	9	10	11	12	13
Total, all institutions	**2,545,235**	**100.0**	**1,227,591**	**1,317,644**	**51.8**	**1,812,912**	**71.2**	**868,767**	**944,145**	**732,323**	**358,824**	**373,499**
Professional staff	1,595,460	62.7	895,591	699,869	43.9	1,031,797	64.7	591,315	440,482	563,663	304,276	259,387
Executive/administrative/managerial	144,755	5.7	85,423	59,332	41.0	139,116	96.1	82,875	56,241	5,639	2,548	3,091
Faculty (instruction and research)	826,252	32.5	525,599	300,653	36.4	535,623	64.8	366,213	169,410	290,629	159,386	131,243
Instruction and research assistants	197,751	7.8	119,125	78,626	39.8	—	—	—	—	197,751	119,125	78,626
Non-faculty professionals	426,702	16.8	165,444	261,258	61.2	357,058	83.7	142,227	214,831	69,644	23,217	46,427
Nonprofessional staff	949,775	37.3	332,000	617,775	65.0	781,115	82.2	277,452	503,663	168,660	54,548	114,112
Technical and paraprofessionals	230,588	9.1	78,693	151,895	65.9	144,967	62.9	61,100	83,867	85,621	17,593	68,028
Clerical and secretarial	412,852	16.2	46,168	366,684	88.8	371,225	89.9	31,937	339,288	41,627	14,231	27,396
Skilled crafts	66,522	2.6	62,048	4,474	6.7	63,327	95.2	59,866	3,461	3,195	2,182	1,013
Service and maintenance	239,813	9.4	145,091	94,722	39.5	201,596	84.1	124,549	77,047	38,217	20,542	17,675
Public, total	1,783,328	100.0	867,578	915,750	51.4	1,242,081	69.6	602,106	639,975	541,247	265,472	275,775
Professional staff	1,133,264	63.5	637,718	495,546	43.7	707,456	62.4	409,659	297,797	425,808	228,059	197,749
Executive/administrative/managerial	84,446	4.7	53,025	31,421	37.2	81,536	96.6	51,670	29,866	2,910	1,355	1,555
Faculty (instruction and research)	580,908	32.6	364,751	216,157	37.2	380,333	65.5	258,366	121,967	200,575	106,385	94,190
Instruction and research assistants	173,560	9.7	104,186	69,374	40.0	—	—	—	—	173,560	104,186	69,374
Non-faculty professionals	294,350	16.5	115,756	178,594	60.7	245,587	83.4	99,623	145,964	48,763	16,133	32,630
Nonprofessional staff	650,064	36.5	229,860	420,204	64.6	534,625	82.2	192,447	342,178	115,439	37,413	78,026
Technical and paraprofessionals	160,509	9.0	55,218	105,291	65.6	101,450	63.2	42,784	58,666	59,059	12,434	46,625
Clerical and secretarial	279,855	15.7	31,162	248,693	88.9	248,907	88.9	20,303	228,604	30,948	10,859	20,089
Skilled crafts	48,444	2.7	45,243	3,201	6.6	46,490	96.0	43,879	2,611	1,954	1,364	590
Service and maintenance	161,256	9.0	98,237	63,019	39.1	137,778	85.4	85,481	52,297	23,478	12,756	10,722
Private, total	761,907	100.0	360,013	401,894	52.7	570,831	74.9	266,661	304,170	191,076	93,352	97,724
Professional staff	462,196	60.7	257,873	204,323	44.2	324,341	70.2	181,656	142,685	137,855	76,217	61,638
Executive/administrative/managerial	60,309	7.9	32,398	27,911	46.3	57,580	95.5	31,205	26,375	2,729	1,193	1,536
Faculty (instruction and research)	245,344	32.2	160,848	84,496	34.4	155,290	63.3	107,847	47,443	90,054	53,001	37,053
Instruction and research assistants	24,191	3.2	14,939	9,252	38.2	—	—	—	—	24,191	14,939	9,252
Non-faculty professionals	132,352	17.4	49,688	82,664	62.5	111,471	84.2	42,604	68,867	20,881	7,084	13,797
Nonprofessional staff	299,711	39.3	102,140	197,571	65.9	246,490	82.2	85,005	161,485	53,221	17,135	36,086
Technical and paraprofessionals	70,079	9.2	23,475	46,604	66.5	43,517	62.1	18,316	25,201	26,562	5,159	21,403
Clerical and secretarial	132,997	17.5	15,006	117,991	88.7	122,318	92.0	11,634	110,684	10,679	3,372	7,307
Skilled crafts	18,078	2.4	16,805	1,273	7.0	16,837	93.1	15,987	850	1,241	818	423
Service and maintenance	78,557	10.3	46,854	31,703	40.4	63,818	81.2	39,068	24,750	14,739	7,786	6,953
4-year, total	2,076,423	100.0	1,007,482	1,068,941	51.5	1,560,254	75.1	751,242	809,012	516,169	256,240	259,929
Professional staff	1,269,157	61.1	724,100	545,057	42.9	877,742	69.2	507,728	370,014	391,415	216,372	175,043
Executive/administrative/managerial	120,822	5.8	70,923	49,899	41.3	116,455	96.4	68,972	47,483	4,367	1,951	2,416
Faculty (instruction and research)	591,269	28.5	399,738	191,531	32.4	433,483	73.3	308,203	125,280	157,786	91,535	66,251
Instruction and research assistants	168,333	8.1	103,004	65,329	38.8	—	—	—	—	168,333	103,004	65,329
Non-faculty professionals	388,733	18.7	150,435	238,298	61.3	327,804	84.3	130,553	197,251	60,929	19,882	41,047
Nonprofessional staff	807,266	38.9	283,382	523,884	64.9	682,512	84.5	243,514	438,998	124,754	39,868	84,886
Technical and paraprofessionals	188,435	9.1	65,889	122,546	65.0	126,508	67.1	53,694	72,814	61,927	12,195	49,732
Clerical and secretarial	351,177	16.9	39,164	312,013	88.8	321,374	91.5	29,011	292,363	29,803	10,153	19,650
Skilled crafts	59,892	2.9	56,140	3,752	6.3	57,460	95.9	54,407	3,053	2,432	1,733	699
Service and maintenance	207,762	10.0	122,189	85,573	41.2	177,170	85.3	106,402	70,768	30,592	15,787	14,805
2-year, total	468,812	100.0	220,109	248,703	53.0	252,658	53.9	117,525	135,133	216,154	102,584	113,570
Professional staff	326,303	69.6	171,491	154,812	47.4	154,055	47.2	83,587	70,468	172,248	87,904	84,344
Executive/administrative/managerial	23,933	5.1	14,500	9,433	39.4	22,661	94.7	13,903	8,758	1,272	597	675
Faculty (instruction and research)	234,983	50.1	125,861	109,122	46.4	102,140	43.5	58,010	44,130	132,843	67,851	64,992
Instruction and research assistants	29,418	6.3	16,121	13,297	45.2	—	—	—	—	29,418	16,121	13,297
Non-faculty professionals	37,969	8.1	15,009	22,960	60.5	29,254	77.0	11,674	17,580	8,715	3,335	5,380
Nonprofessional staff	142,509	30.4	48,618	93,891	65.9	98,603	69.2	33,938	64,665	43,906	14,680	29,226
Technical and paraprofessionals	42,153	9.0	12,804	29,349	69.6	18,459	43.8	7,406	11,053	23,694	5,398	18,296
Clerical and secretarial	61,675	13.2	7,004	54,671	88.6	49,851	80.8	2,926	46,925	11,824	4,078	7,746
Skilled crafts	6,630	1.4	5,908	722	10.9	5,867	88.5	5,459	408	763	449	314
Service and maintenance	32,051	6.8	22,902	9,149	28.5	24,426	76.2	18,147	6,279	7,625	4,755	2,870

—Not applicable.

SOURCE: U.S. Department of Education, National Center for Education Statistics, Integrated Postsecondary Education Data System (IPEDS), "Staff" survey. (This table was prepared April 1994.)

Table 216.—Employees in institutions of higher education, by primary occupation, sex, employment status, and by type and control of institution: Fall 1991

Primary occupation and type and control of institution	Full-time and part-time					Full-time				Part-time		
	Total		Men	Women		Total		Men	Women	Total	Men	Women
	Number	Percent		Number	Percent woman	Number	Percent full-time					
1	2	3	4	5	6	7	8	9	10	11	12	13
Total, all employees	**2,545,235**	**100.0**	**1,227,591**	**1,317,644**	**51.8**	**1,812,912**	**71.2**	**868,767**	**944,145**	**732,323**	**358,824**	**373,499**
Professional staff	1,595,460	62.7	895,591	699,869	43.9	1,031,797	64.7	591,315	440,482	563,663	304,276	259,387
Executive/administrative/managerial	144,755	5.7	85,423	59,332	41.0	139,116	96.1	82,875	56,241	5,639	2,548	3,091
Faculty (instruction and research)	826,252	32.5	525,599	300,653	36.4	535,623	64.8	366,213	169,410	290,629	159,386	131,243
Instruction and research assistants	197,751	7.8	119,125	78,626	39.8	—	—	—	—	197,751	119,125	78,626
Non-faculty professionals	426,702	16.8	165,444	261,258	61.2	357,058	83.7	142,227	214,831	69,644	23,217	46,427
Nonprofessional staff	949,775	37.3	332,000	617,775	65.0	781,115	82.2	277,452	503,663	168,660	54,548	114,112
Technical and paraprofessionals	230,588	9.1	78,693	151,895	65.9	144,967	62.9	61,100	83,867	85,621	17,593	68,028
Clerical and secretarial	412,852	16.2	46,168	366,684	88.8	371,225	89.9	31,937	339,288	41,627	14,231	27,396
Skilled crafts	66,522	2.6	62,048	4,474	6.7	63,327	95.2	59,866	3,461	3,195	2,182	1,013
Service and maintenance	239,813	9.4	145,091	94,722	39.5	201,596	84.1	124,549	77,047	38,217	20,542	17,675
Public 4-year, total	1,341,914	100.0	659,625	682,289	50.8	1,007,874	75.1	492,676	515,198	334,040	166,949	167,091
Professional staff	826,633	61.6	475,814	350,819	42.4	566,184	68.5	332,286	233,898	260,449	143,528	116,921
Executive/administrative/managerial	63,674	4.7	40,186	23,488	36.9	61,765	97.0	39,286	22,479	1,909	900	1,009
Faculty (instruction and research)	358,376	26.7	245,343	113,033	31.5	284,770	79.5	203,872	80,898	73,606	41,471	32,135
Instruction and research assistants	144,344	10.8	88,187	56,157	38.9	—	—	—	—	144,344	88,187	56,157
Non-faculty professionals	260,239	19.4	102,098	158,141	60.8	219,649	84.4	89,128	130,521	40,590	12,970	27,620
Nonprofessional staff	515,281	38.4	183,811	331,470	64.3	441,690	85.7	160,390	281,300	73,591	23,421	50,170
Technical and paraprofessionals	119,873	8.9	42,869	77,004	64.2	83,565	69.7	35,638	47,927	36,308	7,231	29,077
Clerical and secretarial	221,687	16.5	24,465	197,222	89.0	202,130	91.2	17,571	184,559	19,557	6,894	12,663
Skilled crafts	42,311	3.2	39,719	2,592	6.1	40,997	96.9	38,744	2,253	1,314	975	339
Service and maintenance	131,410	9.8	76,758	54,652	41.6	114,998	87.5	68,437	46,561	16,412	8,321	8,091
Public 2-year, total	441,414	100.0	207,953	233,461	52.9	234,207	53.1	109,430	124,777	207,207	98,523	108,684
Professional staff	306,631	69.5	161,904	144,727	47.2	141,272	46.1	77,373	63,899	165,359	84,531	80,828
Executive/administrative/managerial	20,772	4.7	12,839	7,933	38.2	19,771	95.2	12,384	7,387	1,001	455	546
Faculty (instruction and research)	222,532	50.4	119,408	103,124	46.3	95,563	42.9	54,494	41,069	126,969	64,914	62,055
Instruction and research assistants	29,216	6.6	15,999	13,217	45.2	—	—	—	—	29,216	15,999	13,217
Non-faculty professionals	34,111	7.7	13,658	20,453	60.0	25,938	76.0	10,495	15,443	8,173	3,163	5,010
Nonprofessional staff	134,783	30.5	46,049	88,734	65.8	92,935	69.0	32,057	60,878	41,848	13,992	27,856
Technical and paraprofessionals	40,636	9.2	12,349	28,287	69.6	17,885	44.0	7,146	10,739	22,751	5,203	17,548
Clerical and secretarial	58,168	13.2	6,697	51,471	88.5	46,777	80.4	2,732	44,045	11,391	3,965	7,426
Skilled crafts	6,133	1.4	5,524	609	9.9	5,493	89.6	5,135	358	640	389	251
Service and maintenance	29,846	6.8	21,479	8,367	28.0	22,780	76.3	17,044	5,736	7,066	4,435	2,631
Private 4-year, total	734,509	100.0	347,857	386,652	52.6	552,380	75.2	258,566	293,814	182,129	89,291	92,838
Professional staff	442,524	60.2	248,286	194,238	43.9	311,558	70.4	175,442	136,116	130,966	72,844	58,122
Executive/administrative/managerial	57,148	7.8	30,737	26,411	46.2	54,690	95.7	29,686	25,004	2,458	1,051	1,407
Faculty (instruction and research)	232,893	31.7	154,395	78,498	33.7	148,713	63.9	104,331	44,382	84,180	50,064	34,116
Instruction and research assistants	23,989	3.3	14,817	9,172	38.2	—	—	—	—	23,989	14,817	9,172
Non-faculty professionals	128,494	17.5	48,337	80,157	62.4	108,155	84.2	41,425	66,730	20,339	6,912	13,427
Nonprofessional staff	291,985	39.8	99,571	192,414	65.9	240,822	82.5	83,124	157,698	51,163	16,447	34,716
Technical and paraprofessionals	68,562	9.3	23,020	45,542	66.4	42,943	62.6	18,056	24,887	25,619	4,964	20,655
Clerical and secretarial	129,490	17.6	14,699	114,791	88.6	119,244	92.1	11,440	107,804	10,246	3,259	6,987
Skilled crafts	17,581	2.4	16,421	1,160	6.6	16,463	93.6	15,663	800	1,118	758	360
Service and maintenance	76,352	10.4	45,431	30,921	40.5	62,172	81.4	37,965	24,207	14,180	7,466	6,714
Private 2-year, total	27,398	100.0	12,156	15,242	55.6	18,451	67.3	8,095	10,356	8,947	4,061	4,886
Professional staff	19,672	71.8	9,587	10,085	51.3	12,783	65.0	6,214	6,569	6,889	3,373	3,516
Executive/administrative/managerial	3,161	11.5	1,661	1,500	47.5	2,890	91.4	1,519	1,371	271	142	129
Faculty (instruction and research)	12,451	45.4	6,453	5,998	48.2	6,577	52.8	3,516	3,061	5,874	2,937	2,937
Instruction and research assistants	202	0.7	122	80	39.6	—	—	—	—	202	122	80
Non-faculty professionals	3,858	14.1	1,351	2,507	65.0	3,316	86.0	1,179	2,137	542	172	370
Nonprofessional staff	7,726	28.2	2,569	5,157	66.7	5,668	73.4	1,881	3,787	2,058	688	1,370
Technical and paraprofessionals	1,517	5.5	455	1,062	70.0	574	37.8	260	314	943	195	748
Clerical and secretarial	3,507	12.8	307	3,200	91.2	3,074	87.7	194	2,880	433	113	320
Skilled crafts	497	1.8	384	113	22.7	374	75.3	324	50	123	60	63
Service and maintenance	2,205	8.0	1,423	782	35.5	1,646	74.6	1,103	543	559	320	239

—Not applicable.

SOURCE: U.S. Department of Education, National Center for Education Statistics, Integrated Postsecondary Education Data System (IPEDS), "Staff" survey. (This table was prepared April 1994.)

Table 217.—Full-time and part-time senior instructional faculty [1] in institutions of higher education, by employment status, control, and type of institution: Fall 1970 to fall 1991

[In thousands]

Year	Total	Employment status		Control		Type	
		Full-time	Part-time	Public	Private	4-year	2-year
1	2	3	4	5	6	7	8
1970	474	369	104	314	160	382	92
1971 [2]	492	379	113	333	159	387	105
1972	500	380	120	343	157	384	116
1973 [2]	527	389	138	365	162	401	126
1974 [2]	567	406	161	397	170	427	140
1975 [2]	628	440	188	443	185	467	161
1976	633	434	199	449	184	467	166
1977	678	448	230	492	186	485	193
1979 [2]	675	445	230	488	187	494	182
1980 [2]	686	450	236	495	191	494	192
1981	705	461	244	509	196	493	212
1982 [2]	710	462	248	506	204	493	217
1983	724	471	254	512	212	504	220
1984 [2]	717	462	255	505	212	504	213
1985 [2]	715	459	256	503	212	504	211
1986 [2]	722	459	263	510	212	506	216
1987 [3]	793	523	270	553	240	548	246
1989 [3]	824	524	300	577	247	584	241
1991 [3]	826	536	291	581	245	591	235

[1] Includes faculty members with the title of professor, associate professor, assistant professor, instructor, lecturer, assisting professor, adjunct professor, or interim professor (or the equivalent). Excluded are graduate students with titles such as graduate or teaching fellow who assist senior faculty.
[2] Estimated on the basis of enrollment.
[3] Because of revised survey methods, data are not directly comparable with figures for years prior to 1987.

NOTE.—Data exclude faculty employed by system offices. Some data have been revised from previously published figures. For methodological details on estimates and pro-

jections, see *Projections of Education Statistics to 2000*. Because of rounding, details may not add to totals.

SOURCE: U.S. Department of Education, National Center for Education Statistics, *Employees in Institutions of Higher Education*, various years; *Projections of Education Statistics to 2000*; Integrated Postsecondary Education Data System (IPEDS), "Staff" survey; and U.S. Equal Employment Opportunity Commission, Higher Education Staff Information Report File, 1977, 1981, and 1983. (This table was prepared April 1994.)

Table 218.—Full-time instructional faculty in institutions of higher education, by race/ethnicity, academic rank, and sex: Fall 1991

Academic rank and sex	Total	Race/ethnicity				
		White, non-Hispanic	Black, non-Hispanic	Hispanic	Asian or Pacific Islander	American Indian/Alaskan Native
1	2	3	4	5	6	7
Men and women, all ranks	**520,324**	**456,222**	**24,516**	**11,422**	**26,510**	**1,654**
Professors	144,341	132,065	3,572	2,038	6,371	295
Associate professors	116,631	103,918	4,942	2,107	5,391	273
Assistant professors	126,344	106,557	7,524	3,246	8,649	368
Instructors	78,082	67,539	5,223	2,532	2,326	462
Lecturers	11,275	9,603	739	397	483	53
Other faculty	43,651	36,540	2,516	1,102	3,290	203
Men, all ranks	**355,111**	**313,205**	**13,056**	**7,353**	**20,481**	**1,016**
Professors	123,173	113,097	2,466	1,654	5,721	235
Associate professors	84,311	75,341	2,924	1,490	4,363	193
Assistant professors	76,129	63,573	3,884	1,964	6,511	197
Instructors	41,124	35,776	2,328	1,421	1,339	260
Lecturers	5,362	4,599	326	183	225	29
Other faculty	25,012	20,819	1,128	641	2,322	102
Women, all ranks	**165,213**	**143,017**	**11,460**	**4,069**	**6,029**	**638**
Professors	21,168	18,968	1,106	384	650	60
Associate professors	32,320	28,577	2,018	617	1,028	80
Assistant professors	50,215	42,984	3,640	1,282	2,138	171
Instructors	36,958	31,763	2,895	1,111	987	202
Lecturers	5,913	5,004	413	214	258	24
Other faculty	18,639	15,721	1,388	461	968	101

NOTE.—Data exclude faculty employed by system offices. Totals may differ from figures reported in other tables because of varying survey methodologies.

SOURCE: U.S. Equal Employment Opportunity Commission, *EEO–6 Higher Education Staff Information, 1991*. (This table was prepared November 1993.)

Table 219.—Full-time instructional faculty and staff in institutions of higher education, by selected characteristics and type and control of institution: Fall 1992

Selected characteristics	Number in thousands	Percent total	Public research	Private research	Public doctoral	Private doctoral	Public comprehensive	Private comprehensive	Private liberal arts	Public 2-year	Other
1	2	3	4	5	6	7	8	9	10	11	12
Total (in thousands)	526	—	108	32	54	25	96	37	39	110	24
Percent	—	100.0	20.6	6.1	10.3	4.8	18.3	6.9	7.4	20.8	4.6

Percentage distribution

Selected characteristics											
Total	—	100.0	100.0	100.0	100.0	100.0	100.0	100.0	100.0	100.0	100.0
Sex											
Male	355	67.5	77.3	70.1	70.9	76.9	66.5	65.4	61.6	55.4	73.6
Female	171	32.5	22.7	29.9	29.1	23.1	33.5	34.6	38.5	44.6	26.4
Race											
White, non-Hispanic	457	86.8	88.3	84.2	87.8	86.0	83.0	91.8	90.0	85.5	90.9
Black, non-Hispanic	26	4.9	2.7	4.7	2.9	4.2	8.8	3.1	5.4	6.1	2.7
Hispanic	13	2.5	2.0	1.8	2.3	3.2	2.6	1.6	1.3	4.2	1.3
Asian	28	5.2	6.9	9.1	6.3	6.5	5.1	3.4	2.8	3.3	4.6
American Indian	3	0.5	0.1	0.2	0.8	0.2	0.5	0.2	0.5	0.1	0.5
Age											
29 or younger	8	1.4	1.0	1.8	1.2	0.7	1.5	1.4	2.1	1.7	2.0
30–34	35	6.7	7.2	7.8	8.4	9.7	5.9	6.9	7.0	5.3	5.3
35–39	66	12.6	14.2	20.3	14.4	14.8	10.6	10.4	13.9	9.7	11.3
40–44	90	17.0	18.1	19.9	17.4	17.5	15.0	16.4	17.4	16.8	16.6
45–49	97	18.5	17.1	15.2	16.8	19.6	18.8	18.9	19.7	20.8	18.1
50–54	95	18.0	16.0	11.5	17.4	13.3	21.6	16.7	14.7	21.9	18.0
55–59	67	12.7	12.9	9.2	11.7	9.5	14.4	12.8	12.0	13.5	13.3
60 to 64	45	8.5	9.0	8.4	8.3	8.8	8.3	11.4	8.5	7.2	9.4
65 or older	24	4.5	4.8	5.9	4.5	6.0	4.0	5.1	4.8	3.2	6.0
Highest degree											
Doctoral	285	54.5	71.0	63.9	62.1	63.0	68.3	61.2	58.5	16.7	40.8
Professional	57	10.9	17.0	25.0	20.8	24.4	4.3	7.7	3.2	2.3	10.5
Master's	154	29.4	10.5	10.1	15.8	10.4	26.2	28.9	35.2	63.8	40.9
Bachelor's	21	4.0	1.6	1.1	1.4	2.1	1.1	2.1	3.1	11.9	6.8
Less than bachelor's	6	1.2	1.0	0.1	(¹)	(¹)	0.2	0.1	(¹)	5.4	0.9
Academic rank											
Full professor	161	30.6	40.0	33.6	31.5	30.2	34.5	26.9	28.8	19.3	28.6
Associate professor	123	23.5	26.4	22.6	26.2	27.9	26.9	29.1	25.3	12.9	23.3
Assistant professor	123	23.4	22.6	26.9	31.1	29.6	26.0	31.8	29.8	11.2	21.0
Instructor	73	13.9	3.9	4.5	7.6	8.5	8.5	7.9	9.1	39.7	12.1
Lecturer	12	2.2	3.8	6.6	1.6	1.3	2.6	1.2	1.6	0.4	0.7
Other	17	3.2	3.2	4.8	1.7	2.4	1.3	1.9	3.7	5.6	2.5
No rank	17	3.2	0.2	1.0	0.2	0.1	0.2	1.3	1.7	11.0	11.8
Base salary											
Under $10,000	14	1.8	2.0	3.0	2.1	2.5	2.1	2.6	2.5	3.5	3.8
$10,000 to 24,999	29	5.5	3.5	5.2	4.7	2.8	5.5	5.3	10.1	6.1	10.3
$25,000–39,999	180	34.4	19.4	14.5	28.6	22.9	37.1	44.1	53.8	47.3	38.5
$40,000–54,999	164	31.4	29.6	28.8	29.8	27.3	34.2	32.7	24.8	34.1	35.3
$55,000–69,999	77	14.8	23.0	16.0	17.3	21.4	17.1	10.3	6.1	8.1	6.5
$70,000–84,999	32	6.2	12.3	13.3	9.3	9.8	3.3	3.8	2.2	0.8	4.1
$85,000–99,999	11	2.1	4.4	3.8	2.4	7.2	0.7	0.1	0.6	0.1	1.6
$100,000 or more	20	3.8	6.6	17.2	6.5	7.5	0.4	1.5	0.5	0.4	1.5

¹ Less than 0.1 percent.
—Data not applicable.

NOTE.—Data may not add to totals because of rounding or missing data.

SOURCE: U.S. Department of Education, National Center for Education Statistics, National Study of Postsecondary Faculty (NSOPF), 1993. (This table was prepared May 1995.)

Table 220.—Full-time instructional faculty and staff in institutions of higher education, by instruction activities and type and control of institution: Fall 1992

Instruction activities	Average all institutions	Public research	Private research	Public doctoral	Private doctoral	Public comprehensive	Private comprehensive	Private liberal arts	Public 2-year	Other
1	2	3	4	5	6	7	8	9	10	11
Number of full-time instructional faculty and staff	526,222	108,493	32,350	54,433	25,397	96,350	36,548	39,018	109,552	24,081
Percentage distribution	100.0	20.6	6.1	10.3	4.8	18.3	6.9	7.4	20.8	4.6
Hours worked per week										
Average hours worked per week	52.6	56.4	57.7	55.1	54.1	52.4	51.8	52.5	46.9	49.3
Paid activities	42.7	48.0	48.7	46.3	45.3	41.3	40.9	42.4	36.0	39.7
Unpaid activities	5.1	4.3	4.1	4.3	3.4	5.9	5.8	5.8	6.0	5.1
Outside paid activities	2.8	2.4	2.6	2.5	3.5	2.8	3.0	2.7	3.1	2.8
Unpaid activities outside institution	2.0	1.8	2.2	2.1	1.8	2.3	2.1	1.6	1.9	1.7
Work time distribution (percent)										
Total	100.0	100.0	100.0	100.0	100.0	100.0	100.0	100.0	100.0	100.0
Teaching	54.3	40.3	34.7	46.4	43.8	60.2	59.5	63.7	68.7	60.8
Research/scholarship	17.8	31.6	35.6	23.8	22.6	14.0	11.9	9.7	4.6	10.9
Professional growth	4.6	3.7	3.2	4.1	4.3	5.0	4.8	4.7	5.8	5.2
Administration	13.0	12.9	12.9	13.2	16.1	11.9	14.6	14.7	12.0	14.7
Outside consulting	2.7	2.5	3.0	2.5	2.6	2.7	3.1	2.3	2.7	2.8
Service/non-teaching	7.4	8.9	10.6	9.8	10.5	6.0	5.9	4.9	6.1	5.5
Preferred work time distribution (percent)										
Total	100.0	100.0	100.0	100.0	100.0	100.0	100.0	100.0	100.0	100.0
Teaching	49.0	36.5	33.2	41.5	39.1	52.3	52.7	56.1	64.1	54.0
Research/scholarship	24.9	38.5	41.9	31.1	31.4	22.4	19.9	18.9	9.2	17.8
Professional growth	8.1	6.5	6.2	7.2	6.8	8.5	8.6	8.8	9.8	9.4
Administration	8.1	7.7	7.1	8.0	9.9	7.7	9.1	8.6	8.1	9.4
Outside consulting	3.3	3.2	3.4	3.3	3.3	3.5	3.9	2.9	3.1	3.8
Service/non-teaching	6.6	7.4	8.3	8.8	9.4	5.6	5.6	4.8	5.7	5.6
Distribution of hours taught per week (percent)										
Total hours taught per week	100.0	100.0	100.0	100.0	100.0	100.0	100.0	100.0	100.0	100.0
Less than 4.0	15.2	30.5	36.9	19.1	22.8	8.2	8.2	6.3	6.2	10.7
4.0 to 5.9	8.1	15.0	18.9	10.5	10.3	4.9	5.2	6	3.2	5.9
6.0 to 7.9	15.9	26.5	20.9	21.1	24.4	12.6	14.6	13.1	6.0	14.7
8.0 to 9.9	14.6	11.9	6.9	18.8	19.6	20.0	22.1	22.2	6.6	11.6
10.0 to 14.9	22.5	8.9	8.4	16.9	14.6	36.5	34.5	34.2	19.8	27.8
15.0 or more	23.8	7.3	8.1	13.7	8.4	17.8	15.4	18.5	58.3	29.3
Distribution of number of students taught (percent)										
Total students taught	100.0	100.0	100.0	100.0	100.0	100.0	100.0	100.0	100.0	100.0
Less than 25	13.1	21.8	33.3	16.0	19.2	7.3	8.2	11.7	5.8	13.1
25 to 49	19.9	23.0	24.1	22.1	23.6	15.1	20.4	29.8	14.3	23.0
50 to 74	19.5	18.6	11.6	16.5	14.2	20.2	27.8	26.7	17.4	24.6
75 to 99	15.8	11.0	8.9	13.7	12.3	19.4	21.3	15.8	18.7	14.6
100 to 149	18.8	10.9	10.3	15.4	15.7	25.2	17.4	12.0	27.7	16.8
150 or more	12.8	14.8	11.8	16.3	15.1	12.9	4.9	4.0	16.1	7.9
Distribution of student classroom contact hours/week [1] (percent)										
Total contact hours	100.0	100.0	100.0	100.0	100.0	100.0	100.0	100.0	100.0	100.0
Less than 50	8.4	16.6	25.7	10.5	14.0	3.2	4.6	6.1	2.4	6.6
50 to 99	10.6	16.2	18.3	13.5	13.2	7.6	9.9	11.8	4.5	11.9
100 to 199	21.9	25.7	21.9	22.3	27.3	20.0	27.5	34.8	11.8	25.5
200 to 349	27.7	20.1	18.4	25.7	20.0	34.0	38.5	30.2	28.2	29.4
350 to 499	15.7	8.4	4.8	11.3	11.7	20.4	11.8	10.4	26.5	14.8
500 or more	15.7	13.0	11.1	16.8	13.8	14.7	7.8	6.9	26.6	11.9
Distribution of total classroom credit hours (percent)										
Total classroom credit hours	100.0	100.0	100.0	100.0	100.0	100.0	100.0	100.0	100.0	100.0
Less than 4.0	14.2	26.3	28.6	15.5	20.6	8.0	8.5	11.7	7.1	11.8
4.0 to 5.9	8.6	14.6	14.9	12.7	10.5	5.8	5.9	5.9	4.1	7.6
6.0 to 7.9	18.4	31.0	24.9	25.9	26.8	15.0	13.6	13.2	8.0	15.5
8.0 to 9.9	18.6	15.0	16.1	22.4	20.7	23.6	28.4	24.3	10.7	18.2
10.0 to 14.9	24.9	9.5	7.4	17.8	15.5	37.3	34.5	35.0	28.5	29.2
15.0 or more	15.4	3.7	8.1	5.7	6.0	10.3	9.1	9.9	41.6	17.8
Number of classes taught for credit										
Faculty with undergraduate classes only (percent)										
Total undergraduate credit courses	100.0	100.0	100.0	100.0	100.0	100.0	100.0	100.0	100.0	100.0
1	16.0	34.5	41.0	20.7	22.9	11.4	11.4	9.9	12.2	13.1
2	23.1	42.9	37.1	34.2	38.9	20.8	20.8	21.6	13.8	18.0
3	23.6	14.4	7.8	27.4	26.3	32.0	32.0	35.0	15.4	27.1
4	20.1	6.1	7.4	13.3	6.7	26.7	26.7	20.8	21.9	26.1
5 or more	17.2	2.1	6.6	4.5	5.2	9.1	9.1	12.8	36.7	15.8
Faculty with graduate classes only (percent)										
Total graduate credit courses	100.0	100.0	100.0	100.0	100.0	100.0	100.0	100.0	100.0	100.0
1	48.7	57.2	53.3	45.5	52.3	30.4	30.4	30.8	100.0	33.2
2	33.0	33.6	38.6	34.9	27.3	22.8	22.8	12.1	0.0	35.5
3	12.3	6.7	4.5	13.3	16.5	28.2	28.2	42.3	0.0	17.0
4	4.0	1.9	1.6	3.6	2.2	13.4	13.4	9.3	0.0	9.8
5 or more	2.0	0.6	2.1	2.7	1.7	5.3	5.3	5.6	0.0	4.5
Faculty with both undergraduate and graduate classes (percent)										
Total graduate and undergraduate courses	99.9	100.0	100.0	100.0	100.0	100.0	100.0	100.0	100.0	100.0
2	42.5	58.9	67.8	48.4	42.7	25.0	17.6	22.0	18.9	12.8
3	32.1	29.8	22.6	31.1	37.8	34.0	46.2	21.7	21.7	35.3
4	15.9	5.6	7.4	14.5	10.7	25.7	27.2	37.0	20.7	30.0
5 or more	9.4	5.8	2.1	6.0	8.7	15.3	9.0	19.3	38.8	22.0

[1] Hours that faculty and instructional staff spend each week with students during classroom instruction multiplied by the number of students taught.

NOTE.—Because of rounding, details may not add to totals.

SOURCE: U.S. Department of Education, National Center for Education Statistics, *National Survey of Postsecondary Faculty (NSOPF), 1993*. (This table was prepared May 1995.)

Table 221.—Part-time instructional faculty and staff in institutions of higher education, by instruction activities and type and control of institution: Fall 1992

Instruction activities	All institutions	Public research	Private research	Public doctoral	Private doctoral	Public comprehensive	Private comprehensive	Private liberal arts	Public 2-year	Other
1	2	3	4	5	6	7	8	9	10	11
Number of full-time instructional faculty and staff	263,215	16,071	10,924	13,087	11,752	32,367	25,346	19,633	120,797	13,239
Percentage distribution	100.0	6.1	4.2	5.0	4.5	12.3	9.6	7.5	45.9	5.0
Hours worked per week										
Average hours worked per week	33.7	39.0	40.3	34.6	36.0	34.8	35.5	33.4	31.5	32.7
Paid activities	11.7	20.0	11.6	14.2	11.1	13.5	10.3	12.8	10.1	10.3
Unpaid activities	3.2	4.2	4.3	3.9	3.3	3.5	2.3	2.4	3.1	2.9
Outside paid activities	16.9	12.5	22.7	14.5	19.7	15.6	20.9	16.2	16.5	17.1
Unpaid activities outside institution	1.9	2.3	1.7	2.0	1.9	2.2	2.1	1.9	1.8	2.4
Work time distribution (percent)										
Total	100.0	100.0	100.0	100.0	100.0	100.0	100.0	100.0	100.0	100.0
Teaching	60.0	52.0	38.6	60.6	42.0	61.4	56.6	61.5	64.9	58.0
Research/scholarship	7.0	15.7	17.8	8.8	9.1	8.2	6.0	6.6	4.4	7.5
Professional growth	5.8	5.1	8.2	7.4	6.0	6.0	5.8	6.1	5.5	5.2
Administration	5.8	5.4	12.7	5.2	4.6	6.2	6.3	6.9	5.0	5.6
Outside consulting	10.4	10.4	11.1	8.7	17.5	8.2	12.5	10.6	10.0	10.9
Service/non-teaching	11.0	11.2	11.5	9.2	20.5	9.6	12.9	8.3	10.3	12.9
Preferred work time distribution (percent)										
Total	100.0	100.0	100.0	100.0	100.0	100.0	100.0	100.0	100.0	100.0
Teaching	57.9	51.8	37.4	58.0	40.2	56.9	56.1	58.8	62.9	55.1
Research/scholarship	11.1	18.8	21.2	13.2	12.9	13.3	10.2	11.4	8.1	12.1
Professional growth	9.0	7.6	9.4	9.6	8.9	9.3	8.4	9.0	9.1	8.8
Administration	4.3	3.8	9.7	3.3	3.9	5.0	5.1	4.7	3.9	4.1
Outside consulting	8.6	7.6	10.0	7.3	16.8	7.2	9.4	8.8	8.0	9.0
Service/non-teaching	9.2	10.3	12.3	8.4	17.0	8.3	10.8	7.3	8.0	11.0
Distribution of hours taught per week (percent)										
Total hours taught per week	100.0	100.0	100.0	100.0	100.0	100.0	100.0	100.0	100.0	100.0
Less than 4.0	34.4	44.3	60.6	36.3	51.6	35.9	41.9	36.7	26.7	39.9
4.0 to 5.9	15.3	11.0	14.8	15.3	15.4	15.7	13.2	16.7	15.8	16.6
6.0 to 7.9	20.3	15.7	14.5	19.5	14.8	20.9	17.9	20.2	22.9	13.3
8.0 to 9.9	12.3	13.0	4.6	14.8	6.0	11.6	9.7	8.7	14.6	10.7
10.0 to 14.9	9.8	5.8	3.4	8.4	4.1	9.7	8.6	9.2	11.6	10.5
15.0 or more	7.9	10.2	2.2	5.7	8.2	6.2	8.7	8.5	8.4	9.0
Distribution of number of students taught (percent)										
Total students taught	100.0	100.0	100.0	100.0	100.0	100.0	100.0	100.0	100.0	100.0
Less than 25	36.6	36.0	57.5	27.3	51.3	26.1	47.1	50.2	31.7	51.3
25 to 49	33.8	22.9	25.5	29.4	29.9	33.7	28.9	32.6	38.8	23.0
50 to 74	16.0	15.6	11.1	20.1	9.4	21.2	13.2	10.1	17.0	14.0
75 to 99	6.2	5.9	3.1	8.6	2.5	8.0	5.4	3.5	6.7	5.4
100 to 149	5.0	8.5	2.6	8.3	0.7	8.3	4.0	3.1	4.4	6.0
150 or more	2.4	11.1	0.2	6.2	6.2	2.7	1.4	0.6	1.5	0.5
Distribution of student classroom contact hours per week [1] (percent)										
Total contact hours	100.0	100.0	100.0	100.0	100.0	100.0	100.0	100.0	100.0	100.0
Less than 50	18.4	23.9	45.3	13.3	36.5	12.3	27.3	27.2	11.6	32.7
50 to 99	27.1	18.8	34.6	21.8	27.1	24.0	30.0	33.3	27.7	21.3
100 to 199	30.4	25.0	9.5	35.7	22.6	37.1	25.6	25.6	33.6	23.0
200 to 349	15.3	14.4	7.8	17.5	5.0	14.8	9.6	8.9	18.8	17.0
350 to 499	4.6	6.7	2.6	5.0	2.7	6.7	2.7	4.0	4.6	4.1
500 or more	4.2	11.1	0.2	6.7	6.0	5.3	4.8	1.1	3.7	2.1
Distribution of total classroom credit hours (percent)										
Total classroom credit hours	100.0	100.0	100.0	100.0	100.0	100.0	100.0	100.0	100.0	100.0
Less than 4.0	40.3	48.6	51.5	37.0	52.6	39.8	48.3	47.9	35.0	40.1
4.0 to 5.9	15.6	12.8	27.9	17.2	12.3	13.8	9.6	14.2	16.4	21.4
6.0 to 7.9	21.6	16.8	8.9	21.5	16.2	24.9	20.9	18.8	23.8	16.3
8.0 to 9.9	12.3	16.9	5.5	9.2	11.1	14.0	8.8	9.5	13.5	12.5
10.0 to 14.9	7.0	3.2	6.3	8.1	5.1	5.4	7.9	7.3	8.0	5.2
15.0 or more	3.2	1.6	0.0	7.0	2.8	2.2	4.5	2.5	3.3	4.5
Number of classes taught for credit (percent)										
Faculty with undergraduate classes only										
Total undergraduate credit courses	100.0	100.0	100.0	100.0	100.0	100.0	100.0	100.0	100.0	100.0
1	50.1	49.3	69.1	48.8	62.2	49.6	54.4	50.7	48.0	53.3
2	32.1	26.8	26.0	34.6	25.0	32.7	27.9	30.7	33.9	28.2
3	11.2	12.8	0.8	10.9	9.4	12.6	10.7	9.3	11.6	11.2
4	4.0	6.6	4.1	4.6	1.5	3.6	4.1	4.1	3.8	5.8
5 or more	2.7	4.6	0.0	1.1	1.9	1.7	3.0	5.2	2.8	1.4
Faculty with graduate classes only										
Total graduate credit courses	100.0	100.0	100.0	100.0	100.0	100.0	100.0	100.0	100.0	100.0
1	72.5	70.4	77.7	62.8	72.5	57.7	74.4	85.0	36.0	83.9
2	17.8	13.3	14.4	32.9	13.6	33.0	18.9	10.7	39.7	7.6
3	7.0	12.8	6.0	4.1	10.0	8.2	3.0	3.4	24.4	4.9
4	1.4	0.8	2.0	0.0	2.7	1.1	1.4	0.9	0.0	1.7
5 or more	1.2	2.7	0.0	0.2	1.2	0.0	2.2	0.0	0.0	1.9
Faculty with both undergraduate and graduate classes										
Total graduate and undergraduate courses	100.0	100.0	100.0	100.0	100.0	100.0	100.0	100.0	100.0	100.0
2	47.8	86.2	0.0	2.6	7.3	62.9	42.2	32.8	54.2	19.3
3	35.0	13.8	100.0	87.8	31.7	11.1	45.4	27.3	25.2	53.7
4	10.9	0.0	0.0	6.2	17.1	16.6	12.4	21.6	9.0	27.1
5 or more	6.3	0.0	0.0	3.4	43.9	9.4	0.0	18.4	11.6	0.0

[1] Hours that faculty and instructional staff spend each week with students during classroom instruction multiplied by the number of students taught.

NOTE.—Because of rounding, details may not add to totals.

SOURCE: U.S. Department of Education, National Center for Education Statistics, *National Study of Postsecondary Faculty (NSOPF), 1993.* (This table was prepared June 1995.)

Table 222.—Percentage distribution of full-time and part-time instructional faculty and staff in institutions of higher education, by program area, race/ethnicity, and sex: Fall 1992

Program area	Number	Percent	White, non-Hispanic		Black, non-Hispanic		Hispanic		Asian/Pacific Islander		American Indian/Alaskan Native	
			Male	Female	Male	Female	Male	Female	Male	Female	Male	Female
1	2	3	4	5	6	7	8	9	10	11	12	13
					Full-time instructional faculty and staff							
Total	526,222	100.0	58.9	27.9	2.6	2.3	1.7	0.8	4.0	1.3	0.3	0.2
Agriculture and home economics	11,466	100.0	71.3	19.6	2.2	1.5	1.6	0.2	1.0	1.8	—	0.7
Business	39,848	100.0	62.3	26.6	1.9	2.0	0.9	0.4	4.0	0.8	0.6	0.3
Communications	10,344	100.0	56.3	29.8	2.8	2.8	1.6	—	4.3	1.2	0.9	0.3
Education	36,851	100.0	43.9	41.2	3.9	5.1	0.9	2.4	0.5	1.1	0.7	0.3
Teacher education	12,429	100.0	40.6	49.8	2.0	4.6	0.1	0.7	0.3	1.0	0.6	0.2
Other education	24,422	100.0	45.6	36.9	4.8	5.4	1.3	3.2	0.7	1.1	0.8	0.3
Engineering	24,680	100.0	73.0	3.8	2.1	0.6	2.8	0.2	15.6	1.3	0.7	—
Fine arts	31,682	100.0	60.4	28.3	3.8	1.8	2.1	0.3	1.2	1.6	0.3	0.2
Health sciences	77,996	100.0	43.1	43.5	2.0	3.2	1.3	0.7	4.0	2.0	0.1	0.1
First-professional	36,854	100.0	64.7	18.8	3.1	0.9	2.4	0.8	7.2	2.0	0.2	—
Nursing	20,931	100.0	0.9	88.3	0.5	6.7	—	0.9	0.1	2.3	—	0.2
Other health sciences	20,211	100.0	47.4	42.1	1.8	3.6	0.8	0.3	2.1	1.6	0.2	0.2
Humanities	74,086	100.0	53.5	34.8	2.1	2.0	2.0	2.0	1.3	1.9	0.3	0.1
English and literature	37,476	100.0	45.2	45.0	2.1	2.8	1.3	1.0	0.8	1.3	0.5	0.1
Foreign languages	13,684	100.0	40.0	36.6	1.2	0.6	5.4	7.4	1.8	6.4	—	0.4
History	14,644	100.0	70.6	20.0	3.0	2.2	1.2	0.4	1.8	0.4	0.3	—
Philosophy	8,283	100.0	82.5	12.3	1.6	0.2	1.1	0.3	1.5	0.3	0.2	—
Law	7,337	100.0	57.8	30.0	5.8	2.9	1.3	1.1	0.2	0.7	—	—
Natural sciences	101,681	100.0	69.0	17.4	2.5	0.9	1.5	0.3	7.2	0.9	0.2	0.1
Biological sciences	34,303	100.0	68.4	20.5	2.9	1.2	1.0	0.5	4.3	0.9	0.3	0.1
Physical sciences	28,299	100.0	77.4	10.1	2.0	0.3	1.9	0.1	7.3	0.8	—	—
Mathematics	25,407	100.0	61.7	21.2	2.6	1.0	1.7	0.6	9.2	1.2	0.5	0.4
Computer sciences	13,671	100.0	66.5	17.2	2.1	1.3	1.7	0.1	10.4	0.8	—	—
Social sciences	58,526	100.0	65.4	22.3	2.9	2.9	1.9	0.8	2.6	0.7	0.3	0.2
Economics	9,881	100.0	70.4	11.9	3.8	0.3	3.0	1.1	7.9	1.6	—	—
Political sciences	9,434	100.0	75.7	14.5	3.4	1.9	2.6	0.4	1.1	0.2	0.1	—
Psychology	17,692	100.0	58.0	31.8	2.1	3.9	1.5	0.8	1.1	0.3	0.1	0.2
Sociology	9,586	100.0	68.2	20.1	2.7	3.2	2.3	0.5	1.4	0.8	0.9	—
Other social sciences	11,934	100.0	62.1	24.5	3.2	4.1	0.8	1.1	2.7	0.6	0.3	0.6
Occupationally specific programs	15,395	100.0	75.9	13.5	3.5	0.9	3.1	0.3	1.9	0.2	0.5	0.2
All other programs	27,466	100.0	58.1	30.1	2.8	3.3	2.0	0.7	2.3	0.6	—	0.1
					Part-time instructional faculty and staff							
Total	263,215	100.0	48.7	40.1	2.6	1.9	1.8	1.1	1.8	1.3	0.4	0.2
Agriculture and home economics	1,936	100.0	47.8	51.2	—	—	1.0	—	—	—	—	—
Business	24,291	100.0	63.6	26.3	3.1	1.7	2.0	0.7	1.0	1.1	0.2	0.4
Communications	7,132	100.0	42.6	51.1	3.5	0.7	—	0.6	0.6	0.3	0.3	0.1
Education	21,821	100.0	29.2	59.2	2.3	5.1	0.7	1.3	0.3	1.1	0.3	0.6
Teacher education	8,791	100.0	20.1	69.2	2.1	6.0	0.6	0.8	0.5	0.8	—	0.6
Other education	13,030	100.0	35.3	52.5	2.4	4.4	0.7	1.6	0.3	1.3	0.5	1.0
Engineering	7,872	100.0	79.3	7.6	1.7	—	1.8	—	6.7	0.7	2.1	—
Fine arts	23,228	100.0	46.5	43.5	3.0	1.7	1.4	1.1	0.4	1.9	0.4	0.2
Health sciences	30,336	100.0	36.6	51.9	3.1	2.3	0.9	0.7	2.1	1.9	0.4	0.2
First-professional	12,070	100.0	58.0	27.0	6.3	1.0	0.6	0.2	4.6	2.3	—	—
Nursing	7,398	100.0	5.6	85.0	—	5.4	-	0.9	—	2.4	—	0.6
Other health sciences	10,869	100.0	33.8	57.1	1.6	1.6	2.0	1.0	0.9	1.0	1.0	—
Humanities	42,562	100.0	36.0	51.6	1.0	2.0	2.8	3.2	1.2	1.6	0.3	0.4
English and literature	26,525	100.0	29.5	61.0	0.5	2.6	2.0	1.6	0.6	1.1	0.4	0.5
Foreign languages	7,408	100.0	26.7	44.8	0.9	1.5	6.0	12.3	2.3	4.9	—	0.5
History	5,561	100.0	62.7	30.0	2.5	0.7	1.7	0.2	1.8	—	0.4	—
Philosophy	3,068	100.0	65.4	25.0	2.7	0.3	3.0	—	2.2	1.2	—	—
Law	8,608	100.0	68.8	23.0	3.7	2.5	0.3	0.3	1.4	—	—	—
Natural sciences	42,544	100.0	58.6	29.6	2.9	0.9	2.0	0.4	3.5	1.5	0.6	—
Biological sciences	8,322	100.0	49.8	38.3	2.9	1.0	2.1	0.6	1.9	3.4	—	—
Physical sciences	7,555	100.0	68.2	21.4	1.9	0.3	0.9	0.8	5.2	1.3	—	—
Mathematics	17,373	100.0	53.4	35.0	4.1	0.8	2.2	0.2	3.3	0.7	0.2	0.1
Computer sciences	9,294	100.0	68.6	18.2	1.7	1.4	2.2	0.4	3.9	1.2	2.4	—
Social sciences	23,556	100.0	49.4	38.3	3.4	2.7	1.8	0.9	2.1	0.9	0.4	0.1
Economics	2,166	100.0	69.2	14.0	1.4	0.9	2.8	—	9.1	2.5	—	—
Political sciences	2,106	100.0	73.6	17.5	4.5	0.4	3.3	0.7	—	—	—	—
Psychology	10,973	100.0	45.9	46.0	2.2	1.3	1.5	0.5	1.7	0.3	0.3	0.3
Sociology	3,029	100.0	35.0	50.7	6.0	3.9	1.2	0.2	1.6	1.4	—	—
Other social sciences	5,282	100.0	47.1	33.4	4.8	6.5	1.9	2.4	1.1	1.8	1.2	—
Occupationally specific programs	11,757	100.0	71.8	17.6	3.3	0.7	5.2	—	1.3	—	0.1	—
All other programs	14,033	100.0	45.1	43.6	1.8	1.3	2.3	1.5	2.4	1.9	—	—

—Data not available

NOTE.—Because of rounding and nonresponse to program area question, details may not add to totals.

SOURCE: U.S. Department of Education, National Center for Education Statistics, *National Study of Postsecondary Faculty (NSOPF), 1993.* (This table was prepared May 1995.)

Table 223.—Full-time and part-time instructional faculty and staff in institutions of higher education, by type and control, academic rank, age, salary, race/ethnicity, and sex: Fall 1992

Selected characteristics	Number	Percent	White, non-Hispanic		Black, non-Hispanic		Hispanic		Asian/Pacific Islander		American Indian/Alaskan Native	
			Male	Female	Male	Female	Male	Female	Male	Female	Male	Female
1	2	3	4	5	6	7	8	9	10	11	12	13
Full-time instructional faculty and staff												
All institutions	526,222	—	309,815	146,996	13,878	12,149	8,871	4,408	20,932	6,614	1,663	895
Percent distribution	—	100.0	58.9	27.9	2.6	2.3	1.7	0.8	4.0	1.3	0.3	0.2
Type and control												
Public research	108,493	100.0	68.7	19.7	1.5	1.2	1.5	0.5	5.7	1.3	0.1	0.1
Private research	32,350	100.0	59.2	25.0	2.8	1.9	1.2	0.7	6.7	2.4	0.2	—
Public doctoral	54,433	100.0	62.1	25.7	1.6	1.3	1.7	0.6	4.9	1.4	0.6	0.2
Private doctoral	25,397	100.0	66.5	19.4	2.9	1.2	2.3	1.0	5.1	1.4	0.1	0.1
Public comprehensive	96,350	100.0	55.5	27.5	4.9	3.9	1.8	0.8	4.1	1.1	0.2	0.3
Private comprehensive	36,548	100.0	60.5	31.3	1.4	1.6	1.0	0.6	2.5	0.9	—	0.1
Private liberal arts	39,018	100.0	54.9	35.2	3.7	1.7	0.8	0.5	1.9	0.9	0.3	0.2
Public 2–year	109,552	100.0	47.8	37.7	2.5	3.6	2.5	1.6	1.9	1.4	0.7	0.3
Other	24,081	100.0	67.1	23.9	1.5	1.2	0.9	0.4	3.8	0.8	0.4	0.1
Academic rank												
Full professor	161,252	100.0	75.7	14.3	2.1	1.1	1.4	0.3	4.5	0.4	0.2	0.1
Associate professor	123,471	100.0	63.1	24.7	2.9	2.1	1.3	0.8	3.6	1.0	0.3	0.1
Assistant professor	123,285	100.0	47.5	36.0	2.8	3.0	2.0	1.2	5.0	2.1	0.2	0.2
Instructor	72,986	100.0	44.1	40.8	3.1	3.8	2.2	1.1	2.2	1.7	0.7	0.3
Lecturer	11,655	100.0	29.6	53.4	2.6	3.7	2.0	1.2	4.0	2.6	—	1.1
Other	16,753	100.0	41.5	39.5	4.2	4.6	2.2	1.8	4.2	1.7	0.2	0.1
No rank	16,820	100.0	51.6	38.3	1.2	1.3	1.9	0.9	2.0	1.6	0.9	0.3
Age												
Under 30	7,599	100.0	40.5	38.7	2.3	5.2	2.0	1.8	6.2	3.0	0.3	0.1
30 to 34	35,298	100.0	46.7	32.7	3.7	3.5	3.0	1.2	6.6	2.5	0.3	0.0
35 to 39	66,304	100.0	50.7	33.5	2.6	2.3	1.8	1.0	5.5	2.1	0.5	0.2
40 to 44	89,575	100.0	51.7	32.9	2.5	3.0	2.0	1.4	4.3	1.6	0.2	0.5
45 to 49	97,257	100.0	57.0	31.0	2.3	2.8	1.8	0.8	2.7	1.2	0.3	0.1
50 to 54	94,884	100.0	64.2	25.7	2.4	1.7	1.2	0.6	3.1	0.7	0.3	0.2
55 to 59	66,933	100.0	68.3	20.5	2.7	1.6	1.3	0.3	3.9	0.7	0.7	0.1
60 to 64	44,784	100.0	71.1	17.6	2.7	1.6	1.3	0.5	4.2	0.7	0.2	0.1
65 or older	23,589	100.0	69.8	19.8	3.9	1.0	1.6	0.6	2.4	0.5	0.1	0.3
Base salary												
Under $10,000	13,607	100.0	54.5	29.7	6.7	4.7	0.9	0.3	1.9	1.0	0.3	0.1
10,000 to 24,999	28,818	100.0	36.6	50.0	1.7	3.5	1.3	1.3	2.6	2.3	0.1	0.6
25,000 to 39,999	179,758	100.0	46.1	40.3	2.7	3.3	1.7	1.2	2.5	1.6	0.4	0.2
40,000 to 54,999	163,729	100.0	62.7	23.2	2.8	1.9	1.8	1.0	5.1	1.1	0.4	0.1
55,000 to 69,999	77,375	100.0	74.1	14.9	2.2	1.3	2.1	0.4	4.1	0.9	0.2	0.1
70,000 to 84,999	32,287	100.0	79.9	10.6	2.0	0.7	1.6	0.1	4.6	0.5	0.2	—
85,000 to 99,999	10,822	100.0	71.6	12.7	4.6	0.3	0.7	—	9.3	0.9	—	—
100,000 or more	19,827	100.0	78.8	9.2	1.4	0.6	0.6	0.1	7.3	1.4	0.6	0.2
Total income												
Under $10,000	6,710	100.0	48.5	37.9	3.1	4.9	0.6	0.5	2.4	2.0	0.0	0.3
10,000 to 24,999	17,168	100.0	33.4	49.7	3.3	4.2	1.7	1.6	2.9	1.9	0.4	1.0
25,000 to 39,999	128,179	100.0	40.9	45.8	2.6	3.4	1.1	1.2	2.7	1.8	0.2	0.3
40,000 to 54,999	157,513	100.0	56.0	29.7	2.9	2.6	2.2	1.0	3.9	1.2	0.4	0.1
55,000 to 69,999	95,330	100.0	70.3	17.2	2.6	1.8	1.6	0.7	4.5	0.9	0.4	0.2
70,000 to 84,999	49,856	100.0	75.9	12.7	2.0	1.2	1.7	0.4	4.8	1.0	0.3	—
85,000 to 99,999	23,848	100.0	76.9	10.7	3.9	0.6	1.8	0.1	5.4	0.4	0.3	—
100,000 or more	47,618	100.0	77.7	10.8	1.8	0.6	1.9	0.1	5.8	1.0	0.2	0.1
Part-time instructional faculty and staff												
All institutions	263,215	—	128,201	105,508	6,730	5,054	4,845	2,972	4,822	3,549	984	550
Percent distribution	—	100.0	48.7	40.1	2.6	1.9	1.8	1.1	1.8	1.3	0.4	0.2
Type and control												
Public research	16,071	100.0	49.2	38.7	0.8	1.6	2.1	1.1	4.8	1.7	—	—
Private research	10,924	100.0	50.8	39.0	3.1	1.1	2.7	—	1.8	1.2	0.4	—
Public doctoral	13,087	100.0	50.9	40.9	1.6	1.4	1.1	0.5	1.9	1.5	0.2	0.3
Private doctoral	11,752	100.0	54.5	32.4	6.5	1.1	1.2	0.2	1.0	3.0	0.2	—
Public comprehensive	32,367	100.0	41.0	45.2	3.7	2.5	1.0	1.8	2.7	1.4	0.5	0.2
Private comprehensive	25,346	100.0	51.5	39.5	2.1	2.7	0.9	0.3	1.7	0.9	0.4	0.1
Private liberal arts	19,633	100.0	40.7	49.3	3.7	1.9	1.3	1.5	0.8	0.8	0.1	—
Public 2–year	120,797	100.0	49.9	38.5	2.3	1.8	2.5	1.4	1.5	2.1	0.5	0.3
Other	13,239	100.0	53.6	38.0	0.6	2.2	0.7	0.3	1.8	2.1	0.5	0.3

Table 223.—Full-time and part-time instructional faculty and staff in institutions of higher education, by type and control, academic rank, age, salary, race/ethnicity, and sex: Fall 1992—Continued

Selected characteristics	Number	Percent	White, non-Hispanic		Black, non-Hispanic		Hispanic		Asian/Pacific Islander		American Indian/Alaskan Native	
			Male	Female	Male	Female	Male	Female	Male	Female	Male	Female
1	2	3	4	5	6	7	8	9	10	11	12	13
Academic rank												
Full professor	22,026	100.0	63.7	24.9	3.2	1.6	1.7	0.4	2.8	0.7	0.7	0.3
Associate professor	15,286	100.0	59.2	30.1	1.4	1.2	1.6	0.4	3.7	1.7	0.4	0.4
Assistant professor	16,897	100.0	48.9	38.4	5.6	2.1	0.6	0.4	2.3	1.7	—	0.1
Instructor	152,539	100.0	46.5	42.5	2.3	2.0	2.3	1.2	1.4	1.2	0.5	0.2
Lecturer	31,159	100.0	48.3	40.3	2.0	1.8	1.3	1.6	2.5	1.8	0.2	0.2
Other	18,800	100.0	42.8	45.8	3.5	2.2	0.8	1.3	1.2	1.9	—	0.5
No rank	6,507	100.0	43.1	45.4	1.9	2.6	—	2.0	3.0	1.4	0.6	—
Age												
Under 30	14,181	100.0	41.8	46.4	1.9	1.9	1.6	1.6	1.5	2.4	0.3	0.5
30 to 34	25,013	100.0	42.4	44.7	2.0	1.9	2.4	1.6	2.1	2.4	0.4	0.2
35 to 39	40,902	100.0	42.8	44.3	3.9	2.0	2.1	1.1	1.9	1.1	0.6	0.2
40 to 44	49,290	100.0	47.7	41.9	2.0	1.7	1.7	1.4	1.5	1.6	0.2	0.2
45 to 49	47,751	100.0	48.2	42.0	2.0	1.5	1.5	1.4	2.2	1.0	0.0	0.3
50 to 54	31,641	100.0	49.1	36.8	3.5	2.6	2.3	0.6	2.3	1.6	1.0	0.3
55 to 59	20,116	100.0	55.2	35.2	3.1	1.4	1.4	0.7	1.9	1.0	0.2	0.0
60 to 64	15,926	100.0	55.7	34.5	2.0	2.1	2.2	0.6	1.3	0.9	0.8	0.1
65 or older	18,396	100.0	65.8	25.6	2.2	2.7	1.1	0.9	1.2	0.4	0.0	0.0
Base salary												
Under $10,000	196,455	100.0	49.7	39.4	2.5	2.1	1.7	1.1	1.6	1.3	0.3	0.2
10,000 to 24,999	47,568	100.0	43.2	45.1	2.1	1.3	2.7	1.3	2.4	1.5	0.3	0.2
25,000 to 39,999	10,927	100.0	49.9	37.7	4.3	1.9	1.4	0.3	2.5	1.2	0.8	—
40,000 to 54,999	3,630	100.0	55.0	34.4	1.7	2.1	1.4	2.9	0.1	1.7	0.7	—
55,000 to 69,999	1,455	100.0	50.5	16.7	3.5	—	0.7	—	20.8	7.8	—	—
70,000 to 84,999	672	100.0	52.0	26.5	7.6	4.1	—	—	2.9	—	6.9	—
85,000 to 99,999	619	100.0	87.7	12.4	—	—	—	—	—	—	—	—
100,000 or more	1,889	100.0	45.5	40.0	10.8	0.4	1.2	—	—	2.0	—	—
Total income												
Under $10,000	49,601	100.0	35.4	53.1	2.1	2.6	1.9	1.3	1.7	1.6	0.0	0.4
10,000 to 24,999	59,721	100.0	33.4	57.3	1.2	1.7	1.2	1.7	1.3	1.7	0.4	0.1
25,000 to 39,999	53,066	100.0	49.1	39.4	2.3	2.6	2.0	1.2	1.6	1.4	0.2	0.3
40,000 to 54,999	40,682	100.0	55.9	32.4	3.2	1.7	1.6	1.2	1.7	0.7	1.2	0.4
55,000 to 69,999	22,180	100.0	69.8	17.6	3.3	1.5	3.0	0.5	2.9	1.2	0.3	—
70,000 to 84,999	11,858	100.0	70.9	16.9	4.3	0.6	2.9	0.7	2.8	0.6	0.4	—
85,000 to 99,999	5,505	100.0	69.6	18.5	4.9	0.8	4.8	—	1.4	—	—	—
100,000 or more	20,603	100.0	68.9	19.0	4.6	1.2	1.0	—	3.2	1.9	0.1	—

—Data not available or not applicable.

NOTE.—Because of rounding, details may not add to totals.

SOURCE: U.S. Department of Education, National Center for Education Statistics, *National Study of Postsecondary Faculty (NSOPF), 1993.* (This table was prepared May 1995.)

Table 224.—Full-time instructional faculty and staff in institutions of higher education, by faculty characteristics and field: Fall 1992

Faculty characteristics	Number in thousands	All fields	Agriculture and home economics	Business	Education	Engineering	Fine arts	Health	Humanities	Natural sciences	Social sciences	Other and not reported
1	2	3	4	5	6	7	8	9	10	11	12	13
Total, in thousands	526	—	11	40	37	25	32	78	74	102	59	61
Percent	—	100.0	2.2	7.6	7.0	4.7	6.0	14.8	14.1	19.3	11.1	11.5
						Percentage distribution						
Total	526	100.0	100.0	100.0	100.0	100.0	100.0	100.0	100.0	100.0	100.0	100.0
Sex												
Male	355	67.5	76.1	69.8	49.9	94.1	67.8	50.6	59.1	80.3	73.2	70.3
Female	171	32.5	23.9	30.2	50.1	5.9	32.2	49.4	40.9	19.7	26.8	29.7
Race/ethnicity												
White, non-Hispanic	457	86.8	90.9	88.9	85.1	76.8	88.7	86.6	88.3	86.3	87.7	88.1
Black, non-Hispanic	26	4.9	3.8	3.9	9.0	2.7	5.7	5.2	4.1	3.4	5.9	5.9
Hispanic	13	2.5	1.8	1.4	3.3	2.9	2.4	2.0	4.0	1.8	2.7	2.6
Asian	28	5.2	2.9	4.9	1.6	16.9	2.7	6.0	3.2	8.1	3.3	2.9
American Indian	3	0.5	0.7	1.0	1.0	0.7	0.5	0.2	0.5	0.3	0.5	0.4
Age												
Under 30	8	1.4	0.4	1.2	1.1	1.3	1.3	1.1	1.6	1.5	0.8	2.4
30 to 34	35	6.7	7.1	6.3	3.5	11.1	6.1	8.5	4.7	6.7	7.3	6.7
35 to 39	66	12.6	9.1	13.5	7.8	13.2	13.0	16.2	9.5	13.9	12.9	12.1
40 to 44	90	17.0	15.8	16.4	17.5	16.8	17.7	21.7	13.3	17.1	17.8	17.9
45 to 49	97	18.5	17.6	20.9	19.6	14.7	18.4	19.3	20.0	19.3	19.2	18.5
50 to 54	95	18.0	18.5	16.1	21.1	12.2	17.4	13.4	21.6	19.3	19.2	12.3
55 to 59	67	12.7	14.5	11.9	14.2	15.0	14.1	9.5	14.6	13.3	12.3	7.4
60 to 64	45	8.5	11.4	8.0	10.6	10.7	7.9	7.6	9.9	7.5	9.2	7.4
65 or older	24	4.5	5.7	5.8	4.7	5.1	4.0	2.7	4.8	4.7	4.2	4.7
Degree												
Less than bachelor's	6	1.2	0.2	0.5	0.3	2.0	0.7	1.2	(1)	0.2	0.1	6.3
Bachelor's	21	4.0	5.5	4.5	2.9	5.1	5.3	5.9	1.2	2.8	0.7	8.4
Master's	154	29.4	21.7	37.9	30.3	18.4	56.0	29.6	31.6	21.9	18.9	34.1
Professional	57	10.9	4.4	4.5	3.0	2.3	4.4	43.3	2.4	4.5	3.5	15.8
Doctoral	285	54.5	68.2	52.6	63.6	72.2	33.6	20.0	64.8	70.7	76.8	35.4
Rank												
Full professor	161	30.6	41.8	24.9	24.6	36.9	32.3	21.5	33.3	37.3	37.2	26.4
Associate professor	123	23.5	22.6	25.7	29.6	28.0	25.5	23.0	22.2	22.6	24.7	19.5
Assistant professor	123	23.4	19.3	25.5	22.8	22.4	21.4	32.8	19.3	20.6	24.1	23.1
Instructor	73	13.9	10.5	16.5	13.2	10.4	10.1	16.6	14.8	11.6	7.9	22.1
Lecturer	12	2.2	0.9	1.3	2.5	0.9	2.9	2.3	3.8	1.8	1.7	2.4
Other	17	3.2	3.2	2.1	5.5	0.5	3.2	2.4	1.9	2.4	2.0	3.5
No rank	17	3.2	1.7	4.0	1.9	1.0	4.6	1.4	4.7	3.9	2.5	3.0

[1] Less than 0.05 percent.
— Not applicable.

SOURCE: U. S. Department of Education, *National Study of Postsecondary Faculty (NSOPF), 1993.* (This table was prepared May 1995.)

NOTE.—Because of rounding and survey item nonresponse, details may not add to totals.

Table 225.—Average base salaries of full-time instructional faculty and staff in institutions of higher education, by type and control of institution and by field of instruction: 1987–88 and 1992–93

Field of instruction	All institutions	Total public	Total private	Public research	Private research	Public doctoral	Private doctoral	Public comprehensive	Private comprehensive	Private liberal arts	Public 2-year	Other
1	2	3	4	5	6	7	8	9	10	11	12	13
1987–88												
Instructional faculty, in thousands	515	356	159	102	42	56	25	97	37	38	96	22
All fields	$39,323	$39,685	$38,515	$47,237	$51,749	$43,913	$46,503	$36,853	$32,157	$28,823	$32,387	$30,641
Agriculture and home economics	39,381	39,593	—	44,241	—	35,357	—	38,147	—	—	—	—
Business	36,773	37,213	35,826	47,319	—	39,958	—	35,285	36,835	—	33,086	28,685
Education	32,916	34,557	27,252	37,275	—	35,206	—	33,947	27,227	23,896	33,432	—
Engineering	42,438	41,787	44,780	49,875	—	43,186	—	40,896	41,843	—	29,906	—
Fine arts	30,756	32,143	27,934	32,753	—	31,012	—	31,997	26,960	28,028	32,687	—
Health	52,717	52,381	53,391	59,702	62,702	57,760	54,682	46,429	38,756	—	30,087	—
Humanities	34,478	35,837	32,403	37,653	39,817	31,965	37,642	36,251	30,145	30,989	35,324	28,271
Natural sciences	38,860	39,338	37,790	47,098	50,174	40,571	38,129	37,944	31,506	30,691	32,261	30,479
Social sciences	37,578	37,799	37,169	42,949	49,614	38,964	—	36,521	31,384	29,039	33,366	—
Other	36,341	35,957	37,253	42,790	—	36,922	—	34,017	29,043	—	30,692	36,032
1992–93												
Instructional faculty, in thousands	475	340	135	90	25	47	21	92	35	37	105	23
All fields	$46,966	$46,958	$46,984	$56,719	$64,306	$51,858	$56,018	$43,575	$43,424	$37,660	$39,415	$40,333
Agriculture and home economics	48,175	48,874	—	55,506	—	44,530	—	43,507	—	—	39,859	—
Business	49,392	50,100	47,494	65,282	—	59,018	56,399	47,792	53,855	32,353	42,003	33,877
Education	42,148	43,329	37,653	50,118	—	42,280	49,440	41,475	37,964	32,422	41,182	—
Engineering	55,634	56,005	54,190	66,887	60,999	53,583	54,945	48,778	46,083	—	38,716	55,684
Fine arts	40,714	39,389	42,726	41,460	87,606	39,463	37,963	39,169	35,956	37,816	37,638	33,761
Health	56,079	54,572	60,616	74,158	74,041	64,120	69,211	38,333	46,058	42,354	35,828	40,748
Humanities	41,058	41,679	39,723	44,006	44,762	39,931	43,171	40,881	41,176	37,723	41,266	36,344
Natural sciences	48,445	47,670	50,464	55,520	67,333	52,072	59,281	46,013	46,792	37,559	39,715	41,875
Social sciences	46,128	46,238	45,897	53,286	59,504	48,989	49,834	43,753	40,118	40,509	40,322	44,528
Other	44,352	43,699	45,820	51,568	65,896	43,957	56,689	45,558	41,843	36,498	37,811	39,468

—Too few sample cases (fewer than 30) for a reliable estimate.

NOTE.— Data for 1992–93 differ from other tables because of adjustments to maintain consistency with the 1987–88 data. Because of rounding, details may not add to totals.

SOURCE: U.S. Department of Education, National Center for Education Statistics, *National Study of Postsecondary Faculty (NSOPF), 1987–88 and 1992–93*. (This table was prepared August 1995.)

Table 226.—Average salary of full-time instructional faculty on 9-month contracts in institutions of higher education, by academic rank, sex, and control and type of institution: 1970–71 to 1993–94

Academic year and sex	All faculty	Academic rank						Public institutions			Private institutions		
		Professor	Associate professor	Assistant professor	Instructor	Lecturer	No rank	Total	4-year	2-year	Total	4-year	2-year
1	2	3	4	5	6	7	8	9	10	11	12	13	14
Current dollars													
Total													
1970–71	$12,710	$17,958	$13,563	$11,176	$9,360	$11,196	$12,333	$12,953	$13,121	$12,644	$11,619	$11,824	$8,664
1972–73	13,856	19,191	14,580	12,032	10,737	11,637	12,676	14,016	14,417	12,919	13,452	13,622	9,288
1974–75	15,622	21,277	16,146	13,295	12,691	12,575	13,532	15,879	16,271	14,897	14,912	15,092	10,242
1975–76	16,659	22,649	17,065	13,986	13,672	12,906	15,196	16,942	17,400	15,820	15,921	16,116	10,901
1976–77	17,560	23,792	17,905	14,662	11,835	13,431	16,634	17,845	18,313	16,685	16,787	16,977	11,637
1977–78	18,709	25,133	18,987	15,530	12,504	14,528	17,831	19,045	19,517	17,895	17,773	17,966	12,191
1978–79	19,820	26,470	20,047	16,374	13,193	15,281	18,725	20,179	20,722	18,844	18,807	19,010	12,496
1979–80	21,348	28,388	21,451	17,465	14,023	16,122	20,262	21,798	22,349	20,429	20,105	20,318	13,250
1980–81	23,302	30,753	23,214	18,901	15,178	17,301	22,334	23,745	24,373	22,177	22,093	22,325	15,065
1981–82	25,449	33,437	25,278	20,608	16,450	18,756	24,331	25,886	26,591	24,193	24,255	24,509	15,926
1982–83	27,196	35,540	26,921	22,056	17,601	20,072	25,557	27,488	28,293	25,567	26,393	26,691	16,595
1984–85	30,447	39,743	29,945	24,668	20,230	22,334	27,683	30,646	31,764	27,864	29,910	30,247	18,510
1985–86	32,392	42,268	31,787	26,277	20,918	23,770	29,088	32,750	34,033	29,590	31,402	31,732	19,436
1987–88	35,897	47,040	35,231	29,110	22,728	25,977	31,532	36,231	37,840	32,209	35,049	35,346	21,867
1989–90	40,133	52,810	39,392	32,689	25,030	28,990	34,559	40,416	42,365	35,516	39,464	39,817	24,601
1990–91	42,165	55,540	41,414	34,434	26,332	30,097	36,395	42,317	44,510	37,055	41,788	42,224	24,088
1991–92	43,851	57,433	42,929	35,745	30,916	30,456	37,783	43,641	45,638	38,959	44,376	44,793	25,673
1992–93	44,714	58,788	43,945	36,625	28,499	30,543	37,771	44,197	46,515	38,935	45,985	46,427	26,105
1993–94 [1]	46,364	60,649	45,278	37,630	28,828	32,729	40,584	45,920	48,019	41,040	47,465	47,880	28,435
Men													
1972–73	14,422	19,414	14,723	12,193	11,147	12,106	13,047	14,545	14,944	13,268	14,116	14,253	9,571
1974–75	16,303	21,532	16,282	13,458	13,350	13,232	14,008	16,522	16,918	15,350	15,709	15,852	10,633
1975–76	17,414	22,902	17,209	14,174	14,430	13,579	15,761	17,661	18,121	16,339	16,784	16,946	11,378
1976–77	18,378	24,029	18,055	14,851	12,085	14,147	17,253	18,620	19,091	17,235	17,736	17,891	12,193
1977–78	19,575	25,370	19,133	15,726	12,729	15,181	18,459	19,867	20,347	18,479	18,783	18,935	12,759
1978–79	20,777	26,727	20,221	16,602	13,441	15,927	19,400	21,080	21,628	19,475	19,935	20,086	13,048
1979–80	22,394	28,672	21,651	17,720	14,323	16,932	20,901	22,789	23,350	21,131	21,317	21,472	13,938
1980–81	24,499	31,082	23,451	19,227	15,545	18,281	23,170	24,873	25,509	22,965	23,493	23,669	16,075
1981–82	26,796	33,799	25,553	21,025	16,906	19,721	25,276	27,149	27,864	25,085	25,849	26,037	16,834
1982–83	28,664	35,956	27,262	22,586	18,160	21,225	26,541	28,851	29,661	26,524	28,159	28,380	17,346
1984–85	32,182	40,269	30,392	25,330	21,159	23,557	28,670	32,240	33,344	28,891	32,028	32,278	19,460
1985–86	34,294	42,833	32,273	27,094	21,693	25,238	30,267	34,528	35,786	30,758	33,656	33,900	20,412
1987–88	38,112	47,735	35,823	30,086	23,645	27,652	32,747	38,314	39,898	33,477	37,603	37,817	22,641
1989–90	42,763	53,650	40,131	33,781	25,933	31,162	35,980	42,959	44,834	37,081	42,312	42,595	25,218
1990–91	45,065	56,549	42,239	35,636	27,388	32,398	38,036	45,084	47,168	38,787	45,019	45,319	25,937
1991–92	46,848	58,494	43,814	36,969	33,359	32,843	39,422	46,483	48,401	40,811	47,733	48,042	26,825
1992–93	47,866	59,972	44,855	37,842	29,583	32,512	39,365	47,175	49,392	40,725	49,518	49,837	27,402
1993–94 [1]	49,579	61,857	46,229	38,794	29,815	34,796	42,251	48,956	50,989	42,938	51,076	51,397	30,783
Women													
1972–73	11,925	17,123	13,827	11,510	10,098	10,775	11,913	12,250	12,300	12,165	11,044	11,219	8,888
1974–75	13,471	19,012	15,481	12,858	11,740	11,543	12,619	13,892	13,831	13,987	12,233	12,423	9,735
1975–76	14,308	20,308	16,364	13,522	12,572	11,901	14,094	14,762	14,758	14,769	13,030	13,231	10,201
1976–77	15,100	21,536	17,189	14,225	11,589	12,397	15,467	15,573	15,539	15,628	13,709	13,899	10,850
1977–78	16,159	22,943	18,325	15,109	12,288	13,688	16,637	16,684	16,619	16,785	14,597	14,799	11,470
1978–79	17,080	24,143	19,300	15,914	12,966	14,465	17,482	17,646	17,627	17,676	15,388	15,611	11,898
1979–80	18,396	25,910	20,642	16,974	13,750	15,142	19,069	19,042	18,985	19,134	16,539	16,787	12,541
1980–81	19,996	27,959	22,295	18,302	14,854	16,168	20,843	20,673	20,608	20,778	18,073	18,326	13,892
1981–82	21,802	30,438	24,271	19,866	16,054	17,676	22,672	22,524	22,454	22,632	19,743	20,024	14,984
1982–83	23,261	32,221	25,738	21,130	17,102	18,830	23,855	23,892	23,876	23,917	21,451	21,785	15,845
1984–85	25,941	35,824	28,517	23,575	19,362	21,004	26,050	26,566	26,813	26,172	24,186	24,560	17,575
1985–86	27,576	38,252	30,300	24,966	20,237	22,273	27,171	28,299	28,680	27,693	25,523	25,889	18,504
1987–88	30,499	42,371	33,528	27,600	21,962	24,370	29,605	31,215	31,820	30,228	28,621	28,946	21,215
1989–90	34,183	47,663	37,469	31,090	24,320	26,995	32,528	34,796	35,704	33,307	32,650	33,010	24,002
1990–91	35,881	49,728	39,329	32,724	25,534	28,111	34,179	36,459	37,573	34,720	34,359	34,898	22,585
1991–92	37,534	51,621	40,766	34,063	28,873	28,550	35,622	37,800	38,634	36,517	36,828	37,309	24,683
1992–93	38,385	52,755	41,861	35,032	27,700	28,922	35,792	38,356	39,470	36,710	38,460	38,987	25,068
1993–94 [1]	40,058	54,746	43,178	36,169	28,136	31,048	38,474	40,118	41,031	38,707	39,902	40,378	26,142
Constant 1993–94 dollars [2]													
Total													
1970–71	46,781	66,097	49,923	41,136	34,450	41,210	45,395	47,678	48,297	46,539	42,765	43,522	31,890
1972–73	47,328	65,548	49,801	41,096	36,673	39,746	43,296	47,873	49,242	44,125	45,947	46,527	31,726
1974–75	44,103	60,068	45,583	37,533	35,827	35,502	38,203	44,828	45,937	42,058	42,098	42,607	28,914
1975–76	43,921	59,715	44,993	36,875	36,048	34,027	40,065	44,668	45,876	41,709	41,976	42,492	28,740
1976–77	43,748	59,272	44,606	36,528	29,484	33,460	41,439	44,456	45,623	41,567	41,820	42,293	28,991
1977–78	43,675	58,674	44,326	36,256	29,190	33,915	41,627	44,461	45,563	41,775	41,492	41,941	28,459
1978–79	42,308	56,503	42,792	34,952	28,161	32,618	39,969	43,073	44,232	40,223	40,145	40,577	26,673
1979–80	40,208	53,468	40,401	32,895	26,411	30,364	38,161	41,056	42,092	38,477	37,866	38,267	24,956
1980–81	39,332	51,909	39,184	31,904	25,619	29,203	37,698	40,080	41,140	37,433	37,291	37,683	25,429
1981–82	39,540	51,952	39,275	32,019	25,559	29,141	37,803	40,219	41,315	37,589	37,686	38,081	24,744
1982–83	40,515	52,945	40,105	32,857	26,221	29,902	38,073	40,950	42,149	38,088	39,318	39,762	24,722
1984–85	42,091	54,942	41,397	34,102	27,967	30,876	38,270	42,366	43,912	38,520	41,349	41,815	25,589
1985–86	43,525	56,795	42,712	35,308	28,107	31,940	39,085	44,006	45,730	39,760	42,195	42,638	26,116
1987–88	45,310	59,375	44,469	36,743	28,687	32,788	39,800	45,731	47,762	40,655	44,239	44,614	27,601
1989–90	46,215	60,812	45,362	37,643	28,823	33,383	39,796	46,541	48,785	40,898	45,444	45,851	28,329

Table 226.—Average salary of full-time instructional faculty on 9-month contracts in institutions of higher education, by academic rank, sex, and control and type of institution: 1970–71 to 1993–94—Continued

Academic year and sex	All faculty	Academic rank						Public institutions			Private institutions		
		Professor	Associate professor	Assistant professor	Instructor	Lecturer	No rank	Total	4-year	2-year	Total	4-year	2-year
1	2	3	4	5	6	7	8	9	10	11	12	13	14
1990–91	46,038	60,641	45,217	37,597	28,750	32,862	39,738	46,204	48,598	40,458	45,626	46,103	26,301
1991–92	46,393	60,761	45,416	37,817	32,707	32,220	39,973	46,170	48,282	41,217	46,947	47,388	27,161
1992–93	45,872	60,310	45,083	37,574	29,238	31,334	38,749	45,342	47,720	39,943	47,176	47,630	26,781
1993–94[1]	46,364	60,649	45,278	37,630	28,828	32,729	40,584	45,920	48,019	41,040	47,465	47,880	28,435
Men													
1972–73	49,261	66,312	50,289	41,647	38,075	41,348	44,564	49,682	51,043	45,319	48,215	48,683	32,691
1974–75	46,025	60,788	45,966	37,995	37,688	37,355	39,546	46,644	47,762	43,335	44,350	44,751	30,019
1975–76	45,912	60,382	45,371	37,371	38,045	35,801	41,554	46,564	47,776	43,079	44,252	44,678	29,998
1976–77	45,784	59,862	44,981	36,999	30,108	35,243	42,983	46,387	47,561	42,937	44,184	44,571	30,376
1977–78	45,699	59,226	44,667	36,713	29,717	35,439	43,092	46,379	47,499	43,140	43,850	44,203	29,785
1978–79	44,349	57,051	43,162	35,437	28,690	33,998	41,410	44,997	46,167	41,571	42,552	42,875	27,851
1979–80	42,177	54,002	40,778	33,374	26,977	31,890	39,366	42,922	43,979	39,798	40,150	40,441	26,252
1980–81	41,353	52,464	39,584	32,454	26,239	30,857	39,109	41,984	43,057	38,763	39,655	39,952	27,133
1981–82	41,633	52,514	39,702	32,667	26,267	30,641	39,272	42,181	43,293	38,975	40,162	40,454	26,155
1982–83	42,702	53,565	40,613	33,647	27,053	31,620	39,539	42,980	44,187	39,514	41,949	42,279	25,841
1984–85	44,490	55,670	42,015	35,017	29,251	32,566	39,635	44,570	46,096	39,940	44,277	44,623	26,902
1985–86	46,081	57,555	43,365	36,406	29,149	33,912	40,670	46,395	48,086	41,329	45,223	45,551	27,428
1987–88	48,105	60,251	45,216	37,975	29,845	34,903	41,333	48,360	50,360	42,255	47,463	47,733	28,578
1989–90	49,244	61,780	46,212	38,900	29,862	35,884	41,432	49,469	51,628	42,701	48,725	49,049	29,040
1990–91	49,204	61,743	46,118	38,909	29,904	35,373	41,529	49,225	51,500	42,350	49,154	49,482	28,319
1991–92	49,563	61,883	46,353	39,111	35,292	34,747	41,706	49,177	51,206	43,176	50,499	50,826	28,379
1992–93	49,105	61,525	46,017	38,822	30,349	33,354	40,385	48,397	50,672	41,780	50,801	51,128	28,111
1993–94[1]	49,579	61,857	46,229	38,794	29,815	34,796	42,251	48,956	50,989	42,938	51,076	51,397	30,783
Women													
1972–73	40,730	58,485	47,227	39,313	34,492	36,802	40,692	41,843	42,013	41,550	37,723	38,319	30,357
1974–75	38,030	53,673	43,707	36,299	33,145	32,587	35,624	39,218	39,047	39,488	34,536	35,072	27,483
1975–76	37,722	53,543	43,144	35,651	33,146	31,376	37,159	38,922	38,911	38,938	34,355	34,883	26,894
1976–77	37,617	53,651	42,823	35,439	28,871	30,884	38,531	38,796	38,711	38,932	34,152	34,627	27,029
1977–78	37,723	53,560	42,780	35,272	28,686	31,955	38,840	38,948	38,798	39,185	34,077	34,549	26,778
1978–79	36,458	51,534	41,198	33,968	27,676	30,876	37,317	37,666	37,626	37,730	32,847	33,323	25,396
1979–80	34,648	48,801	38,878	31,969	25,898	28,520	35,916	35,864	35,757	36,039	31,150	31,617	23,619
1980–81	33,752	47,193	37,632	30,893	25,073	27,290	35,182	34,895	34,785	35,072	30,506	30,933	23,449
1981–82	33,874	47,292	37,710	30,866	24,943	27,463	35,226	34,995	34,887	35,164	30,675	31,111	23,281
1982–83	34,653	48,001	38,343	31,478	25,477	28,052	35,538	35,593	35,569	35,630	31,956	32,454	23,605
1984–85	35,862	49,525	39,423	32,591	26,767	29,037	36,013	36,726	37,067	36,181	33,436	33,953	24,296
1985–86	37,054	51,399	40,714	33,547	27,192	29,928	36,510	38,025	38,537	37,211	34,295	34,787	24,864
1987–88	38,497	53,481	42,319	34,837	27,720	30,760	37,368	39,400	40,164	38,154	36,126	36,536	26,778
1989–90	39,363	54,886	43,147	35,801	28,005	31,086	37,458	40,069	41,115	38,354	37,597	38,012	27,639
1990–91	39,176	54,296	42,942	35,730	27,879	30,693	37,318	39,808	41,024	37,909	37,515	38,103	24,660
1991–92	39,709	54,612	43,128	36,037	30,546	30,204	37,687	39,991	40,873	38,633	38,962	39,471	26,114
1992–93	39,379	54,122	42,945	35,940	28,418	29,672	36,719	39,349	40,492	37,661	39,456	39,997	25,717
1993–94[1]	40,058	54,746	43,178	36,169	28,136	31,048	38,474	40,118	41,031	38,707	39,902	40,378	26,142

[1] Preliminary data.

[2] Data adjusted, using the Consumer Price Index prepared by the Bureau of Labor Statistics, averaged on an academic year time frame.

NOTE.—Data for 1987–88 to 1993–94 include imputations for nonrespondent institutions.

SOURCE: U.S. Department of Education, National Center for Education Statistics, *Faculty Salaries, Tenure, and Fringe Benefits;* and Integrated Postsecondary Education Data System (IPEDS), "Salaries, Tenure, and Fringe Benefits of Full-Time Instructional Faculty" surveys. (This table was prepared November 1994.)

Table 227.—Average salary of full-time instructional faculty on 9-month contracts in institutions of higher education, by academic rank, sex, and by type and control of institution: 1980–81, 1990–91, 1992–93, and 1993–94

Academic year, control, and type of institution	All faculty	Academic rank						Sex	
		Professor	Associate professor	Assistant professor	Instructor	Lecturer	No academic rank	Men	Women
1	2	3	4	5	6	7	8	9	10
1980–81									
All institutions	$23,302	$30,753	$23,214	$18,901	$15,178	$17,301	$22,334	$24,499	$19,996
4-year	23,693	31,016	23,265	18,867	15,056	17,375	17,380	24,909	19,809
University	25,949	33,622	24,392	19,684	15,530	17,327	17,856	27,206	20,736
Other 4-year	22,230	28,798	22,558	18,398	14,887	17,425	17,334	23,271	19,372
2-year	21,898	26,528	22,750	19,166	15,621	16,222	22,615	22,736	20,434
Public institutions	23,745	31,077	23,772	19,431	15,613	17,620	22,820	24,873	20,673
4-year	24,373	31,442	23,898	19,442	15,486	17,712	19,240	25,509	20,608
University	25,571	32,945	24,268	19,637	15,305	17,426	17,358	26,788	20,564
Other 4-year	23,500	30,097	23,639	19,315	15,567	17,997	19,798	24,499	20,633
2-year	22,177	26,880	22,947	19,370	15,928	16,458	22,875	22,965	20,778
Private institutions	22,093	29,994	21,833	17,767	14,192	15,899	15,946	23,493	18,073
4-year	22,325	30,089	21,887	17,816	14,316	15,971	16,706	23,669	18,326
University	26,897	35,227	24,730	19,792	16,197	16,956	18,933	28,251	21,176
Other 4-year	19,996	26,173	20,502	16,939	13,905	14,741	16,617	21,040	17,342
2-year	15,065	18,645	17,685	14,663	12,155	12,441	14,993	16,075	13,892
1990–91									
All institutions	42,165	55,540	41,414	34,434	26,332	30,097	36,395	45,065	35,881
4-year	43,693	56,485	41,811	34,657	25,772	30,209	31,494	46,519	36,574
University	49,430	63,437	44,877	37,838	27,105	31,748	31,533	52,426	39,788
Other 4-year	40,313	51,467	39,994	33,020	25,370	29,009	31,488	42,660	35,135
2-year	36,642	44,916	37,650	32,253	27,933	28,048	36,752	38,465	34,224
Public institutions	42,317	55,371	42,101	35,137	26,907	29,881	36,990	45,084	36,459
4-year	44,510	56,668	42,742	35,520	26,134	29,956	32,349	47,168	37,573
University	47,499	60,536	43,851	36,889	25,647	30,429	30,412	50,405	38,363
Other 4-year	42,499	53,704	41,969	34,680	26,316	29,664	33,507	44,804	37,147
2-year	37,055	45,411	38,051	32,673	28,389	28,780	37,096	38,787	34,720
Private institutions	41,788	55,911	39,983	33,116	24,928	30,864	28,523	45,019	34,359
4-year	42,224	56,127	40,122	33,235	25,159	31,053	31,122	45,319	34,898
University	53,875	69,732	47,405	40,013	31,239	34,444	36,211	56,989	43,273
Other 4-year	36,888	47,405	36,965	30,688	23,973	25,416	30,915	39,162	32,251
2-year	24,088	29,520	26,353	24,587	20,911	6,165	23,187	25,937	22,585
1992-93									
All institutions	44,714	58,788	43,945	36,625	28,499	30,543	37,771	47,866	38,385
4-year	46,483	59,988	44,317	36,872	27,415	31,349	33,922	49,551	39,285
University	52,703	67,635	47,484	40,354	28,545	32,812	32,850	55,980	42,920
Other 4-year	42,811	54,417	42,428	35,119	27,074	30,167	34,079	45,326	37,639
2-year	38,574	47,965	40,704	34,305	30,753	20,136	38,069	40,422	36,305
Public institutions	44,197	57,534	43,995	36,873	28,827	29,838	38,311	47,175	38,356
4-year	46,515	59,066	44,500	37,228	27,214	30,832	34,288	49,392	39,470
University	49,906	63,452	45,746	38,878	26,693	31,853	30,533	52,997	40,808
Other 4-year	44,212	55,642	43,622	36,226	27,413	30,205	36,141	46,726	38,737
2-year	38,935	48,286	41,094	34,713	31,039	20,116	38,405	40,725	36,710
Private institutions	45,985	61,538	43,842	36,171	27,560	32,910	30,810	49,518	38,460
4-year	46,427	61,735	43,994	36,305	27,763	32,924	33,767	49,837	38,987
University	59,005	76,561	51,654	43,686	34,369	34,527	40,498	62,622	47,849
Other 4-year	40,692	52,283	40,659	33,625	26,570	29,959	33,469	43,107	36,126
2-year	26,105	33,757	28,960	26,921	23,505	24,006	23,848	27,402	25,068
1993–94 [1]									
All institutions	46,364	60,649	45,278	37,630	28,828	32,729	40,584	49,579	40,058
4-year	47,969	61,824	45,656	37,901	28,226	32,620	34,099	51,133	40,785
University	54,357	69,644	48,856	41,367	29,174	34,077	34,196	57,799	44,410
Other 4-year	44,235	56,170	43,759	36,208	27,935	31,496	34,084	46,786	39,154
2-year	40,689	49,173	41,534	35,117	30,279	34,542	41,040	42,634	38,314
Public institutions	45,920	59,354	45,375	37,913	29,003	31,887	41,229	48,956	40,118
4-year	48,019	60,869	45,903	38,323	28,039	31,652	34,733	50,989	41,031
University	51,493	65,327	47,089	39,979	27,503	32,455	32,219	54,734	42,322
Other 4-year	45,677	57,406	45,064	37,344	28,247	31,174	35,772	48,232	40,328
2-year	41,040	49,435	41,922	35,448	30,531	34,943	41,372	42,938	38,707
Private institutions	47,465	63,503	45,080	37,100	28,356	35,472	31,854	51,076	39,902
4-year	47,880	63,661	45,219	37,214	28,550	35,572	33,820	51,397	40,378
University	60,962	79,043	53,219	44,628	34,299	37,014	38,163	64,745	49,484
Other 4-year	42,028	53,993	41,829	34,649	27,474	33,147	33,524	44,477	37,501
2-year	28,435	35,540	30,200	27,901	23,813	19,933	27,978	30,783	26,142

[1] Preliminary data.

NOTE.—Data for 1990–91 through 1993–94 include imputations for nonrespondent institutions.

SOURCE: U.S. Department of Education, National Center for Education Statistics, *Faculty Salaries, Tenure, and Fringe Benefits, 1980–81*; and Integrated Postsecondary Education Data System (IPEDS), "Salaries, Tenure, and Fringe Benefits of Full-Time Instructional Faculty" surveys. (This table was prepared November 1994.)

Table 228.—Average salary of full-time instructional faculty on 9–month contracts in institutions of higher education, by type and control of institution and by state: 1993–94 [1]

State or other area	All institutions	Public institutions					Private institutions				
		Total	4-year institutions			2-year	Total	4-year institutions			2-year
			Total	University	Other 4-year			Total	University	Other 4-year	
1	2	3	4	5	6	7	8	9	10	11	12
United States	$46,364	$45,920	$48,019	$51,493	$45,677	$41,040	$47,465	$47,880	$60,962	$42,028	$28,435
Alabama	38,418	39,268	41,248	44,780	38,941	34,037	33,942	34,129	—	34,129	28,181
Alaska	47,917	48,585	48,556	48,470	48,613	51,052	37,705	37,705	—	37,705	—
Arizona	46,825	47,076	49,225	51,258	40,646	43,395	39,994	41,724	—	41,724	24,121
Arkansas	37,222	37,720	39,498	44,127	38,066	29,506	34,794	35,241	—	35,241	13,109
California	54,259	53,999	57,051	65,132	55,493	50,368	55,418	56,089	68,310	48,937	30,608
Colorado	44,008	43,590	46,709	52,388	42,183	31,598	47,060	47,060	50,592	43,466	—
Connecticut	55,483	55,243	58,001	62,965	53,374	46,813	55,757	56,572	71,857	50,236	26,857
Delaware	49,780	49,728	51,371	54,289	36,012	40,011	50,219	50,219	—	50,219	—
District of Columbia	52,586	49,114	49,114	—	49,114	—	53,046	53,046	54,640	40,297	—
Florida	41,543	41,129	45,865	49,280	43,619	35,795	43,131	43,204	52,248	40,176	29,530
Georgia	40,707	40,525	42,401	47,035	41,272	32,096	41,229	41,687	61,822	35,941	27,568
Hawaii	49,958	50,531	55,155	56,327	46,341	42,967	43,631	43,631	—	43,631	—
Idaho	38,813	39,015	39,680	43,464	37,993	33,977	38,066	34,194	—	34,194	39,034
Illinois	47,435	45,766	46,076	49,697	42,769	45,283	50,458	50,700	66,146	40,698	29,700
Indiana	44,921	45,024	45,902	48,205	41,216	34,211	44,710	44,870	63,709	39,546	29,172
Iowa	43,491	46,686	51,711	54,011	44,717	34,329	38,124	38,326	47,950	36,907	30,160
Kansas	38,481	40,160	42,973	44,837	38,309	33,478	28,236	28,687	—	28,687	22,054
Kentucky	39,393	40,934	43,646	49,500	40,181	31,339	33,591	33,756	—	33,756	25,846
Louisiana	39,304	37,787	38,643	46,409	36,596	30,464	46,497	46,497	53,436	34,892	—
Maine	41,232	40,509	42,521	45,096	40,753	32,514	43,257	43,663	—	43,663	24,047
Maryland	46,212	45,642	47,376	52,906	44,639	42,617	48,177	48,225	65,478	40,466	25,839
Massachusetts	54,233	49,015	52,946	60,961	49,899	39,721	57,133	57,561	64,905	49,318	31,709
Michigan	49,152	51,188	51,919	56,910	47,692	48,882	38,783	39,293	42,240	38,941	26,828
Minnesota	44,617	46,077	48,805	57,010	44,766	41,376	40,980	41,221	—	41,221	32,702
Mississippi	35,214	35,575	39,433	43,214	37,213	30,636	32,569	33,570	—	33,570	21,406
Missouri	41,786	41,874	43,187	49,124	42,027	37,318	41,608	42,306	55,217	34,796	28,468
Montana	36,549	37,365	38,357	39,587	35,662	27,701	30,054	30,417	—	30,417	23,373
Nebraska	41,663	43,172	45,931	52,303	41,371	30,879	37,079	37,079	—	33,629	—
Nevada	45,505	45,620	47,239	50,984	44,966	40,736	33,359	37,401	43,672	37,401	21,233
New Hampshire	45,173	43,148	45,409	48,114	41,276	33,682	47,730	48,338	—	48,338	22,760
New Jersey	55,629	55,678	59,045	67,727	55,879	48,185	55,507	55,713	68,492	45,964	17,098
New Mexico	40,008	40,089	43,306	45,297	37,461	30,270	38,308	38,308	—	38,308	—
New York	52,498	52,636	55,176	59,195	54,560	48,027	52,348	52,819	61,520	47,194	22,617
North Carolina	42,202	42,818	45,208	52,389	42,183	27,454	40,817	41,403	59,302	33,633	28,460
North Dakota	34,379	35,205	36,618	37,926	33,880	29,874	28,559	30,261	—	30,261	20,426
Ohio	45,830	47,276	49,841	51,080	45,484	38,902	42,449	42,590	59,605	40,681	19,744
Oklahoma	39,255	38,859	40,796	44,922	37,472	32,769	41,001	41,668	51,340	36,420	22,867
Oregon	42,161	41,800	44,890	46,806	42,473	38,321	43,796	43,796	—	43,796	—
Pennsylvania	50,390	51,461	52,646	56,677	50,378	45,218	49,116	49,629	64,430	44,656	27,109
Rhode Island	49,560	48,469	51,037	54,472	45,257	40,398	50,429	50,429	—	50,429	—
South Carolina	37,101	37,697	42,078	47,035	37,019	28,085	34,530	34,640	—	34,640	29,494
South Dakota	34,877	35,818	35,929	36,310	35,347	24,780	31,222	31,243	—	31,243	28,500
Tennessee	41,382	41,716	44,485	49,563	42,688	32,652	40,622	41,014	62,247	33,234	24,810
Texas	43,158	42,461	45,110	50,632	40,248	37,760	46,119	46,294	54,490	40,155	22,681
Utah	42,111	40,120	42,330	46,380	36,177	31,244	46,533	46,664	47,568	35,403	33,209
Vermont	40,842	42,792	43,599	45,743	35,972	33,087	39,036	39,953	—	39,953	19,700
Virginia	44,226	45,154	48,313	52,696	45,345	35,503	41,028	41,257	—	41,257	26,573
Washington	43,782	44,231	49,187	52,251	43,953	37,607	41,930	41,930	—	41,930	—
West Virginia	36,486	37,247	37,806	43,704	34,959	29,378	32,173	32,173	—	32,173	—
Wisconsin	45,306	46,306	48,040	58,260	44,231	43,548	40,524	40,524	51,882	36,766	—
Wyoming	37,422	37,422	44,923	44,923	—	30,162	—	—	—	—	—
U.S. Service Schools	56,789	56,789	56,789	—	56,789	—	—	—	—	—	—
Outlying areas	24,793	32,683	32,075	29,952	35,466	35,715	8,238	9,062	—	9,062	6,413
American Samoa	37,530	37,530	—	—	—	37,530	—	—	—	—	—
Federated States of Micronesia	20,001	20,001	—	—	—	20,001	—	—	—	—	—
Guam	46,374	46,374	50,001	—	50,001	41,877	—	—	—	—	—
Marshall Islands	—	—	—	—	—	—	—	—	—	—	—
Northern Marianas	30,005	30,005	—	—	—	30,005	—	—	—	—	—
Palau	36,360	36,360	—	—	—	36,360	—	—	—	—	—
Puerto Rico	21,222	29,523	29,279	29,952	27,489	33,783	8,238	9,062	—	9,062	6,413
Virgin Islands	43,801	43,801	43,801	—	43,801	—	—	—	—	—	—

[1] Preliminary data.

—Data not reported or not applicable.

NOTE.—Data include imputations for nonrespondent institutions.

SOURCE: U.S. Department of Education, National Center for Education Statistics, Integrated Postsecondary Education Data System (IPEDS), "Salaries, Tenure, and Fringe Benefits of Full-Time Instructional Faculty, 1993–94" survey. (This table was prepared November 1994.)

Table 229.—Average salary of full-time instructional faculty on 9-month contracts in institutions of higher education, by type and control of institution and by state: 1992–93

State or other area	All institutions	Public institutions					Private institutions				
		Total	4-year institutions			2-year	Total	4-year institutions			2-year
			Total	University	Other 4-year			Total	University	Other 4-year	
1	2	3	4	5	6	7	8	9	10	11	12
United States	$44,714	$44,197	$46,515	$49,906	$44,212	$38,935	$45,985	$46,427	$59,005	$40,692	$26,105
Alabama	36,813	37,430	39,472	42,913	37,150	32,293	33,425	33,572	—	33,572	28,649
Alaska	45,765	46,281	46,281	44,193	47,643	—	37,718	38,497	—	38,497	20,579
Arizona	43,030	43,340	46,584	48,184	40,087	38,487	35,973	36,984	—	36,984	24,614
Arkansas	36,127	36,684	38,169	41,984	36,979	29,051	33,420	33,854	—	33,854	12,727
California	51,516	51,102	57,546	66,047	55,873	44,495	53,510	54,156	65,978	47,190	28,480
Colorado	43,474	43,315	46,391	52,270	41,711	31,123	44,627	44,911	48,526	41,132	20,579
Connecticut	53,238	52,540	55,260	60,556	50,151	44,000	54,005	54,436	68,463	48,534	28,289
Delaware	48,247	48,557	49,987	52,429	36,879	38,898	45,710	45,710	—	45,710	—
District of Columbia	51,556	47,153	47,153	—	47,153	—	52,178	52,178	53,710	40,007	—
Florida	39,989	39,522	44,117	47,492	41,888	34,265	41,675	41,821	49,689	39,269	23,607
Georgia	39,738	39,760	41,549	45,855	40,427	31,770	39,674	40,374	58,430	35,038	26,771
Hawaii	50,519	50,932	55,493	56,628	47,091	43,276	44,852	44,852	—	44,852	—
Idaho	35,626	38,046	38,728	42,520	37,064	32,783	27,281	31,379	—	31,379	26,390
Illinois	46,055	44,878	45,087	48,441	41,942	44,552	48,204	48,461	63,628	38,442	28,035
Indiana	43,734	43,722	44,768	46,945	40,196	31,833	43,759	43,933	61,509	38,572	27,833
Iowa	42,349	45,660	51,265	53,458	44,633	32,973	36,598	37,008	45,407	35,756	23,224
Kansas	37,433	39,138	41,818	43,546	37,468	32,509	27,528	27,883	—	27,883	22,660
Kentucky	38,101	39,542	42,088	48,061	38,598	30,310	32,606	32,984	—	32,984	21,379
Louisiana	38,989	37,769	38,493	46,209	36,380	30,848	44,900	44,900	51,769	33,395	.
Maine	40,621	40,032	42,062	45,000	40,121	31,710	42,365	42,442	—	42,442	24,702
Maryland	45,307	44,961	46,667	51,861	44,094	42,007	46,530	46,613	63,321	39,327	23,912
Massachusetts	51,232	43,411	47,012	53,463	44,545	34,970	55,400	55,876	63,071	47,569	30,892
Michigan	47,606	49,471	49,948	54,408	46,122	48,097	38,114	38,626	41,195	38,326	25,507
Minnesota	44,328	46,430	47,995	57,005	43,581	41,918	39,749	39,965	—	39,965	29,316
Mississippi	33,516	33,679	37,782	41,693	35,506	28,553	32,345	33,292	—	33,292	21,440
Missouri	40,306	40,216	41,296	45,841	40,385	36,323	40,508	40,805	53,143	33,021	28,311
Montana	36,545	37,490	38,481	39,797	35,544	27,120	28,802	29,247	—	29,247	22,710
Nebraska	41,051	42,543	45,551	51,866	41,001	31,325	36,273	36,273	41,851	33,165	—
Nevada	44,959	45,049	47,110	49,913	45,325	38,991	32,910	32,910	—	32,910	—
New Hampshire	45,448	44,923	47,076	50,542	41,594	36,096	46,054	46,746	—	46,746	22,118
New Jersey	53,308	53,252	56,904	63,325	54,320	45,854	53,433	53,745	65,362	45,067	22,670
New Mexico	38,749	38,815	42,031	43,962	36,062	29,047	37,185	37,185	—	37,185	—
New York	50,015	49,611	51,649	56,618	50,847	45,891	50,421	50,722	59,604	45,214	24,931
North Carolina	40,473	40,753	43,230	49,397	40,569	26,113	39,854	40,460	57,436	33,490	27,683
North Dakota	34,113	35,007	36,323	37,394	33,846	29,872	27,509	29,040	—	29,040	20,400
Ohio	44,558	46,131	48,497	49,635	44,614	37,891	40,933	41,094	57,681	39,355	25,339
Oklahoma	37,899	38,092	39,972	43,643	36,928	32,142	37,067	37,572	47,894	32,104	22,312
Oregon	39,950	39,769	42,466	44,626	39,986	36,609	40,761	40,810	—	40,810	20,579
Pennsylvania	47,856	47,794	48,684	53,668	45,963	42,976	47,930	48,635	64,470	43,300	26,238
Rhode Island	48,679	45,972	48,313	51,320	43,187	38,515	50,607	50,607	—	50,607	—
South Carolina	36,789	37,475	41,738	46,361	36,910	27,928	33,788	33,883	—	33,883	29,466
South Dakota	34,269	35,303	35,303	35,450	35,070	35,627	30,730	30,730	—	30,730	—
Tennessee	38,820	38,777	41,280	45,796	39,708	30,401	38,917	39,453	59,301	31,882	20,416
Texas	40,869	40,205	43,199	48,565	38,354	35,085	43,802	43,944	52,384	37,282	22,846
Utah	42,688	38,917	42,048	44,914	35,846	30,876	47,828	47,898	48,529	33,259	32,525
Vermont	40,517	43,030	43,874	46,562	34,695	33,276	38,330	39,245	—	39,245	19,078
Virginia	43,227	44,265	47,241	51,365	44,461	35,172	39,711	39,872	—	39,872	27,836
Washington	42,428	42,886	47,922	50,963	42,936	36,215	40,483	40,483	—	40,483	—
West Virginia	34,646	35,268	35,793	41,606	32,932	27,565	30,994	30,994	—	30,994	—
Wisconsin	43,961	44,921	46,792	56,876	43,044	41,866	39,349	39,383	50,650	35,592	24,702
Wyoming	37,397	37,430	44,865	44,865	—	29,893	20,579	—	—	—	20,579
U.S. Service Schools	53,230	53,230	53,230	—	53,230	—	—	—	—	—	—
Outlying areas	22,421	30,392	30,086	27,042	34,051	32,501	7,634	7,915	—	7,915	6,778
American Samoa	34,170	34,170	—	—	—	34,170	—	—	—	—	—
Federated States of Micronesia	18,520	18,520	—	—	—	18,520	—	—	—	—	—
Guam	47,510	47,510	49,431	—	49,431	41,077	—	—	—	—	—
Northern Marianas	30,526	30,526	—	—	—	30,526	—	—	—	—	—
Palau	34,160	34,160	—	—	—	34,160	—	—	—	—	—
Puerto Rico	19,233	27,293	27,038	27,042	27,032	32,306	7,634	7,915	—	7,915	6,778
Virgin Islands	43,161	43,161	43,161	—	43,161	—	—	—	—	—	—

—Data not reported or not applicable.

NOTE.—Data include imputations for nonrespondent institutions.

SOURCE: U.S. Department of Education, National Center for Education Statistics, Integrated Postsecondary Education Data System (IPEDS), "Salaries, Tenure, and Fringe Benefits of Full-Time Instructional Faculty, 1992–93" survey. (This table was prepared October 1993.)

Table 230.—Average salary of full-time instructional faculty on 9-month contracts in 4-year institutions of higher education, by type and control of institution and rank of faculty and by state: 1993–94 [1]

State or other area	Public university			Public other 4-year			Private university			Private other 4-year		
	Professor	Associate professor	Assistant professor	Professor	Associate professor	Assistant professor	Professor	Associate professor	Assistant professor	Professor	Associate professor	Assistant professor
1	2	3	4	5	6	7	8	9	10	11	12	13
United States	$65,327	$47,089	$39,979	$57,406	$45,064	$37,344	$79,043	$53,219	$44,628	$53,993	$41,829	$34,649
Alabama	59,077	43,852	37,457	50,627	40,890	34,712	—	—	—	44,521	34,605	30,165
Alaska	64,546	55,213	43,409	60,461	50,407	40,480	—	—	—	45,495	40,620	33,878
Arizona	62,975	45,610	40,888	50,652	42,069	35,879	—	—	—	49,241	46,583	31,267
Arkansas	56,376	44,331	38,641	49,716	39,780	34,153	—	—	—	40,839	35,320	30,543
California	78,006	52,343	44,316	63,097	48,507	40,196	83,693	57,491	48,334	61,627	46,476	38,490
Colorado	62,386	47,597	41,466	50,666	42,123	36,049	62,487	47,522	43,239	56,219	44,442	33,532
Connecticut	75,702	57,316	46,848	65,663	52,586	39,818	93,045	52,638	44,852	62,839	47,413	40,039
Delaware	71,397	53,332	42,254	52,482	41,568	34,501	—	—	—	59,579	53,164	40,318
District of Columbia	—	—	—	55,909	47,596	39,006	72,384	50,476	41,412	57,389	43,947	35,365
Florida	59,590	40,881	38,660	54,753	41,546	37,623	70,338	51,015	42,251	54,444	39,755	33,869
Georgia	61,765	44,702	37,255	53,265	42,805	35,687	80,171	54,375	45,421	45,899	37,111	30,908
Hawaii	70,790	52,743	45,802	56,030	45,164	41,975	—	—	—	53,081	43,069	40,098
Idaho	50,767	41,122	38,239	44,770	37,490	33,612	—	—	—	36,615	30,598	
Illinois	63,915	46,246	38,932	52,301	42,322	36,956	85,031	56,547	47,430	50,643	41,369	34,974
Indiana	62,435	45,706	37,946	56,181	43,093	37,051	79,751	56,189	46,958	48,402	38,924	33,417
Iowa	69,191	50,189	41,325	58,595	46,905	38,948	59,938	45,936	40,069	45,834	37,079	31,919
Kansas	56,144	41,678	36,284	47,921	39,014	33,114	—	—	—	33,801	30,157	25,542
Kentucky	61,932	45,157	39,763	49,852	41,077	34,744	—	—	—	42,415	34,402	29,584
Louisiana	61,831	44,225	38,465	47,418	38,561	33,335	67,736	49,054	41,206	44,579	35,622	32,304
Maine	57,428	43,726	36,612	50,387	40,361	32,664	—	—	—	60,495	43,785	34,564
Maryland	69,306	48,268	40,677	57,316	45,548	38,906	80,605	55,537	45,475	51,040	41,282	35,431
Massachusetts	70,492	53,782	44,135	56,923	48,387	40,052	84,963	54,840	46,438	64,164	47,017	38,781
Michigan	70,682	52,894	44,471	57,635	47,220	39,696	52,729	42,785	35,623	47,369	38,484	33,676
Minnesota	67,802	47,181	42,305	54,730	42,598	35,903	—	—	—	52,926	40,546	34,364
Mississippi	53,665	42,346	38,673	47,854	39,898	33,800	—	—	—	41,324	34,747	29,295
Missouri	60,636	44,861	40,838	53,017	43,036	36,472	71,532	49,388	43,278	42,920	36,491	31,192
Montana	46,327	38,625	33,565	43,496	35,792	30,313	—	—	—	36,640	30,681	27,199
Nebraska	66,907	47,162	42,189	51,169	43,190	36,646	64,553	45,408	33,618	40,667	34,356	30,145
Nevada	64,850	48,276	39,386	59,828	47,758	39,246	—	—	—	62,191	30,484	28,306
New Hampshire	59,173	45,419	37,435	50,525	40,793	34,502	—	—	—	66,038	43,203	35,990
New Jersey	86,228	61,194	48,353	70,270	55,286	43,519	91,961	56,417	42,778	56,206	45,681	37,303
New Mexico	56,630	43,273	37,243	48,147	38,404	32,550	—	—	—	39,039	33,610	28,387
New York	74,644	53,322	42,016	67,718	51,794	41,590	77,729	54,211	44,968	60,798	47,132	38,262
North Carolina	67,498	47,791	40,812	53,642	43,318	37,609	74,895	53,254	44,528	42,043	34,611	29,902
North Dakota	46,554	39,102	34,626	43,210	37,132	31,898	—	—	—	39,091	33,087	29,707
Ohio	64,742	47,593	39,392	59,583	44,713	37,475	75,846	51,757	47,831	51,208	40,332	33,770
Oklahoma	55,935	42,396	37,217	46,104	39,472	35,490	68,645	49,995	40,423	46,371	37,685	27,983
Oregon	59,039	45,658	38,801	50,028	40,499	35,496	—	—	—	55,096	39,644	34,825
Pennsylvania	73,358	53,087	43,210	66,108	51,990	41,496	81,900	56,501	47,248	57,222	44,331	36,645
Rhode Island	63,458	47,921	42,242	51,746	44,194	38,116	—	—	—	69,010	47,366	39,712
South Carolina	59,098	43,598	38,271	45,903	38,847	32,118	—	—	—	45,176	35,069	29,315
South Dakota	45,479	36,471	33,481	44,218	36,552	31,155	—	—	—	40,775	32,683	29,177
Tennessee	58,944	45,440	40,307	52,578	42,486	35,420	80,778	52,279	44,095	41,294	33,883	29,468
Texas	66,476	45,013	39,529	51,168	42,022	35,654	70,894	49,814	44,175	51,118	40,170	32,784
Utah	58,325	41,988	37,594	44,947	36,320	32,597	59,276	45,197	38,079	44,249	36,680	32,330
Vermont	60,339	44,704	36,916	43,263	36,073	29,975	—	—	—	52,382	39,116	34,254
Virginia	68,022	47,715	40,888	57,150	45,441	37,046	—	—	—	52,849	40,432	33,454
Washington	65,675	46,837	40,825	50,395	41,920	35,225	—	—	—	51,723	41,889	35,502
West Virginia	54,422	43,124	36,269	43,582	35,369	29,418	—	—	—	39,428	34,017	29,212
Wisconsin	67,082	49,677	44,196	52,760	43,073	37,679	69,536	51,141	41,485	45,438	37,507	31,359
Wyoming	54,441	41,744	37,655	—	—	—	—	—	—	—	—	—
U.S. Service Schools	—	—	—	67,502	53,576	44,480	—	—	—	—	—	—
Outlying areas	36,996	30,384	25,469	45,814	37,485	32,176	—	—	—	30,552	26,452	22,858
American Samoa	—	—	—	—	—	—	—	—	—	—	—	—
Federated States of Micronesia	—	—	—	—	—	—	—	—	—	—	—	—
Guam	—	—	—	68,717	54,827	43,464	—	—	—	—	—	—
Marshall Islands	—	—	—	—	—	—	—	—	—	—	—	—
Northern Marianas	—	—	—	—	—	—	—	—	—	—	—	—
Palau	—	—	—	—	—	—	—	—	—	—	—	—
Puerto Rico	36,996	30,384	25,469	36,042	29,218	24,719	—	—	—	30,552	26,452	22,858
Virgin Islands	—	—	—	55,512	45,173	38,194	—	—	—	—	—	—

[1] Preliminary data.

—Data not reported or not applicable.

NOTE.—Data include imputations for nonrespondent institutions.

SOURCE: U.S. Department of Education, National Center for Education Statistics, Integrated Postsecondary Education Data System (IPEDS), "Salaries, Tenure, and Fringe Benefits of Full-Time Instructional Faculty, 1993–94" survey. (This table was prepared November 1994.)

Table 231.—Average salary of full-time instructional faculty on 9-month contracts in 4-year institutions of higher education, by type and control of institution and rank of faculty and by state: 1992–93

State or other area	Public university			Public other 4-year			Private university			Private other 4-year		
	Professor	Associate professor	Assistant professor	Professor	Associate professor	Assistant professor	Professor	Associate professor	Assistant professor	Professor	Associate professor	Assistant professor
1	2	3	4	5	6	7	8	9	10	11	12	13
United States	**$63,452**	**$45,746**	**$38,878**	**$55,642**	**$43,622**	**$36,226**	**$76,561**	**$51,654**	**$43,686**	**$52,283**	**$40,659**	**$33,625**
Alabama	56,203	41,925	35,555	48,287	39,003	33,323	—	—	—	43,531	34,750	28,973
Alaska	59,459	50,916	39,077	60,205	50,345	40,534	—	—	—	49,461	40,648	32,260
Arizona	61,566	44,772	39,696	50,585	41,215	34,497	—	—	—	47,211	41,700	30,051
Arkansas	55,394	42,448	37,170	48,556	39,285	33,500	—	—	—	39,755	34,225	28,342
California	79,248	53,468	44,715	63,656	49,340	40,922	81,069	56,745	46,489	60,201	44,848	37,332
Colorado	61,808	46,942	41,048	49,901	41,046	35,722	60,657	45,002	41,311	53,267	42,979	32,491
Connecticut	72,792	55,112	45,046	61,832	49,460	38,355	90,288	53,253	43,865	60,313	46,472	39,208
Delaware	69,284	51,242	40,841	50,666	45,213	35,273	—	—	—	58,647	50,087	34,399
District of Columbia	—	—	—	55,363	47,434	34,508	70,861	49,439	40,153	56,980	43,045	35,086
Florida	57,458	39,289	37,275	52,754	40,005	36,246	67,667	48,318	39,959	52,238	38,595	32,413
Georgia	60,636	43,373	36,728	51,844	41,294	35,038	75,051	51,478	43,486	45,066	36,563	30,381
Hawaii	71,725	53,134	46,177	56,886	45,171	41,354	—	—	—	57,448	39,909	35,467
Idaho	49,318	40,049	38,379	43,391	36,517	32,879	—	—	—	29,173	23,850	—
Illinois	62,394	45,134	37,813	50,872	41,078	35,922	82,155	54,362	46,238	47,792	39,854	33,575
Indiana	60,630	45,101	36,901	54,567	42,247	35,894	77,373	54,390	45,552	47,224	37,775	32,890
Iowa	68,291	49,633	41,028	57,508	46,754	38,881	55,725	42,096	37,970	44,635	36,148	30,801
Kansas	54,318	40,823	35,255	46,470	38,224	32,197	—	—	—	32,901	29,072	25,111
Kentucky	60,177	43,967	37,942	47,227	39,619	33,957	—	—	—	41,756	33,681	28,716
Louisiana	61,807	44,741	38,558	46,926	38,614	33,238	66,659	47,889	39,350	42,716	34,123	30,814
Maine	57,323	43,717	36,785	50,047	40,791	32,564	—	—	—	57,614	41,863	33,954
Maryland	67,609	47,650	40,118	56,981	45,335	38,383	77,515	51,661	43,929	49,895	40,306	34,783
Massachusetts	62,201	46,457	38,369	50,735	43,212	35,711	82,067	53,742	45,900	62,223	46,014	37,677
Michigan	67,440	50,618	43,271	55,980	45,581	38,536	51,082	41,924	35,000	46,850	38,452	32,390
Minnesota	67,600	47,617	42,545	52,431	42,779	35,724	—	—	—	51,598	39,442	33,135
Mississippi	50,453	40,794	37,568	45,989	37,477	32,328	—	—	—	43,440	33,574	28,467
Missouri	57,077	42,148	39,090	50,787	41,289	35,234	68,480	47,432	41,884	40,503	34,389	29,726
Montana	46,935	38,991	34,618	43,484	36,587	30,030	—	—	—	34,723	30,503	25,248
Nebraska	66,061	46,812	41,866	50,922	42,804	36,826	61,822	43,392	33,255	40,208	33,586	29,927
Nevada	63,556	47,394	39,157	59,838	48,345	39,449	—	—	—	54,593	30,185	31,246
New Hampshire	63,306	46,773	39,411	50,536	40,776	35,033	—	—	—	64,553	41,965	34,789
New Jersey	80,474	57,349	45,475	68,412	53,868	42,490	88,554	53,998	42,363	55,508	45,054	36,033
New Mexico	54,583	41,867	36,092	45,466	37,390	31,223	—	—	—	36,779	31,126	26,783
New York	72,143	51,341	39,790	63,256	48,347	39,157	75,407	52,366	44,245	58,588	45,217	36,603
North Carolina	64,884	44,309	37,316	51,436	41,435	35,818	72,746	51,601	42,876	41,384	34,217	29,495
North Dakota	46,426	38,806	33,827	42,310	36,654	31,307	—	—	—	37,745	31,929	29,158
Ohio	63,038	46,350	38,645	58,164	44,076	36,575	73,349	51,205	45,239	49,351	39,081	33,205
Oklahoma	54,638	41,731	36,346	45,515	39,097	35,044	64,105	46,553	38,862	41,159	34,203	26,073
Oregon	55,476	42,925	37,011	47,627	38,815	34,350	—	—	—	52,221	39,489	33,904
Pennsylvania	69,526	50,902	41,652	60,258	47,696	38,133	81,989	56,183	47,336	55,735	42,970	35,708
Rhode Island	60,150	45,594	40,209	50,081	42,105	36,436	—	—	—	65,719	47,529	39,670
South Carolina	58,801	43,135	38,163	45,813	39,136	32,315	—	—	—	43,102	34,733	28,223
South Dakota	44,371	36,274	32,669	44,054	35,734	30,558	—	—	—	38,769	32,632	28,322
Tennessee	54,148	41,136	36,273	48,719	40,930	31,997	78,645	49,950	43,100	39,711	32,141	28,491
Texas	63,754	43,413	37,816	48,752	40,134	34,572	68,363	48,267	42,448	45,942	38,121	31,259
Utah	56,211	40,618	36,297	45,184	36,059	31,413	60,654	45,001	41,311	41,277	34,312	30,050
Vermont	61,047	44,848	37,402	42,270	35,563	29,502	—	—	—	52,067	38,654	33,512
Virginia	66,091	46,778	39,220	56,544	44,535	36,092	—	—	—	51,330	39,024	32,272
Washington	64,415	45,340	40,302	49,302	41,093	34,092	—	—	—	49,863	40,353	34,223
West Virginia	52,189	40,948	34,746	41,069	33,650	27,584	—	—	—	38,066	32,396	28,158
Wisconsin	65,963	48,310	42,838	51,236	41,875	37,344	67,209	49,926	41,094	44,631	36,317	30,021
Wyoming	53,753	42,276	37,467	—	—	—	—	—	—	—	—	—
U.S. Service Schools	—	—	—	65,018	50,492	41,001	—	—	—	—	—	—
Outlying areas	34,103	28,038	23,613	45,823	35,948	30,924	—	—	—	31,958	24,891	11,940
American Samoa	—	—	—	—	—	—	—	—	—	—	—	—
Federated States of Micronesia	—	—	—	—	—	—	—	—	—	—	—	—
Guam	—	—	—	69,457	51,400	45,053	—	—	—	—	—	—
Northern Marianas	—	—	—	—	—	—	—	—	—	—	—	—
Palau	—	—	—	—	—	—	—	—	—	—	—	—
Puerto Rico	34,103	28,038	23,613	36,127	29,602	24,475	—	—	—	31,958	24,891	11,940
Virgin Islands	—	—	—	54,560	43,560	37,661	—	—	—	—	—	—

—Data not reported or not applicable.

NOTE.—Data include imputations for nonrespondent institutions.

SOURCE: U.S. Department of Education, National Center for Education Statistics, Integrated Postsecondary Education Data System (IPEDS), "Salaries, Tenure, and Fringe Benefits of Full-Time Instructional Faculty, 1992–93" survey. (This table was prepared October 1993.)

Table 232.—Full-time instructional faculty with tenure for institutions reporting tenure status, by academic rank, sex, and type and control of institution: 1980–81, 1990–91, 1992–93, and 1993–94

Academic year, type, and control of institution	Percent with tenure, by rank							Percent with tenure, by sex	
	All ranks	Professor	Associate professor	Assistant professor	Instructor	Lecturer	No academic rank	Men	Women
1	2	3	4	5	6	7	8	9	10
1980–81									
All institutions	64.8	95.8	82.9	27.9	9.2	11.9	77.4	70.0	49.7
4-year	62.7	95.8	82.2	24.1	6.6	10.7	24.7	68.3	44.0
University	64.5	96.7	83.7	15.3	5.4	4.3	3.5	70.0	41.0
Other 4-year	61.3	94.9	81.2	29.7	7.1	17.8	32.4	67.0	45.5
2-year	74.5	95.6	89.2	58.9	19.8	34.8	81.1	78.8	66.6
Public institutions	68.0	96.6	85.9	32.5	11.8	14.3	79.4	72.8	54.0
4-year	65.7	96.6	85.3	27.6	8.7	12.8	12.2	71.1	47.5
University	66.0	96.9	86.5	16.8	6.1	4.9	4.5	71.3	42.8
Other 4-year	65.5	96.3	84.4	35.5	10.0	21.4	17.2	70.9	50.2
2-year	75.2	95.9	89.5	59.5	20.3	35.8	81.8	79.3	67.5
Private institutions	55.9	93.8	75.2	17.5	3.0	1.5	43.4	62.2	37.2
4-year	56.0	93.8	75.2	17.4	2.8	1.5	37.5	62.2	37.2
University	60.4	96.3	75.8	11.5	3.5	1.8	0.6	66.3	36.5
Other 4-year	53.6	92.0	74.9	20.2	2.6	1.2	43.4	59.8	37.4
2-year	49.5	84.7	77.3	35.2	8.8	—	52.2	57.3	39.5
1990–91									
All institutions	61.2	95.6	80.8	18.6	6.8	6.9	36.3	67.8	45.3
4-year	61.7	95.7	80.4	15.8	4.1	6.0	19.1	68.6	43.9
University	65.2	97.2	85.4	9.0	3.5	2.1	1.4	71.6	43.6
Other 4-year	59.4	94.6	77.1	19.7	4.3	9.2	30.2	66.3	44.0
2-year	57.1	93.7	85.3	50.7	16.3	26.6	39.8	60.9	51.9
Public institutions	62.9	96.3	83.7	21.7	8.6	8.4	36.6	69.4	47.4
4-year	64.0	96.5	83.5	18.0	5.3	7.3	11.3	70.8	45.9
University	66.3	97.3	88.3	9.7	4.2	2.4	0.4	72.8	44.5
Other 4-year	62.3	95.9	79.9	23.4	5.7	10.6	23.5	69.1	46.7
2-year	57.3	93.7	85.6	51.4	16.7	26.7	39.7	61.0	52.2
Private institutions	56.7	93.9	73.8	11.8	1.5	1.0	33.3	63.7	39.8
4-year	56.8	93.9	73.8	11.6	1.4	1.0	31.2	63.7	39.8
University	62.2	96.9	77.4	7.3	1.4	1.4	6.5	68.5	41.3
Other 4-year	53.9	91.9	72.0	13.5	1.5	0.5	36.3	60.9	39.2
2-year	45.7	90.2	70.9	29.0	4.3	—	49.7	53.1	39.3
1992–93									
All institutions	63.4	95.8	81.3	17.3	9.0	6.4	71.4	70.1	48.9
4-year	61.7	95.9	80.8	14.1	4.2	5.3	21.3	68.9	44.1
University	65.4	97.3	85.7	7.4	3.1	1.7	1.5	72.3	44.2
Other 4-year	59.2	94.8	77.6	17.9	4.6	8.4	28.9	66.5	44.0
2-year	71.2	94.6	86.3	51.1	20.4	21.0	75.9	76.8	63.9
Public institutions	66.3	96.7	84.8	20.7	11.2	7.8	74.1	72.8	52.4
4-year	64.4	97.0	84.6	16.2	5.4	6.5	12.9	71.6	46.3
University	67.2	97.7	89.1	8.0	3.8	1.8	2.0	74.0	45.7
Other 4-year	62.4	96.3	81.0	21.5	6.0	9.8	19.3	69.6	46.7
2-year	72.0	94.7	86.5	52.5	20.8	21.2	77.0	77.5	64.9
Private institutions	56.1	93.6	73.6	10.7	2.2	1.2	37.7	63.5	40.0
4-year	56.4	93.6	73.6	10.6	2.1	1.2	30.3	63.6	40.1
University	61.0	96.1	76.8	5.9	1.0	1.6	0.4	67.8	40.8
Other 4-year	54.0	92.0	72.1	12.6	2.3	0.6	36.7	61.2	39.8
2-year	44.8	89.1	75.5	17.6	6.7	—	46.6	52.0	37.4
1993–94 [1]									
All institutions	64.2	96.0	81.8	17.0	7.0	2.2	76.2	71.0	49.9
4-year	62.3	96.3	81.6	14.2	4.0	1.8	22.8	69.8	44.8
University	66.4	97.6	86.5	7.9	2.6	1.8	3.8	73.5	45.2
Other 4-year	59.7	95.3	78.4	17.6	4.5	1.9	30.7	67.1	44.6
2-year	72.9	92.6	84.1	46.9	15.9	8.4	80.4	78.1	66.2
Public institutions	67.0	96.9	85.5	20.2	8.9	2.4	78.0	73.7	53.3
4-year	65.1	97.4	85.7	16.3	5.2	2.0	13.6	72.5	47.1
University	68.2	98.0	90.0	8.6	3.2	1.9	2.0	75.3	46.7
Other 4-year	62.8	96.9	82.4	21.1	6.1	2.0	20.0	70.2	47.3
2-year	73.2	93.0	84.4	47.8	16.2	8.4	80.6	78.4	66.6
Private institutions	57.0	93.9	73.7	10.6	1.6	1.4	52.8	64.4	40.9
4-year	56.9	94.0	73.8	10.6	1.6	1.4	32.5	64.4	40.7
University	61.9	96.4	77.4	6.2	0.8	1.5	6.8	68.9	41.6
Other 4-year	54.5	92.5	72.1	12.3	1.8	1.1	40.0	61.8	40.4
2-year	61.9	66.7	67.3	19.2	1.8	—	73.6	70.2	49.8

[1] Preliminary data.
—Data not available or not applicable.

SOURCE: U.S. Department of Education, National Center for Education Statistics, Faculty Salaries, Tenure, and Fringe Benefits; and Integrated Postsecondary Education Data System (IPEDS), "Salaries, Tenure, and Fringe Benefits of Full-Time Instructional Faculty" surveys. (This table was prepared April 1995.)

Table 233.—Institutions of higher education, by control and type of institution: 1949–50 to 1994–95

Year	All institutions			Public			Private		
	Total	4-year	2-year	Total	4-year	2-year	Total	4-year	2-year
1	2	3	4	5	6	7	8	9	10
Excluding branch campuses									
1949–50	1,851	1,327	524	641	344	297	1,210	983	227
1950–51	1,852	1,312	540	636	341	295	1,216	971	245
1951–52	1,832	1,326	506	641	350	291	1,191	976	215
1952–53	1,882	1,355	527	639	349	290	1,243	1,006	237
1953–54	1,863	1,345	518	662	369	293	1,201	976	225
1954–55	1,849	1,333	516	648	353	295	1,201	980	221
1955–56	1,850	1,347	503	650	360	290	1,200	987	213
1956–57	1,878	1,355	523	656	359	297	1,222	996	226
1957–58	1,930	1,390	540	666	366	300	1,264	1,024	240
1958–59	1,947	1,394	553	673	366	307	1,274	1,028	246
1959–60	2,004	1,422	582	695	367	328	1,309	1,055	254
1960–61	2,021	1,431	590	700	368	332	1,321	1,063	258
1961–62	2,033	1,443	590	718	374	344	1,315	1,069	246
1962–63	2,093	1,468	625	740	376	364	1,353	1,092	261
1963–64	2,132	1,499	633	760	386	374	1,372	1,113	259
1964–65	2,175	1,521	654	799	393	406	1,376	1,128	248
1965–66	2,230	1,551	679	821	401	420	1,409	1,150	259
1966–67	2,329	1,577	752	880	403	477	1,449	1,174	275
1967–68	2,374	1,588	786	934	414	520	1,440	1,174	266
1968–69	2,483	1,619	864	1,011	417	594	1,472	1,202	270
1969–70	2,525	1,639	886	1,060	426	634	1,465	1,213	252
1970–71	2,556	1,665	891	1,089	435	654	1,467	1,230	237
1971–72	2,606	1,675	931	1,137	440	697	1,469	1,235	234
1972–73	2,665	1,701	964	1,182	449	733	1,483	1,252	231
1973–74	2,720	1,717	1,003	1,200	440	760	1,520	1,277	243
1974–75	2,747	1,744	1,003	1,214	447	767	1,533	1,297	236
1975–76	2,765	1,767	998	1,219	447	772	1,546	1,320	226
1976–77	2,785	1,783	1,002	1,231	452	779	1,554	1,331	223
1977–78	2,826	1,808	1,018	1,241	454	787	1,585	1,354	231
1978–79	2,954	1,843	1,111	1,308	463	845	1,646	1,380	266
1979–80	2,975	1,863	1,112	1,310	464	846	1,665	1,399	266
1980–81	3,056	1,861	1,195	1,334	465	869	1,722	1,396	[1]326
1981–82	3,083	1,883	1,200	1,340	471	869	1,743	1,412	[1]331
1982–83	3,111	1,887	1,224	1,336	472	864	1,775	1,415	[1]360
1983–84	3,117	1,914	1,203	1,325	474	851	1,792	1,440	352
1984–85	3,146	1,911	1,235	1,329	461	868	1,817	1,450	367
1985–86	3,155	1,915	1,240	1,326	461	865	1,829	1,454	375
Including branch campuses									
1974–75	3,004	1,866	1,138	1,433	537	896	1,571	1,329	242
1975–76	3,026	1,898	1,128	1,442	545	897	1,584	1,353	231
1976–77	3,046	1,913	1,133	1,455	550	905	1,591	1,363	228
1977–78	3,095	1,938	1,157	1,473	552	921	1,622	1,386	236
1978–79	3,134	1,941	1,193	1,474	550	924	1,660	1,391	269
1979–80	3,152	1,957	1,195	1,475	549	926	1,677	1,408	269
1980–81	3,231	1,957	1,274	1,497	552	945	1,734	1,405	[1]329
1981–82	3,253	1,979	1,274	1,498	558	940	1,755	1,421	[1]334
1982–83	3,280	1,984	1,296	1,493	560	933	1,787	1,424	[1]363
1983–84	3,284	2,013	1,271	1,481	565	916	1,803	1,448	355
1984–85	3,331	2,025	1,306	1,501	566	935	1,830	1,459	371
1985–86	3,340	2,029	1,311	1,498	566	932	1,842	1,463	379
1986–87 [2]	3,406	2,070	1,336	1,533	573	960	1,873	1,497	376
1987–88 [2]	3,587	2,135	1,452	1,591	599	992	1,996	1,536	460
1988–89 [2]	3,565	2,129	1,436	1,582	598	984	1,983	1,531	452
1989–90 [2]	3,535	2,127	1,408	1,563	595	968	1,972	1,532	440
1990–91 [2]	3,559	2,141	1,418	1,567	595	972	1,992	1,546	446
1991–92 [2]	3,601	2,157	1,444	1,598	599	999	2,003	1,558	445
1992–93 [2]	3,638	2,169	1,469	1,624	600	1,024	2,014	1,569	445
1993–94 [2]	3,632	2,190	1,442	1,625	604	1,021	2,007	1,586	421
1994–95 [2]	3,688	2,215	1,473	1,641	605	1,036	2,047	1,610	437

[1] Large increases are due to the addition of schools accredited by the Accrediting Commission of Career Schools and Colleges of Technology.

[2] Because of revised survey procedures, data are not entirely comparable with figures for earlier years. The number of branch campuses reporting separately has increased since 1986–87.

NOTE.—Includes those colleges designated as institutions of higher education by the Higher Education General Information Survey system, even if they have a less than 2-year program.

SOURCE: U.S. Department of Education, National Center for Education Statistics, *Education Directory, Colleges and Universities;* "Fall Enrollment in Higher Education" and "Institutional Characteristics of Colleges and Universities" surveys; and Integrated Post-secondary Education Data System (IPEDS), "Institutional Characteristics" surveys. (This table was prepared August 1995.)

Table 234.—Institutions of higher education and branches, by type, control of institution, and state: 1994–95

State or other area	All institutions			4-year institutions							2-year institutions		
	Total	Public	Private	All 4-year institutions			Universities		Other 4-year institutions		Total	Public	Private
				Total	Public	Private	Public	Private	Public	Private			
1	2	3	4	5	6	7	8	9	10	11	12	13	14
United States	3,688	1,641	2,047	2,215	605	1,610	94	62	511	1,548	1,473	1,036	437
Alabama	80	53	27	35	18	17	2	0	16	17	45	35	10
Alaska	9	4	5	6	3	3	1	0	2	3	3	1	2
Arizona	43	22	21	21	4	17	2	0	2	17	22	18	4
Arkansas	35	22	13	20	10	10	1	0	9	10	15	12	3
California	336	138	198	190	31	159	2	4	29	155	146	107	39
Colorado	61	29	32	36	14	22	2	1	12	21	25	15	10
Connecticut	43	19	24	26	7	19	1	1	6	18	17	12	5
Delaware	9	5	4	6	2	4	1	0	1	4	3	3	0
District of Columbia	19	2	17	19	2	17	0	5	2	12	0	0	0
Florida	111	38	73	65	9	56	2	1	7	55	46	29	17
Georgia	119	72	47	55	19	36	1	1	18	35	64	53	11
Hawaii	16	10	6	9	3	6	1	0	2	6	7	7	0
Idaho	11	6	5	7	4	3	1	0	3	3	4	2	2
Illinois	167	61	106	104	12	92	3	4	9	88	63	49	14
Indiana	78	28	50	54	14	40	4	1	10	39	24	14	10
Iowa	60	20	40	39	3	36	2	1	1	35	21	17	4
Kansas	52	29	23	29	8	21	3	0	5	21	23	21	2
Kentucky	62	22	40	36	8	28	2	0	6	28	26	14	12
Louisiana	35	20	15	26	14	12	1	2	13	10	9	6	3
Maine	33	14	19	21	8	13	1	0	7	13	12	6	6
Maryland	57	33	24	34	13	21	1	1	12	20	23	20	3
Massachusetts	118	32	86	87	14	73	1	7	13	66	31	18	13
Michigan	109	45	64	71	15	56	3	1	12	55	38	30	8
Minnesota	109	64	45	48	11	37	1	0	10	37	61	53	8
Mississippi	46	31	15	21	9	12	2	0	7	12	25	22	3
Missouri	102	30	72	70	13	57	1	2	12	55	32	17	15
Montana	21	15	6	10	6	4	2	0	4	4	11	9	2
Nebraska	35	18	17	22	7	15	1	1	6	14	13	11	2
Nevada	10	6	4	5	2	3	1	0	1	3	5	4	1
New Hampshire	30	12	18	19	5	14	1	0	4	14	11	7	4
New Jersey	61	33	28	35	14	21	1	2	13	19	26	19	7
New Mexico	35	24	11	15	6	9	2	0	4	9	20	18	2
New York	314	89	225	214	42	172	2	12	40	160	100	47	53
North Carolina	123	75	48	57	17	40	2	2	15	38	66	58	8
North Dakota	20	15	5	10	6	4	2	0	4	4	10	9	1
Ohio	157	61	96	92	24	68	8	1	16	67	65	37	28
Oklahoma	46	29	17	26	14	12	2	1	12	11	20	15	5
Oregon	44	21	23	30	8	22	2	0	6	22	14	13	1
Pennsylvania	218	65	153	146	45	101	3	4	42	97	72	20	52
Rhode Island	13	3	10	11	2	9	1	0	1	9	2	1	1
South Carolina	59	33	26	34	12	22	2	0	10	22	25	21	4
South Dakota	21	9	12	18	8	10	2	0	6	10	3	1	2
Tennessee	78	25	53	51	10	41	1	1	9	40	27	15	12
Texas	178	105	73	97	40	57	6	4	34	53	81	65	16
Utah	16	9	7	9	5	4	2	1	3	3	7	4	3
Vermont	22	6	16	19	5	14	1	0	4	14	3	1	2
Virginia	93	39	54	54	15	39	3	0	12	39	39	24	15
Washington	62	36	26	31	8	23	2	0	6	23	31	28	3
West Virginia	28	16	12	23	13	10	1	0	12	10	5	3	2
Wisconsin	65	30	35	42	13	29	1	1	12	28	23	17	6
Wyoming	9	8	1	1	1	0	1	0	0	0	8	7	1
U.S. Service Schools	10	10	0	9	9	0	0	0	9	0	1	1	0
Outlying areas	69	23	46	49	13	36	1	0	12	36	20	10	10
American Samoa	1	1	0	0	0	0	0	0	0	0	1	1	0
Guam	2	2	0	1	1	0	0	0	1	0	1	1	0
Marshall Islands	1	1	0	0	0	0	0	0	0	0	1	1	0
Micronesia	1	1	0	0	0	0	0	0	0	0	1	1	0
Northern Marianas	1	1	0	0	0	0	0	0	0	0	1	1	0
Palau	1	1	0	0	0	0	0	0	0	0	1	1	0
Puerto Rico	60	14	46	46	10	36	1	0	9	36	14	4	10
Virgin Islands	2	2	0	2	2	0	0	0	2	0	0	0	0

NOTE.—Because of revised survey procedures, data are not entirely comparable with figures for years prior to 1986–87. The number of branch campuses reporting separately has increased since 1986–87.

SOURCE: U.S. Department of Education, National Center for Education Statistics, Integrated Postsecondary Education Data System (IPEDS), "Institutional Characteristics, 1994–95" survey. (This table was prepared August 1995.)

Table 235.—Institutions of higher education that have closed their doors, by control and type of institution: 1960–61 to 1992–93

Year	All institutions			Public			Private		
	Total	4-year	2-year	Total	4-year	2-year	Total	4-year	2-year
1	2	3	4	5	6	7	8	9	10
Excluding branch campuses:									
Total, 1960–61 to 1992–93	**364**	**185**	**179**	**38**	**1**	**37**	**326**	**184**	**142**
1960–61	8	1	7	1	—	1	7	1	6
1961–62	2	1	1	—	—	—	2	1	1
1962–63	—	—	—	—	—	—	—	—	—
1963–64	7	1	6	1	—	1	6	1	5
1964–65	8	1	7	4	—	4	4	1	3
1965–66	8	2	6	4	—	4	4	2	2
1966–67	9	2	7	3	—	3	6	2	4
1967–68	14	6	8	—	—	—	14	6	8
1968–69	21	11	10	1	—	1	20	11	9
1969–70	18	8	10	3	—	3	15	8	7
1970–71	32	9	23	9	—	9	23	9	14
1971–72	12	3	9	3	—	3	9	3	6
1972–73	19	12	7	2	—	2	17	12	5
1973–74	18	11	7	—	—	—	18	11	7
1974–75	17	13	4	3	—	3	14	13	1
1975–76	8	6	2	2	1	1	6	5	1
1976–77	8	5	3	—	—	—	8	5	3
1977–78	12	9	3	—	—	—	12	9	3
1978–79	9	4	5	—	—	—	9	4	5
1979–80	6	5	1	—	—	—	6	5	1
1980–81	4	3	1	—	—	—	4	3	1
1981–82	7	6	1	—	—	—	7	6	1
1982–83	7	4	3	—	—	—	7	4	3
1983–84	4	4	—	—	—	—	4	4	—
1984–85	4	4	—	—	—	—	4	4	—
1985–86	10	6	4	1	—	1	9	6	3
1986–87 and 1987–88	25	19	6	1	—	1	24	19	5
1988–89	14	6	8	—	—	—	14	6	8
1989–90	12	6	6	—	—	—	12	6	6
1990–91	10	4	6	—	—	—	10	4	6
1991–92	10	7	3	—	—	—	10	7	3
1992–93	21	6	15	—	—	—	21	6	15
Including branch campuses:									
Total, 1969–70 to 1992–93	**346**	**178**	**168**	**34**	**4**	**30**	**312**	**174**	**138**
1969–70	24	10	14	5	1	4	19	9	10
1970–71	35	10	25	11	—	11	24	10	14
1971–72	14	5	9	3	—	3	11	5	6
1972–73	21	12	9	4	—	4	17	12	5
1973–74	20	12	8	1	—	1	19	12	7
1974–75	18	13	5	4	—	4	14	13	1
1975–76	9	7	2	2	1	1	7	6	1
1976–77	9	6	3	—	—	—	9	6	3
1977–78	12	9	3	—	—	—	12	9	3
1978–79	9	4	5	—	—	—	9	4	5
1979–80	6	5	1	—	—	—	6	5	1
1980–81	4	3	1	—	—	—	4	3	1
1981–82	7	6	1	—	—	—	7	6	1
1982–83	7	4	3	—	—	—	7	4	3
1983–84	5	5	—	1	1	—	4	4	—
1984–85	4	4	—	—	—	—	4	4	—
1985–86	12	8	4	1	1	—	11	7	4
1986–87 and 1987–88	26	19	7	1	—	1	25	19	6
1988–89	14	6	8	—	—	—	14	6	8
1989–90	19	8	11	—	—	—	19	8	11
1990–91	18	6	12	—	—	—	18	6	12
1991–92	26	8	18	1	—	1	25	8	17
1992–93	27	8	19	—	—	—	27	8	19

—Data not applicable or not available.

NOTE.—This table indicates the year in which the institution closed.

SOURCE: U.S. Department of Education, National Center for Education Statistics, *Education Directory, Higher Education*, 1960–61 to 1974–75; *Education Directory, Colleges and Universities*, 1975–76 to 1983–84; *1982–83 Supplement to the Education Directory, Colleges and Universities*; and Integrated Postsecondary Education Data System, "Institutional Characteristics" surveys, unpublished data. (This table was prepared May 1994.)

Table 236.—Earned degrees conferred by institutions of higher education, by level of degree and sex of student: 1869–70 to 2004–05

Year	Associate degrees			Bachelor's degrees			Master's degrees			First-professional degrees			Doctor's degrees		
	Total	Men	Women	Total	Men	Women	Total	Men	Women	Total	Men	Women	Total	Men	Women
1	2	3	4	5	6	7	8	9	10	11	12	13	14	15	16
1869–70	—	—	—	[1]9,371	[1]7,993	[1]1,378	0	0	0	[2]	[2]	[2]	1	1	0
1879–80	—	—	—	[1]12,896	[1]10,411	[1]2,485	879	868	11	[2]	[2]	[2]	54	51	3
1889–90	—	—	—	[1]15,539	[1]12,857	[1]2,682	1,015	821	194	[2]	[2]	[2]	149	147	2
1899–1900	—	—	—	[1]27,410	[1]22,173	[1]5,237	1,583	1,280	303	[2]	[2]	[2]	382	359	23
1909–10	—	—	—	[1]37,199	[1]28,762	[1]8,437	2,113	1,555	558	[2]	[2]	[2]	443	399	44
1919–20	—	—	—	[1]48,622	[1]31,980	[1]16,642	4,279	2,985	1,294	[2]	[2]	[2]	615	522	93
1929–30	—	—	—	[1]122,484	[1]73,615	[1]48,869	14,969	8,925	6,044	[2]	[2]	[2]	2,299	1,946	353
1939–40	—	—	—	[1]186,500	[1]109,546	[1]76,954	26,731	16,508	10,223	[2]	[2]	[2]	3,290	2,861	429
1949–50	—	—	—	[1]432,058	[1]328,841	[1]103,217	58,183	41,220	16,963	[2]	[2]	[2]	6,420	5,804	616
1959–60	—	—	—	[1]392,440	[1]254,063	[1]138,377	74,435	50,898	23,537	[2]	[2]	[2]	9,829	8,801	1,028
1960–61	—	—	—	365,174	224,538	140,636	84,609	57,830	26,779	25,253	24,577	676	10,575	9,463	1,112
1961–62	—	—	—	383,961	230,456	153,505	91,418	62,603	28,815	25,607	24,836	771	11,622	10,377	1,245
1962–63	—	—	—	411,420	241,309	170,111	98,684	67,302	31,382	26,590	25,753	837	12,822	11,448	1,374
1963–64	—	—	—	461,266	265,349	195,917	109,183	73,850	35,333	27,209	26,357	852	14,490	12,955	1,535
1964–65	—	—	—	493,757	282,173	211,584	121,167	81,319	39,848	28,290	27,283	1,007	16,467	14,692	1,775
1965–66	111,607	63,779	47,828	520,115	299,287	220,828	140,602	93,081	47,521	30,124	28,982	1,142	18,237	16,121	2,116
1966–67	139,183	78,356	60,827	558,534	322,711	235,823	157,726	103,109	54,617	31,695	30,401	1,294	20,617	18,163	2,454
1967–68	159,441	90,317	69,124	632,289	357,682	274,607	176,749	113,552	63,197	33,939	32,402	1,537	23,089	20,183	2,906
1968–69	183,279	105,661	77,618	728,845	410,595	318,250	193,756	121,531	72,225	35,114	33,595	1,519	26,158	22,722	3,436
1969–70[3]	206,023	117,432	88,591	792,316	451,097	341,219	208,291	125,624	82,667	34,918	33,077	1,841	29,866	25,890	3,976
1970–71[3]	252,311	144,144	108,167	839,730	475,594	364,136	230,509	138,146	92,363	37,946	35,544	2,402	32,107	27,530	4,577
1971–72[3]	292,014	166,227	125,787	887,273	500,590	386,683	251,633	149,550	102,083	43,411	40,723	2,688	33,363	28,090	5,273
1972–73	316,174	175,413	140,761	922,362	518,191	404,171	263,371	154,468	108,903	50,018	46,489	3,529	34,777	28,571	6,206
1973–74	343,924	188,591	155,333	945,776	527,313	418,463	277,033	157,842	119,191	53,816	48,530	5,286	33,816	27,365	6,451
1974–75	360,171	191,017	169,154	922,933	504,841	418,092	292,450	161,570	130,880	55,916	48,956	6,960	34,083	26,817	7,266
1975–76	391,454	209,996	181,458	925,746	504,925	420,821	311,771	167,248	144,523	62,649	52,892	9,757	34,064	26,267	7,797
1976–77	406,377	210,842	195,535	919,549	495,545	424,004	317,164	167,783	149,381	64,359	52,374	11,985	33,232	25,142	8,090
1977–78	412,246	204,718	207,528	921,204	487,347	433,857	311,620	161,212	150,408	66,581	52,270	14,311	32,131	23,658	8,473
1978–79	402,702	192,091	210,611	921,390	477,344	444,046	301,079	153,370	147,709	68,848	52,652	16,196	32,730	23,541	9,189
1979–80	400,910	183,737	217,173	929,417	473,611	455,806	298,081	150,749	147,332	70,131	52,716	17,415	32,615	22,943	9,672
1980–81	416,377	188,638	227,739	935,140	469,883	465,257	295,739	147,043	148,696	71,956	52,792	19,164	32,958	22,711	10,247
1981–82[3]	434,526	196,944	237,582	952,998	473,364	479,634	295,546	145,532	150,014	72,032	52,223	19,809	32,707	22,224	10,483
1982–83[3]	449,620	203,991	245,629	969,510	479,140	490,370	289,921	144,697	145,224	73,054	51,250	21,804	32,775	21,902	10,873
1983–84[3]	452,240	202,704	249,536	974,309	482,319	491,990	284,263	143,595	140,668	74,468	51,378	23,090	33,209	22,064	11,145
1984–85	454,712	202,932	251,780	979,477	482,528	496,949	286,251	143,390	142,861	75,063	50,455	24,608	32,943	21,700	11,243
1985–86	446,047	196,166	249,881	987,823	485,923	501,900	288,567	143,508	145,059	73,910	49,261	24,649	33,653	21,819	11,834
1986–87[3]	436,304	190,839	245,465	991,264	480,782	510,482	289,349	141,269	148,080	71,617	46,523	25,094	34,041	22,061	11,980
1987–88	435,085	190,047	245,038	994,829	477,203	517,626	299,317	145,163	154,154	70,735	45,484	25,251	34,870	22,615	12,255
1988–89	436,764	186,316	250,448	1,018,755	483,346	535,409	310,621	149,354	161,267	70,856	45,046	25,810	35,720	22,648	13,072
1989–90	455,102	191,195	263,907	1,051,344	491,696	559,648	324,301	153,653	170,648	70,988	43,961	27,027	38,371	24,401	13,970
1990–91	481,720	198,634	283,086	1,094,538	504,045	590,493	337,168	156,482	180,686	71,948	43,846	28,102	39,294	24,756	14,538
1991–92	504,231	207,481	296,750	1,136,553	520,811	615,742	352,838	161,842	190,996	74,146	45,071	29,075	40,659	25,557	15,102
1992–93	514,756	211,964	302,792	1,165,178	532,881	632,297	369,585	169,258	200,327	75,387	45,153	30,234	42,132	26,073	16,059
1993–94[4]	535,000	214,000	321,000	1,165,000	526,000	638,000	386,000	183,000	203,000	75,400	45,100	30,200	42,900	26,800	16,100
1994–95[4]	536,000	213,000	324,000	1,179,000	528,000	651,000	399,000	192,000	207,000	78,400	44,900	33,500	43,000	26,400	16,600
1995–96[4]	524,000	210,000	314,000	1,198,000	541,000	657,000	393,000	184,000	209,000	83,000	48,700	34,300	43,000	26,000	17,000
1996–97[4]	525,000	210,000	315,000	1,201,000	540,000	661,000	393,000	183,000	210,000	83,500	49,100	34,400	43,000	25,600	17,400
1997–98[4]	534,000	211,000	324,000	1,204,000	543,000	661,000	389,000	178,000	212,000	83,000	49,000	34,100	43,100	25,200	17,900
1998–99[4]	526,000	211,000	315,000	1,232,000	541,000	691,000	379,000	168,000	212,000	82,000	48,200	33,800	43,100	24,800	18,300
1999–2000[4]	530,000	212,000	318,000	1,196,000	541,000	655,000	370,000	159,000	211,000	81,300	47,600	33,700	43,100	24,400	18,700
2000–01[4]	534,000	213,000	321,000	1,198,000	544,000	654,000	366,000	155,000	211,000	80,900	47,200	33,600	43,100	24,000	19,100
2001–02[4]	541,000	215,000	326,000	1,210,000	552,000	658,000	362,000	152,000	210,000	80,500	46,900	33,700	43,100	23,600	19,500
2002–03[4]	547,000	217,000	331,000	1,227,000	562,000	666,000	361,000	153,000	208,000	80,500	46,900	33,700	43,100	23,200	19,900
2003–04[4]	552,000	218,000	334,000	1,248,000	572,000	676,000	360,000	153,000	207,000	80,400	46,700	33,700	43,100	22,800	20,300
2004–05[4]	556,000	220,000	337,000	1,264,000	581,000	683,000	362,000	156,000	206,000	80,000	46,800	33,200	43,100	22,400	20,700

[1] Includes first-professional degrees.

[2] First-professional degrees are included with bachelor's degrees.

[3] Revised from previously published data.

[4] Projected.

—Data not available.

NOTE.—Some data have been revised from previously published figures. Because of rounding, details may not add to totals.

SOURCE: U.S. Department of Education, National Center for Education Statistics, Earned Degrees Conferred; Projections of Education Statistics to 2005; and Integrated Postsecondary Education Data System (IPEDS), "Completions" surveys. (This table was prepared January 1995.)

Table 237.—Earned degrees conferred by institutions of higher education, by level of degree and by state: 1991–92 and 1992–93

State or other area	1991–92					1992–93				
	Associate degrees	Bachelor's degrees	First-professional degrees[1]	Master's degrees	Doctor's degrees (Ph.D., Ed.D., etc.)	Associate degrees	Bachelor's degrees	First-professional degrees[1]	Master's degrees	Doctor's degrees (Ph.D., Ed.D., etc.)
1	2	3	4	5	6	7	8	9	10	11
United States	504,231	1,136,553	74,146	352,838	40,659	514,756	1,165,178	75,387	369,585	42,132
Alabama	7,257	19,628	850	5,544	374	7,484	20,525	866	5,636	406
Alaska	753	1,114	—	367	13	940	1,260	—	363	10
Arizona	6,776	14,680	424	5,093	633	6,928	15,807	436	5,694	690
Arkansas	2,592	8,133	363	1,774	112	2,618	8,449	449	1,836	120
California	53,008	107,462	8,918	35,429	4,703	54,688	111,010	9,195	37,046	4,987
Colorado	6,301	17,646	788	5,655	707	6,294	18,925	813	6,391	768
Connecticut	4,994	15,019	896	6,563	604	5,094	14,931	679	6,590	630
Delaware	1,152	4,121	578	857	167	1,313	4,119	550	954	144
District of Columbia	399	8,206	2,254	5,447	473	435	8,095	2,321	6,059	562
Florida	39,062	41,090	2,312	11,864	1,430	39,405	43,212	2,322	13,145	1,661
Georgia	8,480	23,493	1,833	7,022	880	8,316	25,390	1,949	7,958	899
Hawaii	2,466	3,821	116	1,199	145	2,515	4,186	176	1,383	168
Idaho	3,243	3,529	135	921	76	3,544	3,923	146	1,005	65
Illinois	26,276	53,263	4,364	21,674	2,581	27,620	51,482	4,410	22,440	2,601
Indiana	8,770	30,770	1,512	6,650	1,114	9,236	31,453	1,496	6,874	1,107
Iowa	8,859	17,162	1,493	3,369	698	8,344	17,598	1,534	3,517	683
Kansas	6,371	13,690	614	3,791	447	6,312	14,282	601	3,920	387
Kentucky	5,930	13,861	896	4,059	311	6,546	14,396	985	4,195	328
Louisiana	2,660	16,985	1,562	4,235	423	2,865	17,825	1,502	4,723	428
Maine	2,471	5,778	179	890	51	2,433	5,976	168	917	40
Maryland	8,166	20,324	946	7,496	928	8,425	20,427	1,050	8,006	963
Massachusetts	13,434	45,051	3,651	19,740	2,256	13,354	42,747	3,677	19,215	2,276
Michigan	23,108	44,789	2,575	14,374	1,549	24,231	45,711	2,581	14,944	1,513
Minnesota	9,183	24,453	1,829	4,853	684	9,766	24,762	1,854	5,217	674
Mississippi	5,431	10,054	513	2,547	302	5,575	10,673	466	2,672	303
Missouri	7,818	26,552	2,157	9,405	764	8,023	26,954	2,171	9,303	711
Montana	883	4,161	70	730	65	801	4,194	68	756	57
Nebraska	3,730	9,417	732	1,909	236	2,494	9,522	806	2,007	238
Nevada	1,171	2,694	44	710	45	1,311	3,029	54	845	39
New Hampshire	2,943	7,430	185	2,101	79	3,343	7,524	195	2,267	118
New Jersey	12,287	24,207	1,719	7,901	994	12,299	25,185	1,679	8,110	965
New Mexico	2,874	5,501	176	2,224	229	3,007	5,667	178	2,142	243
New York	53,043	95,611	7,543	41,213	3,816	53,393	97,104	7,476	42,539	4,045
North Carolina	11,865	30,826	1,537	6,644	923	12,164	31,852	1,709	6,864	980
North Dakota	1,615	4,755	127	572	79	1,696	4,555	142	649	74
Ohio	19,589	50,557	3,176	13,760	1,766	19,881	51,487	3,225	14,613	1,973
Oklahoma	6,175	14,542	989	4,267	398	6,304	15,002	928	4,457	416
Oregon	4,829	13,375	1,032	3,918	511	5,676	13,139	988	3,650	535
Pennsylvania	20,932	64,304	3,561	16,899	2,201	20,091	65,073	3,774	17,649	2,267
Rhode Island	4,043	9,249	86	2,038	241	4,156	9,341	81	2,070	269
South Carolina	6,191	14,219	621	3,911	374	5,953	15,254	604	4,245	408
South Dakota	798	4,075	135	785	60	848	4,252	130	913	52
Tennessee	6,661	19,139	1,352	4,946	741	6,801	20,371	1,341	5,016	721
Texas	23,056	64,313	4,817	19,749	2,481	24,804	67,598	4,882	20,887	2,546
Utah	4,556	12,016	364	2,550	378	4,839	12,901	388	2,868	376
Vermont	1,317	4,521	91	1,056	47	1,264	4,707	96	1,103	53
Virginia	9,735	30,320	1,627	8,339	963	10,232	30,858	1,811	9,325	998
Washington	16,436	19,737	886	6,088	594	16,619	20,829	920	6,745	618
West Virginia	2,803	8,191	329	1,912	116	2,919	8,606	320	1,916	99
Wisconsin	9,622	27,542	946	6,252	830	9,481	27,709	971	6,340	851
Wyoming	1,891	1,781	64	350	50	1,850	1,856	69	342	50
U.S. Service Schools	10,226	3,396	179	1,196	17	10,226	3,445	155	1,264	17
Outlying areas	4,473	13,519	655	1,369	68	4,342	14,100	681	1,388	74
American Samoa	41	—	—	—	—	43	—	—	—	—
Federated States of Micronesia	56	—	—	—	—	56	—	—	—	—
Guam	52	198	—	16	—	36	178	—	15	—
Marshall Islands	21	—	—	—	—	35	—	—	—	—
Northern Marianas	52	—	—	—	—	87	—	—	—	—
Palau	4	—	—	—	—	4	—	—	—	—
Puerto Rico	4,180	13,182	655	1,301	68	4,017	13,746	681	1,330	74
Virgin Islands	67	139	—	52	—	64	176	—	43	—

[1] Includes degrees which require at least 6 years of college work for completion (including at least 2 years of preprofessional training).

—Data not available or not applicable.

SOURCE: U.S. Department of Education, National Center for Education Statistics, Integrated Postsecondary Education Data System (IPEDS), "Completions" surveys. (This table was prepared January 1995.)

Table 238.—Associate degrees conferred by institution of higher education, by sex and field of study: 1986–87 to 1990–91

Field of study	Total					Women				
	1986–87	1987–88	1988–89	1989–90	1990–91	1986–87	1987–88	1988–89	1989–90	1990–91
1	2	3	4	5	6	7	8	9	10	11
Total	436,304	435,085	436,764	455,102	481,720	245,465	245,038	250,448	263,907	283,086
Agriculture and natural resources, total	5,460	5,029	4,725	4,832	4,910	1,768	1,658	1,655	1,600	1,588
Agricultural business and production	3,655	3,003	2,884	2,894	2,905	1,182	960	969	930	962
Agricultural sciences	808	1,015	963	925	879	436	543	543	507	444
Conservation and renewable natural resources	997	1,011	878	1,013	1,126	150	155	143	163	182
Architecture and related programs	1,666	1,809	1,815	2,013	2,031	1,436	1,591	1,559	1,745	1,741
Area, ethnic, and cultural studies	14	18	16	68	19	8	14	8	56	13
Biological/life sciences	893	854	982	1,023	1,119	495	506	568	593	667
Business management and administrative services	114,501	110,064	106,819	106,405	102,250	77,999	75,412	73,706	73,992	71,619
Accounting	14,569	14,221	14,266	14,858	14,577	10,760	10,615	10,690	11,275	11,111
Business, general	12,357	12,458	11,929	11,878	11,618	7,474	7,295	6,940	7,095	7,188
Business administration and management	24,856	26,791	27,252	28,292	26,625	14,029	15,392	15,782	16,753	15,863
Business and management, other	12,002	11,936	11,162	11,691	11,663	6,391	6,399	6,130	6,480	6,655
Business data processing	13,446	10,544	9,831	8,532	8,182	7,396	5,861	5,501	4,733	4,775
Secretarial and related programs	20,365	19,059	18,041	17,139	16,872	20,037	18,732	17,660	16,827	16,517
Marketing and distribution	16,906	15,055	14,338	14,015	12,713	11,912	11,118	11,003	10,829	9,510
Communications	1,591	1,919	1,777	1,657	1,847	695	915	955	910	966
Communications technologies	1,944	1,507	1,993	2,027	2,032	779	592	681	678	681
Computer and information sciences	9,101	8,628	7,900	7,574	7,677	4,310	4,154	3,908	3,768	3,770
Construction trades	2,082	2,020	1,731	1,765	1,793	75	64	75	68	78
Consumer and personal services	2,165	2,542	2,815	2,121	2,494	820	985	1,028	843	887
Education	7,333	7,219	7,445	8,061	7,842	5,220	4,904	5,285	5,731	5,640
Engineering	4,539	3,850	2,676	2,345	2,451	478	413	310	279	268
Engineering-related technologies	43,189	44,019	42,593	40,033	37,890	4,078	4,265	4,237	4,006	3,724
English language and literature/letters	507	484	468	527	426	348	321	330	358	302
Foreign languages and literatures	424	418	324	329	327	192	193	214	251	210
Health professions and related sciences	62,532	59,692	59,535	64,113	70,833	55,322	52,759	52,495	56,125	61,495
Dental assisting	4,018	3,675	3,650	3,697	3,810	3,703	3,425	3,427	3,502	3,612
Emergency medical technician-ambulance and paramedic	370	356	354	332	371	107	110	99	100	116
Medical lab technician	2,205	1,839	1,724	1,627	1,731	1,793	1,436	1,339	1,284	1,311
Medical assisting	1,862	1,701	1,786	1,404	1,496	1,828	1,659	1,695	1,375	1,451
Nursing assisting	24	8	12	0	5	14	6	11	0	4
Practical nursing	603	561	591	589	797	567	522	539	535	692
Nursing, R.N. and other	38,198	36,945	36,475	40,212	45,317	35,538	34,338	33,904	36,915	41,261
Health sciences, other	15,252	14,607	14,943	16,252	17,306	11,772	11,263	11,481	12,414	13,048
Home economics and vocational home economics	7,309	7,043	7,559	7,798	8,067	5,572	5,369	5,745	6,080	6,243
Law and legal studies	2,498	3,139	3,742	4,552	5,484	2,211	2,770	3,271	3,967	4,892
Liberal/general studies and humanities	111,218	116,411	121,988	133,466	142,722	63,773	67,172	71,588	78,768	84,977
Library science	117	67	101	107	111	98	61	90	95	102
Mathematics	667	765	654	756	670	248	295	239	270	264
Mechanics and repairers	10,806	10,473	7,769	7,704	7,640	584	588	427	431	445
Multi/interdisciplinary studies	6,676	7,477	7,737	8,176	7,454	3,220	3,719	3,888	4,156	3,998
Parks, recreation, leisure, and fitness studies	573	647	641	485	425	289	350	329	200	177
Philosophy and religion	100	94	81	93	89	36	30	23	34	28
Physical sciences	2,012	1,856	1,838	2,021	2,091	799	774	806	811	901
Physical sciences, other	1,156	1,176	1,090	1,279	1,281	448	480	487	539	562
Science technologies	856	680	748	742	810	351	294	319	272	339
Precision production trades	7,981	7,734	7,414	8,616	9,093	1,683	1,720	1,584	1,898	1,975
Protective services	11,909	11,829	11,682	12,855	13,564	3,199	3,157	3,292	3,402	3,599
Criminal justice and corrections	10,012	9,901	9,663	10,658	11,358	3,006	2,949	3,079	3,137	3,367
Fire control and safety	1,449	1,397	1,493	1,621	1,634	59	53	78	91	92
Protective services, other	448	531	526	576	572	134	155	135	174	140
Psychology	1,016	1,000	1,090	1,115	997	722	701	811	829	740
Public administration and services	2,257	2,317	2,493	2,613	2,779	1,783	1,823	1,959	2,076	2,243
R.O.T.C. and military technologies	50	138	164	129	85	2	20	31	15	8
Social sciences and history	2,582	2,709	2,741	2,872	2,505	1,489	1,556	1,544	1,611	1,494
Theological studies/religious vocations	595	627	568	653	578	240	239	248	264	243
Transportation and material moving	1,294	1,327	2,090	2,619	2,609	223	202	340	395	469
Visual and performing arts	8,703	8,998	8,178	8,740	9,126	5,271	5,495	4,952	5,327	5,362
Fine arts, general	1,012	1,123	1,091	1,150	1,166	652	742	719	729	766
Design and music	4,497	5,677	5,340	5,900	5,986	2,611	3,510	3,218	3,588	3,499
Visual and performing arts, other	3,194	2,198	1,747	1,690	1,974	2,008	1,243	1,015	1,010	1,097
Unclassified by field of study	0	362	4,620	4,839	19,690	0	251	2,267	2,275	11,277

SOURCE: U.S. Department of Education, National Center for Education Statistics, "Degrees and Other Formal Awards Conferred" survey and Integrated Postsecondary Education Data System (IPEDS), "Completions" surveys. (This table was prepared February 1995.)

Table 239.—Associate degrees and other subbaccalaureate awards conferred by institutions of higher education, by length of curriculum, sex of student, and field of study: 1992–93

Field of study	Less than 1-year awards			1- to less than 4-year awards			Associate degrees		
	Total	Men	Women	Total	Men	Women	Total	Men	Women
1	2	3	4	5	6	7	8	9	10
Total	70,922	34,981	35,941	146,859	60,828	86,031	514,756	211,964	302,792
Agriculture and natural resources, total	1,778	1,369	409	4,741	2,214	2,527	5,398	3,750	1,648
Agricultural business and production	1,523	1,152	371	1,348	964	384	3,222	2,204	1,018
Agricultural sciences	194	160	34	2,138	348	1,790	837	465	372
Conservation and renewable natural resources	61	57	4	1,255	902	353	1,339	1,081	258
Architecture and related programs	2	0	2	56	8	48	372	119	253
Area, ethnic, and cultural studies	105	29	76	414	138	276	33	10	23
Biological/life sciences	116	85	31	20	9	11	1,435	588	847
Business management and administrative services	13,373	3,620	9,753	29,291	5,058	24,233	99,164	30,154	69,010
Accounting	1,246	275	971	4,081	687	3,394	15,115	3,528	11,587
Business, general	445	209	236	1,432	422	1,010	11,190	4,144	7,046
Business administration and management	1,590	622	968	2,017	738	1,279	29,556	11,624	17,932
Business and management, other	1,589	799	790	3,136	1,200	1,936	12,285	5,640	6,645
Business data processing	973	330	643	2,460	797	1,663	6,405	2,712	3,693
Secretarial and related programs	4,609	358	4,251	14,111	720	13,391	17,168	707	16,461
Marketing and distribution	2,921	1,027	1,894	2,054	494	1,560	7,445	1,799	5,646
Communications	398	230	168	391	137	254	1,904	945	959
Communications technologies	118	82	36	291	160	131	1,828	1,196	632
Computer and information sciences	1,859	940	919	4,594	2,065	2,529	9,196	4,541	4,655
Construction trades	1,497	1,407	90	4,062	3,859	203	1,653	1,581	72
Consumer and personal services	855	237	618	5,591	1,315	4,276	4,692	3,120	1,572
Education	510	131	379	954	106	848	9,315	3,031	6,284
Engineering	261	237	24	93	76	17	2,478	2,169	309
Engineering-related technologies	2,070	1,768	302	8,514	7,659	855	36,321	32,631	3,690
English language and literature/letters	165	74	91	53	5	48	1,320	469	851
Foreign languages and literatures	339	121	218	27	4	23	511	153	358
Health professions and related sciences	23,278	6,640	16,638	38,933	6,041	32,892	86,237	12,971	73,266
Dental assisting	246	17	229	2,522	134	2,388	4,165	236	3,929
Emergency medical technician-ambulance and paramedic	5,819	3,919	1,900	1,868	1,336	532	442	303	139
Medical lab technician	81	14	67	191	68	123	2,172	571	1,601
Medical assisting	1,407	77	1,330	2,664	76	2,588	2,130	223	1,907
Nursing assisting	7,649	1,003	6,646	151	11	140	86	16	70
Practical nursing	587	85	502	18,153	1,835	16,318	890	86	804
Nursing, R.N. and other	2,175	295	1,880	3,050	330	2,720	54,085	5,796	48,289
Health sciences, other	5,314	1,230	4,084	10,334	2,251	8,083	22,267	5,740	16,527
Home economics and vocational home economics	3,214	1,118	2,096	7,512	1,019	6,493	6,914	655	6,259
Law and legal studies	866	142	724	2,447	473	1,974	8,028	959	7,069
Liberal/general studies and humanities	132	40	92	808	324	484	158,040	63,867	94,173
Library science	97	6	91	53	4	49	85	9	76
Mathematics	0	0	0	15	9	6	743	428	315
Mechanics and repairers	3,613	3,488	125	18,417	17,243	1,174	10,966	10,280	686
Multi/interdisciplinary studies	246	119	127	133	57	76	8,486	4,075	4,411
Parks, recreation, leisure, and fitness studies	29	8	21	126	59	67	717	429	288
Philosophy and religion	6	3	3	668	274	394	111	76	35
Physical sciences	30	15	15	81	56	25	2,241	1,296	945
Physical sciences, other	13	4	9	3	0	3	1,390	792	598
Science technologies	17	11	6	78	56	22	851	504	347
Precision production trades	2,552	2,155	397	7,408	6,333	1,075	9,204	7,393	1,811
Protective services	6,664	5,498	1,166	4,330	3,512	818	16,834	12,289	4,545
Criminal justice and corrections	5,633	4,537	1,096	2,382	1,724	658	14,295	10,030	4,265
Fire control and safety	1,031	961	70	380	351	29	2,020	1,883	137
Protective services, other	0	0	0	1,568	1,437	131	519	376	143
Psychology	33	10	23	47	9	38	1,237	282	955
Public administration and services	235	66	169	589	214	375	3,301	648	2,653
R.O.T.C. and military technologies	0	0	0	0	0	0	52	44	8
Social sciences and history	22	8	14	117	45	72	3,930	1,678	2,252
Theological studies/religious vocations	88	27	61	582	245	337	508	281	227
Transportation and material moving	5,525	4,927	598	437	367	70	2,210	1,850	360
Visual and performing arts	279	104	175	3,913	1,232	2,681	12,690	5,084	7,606
Fine arts, general	17	3	14	725	241	484	1,346	460	886
Design and music	255	98	157	2,402	639	1,763	9,699	3,833	5,866
Visual and performing arts, other	7	3	4	786	352	434	1,645	791	854
Unclassified by field of study	567	277	290	1,151	499	652	6,602	2,913	3,689

SOURCE: U.S. Department of Education, National Center for Education Statistics, Integrated Postsecondary Education Data System (IPEDS), "Completions" survey. (This table was prepared February 1995.)

Table 240.—Associate degrees and other subbaccalaureate awards conferred by institutions of higher education, by length of curriculum, sex of student, and field of study: 1991–92

Field of study	Less than 1-year awards			1- to less than 4-year awards			Associate degrees		
	Total	Men	Women	Total	Men	Women	Total	Men	Women
1	2	3	4	5	6	7	8	9	10
Total	**64,647**	**30,492**	**34,155**	**133,792**	**54,536**	**79,256**	**504,231**	**207,481**	**296,750**
Agriculture and natural resources, total	1,432	1,106	326	3,057	1,405	1,652	5,251	3,576	1,675
Agricultural business and production	1,163	895	268	1,361	978	383	3,046	2,035	1,011
Agricultural sciences	205	161	44	1,523	292	1,231	951	519	432
Conservation and renewable natural resources	64	50	14	173	135	38	1,254	1,022	232
Architecture and related programs	2	0	2	93	31	62	443	106	337
Area, ethnic, and cultural studies	116	39	77	160	15	145	29	9	20
Biological/life sciences	72	55	17	119	83	36	1,361	564	797
Business management and administrative services	13,337	3,357	9,980	27,417	5,175	22,242	102,227	30,274	71,953
Accounting	1,139	224	915	3,568	626	2,942	15,687	3,799	11,888
Business, general	544	217	327	1,307	473	834	11,823	4,530	7,293
Business administration and management	1,430	592	838	2,807	1,023	1,784	31,185	12,283	18,902
Business and management, other	1,322	694	628	3,158	1,174	1,984	11,089	4,320	6,769
Business data processing	1,023	348	675	2,345	811	1,534	6,394	2,715	3,679
Secretarial and related programs	4,672	269	4,403	12,341	625	11,716	17,584	656	16,928
Marketing and distribution	3,207	1,013	2,194	1,891	443	1,448	8,465	1,971	6,494
Communications	354	260	94	395	151	244	1,886	890	996
Communications technologies	160	93	67	354	196	158	1,794	1,145	649
Computer and information sciences	1,563	754	809	3,445	1,407	2,038	9,290	4,565	4,725
Construction trades	944	910	34	3,735	3,560	175	1,560	1,491	69
Consumer and personal services	664	220	444	5,220	1,089	4,131	4,420	2,901	1,519
Education	420	150	270	671	73	598	10,267	3,708	6,559
Engineering	75	67	8	82	75	7	2,685	2,341	344
Engineering-related technologies	2,286	1,998	288	7,632	6,818	814	35,861	32,104	3,757
English language and literature/letters	109	31	78	62	17	45	1,019	348	671
Foreign languages and literatures	328	124	204	36	6	30	433	128	305
Health professions and related sciences	21,234	5,727	15,507	33,789	5,153	28,636	79,453	10,805	68,648
Dental assisting	256	8	248	2,230	124	2,106	4,013	191	3,822
Emergency medical technician-ambulance and paramedic	4,422	3,096	1,326	1,523	1,066	457	378	264	114
Medical lab technician	44	5	39	224	37	187	1,874	449	1,425
Medical assisting	1,253	49	1,204	2,195	74	2,121	1,960	219	1,741
Nursing assisting	7,254	915	6,339	230	26	204	19	6	13
Practical nursing	508	73	435	16,319	1,452	14,867	795	53	742
Nursing, R.N. and other	1,683	209	1,474	3,442	330	3,112	51,193	4,976	46,217
Health sciences, other	5,814	1,372	4,442	7,626	2,044	5,582	19,221	4,647	14,574
Home economics and vocational home economics	2,880	1,035	1,845	8,079	1,004	7,075	6,436	687	5,749
Law and legal studies	936	147	789	2,252	382	1,870	7,053	907	6,146
Liberal/general studies and humanities	71	34	37	1,048	420	628	154,594	62,817	91,777
Library science	77	13	64	50	0	50	103	18	85
Mathematics	0	0	0	33	23	10	744	464	280
Mechanics and repairers	3,083	2,960	123	16,202	14,965	1,237	10,264	9,593	671
Multi/interdisciplinary studies	59	10	49	105	44	61	7,841	3,782	4,059
Parks, recreation, leisure, and fitness studies	38	18	20	100	46	54	620	369	251
Philosophy and religion	10	2	8	1,019	372	647	60	43	17
Physical sciences	58	32	26	306	279	27	2,066	1,205	861
Physical sciences, other	33	14	19	17	17	0	1,228	706	522
Science technologies	25	18	7	289	262	27	838	499	339
Precision production trades	2,385	2,011	374	7,114	6,042	1,072	9,005	7,133	1,872
Protective services	4,345	3,534	811	2,260	1,689	571	15,117	11,241	3,876
Criminal justice and corrections	3,644	2,876	768	1,588	1,092	496	12,649	9,021	3,628
Fire control and safety	700	657	43	589	557	32	1,989	1,873	116
Protective services, other	1	1	0	83	40	43	479	347	132
Psychology	33	8	25	16	4	12	1,209	338	871
Public administration and services	94	33	61	333	109	224	3,162	639	2,523
R.O.T.C. and military technologies	2	2	0	0	0	0	172	156	16
Social sciences and history	12	5	7	94	38	56	3,160	1,400	1,760
Theological studies/religious vocations	109	21	88	530	266	264	496	280	216
Transportation and material moving	4,900	4,373	527	451	361	90	2,418	1,978	440
Visual and performing arts	223	76	147	4,079	1,417	2,662	11,888	4,803	7,085
Fine arts, general	12	3	9	805	260	545	1,159	392	767
Design and music	191	65	126	2,492	803	1,689	9,142	3,606	5,536
Visual and performing arts, other	20	8	12	782	354	428	1,587	805	782
Unclassified by field of study	2,236	1,287	949	3,454	1,821	1,633	9,844	4,673	5,171

SOURCE: U.S. Department of Education, National Center for Education Statistics, Integrated Postsecondary Education Data System (IPEDS), "Completions" survey. (This table was prepared March 1994.)

Table 241.—Bachelor's, master's, and doctor's degrees conferred by institutions of higher education, by sex of student and field of study: 1992–93

Field of study	Bachelor's degrees requiring 4 or 5 years			Master's degrees			Doctor's degrees (Ph.D., Ed.D., etc.)		
	Total	Men	Women	Total	Men	Women	Total	Men	Women
1	2	3	4	5	6	7	8	9	10
All fields	1,165,178	532,881	632,297	369,585	169,258	200,327	42,132	26,073	16,059
Agriculture and natural resources, total	16,778	11,080	5,698	3,965	2,477	1,488	1,173	879	294
Agricultural business and production, total	4,995	3,661	1,334	679	460	219	195	149	46
Agricultural business and management, total	3,368	2,532	836	512	355	157	146	112	34
Agricultural business and management, general	789	562	227	48	32	16	0	0	0
Agricultural business/agribusiness operations	865	688	177	31	26	5	2	2	0
Agricultural economics	1,566	1,159	407	425	291	134	144	110	34
Agricultural business and management, other	148	123	25	8	6	2	0	0	0
Agricultural mechanization	242	220	22	5	5	0	1	1	0
Agricultural production workers and managers	114	89	25	65	47	18	9	8	1
Horticulture service operations and management	479	329	150	35	21	14	19	15	4
International agriculture	19	12	7	18	9	9	0	0	0
Agricultural business and production, other	773	479	294	44	23	21	13	13	7
Agricultural sciences, total	5,918	3,457	2,461	1,583	985	598	708	522	186
Agriculture/agricultural sciences, general	953	670	283	174	129	45	5	5	0
Animal sciences, total	2,811	1,369	1,442	422	286	136	193	144	49
Animal sciences, general	2,359	1,112	1,247	331	219	112	139	106	33
Agricultural animal breeding and genetics	22	7	15	13	10	3	5	3	2
Agricultural animal health	7	3	4	8	5	3	0	0	0
Agricultural animal nutrition	0	0	0	2	2	0	12	11	1
Dairy science	99	65	34	19	16	3	6	5	1
Poultry science	107	89	18	24	18	6	12	7	5
Animal sciences, other	217	93	124	25	16	9	19	12	7
Food sciences and technology	449	197	252	317	134	183	138	75	63
Plant sciences, total	1,447	1,066	381	513	345	168	299	237	62
Plant sciences, general	216	161	55	75	48	27	48	38	10
Agronomy and crop science	539	458	81	228	175	53	154	127	27
Horticulture science	508	322	186	125	68	57	53	37	16
Plant breeding and genetics	0	0	0	16	12	4	7	6	1
Agricultural plant pathology	0	0	0	4	2	2	8	6	2
Plant protection (pest management)	18	12	6	22	11	11	1	0	1
Range science and management	112	78	34	30	18	12	22	17	5
Plant sciences, other	54	35	19	13	11	2	6	6	0
Soil sciences	92	69	23	86	54	32	60	53	7
Agriculture/agricultural sciences, other	166	86	80	71	37	34	13	8	5
Conservation and renewable natural resources, total	5,865	3,962	1,903	1,703	1,032	671	270	208	62
Natural resources conservation, general	2,789	1,700	1,089	768	431	337	79	51	28
Natural resources management and policy	341	236	105	96	58	38	1	1	0
Fishing and fisheries sciences and management	207	169	38	98	66	32	24	22	2
Forest harvesting and production technology/technician	195	149	46	27	22	5	12	10	2
Forestry, general	1,082	887	195	493	314	179	124	104	20
Wildlife and wildlands management	912	606	306	166	112	54	17	11	6
Conservation and renewable natural resources, other	339	215	124	55	29	26	13	9	4
Architecture and related programs, total	9,167	5,940	3,227	3,808	2,376	1,432	148	105	43
Architecture	5,267	3,765	1,502	1,950	1,326	624	48	37	11
City/urban, community, and regional planning	487	349	138	1,272	739	533	79	52	27
Architectural environmental design	722	479	243	36	14	22	6	5	1
Interior architecture	995	144	851	21	4	17	0	0	0
Landscape architecture	1,033	716	317	327	163	164	2	1	1
Architectural urban design and planning	30	18	12	69	47	22	1	1	0
Architecture and related programs, other	633	469	164	133	83	50	12	9	3
Area, ethnic, and cultural studies, total	5,481	1,977	3,504	1,523	732	791	178	90	88
Area studies, total	3,978	1,564	2,414	1,164	568	596	154	77	77
African studies	41	16	25	15	9	6	3	2	1
American studies/civilization	1,558	580	978	251	100	151	87	36	51
Latin American studies	389	122	267	219	114	105	8	6	2
Middle Eastern studies	89	40	49	95	45	50	18	10	8
Russian and Slavic studies	292	124	168	126	60	66	2	2	0
Asian studies	934	444	490	311	155	156	24	14	10
European studies	246	88	158	64	34	30	8	4	4
Area studies, other	429	150	279	83	51	32	4	3	1
Ethnic and cultural studies, total	1,263	332	931	214	58	156	18	10	8
Afro-American (black) studies	433	159	274	68	21	47	8	4	4
Hispanic-American studies	133	38	95	28	3	25	0	0	0
Women's studies	411	11	400	33	0	33	0	0	0
Ethnic studies, other	286	124	162	85	34	51	10	6	4
Area, ethnic and cultural studies, other	240	81	159	145	106	39	6	3	3
Biological sciences/life sciences, total	47,038	22,842	24,196	4,756	2,343	2,413	4,435	2,664	1,771
Biology, general	34,932	16,500	18,432	2,000	1,001	999	671	398	273

Table 241.—Bachelor's, master's, and doctor's degrees conferred by institutions of higher education, by sex of student and field of study: 1992–93—Continued

Field of study	Bachelor's degrees requiring 4 or 5 years			Master's degrees			Doctor's degrees (Ph.D., Ed.D., etc.)		
	Total	Men	Women	Total	Men	Women	Total	Men	Women
1	2	3	4	5	6	7	8	9	10
Biochemistry and biophysics	2,327	1,370	957	207	108	99	692	448	244
Botany, total	263	135	128	224	111	113	223	140	83
Botany, general	249	128	121	137	68	69	119	66	53
Plant pathology	11	5	6	76	36	40	78	55	23
Botany, other	3	2	1	11	7	4	26	19	7
Cell and molecular biology, total	1,222	688	534	160	72	88	405	235	170
Cell biology	157	87	70	64	28	36	138	74	64
Molecular biology	424	244	180	76	37	39	188	111	77
Cell and molecular biology, other	641	357	284	20	7	13	79	50	29
Microbiology/bacteriology	1,769	872	897	328	153	175	520	290	230
Miscellaneous biological specializations, total	2,098	1,045	1,053	1,086	472	614	945	551	394
Anatomy	102	62	40	43	21	22	107	55	52
Ecology	485	286	199	240	144	96	83	55	28
Marine/aquatic biology	513	257	256	96	56	40	30	20	10
Neurosciences	141	75	66	52	35	17	154	99	55
Nutritional sciences	254	57	197	234	27	207	100	36	64
Toxicology	45	20	25	61	30	31	53	30	23
Genetics, plant and animal	160	78	82	123	47	76	219	135	84
Biometrics	18	8	10	31	15	16	24	20	4
Miscellaneous specialized areas, other	380	202	178	206	97	109	175	101	74
Zoology, total	3,071	1,563	1,508	637	372	265	786	494	292
Zoology, general	2,552	1,268	1,284	208	118	90	134	87	47
Entomology	70	54	16	122	86	36	116	86	30
Pathology, human and animal	11	3	8	29	16	13	110	72	38
Pharmacology, human and animal	33	21	12	51	25	26	215	116	99
Physiology, human and animal	404	217	187	226	127	99	211	133	78
Zoology, other	1	0	1	1	0	1	0	0	0
Biological sciences/life sciences, other	1,356	669	687	114	54	60	193	108	85
Business management, administrative services and marketing operations/marketing and distribution, total	256,842	135,573	121,269	89,615	57,651	31,964	1,346	969	377
Business management and administrative services, total	249,871	132,674	117,197	89,064	57,327	31,737	1,339	968	371
Business, general	26,786	14,655	12,131	12,517	8,373	4,144	271	190	81
Business administration and management, total	89,390	47,741	41,649	48,695	31,831	16,864	662	488	174
Office supervision and management	854	109	745	41	23	18	0	0	0
Operations management and supervision	1,855	1,390	465	565	434	131	0	0	0
Business administration and management, other	86,681	46,242	40,439	48,089	31,374	16,715	662	488	174
Accounting	48,853	22,371	26,482	3,887	2,111	1,776	69	45	24
Secretarial and related programs	443	65	378	1	0	1	0	0	0
Business/managerial economics	3,740	2,452	1,288	209	146	63	42	33	9
Small business management and ownership	434	288	146	53	37	16	0	0	0
Finance, general and banking and financial support services	22,903	15,602	7,301	4,942	3,573	1,369	53	45	8
Actuarial sciences	393	243	150	62	38	24	0	0	0
Insurance and risk management	658	403	255	108	79	29	4	3	1
Investments and securities and financial planning	324	197	127	217	152	65	0	0	0
Hospitality services management	5,945	2,737	3,208	533	277	256	4	3	1
Human resources management	5,139	1,972	3,167	2,023	916	1,107	19	10	9
Labor/personnel relations and studies	1,180	579	601	816	325	491	16	8	8
Organizational behavior studies	902	389	513	813	460	353	19	6	13
International business	2,584	1,236	1,348	2,787	1,713	1,074	12	10	2
Business information systems, total	5,570	3,258	2,312	1,800	1,269	531	7	5	2
Management information systems and data processing, general	5,174	3,014	2,160	1,592	1,110	482	7	5	2
Business information systems, other	396	244	152	208	159	49	0	0	0
Quantitative methods and management science, total	2,090	1,206	884	921	651	270	32	24	8
Business statistics	38	22	16	29	18	11	8	5	3
Management science, other	2,052	1,184	868	892	633	259	24	19	5
Marketing management and research	27,437	14,424	13,013	2,131	1,161	970	39	29	10
Real estate	660	482	178	348	286	62	1	1	0
Taxation	2	1	1	1,559	934	625	0	0	0
Consumer and personal services	160	113	47	0	0	0	0	0	0
Business management and administrative services, other	4,278	2,260	2,018	4,642	2,995	1,647	89	68	21
Marketing operations/marketing and distribution, total	6,971	2,899	4,072	551	324	227	7	1	6
Apparel and accessories marketing operations	1,624	71	1,553	0	0	0	5	0	5
Business and personal services marketing operations	561	331	230	7	3	4	0	0	0
General/retailing and wholesaling operations and skills	3,728	1,885	1,843	393	218	175	2	1	1
Transportation and travel marketing	284	87	197	20	6	14	0	0	0
Marketing and distribution, other	774	525	249	131	97	34	0	0	0
Communications and communications technologies, total	54,706	22,028	32,678	5,209	1,980	3,229	301	146	155
Communications, total	53,874	21,601	32,273	4,754	1,725	3,029	293	143	150
Communications, general	25,308	9,876	15,432	1,565	569	996	184	81	103
Advertising	3,109	1,244	1,865	239	83	156	0	0	0
Journalism	11,443	4,128	7,315	1,528	518	1,010	26	13	13
Broadcast journalism	495	203	292	12	6	6	0	0	0

Table 241.—Bachelor's, master's, and doctor's degrees conferred by institutions of higher education, by sex of student and field of study: 1992–93—Continued

Field of study	Bachelor's degrees requiring 4 or 5 years			Master's degrees			Doctor's degrees (Ph.D., Ed.D., etc.)		
	Total	Men	Women	Total	Men	Women	Total	Men	Women
1	2	3	4	5	6	7	8	9	10
Public relations and organizational communications	2,255	695	1,560	231	49	182	0	0	0
Radio and television broadcasting	6,469	3,374	3,095	365	188	177	14	8	6
Communications, other	4,795	2,081	2,714	814	312	502	69	41	28
Communications technologies, total	832	427	405	455	255	200	8	3	5
Photographic technology	23	10	13	0	0	0	0	0	0
Radio and television technology	725	370	355	327	177	150	8	3	5
Communications technologies, other	84	47	37	128	78	50	0	0	0
Computer and information sciences, total	24,200	17,403	6,797	10,163	7,410	2,753	805	689	116
Computer and information sciences, general	15,997	11,914	4,083	7,438	5,554	1,884	686	587	99
Computer programming	145	107	38	15	13	2	0	0	0
Data processing technology/technician	225	127	98	62	44	18	0	0	0
Information science and systems	3,644	2,184	1,460	1,301	790	511	15	11	4
Computer systems analysis	231	156	75	78	60	18	8	7	1
Computer and information sciences, other	3,958	2,915	1,043	1,269	949	320	96	84	12
Education, total	107,781	23,233	84,548	96,028	22,197	73,831	7,030	2,867	4,163
Education, general	2,009	287	1,722	10,127	2,379	7,748	1,196	455	741
Bilingual/bicultural education	56	5	51	227	38	189	11	6	5
Curriculum and instruction	9	4	5	7,694	1,430	6,264	785	269	516
Education administration and supervision, total	6	1	5	10,638	4,142	6,496	2,248	1,046	1,202
Education administration and supervision, general	4	0	4	7,030	2,776	4,254	1,620	772	848
Administration of special education	0	0	0	10	2	8	11	0	11
Adult and continuing education administration	0	0	0	217	49	168	61	21	40
Educational supervision	0	0	0	724	203	521	24	5	19
Elementary, middle, and secondary education administration	0	0	0	1,644	721	923	41	23	18
Higher education administration	1	0	1	406	147	259	391	176	215
Community and junior college education administration	0	0	0	71	31	40	7	4	3
Education administration and supervision, other	1	1	0	536	213	323	93	45	48
Educational/instructional media design	27	12	15	939	279	660	62	32	30
Educational evaluation and research, general	18	7	11	31	7	24	26	10	16
Educational statistics and research methods	1	0	1	35	13	22	41	23	18
Educational assessment, testing and measurement	0	0	0	89	18	71	23	13	10
Social and philosophical foundations of education	24	7	17	250	69	181	102	46	56
Special education, total	8,657	674	7,983	9,765	1,324	8,441	249	67	182
Special education, general	5,835	460	5,375	7,545	1,059	6,486	233	62	171
Education of the deaf and hearing impaired	203	11	192	235	25	210	0	0	0
Education of the gifted and talented	1	0	1	171	20	151	0	0	0
Education of the emotionally handicapped	297	41	256	218	52	166	2	0	2
Education of the mentally handicapped	627	46	581	147	25	122	0	0	0
Education of the multiple handicapped	113	5	108	99	3	96	0	0	0
Education of the physically handicapped	28	3	25	63	11	52	0	0	0
Education of the blind and visually handicapped	27	0	27	28	5	23	0	0	0
Education of the specific learning disabled	573	48	525	659	50	609	9	3	6
Education of the speech impaired	672	21	651	295	22	273	0	0	0
Special education, other	281	39	242	305	52	253	5	2	3
Counselor education/counseling and guidance services	76	18	58	11,555	2,502	9,053	375	135	240
General teacher education, total	61,244	5,860	55,384	22,127	3,470	18,657	433	144	289
Adult and continuing education	24	10	14	927	259	668	148	58	90
Elementary education	49,485	3,881	45,604	13,234	1,250	11,984	76	17	59
Junior high/intermediate/middle school education	1,308	254	1,054	563	86	477	0	0	0
Pre-elementary/early childhood/kindergarten education	6,154	163	5,991	1,893	43	1,850	45	2	43
Secondary education	3,773	1,522	2,251	3,707	1,387	2,320	76	32	44
Teacher education, general programs, other	500	30	470	1,803	445	1,358	88	35	53
Teacher education, academic and vocational programs	34,742	16,059	18,683	16,467	5,124	11,343	821	381	440
Agricultural education (vocational)	427	312	115	234	164	70	48	37	11
Art education	1,804	310	1,494	656	94	562	27	8	19
Business education (vocational)	1,572	371	1,201	525	133	392	16	6	10
Driver and safety education	35	29	6	60	42	18	1	1	0
English education	2,895	596	2,299	739	161	578	21	5	16
Foreign languages education	399	79	320	242	39	203	9	1	8
Health education	1,540	432	1,108	841	181	660	87	24	63
Home economics education (vocational)	340	8	332	177	6	171	10	0	10
Technology/industrial arts education	1,506	1,307	199	495	361	134	22	19	3
Marketing operations/marketing and distribution education	99	43	56	17	3	14	2	1	1
Mathematics education	1,953	710	1,243	912	282	630	35	11	24
Music education	2,821	1,175	1,646	896	375	521	74	35	39
Physical education and coaching	11,553	6,578	4,975	3,044	1,594	1,450	174	96	78
Reading education	152	15	137	3,935	183	3,752	71	11	60
Science education	1,138	468	670	720	313	407	36	22	14
Social science education	855	460	395	118	60	58	6	1	5
Social studies education	2,402	1,416	986	453	260	193	5	4	1
Technical education (vocational)	223	148	75	275	113	162	42	16	26
Trade and industrial education (vocational)	1,100	777	323	458	222	236	75	51	24
Teacher education, academic and vocational programs, other	1,928	825	1,103	1,670	538	1,132	60	32	28

Table 241.—Bachelor's, master's, and doctor's degrees conferred by institutions of higher education, by sex of student and field of study: 1992–93—Continued

Field of study	Bachelor's degrees requiring 4 or 5 years			Master's degrees			Doctor's degrees (Ph.D., Ed.D., etc.)		
	Total	Men	Women	Total	Men	Women	Total	Men	Women
1	2	3	4	5	6	7	8	9	10
Teaching English as a second language/foreign language	39	14	25	1,544	365	1,179	2	2	0
Education, other	873	285	588	4,540	1,037	3,503	656	238	418
Engineering and engineering-related technologies, total	78,051	66,836	11,215	28,726	24,454	4,272	5,843	5,283	560
Engineering, total	61,973	52,185	9,788	27,626	23,537	4,089	5,823	5,265	558
Engineering, general	2,128	1,802	326	1,338	1,142	196	274	249	25
Aerospace, aeronautical, and astronautical engineering	2,735	2,419	316	1,047	941	106	203	197	6
Agricultural engineering	512	432	80	150	122	28	80	73	7
Architectural engineering	497	400	97	29	23	6	0	0	0
Bioengineering and biomedical engineering	706	480	226	469	322	147	150	121	29
Ceramic sciences and engineering	287	234	53	92	69	23	60	52	8
Chemical engineering	4,459	2,995	1,464	990	792	198	595	516	79
Civil engineering	8,868	7,291	1,577	3,610	3,003	607	577	527	50
Computer engineering	2,138	1,888	250	955	817	138	123	108	15
Electrical, electronics, and communications engineering	17,281	15,314	1,967	7,870	6,957	913	1,413	1,295	118
Engineering mechanics	134	116	18	186	170	16	98	90	8
Engineering physics	295	253	42	68	65	3	50	46	4
Engineering science	286	215	71	357	285	72	49	41	8
Environmental/environmental health engineering	262	180	82	783	566	217	40	37	3
Geological engineering	104	71	33	46	40	6	11	10	1
Geophysical engineering	8	5	3	10	9	1	1	1	0
Industrial/manufacturing engineering	3,300	2,354	946	2,058	1,622	436	267	235	32
Material engineering	588	447	141	537	434	103	336	275	61
Mechanical engineering	14,464	12,863	1,601	3,982	3,598	384	871	823	48
Metallurgical engineering	298	241	57	171	139	32	93	86	7
Mining and mineral engineering	111	100	11	66	61	5	25	25	0
Naval architecture and marine engineering	275	259	16	31	27	4	6	5	1
Nuclear engineering	234	207	27	269	236	33	115	108	7
Ocean engineering	99	78	21	94	81	13	29	28	1
Petroleum engineering	256	226	30	139	128	11	50	44	6
Systems engineering	411	342	69	403	318	85	31	25	6
Textile sciences and engineering	34	21	13	19	12	7	1	1	0
Engineering, other	1,203	952	251	1,857	1,558	299	275	247	28
Engineering-related technologies, total	16,078	14,651	1,427	1,100	917	183	20	18	2
Architectural engineering technologies	600	530	70	1	1	0	0	0	0
Civil technologies	435	387	48	0	0	0	0	0	0
Electrical and electronic technologies	3,986	3,705	281	37	34	3	0	0	0
Electromechanical instrumentation and maintenance technologies	316	303	13	10	9	1	3	2	1
Environmental control technologies	253	199	54	58	38	20	1	1	0
Industrial production technologies	4,377	3,905	472	295	258	37	5	5	0
Quality control and safety technologies	395	310	85	265	202	63	4	4	0
Mechanical and related technologies	1,836	1,715	121	0	0	0	0	0	0
Mining and petroleum technologies	24	24	0	0	0	0	0	0	0
Surveying	125	115	10	26	19	7	7	6	1
Mechanics and repairers	69	64	5	0	0	0	0	0	0
Construction trades	105	102	3	0	0	0	0	0	0
Engineering and related technologies, other	3,557	3,292	265	408	356	52	0	0	0
English language and literature/letters, total	56,133	19,247	36,886	7,790	2,667	5,123	1,341	550	791
English language and literature, general	41,564	13,822	27,742	5,287	1,812	3,475	949	388	561
Comparative literature	844	240	604	253	97	156	140	55	85
English composition	307	145	162	12	4	8	7	2	5
English creative writing	872	363	509	749	305	444	7	5	2
American literature (United States)	135	48	87	23	5	18	12	3	9
English literature (British and Commonwealth)	1,493	535	958	332	104	228	69	28	41
Speech and rhetorical studies	9,605	3,630	5,975	833	261	572	108	53	55
English technical and business writing	106	44	62	158	45	113	0	0	0
English language and literature/letters, other	1,207	420	787	143	34	109	49	16	33
Foreign languages and literatures, total	14,387	4,158	10,229	3,198	1,062	2,136	830	355	475
Foreign languages and literatures, total	1,481	411	1,070	926	310	616	235	103	132
Foreign languages and literatures, general	928	252	676	318	93	225	53	19	34
Linguistics	553	159	394	608	217	391	182	84	98
East and Southeast Asian languages and literatures, total	585	294	291	142	57	85	20	13	7
Chinese	129	67	62	54	26	28	8	7	1
Japanese	327	151	176	57	13	44	2	1	1
East and Southeast Asian languages, other	129	76	53	31	18	13	10	5	5
East European languages and literatures, total	693	266	427	166	62	104	28	14	14
Russian languages	612	231	381	68	20	48	4	0	4
Slavic languages (other than Russian)	77	33	44	93	39	54	24	14	10
East European languages, other	4	2	2	5	3	2	0	0	0
Germanic languages and literatures, total	1,611	640	971	346	133	213	97	42	55
German	1,572	629	943	317	123	194	86	37	49

Table 241.—Bachelor's, master's, and doctor's degrees conferred by institutions of higher education, by sex of student and field of study: 1992–93—Continued

Field of study	Bachelor's degrees requiring 4 or 5 years			Master's degrees			Doctor's degrees (Ph.D., Ed.D., etc.)		
	Total	Men	Women	Total	Men	Women	Total	Men	Women
1	2	3	4	5	6	7	8	9	10
Scandinavian languages	20	5	15	8	2	6	1	1	0
Germanic languages, other	19	6	13	21	8	13	10	4	6
South Asian languages and literatures	4	2	2	1	0	1	5	3	2
Romance languages and literatures, total	8,916	2,047	6,869	1,329	364	965	312	107	205
French	3,280	634	2,646	513	125	388	98	34	64
Italian	274	62	212	50	18	32	13	5	8
Portuguese	41	27	14	9	3	6	1	1	0
Spanish	5,233	1,309	3,924	667	194	473	145	47	98
Romance languages, other	88	15	73	90	24	66	55	20	35
Middle Eastern languages and literatures, total	82	36	46	51	35	16	20	12	8
Arabic	8	3	5	3	2	1	2	1	1
Hebrew	54	22	32	33	26	7	7	6	1
Middle East languages, other	20	11	9	15	7	8	11	5	6
Classical and ancient Near East languages and literatures, total .	741	371	370	144	77	67	60	34	26
Classics	598	300	298	128	69	59	58	33	25
Greek (ancient and medieval)	35	18	17	3	1	2	1	0	1
Latin (ancient and medieval)	108	53	55	13	7	6	1	1	0
Foreign languages, other	274	91	183	93	24	69	53	27	26
Health professions and related sciences, total	67,089	11,347	55,742	25,718	5,227	20,491	1,767	753	1,014
Communication disorders sciences and services	4,814	252	4,562	4,002	171	3,831	102	23	79
Community health liaison	460	86	374	121	37	84	2	2	0
Dentistry	0	0	0	352	221	131	27	21	6
Dental services	927	25	902	48	27	21	0	0	0
Epidemiology	0	0	0	239	96	143	82	34	48
Health services administration, total	3,341	821	2,520	3,303	1,155	2,148	51	26	25
Health services administration	1,681	456	1,225	1,774	655	1,119	30	11	19
Medical records administration	635	49	586	0	0	0	0	0	0
Medical records technology/technician	3	0	3	5	3	2	6	5	1
Health and medical administrative services, other	1,022	316	706	1,524	497	1,027	15	10	5
Health and medical assistants, total	967	468	499	184	48	136	0	0	0
Medical assistant	2	0	2	0	0	0	0	0	0
Physician assistant	858	441	417	171	44	127	0	0	0
Health and medical assistants, other	107	27	80	13	4	9	0	0	0
Health and medical diagnostic and treatment services, total	1,255	467	788	56	30	26	0	0	0
Respiratory therapy technology/technician ...	322	112	210	0	0	0	0	0	0
Health and medical diagnostic and treatment services, other ...	933	355	578	56	30	26	0	0	0
Medical laboratory technologies, total	2,458	700	1,758	380	159	221	111	52	59
Medical technology	2,135	593	1,542	61	21	40	3	2	1
Health and medical laboratory technologies/technicians, other .	323	107	216	319	138	181	108	50	58
Pre-dentistry studies	176	102	74	3	2	1	0	0	0
Pre-medicine studies	690	382	308	0	0	0	0	0	0
Pre-pharmacy studies	400	161	239	0	0	0	0	0	0
Pre-veterinary studies	265	103	162	2	1	1	0	0	0
Medical basic sciences	216	84	132	249	116	133	313	192	121
Mental health services, total	537	86	451	383	90	293	6	2	4
Alcohol/drug abuse counseling	88	29	59	52	15	37	0	0	0
Psychiatric/mental health services technician	153	26	127	48	21	27	0	0	0
Clinical and medical social work	82	9	73	97	24	73	6	2	4
Mental health services, other	214	22	192	186	30	156	0	0	0
Nursing	34,792	2,934	31,858	8,151	527	7,624	396	20	376
Optometry	183	81	102	7	2	5	1	1	0
Pharmacy	5,489	2,071	3,418	257	115	142	203	124	79
Rehabilitation/therapeutic services, total	6,625	1,276	5,349	3,889	902	2,987	37	13	24
Art therapy	58	3	55	202	12	190	0	0	0
Dance therapy	1	0	1	34	0	34	0	0	0
Music therapy	155	19	136	16	4	12	0	0	0
Occupational therapy	2,500	241	2,259	521	51	470	3	1	2
Orthotics/prosthetics	34	25	9	0	0	0	0	0	0
Physical therapy	2,928	792	2,136	2,202	586	1,616	9	5	4
Recreational therapy	125	24	101	3	1	2	5	0	5
Vocational rehabilitation counseling	178	46	132	578	155	423	5	2	3
Rehabilitative services, other	646	126	520	333	93	240	15	5	10
Veterinary medicine	126	53	73	153	87	66	132	87	45
Miscellaneous health professions	297	160	137	201	92	109	28	24	4
Health professions and related sciences, other	3,071	1,035	2,036	3,738	1,349	2,389	276	132	144
Home economics and vocational home economics, total	15,100	1,638	13,462	2,479	422	2,057	345	97	248
Home economics, total	14,444	1,382	13,062	2,440	417	2,023	335	95	240
Home economics, general	2,974	201	2,773	300	23	277	42	14	28
Home economics business services	156	10	146	2	0	2	0	0	0
Family and community studies	185	24	161	65	16	49	2	2	0
Family and consumer resource management	1,285	368	917	60	9	51	22	2	20
Food and nutrition studies	2,735	343	2,392	534	61	473	60	13	47
Housing studies	576	65	511	51	19	32	1	0	1
Individual and family development studies	4,422	279	4,143	1,287	276	1,011	190	58	132

Table 241.—Bachelor's, master's, and doctor's degrees conferred by institutions of higher education, by sex of student and field of study: 1992–93—Continued

Field of study	Bachelor's degrees requiring 4 or 5 years			Master's degrees			Doctor's degrees (Ph.D., Ed.D., etc.)		
	Total	Men	Women	Total	Men	Women	Total	Men	Women
1	2	3	4	5	6	7	8	9	10
Clothing/apparel and textile studies	1,960	77	1,883	110	12	98	14	5	9
Home economics, other	151	15	136	31	1	30	4	1	3
Vocational home economics, total	656	256	400	39	5	34	10	2	8
Child care and guidance management	180	0	180	34	1	33	4	0	4
Custodial, housekeeping and home services workers and managers	5	3	2	4	4	0	0	0	0
Vocational home economics, other	471	253	218	1	0	1	6	2	4
Law and legal studies, total	2,056	667	1,389	2,197	1,481	716	86	65	21
Pre-law studies	262	140	122	12	4	8	0	0	0
Paralegal/legal assistant	913	143	770	13	5	8	0	0	0
Law and legal studies, other	881	384	497	2,172	1,472	700	86	65	21
Liberal arts and sciences, general studies, and humanities, total	33,456	13,275	20,181	2,416	840	1,576	81	38	43
Liberal arts and sciences/liberal studies	21,044	7,655	13,389	1,630	548	1,082	18	9	9
Humanities/humanistic studies	2,898	1,011	1,887	491	188	303	32	17	15
Liberal arts and sciences, general studies, other	9,514	4,609	4,905	295	104	191	31	12	19
Library science, total	83	9	74	4,871	961	3,910	77	26	51
Library science/librarianship	81	9	72	4,767	950	3,817	72	22	50
Library science, other	2	0	2	104	11	93	5	4	1
Mathematics, total	14,812	7,827	6,985	4,067	2,455	1,612	1,189	906	283
Mathematics	12,635	6,522	6,113	2,423	1,449	974	808	623	185
Applied mathematics, total	1,285	758	527	822	553	269	159	116	43
Applied mathematics, general and other	857	497	360	399	249	150	108	77	31
Operations research (quantitative methods)	428	261	167	423	304	119	51	39	12
Mathematical statistics	520	296	224	763	420	343	214	160	54
Mathematics, other	372	251	121	59	33	26	8	7	1
Multi/interdisciplinary studies, total	23,955	8,917	15,038	2,498	1,221	1,277	196	115	81
Biological and physical sciences	2,007	1,115	892	163	92	71	24	14	10
Systems science and theory	121	70	51	276	163	113	12	11	1
Museology/museum studies	2	1	1	103	24	79	0	0	0
Multi/interdisciplinary studies, other	21,825	7,731	14,094	1,956	942	1,014	160	90	70
Parks, recreation, leisure, and fitness studies, total	9,859	4,885	4,974	1,434	714	720	108	75	33
Parks, recreation and leisure studies	2,040	871	1,169	222	107	115	23	16	7
Parks, recreation and leisure facilities management	2,455	1,095	1,360	249	107	142	10	6	4
Health and physical education/fitness	5,230	2,832	2,398	940	493	447	73	52	21
Parks, recreation, leisure and fitness studies, other	134	87	47	23	7	16	2	1	1
Philosophy and religion, total	7,781	4,938	2,843	1,425	988	437	448	323	125
Philosophy	4,842	3,310	1,532	707	519	188	266	199	67
Religion/religious studies	2,569	1,415	1,154	680	459	221	177	120	57
Philosophy and religion, other	370	213	157	38	10	28	5	4	1
Physical sciences and science technologies, total	17,545	11,825	5,720	5,366	3,808	1,558	4,393	3,432	961
Physical sciences, total	17,462	11,773	5,689	5,347	3,793	1,554	4,376	3,419	957
Physical sciences, general	380	270	110	68	52	16	0	0	0
Astronomy	116	89	27	89	66	23	82	68	14
Astrophysics	51	31	20	46	40	6	16	13	3
Atmospheric science and meteorology	369	305	64	202	161	41	65	55	10
Chemistry, total	8,914	5,288	3,626	1,842	1,105	737	2,261	1,623	638
Chemistry, general	8,674	5,148	3,526	1,713	1,040	673	2,081	1,494	587
Analytical chemistry	0	0	0	19	8	11	22	16	6
Inorganic chemistry	0	0	0	0	0	0	7	6	1
Organic chemistry	11	2	9	11	3	8	14	9	5
Medicinal/pharmaceutical chemistry	11	6	5	20	5	15	45	28	17
Chemistry, other	218	132	86	79	49	30	92	70	22
Geological and related sciences, total	2,299	1,554	745	925	670	255	406	334	72
Geology	2,136	1,446	690	793	565	228	314	254	60
Geochemistry	6	3	3	5	3	2	10	8	2
Geophysics and seismology	45	32	13	69	59	10	53	48	5
Geological and related sciences, other	112	73	39	58	43	15	29	24	5
Miscellaneous physical sciences, total	924	639	285	335	213	122	233	187	46
Metallurgy	0	0	0	3	3	0	0	0	0
Oceanography	233	170	63	143	89	54	112	85	27
Earth and planetary sciences	591	415	176	127	86	41	108	90	18
Miscellaneous physical sciences, other	100	54	46	62	35	27	13	12	1
Physics, total	4,063	3,390	673	1,777	1,460	317	1,277	1,107	170
Physics, general	3,892	3,249	643	1,643	1,356	287	1,210	1,051	159

Table 241.—Bachelor's, master's, and doctor's degrees conferred by institutions of higher education, by sex of student and field of study: 1992–93—Continued

Field of study	Bachelor's degrees requiring 4 or 5 years			Master's degrees			Doctor's degrees (Ph.D., Ed.D., etc.)		
	Total	Men	Women	Total	Men	Women	Total	Men	Women
1	2	3	4	5	6	7	8	9	10
Physics, other	171	141	30	134	104	30	67	56	11
Physical sciences, other	346	207	139	63	26	37	36	32	4
Science technologies, total	83	52	31	19	15	4	17	13	4
Precision production trades, total	388	281	107	2	2	0	0	0	0
Drafting, general	149	127	22	0	0	0	0	0	0
Precision production trades, other	239	154	85	2	2	0	0	0	0
Protective services, total	20,902	13,020	7,882	1,357	837	520	32	23	9
Criminal justice and corrections, total	20,623	12,774	7,849	1,323	806	517	32	23	9
Corrections/correctional administration	666	363	303	56	42	14	0	0	0
Criminal justice/law enforcement administration	6,642	4,178	2,464	472	288	184	6	4	2
Criminal justice studies	10,436	6,277	4,159	683	416	267	26	19	7
Forensic studies	163	91	72	38	20	18	0	0	0
Law enforcement/police science	1,712	1,287	425	47	24	23	0	0	0
Criminal justice, other	1,004	578	426	27	16	11	0	0	0
Fire control and safety	230	218	12	25	23	2	0	0	0
Protective services, other	49	28	21	9	8	1	0	0	0
Psychology, total	66,728	17,908	48,820	10,957	3,029	7,928	3,651	1,415	2,236
Psychology, general	63,247	17,021	46,226	4,265	1,323	2,942	1,575	659	916
Clinical psychology	64	14	50	1,319	345	974	1,205	426	779
Counseling psychology	261	57	204	3,117	761	2,356	236	88	148
Developmental and child psychology	732	79	653	115	26	89	57	15	42
Experimental psychology	251	57	194	82	29	53	90	38	52
Industrial and organizational psychology	156	62	94	309	124	185	63	28	35
Physiological psychology/psychobiology	172	75	97	7	4	3	26	12	14
Social psychology	195	40	155	110	19	91	34	11	23
School psychology	0	0	0	609	114	495	108	30	78
Psychology, other	1,650	503	1,147	1,024	284	740	257	108	149
Public administration and services, total	16,775	3,801	12,974	20,634	6,105	14,529	459	215	244
Public administration	2,607	1,384	1,223	6,347	3,340	3,007	120	82	38
Community organization, resources and services	1,241	312	929	210	72	138	4	1	3
Public policy analysis	382	210	172	670	330	340	70	42	28
Social work	12,090	1,663	10,427	13,032	2,223	10,809	233	81	152
Public affairs, other	455	232	223	375	140	235	32	9	23
R.O.T.C. and military technologies, total	11	11	0	108	100	8	0	0	0
Social sciences and history, total	135,703	73,589	62,114	13,471	7,671	5,800	3,460	2,203	1,257
Social sciences, general	7,390	3,188	4,202	473	213	260	70	39	31
Anthropology	5,098	1,819	3,279	913	388	525	359	138	221
Archeology	95	41	54	14	5	9	11	5	6
Criminology	1,772	1,005	767	83	48	35	8	2	6
Demography and population studies	0	0	0	38	13	25	13	8	5
Economics	21,321	14,965	6,356	2,292	1,611	681	879	674	205
Geography, total	4,151	2,752	1,399	646	423	223	150	105	45
Geography	4,116	2,724	1,392	643	421	222	150	105	45
Cartography	35	28	7	3	2	1	0	0	0
History	27,774	17,212	10,562	2,952	1,812	1,140	690	451	239
International relations and affairs	6,361	2,721	3,640	1,859	994	865	79	55	24
Political science and government, general	37,931	22,052	15,879	1,943	1,239	704	529	389	140
Sociology	20,896	6,605	14,291	1,521	591	930	536	272	264
Urban affairs/studies	699	370	329	291	148	143	74	43	31
Social sciences and history, other	2,215	859	1,356	446	186	260	62	22	40
Theological studies/religious vocations, total	5,433	4,168	1,265	4,985	2,989	1,996	1,417	1,219	198
Biblical and other theological languages and literatures	52	37	15	62	23	39	7	7	0
Bible/biblical studies	1,439	1,112	327	275	221	54	11	11	0
Missions/missionary studies and misology	312	185	127	195	111	84	45	41	4
Religious education	832	507	325	788	391	397	55	48	7
Religious/sacred music	173	90	83	102	52	50	17	15	2
Theology/theological studies	2,131	1,883	248	2,546	1,682	864	922	812	110
Pastoral counseling and specialized ministries	101	75	26	680	298	382	198	155	43
Theological studies and religious vocations, other	393	279	114	337	211	126	162	130	32
Transportation and materials moving workers, total	3,930	3,508	422	495	456	39	0	0	0
Water transportation workers	286	264	22	0	0	0	0	0	0
Transportation and material moving, other	3,644	3,244	400	495	456	39	0	0	0
Visual and performing arts, total	47,761	18,610	29,151	9,440	4,099	5,341	882	478	404

Table 241.—Bachelor's, master's, and doctor's degrees conferred by institutions of higher education, by sex of student and field of study: 1992–93—Continued

Field of study	Bachelor's degrees requiring 4 or 5 years			Master's degrees			Doctor's degrees (Ph.D., Ed.D., etc.)		
	Total	Men	Women	Total	Men	Women	Total	Men	Women
1	2	3	4	5	6	7	8	9	10
Visual and performing arts, general	1,477	559	918	120	45	75	9	7	2
Crafts, folk art, and artisanry	99	37	62	7	2	5	0	0	0
Dance	812	79	733	204	38	166	3	0	3
Design and applied art	7,914	2,929	4,985	431	185	246	1	0	1
Dramatic/theater arts and stagecraft	5,891	2,357	3,534	1,290	626	664	76	47	29
Film/video and photographic arts, total	2,681	1,664	1,017	566	347	219	14	9	5
Film-video making/cinematography and production	868	575	293	284	182	102	5	2	3
Photography	987	527	460	150	83	67	1	1	0
Film arts, other	826	562	264	132	82	50	8	6	2
Fine arts and art studies, total	20,526	6,825	13,701	3,090	1,143	1,947	137	49	88
Art, general	11,347	4,039	7,308	980	384	596	39	14	25
Art history, criticism and conservation	4,192	998	3,194	798	232	566	97	34	63
Arts management	119	27	92	111	25	86	0	0	0
Painting	846	316	530	214	97	117	0	0	0
Ceramic arts and ceramics	212	73	139	44	21	23	0	0	0
Fiber, textile and weaving arts	118	9	109	37	7	30	1	1	0
Metal and jewelry arts	75	23	52	20	5	15	0	0	0
Fine arts and art studies, other	3,617	1,340	2,277	886	372	514	0	0	0
Music, total	7,853	3,962	3,891	3,488	1,629	1,859	609	357	252
Music, general	3,836	1,856	1,980	1,090	511	579	238	136	102
Music history and literature	58	18	40	37	18	19	33	21	12
Music, general performance	2,683	1,271	1,412	1,862	826	1,036	219	125	94
Music theory and composition	209	161	48	151	111	40	62	44	18
Music, other	1,067	656	411	348	163	185	57	31	26
Visual and performing arts, other	508	198	310	244	84	160	33	9	24
Not classified by field of study	5,247	2,340	2,907	884	504	380	111	93	18

NOTE.—Aggregations by field of study derived from the *Classification of Instructional Programs* developed by the National Center for Education Statistics.

SOURCE: U.S. Department of Education, National Center for Education Statistics, Integrated Postsecondary Education Data System (IPEDS), "Completions" survey. (This table was prepared January 1995.)

Table 242.—Bachelor's, master's, and doctor's degrees conferred by institutions of higher education, by sex of student and field of study: 1991–92

Field of study	Bachelor's degrees requiring 4 or 5 years			Master's degrees			Doctor's degrees (Ph.D., Ed.D., etc.)		
	Total	Men	Women	Total	Men	Women	Total	Men	Women
1	2	3	4	5	6	7	8	9	10
All fields	1,136,553	520,811	615,742	352,838	161,842	190,996	40,659	25,557	15,102
Agriculture and natural resources, total	15,124	9,869	5,255	3,735	2,413	1,322	1,214	963	251
Agricultural business and production, total	4,682	3,392	1,290	687	490	197	176	147	29
Agricultural business and management, total	3,349	2,458	891	534	385	149	139	115	24
Agricultural business and management, general	692	450	242	56	36	20	0	0	0
Agricultural business/agribusiness operations	1,014	783	231	18	15	3	0	0	0
Agricultural economics	1,487	1,103	384	449	326	123	139	115	24
Agricultural business and management, other	156	122	34	11	8	3	0	0	0
Agricultural mechanization	177	172	5	7	7	0	0	0	0
Agricultural production workers and managers	106	82	24	56	50	6	12	11	1
Horticulture service operations and management	370	266	104	25	15	10	13	12	1
International agriculture	15	9	6	15	7	8	0	0	0
Agricultural business and production, other	665	405	260	50	26	24	12	9	3
Agricultural sciences, total	5,793	3,384	2,409	1,592	1,012	580	773	601	172
Agriculture/agricultural sciences, general	847	600	247	132	87	45	2	2	0
Animal sciences, total	2,858	1,429	1,429	454	291	163	228	182	46
Animal sciences, general	2,369	1,151	1,218	343	217	126	169	134	35
Agricultural animal breeding and genetics	11	2	9	8	5	3	8	8	0
Agricultural animal health	8	1	7	15	6	9	9	9	0
Agricultural animal nutrition	0	0	0	3	1	2	4	2	2
Dairy science	124	94	30	34	22	12	10	8	2
Poultry science	100	73	27	28	21	7	17	13	4
Animal sciences, other	246	108	138	23	19	4	11	8	3
Food sciences and technology	449	198	251	306	143	163	133	83	50
Plant sciences, total	1,362	983	379	531	378	153	329	266	63
Plant sciences, general	201	130	71	60	39	21	28	20	8
Agronomy and crop science	438	376	62	255	203	52	188	154	34
Horticulture science	477	295	182	146	82	64	60	46	14
Plant breeding and genetics	0	0	0	9	9	0	15	13	2
Agricultural plant pathology	1	0	1	4	3	1	9	8	1
Plant protection (pest management)	17	15	2	18	11	7	3	3	0
Range science and management	111	78	33	39	31	8	26	22	4
Plant sciences, other	117	89	28	0	0	0	0	0	0
Soil sciences	94	70	24	91	67	24	59	53	6
Agriculture/agricultural sciences, other	183	104	79	78	46	32	22	15	7
Conservation and renewable natural resources, total	4,649	3,093	1,556	1,456	911	545	265	215	50
Natural resources conservation, general	2,005	1,130	875	627	362	265	72	50	22
Natural resources management and policy	280	186	94	101	67	34	3	3	0
Fishing and fisheries sciences and management	183	153	30	88	62	26	21	18	3
Forest harvesting and production technology/technician	191	160	31	21	19	2	20	17	3
Forestry, general	946	749	197	423	282	141	123	105	18
Wildlife and wildlands management	808	571	237	127	83	44	15	13	2
Conservation and renewable natural resources, other	236	144	92	69	36	33	11	9	2
Architecture and related programs, total	8,753	5,805	2,948	3,640	2,271	1,369	132	93	39
Architecture	5,001	3,598	1,403	1,832	1,258	574	50	35	15
City/urban, community, and regional planning	481	349	132	1,212	712	500	75	53	22
Architectural environmental design	799	551	248	74	33	41	2	1	1
Interior architecture	844	117	727	19	3	16	4	3	1
Landscape architecture	1,064	782	282	323	169	154	0	0	0
Architectural urban design and planning	0	0	0	63	37	26	0	0	0
Architecture and related programs, other	564	408	156	117	59	58	1	1	0
Area, ethnic, and cultural studies, total	5,342	1,907	3,435	1,385	688	697	155	90	65
Area studies, total	4,029	1,514	2,515	1,057	515	542	123	68	55
African studies	45	20	25	24	9	15	5	4	1
American studies/civilization	1,597	577	1,020	238	98	140	72	32	40
Latin American studies	339	104	235	220	122	98	5	4	1
Middle Eastern studies	63	29	34	73	32	41	16	12	4
Russian and Slavic studies	321	120	201	120	66	54	0	0	0
Asian studies	991	470	521	278	133	145	11	9	2
European studies	257	85	172	46	20	26	9	3	6
Area studies, other	416	109	307	58	35	23	5	4	1
Ethnic and cultural studies, total	1,063	316	747	169	62	107	11	5	6
Afro-American (black) studies	410	148	262	62	28	34	5	2	3
Hispanic-American studies	87	36	51	24	11	13	0	0	0
Women's studies	330	4	326	24	0	24	0	0	0
Ethnic studies, other	236	128	108	59	23	36	6	3	3
Area, ethnic and cultural studies, other	250	77	173	159	111	48	21	17	4
Biological sciences/life sciences, total	42,941	20,798	22,143	4,785	2,301	2,484	4,243	2,620	1,623
Biology, general	31,909	15,109	16,800	1,995	1,001	994	657	404	253

Table 242.—Bachelor's, master's, and doctor's degrees conferred by institutions of higher education, by sex of student and field of study: 1991–92—Continued

Field of study	Bachelor's degrees requiring 4 or 5 years			Master's degrees			Doctor's degrees (Ph.D., Ed.D., etc.)		
	Total	Men	Women	Total	Men	Women	Total	Men	Women
1	2	3	4	5	6	7	8	9	10
Biochemistry and biophysics	2,148	1,204	944	239	120	119	620	382	238
Botany, total	222	93	129	220	111	109	293	194	99
Botany, general	207	88	119	130	69	61	156	95	61
Plant pathology	12	5	7	79	37	42	85	59	26
Botany, other	3	0	3	11	5	6	52	40	12
Cell and molecular biology, total	1,108	638	470	180	93	87	323	198	125
Cell biology	122	67	55	75	33	42	103	56	47
Molecular biology	425	252	173	80	47	33	157	101	56
Cell and molecular biology, other	561	319	242	25	13	12	63	41	22
Microbiology/bacteriology	1,722	842	880	336	164	172	454	251	203
Miscellaneous biological specializations, total	1,853	871	982	1,062	396	666	872	504	368
Anatomy	31	10	21	59	29	30	95	53	42
Ecology	438	235	203	194	106	88	80	49	31
Marine/aquatic biology	394	196	198	100	59	41	29	21	8
Neurosciences	111	68	43	46	26	20	119	73	46
Nutritional sciences	284	53	231	288	30	258	115	38	77
Toxicology	60	29	31	65	30	35	70	46	24
Genetics, plant and animal	147	73	74	123	32	91	170	105	65
Biometrics	23	16	7	30	10	20	20	13	7
Miscellaneous specialized areas, other	365	191	174	157	74	83	174	106	68
Zoology, total	2,840	1,466	1,374	620	335	285	818	563	255
Zoology, general	2,350	1,183	1,167	214	103	111	161	112	49
Entomology	65	49	16	120	79	41	132	98	34
Pathology, human and animal	12	7	5	33	15	18	101	65	36
Pharmacology, human and animal	27	16	11	58	28	30	223	147	76
Physiology, human and animal	353	188	165	195	110	85	201	141	60
Zoology, other	33	23	10	0	0	0	0	0	0
Biological sciences/life sciences, other	1,139	575	564	133	81	52	206	124	82
Business management, administrative services and marketing operations/marketing and distribution, total	256,603	135,440	121,163	84,642	54,705	29,937	1,242	953	289
Business management and administrative services, total	249,062	132,450	116,612	84,047	54,369	29,678	1,238	952	286
Business, general	27,742	14,777	12,965	12,424	8,300	4,124	241	177	64
Business administration and management, total	87,652	46,864	40,788	46,752	30,463	16,289	608	470	138
Office supervision and management	953	86	867	0	0	0	0	0	0
Operations management and supervision	1,532	1,137	395	455	343	112	9	8	1
Business administration and management, other	85,167	45,641	39,526	46,297	30,120	16,177	599	462	137
Accounting	47,606	21,956	25,650	3,287	1,778	1,509	73	59	14
Secretarial and related programs	636	137	499	1	0	1	9	8	1
Business/managerial economics	3,779	2,444	1,335	159	108	51	20	14	6
Small business management and ownership	282	184	98	18	11	7	0	0	0
Finance, general and banking and financial support services	24,375	16,633	7,742	5,068	3,661	1,407	55	51	4
Actuarial sciences	351	218	133	76	43	33	0	0	0
Insurance and risk management and financial planning	610	389	221	70	46	24	12	9	3
Investments and securities	327	179	148	253	173	80	0	0	0
Hospitality services management	5,929	2,731	3,198	460	260	200	0	0	0
Human resources management	4,549	1,840	2,709	1,202	488	714	8	5	3
Labor/personnel relations and studies	1,218	556	662	759	308	451	12	5	7
Organizational behavior studies	805	352	453	199	88	111	15	9	6
International business	1,978	901	1,077	2,532	1,656	876	21	16	5
Business information systems, total	4,878	2,838	2,040	1,565	1,078	487	8	6	2
Management information systems and data processing, general	4,528	2,611	1,917	1,440	982	458	8	6	2
Business information systems, other	350	227	123	125	96	29	0	0	0
Quantitative methods and management science, total	1,881	1,118	763	747	563	184	45	35	10
Business statistics	44	24	20	23	20	3	7	5	2
Management science, other	1,837	1,094	743	724	543	181	38	30	8
Marketing management and research	28,390	14,741	13,649	2,223	1,242	981	42	29	13
Real estate	752	577	175	355	287	68	0	0	0
Taxation	4	3	1	1,479	905	574	0	0	0
Consumer and personal services	155	111	44	3	0	3	0	0	0
Business management and administrative services, other	5,163	2,901	2,262	4,415	2,911	1,504	69	59	10
Marketing operations/marketing and distribution, total	7,541	2,990	4,551	595	336	259	4	1	3
Apparel and accessories marketing operations	1,799	63	1,736	1	0	1	2	0	2
Business and personal services marketing operations	576	341	235	5	3	2	0	0	0
General/retailing and wholesaling operations and skills	4,292	2,089	2,203	452	231	221	2	1	1
Transportation and travel marketing	173	41	132	19	11	8	0	0	0
Marketing and distribution, other	701	456	245	118	91	27	0	0	0
Communications and communications technologies, total	54,977	21,497	33,480	4,464	1,692	2,772	255	132	123
Communications, total	54,257	21,150	33,107	4,180	1,537	2,643	252	131	121
Communications, general	25,363	9,522	15,841	1,445	509	936	158	78	80
Advertising	3,342	1,172	2,170	182	42	140	4	2	2
Journalism	11,835	4,162	7,673	1,445	546	899	33	18	15
Broadcast journalism	537	226	311	0	0	0	0	0	0

Table 242.—Bachelor's, master's, and doctor's degrees conferred by institutions of higher education, by sex of student and field of study: 1991–92—Continued

Field of study	Bachelor's degrees requiring 4 or 5 years			Master's degrees			Doctor's degrees (Ph.D., Ed.D., etc.)		
	Total	Men	Women	Total	Men	Women	Total	Men	Women
1	2	3	4	5	6	7	8	9	10
Public relations and organizational communications	2,138	669	1,469	122	28	94	0	0	0
Radio and television broadcasting	6,398	3,462	2,936	351	177	174	18	10	8
Communications, other	4,644	1,937	2,707	635	235	400	39	23	16
Communications technologies, total	720	347	373	284	155	129	3	1	2
Photographic technology	19	7	12	0	0	0	0	0	0
Radio and television technology	648	313	335	226	113	113	3	1	2
Communications technologies, other	53	27	26	58	42	16	0	0	0
Computer and information sciences, total	24,557	17,510	7,047	9,530	6,884	2,646	772	669	103
Computer and information sciences, general	16,004	11,688	4,316	6,985	5,210	1,775	667	590	77
Computer programming	375	233	142	71	45	26	0	0	0
Data processing technology/technician	288	163	125	76	56	20	0	0	0
Information science and systems	3,556	2,225	1,331	1,203	703	500	22	9	13
Computer systems analysis	279	186	93	73	60	13	6	6	0
Computer and information sciences, other	4,055	3,015	1,040	1,122	810	312	77	64	13
Education, total	108,006	22,686	85,320	92,668	21,244	71,424	6,864	2,783	4,081
Education, general	2,176	346	1,830	10,167	2,471	7,696	1,141	420	721
Bilingual/bicultural education	63	4	59	153	24	129	10	5	5
Curriculum and instruction	42	6	36	6,957	1,340	5,617	863	280	583
Education administration and supervision, total	20	4	16	10,329	4,026	6,303	2,131	1,002	1,129
Education administration and supervision, general	3	1	2	6,849	2,740	4,109	1,502	729	773
Administration of special education	12	2	10	9	1	8	15	2	13
Adult and continuing education administration	0	0	0	129	26	103	61	25	36
Educational supervision	0	0	0	725	214	511	26	11	15
Elementary, middle, and secondary education administration	5	1	4	1,726	701	1,025	33	14	19
Higher education administration	0	0	0	384	145	239	359	158	201
Community and junior college education administration	0	0	0	85	23	62	2	2	0
Education administration and supervision, other	0	0	0	422	176	246	133	61	72
Educational/instructional media design	9	2	7	931	239	692	64	24	40
Educational evaluation and research, general	19	3	16	44	17	27	30	14	16
Educational statistics and research methods	0	0	0	38	21	17	28	8	20
Educational assessment, testing and measurement	0	0	0	79	16	63	39	18	21
Social and philosophical foundations of education	0	0	0	243	64	179	125	52	73
Special education, total	7,867	597	7,270	9,420	1,214	8,206	192	51	141
Special education, general	5,332	449	4,883	7,194	938	6,256	173	48	125
Education of the deaf and hearing impaired	236	4	232	175	25	150	0	0	0
Education of the gifted and talented	1	0	1	184	19	165	0	0	0
Education of the emotionally handicapped	240	31	209	207	52	155	1	1	0
Education of the mentally handicapped	551	27	524	221	30	191	2	1	1
Education of the multiple handicapped	85	7	78	114	19	95	0	0	0
Education of the physically handicapped	29	6	23	47	7	40	0	0	0
Education of the blind and visually handicapped	25	3	22	17	2	15	0	0	0
Education of the specific learning disabled	468	19	449	661	61	600	7	0	7
Education of the speech impaired	653	19	634	288	22	266	0	0	0
Special education, other	247	32	215	312	39	273	9	1	8
Counselor education/counseling and guidance services	44	12	32	11,429	2,515	8,914	372	159	213
General teacher education, total	62,688	5,923	56,765	21,779	3,191	18,588	441	139	302
Adult and continuing education	99	25	74	805	236	569	145	56	89
Elementary education	50,619	3,856	46,763	13,122	1,191	11,931	88	18	70
Junior high/intermediate/middle school education	1,247	233	1,014	568	82	486	0	0	0
Pre-elementary/early childhood/kindergarten education	6,179	130	6,049	1,913	39	1,874	27	1	26
Secondary education	4,153	1,631	2,522	3,598	1,263	2,335	73	25	48
Teacher education, general programs, other	391	48	343	1,773	380	1,393	108	39	69
Teacher education, academic and vocational programs	34,273	15,619	18,654	16,413	5,084	11,329	865	422	443
Agricultural education (vocational)	408	301	107	237	169	68	39	27	12
Art education	1,371	249	1,122	580	99	481	40	11	29
Business education (vocational)	1,723	380	1,343	557	107	450	13	7	6
Driver and safety education	42	33	9	61	44	17	1	1	0
English education	2,638	475	2,163	663	142	521	23	10	13
Foreign languages education	330	44	286	203	37	166	19	9	10
Health education	1,655	440	1,215	804	178	626	107	38	69
Home economics education (vocational)	408	12	396	161	5	156	10	1	9
Technology/industrial arts education	1,495	1,266	229	515	372	143	20	16	4
Marketing operations/marketing and distribution education	122	57	65	27	6	21	0	0	0
Mathematics education	1,834	661	1,173	850	281	569	27	15	12
Music education	2,885	1,198	1,687	796	341	455	84	44	40
Physical education and coaching	11,792	6,676	5,116	3,003	1,598	1,405	173	96	77
Reading education	210	25	185	4,097	179	3,918	83	12	71
Science education	1,138	487	651	789	336	453	47	28	19
Social science education	725	363	362	129	55	74	4	3	1
Social studies education	2,270	1,282	988	417	239	178	3	2	1
Technical education (vocational)	231	145	86	296	149	147	41	24	17
Trade and industrial education (vocational)	1,080	762	318	459	194	265	69	46	23
Teacher education, academic and vocational programs, other	1,916	763	1,153	1,769	553	1,216	62	32	30

Table 242.—Bachelor's, master's, and doctor's degrees conferred by institutions of higher education, by sex of student and field of study: 1991–92—Continued

Field of study	Bachelor's degrees requiring 4 or 5 years			Master's degrees			Doctor's degrees (Ph.D., Ed.D., etc.)		
	Total	Men	Women	Total	Men	Women	Total	Men	Women
1	2	3	4	5	6	7	8	9	10
Teaching English as a second language/foreign language	48	12	36	1,305	289	1,016	3	2	1
Education, other	757	158	599	3,381	733	2,648	560	187	373
Engineering and engineering-related technologies, total	77,541	66,716	10,825	25,977	22,143	3,834	5,499	4,972	527
Engineering, total	61,206	51,768	9,438	24,983	21,327	3,656	5,488	4,961	527
Engineering, general	2,090	1,769	321	1,165	983	182	268	241	27
Aerospace, aeronautical, and astronautical engineering	2,996	2,658	338	933	850	83	226	216	10
Agricultural engineering	500	431	69	161	143	18	83	76	7
Architectural engineering	532	421	111	31	27	4	0	0	0
Bioengineering and biomedical engineering	623	402	221	407	283	124	137	107	30
Ceramic sciences and engineering	288	235	53	93	77	16	38	31	7
Chemical engineering	3,754	2,576	1,178	956	740	216	590	491	99
Civil engineering	8,034	6,712	1,322	3,113	2,648	465	540	498	42
Computer engineering	2,093	1,826	267	908	756	152	91	83	8
Electrical, electronics, and communications engineering	17,958	15,811	2,147	7,360	6,468	892	1,282	1,182	100
Engineering mechanics	150	131	19	171	155	16	102	92	10
Engineering physics	342	289	53	91	80	11	50	48	2
Engineering science	254	206	48	249	197	52	33	30	3
Environmental/environmental health engineering	214	152	62	604	440	164	72	51	21
Geological engineering	90	68	22	32	26	6	11	10	1
Geophysical engineering	13	8	5	8	5	3	4	4	0
Industrial/manufacturing engineering	3,679	2,623	1,056	2,012	1,596	416	220	191	29
Material engineering	526	385	141	482	389	93	304	261	43
Mechanical engineering	14,067	12,545	1,522	3,653	3,298	355	851	814	37
Metallurgical engineering	255	208	47	159	136	23	80	74	6
Mining and mineral engineering	101	89	12	65	53	12	28	26	2
Naval architecture and marine engineering	328	312	16	26	26	0	10	10	0
Nuclear engineering	256	226	30	209	178	31	122	113	9
Ocean engineering	108	86	22	103	88	15	24	22	2
Petroleum engineering	238	212	26	123	115	8	50	46	4
Systems engineering	333	270	63	330	260	70	30	28	2
Textile sciences and engineering	54	27	27	25	19	6	2	2	0
Engineering, other	1,330	1,090	240	1,514	1,291	223	240	214	26
Engineering-related technologies, total	16,335	14,948	1,387	994	816	178	11	11	0
Architectural engineering technologies	664	597	67	0	0	0	0	0	0
Civil technologies	401	370	31	1	1	0	0	0	0
Electrical and electronic technologies	4,364	4,091	273	34	32	2	0	0	0
Electromechanical instrumentation and maintenance technologies	345	315	30	11	9	2	2	2	0
Environmental control technologies	164	122	42	58	37	21	0	0	0
Industrial production technologies	4,352	3,902	450	331	283	48	5	5	0
Quality control and safety technologies	350	276	74	218	165	53	0	0	0
Mechanical and related technologies	1,668	1,599	69	0	0	0	0	0	0
Mining and petroleum technologies	36	32	4	0	0	0	0	0	0
Surveying	107	97	10	25	20	5	4	4	0
Mechanics and repairers	78	77	1	0	0	0	0	0	0
Construction trades	67	65	2	0	0	0	0	0	0
Engineering and related technologies, other	3,739	3,405	334	316	269	47	0	0	0
English language and literature/letters, total	54,951	18,536	36,415	7,450	2,513	4,937	1,273	537	736
English language and literature, general	40,514	13,191	27,323	5,037	1,716	3,321	893	370	523
Comparative literature	701	222	479	235	72	163	131	53	78
English composition	307	145	162	14	6	8	7	4	3
English creative writing	783	322	461	720	305	415	3	0	3
American literature (United States)	26	13	13	1	0	1	3	0	3
English literature (British and Commonwealth)	1,513	538	975	373	110	263	64	28	36
Speech and rhetorical studies	9,650	3,584	6,066	768	218	550	121	61	60
English technical and business writing	115	41	74	110	35	75	0	0	0
English language and literature/letters, other	1,342	480	862	192	51	141	51	21	30
Foreign languages and literatures, total	13,903	3,985	9,918	2,926	971	1,955	850	378	472
Foreign languages and literatures, total	1,488	432	1,056	872	294	578	252	120	132
Foreign languages and literatures, general	919	262	657	289	89	200	45	18	27
Linguistics	569	170	399	583	205	378	207	102	105
East and Southeast Asian languages and literatures, total	554	288	266	87	28	59	28	18	10
Chinese	183	82	101	36	14	22	14	11	3
Japanese	257	132	125	30	5	25	6	5	1
East and Southeast Asian languages, other	114	74	40	21	9	12	8	2	6
East European languages and literatures, total	703	271	432	140	60	80	34	12	22
Russian languages	629	244	385	68	31	37	7	3	4
Slavic languages (other than Russian)	67	25	42	66	26	40	27	9	18
East European languages, other	7	2	5	6	3	3	0	0	0
Germanic languages and literatures, total	1,657	596	1,061	312	122	190	95	34	61
German	1,616	583	1,033	273	104	169	85	29	56

Table 242.—Bachelor's, master's, and doctor's degrees conferred by institutions of higher education, by sex of student and field of study: 1991–92—Continued

Field of study	Bachelor's degrees requiring 4 or 5 years			Master's degrees			Doctor's degrees (Ph.D., Ed.D., etc.)		
	Total	Men	Women	Total	Men	Women	Total	Men	Women
1	2	3	4	5	6	7	8	9	10
Scandinavian languages	31	7	24	10	4	6	2	1	1
Germanic languages, other	10	6	4	29	14	15	8	4	4
South Asian languages and literatures	5	3	2	1	0	1	4	3	1
Romance languages and literatures, total	8,450	1,940	6,510	1,247	326	921	314	123	191
French	3,371	637	2,734	465	101	364	112	41	71
Italian	238	67	171	55	17	38	18	8	10
Portuguese	27	15	12	8	5	3	2	0	2
Spanish	4,768	1,214	3,554	647	185	462	143	64	79
Romance languages, other	46	7	39	72	18	54	39	10	29
Middle Eastern languages and literatures, total	79	30	49	43	27	16	17	14	3
Arabic	13	6	7	0	0	0	0	0	0
Hebrew	50	14	36	29	19	10	8	6	2
Middle East languages, other	16	10	6	14	8	6	9	8	1
Classical and ancient Near East languages and literatures, total	714	345	369	163	92	71	58	36	22
Classics	563	259	304	142	82	60	57	35	22
Greek (ancient and medieval)	41	26	15	10	3	7	1	1	0
Latin (ancient and medieval)	110	60	50	11	7	4	0	0	0
Foreign languages, other	253	80	173	61	22	39	48	18	30
Health professions and related sciences, total	61,720	10,189	51,531	23,065	4,691	18,374	1,661	698	963
Communication disorders sciences and services	4,157	177	3,980	3,541	155	3,386	81	22	59
Community health liaison	327	78	249	130	34	96	23	15	8
Dentistry	85	46	39	325	222	103	13	11	2
Dental services	732	34	698	72	48	24	0	0	0
Epidemiology	0	0	0	210	94	116	69	27	42
Health services administration, total	3,222	697	2,525	3,103	1,030	2,073	57	25	32
Health services administration	1,641	405	1,236	1,485	544	941	22	9	13
Medical records administration	587	54	533	0	0	0	0	0	0
Medical records technology/technician	22	1	21	8	4	4	4	4	0
Health and medical administrative services, other	972	237	735	1,610	482	1,128	31	12	19
Health and medical assistants, total	897	442	455	136	40	96	0	0	0
Medical assistant	15	11	4	19	7	12	0	0	0
Physician assistant	788	407	381	105	30	75	0	0	0
Health and medical assistants, other	94	24	70	12	3	9	0	0	0
Health and medical diagnostic and treatment services, total	1,159	434	725	23	14	9	0	0	0
Respiratory therapy technology/technician	292	113	179	0	0	0	0	0	0
Health and medical diagnostic and treatment services, other	867	321	546	23	14	9	0	0	0
Medical laboratory technologies, total	2,375	651	1,724	464	208	256	89	46	43
Medical technology	2,081	543	1,538	62	21	41	2	2	0
Health and medical laboratory technologies/technicians, other	294	108	186	402	187	215	87	44	43
Pre-dentistry studies	92	63	29	0	0	0	0	0	0
Pre-medicine studies	611	368	243	6	1	5	10	8	2
Pre-pharmacy studies	4,421	1,735	2,686	94	53	41	63	34	29
Pre-veterinary studies	184	78	106	33	23	10	0	0	0
Medical basic sciences	224	69	155	153	65	88	232	128	104
Mental health services, total	483	74	409	411	89	322	14	6	8
Alcohol/drug abuse counseling	127	31	96	60	18	42	0	0	0
Psychiatric/mental health services technician	137	18	119	53	15	38	0	0	0
Clinical and medical social work	83	13	70	64	15	49	6	0	6
Mental health services, other	136	12	124	234	41	193	8	6	2
Nursing	31,029	2,381	28,648	7,512	507	7,005	408	21	387
Optometry	140	63	77	12	4	8	6	4	2
Pharmacy [1]	1,280	486	794	118	70	48	201	118	83
Rehabilitation/therapeutic services, total	6,318	1,134	5,184	3,067	698	2,369	28	12	16
Art therapy	49	1	48	172	24	148	0	0	0
Dance therapy	5	0	5	46	4	42	0	0	0
Music therapy	153	16	137	33	8	25	0	0	0
Occupational therapy	2,149	182	1,967	466	46	420	2	0	2
Orthotics/prosthetics	29	18	11	0	0	0	0	0	0
Physical therapy	3,111	763	2,348	1,533	413	1,120	7	4	3
Recreational therapy	124	14	110	3	0	3	2	1	1
Vocational rehabilitation counseling	93	21	72	515	121	394	7	3	4
Rehabilitative services, other	605	119	486	299	82	217	10	4	6
Veterinary medicine	69	36	33	145	76	69	112	82	30
Miscellaneous health professions	341	205	136	68	43	25	25	17	8
Health professions and related sciences, other	3,574	938	2,636	3,442	1,217	2,225	230	122	108
Home economics and vocational home economics, total	14,898	1,687	13,211	2,412	409	2,003	293	71	222
Home economics, total	14,139	1,377	12,762	2,389	408	1,981	288	70	218
Home economics, general	3,064	203	2,861	303	22	281	42	9	33
Home economics business services	163	16	147	5	0	5	0	0	0
Family and community studies	219	20	199	65	10	55	2	2	0
Family and consumer resource management	1,124	334	790	54	11	43	15	4	11
Food and nutrition studies	2,623	318	2,305	559	71	488	58	17	41
Housing studies	608	84	524	44	10	34	5	1	4
Individual and family development studies	4,020	290	3,730	1,217	268	949	134	35	99

Table 242.—Bachelor's, master's, and doctor's degrees conferred by institutions of higher education, by sex of student and field of study: 1991–92—Continued

Field of study	Bachelor's degrees requiring 4 or 5 years			Master's degrees			Doctor's degrees (Ph.D., Ed.D., etc.)		
	Total	Men	Women	Total	Men	Women	Total	Men	Women
1	2	3	4	5	6	7	8	9	10
Clothing/apparel and textile studies	2,155	91	2,064	86	13	73	23	2	21
Home economics, other	163	21	142	56	3	53	9	0	9
Vocational home economics, total	759	310	449	23	1	22	5	1	4
Child care and guidance management	196	6	190	19	1	18	0	0	0
Custodial, housekeeping and home services workers and managers	9	1	8	1	0	1	0	0	0
Vocational home economics, other	554	303	251	3	0	3	5	1	4
Law and legal studies, total	2,144	701	1,443	2,369	1,597	772	68	50	18
Pre-law studies	566	272	294	102	54	48	5	3	2
Paralegal/legal assistant	776	112	664	4	1	3	0	0	0
Law and legal studies, other	802	317	485	2,263	1,542	721	63	47	16
Liberal arts and sciences, general studies, and humanities, total	32,174	12,784	19,390	2,394	870	1,524	67	30	37
Liberal arts and sciences/liberal studies	20,569	7,438	13,131	1,577	566	1,011	28	10	18
Humanities/humanistic studies	3,083	1,014	2,069	492	189	303	32	13	19
Liberal arts and sciences, general studies, other	8,522	4,332	4,190	325	115	210	7	7	0
Library science, total	97	8	89	4,893	992	3,901	50	16	34
Library science/librarianship	90	8	82	4,783	972	3,811	49	16	33
Library science, other	7	0	7	110	20	90	1	0	1
Mathematics, total	14,783	7,888	6,895	4,011	2,452	1,559	1,082	851	231
Mathematics	12,679	6,588	6,091	2,329	1,388	941	755	595	160
Applied mathematics, total	1,200	778	422	846	547	299	151	123	28
Applied mathematics, general and other	885	558	327	393	246	147	117	97	20
Operations research (quantitative methods)	315	220	95	453	301	152	34	26	8
Mathematical statistics	554	296	258	751	457	294	170	129	41
Mathematics, other	350	226	124	85	60	25	6	4	2
Multi/interdisciplinary studies, total	20,647	8,628	12,019	2,126	995	1,131	231	144	87
Biological and physical sciences	2,094	1,119	975	230	129	101	30	20	10
Systems science and theory	75	46	29	107	60	47	9	6	3
Museology/museum studies	2	0	2	67	11	56	0	0	0
Multi/interdisciplinary studies, other	18,476	7,463	11,013	1,722	795	927	192	118	74
Parks, recreation, leisure, and fitness studies, total	8,446	4,144	4,302	1,358	650	708	61	41	20
Parks, recreation and leisure studies	2,220	970	1,250	183	91	92	20	14	6
Parks, recreation and leisure facilities management	2,253	1,084	1,169	253	110	143	7	5	2
Health and physical education/fitness	3,808	1,978	1,830	893	431	462	33	21	12
Parks, recreation, leisure and fitness studies, other	165	112	53	29	18	11	1	1	0
Philosophy and religion, total	7,526	4,752	2,774	1,146	731	415	475	365	110
Philosophy	4,846	3,293	1,553	555	399	156	282	218	64
Religion/religious studies	2,372	1,272	1,100	521	300	221	191	145	46
Philosophy and religion, other	308	187	121	70	32	38	2	2	0
Physical sciences and science technologies, total	16,960	11,431	5,529	5,374	3,909	1,465	4,391	3,429	962
Physical sciences, total	16,871	11,370	5,501	5,339	3,889	1,450	4,378	3,418	960
Physical sciences, general	407	263	144	45	33	12	0	0	0
Astronomy	93	67	26	97	71	26	69	56	13
Astrophysics	45	30	15	16	10	6	27	23	4
Atmospheric science and meteorology	412	331	81	180	147	33	70	49	21
Chemistry, total	8,641	5,155	3,486	1,780	1,085	695	2,280	1,648	632
Chemistry, general	8,407	5,006	3,401	1,653	1,007	646	2,113	1,525	588
Analytical chemistry	0	0	0	20	12	8	12	11	1
Inorganic chemistry	0	0	0	2	1	1	7	5	2
Organic chemistry	13	9	4	10	7	3	12	12	0
Medicinal/pharmaceutical chemistry	12	6	6	34	21	13	47	27	20
Chemistry, other	209	134	75	61	37	24	89	68	21
Geological and related sciences, total	2,078	1,382	696	990	735	255	413	314	99
Geology	1,928	1,286	642	853	633	220	319	241	78
Geochemistry	8	2	6	9	7	2	12	7	5
Geophysics and seismology	53	40	13	69	58	11	43	35	8
Geological and related sciences, other	89	54	35	59	37	22	39	31	8
Miscellaneous physical sciences, total	759	495	264	318	217	101	147	117	30
Metallurgy	0	0	0	5	4	1	3	3	0
Oceanography	216	137	79	143	105	38	73	57	16
Earth and planetary sciences	490	323	167	112	70	42	63	50	13
Miscellaneous physical sciences, other	53	35	18	58	38	20	8	7	1
Physics, total	4,098	3,427	671	1,834	1,539	295	1,337	1,182	155
Physics, general	3,907	3,268	639	1,705	1,440	265	1,233	1,088	145

Table 242.—Bachelor's, master's, and doctor's degrees conferred by institutions of higher education, by sex of student and field of study: 1991–92—Continued

Field of study	Bachelor's degrees requiring 4 or 5 years			Master's degrees			Doctor's degrees (Ph.D., Ed.D., etc.)		
	Total	Men	Women	Total	Men	Women	Total	Men	Women
1	2	3	4	5	6	7	8	9	10
Physics, other	191	159	32	129	99	30	104	94	10
Physical sciences, other	338	220	118	79	52	27	35	29	6
Science technologies, total	89	61	28	35	20	15	13	11	2
Precision production trades, total	378	280	98	0	0	0	0	0	0
Drafting, general	193	162	31	0	0	0	0	0	0
Precision production trades, other	185	118	67	0	0	0	0	0	0
Protective services, total	18,855	11,659	7,196	1,249	797	452	24	13	11
Criminal justice and corrections, total	18,626	11,462	7,164	1,240	789	451	24	13	11
Corrections/correctional administration	678	350	328	94	57	37	0	0	0
Criminal justice/law enforcement administration	5,889	3,664	2,225	405	238	167	3	2	1
Criminal justice studies	9,492	5,682	3,810	624	432	192	21	11	10
Forensic studies	128	73	55	39	24	15	0	0	0
Law enforcement/police science	1,623	1,213	410	41	18	23	0	0	0
Criminal justice, other	816	480	336	37	20	17	0	0	0
Fire control and safety	197	185	12	9	8	1	0	0	0
Protective services, other	32	12	20	0	0	0	0	0	0
Psychology, total	63,513	17,031	46,482	10,215	2,988	7,227	3,373	1,359	2,014
Psychology, general	60,168	16,154	44,014	4,322	1,357	2,965	1,583	700	883
Clinical psychology	43	8	35	1,135	315	820	1,024	356	668
Counseling psychology	205	52	153	2,574	650	1,924	265	107	158
Developmental and child psychology	768	111	657	98	18	80	57	18	39
Experimental psychology	235	61	174	77	34	43	82	37	45
Industrial and organizational psychology	138	36	102	562	253	309	61	29	32
Physiological psychology/psychobiology	140	57	83	8	3	5	16	7	9
Social psychology	268	81	187	84	23	61	26	9	17
School psychology	39	11	28	458	85	373	85	26	59
Psychology, other	1,509	460	1,049	897	250	647	174	70	104
Public administration and services, total	15,987	3,479	12,508	19,243	5,769	13,474	432	204	228
Public administration	2,558	1,330	1,228	6,039	3,186	2,853	105	78	27
Community organization, resources and services	1,203	261	942	203	83	120	7	4	3
Public policy analysis	435	200	235	590	302	288	59	33	26
Social work	11,427	1,528	9,899	11,993	2,028	9,965	242	82	160
Public affairs, other	364	160	204	418	170	248	19	7	12
R.O.T.C. and military technologies, total	184	158	26	0	0	0	0	0	0
Social sciences and history, total	133,974	73,001	60,973	12,702	7,237	5,465	3,218	2,126	1,092
Social sciences, general	7,024	3,032	3,992	462	209	253	36	15	21
Anthropology	4,648	1,535	3,113	895	341	554	324	168	156
Archeology	102	40	62	18	7	11	10	5	5
Criminology	1,756	947	809	67	35	32	6	4	2
Demography and population studies	0	0	0	28	20	8	5	4	1
Economics	23,423	16,416	7,007	2,106	1,520	586	866	690	176
Geography, total	3,851	2,627	1,224	642	419	223	122	90	32
Geography	3,808	2,592	1,216	639	419	220	122	90	32
Cartography	43	35	8	3	0	3	0	0	0
History	26,966	16,434	10,532	2,754	1,645	1,109	644	419	225
International relations and affairs	5,860	2,484	3,376	1,715	933	782	58	38	20
Political science and government, general	37,805	22,044	15,761	1,908	1,218	690	535	385	150
Sociology	19,568	6,096	13,472	1,347	540	807	501	260	241
Urban affairs/studies	654	357	297	249	123	126	48	21	27
Social sciences and history, other	2,317	989	1,328	511	227	284	63	27	36
Theological studies/religious vocations, total	4,729	3,552	1,177	5,185	3,199	1,986	1,259	1,077	182
Biblical and other theological languages and literatures	16	15	1	68	31	37	3	3	0
Bible/biblical studies	1,454	1,122	332	373	310	63	11	11	0
Missions/missionary studies and misology	317	176	141	197	123	74	36	33	3
Religious education	825	477	348	942	448	494	41	33	8
Religious/sacred music	190	126	64	108	76	32	11	6	5
Theology/theological studies	1,539	1,324	215	2,476	1,598	878	856	739	117
Pastoral counseling and specialized ministries	65	57	8	506	227	279	152	126	26
Theological studies and religious vocations, other	323	255	68	515	386	129	149	126	23
Transportation and materials moving workers, total	3,598	3,239	359	385	354	31	0	0	0
Water transportation workers	236	209	27	0	0	0	0	0	0
Transportation and material moving, other	3,362	3,030	332	385	354	31	0	0	0
Visual and performing arts, total	46,522	17,616	28,906	9,353	4,078	5,275	906	504	402

Table 242.—Bachelor's, master's, and doctor's degrees conferred by institutions of higher education, by sex of student and field of study: 1991–92—Continued

Field of study	Bachelor's degrees requiring 4 or 5 years			Master's degrees			Doctor's degrees (Ph.D., Ed.D., etc.)		
	Total	Men	Women	Total	Men	Women	Total	Men	Women
1	2	3	4	5	6	7	8	9	10
Visual and performing arts, general	1,494	555	939	128	58	70	1	1	0
Crafts, folk art, and artisanry	104	34	70	4	1	3	0	0	0
Dance	785	90	695	224	28	196	4	0	4
Design and applied art	8,014	2,812	5,202	354	147	207	5	0	5
Dramatic/theater arts and stagecraft	5,486	2,245	3,241	1,307	621	686	91	50	41
Film/video and photographic arts, total	2,517	1,455	1,062	501	292	209	7	5	2
Film-video making/cinematography and production	882	561	321	280	175	105	4	2	2
Photography	988	488	500	123	57	66	0	0	0
Film arts, other	647	406	241	98	60	38	3	3	0
Fine arts and art studies, total	19,928	6,449	13,479	3,074	1,165	1,909	149	50	99
Art, general	10,957	3,717	7,240	1,045	409	636	28	11	17
Art history, criticism and conservation	4,871	1,264	3,607	832	245	587	120	38	82
Arts management	104	23	81	90	29	61	0	0	0
Painting	771	317	454	221	84	137	0	0	0
Ceramic arts and ceramics	171	58	113	51	24	27	0	0	0
Fiber, textile and weaving arts	123	12	111	18	2	16	1	1	0
Metal and jewelry arts	85	18	67	16	6	10	0	0	0
Fine arts and art studies, other	2,846	1,040	1,806	801	366	435	0	0	0
Music, total	7,724	3,805	3,919	3,458	1,651	1,807	623	391	232
Music, general	3,863	1,818	2,045	1,070	539	531	263	154	109
Music history and literature	58	31	27	55	26	29	26	14	12
Music, general performance	2,696	1,246	1,450	1,924	854	1,070	215	130	85
Music theory and composition	209	160	49	156	109	47	63	55	8
Music, other	898	550	348	253	123	130	56	38	18
Visual and performing arts, other	470	171	299	303	115	188	26	7	19
Not classified by field of study	6,720	3,835	2,885	4,156	2,299	1,857	569	389	180

[1] Because of the change in the Classification of Instructional Programs most pharmacy degrees are now in pre-pharmacy studies for 1991–92.

NOTE.—Aggregations by field of study derived from the *Classification of Instructional Programs* developed by the National Center for Education Statistics.

SOURCE: U.S. Department of Education, National Center for Education Statistics, Integrated Postsecondary Education Data System (IPEDS), "Completions" survey. (This table was prepared February 1994.)

Table 243.—Bachelor's degrees conferred by institutions of higher education, by discipline division: 1970-71 to 1992-93

Discipline division	1970-71	1975-76	1979-80	1980-81	1981-82	1982-83	1983-84	1984-85	1985-86	1986-87	1987-88	1988-89	1989-90	1990-91	1991-92	1992-93
1	2	3	4	5	6	7	8	9	10	11	12	13	14	15	16	17
Total	839,730	925,746	929,417	935,140	952,998	969,510	974,309	979,477	987,823	991,264	994,829	1,018,755	1,051,344	1,094,538	1,136,553	1,165,178
Agriculture and natural resources	12,672	19,402	22,802	21,886	21,029	20,909	19,317	18,107	16,823	14,991	14,222	13,492	12,900	13,124	15,124	16,778
Architecture and related programs	5,570	9,146	9,132	9,455	9,728	9,823	9,186	9,325	9,119	8,950	8,603	9,150	9,364	9,781	8,753	9,167
Area, ethnic and cultural studies	2,582	3,577	2,840	2,887	2,862	3,068	3,005	2,985	3,178	3,427	3,601	4,102	4,613	4,884	5,342	5,481
Biological sciences/life sciences	35,743	54,275	46,370	43,216	41,639	39,982	38,640	38,445	38,524	38,121	36,755	36,059	37,204	39,530	42,941	47,038
Business management and administrative services	114,729	142,034	184,867	198,983	213,374	226,627	229,478	232,636	237,319	240,546	243,021	246,399	248,698	249,311	256,603	256,842
Communications	10,324	20,045	26,927	29,428	32,428	36,954	38,586	40,358	41,666	43,953	45,410	47,405	50,114	51,650	54,257	53,874
Communications technologies	478	1,237	1,689	1,854	1,794	1,613	1,527	1,644	1,410	1,384	1,239	1,204	1,194	1,123	720	832
Computer and information sciences	2,388	5,652	11,154	15,121	20,267	24,510	32,172	38,878	41,889	39,589	34,523	30,454	27,257	25,083	24,557	24,200
Education	176,307	154,437	118,038	108,074	100,932	97,895	92,299	88,072	87,114	86,936	91,112	96,913	105,112	110,807	108,006	107,781
Engineering	44,898	38,388	58,402	63,287	67,021	72,163	75,638	77,066	76,225	73,747	69,380	66,099	63,609	61,531	61,206	61,973
Engineering-related technologies	5,148	7,943	10,491	11,713	12,984	16,855	18,547	18,762	19,435	19,069	19,126	18,903	17,713	17,119	16,335	16,078
English language and literature/letters	64,342	42,006	32,541	32,254	33,419	31,829	32,834	33,218	34,552	36,284	38,661	42,470	47,519	51,841	54,951	56,133
Foreign languages and literatures	20,536	16,484	12,089	11,273	10,756	10,599	10,384	10,827	10,984	11,034	10,926	11,693	12,386	13,133	13,903	14,387
Health professions and related sciences	25,226	53,958	63,920	63,649	63,653	64,685	64,288	64,422	64,396	63,103	60,644	59,005	58,302	59,070	61,720	67,089
Home economics and vocational home economics	11,167	17,409	18,411	18,370	17,872	16,296	15,948	15,157	14,889	14,417	14,320	14,160	14,491	14,892	14,898	15,100
Law and legal studies	545	531	683	776	846	1,099	1,272	1,157	1,197	1,178	1,303	1,976	1,592	1,758	2,144	2,056
Liberal arts and sciences, general studies, and humanities	7,481	18,855	23,196	21,643	21,089	21,603	21,479	21,818	21,336	23,717	24,274	26,388	27,985	30,526	32,174	33,456
Library science	1,013	843	398	375	307	254	252	197	155	136	119	121	77	90	97	83
Mathematics	24,937	16,329	11,872	11,433	12,226	12,719	13,764	15,861	17,147	16,999	16,608	15,994	15,176	15,310	14,783	14,812
Multi/interdisciplinary studies	6,286	13,588	11,277	12,848	14,707	14,107	13,940	12,978	13,489	13,933	14,723	15,168	16,267	17,561	20,647	23,955
Parks, recreation, leisure and fitness studies	1,621	5,182	5,753	5,729	5,335	5,214	4,850	4,725	4,620	4,264	4,235	4,376	4,582	4,315	8,446	9,859
Philosophy and religion	8,146	8,447	7,069	6,776	6,309	6,483	6,435	6,400	6,239	5,984	5,963	6,425	6,868	7,315	7,526	7,781
Physical sciences and science technologies	21,412	21,465	23,410	23,952	24,052	23,381	23,651	23,704	21,717	20,070	17,806	17,186	16,066	16,344	16,960	17,545
Precision production trades	0	0	0	0	0	384	371	553	400	455	481	482	528	460	378	388
Protective services	2,045	12,507	15,015	13,707	12,438	12,579	12,654	12,510	12,704	12,930	13,367	14,698	15,354	16,806	18,855	20,902
Psychology	38,187	50,278	42,093	41,068	41,212	40,460	39,955	39,900	40,628	42,994	45,187	48,910	53,952	58,655	63,513	66,728
Public administration and services	5,466	15,440	16,644	16,707	16,495	14,414	12,570	11,754	11,887	12,328	12,385	13,162	13,908	14,350	15,987	16,775
R.O.T.C. and military technologies	357	952	38	42	55	267	195	299	256	384	82	198	196	183	184	11
Social sciences and history	155,324	126,396	103,662	100,513	99,705	95,228	93,323	91,570	93,840	96,342	100,460	108,151	118,083	125,107	133,974	135,703
Theological studies/religious vocations	3,744	5,520	6,207	5,841	5,998	6,054	5,920	6,047	5,607	5,730	5,565	5,318	5,200	4,813	4,729	5,433
Transportation and material moving	662	1,282	1,535	1,801	2,044	1,662	1,698	1,962	1,837	1,654	1,983	2,062	2,387	2,622	3,598	3,930
Visual and performing arts	30,394	42,138	40,892	40,479	40,422	39,794	40,131	38,140	37,241	36,615	36,944	38,227	39,934	42,186	46,522	47,761
Not classified by field of study	0	0	0	0	0	0	0	0	0	0	1,801	2,405	2,713	13,258	6,720	5,247

NOTE.—The new Classification of Instructional Programs was initiated in 1991-92. The figures for earlier years have been reclassified when necessary to make them conform to the new taxonomy. To facilitate trend comparisons, certain aggregations have been made of the degree fields as reported in the IPEDS "Completions" survey: "Agriculture and natural resources" includes Agribusiness and agriculture production, Agricultural sciences, and Conservation and renewable natural resources; "Business management and administrative services" includes Business and management, Business (administrative support), Marketing and distribution, and Consumer, personal, and miscellaneous services; and "Engineering-related technologies" includes Engineering-related technologies, Mechanics and repairers, and Construction trades.

SOURCE: U.S. Department of Education, National Center for Education Statistics, "Degrees and Other Formal Awards Conferred" surveys, and Integrated Postsecondary Education Data System (IPEDS), "Completions" surveys. (This table was prepared January 1995.)

Table 244.—Master's degrees conferred by institutions of higher education, by discipline division: 1970–71 to 1992–93

Discipline division	1970–71	1975–76	1979–80	1980–81	1981–82	1982–83	1983–84	1984–85	1985–86	1986–87	1987–88	1988–89	1989–90	1990–91	1991–92	1992–93
1	2	3	4	5	6	7	8	9	10	11	12	13	14	15	16	17
Total	230,509	311,771	298,081	295,739	295,546	289,921	284,263	286,251	288,567	289,349	299,317	310,621	324,301	337,168	352,838	369,585
Agriculture and natural resources	2,457	3,340	3,976	4,003	4,163	4,254	4,178	3,928	3,801	3,522	3,479	3,245	3,382	3,295	3,735	3,965
Architecture and related programs	1,705	3,215	3,139	3,153	3,327	3,357	3,223	3,275	3,260	3,163	3,159	3,383	3,499	3,490	3,640	3,808
Area, ethnic, and cultural studies	1,032	995	852	804	809	845	897	904	945	864	911	1,016	1,212	1,263	1,385	1,523
Biological sciences/life sciences	5,728	6,582	6,510	5,978	5,874	5,696	5,406	5,059	5,013	4,952	4,784	4,961	4,869	4,765	4,785	4,756
Business management and administrative services	25,977	42,054	54,484	57,391	60,763	64,758	66,150	66,996	66,689	67,093	69,230	73,065	76,676	78,255	84,642	89,615
Communications	1,770	2,961	2,911	2,896	3,104	3,502	3,513	3,460	3,500	3,622	3,678	3,940	4,063	4,123	4,180	4,754
Communications technologies	86	165	171	209	223	102	143	209	323	271	247	317	299	213	284	455
Computer and information sciences	1,588	2,603	3,647	4,218	4,935	5,321	6,190	7,101	8,070	8,481	9,197	9,414	9,677	9,324	9,530	10,163
Education	87,666	126,061	101,819	96,713	91,601	83,250	75,664	74,654	74,801	74,045	76,566	81,174	84,881	87,343	92,668	96,028
Engineering	16,309	16,014	15,904	16,386	17,526	18,807	20,078	20,905	21,040	22,015	22,627	23,740	23,863	23,962	24,983	27,626
Engineering-related technologies	134	328	339	323	413	537	577	650	617	639	758	828	909	996	994	1,100
English language and literature/letters	10,686	8,809	6,189	5,929	5,772	5,048	5,010	5,187	5,518	5,483	5,562	5,950	6,567	7,026	7,450	7,790
Foreign languages and literatures	5,217	4,190	2,854	2,690	2,657	2,478	2,581	2,471	2,494	2,379	2,469	2,595	2,760	2,800	2,926	3,198
Health professions and related sciences	5,749	12,556	15,704	16,515	16,503	17,047	17,411	17,385	18,573	18,394	18,657	19,268	20,321	21,200	23,065	25,718
Home economics and vocational home economics	1,452	2,179	2,690	2,570	2,355	2,385	2,416	2,375	2,294	2,064	2,047	2,164	2,100	2,019	2,412	2,479
Law and legal studies	955	1,442	1,817	1,832	1,893	2,091	1,802	1,796	1,924	1,943	1,880	2,013	1,888	2,057	2,369	2,197
Liberal arts and sciences, general studies, and humanities	885	2,633	2,646	2,375	2,425	1,286	1,796	1,696	1,586	1,581	1,814	1,850	1,999	2,213	2,394	2,416
Library science	7,001	8,037	5,374	4,859	4,506	3,904	3,782	3,870	3,564	3,783	3,674	3,906	4,341	4,763	4,893	4,871
Mathematics	5,695	4,315	3,382	3,074	3,263	3,398	3,244	3,413	3,607	3,730	3,867	3,903	4,146	4,041	4,011	4,067
Multi/interdisciplinary studies	821	1,158	2,306	2,144	2,553	2,499	2,431	2,583	2,625	2,482	2,575	2,762	2,834	1,796	2,126	2,498
Parks, recreation, leisure and fitness studies	218	571	647	643	526	608	603	596	570	560	544	535	529	483	1,358	1,434
Philosophy and religion	1,326	1,356	1,204	1,229	1,152	1,091	1,153	1,167	1,163	1,109	1,099	1,280	1,306	1,441	1,146	1,425
Physical sciences and science technologies	6,367	5,466	5,219	5,284	5,514	5,290	5,576	5,796	5,902	5,629	5,733	5,723	5,449	5,309	5,374	5,366
Precision production trades	0	0	0	0	0	0	0	4	0	0	4	3	3	0	0	2
Protective services	194	1,197	1,805	1,538	1,336	1,300	1,219	1,235	1,074	1,019	1,024	1,047	1,151	1,108	1,249	1,357
Psychology	5,717	10,167	9,938	10,223	9,947	9,981	9,525	9,891	9,845	9,562	9,180	9,940	10,730	11,349	10,215	10,957
Public administration and services	7,785	15,209	17,560	17,803	17,416	16,046	15,060	15,575	15,692	16,432	16,424	17,020	17,399	17,905	19,243	20,634
R.O.T.C. and military technologies	2	0	46	43	49	110	127	119	83	119	49	0	0	0	0	108
Social sciences and history	16,539	15,953	12,176	11,945	12,002	11,205	10,577	10,503	10,564	10,506	10,412	11,023	11,634	12,233	12,702	13,471
Theological studies/religious vocations	2,710	3,290	3,922	4,220	4,064	4,871	5,211	4,435	4,556	4,966	4,905	4,749	4,959	4,810	5,185	4,985
Transportation and material moving	63	108	142	120	129	91	194	295	454	433	679	692	538	406	385	495
Visual and performing arts	6,675	8,817	8,708	8,629	8,746	8,763	8,526	8,718	8,420	8,508	7,939	8,267	8,481	8,657	9,353	9,440
Not classified by field of study	0	0	0	0	0	0	0	0	0	0	4,144	851	1,836	8,523	4,156	884

NOTE.—The new Classification of Instructional Programs was initiated in 1991–92. The figures for earlier years have been reclassified when necessary to make them conform to the new taxonomy. To facilitate trend comparisons, certain aggregations have been made of the degree fields as reported in the IPEDS "Completions" survey. "Agriculture and natural resources" includes Agribusiness and agriculture production, Agricultural sciences, and Conservation and renewable natural resources; "Business management and administrative services" includes Business and management, Business (administrative support), Marketing and distribution, and Consumer, personal, and miscellaneous services; and "Engineering-related technologies" includes Mechanics and repairers, Construction trades, and Engineering-related technologies.

SOURCE: U.S. Department of Education, National Center for Education Statistics, "Degrees and Other Formal Awards Conferred" surveys, and Integrated Postsecondary Education Data System (IPEDS), "Completions" surveys. (This table was prepared January 1995.)

Table 245.—Doctor's degrees conferred by institutions of higher education, by discipline division: 1970–71 to 1992–93

Discipline division	1970–71	1975–76	1979–80	1980–81	1981–82	1982–83	1983–84	1984–85	1985–86	1986–87	1987–88	1988–89	1989–90	1990–91	1991–92	1992–93
1	2	3	4	5	6	7	8	9	10	11	12	13	14	15	16	17
Total	32,107	34,064	32,615	32,958	32,707	32,775	33,209	32,943	33,653	34,041	34,870	35,720	38,371	39,294	40,659	42,132
Agriculture and natural resources	1,086	928	991	1,067	1,079	1,149	1,172	1,213	1,158	1,049	1,142	1,183	1,295	1,185	1,214	1,173
Architecture and related programs	36	82	79	93	80	97	84	89	73	134	98	86	103	135	132	148
Area, ethnic, and cultural studies	144	188	151	162	102	155	141	140	159	134	142	114	131	167	155	178
Biological sciences/life sciences	3,645	3,392	3,636	3,718	3,743	3,341	3,437	3,432	3,358	3,419	3,629	3,520	3,844	4,093	4,243	4,435
Business management and administrative services	757	900	753	795	815	776	929	831	934	1,062	1,063	1,100	1,093	1,185	1,242	1,346
Communications	145	196	182	171	182	205	215	228	212	273	230	247	267	259	252	293
Communications technologies	0	8	11	11	18	9	4	6	11	2	4	6	6	15	3	8
Computer and information sciences	128	244	240	252	251	262	251	248	344	374	428	551	627	676	772	805
Education	6,041	7,202	7,314	7,279	6,999	7,057	6,911	6,612	6,605	6,407	6,060	6,337	6,502	6,187	6,864	7,030
Engineering	3,637	2,819	2,502	2,551	2,621	2,818	2,979	3,221	3,398	3,801	4,174	4,506	4,967	5,258	5,488	5,823
Engineering-related technologies	1	2	5	10	15	13	2	9	12	17	17	17	14	14	11	20
English language and literature/letters	1,650	1,672	1,294	1,164	1,101	991	1,018	1,041	991	961	981	1,022	1,078	1,184	1,273	1,341
Foreign languages and literatures	988	1,076	755	804	748	673	659	635	672	661	602	632	724	758	850	830
Health professions and related sciences	466	577	786	842	925	1,155	1,164	1,199	1,241	1,213	1,261	1,437	1,536	1,613	1,661	1,767
Home economics and vocational home economics	123	178	192	247	247	255	277	273	311	296	307	264	301	253	293	345
Law and legal studies	20	76	40	60	22	72	121	105	54	120	89	76	111	90	68	86
Liberal arts and sciences, general studies, and humanities	32	162	192	121	155	215	173	112	90	56	66	72	63	70	67	81
Library science	39	71	73	71	84	52	74	87	62	57	46	61	42	56	50	77
Mathematics	1,249	909	763	775	721	731	743	734	777	759	796	915	966	1,036	1,082	1,189
Multi/interdisciplinary studies	59	111	209	158	238	225	249	219	263	247	224	212	272	220	231	196
Parks, recreation, leisure, and fitness studies	2	15	21	42	33	33	27	36	39	32	29	35	35	28	61	108
Philosophy and religion	554	554	374	410	364	404	442	468	477	421	405	465	439	456	475	448
Physical sciences and science technologies	4,390	3,431	3,089	3,141	3,286	3,269	3,306	3,403	3,551	3,673	3,809	3,858	4,164	4,290	4,391	4,393
Precision production trades	0	0	0	0	0	0	0	0	0	0	0	0	0	0	0	0
Protective services	1	9	18	21	24	38	31	33	21	18	32	26	38	28	24	32
Psychology	2,144	3,157	3,395	3,576	3,461	3,602	3,535	3,447	3,593	3,560	3,480	3,685	3,811	3,932	3,373	3,651
Public administration and services	174	292	342	362	372	347	420	431	382	398	470	428	508	430	432	459
R.O.T.C. and military technologies	0	0	0	0	0	0	0	0	0	0	0	0	0	0	0	0
Social sciences and history	3,660	4,157	3,230	3,122	3,061	2,931	2,911	2,851	2,955	2,916	2,781	2,885	3,010	3,012	3,218	3,460
Theological studies/religious vocations	312	1,033	1,319	1,276	1,288	1,208	1,204	1,144	1,185	1,230	1,199	1,166	1,317	1,079	1,259	1,417
Transportation and material moving	3	3	4	3	2	0	0	0	3	0	0	0	0	0	0	0
Visual and performing arts	621	620	655	654	670	692	730	696	722	793	727	753	849	838	906	882
Not classified by field of study	0	0	0	0	0	0	0	0	0	0	579	61	258	747	569	111

NOTE.—The new Classification of Instructional Programs was initiated in 1991–92. The figures for earlier years have been reclassified when necessary to make them conform to the new taxonomy. To facilitate trend comparisons, certain aggregations have been made of the degree fields as reported in the IPEDS "Completions" survey: "Agriculture and natural resources" includes Agribusiness and agriculture production, Agricultural sciences, and Conservation and renewable natural resources; "Business management and administrative services" includes Business management, Business (administrative support), Marketing and distribution, and Consumer, personal, and miscellaneous services; and "Engineering-related technologies" includes Engineering-related technologies, Mechanics and repairers, and Construction trades.

SOURCE: U.S. Department of Education, National Center for Education Statistics, "Degrees and Other Formal Awards Conferred" surveys, and Integrated Postsecondary Education Data System (IPEDS), "Completions" surveys. (This table was prepared January 1995.)

Table 246.—Degrees conferred by institutions of higher education, by control of institution: 1969–70 to 1992–93

Year	Public institutions					Private institutions				
	Associate	Bachelor's	Master's	Doctor's	First-profes-sional [1]	Associate	Bachelor's	Master's	Doctor's	First-profes-sional [1]
1	2	3	4	5	6	7	8	9	10	11
1969–70	170,966	519,550	134,545	19,183	14,542	35,057	272,766	73,746	10,683	20,376
1970–71	215,645	557,996	151,603	20,788	16,139	36,666	281,734	78,906	11,319	21,807
1971–72	255,218	599,615	167,075	21,776	18,521	36,796	287,658	84,558	11,587	24,890
1972–73	278,132	630,899	174,405	22,357	21,872	38,042	291,463	88,966	12,420	28,146
1973–74	303,188	651,544	184,632	21,810	23,208	40,736	294,232	92,401	12,006	30,608
1974–75	318,474	634,785	193,804	22,176	23,612	41,697	288,148	98,646	11,907	32,304
1975–76	345,006	635,161	206,298	21,751	25,766	46,448	290,585	105,473	12,313	36,883
1976–77	355,650	630,463	208,901	21,229	26,344	50,727	289,086	108,263	12,003	38,015
1977–78	358,874	627,903	202,099	20,456	27,097	53,372	293,301	109,521	11,675	39,484
1978–79	346,808	621,666	192,016	20,817	27,785	55,894	299,724	109,063	11,913	41,063
1979–80	344,536	624,084	187,499	20,608	27,942	56,374	305,333	110,582	12,007	42,189
1980–81	352,391	626,452	184,384	20,895	29,128	63,986	308,688	111,355	12,063	42,828
1981–82	[2]366,732	636,475	182,295	20,889	29,611	[2]67,794	316,523	113,251	11,818	42,421
1982–83	377,817	646,317	176,246	21,186	29,757	71,803	323,193	113,675	11,589	43,297
1983–84	[2]379,249	646,013	170,693	21,141	29,586	[2]72,991	328,296	113,570	12,068	44,882
1984–85	377,625	652,246	170,000	21,337	30,152	77,087	327,231	116,251	11,606	44,911
1985–86	369,052	658,586	169,903	21,433	29,568	76,995	329,237	118,664	12,220	44,342
1986–87 [3]	358,811	659,260	167,797	21,870	29,346	77,493	332,004	121,552	12,171	42,271
1987–88	354,180	658,491	173,778	22,488	29,153	80,905	336,338	125,539	12,382	41,582
1988–89	357,001	675,675	179,109	22,970	28,993	79,763	343,080	131,512	12,750	41,863
1989–90	375,635	700,015	186,104	24,641	28,810	79,467	351,329	138,197	13,730	42,178
1990–91	398,055	724,062	193,057	25,681	29,554	83,665	370,476	144,111	13,613	42,394
1991–92	420,265	759,475	203,398	26,820	29,366	83,966	377,078	149,440	13,839	44,780
1992–93	430,321	785,112	213,843	27,392	29,628	84,435	380,066	155,742	14,740	45,759

[1] Includes degrees which require at least 6 years of college work for completion (including at least 2 years of preprofessional training).
[2] Data are approximations.
[3] Revised from previously published data.

SOURCE: U.S. Department of Education, National Center for Education Statistics, "Degrees and Other Formal Awards Conferred" surveys, and Integrated Postsecondary Education Data System (IPEDS), "Completions" surveys. (This table was prepared February 1995.)

Table 247.—Degrees conferred by institutions of higher education, by control of institution, level of degree, and discipline division: 1992–93

Discipline division	Public institutions				Private institutions			
	Associate degrees	Bachelor's degrees	Master's degrees	Doctor's degrees	Associate degrees	Bachelor's degrees	Master's degrees	Doctor's degrees
1	2	3	4	5	6	7	8	9
Total	**430,321**	**785,112**	**213,843**	**27,392**	**84,435**	**380,066**	**155,742**	**14,740**
Agriculture and natural resources [1]	5,080	15,977	3,668	1,148	318	801	297	25
Architecture and related programs	322	6,771	2,667	88	50	2,396	1,141	60
Area, ethnic, and cultural studies	23	2,745	908	83	10	2,736	615	95
Biological sciences/life sciences	1,356	30,531	3,525	3,073	79	16,507	1,231	1,362
Business management and administrative services [2]	76,317	160,944	36,624	941	27,539	95,898	52,991	405
Communications	1,413	37,791	2,716	249	491	16,083	2,038	44
Communications technologies	1,386	510	86	0	442	322	369	8
Computer and information sciences	6,821	15,371	5,467	540	2,375	8,829	4,696	265
Construction trades	1,351	24	0	0	302	45	0	0
Education	8,137	82,202	63,805	5,122	1,178	25,579	32,223	1,908
Engineering	2,079	46,118	18,671	4,021	399	15,855	8,955	1,802
Engineering-related technologies	23,830	11,891	965	20	12,491	4,013	135	0
English language and literature/letters	1,264	37,406	5,839	959	56	18,727	1,951	382
Foreign languages and literatures	331	9,123	2,344	483	180	5,264	854	347
Health professions and related sciences	76,461	46,331	15,580	1,328	9,776	20,758	10,138	439
Home economics and vocational home economics	6,464	13,166	1,453	259	450	1,934	1,026	86
Law and legal studies	5,422	1,347	420	8	2,606	709	1,777	78
Liberal/general studies and humanities	147,375	21,637	1,220	28	10,665	11,819	1,196	53
Library science	74	72	4,090	65	11	11	781	12
Mathematics	716	9,737	3,118	855	27	5,075	949	334
Mechanics and repairers	9,426	14	0	0	1,540	91	0	0
Multi/interdisciplinary studies	8,402	18,210	1,653	142	84	5,745	845	54
Parks, recreation, leisure, and fitness studies	635	7,988	1,130	102	82	1,871	304	6
Philosophy and religion	36	3,003	479	164	75	4,778	946	284
Physical sciences and science technologies	2,144	11,372	3,930	3,039	97	6,173	1,436	1,354
Precision production trades	6,585	351	0	0	2,619	37	2	0
Protective services	16,350	16,983	894	31	484	3,919	463	1
Psychology	1,151	44,958	5,220	1,751	86	21,770	5,737	1,900
Public administration and services	2,895	12,173	12,909	240	406	4,602	7,725	219
R.O.T.C. and military technologies	42	0	108	0	10	11	0	0
Social sciences and history	3,560	87,508	8,653	2,101	370	48,195	4,818	1,359
Theological studies/religious vocations	0	0	0	0	508	5,433	4,985	1,417
Transportation and material moving	1,970	1,821	60	0	240	2,109	435	0
Visual and performing arts	6,467	28,055	5,441	552	6,223	19,706	3,999	330
Unclassified by field of study	4,436	2,982	200	0	2,166	2,265	684	111

[1] Includes "Agricultural business and production," "Agricultural sciences," and "Conservation and renewable natural resources."
[2] Includes "Marketing operations/marketing and distribution" and "Consumer and personal services."

SOURCE: U.S. Department of Education, National Center for Education Statistics, Integrated Postsecondary Education Data System, "Completions" survey 1992–93 and "Consolidated" survey 1993. (This table was prepared January 1995.)

Table 248.—Degrees conferred by institutions of higher education, by control of institution, level of degree, and discipline division: 1991–92

Discipline division	Public institutions				Private institutions			
	Associate degrees	Bachelor's degrees	Master's degrees	Doctor's degrees	Associate degrees	Bachelor's degrees	Master's degrees	Doctor's degrees
1	2	3	4	5	6	7	8	9
Total	**420,265**	**759,475**	**203,398**	**26,820**	**83,966**	**377,078**	**149,440**	**13,839**
Agriculture and natural resources [1]	4,967	14,440	3,442	1,196	284	684	293	18
Architecture and related programs	376	6,498	2,531	72	67	2,255	1,109	60
Area, ethnic, and cultural studies	27	2,508	826	76	2	2,834	559	79
Biological sciences/life sciences	1,287	27,712	3,536	3,052	74	15,229	1,249	1,191
Business management and administrative services [2]	79,860	161,699	34,696	895	26,787	94,904	49,946	347
Communications	1,403	38,258	2,489	204	483	15,999	1,691	48
Communications technologies	1,349	503	57	0	445	217	227	3
Computer and information sciences	6,933	15,351	4,997	508	2,357	9,206	4,533	264
Construction trades	1,276	24	0	0	284	43	0	0
Education	9,095	83,018	62,339	5,199	1,172	24,988	30,329	1,665
Engineering	2,209	45,355	16,817	3,847	476	15,851	8,166	1,641
Engineering-related technologies	23,998	12,080	862	11	11,863	4,110	132	0
English language and literature/letters	953	36,234	5,695	934	66	18,717	1,755	339
Foreign languages and literatures	250	8,514	2,154	539	183	5,389	772	311
Health professions and related sciences	71,008	41,967	14,030	1,219	8,445	19,753	9,035	442
Home economics and vocational home economics	6,100	13,082	1,455	256	336	1,816	957	37
Law and legal studies	4,879	1,411	482	9	2,174	733	1,887	59
Liberal/general studies and humanities	143,139	20,934	1,239	29	11,455	11,240	1,155	38
Library science	97	77	4,008	42	6	20	885	8
Mathematics	719	9,597	3,134	764	25	5,186	877	318
Mechanics and repairers	9,086	32	0	0	1,178	46	0	0
Multi/interdisciplinary studies	7,720	15,829	1,358	170	121	4,818	768	61
Parks, recreation, leisure, and fitness studies	529	7,053	1,125	58	91	1,393	233	3
Philosophy and religion	32	2,822	425	163	28	4,704	721	312
Physical sciences and science technologies	1,969	10,646	4,008	3,089	97	6,314	1,366	1,302
Precision production trades	6,417	295	0	0	2,588	83	0	0
Protective services	14,677	15,242	829	23	440	3,613	420	1
Psychology	1,084	42,519	4,901	1,679	125	20,994	5,314	1,694
Public administration and services	2,722	11,421	12,140	225	440	4,566	7,103	207
R.O.T.C. and military technologies	55	0	0	0	117	184	0	0
Social sciences and history	2,824	85,342	8,214	1,968	336	48,632	4,488	1,250
Theological studies/religious vocations	0	1	7	3	496	4,728	5,178	1,256
Transportation and material moving	2,068	1,649	51	0	350	1,949	334	0
Visual and performing arts	6,153	26,947	5,547	590	5,735	19,575	3,806	316
Unclassified by field of study	5,004	415	4	0	4,840	6,305	4,152	569

[1] Includes "Agricultural business and production," "Agricultural sciences," and "Conservation and renewable natural resources."

[2] Includes "Marketing operations/marketing and distribution" and "Consumer and personal services."

SOURCE: U.S. Department of Education, National Center for Education Statistics, Integrated Postsecondary Education Data System, "Completions" survey 1991–92 and "Consolidated" survey 1992. (This table was prepared March 1994.)

Table 249.—Number of institutions of higher education conferring degrees, by level of degree and discipline division: 1992–93

Discipline division	Total number of institutions awarding degrees				Number of public institutions awarding degrees				Number of private institutions awarding degrees			
	Associate degrees	Bachelor's degrees	Master's degrees	Doctor's degrees	Associate degrees	Bachelor's degrees	Master's degrees	Doctor's degrees	Associate degrees	Bachelor's degrees	Master's degrees	Doctor's degrees
1	2	3	4	5	6	7	8	9	10	11	12	13
Total	2,145	1,813	1,310	473	1,229	550	482	209	916	1,263	828	264
Agriculture business and production	297	125	65	34	283	99	61	33	14	26	4	1
Agricultural sciences	101	131	77	51	93	114	74	51	8	17	3	0
Architecture and related programs	57	167	119	25	48	105	88	18	9	62	31	7
Area, ethnic, and cultural studies	16	355	105	35	13	159	62	19	3	196	43	16
Biological sciences/life sciences	166	1,217	422	217	153	463	301	144	13	754	121	73
Business management and administrative services	1,557	1,331	691	111	1,077	483	347	75	480	848	344	36
Communications	225	868	220	44	186	355	153	35	39	513	67	9
Communications technologies	169	42	11	2	145	17	1	0	24	25	10	2
Computer and information sciences	697	1,039	316	112	512	429	208	76	185	610	108	36
Conservation and renewable natural resources	115	187	92	43	103	123	84	39	12	64	8	4
Construction trades	178	5	0	0	165	2	0	0	13	3	0	0
Consumer and personal services	191	10	0	0	163	6	0	0	28	4	0	0
Education	383	1,137	805	201	291	423	409	136	92	714	396	65
Engineering	272	398	264	165	245	214	172	117	27	184	92	48
Engineering-related technologies	961	311	67	6	799	218	57	6	162	93	10	0
English language and literature/letters	125	1,242	405	137	112	470	288	93	13	772	117	44
Foreign languages and literatures	71	837	196	84	67	367	142	55	4	470	54	29
Health professions and related sciences	1,170	903	506	138	925	412	281	101	245	491	225	37
Home economics	77	335	172	37	59	216	115	28	18	119	57	9
Law and legal studies	385	114	61	14	267	41	26	4	118	73	35	10
Liberal/general studies and humanities	1,268	697	141	17	968	291	68	8	300	406	73	9
Library science	29	18	73	18	26	16	62	15	3	2	11	3
Marketing operations/marketing and distribution	527	195	18	1	406	68	2	0	121	127	16	1
Mathematics	134	1,121	333	147	126	463	250	102	8	658	83	45
Mechanics and repairers	509	10	0	0	480	3	0	0	29	7	0	0
Multi/interdisciplinary studies	177	591	170	51	159	259	116	39	18	332	54	12
Parks, recreation, leisure, and fitness studies	113	428	108	23	102	223	92	20	11	205	16	3
Philosophy and religion	29	834	183	88	18	280	82	45	11	554	101	43
Physical sciences	140	1,050	336	204	130	449	243	135	10	601	93	69
Precision production trades	600	26	1	0	532	20	0	0	68	6	1	0
Protective services	739	407	106	8	689	240	80	7	50	167	26	1
Psychology	143	1,222	510	225	128	453	299	124	15	769	211	101
Public administration and services	230	625	337	74	190	288	226	43	40	337	111	31
R.O.T.C. and military technologies	2	2	1	0	1	0	1	0	1	2	0	0
Science technologies	106	16	3	3	97	7	2	3	9	9	1	0
Social sciences and history	213	1,280	404	168	177	481	289	111	36	799	115	57
Theological studies/religious vocations	84	335	268	113	0	0	0	0	84	335	268	113
Transportation and material moving	117	57	6	0	105	28	2	0	12	29	4	0
Visual and performing arts	524	1,177	366	94	389	434	232	60	135	743	134	34
Vocational home economics	490	38	6	3	464	22	4	2	26	16	2	1
Unclassified by field of study	34	27	15	4	10	5	3	0	24	22	12	4

NOTE.—Data represent programs, not organizational units within institutions.

SOURCE: U.S. Department of Education, National Center for Education Statistics, Integrated Postsecondary Education Data System, "Completions" survey, 1992–93 and "Consolidated" survey, 1993. (This table was prepared January 1995.)

Table 250.—Number of institutions of higher education conferring degrees, by level of degree and discipline division: 1991–92

Discipline division	Total number of institutions awarding degrees				Number of public institutions awarding degrees				Number of private institutions awarding degrees			
	Associate degrees	Bachelor's degrees	Master's degrees	Doctor's degrees	Associate degrees	Bachelor's degrees	Master's degrees	Doctor's degrees	Associate degrees	Bachelor's degrees	Master's degrees	Doctor's degrees
1	2	3	4	5	6	7	8	9	10	11	12	13
Total	2,162	1,809	1,297	477	1,241	551	480	209	921	1,258	817	268
Agriculture business and production	298	126	63	35	285	100	60	34	13	26	3	1
Agricultural sciences	105	131	77	50	93	114	73	49	12	17	4	1
Architecture and related programs	60	169	114	19	49	104	87	14	11	65	27	5
Area, ethnic, and cultural studies	19	348	103	36	17	141	61	19	2	207	42	17
Biological sciences/life sciences	158	1,202	436	218	145	464	309	144	13	738	127	74
Business management and administrative services	1,562	1,320	679	110	1,074	487	350	74	488	833	329	36
Communications	227	853	216	40	181	357	154	33	46	496	62	7
Communications technologies	166	41	7	2	142	17	1	0	24	24	6	2
Computer and information sciences	696	1,036	319	103	511	434	202	74	185	602	117	29
Conservation and renewable natural resources	117	168	84	39	105	120	77	36	12	48	7	3
Construction trades	176	7	0	0	165	3	0	0	11	4	0	0
Consumer and personal services	166	9	1	0	142	5	0	0	24	4	1	0
Education	385	1,150	794	199	292	439	410	137	93	711	384	62
Engineering	267	390	259	161	242	211	170	114	25	179	89	47
Engineering-related technologies	964	300	63	3	801	213	53	3	163	87	10	0
English language and literature/letters	117	1,222	409	136	107	476	289	91	10	746	120	45
Foreign languages and literatures	68	830	198	83	61	363	140	54	7	467	58	29
Health professions and related sciences	1,168	896	497	132	925	411	282	97	243	485	215	35
Home economics	97	328	174	38	79	215	124	30	18	113	50	8
Law and legal studies	361	117	59	11	260	45	26	4	101	72	33	7
Liberal/general studies and humanities	1,274	696	143	15	962	291	71	8	312	405	72	7
Library science	32	26	75	15	31	19	62	12	1	7	13	3
Marketing operations/marketing and distribution	541	197	18	2	415	75	5	1	126	122	13	1
Mathematics	136	1,129	335	147	128	470	249	102	8	659	86	45
Mechanics and repairers	504	11	0	0	474	2	0	0	30	9	0	0
Multi/interdisciplinary studies	155	589	174	52	138	256	116	36	17	333	58	16
Parks, recreation, leisure, and fitness studies	105	391	106	21	96	216	92	19	9	175	14	2
Philosophy and religion	25	820	176	91	16	274	84	48	9	546	92	43
Physical sciences	138	1,059	346	198	125	460	247	132	13	599	99	66
Precision production trades	601	35	0	0	532	23	0	0	69	12	0	0
Protective services	736	405	105	6	689	238	79	5	47	167	26	1
Psychology	148	1,218	493	225	128	456	293	127	20	762	200	98
Public administration and services	226	637	332	70	190	294	221	39	36	343	111	31
R.O.T.C. and military technologies	4	2	0	0	2	0	0	0	2	2	0	0
Science technologies	108	20	4	2	97	9	3	2	11	11	1	0
Social sciences and history	208	1,276	405	165	173	482	287	111	35	794	118	54
Theological studies/religious vocations	76	317	249	106	0	1	1	1	76	316	248	105
Transportation and material moving	112	52	6	0	97	28	2	0	15	24	4	0
Visual and performing arts	525	1,179	372	87	381	433	236	56	144	746	136	31
Vocational home economics	464	44	5	2	436	26	4	2	28	18	1	0
Unclassified by field of study	56	43	30	18	17	3	1	0	39	40	29	18

NOTE.—Data represent programs, not organizational units within institutions.

SOURCE: U.S. Department of Education, National Center for Education Statistics, Integrated Postsecondary Education Data System, "Completions" survey, 1991–92 and "Consolidated" survey, 1992. (This table was prepared March 1994.)

Table 251.—First-professional degrees conferred by institutions of higher education in dentistry, medicine, and law, by sex, and number of institutions conferring degrees: 1949–50 to 1992–93

Year	Dentistry (D.D.S. or D.M.D.)				Medicine (M.D.)				Law (LL.B. or J.D.)			
	Number of institutions conferring degrees	Degrees conferred			Number of institutions conferring degrees	Degrees conferred			Number of institutions conferring degrees	Degrees conferred		
		Total	Men	Women		Total	Men	Women		Total	Men	Women
1	2	3	4	5	6	7	8	9	10	11	12	13
1949–50	40	2,579	2,561	18	72	5,612	5,028	584	(1)	(1)	(1)	(1)
1951–52	41	2,918	2,895	23	72	6,201	5,871	330	(1)	(1)	(1)	(1)
1953–54	42	3,102	3,063	39	73	6,712	6,377	335	(1)	(1)	(1)	(1)
1955–56	42	3,009	2,975	34	73	6,810	6,464	346	131	8,262	7,974	288
1957–58	43	3,065	3,031	34	75	6,816	6,469	347	131	9,394	9,122	272
1959–60	45	3,247	3,221	26	79	7,032	6,645	387	134	9,240	9,010	230
1961–62	46	3,183	3,166	17	81	7,138	6,749	389	134	9,364	9,091	273
1963–64	46	3,180	3,168	12	82	7,303	6,878	425	133	10,679	10,372	307
1965–66	47	3,178	3,146	32	84	7,673	7,170	503	136	13,246	12,776	470
1967–68	48	3,422	3,375	47	85	7,944	7,318	626	138	16,454	15,805	649
1969–70	48	3,718	3,684	34	86	8,314	7,615	699	145	14,916	14,115	801
1970–71	48	3,745	3,703	42	89	8,919	8,110	809	147	17,421	16,181	1,240
1971–72	48	3,862	3,819	43	92	9,253	8,423	830	147	21,764	20,266	1,498
1972–73	51	4,047	3,992	55	97	10,307	9,388	919	152	27,205	25,037	2,168
1973–74	52	4,440	4,355	85	99	11,356	10,093	1,263	151	29,326	25,986	3,340
1974–75	52	4,773	4,627	146	104	12,447	10,818	1,629	154	29,296	24,881	4,415
1975–76	56	5,425	5,187	238	107	13,426	11,252	2,174	166	32,293	26,085	6,208
1976–77	57	5,138	4,764	374	109	13,461	10,891	2,570	169	34,104	26,447	7,657
1977–78	57	5,189	4,623	566	109	14,279	11,210	3,069	169	34,402	25,457	8,945
1978–79	58	5,434	4,794	640	109	14,786	11,381	3,405	175	35,206	25,180	10,026
1979–80	58	5,258	4,558	700	112	14,902	11,416	3,486	179	35,647	24,893	10,754
1980–81	58	5,460	4,672	788	116	15,505	11,672	3,833	176	36,331	24,563	11,768
1981–82	59	5,282	4,467	815	119	15,814	11,867	3,947	180	35,991	23,965	12,026
1982–83	59	5,585	4,631	954	118	15,484	11,350	4,134	177	36,853	23,550	13,303
1983–84	60	5,353	4,302	1,051	119	15,813	11,359	4,454	179	37,012	23,382	13,630
1984–85	59	5,339	4,233	1,106	120	16,041	11,167	4,874	181	37,491	23,070	14,421
1985–86	59	5,046	3,907	1,139	120	15,938	11,022	4,916	181	35,844	21,874	13,970
1986–87	58	4,741	3,603	1,138	121	15,428	10,431	4,997	179	36,056	21,561	14,495
1987–88	57	4,477	3,300	1,177	122	15,358	10,278	5,080	180	35,397	21,067	14,330
1988–89	58	4,265	3,124	1,141	124	15,460	10,310	5,150	182	35,634	21,069	14,565
1989–90	57	4,100	2,834	1,266	124	15,075	9,923	5,152	182	36,485	21,079	15,406
1990–91	55	3,699	2,510	1,189	121	15,043	9,629	5,414	179	37,945	21,643	16,302
1991–92	52	3,593	2,431	1,162	120	15,243	9,796	5,447	177	38,848	22,260	16,588
1992–93	55	3,605	2,383	1,222	122	15,531	9,679	5,852	184	40,302	23,182	17,120

[1] Data prior to 1955–56 are not shown because they lack comparability with the figures for subsequent years.

SOURCE: U.S. Department of Education, National Center for Education Statistics, "Degrees and Other Formal Awards Conferred" surveys, and Integrated Postsecondary Education Data System (IPEDS), "Completions" surveys. (This table was prepared January 1995.)

Table 252.—First-professional degrees¹ conferred by institutions of higher education, by sex of student, control of institution, and field of study: 1982-83 to 1992-93

Control of institution and field of study	1982-83 Total	1983-84 Total	1984-85 Total	1985-86 Total	1986-87 Total	1987-88 Total	1988-89 Total	1989-90 Total	1990-91 Total	1990-91 Men	1990-91 Women	1991-92 Total	1991-92 Men	1991-92 Women	1992-93 Total	1992-93 Men	1992-93 Women
1	2	3	4	5	6	7	8	9	10	11	12	13	14	15	16	17	18
Total, all institutions	**73,136**	**74,407**	**75,063**	**73,910**	**71,617**	**70,735**	**70,856**	**70,988**	**71,948**	**43,846**	**28,102**	**74,146**	**45,071**	**29,075**	**75,387**	**45,153**	**30,234**
Dentistry (D.D.S. or D.M.D.)	5,585	5,353	5,339	5,046	4,741	4,477	4,265	4,100	3,699	2,510	1,189	3,593	2,431	1,162	3,605	2,383	1,222
Medicine (M.D.)	15,484	15,813	16,041	15,938	15,428	15,358	15,460	15,075	15,043	9,629	5,414	15,243	9,796	5,447	15,531	9,679	5,852
Optometry (O.D.)	1,116	1,086	1,115	1,029	1,082	1,023	1,093	1,072	1,115	625	490	1,232	676	556	1,148	584	564
Osteopathic medicine (D.O.)	1,319	1,515	1,489	1,547	1,618	1,544	1,635	1,555	1,459	1,029	430	1,326	887	439	1,627	1,091	536
Pharmacy (Pharm.D.)	705	709	861	903	861	962	1,074	1,199	1,244	475	769	1,339	493	846	1,904	673	1,231
Podiatry (Pod.D. or D.P.) or podiatric medicine (D.P.M.)	631	607	582	612	590	645	636	675	589	445	144	504	359	145	476	350	126
Veterinary medicine (D.V.M.)	2,060	2,269	2,178	2,270	2,230	2,235	2,157	2,151	2,032	870	1,162	2,044	850	1,194	2,057	766	1,291
Chiropractic (D.C. or D.C.M.)	2,889	3,105	2,661	3,395	2,493	2,628	2,890	2,581	2,640	1,992	648	2,694	2,012	682	2,799	1,991	808
Law (LL.B. or J.D.)	36,853	37,012	37,491	35,844	36,056	35,397	35,634	36,485	37,945	21,643	16,302	38,848	22,260	16,588	40,302	23,182	17,120
Theology (M. Div., M.H.L., B.D., or Ord. and M.H.L./Rav.)	6,494	6,878	7,221	7,283	6,518	6,466	6,012	5,851	5,695	4,360	1,335	5,251	4,025	1,226	5,447	4,096	1,351
Other	0	60	85	43	0	0	0	244	487	268	219	2,072	1,282	790	491	358	133
Total, public institutions	**29,757**	**29,586**	**30,152**	**29,568**	**29,346**	**29,153**	**28,993**	**28,810**	**29,554**	**17,621**	**11,933**	**29,366**	**17,338**	**12,028**	**29,628**	**17,126**	**12,502**
Dentistry (D.D.S. or D.M.D.)	3,438	3,174	3,051	2,827	2,655	2,524	2,512	2,353	2,308	1,603	705	2,200	1,505	705	2,167	1,462	705
Medicine (M.D.)	9,569	9,674	10,071	9,991	9,711	9,557	9,491	9,108	9,364	6,093	3,271	9,259	5,908	3,351	9,370	5,843	3,527
Optometry (O.D.)	427	384	456	441	454	429	451	444	477	273	204	595	309	286	460	221	239
Osteopathic medicine (D.O.)	386	537	455	486	480	434	500	458	493	354	139	416	290	126	490	336	154
Pharmacy (Pharm.D.)	366	356	416	473	475	615	679	727	808	304	504	852	316	536	1,171	405	766
Podiatry (Pod.D. or D.P.) or podiatric medicine (D.P.M.)	0	0	0	0	0	0	0	0	0	0	0	0	0	0	0	0	0
Veterinary medicine (D.V.M.)	1,828	2,060	1,963	1,931	2,003	2,014	1,943	1,943	1,814	786	1,028	1,831	782	1,049	1,840	701	1,139
Chiropractic (D.C. or D.C.M.)	0	0	0	0	0	0	0	0	0	0	0	0	0	0	0	0	0
Law (LL.B. or J.D.)	13,743	13,380	13,695	13,419	13,568	13,580	13,417	13,585	14,290	8,208	6,082	14,097	8,160	5,937	14,130	8,158	5,972
Theology (M. Div., M.H.L., B.D., or Ord. and M.H.L./Rav.)	0	0	2	0	0	0	0	0	0	0	0	0	0	0	0	0	0
Other	0	21	43	0	0	0	0	192	0	0	0	116	68	48	0	0	0
Total, private institutions	**43,379**	**44,821**	**44,911**	**44,342**	**42,271**	**41,582**	**41,863**	**42,178**	**42,394**	**26,225**	**16,169**	**44,780**	**27,733**	**17,047**	**45,759**	**28,027**	**17,732**
Dentistry (D.D.S. or D.M.D.)	2,147	2,179	2,288	2,219	2,086	1,953	1,753	1,747	1,391	907	484	1,393	926	467	1,438	921	517
Medicine (M.D.)	5,915	6,139	5,970	5,947	5,717	5,801	5,969	5,967	5,679	3,536	2,143	5,984	3,888	2,096	6,161	3,836	2,325
Optometry (O.D.)	689	702	659	588	628	594	642	628	638	352	286	637	367	270	688	363	325
Osteopathic medicine (D.O.)	933	978	1,034	1,061	1,138	1,110	1,135	1,097	966	675	291	910	597	313	1,137	755	382
Pharmacy (Pharm.D.)	339	353	445	430	386	347	395	472	436	171	265	487	177	310	733	268	465
Podiatry (Pod.D. or D.P.) or podiatric medicine (D.P.M.)	631	607	582	612	590	645	636	675	589	445	144	504	359	145	476	350	126
Veterinary medicine (D.V.M.)	232	209	215	339	227	221	214	208	218	84	134	213	68	145	217	65	152
Chiropractic (D.C. or D.C.M.)	2,889	3,105	2,661	3,395	2,493	2,628	2,890	2,581	2,640	1,992	648	2,694	2,012	682	2,799	1,991	808
Law (LL.B. or J.D.)	23,110	23,632	23,796	22,425	22,488	21,817	22,217	22,900	23,655	13,435	10,220	24,751	14,100	10,651	26,172	15,024	11,148
Theology (M. Div., M.H.L., B.D., or Ord. and M.H.L./Rav.)	6,494	6,878	7,219	7,283	6,518	6,466	6,012	5,851	5,695	4,360	1,335	5,251	4,025	1,226	5,447	4,096	1,351
Other	0	39	42	43	0	0	0	52	487	268	219	1,956	1,214	742	491	358	133

¹ Includes degrees which require at least 6 years of college work for completion (including at least 2 years of preprofessional training).

SOURCE: U.S. Department of Education, National Center for Education Statistics, "Degrees and Other Formal Awards Conferred" surveys, and Integrated Postsecondary Education Data System (IPEDS), "Completions" survey. (This table was prepared January 1995.)

Table 253.—Associate degrees conferred by institutions of higher education, by racial/ethnic group and sex of student: 1976–77 to 1992–93

Year and sex of student	Total	White, non-Hispanic	Black, non-Hispanic	Hispanic	Asian or Pacific Islander	American Indian/Alaskan Native	Nonresident alien
1	2	3	4	5	6	7	8
Number of degrees conferred							
1976–77, total [1]	404,956	342,290	33,159	16,636	7,044	2,498	3,329
Men	209,672	178,236	15,330	9,105	3,630	1,216	2,155
Women	195,284	164,054	17,829	7,531	3,414	1,282	1,174
1978–79, total [2]	396,745	331,092	34,979	16,269	7,518	2,336	4,551
Men	187,284	156,671	14,425	8,135	4,058	1,069	2,926
Women	209,461	174,421	20,554	8,134	3,460	1,267	1,625
1980–81, total [3]	410,174	339,167	35,330	17,800	8,650	2,584	6,643
Men	183,819	151,242	14,290	8,327	4,557	1,108	4,295
Women	226,355	187,925	21,040	9,473	4,093	1,476	2,348
1984–85, total [4]	429,815	355,343	35,791	19,407	9,914	2,953	6,407
Men	190,409	157,278	14,184	8,561	5,492	1,198	3,696
Women	239,406	198,065	21,607	10,846	4,422	1,755	2,711
1986–87, total [5]	436,304	361,861	35,447	19,334	11,779	3,195	4,688
Men	190,839	158,132	13,959	8,760	6,169	1,263	2,556
Women	245,465	203,729	21,488	10,574	5,610	1,932	2,132
1988–89, total [6]	432,144	354,865	34,664	20,384	12,519	3,331	6,381
Men	183,963	150,978	12,884	9,217	6,366	1,323	3,195
Women	248,181	203,887	21,780	11,167	6,153	2,008	3,186
1989–90, total [7]	450,263	369,580	35,327	22,195	13,482	3,530	6,149
Men	188,631	154,748	13,147	9,859	6,477	1,433	2,967
Women	261,632	214,832	22,180	12,336	7,005	2,097	3,182
1990–91, total [8]	462,030	376,081	37,657	24,251	13,725	3,672	6,644
Men	190,221	155,330	13,718	10,210	6,440	1,373	3,150
Women	271,809	220,751	23,939	14,041	7,285	2,299	3,494
1991–92, total [9]	494,387	400,530	39,411	26,905	15,596	4,008	7,937
Men	202,808	164,799	14,294	11,536	7,254	1,531	3,394
Women	291,579	235,731	25,117	15,369	8,342	2,477	4,543
1992–93, total [10]	508,154	405,883	42,340	29,991	16,632	4,379	8,929
Men	209,051	167,312	15,497	12,924	7,877	1,663	3,778
Women	299,103	238,571	26,843	17,067	8,755	2,716	5,151
Percentage distribution of degrees conferred							
1976–77, total [1]	100.0	84.5	8.2	4.1	1.7	0.6	0.8
Men	100.0	85.0	7.3	4.3	1.7	0.6	1.0
Women	100.0	84.0	9.1	3.9	1.7	0.7	0.6
1978–79, total [2]	100.0	83.5	8.8	4.1	1.9	0.6	1.1
Men	100.0	83.7	7.7	4.3	2.2	0.6	1.6
Women	100.0	83.3	9.8	3.9	1.7	0.6	0.8
1980–81, total [3]	100.0	82.7	8.6	4.3	2.1	0.6	1.6
Men	100.0	82.3	7.8	4.5	2.5	0.6	2.3
Women	100.0	83.0	9.3	4.2	1.8	0.7	1.0
1984–85, total [4]	100.0	82.7	8.3	4.5	2.3	0.7	1.5
Men	100.0	82.6	7.4	4.5	2.9	0.6	1.9
Women	100.0	82.7	9.0	4.5	1.8	0.7	1.1
1986–87, total [5]	100.0	82.9	8.1	4.4	2.7	0.7	1.1
Men	100.0	82.9	7.3	4.6	3.2	0.7	1.3
Women	100.0	83.0	8.8	4.3	2.3	0.8	0.9
1988–89, total [6]	100.0	82.1	8.0	4.7	2.9	0.8	1.5
Men	100.0	82.1	7.0	5.0	3.5	0.7	1.7
Women	100.0	82.2	8.8	4.5	2.5	0.8	1.3
1989–90, total [7]	100.0	82.1	7.8	4.9	3.0	0.8	1.4
Men	100.0	82.0	7.0	5.2	3.4	0.8	1.6
Women	100.0	82.1	8.5	4.7	2.7	0.8	1.2
1990–91, total [8]	100.0	81.4	8.2	5.2	3.0	0.8	1.4
Men	100.0	81.7	7.2	5.4	3.4	0.7	1.7
Women	100.0	81.2	8.8	5.2	2.7	0.8	1.3
1991–92, total [9]	100.0	81.0	8.0	5.4	3.2	0.8	1.6
Men	100.0	81.3	7.0	5.7	3.6	0.8	1.7
Women	100.0	80.8	8.6	5.3	2.9	0.8	1.6
1992–93, total [10]	100.0	79.9	8.3	5.9	3.3	0.9	1.8
Men	100.0	80.0	7.4	6.2	3.8	0.8	1.8
Women	100.0	79.8	9.0	5.7	2.9	0.9	1.7

[1] Excludes 1,170 men and 251 women whose racial/ethnic group was not available.

[2] Excludes 4,807 men and 1,150 women whose racial/ethnic group was not available.

[3] Excludes 4,819 men and 1,384 women whose racial/ethnic group was not available.

[4] Racial/ethnic data were imputed for approximately 45,400 men and 55,400 women. This tabulation excludes 11,490 men and 10,862 women whose racial/ethnic group could not be imputed. In addition, data for 1,033 men and 1,512 women were not available by field of study and were not imputed by race.

[5] Excludes 3 men and 1 woman whose racial/ethnic group was not available.

[6] Reported racial/ethnic distributions of students by level of degree, field of degree, and sex were used to estimate race/ethnicity for students whose race/ethnicity was not reported. Excludes 2,353 men and 2,267 women whose racial/ethnic group and field of study were not available.

[7] Reported racial/ethnic distributions of students by level of degree, field of degree, and sex were used to estimate race/ethnicity for students whose race/ethnicity was not reported. Excludes 2,564 men and 2,275 women whose racial/ethnic group and field of study were not available.

[8] Reported racial/ethnic distributions of students by level of degree, field of degree, and sex were used to estimate race/ethnicity for students whose race/ethnicity was not reported. Excludes 8,413 men and 11,277 women whose racial/ethnic group and field of study were not available.

[9] Reported racial/ethnic distributions of students by level of degree, field of degree, and sex were used to estimate race/ethnicity for students whose race/ethnicity was not reported. Excludes 4,673 men and 5,171 women whose racial/ethnic group and field of study were not available.

[10] Reported racial/ethnic distributions of students by level of degree, field of degree, and sex were used to estimate race/ethnicity for students whose race/ethnicity was not reported. Excludes 2,913 men and 3,689 women whose racial/ethnic group and field of study were not available.

SOURCE: U.S. Department of Education, National Center for Education Statistics, "Degrees and Other Formal Awards Conferred" surveys, and Integrated Postsecondary Education Data System (IPEDS), "Completions" surveys. (This table was prepared January 1995.)

Table 254.—Associate degrees conferred by institutions of higher education, by racial/ethnic group, major field of study, and sex of student: 1992–93

Major field of study	Total							Men							Women						
	Total	White, non-Hispanic	Black, non-Hispanic	Hispanic	Asian/Pacific Islander	American Indian/Alaskan Native	Nonresident alien	Total	White, non-Hispanic	Black, non-Hispanic	Hispanic	Asian/Pacific Islander	American Indian/Alaskan Native	Nonresident alien	Total	White, non-Hispanic	Black, non-Hispanic	Hispanic	Asian/Pacific Islander	American Indian/Alaskan Native	Nonresident alien
1	2	3	4	5	6	7	8	9	10	11	12	13	14	15	16	17	18	19	20	21	22
All fields, total [1]	508,154	405,883	42,340	29,991	16,632	4,379	8,929	209,051	167,312	15,497	12,924	7,877	1,663	3,778	299,103	238,571	26,843	17,067	8,755	2,716	5,151
Agriculture and natural resources	5,398	5,130	47	75	18	58	70	3,750	3,569	40	46	11	37	47	1,648	1,561	7	29	7	21	23
Architecture and related programs	372	300	12	23	24	1	12	119	83	8	11	12	0	5	253	217	4	12	12	1	7
Area, ethnic, and cultural studies	33	5	10	2	7	7	2	10	1	7	0	0	2	0	23	4	3	2	7	5	2
Biological sciences/life sciences	1,435	1,000	96	131	145	25	38	588	406	31	62	68	7	14	847	594	65	69	77	18	24
Business management and administrative services	103,856	79,407	11,088	6,595	3,629	848	2,289	33,274	25,629	3,084	2,127	1,332	210	892	70,582	53,778	8,004	4,468	2,297	638	1,397
Communications	1,904	1,564	144	79	53	10	54	945	805	68	27	26	4	15	959	759	76	52	27	6	39
Communications technologies	1,828	1,468	178	98	42	7	35	1,196	975	101	65	29	4	22	632	493	77	33	13	3	13
Computer and information sciences	9,196	6,528	1,056	792	480	109	231	4,541	3,322	418	388	248	36	129	4,655	3,206	638	404	232	73	102
Construction trades	1,653	1,399	76	47	86	40	5	1,581	1,339	73	46	79	39	5	72	60	3	1	7	1	0
Education	9,315	7,313	867	732	140	198	65	3,031	2,356	300	221	59	72	23	6,284	4,957	567	511	81	126	42
Engineering	2,478	1,936	207	109	139	8	79	2,169	1,699	178	86	127	7	72	309	237	29	23	12	1	7
Engineering-related technologies	36,321	29,417	2,750	2,157	1,431	221	345	32,631	26,531	2,306	1,989	1,317	188	300	3,690	2,886	444	168	114	33	45
English language and literature/letters	1,320	758	104	138	59	19	242	469	243	57	49	20	9	91	851	515	47	89	39	10	151
Foreign languages and literatures	511	373	9	83	12	4	30	153	116	2	24	5	1	5	358	257	7	59	7	3	25
Health professions and related sciences	86,237	73,795	6,187	3,032	1,915	662	646	12,971	10,613	869	706	524	115	144	73,266	63,182	5,318	2,326	1,391	547	502
Home economics and vocational home economics	6,914	5,329	767	417	248	47	106	655	485	66	32	62	2	8	6,259	4,844	701	385	186	45	98
Law and legal studies	8,028	6,617	751	506	91	45	18	959	719	127	83	21	5	4	7,069	5,898	624	423	70	40	14
Liberal arts and sciences, general studies, and humanities	158,040	124,989	12,593	10,359	5,441	1,287	3,371	63,867	50,543	4,860	4,156	2,369	477	1,462	94,173	74,446	7,733	6,203	3,072	810	1,909
Library science	85	79	2	3	1			9	7	2					76	72		3	1		
Mathematics	743	516	26	69	70	15	47	428	295	10	40	46	12	25	315	221	16	29	24	3	22
Mechanics and repairers	10,966	8,878	670	634	548	119	117	10,280	8,380	595	596	493	109	107	686	498	75	38	55	10	10
Multi/interdisciplinary studies	8,486	7,089	621	361	302	39	74	4,075	3,430	273	169	145	20	38	4,411	3,659	348	192	157	19	36
Parks, recreation, leisure and fitness studies	717	549	98	37	19	6	8	429	309	71	27	15	4	3	288	240	27	10	4	2	5
Philosophy and religion	111	95	6	8	0	0	2	76	68	3	3	0	0	2	35	27	3	5	0	0	0
Physical sciences and science technologies	2,241	1,784	143	100	123	12	79	1,296	1,072	62	55	59	7	41	945	712	81	45	64	5	38
Precision production trades	9,204	7,654	411	642	349	86	62	7,393	6,174	326	533	254	66	40	1,811	1,480	85	109	95	20	22
Protective services	16,834	14,077	1,382	952	215	163	45	12,289	10,593	724	666	173	101	32	4,545	3,484	658	286	42	62	13
Psychology	1,237	913	111	144	34	18	17	282	197	33	38	7	6	1	955	716	78	106	27	12	16
Public administration and services	3,301	2,240	635	296	47	69	14	648	446	115	55	17	11	4	2,653	1,794	520	241	30	58	10
R.O.T.C. and military technologies	52	28	21	1	2	0	0	44	25	17	1	1	0	0	8	3	4	0	1	0	0
Social sciences and history	3,930	2,555	507	458	192	100	118	1,678	1,086	255	174	82	33	48	2,252	1,469	252	284	110	67	70
Theological studies/religious vocations	508	438	33	12	5	5	15	281	237	20	12	2	3	7	227	201	13	0	3	2	8
Transportation and material moving	2,210	1,927	68	98	60	18	39	1,850	1,633	56	84	42	12	23	360	294	12	14	18	6	16
Visual and performing arts	12,690	9,733	664	801	703	133	656	5,084	3,924	342	353	230	64	171	7,606	5,809	322	448	473	69	485

[1] Reported racial/ethnic distributions of students by level of degree, field of degree, and sex were used to estimate race/ethnicity for students whose race/ethnicity was not reported. Excludes 2,913 men and 3,689 women whose racial/ethnic group and field of study were not available.

NOTE.—To facilitate trend comparisons, certain aggregations have been made of the degree fields as reported in the IPEDS "Completions" survey. "Agriculture and natural resources" includes Agribusiness and agriculture production, Agricultural sciences, and Conservation and renewable natural resources; and "Business management and administrative services" includes Business and management; Business and office, Marketing and distribution, and Consumer and personal services.

SOURCE: U.S. Department of Education, National Center for Education Statistics, Integrated Postsecondary Education Data System (IPEDS), "Completions" survey. (This table was prepared January 1995.)

Table 255.—Associate degrees conferred by institutions of higher education, by racial/ethnic group, major field of study, and sex of student: 1991–92

Major field of study	Total							Men							Women						
	Total	White, non-His-panic	Black, non-His-panic	His-panic	Asian/Pacific Islander	Amer-ican Indian/Alas-kan Native	Non-resi-dent alien	Total	White, non-His-panic	Black, non-His-panic	His-panic	Asian/Pacific Is-lander	Amer-ican Indian/Alas-kan Native	Non-resi-dent alien	Total	White, non-His-panic	Black, non-His-panic	His-panic	Asian/Pacific Is-lander	Amer-ican Indian/Alas-kan Native	Non-resi-dent alien
1	2	3	4	5	6	7	8	9	10	11	12	13	14	15	16	17	18	19	20	21	22
All fields, total[1]	494,387	400,530	39,411	26,905	15,596	4,008	7,937	202,808	164,799	14,294	11,536	7,254	1,531	3,394	291,579	235,731	25,117	15,369	8,342	2,477	4,543
Agriculture and natural resources	5,251	4,970	39	61	29	53	99	3,576	3,393	24	43	18	38	60	1,675	1,577	15	18	11	15	39
Architecture and related programs	443	344	9	34	42	3	11	106	65	3	18	17	1	2	337	279	6	16	25	2	9
Area, ethnic, and cultural studies	29	15	6	5	1	2	0	9	6	2	0	0	1	0	20	9	4	5	1	1	0
Biological sciences/life sciences	1,361	992	76	113	133	15	32	564	404	32	54	57	5	12	797	588	44	59	76	10	20
Business management and administrative services	106,647	83,347	10,703	5,972	3,737	824	2,064	33,175	26,256	2,948	1,750	1,269	201	751	73,472	57,091	7,755	4,222	2,468	623	1,313
Communications	1,886	1,594	145	66	34	14	33	890	761	74	26	13	7	9	996	833	71	40	21	7	24
Communications technologies	1,794	1,455	170	97	32	4	36	1,145	954	90	60	17	7	22	649	501	80	37	15	2	14
Computer and information sciences	9,290	6,716	1,162	624	509	67	212	4,565	3,443	414	312	263	26	107	4,725	3,273	748	312	246	41	105
Construction trades	1,560	1,322	64	52	90	26	6	1,491	1,268	60	45	86	26	6	69	54	4	7	4	0	0
Education	10,267	8,037	999	775	168	200	88	3,708	2,869	406	248	79	79	27	6,559	5,168	593	527	89	121	61
Engineering	2,685	2,154	139	105	191	15	81	2,341	1,896	107	92	169	13	64	344	258	32	13	22	2	17
Engineering-related technologies	35,861	29,288	2,491	2,044	1,385	185	468	32,104	26,342	2,108	1,850	1,236	152	416	3,757	2,946	383	194	149	33	52
English language and literature/letters	1,019	618	74	78	59	6	184	348	193	31	29	19	6	70	671	425	43	49	40	0	114
Foreign languages and literatures	433	334	6	58	14	4	17	128	101	1	19	2	0	5	305	233	5	39	12	4	12
Health professions and related sciences	79,453	68,000	5,865	2,745	1,644	559	640	10,805	8,864	750	601	368	100	122	68,648	59,136	5,115	2,144	1,276	459	518
Home economics and vocational home economics	6,436	5,025	681	409	152	39	130	687	519	78	33	41	2	14	5,749	4,506	603	376	111	37	116
Law and legal studies	7,053	5,902	653	334	95	50	95	907	676	140	63	18	8	14	6,146	5,226	513	271	77	42	17
Liberal arts and sciences, general studies, and humanities	154,594	124,653	11,607	9,362	4,809	1,245	2,918	62,817	50,642	4,515	3,815	2,094	465	1,286	91,777	74,011	7,092	5,547	2,715	780	1,632
Library science	103	94	5	3	1	0	0	18	13	2	3	0	0	0	85	81	4	3	0	0	0
Mathematics	744	539	27	65	67	8	38	464	343	9	43	41	3	25	280	196	18	22	26	5	13
Mechanics and repairers	10,264	8,338	600	652	494	91	89	9,593	7,873	543	575	438	79	85	671	465	57	77	56	12	4
Multi/interdisciplinary studies	7,841	6,932	392	208	211	26	72	3,782	3,349	181	99	104	8	41	4,059	3,583	211	109	107	18	31
Parks, recreation, leisure and fitness studies	620	542	53	7	5	5	8	369	320	36	3	3	2	5	251	222	17	4	2	3	3
Philosophy and religion	60	51	3	4	2	0	0	43	36	3	3	1	0	0	17	15	0	1	0	0	0
Physical sciences and science technologies	2,066	1,611	140	110	147	8	50	1,205	954	69	72	75	4	31	861	657	71	38	72	4	19
Precision production trades	9,005	7,510	413	521	409	75	77	7,133	5,978	309	423	305	59	59	1,872	1,532	104	98	104	16	18
Protective services	15,117	12,766	1,102	851	216	132	50	11,241	9,722	614	606	176	90	33	3,876	3,044	488	245	40	42	17
Psychology	1,209	933	79	119	34	31	13	338	251	29	31	16	9	2	871	682	50	88	18	22	11
Public administration and services	3,162	2,193	570	258	63	64	14	639	452	90	62	17	15	3	2,523	1,741	480	196	46	49	11
R.O.T.C. and military technologies	172	132	21	14	4	0	1	156	121	19	11	4	0	1	16	11	2	3	0	0	0
Social sciences and history	3,160	2,176	375	354	108	80	67	1,400	974	188	137	50	24	27	1,760	1,202	187	217	58	56	40
Theological studies/religious vocations	496	417	40	8	18	2	11	280	238	22	5	1	1	5	216	179	18	3	9	1	6
Transportation and material moving	2,418	2,108	88	101	50	38	33	1,978	1,746	72	83	30	29	18	440	362	16	18	20	9	15
Visual and performing arts	11,888	9,422	614	696	643	137	376	4,803	3,777	325	322	219	76	84	7,085	5,645	289	374	424	61	292

[1] Reported racial/ethnic distributions of students by level of degree, field of degree, and sex were used to estimate race/ethnicity for students whose race/ethnicity was not reported. Excludes 4,673 men and 5,171 women whose racial/ethnic group and field of study were not available.

NOTE.—To facilitate trend comparisons, certain aggregations have been made of the degree fields as reported in the IPEDS "Completions" survey: "Agriculture and natural resources" includes Agribusiness and agriculture production, Agricultural sciences, and Conservation and renewable natural resources; and "Business management and administrative services" includes Business and management, Business and office, Marketing and distribution, and Consumer and personal services.

SOURCE: U.S. Department of Education, National Center for Education Statistics, Integrated Postsecondary Education Data System (IPEDS), "Completions" survey. (This table was prepared April 1994.)

Table 256.—Bachelor's degrees conferred by institutions of higher education, by racial/ethnic group and sex of student: 1976–77 to 1992–93

Year and sex of student	Total	White, non-Hispanic	Black, non-Hispanic	Hispanic	Asian or Pacific Islander	American Indian/Alaskan Native	Nonresident alien
1	2	3	4	5	6	7	8
			Number of degrees conferred				
1976–77, total [1]	917,900	807,688	58,636	18,743	13,793	3,326	15,714
Men	494,424	438,161	25,147	10,318	7,638	1,804	11,356
Women	423,476	369,527	33,489	8,425	6,155	1,522	4,358
1978–79, total [2]	919,540	802,542	60,246	20,096	15,407	3,410	17,839
Men	476,065	418,215	24,659	10,418	8,261	1,736	12,776
Women	443,475	384,327	35,587	9,678	7,146	1,674	5,063
1980–81, total [3]	934,800	807,319	60,673	21,832	18,794	3,593	22,589
Men	469,625	406,173	24,511	10,810	10,107	1,700	16,324
Women	465,175	401,146	36,162	11,022	8,687	1,893	6,265
1984–85, total [4]	968,311	826,106	57,473	25,874	25,395	4,246	29,217
Men	476,148	405,085	23,018	12,402	13,554	1,998	20,091
Women	492,163	421,021	34,455	13,472	11,841	2,248	9,126
1986–87, total [5]	991,264	841,818	56,560	26,988	32,624	3,968	29,306
Men	480,782	406,749	22,501	12,865	17,253	1,817	19,597
Women	510,482	435,069	34,059	14,123	15,371	2,151	9,709
1988–89, total [5,6]	1,016,350	859,703	58,078	29,918	37,674	3,951	27,026
Men	481,946	407,154	22,370	13,950	19,260	1,730	17,482
Women	534,404	452,549	35,708	15,968	18,414	2,221	9,544
1989–90, total [5,7]	1,048,631	884,376	61,063	32,844	39,248	4,392	26,708
Men	490,317	413,573	23,262	14,941	19,721	1,859	16,961
Women	558,314	470,803	37,801	17,903	19,527	2,533	9,747
1990–91, total [5,8]	1,081,280	904,062	65,341	36,612	41,618	4,513	29,134
Men	496,424	415,505	24,328	16,158	20,678	1,901	17,854
Women	584,856	488,557	41,013	20,454	20,940	2,612	11,280
1991–92, total [5,9]	1,129,833	936,771	72,326	40,761	46,720	5,176	28,079
Men	516,976	429,842	26,956	17,976	23,248	2,182	16,772
Women	612,857	506,929	45,370	22,785	23,472	2,994	11,307
1992–93, total [5,10]	1,159,931	947,309	77,872	45,376	51,463	5,671	32,240
Men	530,541	435,084	28,883	19,865	25,293	2,449	18,967
Women	629,390	512,225	48,989	25,511	26,170	3,222	13,273
			Percentage distribution of degrees conferred				
1976–77, total [1]	100.0	88.0	6.4	2.0	1.5	0.4	1.7
Men	100.0	88.6	5.1	2.1	1.5	0.4	2.3
Women	100.0	87.3	7.9	2.0	1.5	0.4	1.0
1978–79, total [2]	100.0	87.3	6.6	2.2	1.7	0.4	1.9
Men	100.0	87.8	5.2	2.2	1.7	0.4	2.7
Women	100.0	86.7	8.0	2.2	1.6	0.4	1.1
1980–81, total [3]	100.0	86.4	6.5	2.3	2.0	0.4	2.4
Men	100.0	86.5	5.2	2.3	2.2	0.4	3.5
Women	100.0	86.2	7.8	2.4	1.9	0.4	1.3
1984–85, total [4]	100.0	85.3	5.9	2.7	2.6	0.4	3.0
Men	100.0	85.1	4.8	2.6	2.8	0.4	4.2
Women	100.0	85.5	7.0	2.7	2.4	0.5	1.9
1986–87, total [5]	100.0	84.9	5.7	2.7	3.3	0.4	3.0
Men	100.0	84.6	4.7	2.7	3.6	0.4	4.1
Women	100.0	85.2	6.7	2.8	3.0	0.4	1.9
1988–89, total [5,6]	100.0	84.6	5.7	2.9	3.7	0.4	2.7
Men	100.0	84.5	4.6	2.9	4.0	0.4	3.6
Women	100.0	84.7	6.7	3.0	3.4	0.4	1.8
1989–90, total [5,7]	100.0	84.3	5.8	3.1	3.7	0.4	2.5
Men	100.0	84.3	4.7	3.0	4.0	0.4	3.5
Women	100.0	84.3	6.8	3.2	3.5	0.5	1.7
1990–91, total [5,8]	100.0	83.6	6.0	3.4	3.8	0.4	2.7
Men	100.0	83.7	4.9	3.3	4.2	0.4	3.6
Women	100.0	83.5	7.0	3.5	3.6	0.4	1.9
1991–92, total [5,9]	100.0	82.9	6.4	3.6	4.1	0.5	2.5
Men	100.0	83.1	5.2	3.5	4.5	0.4	3.2
Women	100.0	82.7	7.4	3.7	3.8	0.5	1.8
1992–93, total [5,10]	100.0	81.7	6.7	3.9	4.4	0.5	2.8
Men	100.0	82.0	5.4	3.7	4.8	0.5	3.6
Women	100.0	81.4	7.8	4.1	4.2	0.5	2.1

[1] Excludes 1,121 men and 528 women whose racial/ethnic group was not available.
[2] Excludes 1,279 men and 571 women whose racial/ethnic group was not available.
[3] Excludes 258 men and 82 women whose racial/ethnic group was not available.
[4] Excludes 6,380 men and 4,786 women whose racial/ethnic group was not available.
[5] Reported racial/ethnic distributions of students by level of degree, field of degree, and sex were used to estimate race/ethnicity for students whose race/ethnicity was not reported.
[6] Excludes 1,400 men and 1,005 women whose racial/ethnic group was not available.
[7] Excludes 1,379 men and 1,334 women whose racial/ethnic group was not available.

[8] Excludes 7,621 men and 5,637 women whose racial/ethnic group was not available.
[9] Excludes 3,835 men and 2,885 women whose racial/ethnic group was not available.
[10] Excludes 2,340 men and 2,907 women whose racial/ethnic group was not available.

SOURCE: U.S. Department of Education, National Center for Education Statistics, "Degrees and Other Formal Awards Conferred" surveys, and Integrated Postsecondary Education Data System (IPEDS), "Completions" surveys. (This table was prepared January 1995.)

Table 257.—Bachelor's degrees conferred by institutions of higher education, by racial/ethnic group, major field of study, and sex of student: 1992–93

Major field of study	Total							Men							Women						
	Total	White, non-His-panic	Black, non-His-panic	His-panic	Asian/ Pacific Islander	Amer-ican Indian/ Alas-kan Native	Non-resi-dent alien	Total	White, non-His-panic	Black, non-His-panic	His-panic	Asian/ Pacific Is-lander	Amer-ican Indian/ Alas-kan Native	Non-resi-dent alien	Total	White, non-His-panic	Black, non-His-panic	His-panic	Asian/ Pacific Is-lander	Amer-ican Indian/ Alas-kan Native	Non-resi-dent alien
1	2	3	4	5	6	7	8	9	10	11	12	13	14	15	16	17	18	19	20	21	22
All fields, total [1]	1,159,931	947,309	77,872	45,376	51,463	5,671	32,240	530,541	435,084	28,883	19,865	25,293	2,449	18,967	629,390	512,225	48,989	25,511	26,170	3,222	13,273
Agriculture and natural resources	16,778	15,152	435	325	318	90	458	11,080	10,101	233	210	168	63	305	5,698	5,051	202	115	150	27	153
Architecture and related programs	9,167	7,289	293	461	667	35	422	5,940	4,762	200	313	373	23	269	3,227	2,527	93	148	294	12	153
Area, ethnic, and cultural studies	5,481	3,864	530	437	463	51	136	1,977	1,430	191	140	150	17	49	3,504	2,434	339	297	313	34	87
Biological/life sciences	47,038	35,766	2,784	1,855	5,203	215	1,215	22,842	17,673	898	909	2,690	105	567	24,196	18,093	1,886	946	2,513	110	648
Business management and administrative services	256,842	205,083	19,187	9,588	11,780	1,051	10,153	135,573	111,478	7,644	4,711	5,249	530	5,961	121,269	93,605	11,543	4,877	6,531	521	4,192
Communications	53,874	45,480	4,164	1,883	1,178	201	968	21,601	18,621	1,435	706	399	86	354	32,273	26,859	2,729	1,177	779	115	614
Communications technologies	832	666	93	26	12	10	25	427	359	35	12	4	3	14	405	307	58	14	8	7	11
Computer and information sciences	24,200	16,502	2,261	860	2,294	83	2,200	17,403	12,591	1,071	565	1,524	54	1,598	6,797	3,911	1,190	295	770	29	602
Construction trades	69	58	7	1	2	1	0	64	53	7	1	1	1	1	5	5	0	0	0	0	0
Education	107,781	96,857	5,590	2,973	1,100	644	617	23,233	20,538	1,380	657	288	154	216	84,548	76,319	4,210	2,316	812	490	401
Engineering	61,973	45,803	2,630	2,312	6,542	180	4,506	52,185	39,071	1,802	1,884	5,241	145	4,042	9,788	6,732	828	428	1,301	35	464
Engineering-related technologies	15,904	12,929	1,068	622	765	103	417	14,485	11,878	882	553	692	91	389	1,419	1,051	186	69	73	12	28
English language and literature/letters	56,133	48,957	3,065	1,756	1,583	235	537	19,247	17,129	751	605	492	94	176	36,886	31,828	2,314	1,151	1,091	141	361
Foreign languages and literatures	14,387	11,240	477	1,647	526	53	444	4,158	3,315	123	417	148	21	134	10,229	7,925	354	1,230	378	32	310
Health professions and related sciences	67,089	56,464	4,744	2,009	2,513	348	1,011	11,347	9,282	688	457	573	69	278	55,742	47,182	4,056	1,552	1,940	279	733
Home economics and vocational home economics	15,100	13,019	945	400	475	59	202	1,638	1,371	137	43	53	6	28	13,462	11,648	808	357	422	53	174
Law and legal studies	2,056	1,678	192	100	71	12	3	667	520	54	52	37	4	0	1,389	1,158	138	48	34	8	3
Liberal arts and sciences, general studies, and humanities	33,456	26,965	2,725	1,892	1,004	258	612	13,275	10,916	992	639	361	94	273	20,181	16,049	1,733	1,253	643	164	339
Library science	83	74	4	2	0	1	2	9	8	0	0	0	0	1	74	66	4	2	0	1	1
Mathematics	14,812	11,867	978	437	929	56	545	7,827	6,244	450	254	510	27	342	6,985	5,623	528	183	419	29	203
Mechanics and repairers	105	76	6	5	14	0	4	102	74	5	5	14	0	4	3	2	1	0	0	0	0
Multi/interdisciplinary studies	23,955	19,207	1,495	1,556	1,188	117	392	8,917	7,140	551	411	561	54	200	15,038	12,067	944	1,145	627	63	192
Parks, recreation, leisure and fitness studies	9,859	8,885	447	285	103	36	103	4,885	4,317	258	183	53	15	59	4,974	4,568	189	102	50	21	44
Philosophy and religion	7,781	6,693	333	244	314	46	151	4,938	4,259	197	168	173	29	112	2,843	2,434	136	76	141	17	39
Physical sciences and science technologies	17,545	14,275	850	438	1,124	93	765	11,825	9,865	379	300	695	62	524	5,720	4,410	471	138	429	31	241
Precision production trades	388	331	34	4	4	2	13	281	240	23	3	3	1	11	107	91	11	1	1	1	2
Protective services	20,902	15,952	3,099	1,265	325	130	131	13,020	10,478	1,448	724	223	71	76	7,882	5,474	1,651	541	102	59	55
Psychology	66,728	55,057	4,727	3,175	2,596	344	829	17,908	14,876	1,127	833	756	96	220	48,820	40,181	3,600	2,342	1,840	248	609
Public administration and services	16,775	12,716	2,506	886	327	187	153	3,801	2,819	547	229	109	46	51	12,974	9,897	1,959	657	218	141	102
R.O.T.C. and military sciences	11	11	0	0	0	0	0	11	11	0	0	0	0	0	0	0	0	0	0	0	0
Social sciences and history	135,703	109,942	9,964	6,067	5,712	772	3,246	73,589	61,332	4,277	2,992	2,802	372	1,814	62,114	48,610	5,687	3,075	2,910	400	1,432
Theological studies/religious vocations	5,433	4,841	151	111	128	27	175	4,168	3,734	117	82	88	18	129	1,265	1,107	34	29	40	9	46
Transportation and material moving	3,930	3,482	163	136	73	18	58	3,508	3,121	131	120	66	15	55	422	361	32	16	7	3	3
Visual and performing arts	47,761	40,128	1,925	1,618	2,130	213	1,747	18,610	15,478	850	687	796	83	716	29,151	24,650	1,075	931	1,334	130	1,031

[1] Reported racial/ethnic distributions of students by level of degree, field of degree, and sex were used to estimate race/ethnicity for students whose race/ethnicity was not reported. Excludes 2,340 men and 2,907 women whose racial/ethnic group and field of study were not available.

NOTE.—To facilitate trend comparisons, certain aggregations have been made of the degree fields as reported in the IPEDS "Completions" survey: "Agriculture and natural resources" includes Agribusiness and agriculture production, Agricultural sciences, and Conservation and renewable natural resources; and "Business management and administrative services" includes Business and management, Business and office, Marketing and distribution, and Consumer and personal services.

SOURCE: U.S. Department of Education, National Center for Education Statistics, Integrated Postsecondary Education Data System (IPEDS), "Completions" survey. (This table was prepared January 1995.)

Table 258.—Bachelor's degrees conferred by institutions of higher education, by racial/ethnic group, major field of study, and sex of student: 1991–92

Major field of study	Total							Men							Women						
	Total	White, non-His-panic	Black, non-His-panic	His-panic	Asian/ Pacific Is-lander	Amer-ican Indian/ Alas-kan Native	Non-resi-dent alien	Total	White, non-His-panic	Black, non-His-panic	His-panic	Asian/ Pacific Is-lander	Amer-ican Indian/ Alas-kan Native	Non-resi-dent alien	Total	White, non-His-panic	Black, non-His-panic	His-panic	Asian/ Pacific Is-lander	Amer-ican Indian/ Alas-kan Native	Non-resi-dent alien
1	2	3	4	5	6	7	8	9	10	11	12	13	14	15	16	17	18	19	20	21	22
All fields, total [1]	1,129,833	936,771	72,326	40,761	46,720	5,176	28,079	516,976	429,842	26,956	17,976	23,248	2,182	16,772	612,857	506,929	45,370	22,785	23,472	2,994	11,307
Agriculture and natural resources	15,124	13,743	413	296	300	83	289	9,869	9,054	229	178	149	59	200	5,255	4,689	184	118	151	24	89
Architecture and related programs	8,753	7,050	294	407	551	33	418	5,805	4,715	211	268	323	21	267	2,948	2,335	83	139	228	12	151
Area, ethnic, and cultural studies	5,342	3,875	517	355	382	48	165	1,907	1,384	185	132	126	16	64	3,435	2,491	332	223	256	32	101
Biological/life sciences	42,941	33,179	2,428	1,673	4,488	185	988	20,798	16,386	764	797	2,278	95	478	22,143	16,793	1,664	876	2,210	90	510
Business management and administrative services	256,603	209,768	18,304	8,466	10,592	949	8,524	135,440	113,660	7,167	4,194	4,761	462	5,196	121,163	96,108	11,137	4,272	5,831	487	3,328
Communications	54,257	46,554	3,970	1,650	1,088	177	818	21,150	18,473	1,331	604	359	70	313	33,107	28,081	2,639	1,046	729	107	505
Communications technologies	720	588	99	14	6	2	11	347	288	41	9	2	2	5	373	300	58	5	4	0	6
Computer and information sciences	24,557	17,311	2,147	901	2,140	81	1,977	17,510	12,924	1,123	581	1,412	49	1,421	7,047	4,387	1,024	320	728	32	556
Construction trades	67	52	11	1	1	1	1	65	51	10	1	1	0	2	2	1	0	0	0	0	0
Education	108,006	97,460	5,226	3,116	977	654	573	22,686	20,096	1,266	717	246	155	206	85,320	77,364	3,960	2,399	731	499	367
Engineering	61,206	45,923	2,406	2,087	6,387	186	4,217	51,768	39,321	1,648	1,724	5,173	154	3,748	9,438	6,602	758	363	1,214	32	469
Engineering-related technologies	16,190	13,071	1,174	558	794	88	505	14,806	12,129	935	490	708	81	463	1,384	942	239	68	86	7	42
English language and literature/letters	54,951	48,543	2,658	1,623	1,447	222	458	18,536	16,687	703	516	431	72	127	36,415	31,856	1,955	1,107	1,016	150	331
Foreign languages and literatures	13,903	11,157	427	1,426	480	46	367	3,985	3,253	104	387	127	15	99	9,918	7,904	323	1,039	353	31	268
Health professions and related sciences	61,720	52,281	4,222	1,765	2,261	332	859	10,189	8,428	543	355	554	62	247	51,531	43,853	3,679	1,410	1,707	270	612
Home economics and vocational home economics	14,898	12,980	868	340	425	67	218	1,687	1,400	121	59	56	6	45	13,211	11,580	747	281	369	61	173
Law and legal studies	2,144	1,835	149	69	67	16	8	701	593	38	33	26	6	5	1,443	1,242	111	36	41	10	3
Liberal arts and sciences, general studies, and humanities	32,174	26,457	2,670	1,581	817	205	444	12,784	10,655	992	539	310	84	204	19,390	15,802	1,678	1,042	507	121	240
Library science	97	85	5	1	2	0	4	8	7	0	0	1	0	1	89	78	5	1	1	0	4
Mathematics	14,783	11,906	916	455	868	46	592	7,888	6,369	381	264	494	22	358	6,895	5,537	535	191	374	24	234
Mechanics and repairers	78	70	4	0	1	0	2	77	69	4	1	1	0	2	1	1	0	0	0	0	0
Multi/interdisciplinary studies	20,647	16,853	1,290	957	1,056	126	365	8,628	7,037	522	346	476	46	201	12,019	9,816	768	611	580	80	164
Parks, recreation, leisure and fitness studies	8,446	7,679	393	181	262	38	70	4,144	3,681	255	105	48	16	39	4,302	3,998	138	76	76	22	31
Philosophy and religion	7,526	6,559	311	229	276	27	124	4,752	4,143	193	148	173	16	79	2,774	2,416	118	81	103	11	45
Physical sciences and science technologies	16,960	14,044	836	382	1,025	66	607	11,431	9,696	392	254	632	40	417	5,529	4,348	444	128	393	26	190
Precision production trades	378	303	42	2	11	6	14	280	221	29	2	10	6	12	98	82	13	0	0	0	2
Protective services	18,855	14,574	2,699	1,075	262	135	110	11,659	9,435	1,281	610	186	76	71	7,196	5,139	1,418	465	76	59	39
Psychology	63,513	53,242	4,271	2,827	2,194	319	660	17,031	14,377	1,008	745	633	93	175	46,482	38,865	3,263	2,082	1,561	226	485
Public administration and services	15,987	12,169	2,369	798	302	174	175	3,479	2,609	504	189	95	34	48	12,508	9,560	1,865	609	207	140	127
R.O.T.C. and military sciences	184	149	20	14	1	1	0	158	127	17	13	0	1	0	26	22	3	1	1	0	0
Social sciences and history	133,974	110,086	9,188	5,808	5,470	606	2,816	73,001	61,613	3,978	2,914	2,661	291	1,544	60,973	48,473	5,210	2,894	2,809	315	1,272
Theological studies/religious vocations	4,729	4,143	159	102	136	21	168	3,552	3,118	125	77	93	16	123	1,177	1,025	34	25	43	5	45
Transportation and material moving	3,598	3,156	174	123	55	28	62	3,239	2,852	147	104	52	26	58	359	304	27	19	2	2	4
Visual and performing arts	46,522	39,926	1,666	1,478	1,774	208	1,470	17,616	14,991	709	620	651	89	556	28,906	24,935	957	858	1,123	119	914

[1] Reported racial/ethnic distributions of students by level of degree, field of degree, and sex were used to estimate race/ethnicity for students whose race/ethnicity was not reported. Excludes 3,835 men and 2,885 women whose racial/ethnic group and field of study were not available.

NOTE.—To facilitate trend comparisons, certain aggregations have been made of the degree fields as reported in the IPEDS "Completions" survey. "Agriculture and natural resources" includes Agribusiness and agriculture production, Agricultural sciences, and Conservation and renewable natural resources; and "Business management and administrative services" includes Business and management, Business and office, Marketing and distribution, and Consumer and personal services.

SOURCE: U.S. Department of Education, National Center for Education Statistics, Integrated Postsecondary Education Data System (IPEDS), "Completions" survey. (This table was prepared April 1994.)

Table 259.—Master's degrees conferred by institutions of higher education, by racial/ethnic group and sex of student: 1976–77 to 1992–93

Year and sex of student	Total	White, non-Hispanic	Black, non-Hispanic	Hispanic	Asian or Pacific Islander	American Indian/Alaskan Native	Nonresident alien
1	2	3	4	5	6	7	8

				Number of degrees conferred			
1976–77, total [1]	316,602	266,061	21,037	6,071	5,122	967	17,344
Men	167,396	139,210	7,781	3,268	3,123	521	13,493
Women	149,206	126,851	13,256	2,803	1,999	446	3,851
1978–79, total [2]	300,255	249,360	19,418	5,555	5,496	999	19,427
Men	152,637	124,058	7,070	2,786	3,325	495	14,903
Women	147,618	125,302	12,348	2,769	2,171	504	4,524
1980–81, total [3]	294,183	241,216	17,133	6,461	6,282	1,034	22,057
Men	145,666	115,562	6,158	3,085	3,773	501	16,587
Women	148,517	125,654	10,975	3,376	2,509	533	5,470
1984–85, total [4]	280,421	223,628	13,939	6,864	7,782	1,256	26,952
Men	139,417	106,059	5,200	3,059	4,842	583	19,674
Women	141,004	117,569	8,739	3,805	2,940	673	7,278
1986–87, total [5]	289,349	228,874	13,873	7,044	8,559	1,103	29,896
Men	141,269	105,572	5,153	3,331	5,239	518	21,456
Women	148,080	123,302	8,720	3,713	3,320	585	8,440
1988–89, total [5,6]	309,770	242,764	14,095	7,277	10,335	1,086	34,213
Men	148,872	109,715	5,175	3,325	6,048	476	24,133
Women	160,898	133,049	8,920	3,952	4,287	610	10,080
1989–90, total [5,7]	322,465	251,690	15,446	7,950	10,577	1,101	35,701
Men	152,926	112,877	5,539	3,586	6,002	463	24,459
Women	169,539	138,813	9,907	4,364	4,575	638	11,242
1990–91, total [5,8]	328,645	255,281	16,139	8,386	11,180	1,136	36,523
Men	151,796	111,224	5,709	3,670	6,319	459	24,415
Women	176,849	144,057	10,430	4,716	4,861	677	12,108
1991–92, total [5,9]	348,682	268,371	18,116	9,358	12,658	1,273	38,906
Men	159,543	116,096	6,054	4,132	7,062	523	25,676
Women	189,139	152,275	12,062	5,226	5,596	750	13,230
1992–93, total [5,10]	368,701	278,829	19,780	10,665	13,866	1,407	44,154
Men	168,754	120,225	6,821	4,735	7,544	586	28,843
Women	199,947	158,604	12,959	5,930	6,322	821	15,311

				Percentage distribution of degrees conferred			
1976–77, total [1]	100.0	84.0	6.6	1.9	1.6	0.3	5.5
Men	100.0	83.2	4.6	2.0	1.9	0.3	8.1
Women	100.0	85.0	8.9	1.9	1.3	0.3	2.6
1978–79, total [2]	100.0	83.0	6.5	1.9	1.8	0.3	6.5
Men	100.0	81.3	4.6	1.8	2.2	0.3	9.8
Women	100.0	84.9	8.4	1.9	1.5	0.3	3.1
1980–81, total [3]	100.0	82.0	5.8	2.2	2.1	0.4	7.5
Men	100.0	79.3	4.2	2.1	2.6	0.3	11.4
Women	100.0	84.6	7.4	2.3	1.7	0.4	3.7
1984–85, total [4]	100.0	79.7	5.0	2.4	2.8	0.4	9.6
Men	100.0	76.1	3.7	2.2	3.5	0.4	14.1
Women	100.0	83.4	6.2	2.7	2.1	0.5	5.2
1986–87, total [5]	100.0	79.1	4.8	2.4	3.0	0.4	10.3
Men	100.0	74.7	3.6	2.4	3.7	0.4	15.2
Women	100.0	83.3	5.9	2.5	2.2	0.4	5.7
1988–89, total [5,6]	100.0	78.4	4.6	2.3	3.3	0.4	11.0
Men	100.0	73.7	3.5	2.2	4.1	0.3	16.2
Women	100.0	82.7	5.5	2.5	2.7	0.4	6.3
1989–90, total [5,7]	100.0	78.1	4.8	2.5	3.3	0.3	11.1
Men	100.0	73.8	3.6	2.3	3.9	0.3	16.0
Women	100.0	81.9	5.8	2.6	2.7	0.4	6.6
1990–91, total [5,8]	100.0	77.7	4.9	2.6	3.4	0.3	11.1
Men	100.0	73.3	3.8	2.4	4.2	0.3	16.1
Women	100.0	81.5	5.9	2.7	2.7	0.4	6.8
1991–92, total [5,9]	100.0	77.0	5.2	2.7	3.6	0.4	11.2
Men	100.0	72.8	3.8	2.6	4.4	0.3	16.1
Women	100.0	80.5	6.4	2.8	3.0	0.4	7.0
1992–93, total [5,10]	100.0	75.6	5.4	2.9	3.8	0.4	12.0
Men	100.0	71.2	4.0	2.8	4.5	0.3	17.1
Women	100.0	79.3	6.5	3.0	3.2	0.4	7.7

[1] Excludes 387 men and 175 women whose racial/ethnic group was not available.
[2] Excludes 733 men and 91 women whose racial/ethnic group was not available.
[3] Excludes 1,377 men and 179 women whose racial/ethnic group was not available.
[4] Excludes 3,973 men and 1,857 women whose racial/ethnic group was not available.
[5] Reported racial/ethnic distributions of students by level of degree, field of degree, and sex were used to estimate race/ethnicity for students whose race/ethnicity was not reported.
[6] Excludes 482 men and 369 women whose racial/ethnic group was not available.
[7] Excludes 727 men and 1,109 women whose racial/ethnic group was not available.

[8] Excludes 4,686 men and 3,837 women whose racial/ethnic group was not available.
[9] Excludes 2,299 men and 1,857 women whose racial/ethnic group was not available.
[10] Excludes 504 men and 380 women whose racial/ethnic group was not available.

SOURCE: U.S. Department of Education, National Center for Education Statistics, "Degrees and Other Formal Awards Conferred" surveys, and Integrated Postsecondary Education Data System (IPEDS), "Completions" surveys. (This table was prepared January 1995.)

Table 260.—Master's degrees conferred by institutions of higher education, by racial/ethnic group, major field of study, and sex of student: 1992–93

Major field of study	Total							Men							Women						
	Total	White, non-His-panic	Black, non-His-panic	His-panic	Asian/ Pacific Is-lander	Amer-ican Indian/ Alas-kan Native	Non-resi-dent alien	Total	White, non-His-panic	Black, non-His-panic	His-panic	Asian/ Pacific Is-lander	Amer-ican Indian/ Alas-kan Native	Non-resi-dent alien	Total	White, non-His-panic	Black, non-His-panic	His-panic	Asian/ Pacific Is-lander	Amer-ican Indian/ Alas-kan Native	Non-resi-dent alien
1	2	3	4	5	6	7	8	9	10	11	12	13	14	15	16	17	18	19	20	21	22
All fields, total[1]	368,701	278,829	19,780	10,665	13,866	1,407	44,154	168,754	120,225	6,821	4,735	7,544	586	28,843	199,947	158,604	12,959	5,930	6,322	821	15,311
Agriculture and natural resources	3,965	2,743	93	85	80	10	954	2,477	1,655	56	44	40	7	675	1,488	1,088	37	41	40	3	279
Architecture and related programs	3,808	2,586	145	148	206	12	711	2,376	1,604	80	95	124	7	466	1,432	982	65	53	82	5	245
Area, ethnic, and cultural studies	1,523	1,040	131	77	86	10	179	732	531	38	38	30	5	90	791	509	93	39	56	5	89
Biological sciences/life sciences	4,756	3,281	141	140	317	27	850	2,343	1,663	49	74	141	9	407	2,413	1,618	92	66	176	18	443
Business management and administrative services	89,615	66,535	4,474	2,241	4,304	269	11,792	57,651	43,235	2,184	1,432	2,627	158	8,015	31,964	23,300	2,290	809	1,677	111	3,777
Communications	4,754	3,461	273	122	151	10	737	1,725	1,284	80	42	56	5	258	3,029	2,177	193	80	95	5	479
Communications technologies	455	307	25	10	10		105	255	176	11	5	7		58	200	131	14	5	3	0	47
Computer and information sciences	10,163	4,700	324	167	1,163	15	3,794	7,410	3,513	204	109	750	12	2,822	2,753	1,187	120	58	413	3	972
Education	96,028	81,290	6,725	3,181	1,391	459	2,982	22,197	18,341	1,523	835	369	142	987	73,831	62,949	5,202	2,346	1,022	317	1,995
Engineering	27,626	14,827	600	618	2,405	53	9,123	23,537	12,580	435	512	1,943	39	8,028	4,089	2,247	165	106	462	14	1,095
Engineering-related technologies	1,100	824	40	17	36	8	175	917	690	24	15	27	7	154	183	134	16	2	9	1	21
English language and literature/letters	7,790	6,732	269	174	158	37	420	2,667	2,341	66	67	46	17	130	5,123	4,391	203	107	112	20	290
Foreign languages and literatures	3,198	2,060	44	262	108	6	718	1,062	718	9	82	26	2	225	2,136	1,342	35	180	82	4	493
Health professions and related sciences	25,718	21,328	1,301	638	864	120	1,467	5,227	3,987	217	158	233	21	611	20,491	17,341	1,084	480	631	99	856
Home economics and vocational home economics	2,479	1,935	153	105	52	9	225	422	310	27	27	6	2	50	2,057	1,625	126	78	46	7	175
Law and legal studies	2,197	1,188	41	84	66	5	813	1,481	814	22	45	37	3	560	716	374	19	39	29	2	253
Liberal arts and sciences, general studies, and humanities	2,416	2,076	106	50	34	7	143	840	709	35	21	13	3	59	1,576	1,367	71	29	21	4	84
Library science	4,871	4,154	187	118	118	16	278	961	807	30	23	20	3	78	3,910	3,347	157	95	98	13	200
Mathematics	4,067	2,530	105	69	212	8	1,143	2,455	1,467	53	43	133	4	755	1,612	1,063	52	26	79	4	388
Multi/interdisciplinary studies	2,498	2,100	96	65	63	14	160	1,221	1,018	39	31	34	4	95	1,277	1,082	57	34	29	10	65
Parks, recreation, leisure and fitness studies	1,434	1,227	80	25	14	4	84	714	603	38	14	10	2	47	720	624	42	11	4	2	37
Philosophy and religion	1,425	1,170	57	26	50	5	117	988	802	37	16	37	4	92	437	368	20	10	13	1	25
Physical sciences and science technologies	5,366	3,262	112	107	262	13	1,610	3,808	2,379	63	98	140	4	1,124	1,558	883	49	9	122	9	486
Precision production trades	2		0	0		1	1	2	0	0	0		1	1	0	0	0	0		0	
Protective services	1,357	1,024	214	45	17	6	51	837	663	99	26	13	3	33	520	361	115	19	4	3	18
Psychology	10,957	9,357	578	425	203	61	333	3,029	2,583	123	148	53	11	111	7,928	6,774	455	277	150	50	222
Public administration and services	20,634	16,130	2,271	890	466	92	785	6,105	4,536	633	294	143	31	468	14,529	11,594	1,638	596	323	61	317
R.O.T.C. and military technologies	108	93	6	3	5	1	0	100	86	5	3	5	1	0	8	7	1	0	0	0	0
Social sciences and history	13,471	9,474	645	396	422	72	2,462	7,671	5,276	330	247	205	43	1,570	5,800	4,198	315	149	217	29	892
Theological studies/religious vocations	4,985	3,836	227	123	207	9	583	2,989	2,274	143	74	133	5	360	1,996	1,562	84	49	74	4	223
Transportation and material moving	495	439	22	19	6	1	8	456	401	22	18	6	1	8	39	38	0	1	0	0	0
Visual and performing arts	9,440	7,118	295	235	393	47	1,352	4,099	3,177	146	123	121	25	507	5,341	3,941	149	112	272	22	845

[1] Reported racial/ethnic distributions of students by level of degree, field of degree, and sex were used to estimate race/ethnicity for students whose race/ethnicity was not reported. Excludes 504 men and 380 women whose racial/ethnic group and field of study were not available.

Agricultural sciences, and Conservation and renewable natural resources; and "Business management and administrative services" includes Business and management, Business and office, Marketing and distribution, and Consumer and personal services.

NOTE.—To facilitate trend comparisons, certain aggregations have been made of the degree fields as reported in the IPEDS "Completions" survey: "Agriculture and natural resources" includes Agribusiness and agriculture production,

SOURCE: U.S. Department of Education, National Center for Education Statistics, Integrated Postsecondary Education Data System (IPEDS), "Completions" survey. (This table was prepared January 1995.)

Table 261.—Master's degrees conferred by institutions of higher education, by racial/ethnic group, major field of study, and sex of student: 1991–92

Major field of study	Total							Men							Women						
	Total	White, non-His-panic	Black, non-His-panic	His-panic	Asian/ Pacific Islander	Amer-ican Indian/ Alas-kan Native	Non-resi-dent alien	Total	White, non-His-panic	Black, non-His-panic	His-panic	Asian/ Pacific Is-lander	Amer-ican Indian/ Alas-kan Native	Non resi-dent alien	Total	White, non-His-panic	Black, non-His-panic	His-panic	Asian/ Pacific Is-lander	Amer-ican Indian/ Alas-kan Native	Non-resi-dent alien
1	2	3	4	5	6	7	8	9	10	11	12	13	14	15	16	17	18	19	20	21	22
All fields, total [1]	348,682	268,371	18,116	9,358	12,658	1,273	38,906	159,543	116,096	6,054	4,132	7,062	523	25,676	189,139	152,275	12,062	5,226	5,596	750	13,230
Agriculture and natural resources	3,735	2,546	82	61	74	7	965	2,413	1,582	50	43	46	5	687	1,322	964	32	18	28	2	278
Architecture and related programs	3,640	2,530	135	121	191	10	653	2,271	1,552	79	74	112	7	447	1,369	978	56	47	79	3	206
Area, ethnic, and cultural studies	1,385	957	91	86	69	16	166	688	493	41	52	27	7	68	697	464	50	34	42	9	98
Biological sciences/life sciences	4,785	3,404	156	141	276	13	795	2,301	1,645	64	68	131	8	385	2,484	1,759	92	73	145	5	410
Business management and administrative services	84,642	65,320	3,966	1,944	3,635	220	9,557	54,705	42,668	1,900	1,223	2,175	123	6,616	29,937	22,652	2,066	721	1,460	97	2,941
Communications	4,180	3,109	258	78	110	15	610	1,537	1,175	57	27	33	5	240	2,643	1,934	201	51	77	10	370
Communications technologies	284	170	18	5	9	0	82	155	95	9	3	7	0	41	129	75	9	2	2	0	41
Computer and information sciences	9,530	4,678	334	158	1,171	16	3,173	6,884	3,448	186	104	751	11	2,384	2,646	1,230	148	54	420	5	789
Education	92,668	78,874	6,444	2,838	1,192	457	2,863	21,244	17,653	1,345	745	308	136	1,057	71,424	61,221	5,099	2,093	884	321	1,806
Engineering	24,983	13,640	498	521	2,377	45	7,902	21,327	11,552	356	437	1,947	38	6,997	3,656	2,088	142	84	430	7	905
Engineering-related technologies	994	728	52	20	55	6	133	816	596	42	15	43	5	115	178	132	10	5	12	1	18
English language and literature/letters	7,450	6,462	220	152	146	37	433	2,513	2,208	60	48	48	17	132	4,937	4,254	160	104	98	20	301
Foreign languages and literatures	2,926	1,896	37	280	101	6	606	971	646	10	101	20	3	191	1,955	1,250	27	179	81	3	415
Health professions and related sciences	23,065	19,220	1,136	559	739	94	1,317	4,691	3,575	180	142	226	24	544	18,374	15,645	956	417	513	70	773
Home economics and vocational home economics	2,412	1,920	121	61	45	6	259	409	295	12	10	12	0	80	2,003	1,625	109	51	33	6	179
Law and legal studies	2,369	1,253	46	76	77	2	915	1,597	847	24	49	52	0	625	772	406	22	27	25	2	290
Liberal arts and sciences, general studies, and humanities	2,394	2,057	107	48	36	8	138	870	736	36	11	15	2	70	1,524	1,321	71	37	21	6	68
Library science	4,893	4,230	159	106	148	8	242	992	846	30	29	20	2	65	3,901	3,384	129	77	128	6	177
Mathematics	4,011	2,523	84	64	216	4	1,120	2,452	1,524	49	47	113	1	718	1,559	999	35	17	103	3	402
Multi/interdisciplinary studies	2,126	1,721	87	60	63	8	187	995	787	35	32	36	2	103	1,131	934	52	28	27	6	84
Parks, recreation, leisure and fitness studies	1,358	1,191	49	32	11	2	73	650	556	25	22	7	0	40	708	635	24	10	4	2	33
Philosophy and religion	1,146	931	50	26	39	7	93	731	586	27	21	25	7	67	415	345	23	5	14	0	26
Physical sciences and science technologies	5,374	3,296	105	91	318	19	1,545	3,909	2,419	71	66	222	15	1,116	1,465	877	34	25	96	4	429
Precision production trades	0	0	0	0	0	0	0	0	0	0	0	0	0	0	0	0	0	0	0	0	0
Protective services	1,249	973	182	35	15	6	38	797	646	85	23	10	4	29	452	327	97	12	5	2	9
Psychology	10,215	8,737	562	379	194	41	302	2,988	2,544	146	123	66	14	95	7,227	6,193	416	256	128	27	207
Public administration and services	19,243	15,231	2,001	771	422	124	694	5,769	4,386	527	253	150	47	406	13,474	10,845	1,474	518	272	77	288
R.O.T.C. and military technologies	0	0	0	0	0	0	0	0	0	0	0	0	0	0	0	0	0	0	0	0	0
Social sciences and history	12,702	9,034	602	301	396	50	2,319	7,237	5,084	293	168	216	18	1,458	5,465	3,950	309	133	180	32	861
Theological studies/religious vocations	5,185	4,085	240	116	189	12	543	3,199	2,441	156	70	126	9	397	1,986	1,644	84	46	63	3	146
Transportation and material moving	385	340	22	9	8	3	3	354	311	22	8	8	2	3	31	29	0	1	0	1	0
Visual and performing arts	9,353	7,315	272	219	336	31	1,180	4,078	3,200	137	118	110	13	500	5,275	4,115	135	101	226	18	680

[1] Reported racial/ethnic distributions of students by level of degree, field of degree, and sex were used to estimate race/ethnicity for students whose race/ethnicity was not reported. Excludes 2,299 men and 1,857 women whose racial/ethnic group and field of study were not available.

NOTE.—To facilitate trend comparisons, certain aggregations have been made of the degree fields as reported in the IPEDS "Completions" survey. "Agriculture and natural resources" includes Agribusiness and agriculture production, Agricultural sciences, and Conservation and renewable natural resources; and "Business management and administrative services" includes Business and management, Business and office, Marketing and distribution, and Consumer and personal services.

SOURCE: U.S. Department of Education, National Center for Education Statistics, Integrated Postsecondary Education Data System (IPEDS), "Completions" survey. (This table was prepared April 1994.)

Table 262.—Doctor's degrees [1] conferred by institutions of higher education, by racial/ethnic group and sex of student: 1976–77 to 1992–93

Year and sex of student	Total	White, non-Hispanic	Black, non-Hispanic	Hispanic	Asian or Pacific Islander	American Indian/Alaskan Native	Nonresident alien
1	2	3	4	5	6	7	8
Number of degrees conferred							
1976–77, total [2]	33,126	26,851	1,253	522	658	95	3,747
Men	25,036	20,032	766	383	540	67	3,248
Women	8,090	6,819	487	139	118	28	499
1978–79, total [3]	32,675	26,138	1,268	439	811	104	3,915
Men	23,488	18,433	734	294	646	69	3,312
Women	9,187	7,705	534	145	165	35	603
1980–81, total [4]	32,839	25,908	1,265	456	877	130	4,203
Men	22,595	17,310	694	277	655	95	3,564
Women	10,244	8,598	571	179	222	35	639
1984–85, total [5]	32,307	23,934	1,154	677	1,106	119	5,317
Men	21,296	15,017	561	431	802	64	4,421
Women	11,011	8,917	593	246	304	55	896
1986–87, total [6]	34,041	24,434	1,057	751	1,098	105	6,596
Men	22,061	14,812	485	441	794	57	5,472
Women	11,980	9,622	572	310	304	48	1,124
1988–89, total [6,7]	35,659	24,884	1,066	629	1,323	85	7,672
Men	22,597	14,541	491	350	945	50	6,220
Women	13,062	10,343	575	279	378	35	1,452
1989–90, total [6,8]	38,113	25,880	1,153	788	1,235	99	8,958
Men	24,248	15,105	533	423	871	49	7,267
Women	13,865	10,775	620	365	364	50	1,691
1990–91, total [6,9]	38,547	25,328	1,211	732	1,459	102	9,715
Men	24,333	14,565	581	387	987	58	7,755
Women	14,214	10,763	630	345	472	44	1,960
1991–92, total [6,10]	40,090	25,813	1,223	811	1,559	118	10,566
Men	25,168	14,674	576	458	1,062	65	8,333
Women	14,922	11,139	647	353	497	53	2,233
1992–93, total [6,11]	42,021	26,700	1,352	827	1,582	106	11,454
Men	25,980	14,902	615	439	1,041	51	8,932
Women	16,041	11,798	737	388	541	55	2,522
Percentage distribution of degrees conferred							
1976–77, total [2]	100.0	81.1	3.8	1.6	2.0	0.3	11.3
Men	100.0	80.0	3.1	1.5	2.2	0.3	13.0
Women	100.0	84.3	6.0	1.7	1.5	0.3	6.2
1978–79, total [3]	100.0	80.0	3.9	1.3	2.5	0.3	12.0
Men	100.0	78.5	3.1	1.3	2.8	0.3	14.1
Women	100.0	83.9	5.8	1.6	1.8	0.4	6.6
1980–81, total [4]	100.0	78.9	3.9	1.4	2.7	0.4	12.8
Men	100.0	76.6	3.1	1.2	2.9	0.4	15.8
Women	100.0	83.9	5.6	1.7	2.2	0.3	6.2
1984–85, total [5]	100.0	74.1	3.6	2.1	3.4	0.4	16.5
Men	100.0	70.5	2.6	2.0	3.8	0.3	20.8
Women	100.0	81.0	5.4	2.2	2.8	0.5	8.1
1986–87, total [6]	100.0	71.8	3.1	2.2	3.2	0.3	19.4
Men	100.0	67.1	2.2	2.0	3.6	0.3	24.8
Women	100.0	80.3	4.8	2.6	2.5	0.4	9.4
1988–89, total [6,7]	100.0	69.8	3.0	1.8	3.7	0.2	21.5
Men	100.0	64.3	2.2	1.5	4.2	0.2	27.5
Women	100.0	79.2	4.4	2.1	2.9	0.3	11.1
1989–90, total [6,8]	100.0	67.9	3.0	2.1	3.2	0.3	23.5
Men	100.0	62.3	2.2	1.7	3.6	0.2	30.0
Women	100.0	77.7	4.5	2.6	2.6	0.4	12.2
1990–91, total [6,9]	100.0	65.7	3.1	1.9	3.8	0.3	25.2
Men	100.0	59.9	2.4	1.6	4.1	0.2	31.9
Women	100.0	75.7	4.4	2.4	3.3	0.3	13.8
1991–92, total [6,10]	100.0	64.4	3.1	2.0	3.9	0.3	26.4
Men	100.0	58.3	2.3	1.8	4.2	0.3	33.1
Women	100.0	74.6	4.3	2.4	3.3	0.4	15.0
1992–93, total [6,11]	100.0	63.5	3.2	2.0	3.8	0.3	27.3
Men	100.0	57.4	2.4	1.7	4.0	0.2	34.4
Women	100.0	73.5	4.6	2.4	3.4	0.3	15.7

[1] Includes Ph.D., Ed.D, and comparable degrees at the doctoral level. Excludes first-professional degrees.
[2] Excludes 106 men whose racial/ethnic group was not available.
[3] Excludes 53 men and 2 women whose racial/ethnic group was not available.
[4] Excludes 116 men and 3 women whose racial/ethnic group was not available.
[5] Excludes 404 men and 232 women whose racial/ethnic group was not available.
[6] Reported racial/ethnic distributions of students by level of degree, field of degree, and sex were used to estimate race/ethnicity for students whose race/ethnicity was not reported.
[7] Excludes 51 men and 10 women whose racial/ethnic group was not available.

[8] Excludes 153 men and 105 women whose racial/ethnic group was not available.
[9] Excludes 423 men and 324 women whose racial/ethnic group was not available.
[10] Excludes 389 men and 180 women whose racial/ethnic group was not available.
[11] Excludes 93 men and 18 women whose racial/ethnic group was not available.

SOURCE: U.S. Department of Education, National Center for Education Statistics, "Degrees and Other Formal Awards Conferred" surveys, and Integrated Postsecondary Education Data System (IPEDS), "Completions" surveys. (This table was prepared January 1995.)

Table 263.—Doctor's degrees conferred by institutions of higher education, by racial/ethnic group, major field of study, and sex of student: 1992–93

Major field of study	Total							Men							Women						
	Total	White, non-His-panic	Black, non-His-panic	His-panic	Asian/ Pacific Islander	Amer-ican Indian/ Alas-kan Native	Non-resi-dent alien	Total	White, non-His-panic	Black, non-His-panic	His-panic	Asian/ Pacific Is-lander	Amer-ican Indian/ Alas-kan Native	Non-resi-dent alien	Total	White, non-His-panic	Black, non-His-panic	His-panic	Asian/ Pacific Is-lander	Amer-ican Indian/ Alas-kan Native	Non-resi-dent alien
1	2	3	4	5	6	7	8	9	10	11	12	13	14	15	16	17	18	19	20	21	22
All fields, total[1]	42,021	26,700	1,352	827	1,582	106	11,454	25,980	14,902	615	439	1,041	51	8,932	16,041	11,798	737	388	541	55	2,522
Agriculture and natural resources	1,173	564	13	20	23	0	553	879	416	10	14	15	0	424	294	148	6	6	8	0	129
Architecture and related programs	148	61	11	5	5	0	66	105	36	8	5	4	0	52	43	25	3	0	1	0	14
Area, ethnic, and cultural studies	178	114	11	5	13	1	34	90	54	3	3	6	0	24	88	60	8	2	7	1	10
Biological sciences/life sciences	4,435	2,810	63	84	265	5	1,208	2,664	1,652	37	50	136	3	786	1,771	1,158	26	34	129	2	422
Business management and administrative services	1,346	815	29	10	45	3	444	969	521	17	7	34	2	388	377	294	12	3	11	1	56
Communications	293	196	21	8	12	3	53	143	87	6	2	7	2	39	150	109	15	6	5	1	14
Communications technologies	8	5	0	0	0	0	3	3	2	0	0	0	0	1	5	3	0	0	0	0	2
Computer and information sciences	805	383	6	7	56	1	352	689	309	3	7	44	1	325	116	74	3	0	12	0	27
Education	7,030	5,497	552	185	123	35	638	2,867	2,175	193	86	53	16	344	4,163	3,322	359	99	70	19	294
Engineering	5,823	2,210	42	51	379	2	3,139	5,265	1,932	31	39	343	1	2,919	558	278	11	12	36	1	220
Engineering-related technologies	20	9	1	1	2	0	7	18	8	1	1	2	0	6	2	1	0	0	0	0	1
English language and literature/letters	1,341	1,094	32	22	23	7	163	550	432	14	12	7	3	82	791	662	18	10	16	4	81
Foreign languages and literatures	830	488	8	65	26	3	240	355	200	6	19	5	0	125	475	288	2	46	21	3	115
Health professions and related sciences	1,767	1,205	66	26	64	4	402	753	432	18	6	32	1	264	1,014	773	48	20	32	3	138
Home economics and vocational home economics	345	255	16	3	6	0	65	97	69	5	0	3	0	20	248	186	11	3	3	0	45
Law and legal studies	86	11	1	0	0	1	73	65	8	0	0	0	1	56	21	3	1	0	0	0	17
Liberal arts and sciences, general studies, and humanities	81	65	9	1	0	1	5	38	32	3	0	0	0	3	43	33	6	1	0	1	2
Library science	77	46	6	2	2	0	21	26	17	0	2	2	0	7	51	29	6	2	0	0	14
Mathematics	1,189	484	7	8	57	0	632	906	353	6	7	39	0	501	283	131	2	1	18	0	131
Multi/interdisciplinary studies	196	140	1	4	2	0	49	115	72	0	3	2	0	38	81	68	1	1	0	0	11
Parks, recreation, leisure and fitness studies	108	77	3	0	2	0	26	75	48	3	0	2	0	22	33	29	0	0	0	0	4
Philosophy and religion	448	340	17	5	12	0	74	323	233	14	3	10	0	63	125	107	3	2	2	0	11
Physical sciences and science technologies	4,393	2,405	37	68	215	4	1,664	3,432	1,874	29	49	154	2	1,324	961	531	8	19	61	2	340
Precision production trades	0	0	0	0	0	0	0	0	0	0	0	0	0	0	0	0	0	0	0	0	0
Protective services	32	22	2	0	0	0	8	23	16	1	0	0	0	6	9	6	1	0	0	0	2
Psychology	3,651	3,125	134	125	63	22	182	1,415	1,214	44	45	23	9	80	2,236	1,911	90	80	40	13	102
Public administration and services	459	318	47	9	10	2	73	215	135	15	3	6	2	54	244	183	32	6	4	0	19
R.O.T.C. and military technologies	0	0	0	0	0	0	0	0	0	0	0	0	0	0	0	0	0	0	0	0	0
Social sciences and history	3,460	2,201	91	85	111	7	965	2,203	1,284	46	55	73	3	742	1,257	917	45	30	38	4	223
Theological studies/religious vocations	1,417	1,065	102	12	38	4	196	1,219	905	88	10	28	4	184	198	160	14	2	10	0	12
Transportation and material moving	0	0	0	0	0	0	0	0	0	0	0	0	0	0	0	0	0	0	0	0	0
Visual and performing arts	882	695	23	16	28	1	119	478	386	14	13	11	1	53	404	309	9	3	17	0	66

[1] Reported racial/ethnic distributions of students by level of degree, field of degree, and sex were used to estimate race/ethnicity for students whose race/ethnicity was not reported. Excludes 93 men and 18 women whose racial/ethnic group and field of study were not available.

NOTE.—To facilitate trend comparisons, certain aggregations have been made of the degree fields as reported in the IPEDS "Completions" survey: "Agriculture and natural resources" includes Agribusiness and agriculture production, Agricultural sciences, and Conservation and renewable natural resources; and "Business management and administrative services" includes Business and management, Business and office, Marketing and distribution, and Consumer and personal services.

SOURCE: U.S. Department of Education, National Center for Education Statistics, Integrated Postsecondary Education Data System (IPEDS), "Completions" survey. (This table was prepared January 1995.)

Table 264.—Doctor's degrees conferred by institutions of higher education, by racial/ethnic group, major field of study, and sex of student: 1991–92

Major field of study	Total							Men							Women						
	Total	White, non-His-panic	Black, non-His-panic	His-panic	Asian/ Pacific Islander	American Indian/ Alaskan Native	Non-resi-dent alien	Total	White, non-His-panic	Black, non-His-panic	His-panic	Asian/ Pacific Is-lander	American Indian/ Alas-kan Native	Non-resi-dent alien	Total	White, non-His-panic	Black, non-His-panic	His-panic	Asian/ Pacific Is-lander	American Indian/ Alas-kan Native	Non-resi-dent alien
1	2	3	4	5	6	7	8	9	10	11	12	13	14	15	16	17	18	19	20	21	22
All fields, total [1]	40,090	25,813	1,223	811	1,559	118	10,566	25,168	14,674	576	458	1,062	65	8,333	14,922	11,139	647	353	497	53	2,233
Agriculture and natural resources	1,214	590	10	14	35	1	564	963	443	9	13	26	1	471	251	147	1	1	9	0	93
Architecture and related programs	132	68	3	5	3	0	53	93	43	2	1	3	1	44	39	25	1	4	0	0	9
Area, ethnic, and cultural studies	155	105	18	0	4	0	28	90	60	9	0	3	0	18	65	45	9	0	1	0	10
Biological sciences/life sciences	4,243	2,785	57	89	214	11	1,087	2,620	1,683	34	53	123	8	719	1,623	1,102	23	36	91	3	368
Business management and administrative services	1,242	700	27	11	63	2	439	953	484	17	9	54	1	388	289	216	10	2	9	1	51
Communications	252	177	18	6	9	1	41	131	84	10	4	7	0	26	121	93	8	2	2	1	15
Communications technologies	3	3	0	0	0	0	0	1	1	0	0	0	0	0	2	2	0	0	0	0	0
Computer and information sciences	772	366	0	6	45	1	349	669	301	3	6	40	1	318	103	65	2	0	5	0	31
Education	6,864	5,404	513	187	100	36	624	2,783	2,149	175	86	32	16	325	4,081	3,255	338	101	68	20	299
Engineering	5,488	2,102	44	58	414	11	2,859	4,961	1,840	38	49	364	6	2,664	527	262	6	9	50	5	195
Engineering-related technologies	11	5	0	0	0	0	4	11	5	1	0	1	0	4	0	0	0	0	0	0	0
English language and literature/letters	1,273	1,034	32	12	28	4	163	537	425	13	7	13	2	77	736	609	19	5	15	2	86
Foreign languages and literatures	850	514	13	66	18	1	238	378	218	4	27	8	1	120	472	296	9	39	10	3	118
Health professions and related sciences	1,661	1,161	45	26	68	3	358	698	396	15	15	34	0	238	963	765	30	11	34	3	120
Home economics and vocational home economics	293	209	12	5	6	0	61	71	45	5	1	0	0	20	222	164	7	4	6	0	41
Law and legal studies	68	15	0	5	2	0	46	50	11	0	4	1	0	34	18	4	0	1	1	0	12
Liberal arts and sciences, general studies, and humanities	67	55	4	1	0	0	7	30	23	0	1	0	0	6	37	32	4	0	0	0	1
Library science	50	36	2	2	2	0	8	16	11	2	1	2	0	1	34	25	1	1	0	0	7
Mathematics	1,082	460	3	11	55	2	552	851	350	2	8	40	0	451	231	110	0	3	15	2	101
Multi/interdisciplinary studies	231	153	3	5	8	1	61	144	89	0	4	7	1	43	87	64	3	1	1	0	18
Parks, recreation, leisure and fitness studies	61	34	5	0	3	0	19	41	23	3	0	0	0	14	20	11	2	0	2	0	5
Philosophy and religion	475	376	10	6	14	2	67	365	287	9	3	11	1	54	110	89	1	3	3	1	13
Physical sciences and science technologies	4,391	2,470	31	75	224	6	1,585	3,429	1,923	23	51	158	5	1,269	962	547	8	24	66	1	316
Precision production trades	0	0	0	0	0	0	0	0	0	0	0	0	0	0	0	0	0	0	0	0	0
Protective services	24	18	0	0	0	0	5	13	10	0	0	0	0	3	11	8	0	0	1	0	2
Psychology	3,373	2,931	118	102	58	12	152	1,359	1,177	36	39	21	3	83	2,014	1,754	82	63	37	9	69
Public administration and services	432	306	36	9	14	2	65	204	131	16	1	4	2	50	228	175	20	8	10	0	15
R.O.T.C. and military technologies	0	0	0	0	0	0	0	0	0	0	0	0	0	0	0	0	0	0	0	0	0
Social sciences and history	3,218	2,052	107	63	112	13	871	2,126	1,242	63	41	71	9	700	1,092	810	44	22	41	4	171
Theological studies/religious vocations	1,259	958	88	25	39	5	144	1,077	815	74	21	31	5	131	182	143	14	4	8	0	13
Transportation and material moving	0	0	0	0	0	0	0	0	0	0	0	0	0	0	0	0	0	0	0	0	0
Visual and performing arts	906	726	19	22	19	4	116	504	405	14	13	7	3	62	402	321	5	9	12	1	54

[1] Reported racial/ethnic distributions of students by level of degree, field of degree, and sex were used to estimate race/ethnicity for students whose race/ethnicity was not reported. Excludes 389 men and 180 women whose racial/ethnic group and field of study were not available.

NOTE.—To facilitate trend comparisons, certain aggregations have been made of the degree fields as reported in the IPEDS "Completions" survey. "Agriculture and natural resources" includes Agribusiness and agriculture production, Agricultural sciences, and Conservation and renewable natural resources; and "Business management and administrative services" includes Business and management, Business and office, Marketing and distribution, and Consumer and personal services.

SOURCE: U.S. Department of Education, National Center for Education Statistics, Integrated Postsecondary Education Data System (IPEDS), "Completions" survey. (This table was prepared April 1994.)

Table 265.—First-professional degrees conferred by institutions of higher education, by racial/ethnic group and sex of student: 1976–77 to 1992–93

Year and sex of student	Total	White, non-Hispanic	Black, non-Hispanic	Hispanic	Asian or Pacific Islander	American Indian/Alaskan Native	Nonresident alien
1	2	3	4	5	6	7	8
			Number of degrees conferred				
1976–77, total [1]	63,953	58,422	2,537	1,076	1,021	196	701
Men	51,980	47,777	1,761	893	776	159	614
Women	11,973	10,645	776	183	245	37	87
1978–79, total [2]	68,611	62,430	2,836	1,283	1,205	216	641
Men	52,425	48,123	1,783	989	860	150	520
Women	16,186	14,307	1,053	294	345	66	121
1980–81, total [3]	71,340	64,551	2,931	1,541	1,456	192	669
Men	52,194	47,629	1,772	1,131	991	134	537
Women	19,146	16,922	1,159	410	465	58	132
1984–85, total [4]	71,057	63,219	3,029	1,884	1,816	248	861
Men	47,501	42,630	1,623	1,239	1,152	176	681
Women	23,556	20,589	1,406	645	664	72	180
1986–87, total	71,617	62,688	3,420	2,051	2,270	304	884
Men	46,523	41,149	1,835	1,303	1,420	183	633
Women	25,094	21,539	1,585	748	850	121	251
1988–89, total	70,856	61,214	3,148	2,269	2,976	264	985
Men	45,046	39,399	1,618	1,374	1,819	148	688
Women	25,810	21,815	1,530	895	1,157	116	297
1989–90, total [5]	70,744	60,240	3,410	2,427	3,362	257	1,048
Men	43,778	37,850	1,672	1,450	1,963	135	708
Women	26,966	22,390	1,738	977	1,399	122	340
1990–91, total [6]	71,515	60,327	3,575	2,527	3,755	261	1,070
Men	43,601	37,348	1,672	1,506	2,178	144	753
Women	27,914	22,979	1,903	1,021	1,577	117	317
1991–92, total [7]	72,129	59,800	3,560	2,766	4,455	296	1,252
Men	43,812	36,939	1,603	1,635	2,593	157	885
Women	28,317	22,861	1,957	1,131	1,862	139	367
1992–93, total [8]	74,960	60,830	4,100	2,984	5,160	368	1,518
Men	44,821	37,157	1,777	1,762	2,858	190	1,077
Women	30,139	23,673	2,323	1,222	2,302	178	441
			Percentage distribution of degrees conferred				
1976–77, total [1]	100.0	91.4	4.0	1.7	1.6	0.3	1.1
Men	100.0	91.9	3.4	1.7	1.5	0.3	1.2
Women	100.0	88.9	6.5	1.5	2.0	0.3	0.7
1978–79, total [2]	100.0	91.0	4.1	1.9	1.8	0.3	0.9
Men	100.0	91.8	3.4	1.9	1.6	0.3	1.0
Women	100.0	88.4	6.5	1.8	2.1	0.4	0.7
1980–81, total [3]	100.0	90.5	4.1	2.2	2.0	0.3	0.9
Men	100.0	91.3	3.4	2.2	1.9	0.3	1.0
Women	100.0	88.4	6.1	2.1	2.4	0.3	0.7
1984–85, total [4]	100.0	89.0	4.3	2.7	2.6	0.3	1.2
Men	100.0	89.7	3.4	2.6	2.4	0.4	1.4
Women	100.0	87.4	6.0	2.7	2.8	0.3	0.8
1986–87, total	100.0	87.5	4.8	2.9	3.2	0.4	1.2
Men	100.0	88.4	3.9	2.8	3.1	0.4	1.4
Women	100.0	85.8	6.3	3.0	3.4	0.5	1.0
1988–89, total	100.0	86.4	4.4	3.2	4.2	0.4	1.4
Men	100.0	87.5	3.6	3.1	4.0	0.3	1.5
Women	100.0	84.5	5.9	3.5	4.5	0.4	1.2
1989–90, total [5]	100.0	85.2	4.8	3.4	4.8	0.4	1.5
Men	100.0	86.5	3.8	3.3	4.5	0.3	1.6
Women	100.0	83.0	6.4	3.6	5.2	0.5	1.3
1990–91, total [6]	100.0	84.4	5.0	3.5	5.3	0.4	1.5
Men	100.0	85.7	3.8	3.5	5.0	0.3	1.7
Women	100.0	82.3	6.8	3.7	5.6	0.4	1.1
1991–92, total [7]	100.0	82.9	4.9	3.8	6.2	0.4	1.7
Men	100.0	84.3	3.7	3.7	5.9	0.4	2.0
Women	100.0	80.7	6.9	4.0	6.6	0.5	1.3
1992–93, total [8]	100.0	81.1	5.5	4.0	6.9	0.5	2.0
Men	100.0	82.9	4.0	3.9	6.4	0.4	2.4
Women	100.0	78.5	7.7	4.1	7.6	0.6	1.5

[1] Excludes 394 men and 12 women whose racial/ethnic group was not available.
[2] Excludes 227 men and 10 women whose racial/ethnic group was not available.
[3] Excludes 598 men and 18 women whose racial/ethnic group was not available.
[4] Excludes 2,954 men and 1,052 women whose racial/ethnic group was not available.
[5] Excludes 183 men and 61 women whose racial/ethnic group was not available.
[6] Excludes 245 men and 188 women whose racial/ethnic group was not available.
[7] Excludes 1,259 men and 758 women whose racial/ethnic group was not available.
[8] Excludes 332 men and 95 women whose racial/ethnic group was not available.

NOTE.—For years 1984–85 to 1992–93, reported racial/ethnic distributions of students by level of degree, field of degree, and sex were used to estimate race/ethnicity for students whose race/ethnicity was not reported.

SOURCE: U.S. Department of Education, National Center for Education Statistics, "Degrees and Other Formal Awards Conferred" surveys, and Integrated Postsecondary Education Data System (IPEDS), "Completions" surveys. (This table was prepared January 1995.)

Table 266.—First-professional degrees conferred by institutions of higher education, by racial/ethnic group, major field of study, and sex of student: 1992–93

Major field of study	Total							Men							Women						
	Total	White, non-Hispanic	Black, non-Hispanic	Hispanic	Asian/Pacific Islander	American Indian/Alaskan Native	Non-resident alien	Total	White, non-Hispanic	Black, non-Hispanic	Hispanic	Asian/Pacific Islander	American Indian/Alaskan Native	Non-resident alien	Total	White, non-Hispanic	Black, non-Hispanic	Hispanic	Asian/Pacific Islander	American Indian/Alaskan Native	Non-resident alien
1	2	3	4	5	6	7	8	9	10	11	12	13	14	15	16	17	18	19	20	21	22
All fields [1]	74,960	60,830	4,100	2,984	5,160	368	1,518	44,821	37,157	1,777	1,762	2,858	190	1,077	30,139	23,673	2,323	1,222	2,302	178	441
Dentistry (D.D.S. or D.M.D.)	3,605	2,451	159	212	532	10	241	2,383	1,705	74	131	305	7	161	1,222	746	85	81	227	3	80
Medicine (M.D.)	15,531	11,729	900	610	2,001	73	218	9,679	7,512	378	372	1,226	34	157	5,852	4,217	522	238	775	39	61
Optometry (O.D.)	1,148	903	24	31	139	3	48	584	492	5	20	38	3	26	564	411	19	11	101	0	22
Osteopathic medicine (D.O.)	1,627	1,359	45	69	132	9	13	1,091	924	21	47	85	8	6	536	435	24	22	47	1	7
Pharmacy (Pharm.D.)	1,904	1,263	109	56	369	7	100	673	461	28	24	110	4	46	1,231	802	81	32	259	3	54
Podiatry (Pod.D. or D.P.) or podiatric medicine (D.P.M.)	476	350	42	30	35	1	18	350	266	20	21	26	1	16	126	84	22	9	9	0	2
Veterinary medicine (D.V.M.)	2,057	1,888	51	60	39	12	7	766	710	14	25	11	3	3	1,291	1,178	37	35	28	9	4
Chiropractic medicine (D.C. or D.C.M.)	2,799	2,383	38	113	115	23	127	1,991	1,709	23	69	86	16	88	808	674	15	44	29	7	39
Law (LL.B. or J.D.)	40,302	34,267	2,284	1,665	1,550	213	323	23,182	20,263	914	935	756	104	210	17,120	14,004	1,370	730	794	109	113
Theology (M.Div., M.H.L., B.D. or Ord.)	5,447	4,189	447	137	246	15	413	4,096	3,097	299	118	215	10	357	1,351	1,092	148	19	31	5	56
Other	64	48	1	1	2	2	10	26	18	1	0	0	0	7	38	30	0	1	1	2	3

[1] Reported racial/ethnic distributions of students by level of degree, field of degree, and sex were used to estimate race/ethnicity for students whose race/ethnicity was not reported. Excludes 332 men and 95 women whose racial/ethnic group and field of study were not available.

SOURCE: U.S. Department of Education, National Center for Education Statistics, Integrated Postsecondary Education Data System (IPEDS), "Completions" survey. (This table was prepared January 1995.)

Table 267.—First-professional degrees conferred by institutions of higher education, by racial/ethnic group, major field of study, and sex of student: 1991–92

Major field of study	Total							Men							Women						
	Total	White, non-Hispanic	Black, non-Hispanic	Hispanic	Asian/Pacific Islander	American Indian/Alaskan Native	Non-resident alien	Total	White, non-Hispanic	Black, non-Hispanic	Hispanic	Asian/Pacific Islander	American Indian/Alaskan Native	Non-resident alien	Total	White, non-Hispanic	Black, non-Hispanic	Hispanic	Asian/Pacific Islander	American Indian/Alaskan Native	Non-resident alien
1	2	3	4	5	6	7	8	9	10	11	12	13	14	15	16	17	18	19	20	21	22
All fields [1]	72,129	59,800	3,560	2,766	4,455	296	1,252	43,812	36,939	1,603	1,635	2,593	157	885	28,317	22,861	1,957	1,131	1,862	139	367
Dentistry (D.D.S. or D.M.D.)	3,593	2,415	180	244	535	15	204	2,431	1,691	97	174	324	13	132	1,162	724	83	70	211	2	72
Medicine (M.D.)	15,243	11,658	850	638	1,827	67	203	9,796	7,666	395	410	1,147	34	144	5,447	3,992	455	228	680	33	59
Optometry (O.D.)	1,232	972	34	44	144	7	31	676	569	7	20	57	4	19	556	403	27	24	87	3	12
Osteopathic medicine (D.O.)	1,326	1,102	55	57	99	5	8	887	750	21	41	68	2	5	439	352	34	16	31	3	3
Pharmacy (Pharm.D.)	1,339	939	66	42	222	4	66	493	355	22	22	63	1	30	846	584	44	20	159	3	36
Podiatry (Pod.D. or D.P.) or podiatric medicine (D.P.M.)	504	396	44	22	32	2	8	359	288	28	13	22	2	6	145	108	16	9	10	0	2
Veterinary medicine (D.V.M.)	2,044	1,887	51	60	32	9	5	850	790	19	23	10	3	5	1,194	1,097	32	37	22	3	3
Chiropractic medicine (D.C. or D.C.M.)	2,694	2,316	35	63	81	27	172	2,012	1,720	27	53	63	15	134	682	596	8	10	18	12	38
Law (LL.B. or J.D.)	38,848	33,807	1,908	1,473	1,250	151	259	22,260	19,836	766	781	640	75	162	16,588	13,971	1,142	692	610	76	97
Theology (M.Div., M.H.L., B.D., or Ord.)	5,251	4,263	336	122	233	8	289	4,025	3,253	221	98	199	5	249	1,226	1,010	115	24	34	5	40
Other	55	45	1	1	0	1	7	23	21	0	0	0	1	1	32	24	1	0	0	1	5

[1] Reported racial/ethnic distributions of students by level of degree, field of degree, and sex were used to estimate race/ethnicity for students whose race/ethnicity was not reported. Excludes 1,259 men and 758 women whose racial/ethnic group and field of study were not available.

SOURCE: U.S. Department of Education, National Center for Education Statistics, Integrated Postsecondary Education Data System (IPEDS), "Completions" survey. (This table was prepared April 1994.)

Table 268.—Earned degrees in agriculture and natural resources [1] conferred by institutions of higher education, by level of degree and sex of student: 1970–71 to 1992–93

Year	Bachelor's degrees			Master's degrees			Doctor's degrees		
	Total	Men	Women	Total	Men	Women	Total	Men	Women
1	2	3	4	5	6	7	8	9	10
1970–71	12,672	12,136	536	2,457	2,313	144	1,086	1,055	31
1971–72	13,516	12,779	737	2,680	2,490	190	971	945	26
1972–73	14,756	13,661	1,095	2,807	2,588	219	1,059	1,031	28
1973–74	16,253	14,684	1,569	2,928	2,640	288	930	897	33
1974–75	17,528	15,061	2,467	3,067	2,703	364	991	958	33
1975–76	19,402	15,845	3,557	3,340	2,862	478	928	867	61
1976–77	21,467	16,690	4,777	3,724	3,177	547	893	831	62
1977–78	22,650	17,069	5,581	4,023	3,268	755	971	909	62
1978–79	23,134	16,854	6,280	3,994	3,187	807	950	877	73
1979–80	22,802	16,045	6,757	3,976	3,082	894	991	879	112
1980–81	21,886	15,154	6,732	4,003	3,061	942	1,067	940	127
1981–82	21,029	14,443	6,586	4,163	3,114	1,049	1,079	925	154
1982–83	20,909	14,085	6,824	4,254	3,129	1,125	1,149	1,004	145
1983–84	19,317	13,206	6,111	4,178	2,989	1,189	1,172	1,001	171
1984–85	18,107	12,477	5,630	3,928	2,846	1,082	1,213	1,036	177
1985–86	16,823	11,544	5,279	3,801	2,701	1,100	1,158	966	192
1986–87	14,991	10,314	4,677	3,522	2,460	1,062	1,049	871	178
1987–88	14,222	9,744	4,478	3,479	2,427	1,052	1,142	926	216
1988–89	13,492	9,298	4,194	3,245	2,231	1,014	1,183	950	233
1989–90	12,900	8,822	4,078	3,382	2,239	1,143	1,295	1,038	257
1990–91	13,124	8,832	4,292	3,295	2,160	1,135	1,185	953	232
1991–92	15,124	9,869	5,255	3,735	2,413	1,322	1,214	963	251
1992–93	16,778	11,080	5,698	3,965	2,477	1,488	1,173	879	294

[1] Includes degrees in agricultural business and production; agricultural sciences; and conservation and renewable natural resources.

SOURCE: U.S. Department of Education, National Center for Education Statistics, "Degrees and Other Formal Awards Conferred" surveys, and Integrated Postsecondary Education Data System (IPEDS), "Completions" surveys. (This table was prepared January 1995.)

Table 269.—Earned degrees in architecture and related programs [1] conferred by institutions of higher education, by level of degree and sex of student: 1949–50 to 1992–93

Year	Bachelor's degrees			Master's degrees			Doctor's degrees		
	Total	Men	Women	Total	Men	Women	Total	Men	Women
1	2	3	4	5	6	7	8	9	10
1949–50	2,563	2,441	122	166	159	7	1	1	0
1959–60	1,801	1,744	57	319	305	14	17	17	0
1967–68	3,057	2,931	126	1,021	953	68	15	15	0
1969–70	4,105	3,888	217	1,427	1,260	167	35	33	2
1970–71	5,570	4,906	664	1,705	1,469	236	36	33	3
1971–72	6,440	5,667	773	1,899	1,626	273	50	43	7
1972–73	6,962	6,042	920	2,307	1,943	364	58	54	4
1973–74	7,822	6,665	1,157	2,702	2,208	494	69	65	4
1974–75	8,226	6,791	1,435	2,938	2,343	595	69	58	11
1975–76	9,146	7,396	1,750	3,215	2,545	670	82	69	13
1976–77	9,222	7,249	1,973	3,213	2,489	724	73	62	11
1977–78	9,250	7,054	2,196	3,115	2,304	811	73	57	16
1978–79	9,273	6,876	2,397	3,113	2,226	887	96	74	22
1979–80	9,132	6,596	2,536	3,139	2,245	894	79	66	13
1980–81	9,455	6,800	2,655	3,153	2,234	919	93	73	20
1981–82	9,728	6,825	2,903	3,327	2,242	1,085	80	58	22
1982–83	9,823	6,403	3,420	3,357	2,224	1,133	97	74	23
1983–84	9,186	5,895	3,291	3,223	2,197	1,026	84	62	22
1984–85	9,325	6,019	3,306	3,275	2,148	1,127	89	66	23
1985–86	9,119	5,824	3,295	3,260	2,129	1,131	73	56	17
1986–87	8,950	5,617	3,333	3,163	2,086	1,077	92	66	26
1987–88	8,603	5,271	3,332	3,159	2,042	1,117	98	66	32
1988–89	9,150	5,545	3,605	3,383	2,192	1,191	86	63	23
1989–90	9,364	5,703	3,661	3,499	2,228	1,271	103	73	30
1990–91	9,781	5,788	3,993	3,490	2,244	1,246	135	101	34
1991–92	8,753	5,805	2,948	3,640	2,271	1,369	132	93	39
1992–93	9,167	5,940	3,227	3,808	2,376	1,432	148	105	43

[1] Prior to 1967–68, includes degrees in architecture. From 1967–68, includes degrees in architecture; city/urban, community, and regional planning; architectural environmental design; interior architecture; landscape architecture; architectural urban design and planning; and architecture and related programs, other.

SOURCE: U.S. Department of Education, National Center for Education Statistics, "Degrees and Other Formal Awards Conferred" surveys, and Integrated Postsecondary Education Data System (IPEDS), "Completions" surveys. (This table was prepared January 1995.)

Table 270.—Earned degrees in the biological/life sciences [1] conferred by institutions of higher education, by level of degree and sex of student: 1951–52 to 1992–93

Year	Bachelor's degrees			Master's degrees			Doctor's degrees		
	Total	Men	Women	Total	Men	Women	Total	Men	Women
1	2	3	4	5	6	7	8	9	10
1951–52	11,094	8,212	2,882	2,307	1,908	399	764	680	84
1953–54	9,279	6,710	2,569	1,610	1,287	323	1,077	977	100
1955–56	12,423	9,515	2,908	1,759	1,379	380	1,025	908	117
1957–58	14,308	11,159	3,149	1,852	1,448	404	1,125	987	138
1959–60	15,576	11,654	3,922	2,154	1,668	486	1,205	1,086	119
1961–62	16,915	12,136	4,779	2,642	1,982	660	1,338	1,179	159
1963–64	22,723	16,321	6,402	3,296	2,348	948	1,625	1,432	193
1965–66	26,916	19,368	7,548	4,232	3,085	1,147	2,097	1,792	305
1967–68	31,826	22,986	8,840	5,506	3,959	1,547	2,784	2,345	439
1969–70	34,034	23,919	10,115	5,800	3,975	1,825	3,289	2,820	469
1970–71	35,743	25,333	10,410	5,728	3,805	1,923	3,645	3,050	595
1971–72	37,293	26,323	10,970	6,101	4,087	2,014	3,653	3,031	622
1972–73	42,233	29,636	12,597	6,263	4,354	1,909	3,636	2,926	710
1973–74	48,340	33,245	15,095	6,552	4,555	1,997	3,439	2,740	699
1974–75	51,741	34,612	17,129	6,550	4,587	1,963	3,384	2,641	743
1975–76	54,275	35,520	18,755	6,582	4,497	2,085	3,392	2,663	729
1976–77	53,605	34,218	19,387	7,114	4,718	2,396	3,397	2,671	726
1977–78	51,502	31,705	19,797	6,806	4,400	2,406	3,309	2,511	798
1978–79	48,846	29,191	19,655	6,831	4,265	2,566	3,542	2,636	906
1979–80	46,370	26,828	19,542	6,510	4,098	2,412	3,636	2,690	946
1980–81	43,216	24,149	19,067	5,978	3,654	2,324	3,718	2,666	1,052
1981–82	41,639	22,754	18,885	5,874	3,426	2,448	3,743	2,654	1,089
1982–83	39,982	21,564	18,418	5,696	3,214	2,482	3,341	2,266	1,075
1983–84	38,640	20,558	18,082	5,406	2,996	2,410	3,437	2,381	1,056
1984–85	38,445	20,064	18,381	5,059	2,647	2,412	3,432	2,307	1,125
1985–86	38,524	19,993	18,531	5,013	2,616	2,397	3,358	2,229	1,129
1986–87	38,121	19,657	18,464	4,952	2,538	2,414	3,419	2,225	1,194
1987–88	36,755	18,245	18,510	4,784	2,423	2,361	3,629	2,349	1,280
1988–89	36,059	17,953	18,106	4,961	2,492	2,469	3,520	2,234	1,286
1989–90	37,204	18,312	18,892	4,869	2,395	2,474	3,844	2,394	1,450
1990–91	39,530	19,412	20,118	4,765	2,302	2,463	4,093	2,577	1,516
1991–92	42,941	20,798	22,143	4,785	2,301	2,484	4,243	2,620	1,623
1992–93	47,038	22,842	24,196	4,756	2,343	2,413	4,435	2,664	1,771

[1] Includes degrees in biology; biochemistry and biophysics; botany; cell and molecular biology; microbiology/bacteriology; zoology; and other biological sciences.

SOURCE: U.S. Department of Education, National Center for Education Statistics, "Degrees and Other Formal Awards Conferred" surveys, and Integrated Postsecondary Education Data System (IPEDS), "Completions" surveys. (This table was prepared January 1995.)

Table 271.—Earned degrees in biology, microbiology, and zoology conferred by institutions of higher education, by level of degree: 1970–71 to 1992–93

Year	Biology, general			Microbiology [1]			Zoology [2]		
	Bachelor's	Master's	Doctor's	Bachelor's	Master's	Doctor's	Bachelor's	Master's	Doctor's
1	2	3	4	5	6	7	8	9	10
1970–71	26,294	2,665	536	1,475	456	365	5,722	1,167	1,107
1971–72	27,473	2,943	580	1,548	470	351	5,522	1,189	1,094
1972–73	31,185	2,959	627	1,940	517	344	5,770	1,191	1,008
1973–74	36,188	3,186	657	2,311	505	384	6,192	1,250	919
1974–75	38,748	3,109	637	2,767	552	345	6,116	1,216	920
1975–76	40,163	3,177	624	2,927	585	364	6,105	1,153	909
1976–77	39,530	3,322	608	2,884	659	325	5,608	1,168	950
1977–78	37,598	3,094	664	2,695	615	353	5,139	1,160	885
1978–79	35,962	3,093	663	2,670	597	395	4,913	1,109	938
1979–80	33,523	2,911	718	2,631	596	376	4,374	1,078	955
1980–81	31,323	2,598	734	2,414	482	370	3,946	1,090	946
1981–82	29,651	2,579	678	2,377	470	350	3,664	1,028	936
1982–83	28,022	2,354	521	2,306	446	331	3,453	918	809
1983–84	27,379	2,313	617	2,329	447	360	3,294	867	826
1984–85	27,593	2,130	658	2,180	413	302	3,128	778	802
1985–86	27,618	2,173	574	2,217	353	336	2,940	723	844
1986–87	27,465	2,022	537	2,098	390	337	2,858	740	787
1987–88	26,838	1,981	576	2,014	357	386	2,580	725	786
1988–89	26,229	2,097	527	1,780	411	356	2,582	736	744
1989–90	27,213	1,998	551	1,814	366	409	2,501	638	810
1990–91	29,285	1,956	632	1,757	324	419	2,673	640	833
1991–92	31,909	1,995	657	1,722	336	454	2,840	620	818
1992–93	34,932	2,000	671	1,769	328	520	3,071	637	786

[1] Includes bacteriology.
[2] Includes general zoology; entomology; pathology; pharmacology; physiology; and zoology, other.

SOURCE: U.S. Department of Education, National Center for Education Statistics, "Degrees and Other Formal Awards Conferred" surveys, and Integrated Postsecondary Education Data System (IPEDS), "Completions" surveys. (This table was prepared January 1995.)

Table 272.—Earned degrees in business management and administrative services [1] conferred by institutions of higher education, by level of degree and sex of student: 1955–56 to 1992–93

Year	Bachelor's degrees			Master's degrees			Doctor's degrees		
	Total	Men	Women	Total	Men	Women	Total	Men	Women
1	2	3	4	5	6	7	8	9	10
1955–56	42,813	38,706	4,107	3,280	3,118	162	129	127	2
1957–58	51,991	48,063	3,928	4,223	4,072	151	110	105	5
1959–60	51,076	47,262	3,814	4,643	4,476	167	135	133	2
1961–62	49,017	45,184	3,833	7,691	7,484	207	226	221	5
1963–64	55,474	51,056	4,418	9,251	9,008	243	275	268	7
1965–66	62,721	57,516	5,205	12,959	12,628	331	387	370	17
1967–68	79,074	72,126	6,948	17,795	17,186	609	441	427	14
1969–70	105,580	96,346	9,234	21,561	20,792	769	620	610	10
1970–71	114,729	104,275	10,454	25,977	24,967	1,010	757	736	21
1971–72	121,266	109,688	11,578	30,028	28,845	1,183	859	840	19
1972–73	126,144	112,783	13,361	30,638	29,128	1,510	902	850	52
1973–74	131,640	114,729	16,911	32,172	30,044	2,128	919	870	49
1974–75	132,731	111,144	21,587	35,758	32,732	3,026	936	897	39
1975–76	142,034	113,954	28,080	42,054	37,145	4,909	900	851	49
1976–77	150,765	115,353	35,412	46,006	39,400	6,606	827	775	52
1977–78	159,691	116,171	43,520	47,837	39,743	8,094	823	753	70
1978–79	171,241	118,825	52,416	49,855	40,274	9,581	821	724	97
1979–80	184,867	122,508	62,359	54,484	42,288	12,196	753	642	111
1980–81	198,983	125,523	73,460	57,391	42,980	14,411	795	675	120
1981–82	213,374	129,262	84,112	60,763	43,807	16,956	815	668	147
1982–83	226,627	131,538	95,089	64,758	45,999	18,759	776	644	132
1983–84	229,478	129,559	99,919	66,150	46,178	19,972	929	730	199
1984–85	232,636	127,659	104,977	66,996	46,209	20,787	831	688	143
1985–86	237,319	128,780	108,539	66,689	45,938	20,751	934	729	205
1986–87	240,546	128,603	111,943	67,093	44,913	22,180	1,062	808	254
1987–88	243,021	129,552	113,469	69,230	45,980	23,250	1,063	810	253
1988–89	246,399	131,157	115,242	73,065	48,540	24,525	1,100	800	300
1989–90	248,698	132,329	116,369	76,676	50,585	26,091	1,093	818	275
1990–91	249,311	131,624	117,687	78,255	50,883	27,372	1,185	876	309
1991–92	256,603	135,440	121,163	84,642	54,705	29,937	1,242	953	289
1992–93	256,842	135,573	121,269	89,615	57,651	31,964	1,346	969	377

[1] Includes degrees in business management/administrative services; marketing operations/marketing and distribution; and consumer and personal services.

SOURCE: U.S. Department of Education, National Center for Education Statistics, "Degrees and Other Formal Awards Conferred" surveys, and Integrated Postsecondary Education Data System (IPEDS), "Completions" surveys. (This table was prepared January 1995.)

Table 273.—Earned degrees in communications [1] conferred by institutions of higher education, by level of degree and sex of student: 1970–71 to 1992–93

Year	Bachelor's degrees			Master's degrees			Doctor's degrees		
	Total	Men	Women	Total	Men	Women	Total	Men	Women
1	2	3	4	5	6	7	8	9	10
1970–71	10,802	6,989	3,813	1,856	1,214	642	145	126	19
1971–72	12,340	7,964	4,376	2,200	1,443	757	111	96	15
1972–73	14,317	9,074	5,243	2,406	1,546	860	139	114	25
1973–74	17,096	10,536	6,560	2,640	1,668	972	175	146	29
1974–75	19,248	11,455	7,793	2,794	1,618	1,176	165	119	46
1975–76	21,282	12,458	8,824	3,126	1,818	1,308	204	154	50
1976–77	23,214	12,932	10,282	3,091	1,719	1,372	171	130	41
1977–78	25,400	13,480	11,920	3,296	1,673	1,623	191	138	53
1978–79	26,457	13,266	13,191	2,882	1,483	1,399	192	138	54
1979–80	28,616	13,656	14,960	3,082	1,527	1,555	193	121	72
1980–81	31,282	14,179	17,103	3,105	1,448	1,657	182	107	75
1981–82	34,222	14,917	19,305	3,327	1,578	1,749	200	136	64
1982–83	38,567	16,161	22,406	3,604	1,661	1,943	214	126	88
1983–84	40,113	16,604	23,509	3,656	1,600	2,056	219	131	88
1984–85	42,002	17,175	24,827	3,669	1,576	2,093	234	143	91
1985–86	43,076	17,639	25,437	3,823	1,610	2,213	223	116	107
1986–87	45,337	18,110	27,227	3,893	1,590	2,303	275	158	117
1987–88	46,649	18,527	28,122	3,925	1,568	2,357	234	134	100
1988–89	48,609	19,215	29,394	4,257	1,737	2,520	253	138	115
1989–90	51,308	20,218	31,090	4,362	1,707	2,655	273	145	128
1990–91	52,773	20,645	32,128	4,336	1,711	2,625	274	151	123
1991–92	54,977	21,497	33,480	4,464	1,692	2,772	255	132	123
1992–93	54,706	22,028	32,678	5,209	1,980	3,229	301	146	155

[1] Includes degrees in communications, general; advertising; journalism; broadcast journalism; public relations and organizational communications; radio and television broadcasting; other communications; and communications technology.

SOURCE: U.S. Department of Education, National Center for Education Statistics, "Degrees and Other Formal Awards Conferred" surveys, and Integrated Postsecondary Education Data System (IPEDS), "Completions" surveys. (This table was prepared January 1995.)

Table 274.—Earned degrees in computer and information sciences [1] conferred by institutions of higher education, by level of degree and sex of student: 1970–71 to 1992–93

Year	Bachelor's degrees			Master's degrees			Doctor's degrees		
	Total	Men	Women	Total	Men	Women	Total	Men	Women
1	2	3	4	5	6	7	8	9	10
1970–71	2,388	2,064	324	1,588	1,424	164	128	125	3
1971–72	3,402	2,941	461	1,977	1,752	225	167	155	12
1972–73	4,304	3,664	640	2,113	1,888	225	196	181	15
1973–74	4,756	3,976	780	2,276	1,983	293	198	189	9
1974–75	5,033	4,080	953	2,299	1,961	338	213	199	14
1975–76	5,652	4,534	1,118	2,603	2,226	377	244	221	23
1976–77	6,407	4,876	1,531	2,798	2,332	466	216	197	19
1977–78	7,201	5,349	1,852	3,038	2,471	567	196	181	15
1978–79	8,719	6,272	2,447	3,055	2,480	575	236	206	30
1979–80	11,154	7,782	3,372	3,647	2,883	764	240	213	27
1980–81	15,121	10,202	4,919	4,218	3,247	971	252	227	25
1981–82	20,267	13,218	7,049	4,935	3,625	1,310	251	230	21
1982–83	24,510	15,606	8,904	5,321	3,813	1,508	262	228	34
1983–84	32,172	20,246	11,926	6,190	4,379	1,811	251	225	26
1984–85	38,878	24,579	14,299	7,101	5,064	2,037	248	223	25
1985–86	41,889	26,923	14,966	8,070	5,658	2,412	344	299	45
1986–87	39,589	25,865	13,724	8,481	5,985	2,496	374	322	52
1987–88	34,523	23,331	11,192	9,197	6,726	2,471	428	380	48
1988–89	30,454	21,087	9,367	9,414	6,775	2,639	551	466	85
1989–90	27,257	19,117	8,140	9,677	6,960	2,717	627	534	93
1990–91	25,083	17,726	7,357	9,324	6,563	2,761	676	584	92
1991–92	24,557	17,510	7,047	9,530	6,884	2,646	772	669	103
1992–93	24,200	17,403	6,797	10,163	7,410	2,753	805	689	116

[1] Includes degrees in computer and information sciences, general; computer programming; data processing technology/technician; information science and systems; computer systems analysis; and other computer and information sciences.

SOURCE: U.S. Department of Education, National Center for Education Statistics, "Degrees and Other Formal Awards Conferred" surveys, and Integrated Postsecondary Education Data System (IPEDS), "Completions" surveys. (This table was prepared January 1995.)

Table 275.—Earned degrees in education conferred by institutions of higher education, by level of degree and sex of student: 1949–50 to 1992–93

Year	Bachelor's degrees			Master's degrees			Doctor's degrees		
	Total	Men	Women	Total	Men	Women	Total	Men	Women
1	2	3	4	5	6	7	8	9	10
1949–50	61,472	31,398	30,074	20,069	12,025	8,044	953	797	156
1959–60	89,002	25,556	63,446	33,433	18,057	15,376	1,591	1,279	312
1967–68	133,965	31,926	102,039	63,399	30,672	32,727	4,078	3,250	828
1969–70	163,964	40,420	123,544	78,020	34,832	43,188	5,588	4,479	1,109
1970–71	176,307	44,896	131,411	87,666	38,365	49,301	6,041	4,771	1,270
1971–72	190,880	49,344	141,536	96,668	41,141	55,527	6,648	5,104	1,544
1972–73	193,984	51,300	142,684	103,777	43,298	60,479	6,857	5,191	1,666
1973–74	184,907	48,997	135,910	110,402	44,112	66,290	6,757	4,974	1,783
1974–75	166,758	44,463	122,295	117,841	44,430	73,411	6,975	4,856	2,119
1975–76	154,437	42,004	112,433	126,061	44,831	81,230	7,202	4,826	2,376
1976–77	143,234	39,867	103,367	124,267	42,308	81,959	7,338	4,832	2,506
1977–78	135,821	37,410	98,411	116,916	37,662	79,254	7,018	4,281	2,737
1978–79	125,873	33,743	92,130	109,866	34,410	75,456	7,170	4,174	2,996
1979–80	118,038	30,901	87,137	101,819	30,300	71,519	7,314	4,100	3,214
1980–81	108,074	27,039	81,035	96,713	27,548	69,165	7,279	3,843	3,436
1981–82	100,932	24,380	76,552	91,601	25,339	66,262	6,999	3,612	3,387
1982–83	97,895	23,644	74,251	83,250	22,823	60,427	7,057	3,547	3,510
1983–84	92,299	22,195	70,104	75,664	21,142	54,522	6,911	3,446	3,465
1984–85	88,072	21,252	66,820	74,654	20,537	54,117	6,612	3,172	3,440
1985–86	87,114	20,959	66,155	74,801	20,295	54,506	6,605	3,088	3,517
1986–87	86,936	20,729	66,207	74,045	19,293	54,752	6,407	2,931	3,476
1987–88	91,112	20,988	70,124	76,566	19,108	57,458	6,060	2,739	3,321
1988–89	96,913	21,662	75,251	81,174	19,956	61,218	6,337	2,704	3,633
1989–90	105,112	23,007	82,105	84,881	20,467	64,414	6,502	2,776	3,726
1990–91	110,807	23,417	87,390	87,343	20,448	66,895	6,187	2,613	3,574
1991–92	108,006	22,686	85,320	92,668	21,244	71,424	6,864	2,783	4,081
1992–93	107,781	23,233	84,548	96,028	22,197	73,831	7,030	2,867	4,163

SOURCE: U.S. Department of Education, National Center for Education Statistics, "Degrees and Other Formal Awards Conferred" surveys, and Integrated Postsecondary Education Data System (IPEDS), "Completions" surveys. (This table was prepared January 1995.)

Table 276.—Earned degrees in engineering [1] conferred by institutions of higher education, by level of degree and sex of student: 1949–50 to 1992–93

Year	Bachelor's degrees			Master's degrees			Doctor's degrees		
	Total	Men	Women	Total	Men	Women	Total	Men	Women
1	2	3	4	5	6	7	8	9	10
1949–50	52,246	52,071	175	4,496	4,481	15	417	416	1
1959–60	37,679	37,537	142	7,159	7,133	26	786	783	3
1963–64	35,226	35,067	159	10,827	10,793	34	1,693	1,686	7
1965–66	35,615	35,472	143	13,675	13,599	76	2,304	2,295	9
1967–68	37,368	37,159	209	15,182	15,083	99	2,932	2,920	12
1969–70	44,479	44,149	330	15,593	15,421	172	3,681	3,657	24
1970–71	50,046	49,646	400	16,443	16,258	185	3,638	3,615	23
1971–72	51,164	50,638	526	16,960	16,688	272	3,671	3,649	22
1972–73	51,265	50,652	613	16,619	16,341	278	3,492	3,438	54
1973–74	50,286	49,490	796	15,379	15,023	356	3,312	3,257	55
1974–75	46,852	45,838	1,014	15,348	14,973	375	3,108	3,042	66
1975–76	46,331	44,871	1,460	16,342	15,760	582	2,821	2,755	66
1976–77	49,283	47,065	2,218	16,245	15,525	720	2,586	2,513	73
1977–78	55,654	51,945	3,709	16,398	15,533	865	2,440	2,383	57
1978–79	62,375	57,201	5,174	15,495	14,544	951	2,506	2,423	83
1979–80	68,893	62,488	6,405	16,243	15,101	1,142	2,507	2,412	95
1980–81	75,000	67,301	7,699	16,709	15,347	1,362	2,561	2,457	104
1981–82	80,005	70,899	9,106	17,939	16,311	1,628	2,636	2,496	140
1982–83	89,018	78,096	10,922	19,344	17,548	1,796	2,831	2,706	125
1983–84	94,185	82,092	12,093	20,655	18,500	2,155	2,981	2,816	165
1984–85	95,828	83,232	12,596	21,555	19,247	2,308	3,230	3,022	208
1985–86	95,660	83,117	12,543	21,657	19,165	2,492	3,410	3,181	229
1986–87	92,816	80,104	12,712	22,654	19,804	2,850	3,818	3,555	263
1987–88	88,506	76,372	12,134	23,385	20,476	2,909	4,191	3,898	293
1988–89	85,002	73,436	11,566	24,568	21,374	3,194	4,523	4,123	400
1989–90	81,322	70,071	11,251	24,772	21,357	3,415	4,981	4,536	445
1990–91	78,650	67,738	10,912	24,958	21,430	3,528	5,272	4,787	485
1991–92	77,541	66,716	10,825	25,977	22,143	3,834	5,499	4,972	527
1992–93	78,051	66,836	11,215	28,726	24,454	4,272	5,843	5,283	560

[1] Includes degrees in engineering and engineering-related technologies from 1969–70 through 1992–93.

SOURCE: U.S. Department of Education, National Center for Education Statistics, "Degrees and Other Formal Awards Conferred" surveys, and Integrated Postsecondary Education Data System (IPEDS), "Completions" surveys. (This table was prepared January 1995.)

Table 277.—Earned degrees in chemical, civil, electrical, and mechanical engineering conferred by institutions of higher education, by level of degree: 1970–71 to 1992–93

Year	Chemical engineering			Civil engineering			Electrical engineering [1]			Mechanical engineering		
	Bachelor's	Master's	Doctor's	Bachelor's	Master's	Doctor's	Bachelor's	Master's	Doctor's	Bachelor's	Master's	Doctor's
1	2	3	4	5	6	7	8	9	10	11	12	13
1970–71	3,579	1,100	406	6,526	2,425	446	12,198	4,282	879	8,858	2,237	438
1971–72	3,625	1,154	394	6,803	2,487	415	12,101	4,206	824	8,530	2,282	411
1972–73	3,578	1,051	397	7,390	2,627	397	12,313	3,895	791	8,523	2,141	370
1973–74	3,399	1,044	400	8,017	2,652	368	11,316	3,499	705	7,677	1,843	385
1974–75	3,070	990	346	7,651	2,769	356	10,161	3,469	701	6,890	1,858	340
1975–76	3,140	1,031	308	7,923	2,999	370	9,791	3,774	649	6,800	1,907	305
1976–77	3,524	1,086	291	8,228	2,964	309	9,936	3,788	566	7,703	1,952	283
1977–78	4,569	1,235	259	9,135	2,685	277	11,133	3,740	503	8,875	1,942	279
1978–79	5,568	1,149	304	9,809	2,646	253	12,338	3,591	586	10,107	1,877	271
1979–80	6,320	1,270	284	10,326	2,683	270	13,821	3,836	525	11,808	2,060	281
1980–81	6,527	1,267	300	10,678	2,891	325	14,938	3,901	535	13,329	2,291	276
1981–82	6,740	1,285	311	10,524	2,995	329	16,455	4,462	526	13,922	2,399	333
1982–83	7,185	1,368	319	9,989	3,074	340	18,049	4,531	550	15,675	2,511	299
1983–84	7,475	1,514	330	9,693	3,146	369	19,943	5,078	585	16,629	2,797	319
1984–85	7,146	1,544	418	9,162	3,172	377	21,691	5,153	660	16,794	3,053	409
1985–86	5,877	1,361	446	8,679	2,926	395	23,742	5,534	722	16,194	3,075	426
1986–87	4,991	1,184	497	8,147	2,901	451	24,547	6,183	724	15,450	3,198	528
1987–88	3,917	1,088	579	7,488	2,836	481	23,597	6,688	860	14,900	3,329	596
1988–89	3,663	1,093	602	7,312	2,903	505	21,908	7,028	998	14,843	3,498	633
1989–90	3,430	1,035	562	7,252	2,812	516	20,711	7,225	1,162	14,336	3,424	742
1990–91	3,444	903	611	7,314	2,927	536	19,320	7,095	1,220	13,977	3,516	757
1991–92	3,754	956	590	8,034	3,113	540	17,958	7,360	1,282	14,067	3,653	851
1992–93	4,459	990	595	8,868	3,610	577	17,281	7,870	1,413	14,464	3,982	871

[1] From 1970–71 to 1981–82 includes "construction and transportation engineering."

NOTE.—Degrees in engineering-related technologies are not included in this tabulation.

SOURCE: U.S. Department of Education, National Center for Education Statistics, "Degrees and Other Formal Awards Conferred" surveys, and Integrated Postsecondary Education Data System (IPEDS), "Completions" surveys. (This table was prepared January 1995.)

Table 278.—Earned degrees in English language and literature/letters [1] conferred by institutions of higher education, by level of degree and sex of student: 1949–50 to 1992–93

Year	Bachelor's degrees			Master's degrees			Doctor's degrees		
	Total	Men	Women	Total	Men	Women	Total	Men	Women
1	2	3	4	5	6	7	8	9	10
1949–50	17,240	8,221	9,019	2,259	1,320	939	230	181	49
1959–60	20,128	7,580	12,548	2,931	1,458	1,473	397	314	83
1967–68	47,977	15,700	32,277	7,916	3,434	4,482	977	717	260
1969–70	56,410	18,650	37,760	8,517	3,326	5,191	1,213	837	376
1970–71	64,342	22,155	42,187	10,686	4,211	6,475	1,650	1,175	475
1971–72	63,976	22,657	41,319	10,579	4,123	6,456	1,826	1,233	593
1972–73	61,003	22,156	38,847	10,239	4,063	6,176	1,935	1,258	677
1973–74	54,590	20,214	34,376	9,803	3,917	5,886	1,885	1,208	677
1974–75	47,619	17,880	29,739	9,444	3,569	5,875	1,711	1,025	686
1975–76	42,006	16,073	25,933	8,809	3,383	5,426	1,672	967	705
1976–77	37,794	14,295	23,499	8,016	2,985	5,031	1,508	841	667
1977–78	35,328	13,137	22,191	7,655	2,706	4,949	1,400	758	642
1978–79	33,561	12,198	21,363	6,684	2,369	4,315	1,314	708	606
1979–80	32,541	11,380	21,161	6,189	2,233	3,956	1,294	686	608
1980–81	32,254	11,198	21,056	5,929	2,092	3,837	1,164	553	611
1981–82	33,419	11,414	22,005	5,772	1,983	3,789	1,101	511	590
1982–83	31,829	10,859	20,970	5,048	1,710	3,338	991	471	520
1983–84	32,834	11,170	21,664	5,010	1,736	3,274	1,018	459	559
1984–85	33,218	11,334	21,884	5,187	1,786	3,401	1,041	470	571
1985–86	34,552	11,819	22,733	5,518	1,881	3,637	991	428	563
1986–87	36,284	12,353	23,931	5,483	1,891	3,592	961	415	546
1987–88	38,661	12,836	25,825	5,562	1,870	3,692	981	428	553
1988–89	42,470	13,927	28,543	5,950	2,002	3,948	1,022	458	564
1989–90	47,519	15,662	31,857	6,567	2,205	4,362	1,078	480	598
1990–91	51,841	17,146	34,695	7,026	2,296	4,730	1,184	517	667
1991–92	54,951	18,536	36,415	7,450	2,513	4,937	1,273	537	736
1992–93	56,133	19,247	36,886	7,790	2,667	5,123	1,341	550	791

[1] Includes degrees conferred in English language and literature, general; comparative literature; English composition; English creative writing; American literature; English literature; speech and rhetorical studies; English technical and business writing; and English language and literature/letters, other.

SOURCE: U.S. Department of Education, National Center for Education Statistics, "Degrees and Other Formal Awards Conferred" surveys, and Integrated Postsecondary Education Data System (IPEDS), "Completions" surveys. (This table was prepared January 1995.)

Table 279.—Earned degrees in modern foreign languages and literatures [1] conferred by institutions of higher education, by level of degree and sex of student: 1949–50 to 1992–93

Year	Bachelor's degrees			Master's degrees			Doctor's degrees		
	Total	Men	Women	Total	Men	Women	Total	Men	Women
1	2	3	4	5	6	7	8	9	10
1949–50	4,477	1,746	2,731	919	456	463	168	135	33
1959–60	4,527	1,548	2,979	832	392	440	150	100	50
1967–68	17,499	4,450	13,049	3,911	1,555	2,356	491	336	155
1969–70	19,457	4,921	14,536	4,154	1,476	2,678	590	369	221
1970–71	19,055	4,734	14,321	4,407	1,492	2,915	703	425	278
1971–72	18,137	4,445	13,692	4,277	1,449	2,828	753	466	287
1972–73	18,232	4,347	13,885	3,992	1,407	2,585	889	519	370
1973–74	18,252	4,276	13,976	3,793	1,252	2,541	875	487	388
1974–75	17,115	3,912	13,203	3,672	1,179	2,493	829	442	387
1975–76	15,079	3,495	11,584	3,359	1,095	2,264	830	429	401
1976–77	13,626	3,225	10,401	2,986	886	2,100	728	347	381
1977–78	12,448	2,938	9,510	2,653	768	1,885	626	282	344
1978–79	11,531	2,705	8,826	2,338	685	1,653	625	287	338
1979–80	10,816	2,583	8,233	2,152	628	1,524	522	217	305
1980–81	10,050	2,402	7,648	2,018	657	1,361	556	259	297
1981–82	9,576	2,278	7,298	1,913	571	1,342	495	220	275
1982–83	9,334	2,343	6,991	1,597	528	1,069	451	183	268
1983–84	9,152	2,399	6,753	1,640	512	1,128	424	191	233
1984–85	9,675	2,529	7,146	1,611	503	1,108	387	156	231
1985–86	9,808	2,685	7,123	1,655	482	1,173	426	173	253
1986–87	9,858	2,655	7,203	1,692	491	1,201	403	162	241
1987–88	9,790	2,628	7,162	1,795	564	1,231	380	159	221
1988–89	10,498	2,767	7,731	1,821	552	1,269	389	145	244
1989–90	11,092	2,902	8,190	1,931	584	1,347	475	183	292
1990–91	11,724	3,207	8,517	1,973	595	1,378	477	200	277
1991–92	12,367	3,390	8,977	2,119	652	1,467	537	222	315
1992–93	12,819	3,537	9,282	2,353	744	1,609	535	210	325

[1] Includes degrees conferred in a single language or a combination of modern foreign languages. Excludes degrees in linguistics, Latin, classical Greek, and "other" foreign languages.

SOURCE: U.S. Department of Education, National Center for Education Statistics, "Degrees and Other Formal Awards Conferred" surveys, and Integrated Postsecondary Education Data System (IPEDS), "Completions" surveys. (This table was prepared January 1995.)

Table 280.—Earned degrees in French, German, and Spanish conferred by institutions of higher education, by level of degree: 1949–50 to 1992–93

Year	French			German			Spanish		
	Bachelor's	Master's	Doctor's	Bachelor's	Master's	Doctor's	Bachelor's	Master's	Doctor's
1	2	3	4	5	6	7	8	9	10
1949–50	1,471	299	53	540	121	40	2,122	373	34
1959–60	1,927	316	58	659	126	21	1,610	261	31
1967–68	7,068	1,301	152	2,368	771	117	6,381	1,188	123
1969–70	7,624	1,409	181	2,652	669	118	7,226	1,372	139
1970–71	7,306	1,437	192	2,601	690	144	7,068	1,456	168
1971–72	6,822	1,421	193	2,477	608	167	6,847	1,421	152
1972–73	6,705	1,277	203	2,520	598	176	7,209	1,298	206
1973–74	6,263	1,195	213	2,425	550	149	7,250	1,217	203
1974–75	5,745	1,077	200	2,289	480	147	6,719	1,228	202
1975–76	4,783	914	190	1,983	471	164	5,984	1,080	176
1976–77	4,228	875	177	1,820	394	126	5,359	930	153
1977–78	3,708	692	155	1,647	357	101	4,832	822	113
1978–79	3,558	576	143	1,524	344	106	4,563	720	118
1979–80	3,285	513	128	1,466	309	94	4,331	685	103
1980–81	3,178	460	115	1,286	294	79	3,870	592	131
1981–82	3,054	485	92	1,327	324	76	3,633	568	140
1982–83	2,871	360	106	1,367	281	68	3,349	506	129
1983–84	2,876	418	86	1,292	241	63	3,254	537	102
1984–85	2,991	385	74	1,411	240	58	3,415	505	115
1985–86	3,015	409	86	1,396	249	73	3,385	521	95
1986–87	3,062	421	85	1,366	234	70	3,450	504	104
1987–88	3,082	437	89	1,350	244	71	3,416	553	93
1988–89	3,297	444	83	1,428	263	59	3,748	552	101
1989–90	3,259	478	115	1,437	253	67	4,176	573	108
1990–91	3,355	480	98	1,543	242	58	4,480	609	125
1991–92	3,371	465	112	1,616	273	85	4,768	647	143
1992–93	3,280	513	98	1,572	346	97	5,233	667	145

SOURCE: U.S. Department of Education, National Center for Education Statistics, "Degrees and Other Formal Awards Conferred" surveys, and Integrated Postsecondary Education Data System (IPEDS), "Completions" surveys. (This table was prepared January 1995.)

Table 281.—Earned degrees in the health professions and related sciences [1] conferred by institutions of higher education, by level of degree and sex of student: 1970–71 to 1992–93

Year	Bachelor's degrees			Master's degrees			Doctor's degrees		
	Total	Men	Women	Total	Men	Women	Total	Men	Women
1	2	3	4	5	6	7	8	9	10
1970–71	25,226	5,788	19,438	5,749	2,567	3,182	466	389	77
1971–72	28,611	7,005	21,606	7,207	3,141	4,066	442	362	80
1972–73	33,564	7,754	25,810	8,362	3,567	4,795	646	485	161
1973–74	41,459	9,388	32,071	9,599	3,819	5,780	578	447	131
1974–75	49,090	10,930	38,160	10,692	4,092	6,600	618	441	177
1975–76	53,958	11,456	42,502	12,556	4,217	8,339	577	411	166
1976–77	57,328	11,947	45,381	12,951	4,163	8,788	538	366	172
1977–78	59,434	11,593	47,841	14,325	4,265	10,060	654	402	252
1978–79	62,085	11,205	50,880	15,485	4,494	10,991	718	454	264
1979–80	63,920	11,391	52,529	15,704	4,357	11,347	786	435	351
1980–81	63,649	10,519	53,130	16,515	4,316	12,199	842	475	367
1981–82	63,653	10,105	53,548	16,503	4,006	12,497	925	503	422
1982–83	64,685	10,218	54,467	17,047	4,235	12,812	1,155	649	506
1983–84	64,288	10,040	54,248	17,411	4,251	13,160	1,164	574	590
1984–85	64,422	9,741	54,681	17,385	4,119	13,266	1,199	565	634
1985–86	64,396	9,630	54,766	18,573	4,428	14,145	1,241	604	637
1986–87	63,103	9,134	53,969	18,394	3,874	14,520	1,213	564	649
1987–88	60,644	8,929	51,715	18,657	4,047	14,610	1,261	548	713
1988–89	59,005	8,872	50,133	19,268	4,226	15,042	1,437	609	828
1989–90	58,302	9,118	49,184	20,321	4,534	15,787	1,536	704	832
1990–91	59,070	9,596	49,474	21,200	4,444	16,756	1,613	694	919
1991–92	61,720	10,189	51,531	23,065	4,691	18,374	1,661	698	963
1992–93	67,089	11,347	55,742	25,718	5,227	20,491	1,767	753	1,014

[1] Includes degrees in chiropractic; communication disorders sciences; community health liaison; dentistry; dental services; health services administration; health and medical assistants; health and medical diagnostic and treatment services; medical laboratory technologies; predentistry; premedicine; prepharmacy; preveterinary; medical basic sciences; mental health services; nursing; optometry; pharmacy; epidemiology; rehabilitation and therapeutic services; veterinary medicine; and other health professions.

SOURCE: U.S. Department of Education, National Center for Education Statistics, "Degrees and Other Formal Awards Conferred" surveys, and Integrated Postsecondary Education Data System (IPEDS), "Completions" surveys. (This table was prepared January 1995.)

Table 282.—Earned degrees in mathematics [1] conferred by institutions of higher education, by level of degree and sex of student: 1949–50 to 1992–93

Year	Bachelor's degrees			Master's degrees			Doctor's degrees		
	Total	Men	Women	Total	Men	Women	Total	Men	Women
1	2	3	4	5	6	7	8	9	10
1949–50	6,382	4,942	1,440	974	784	190	160	151	9
1959–60	11,399	8,293	3,106	1,757	1,422	335	303	285	18
1967–68	23,513	14,782	8,731	5,527	4,199	1,328	947	895	52
1969–70	27,442	17,177	10,265	5,636	3,966	1,670	1,236	1,140	96
1970–71	24,937	15,498	9,439	5,695	4,149	1,546	1,249	1,154	95
1971–72	23,807	14,542	9,265	5,537	3,976	1,561	1,165	1,075	90
1972–73	23,186	13,910	9,276	5,397	3,878	1,519	1,089	987	102
1973–74	21,761	12,912	8,849	5,306	3,784	1,522	1,093	992	101
1974–75	18,460	10,853	7,607	4,816	3,358	1,458	1,048	936	112
1975–76	16,329	9,788	6,541	4,315	2,961	1,354	909	812	97
1976–77	14,395	8,476	5,919	4,109	2,762	1,347	859	748	111
1977–78	13,065	7,806	5,259	3,862	2,635	1,227	848	722	126
1978–79	12,329	7,301	5,028	3,553	2,412	1,141	769	644	125
1979–80	11,872	6,951	4,921	3,382	2,262	1,120	763	659	104
1980–81	11,433	6,614	4,819	3,074	2,106	968	775	656	119
1981–82	12,226	6,999	5,227	3,263	2,257	1,006	721	623	98
1982–83	12,719	7,175	5,544	3,398	2,316	1,082	731	611	120
1983–84	13,764	7,716	6,048	3,244	2,178	1,066	743	614	129
1984–85	15,861	8,537	7,324	3,413	2,289	1,124	734	620	114
1985–86	17,147	9,216	7,931	3,607	2,397	1,210	777	648	129
1986–87	16,999	9,110	7,889	3,730	2,328	1,402	759	628	131
1987–88	16,608	8,919	7,689	3,867	2,391	1,476	796	668	128
1988–89	15,994	8,662	7,332	3,903	2,418	1,485	915	737	178
1989–90	15,176	8,236	6,940	4,146	2,568	1,578	966	794	172
1990–91	15,310	8,178	7,132	4,041	2,446	1,595	1,036	837	199
1991–92	14,783	7,888	6,895	4,011	2,452	1,559	1,082	851	231
1992–93	14,812	7,827	6,985	4,067	2,455	1,612	1,189	906	283

[1] Includes degrees conferred in statistics.

SOURCE: U.S. Department of Education, National Center for Education Statistics, "Degrees and Other Formal Awards Conferred" surveys, and Integrated Postsecondary Education Data System (IPEDS), "Completions" surveys. (This table was prepared January 1995.)

Table 283.—Earned degrees in the physical sciences [1] conferred by institutions of higher education, by level of degree and sex of student: 1959–60 to 1992–93

Year	Bachelor's degrees			Master's degrees			Doctor's degrees		
	Total	Men	Women	Total	Men	Women	Total	Men	Women
1	2	3	4	5	6	7	8	9	10
1959–60	16,007	14,013	1,994	3,376	3,049	327	1,838	1,776	62
1967–68	19,380	16,739	2,641	5,499	4,869	630	3,593	3,405	188
1969–70	21,439	18,522	2,917	5,935	5,093	842	4,312	4,077	235
1970–71	21,412	18,459	2,953	6,367	5,521	846	4,390	4,144	246
1971–72	20,745	17,663	3,082	6,287	5,404	883	4,103	3,830	273
1972–73	20,696	17,626	3,070	6,257	5,414	843	4,006	3,738	268
1973–74	21,178	17,674	3,504	6,062	5,186	876	3,626	3,373	253
1974–75	20,778	16,992	3,786	5,807	4,969	838	3,626	3,325	301
1975–76	21,465	17,353	4,112	5,466	4,648	818	3,431	3,132	299
1976–77	22,497	17,996	4,501	5,331	4,450	881	3,341	3,022	319
1977–78	22,986	18,090	4,896	5,561	4,620	941	3,133	2,821	312
1978–79	23,207	17,985	5,222	5,451	4,461	990	3,102	2,752	350
1979–80	23,410	17,864	5,546	5,219	4,248	971	3,089	2,705	384
1980–81	23,952	18,064	5,888	5,284	4,200	1,084	3,141	2,765	376
1981–82	24,052	17,866	6,186	5,514	4,318	1,196	3,286	2,835	451
1982–83	23,381	16,993	6,388	5,290	4,157	1,133	3,269	2,811	458
1983–84	23,651	17,116	6,535	5,576	4,268	1,308	3,306	2,815	491
1984–85	23,704	17,069	6,635	5,796	4,452	1,344	3,403	2,851	552
1985–86	21,717	15,755	5,962	5,902	4,470	1,432	3,551	2,963	588
1986–87	20,070	14,372	5,698	5,629	4,219	1,410	3,673	3,039	634
1987–88	17,806	12,389	5,417	5,733	4,324	1,409	3,809	3,123	686
1988–89	17,186	12,077	5,109	5,723	4,199	1,524	3,858	3,088	770
1989–90	16,066	11,031	5,035	5,449	4,010	1,439	4,164	3,356	808
1990–91	16,344	11,176	5,168	5,309	3,837	1,472	4,290	3,447	843
1991–92	16,960	11,431	5,529	5,374	3,909	1,465	4,391	3,429	962
1992–93	17,545	11,825	5,720	5,366	3,808	1,558	4,393	3,432	961

[1] Includes degrees in physical sciences, general; astronomy, astrophysics; atmospheric science and meterorology; chemistry, geology, miscellaneous physical sciences; physics, science technologies, and other physical sciences.

SOURCE: U.S. Department of Education, National Center for Education Statistics, "Degrees and Other Formal Awards Conferred" surveys, and Integrated Postsecondary Education Data System (IPEDS), "Completions" surveys. (This table was prepared January 1995.)

Table 284.—Earned degrees in chemistry, geology, and physics conferred by institutions of higher education, by level of degree: 1970–71 to 1992–93

Year	Chemistry			Geology [1]			Physics		
	Bachelor's	Master's	Doctor's	Bachelor's	Master's	Doctor's	Bachelor's	Master's	Doctor's
1	2	3	4	5	6	7	8	9	10
1970–71	11,063	2,275	2,159	2,414	651	324	5,071	2,188	1,482
1971–72	10,590	2,248	1,971	2,573	841	310	4,634	2,033	1,344
1972–73	10,128	2,225	1,872	2,923	827	305	4,259	1,747	1,338
1973–74	10,438	2,125	1,823	3,253	938	315	3,952	1,655	1,115
1974–75	10,549	1,986	1,822	3,319	932	292	3,706	1,574	1,080
1975–76	11,022	1,783	1,621	3,358	1,003	313	3,544	1,451	997
1976–77	11,215	1,767	1,568	3,879	1,047	325	3,420	1,319	945
1977–78	11,315	1,886	1,521	4,342	1,239	268	3,330	1,294	873
1978–79	11,509	1,757	1,516	4,502	1,300	286	3,337	1,319	918
1979–80	11,232	1,723	1,545	4,597	1,295	313	3,396	1,192	830
1980–81	11,347	1,654	1,622	5,202	1,396	294	3,441	1,294	866
1981–82	11,062	1,751	1,722	5,538	1,540	282	3,472	1,284	873
1982–83	10,796	1,622	1,746	6,102	1,552	295	3,793	1,369	873
1983–84	10,704	1,667	1,744	6,549	1,514	315	3,907	1,532	953
1984–85	10,482	1,719	1,789	6,308	1,692	289	4,097	1,523	951
1985–86	10,116	1,754	1,908	4,974	1,767	271	4,180	1,501	1,010
1986–87	9,670	1,738	1,976	3,665	1,603	280	4,318	1,543	1,074
1987–88	9,052	1,708	1,995	2,551	1,523	350	4,100	1,675	1,093
1988–89	8,625	1,774	2,037	2,252	1,404	358	4,352	1,736	1,112
1989–90	8,132	1,682	2,183	1,767	1,200	414	4,155	1,831	1,192
1990–91	8,321	1,665	2,238	1,784	1,089	446	4,236	1,725	1,209
1991–92	8,641	1,780	2,280	2,078	990	413	4,098	1,834	1,337
1992–93	8,914	1,842	2,261	2,299	925	406	4,063	1,777	1,277

[1] Includes geology, geochemistry, and geophysics and seismology. Beginning in 1982–83, also includes other geological sciences.

SOURCE: U.S. Department of Education, National Center for Education Statistics, "Degrees and Other Formal Awards Conferred" surveys, and Integrated Postsecondary Education Data System (IPEDS), "Completions" surveys. (This table was prepared January 1995.)

Table 285.—Earned degrees in psychology conferred by institutions of higher education, by level of degree and by sex of student: 1949–50 to 1992–93

Year	Bachelor's degrees			Master's degrees			Doctor's degrees		
	Total	Men	Women	Total	Men	Women	Total	Men	Women
1	2	3	4	5	6	7	8	9	10
1949–50	9,569	6,055	3,514	1,316	948	368	283	241	42
1959–60	8,061	4,773	3,288	1,406	981	425	641	544	97
1967–68	23,819	13,792	10,027	3,479	2,321	1,158	1,268	982	286
1969–70	33,679	19,077	14,602	5,158	2,975	2,183	1,962	1,505	457
1970–71	38,187	21,227	16,960	5,717	3,395	2,322	2,144	1,629	515
1971–72	43,433	23,352	20,081	6,764	3,934	2,830	2,277	1,694	583
1972–73	47,940	25,117	22,823	7,619	4,325	3,294	2,550	1,797	753
1973–74	52,139	25,868	26,271	8,796	4,983	3,813	2,872	1,987	885
1974–75	51,245	24,284	26,961	9,394	5,035	4,359	2,913	1,979	934
1975–76	50,278	22,898	27,380	10,167	5,136	5,031	3,157	2,115	1,042
1976–77	47,861	20,627	27,234	10,859	5,293	5,566	3,386	2,127	1,259
1977–78	44,879	18,422	26,457	10,282	4,670	5,612	3,164	1,974	1,190
1978–79	42,697	16,540	26,157	10,132	4,405	5,727	3,228	1,895	1,333
1979–80	42,093	15,440	26,653	9,938	4,096	5,842	3,395	1,921	1,474
1980–81	41,068	14,332	26,736	10,223	4,066	6,157	3,576	2,002	1,574
1981–82	41,212	13,645	27,567	9,947	3,823	6,124	3,461	1,856	1,605
1982–83	40,460	13,131	27,329	9,981	3,647	6,334	3,602	1,838	1,764
1983–84	39,955	12,812	27,143	9,525	3,400	6,125	3,535	1,774	1,761
1984–85	39,900	12,706	27,194	9,891	3,452	6,439	3,447	1,739	1,708
1985–86	40,628	12,605	28,023	9,845	3,347	6,498	3,593	1,724	1,869
1986–87	42,994	13,362	29,632	9,562	3,172	6,390	3,560	1,615	1,945
1987–88	45,187	13,538	31,649	9,180	2,923	6,257	3,480	1,573	1,907
1988–89	48,910	14,246	34,664	9,940	3,122	6,818	3,685	1,590	2,095
1989–90	53,952	15,336	38,616	10,730	3,377	7,353	3,811	1,566	2,245
1990–91	58,655	16,067	42,588	11,349	3,329	8,020	3,932	1,520	2,412
1991–92	63,513	17,031	46,482	10,215	2,988	7,227	3,373	1,359	2,014
1992–93	66,728	17,908	48,820	10,957	3,029	7,928	3,651	1,415	2,236

SOURCE: U.S. Department of Education, National Center for Education Statistics, "Degrees and Other Formal Awards Conferred" surveys, and Integrated Postsecondary Education Data System (IPEDS), "Completions" surveys. (This table was prepared January 1995.)

Table 286.—Earned degrees in public administration and services [1] conferred by institutions of higher education, by level of degree and sex of student: 1970–71 to 1992–93

Year	Bachelor's degrees			Master's degrees			Doctor's degrees		
	Total	Men	Women	Total	Men	Women	Total	Men	Women
1	2	3	4	5	6	7	8	9	10
1970–71	5,466	1,726	3,740	7,785	3,893	3,892	174	132	42
1971–72	7,508	2,588	4,920	8,756	4,537	4,219	193	150	43
1972–73	10,690	3,998	6,692	10,068	5,271	4,797	198	160	38
1973–74	11,966	4,266	7,700	11,415	6,028	5,387	201	154	47
1974–75	13,661	4,630	9,031	13,617	7,200	6,417	257	192	65
1975–76	15,440	5,706	9,734	15,209	7,969	7,240	292	192	100
1976–77	16,136	5,544	10,592	17,026	8,810	8,216	292	197	95
1977–78	16,607	5,096	11,511	17,337	8,513	8,824	357	237	120
1978–79	17,328	4,938	12,390	17,306	8,051	9,255	315	215	100
1979–80	16,644	4,451	12,193	17,560	7,866	9,694	342	216	126
1980–81	16,707	4,248	12,459	17,803	7,460	10,343	362	212	150
1981–82	16,495	4,176	12,319	17,416	6,975	10,441	372	205	167
1982–83	14,414	3,343	11,071	16,046	5,961	10,085	347	184	163
1983–84	12,570	2,998	9,572	15,060	5,634	9,426	420	230	190
1984–85	11,754	2,829	8,925	15,575	5,573	10,002	431	213	218
1985–86	11,887	2,966	8,921	15,692	5,594	10,098	382	171	211
1986–87	12,328	2,993	9,335	16,432	5,673	10,759	398	216	182
1987–88	12,385	2,923	9,462	16,424	5,631	10,793	470	238	232
1988–89	13,162	3,214	9,948	17,020	5,615	11,405	428	210	218
1989–90	13,908	3,334	10,574	17,399	5,634	11,765	508	235	273
1990–91	14,350	3,215	11,135	17,905	5,679	12,226	430	190	240
1991–92	15,987	3,479	12,508	19,243	5,769	13,474	432	204	228
1992–93	16,775	3,801	12,974	20,634	6,105	14,529	459	215	244

[1] Includes degrees in public administration; community organization, resources and services; public policy analysis; social work; and public affairs, other.

SOURCE: U.S. Department of Education, National Center for Education Statistics, "Degrees and Other Formal Awards Conferred" surveys, and Integrated Postsecondary Education Data System (IPEDS), "Completions" surveys. (This table was prepared January 1995.)

Table 287.—Earned degrees in the social sciences [1] and history conferred by institutions of higher education, by level of degree and sex of student: 1970–71 to 1992–93

Year	Bachelor's degrees			Master's degrees			Doctor's degrees		
	Total	Men	Women	Total	Men	Women	Total	Men	Women
1	2	3	4	5	6	7	8	9	10
1970–71	155,324	98,173	57,151	16,539	11,833	4,706	3,660	3,153	507
1971–72	158,060	100,895	57,165	17,445	12,540	4,905	4,081	3,483	598
1972–73	155,970	99,735	56,235	17,477	12,605	4,872	4,234	3,573	661
1973–74	150,320	95,650	54,670	17,293	12,321	4,972	4,124	3,383	741
1974–75	135,190	84,826	50,364	16,977	11,875	5,102	4,212	3,334	878
1975–76	126,396	78,691	47,705	15,953	10,918	5,035	4,157	3,262	895
1976–77	117,040	71,128	45,912	15,533	10,413	5,120	3,802	2,957	845
1977–78	112,952	67,217	45,735	14,718	9,845	4,873	3,594	2,722	872
1978–79	108,059	62,852	45,207	12,963	8,395	4,568	3,371	2,501	870
1979–80	103,662	58,511	45,151	12,176	7,794	4,382	3,230	2,357	873
1980–81	100,513	56,131	44,382	11,945	7,457	4,488	3,122	2,274	848
1981–82	99,705	55,196	44,509	12,002	7,468	4,534	3,061	2,237	824
1982–83	95,228	52,771	42,457	11,205	6,974	4,231	2,931	2,042	889
1983–84	93,323	52,154	41,169	10,577	6,551	4,026	2,911	2,030	881
1984–85	91,570	51,226	40,344	10,503	6,475	4,028	2,851	1,933	918
1985–86	93,840	52,724	41,116	10,564	6,419	4,145	2,955	1,970	985
1986–87	96,342	53,949	42,393	10,506	6,373	4,133	2,916	2,026	890
1987–88	100,460	56,377	44,083	10,412	6,310	4,102	2,781	1,849	932
1988–89	108,151	60,121	48,030	11,023	6,599	4,424	2,885	1,949	936
1989–90	118,083	65,887	52,196	11,634	6,898	4,736	3,010	2,019	991
1990–91	125,107	68,701	56,406	12,233	7,016	5,217	3,012	1,956	1,056
1991–92	133,974	73,001	60,973	12,702	7,237	5,465	3,218	2,126	1,092
1992–93	135,703	73,589	62,114	13,471	7,671	5,800	3,460	2,203	1,257

[1] Includes degrees in social sciences, general; anthropology; archeology; criminology; demography and population studies; economics; geography; history; international relations and affairs; political science and government; sociology; urban affairs/studies; and social sciences and history, other.

SOURCE: U.S. Department of Education, National Center for Education Statistics, "Degrees and Other Formal Awards Conferred" surveys, and Integrated Postsecondary Education Data System (IPEDS), "Completions" surveys. (This table was prepared January 1995.)

Table 288.—Earned degrees in economics, history, political science and government, and sociology conferred by institutions of higher education, by level of degree: 1949–50 to 1992–93

Year	Economics			History			Political science and government [1]			Sociology		
	Bach-elor's	Master's	Doctor's	Bach-elor's	Master's	Doctor's	Bach-elor's	Master's	Doctor's	Bach-elor's	Master's	Doctor's
1	2	3	4	5	6	7	8	9	10	11	12	13
1949–50	14,568	921	200	13,542	1,801	275	6,336	710	127	7,870	552	98
1951–52	8,593	695	239	10,187	1,445	317	4,911	525	147	6,648	517	141
1953–54	6,719	609	245	9,363	1,220	355	5,314	534	153	5,692	440	184
1955–56	6,555	581	232	10,510	1,114	259	5,633	509	203	5,878	402	170
1957–58	7,457	669	239	12,840	1,397	297	6,116	665	170	6,568	397	150
1959–60	7,453	708	237	14,737	1,794	342	6,596	722	201	7,147	440	161
1961–62	8,366	853	268	17,340	2,163	343	8,326	839	214	8,120	578	173
1963–64	10,583	1,104	385	23,668	2,705	507	12,126	1,163	263	10,943	646	198
1965–66	11,555	1,522	458	28,612	3,883	599	15,242	1,429	336	15,038	981	244
1967–68	15,193	1,916	600	35,291	4,845	688	20,387	1,937	457	21,710	1,193	367
1969–70	17,197	1,988	794	43,386	5,049	1,038	25,713	2,105	525	30,436	1,813	534
1970–71	15,758	1,995	721	44,663	5,157	991	27,482	2,318	700	33,263	1,808	574
1971–72	15,231	2,224	794	43,695	5,217	1,133	28,135	2,451	758	35,216	1,944	636
1972–73	14,770	2,225	845	40,943	5,030	1,140	30,100	2,398	747	35,436	1,923	583
1973–74	14,285	2,141	788	37,049	4,533	1,114	30,744	2,448	766	35,491	2,196	632
1974–75	14,046	2,127	815	31,470	4,226	1,117	29,126	2,333	680	31,488	2,112	693
1975–76	14,741	2,087	763	28,400	3,658	1,014	28,302	2,191	723	27,634	2,009	729
1976–77	15,296	2,158	758	25,433	3,393	921	26,411	2,222	641	24,713	1,830	714
1977–78	15,661	1,995	706	23,004	3,033	813	26,069	2,069	636	22,750	1,611	599
1978–79	16,409	1,955	712	21,019	2,536	756	25,628	2,037	563	20,285	1,415	612
1979–80	17,863	1,821	677	19,301	2,367	712	25,457	1,938	535	18,881	1,341	583
1980–81	18,753	1,911	727	18,301	2,237	643	24,977	1,875	484	17,272	1,240	610
1981–82	19,876	1,964	677	17,146	2,210	636	25,658	1,954	513	16,042	1,145	558
1982–83	20,517	1,972	734	16,467	2,041	575	25,791	1,829	435	14,105	1,112	522
1983–84	20,719	1,891	729	16,643	1,940	561	25,719	1,769	457	13,145	1,008	520
1984–85	20,711	1,992	749	16,049	1,921	468	25,834	1,500	441	11,968	1,022	480
1985–86	21,602	1,937	789	16,415	1,961	497	26,439	1,704	439	12,271	965	504
1986–87	22,378	1,855	750	16,997	2,021	534	26,817	1,618	435	12,239	950	451
1987–88	22,911	1,847	770	18,207	2,093	517	27,207	1,579	391	13,024	984	452
1988–89	23,454	1,886	827	20,159	2,121	487	30,450	1,598	452	14,435	1,135	451
1989–90	23,923	1,950	806	22,476	2,369	570	33,560	1,580	480	16,035	1,198	432
1990–91	23,488	1,951	802	24,541	2,591	606	35,737	1,772	468	17,550	1,260	465
1991–92	23,423	2,106	866	26,966	2,754	644	37,805	1,908	535	19,568	1,347	501
1992–93	21,321	2,292	879	27,774	2,952	690	37,931	1,943	529	20,896	1,521	536

[1] Excludes degrees in public administration and international relations.

SOURCE: U.S. Department of Education, National Center for Education Statistics, "Degrees and Other Formal Awards Conferred" surveys, and Integrated Postsecondary Education Data System (IPEDS), "Completions" surveys. (This table was prepared January 1995.)

Table 289.—Earned degrees in visual and performing arts [1] conferred by institutions of higher education, by level of degree and sex of student: 1970–71 to 1992–93

Year	Bachelor's degrees			Master's degrees			Doctor's degrees		
	Total	Men	Women	Total	Men	Women	Total	Men	Women
1	2	3	4	5	6	7	8	9	10
1970–71	30,394	12,256	18,138	6,675	3,510	3,165	621	483	138
1971–72	33,831	13,580	20,251	7,537	4,049	3,488	572	428	144
1972–73	36,017	14,267	21,750	7,254	4,005	3,249	616	449	167
1973–74	39,730	15,821	23,909	8,001	4,325	3,676	585	440	145
1974–75	40,782	15,532	25,250	8,362	4,448	3,914	649	446	203
1975–76	42,138	16,491	25,647	8,817	4,507	4,310	620	447	173
1976–77	41,793	16,166	25,627	8,636	4,211	4,425	662	447	215
1977–78	40,951	15,572	25,379	9,036	4,327	4,709	708	448	260
1978–79	40,969	15,380	25,589	8,524	3,933	4,591	700	454	246
1979–80	40,892	15,065	25,827	8,708	4,067	4,641	655	413	242
1980–81	40,479	14,798	25,681	8,629	4,056	4,573	654	396	258
1981–82	40,422	14,819	25,603	8,746	3,866	4,880	670	380	290
1982–83	39,794	14,690	25,104	8,763	4,013	4,750	692	404	288
1983–84	40,131	15,089	25,042	8,526	3,897	4,629	730	406	324
1984–85	38,140	14,462	23,678	8,718	3,894	4,824	696	407	289
1985–86	37,241	14,236	23,005	8,420	3,775	4,645	722	396	326
1986–87	36,615	13,751	22,864	8,508	3,756	4,752	793	447	346
1987–88	36,944	14,068	22,876	7,939	3,442	4,497	727	424	303
1988–89	38,227	14,539	23,688	8,267	3,611	4,656	753	446	307
1989–90	38,934	15,189	23,745	8,481	3,706	4,775	849	472	377
1990–91	42,186	15,761	26,425	8,657	3,830	4,827	838	466	372
1991–92	46,522	17,616	28,906	9,353	4,078	5,275	906	504	402
1992–93	47,761	18,610	29,151	9,440	4,099	5,341	882	478	404

[1] Prior to 1982–83: Includes visual and performing arts, general; crafts, folk art, and artisanry; dance; design and applied art; theatre arts; film and photographic arts; fine arts; graphic arts technology; music; and precision production. From 1982–83: Includes visual and performing arts, general; crafts, folk art, and artisanry; dance; design and applied art; theatre arts and stagecraft; film/video and photographic arts; fine arts and art studies; music; and visual performing arts, other.

SOURCE: U.S. Department of Education, National Center for Education Statistics, "Degrees and Other Formal Awards Conferred" surveys, and Integrated Postsecondary Education Data System (IPEDS), "Completions" surveys. (This table was prepared January 1995.)

Table 290.—Statistical profile of persons receiving doctor's degrees,[1] by field of study: 1992–93

Item	All fields	Education	Engineering	Humanities	Life sciences	Physical sciences [2] Total	Mathematics	Business and management	Social sciences and psychology	Other professional fields
1	2	3	4	5	6	7	8	9	10	11
Doctor's degrees conferred (number)	**39,754**	**6,647**	**5,696**	**4,481**	**7,397**	**6,496**	**1,146**	**1,280**	**6,545**	**1,212**
Sex (percent)										
Men	62.0	41.3	90.9	52.5	58.3	79.3	77.0	72.3	50.7	55.4
Women	38.0	58.7	9.1	47.5	41.7	20.7	23.0	27.7	49.3	44.6
Racial/ethnic group (percent) [3]										
American Indian	0.4	0.8	0.1	0.3	0.3	0.3	0.2	0.6	0.4	0.5
Asian	7.1	2.4	19.7	3.6	8.7	11.4	13.6	8.2	4.0	4.3
Black	4.5	9.4	1.9	3.0	2.9	1.5	1.4	3.1	4.7	8.4
Hispanic	3.4	3.7	2.4	4.2	3.0	3.0	2.8	1.7	4.1	3.2
White	84.6	83.7	75.9	88.9	85.1	83.8	82.1	86.5	86.9	83.6
Citizenship (percent)										
United States	66.4	86.4	39.1	78.3	65.3	53.5	43.3	59.7	75.5	73.9
Non-U.S., permanent visa	5.7	2.6	8.2	6.0	5.7	7.0	8.2	6.0	4.9	5.6
Non-U.S., temporary visa	25.0	8.2	48.9	12.7	26.9	36.4	45.1	30.7	16.4	17.1
Unknown	3.0	2.7	3.9	3.0	2.2	3.1	3.4	3.6	3.1	3.4
Median age at doctorate (years)	34.1	43.0	31.6	35.6	32.5	30.9	31.1	35.5	34.3	39.4
Percent with bachelor's degree in same field as doctorate	55.6	37.4	80.1	56.4	51.9	67.9	73.3	36.6	53.7	25.9
Median time lapse from bachelor's to doctorate (years)										
Total time	10.5	19.2	8.8	11.9	9.4	8.3	8.5	11.9	10.4	14.8
Registered time	7.1	8.2	6.3	8.3	6.8	6.5	6.7	7.2	7.5	7.8
Postdoctoral plans (percent)										
Postdoctoral study plans	26.4	4.1	25.1	7.3	58.6	43.8	24.3	2.7	18.2	5.8
Fellowship	13.8	1.8	8.5	4.1	34.6	19.8	12.7	0.8	12.3	3.1
Research associateship	10.1	1.2	15.1	1.0	17.8	22.4	9.0	1.2	3.5	1.4
Traineeship	0.9	0.3	0.8	0.4	1.6	0.8	1.4	0.6	1.3	0.8
Other	1.6	0.7	0.6	1.8	4.6	0.8	1.3	0.2	1.1	0.4
Postdoctoral employment	65.6	87.5	66.7	84.1	35.3	47.9	66.1	89.7	73.3	84.1
Educational institution [4]	39.3	67.7	20.5	70.4	17.5	20.6	48.6	74.7	39.4	52.9
Industry, business	12.9	4.6	34.0	3.7	7.6	19.8	10.0	9.6	10.5	6.7
Government	5.4	5.8	6.8	1.5	5.4	3.5	2.3	2.0	8.3	7.6
Nonprofit organization	3.4	3.8	1.1	3.6	2.1	0.7	1.0	0.8	7.8	12.1
Other and unknown	4.6	5.5	4.4	5.0	2.8	3.3	4.2	2.6	7.2	4.9
Postdoctoral plans unknown	8.0	8.5	8.3	8.6	6.1	8.3	9.6	7.6	8.5	10.1
Definite postdoctoral study	17.6	1.9	12.7	3.8	43.5	29.8	14.4	0.9	12.0	2.8
Seeking postdoctoral study	8.8	2.2	12.4	3.5	15.1	14.0	9.9	1.8	6.2	2.8
Definite employment	43.4	64.1	37.5	51.1	24.3	30.1	39.1	71.1	47.9	61.3
Seeking employment	22.2	23.3	29.2	33.1	11.0	17.8	27.0	18.6	25.3	22.9
Primary postdoctoral activity (percent) [5]										
Research and development	27.1	5.7	63.4	7.7	42.9	55.1	34.8	26.9	23.1	11.7
Teaching	33.4	31.2	15.3	65.3	25.7	25.3	46.2	51.0	27.1	44.4
Administration	11.4	32.5	2.1	4.0	6.7	1.2	0.9	3.8	4.8	14.7
Professional services	10.3	8.1	5.2	3.0	9.7	4.7	4.7	2.2	27.5	11.7
Other	2.7	2.2	2.8	3.2	3.4	1.8	1.3	2.0	2.8	4.3
Activity unknown	15.1	20.1	11.2	16.7	11.6	11.8	12.1	14.1	14.7	13.1
Region of employment after doctorate (percent) [5]										
New England	5.8	5.2	6.2	7.1	4.5	6.9	4.9	5.5	5.8	4.7
Middle Atlantic	13.4	12.5	11.9	15.0	10.1	15.5	12.1	12.5	15.0	13.9
East North Central	12.8	13.6	11.5	14.5	11.2	12.9	15.0	13.1	12.3	12.7
West North Central	6.9	8.5	4.4	7.2	6.3	6.2	6.0	7.0	6.9	6.4
South Atlantic	15.4	17.8	11.0	15.6	15.7	13.0	16.5	15.4	16.4	14.4
East South Central	4.4	5.4	4.1	4.7	4.5	3.6	3.8	5.1	3.0	4.7
West South Central	8.3	10.3	6.5	8.1	8.2	6.5	5.6	10.1	6.4	13.2
Mountain	4.7	5.0	5.8	4.2	4.4	5.2	6.0	4.2	4.3	3.8
Pacific and insular	11.0	10.6	13.0	10.5	11.0	11.7	9.6	7.5	11.9	8.1
U.S., region unknown	3.9	5.0	2.5	3.3	3.8	3.5	2.7	2.9	4.4	3.7
Foreign	13.1	5.7	22.6	9.4	19.9	14.8	17.4	16.6	13.4	14.1
Region unknown	0.3	0.2	0.5	0.3	0.4	0.3	0.4	0.2	0.3	0.2

[1] Includes Ph.D., Ed.D., and comparable degrees at the doctoral level. Excludes first-professional degrees, such as M.D., D.D.S., and D.V.M.

[2] Includes mathematics, computer science, physics, astronomy, chemistry, and earth, atmospheric, and marine sciences.

[3] Distribution by race/ethnicity based on U.S. citizens and those with permanent visas only.

[4] Includes 2–year, 4–year, and foreign colleges and universities, medical schools, and elementary/secondary schools.

[5] Includes only recipients with definite employment plans.

NOTE.—The above classification of degrees by field differs somewhat from that in most publications of the National Center for Education Statistics (NCES). The major differences are that history is included under humanities rather than social sciences and that psychology is included under social sciences. The number of degrees also differs slightly from that reported in the NCES "Degrees and Other Formal Awards Conferred" survey. The above tabulation excludes some non-research doctorate degrees such as doctor's degrees in theology. Because of rounding, percents may not add to 100.0.

SOURCE: National Academy of Sciences, National Research Council, Office of Scientific and Engineering Personnel, *Summary Report 1993: Doctorate Recipients from United States Universities.* (This table was prepared June 1995.)

Table 291.—Statistical profile of persons receiving doctor's degrees in education: 1979–80 to 1992–93

Item	1979–80	1980–81	1981–82	1982–83	1983–84	1984–85	1985–86	1986–87	1987–88	1988–89	1989–90	1990–91	1991–92	1992–93
1	2	3	4	5	6	7	8	9	10	11	12	13	14	15
Number of doctorates	7,576	7,489	7,226	7,147	6,780	6,717	6,602	6,447	6,349	6,265	6,484	6,397	6,622	6,647
Sex (percent)														
Men	55.5	52.8	51.2	49.6	49.0	48.2	45.6	44.9	44.8	42.5	42.4	41.9	40.5	41.3
Women	44.5	47.2	48.8	50.4	51.0	51.8	54.4	55.1	55.2	57.5	57.6	58.1	59.5	58.7
Racial/ethnic group (percent) [1]														
American Indian	0.8	0.6	0.5	0.7	0.5	0.7	0.5	0.7	0.6	0.4	0.6	1.0	0.8	0.8
Asian	1.3	1.9	1.7	1.9	1.5	1.7	1.6	1.7	2.4	1.9	1.8	2.2	2.4	2.4
Black	9.1	9.1	9.7	8.2	8.7	8.7	8.1	7.4	7.6	8.1	8.2	7.9	8.4	9.4
Hispanic	2.4	2.5	3.0	2.9	2.6	3.2	3.7	3.6	2.9	3.1	3.3	3.3	3.5	3.7
White	86.3	85.9	85.1	86.2	86.7	85.6	86.1	86.6	86.4	86.5	86.0	85.6	84.8	83.7
Citizenship (percent)														
United States	88.7	87.7	86.6	87.1	86.8	85.5	84.7	84.9	83.1	82.9	84.4	84.8	86.8	86.4
Foreign	8.2	8.8	9.9	9.8	9.8	10.4	9.6	9.2	10.2	9.7	9.7	10.2	10.7	10.8
Unknown	3.1	3.6	3.5	3.1	3.4	4.1	5.6	6.0	6.7	7.4	5.8	5.0	2.4	2.7
Median age at doctorate (years)	37.0	37.3	37.4	37.8	38.4	38.7	39.4	39.8	40.5	41.1	41.6	42.1	42.7	43.0
Percent with bachelor's degree in same field as doctorate	39.0	38.9	39.9	39.5	39.6	38.7	39.0	37.8	36.9	38.5	37.5	39.3	38.7	37.4
Median time lapse from bachelor's to doctorate (years)														
Total time	13.1	13.5	13.6	14.1	14.6	15.1	15.7	16.2	16.9	17.3	17.9	18.4	18.9	19.2
Registered time	6.9	7.0	7.2	7.4	7.6	7.6	7.8	7.9	8.1	8.2	8.1	8.1	8.2	8.2

[1] Longitudinal comparisons by race/ethnicity should be done with extreme care, due to periodic changes in the survey. Distribution by race/ethnicity based on U.S. citizens and those with permanent visas only.

NOTE.—The National Research Council's classification of degrees by field differs somewhat from that in most publications of the National Center for Education Statistics (NCES). The number of degrees also differs slightly from that reported in the NCES "Completions" survey. Because of rounding, percents may not add to 100.0.

SOURCE: National Academy of Sciences, National Research Council, Office of Scientific and Engineering Personnel, Doctorate Records File. (This table was prepared May 1995.)

Table 292.—Statistical profile of persons receiving doctor's degrees in engineering: 1979–80 to 1992–93

Item	1979–80	1980–81	1981–82	1982–83	1983–84	1984–85	1985–86	1986–87	1987–88	1988–89	1989–90	1990–91	1991–92	1992–93
1	2	3	4	5	6	7	8	9	10	11	12	13	14	15
Number of doctorates	2,479	2,528	2,644	2,780	2,915	3,165	3,376	3,716	4,190	4,536	4,892	5,212	5,437	5,696
Sex (percent)														
Men	96.4	96.1	95.3	95.5	94.8	93.7	93.3	93.5	93.2	91.8	91.5	91.3	90.7	90.9
Women	3.6	3.9	4.7	4.5	5.2	6.3	6.7	6.6	6.8	8.2	8.5	8.7	9.3	9.1
Racial/ethnic group (percent) [1]														
American Indian	0.2	0.3	0.2	0.1	0.2	0.1	0.3	0.4	0.2	0.3	0.2	0.3	0.4	0.1
Asian	18.9	20.0	17.5	17.3	17.1	18.4	15.6	17.7	16.0	16.6	15.3	17.4	18.2	19.7
Black	1.2	1.4	1.5	2.0	1.0	2.2	1.4	1.3	1.4	1.4	1.8	2.4	1.9	1.9
Hispanic	1.9	1.0	2.5	2.1	2.4	1.5	2.1	1.8	3.0	2.2	2.4	2.6	3.0	2.4
White	77.8	77.3	78.3	78.6	79.3	77.8	80.6	78.8	79.4	79.5	80.4	77.4	76.5	75.9
Citizenship (percent)														
United States	50.6	46.2	44.1	41.8	42.5	40.4	40.8	41.8	42.4	40.9	39.4	37.9	38.7	39.1
Foreign	46.3	49.1	50.1	53.5	52.9	54.6	50.8	50.7	49.8	50.4	52.5	54.7	57.8	57.1
Unknown	3.1	4.7	5.9	4.7	4.6	5.0	8.4	7.4	7.7	8.8	8.1	7.3	3.5	3.9
Median age at doctorate (years)	30.3	30.5	30.7	30.8	30.7	30.9	31.0	31.0	31.0	31.1	31.2	31.4	31.5	31.6
Percent with bachelor's degree in same field as doctorate	75.2	74.1	72.4	74.0	74.3	74.2	73.0	75.2	76.4	76.2	76.9	79.0	81.8	80.1
Median time lapse from bachelor's to doctorate (years)														
Total time	7.6	7.9	8.0	8.0	8.0	8.1	8.1	8.1	8.1	8.1	8.2	8.5	8.7	8.8
Registered time	5.6	5.6	5.8	5.7	5.8	5.8	5.9	5.9	5.9	6.0	6.0	6.1	6.2	6.3

[1] Longitudinal comparisons by race/ethnicity should be done with extreme care, due to periodic changes in the survey. Distribution by race/ethnicity based on U.S. citizens and those with permanent visas only.

NOTE.—The National Research Council's classification of degrees by field differs somewhat from that in most publications of the National Center for Education Statistics (NCES). The number of degrees also differs slightly from that reported in the NCES "Completions" survey. Because of rounding, percents may not add to 100.0.

SOURCE: National Academy of Sciences, National Research Council, Office of Scientific and Engineering Personnel, Doctorate Records File. (This table was prepared May 1995.)

Table 293.—Statistical profile of persons receiving doctor's degrees in the humanities: [1] **1979–80 to 1992–93**

Item	1979–80	1980–81	1981–82	1982–83	1983–84	1984–85	1985–86	1986–87	1987–88	1988–89	1989–90	1990–91	1991–92	1992–93
1	2	3	4	5	6	7	8	9	10	11	12	13	14	15
Number of doctorates	3,863	3,745	3,560	3,494	3,528	3,428	3,461	3,504	3,553	3,558	3,820	4,094	4,444	4,481
Sex (percent)														
Men	60.4	58.7	57.6	56.2	55.0	56.6	54.8	55.1	55.7	54.5	54.4	53.5	53.7	52.5
Women	39.6	41.3	42.4	43.8	45.0	43.4	45.2	44.9	44.3	45.5	45.6	46.5	46.3	47.5
Racial/ethnic group (percent) [2]														
American Indian	0.3	0.4	0.2	0.2	0.2	0.3	0.2	0.4	0.2	0.2	0.3	0.3	0.5	0.3
Asian	2.0	1.8	1.7	1.5	1.8	2.3	1.8	2.1	2.3	3.0	2.4	2.5	3.0	3.6
Black	3.0	2.9	3.4	2.6	3.4	2.6	2.9	2.9	3.0	2.9	2.3	3.0	2.7	3.0
Hispanic	3.0	3.2	4.3	3.7	3.7	3.8	3.5	4.3	3.9	3.8	4.2	4.3	3.9	4.2
White	91.6	91.7	90.3	92.0	90.9	91.1	91.6	90.3	90.5	90.2	90.9	89.9	89.9	88.9
Citizenship (percent)														
United States	87.3	85.7	84.7	85.3	83.7	83.1	78.8	78.0	78.4	76.4	78.3	77.0	77.7	78.3
Foreign	8.8	10.2	10.2	10.7	11.2	12.1	13.7	14.3	14.4	15.5	15.2	18.3	19.2	18.7
Unknown	3.9	4.1	5.1	4.0	5.2	4.8	7.4	7.7	7.1	8.1	6.5	4.7	3.2	3.0
Median age at doctorate (years)	33.4	33.5	34.0	34.0	34.5	34.7	35.0	35.0	35.4	35.7	35.7	35.8	35.6	35.6
Percent with bachelor's degree in same field as doctorate	64.2	61.0	61.1	58.4	60.2	58.8	58.2	58.5	56.7	55.5	57.1	57.7	56.5	56.4
Median time lapse from bachelor's to doctorate (years)														
Total time	10.6	10.8	11.2	11.1	11.5	11.7	12.1	12.0	12.2	12.5	12.2	12.3	12.0	11.9
Registered time	7.7	7.7	8.0	8.0	8.2	8.3	8.2	8.4	8.5	8.4	8.3	8.4	8.3	8.3

[1] Includes American studies, archeology, art history, classics, history, letters, literature, music, philosophy, religion, and theatre.

[2] Longitudinal comparisons by race/ethnicity should be done with extreme care, due to periodic changes in the survey. Distribution by race/ethnicity based on U.S. citizens and those with permanent visas only.

NOTE.—The National Research Council's classification of degrees by field differs somewhat from that in most publications of the National Center for Education Statistics (NCES). The major differences are that history is included under humanities rather than social sciences and that psychology is included under social sciences. The number of degrees also differs slightly from that reported in the NCES "Completions" survey. Because of rounding, percents may not add to 100.0.

SOURCE: National Academy of Sciences, National Research Council, Office of Scientific and Engineering Personnel, Doctorate Records File. (This table was prepared May 1995.)

Table 294.—Statistical profile of persons receiving doctor's degrees in the life sciences: [1] **1979–80 to 1992–93**

Item	1979–80	1980–81	1981–82	1982–83	1983–84	1984–85	1985–86	1986–87	1987–88	1988–89	1989–90	1990–91	1991–92	1992–93
1	2	3	4	5	6	7	8	9	10	11	12	13	14	15
Number of doctorates	5,325	5,461	5,565	5,540	5,745	5,748	5,720	5,742	6,143	6,343	6,613	6,928	7,108	7,397
Sex (percent)														
Men	74.8	73.6	72.3	69.0	68.9	67.7	66.0	64.8	63.2	61.8	62.6	61.4	60.7	58.3
Women	25.2	26.4	27.7	31.0	31.1	32.3	34.0	35.2	36.8	38.2	37.4	38.6	39.3	41.7
Racial/ethnic group (percent) [2]														
American Indian	0.2	0.2	0.3	0.2	0.3	0.4	0.5	0.4	0.4	0.3	0.2	0.4	0.4	0.3
Asian	5.3	4.8	4.6	5.3	4.7	4.7	4.9	5.7	5.0	5.3	5.6	6.6	7.1	8.7
Black	1.6	1.9	1.5	1.6	2.1	2.1	1.9	2.5	2.2	2.1	1.9	2.4	2.3	2.9
Hispanic	1.1	1.4	1.5	1.2	1.4	1.9	2.1	2.0	2.3	2.1	2.7	2.6	2.8	3.0
White	91.8	91.7	92.0	91.6	91.5	90.8	90.5	89.4	90.0	90.1	89.6	88.0	87.3	85.1
Citizenship (percent)														
United States	80.4	80.3	80.4	79.9	79.4	77.1	75.9	73.5	71.3	71.1	68.0	66.8	65.7	65.3
Foreign	17.6	17.1	16.6	17.4	17.6	19.3	18.8	20.5	22.2	22.1	26.3	29.1	31.8	32.6
Unknown	2.0	2.6	3.0	2.6	3.0	3.6	5.3	6.1	6.4	6.9	5.6	4.0	2.5	2.2
Median age at doctorate (years)	30.0	30.1	30.3	30.6	31.0	31.3	31.6	31.7	31.9	32.2	32.3	32.4	32.7	32.5
Percent with bachelor's degree in same field as doctorate	40.9	40.7	41.4	56.3	58.1	58.3	57.1	55.6	55.4	53.4	53.8	54.1	53.5	51.9
Median time lapse from bachelor's to doctorate (years)														
Total time	7.3	7.3	7.6	7.9	8.2	8.4	8.7	8.7	8.9	9.1	9.1	9.1	9.4	9.4
Registered time	5.8	5.9	6.0	6.1	6.3	6.3	6.4	6.5	6.5	6.5	6.7	6.7	6.7	6.8

[1] Includes agricultural, biological, and health sciences.

[2] Longitudinal comparisons by race/ethnicity should be done with extreme care, due to periodic changes in the survey. Distribution by race/ethnicity based on U.S. citizens and those with permanent visas only.

NOTE.—The National Research Council's classification of degrees by field differs somewhat from that in most publications of the National Center for Education Statistics (NCES). The number of degrees also differs slightly from that reported in the NCES "Completions" survey. Because of rounding, percents may not add to 100.0.

SOURCE: National Academy of Sciences, National Research Council, Office of Scientific and Engineering Personnel, Doctorate Records File. (This table was prepared May 1995.)

Table 295.—Statistical profile of persons receiving doctor's degrees in the physical sciences:[1] 1979–80 to 1992–93

Item	1979–80	1980–81	1981–82	1982–83	1983–84	1984–85	1985–86	1986–87	1987–88	1988–89	1989–90	1990–91	1991–92	1992–93
1	2	3	4	5	6	7	8	9	10	11	12	13	14	15
Number of doctorates	**3,151**	**3,208**	**3,348**	**3,438**	**3,459**	**3,531**	**3,679**	**3,837**	**4,046**	**3,987**	**4,263**	**4,439**	**4,573**	**4,472**
Sex (percent)														
Men	87.7	88.7	86.3	86.4	85.4	83.7	83.6	83.3	82.6	80.9	81.2	81.0	79.1	69.9
Women	12.3	11.3	13.7	13.6	14.6	16.3	16.4	16.7	17.4	19.1	18.8	19.0	20.9	30.1
Racial/ethnic group (percent)[2]														
American Indian	0.2	0.1	0.2	0.3	0.2	0.1	0.2	0.3	0.3	0.6	0.1	0.5	0.5	0.3
Asian	7.7	6.9	6.2	6.6	6.6	6.9	7.1	7.0	5.7	6.7	6.6	6.6	8.9	10.2
Black	1.0	1.3	1.1	1.0	1.3	1.2	1.0	1.0	1.3	1.3	1.0	1.2	1.1	1.6
Hispanic	1.1	1.3	1.2	1.3	2.0	1.7	2.1	2.4	2.6	2.6	3.1	2.9	3.2	3.4
White	90.0	90.5	91.2	90.7	89.9	90.1	89.5	89.3	90.1	88.8	89.3	88.8	86.4	84.5
Citizenship (percent)														
United States	75.9	75.4	75.0	74.0	73.6	70.3	66.1	65.1	64.3	62.5	61.0	59.3	57.9	57.1
Foreign	21.6	21.3	21.9	23.1	23.5	25.5	27.8	28.5	28.8	29.8	32.4	35.9	39.6	39.7
Unknown	2.4	3.3	3.1	2.9	2.9	4.1	6.1	6.4	6.9	7.8	6.7	4.8	2.5	3.2
Median age at doctorate (years)	29.1	29.0	29.2	29.3	29.5	29.5	29.9	29.8	30.1	30.0	30.7	30.2	30.3	30.6
Percent with bachelor's degree in same field as doctorate	76.5	76.6	77.2	75.4	77.7	75.0	73.4	72.6	72.6	72.6	80.0	76.9	74.5	72.9
Median time lapse from bachelor's to doctorate (years)														
Total time	6.8	6.7	6.8	7.0	7.0	7.1	7.1	7.1	7.2	7.2	7.8	7.5	7.8	8.0
Registered time	5.7	5.7	5.8	5.9	6.0	6.0	6.0	5.9	6.1	6.0	6.3	6.2	6.4	6.4

[1] Includes physics, astronomy, chemistry, and earth, atmospheric, and marine sciences. Excludes mathematics and computer science.

[2] Longitudinal comparisons by race/ethnicity should be done with extreme care, due to periodic changes in the survey. Distribution by race/ethnicity based on U.S. citizens and those with permanent visas only.

NOTE.—The National Research Council's classification of degrees by field differs somewhat from that in most publications of the National Center for Education Statistics (NCES). The number of degrees also differs slightly from that reported in the NCES "Completions" survey. Because of rounding, percents may not add to 100.0.

SOURCE: National Academy of Sciences, National Research Council, Office of Scientific and Engineering Personnel, Doctorate Records File. (This table was prepared May 1995.)

Table 296.—Statistical profile of persons receiving doctor's degrees in the social sciences:[1] 1979–80 to 1992–93

Item	1979–80	1980–81	1981–82	1982–83	1983–84	1984–85	1985–86	1986–87	1987–88	1988–89	1989–90	1990–91	1991–92	1992–93
1	2	3	4	5	6	7	8	9	10	11	12	13	14	15
Number of doctorates	**6,253**	**6,505**	**6,250**	**6,055**	**5,895**	**5,720**	**5,841**	**5,718**	**5,769**	**5,955**	**6,076**	**6,127**	**6,205**	**6,545**
Sex (percent)														
Men	65.4	64.4	63.3	60.7	59.2	58.9	57.6	57.2	55.0	54.8	53.7	50.6	52.6	50.7
Women	34.6	35.6	36.7	39.3	40.8	41.1	42.4	42.8	45.0	45.2	46.3	49.4	47.4	49.3
Racial/ethnic group (percent)[2]														
American Indian	0.3	0.2	0.4	0.2	0.2	0.4	0.4	0.5	0.3	0.4	0.5	0.4	0.5	0.4
Asian	2.8	2.5	2.5	2.2	2.5	2.6	2.6	3.2	3.3	3.1	3.0	3.3	3.6	4.0
Black	4.2	4.0	4.7	3.9	4.6	4.4	4.1	3.8	4.4	4.4	4.4	4.9	4.5	4.7
Hispanic	2.0	2.3	2.7	3.0	2.8	2.9	3.3	3.6	3.3	3.3	3.9	4.2	3.8	4.1
White	90.7	91.0	89.8	90.7	90.0	89.8	89.7	89.0	88.8	88.7	88.2	87.2	87.7	86.9
Citizenship (percent)														
United States	84.7	84.0	81.8	82.9	80.6	79.3	77.9	76.1	74.8	70.4	73.8	73.4	74.3	75.5
Foreign	11.6	11.9	12.6	12.5	14.1	15.3	15.3	15.7	16.1	17.3	18.0	19.8	21.2	21.3
Unknown	3.7	4.2	5.6	4.5	5.4	5.4	6.9	8.3	9.1	12.2	8.2	6.8	4.4	3.1
Median age at doctorate (years)	31.6	32.0	32.3	32.4	32.7	33.0	33.4	33.5	34.1	33.9	34.2	34.1	34.3	34.3
Percent with bachelor's degree in same field as doctorate	58.6	59.1	57.4	58.9	59.3	58.5	57.0	56.4	54.5	52.3	55.4	54.2	53.1	53.7
Median time lapse from bachelor's to doctorate (years)														
Total time	8.7	9.0	9.2	9.3	9.7	9.9	10.0	10.3	10.5	10.3	10.6	10.5	10.6	10.4
Registered time	6.4	6.5	6.7	6.8	7.1	7.1	7.2	7.4	7.4	7.4	7.5	7.5	7.5	7.5

[1] Includes anthropology, area studies, criminology, economics, geography, political science, public policy, psychology, and sociology.

[2] Longitudinal comparisons by race/ethnicity should be done with extreme care, due to periodic changes in the survey. Distribution by race/ethnicity based on U.S. citizens and those with permanent visas only.

NOTE.—The National Research Council's classification of degrees by field differs somewhat from that in most publications of the National Center for Education Statistics (NCES). The major differences are that history is included under humanities rather than social sciences and that psychology is included under social sciences. The number of degrees also differs slightly from that reported in the NCES "Completions" survey. Because of rounding, percents may not add to 100.0.

SOURCE: National Academy of Sciences, National Research Council, Office of Scientific and Engineering Personnel, Doctorate Records File. (This table was prepared May 1995.)

Table 297.—Doctor's degrees [1] conferred by 60 large institutions of higher education: 1983–84 to 1992–93

Institution	Rank order [2]	Total, 1983–84 to 1992–93	1983–84	1984–85	1985–86	1986–87	1987–88	1988–89	1989–90	1990–91	1991–92	1992–93
1	2	3	4	5	6	7	8	9	10	11	12	13
United States, all institutions	—	364,892	33,209	32,943	33,653	34,041	34,870	35,720	38,371	39,294	40,659	42,132
Total, 60 large institutions	—	212,469	19,535	19,409	19,547	19,884	20,320	20,984	22,182	22,919	23,469	24,220
University of California-Berkeley	1	7,655	698	689	753	727	742	838	800	800	798	810
University of Wisconsin-Madison	2	6,709	630	674	606	667	684	667	717	708	680	676
University of Illinois, Urbana Campus	3	6,553	538	622	560	616	646	647	707	737	775	705
Columbia University in the City of New York [3]	4	6,455	603	625	610	593	567	615	723	802	630	687
University of Michigan-Ann Arbor	5	6,197	738	607	598	589	564	527	583	661	676	654
University of Texas at Austin	6	5,943	427	474	545	612	588	583	647	710	671	686
Ohio State University-Main Campus	7	5,900	521	543	512	570	542	608	604	644	671	685
University of Minnesota, Twin Cities	8	5,761	495	515	556	508	527	543	633	706	651	627
Stanford University (Calif.)	9	5,355	497	497	530	562	560	540	532	487	569	581
University of California-Los Angeles	10	5,148	465	449	433	448	508	459	558	558	613	657
Cornell University (N.Y.) [4]	11	4,847	432	433	456	445	454	481	555	531	540	520
Massachusetts Institute of Technology	12	4,819	415	447	455	458	516	492	509	497	514	516
Harvard University (Mass.)	13	4,705	457	385	452	434	465	461	505	505	501	540
Michigan State University	14	4,269	395	405	438	464	427	434	432	397	476	401
Purdue University-Main Campus (Ind.)	15	4,186	383	389	379	370	366	420	467	430	478	504
University of Maryland, College Park Campus	16	4,182	387	373	370	378	364	393	468	453	506	490
Pennsylvania State University-Main Campus	17	4,141	364	371	350	341	379	417	420	463	541	495
University of Pennsylvania	18	4,094	406	367	341	307	319	414	462	495	477	506
University of Washington	19	3,979	358	342	345	411	392	403	457	459	396	416
New York University	20	3,967	418	391	377	392	421	376	392	392	404	404
Texas A & M University	21	3,945	298	315	336	369	382	420	411	446	472	496
University of Southern California	22	3,906	424	424	363	354	354	429	429	359	355	415
University of Pittsburgh-Main Campus	23	3,685	389	398	390	394	390	367	337	344	343	333
Indiana University, Bloomington	24	3,582	417	397	353	374	319	313	321	342	398	348
Rutgers University, New Brunswick (N.J.)	25	3,429	362	343	320	320	311	327	342	326	402	376
University of Florida	26	3,327	294	301	290	313	315	342	366	370	364	372
University of Massachusetts at Amherst	27	3,320	268	300	290	311	281	329	362	400	409	370
Northwestern University (Ill.)	28	3,287	310	326	312	319	313	358	327	308	351	363
University of Chicago (Ill.)	29	3,216	329	291	329	319	318	310	335	317	322	346
University of Georgia	30	3,193	270	355	309	275	316	340	313	332	331	352
University of North Carolina at Chapel Hill	31	3,136	283	260	283	311	301	299	337	336	338	388
Yale University (Conn.)	32	3,118	299	276	259	305	290	317	312	344	347	369
University of Arizona	33	3,112	259	261	260	298	290	326	311	382	352	373
Virginia Polytechnic Institute and State University	34	3,099	271	260	274	295	287	303	342	332	366	369
University of Iowa	35	3,071	273	284	258	287	312	287	299	360	380	331
Nova University (Fla.)	36	2,926	210	209	263	271	292	306	316	290	336	433
Boston University (Mass.)	37	2,850	333	276	307	299	245	304	277	258	280	271
Iowa State University	38	2,769	228	245	256	296	309	257	282	297	277	322
Temple University (Pa.)	39	2,700	243	264	277	290	277	285	249	251	282	282
City University of New York Graduate School and University Center	40	2,535	200	234	232	232	258	225	259	320	257	318
Johns Hopkins University (Md.)	41	2,535	212	254	220	213	267	229	240	285	297	318
Florida State University	42	2,530	273	257	224	226	250	246	249	257	286	262
University of California-Davis	43	2,515	253	224	245	228	238	221	258	258	284	306
University of Virginia-Main Campus	44	2,467	190	221	217	218	229	242	253	291	291	315
State University of New York at Buffalo	45	2,455	208	194	206	209	240	274	249	265	290	320
North Carolina State University at Raleigh	46	2,408	210	204	219	200	239	224	294	256	279	283
University of Colorado at Boulder	47	2,394	258	198	198	229	231	221	248	263	249	299
Princeton University (N.J.)	48	2,355	226	211	216	218	269	227	240	244	255	249
University of Missouri-Columbia	49	2,287	245	230	202	181	227	236	236	212	258	260
University of Tennessee-Knoxville	50	2,275	250	223	233	206	217	209	214	214	260	249
Oklahoma State University-Main Campus	51	2,068	197	220	224	189	184	211	229	206	183	225
University of Cincinnati-Main Campus (Ohio)	52	2,002	202	171	187	182	188	182	213	231	220	226
University of South Carolina at Columbia	53	1,977	138	156	168	169	191	169	215	248	242	281
University of Rochester (N.Y.)	54	1,965	154	168	195	198	167	208	226	194	231	224
State University of New York at Stony Brook	55	1,958	169	147	144	156	196	190	200	248	225	283
University of Oregon	56	1,915	208	173	197	140	167	196	184	196	217	237
Wayne State University	57	1,895	147	150	156	123	137	193	178	290	222	299
University of California, San Diego	58	1,895	166	151	163	163	186	189	185	185	227	280
Arizona State University-Main Campus	59	1,823	130	128	157	146	158	194	191	227	222	270
University of Illinois at Chicago	60	1,679	112	112	149	166	148	161	182	200	202	247

[1] Includes Ph.D., Ed.D., and comparable degrees at the doctoral level. Excludes first-professional degrees (e.g., M.D., D.D.S., and D.V.M.).
[2] Institutions are ranked by the total number of doctor's degrees conferred during the designated 10-year period.
[3] Includes degrees conferred by the Main Division and Teachers College.
[4] Includes degrees conferred by the Endowed and Statutory Colleges.

—Not applicable.

SOURCE: U.S. Department of Education, National Center for Education Statistics, Higher Education General Information Survey (HEGIS), "Degrees and Other Formal Awards Conferred" survey, and Integrated Postsecondary Education Data System (IPEDS), "Completions" survey. (This table was prepared February 1995.)

Table 298.—Percentage distribution of 1980 high school sophomores by the timing of their first postsecondary enrollment, by selected characteristics: 1982 to 1992

Student and institution characteristics	All 1980 sophomores	Never enrolled	Before November 1982	November 1982 to May 1983	June 1983 to May 1984	June 1984 to May 1985	June 1985 to May 1986	June 1986 to May 1987	June 1987 to May 1988	June 1988 to May 1989	June 1989 to May 1990	June 1990 to May 1991	June 1991 or later
1	2	3	4	5	6	7	8	9	10	11	12	13	14
Total	100.0	35.5	44.1	3.5	6.5	2.7	2.4	1.3	1.1	0.9	1.0	0.6	0.5
College expectations in sixth grade													
Decided to go	100.0	18.0	64.4	3.4	6.1	2.1	2.3	1.2	0.7	0.8	0.5	0.3	0.2
Planned not to go	100.0	54.4	24.6	3.3	6.4	2.6	2.6	1.4	1.4	0.9	1.0	0.9	0.6
Not sure	100.0	35.9	43.7	4.3	6.5	2.6	2.0	1.5	1.0	0.4	1.3	0.6	0.3
Hadn't thought about it	100.0	30.6	46.3	4.2	6.4	3.7	2.8	1.4	1.1	1.3	1.2	0.5	0.5
Postsecondary expectations in 1982													
None	100.0	75.7	4.7	1.8	4.5	2.5	3.0	1.5	1.6	1.3	1.5	1.0	0.9
Vocational/technical	100.0	43.6	27.1	5.5	8.7	4.2	3.6	1.8	1.6	1.6	1.1	0.7	0.5
Less-than-4-year degree	100.0	23.5	51.8	5.2	8.8	2.9	2.9	1.3	1.0	0.6	1.0	0.4	0.7
Bachelor's degree	100.0	9.0	76.7	3.1	5.0	2.2	1.4	1.3	0.4	0.6	0.3	0.1	0.1
Advanced degree	100.0	7.3	80.4	2.5	5.5	1.5	1.2	0.4	0.4	0.2	0.4	0.2	—
First postsecondary institution type													
Never enrolled	100.0	100.0	—	—	—	—	—	—	—	—	—	—	—
Private for-profit	100.0	—	39.6	10.1	15.8	10.7	7.8	3.6	4.1	1.1	3.9	2.3	1.0
Private not-for-profit less-than-4-year	100.0	—	66.2	3.8	15.0	5.9	2.7	0.3	0.3	2.4	2.7	0.9	—
Public less-than-2-year	100.0	—	48.5	8.3	13.6	8.8	7.2	4.7	2.6	0.7	3.5	1.6	0.4
Public 2-year	100.0	—	58.6	7.7	12.5	4.5	5.2	2.4	2.2	2.5	1.8	1.3	1.2
Public 4-year	100.0	—	84.5	2.2	6.4	2.2	1.3	1.2	0.5	0.8	0.4	0.4	0.2
Private not-for-profit 4-year	100.0	—	86.9	2.3	5.3	1.7	1.2	0.9	0.7	0.3	0.2	0.1	0.5
Number of applications to college in 1982													
Did not apply	100.0	56.3	17.9	3.7	7.8	3.4	3.5	1.8	1.6	1.3	1.3	0.9	0.6
1 college	100.0	9.9	77.0	3.8	4.6	1.6	1.1	0.6	0.3	0.3	0.3	0.3	0.2
2 or 3 colleges	100.0	5.6	82.7	2.8	3.9	2.3	1.0	0.7	0.2	0.5	0.3	—	0.1
4 or more colleges	100.0	5.0	89.9	0.7	3.2	0.3	0.8	—	0.1	—	—	0.1	—
Accepted at 1982 first choice college													
No applications	100.0	62.4	10.2	3.3	7.1	4.0	4.1	2.1	1.9	1.7	1.4	1.1	0.9
Attended first choice	100.0	—	89.7	3.8	5.0	0.8	0.3	0.2	0.1	—	0.1	0.1	—
Accepted, but did not attend first choice	100.0	23.3	51.0	5.3	8.2	4.3	2.3	1.8	1.2	1.0	0.9	0.4	0.3
Was not accepted at first choice	100.0	12.8	73.1	2.7	7.1	1.9	1.0	0.4	0.1	0.4	—	0.5	—

—Data not available or not applicable.

NOTE.—Because of rounding, details may not add to 100.0 percent.

SOURCE: National Center for Education Statistics, *High School and Beyond, Educational Attainment of 1980 High School Sophomores by 1992.* (This table was prepared May 1995.)

Table 299.—Percentage distribution of 1980 high school sophomores, by highest level of education completed through 1992, by selected student characteristics: 1980 to 1992

Student characteristics	All 1980 sopho-mores	Less than high school	High school	Certificate	Associate degree	Bachelor's degree	Master's degree	Professional degree	Doctor's degree
1	2	3	4	5	6	7	8	9	10
Total	100.0	5.8	51.5	11.0	7.9	20.0	2.7	0.9	0.2
Sex									
Male	100.0	6.5	53.5	9.7	6.7	19.5	2.6	1.3	0.2
Female	100.0	5.0	49.5	12.4	9.1	20.5	2.8	0.5	0.1
Race/ethnicity									
White, non-Hispanic	100.0	4.9	49.1	10.1	8.4	23.1	3.2	1.0	0.2
Black, non-Hispanic	100.0	6.9	59.6	16.3	5.2	10.0	1.5	0.5	0.2
Hispanic	100.0	11.9	59.6	11.2	7.3	9.0	0.6	0.3	—
Asian/Pacific Islander	100.0	0.6	40.9	6.9	6.2	32.7	4.7	7.5	0.7
American Indian/Alaskan Native ...	100.0	17.8	58.2	11.8	5.0	6.7	0.5	—	—
Socioeconomic status (1980)									
Low quartile	100.0	9.0	64.6	12.3	6.9	6.4	0.7	0.1	—
Middle two quartiles	100.0	3.9	53.8	11.5	9.1	19.0	2.0	0.5	0.1
High quartile	100.0	1.4	32.7	7.0	7.6	41.2	6.9	2.7	0.5
Test score composite (1982)									
Low quartile	100.0	15.6	64.0	13.0	4.1	3.0	0.2	—	0.1
Middle two quartiles	100.0	3.1	56.2	12.8	10.1	16.1	1.5	0.3	—
High quartile	100.0	0.1	26.5	4.8	7.2	49.2	8.7	3.0	0.6
Parents' educational attainment in 1980									
No high school diploma	100.0	6.5	59.8	12.8	8.6	10.8	1.2	0.3	0.1
High school graduate	100.0	5.2	59.1	12.4	6.0	16.6	0.3	0.4	—
Vocational/technical	100.0	3.0	49.2	15.4	10.2	19.1	2.4	0.5	0.1
Some college	100.0	2.1	43.7	8.4	8.4	32.0	4.3	1.0	0.2
Bachelor's degree	100.0	1.4	32.6	4.9	8.1	42.4	6.9	3.1	0.5
Advanced degree	100.0	3.5	23.9	8.6	4.9	44.1	10.0	4.3	0.7
High school diploma status									
Regular diploma in 1982	100.0	0.3	51.9	10.8	8.7	23.9	3.2	1.1	0.2
Returned for diploma	100.0	6.8	68.3	14.4	7.0	3.4	0.1	0.1	—
Returned but no diploma	100.0	27.1	47.7	19.9	3.4	1.9	—	—	—
Never returned	100.0	51.5	35.7	9.5	2.1	0.9	0.3	—	—
Postsecondary expectations in 1982									
None	100.0	15.5	71.1	9.3	3.0	1.0	0.1	—	0.1
Vocational/technical	100.0	4.6	61.6	19.8	10.7	3.3	0.1	—	—
Less-than-4-year degree	100.0	1.6	53.2	13.3	15.6	15.0	1.1	0.2	—
Bachelor's degree	100.0	0.9	35.3	6.8	6.3	44.9	5.0	0.8	0.1
Advanced degree	100.0	0.8	28.9	5.2	5.7	45.1	9.0	4.4	0.8
Type of start in postsecondary education									
Fall 1982 full-time 4-year	100.0	—	21.2	3.5	4.6	57.8	9.0	3.4	0.5
Fall 1982 full-time public 2-year	100.0	0.3	36.5	11.9	24.4	24.6	2.1	0.2	—
Fall 1982 part-time 4-year	100.0	—	52.2	6.7	10.0	27.2	3.5	0.1	0.4
Fall 1982 part-time public 2-year	100.0	1.6	59.5	13.4	9.4	14.4	0.9	0.8	—
Fall 1982 other	100.0	0.2	23.0	34.3	24.5	15.7	1.9	0.4	—
Delayed 4-year	100.0	0.4	55.6	8.1	7.4	24.0	3.7	0.4	0.4
Delayed public 2-year	100.0	1.7	63.0	16.9	12.0	6.2	0.2	—	—
Delayed other	100.0	1.9	31.4	48.4	14.4	3.8	0.1	0.1	—
Other enrollment	100.0	—	—	86.5	5.1	6.0	1.1	0.4	0.8
Never enrolled	100.0	16.1	83.9	—	—	—	—	—	—

—Data not applicable or not available.

NOTE.—Because of rounding, details may not add to 100.0 percent.

SOURCE: National Center for Education Statistics, *High School and Beyond, Educational Attainment of High School Sophomores by 1992.* (This table was prepared May 1995.)

Table 300.—Mean number of semester credits completed by bachelor's degree recipients, by major and course area: 1972 to 1976 and 1980 to 1984

Selected college majors	Course areas									
	Total	Business	Computer science	Education	Engineering	Mathematics	Biological sciences	Physical sciences	Social sciences	Other
1	2	3	4	5	6	7	8	9	10	11
1972–76 [1]										
Mean, all majors	**124.0**	**7.8**	**1.0**	**9.7**	**2.3**	**7.4**	**7.6**	**9.0**	**30.3**	**48.8**
Business and management	124.4	41.2	2.3	0.5	0.4	10.2	2.5	4.8	30.4	32.0
Computer science	133.3	6.6	33.5	0.4	5.3	22.4	1.9	7.8	20.6	34.8
Education	126.4	0.9	0.3	40.2	—	5.0	5.5	4.3	23.9	46.4
Engineering	134.8	1.6	2.0	0.1	50.0	18.2	1.3	20.5	14.0	27.1
English	117.8	0.5	0.1	7.8	0.1	3.2	3.4	3.4	24.2	75.2
Fine arts	124.9	0.3	0.1	6.6	—	1.3	2.5	2.1	13.6	98.4
Life sciences	122.2	0.4	0.8	1.7	—	8.4	35.6	26.2	17.8	31.3
Physical sciences	122.7	0.8	1.4	0.9	1.9	16.2	9.6	49.5	13.1	29.2
Psychology	119.1	2.0	0.5	5.9	0.3	5.5	6.2	5.9	56.0	36.9
Social sciences	120.6	3.4	0.4	3.3	0.4	5.3	3.2	4.3	60.3	40.1
1980–84 [2]										
Mean, all majors	**123.5**	**12.8**	**3.3**	**6.2**	**4.6**	**8.4**	**5.3**	**8.1**	**27.5**	**47.2**
Business and management	122.8	41.2	4.5	0.6	1.1	8.9	2.2	3.9	27.5	32.7
Computer science	129.3	11.8	27.9	0.3	4.7	21.3	1.8	8.5	19.0	33.9
Education	127.4	0.7	0.3	45.5	0.1	4.4	4.4	3.8	20.8	47.3
Engineering	132.3	1.0	2.3	0.8	52.5	16.2	1.1	20.2	12.3	25.9
English	114.8	1.7	1.5	6.9	—	2.2	2.1	4.7	21.4	74.4
Fine arts	120.5	1.7	0.6	5.1	—	1.7	2.7	1.5	14.1	93.1
Life sciences	121.9	0.7	1.5	1.9	0.2	10.1	33.5	22.6	18.1	33.3
Physical sciences	124.3	0.2	4.9	0.1	2.0	14.1	12.9	48.7	11.6	30.0
Psychology	120.7	3.0	2.7	2.1	—	6.5	5.8	4.2	55.2	41.2
Social sciences	119.2	6.0	1.4	1.0	0.5	5.4	4.4	5.1	52.0	43.3

[1] Sample survey based on 1972 high school seniors who completed bachelor's degrees by 1976.
[2] Sample survey based on 1980 high school seniors who completed bachelor's degrees by 1984.
—Data not available.

NOTE.—Because of rounding, details may not add to totals.

SOURCE: U.S. Department of Education, National Center for Education Statistics, High School and Beyond survey. (This table was prepared April 1986.)

Table 301.—Colleges and universities offering remedial services, by type and control of institution: 1987–88 to 1992–93

Type and control of institution	Percent of colleges offering remedial instruction or tutoring						Change in percentage points				
	1987–88	1988–89	1989–90	1990–91	1991–92	1992–93	1987–88 to 1988–89	1988–89 to 1989–90	1989–90 to 1990–91	1990–91 to 1991–92	1991–92 to 1992–93
1	2	3	4	5	6	7	8	9	10	11	12
Total	72.7	74.9	76.6	77.7	78.6	76.6	2.1	1.8	1.0	0.9	−2.0
All 4-year colleges	66.0	68.2	69.6	70.6	71.4	69.7	2.3	1.4	1.0	0.9	−1.7
All 2-year colleges	82.7	84.7	87.2	88.4	89.2	86.6	2.0	2.5	1.1	0.8	−2.6
Public institutions											
4-year colleges	80.5	81.8	82.9	83.5	84.5	78.4	1.3	1.1	0.7	0.9	−6.1
2-year colleges	96.4	96.6	98.2	98.9	99.6	95.6	0.3	1.6	0.6	0.7	−4.0
Private institutions											
4-year colleges	60.3	63.0	64.5	65.6	66.4	66.2	2.7	1.5	1.1	0.8	−0.2
2-year colleges	53.0	58.6	63.0	65.5	65.8	65.4	5.6	4.3	2.5	0.4	−0.4

SOURCE: U.S. Department of Education, National Center for Education Statistics, Integrated Postsecondary Education Data System (IPEDS), "Institutional Characteristics" surveys. (This table was prepared May 1995.)

Table 302.—Highest level of education attained by 1980 high school seniors, by selected student and school characteristics: Spring 1986

Student and school characteristics	Highest educational attainment of 1980 high school seniors in 1986						
	Total	No high school diploma [1]	High school diploma	License [2]	Associate degree	Bachelor's degree	Graduate/ professional degree
1	2	3	4	5	6	7	8
Total	**100.0**	**0.9**	**61.8**	**11.9**	**6.5**	**18.2**	**0.7**
Sex							
Men	100.0	1.0	64.0	10.5	5.9	17.6	0.9
Women	100.0	0.8	59.6	13.3	7.0	18.8	0.6
Race/ethnicity							
White, non-Hispanic	100.0	0.8	60.0	11.5	6.6	20.2	0.9
Black, non-Hispanic	100.0	1.2	69.4	13.9	5.3	9.9	0.2
Hispanic	100.0	1.7	70.2	13.8	7.3	6.8	0.1
Asian	100.0	([3])	49.6	12.6	8.7	27.3	1.7
American Indian	100.0	([3])	61.3	18.6	9.3	10.8	([3])
Socioeconomic status quartile [4]							
Low	100.0	1.2	74.1	12.3	5.5	6.6	0.2
Low-middle	100.0	0.5	66.7	13.6	8.0	11.1	0.2
High-middle	100.0	0.1	58.4	12.9	7.7	20.4	0.6
High	100.0	([3])	45.7	8.7	6.3	37.1	2.2
High school program [5]							
General	100.0	0.8	69.7	12.6	6.5	10.2	0.2
Academic	100.0	0.1	45.6	8.8	7.2	36.6	1.8
Vocational	100.0	0.6	72.8	16.2	6.9	3.6	0.0
Postsecondary education plans [6]							
No plans	100.0	1.4	83.5	12.7	2.1	0.2	([3])
Attend vocational/technical school	100.0	0.3	72.5	17.7	8.4	1.1	([3])
Attend college less than 4 years .	100.0	0.2	65.5	14.4	13.1	6.8	([3])
Earn bachelor's degree	100.0	([3])	48.3	8.2	6.9	35.8	0.7
Earn advanced degree	100.0	0.1	43.5	7.9	4.9	40.6	3.0
Type of high school							
Public	100.0	1.0	63.2	12.1	6.6	16.4	0.7
Catholic	100.0	([3])	47.4	11.9	6.4	32.8	1.6
Other private	100.0	([3])	52.3	7.0	3.9	36.7	0.1

[1] Seniors who dropped out of high school after spring 1980 survey and had not completed high school by 1986.
[2] Persons who earned a certificate for completing a program of study.
[3] Less than .05 percent.
[4] Socioeconomic status was measured by a composite score on parental education, family income, father's occupation, and household characteristics in 1980.
[5] Students' self-reported high school program.
[6] During their senior year of high school, students were asked about the highest level of education they planned to attain. Students who planned to get less than a high school education or a high school education only were classified as having no postsecondary education plans.

NOTE.—Because of rounding, percents may not add to 100.0.

SOURCE: U.S. Department of Education, National Center for Education Statistics, High School and Beyond survey. (This table was prepared September 1987.)

Table 303.—Highest level of education attained by 1980 high school seniors, by race/ethnicity and October 1980 postsecondary education attendance status: Spring 1986

Race/ethnicity and October 1980 postsecondary education attendance status	Highest educational attainment of 1980 high school seniors in 1986						
	Total	No high school diploma [1]	High school diploma	License [2]	Associate degree	Bachelor's degree	Graduate/ professional degree
1	2	3	4	5	6	7	8
Total							
Part-time 2-year public college	100.0	0.7	66.4	17.7	8.8	6.5	(3)
Part-time 4-year public college	100.0	2.7	57.1	15.4	1.6	22.6	0.6
Full-time 2-year public college	100.0	(3)	49.5	11.7	20.7	17.6	0.5
Full-time 4-year public college	100.0	(3)	41.7	7.6	4.5	44.9	1.3
Full-time 4-year private college	100.0	(3)	31.1	8.8	5.1	51.9	3.0
Not a student	100.0	1.8	78.2	12.8	3.6	3.5	0.2
White, non-Hispanic							
Part-time 2-year public college	100.0	0.8	67.7	17.9	6.9	6.7	(3)
Part-time 4-year public college	100.0	3.4	54.8	14.5	0.3	27.0	(3)
Full-time 2-year public college	100.0	(3)	48.6	10.8	20.7	19.3	0.7
Full-time 4-year public college	100.0	(3)	39.0	6.8	4.8	48.0	1.5
Full-time 4-year private college	100.0	(3)	28.1	7.9	5.1	55.7	3.3
Not a student	100.0	1.6	78.5	12.7	3.5	3.5	0.2
Black, non-Hispanic							
Part-time 2-year public college	100.0	(3)	65.8	22.1	9.8	2.3	(3)
Part-time 4-year public college	100.0	(3)	58.5	25.1	6.0	8.5	1.8
Full-time 2-year public college	100.0	(3)	52.8	19.2	18.9	9.1	(3)
Full-time 4-year public college	100.0	(3)	59.4	11.2	3.4	25.6	0.5
Full-time 4-year private college	100.0	(3)	50.5	15.0	5.5	28.5	0.6
Not a student	100.0	2.2	78.1	13.3	3.6	2.8	(3)
Hispanic							
Part-time 2-year public college	100.0	(3)	57.4	14.9	23.4	4.4	(3)
Part-time 4-year public college	(4)	(4)	(4)	(4)	(4)	(4)	(4)
Full-time 2-year public college	100.0	(3)	53.9	14.9	22.7	8.5	(3)
Full-time 4-year public college	100.0	(3)	51.1	18.4	4.1	25.6	0.9
Full-time 4-year private college	100.0	(3)	46.8	19.4	6.1	26.8	1.0
Not a student	100.0	3.1	83.2	10.3	2.4	0.9	(3)

[1] Seniors who dropped out of high school after spring 1980 survey and had not completed high school by 1986.
[2] Includes persons who earned a certificate for completing a program of study.
[3] Less than .05 percent.

[4] Fewer than 30 cases available for analysis. Estimates are suppressed because they are unreliable.

NOTE.—Because of rounding, percents may not add to 100.0.

SOURCE: U.S. Department of Education, National Center for Education Statistics, High School and Beyond survey. (This table was prepared September 1987.)

Table 304.—Enrollment and completion status of first-time postsecondary students starting during the 1989–90 academic year, by degree objective and other student characteristics: Spring 1992

Student characteristics	Vocational certificate					Associate degree						Bachelor's degree				
	Number, in thousands	Total	Completed nine months or less	Completed in over nine months	Not completed	Number, in thousands	Total	Completed	Continuously enrolled	Stopped and reenrolled [1]	Stopped, no reenrollment [2]	Number, in thousands	Total	Continuously enrolled	Stopped and reenrolled [1]	Stopped, no reenrollment [2]
1	2	3	4	5	6	7	8	9	10	11	12	13	14	15	16	17
Total	**376**	**100.0**	**29.2**	**21.3**	**49.5**	**708**	**100.0**	**12.3**	**19.1**	**22.5**	**46.1**	**1,162**	**100.0**	**56.8**	**18.9**	**24.2**
Male	153	100.0	30.8	18.2	51.0	315	100.0	11.0	23.4	21.0	44.6	573	100.0	52.8	19.9	27.3
Female	223	100.0	28.1	23.5	48.5	393	100.0	13.3	15.6	23.7	47.4	589	100.0	60.7	18.0	21.3
Race																
White, non-Hispanic	270	100.0	29.6	23.1	47.3	566	100.0	12.8	18.5	21.6	47.2	920	100.0	57.6	17.9	24.5
Black, non-Hispanic	55	100.0	26.4	17.5	56.1	70	100.0	7.9	12.2	27.1	52.9	92	100.0	50.3	23.4	26.3
Hispanic	36	100.0	23.2	9.2	67.6	52	100.0	16.6	27.0	28.0	28.4	76	100.0	46.0	27.7	26.3
Socioeconomic status																
Low (25 percent)	126	100.0	36.6	16.2	47.2	124	100.0	4.6	22.7	20.0	52.7	75	100.0	50.4	18.8	30.9
Middle (50 percent)	195	100.0	28.0	23.1	48.9	374	100.0	12.3	15.7	24.9	47.1	434	100.0	53.8	18.8	27.4
High (25 percent)	56	100.0	16.4	26.8	56.9	210	100.0	16.7	23.1	19.8	40.5	653	100.0	59.6	19.0	21.4
Dependent student family income																
Less than $20,000	269	100.0	35.3	18.2	46.5	347	100.0	7.8	17.1	23.0	52.1	294	100.0	47.6	20.2	32.3
$20,000 to $39,999	56	100.0	10.8	26.3	62.9	162	100.0	18.3	22.0	21.0	38.4	300	100.0	57.4	19.6	23.1
$40,000 to $59,999	30	100.0	16.3	44.8	39.0	128	100.0	15.8	22.0	20.5	41.7	288	100.0	56.2	19.7	24.2
$60,000 or more	(3)	(3)	(3)	(3)	(3)	71	100.0	14.6	16.5	26.5	42.5	280	100.0	66.7	16.2	17.2
Time between high school graduation and entering postsecondary education																
12 months or less	154	100.0	36.1	20.7	43.2	444	100.0	5.1	11.6	23.4	60.0	1,020	100.0	37.7	25.3	37.0
More than 12 months	221	100.0	19.4	22.2	58.4	263	100.0	16.6	23.5	22.0	37.9	142	100.0	59.5	18.0	22.5
Marital/family status as of spring 1992 [4]																
Married, no children	38	100.0	22.6	23.9	53.6	57	100.0	7.6	19.7	16.1	56.6	40	100.0	34.3	20.6	45.1
Married, with children	119	100.0	42.2	19.0	38.7	133	100.0	3.6	11.2	23.5	61.7	58	100.0	22.1	21.5	56.4
Single, no children	148	100.0	22.6	26.2	51.3	436	100.0	17.2	24.4	25.5	33.0	964	100.0	63.0	19.7	17.3
Single, with children	31	100.0	17.6	18.0	64.4	29	100.0	9.7	7.1	22.9	60.3	(3)	(3)	(3)	(3)	(3)
Expected degree level [4]																
Less than 2 years	126	100.0	33.7	26.9	39.4	(3)	(3)	(3)	(3)	(3)	(3)	(3)	(3)	(3)	(3)	(3)
2 to 4 years	98	100.0	23.4	14.3	62.3	193	100.0	9.3	14.6	24.5	51.7	(3)	(3)	(3)	(3)	(3)
Bachelor's or higher	118	100.0	29.0	20.1	50.9	479	100.0	13.9	21.8	22.2	42.1	1,117	100.0	58.0	18.8	23.2
Average hours worked per week while enrolled																
None	117	100.0	30.8	22.7	46.5	121	100.0	11.2	23.7	19.4	45.7	236	100.0	56.7	20.7	22.5
1 to 20 hours	37	100.0	23.5	36.2	40.3	144	100.0	16.8	20.7	24.3	38.4	366	100.0	63.2	14.9	21.9
More than 20 hours	221	100.0	29.3	18.1	52.6	443	100.0	11.2	17.3	22.8	48.7	560	100.0	52.7	20.8	26.5
Involvement in school activities [4]																
Never involved	141	100.0	34.7	14.4	50.9	193	100.0	7.4	14.6	24.7	53.3	337	100.0	35.1	25.5	39.4
Once	123	100.0	24.2	26.3	49.6	273	100.0	13.8	21.2	22.9	42.2	454	100.0	52.5	19.3	28.2
Sometimes	71	100.0	26.1	24.8	49.1	180	100.0	15.2	21.0	20.2	43.8	209	100.0	61.0	19.3	19.7
Often	(3)	(3)	(3)	(3)	(3)	42	100.0	15.3	21.0	16.2	47.5		100.0	66.4	14.4	19.2
Received financial aid during 1989–90 [4]																
Yes	197	100.0	33.6	23.6	42.8	277	100.0	14.4	20.6	18.3	46.8	553	100.0	61.9	15.4	22.7
No	173	100.0	24.8	18.6	56.7	423	100.0	10.9	18.0	24.9	46.2	562	100.0	52.1	22.2	25.7

[1] Includes those students who were not enrolled for more than 4 months out of the year. Some students may not be enrolled at the time of the follow-up survey.

[2] Includes those students who stopped enrolling for more than 4 months and did not re-enroll during the survey period.

[3] Too few observations for a reliable estimate.

[4] Because of survey item nonresponse, sum of details is less than total number.

NOTE.—Data reflect completion and enrollment status by spring 1992 of first-time postsecondary students starting academic year 1989–90. Due to the limited time period covered by the survey, it was inappropriate to calculate bachelor's degree completion rates. Some cells in this table have relatively large sampling errors. See sampling error table in appendix.

SOURCE: U.S. Department of Education, National Center for Education Statistics, Beginning Postsecondary Student Longitudinal Survey, 1992. (This table was prepared in June 1994.)

Table 305.—Scores on Graduate Record Examination (GRE) and subject matter tests: 1965 to 1992

Academic year ending	Number of GRE takers	GRE takers as a percent of bachelor's degrees	Verbal Mean	Verbal Standard deviation	Quantitative Mean	Quantitative Standard deviation	Analytical Mean	Analytical Standard deviation	Biology Mean	Biology Standard deviation	Chemistry Mean	Chemistry Standard deviation	Education Mean	Education Standard deviation	Engineering Mean	Engineering Standard deviation	Literature Mean	Literature Standard deviation	Psychology Mean	Psychology Standard deviation
1	2	3	4	5	6	7	8	9	10	11	12	13	14	15	16	17	18	19	20	21
1965	93,792	18.7	530	124	533	137	—	—	617	117	628	114	481	86	618	108	591	95	556	91
1966	123,960	23.8	520	124	528	133	—	—	610	115	618	110	474	87	609	106	588	94	552	91
1967	151,134	27.0	519	125	528	134	—	—	613	114	615	104	476	90	603	104	582	91	553	93
1968	182,432	28.8	520	124	527	135	—	—	614	114	617	104	478	87	601	105	572	91	547	93
1969	206,113	28.3	515	124	524	132	—	—	613	112	613	104	477	88	591	103	569	89	543	89
1970	265,359	33.5	503	123	516	132	—	—	603	111	613	113	462	92	586	110	556	90	532	91
1971	293,600	35.0	497	125	512	134	—	—	603	114	618	117	457	95	587	115	546	91	530	92
1972	293,506	33.1	494	126	508	136	—	—	606	115	624	124	446	93	594	119	544	96	528	92
1973	290,104	31.5	497	125	512	135	—	—	619	110	630	114	459	96	593	114	545	96	529	92
1974	301,070	31.8	492	126	509	137	—	—	624	110	634	115	452	93	591	121	547	99	530	95
1975	298,335	32.3	493	125	508	137	—	—	—	—	—	—	—	—	—	—	—	—	—	—
1976	299,292	32.3	492	127	510	138	—	—	627	112	627	107	454	93	594	119	539	101	531	93
1977	287,715	31.3	490	129	514	139	—	—	625	113	630	109	453	93	592	115	532	101	532	95
1978	286,383	31.1	484	128	518	135	—	—	622	113	624	108	452	91	594	114	530	102	529	97
1979	282,482	30.7	476	130	517	135	—	—	621	117	623	104	451	89	592	115	525	102	530	97
1980	272,281	29.3	474	131	522	136	—	—	619	115	618	105	449	90	590	116	521	105	534	98
1981	262,855	28.1	473	128	523	136	—	—	617	115	615	103	453	90	590	116	520	99	532	97
1982	256,381	26.9	469	130	533	137	498	126	616	114	616	105	456	89	593	115	521	100	532	97
1983	263,674	27.2	473	131	541	138	504	128	623	115	620	105	459	89	599	114	527	98	542	95
1984	265,221	27.2	475	130	541	139	512	129	622	115	619	102	461	90	604	114	530	97	543	96
1985	271,972	27.8	474	126	545	140	516	129	619	114	621	101	459	89	615	120	531	95	541	95
1986	279,428	28.3	475	126	552	140	520	129	612	114	628	106	464	87	616	119	527	96	542	97
1987	293,560	29.6	477	126	550	140	521	128	616	116	629	104	465	86	619	119	526	95	536	95
1988	303,703	30.5	483	123	557	140	528	128	615	114	631	108	467	85	622	120	525	94	537	94
1989	326,096	32.0	484	125	560	142	530	129	612	114	642	117	465	87	626	116	528	91	538	95
1990	344,572	32.8	486	123	562	143	534	128	612	114	662	123	461	84	617	111	523	92	537	95
1991	379,882	34.7	485	122	562	141	536	129	609	113	660	123	457	85	611	111	523	93	535	95
1992	411,528	36.2	483	120	561	140	537	129	605	113	654	128	462	82	610	117	525	92	536	95

—Data not reported or not applicable.

NOTE.—GRE scores for the verbal, quantitative, and analytical sections range from 200 to 800. Subject matter test scores range from 200 to 990.

SOURCE: Graduate Record Examination Board, Examinee and Score Trends for the GRE General Test, various years; and A Summary of Data Collected From Graduate Record Examinations Test-Takers During 1986–87; and U.S. Department of Education, National Center for Education Statistics, "Degrees and Other Formal Awards Conferred" surveys, and Integrated Postsecondary Education Data System (IPEDS), "Completions" surveys. (This table was prepared April 1993.)

Table 306.—Average undergraduate tuition and fees and room and board rates paid by students in institutions of higher education, by type and control of institution: 1964–65 to 1994–95

Year and control of institution	Total tuition, room, and board					Tuition and required fees (in-state)					Dormitory rooms					Board (7-day basis)[1]				
	All institutions	4-year institutions			2-year	All institutions	4-year institutions			2-year	All institutions	4-year institutions			2-year	All institutions	4-year institutions			2-year
		All 4-year	Universities	Other 4-year			All 4-year	Universities	Other 4-year			All 4-year	Universities	Other 4-year			All 4-year	Universities	Other 4-year	
1	2	3	4	5	6	7	8	9	10	11	12	13	14	15	16	17	18	19	20	21
All institutions																				
1976–77	$2,275	$2,577	$2,647	$2,527	$1,598	$924	$1,218	$1,210	$1,223	$346	$603	$611	$649	$584	$503	$748	$748	$788	$719	$750
1977–78	2,411	2,725	2,777	2,685	1,703	984	1,291	1,269	1,305	378	645	654	691	628	525	781	780	818	752	801
1978–79	2,587	2,917	2,967	2,879	1,828	1,073	1,397	1,370	1,413	411	688	696	737	667	575	826	825	860	800	842
1979–80	2,809	3,167	3,223	3,124	1,979	1,163	1,513	1,484	1,530	451	751	759	803	729	628	895	895	936	865	900
1980–81	3,101	3,499	3,535	3,469	2,230	1,289	1,679	1,634	1,705	526	836	846	881	821	705	976	975	1,020	943	1,000
1981–82	3,489	3,951	4,005	3,908	2,476	1,457	1,907	1,860	1,935	590	950	961	1,023	919	793	1,083	1,082	1,121	1,055	1,094
1982–83	3,877	4,406	4,466	4,356	2,713	1,626	2,139	2,081	2,173	675	1,064	1,078	1,150	1,028	873	1,187	1,189	1,235	1,155	1,165
1983–84	4,167	4,747	4,793	4,712	2,854	1,783	2,344	2,300	2,368	730	1,145	1,162	1,211	1,130	916	1,239	1,242	1,282	1,214	1,208
1984–85	4,563	5,160	5,236	5,107	3,179	1,985	2,567	2,539	2,583	821	1,267	1,282	1,343	1,242	1,058	1,310	1,311	1,353	1,282	1,301
1985–86[2]	4,885	5,504	5,597	5,441	3,367	2,181	2,784	2,770	2,793	888	1,338	1,355	1,424	1,309	1,107	1,365	1,365	1,403	1,339	1,372
1986–87[3]	5,206	5,964	6,124	5,857	3,295	2,312	3,042	3,042	3,042	897	1,405	1,427	1,501	1,376	1,034	1,489	1,495	1,581	1,439	1,364
1987–88	5,494	6,272	6,339	6,226	3,263	2,458	3,201	3,168	3,220	809	1,488	1,516	1,576	1,478	1,017	1,549	1,555	1,596	1,529	1,437
1988–89	5,869	6,725	6,801	6,673	3,573	2,658	3,472	3,422	3,499	979	1,575	1,609	1,665	1,573	1,085	1,636	1,644	1,715	1,601	1,509
1989–90	6,207	7,212	7,347	7,120	3,705	2,839	3,800	3,765	3,819	978	1,638	1,675	1,732	1,638	1,105	1,730	1,737	1,850	1,663	1,622
1990–91	6,562	7,602	7,709	7,528	3,930	3,016	4,009	3,958	4,036	1,087	1,743	1,782	1,848	1,740	1,182	1,802	1,811	1,903	1,751	1,660
1991–92	7,074	8,252	8,389	8,164	4,089	3,282	4,399	4,366	4,417	1,186	1,874	1,921	1,998	1,874	1,210	1,918	1,931	2,026	1,873	1,692
1992–93	7,452	8,758	8,934	8,648	4,207	3,517	4,752	4,665	4,795	1,276	1,939	1,991	2,104	1,926	1,240	1,996	2,015	2,165	1,927	1,692
1993–94	7,931	9,296	9,495	9,186	4,449	3,827	5,119	5,104	5,127	1,399	2,057	2,111	2,190	2,068	1,332	2,067	2,067	2,201	1,992	1,718
1994–95[4]	8,286	9,723	9,852	9,644	4,644	4,030	5,391	5,281	5,445	1,492	2,143	2,198	2,279	2,153	1,395	2,113	2,134	2,292	2,046	1,756
Public institutions																				
1964–65	950	—	1,051	867	638	243	—	298	224	99	271	—	291	241	178	436	—	462	402	361
1965–66	983	—	1,105	904	670	257	—	327	241	109	281	—	304	255	194	445	—	474	408	367
1966–67	1,026	—	1,171	947	710	275	—	360	259	121	294	—	321	271	213	457	—	490	417	376
1967–68	1,064	—	1,199	997	789	283	—	366	268	144	313	—	337	292	243	468	—	496	437	402
1968–69	1,117	—	1,245	1,063	883	295	—	377	281	170	337	—	359	318	278	485	—	509	464	435
1969–70	1,203	—	1,362	1,135	951	323	—	427	306	178	369	—	395	346	308	511	—	540	483	465
1970–71	1,287	—	1,477	1,206	998	351	—	478	332	187	401	—	431	375	338	535	—	568	499	473
1971–72	1,357	—	1,579	1,263	1,073	376	—	526	354	192	430	—	463	400	366	551	—	590	509	515
1972–73	1,458	—	1,668	1,460	1,197	407	—	566	455	233	476	—	500	455	398	575	—	602	550	566
1973–74	1,517	—	1,707	1,506	1,274	438	—	581	463	274	480	—	505	464	409	599	—	621	579	591
1974–75	1,563	—	1,760	1,558	1,339	432	—	599	448	277	506	—	527	497	424	625	—	634	613	638
1975–76	1,666	—	1,935	1,657	1,386	433	—	642	469	245	544	—	573	533	442	689	—	720	655	699
1976–77	1,789	1,935	2,067	1,827	1,491	479	617	689	564	283	582	592	614	572	465	728	727	763	692	742
1977–78	1,888	2,038	2,170	1,931	1,590	512	655	736	596	306	621	631	649	616	486	755	752	785	720	797
1978–79	1,994	2,145	2,289	2,027	1,691	543	688	777	622	327	655	664	689	641	527	796	793	823	764	837
1979–80	2,165	2,327	2,487	2,198	1,822	583	738	840	662	355	715	725	750	703	574	867	865	898	833	893
1980–81	2,373	2,550	2,712	2,421	2,027	635	804	915	722	391	799	811	827	796	642	940	936	969	904	994
1981–82	2,663	2,871	3,079	2,705	2,224	714	909	1,042	813	434	909	925	970	885	703	1,039	1,036	1,067	1,006	1,086
1982–83	2,945	3,196	3,403	3,032	2,390	798	1,031	1,164	936	473	1,010	1,030	1,072	993	755	1,136	1,134	1,167	1,103	1,162
1983–84	3,156	3,433	3,628	3,285	2,534	891	1,148	1,284	1,052	528	1,087	1,110	1,131	1,092	801	1,178	1,175	1,213	1,141	1,205
1984–85	3,408	3,682	3,899	3,518	2,807	971	1,228	1,386	1,117	584	1,196	1,217	1,237	1,200	921	1,241	1,237	1,276	1,201	1,302
1985–86[2]	3,571	3,859	4,146	3,637	2,981	1,045	1,318	1,536	1,157	641	1,242	1,263	1,290	1,240	960	1,285	1,278	1,320	1,240	1,380
1986–87[3]	3,805	4,138	4,469	3,891	2,989	1,106	1,414	1,651	1,248	660	1,301	1,323	1,355	1,295	979	1,398	1,401	1,464	1,348	1,349
1987–88	4,050	4,403	4,619	4,250	3,066	1,218	1,537	1,726	1,407	706	1,378	1,410	1,410	1,409	943	1,454	1,456	1,482	1,434	1,417
1988–89	4,274	4,678	4,905	4,526	3,183	1,285	1,646	1,846	1,515	730	1,457	1,496	1,483	1,506	965	1,533	1,536	1,576	1,504	1,488
1989–90	4,504	4,975	5,324	4,723	3,299	1,356	1,780	2,035	1,608	756	1,513	1,557	1,561	1,554	962	1,635	1,638	1,728	1,561	1,581
1990–91	4,757	5,243	5,585	5,004	3,467	1,454	1,888	2,159	1,707	824	1,612	1,657	1,658	1,655	1,050	1,691	1,698	1,767	1,641	1,594

Table 306.—Average undergraduate tuition and fees and room and board rates paid by students in institutions of higher education, by type and control of institution: 1964–65 to 1994–95—Continued

Year and control of institution	Total tuition, room, and board					Tuition and required fees (in-state)					Dormitory rooms					Board (7-day basis) [1]				
	All institutions	4-year institutions			2-year	All institutions	4-year institutions			2-year	All institutions	4-year institutions			2-year	All institutions	4-year institutions			2-year
		All 4-year	Universities	Other 4-year			All 4-year	Universities	Other 4-year			All 4-year	Universities	Other 4-year			All 4-year	Universities	Other 4-year	
1	2	3	4	5	6	7	8	9	10	11	12	13	14	15	16	17	18	19	20	21
1991–92	5,135	5,695	6,051	5,459	3,623	1,624	2,119	2,410	1,933	937	1,731	1,785	1,789	1,782	1,074	1,780	1,792	1,852	1,745	1,612
1992–93	5,379	6,020	6,442	5,740	3,799	1,782	2,349	2,604	2,192	1,025	1,756	1,816	1,856	1,787	1,106	1,841	1,854	1,982	1,761	1,668
1993–94	5,694	6,365	6,710	6,146	3,996	1,942	2,537	2,820	2,360	1,125	1,873	1,934	1,897	1,958	1,190	1,880	1,895	1,993	1,828	1,681
1994–95 [4]	5,962	6,674	7,082	6,411	4,149	2,057	2,689	2,982	2,507	1,194	1,959	2,021	1,993	2,041	1,239	1,947	1,964	2,107	1,863	1,716
Private institutions																				
1964–65	1,907	—	2,202	1,810	1,455	1,088	—	1,297	1,023	702	331	—	390	308	289	488	—	515	479	464
1965–66	2,005	—	2,316	1,899	1,557	1,154	—	1,369	1,086	768	356	—	418	330	316	495	—	529	483	473
1966–67	2,124	—	2,456	2,007	1,679	1,233	—	1,456	1,162	845	385	—	452	355	347	506	—	548	490	487
1967–68	2,205	—	2,545	2,104	1,762	1,297	—	1,534	1,237	892	392	—	455	366	366	516	—	556	501	504
1968–69	2,321	—	2,673	2,237	1,876	1,383	—	1,638	1,335	956	404	—	463	382	391	534	—	572	520	529
1969–70	2,530	—	2,920	2,420	1,993	1,533	—	1,809	1,468	1,034	436	—	503	409	413	561	—	608	543	546
1970–71	2,738	—	3,163	2,599	2,103	1,684	—	1,980	1,603	1,109	468	—	542	434	434	586	—	641	562	560
1971–72	2,917	—	3,375	2,748	2,186	1,820	—	2,133	1,721	1,172	494	—	576	454	449	603	—	666	573	565
1972–73	3,038	—	3,512	2,934	2,273	1,898	—	2,226	1,846	1,221	524	—	622	490	457	616	—	664	598	595
1973–74	3,164	—	3,717	3,040	2,410	1,989	—	2,375	1,925	1,303	533	—	622	502	483	642	—	720	613	624
1974–75	3,403	—	4,076	3,156	2,591	2,117	—	2,614	1,954	1,367	586	—	691	536	564	700	—	771	666	660
1975–76	3,663	—	4,467	3,385	2,711	2,272	—	2,881	2,084	1,427	636	—	753	583	572	755	—	833	718	712
1976–77	3,906	3,977	4,715	3,714	2,971	2,467	2,534	3,051	2,351	1,592	649	651	783	604	607	790	791	882	759	772
1977–78	4,158	4,240	5,033	3,967	3,148	2,624	2,700	3,240	2,520	1,706	698	702	850	648	631	836	838	943	800	811
1978–79	4,514	4,609	5,403	4,327	3,389	2,867	2,958	3,487	2,771	1,831	758	761	916	704	700	889	890	1,000	851	858
1979–80	4,912	5,013	5,891	4,700	3,751	3,130	3,225	3,811	3,020	2,062	827	831	1,001	768	766	955	957	1,078	912	923
1980–81	5,470	5,594	6,569	5,249	4,303	3,498	3,617	4,275	3,390	2,413	918	921	1,086	859	871	1,054	1,056	1,209	1,000	1,019
1981–82	6,166	6,330	7,443	5,947	4,746	3,953	4,113	4,887	3,853	2,605	1,038	1,039	1,229	970	1,022	1,175	1,178	1,327	1,124	1,119
1982–83	6,920	7,126	8,536	6,646	5,364	4,439	4,639	5,583	4,329	3,008	1,181	1,181	1,453	1,083	1,177	1,300	1,306	1,501	1,234	1,179
1983–84	7,508	7,759	9,308	7,244	5,571	4,851	5,093	6,217	4,726	3,099	1,278	1,279	1,531	1,191	1,253	1,380	1,387	1,559	1,327	1,219
1984–85	8,202	8,451	10,243	7,849	6,203	5,315	5,556	6,843	5,135	3,485	1,426	1,426	1,753	1,309	1,424	1,462	1,469	1,647	1,405	1,294
1985–86 [2]	8,885	9,228	11,034	8,551	6,512	5,789	6,121	7,374	5,641	3,672	1,553	1,557	1,940	1,420	1,500	1,542	1,551	1,720	1,490	1,340
1986–87 [3]	9,676	10,039	12,278	9,276	6,384	6,316	6,658	8,118	6,171	3,684	1,658	1,673	2,097	1,518	1,266	1,702	1,708	2,063	1,587	1,434
1987–88	10,512	10,659	13,075	9,854	7,078	6,988	7,116	8,771	6,574	4,161	1,748	1,760	2,244	1,593	1,380	1,775	1,783	2,060	1,687	1,537
1988–89	11,189	11,474	14,073	10,620	7,967	7,461	7,722	9,451	7,172	4,817	1,849	1,863	2,353	1,686	1,540	1,880	1,889	2,269	1,762	1,609
1989–90	12,018	12,284	15,098	11,374	8,670	8,147	8,396	10,348	7,778	5,196	1,923	1,935	2,411	1,774	1,663	1,948	1,953	2,339	1,823	1,811
1990–91	12,910	13,237	16,503	12,220	9,302	8,772	9,083	11,379	8,389	5,570	2,063	2,077	2,654	1,889	1,744	2,052	2,077	2,470	1,943	1,989
1991–92	13,907	14,273	17,779	13,189	9,631	9,434	9,775	12,192	9,053	5,752	2,221	2,241	2,860	2,038	1,789	2,252	2,257	2,727	2,098	2,090
1992–93	14,634	15,009	18,898	13,882	9,903	9,942	10,294	13,055	9,533	6,059	2,348	2,362	3,018	2,151	1,970	2,344	2,354	2,825	2,197	1,875
1993–94	15,496	15,904	20,097	14,640	10,406	10,572	10,952	13,874	10,100	6,370	2,490	2,506	3,277	2,261	2,067	2,434	2,445	2,946	2,278	1,970
1994–95 [4]	16,222	16,645	21,010	15,410	11,059	11,128	11,522	14,510	10,698	6,865	2,586	2,604	3,468	2,350	2,166	2,508	2,520	3,032	2,363	2,028

[1] Data for 1986–87 and later years reflect 20 meals per week rather than meals 7 days per week.

[2] Room and board data are estimated.

[3] Because of revisions in data collection procedures, figures are not entirely comparable with those for previous years. In particular, data on board rates are somewhat higher than earlier years because they reflect a basis of 20 meals per week rather than meals served 7 days per week. Since many institutions serve fewer than 3 meals each day, the 1986–87 and later data reflect a more accurate accounting of total board costs. Because of their low response rate, data for private 2-year colleges must be interpreted with caution.

[4] Preliminary data based on fall 1993 enrollment weights.

—Data not available.

NOTE.—Data are for the entire academic year and are average charges paid by students. Tuition and fees were weighted by the number of full-time-equivalent undergraduates but were not adjusted to reflect student residency. Room and board were based on full-time students. The data have not been adjusted for changes in the purchasing power of the dollar. Some data have been revised from previously published figures. Because of rounding, details may not add to totals.

SOURCE: U.S. Department of Education, National Center for Education Statistics, "Institutional Characteristics of Colleges and Universities" and "Fall Enrollment in Institutions of Higher Education" surveys; Integrated Postsecondary Education Data System (IPEDS), "Fall Enrollment" and "Institutional Characteristics" surveys. (This table was prepared August 1995.)

Table 307.—Average undergraduate tuition and fees and room and board rates paid by students in institutions of higher education, by control of institution and by state: 1993–94 and 1994–95

State or other area	Public 4-year, 1993–94		Public 4-year, 1994–95 [1]				Private 4-year, 1993–94		Private 4-year, 1994–95 [1]				Public 2-year, tuition only (in-state)	
	Total	Tuition (in-state)	Total	Tuition (in-state)	Room	Board	Total	Tuition	Total	Tuition (in-state)	Room	Board	1993–94	1994–95 [1]
1	2	3	4	5	6	7	8	9	10	11	12	13	14	15
United States	$6,365	$2,537	$6,674	$2,689	$2,021	$1,964	$15,904	$10,952	$16,645	$11,522	$2,604	$2,520	$1,125	$1,194
Alabama	5,295	1,986	5,432	2,106	1,674	1,652	10,551	6,905	11,321	7,404	1,699	2,219	1,107	1,123
Alaska	5,978	1,909	6,156	2,045	2,227	1,884	12,134	7,637	12,448	7,950	1,835	2,662	1,268	1,320
Arizona	5,463	1,819	5,829	1,894	1,956	1,979	9,406	5,716	10,179	6,076	1,990	2,113	727	734
Arkansas	5,296	1,805	4,926	1,955	1,584	1,387	8,866	5,721	9,577	6,162	1,419	1,997	842	888
California	7,524	2,388	7,922	2,703	2,881	2,338	19,277	13,249	18,631	12,748	2,980	2,903	345	365
Colorado	6,190	2,267	6,523	2,377	1,887	2,259	15,960	11,007	16,908	11,710	2,590	2,608	1,201	1,279
Connecticut	7,915	3,476	8,505	3,746	2,526	2,234	20,740	14,785	21,923	15,704	3,461	2,757	1,398	1,520
Delaware	7,790	3,663	8,131	3,817	2,290	2,023	10,595	6,817	11,356	7,187	2,710	1,458	—	1,266
District of Columbia	—	974	—	1,046	—	—	18,581	12,573	19,637	13,367	3,706	2,565	—	—
Florida	5,861	1,784	6,192	1,786	2,112	2,294	13,778	9,422	14,480	9,941	2,316	2,223	1,074	1,112
Georgia	5,063	1,886	5,381	1,965	1,590	1,826	13,696	9,040	14,369	9,571	2,522	2,276	974	1,015
Hawaii	1,452	1,452	—	1,508	—	—	10,185	5,578	11,000	5,951	2,920	2,129	480	500
Idaho	4,977	1,497	5,205	1,583	1,507	2,115	14,176	10,103	14,583	11,246	1,330	2,007	914	990
Illinois	6,999	3,031	7,482	3,197	1,972	2,312	15,242	10,471	15,986	11,070	2,609	2,307	1,134	1,194
Indiana	6,640	2,621	6,921	2,864	1,757	2,300	14,974	11,094	15,923	11,848	1,879	2,195	1,743	1,854
Iowa	5,439	2,352	5,699	2,462	1,613	1,623	14,499	10,820	15,274	11,430	1,789	2,054	1,615	1,699
Kansas	5,137	1,890	5,442	2,019	1,656	1,767	11,138	7,602	11,736	8,079	1,517	2,140	982	1,044
Kentucky	5,027	1,914	5,324	2,056	1,465	1,802	10,019	6,519	10,665	7,038	1,680	1,948	966	1,080
Louisiana	5,214	2,177	5,275	2,214	1,470	1,591	16,150	11,179	16,764	11,769	2,601	2,394	955	1,027
Maine	7,503	3,131	7,794	3,319	2,247	2,229	19,827	14,421	20,853	15,383	2,679	2,791	1,907	2,137
Maryland	8,147	3,111	8,297	3,318	2,631	2,348	18,962	12,847	20,053	13,762	3,342	2,949	1,676	1,848
Massachusetts	8,503	4,163	8,536	4,131	2,331	2,073	21,384	14,826	22,322	15,685	3,526	3,112	2,344	2,441
Michigan	7,668	3,492	7,949	3,729	2,041	2,178	12,253	8,362	12,815	8,739	1,926	2,150	1,357	1,432
Minnesota	5,929	2,783	6,182	2,919	1,818	1,445	15,594	11,637	16,348	12,233	1,975	2,141	1,845	1,928
Mississippi	5,088	2,368	5,248	2,448	1,350	1,451	8,763	5,960	9,179	6,289	1,458	1,433	937	935
Missouri	5,833	2,476	6,326	2,787	1,908	1,632	13,005	8,722	14,069	9,607	2,165	2,297	1,138	1,203
Montana	5,668	1,889	5,996	2,110	1,745	2,141	9,446	6,084	10,406	6,993	1,315	2,098	1,162	1,329
Nebraska	4,925	1,936	5,186	2,058	1,340	1,788	11,811	8,338	12,573	8,897	1,709	1,966	1,088	1,097
Nevada	6,379	1,532	6,908	1,601	3,009	2,298	9,773	7,173	—	7,494	3,050	—	817	842
New Hampshire	7,801	3,835	8,145	4,003	2,478	1,665	18,738	13,359	17,162	12,143	2,530	2,490	2,259	2,316
New Jersey	8,251	3,517	8,714	3,773	2,945	1,997	18,208	12,375	18,983	12,951	3,124	2,909	1,540	1,755
New Mexico	5,062	1,726	5,373	1,836	1,631	1,906	14,637	10,261	16,004	11,549	2,226	2,228	620	678
New York	7,721	2,920	7,952	2,957	2,780	2,215	18,364	12,161	19,481	12,892	3,484	3,106	2,112	2,152
North Carolina	4,706	1,408	4,858	1,503	1,686	1,670	13,543	9,635	14,544	10,406	1,963	2,176	578	582
North Dakota	5,253	2,124	5,513	2,245	967	2,301	9,194	6,437	9,505	6,653	1,229	1,623	1,637	1,689
Ohio	6,992	3,265	7,733	3,405	2,262	2,066	15,396	11,055	16,334	11,782	2,253	2,299	2,088	2,164
Oklahoma	4,027	1,643	4,205	1,675	964	1,566	10,706	7,126	11,859	8,078	1,731	2,049	1,107	1,153
Oregon	6,630	2,831	6,929	3,063	1,557	2,309	16,617	12,311	17,577	12,969	2,028	2,580	1,185	1,324
Pennsylvania	8,277	4,316	8,665	4,512	2,152	2,000	18,137	12,710	19,035	13,457	2,823	2,755	1,672	1,751
Rhode Island	8,604	3,404	9,080	3,718	2,849	2,513	19,695	13,617	20,799	14,445	3,417	2,937	1,546	1,686
South Carolina	6,206	2,895	6,758	3,021	1,904	1,833	12,138	8,570	12,709	9,122	1,741	1,847	1,058	1,048
South Dakota	4,917	2,338	5,319	2,557	1,123	1,639	11,652	8,019	12,385	8,574	1,482	2,329	2,640	3,430
Tennessee	5,019	1,796	5,130	1,897	1,553	1,680	11,967	8,579	13,176	9,210	2,036	1,930	950	975
Texas	4,934	1,504	5,175	1,608	1,838	1,729	11,847	7,936	12,417	8,410	1,860	2,147	625	680
Utah	5,125	1,868	5,349	1,960	1,390	2,000	6,796	2,679	7,112	2,814	1,340	2,959	1,289	1,340
Vermont	10,054	5,532	10,401	5,752	2,998	1,652	19,555	14,263	20,675	15,032	3,172	2,471	2,726	2,877
Virginia	7,725	3,645	7,951	3,769	2,221	1,961	13,852	9,679	14,519	10,309	2,018	2,192	1,332	1,384
Washington	6,476	2,334	7,070	2,686	1,930	2,454	16,108	11,713	16,996	12,412	2,483	2,101	1,143	1,314
West Virginia	5,687	1,875	5,912	1,963	1,908	2,042	13,179	9,284	13,835	9,889	1,681	2,265	1,237	1,312
Wisconsin	5,249	2,316	5,615	2,470	1,681	1,464	13,872	10,160	14,766	10,835	1,668	2,263	1,527	1,649
Wyoming	4,900	1,648	5,237	1,908	1,462	1,867	—	—	—	—	—	—	874	893

[1] Preliminary data based on fall 1993 enrollments.

—Data not reported or not applicable.

NOTE.—Data are for the entire academic year and are average charges. Tuition and fees were weighted by the number of full-time-equivalent undergraduates in 1993, but are not adjusted to reflect student residency. Room and board are based on full-time students.

SOURCE: U.S. Department of Education, National Center for Education Statistics, Integrated Postsecondary Education Data System (IPEDS), "Fall Enrollment" and "Institutional Characteristics" surveys. (This table was prepared August 1995.)

Table 308.—Average graduate and first-professional tuition paid by students in institutions of higher education: 1987–88 to 1994–95

Year	Average full-time graduate tuition	Average full-time first-professional tuition									
		Chiropractic	Dentistry	Medicine	Optometry	Osteopathic medicine	Pharmacy	Podiatry	Veterinary medicine	Law	Theology
1	2	3	4	5	6	7	8	9	10	11	12
All institutions											
1987–88	$3,599	$6,996	$9,399	$9,034	$7,926	$10,674	$5,201	$12,736	$4,503	$6,636	$3,572
1988–89	3,728	7,972	9,324	9,439	8,503	11,462	4,952	13,232	4,856	7,099	3,911
1989–90	4,135	8,315	10,515	10,597	9,469	11,888	5,890	14,611	5,470	8,059	4,079
1990–91	4,488	9,108	10,270	10,571	9,512	12,830	5,889	15,143	5,396	8,708	4,569
1991–92	5,116	10,226	12,049	11,646	9,610	13,004	6,731	16,257	6,367	9,469	4,876
1992–93	5,475	11,117	12,710	12,265	11,146	14,297	6,635	17,426	6,771	10,463	5,331
1993–94 [1]	5,973	11,542	13,993	13,075	11,129	14,903	7,992	17,860	7,242	11,479	5,647
1994–95 [2]	6,177	12,329	14,398	13,666	11,811	15,665	8,546	18,189	7,850	12,194	6,032
Public [3]											
1987–88	1,827	—	4,614	5,245	2,789	5,125	2,462	—	3,523	2,810	—
1988–89	1,913	—	5,286	5,669	3,455	6,269	2,218	—	3,889	2,766	—
1989–90	1,999	—	5,728	6,259	3,569	6,521	2,816	—	4,505	3,196	—
1990–91	2,206	—	5,927	6,437	3,821	7,188	2,697	—	4,840	3,430	—
1991–92	2,524	—	6,595	7,106	4,161	7,699	2,871	—	5,231	3,933	—
1992–93	2,791	—	7,006	7,867	5,106	8,404	2,987	—	5,553	4,261	—
1993–94 [1]	3,050	—	7,576	8,337	5,322	8,723	3,615	—	5,997	4,842	—
1994–95 [2]	3,202	—	8,064	8,768	5,781	8,987	3,874	—	6,500	5,304	—
Private											
1987–88	6,769	6,996	16,201	14,945	11,635	13,311	8,834	12,736	12,544	9,048	3,572
1988–89	6,945	7,972	16,127	15,610	12,050	13,536	9,692	13,232	13,285	9,892	3,911
1989–90	7,881	8,315	16,800	16,826	13,640	14,117	10,656	14,611	14,184	10,901	4,079
1990–91	8,507	9,108	18,270	17,899	13,767	15,009	11,546	15,143	14,159	12,247	4,569
1991–92	9,592	10,226	20,318	19,225	14,366	16,098	12,937	16,257	15,816	12,946	4,876
1992–93	10,008	11,117	21,309	19,585	14,964	17,098	13,373	17,426	17,103	13,975	5,331
1993–94 [1]	10,790	11,542	23,323	20,804	15,012	17,700	14,981	17,860	17,799	15,197	5,647
1994–95 [2]	11,079	12,329	24,318	21,740	15,779	18,829	16,677	18,189	18,551	16,089	6,032

[1] Preliminary first-professional figures based on 1992–93 graduates.
[2] Preliminary graduate figures based on fall 1993 data and first-professional figures based on 1992–93 graduates.
[3] Data are for in-state students only.
—Data not available or not applicable.

NOTE.—Average graduate student tuition weighted by fall enrollment. Average first-professional tuition weighted by number of degrees conferred during the academic year.

Some year-to-year fluctuations in tuition data may reflect nonreporting by individual institutions. Some data have been revised from previously published figures.

SOURCE: U.S. Department of Education, National Center for Education Statistics, Integrated Postsecondary Education Data System (IPEDS), "Institutional Characteristics," "Fall Enrollment," and "Degrees Conferred" surveys. (This table was prepared August 1995.)

Table 309.—Percent of undergraduates enrolled in fall 1992 receiving aid and average amount awarded in 1992–93 per student, by type and source of aid and selected student characteristics

Selected student characteristics	Enrollment of under-graduates,[1] in thousands	Any aid			Grants			Loans			Work study	Other		
		Total[2]	Federal	Non-federal	Total	Federal	Non-federal	Total	Federal	Non-federal	Total[3]	Total	Federal	Non-federal
1	2	3	4	5	6	7	8	9	10	11	12	13	14	15
		Percent of all undergraduates receiving aid												
All undergraduates	**18,478**	**41.4**	**32.1**	**23.6**	**36.6**	**22.6**	**20.9**	**20.4**	**19.9**	**1.4**	**4.8**	**5.8**	**2.7**	**3.3**
Sex														
Men	8,166	39.1	29.5	23.3	31.8	19.2	20.6	19.7	19.1	1.5	4.6	6.9	2.9	4.2
Women	10,188	42.9	33.7	23.7	36.6	25.0	21.1	20.7	20.1	1.4	5.0	4.9	2.6	2.5
Race/ethnicity														
White, non-Hispanic	13,818	39.3	29.2	23.3	32.1	19.2	20.8	20.0	19.4	1.4	4.5	5.6	2.7	3.1
Black, non-Hispanic	1,847	54.1	47.6	24.7	47.2	38.2	20.9	26.8	26.4	1.3	6.8	8.2	3.9	4.7
Hispanic	1,432	43.0	36.3	21.5	38.8	30.7	19.1	15.2	14.5	1.2	4.0	4.9	1.6	3.4
Asian American	718	30.8	25.1	20.1	26.8	18.7	18.2	15.3	15.0	0.9	5.8	2.7	1.1	1.7
American Indian	172	47.8	35.2	28.7	42.6	29.2	25.1	15.4	15.0	0.9	4.4	8.4	1.6	6.7
Age														
23 years old or younger	10,163	45.6	35.5	27.3	37.4	23.1	24.3	24.8	24.0	2.0	7.0	7.3	4.6	2.9
24 to 29 years old	3,159	41.2	35.3	18.7	35.1	27.3	16.5	19.9	19.7	0.7	2.8	5.0	0.5	4.6
30 years old or over	5,116	33.3	23.5	19.1	28.8	18.5	16.9	12.1	11.9	0.7	1.7	3.5	0.3	3.2
Marital status														
Married	4,481	32.4	22.9	17.8	26.8	16.1	15.9	13.3	13.0	0.7	1.5	3.6	0.4	3.3
Not married[4]	12,744	44.5	35.5	25.8	37.1	24.6	22.9	23.4	22.8	1.7	6.1	6.6	3.6	3.2
Separated	322	61.6	56.1	27.8	59.2	52.5	22.9	23.1	23.0	0.7	4.7	5.7	0.2	5.5
Attendance status[5]														
Full-time	6,000	57.9	45.6	37.9	48.1	29.4	34.0	33.6	32.7	2.7	10.2	9.5	5.2	4.6
Part-time	12,293	32.9	25.0	16.5	27.7	18.8	14.5	13.6	13.2	0.8	2.1	4.0	1.4	2.7
Dependency status														
Dependent	8,858	41.7	31.2	26.7	33.5	18.6	23.8	23.0	22.2	2.1	7.1	7.1	5.0	2.3
Independent	9,620	41.2	33.0	20.7	35.7	26.3	18.2	18.0	17.8	0.8	2.7	4.7	0.6	4.2
Housing status														
School-owned	2,369	63.0	47.7	46.0	52.5	26.7	41.6	40.7	39.4	3.5	17.5	12.0	8.3	4.2
Off-campus, not with parents	10,163	39.8	30.6	21.4	33.0	22.1	18.8	18.9	18.6	1.2	3.2	5.1	1.7	3.5
With parents	4,793	35.0	28.1	17.8	29.7	21.4	15.8	14.2	13.7	1.1	2.3	4.5	2.3	2.3
With relatives	406	36.7	30.6	16.9	32.3	24.9	14.3	16.0	15.6	1.0	2.9	4.4	1.6	2.9
Other	38	40.9	28.6	26.4	38.2	24.1	26.3	8.4	7.9	0.4	2.2	1.5	1.3	0.2
		Average 1992–93 award for full-time, full-year undergraduates enrolled in fall 1992 (Award averages are computed for students participating in the designated program.)												
All full-time, full-year undergraduates	**6,000**	**$5,543**	**$4,257**	**$3,347**	**$3,487**	**$2,003**	**$3,201**	**$3,834**	**$3,723**	**$2,639**	**$1,357**	**$2,932**	**$3,340**	**$2,289**
Sex														
Men	2,838	5,759	4,407	3,499	3,616	1,990	3,372	3,944	3,839	2,626	1,372	3,061	3,452	2,539
Women	3,145	5,370	4,137	3,226	3,391	2,016	3,064	3,740	3,625	2,656	1,348	2,793	3,238	1,951
Race/ethnicity														
White, non-Hispanic	4,542	5,495	4,297	3,312	3,438	1,955	3,154	3,879	3,761	2,671	1,362	2,978	3,407	2,304
Black, non-Hispanic	553	5,738	4,329	3,439	3,424	2,094	3,411	3,619	3,538	2,359	1,324	2,809	3,061	2,174
Hispanic	384	4,960	3,666	2,843	3,302	2,079	2,659	3,655	3,597	—	1,301	2,587	3,294	2,090
Asian American	268	6,454	4,111	4,127	4,569	2,067	4,073	3,827	3,667	—	1,542	3,078	—	—
American Indian	48	5,072	4,047	2,752	3,181	2,231	2,368	3,568	3,475	—	—	2,800	—	—
Age														
23 years old or younger	4,785	5,622	4,147	3,629	3,697	1,947	3,470	3,722	3,588	2,744	1,323	3,205	3,379	2,568
24 to 29 years old	606	5,528	4,710	2,337	2,944	2,125	2,191	4,269	4,216	1,976	1,495	2,223	3,029	2,120
30 years old or over	605	5,062	4,383	2,035	2,718	2,107	1,820	4,091	4,050	2,100	1,674	1,802	—	1,712
Marital status														
Married	608	4,872	4,355	2,106	2,537	1,965	1,905	3,797	3,676	2,650	1,341	3,011	3,362	2,294
Not married[4]	4,917	5,706	4,254	3,479	3,631	2,004	3,328	4,147	4,114	2,046	1,409	2,215	—	2,156
Separated	63	4,914	3,981	1,978	2,858	2,275	1,711	3,678	3,548	—	—	—	—	—
Dependency status														
Dependent	4,334	5,676	4,094	3,766	3,819	1,874	3,611	3,716	3,570	2,753	1,319	3,289	3,389	2,658
Independent	1,666	5,298	4,495	2,287	2,906	2,130	2,107	4,046	3,994	2,231	1,491	2,165	2,879	1,999
Housing status														
School-owned	1,643	7,103	4,631	4,723	4,822	2,093	4,540	3,732	3,581	2,906	1,275	3,395	3,412	2,930
Off-campus, not with parents	2,717	5,194	4,413	2,613	2,961	2,035	2,437	3,998	3,902	2,558	1,458	2,689	3,283	2,173
With parents	1,549	4,044	3,369	2,363	2,681	1,836	2,265	3,525	3,455	2,152	1,406	2,640	3,272	1,788
With relatives	85	4,948	4,225	2,279	2,687	2,027	2,043	4,129	4,035	—	1,633	—	—	—
Other	7	—	—	—	—	—	—	—	—	—	—	—	—	—
		Average 1992–93 award for other undergraduates enrolled in fall 1992 (Award averages are computed for students participating in the designated program.)												
All other undergraduates[6]	**12,293**	**2,976**	**2,916**	**1,521**	**1,711**	**1,435**	**1,407**	**3,256**	**3,219**	**2,017**	**1,353**	**1,942**	**3,094**	**1,274**
Sex														
Men	5,282	3,108	3,067	1,646	1,776	1,438	1,550	3,418	3,371	2,109	1,322	1,959	3,308	1,308
Women	6,958	2,886	2,824	1,428	1,672	1,432	1,302	3,150	3,122	1,924	1,373	1,942	2,909	1,243
Race/ethnicity														
White, non-Hispanic	9,152	3,007	3,040	1,515	1,691	1,412	1,407	3,311	3,268	2,108	1,353	1,968	3,085	1,281
Black, non-Hispanic	1,271	2,928	2,686	1,478	1,753	1,478	1,375	3,052	3,008	1,779	1,192	2,052	3,122	1,387
Hispanic	1,042	2,598	2,479	1,356	1,686	1,518	1,234	3,059	3,187	944	1,805	1,683	3,218	1,199
Asian American	449	3,664	3,159	1,896	2,142	1,590	1,690	3,125	3,131	—	1,282	1,833	—	—
American Indian	123	2,441	2,327	1,514	1,622	1,260	1,488	3,073	2,939	—	—	—	—	—

Table 309.—Percent of undergraduates enrolled in fall 1992 receiving aid and average amount awarded in 1992–93 per student, by type and source of aid and selected student characteristics—Continued

Selected student characteristics	Enrollment of under-graduates,[1] in thousands	Any aid			Grants			Loans			Work study	Other		
		Total[2]	Federal	Non-federal	Total	Federal	Non-federal	Total	Federal	Non-federal	Total[3]	Total	Federal	Non-federal
1	2	3	4	5	6	7	8	9	10	11	12	13	14	15
Age														
23 years old or younger	5,277	3,320	2,989	1,878	1,908	1,435	1,747	3,199	3,154	2,172	1,195	2,385	3,224	1,262
24 to 29 years old	2,523	2,920	2,925	1,189	1,560	1,446	1,075	3,282	3,257	1,766	1,625	1,357	2,207	1,284
30 years old or over	4,465	2,498	2,775	1,249	1,538	1,424	1,175	3,380	3,352	1,552	1,672	1,339	1,712	1,291
Marital status														
Married	3,847	2,484	2,804	1,214	1,447	1,367	1,162	3,256	3,246	1,680	1,477	1,356	2,656	1,222
Not married[4]	7,709	3,181	2,970	1,650	1,817	1,449	1,517	3,273	3,231	2,018	1,343	2,135	3,160	1,293
Separated	257	2,649	2,498	1,046	1,619	1,472	928	2,857	2,846	—	—	1,194	—	1,124
Dependency status														
Dependent	4,440	3,457	3,039	2,097	2,018	1,391	1,961	3,275	3,216	2,318	1,191	2,648	3,217	1,370
Independent	7,854	2,729	2,849	1,216	1,569	1,455	1,126	3,243	3,222	1,632	1,552	1,354	2,344	1,242
Housing status														
School-owned	709	4,811	3,640	3,148	2,881	1,580	2,961	3,443	3,305	3,020	1,007	2,965	3,195	2,049
Off-campus, not with parents	8,040	2,834	2,969	1,316	1,583	1,435	1,212	3,313	3,270	2,006	1,575	1,664	2,989	1,229
With parents	3,195	2,615	2,475	1,333	1,617	1,379	1,232	2,961	2,999	1,445	1,383	2,038	3,155	1,063
With relatives	319	2,894	2,943	1,159	1,648	1,560	1,127	3,151	3,186	—	—	1,717	—	—
Other	31	—	—	—	—	—	—	—	—	—	—	—	—	—

[1] Numbers of undergraduates may not equal figures reported in other tables, since these data are based on a sample survey of students who enrolled at any time during the academic year.

[2] Includes students who reported they were awarded aid, but did not specify the source or type of aid.

[3] Details on nonfederal Work Study participants are not available.

[4] Includes students who were single, divorced, or widowed.

[5] Excludes persons whose attendance status was not reported.

[6] Enrollment data include persons whose attendance status was not reported.

NOTE.—Because of rounding and/or the fact that some students receive aid from multiple sources, row details may not add to totals. Because of rounding and survey item nonresponse, enrollment data may not add to totals. Data include undergraduates in noncollegiate and collegiate institutions.

SOURCE: U.S. Department of Education, National Center for Education Statistics, National Postsecondary Student Aid Study, 1992–93. (This table was prepared August 1995.)

Table 310.—Undergraduates enrolled full-time and part-time in fall 1992, by aid status and source of aid during 1992–93, and control and level of institution

Control and level of institution	Number of undergraduates, fall 1992,[1] in thousands	Aid status, 1992–93, in percents					
		Nonaided	Receiving aid, by source				
			Any aid[2]	Federal	State	Institutional	Other[2]
1	2	3	4	5	6	7	8
Full-time students[3]							
All institutions	6,000	42.1	57.9	45.6	17.9	23.4	9.7
Public	4,110	48.1	51.9	40.0	16.5	16.2	8.8
4-year doctoral	1,772	46.3	53.7	39.3	14.9	20.8	9.7
Other 4-year	1,087	43.6	56.4	46.1	21.6	16.1	8.1
2-year	1,196	54.1	45.9	36.0	14.6	10.1	8.2
Less than 2-year	55	65.0	35.0	31.6	10.9	0.4	7.7
Private, nonprofit	1,469	30.5	69.5	53.4	24.6	48.5	13.2
4-year doctoral	681	37.3	62.7	44.5	17.9	48.2	13.4
Other 4-year	719	24.5	75.5	60.8	31.0	51.2	13.3
2-year or less	70	26.1	73.9	63.9	23.2	23.8	10.4
Private, proprietary	421	23.9	76.1	72.4	8.1	6.1	6.9
2-year and above	182	19.4	80.6	77.4	14.1	7.5	10.6
Less than 2-year	238	27.3	72.7	68.6	3.5	5.0	4.1
Part-time students[3]							
All institutions	12,293	67.1	32.9	25.0	6.7	6.6	6.6
Public	9,911	72.9	27.1	19.8	6.2	4.9	6.1
4-year doctoral	1,504	63.5	36.5	27.5	7.6	9.5	6.9
Other 4-year	1,330	64.4	35.6	28.4	10.0	6.7	6.2
2-year	6,850	76.4	23.6	16.5	5.3	3.7	5.9
Less than 2-year	227	80.8	19.2	15.1	1.5	1.0	5.3
Private, nonprofit	1,431	50.6	49.4	35.1	11.6	20.2	11.0
4-year doctoral	391	55.6	44.4	28.3	8.8	23.7	8.9
Other 4-year	818	47.8	52.2	38.1	13.4	19.8	13.3
2-year or less	223	52.4	47.6	35.8	10.0	15.3	6.4
Private, proprietary	951	31.0	69.0	64.4	4.7	3.8	5.0
2-year and above	383	39.6	60.4	54.9	6.4	2.9	6.8
Less than 2-year	568	25.2	74.8	70.8	3.5	4.3	3.8

[1] Numbers of undergraduates may not equal figures reported in other tables, since these data are based on a sample survey. Includes students who enrolled at any time during the academic year.

[2] Includes students who reported that they were awarded aid but did not specify the source of the aid.

[3] Full-time students are students who attend full-time for the entire academic year. All other students, including those who attend full-time for part of the academic year, are counted as part-time students.

NOTE.—Because some students receive aid from multiple sources, percents do not add to totals. Excludes students whose attendance status was not reported. Data have been revised from previously published figures.

SOURCE: U.S. Department of Education, National Center for Education Statistics, National Postsecondary Student Aid Study, 1992–93. (This table was prepared July 1995.)

Table 311.—Undergraduates enrolled full-time and part-time in fall 1992, by type and source of aid received during 1992–93, and by control and level of institution

Control and level of institution	Number of undergraduates, fall 1992,[1] in thousands	Percent receiving aid in 1992–93, by type and source													
		Any aid			Grants			Loans			Work-study		Other		
		Total[2]	Federal	Nonfederal	Total	Federal	Nonfederal	Total	Federal	Nonfederal	Total	Federal	Total	Federal	Nonfederal
1	2	3	4	5	6	7	8	9	10	11	12	13	14	15	16
Full-time students [4]															
All institutions	**6,000**	**57.9**	**45.6**	**37.9**	**48.1**	**29.4**	**34.0**	**33.6**	**32.7**	**2.7**	**10.2**	**6.8**	**9.5**	**5.2**	**4.6**
Public	4,110	51.9	40.0	33.0	42.3	27.8	29.1	26.9	26.1	2.0	6.8	4.2	7.9	3.7	4.4
4-year doctoral	1,772	53.7	39.3	34.8	41.9	23.8	30.8	33.0	32.2	2.4	7.1	4.3	8.6	5.0	3.9
Other 4-year	1,087	56.4	46.1	37.4	45.5	32.1	32.4	33.7	32.7	2.8	9.5	5.5	7.9	4.2	3.8
2-year	1,196	45.9	36.0	27.0	40.6	29.9	24.3	12.7	12.3	0.7	4.1	3.0	7.0	1.3	5.7
Less than 2-year	55	35.0	31.6	15.7	29.9	26.6	12.8	3.0	3.0	0.6	1.5	1.4	5.1	0.8	4.4
Private, nonprofit	1,469	69.5	53.4	58.0	62.1	27.7	54.1	46.5	44.9	4.9	22.2	15.9	12.1	7.7	5.0
4-year doctoral	681	62.7	44.5	54.8	55.2	17.3	51.8	41.6	39.7	6.1	18.9	13.2	11.6	7.4	4.5
Other 4-year	719	75.5	60.8	62.7	68.7	35.6	58.1	51.7	50.3	4.1	27.0	19.7	12.2	7.9	5.3
2-year or less	70	73.9	63.9	42.0	61.3	47.3	35.4	41.1	39.5	2.5	4.6	3.0	17.2	9.4	7.8
Private, proprietary	421	76.1	72.4	16.4	55.3	50.9	11.4	54.1	53.8	2.1	1.9	0.7	15.6	11.3	4.5
2-year and above	182	80.6	77.4	22.7	49.5	43.4	16.4	65.2	65.2	3.0	3.5	1.4	24.6	18.8	6.5
Less than 2-year	238	72.7	68.6	11.5	59.7	56.7	7.5	45.6	45.1	1.5	0.7	0.2	8.7	5.6	3.1
Part-time students [4]															
All institutions	**12,293**	**32.9**	**25.0**	**16.5**	**27.7**	**18.8**	**14.5**	**13.6**	**13.2**	**0.8**	**2.1**	**1.2**	**4.0**	**1.4**	**2.7**
Public	9,911	27.1	19.8	14.5	23.0	15.3	12.6	9.4	9.1	0.6	1.7	0.9	3.5	1.0	2.6
4-year doctoral	1,504	36.5	27.5	19.5	27.2	17.1	16.6	21.5	21.1	1.1	3.6	2.1	6.2	3.1	3.4
Other 4-year	1,330	35.6	28.4	19.2	29.9	22.0	16.1	16.5	15.9	1.3	3.1	1.6	4.1	1.5	2.6
2-year	6,850	23.6	16.5	12.7	20.9	13.7	11.2	5.6	5.4	0.4	1.1	0.6	2.9	0.4	2.5
Less than 2-year	227	19.2	15.1	6.9	17.3	13.8	6.0	0.6	0.6	0.0	0.6	0.4	1.7	0.3	1.3
Private, nonprofit	1,431	49.4	35.1	33.7	43.1	23.2	31.7	24.0	23.4	1.8	5.9	3.8	5.3	2.6	2.9
4-year doctoral	391	44.4	28.3	33.0	37.3	12.8	31.7	24.3	23.4	2.7	5.4	3.1	4.2	2.9	1.5
Other 4-year	818	52.2	38.1	35.6	46.4	26.8	33.6	24.8	24.2	1.5	7.3	4.8	5.7	2.5	3.4
2-year or less	223	47.6	35.8	28.4	41.4	28.3	24.4	20.7	20.3	1.2	1.2	1.2	5.8	2.2	3.6
Private, proprietary	951	69.0	64.4	11.8	53.2	48.8	8.6	42.0	41.5	1.5	0.9	0.4	6.8	4.4	2.5
2-year and above	383	60.4	54.9	14.3	42.0	35.0	12.1	45.4	45.3	0.9	1.4	0.6	8.0	6.0	2.1
Less than 2-year	568	74.8	70.8	10.2	60.8	58.1	6.3	39.6	39.0	1.8	0.5	0.3	5.9	3.2	2.7

[1] Numbers of undergraduates may not equal figures reported in other tables, since these data are based on a sample survey. Includes students who enrolled at any time during the academic year.

[2] Includes students who reported they were awarded aid but did not specify the source of aid.

[3] Details on nonfederal work study participants are not available.

[4] Full-time students are students who attend full-time for the entire academic year. All other students, including those who attend full-time for part of the academic year, are counted as part-time students.

NOTE.—Excludes students whose attendance status was not reported. Because some students receive multiple types and sources of aid, details may not add to totals.

SOURCE: U.S. Department of Education, National Center for Education Statistics, National Postsecondary Student Aid Study, 1992–93. (This table was prepared July 1995.)

Table 312.—Undergraduates enrolled full-time and part-time in fall 1992, by federal aid program and by control and level of institution: 1992–93

Control and level of institution	Number of undergraduates, fall 1992 [1]	Percent receiving federal aid in 1992–93, by type										
		Any federal aid	Selected Title IV programs [2]									Any other federal aid [9]
			Any Title IV aid	Pell	SEOG [3]	CWS [4]	Per-kins [5]	Stafford [6]	Plus [7]	SLS [8]	
1	2	3	4	5	6	7	8	9	10	11	12
					Full-time students [10]						
All institutions	6,000	45.6	44.5	28.2	8.5	10.2	6.6	29.5	5.0	3.4	5.2
Public	4,110	40.0	38.7	26.8	6.7	6.8	4.4	23.0	3.5	2.1	3.7
4-year doctoral	1,772	39.3	38.5	23.0	6.1	7.1	5.9	28.4	5.0	2.7	5.0
Other 4-year	1,087	46.1	45.3	31.1	8.4	9.5	5.6	28.7	4.2	2.2	4.2
2-year	1,196	36.0	33.4	28.5	6.3	4.1	1.4	10.6	0.8	1.2	1.3
Less than 2-year	55	31.6	27.2	24.9	0.8	1.5	0.1	3.0	0.0	0.9	0.8
Private, nonprofit	1,469	53.4	52.8	26.0	12.4	22.2	13.6	41.6	7.6	4.0	7.7
4-year doctoral	681	44.5	43.8	15.2	8.9	18.9	15.0	36.7	7.4	3.9	7.4
Other 4-year	719	60.8	60.3	34.1	15.7	27.0	13.5	46.6	7.8	4.1	7.9
2-year or less	70	63.9	63.4	46.4	12.0	4.6	0.6	37.6	8.2	3.6	9.4
Private, proprietary	421	72.4	71.9	49.6	12.5	1.9	3.1	51.5	11.3	14.1	11.3
2-year and above	182	77.4	76.7	42.1	14.0	3.5	4.0	62.7	18.8	18.6	18.8
Less than 2-year	238	68.6	68.1	55.3	11.4	0.7	2.3	43.0	5.5	10.6	5.6
					Part-time students [10]						
All institutions	12,293	25.0	23.9	18.0	3.5	2.1	1.6	12.2	1.3	2.0	1.4
Public	9,911	19.8	18.5	14.5	2.6	1.7	1.1	8.2	0.8	1.0	1.0
4-year doctoral	1,504	27.5	26.4	16.1	3.8	3.6	3.5	19.2	2.9	2.2	3.1
Other 4-year	1,330	28.4	27.5	21.3	3.7	3.1	2.2	14.0	1.4	1.4	1.5
2-year	6,850	16.5	15.2	13.0	2.1	1.1	0.5	4.9	0.3	0.7	0.4
Less than 2-year	227	15.1	13.5	10.8	2.4	0.6	—	0.6	—	0.1	0.3
Private, nonprofit	1,431	35.1	34.3	21.9	5.4	5.9	3.8	21.8	2.5	3.4	2.6
4-year doctoral	391	28.3	27.6	11.1	3.6	5.4	4.5	21.5	2.8	5.0	2.9
Other 4-year	818	38.1	37.2	25.7	6.2	7.3	4.3	22.8	2.5	3.0	2.5
2-year or less	223	35.8	35.4	27.1	5.7	1.2	0.9	19.0	2.0	2.1	2.2
Private, proprietary	951	64.4	64.0	47.8	9.9	0.9	2.5	40.1	4.3	10.8	4.4
2-year and above	383	54.9	54.8	34.2	9.9	1.4	3.7	44.3	6.0	13.6	6.0
Less than 2-year	568	70.8	70.3	56.9	9.9	0.5	1.6	37.4	3.2	8.9	3.2

[1] Numbers of undergraduates may not equal figures reported in other tables, since these data are based on a sample survey. Includes students who enrolled at any time during the academic year.
[2] Title IV of the Higher Education Act.
[3] Supplemental Educational Opportunity Grants.
[4] College Work Study (CWS). Prior to October 17, 1986, private, proprietary institutions were prohibited by law from spending CWS funds for on-campus work. Includes persons who participated in the program, but had no earnings.
[5] Formerly National Direct Student Loans (NDSL).
[6] Formerly Guaranteed Student Loans (GSL).
[7] Parent Loans for Undergraduate Students.
[8] Supplementary Loans for Students.

[9] Includes aid from all federal departments and agencies except Title IV aid.
[10] Full-time students are students who attend full-time for the entire academic year. All other students, including those who attend full-time for part of the academic year, are counted as part-time students.

—Less than .05 percent.

NOTE.—Excludes students whose attendance status was not reported. Because some students receive aid from multiple sources, percents do not add to totals.

SOURCE: U.S. Department of Education, National Center for Education Statistics, National Postsecondary Student Aid Study, 1992–93. (This table was prepared July 1995.)

Table 313.—Postbaccalaureate students enrolled full-time and part-time in fall 1992, by aid status and source of aid during 1992–93, by level of study and by control and level of institution

Level of degree, control and type of institution	Postbaccalaureate students,[1] fall 1992, in thousands	Aid status, 1992–93, in percents						
		Nonaided	Receiving aid, by source					
			Any aid[2]	Federal	State	Institutional	Employer	Other[3]
1	2	3	4	5	6	7	8	9
		Full-time students[4]						
All institutions	673	31.9	68.1	44.4	7.0	40.6	3.3	14.6
Master's degree	281	37.5	62.5	33.8	5.8	42.4	5.1	12.0
Public	163	34.6	65.4	33.9	7.8	44.0	4.8	9.7
4-year doctoral	139	34.3	65.7	32.4	6.7	46.3	4.7	10.1
Other 4-year	24	36.1	63.9	42.5	14.4	30.4	5.3	7.5
Private	118	41.6	58.4	33.7	3.2	40.2	5.6	15.2
4-year doctoral	102	39.3	60.7	34.2	2.9	42.9	5.7	16.4
Other 4-year	16	56.5	43.5	30.5	5.1	22.8	4.7	7.4
Doctor's degree	120	30.4	69.6	28.3	4.4	51.6	2.2	13.2
Public	73	30.3	69.7	22.3	6.5	55.5	3.1	11.7
Private	46	30.4	69.6	37.8	1.1	45.5	0.9	15.7
First-professional	211	23.0	77.0	68.2	10.0	37.0	1.2	20.3
Public	101	20.7	79.3	72.5	13.4	37.7	1.3	15.8
Private	110	25.1	74.9	64.3	6.8	36.4	1.2	24.4
Other graduate	61	39.3	60.7	42.4	6.7	22.9	3.7	9.1
		Part-time students[4]						
All institutions	1,980	71.3	28.7	10.8	1.9	12.7	7.9	9.9
Master's degree	1,322	71.7	28.3	10.5	1.6	11.1	8.8	10.8
Public	773	73.9	26.1	10.1	2.5	11.7	6.7	8.0
4-year doctoral	489	69.6	30.4	11.9	2.5	15.3	6.7	8.2
Other 4-year	284	81.2	18.8	6.9	2.4	5.5	6.5	7.5
Private	549	68.6	31.4	11.1	0.4	10.3	11.8	14.9
4-year doctoral	357	66.9	33.1	12.1	0.4	12.1	12.1	15.0
Other 4-year	192	71.7	28.3	9.3	0.6	6.9	11.2	14.7
Doctor's degree	149	56.2	43.8	8.6	3.5	33.1	5.4	9.9
Public	97	56.1	43.9	8.5	4.4	33.3	6.4	8.9
Private	51	56.4	43.6	8.9	1.6	32.6	3.7	11.8
First-professional	64	42.6	57.4	44.9	3.3	25.7	3.4	13.9
Public	24	50.8	49.2	42.9	3.6	22.2	2.5	7.5
Private	40	37.8	62.2	46.1	3.2	27.8	3.9	17.6
Other graduate	446	79.7	20.3	7.7	1.7	8.4	6.4	6.5

[1] Numbers of postbaccalaureate students may not equal figures reported in other tables, since these data are based on a sample survey of all postbaccalaureate students. Includes students who enrolled at any time during the academic year.

[2] Includes students who reported they were awarded aid but did not specify the source of aid.

[3] Includes aid provided by corporations, unions, foundations, fraternal organizations, community organizations, etc.

[4] Full-time students are students who attend full-time for the entire academic year. All other students, including those who attend full-time for part of the academic year, are counted as part-time students.

NOTE.—Excludes students whose attendance status was not reported. Because some students receive aid from multiple sources, percents do not add to totals.

SOURCE: U.S. Department of Education, National Center for Education Statistics, National Postsecondary Student Aid Study, 1992–93. (This table was prepared July 1995.)

Table 314.—Postbaccalaureate students enrolled full-time and part-time in fall 1992, by type of aid received during 1992–93, by level of study and by control and level of institution

Level of degree, control and type of institution	Postbaccalaureate students,[1] fall 1992, in thousands	Type of aid, 1992–93, in percents							
		Any aid[2]	Fellowship grants	Tuition waivers	Assistantships[3]	Employer	Loans		
							Any loans	Stafford[4]	SLS[5]
1	2	3	4	5	6	7	8	9	10
Full-time students[6]									
All institutions	**673**	**68.1**	**3.5**	**12.4**	**14.3**	**3.3**	**43.5**	**41.1**	**19.2**
Master's degree	281	62.5	3.5	15.6	18.1	5.1	32.5	30.5	10.0
Public	163	65.4	2.2	20.5	22.4	4.8	32.2	30.8	7.3
4-year doctoral	139	65.7	2.4	23.3	23.5	4.7	30.6	29.6	7.4
Other 4-year	24	63.9	1.0	4.4	15.8	5.3	41.5	38.4	6.8
Private	118	58.4	5.3	8.9	12.1	5.6	32.9	30.0	13.6
4-year doctoral	103	60.7	6.2	9.5	13.6	5.7	33.6	30.8	14.9
Other 4-year	16	43.5	0.0	5.4	3.0	4.7	28.7	24.6	5.6
Doctor's degree	120	69.6	9.3	19.4	27.0	2.2	25.8	23.9	10.0
Public	73	69.7	4.2	23.1	31.6	3.1	20.6	18.9	5.6
Private	46	69.6	17.5	13.6	19.9	0.9	34.1	31.9	17.0
First-professional	211	77.0	0.9	5.6	4.4	1.2	67.8	65.5	38.3
Public	101	79.3	0.4	5.4	4.3	1.3	71.8	69.9	37.5
Private	110	74.9	1.2	5.8	4.5	1.2	64.1	61.6	39.1
Other graduate	61	60.7	1.1	7.5	6.2	3.7	44.4	39.6	14.2
Part-time students[6]									
All institutions	**1,980**	**28.7**	**0.6**	**5.1**	**4.3**	**7.9**	**10.5**	**9.4**	**2.8**
Master's degree	1,322	28.3	0.6	4.6	3.8	8.8	10.3	9.3	2.1
Public	773	26.1	0.9	4.9	5.2	6.7	9.9	9.0	1.7
4-year doctoral	489	30.4	1.4	6.5	6.7	6.7	11.8	10.7	2.3
Other 4-year	284	18.8	0.1	2.3	2.6	6.5	6.5	6.0	0.8
Private	549	31.4	0.2	4.2	1.8	11.8	11.0	9.7	2.6
4-year doctoral	357	33.1	0.3	4.4	2.5	12.1	11.9	10.5	3.3
Other 4-year	192	28.3	0.2	3.8	0.7	11.2	9.3	8.1	1.3
Doctor's degree	149	43.8	2.4	12.7	17.0	5.4	7.3	6.9	1.6
Public	97	43.9	2.1	15.0	17.0	6.4	7.1	6.5	0.6
Private	51	43.6	3.1	8.3	17.0	3.7	7.7	7.5	3.6
First-professional	64	57.4	0.3	5.9	3.1	3.4	45.6	42.0	22.8
Public	24	49.2	0.0	6.8	6.1	2.5	42.4	41.4	19.6
Private	40	62.2	0.5	5.4	1.4	3.9	47.5	42.3	24.8
Other graduate	446	20.3	0.1	3.4	1.6	6.4	7.1	6.0	2.2

[1] Numbers of postbaccalaureate students may not equal figures reported in other tables, since these data are based on a sample survey of all postbaccalaureate students. Includes students who enrolled at any time during the academic year.

[2] Includes students who reported they were awarded aid but did not specify the source of aid.

[3] Includes students who received teaching or research assistantships and/or participated in work-study programs.

[4] Stafford loans, formerly Graduate Student Loans (GSL).

[5] Supplementary Loans for Students.

[6] Full-time students are students who attend full-time for the entire academic year. All other students, including those who attend full-time for part of the academic year, are counted as part-time students.

NOTE.—Excludes students whose attendance status was not reported. Because some students receive aid from multiple sources, percents do not add to totals.

SOURCE: U.S. Department of Education, National Center for Education Statistics, National Postsecondary Student Aid Study, 1992–93. (This table was prepared July 1995.)

Table 315.—Scholarship and fellowship awards [1] of institutions of higher education, by control of institution: 1959–60 to 1992–93

[In thousands]

Year	Total scholarship and fellowship awards			Scholarship and fellowship awards from unrestricted funds			Scholarship and fellowship awards from restricted funds		
	All institutions	Public	Private	All institutions	Public	Private	All institutions	Public	Private
1	2	3	4	5	6	7	8	9	10
1959–60	$172,051	$59,673	$112,377	—	—	—	—	—	—
1961–62	228,765	78,255	150,510	—	—	—	—	—	—
1963–64	300,370	107,767	192,603	—	—	—	—	—	—
1965–66	425,524	153,256	272,269	—	—	—	—	—	—
1966–67	583,390	248,077	335,311	—	—	—	—	—	—
1967–68	712,425	326,915	385,510	—	—	—	—	—	—
1968–69	814,755	367,433	447,322	—	—	—	—	—	—
1969–70	984,594	456,977	527,617	—	—	—	—	—	—
1970–71	1,098,198	528,243	569,955	—	—	—	—	—	—
1971–72	1,241,372	621,387	619,986	—	—	—	—	—	—
1972–73	1,322,411	656,054	666,357	—	—	—	—	—	—
1973–74	1,396,488	705,691	690,797	$631,801	$267,191	$364,610	$817,741	$451,589	$366,152
1974–75	1,449,542	718,780	730,762	686,604	276,334	410,269	949,255	522,181	427,074
1975–76	1,635,859	798,515	837,343	748,763	291,073	457,690	1,021,451	567,938	453,514
1976–77	1,770,215	859,011	911,204						
1977–78	1,839,298	840,666	998,632	818,101	305,563	512,537	1,021,197	535,102	486,095
1978–79	1,944,599	861,578	1,083,021	883,213	326,201	557,012	1,061,386	535,377	526,009
1979–80	2,200,468	970,363	1,230,106	904,876	324,224	580,652	1,295,592	646,138	649,454
1980–81	2,504,525	1,064,864	1,439,661	1,080,614	367,476	713,138	1,423,911	697,388	726,523
1981–82	2,684,945	1,088,717	1,596,228	1,236,081	374,632	861,449	1,448,864	714,085	734,779
1982–83	2,922,897	1,188,383	1,734,514	1,478,762	460,291	1,018,470	1,444,136	728,092	716,044
1983–84	3,301,673	1,276,644	2,025,028	1,738,188	518,626	1,219,562	1,563,485	758,018	805,466
1984–85	3,670,355	1,374,803	2,295,551	1,961,597	569,058	1,392,539	1,708,758	805,745	903,012
1985–86	4,160,174	1,575,909	2,584,266	2,285,116	696,973	1,588,143	1,875,059	878,935	996,123
1986–87	4,776,100	1,751,671	3,024,430	2,644,615	750,931	1,893,684	2,131,486	1,000,740	1,130,746
1987–88	5,325,358	1,941,389	3,383,968	2,941,143	830,195	2,110,948	2,384,215	1,111,194	1,273,021
1988–89	5,918,666	2,150,350	3,768,316	3,282,698	944,001	2,338,697	2,635,969	1,206,349	1,429,619
1989–90	6,655,544	2,386,493	4,269,051	3,853,904	1,099,425	2,754,479	2,801,640	1,287,068	1,514,572
1990–91	7,551,184	2,688,532	4,862,651	4,445,106	1,270,158	3,174,947	3,106,078	1,418,374	1,687,704
1991–92	9,060,000	3,255,660	5,804,340	5,205,797	1,523,721	3,682,076	3,854,203	1,731,939	2,122,264
1992–93 [2]	10,148,373	3,727,838	6,420,536	5,949,037	1,745,339	4,203,697	4,199,337	1,982,498	2,216,838

[1] Includes Supplemental Educational Opportunity Grants and State Student Incentive Grants, but excludes Pell Grants.

[2] Preliminary data.

—Data not collected.

NOTE.—Because of rounding, details may not add to totals.

SOURCE: U.S. Department of Education, National Center for Education Statistics, "Financial Statistics of Institutions of Higher Education" surveys and Integrated Postsecondary Education Data System (IPEDS), "Finance" surveys. (This table was prepared May 1995.)

Table 316.—Pell Grant revenue of institutions of higher education compared to current-fund revenue and tuition, by type and control of institution: 1985–86 to 1992–93

[Amounts in thousands]

Year and type of control of institution	Total				Public				Private			
	Current-fund revenue	Tuition	Pell Grant revenue	Pell Grants as a percent of current-fund revenue	Current-fund revenue	Tuition	Pell Grant revenue	Pell Grants as a percent of current-fund revenue	Current-fund revenue	Tuition	Pell Grant revenue	Pell Grants as a percent of current-fund revenue
1	2	3	4	5	6	7	8	9	10	11	12	13
1985–86	$100,437,616	$23,116,605	$2,565,048	2.6	$65,004,632	$9,439,177	$1,873,456	2.9	$35,432,985	$13,677,429	$691,592	2.0
4-year	88,144,386	20,498,399	1,770,042	2.0	53,746,503	7,539,717	1,214,303	2.3	34,397,882	12,958,683	555,739	1.6
2-year	12,293,231	2,618,206	795,006	6.5	11,258,128	1,899,460	659,153	5.9	1,035,102	718,746	135,853	13.1
1987–88	117,340,109	27,836,781	2,496,133	2.1	74,771,255	11,184,657	1,876,777	2.5	42,568,854	16,652,124	619,355	1.5
4-year	103,280,070	24,779,364	1,714,118	1.7	61,958,780	9,032,936	1,207,418	1.9	41,321,290	15,746,428	506,700	1.2
2-year	14,060,039	3,057,417	782,015	5.6	12,812,475	2,151,721	669,359	5.2	1,247,564	905,696	112,656	9.0
1989–90	139,635,477	33,926,060	3,348,018	2.4	88,911,433	13,820,240	2,566,209	2.9	50,724,044	20,105,820	781,809	1.5
4-year	122,858,290	30,302,689	2,253,803	1.8	73,415,696	11,090,012	1,591,684	2.2	49,442,595	19,212,677	662,119	1.3
2-year	16,777,187	3,623,371	1,094,215	6.5	15,495,738	2,730,229	974,525	6.3	1,281,449	893,143	119,690	9.3
1990–91	149,766,051	37,434,462	3,510,537	2.3	94,904,506	15,258,024	2,725,357	2.9	54,861,545	22,176,439	785,180	1.4
4-year	131,743,973	33,405,241	2,312,931	1.8	78,272,989	12,188,851	1,647,376	2.1	53,470,984	21,216,389	665,554	1.2
2-year	18,022,078	4,029,222	1,197,606	6.6	16,631,517	3,069,173	1,077,981	6.5	1,390,562	960,049	119,625	8.6
1991–92	161,395,896	41,559,037	4,238,047	2.6	102,202,890	17,460,263	3,312,386	3.2	59,193,006	24,098,774	925,661	1.6
4-year	141,700,893	36,910,390	2,710,510	1.9	83,969,040	13,827,245	1,928,623	2.3	57,731,852	23,083,145	781,887	1.4
2-year	19,695,003	4,648,647	1,527,537	7.8	18,233,850	3,633,018	1,383,763	7.6	1,461,153	1,015,629	143,774	9.8
1992–93 [1]	170,880,503	45,346,071	4,701,905	2.8	108,186,484	19,490,221	3,663,529	3.4	62,694,018	25,855,850	1,038,377	1.7
4-year	150,075,119	40,127,624	2,982,999	2.0	88,952,983	15,406,746	2,097,638	2.4	61,122,135	24,720,878	885,360	1.4
2-year	20,805,384	5,218,447	1,718,907	8.3	19,233,501	4,083,475	1,565,890	8.1	1,571,883	1,134,972	153,017	9.7

[1] Preliminary data.

NOTE.—Pell Grants which are spent on campus for tuition, room, board or other college expenses are included in current-fund revenue. Because of rounding, details may not add to totals.

SOURCE: U.S. Department of Education, National Center for Education Statistics, "Financial Statistics of Institutions of Higher Education" surveys; and Integrated Postsecondary Education Data System (IPEDS), "Finance" surveys. (This table was prepared May 1995.)

Table 317.—State awards for need-based [1] undergraduate scholarship and grant programs, by state: 1983–84 to 1993–94

[In thousands]

State	1983–84	1985–86	1986–87	1987–88	1988–89	1989–90	1990–91	1991–92	1992–93 [2]	1993–94 [2]	Percent change, 1983–84 to 1993–94 [3]
1	2	3	4	5	6	7	8	9	10	11	12
United States	$1,024,206	$1,222,112	$1,325,984	$1,377,996	$1,423,743	$1,529,421	$1,658,221	$1,781,820	$1,923,720	$2,195,993	114.4
Alabama	1,731	2,242	2,120	2,260	2,196	2,984	2,878	2,183	2,271	2,283	31.9
Alaska	189	241	229	240	234	228	464	475	470	454	140.2
Arizona	2,027	2,401	2,437	3,222	3,508	3,420	3,318	2,278	2,437	3,476	71.5
Arkansas	2,226	4,108	3,800	3,759	3,903	3,946	3,885	4,742	6,319	7,701	246.0
California	86,031	112,373	112,770	118,819	129,264	153,045	161,642	172,852	151,379	207,969	141.7
Colorado	7,341	9,282	9,491	9,327	9,395	10,349	11,276	12,380	14,812	16,480	124.5
Connecticut	9,371	11,095	9,094	14,650	21,149	19,915	20,580	20,595	20,805	20,641	120.3
Delaware	548	756	875	807	829	956	1,066	906	1,121	1,270	131.8
District of Columbia .	759	1,106	1,059	1,106	1,075	1,069	947	978	1,015	1,022	34.7
Florida	12,515	14,819	14,151	15,245	16,522	20,134	24,729	29,279	29,628	31,277	149.9
Georgia	3,683	4,510	4,946	4,599	5,197	4,607	5,070	5,084	4,951	26,853	629.1
Hawaii	493	604	595	563	598	726	612	632	724	748	51.7
Idaho	378	509	487	343	348	346	350	483	580	634	67.7
Illinois	104,384	122,300	131,788	135,880	143,373	171,361	183,508	184,753	203,532	214,809	105.8
Indiana	20,380	26,448	30,512	45,408	35,692	41,874	46,756	[4]50,441	55,814	55,814	173.9
Iowa	20,263	22,379	22,378	25,960	30,050	32,467	35,586	34,654	34,067	34,718	71.3
Kansas	4,664	5,609	5,250	5,337	5,540	6,478	6,462	6,587	6,894	9,060	94.3
Kentucky	7,886	8,758	12,139	12,161	12,522	12,605	19,866	16,996	20,520	20,619	161.5
Louisiana	1,693	2,003	1,818	1,880	1,947	2,786	3,827	4,446	5,125	6,374	276.5
Maine	477	809	1,151	1,418	1,408	1,877	4,802	5,002	5,200	5,170	983.9
Maryland	5,459	6,859	7,822	8,737	12,841	14,800	15,607	16,253	20,828	23,713	334.4
Massachusetts	25,655	43,466	56,995	61,600	62,443	50,844	46,000	23,690	45,989	45,059	75.6
Michigan	30,753	57,645	66,864	70,099	75,467	70,721	68,918	78,116	75,469	79,735	159.3
Minnesota	46,600	45,486	65,473	63,300	68,293	58,136	74,656	81,322	83,170	102,920	120.9
Mississippi	1,015	1,288	1,287	1,230	1,251	1,243	1,136	1,131	1,244	1,255	23.6
Missouri	8,766	9,645	9,692	8,394	10,234	10,796	11,078	10,142	11,097	11,124	26.9
Montana	353	440	401	419	420	415	383	414	418	401	13.6
Nebraska	860	1,093	1,042	1,094	1,052	1,276	2,192	2,370	2,613	2,686	212.3
Nevada	327	414	326	352	352	[4]352	321	326	341	342	4.6
New Hampshire	536	660	623	810	886	918	770	825	1,253	840	56.7
New Jersey	47,980	65,173	63,978	70,298	76,204	84,347	87,054	100,220	118,868	135,251	181.9
New Mexico	695	1,461	1,461	4,107	5,024	5,601	6,479	[4]7,293	8,295	9,266	1,233.2
New York	327,320	363,949	391,989	372,363	355,192	382,655	428,358	504,195	554,803	618,849	89.1
North Carolina	3,974	4,440	4,386	4,559	4,489	3,046	2,519	2,908	3,163	14,436	263.3
North Dakota	635	808	503	490	976	1,242	1,177	1,475	2,162	2,036	220.6
Ohio	41,974	45,000	47,846	49,200	50,865	53,848	54,600	57,275	66,000	77,940	85.7
Oklahoma	6,561	8,242	8,630	10,245	9,861	11,591	11,871	12,612	13,286	13,405	104.3
Oregon	8,546	9,514	9,204	9,959	10,108	10,092	11,809	12,023	12,606	12,903	51.0
Pennsylvania	83,474	96,800	103,401	110,992	118,986	132,344	142,389	158,092	173,214	188,751	126.1
Rhode Island	6,745	7,856	8,930	8,138	8,967	9,917	9,522	9,141	9,586	6,500	3.6
South Carolina	12,588	15,146	16,348	16,346	17,810	18,150	17,901	16,800	17,105	16,795	33.4
South Dakota	440	624	563	516	506	504	468	480	587	589	33.9
Tennessee	6,700	9,434	10,618	12,591	11,977	12,977	13,487	12,793	13,723	16,755	150.1
Texas	21,438	19,033	20,990	22,705	22,266	24,784	24,135	27,385	27,467	29,102	35.7
Utah	1,538	1,131	1,080	1,133	1,081	1,091	1,001	1,034	1,115	1,132	26.4
Vermont	7,039	7,724	8,088	8,414	9,264	11,137	10,184	11,019	11,120	11,167	58.6
Virginia	4,075	4,415	4,349	4,414	8,062	7,966	7,351	4,892	6,654	6,408	57.3
Washington	7,530	8,827	10,022	12,425	12,858	13,925	21,095	23,527	23,571	46,617	519.1
West Virginia	4,376	5,167	5,157	5,189	5,204	5,217	5,559	5,781	5,868	5,802	32.6
Wisconsin	23,011	27,816	30,622	34,653	35,842	38,072	42,365	42,324	44,216	46,592	102.5
Wyoming	204	204	204	240	212	[4]241	[4]212	216	225	250	22.5

[1] In 1987–88, 1988–89, 1989–90, 1990–91, 1991–92, and 1992–93 need-based aid to undergraduates comprised 81.0, 78.2, 76.8, 77.4, 74.7, and 75.7 percent of all aid, respectively, compared with non-need-based aid or other types of aid to all undergraduate and graduate students. This table excludes loans.

[2] Estimated.

[3] Changes may reflect introduction of new programs or discontinuation of existing programs.

[4] Data are estimated based on prior year's report.

NOTE.—Some data have been revised from previously published figures. Because of rounding, details may not add to totals.

SOURCE: National Association of State Scholarship and Grant Programs, *Annual Survey Report,* various years. (This table was prepared June 1995.)

Table 318.—Current-fund revenue of institutions of higher education, by source: 1980–81 to 1992–93

Source	1980–81	1985–86	1986–87	1987–88	1988–89	1989–90	1990–91	1991–92[1]	1992–93[2]
1	2	3	4	5	6	7	8	9	10

	In thousands								
Total current-fund revenue	$65,584,789	$100,437,616	$108,809,827	$117,340,109	$128,501,638	$139,635,477	$149,766,051	$161,395,896	$170,880,503
Tuition and fees	13,773,259	23,116,605	25,705,827	27,836,781	30,806,566	33,926,060	37,434,462	41,559,037	45,346,071
Federal government	9,747,586	12,704,750	13,904,049	14,771,954	15,893,978	17,254,874	18,236,082	19,833,317	21,014,564
Appropriations	1,346,835	1,617,510	1,656,245	1,664,054	1,677,430	1,890,046	1,840,694	1,907,403	1,872,840
Unrestricted grants and contracts	1,126,558	1,658,636	1,878,202	1,980,749	2,150,079	2,353,119	2,504,859	2,703,590	2,913,256
Restricted grants and contracts[3]	6,005,317	7,190,345	7,690,232	8,225,129	9,009,709	9,773,266	10,443,977	11,561,444	12,589,727
Independent operations (FFRDC)[4]	1,268,877	2,238,259	2,679,369	2,902,022	3,056,760	3,238,442	3,446,552	3,660,881	3,638,741
State governments	20,106,222	29,911,500	31,309,303	33,517,166	36,031,208	38,349,239	39,480,874	40,586,907	41,247,955
Appropriations	19,266,186	28,402,288	29,337,120	31,298,537	33,287,034	35,223,174	36,255,090	36,884,957	37,314,176
Unrestricted grants and contracts	84,848	154,109	213,461	217,208	357,221	411,757	366,206	376,176	382,204
Restricted grants and contracts	755,188	1,355,102	1,758,722	2,001,421	2,386,953	2,714,309	2,859,577	3,325,774	3,551,575
Local governments	1,790,740	2,544,506	2,799,321	3,006,263	3,363,676	3,639,902	3,931,239	4,159,876	4,444,875
Appropriations	1,482,536	2,153,160	2,294,133	2,470,439	2,758,086	2,919,447	3,177,696	3,336,012	3,599,983
Unrestricted grants and contracts	29,629	56,975	92,724	76,638	98,787	122,404	116,982	140,135	139,881
Restricted grants and contracts	278,575	334,371	412,465	459,186	506,803	598,051	636,561	683,729	705,011
Private gifts, grants, and contracts	3,176,670	5,410,905	5,952,682	6,359,282	7,060,730	7,781,422	8,361,265	8,977,271	9,659,977
Unrestricted	1,210,903	2,111,972	2,234,942	2,235,096	2,429,579	2,634,974	2,720,233	2,921,997	3,229,718
Restricted	1,965,766	3,298,933	3,717,741	4,124,186	4,631,151	5,146,448	5,641,032	6,055,274	6,430,259
Endowment income	1,364,443	2,275,898	2,377,958	2,586,441	2,914,396	3,143,696	3,268,629	3,442,009	3,627,773
Unrestricted	770,358	1,285,194	1,229,943	1,340,788	1,498,703	1,614,088	1,521,940	1,549,930	1,536,511
Restricted	594,085	990,704	1,148,015	1,245,654	1,415,694	1,529,608	1,746,690	1,892,079	2,091,262
Sales and services	13,677,366	21,274,265	23,283,927	25,492,435	28,162,465	30,787,233	34,107,502	37,519,828	39,824,766
Educational activities	1,409,730	2,373,494	2,641,906	2,918,090	3,315,620	3,632,100	4,054,703	4,520,890	5,037,901
Auxiliary enterprises	7,287,290	10,674,136	11,364,188	11,947,778	12,855,580	13,938,469	14,903,127	15,758,599	16,662,850
Hospitals	4,980,346	8,226,635	9,277,834	10,626,566	11,991,265	13,216,664	15,149,672	17,240,338	18,124,015
Other sources	1,948,503	3,199,186	3,476,760	3,769,787	4,268,618	4,753,051	4,945,998	5,317,651	5,714,523

	Percentage distribution								
Total current-fund revenue	100.0	100.0	100.0	100.0	100.0	100.0	100.0	100.0	100.0
Tuition and fees	21.0	23.0	23.6	23.7	24.0	24.3	25.0	25.7	26.5
Federal government	14.9	12.6	12.8	12.6	12.4	12.4	12.2	12.3	12.3
Appropriations	2.1	1.6	1.5	1.4	1.3	1.4	1.2	1.2	1.1
Unrestricted grants and contracts	1.7	1.7	1.7	1.7	1.7	1.7	1.7	1.7	1.7
Restricted grants and contracts[3]	9.2	7.2	7.1	7.0	7.0	7.0	7.0	7.2	7.4
Independent operations (FFRDC)[4]	1.9	2.2	2.5	2.5	2.4	2.3	2.3	2.3	2.1
State governments	30.7	29.8	28.8	28.6	28.0	27.5	26.4	25.1	24.1
Appropriations	29.4	28.3	27.0	26.7	25.9	25.2	24.2	22.9	21.8
Unrestricted grants and contracts	0.1	0.2	0.2	0.2	0.3	0.3	0.2	0.2	0.2
Restricted grants and contracts	1.2	1.3	1.6	1.7	1.9	1.9	1.9	2.1	2.1
Local governments	2.7	2.5	2.6	2.6	2.6	2.6	2.6	2.6	2.6
Appropriations	2.3	2.1	2.1	2.1	2.1	2.1	2.1	2.1	2.1
Unrestricted grants and contracts	(5)	0.1	0.1	0.1	0.1	0.1	0.1	0.1	0.1
Restricted grants and contracts	0.4	0.3	0.4	0.4	0.4	0.4	0.4	0.4	0.4
Private gifts, grants, and contracts	4.8	5.4	5.5	5.4	5.5	5.6	5.6	5.6	5.7
Unrestricted	1.8	2.1	2.1	1.9	1.9	1.9	1.8	1.8	1.9
Restricted	3.0	3.3	3.4	3.5	3.6	3.7	3.8	3.8	3.8
Endowment income	2.1	2.3	2.2	2.2	2.3	2.3	2.2	2.1	2.1
Unrestricted	1.2	1.3	1.1	1.1	1.2	1.2	1.0	1.0	0.9
Restricted	0.9	1.0	1.1	1.1	1.1	1.1	1.2	1.2	1.2
Sales and services	20.9	21.2	21.4	21.7	21.9	22.0	22.8	23.2	23.3
Educational activities	2.1	2.4	2.4	2.5	2.6	2.6	2.7	2.8	2.9
Auxiliary enterprises	11.1	10.6	10.4	10.2	10.0	10.0	10.0	9.8	9.8
Hospitals	7.6	8.2	8.5	9.1	9.3	9.5	10.1	10.7	10.6
Other sources	3.0	3.2	3.2	3.2	3.3	3.4	3.3	3.3	3.3

[1] Revised from previously published data.
[2] Preliminary data.
[3] Excludes Pell Grants. Federally supported student aid that is received through students is included under tuition and auxiliary enterprises.
[4] Generally includes only those revenues associated with major federally funded research and development centers (FFRDC).
[5] Less than 0.05 percent.

NOTE.—Because of rounding, details may not add to totals.

SOURCE: U.S. Department of Education, National Center for Education Statistics, "Financial Statistics of Institutions of Higher Education" surveys; and Integrated Postsecondary Education Data System (IPEDS), "Finance" surveys. (This table was prepared April 1995.)

Table 319.—Current-fund revenue of public institutions of higher education, by source: 1980–81 to 1992–93

Source	1980–81	1985–86	1986–87	1987–88	1988–89	1989–90	1990–91	1991–92[1]	1992–93[2]
1	2	3	4	5	6	7	8	9	10
					In thousands				
Total current-fund revenue	$43,195,617	$65,004,632	$69,613,289	$74,771,255	$81,927,371	$88,911,433	$94,904,506	$102,202,890	$108,186,484
Tuition and fees	5,570,404	9,439,177	10,198,633	11,184,657	12,435,763	13,820,240	15,258,024	17,460,263	19,490,221
Federal government	5,540,101	6,852,370	7,227,995	7,714,261	8,412,582	9,171,488	9,763,427	10,783,842	11,655,011
Appropriations	1,128,101	1,401,367	1,434,295	1,434,906	1,443,539	1,636,047	1,604,548	1,662,229	1,658,052
Unrestricted grants and contracts	529,424	816,364	907,299	989,781	1,083,575	1,214,836	1,319,035	1,462,372	1,601,201
Restricted grants and contracts[3]	3,812,197	4,481,723	4,662,798	5,095,910	5,656,468	6,106,112	6,629,484	7,426,627	8,155,317
Independent operations (FFRDC)[4]	70,379	152,916	223,602	193,664	228,999	214,493	210,360	232,613	240,441
State governments	19,675,968	29,220,586	30,439,878	32,437,504	34,835,716	37,052,307	38,239,978	39,107,560	39,789,641
Appropriations	19,006,716	28,071,070	28,974,665	30,917,354	32,929,719	34,858,904	35,898,653	36,612,540	37,073,932
Unrestricted grants and contracts	45,390	88,779	139,059	113,204	240,028	297,338	250,168	253,184	259,046
Restricted grants and contracts	623,863	1,060,737	1,326,154	1,406,946	1,665,969	1,896,065	2,091,157	2,241,836	2,456,663
Local governments	1,622,938	2,325,844	2,535,014	2,731,862	3,025,703	3,264,303	3,531,714	3,778,615	4,040,897
Appropriations	1,478,001	2,150,459	2,289,420	2,465,172	2,751,704	2,910,444	3,159,789	3,319,119	3,594,207
Unrestricted grants and contracts	9,915	27,852	56,781	41,940	64,455	82,405	73,281	90,257	84,974
Restricted grants and contracts	135,022	147,533	188,813	224,751	209,544	271,453	298,644	369,239	361,717
Private gifts, grants, and contracts	1,100,084	2,109,782	2,292,985	2,517,422	2,948,827	3,368,635	3,651,107	4,039,212	4,330,112
Unrestricted	110,462	279,381	297,163	305,457	362,011	436,028	529,496	650,468	686,214
Restricted	989,622	1,830,401	1,995,822	2,211,966	2,586,815	2,932,607	3,121,611	3,388,743	3,643,898
Endowment income	214,561	398,603	349,779	361,545	422,252	461,701	431,235	593,998	667,711
Unrestricted	102,888	181,624	125,165	127,861	149,650	164,242	147,368	248,770	257,113
Restricted	111,673	216,979	224,614	233,684	272,602	297,459	283,867	345,228	410,598
Sales and services	8,455,449	12,990,670	14,775,531	15,851,714	17,586,819	19,330,429	21,546,202	23,738,382	25,282,113
Educational activities	943,737	1,596,946	1,771,760	1,948,679	2,186,448	2,423,779	2,700,185	2,960,980	3,236,037
Auxiliary enterprises	4,614,561	6,684,794	7,092,985	7,306,302	7,809,284	8,473,282	9,058,745	9,655,373	10,255,044
Hospitals	2,897,151	4,708,930	5,910,785	6,596,733	7,591,087	8,433,369	9,787,271	11,122,029	11,791,033
Other sources	1,016,110	1,667,600	1,793,474	1,972,290	2,259,709	2,442,330	2,482,819	2,701,019	2,930,778
					Percentage distribution				
Total current-fund revenue	100.0	100.0	100.0	100.0	100.0	100.0	100.0	100.0	100.0
Tuition and fees	12.9	14.5	14.7	15.0	15.2	15.5	16.1	17.1	18.0
Federal government	12.8	10.5	10.4	10.3	10.3	10.3	10.3	10.6	10.8
Appropriations	2.6	2.2	2.1	1.9	1.8	1.8	1.7	1.6	1.5
Unrestricted grants and contracts	1.2	1.3	1.3	1.3	1.3	1.4	1.4	1.4	1.5
Restricted grants and contracts[3]	8.8	6.9	6.7	6.8	6.9	6.9	7.0	7.3	7.5
Independent operations (FFRDC)[4]	0.2	0.2	0.3	0.3	0.3	0.2	0.2	0.2	0.2
State governments	45.6	45.0	43.7	43.4	42.5	41.7	40.3	38.3	36.8
Appropriations	44.0	43.2	41.6	41.3	40.2	39.2	37.8	35.8	34.3
Unrestricted grants and contracts	0.1	0.1	0.2	0.2	0.3	0.3	0.3	0.2	0.2
Restricted grants and contracts	1.4	1.6	1.9	1.9	2.0	2.1	2.2	2.2	2.3
Local governments	3.8	3.6	3.6	3.7	3.7	3.7	3.7	3.7	3.7
Appropriations	3.4	3.3	3.3	3.3	3.4	3.3	3.3	3.2	3.3
Unrestricted grants and contracts	(5)	(5)	0.1	0.1	0.1	0.1	0.1	0.1	0.1
Restricted grants and contracts	0.3	0.2	0.3	0.3	0.3	0.3	0.3	0.4	0.3
Private gifts, grants, and contracts	2.5	3.2	3.3	3.4	3.6	3.8	3.8	4.0	4.0
Unrestricted	0.3	0.4	0.4	0.4	0.4	0.5	0.6	0.6	0.6
Restricted	2.3	2.8	2.9	3.0	3.2	3.3	3.3	3.3	3.4
Endowment income	0.5	0.6	0.5	0.5	0.5	0.5	0.5	0.6	0.6
Unrestricted	0.2	0.3	0.2	0.2	0.2	0.2	0.2	0.2	0.2
Restricted	0.3	0.3	0.3	0.3	0.3	0.3	0.3	0.3	0.4
Sales and services	19.6	20.0	21.2	21.2	21.5	21.7	22.7	23.2	23.4
Educational activities	2.2	2.5	2.5	2.6	2.7	2.7	2.8	2.9	3.0
Auxiliary enterprises	10.7	10.3	10.2	9.8	9.5	9.5	9.5	9.4	9.5
Hospitals	6.7	7.2	8.5	8.8	9.3	9.5	10.3	10.9	10.9
Other sources	2.4	2.6	2.6	2.6	2.8	2.7	2.6	2.6	2.7

[1] Revised from previously published data.

[2] Preliminary data.

[3] Excludes Pell Grants. Federally supported student aid that is received through students is included under tuition and auxiliary enterprises.

[4] Generally includes only those revenues associated with major federally funded research and development centers (FFRDC).

[5] Less than 0.05 percent.

NOTE.—Because of rounding, details may not add to totals.

SOURCE: U.S. Department of Education, National Center for Education Statistics, "Financial Statistics of Institutions of Higher Education" surveys; and Integrated Postsecondary Education Data System (IPEDS), "Finance" surveys. (This table was prepared April 1995.)

Table 320.—Current-fund revenue of private institutions of higher education, by source: 1980–81 to 1992–93

Source	1980–81	1985–86	1986–87	1987–88	1988–89	1989–90	1990–91	1991–92[1]	1992–93[2]
1	2	3	4	5	6	7	8	9	10
	In thousands								
Total current-fund revenue	$22,389,172	$35,432,985	$39,196,539	$42,568,854	$46,574,267	$50,724,044	$54,861,545	$59,193,006	$62,694,018
Tuition and fees	8,202,855	13,677,429	15,507,194	16,652,124	18,370,803	20,105,820	22,176,439	24,098,774	25,855,850
Federal government	4,207,485	5,852,380	6,676,054	7,057,693	7,481,396	8,083,386	8,472,654	9,049,476	9,359,554
Appropriations	218,733	216,143	221,950	229,148	233,891	254,000	236,146	245,173	214,788
Unrestricted grants and contracts	597,134	842,272	970,903	990,968	1,066,504	1,138,283	1,185,824	1,241,218	1,312,056
Restricted grants and contracts[3]	2,193,119	2,708,622	3,027,434	3,129,219	3,353,241	3,667,154	3,814,493	4,134,817	4,434,410
Independent operations (FFRDC)[4]	1,198,498	2,085,343	2,455,767	2,708,358	2,827,761	3,023,949	3,236,192	3,428,267	3,398,300
State governments	430,253	690,914	869,424	1,079,662	1,195,492	1,296,932	1,240,896	1,479,347	1,458,314
Appropriations	259,470	331,219	362,454	381,183	357,315	364,270	356,437	272,417	240,244
Unrestricted grants and contracts	39,458	65,330	74,402	104,004	117,193	114,419	116,038	122,992	123,158
Restricted grants and contracts	131,326	294,365	432,568	594,475	720,984	818,244	768,421	1,083,938	1,094,912
Local governments	167,801	218,662	264,307	274,400	337,973	375,599	399,525	381,261	403,977
Appropriations	4,535	2,701	4,713	5,267	6,383	9,003	17,907	16,893	5,776
Unrestricted grants and contracts	19,714	29,123	35,943	34,698	34,332	39,999	43,701	49,878	54,907
Restricted grants and contracts	143,552	186,838	223,651	234,435	297,258	326,598	337,917	314,490	343,294
Private gifts, grants, and contracts	2,076,585	3,301,124	3,659,697	3,841,860	4,111,904	4,412,787	4,710,158	4,938,060	5,329,865
Unrestricted	1,100,441	1,832,592	1,937,778	1,929,639	2,067,568	2,198,946	2,190,736	2,271,529	2,543,504
Restricted	976,144	1,468,532	1,721,919	1,912,220	2,044,336	2,213,841	2,519,421	2,666,531	2,786,361
Endowment income	1,149,883	1,877,295	2,028,179	2,224,896	2,492,144	2,681,995	2,837,394	2,848,012	2,960,062
Unrestricted	667,471	1,103,570	1,104,778	1,212,926	1,349,053	1,449,846	1,374,572	1,301,160	1,279,398
Restricted	482,412	773,725	923,400	1,011,970	1,143,091	1,232,149	1,462,822	1,546,851	1,680,664
Sales and services	5,221,917	8,283,595	8,508,396	9,640,720	10,575,646	11,456,804	12,561,301	13,781,446	14,542,653
Educational activities	465,993	776,548	870,145	969,411	1,129,171	1,208,322	1,354,518	1,559,910	1,801,865
Auxiliary enterprises	2,672,729	3,989,342	4,271,203	4,641,476	5,046,296	5,465,187	5,844,382	6,103,226	6,407,806
Hospitals	2,083,195	3,517,705	3,367,048	4,029,833	4,400,178	4,783,295	5,362,401	6,118,309	6,332,982
Other sources	932,392	1,531,586	1,683,287	1,797,498	2,008,909	2,310,720	2,463,178	2,616,632	2,783,744
	Percentage distribution								
Total current-fund revenue	100.0	100.0	100.0	100.0	100.0	100.0	100.0	100.0	100.0
Tuition and fees	36.6	38.6	39.6	39.1	39.4	39.6	40.4	40.7	41.2
Federal government	18.8	16.5	17.0	16.6	16.1	15.9	15.4	15.3	14.9
Appropriations	1.0	0.6	0.6	0.5	0.5	0.5	0.4	0.4	0.3
Unrestricted grants and contracts	2.7	2.4	2.5	2.3	2.3	2.2	2.2	2.1	2.1
Restricted grants and contracts[3]	9.8	7.6	7.7	7.4	7.2	7.2	7.0	7.0	7.1
Independent operations (FFRDC)[4]	5.4	5.9	6.3	6.4	6.1	6.0	5.9	5.8	5.4
State governments	1.9	1.9	2.2	2.5	2.6	2.6	2.3	2.5	2.3
Appropriations	1.2	0.9	0.9	0.9	0.8	0.7	0.6	0.5	0.4
Unrestricted grants and contracts	0.2	0.2	0.2	0.2	0.3	0.2	0.2	0.2	0.2
Restricted grants and contracts	0.6	0.8	1.1	1.4	1.5	1.6	1.4	1.8	1.7
Local governments	0.7	0.6	0.7	0.6	0.7	0.7	0.7	0.6	0.6
Appropriations	(5)	(5)	(5)	(5)	(5)	(5)	(5)	(5)	(5)
Unrestricted grants and contracts	0.1	0.1	0.1	0.1	0.1	0.1	0.1	0.1	0.1
Restricted grants and contracts	0.6	0.5	0.6	0.6	0.6	0.6	0.6	0.5	0.5
Private gifts, grants, and contracts	9.3	9.3	9.3	9.0	8.8	8.7	8.6	8.3	8.5
Unrestricted	4.9	5.2	4.9	4.5	4.4	4.3	4.0	3.8	4.1
Restricted	4.4	4.1	4.4	4.5	4.4	4.4	4.6	4.5	4.4
Endowment income	5.1	5.3	5.2	5.2	5.4	5.3	5.2	4.8	4.7
Unrestricted	3.0	3.1	2.8	2.8	2.9	2.9	2.5	2.2	2.0
Restricted	2.2	2.2	2.4	2.4	2.5	2.4	2.7	2.6	2.7
Sales and services	23.3	23.4	21.7	22.6	22.7	22.6	22.9	23.3	23.2
Educational activities	2.1	2.2	2.2	2.3	2.4	2.4	2.5	2.6	2.9
Auxiliary enterprises	11.9	11.3	10.9	10.9	10.8	10.8	10.7	10.3	10.2
Hospitals	9.3	9.9	8.6	9.5	9.4	9.4	9.8	10.3	10.1
Other sources	4.2	4.3	4.3	4.2	4.3	4.6	4.5	4.4	4.4

[1] Revised from previously published data.
[2] Preliminary data.
[3] Excludes Pell Grants. Federally supported student aid that is received through students is included under tuition and auxiliary enterprises.
[4] Generally includes only those revenues associated with major federally funded research and development centers (FFRDC).
[5] Less than 0.05 percent.

NOTE.—Because of rounding, details may not add to totals.

SOURCE: U.S. Department of Education, National Center for Education Statistics, "Financial Statistics of Institutions of Higher Education" surveys; and Integrated Postsecondary Education Data System (IPEDS), "Finance" surveys. (This table was prepared April 1995.)

Table 321.—Revenue of institutions of higher education, by source of funds: 1919–20 to 1992–93

[In thousands]

Year	Current-fund revenue	Student tuition and fees [1]	Federal government [2]	State governments [3]	Local governments	Endowment earnings	Private gifts and grants [4]	Sales and services of educational activities	Auxiliary enterprises	Hospitals [5]	Other current income
1	2	3	4	5	6	7	8	9	10	11	12
1919–20	$199,922	$42,255	$12,783	$61,690	(6)	$26,482	$7,584	—	$26,993	—	$22,135
1929–30	554,511	144,126	20,658	150,847	(6)	68,605	26,172	—	60,419	—	83,684
1939–40	715,211	200,897	38,860	151,222	$24,392	71,304	40,453	$32,777	143,923	—	11,383
1949–50	2,374,645	394,610	524,319	491,636	61,700	96,341	118,627	111,987	511,265	$187,769	64,160
1959–60	5,785,537	1,157,482	1,036,990	1,374,476	151,715	206,619	382,569	102,525	1,004,283		181,110
1969–70	21,515,242	4,419,845	4,130,066	5,873,626	778,162	516,038	1,129,438	612,777	2,900,390	619,578	535,323
1975–76	39,703,166	8,171,942	6,477,178	12,260,885	1,616,975	687,470	1,917,036	645,420	4,547,622	2,494,340	884,298
1976–77	43,436,827	9,024,932	7,169,031	13,285,684	1,626,908	764,788	2,105,070	779,058	4,919,602	2,859,376	902,377
1977–78	47,034,032	9,855,270	6,968,501	14,746,166	1,744,230	832,286	2,320,368	882,715	5,327,821	3,268,956	1,087,719
1978–79	51,837,789	10,704,171	7,851,326	16,363,784	1,573,018	985,242	2,489,366	1,037,130	5,741,309	3,763,453	1,328,991
1979–80	58,519,982	11,930,340	8,902,844	18,378,299	1,587,552	1,176,627	2,808,075	1,239,439	6,481,458	4,373,384	1,641,965
1980–81	65,584,789	13,773,259	9,747,586	20,106,222	1,790,740	1,364,443	3,176,670	1,409,730	7,287,290	4,980,346	1,948,503
1981–82	72,190,856	15,774,038	9,591,805	21,848,791	1,937,669	1,596,813	3,563,558	1,582,922	8,121,611	5,838,565	2,335,084
1982–83	77,595,726	17,776,041	9,631,097	23,065,636	2,031,353	1,720,677	4,052,649	1,723,484	8,769,521	6,531,562	2,293,706
1983–84	84,417,287	19,714,884	10,406,166	24,706,990	2,192,275	1,873,945	4,415,275	1,970,747	9,456,369	7,040,662	2,639,973
1984–85	92,472,694	21,283,329	11,509,125	27,583,011	2,387,212	2,096,298	4,896,325	2,126,927	10,100,410	7,474,575	3,015,483
1985–86	100,437,616	23,116,605	12,704,750	29,911,500	2,544,506	2,275,898	5,410,905	2,373,494	10,674,136	8,226,635	3,199,186
1986–87	108,809,827	25,705,827	13,904,049	31,309,303	2,799,321	2,377,958	5,952,682	2,641,906	11,364,188	9,277,834	3,476,760
1987–88	117,340,109	27,836,781	14,771,954	33,517,166	3,006,263	2,586,441	6,359,282	2,918,090	11,947,778	10,626,566	3,769,787
1988–89	128,501,638	30,806,566	15,893,978	36,031,208	3,363,676	2,914,396	7,060,730	3,315,620	12,855,580	11,991,265	4,268,618
1989–90	139,635,477	33,926,060	17,254,874	38,349,239	3,639,902	3,143,696	7,781,422	3,632,100	13,938,469	13,216,664	4,753,051
1990–91	149,766,051	37,434,462	18,236,082	39,480,874	3,931,239	3,268,629	8,361,265	4,054,703	14,903,127	15,149,672	4,945,998
1991–92 [7]	161,395,896	41,559,037	19,833,317	40,586,907	4,159,876	3,442,009	8,977,271	4,520,890	15,758,599	17,240,338	5,317,651
1992–93 [8]	170,880,503	45,346,071	21,014,564	41,247,955	4,444,875	3,627,773	9,659,977	5,037,901	16,662,850	18,124,015	5,714,523

[1] Tuition and fees received from veterans under Public Law 550 are reported under student fees and are not under income from the federal government.
[2] Federally supported student aid that is received through students is included under tuition and auxiliary enterprises.
[3] Includes federal aid received through state channels and regional compacts, through 1959–60.
[4] Beginning in 1969–70, the private grants represent nongovernmental revenue for sponsored research, student aid, and other sponsored programs.
[5] Prior to 1959–60, data for hospitals are included under sales and services of educational activities.
[6] Income from state and local governments tabulated under "State governments."
[7] Data revised from previously published figures.
[8] Preliminary data.
— Data not available.

NOTE.—Data for years prior to 1969–70 are not entirely comparable with data for later years. Also, some details for 1969–70 are not directly comparable with data for later years. Because of rounding, details may not add to totals.

SOURCE: U.S. Department of Education, National Center for Education Statistics, "Financial Statistics of Institutions of Higher Education" surveys; and Integrated Postsecondary Education Data System (IPEDS), "Finance" surveys. (This table was prepared April 1995.)

Table 322.—Revenue of institutions of higher education, by source of funds and by control and type of institution: 1992–93 [1]

In thousands

Control and type of institution	Current-fund revenue	Student tuition and fees [2]	Federal government [3]	State governments	Local governments	Private gifts and grants	Endowment earnings	Educational activities	Auxiliary enterprises	Hospitals	Other current income
1	2	3	4	5	6	7	8	9	10	11	12
Total	$170,880,503	$45,346,071	$21,014,564	$41,247,955	$4,444,875	$9,659,977	$3,627,773	$5,037,901	$16,662,850	$18,124,015	$5,714,523
Public	108,186,484	19,490,221	11,655,011	39,789,641	4,040,897	4,330,112	667,711	3,236,037	10,255,044	11,791,033	2,930,778
Research I universities [4]	40,633,583	5,800,203	6,183,151	11,845,549	186,856	2,471,779	354,719	1,804,911	3,964,508	7,233,644	788,251
Research II universities [4]	6,620,287	1,471,427	752,747	2,734,833	22,800	305,937	88,673	202,359	886,514	0	154,997
Doctoral universities	11,834,261	2,558,507	911,460	5,175,582	86,286	488,164	129,083	251,176	1,344,516	372,952	516,535
Master's	17,218,472	4,512,471	796,055	8,216,784	131,645	336,798	44,725	354,150	2,215,912	218,508	391,423
Baccalaureate	1,886,541	586,954	83,810	842,299	12,285	41,512	4,362	24,497	256,282	0	34,539
Associate of arts	19,485,234	4,175,541	991,216	8,682,946	3,530,527	170,055	15,113	128,862	1,272,550	0	518,425
Specialized institutions [5]											
Health and medicine	8,812,263	235,692	896,857	2,050,940	43,463	490,782	30,182	466,842	202,575	3,895,388	499,542
Engineering	200,948	47,121	13,879	107,668	5	11,888	17	1,254	16,445	0	2,573
Business	20,833	5,714	1,352	9,898	41	434	7	1,713	1,542	0	132
Fine arts	105,984	25,061	810	31,170	22,365	1,756	10	80	10,039	0	14,693
Other specialized [6]	1,295,686	65,258	974,497	90,156	2,314	5,138	215	136	81,256	70,539	6,176
Tribal colleges [6]	72,392	6,162	49,177	1,816	2,310	5,869	605	55	2,906	0	3,492
Private	62,694,018	25,855,850	9,359,554	1,458,314	403,977	5,329,865	2,960,062	1,801,865	6,407,806	6,332,982	2,783,744
Research I universities [4]	24,219,105	5,414,111	6,943,108	392,751	201,827	2,284,765	1,338,846	1,235,810	1,705,809	3,771,507	930,570
Research II universities [4]	3,781,529	1,409,273	292,034	48,002	63	365,611	162,123	88,878	503,982	759,375	152,188
Doctoral universities	5,957,910	3,121,168	391,773	145,058	6,843	318,466	197,973	96,970	1,185,657	757,979	354,155
Master's	8,669,513	5,711,491	410,236	278,067	9,152	494,359	218,205	119,574	1,863,052	7,925	234,847
Baccalaureate	10,908,864	6,334,672	366,199	308,879	1,766	999,436	729,723	30,675	147,834	0	274,461
Associate of arts	1,780,848	1,291,977	53,498	110,963	3,411	82,381	21,030	15,322	54,434	0	54,434
Specialized institutions [5]											
Religion and theology	959,565	291,163	13,049	4,716	1,260	340,458	120,742	7,252	139,382	0	41,544
Health and medicine	4,076,835	610,229	783,649	114,020	175,455	310,464	86,748	174,552	96,513	1,036,196	689,010
Engineering	365,580	218,765	22,622	9,533	0	39,945	30,410	7,185	27,415	0	9,705
Business	851,135	641,125	14,614	23,574	214	18,306	11,475	17,750	104,914	0	19,163
Fine arts	621,442	442,923	21,624	17,110	1,544	45,699	31,756	2,442	46,700	0	11,644
Other specialized	480,450	563,303	35,921	5,410	2,101	28,036	10,924	5,375	18,043	0	11,337
Tribal colleges [6]	21,242	5,651	11,229	232	341	1,939	107	79	979	0	687

Percentage distribution

Control and type of institution	Current-fund revenue	Student tuition and fees [2]	Federal government [3]	State governments	Local governments	Private gifts and grants	Endowment earnings	Educational activities	Auxiliary enterprises	Hospitals	Other current income
Total	100.00	26.54	12.30	24.14	2.60	5.65	2.12	2.95	9.75	10.61	3.34
Public											
Research I universities [4]	100.00	18.02	10.77	36.78	3.74	4.00	0.62	2.99	9.48	10.90	2.71
Research II universities [4]	100.00	14.27	15.22	29.15	0.46	6.08	0.87	4.44	9.76	17.80	1.94
Doctoral universities	100.00	22.23	11.37	41.31	0.34	4.62	1.34	3.06	13.39	0.00	2.34
Master's	100.00	21.62	7.70	43.73	0.73	4.13	1.09	2.12	11.36	3.15	4.36
Baccalaureate	100.00	26.21	4.62	47.72	0.76	1.96	0.26	2.06	12.87	1.27	2.27
Associate of arts	100.00	31.11	4.44	44.65	0.65	2.20	0.23	1.30	13.58	0.00	1.83
Specialized institutions [5]	100.00	21.43	5.09	44.56	18.12	0.87	0.08	0.66	6.53	0.00	2.66
Health and medicine	100.00	2.67	10.18	23.27	0.49	5.57	0.34	5.30	2.30	44.20	5.67
Engineering	100.00	23.50	6.91	53.58	0.00	5.92	0.01	0.62	8.18	0.00	1.28
Business	100.00	27.43	6.49	47.51	0.20	2.08	0.03	8.22	7.40	0.00	0.63
Fine arts	100.00	23.65	0.76	29.41	21.10	1.66	0.01	0.08	9.47	0.00	13.86
Other specialized	100.00	5.04	75.21	6.96	0.18	0.40	0.02	0.01	6.27	5.44	0.48
Tribal colleges [6]	100.00	8.51	67.93	2.51	3.19	8.11	0.84	0.08	4.01	0.00	4.82

Table 322.—Revenue of institutions of higher education, by source of funds and by control and type of institution: 1992-93 [1]—Continued

Control and type of institution	Current-fund revenue	Student tuition and fees [2]	Federal government [3]	State governments	Local governments	Private gifts and grants	Endowment earnings	Educational activities	Auxiliary enterprises	Hospitals	Other current income
1	2	3	4	5	6	7	8	9	10	11	12
Private [4]	100.00	41.24	14.93	2.33	0.64	8.50	4.72	2.87	10.22	10.10	4.44
Research I universities [4]	100.00	22.35	28.67	1.62	0.83	9.43	5.53	5.10	7.04	15.57	3.84
Research II universities [4]	100.00	37.27	7.72	1.27	0.00	9.67	4.29	2.35	13.33	20.08	4.02
Doctoral universities	100.00	52.39	6.58	2.43	0.11	5.35	3.32	1.63	9.53	12.72	5.94
Master's	100.00	65.88	4.73	3.21	0.11	5.70	2.52	1.38	13.68	0.09	2.71
Baccalaureate	100.00	58.07	3.36	2.83	0.02	9.16	6.69	0.28	17.08	0.00	2.52
Associate of arts	100.00	72.55	3.00	6.23	0.19	4.63	1.18	0.86	8.30	0.00	3.06
Specialized institutions [5]											
Religion and theology	100.00	30.34	1.36	0.49	0.13	35.48	12.58	0.76	14.53	0.00	4.33
Health and medicine	100.00	14.97	19.22	2.80	4.30	7.62	2.13	4.28	2.37	25.42	16.90
Engineering	100.00	59.84	6.19	2.61	0.00	10.93	8.32	1.97	7.50	0.00	2.65
Business	100.00	75.33	1.72	2.77	0.03	2.15	1.35	2.09	12.33	0.00	2.25
Fine arts	100.00	71.27	3.48	2.75	0.25	7.35	5.11	0.39	7.51	0.00	1.87
Other specialized	100.00	75.62	7.48	1.13	0.44	5.84	2.27	1.12	3.76	0.00	2.36
Tribal colleges [6]	100.00	26.60	52.86	1.09	1.61	9.13	0.50	0.37	4.61	0.00	3.23

[1] Preliminary data.

[2] Includes federally supported aid received through students. Excludes Pell Grants.

[3] Includes appropriations, grants, contracts, and revenues associated with major federally funded research and development centers (FFRDC).

[4] Research institutions are committed to graduate education through the doctorate, and give high priority to research. Research I institutions receive $40 million or more annually in federal support. Research II institutions receive between $15.5 million and $40 million annually.

[5] Specialized institutions award baccalaureate or higher level degrees in specific fields of study.

[6] Tribally controlled colleges are located on reservations and are members of the American Indian Higher Education Consortium.

NOTE.—Because of rounding, details may not add to totals.

SOURCE: U.S. Department of Education, National Center for Education Statistics, Integrated Postsecondary Education Data System (IPEDS), "Finance, 1992-93" survey. (This table was prepared May 1995.)

Table 323.—Current-fund revenue of public institutions of higher education, by state: 1980–81 to 1992–93

[In thousands of dollars]

State	1980–81	1985–86	1986–87	1987–88	1988–89	1989–90	1990–91	1991–92	1992–93[1]	Percent change, 1987–88 to 1992–93
1	2	3	4	5	6	7	8	9	10	11
United States	$43,195,617	$65,004,632	$69,613,289	$74,771,255	$81,927,371	$88,911,433	$94,904,506	$102,202,890	$108,186,484	44.7
Alabama	889,121	1,401,693	1,438,945	1,552,128	1,743,168	1,926,148	2,131,005	2,296,665	2,521,938	62.5
Alaska	159,446	221,837	211,186	220,393	244,857	270,926	291,826	304,857	323,740	46.9
Arizona	719,835	1,049,493	1,119,516	1,221,641	1,353,468	1,483,996	1,596,710	1,655,873	1,677,711	37.3
Arkansas	350,597	539,185	566,317	652,029	716,105	781,375	818,079	920,699	995,482	52.7
California	5,906,729	8,739,396	9,506,244	9,995,464	11,022,341	11,776,298	12,281,700	13,628,928	14,262,239	42.7
Colorado	747,040	1,085,076	1,153,559	1,247,390	1,371,303	1,390,413	1,483,901	1,594,541	1,714,698	37.5
Connecticut	378,527	578,866	636,210	692,830	788,194	833,154	889,831	940,067	976,380	40.9
Delaware	168,522	251,677	275,473	294,347	324,853	354,322	388,635	433,186	446,768	51.8
District of Columbia	66,138	91,842	95,139	99,457	109,167	109,254	109,642	121,991	118,865	19.5
Florida	1,202,788	1,810,090	2,035,008	2,228,502	2,510,894	2,812,644	2,944,935	3,049,921	3,202,499	43.7
Georgia	765,826	1,267,472	1,421,979	1,528,594	1,648,753	1,794,990	1,953,866	2,042,825	2,268,331	48.4
Hawaii	219,633	316,246	323,030	358,754	384,775	433,164	497,495	579,805	594,752	65.8
Idaho	169,274	235,507	243,122	270,133	290,303	320,119	359,710	396,173	416,359	54.1
Illinois	1,809,981	2,560,241	2,722,913	2,812,875	3,067,687	3,370,011	3,566,406	3,659,328	3,924,599	39.5
Indiana	1,094,560	1,701,421	1,800,669	1,910,144	2,083,416	2,302,583	2,494,029	2,767,477	2,882,592	50.9
Iowa	784,950	1,109,681	1,210,284	1,321,697	1,529,907	1,653,221	1,775,267	1,827,776	1,930,399	46.1
Kansas	594,104	864,119	891,746	975,159	1,047,219	1,174,759	1,219,129	1,297,129	1,350,052	38.4
Kentucky	671,414	943,068	1,016,961	1,109,682	1,194,424	1,283,778	1,450,958	1,565,021	1,576,644	42.1
Louisiana	735,374	1,055,941	1,078,664	1,118,919	1,180,464	1,301,127	1,447,772	1,553,258	1,821,190	62.8
Maine	157,370	222,624	253,862	278,078	317,636	352,024	373,770	375,512	384,730	38.4
Maryland	818,850	1,144,230	1,233,023	1,344,947	1,515,369	1,638,822	1,777,841	1,745,479	1,913,029	42.2
Massachusetts	582,873	1,075,348	1,161,694	1,287,595	1,365,350	1,429,770	1,457,142	1,525,943	1,639,854	27.4
Michigan	2,094,394	3,071,172	3,348,947	3,699,398	3,992,084	4,322,956	4,648,488	5,127,892	5,329,224	44.1
Minnesota	894,236	1,373,436	1,530,623	1,631,838	1,880,373	1,916,297	2,080,637	2,261,978	2,363,483	44.8
Mississippi	543,209	734,813	729,024	802,055	903,637	956,300	1,005,448	1,054,530	1,150,201	43.4
Missouri	717,626	1,032,685	1,086,719	1,169,613	1,289,742	1,416,556	1,517,071	1,566,480	1,698,594	45.2
Montana	123,933	181,462	184,812	196,957	197,605	227,403	258,189	334,243	349,102	77.2
Nebraska	390,372	554,814	601,666	628,140	699,859	787,282	870,289	941,062	989,156	57.5
Nevada	113,298	184,883	201,941	221,740	243,208	286,719	336,841	368,245	392,258	76.9
New Hampshire	131,990	190,462	208,577	232,411	255,948	275,121	304,315	324,186	348,839	50.1
New Jersey	917,143	1,446,098	1,657,551	1,853,740	2,065,233	2,253,830	2,413,530	2,610,949	2,745,100	48.1
New Mexico	334,392	473,716	521,547	543,196	786,667	858,989	944,248	1,056,819	1,125,366	107.2
New York	2,519,437	3,830,119	4,321,209	4,553,725	4,772,942	5,014,789	5,424,379	5,616,604	6,117,555	34.3
North Carolina	1,146,931	1,857,124	2,005,207	2,138,818	2,295,295	2,480,396	2,650,124	2,873,684	3,113,193	45.6
North Dakota	196,267	286,550	304,304	303,700	327,293	365,089	377,960	411,293	431,464	42.1
Ohio	1,828,079	2,824,411	3,025,444	3,221,449	3,561,646	3,871,477	4,184,621	4,484,576	4,628,902	43.7
Oklahoma	588,936	873,446	846,389	862,152	902,463	997,781	1,072,967	1,190,393	1,209,863	40.3
Oregon	647,391	899,709	963,153	1,042,939	1,128,211	1,242,595	1,358,244	1,523,505	1,615,882	54.9
Pennsylvania	1,575,104	2,473,794	2,703,292	2,951,559	3,262,178	3,511,535	3,692,745	4,153,483	4,262,533	44.4
Rhode Island	156,451	213,859	227,564	247,606	270,500	291,376	292,404	308,383	325,003	31.3
South Carolina	630,966	957,771	997,857	1,096,800	1,216,468	1,333,941	1,502,709	1,629,876	1,733,468	58.0
South Dakota	127,839	147,699	154,582	160,019	169,210	184,954	198,583	219,751	241,536	50.9
Tennessee	675,770	1,104,118	1,226,302	1,346,786	1,435,262	1,556,416	1,634,491	1,672,605	1,839,384	36.6
Texas	2,858,725	4,558,275	4,437,640	4,814,275	5,204,122	5,777,100	6,015,690	6,664,828	7,126,068	48.0
Utah	431,294	686,817	729,349	794,630	870,334	960,027	1,020,836	1,160,882	1,224,127	54.0
Vermont	127,337	191,559	207,565	223,950	244,836	267,178	281,526	298,524	305,477	36.4
Virginia	1,159,453	1,876,151	2,054,766	2,245,676	2,486,637	2,736,307	2,902,939	3,041,850	3,176,437	41.4
Washington	998,146	1,445,849	1,552,662	1,627,937	1,809,540	1,966,838	2,188,366	2,355,445	2,539,934	56.0
West Virginia	318,915	385,170	398,943	415,387	447,533	502,436	563,796	608,294	631,619	52.1
Wisconsin	1,228,414	1,761,927	1,864,947	2,032,154	2,191,795	2,343,203	2,487,501	2,629,388	2,775,635	36.6
Wyoming	140,520	208,595	204,300	211,403	224,602	237,093	251,760	271,290	270,515	28.0
U.S. Service Schools	586,095	913,092	920,863	980,041	982,495	1,176,548	1,114,245	1,159,395	1,183,716	20.8
Outlying areas	242,380	451,734	446,110	508,034	515,558	573,106	557,655	665,323	704,076	38.6
American Samoa	1,305	2,413	2,568	2,791	3,060	3,585	3,939	4,057	4,428	58.6
Federated States of Micronesia	—	—	—	—	1,789	1,842	2,063	2,078	3,453	—
Guam	14,291	31,139	29,447	35,943	39,282	50,411	61,667	70,658	74,928	108.5
Marshall Islands	—	—	—	—	—	—	—	3,798	1,111	—
Northern Marianas	—	1,350	1,484	774	748	791	1,458	1,715	2,462	218.2
Palau	—	—	—	—	3,643	4,038	4,100	3,948	5,133	—
Puerto Rico	213,012	392,194	388,945	440,382	441,449	487,133	428,768	518,747	581,128	32.0
Trust Territory of the Pacific	1,669	5,681	4,523	4,862	—	—	—	—	—	—
Virgin Islands	12,103	18,957	19,143	23,281	25,587	25,307	55,659	60,322	31,432	35.0

[1] Preliminary data.

—Data not available or not applicable.

NOTE.—Because of rounding, details may not add to totals.

SOURCE: U.S. Department of Education, National Center for Education Statistics, "Financial Statistics of Institutions of Higher Education" survey; and Integrated Postsecondary Education Data System (IPEDS), "Finance" surveys. (This table was prepared March 1995.)

Table 324.—Current-fund revenue of public institutions of higher education, by source of funds and state: 1992–93 [1]

[In thousands of dollars]

State	Total	Tuition and fees	Federal appropriations, grants, and contracts [2]	State appropriations, grants, and contracts	Local appropriations, grants, and contracts	Private gifts, grants, and contracts	Endowment income	Auxiliary enterprises	Hospitals	Educational activities and other
1	2	3	4	5	6	7	8	9	10	11
United States	$108,186,484	$19,490,221	$11,655,011	$39,789,641	$4,040,897	$4,330,112	$667,711	$10,255,044	$11,791,033	$6,166,815
Alabama	2,521,938	364,208	268,543	772,713	10,002	107,008	17,486	181,805	706,423	93,751
Alaska	323,740	37,986	51,315	178,497	1,507	8,326	2,618	18,976	0	24,514
Arizona	1,677,711	347,776	221,936	596,087	173,105	86,518	9,071	190,599	0	52,621
Arkansas	995,482	140,941	71,910	404,957	623	31,953	1,330	90,232	209,169	44,367
California	14,262,239	1,608,616	1,312,300	5,914,065	1,114,074	407,246	90,849	901,061	1,782,484	1,131,545
Colorado	1,714,698	482,504	299,613	476,829	26,995	80,960	8,913	212,062	34,863	91,959
Connecticut	976,380	204,407	70,248	348,823	556	37,220	491	101,017	168,589	45,029
Delaware	446,768	147,230	45,249	130,215	3,867	18,774	21,445	56,700	0	23,289
District of Columbia	118,865	28,859	7,228	0	76,258	308	1,283	603	0	4,327
Florida	3,202,499	592,468	292,452	1,699,701	14,743	189,874	40,253	292,430	0	80,579
Georgia	2,268,331	361,389	228,337	1,030,941	24,620	124,694	4,462	202,427	226,927	64,535
Hawaii	594,752	48,659	92,094	378,384	601	13,503	1,429	49,037	0	11,045
Idaho	416,359	65,232	38,808	197,411	7,794	23,968	8,222	44,483	0	30,441
Illinois	3,924,599	712,345	358,133	1,386,402	379,410	138,448	3,299	407,848	238,786	299,928
Indiana	2,882,592	596,565	218,820	968,430	6,494	137,563	9,197	449,794	341,524	154,206
Iowa	1,930,399	279,291	254,716	590,852	24,503	68,557	1,896	195,320	397,540	117,723
Kansas	1,350,052	231,801	121,960	476,753	105,539	28,060	30,706	118,810	161,835	74,588
Kentucky	1,576,644	261,195	112,124	670,197	7,147	33,926	6,116	131,332	215,173	139,434
Louisiana	1,821,190	319,550	105,079	650,344	2,433	45,836	1,002	197,296	316,185	183,464
Maine	384,730	89,324	33,870	174,502	264	11,598	1,782	52,185	0	21,204
Maryland	1,913,029	468,210	217,724	728,205	113,876	68,669	4,021	233,620	0	78,703
Massachusetts	1,639,854	452,851	135,629	547,420	2,802	51,690	935	140,277	177,105	131,144
Michigan	5,329,224	1,196,982	518,493	1,487,865	197,739	256,593	25,597	771,221	639,010	235,724
Minnesota	2,363,483	404,287	249,881	856,739	9,067	161,832	16,693	204,218	300,179	160,586
Mississippi	1,150,201	203,263	140,205	410,776	30,714	34,923	956	148,437	134,582	46,347
Missouri	1,698,594	386,254	106,934	587,986	61,235	57,598	10,640	168,246	188,077	131,624
Montana	349,102	61,148	56,923	128,445	4,010	9,930	311	64,448	0	23,887
Nebraska	989,156	130,924	78,803	353,186	48,226	50,262	2,873	103,262	187,780	33,840
Nevada	392,258	63,352	50,367	192,460	4,740	22,325	1,393	30,997	0	26,626
New Hampshire	348,839	137,307	37,237	77,595	1,953	14,538	1,794	63,623	0	14,793
New Jersey	2,745,100	567,701	157,525	1,058,237	162,968	90,639	9,769	214,193	358,699	125,369
New Mexico	1,125,366	100,406	217,114	368,785	49,393	58,299	12,954	81,072	176,676	60,667
New York	6,117,555	1,299,154	417,160	2,616,728	387,273	226,438	15,410	359,980	656,593	138,819
North Carolina	3,113,193	350,968	348,575	1,524,786	76,406	152,130	12,222	408,522	0	239,584
North Dakota	431,464	79,459	63,377	151,143	206	17,851	2,023	71,468	11,814	34,122
Ohio	4,628,902	1,222,095	330,888	1,319,208	85,735	182,860	33,532	423,491	835,094	195,999
Oklahoma	1,209,863	183,950	161,067	583,977	14,559	34,727	1,461	192,235	0	37,888
Oregon	1,615,882	249,909	213,499	484,275	128,251	70,106	6,632	146,914	263,063	53,232
Pennsylvania	4,262,533	1,246,946	447,056	1,064,949	75,094	172,137	32,934	449,398	593,632	180,388
Rhode Island	325,003	108,328	39,983	117,062	0	5,902	0	43,184	0	10,544
South Carolina	1,733,468	305,566	138,497	595,843	22,550	71,868	2,147	171,629	372,704	52,665
South Dakota	241,536	56,751	36,104	97,242	22	6,232	16	27,469	0	17,701
Tennessee	1,839,384	290,606	170,501	741,326	11,899	80,643	15,302	158,710	298,253	72,145
Texas	7,126,068	1,009,538	736,402	3,118,048	281,364	328,240	132,436	511,731	240,280	768,030
Utah	1,224,127	154,464	171,830	363,909	21,238	32,778	8,509	99,863	223,361	148,175
Vermont	305,477	132,773	37,559	46,439	78	22,721	3,711	36,338	0	25,857
Virginia	3,176,437	649,903	269,765	836,957	12,796	145,689	28,854	423,486	749,682	59,306
Washington	2,539,934	385,943	433,598	976,065	8,504	123,661	8,788	227,848	240,084	135,442
West Virginia	631,619	154,432	59,574	294,996	1,392	19,258	141	80,510	0	21,316
Wisconsin	2,775,635	480,399	336,220	888,921	233,042	141,567	10,561	201,062	274,329	209,533
Wyoming	270,515	35,419	33,760	123,967	13,234	16,826	3,250	35,850	0	8,209
U.S. Service Schools	1,183,716	584	1,038,028	0	0	6,840	0	67,725	70,539	0
Outlying areas	704,076	65,010	89,042	468,882	22,641	8,121	725	12,066	1,915	35,673
American Samoa	4,428	75	1,944	2,410	0	0	0	0	0	0
Federated States of Micronesia	3,453	1,890	0	0	969	0	0	367	0	227
Guam	74,928	5,358	6,861	41,584	15,366	1,036	519	2,856	0	1,348
Marshall Islands	1,111	695	119	156	0	23	0	113	0	5
Northern Marianas	2,462	1,310	0	0	671	0	0	254	0	227
Palau	5,133	961	2,470	885	0	0	0	726	0	91
Puerto Rico	581,128	51,242	73,969	406,760	2,159	6,321	206	5,344	1,915	33,417
Virgin Islands	31,432	3,480	3,680	17,087	3,475	740	0	2,405	0	359

[1] Preliminary data.
[2] Includes independent operations (federally funded research and development centers).

NOTE.—Because of rounding, details may not add to totals.

SOURCE: U.S. Department of Education, National Center for Education Statistics, Integrated Postsecondary Education Data System (IPEDS), "Finance" survey. (This table was prepared March 1995.)

Table 325.—Current-fund revenue of public institutions of higher education, by source of funds and state: 1991–92

[In thousands of dollars]

State	Total	Tuition and fees	Federal appropriations, grants, and contracts[1]	State appropriations, grants, and contracts	Local appropriations, grants, and contracts	Private gifts, grants, and contracts	Endowment income	Auxiliary enterprises	Hospitals	Educational activities and other
1	2	3	4	5	6	7	8	9	10	11
United States	$102,202,890	$17,460,263	$10,783,842	$39,107,560	$3,778,615	$4,039,212	$593,998	$9,655,373	$11,122,029	$5,661,999
Alabama	2,296,665	325,589	233,615	744,836	9,018	94,636	14,623	175,062	605,282	94,004
Alaska	304,857	34,005	40,796	180,017	1,339	7,130	2,488	16,841	0	22,241
Arizona	1,655,873	336,795	210,432	612,468	166,701	78,854	9,805	195,289	0	45,529
Arkansas	920,699	125,282	62,661	369,525	207	23,919	1,701	86,724	207,454	43,227
California	13,628,928	1,299,169	1,246,685	6,120,436	968,317	386,138	83,244	886,238	1,691,490	947,213
Colorado	1,594,541	433,950	265,136	464,309	39,858	82,828	322	174,671	32,618	100,848
Connecticut	940,067	179,065	67,545	363,606	261	28,215	137	97,715	176,371	27,153
Delaware	433,186	139,782	35,940	137,960	4,491	16,024	22,133	54,091	0	22,766
District of Columbia	121,991	8,061	28,442	0	79,757	476	1,241	649	0	3,364
Florida	3,049,921	526,103	260,538	1,686,698	11,427	205,147	541	285,314	0	74,153
Georgia	2,042,825	305,713	233,408	929,898	24,982	105,028	3,646	177,959	203,804	58,388
Hawaii	579,805	46,242	84,803	380,540	394	12,996	1,643	45,103	0	8,085
Idaho	396,173	54,784	38,441	199,330	7,375	21,358	7,790	41,744	0	25,351
Illinois	3,659,328	646,575	317,037	1,393,254	328,357	135,001	3,476	391,649	170,802	273,177
Indiana	2,767,477	547,232	203,841	973,426	1,797	132,170	9,189	429,826	329,525	140,471
Iowa	1,827,776	261,279	225,780	565,049	23,719	61,798	1,237	183,839	381,943	123,131
Kansas	1,297,129	212,213	108,695	472,575	94,793	26,906	29,500	137,779	146,312	68,356
Kentucky	1,565,021	242,401	101,704	693,883	6,815	38,060	6,354	131,496	216,143	128,165
Louisiana	1,553,258	286,212	98,735	655,975	2,134	40,586	528	190,110	127,130	128,165
Maine	375,512	84,244	32,795	170,337	139	13,544	1,717	52,498	0	20,238
Maryland	1,745,479	423,185	199,481	669,319	120,198	42,221	8,231	217,807	0	65,038
Massachusetts	1,525,943	436,148	128,967	481,111	2,151	50,558	1,021	132,395	177,105	116,487
Michigan	5,127,892	1,080,350	472,951	1,534,869	190,903	245,622	25,770	530,722	821,924	224,781
Minnesota	2,261,978	368,819	231,247	823,271	20,836	158,126	11,685	196,315	304,433	147,246
Mississippi	1,054,530	184,260	128,022	371,401	29,256	31,406	1,137	146,752	114,118	48,178
Missouri	1,566,480	348,272	96,029	552,328	41,273	53,375	9,098	163,610	177,326	125,169
Montana	334,243	45,231	56,444	135,668	3,782	10,470	314	57,746	0	24,588
Nebraska	941,062	120,642	76,908	343,145	43,401	45,638	2,723	94,472	180,488	33,646
Nevada	368,245	52,397	42,834	190,560	711	22,661	2,069	29,306	0	27,707
New Hampshire	324,186	124,832	34,334	73,698	1,863	12,821	3,159	57,879	0	15,601
New Jersey	2,610,949	527,480	142,380	1,057,449	154,177	79,568	11,008	204,450	322,494	111,943
New Mexico	1,056,819	86,849	192,414	349,004	86,971	14,372	7,341	78,208	160,326	81,335
New York	5,616,604	1,080,026	354,840	2,529,869	367,411	233,616	15,250	348,955	571,504	115,132
North Carolina	2,873,684	310,261	304,279	1,437,931	69,807	145,008	11,348	382,736	0	212,315
North Dakota	411,293	75,798	62,911	139,764	109	16,481	2,511	68,627	11,260	33,832
Ohio	4,484,576	1,130,959	334,841	1,368,574	81,228	174,482	33,851	407,457	746,957	206,225
Oklahoma	1,190,393	175,952	163,034	573,833	14,230	39,246	1,322	188,622	0	34,155
Oregon	1,523,505	229,720	194,334	446,307	130,236	66,205	5,948	136,800	256,781	57,174
Pennsylvania	4,153,483	1,179,545	407,745	1,076,522	74,149	161,171	28,109	425,669	652,555	148,017
Rhode Island	308,383	97,159	37,693	114,159	0	5,092	0	43,127	0	11,153
South Carolina	1,629,876	280,325	123,230	575,293	21,300	69,589	2,349	167,344	343,941	46,504
South Dakota	219,751	50,679	29,004	92,764	26	5,617	33	24,729	0	16,899
Tennessee	1,672,605	269,003	153,177	661,610	10,059	71,884	13,733	158,816	263,814	70,510
Texas	6,664,828	865,367	642,847	2,957,902	267,106	295,998	135,253	500,772	287,447	712,136
Utah	1,160,882	136,543	172,020	340,229	19,804	32,750	9,407	94,103	200,723	155,304
Vermont	298,524	122,255	37,465	46,665	45	22,158	4,538	38,018	0	27,380
Virginia	3,041,850	580,217	246,561	847,674	15,148	143,122	26,491	403,330	716,333	62,974
Washington	2,355,445	356,945	413,368	912,578	9,221	107,860	6,283	220,895	208,037	120,260
West Virginia	608,294	135,063	54,080	290,967	1,551	19,457	0	82,856	0	24,320
Wisconsin	2,629,388	459,400	305,832	870,271	214,779	131,306	9,612	195,900	243,651	198,636
Wyoming	271,290	31,451	30,910	128,705	15,005	13,529	3,091	38,955	0	9,644
U.S. Service Schools	1,159,395	434	1,016,630	0	0	6,988	0	63,407	71,935	0
Outlying areas	665,323	50,325	85,555	451,599	24,553	7,971	571	17,704	0	27,044
American Samoa	4,057	69	1,774	2,215	0	0	0	0	0	0
Federated States of Micronesia	2,078	988	128	467	0	0	0	0	0	0
Guam	70,658	4,723	8,020	35,797	16,768	1,364	0	480	0	15
Marshall Islands	3,798	707	1,815	651	0	0	270	2,168	0	1,548
Northern Marianas	1,715	806	122	381	0	0	0	534	0	91
Palau	3,948	735	1,889	677	0	0	0	392	0	15
Puerto Rico	518,747	37,235	67,067	373,640	4,682	5,676	0	555	0	91
Virgin Islands	60,322	5,063	4,738	37,772	3,103	930	301	6,531	0	23,914
								7,043	0	1,370

[1] Includes independent operations (federally funded research and development centers).

NOTE.—Revised from previously published data. Because of rounding, details may not add to totals.

SOURCE: U.S. Department of Education, National Center for Education Statistics, Integrated Postsecondary Education Data System (IPEDS), "Finance" survey. (This table was prepared April 1995.)

Table 326.—Current-fund revenue from state and local governments of institutions of higher education, by state: 1985–86 to 1992–93

[In thousands]

State	Current-fund revenue from state and local governments					Current-fund revenue from state and local governments, 1992–93 [1]					
	1985–86	1988–89	1989–90	1990–91	1991–92	Total	State appro-priations for public institutions	Local appro-priations for public institutions	State and local appro-priations for private institutions	State and local grants and con-tracts for public institutions	State and local grants and con-tracts for private institutions
1	2	3	4	5	6	7	8	9	10	11	12
United States [2]	$32,456,006	$39,394,884	$41,989,141	$43,412,081	$44,746,783	$45,692,830	$37,073,932	$3,594,207	$246,020	$3,162,400	$1,616,271
Alabama	656,823	723,697	727,543	758,900	762,004	791,758	742,649	2,799	4,991	37,266	4,052
Alaska	159,781	159,677	167,360	175,938	181,358	180,110	171,003	641	0	8,361	106
Arizona	539,054	668,016	714,195	768,654	779,292	769,328	574,219	165,307	0	29,665	136
Arkansas	266,898	321,154	326,399	332,367	371,131	407,115	375,474	473	1	29,634	1,533
California	4,943,659	6,202,242	6,425,599	6,628,037	7,127,388	7,072,896	5,424,000	994,791	1,381	609,348	43,376
Colorado	391,468	424,906	474,849	510,649	508,624	508,586	434,984	23,336	313	45,504	4,450
Connecticut	280,012	397,833	400,074	406,306	390,250	379,720	330,918	0	1,876	18,461	28,465
Delaware	88,661	111,407	119,602	124,881	142,638	134,355	123,621	568	0	9,893	273
District of Columbia	71,761	85,554	83,756	84,471	83,808	79,935	0	67,796	0	8,462	3,677
Florida	1,172,112	1,633,819	1,824,902	1,863,133	1,793,785	1,808,015	1,589,960	4,490	11,928	119,994	81,643
Georgia	689,379	857,256	920,901	1,001,889	977,304	1,077,918	985,136	19,747	10,004	50,678	12,353
Hawaii	195,375	233,648	268,859	321,195	381,118	379,025	363,771	0	0	15,214	40
Idaho	125,338	153,111	167,155	193,188	206,819	205,370	186,189	7,703	0	11,312	166
Illinois	1,405,622	1,575,798	1,783,123	1,855,023	1,821,597	1,865,744	1,252,502	368,135	18,888	145,175	81,044
Indiana	645,880	835,387	914,108	984,176	999,381	1,002,215	913,969	1,918	0	59,036	27,291
Iowa	431,840	503,264	545,959	599,407	613,147	635,838	569,216	23,999	3	22,140	20,480
Kansas	422,278	484,697	546,565	556,372	571,270	587,290	450,686	97,787	0	33,819	4,998
Kentucky	483,027	565,168	595,727	665,808	707,859	684,648	633,218	5,015	3	39,111	7,300
Louisiana	562,205	510,286	563,543	634,541	670,183	676,781	578,575	545	2,640	73,656	21,365
Maine	103,724	161,724	178,358	189,099	171,887	176,327	159,944	0	0	14,822	1,561
Maryland	631,471	824,681	890,011	943,620	823,075	876,755	669,597	111,637	23,366	60,847	11,308
Massachusetts	589,876	811,975	758,239	545,606	507,248	580,056	501,604	46	4,168	48,573	25,665
Michigan	1,215,291	1,463,070	1,555,997	1,589,630	1,764,129	1,730,143	1,429,337	187,378	7,549	68,889	36,991
Minnesota	533,573	702,126	760,863	818,117	871,048	893,456	808,314	5,859	559	51,633	27,090
Mississippi	362,517	420,388	421,069	419,177	401,458	441,825	383,114	28,338	0	30,038	336
Missouri	506,246	588,755	636,322	651,819	613,905	655,962	560,521	60,261	181	28,439	6,561
Montana	97,672	98,823	109,282	119,813	139,753	133,037	123,261	2,973	182	6,221	400
Nebraska	248,544	293,836	336,087	374,112	387,688	402,829	339,821	43,720	0	17,871	1,417
Nevada	99,841	128,552	156,966	173,580	191,292	197,213	176,374	0	0	20,825	13
New Hampshire	52,393	72,934	72,201	79,979	80,343	85,033	72,208	0	0	7,339	5,486
New Jersey	837,214	1,161,150	1,218,368	1,190,657	1,280,172	1,285,916	924,404	154,878	13,352	141,922	51,359
New Mexico	221,094	288,222	362,937	413,558	437,925	419,182	334,238	33,124	0	50,815	1,004
New York	2,726,150	3,295,879	3,413,434	3,421,222	3,578,508	3,675,680	2,262,050	330,540	42,477	411,411	629,202
North Carolina	1,074,960	1,461,768	1,561,133	1,633,096	1,703,504	1,810,371	1,481,492	73,868	4,180	45,832	204,999
North Dakota	118,691	120,843	130,672	133,796	140,149	151,668	144,961	15	0	6,374	319
Ohio	1,132,678	1,364,838	1,457,509	1,541,996	1,490,804	1,448,082	1,253,426	76,626	5,434	74,892	37,705
Oklahoma	437,693	422,123	485,273	535,024	590,597	601,040	522,342	13,971	1	62,223	2,503
Oregon	394,899	466,172	509,225	544,631	580,442	616,623	445,081	115,649	147	51,796	3,951
Pennsylvania	961,089	1,180,734	1,259,717	1,276,665	1,334,311	1,298,755	992,733	71,650	48,133	75,659	110,580
Rhode Island	107,265	133,263	136,654	123,502	116,197	118,844	108,136	0	53	8,926	1,730
South Carolina	491,802	551,097	601,516	618,304	601,894	627,013	584,629	20,920	75	12,843	8,546
South Dakota	65,151	74,132	81,315	86,262	93,150	97,575	91,664	0	0	5,600	311
Tennessee	528,933	677,513	712,775	711,103	681,944	763,246	711,844	1,867	1,373	39,514	8,649
Texas	2,521,860	2,810,145	3,051,747	3,069,099	3,315,755	3,496,729	2,959,976	233,781	30,506	205,654	66,811
Utah	256,997	298,068	322,123	346,711	369,253	385,953	347,109	0	0	38,037	807
Vermont	35,334	45,620	46,061	48,485	49,405	49,418	41,429	78	0	5,010	2,901
Virginia	775,474	937,961	995,573	961,845	887,077	873,539	781,956	927	9,550	66,871	14,235
Washington	620,383	769,514	817,265	915,462	922,706	985,218	883,963	0	0	100,606	649
West Virginia	222,693	234,663	263,157	280,199	293,370	297,177	277,219	712	0	18,457	789
Wisconsin	825,610	956,133	986,035	1,053,246	1,094,481	1,134,317	879,607	227,629	2,706	14,727	9,648
Wyoming	127,714	131,261	131,040	137,727	144,360	137,201	121,488	12,709	0	3,004	0

[1] Preliminary data.

[2] Excludes U.S. Service Schools.

NOTE.—Because of rounding, details may not add to totals.

SOURCE: U.S. Department of Education, National Center for Education Statistics, "Financial Statistics of Institutions of Higher Education" surveys and Integrated Postsecondary Education Data System (IPEDS), "Finance" surveys. (This table was prepared March 1995.)

Table 327.—Current-fund revenue received from the federal government by the 120 institutions of higher education receiving the largest amounts: 1992–93

[In thousands]

Institution	Rank order	Current-fund revenue from the federal government [1]	Institution	Rank order	Current-fund revenue from the federal government [1]
1	2	3	1	2	3
United States (all institutions)	—	$21,014,564			
120 institutions receiving the largest amounts	—	16,010,971			
California Institute of Technology	1	1,220,682	University of Hawaii at Manoa	61	82,683
Johns Hopkins University (MD)	2	[2] 734,332	Rutgers University, Central Office (NJ)	62	[2] 79,858
University of Chicago (IL)	3	693,065	University of Colorado, Health Sciences Center	63	79,568
Massachusetts Institute of Technology	4	609,328	Yeshiva University (NY)	64	78,475
Stanford University (CA)	5	437,965	The University of Texas, Southwestern Medical Center, Dallas	65	77,667
University of Washington	6	332,559	North Carolina State University at Raleigh	66	77,373
University of Michigan, Ann Arbor	7	288,978	Oregon State University	67	76,178
United States Military Academy (NY)	8	275,431	University of Oklahoma, Health Sciences Center	68	75,870
University of Southern California	9	265,061	University of Tennessee, Knoxville	69	75,466
University of Wisconsin, Madison	10	263,986	New Mexico State University, Main Campus	70	[2] 74,922
United States Air Force Academy (CO)	11	249,519	University of Georgia	71	74,182
University of Miami (FL)	12	248,240	University of Cincinnati, Main Campus (OH)	72	71,070
University of California, Los Angeles	13	240,428	State University of New York at Stony Brook	73	[3] 70,911
University of California, San Diego	14	[3] 230,400	Colorado State University	74	68,884
Columbia University in the City of New York	15	225,470	University of California, Irvine	75	[3] 67,722
Cornell University Medical Center (NY)	16	221,541	Uniformed Services University of the Health Sciences (MD)	76	67,422
Harvard University (MA)	17	220,370	University of Illinois at Chicago	77	[3] 66,824
United States Naval Academy (MD)	18	213,304	Virginia Polytechnic Institute and State University	78	66,218
University of California, San Francisco	19	[3] 211,731	Cornell University, Statutory Colleges (NY)	79	64,939
University of Pennsylvania	20	206,578	Utah State University	80	61,678
University of Minnesota, Twin Cities	21	203,340	State University of New York at Buffalo	81	[3] 61,431
Rush University (IL)	22	200,113	Mount Sinai School of Medicine (NY)	82	[4] 60,535
Georgetown University (DC)	23	196,255	University of Kentucky	83	59,194
Yale University (CT)	24	194,455	Virginia Commonwealth University	84	58,992
Princeton University (NJ)	25	185,029	University of Texas, Health Science Center, San Antonio	85	58,232
Howard University (DC)	26	181,089	Washington State University	86	58,196
University of Illinois at Urbana	27	[3] 180,335	Wayne State University (MI)	87	55,190
University of California, Berkeley	28	177,842	University of Maryland, Baltimore Professional Schools	88	54,621
University of Pittsburgh, Main Campus (PA)	29	174,923	Indiana University-Purdue University at Indianapolis	89	54,591
University of North Carolina, Chapel Hill	30	168,766	Gallaudet University (DC)	90	54,568
Pennsylvania State University, Main Campus	31	163,254	Tufts University (MA)	91	54,079
University of Texas at Austin	32	158,762	Tulane University of Louisiana	92	53,719
University of Arizona	33	147,430	University of California, Santa Barbara	93	[3] 53,647
Washington University (MO)	34	144,964	Hahnemann University (PA)	94	53,348
Ohio State University, Main Campus	35	141,462	Indiana University, Bloomington	95	51,347
Cornell University, Endowed Colleges (NY)	36	128,807	Air Force Institute of Technology (OH)	96	[4] 50,917
University of Rochester (NY)	37	123,449	Oregon Health Science University	97	50,258
University of Alabama at Birmingham	38	122,097	City University of New York System Office	98	49,766
University of Iowa	39	120,023	Mississippi State University	99	49,411
Carnegie Mellon University (PA)	40	118,854	University of Medicine and Dentistry of New Jersey	100	48,853
Vanderbilt University (TN)	41	112,523	Rochester Institute of Technology (NY)	101	48,591
New York University	42	108,347	Dartmouth College (NH)	102	47,715
University of Colorado at Boulder	43	104,692	University of Massachusetts, Amherst	103	47,337
University of California, Davis	44	[3] 104,521	University of Alaska, Fairbanks	104	46,842
Iowa State University	45	104,476	Florida State University	105	46,063
University of New Mexico, Main Campus	46	104,236	Brown University (RI)	106	45,804
Case Western Reserve University (OH)	47	103,418	University of Massachusetts, Medical School, Worcester	107	[4] 45,315
Michigan State University	48	103,081	Wake Forest University (NC)	108	45,062
Naval Postgraduate School (CA)	49	102,629	West Virginia University	109	44,909
University of Florida	50	101,982	University of Nebraska at Lincoln	110	43,752
Georgia Institute of Technology, Main Campus	51	101,843	University of Texas Health Science Center	111	43,442
Baylor College of Medicine (TX)	52	101,039	United States Coast Guard Academy (CT)	112	43,226
Texas A & M University	53	94,405	Arizona State University, Main Campus	113	42,436
University of Utah	54	94,039	University of Missouri, Columbia	114	41,913
Purdue University, Main Campus (IN)	55	93,494	University of Dayton (OH)	115	39,701
Northwestern University (IL)	56	92,552	State University of New York at Albany	116	[3] 39,557
Boston University (MA)	57	91,702	George Washington University (DC)	117	37,424
University of Maryland, College Park Campus	58	90,613	University of South Florida	118	37,228
University of Virginia, Main Campus	59	86,874	University of South Carolina at Columbia	119	36,951
Emory University (GA)	60	85,362	Rockefeller University (NY)	120	36,854

[1] Includes federal appropriations, unrestricted and restricted federal contracts and grants, and revenue for independent operations. Independent operations generally include only the revenues associated with major federally funded research and development centers. Excludes Pell Grants. Federally supported student aid that is received through students is excluded.

[2] Includes some funds from other branch campuses.

[3] Some funds included with other branch campus reports.

[4] NCES estimate based on prior years' data.

—Not applicable.

SOURCE: U.S. Department of Education, National Center for Education Statistics, Integrated Postsecondary Education Data System (IPEDS), "Finance, 1992–93" survey. (This table was prepared May 1995.)

Table 328.—Current-fund expenditures and expenditures per full-time-equivalent student in institutions of higher education, by type and control of institution: 1970–71 to 1992–93

Control of institution and year	All institutions			4-year institutions			2-year institutions		
	Current-fund expenditures, in millions		Current-fund expenditures per student, in constant 1992–93 dollars [1]	Current-fund expenditures, in millions		Current-fund expenditures per student, in constant 1992–93 dollars [1]	Current-fund expenditures, in millions		Current-fund expenditures per student, in constant 1992–93 dollars [1]
	Unadjusted dollars	Constant 1992–93 dollars [1]		Unadjusted dollars	Constant 1992–93 dollars [1]		Unadjusted dollars	Constant 1992–93 dollars [1]	
1	2	3	4	5	6	7	8	9	10
All institutions									
1970–71	$23,375	$87,837	$13,036	$21,049	$79,094	$15,372	$2,327	$8,743	$5,490
1973–74	30,714	97,373	13,064	26,912	85,320	15,686	3,802	12,052	5,984
1974–75	35,058	102,138	13,085	30,596	89,141	15,900	4,461	12,997	5,910
1975–76	38,903	106,295	12,535	33,811	92,382	15,657	5,092	13,913	5,394
1976–77	42,600	109,227	13,140	37,052	95,001	16,245	5,548	14,226	5,772
1977–78	45,971	110,526	13,134	39,899	95,926	16,163	6,072	14,599	5,886
1978–79	50,721	113,655	13,614	44,163	98,960	16,681	6,558	14,695	6,082
1979–80	56,914	116,177	13,688	49,661	101,372	16,850	7,253	14,805	5,991
1980–81	64,053	117,965	13,376	55,840	102,840	16,691	8,212	15,125	5,691
1981–82	70,339	118,380	13,132	61,333	103,223	16,516	9,006	15,157	5,482
1982–83	75,936	120,130	13,213	66,238	104,789	16,769	9,697	15,341	5,397
1983–84	81,993	123,891	13,516	71,680	108,307	17,123	10,314	15,584	5,485
1984–85	89,951	128,781	14,386	78,744	112,736	17,915	11,207	16,045	6,034
1985–86	97,536	133,479	14,925	85,560	117,090	18,602	11,976	16,389	6,187
1986–87	105,764	138,968	15,332	92,985	122,177	19,209	12,779	16,791	6,210
1987–88	113,786	143,092	15,503	100,143	125,935	19,415	13,644	17,158	6,255
1988–89	123,867	147,226	15,556	109,141	129,723	19,466	14,726	17,503	6,251
1989–90	134,656	151,296	15,469	118,578	133,232	19,554	16,077	18,064	6,088
1990–91	146,088	155,840	15,610	128,594	137,179	19,687	17,494	18,662	6,189
1991–92	156,189	161,392	15,577	137,375	141,951	20,046	18,814	19,441	5,929
1992–93 [2]	165,241	165,241	15,834	145,300	145,300	20,383	19,941	19,941	6,029
Public institutions									
1970–71	14,996	56,351	11,377	12,899	48,471	13,974	2,097	7,880	5,308
1973–74	20,336	64,473	11,453	16,802	53,268	14,315	3,534	11,205	5,871
1974–75	23,490	68,437	11,512	19,309	56,256	14,621	4,181	12,181	5,808
1975–76	26,184	71,542	10,969	21,392	58,449	14,409	4,792	13,093	5,310
1976–77	28,635	73,420	11,562	23,411	60,026	15,012	5,224	13,395	5,696
1977–78	30,725	73,871	11,549	25,013	60,138	14,889	5,712	13,733	5,826
1978–79	33,733	75,588	12,038	27,600	61,847	15,477	6,132	13,742	6,019
1979–80	37,768	77,095	12,060	30,979	63,237	15,578	6,789	13,859	5,939
1980–81	42,280	77,866	11,723	34,677	63,865	15,358	7,602	14,001	5,636
1981–82	46,219	77,786	11,471	37,890	63,767	15,152	8,330	14,019	5,449
1982–83	49,573	78,424	11,448	40,616	64,254	15,224	8,957	14,170	5,388
1983–84	53,087	80,213	11,656	43,588	65,861	15,439	9,499	14,352	5,487
1984–85	58,315	83,487	12,489	48,017	68,745	16,221	10,298	14,743	6,025
1985–86	63,194	86,482	12,970	52,184	71,415	16,845	11,010	15,067	6,205
1986–87	67,654	88,894	13,115	56,003	73,585	17,131	11,651	15,309	6,167
1987–88	72,641	91,350	13,167	60,137	75,625	17,204	12,505	15,725	6,186
1988–89	78,946	93,833	13,222	65,349	77,672	17,238	13,597	16,161	6,237
1989–90	85,771	96,370	13,073	70,865	79,622	17,235	14,906	16,748	6,086
1990–91	92,961	99,167	13,121	76,722	81,844	17,266	16,239	17,323	6,147
1991–92	98,847	102,140	12,990	81,334	84,044	17,525	17,513	18,096	5,900
1992–93 [2]	104,570	104,570	13,217	86,065	86,065	17,938	18,505	18,505	5,943
Private institutions									
1970–71	8,379	31,487	17,643	8,150	30,624	18,263	230	863	8,000
1973–74	10,377	32,900	18,038	10,110	32,052	18,655	267	847	8,015
1974–75	11,568	33,701	18,113	11,287	32,885	18,698	280	817	8,012
1975–76	12,719	34,753	17,755	12,419	33,933	18,403	300	819	7,220
1976–77	13,965	35,806	18,244	13,641	34,975	18,910	324	831	7,352
1977–78	15,246	36,654	18,156	14,885	35,788	18,876	360	866	7,049
1978–79	16,988	38,067	18,396	16,563	37,113	19,168	425	953	7,166
1979–80	19,146	39,082	18,657	18,682	38,135	19,489	464	947	6,864
1980–81	21,773	40,099	18,422	21,163	38,975	19,458	610	1,124	6,472
1981–82	24,120	40,594	18,177	23,444	39,456	19,328	676	1,138	5,932
1982–83	26,363	41,706	18,610	25,623	40,535	19,985	740	1,171	5,503
1983–84	28,907	43,678	19,116	28,092	42,446	20,611	815	1,231	5,460
1984–85	31,637	45,293	19,979	30,727	43,991	21,409	910	1,302	6,137
1985–86	34,342	46,997	20,652	33,376	45,675	22,230	966	1,322	5,983
1986–87	38,110	50,074	21,904	36,982	48,593	23,533	1,128	1,482	6,696
1987–88	41,145	51,742	22,575	40,006	50,310	24,063	1,139	1,433	7,118
1988–89	44,922	53,393	22,554	43,792	52,050	24,116	1,130	1,343	6,424
1989–90	48,885	54,926	22,798	47,713	53,610	24,437	1,172	1,316	6,108
1990–91	53,127	56,673	23,366	51,872	55,335	24,837	1,255	1,338	6,777
1991–92	57,342	59,252	23,722	56,041	57,908	25,334	1,301	1,344	6,341
1992–93 [2]	60,671	60,671	24,037	59,235	59,235	25,418	1,436	1,436	7,417

[1] Dollars adjusted by the Higher Education Price Index.

[2] Preliminary data.

NOTE.—Because of rounding, details may not add to totals.

SOURCE: U.S. Department of Education, National Center for Education Statistics, "Financial Statistics of Institutions of Higher Education" and "Fall Enrollment in Colleges and Universities" surveys; Integrated Postsecondary Education Data System (IPEDS), "Fall Enrollment" and "Finance" surveys; and Research Associates of Washington, unpublished data. (This table was prepared May 1995.)

Table 329.—Current-fund expenditures of institutions of higher education, by purpose: 1980–81 to 1992–93

Purpose	1980–81	1985–86	1986–87	1987–88	1988–89	1989–90	1990–91	1991–92	1992–93[1]
1	2	3	4	5	6	7	8	9	10
	In thousands								
Total current-fund expenditures	$64,052,938	$97,535,742	$105,763,557	$113,786,476	$123,867,184	$134,655,571	$146,087,836	$156,189,161	$165,241,040
Educational and general expenditures	50,073,805	76,127,965	82,955,555	89,157,430	96,803,377	105,585,076	114,139,901	121,567,157	128,977,968
Instruction	20,733,166	31,032,099	33,711,146	35,833,563	38,812,690	42,145,987	45,496,117	47,997,196	50,340,914
Research	5,657,719	8,437,367	9,352,309	10,350,931	11,432,170	12,505,961	13,444,040	14,261,554	15,291,309
Public service	2,057,770	3,119,533	3,448,453	3,786,362	4,227,323	4,689,758	5,076,177	5,489,298	5,935,095
Academic support	4,273,286	6,667,392	7,575,451	8,141,581	8,904,279	9,437,644	10,050,773	10,577,018	11,072,970
Libraries	1,759,784	2,551,331	2,441,184	2,836,498	3,009,870	3,254,239	3,343,892	3,595,834	3,684,852
Student services	2,908,998	4,562,938	4,975,913	5,396,520	5,780,837	6,388,148	7,025,482	7,509,094	8,165,079
Institutional support	5,772,515	9,350,786	10,084,663	10,774,495	11,529,119	12,674,031	13,726,484	14,475,023	15,249,898
Operation and maintenance of plant	5,350,310	7,605,226	7,819,032	8,230,986	8,739,895	9,458,262	10,062,581	10,346,580	10,783,727
Scholarships and fellowships	2,504,525	4,160,174	4,776,100	5,325,358	5,918,666	6,655,544	7,551,184	9,060,000	10,148,373
From unrestricted funds	1,080,614	2,285,116	2,644,615	2,941,143	3,282,698	3,853,904	4,445,106	5,205,797	5,949,037
From restricted funds[2]	1,423,911	1,875,059	2,131,486	2,384,215	2,635,969	2,801,640	3,106,078	3,854,203	4,199,337
Mandatory transfers	815,516	1,192,449	1,212,488	1,317,633	1,458,397	1,629,742	1,707,063	1,851,393	1,990,603
Auxiliary enterprises	7,288,089	10,528,303	11,037,333	11,399,953	12,280,063	13,203,984	14,272,247	14,966,100	15,561,508
Mandatory transfers	508,377	617,171	633,461	629,369	774,752	836,852	936,876	1,003,299	1,109,549
Hospitals	5,433,111	8,692,113	9,173,014	10,406,461	11,824,782	12,679,286	14,325,865	16,104,313	17,049,672
Mandatory transfers	57,963	128,833	151,071	178,472	240,278	222,192	274,452	333,714	308,059
Independent operations (FFRDC)[3]	1,257,934	2,187,361	2,597,655	2,822,632	2,958,962	3,187,224	3,349,824	3,551,592	3,651,891
Mandatory transfers	643	3,432	2,292	4,306	6,987	5,812	5,645	3,396	2,271
	Percentage distribution								
Total current-fund expenditures	100.0	100.0	100.0	100.0	100.0	100.0	100.0	100.0	100.0
Educational and general expenditures	78.2	78.1	78.4	78.4	78.2	78.4	78.1	77.8	78.1
Instruction	32.4	31.8	31.9	31.5	31.3	31.3	31.1	30.7	30.5
Research	8.8	8.7	8.8	9.1	9.2	9.3	9.2	9.1	9.3
Public service	3.2	3.2	3.3	3.3	3.4	3.5	3.5	3.5	3.6
Academic support	6.7	6.8	7.2	7.2	7.2	7.0	6.9	6.8	6.7
Libraries	2.7	2.6	2.3	2.5	2.4	2.4	2.3	2.3	2.2
Student services	4.5	4.7	4.7	4.7	4.7	4.7	4.8	4.8	4.9
Institutional support	9.0	9.6	9.5	9.5	9.3	9.4	9.4	9.3	9.2
Operation and maintenance of plant	8.4	7.8	7.4	7.2	7.1	7.0	6.9	6.6	6.5
Scholarships and fellowships	3.9	4.3	4.5	4.7	4.8	4.9	5.2	5.8	6.1
From unrestricted funds	1.7	2.3	2.5	2.6	2.7	2.9	3.0	3.3	3.6
From restricted funds[2]	2.2	1.9	2.0	2.1	2.1	2.1	2.1	2.5	2.5
Mandatory transfers	1.3	1.2	1.1	1.2	1.2	1.2	1.2	1.2	1.2
Auxiliary enterprises	11.4	10.8	10.4	10.0	9.9	9.8	9.8	9.6	9.4
Mandatory transfers	0.8	0.6	0.6	0.6	0.6	0.6	0.6	0.6	0.7
Hospitals	8.5	8.9	8.7	9.1	9.5	9.4	9.8	10.3	10.3
Mandatory transfers	0.1	0.1	0.1	0.2	0.2	0.2	0.2	0.2	0.2
Independent operations (FFRDC)[3]	2.0	2.2	2.5	2.5	2.4	2.4	2.3	2.3	2.2
Mandatory transfers	(4)	(4)	(4)	(4)	(4)	(4)	(4)	(4)	(4)

[1] Preliminary data.

[2] Excludes Pell Grants.

[3] Generally includes only those expenditures associated with major federally funded research and development centers (FFRDC).

[4] Less than 0.05 percent.

NOTE.—Because of rounding, details may not add to totals.

SOURCE: U.S. Department of Education, National Center for Education Statistics, "Financial Statistics of Institutions of Higher Education" surveys; and Integrated Postsecondary Education Data System (IPEDS), "Finance" surveys. (This table was prepared April 1995.)

Table 330.—Current-fund expenditures of public institutions of higher education, by purpose: 1980–81 to 1992–93

Purpose	1980–81	1985–86	1986–87	1987–88	1988–89	1989–90	1990–91	1991–92	1992–93[1]
1	2	3	4	5	6	7	8	9	10
In thousands									
Total current-fund expenditures	$42,279,806	$63,193,853	$67,653,838	$72,641,301	$78,945,618	$85,770,530	$92,961,093	$98,847,180	$104,570,101
Educational and general expenditures	34,173,013	50,872,962	54,359,434	58,639,468	63,444,908	69,163,958	74,395,428	78,554,534	83,210,979
Instruction	14,849,822	21,880,782	23,359,057	24,954,204	26,893,691	29,257,209	31,371,394	32,828,420	34,260,177
Research	3,813,350	5,705,144	6,258,625	6,976,925	7,796,952	8,542,235	9,364,213	9,948,580	10,604,973
Public service	1,718,924	2,515,734	2,727,593	2,986,164	3,351,950	3,688,664	3,990,232	4,285,501	4,563,397
Academic support	3,029,284	4,693,543	5,048,232	5,436,155	5,941,906	6,535,076	6,933,847	7,274,159	7,613,244
Libraries	1,187,116	1,685,052	1,619,353	1,853,410	1,956,497	2,102,672	2,167,161	2,284,520	2,329,625
Student services	1,950,566	2,921,758	3,158,991	3,482,112	3,678,419	4,021,328	4,398,365	4,690,921	5,173,239
Institutional support	3,563,194	5,667,144	6,042,593	6,470,162	6,876,360	7,490,137	8,030,642	8,423,156	9,049,589
Operation and maintenance of plant	3,681,921	5,177,254	5,308,631	5,601,732	5,913,267	6,333,582	6,655,605	6,790,215	7,076,805
Scholarships and fellowships	1,064,864	1,575,909	1,751,671	1,941,389	2,150,350	2,386,493	2,688,532	3,255,660	3,727,838
From unrestricted funds	367,476	696,973	750,931	830,195	944,001	1,099,425	1,270,158	1,523,721	1,745,339
From restricted funds[2]	697,388	878,935	1,000,740	1,111,194	1,206,349	1,287,068	1,418,374	1,731,939	1,982,498
Mandatory transfers	501,087	735,695	704,040	790,624	842,012	909,234	962,598	1,057,923	1,141,717
Auxiliary enterprises	4,658,140	6,830,235	7,135,393	7,237,866	7,744,725	8,282,332	9,049,935	9,634,131	10,024,352
Mandatory transfers	344,043	410,777	409,726	412,006	512,413	551,331	623,146	655,301	758,644
Hospitals	3,377,972	5,358,699	5,904,212	6,532,905	7,533,912	8,113,989	9,315,902	10,432,773	11,100,602
Mandatory transfers	26,613	75,569	102,623	106,181	159,507	156,029	195,961	224,095	223,241
Independent operations (FFRDC)[3]	70,681	131,956	254,799	231,063	222,072	210,252	199,827	225,742	234,168
Mandatory transfers	322	846	194	2,063	1,787	2,276	1,201	510	462
Percentage distribution									
Total current-fund expenditures	100.0	100.0	100.0	100.0	100.0	100.0	100.0	100.0	100.0
Educational and general expenditures	80.8	80.5	80.3	80.7	80.4	80.6	80.0	79.5	79.6
Instruction	35.1	34.6	34.5	34.4	34.1	34.1	33.7	33.2	32.8
Research	9.0	9.0	9.3	9.6	9.9	10.0	10.1	10.1	10.1
Public service	4.1	4.0	4.0	4.1	4.2	4.3	4.3	4.3	4.4
Academic support	7.2	7.4	7.5	7.5	7.5	7.6	7.5	7.4	7.3
Libraries	2.8	2.7	2.4	2.6	2.5	2.5	2.3	2.3	2.2
Student services	4.6	4.6	4.7	4.8	4.7	4.7	4.7	4.7	4.9
Institutional support	8.4	9.0	8.9	8.9	8.7	8.7	8.6	8.5	8.7
Operation and maintenance of plant	8.7	8.2	7.8	7.7	7.5	7.4	7.2	6.9	6.8
Scholarships and fellowships	2.5	2.5	2.6	2.7	2.7	2.8	2.9	3.3	3.6
From unrestricted funds	0.9	1.1	1.1	1.1	1.2	1.3	1.4	1.5	1.7
From restricted funds[2]	1.6	1.4	1.5	1.5	1.5	1.5	1.5	1.8	1.9
Mandatory transfers	1.2	1.2	1.0	1.1	1.1	1.1	1.0	1.1	1.1
Auxiliary enterprises	11.0	10.8	10.5	10.0	9.8	9.7	9.7	9.7	9.6
Mandatory transfers	0.8	0.7	0.6	0.6	0.6	0.6	0.7	0.7	0.7
Hospitals	8.0	8.5	8.7	9.0	9.5	9.5	10.0	10.6	10.6
Mandatory transfers	0.1	0.1	0.2	0.1	0.2	0.2	0.2	0.2	0.2
Independent operations (FFRDC)[3]	0.2	0.2	0.4	0.3	0.3	0.2	0.2	0.2	0.2
Mandatory transfers	(4)	(4)	(4)	(4)	(4)	(4)	(4)	(4)	(4)

[1] Preliminary data.
[2] Excludes Pell Grants.
[3] Generally includes only those expenditures associated with major federally funded research and development centers (FFRDC).
[4] Less than 0.05 percent.

NOTE.—Because of rounding, details may not add to totals.

SOURCE: U.S. Department of Education, National Center for Education Statistics, "Financial Statistics of Institutions of Higher Education" surveys; and Integrated Postsecondary Education Data System (IPEDS), "Finance" surveys. (This table was prepared April 1995.)

Table 331.—Current-fund expenditures of private institutions of higher education, by purpose: 1980–81 to 1992–93

Purpose	1980–81	1985–86	1986–87	1987–88	1988–89	1989–90	1990–91	1991–92	1992–93[1]
1	2	3	4	5	6	7	8	9	10
	In thousands								
Total current-fund expenditures	$21,773,132	$34,341,889	$38,109,719	$41,145,174	$44,921,566	$48,885,041	$53,126,743	$57,341,982	$60,670,938
Educational and general expenditures	15,900,792	25,255,003	28,596,121	30,517,962	33,358,469	36,421,118	39,744,472	43,012,623	45,766,989
Instruction	5,883,343	9,151,318	10,352,089	10,879,358	11,918,999	12,888,779	14,124,723	15,168,776	16,080,736
Research	1,844,369	2,732,222	3,093,684	3,374,006	3,635,218	3,963,726	4,079,827	4,312,973	4,686,336
Public service	338,845	603,799	720,860	800,198	875,373	1,001,094	1,085,945	1,203,797	1,371,697
Academic support	1,244,002	1,973,849	2,527,219	2,705,426	2,962,374	2,902,568	3,116,927	3,302,859	3,459,726
Libraries	572,667	866,279	821,831	983,087	1,053,372	1,151,567	1,176,731	1,311,314	1,355,227
Student services	958,432	1,641,180	1,816,922	1,914,409	2,102,418	2,366,819	2,627,117	2,818,174	2,991,840
Institutional support	2,209,321	3,683,642	4,042,069	4,304,333	4,652,759	5,183,893	5,695,842	6,051,868	6,200,308
Operation and maintenance of plant	1,668,389	2,427,972	2,510,400	2,629,254	2,826,628	3,124,680	3,406,975	3,556,365	3,706,923
Scholarships and fellowships	1,439,661	2,584,266	3,024,430	3,383,968	3,768,316	4,269,051	4,862,651	5,804,340	6,420,536
From unrestricted funds	713,138	1,588,143	1,893,684	2,110,948	2,338,697	2,754,479	3,174,947	3,682,076	4,203,697
From restricted funds[2]	726,523	996,123	1,130,746	1,273,021	1,429,619	1,514,572	1,687,704	2,122,264	2,216,838
Mandatory transfers	314,429	456,754	508,448	527,009	616,385	720,508	744,465	793,471	848,886
Auxiliary enterprises	2,629,948	3,698,067	3,901,940	4,162,087	4,535,337	4,921,653	5,222,312	5,331,969	5,537,156
Mandatory transfers	164,335	206,394	223,736	217,364	262,339	285,521	313,730	347,999	350,905
Hospitals	2,055,139	3,333,414	3,268,802	3,873,556	4,290,869	4,565,297	5,009,963	5,671,540	5,949,070
Mandatory transfers	31,349	53,264	48,449	72,291	80,771	66,164	78,491	109,619	84,818
Independent operations (FFRDC)[3]	1,187,253	2,055,405	2,342,856	2,591,569	2,736,890	2,976,973	3,149,996	3,325,850	3,417,723
Mandatory transfers	321	2,586	2,098	2,244	5,200	3,535	4,444	2,886	1,808
	Percentage distribution								
Total current-fund expenditures	100.0	100.0	100.0	100.0	100.0	100.0	100.0	100.0	100.0
Educational and general expenditures	73.0	73.5	75.0	74.2	74.3	74.5	74.8	75.0	75.4
Instruction	27.0	26.6	27.2	26.4	26.5	26.4	26.6	26.5	26.5
Research	8.5	8.0	8.1	8.2	8.1	8.1	7.7	7.5	7.7
Public service	1.6	1.8	1.9	1.9	1.9	2.0	2.0	2.1	2.3
Academic support	5.7	5.7	6.6	6.6	6.6	5.9	5.9	5.8	5.7
Libraries	2.6	2.5	2.2	2.4	2.3	2.4	2.2	2.3	2.2
Student services	4.4	4.8	4.8	4.7	4.7	4.8	4.9	4.9	4.9
Institutional support	10.1	10.7	10.6	10.5	10.4	10.6	10.7	10.6	10.2
Operation and maintenance of plant	7.7	7.1	6.6	6.4	6.3	6.4	6.4	6.2	6.1
Scholarships and fellowships	6.6	7.5	7.9	8.2	8.4	8.7	9.2	10.1	10.6
From unrestricted funds	3.3	4.6	5.0	5.1	5.2	5.6	6.0	6.4	6.9
From restricted funds[2]	3.3	2.9	3.0	3.1	3.2	3.1	3.2	3.7	3.7
Mandatory transfers	1.4	1.3	1.3	1.3	1.4	1.5	1.4	1.4	1.4
Auxiliary enterprises	12.1	10.8	10.2	10.1	10.1	10.1	9.8	9.3	9.1
Mandatory transfers	0.8	0.6	0.6	0.5	0.6	0.6	0.6	0.6	0.6
Hospitals	9.4	9.7	8.6	9.4	9.6	9.3	9.4	9.9	9.8
Mandatory transfers	0.1	0.2	0.1	0.2	0.2	0.1	0.1	0.2	0.1
Independent operations (FFRDC)[3]	5.5	6.0	6.1	6.3	6.1	6.1	5.9	5.8	5.6
Mandatory transfers	(4)	(4)	(4)	(4)	(4)	(4)	(4)	(4)	(4)

[1] Preliminary data.
[2] Excludes Pell Grants.
[3] Generally includes only those expenditures associated with major federally funded research and development centers (FFRDC).
[4] Less than 0.05 percent.

NOTE.—Because of rounding, details may not add to totals.

SOURCE: U.S. Department of Education, National Center for Education Statistics, "Financial Statistics of Institutions of Higher Education" surveys; and Integrated Postsecondary Education Data System (IPEDS), "Finance" surveys. (This table was prepared April 1995.)

Table 332.—Voluntary support for institutions of higher education, by source and purpose of support: 1949–50 to 1993–94

[In millions]

Source and purpose of support	1949–50	1959–60	1965–66	1970–71	1975–76	1980–81	1985–86	1989–90	1990–91	1991–92	1992–93	1993–94
1	2	3	4	5	6	7	8	9	10	11	12	13
Total voluntary support[1]	$240	$815	$1,440	$1,860	$2,410	$4,230	$7,400	$9,800	$10,200	$10,700	$11,200	$12,350
Sources												
Alumni	60	191	310	458	588	1,049	1,825	2,540	2,680	2,840	2,980	3,410
Nonalumni individuals	60	194	350	495	569	1,007	1,781	2,230	2,310	2,500	2,530	2,800
Corporations	28	130	230	259	379	778	1,702	2,170	2,230	2,260	2,400	2,510
Foundations	60	163	357	418	549	922	1,363	1,920	2,030	2,090	2,200	2,540
Religious organizations	16	80	108	104	130	140	211	240	240	240	250	240
Other	16	57	85	126	195	334	518	700	710	770	840	850
Purpose												
Current operations	101	385	675	1,050	1,480	2,590	4,022	5,440	5,830	6,100	6,300	6,710
Capital purposes	139	430	765	810	930	1,640	3,378	4,360	4,370	4,600	4,900	5,640
Voluntary support as a percent of total expenditures[2]	9.0	11.4	9.2	6.8	5.5	6.0	6.9	6.5	6.2	6.2	6.1	6.4

[1] Data are based on a sample survey of institutions of higher education.
[2] Total expenditures include current-fund expenditures and additions to plant value.

SOURCE: Council for Aid to Education, Research Report, "Contributions to Colleges Drop for First Time Since 1975;" and "Voluntary Support of Education," various years. (This table was prepared May 1995.)

Table 333.—Current-fund expenditures and educational and general expenditures of institutions of higher education, by purpose and per student: 1929–30 to 1992–93

[Columns 2 through 17 in thousands]

Year	Current-fund expenditures	Educational and general expenditures							
		Total	Administration and general expense	Instruction and departmental research	Organized research	Libraries	Plant operation and maintenance	Organized activities related to instructional departments	Other sponsored programs [1]
1	2	3	4	5	6	7	8	9	10
1929–30	$507,142	$377,903	$42,633	$221,598	[5] $18,007	$9,622	$61,061	[6]	—
1931–32	536,523	420,633	47,232	232,645	[5] 21,978	11,379	56,797	[7] $21,297	—
1933–34	469,329	369,661	43,155	203,332	[5] 17,064	13,387	51,046	[7] 14,155	—
1935–36	541,391	419,883	48,069	225,143	[5] 22,091	15,531	56,802	[7] 20,241	—
1937–38	614,385	475,191	56,406	253,006	[5] 25,213	17,588	62,738	[7] 24,031	—
1939–40	674,688	521,990	62,827	280,248	[5] 27,266	19,487	69,612	[7] 27,225	—
1941–42	738,169	572,465	66,968	298,558	[5] 34,287	19,763	72,594	[7] 37,771	—
1943–44	974,118	753,846	69,668	334,189	[5] 58,456	20,452	81,201	[7] 48,415	[8] $97,044
1945–46	1,088,422	820,326	104,808	375,122	[5] 86,812	26,560	110,947	[7] 60,604	—
1947–48	1,883,269	1,391,594	171,829	657,945	[5] 159,090	44,208	201,996	[7] 85,346	—
1949–50	2,245,661	1,706,444	213,070	780,994	[5] 225,341	56,147	225,110	[7] 119,108	—
1951–52	2,471,008	1,960,481	233,844	823,117	[5] 317,928	60,612	240,446	[7] 147,854	—
1953–54	2,882,864	2,345,331	288,147	960,556	[5] 372,643	72,944	277,874	[7] 186,905	—
1955–56	3,499,463	2,861,858	355,207	1,140,655	[5] 500,793	85,563	324,229	[7] 222,007	—
1957–58	4,509,666	3,734,350	473,945	1,465,603	[5] 727,776	109,715	406,226	[7] 238,455	—
1959–60	5,601,376	4,685,258	583,224	1,793,320	[5] 1,022,353	135,384	469,943	[7] 294,255	—
1961–62	7,154,526	5,997,007	730,429	2,202,443	[5] 1,474,406	177,362	564,225	[7] 375,040	—
1963–64	9,177,677	7,725,433	957,512	2,801,707	[5] 1,973,383	236,718	686,054	[7] 458,507	—
1965–66	12,509,489	10,376,630	1,251,107	3,756,175	[5] 2,448,300	346,248	844,506	[7] 558,170	155,202
1966–67	14,230,341	10,724,974	1,445,074	4,356,413	1,565,102	415,903	969,275	591,848	350,950
1967–68	16,480,786	12,847,350	1,738,946	5,139,179	1,933,473	493,266	1,127,290	350,711	514,294
1968–69	18,481,583	14,718,140	2,277,585	5,941,972	2,034,074	571,572	1,337,903	535,269	668,483
1969–70	21,043,110	16,845,210	2,627,993	6,883,844	2,144,076	652,596	1,541,698	648,089	769,253
1970–71	23,375,197	18,714,642	2,983,911	7,804,410	2,209,338	716,212	1,730,664	693,011	890,507
1971–72	25,559,560	20,441,878	3,344,215	8,443,261	2,265,282	764,481	1,927,553	779,728	1,059,989
1972–73	27,955,624	22,400,379	3,713,068	9,243,641	2,394,261	840,727	2,141,162	791,290	1,284,085
1973–74	30,713,581	24,653,849	4,200,955	10,219,118	2,480,450	939,023	2,494,057	838,170	1,355,027
1974–75	35,057,563	27,547,620	4,495,391	11,797,823	3,132,132	1,001,868	2,786,768	1,253,824	—
1975–76	38,903,177	30,598,685	5,240,066	13,094,943	3,287,364	1,223,723	3,082,959	1,248,670	—
1976–77	42,599,816	33,151,681	5,590,669	14,031,145	3,600,067	1,250,314	3,436,705	1,544,646	—
1977–78	45,970,790	36,256,604	6,177,029	15,336,229	3,919,830	1,348,747	3,795,043	1,781,160	—
1978–79	50,720,984	39,833,116	6,832,004	16,662,820	4,447,760	1,426,614	4,178,574	2,044,386	—
1979–80	56,913,588	44,542,843	7,621,143	18,496,717	5,099,151	1,623,811	4,700,070	2,252,577	—
1980–81	64,052,938	50,073,805	8,681,513	20,733,166	5,657,719	1,759,784	5,350,310	2,513,502	—
1981–82	70,339,448	54,848,752	9,648,069	22,962,527	5,929,894	1,922,416	5,979,281	2,734,038	—
1982–83	75,935,749	58,929,218	10,412,233	24,673,293	6,265,280	2,039,671	6,391,596	3,047,220	—
1983–84	81,993,360	63,741,276	11,561,260	26,436,308	6,723,534	2,231,149	6,729,825	3,300,003	—
1984–85	89,951,263	70,061,324	12,765,452	28,777,183	7,551,892	2,361,793	7,345,482	3,712,460	—
1985–86	97,535,742	76,127,965	13,913,724	31,032,099	8,437,367	2,551,331	7,605,226	4,116,061	—
1986–87	105,763,557	82,955,555	15,060,576	33,711,146	9,352,309	2,441,184	7,819,032	5,134,267	—
1987–88	113,786,476	89,157,430	16,171,015	35,833,563	10,350,931	2,836,498	8,230,986	5,305,083	—
1988–89	123,867,184	96,803,377	17,309,956	38,812,690	11,432,170	3,009,870	8,739,895	5,894,409	—
1989–90	134,655,571	105,585,076	19,062,179	42,145,987	12,505,961	3,254,239	9,458,262	6,183,405	—
1990–91	146,087,836	114,139,901	20,751,966	45,496,117	13,444,040	3,343,892	10,062,581	6,706,881	—
1991–92 [10]	156,189,161	121,567,156	21,984,118	47,997,196	14,261,554	3,595,834	10,346,580	6,981,184	—
1992–93 [11]	165,241,040	128,977,968	23,414,977	50,340,914	15,291,309	3,684,852	10,783,727	7,388,118	—

Table 333.—Current-fund expenditures and educational and general expenditures of institutions of higher education, by purpose and per student: 1929–30 to 1992–93—Continued

[Columns 2 through 17 in thousands]

Year	Educational and general expenditures			Auxiliary enterprises	Independent operations[2]	Hospitals	Other current expenditures	Educational and general expenditures per student in fall enrollment[3]	
	Extension and public service	Scholarships and fellowships	Other general expenditures					Current dollars	Constant 1992–93 dollars[4]
1	11	12	13	14	15	16	17	18	19
1929–30	$24,982	(6)	—	$3,127	(5)	(7)	$126,112	$343	$2,859
1931–32	24,066	(6)	$5,239	90,897	(5)	(7)	24,993	364	3,603
1933–34	20,020	(6)	7,502	78,730	(5)	(7)	20,938	350	3,770
1935–36	29,426	(6)	2,580	95,332	(5)	(7)	26,176	348	3,604
1937–38	34,189	(6)	2,020	115,620	(5)	(7)	23,574	352	3,500
1939–40	35,325	(6)	—	124,184	(5)	(7)	28,514	349	3,563
1941–42	42,525	(6)	—	137,328	(5)	(7)	28,375	408	3,727
1943–44	44,421	(6)	—	199,344	(5)	(7)	20,928	653	5,337
1945–46	55,473	(6)	—	242,028	(5)	(7)	26,068	489	3,822
1947–48	71,180	(6)	—	438,988	(5)	(7)	52,687	595	3,641
1949–50	86,674	(6)	—	476,401	(5)	(7)	62,816	698	4,200
1951–52	97,408	$39,272	—	477,672	(5)	(7)	32,855	933	5,058
1953–54	112,227	74,035	—	537,533	(5)	(7)	—	1,051	5,571
1955–56	137,914	95,490	—	637,605	(5)	(7)	—	1,079	5,719
1957–58	175,256	129,935	7,439	775,316	(5)	(7)	—	1,124	5,607
1959–60	205,595	172,050	9,134	916,117	(5)	(7)	—	1,287	6,244
1961–62	244,337	228,765	—	1,157,517	(5)	(7)	—	1,447	6,860
1963–64	297,350	300,370	13,832	1,452,244	(5)	(7)	—	1,616	7,469
1965–66	438,385	425,524	153,013	1,887,744	(5)	(7)	245,115[9]	1,753	7,828
1966–67	226,566	583,390	220,453	2,060,130	$951,668	$253,790	239,780[9]	1,678	7,267
1967–68	597,544	712,425	240,222	2,302,419	765,495	290,000	275,523[9]	1,859	7,790
1968–69	536,527	814,755	—	2,539,183	697,317	526,943	—	1,959	7,828
1969–70	593,067	984,594	—	2,769,276	757,388	671,236	—	2,104	7,940
1970–71	588,390	1,098,198	—	2,988,407	829,596	842,552	—	2,181	7,825
1971–72	615,997	1,241,372	—	3,178,272	940,825	998,585	—	2,284	7,912
1972–73	669,735	1,322,411	—	3,337,789	1,033,746	1,183,709	—	2,431	8,093
1973–74	730,560	1,396,488	—	3,613,256	1,014,872	1,431,604	—	2,568	7,849
1974–75	1,097,788	1,449,542	532,485	4,073,590	1,085,590	2,350,763	—	2,694	7,415
1975–76	1,238,603	1,635,859	546,498	4,476,841	1,132,016	2,695,635	—	2,736	7,031
1976–77	1,343,404	1,770,214	584,515	4,858,328	1,434,738	3,155,069	—	3,010	7,310
1977–78	1,425,294	1,839,298	633,973	5,261,477	855,054	3,597,655	—	3,213	7,310
1978–79	1,593,097	1,944,599	703,262	5,749,974	1,007,119	4,130,775	—	3,538	7,360
1979–80	1,816,521	2,200,468	732,385	6,485,608	1,127,728	4,757,409	—	3,850	7,068
1980–81	2,057,770	2,504,525	815,516	7,288,089	1,257,934	5,433,111	—	4,139	6,811
1981–82	2,203,726	2,684,945	783,854	7,997,632	1,258,777	6,234,287	—	4,433	6,714
1982–83	2,320,478	2,922,897	856,548	8,614,316	1,406,126	6,986,089	—	4,742	6,887
1983–84	2,499,203	3,301,673	958,321	9,250,196	1,622,233	7,379,654	—	5,114	7,161
1984–85	2,861,095	3,670,355	1,015,613	10,012,248	1,867,550	8,010,141	—	5,723	7,712
1985–86	3,119,533	4,160,174	1,192,449	10,528,303	2,187,361	8,692,113	—	6,216	8,142
1986–87	3,448,453	4,776,100	1,212,488	11,037,333	2,597,655	9,173,014	—	6,635	8,501
1987–88	3,786,362	5,325,358	1,317,633	11,399,953	2,822,632	10,406,461	—	6,984	8,592
1988–89	4,227,323	5,918,666	1,458,397	12,280,063	2,958,962	11,824,782	—	7,415	8,720
1989–90	4,689,758	6,655,544	1,629,742	13,203,984	3,187,224	12,679,286	—	7,799	8,754
1990–91	5,076,177	7,551,184	1,707,063	14,272,247	3,349,824	14,325,865	—	8,259	8,790
1991–92[10]	5,489,298	9,060,000	1,851,393	14,966,100	3,551,592	16,104,313	—	8,466	8,731
1992–93[11]	5,935,095	10,148,373	1,990,603	15,561,508	3,651,891	17,049,672	—	8,903	8,903

[1] Includes all separately budgeted programs, other than research, which are supported by sponsors outside the institution. Examples are training programs, workshops, and training and instructional institutes. For years not shown, most expenditures for these programs are included under "Extension and public service."

[2] Generally includes only those expenditures associated with federally funded research and development centers (FFRDCs).

[3] Data for 1929–30 to 1945–46 are based on school year enrollment.

[4] Data adjusted by the consumer price index computed on a school year basis.

[5] Expenditures for federally funded research and development centers are included under "Organized research."

[6] Included under "Other current expenditures."

[7] Expenditures for hospitals and independent operations included under "Organized activities related to instructional departments."

[8] Expenditures were for federal contract courses.

[9] Includes current expenditures for physical plant assets. In later years, the educational and general expenditures for physical plant assets are included under "Other general expenditures."

[10] Some data have been revised from previously published figures.

[11] Preliminary data.

—Data not available.

NOTE.—The data in this table reflect limitations of data availability and comparability. Major changes in data collection forms in 1965–66 and 1974–75 cause significant data comparability problems among the three mostly consistent time periods, 1929–30 to 1963–64, 1965–66 to 1973–74, and 1974–75 to 1992–93. The largest problems affect Hospitals, Independent operations, Organized research, Other sponsored programs, Extension and public service, and Scholarships and fellowships.

SOURCE: U.S. Department of Education, National Center for Education Statistics, *Biennial Survey of Education in the United States; Financial Statistics of Institutions of Higher Education;* and Integrated Postsecondary Education Data System, "Finance" surveys. (This table was prepared April 1995.)

Table 334.—Expenditures of institutions of higher education, by purpose and by control and type of institution: 1992–93 [1]

Control and type of institution	Current-fund expenditures	Educational and general expenditures					
		Total	Instruction	Research	Public service	Academic support	
						Total	Libraries only
1	2	3	4	5	6	7	8
		In thousands					
Total	$165,241,040	$128,977,968	$50,340,914	$15,291,309	$5,935,095	$11,072,970	$3,684,852
Public	104,570,101	83,210,979	34,260,177	10,604,973	4,563,397	7,613,244	2,329,625
Research I universities [3]	39,104,022	28,564,549	9,821,649	7,172,637	2,200,604	2,709,488	769,397
Research II universities [3]	6,448,911	5,524,396	2,097,126	954,312	445,883	554,033	194,356
Doctoral universities	11,306,580	9,660,646	3,651,275	1,060,650	578,950	969,779	307,513
Master's	16,759,552	14,358,665	6,690,920	438,247	531,327	1,342,345	513,061
Baccalaureate	1,845,161	1,591,098	664,405	19,870	52,886	163,197	63,162
Associate of arts	18,751,372	17,472,704	8,741,191	24,292	404,882	1,422,632	396,321
Specialized institutions [4]							
Health and medicine	8,605,155	4,471,346	2,068,141	838,355	329,730	295,618	57,068
Engineering	194,463	176,065	69,591	20,494	3,240	14,133	5,266
Business	20,717	19,325	9,139	0	1,783	2,202	143
Fine arts	107,656	97,186	40,417	0	1,002	8,098	4,372
Other specialized	1,356,112	1,207,267	382,127	72,256	12,501	125,828	17,304
Tribal colleges [5]	70,399	67,731	24,197	3,860	609	5,891	1,660
Private	60,670,938	45,766,989	16,080,736	4,686,336	1,371,697	3,459,726	1,355,227
Research I universities [3]	23,412,164	15,555,187	5,756,050	3,436,608	487,784	1,086,583	464,543
Research II universities [3]	3,684,935	2,487,186	1,030,399	266,781	17,321	199,222	82,222
Doctoral universities	5,756,308	4,469,324	1,717,454	297,747	70,297	414,749	147,463
Master's	8,422,057	7,388,175	2,668,516	129,301	97,783	577,730	219,284
Baccalaureate	10,577,412	9,031,277	2,854,665	80,900	66,650	648,598	291,179
Associate of arts	1,627,322	1,496,961	423,700	1,860	3,371	139,211	30,232
Specialized institutions [4]							
Religion and theology	945,493	827,418	246,942	2,972	11,240	82,677	44,072
Health and medicine	4,034,338	2,477,204	673,880	438,103	593,856	118,249	27,425
Engineering	340,022	318,949	113,599	24,631	4,008	20,459	4,847
Business	799,090	716,642	214,787	427	2,339	76,196	13,034
Fine arts	614,316	556,270	198,405	158	5,613	40,850	10,281
Other specialized	436,177	422,149	174,881	6,821	9,427	53,381	20,438
Tribal colleges [5]	21,305	20,248	7,457	30	2,009	1,821	207
		Percentage distribution of current-fund expenditures					
Total	100.00	78.05	30.47	9.25	3.59	6.70	2.23
Public	100.00	79.57	32.76	10.14	4.36	7.28	2.23
Research I universities [3]	100.00	73.05	25.12	18.34	5.63	6.93	1.97
Research II universities [3]	100.00	85.66	32.52	14.80	6.91	8.59	3.01
Doctoral universities	100.00	85.44	32.29	9.38	5.12	8.58	2.72
Master's	100.00	85.67	39.92	2.61	3.17	8.01	3.06
Baccalaureate	100.00	86.23	36.01	1.08	2.87	8.84	3.42
Associate of arts	100.00	93.18	46.62	0.13	2.16	7.59	2.11
Specialized institutions [4]							
Health and medicine	100.00	51.96	24.03	9.74	3.83	3.44	0.66
Engineering	100.00	90.54	35.79	10.54	1.67	7.27	2.71
Business	100.00	93.28	44.11	0.00	8.61	10.63	0.69
Fine arts	100.00	90.27	37.54	0.00	0.93	7.52	4.06
Other specialized	100.00	89.02	28.18	5.33	0.92	9.28	1.28
Tribal colleges [5]	100.00	96.21	34.37	5.48	0.87	8.37	2.36
Private	100.00	75.43	26.50	7.72	2.26	5.70	2.23
Research I universities [3]	100.00	66.44	24.59	14.68	2.08	4.64	1.98
Research II universities [3]	100.00	67.50	27.96	7.24	0.47	5.41	2.23
Doctoral universities	100.00	77.64	29.84	5.17	1.22	7.21	2.56
Master's	100.00	87.72	31.68	1.54	1.16	6.86	2.60
Baccalaureate	100.00	85.38	26.99	0.76	0.63	6.13	2.75
Associate of arts	100.00	91.99	26.04	0.11	0.21	8.55	1.86
Specialized institutions [4]							
Religion and theology	100.00	87.51	26.12	0.31	1.19	8.74	4.66
Health and medicine	100.00	61.40	16.70	10.86	14.72	2.93	0.68
Engineering	100.00	93.80	33.41	7.24	1.18	6.02	1.43
Business	100.00	89.68	26.88	0.05	0.29	9.54	1.63
Fine arts	100.00	90.55	32.30	0.03	0.91	6.65	1.67
Other specialized	100.00	96.78	40.09	1.56	2.16	12.24	4.69
Tribal colleges [5]	100.00	95.04	35.00	0.14	9.43	8.55	0.97

Table 334.—Expenditures of institutions of higher education, by purpose and by control and type of institution: 1992–93 [1]—Continued

Control and type of institution	Educational and general expenditures					Auxiliary enterprises	Hospitals	Independent operations [2]
	Student services	Institutional support	Plant operation	Scholarships and fellowships	Mandatory transfers			
1	9	10	11	12	13	14	15	16

	In thousands							
Total	$8,165,079	$15,249,898	$10,783,727	$10,148,373	$1,990,603	$15,561,508	$17,049,672	$3,651,891
Public	5,173,239	9,049,589	7,076,805	3,727,838	1,141,717	10,024,352	11,100,602	234,168
Research I universities [3]	968,446	1,804,111	1,942,321	1,462,499	482,794	3,818,579	6,620,118	100,776
Research II universities [3]	250,888	451,355	412,225	277,406	81,169	923,140	0	1,375
Doctoral universities	537,593	1,454,092	751,963	497,002	159,341	1,317,961	327,973	0
Master's	1,264,681	1,770,066	1,401,239	699,620	220,219	2,169,859	218,296	12,732
Baccalaureate	152,647	225,844	176,599	106,928	28,723	254,063	0	0
Associate of arts	1,813,258	2,620,773	1,772,234	554,924	118,518	1,244,080	2	34,587
Specialized institutions [4]								
Health and medicine	38,968	455,157	348,687	56,093	40,596	188,411	3,863,673	81,725
Engineering	11,464	21,338	19,016	9,671	7,119	15,428	0	2,971
Business	1,263	2,365	2,206	368	0	1,392	0	0
Fine arts	6,112	24,172	12,371	5,012	2	10,470	0	0
Other specialized	120,090	208,472	228,682	54,661	2,650	78,302	70,539	4
Tribal colleges [5]	7,829	11,847	9,260	3,653	585	2,668	0	0
Private	2,991,840	6,200,308	3,706,923	6,420,536	848,886	5,537,156	5,949,070	3,417,723
Research I universities [3]	452,998	1,360,121	1,157,106	1,579,450	238,486	1,547,725	3,438,540	2,870,713
Research II universities [3]	102,665	299,738	182,731	349,021	39,308	450,168	741,837	5,745
Doctoral universities	289,828	606,893	335,391	631,784	105,181	529,585	688,773	68,625
Master's	710,446	1,150,860	580,445	1,291,973	181,122	1,007,826	6,773	19,283
Baccalaureate	954,787	1,487,942	818,295	1,952,389	167,050	1,513,027	0	33,107
Associate of arts	180,081	354,446	187,018	195,881	11,393	130,060	0	301
Specialized institutions [4]								
Religion and theology	56,514	201,524	99,243	114,478	11,828	112,978	0	5,096
Health and medicine	61,535	336,587	146,568	62,749	45,677	88,273	1,073,148	395,713
Engineering	25,752	60,357	33,833	30,641	5,670	21,073	0	0
Business	87,297	150,912	64,403	98,207	22,074	82,448	0	0
Fine arts	43,419	111,669	63,836	80,089	12,229	38,906	0	19,140
Other specialized	24,402	75,471	36,361	32,754	8,653	14,028	0	0
Tribal colleges [5]	2,116	3,790	1,693	1,118	214	1,057	0	0

	Percentage distribution of current-fund expenditures							
Total	4.94	9.23	6.53	6.14	1.20	9.42	10.32	2.21
Public	4.95	8.65	6.77	3.56	1.09	9.59	10.62	0.22
Research I universities [3]	2.48	4.61	4.97	3.74	1.23	9.77	16.93	0.26
Research II universities [3]	3.89	7.00	6.39	4.30	1.26	14.31	0.00	0.02
Doctoral universities	4.75	12.86	6.65	4.40	1.41	11.66	2.90	0.00
Master's	7.55	10.56	8.36	4.17	1.31	12.95	1.30	0.08
Baccalaureate	8.27	12.24	9.57	5.80	1.56	13.77	0.00	0.00
Associate of arts	9.67	13.98	9.45	2.96	0.63	6.63	0.00	0.18
Specialized institutions [4]								
Health and medicine	0.45	5.29	4.05	0.65	0.47	2.19	44.90	0.95
Engineering	5.90	10.97	9.78	4.97	3.66	7.93	0.00	1.53
Business	6.10	11.42	10.65	1.78	0.00	6.72	0.00	0.00
Fine arts	5.68	22.45	11.49	4.66	0.00	9.73	0.00	0.00
Other specialized	8.86	15.37	16.86	4.03	0.20	5.77	5.20	0.00
Tribal colleges [5]	11.12	16.83	13.15	5.19	0.83	3.79	0.00	0.00
Private	4.93	10.22	6.11	10.58	1.40	9.13	9.81	5.63
Research I universities [3]	1.93	5.81	4.94	6.75	1.02	6.61	14.69	12.26
Research II universities [3]	2.79	8.13	4.96	9.47	1.07	12.22	20.13	0.16
Doctoral universities	5.03	10.54	5.83	10.98	1.83	9.20	11.97	1.19
Master's	8.44	13.66	6.89	15.34	2.15	11.97	0.08	0.23
Baccalaureate	9.03	14.07	7.74	18.46	1.58	14.30	0.00	0.31
Associate of arts	11.07	21.78	11.49	12.04	0.70	7.99	0.00	0.02
Specialized institutions [4]								
Religion and theology	5.98	21.31	10.50	12.11	1.25	11.95	0.00	0.54
Health and medicine	1.53	8.34	3.63	1.56	1.13	2.19	26.60	9.81
Engineering	7.57	17.75	9.95	9.01	1.67	6.20	0.00	0.00
Business	10.92	18.89	8.06	12.29	2.76	10.32	0.00	3.12
Fine arts	7.07	18.18	10.39	13.04	1.99	6.33	0.00	0.00
Other specialized	5.59	17.30	8.34	7.51	1.98	3.22	0.00	0.00
Tribal colleges [5]	9.93	17.79	7.95	5.25	1.00	4.96	0.00	0.00

[1] Preliminary data.

[2] Generally includes only those expenditures associated with major federally funded research and development centers (FFRDC).

[3] Research institutions are committed to graduate education through the doctorate, and give high priority to research. Research I institutions receive $40 million or more annually in federal support. Research II institutions receive between $15.5 million and $40 million annually.

[4] Specialized institutions award baccalaureate or higher level degrees in specific fields of study.

[5] Tribally controlled colleges are located on reservations. They are members of the American Indian Higher Education Consortium.

SOURCE: U.S. Department of Education, National Center for Education Statistics, Integrated Postsecondary Education Data System (IPEDS), "Finance, 1992–93" survey. (This table was prepared May 1995.)

Table 335.—Educational and general expenditures of public universities, by purpose: 1976–77 to 1992–93

Year	Educational and general expenditures									
	Total	Instruction	Administration [1]	Student services	Research	Libraries	Public service	Operation and maintenance of plant	Scholarships and fellowships	Mandatory transfers
1	2	3	4	5	6	7	8	9	10	11
Expenditures, in thousands of current dollars										
1976–77	$9,413,626	$3,670,554	$1,222,410	$346,906	$1,727,807	$331,614	$763,809	$857,677	$377,749	$115,099
1977–78	10,220,191	4,009,870	1,344,538	388,262	1,896,578	343,198	803,309	938,952	389,682	105,803
1978–79	11,284,191	4,408,025	1,478,568	419,231	2,136,135	363,875	920,726	1,046,740	396,356	114,533
1979–80	12,540,072	4,860,411	1,572,523	473,460	2,444,471	463,642	1,012,376	1,148,942	439,461	124,786
1980–81	13,951,029	5,374,271	1,795,504	525,891	2,743,145	451,978	1,158,512	1,270,339	492,225	139,164
1981–82	15,077,263	5,852,958	1,974,219	566,366	2,903,178	488,939	1,223,417	1,412,557	525,498	130,131
1982–83	16,089,168	6,247,358	2,107,933	604,657	3,086,846	528,470	1,300,353	1,512,947	562,903	137,702
1983–84	17,234,711	6,646,501	2,263,565	643,614	3,295,053	577,136	1,385,191	1,627,702	624,642	171,306
1984–85	18,960,810	7,257,618	2,598,784	701,451	3,682,755	609,365	1,519,324	1,745,825	677,533	168,155
1985–86	20,716,657	7,807,522	2,882,006	762,324	4,076,258	669,253	1,664,917	1,831,618	780,080	242,679
1986–87	22,023,387	8,368,187	3,088,348	819,829	4,399,405	677,531	1,725,613	1,829,880	847,328	267,266
1987–88	23,848,427	8,902,624	3,311,806	889,528	4,911,929	762,858	1,857,008	1,934,489	949,438	328,746
1988–89	26,138,665	9,623,797	3,638,424	975,801	5,476,936	813,888	2,096,267	2,069,744	1,096,447	347,362
1989–90	28,077,757	10,269,007	3,867,818	1,028,463	5,997,942	860,981	2,263,623	2,200,111	1,199,643	390,170
1990–91	30,367,325	11,012,373	4,157,677	1,103,058	6,599,209	906,506	2,479,956	2,305,115	1,367,754	435,676
1991–92	31,565,791	11,373,749	4,198,990	1,161,633	6,937,360	946,098	2,609,520	2,323,220	1,556,868	458,354
1992–93 [2] ..	32,836,061	11,708,500	4,317,605	1,211,143	7,330,922	959,306	2,714,785	2,365,942	1,734,530	493,328
Percentage distribution										
1976–77	100.0	39.0	13.0	3.7	18.4	3.5	8.1	9.1	4.0	1.2
1977–78	100.0	39.2	13.2	3.8	18.6	3.4	7.9	9.2	3.8	1.0
1978–79	100.0	39.1	13.1	3.7	18.9	3.2	8.2	9.3	3.5	1.0
1979–80	100.0	38.8	12.5	3.8	19.5	3.7	8.1	9.2	3.5	1.0
1980–81	100.0	38.5	12.9	3.8	19.7	3.2	8.3	9.1	3.5	1.0
1981–82	100.0	38.8	13.1	3.8	19.3	3.2	8.1	9.4	3.5	0.9
1982–83	100.0	38.8	13.1	3.8	19.2	3.3	8.1	9.4	3.5	0.9
1983–84	100.0	38.6	13.1	3.7	19.1	3.3	8.0	9.4	3.6	1.0
1984–85	100.0	38.3	13.7	3.7	19.4	3.2	8.0	9.2	3.6	0.9
1985–86	100.0	37.7	13.9	3.7	19.7	3.2	8.0	8.8	3.8	1.2
1986–87	100.0	38.0	14.0	3.7	20.0	3.1	7.8	8.3	3.8	1.2
1987–88	100.0	37.3	13.9	3.7	20.6	3.2	7.8	8.1	4.0	1.4
1988–89	100.0	36.8	13.9	3.7	21.0	3.1	8.0	7.9	4.2	1.3
1989–90	100.0	36.6	13.8	3.7	21.4	3.1	8.1	7.8	4.3	1.4
1990–91	100.0	36.3	13.7	3.6	21.7	3.0	8.2	7.6	4.5	1.4
1991–92	100.0	36.0	13.3	3.7	22.0	3.0	8.3	7.4	4.9	1.5
1992–93 [2] ..	100.0	35.7	13.1	3.7	22.3	2.9	8.3	7.2	5.3	1.5
Expenditure per full-time-equivalent student in constant 1992–93 dollars										
1976–77	$13,751	$5,362	$1,786	$507	$2,524	$484	$1,116	$1,253	$552	$168
1977–78	13,897	5,453	1,828	528	2,579	467	1,092	1,277	530	144
1978–79	14,404	5,627	1,887	535	2,727	464	1,175	1,336	506	146
1979–80	14,271	5,531	1,790	539	2,782	528	1,152	1,307	500	142
1980–81	14,033	5,406	1,806	529	2,759	455	1,165	1,278	495	140
1981–82	13,836	5,371	1,812	520	2,664	449	1,123	1,296	482	119
1982–83	13,820	5,366	1,811	519	2,651	454	1,117	1,300	484	118
1983–84	14,168	5,464	1,861	529	2,709	474	1,139	1,338	513	141
1984–85	14,861	5,689	2,037	550	2,887	478	1,191	1,368	531	132
1985–86	15,491	5,838	2,155	570	3,048	500	1,245	1,370	583	181
1986–87	15,732	5,978	2,206	586	3,143	484	1,233	1,307	605	191
1987–88	16,131	6,022	2,240	602	3,322	516	1,256	1,308	642	222
1988–89	16,359	6,023	2,277	611	3,428	509	1,312	1,295	686	217
1989–90	16,354	5,981	2,253	599	3,494	501	1,318	1,281	699	227
1990–91	16,637	6,033	2,278	604	3,615	497	1,359	1,263	749	239
1991–92	16,596	5,980	2,208	611	3,647	497	1,372	1,221	819	241
1992–93 [2] ..	16,936	6,039	2,227	625	3,781	495	1,400	1,220	895	254

[1] Includes institutional and academic support less libraries.
[2] Preliminary data.

NOTE.—Data in this table may differ slightly from data appearing in other tables. Data for 1976–77 through 1985–86 include only institutions which provided both enrollment and finance data. The Higher Education Price Index was used to convert the per student figures to constant dollars. Because of rounding, details may not add to totals.

SOURCE: U.S. Department of Education, National Center for Education Statistics, "Financial Statistics of Institutions of Higher Education" surveys; Integrated Postsecondary Education Data System (IPEDS), "Finance" surveys; and Research Associates of Washington, unpublished data. (This table was prepared April 1995.)

Table 336.—Educational and general expenditures of public 4-year colleges,[1] by purpose: 1976–77 to 1992–93

Year	Educational and general expenditures									
	Total	Instruction	Administration [2]	Student services	Research	Libraries	Public service	Operation and maintenance of plant	Scholarships and fellowships	Mandatory transfers
1	2	3	4	5	6	7	8	9	10	11
	Expenditures, in thousands of current dollars									
1976–77	$8,682,538	$4,027,051	$1,445,651	$500,832	$607,235	$340,002	$250,152	$1,001,848	$338,432	$171,335
1977–78	9,568,977	4,423,487	1,598,092	572,193	677,414	369,408	274,314	1,118,393	332,899	202,777
1978–79	10,455,134	4,770,598	1,789,534	651,541	786,072	395,299	301,387	1,214,996	337,588	208,119
1979–80	11,750,398	5,271,621	2,029,327	733,557	937,874	448,190	359,467	1,375,308	383,036	212,019
1980–81	13,139,618	5,890,759	2,258,987	807,249	1,043,614	511,817	407,816	1,563,514	412,972	242,890
1981–82	14,321,586	6,537,888	2,518,182	834,225	1,086,146	536,080	440,736	1,738,210	403,069	227,050
1982–83	15,286,145	6,980,269	2,660,360	904,745	1,150,011	559,353	469,841	1,857,151	450,067	254,349
1983–84	16,538,128	7,464,035	3,013,666	1,041,488	1,246,289	622,879	513,732	1,873,628	473,503	288,908
1984–85	18,333,578	8,211,171	3,370,676	1,140,312	1,420,844	669,518	603,018	2,137,225	489,188	291,626
1985–86	19,860,947	8,945,373	3,658,627	1,235,418	1,618,737	712,112	648,178	2,118,522	569,841	354,139
1986–87	21,490,078	9,608,239	4,019,850	1,318,666	1,846,712	695,692	766,865	2,226,599	660,940	346,515
1987–88	23,124,455	10,310,532	4,261,440	1,434,726	2,053,638	774,274	864,347	2,340,495	711,704	373,299
1988–89	24,639,653	10,991,086	4,496,286	1,504,869	2,305,152	813,801	941,434	2,429,103	754,412	403,508
1989–90	27,210,634	12,079,093	5,076,792	1,648,526	2,525,080	888,526	1,088,113	2,607,385	871,944	425,175
1990–91	28,903,790	12,818,677	5,374,417	1,800,723	2,745,613	888,162	1,145,892	2,728,949	963,436	437,921
1991–92	30,720,827	13,270,992	5,805,724	1,868,329	2,986,474	945,097	1,310,700	2,782,200	1,248,220	503,091
1992–93 [3] ..	33,119,294	13,906,211	6,416,859	2,164,309	3,246,542	979,635	1,447,684	2,960,373	1,457,901	539,779
	Percentage distribution									
1976–77	100.0	46.4	16.7	5.8	7.0	3.9	2.9	11.5	3.9	2.0
1977–78	100.0	46.2	16.7	6.0	7.1	3.9	2.9	11.7	3.5	2.1
1978–79	100.0	45.6	17.1	6.2	7.5	3.8	2.9	11.6	3.2	2.0
1979–80	100.0	44.9	17.3	6.2	8.0	3.8	3.1	11.7	3.3	1.8
1980–81	100.0	44.8	17.2	6.1	7.9	3.9	3.1	11.9	3.1	1.8
1981–82	100.0	45.7	17.6	5.8	7.6	3.7	3.1	12.1	2.8	1.6
1982–83	100.0	45.7	17.4	5.9	7.5	3.7	3.1	12.1	2.9	1.7
1983–84	100.0	45.1	18.2	6.3	7.5	3.8	3.1	11.3	2.9	1.7
1984–85	100.0	44.8	18.4	6.2	7.7	3.7	3.3	11.7	2.7	1.6
1985–86	100.0	45.0	18.4	6.2	8.2	3.6	3.3	10.7	2.9	1.8
1986–87	100.0	44.7	18.7	6.1	8.6	3.2	3.6	10.4	3.1	1.6
1987–88	100.0	44.6	18.4	6.2	8.9	3.3	3.7	10.1	3.1	1.6
1988–89	100.0	44.6	18.2	6.1	9.4	3.3	3.8	9.9	3.1	1.6
1989–90	100.0	44.4	18.7	6.1	9.3	3.3	4.0	9.6	3.2	1.6
1990–91	100.0	44.3	18.6	6.2	9.5	3.1	4.0	9.4	3.3	1.5
1991–92	100.0	43.2	18.9	6.1	9.7	3.1	4.3	9.1	4.1	1.6
1992–93 [3] ..	100.0	42.0	19.4	6.5	9.8	3.0	4.4	8.9	4.4	1.6
	Expenditure per full-time-equivalent student in constant 1992–93 dollars									
1976–77	$10,027	$4,651	$1,670	$578	$701	$393	$289	$1,157	$391	$198
1977–78	10,131	4,683	1,692	606	717	391	290	1,184	352	215
1978–79	10,456	4,771	1,790	652	786	395	301	1,215	338	208
1979–80	10,587	4,750	1,828	661	845	404	324	1,239	345	191
1980–81	10,469	4,694	1,800	643	832	408	325	1,246	329	194
1981–82	10,418	4,756	1,832	607	790	390	321	1,264	293	165
1982–83	10,177	4,647	1,771	602	766	372	313	1,236	300	169
1983–84	10,293	4,645	1,876	648	776	388	320	1,166	295	180
1984–85	10,885	4,875	2,001	677	844	398	358	1,269	290	173
1985–86	11,280	5,081	2,078	702	919	404	368	1,203	324	201
1986–87	11,255	5,032	2,105	691	967	364	402	1,166	346	181
1987–88	11,463	5,111	2,112	711	1,018	384	428	1,160	353	185
1988–89	11,235	5,012	2,050	686	1,051	371	429	1,108	344	184
1989–90	11,362	5,044	2,120	688	1,054	371	454	1,089	364	178
1990–91	11,040	4,896	2,053	688	1,049	339	438	1,042	368	167
1991–92	11,215	4,845	2,120	682	1,090	345	479	1,016	456	184
1992–93 [3] ..	11,584	4,864	2,244	757	1,136	343	506	1,035	510	189

[1] Excludes universities. See preceding table.
[2] Includes institutional and academic support less libraries.
[3] Preliminary data.

NOTE.—Data in this table may differ slightly from data appearing in other tables. Data for 1976–77 through 1985–86 include only institutions which provided both enrollment and finance data. The Higher Education Price Index was used to convert the per student figures to constant dollars. Because of rounding, details may not add to totals.

SOURCE: U.S. Department of Education, National Center for Education Statistics, "Financial Statistics of Institutions of Higher Education" surveys; Integrated Postsecondary Education Data System (IPEDS), "Finance" surveys; and Research Associates of Washington, unpublished data. (This table was prepared April 1995.)

Table 337.—Educational and general expenditures of public 2-year colleges, by purpose: 1976–77 to 1992–93

Year	Educational and general expenditures									
	Total	Instruction	Administration [1]	Student services	Research	Libraries	Public service	Operation and maintenance of plant	Scholarships and fellowships	Mandatory transfers
1	2	3	4	5	6	7	8	9	10	11
Expenditures, in thousands of current dollars										
1976–77	$4,875,998	$2,490,274	$882,813	$409,217	$15,698	$171,409	$97,635	$547,515	$142,827	$118,610
1977–78	5,336,153	2,700,489	1,035,206	437,060	9,333	188,201	112,944	605,464	117,996	129,458
1978–79	5,734,611	2,877,651	1,119,840	482,323	21,289	193,703	110,918	650,447	127,633	150,807
1979–80	6,334,777	3,185,815	1,204,082	547,457	26,288	202,583	141,000	743,014	147,865	136,672
1980–81	7,063,474	3,575,743	1,347,020	615,869	26,591	222,391	152,597	844,781	159,474	119,008
1981–82	7,757,435	3,947,065	1,473,733	684,650	15,632	262,697	147,385	952,691	160,109	113,473
1982–83	8,292,446	4,218,388	1,620,644	741,179	18,090	248,682	123,722	1,016,267	175,069	130,403
1983–84	8,820,575	4,481,854	1,748,535	775,084	18,189	263,485	150,109	1,076,371	178,500	128,448
1984–85	9,560,507	4,806,050	1,929,968	841,101	15,591	278,363	193,903	1,156,074	207,975	131,482
1985–86	10,252,955	5,116,884	2,122,060	920,299	10,136	295,691	202,440	1,220,646	225,979	138,820
1986–87	10,845,969	5,382,631	2,363,275	1,020,496	12,508	246,131	235,115	1,252,152	243,402	90,258
1987–88	11,666,586	5,741,049	2,479,661	1,157,858	11,358	316,278	264,809	1,326,748	280,247	88,578
1988–89	12,666,590	6,278,809	2,727,058	1,197,748	14,864	328,809	314,250	1,414,420	299,491	91,142
1989–90	13,875,566	6,909,109	2,977,932	1,344,339	19,213	353,165	336,927	1,526,086	314,906	93,889
1990–91	15,124,313	7,540,344	3,265,233	1,494,583	19,390	372,492	364,384	1,621,542	357,343	89,001
1991–92	16,267,915	8,183,678	3,408,080	1,660,958	24,747	393,325	365,281	1,684,796	450,572	96,477
1992–93 [2] ..	17,255,624	8,645,466	3,598,745	1,797,787	27,510	390,684	400,927	1,750,489	535,406	108,610
Percentage distribution										
1976–77	100.0	51.1	18.1	8.4	0.3	3.5	2.0	11.2	2.9	2.4
1977–78	100.0	50.6	19.4	8.2	0.2	3.5	2.1	11.3	2.2	2.4
1978–79	100.0	50.2	19.5	8.4	0.4	3.4	1.9	11.3	2.2	2.6
1979–80	100.0	50.3	19.0	8.6	0.4	3.2	2.2	11.7	2.3	2.2
1980–81	100.0	50.6	19.1	8.7	0.4	3.1	2.2	12.0	2.3	1.7
1981–82	100.0	50.9	19.0	8.8	0.2	3.4	1.9	12.3	2.1	1.5
1982–83	100.0	50.9	19.5	8.9	0.2	3.0	1.5	12.3	2.1	1.6
1983–84	100.0	50.8	19.8	8.8	0.2	3.0	1.7	12.2	2.0	1.5
1984–85	100.0	50.3	20.2	8.8	0.2	2.9	2.0	12.1	2.2	1.4
1985–86	100.0	49.9	20.7	9.0	0.1	2.9	2.0	11.9	2.2	1.4
1986–87	100.0	49.6	21.8	9.4	0.1	2.3	2.2	11.5	2.2	0.8
1987–88	100.0	49.2	21.3	9.9	0.1	2.7	2.3	11.4	2.4	0.8
1988–89	100.0	49.6	21.5	9.5	0.1	2.6	2.5	11.2	2.4	0.7
1989–90	100.0	49.8	21.5	9.7	0.1	2.5	2.4	11.0	2.3	0.7
1990–91	100.0	49.9	21.6	9.9	0.1	2.5	2.4	10.7	2.4	0.6
1991–92	100.0	50.3	20.9	10.2	0.2	2.4	2.2	10.4	2.8	0.6
1992–93 [2] ..	100.0	50.1	20.9	10.4	0.2	2.3	2.3	10.1	3.1	0.6
Expenditure per full-time-equivalent student in constant 1992–93 dollars										
1976–77	$5,404	$2,760	$978	$454	$17	$190	$108	$607	$158	$131
1977–78	5,442	2,754	1,056	446	10	192	115	617	120	132
1978–79	5,628	2,824	1,099	473	21	190	109	638	125	148
1979–80	5,542	2,787	1,053	479	23	177	123	650	129	120
1980–81	5,305	2,685	1,012	463	20	167	115	634	120	89
1981–82	5,300	2,697	1,007	468	11	179	101	651	109	78
1982–83	5,019	2,553	981	449	11	151	75	615	106	79
1983–84	5,095	2,589	1,010	448	11	152	87	622	103	74
1984–85	5,594	2,812	1,129	492	9	163	113	676	122	77
1985–86	5,779	2,884	1,196	519	6	167	114	688	127	78
1986–87	5,861	2,909	1,277	551	7	133	127	677	132	49
1987–88	5,773	2,841	1,227	573	6	156	131	656	139	44
1988–89	5,810	2,880	1,251	549	7	151	144	649	137	42
1989–90	5,666	2,821	1,216	549	8	144	138	623	129	38
1990–91	5,725	2,854	1,236	566	7	141	138	614	135	34
1991–92	5,481	2,757	1,148	560	8	133	123	568	152	33
1992–93 [2] ..	5,542	2,776	1,156	577	9	125	129	562	172	35

[1] Includes institutional and academic support less libraries.
[2] Preliminary data.

NOTE.—Data in this table may differ slightly from data appearing in other tables. Data for 1976–77 through 1985–86 include only institutions which provided both enrollment and finance data. The Higher Education Price Index was used to convert the per student figures to constant dollars. Because of rounding, details may not add to totals.

SOURCE: U.S. Department of Education, National Center for Education Statistics, "Financial Statistics of Institutions of Higher Education" surveys; Integrated Postsecondary Education Data System (IPEDS), "Finance" surveys; and Research Associates of Washington, unpublished data. (This table was prepared April 1995.)

Table 338.—Educational and general expenditures of private (nonprofit) universities, by purpose: 1976–77 to 1992–93

Year	Educational and general expenditures									
	Total	Instruction	Administration [1]	Student services	Research	Libraries	Public service	Operation and maintenance of plant	Scholarships and fellowships	Mandatory transfers
1	2	3	4	5	6	7	8	9	10	11
Expenditures, in thousands of current dollars										
1976–77	$4,694,593	$1,784,975	$621,733	$156,457	$988,656	$195,146	$105,011	$411,340	$380,821	$50,453
1977–78	5,120,125	1,943,031	683,988	172,261	1,063,906	215,068	108,201	447,743	427,907	58,019
1978–79	5,675,608	2,120,800	796,751	195,238	1,175,657	221,676	119,082	510,819	460,200	75,385
1979–80	6,408,288	2,426,312	908,580	215,646	1,315,469	236,184	148,028	568,806	507,257	82,006
1980–81	7,249,102	2,763,320	1,009,957	254,872	1,436,318	267,142	149,946	660,152	596,241	111,154
1981–82	7,951,934	3,105,731	1,100,088	289,398	1,505,340	294,523	160,496	752,673	650,285	93,401
1982–83	8,198,167	3,227,925	1,214,617	304,617	1,464,809	295,709	169,382	754,480	670,390	96,238
1983–84	9,491,967	3,660,650	1,445,910	350,096	1,683,020	360,238	187,615	859,065	833,108	112,266
1984–85	10,431,950	3,965,165	1,556,854	393,526	1,892,570	366,356	253,010	930,229	931,027	143,212
1985–86	11,407,571	4,308,432	1,711,155	438,678	2,108,731	397,745	271,271	981,131	1,040,677	149,751
1986–87	13,013,183	4,998,565	1,977,175	502,291	2,399,976	397,460	332,223	1,006,334	1,218,002	181,159
1987–88	13,876,586	5,209,101	2,107,206	529,261	2,597,435	484,987	340,475	1,073,880	1,328,775	205,464
1988–89	15,123,369	5,743,104	2,293,256	565,903	2,786,178	510,820	377,820	1,135,273	1,472,675	238,340
1989–90	16,363,342	6,188,447	2,411,051	607,623	3,048,455	555,752	414,916	1,231,028	1,615,096	290,974
1990–91	17,827,649	6,827,220	2,633,605	669,160	3,170,083	567,800	456,615	1,383,686	1,833,124	286,357
1991–92	19,307,030	7,367,629	2,852,739	711,041	3,364,795	624,416	484,871	1,453,365	2,142,466	305,707
1992–93 [2] ..	20,435,319	7,844,576	2,874,208	719,657	3,648,010	644,005	547,159	1,495,825	2,322,331	339,547
Percentage distribution										
1976–77	100.0	38.0	13.2	3.3	21.1	4.2	2.2	8.8	8.1	1.1
1977–78	100.0	37.9	13.4	3.4	20.8	4.2	2.1	8.7	8.4	1.1
1978–79	100.0	37.4	14.0	3.4	20.7	3.9	2.1	9.0	8.1	1.3
1979–80	100.0	37.9	14.2	3.4	20.5	3.7	2.3	8.9	7.9	1.3
1980–81	100.0	38.1	13.9	3.5	19.8	3.7	2.1	9.1	8.2	1.5
1981–82	100.0	39.1	13.8	3.6	18.9	3.7	2.0	9.5	8.2	1.2
1982–83	100.0	39.4	14.8	3.7	17.9	3.6	2.1	9.2	8.2	1.2
1983–84	100.0	38.6	15.2	3.7	17.7	3.8	2.0	9.1	8.8	1.2
1984–85	100.0	38.0	14.9	3.8	18.1	3.5	2.4	8.9	8.9	1.4
1985–86	100.0	37.8	15.0	3.8	18.5	3.5	2.4	8.6	9.1	1.3
1986–87	100.0	38.4	15.2	3.9	18.4	3.1	2.6	7.7	9.4	1.4
1987–88	100.0	37.5	15.2	3.8	18.7	3.5	2.5	7.7	9.6	1.5
1988–89	100.0	38.0	15.2	3.7	18.4	3.4	2.5	7.5	9.7	1.6
1989–90	100.0	37.8	14.7	3.7	18.6	3.4	2.5	7.5	9.9	1.8
1990–91	100.0	38.3	14.8	3.8	17.8	3.2	2.6	7.8	10.3	1.6
1991–92	100.0	38.2	14.8	3.7	17.4	3.2	2.5	7.5	11.1	1.6
1992–93 [2] ..	100.0	38.4	14.1	3.5	17.9	3.2	2.7	7.3	11.4	1.7
Expenditure per full-time-equivalent student in constant 1992–93 dollars										
1976–77	$21,287	$8,094	$2,819	$709	$4,483	$885	$476	$1,865	$1,727	$229
1977–78	21,072	7,997	2,815	709	4,379	885	445	1,843	1,761	239
1978–79	21,341	7,975	2,996	734	4,421	834	448	1,921	1,730	283
1979–80	21,680	8,209	3,074	730	4,450	799	501	1,924	1,716	277
1980–81	21,920	8,356	3,054	771	4,343	808	453	1,996	1,803	336
1981–82	21,837	8,529	3,021	795	4,134	809	441	2,067	1,786	256
1982–83	22,037	8,677	3,265	819	3,937	795	455	2,028	1,802	259
1983–84	23,674	9,130	3,606	873	4,198	898	468	2,143	2,078	280
1984–85	24,681	9,381	3,683	931	4,478	867	599	2,201	2,203	339
1985–86	25,700	9,706	3,855	988	4,751	896	611	2,210	2,345	337
1986–87	27,998	10,755	4,254	1,081	5,164	855	715	2,165	2,621	390
1987–88	28,306	10,626	4,298	1,080	5,298	989	695	2,191	2,710	419
1988–89	28,790	10,933	4,366	1,077	5,304	972	719	2,161	2,804	454
1989–90	29,176	11,034	4,299	1,083	5,435	991	740	2,195	2,880	519
1990–91	30,054	11,509	4,440	1,128	5,344	957	770	2,333	3,090	483
1991–92	31,028	11,840	4,585	1,143	5,407	1,003	779	2,336	3,443	491
1992–93 [2] ..	31,771	12,196	4,469	1,119	5,672	1,001	851	2,326	3,611	528

[1] Includes institutional and academic support less libraries.
[2] Preliminary data.

NOTE.—Data in this table may differ slightly from data appearing in other tables. Data for 1976–77 through 1985–86 include only institutions which provided both enrollment and finance data. The Higher Education Price Index was used to convert the per student figures to constant dollars. Because of rounding, details may not add to totals.

SOURCE: U.S. Department of Education, National Center for Education Statistics, "Financial Statistics of Institutions of Higher Education" surveys; Integrated Postsecondary Education Data System (IPEDS), "Finance" surveys; and Research Associates of Washington, unpublished data. (This table was prepared April 1995.)

Table 339.—Educational and general expenditures of private (nonprofit) 4-year colleges,[1] by purpose: 1976–77 to 1992–93

Year	Educational and general expenditures									
	Total	Instruction	Administration[2]	Student services	Research	Libraries	Public service	Operation and maintenance of plant	Scholarships and fellowships	Mandatory transfers
1	2	3	4	5	6	7	8	9	10	11

				Expenditures, in thousands of current dollars						
1976–77	$5,139,939	$1,919,574	$1,047,932	$381,428	$259,530	$200,844	$123,717	$574,910	$511,907	$120,097
1977–78	5,637,836	2,114,043	1,160,141	428,265	271,637	221,807	123,214	638,330	550,372	130,026
1978–79	6,263,692	2,328,418	1,299,063	483,031	328,042	240,098	136,861	704,180	598,487	145,513
1979–80	7,063,953	2,589,908	1,466,556	549,639	374,520	259,969	153,056	807,943	694,791	167,570
1980–81	8,061,774	2,907,255	1,703,307	639,795	407,622	289,944	186,399	930,075	811,636	185,741
1981–82	9,061,667	3,271,255	1,938,727	727,382	419,283	322,702	228,368	1,036,118	913,999	203,834
1982–83	9,805,459	3,552,387	2,124,446	804,943	437,286	356,768	236,142	1,092,836	983,887	216,764
1983–84	10,845,622	3,900,082	2,347,962	890,707	480,459	388,153	259,932	1,184,788	1,149,813	243,726
1984–85	11,835,351	4,213,485	2,564,844	980,416	539,322	416,539	289,124	1,251,490	1,312,673	267,459
1985–86	12,855,040	4,507,505	2,790,504	1,067,717	623,050	446,766	328,827	1,317,062	1,481,954	291,654
1986–87	14,232,003	4,886,585	3,249,910	1,184,395	693,450	410,013	384,594	1,386,729	1,717,948	318,379
1987–88	15,405,503	5,248,764	3,403,379	1,293,302	776,022	485,517	456,111	1,462,345	1,966,124	313,939
1988–89	16,980,645	5,738,789	3,766,237	1,437,829	848,094	530,032	495,683	1,596,786	2,198,328	368,866
1989–90	18,717,398	6,276,102	4,097,242	1,599,951	909,822	578,520	581,730	1,712,000	2,547,600	414,432
1990–91	20,374,743	6,809,318	4,533,043	1,770,071	901,357	589,052	624,663	1,809,977	2,898,547	438,715
1991–92	22,121,380	7,320,211	4,723,853	1,919,662	942,407	659,416	714,728	1,896,424	3,478,153	466,528
1992–93[3] ..	23,609,625	7,743,656	4,887,700	2,044,830	1,036,676	680,457	821,381	1,995,164	3,900,807	498,954

				Percentage distribution						
1976–77	100.0	37.3	20.4	7.4	5.0	3.9	2.4	11.2	10.0	2.3
1977–78	100.0	37.5	20.6	7.6	4.8	3.9	2.2	11.3	9.8	2.3
1978–79	100.0	37.2	20.7	7.7	5.2	3.8	2.2	11.2	9.6	2.3
1979–80	100.0	36.7	20.8	7.8	5.3	3.7	2.2	11.4	9.8	2.4
1980–81	100.0	36.1	21.1	7.9	5.1	3.6	2.3	11.5	10.1	2.3
1981–82	100.0	36.1	21.4	8.0	4.6	3.6	2.5	11.4	10.1	2.2
1982–83	100.0	36.2	21.7	8.2	4.5	3.6	2.4	11.1	10.0	2.2
1983–84	100.0	36.0	21.6	8.2	4.4	3.6	2.4	10.9	10.6	2.2
1984–85	100.0	35.6	21.7	8.3	4.6	3.5	2.4	10.6	11.1	2.3
1985–86	100.0	35.1	21.7	8.3	4.8	3.5	2.6	10.2	11.5	2.3
1986–87	100.0	34.3	22.8	8.3	4.9	2.9	2.7	9.7	12.1	2.2
1987–88	100.0	34.1	22.1	8.4	5.0	3.2	3.0	9.5	12.8	2.0
1988–89	100.0	33.8	22.2	8.5	5.0	3.1	2.9	9.4	12.9	2.2
1989–90	100.0	33.5	21.9	8.5	4.9	3.1	3.1	9.1	13.6	2.2
1990–91	100.0	33.4	22.2	8.7	4.4	2.9	3.1	8.9	14.2	2.2
1991–92	100.0	33.1	21.4	8.7	4.3	3.0	3.2	8.6	15.7	2.1
1992–93[3] ..	100.0	32.8	20.7	8.7	4.4	2.9	3.5	8.5	16.5	2.1

				Expenditure per full-time-equivalent student in constant 1992–93 dollars						
1976–77	$10,494	$3,919	$2,140	$779	$530	$410	$253	$1,174	$1,045	$245
1977–78	10,465	3,924	2,153	795	504	412	229	1,185	1,022	241
1978–79	10,595	3,939	2,197	817	555	406	232	1,191	1,012	246
1979–80	10,791	3,956	2,240	840	572	397	234	1,234	1,061	256
1980–81	10,829	3,905	2,288	859	548	389	250	1,249	1,090	249
1981–82	10,968	3,959	2,347	880	507	391	276	1,254	1,106	247
1982–83	11,210	4,061	2,429	920	500	408	270	1,249	1,125	248
1983–84	11,598	4,171	2,511	953	514	415	278	1,267	1,230	261
1984–85	12,039	4,286	2,609	997	549	424	294	1,273	1,335	272
1985–86	12,495	4,381	2,712	1,038	606	434	320	1,280	1,440	283
1986–87	13,208	4,535	3,016	1,099	644	381	357	1,287	1,594	295
1987–88	13,514	4,604	2,985	1,134	681	426	400	1,283	1,725	275
1988–89	13,585	4,591	3,013	1,150	679	424	397	1,278	1,759	295
1989–90	13,845	4,642	3,031	1,183	673	428	430	1,266	1,884	307
1990–91	14,064	4,700	3,129	1,222	622	407	431	1,249	2,001	303
1991–92	14,463	4,786	3,088	1,255	616	431	467	1,240	2,274	305
1992–93[3] ..	14,546	4,771	3,011	1,260	639	419	506	1,229	2,403	307

[1] Excludes universities. See preceding table.
[2] Includes institutional and academic support less libraries.
[3] Preliminary data.

NOTE.—Data in this table may differ slightly from data appearing in other tables. Data for 1976–77 through 1985–86 include only institutions which provided both enrollment and finance data. The Higher Education Price Index was used to convert the per student figures to constant dollars. Because of rounding, details may not add to totals.

SOURCE: U.S. Department of Education, National Center for Education Statistics, "Financial Statistics of Institutions of Higher Education" surveys; Integrated Postsecondary Education Data System (IPEDS), "Finance" surveys; and Research Associates of Washington, unpublished data. (This table was prepared April 1995.)

Table 340.—Current-fund expenditures of public institutions of higher education, by state: 1980–81 to 1992–93

[In thousands of dollars]

State	1980–81	1985–86	1986–87	1987–88	1988–89	1989–90	1990–91	1991–92	1992–93 [1]	Percent change, 1987–88 to 1992–93
1	2	3	4	5	6	7	8	9	10	11
United States	$42,279,806	$63,193,853	$67,653,838	$72,641,301	$78,945,618	$85,770,530	$92,961,093	$98,847,180	$104,570,101	44.0
Alabama	839,366	1,324,774	1,351,761	1,511,246	1,669,401	1,831,657	2,054,798	2,189,029	2,428,620	60.7
Alaska	158,700	224,042	213,286	221,296	240,913	268,057	289,606	306,218	322,620	45.8
Arizona	691,481	1,017,203	1,098,146	1,193,765	1,317,954	1,446,388	1,586,891	1,620,019	1,621,716	35.8
Arkansas	340,621	528,831	543,200	622,442	692,970	751,336	797,291	878,783	976,735	56.9
California	5,775,482	8,515,440	9,079,890	9,493,900	10,182,106	11,230,941	12,023,304	12,910,152	13,537,367	42.6
Colorado	738,363	1,057,558	1,123,508	1,225,193	1,331,091	1,374,188	1,452,137	1,546,642	1,670,921	36.4
Connecticut	367,850	562,696	621,183	680,087	774,179	811,282	886,846	957,627	981,286	44.3
Delaware	158,332	229,377	255,335	279,084	314,003	342,119	367,012	396,947	416,699	49.3
District of Columbia	71,791	88,462	92,438	96,642	104,637	111,468	111,469	121,488	119,522	23.7
Florida	1,170,305	1,782,180	1,973,533	2,182,947	2,443,879	2,766,267	2,896,046	2,988,794	3,179,353	45.6
Georgia	754,060	1,255,964	1,404,747	1,507,960	1,622,707	1,769,744	1,929,993	2,015,816	2,227,608	47.7
Hawaii	222,718	312,248	317,294	349,791	379,799	424,473	498,307	575,337	602,346	72.2
Idaho	166,844	238,438	246,847	269,697	289,148	314,398	353,561	391,441	409,167	51.7
Illinois	1,780,403	2,571,409	2,707,123	2,789,932	3,015,395	3,310,763	3,528,967	3,644,740	3,877,243	39.0
Indiana	1,064,395	1,602,203	1,758,524	1,841,317	2,005,740	2,186,604	2,391,173	2,643,997	2,671,055	45.1
Iowa	767,590	1,092,542	1,162,266	1,229,142	1,491,442	1,617,626	1,734,476	1,776,217	1,899,159	54.5
Kansas	579,857	848,602	886,190	928,956	1,028,578	1,131,558	1,190,573	1,262,215	1,329,587	43.1
Kentucky	673,775	898,718	992,842	1,068,927	1,143,612	1,236,680	1,400,529	1,514,985	1,516,017	41.8
Louisiana	716,702	1,039,177	1,065,692	1,112,935	1,172,325	1,286,648	1,439,415	1,541,126	1,800,188	61.8
Maine	153,658	216,737	244,432	271,928	315,700	344,435	355,074	362,905	375,090	37.9
Maryland	795,100	1,064,430	1,144,897	1,249,730	1,389,900	1,522,145	1,684,341	1,674,918	1,829,812	46.4
Massachusetts	553,019	980,585	1,100,445	1,235,566	1,306,814	1,357,588	1,435,063	1,474,589	1,605,121	29.9
Michigan	2,053,795	2,946,336	3,094,481	3,507,141	3,745,488	4,076,519	4,416,914	4,741,682	4,925,759	40.4
Minnesota	876,632	1,324,691	1,427,227	1,565,491	1,809,757	1,802,133	2,012,225	2,219,016	2,286,336	46.0
Mississippi	539,222	706,380	701,795	775,821	864,611	922,574	978,366	1,012,544	1,102,806	42.1
Missouri	687,643	999,869	1,071,224	1,132,628	1,237,603	1,349,451	1,453,608	1,501,166	1,582,746	39.7
Montana	121,894	182,102	182,795	192,382	198,475	218,231	254,175	320,876	337,189	75.3
Nebraska	378,928	537,858	582,939	610,064	676,527	762,480	848,778	916,814	968,407	58.7
Nevada	111,347	180,107	198,714	217,330	240,711	281,018	330,592	363,306	377,786	73.8
New Hampshire	134,391	183,959	200,211	222,842	247,686	259,157	281,542	307,217	335,575	50.6
New Jersey	903,169	1,406,490	1,579,018	1,770,521	1,968,859	2,165,562	2,309,968	2,489,088	2,630,533	48.6
New Mexico	325,960	456,600	500,674	524,181	751,405	828,157	896,299	1,010,859	1,069,497	104.0
New York	2,519,104	3,802,602	4,227,556	4,494,943	4,732,811	5,058,750	5,605,621	5,681,964	6,096,863	35.6
North Carolina	1,128,383	1,799,173	1,955,910	2,076,493	2,238,155	2,420,825	2,581,156	2,770,977	3,002,915	44.6
North Dakota	192,046	288,214	309,961	303,762	319,583	357,832	367,959	408,219	419,268	38.0
Ohio	1,784,754	2,718,408	2,933,615	3,172,348	3,494,228	3,726,135	4,084,840	4,359,943	4,389,408	38.4
Oklahoma	583,174	844,829	826,461	844,428	887,293	973,213	1,057,248	1,158,696	1,177,061	39.4
Oregon	642,411	880,696	959,238	1,023,207	1,116,966	1,219,341	1,329,794	1,484,621	1,560,699	52.5
Pennsylvania	1,544,586	2,392,145	2,608,557	2,874,641	3,147,180	3,390,869	3,602,685	3,904,332	4,004,062	39.3
Rhode Island	158,365	213,253	225,033	246,258	270,411	287,194	292,199	303,606	330,038	34.0
South Carolina	617,963	951,848	980,264	1,079,002	1,179,216	1,324,647	1,475,074	1,595,552	1,702,419	57.8
South Dakota	124,103	149,092	152,274	157,736	169,308	184,153	197,853	217,756	240,061	52.2
Tennessee	665,885	1,081,052	1,275,950	1,311,921	1,411,226	1,519,680	1,585,614	1,621,202	1,776,066	35.4
Texas	2,736,276	4,375,082	4,451,215	4,771,023	5,166,389	5,604,164	5,959,584	6,370,847	6,982,016	46.3
Utah	405,314	669,714	700,774	757,976	835,250	914,771	993,625	1,116,845	1,174,239	54.9
Vermont	122,708	188,112	201,435	216,972	241,314	260,371	274,746	294,045	298,626	37.6
Virginia	1,143,755	1,825,156	2,003,090	2,201,018	2,431,539	2,682,902	2,812,109	2,939,683	3,072,851	39.6
Washington	993,171	1,399,780	1,512,376	1,575,333	1,779,855	1,922,673	2,157,074	2,278,549	2,486,455	57.8
West Virginia	317,482	376,293	392,671	406,170	451,503	493,825	548,802	582,453	609,447	50.0
Wisconsin	1,208,396	1,754,395	1,872,979	2,022,712	2,159,069	2,307,325	2,469,260	2,596,853	2,726,350	34.8
Wyoming	126,082	203,307	198,934	208,663	212,813	227,131	240,216	265,048	260,592	24.9
U.S. Service Schools	592,454	904,695	942,888	1,015,815	728,092	793,082	1,136,296	1,219,439	1,246,801	22.7
Outlying areas	268,310	451,370	429,481	491,892	494,087	543,925	516,958	574,988	654,292	33.0
American Samoa	1,609	1,092	1,162	1,257	2,642	2,879	3,187	3,228	3,356	166.9
Federated States of Micronesia	—	—	—	—	1,789	1,842	3,777	3,765	3,294	—
Guam	16,100	31,310	30,780	33,481	38,488	48,954	57,645	67,220	71,917	114.8
Marshall Islands	—	—	—	—	—	—	—	3,588	1,298	—
Northern Marianas	—	1,350	2,787	2,292	950	1,003	2,798	3,194	2,505	9.3
Palau	—	—	—	—	3,513	3,870	3,837	3,687	4,485	—
Puerto Rico	237,319	394,046	370,455	427,572	424,125	460,897	385,511	434,032	536,917	25.6
Trust Territory of the Pacific	1,447	5,992	5,444	6,455	—	—	—	—	—	—
Virgin Islands	11,835	17,580	18,853	20,834	22,580	24,480	60,202	56,274	30,520	46.5

[1] Preliminary data.

—Data not reported or not applicable.

NOTE.—Because of rounding, details may not add to totals.

SOURCE: U.S. Department of Education, National Center for Education Statistics, "Financial Statistics of Institutions of Higher Education" surveys; and Integrated Postsecondary Education Data System (IPEDS), "Finance" surveys. (This table was prepared March 1995.)

Table 341.—Educational and general expenditures of public institutions of higher education, by state: 1980–81 to 1992–93

[In thousands of dollars]

State	1980–81	1985–86	1986–87	1987–88	1988–89	1989–90	1990–91	1991–92	1992–93 [1]	Percent change, 1987–88 to 1992–93
1	2	3	4	5	6	7	8	9	10	11
United States	**$34,173,013**	**$50,872,962**	**$54,359,434**	**$58,639,468**	**$63,444,908**	**$69,163,958**	**$74,395,428**	**$78,554,534**	**$83,210,979**	**41.9**
Alabama	611,409	979,770	996,174	1,102,484	1,223,329	1,305,463	1,415,440	1,456,605	1,580,484	43.4
Alaska	150,421	210,894	199,147	208,641	227,331	253,392	273,577	288,999	304,137	45.8
Arizona	554,120	862,816	932,162	1,019,287	1,122,890	1,236,696	1,364,060	1,407,819	1,409,122	38.2
Arkansas	266,522	415,800	423,721	477,369	530,691	573,923	633,194	604,885	676,378	41.7
California	4,847,879	7,049,635	7,419,792	7,842,747	8,352,924	9,238,960	9,615,356	10,341,888	11,000,665	40.3
Colorado	561,552	809,621	872,016	956,381	1,052,644	1,167,864	1,258,356	1,363,615	1,452,957	51.9
Connecticut	281,581	439,397	475,714	527,537	605,228	622,298	673,182	736,202	731,570	38.7
Delaware	135,164	202,331	225,753	247,116	277,543	303,220	325,838	349,369	366,801	48.4
District of Columbia	71,245	87,620	91,554	95,569	103,475	109,795	110,324	120,926	118,282	23.8
Florida	1,071,754	1,638,227	1,795,084	2,005,883	2,250,014	2,546,201	2,657,553	2,710,041	2,904,932	44.8
Georgia	628,939	1,046,341	1,178,559	1,265,156	1,364,338	1,482,499	1,617,020	1,665,009	1,834,141	45.0
Hawaii	202,154	282,058	287,357	314,832	341,609	384,535	454,880	526,269	546,473	73.6
Idaho	141,296	202,736	210,186	229,094	244,969	268,690	303,224	334,762	346,932	51.4
Illinois	1,487,123	2,152,955	2,291,593	2,354,360	2,556,337	2,812,244	2,979,768	3,068,891	3,245,802	37.9
Indiana	771,564	1,183,098	1,283,767	1,403,895	1,534,653	1,671,111	1,842,610	1,935,566	2,014,834	43.5
Iowa	512,205	736,894	778,973	883,335	987,522	1,077,810	1,172,328	1,184,382	1,267,646	43.5
Kansas	461,979	660,995	680,799	720,287	801,774	884,775	928,772	994,560	1,059,683	47.1
Kentucky	527,235	737,101	803,423	860,198	916,498	992,403	1,112,190	1,208,448	1,212,211	40.9
Louisiana	557,825	810,479	825,811	865,860	908,303	1,005,278	1,135,955	1,215,771	1,275,446	47.3
Maine	127,983	183,349	210,284	235,916	271,016	297,782	308,699	316,116	324,515	37.6
Maryland	604,419	911,562	982,303	1,063,956	1,186,989	1,299,110	1,443,669	1,428,072	1,564,259	47.0
Massachusetts	441,068	779,341	876,226	1,007,570	1,051,636	1,076,241	1,122,629	1,165,598	1,295,720	28.6
Michigan	1,610,016	2,278,217	2,368,290	2,729,356	2,850,114	3,079,227	3,325,625	3,556,178	3,727,115	36.6
Minnesota	667,119	1,023,324	1,113,161	1,202,304	1,330,114	1,420,124	1,563,054	1,728,356	1,775,640	47.7
Mississippi	409,942	542,022	538,471	602,499	674,608	719,821	756,492	772,618	842,603	39.9
Missouri	553,793	802,936	859,671	899,646	995,472	1,083,473	1,155,531	1,184,338	1,260,304	40.1
Montana	99,990	148,099	150,804	160,413	161,543	179,510	210,813	262,480	279,323	74.1
Nebraska	286,122	397,523	434,585	437,700	489,501	543,341	600,224	639,475	672,427	53.6
Nevada	105,177	163,714	180,492	198,938	220,033	257,526	301,487	332,246	353,875	77.9
New Hampshire	104,285	143,191	158,144	177,908	195,404	206,207	229,360	252,021	275,138	54.7
New Jersey	735,097	1,140,310	1,286,796	1,446,642	1,607,786	1,765,002	1,875,481	2,002,975	2,103,355	45.4
New Mexico	278,960	393,151	436,528	454,493	561,308	626,386	671,206	724,157	769,646	69.3
New York	2,249,821	3,238,773	3,624,574	3,820,677	3,961,073	4,252,153	4,680,376	4,768,772	5,113,506	33.8
North Carolina	971,928	1,527,535	1,656,911	1,799,484	1,941,331	2,101,016	2,227,060	2,406,405	2,600,325	44.5
North Dakota	151,372	228,609	245,905	238,453	248,612	282,247	292,978	328,738	336,361	41.1
Ohio	1,327,483	2,019,351	2,205,567	2,385,244	2,630,782	2,799,829	3,046,603	3,214,612	3,185,955	33.6
Oklahoma	404,178	594,561	586,653	608,121	688,953	762,034	830,929	906,908	930,102	52.9
Oregon	497,593	672,175	734,860	781,964	839,670	911,812	996,887	1,086,673	1,142,781	46.1
Pennsylvania	1,231,502	1,814,384	1,946,738	2,165,078	2,385,349	2,596,987	2,737,817	2,963,168	3,087,186	42.6
Rhode Island	138,965	185,215	195,498	214,627	236,790	250,604	251,992	260,123	284,957	32.8
South Carolina	481,737	741,740	749,845	832,075	903,484	1,012,928	1,065,867	1,100,035	1,172,246	40.9
South Dakota	108,632	130,825	133,995	138,428	149,457	162,001	173,396	192,001	211,716	52.9
Tennessee	515,578	865,946	1,023,986	1,037,718	1,107,583	1,194,378	1,231,619	1,228,340	1,352,125	30.3
Texas	2,278,337	3,674,109	3,733,581	4,038,745	4,394,333	4,816,945	5,105,246	5,439,843	5,961,535	47.6
Utah	320,278	503,557	519,875	552,193	602,628	656,772	730,496	826,170	856,933	55.2
Vermont	101,539	157,266	168,529	182,916	204,586	222,470	238,512	258,150	263,475	44.0
Virginia	796,616	1,241,534	1,372,892	1,500,030	1,647,075	1,807,829	1,852,416	1,892,627	1,991,591	32.8
Washington	837,281	1,143,285	1,235,106	1,270,682	1,450,608	1,564,535	1,757,053	1,837,095	2,007,044	58.0
West Virginia	228,755	310,142	321,492	331,806	371,151	411,950	459,984	494,733	522,173	57.4
Wisconsin	998,862	1,438,918	1,530,657	1,663,132	1,824,067	1,931,561	2,057,786	2,158,188	2,266,312	36.3
Wyoming	111,170	171,335	170,678	179,700	181,985	194,506	204,028	225,238	222,188	23.6
U.S. Service Schools	555,447	798,194	834,751	901,023	677,797	740,496	1,016,486	1,088,075	1,110,052	23.2
Outlying areas	253,820	421,500	396,895	457,094	457,344	501,855	498,958	555,054	607,730	33.0
American Samoa	1,609	1,092	1,162	1,257	2,642	2,879	3,187	3,228	3,356	166.9
Federated States of Micronesia	—	—	—	—	1,474	1,351	3,302	3,286	2,898	—
Guam	15,582	29,916	28,909	31,762	36,276	47,380	55,641	64,772	68,550	115.8
Marshall Islands	—	—	—	—	—	—	—	3,093	1,220	—
Northern Marianas	—	1,328	2,625	2,009	794	766	2,472	2,803	2,230	11.0
Palau	—	—	—	—	2,993	3,297	3,277	3,172	3,808	—
Puerto Rico	224,988	367,523	342,049	397,605	392,814	426,754	378,352	427,021	497,590	25.1
Trust Territory of the Pacific	1,320	5,992	5,302	5,684	—	—	—	—	—	—
Virgin Islands	10,322	15,649	16,849	18,777	20,351	19,427	52,726	47,679	28,078	49.5

[1] Preliminary data.

—Data not reported or not applicable.

NOTE.—Because of rounding, details may not add to totals.

SOURCE: U.S. Department of Education, National Center for Education Statistics, "Financial Statistics of Institutions of Higher Education" surveys; and Integrated Postsecondary Education Data System (IPEDS), "Finance" surveys. (This table was prepared March 1995.)

Table 342.—Current-fund expenditures and educational and general expenditures of private institutions of higher education, by state: 1985–86 to 1992–93

[In thousands of dollars]

State	Current-fund expenditures					Educational and general expenditures				
	1985–86	1989–90	1990–91	1991–92 [1]	1992–93 [2]	1985–86	1989–90	1990–91	1991–92 [1]	1992–93 [2]
1	2	3	4	5	6	7	8	9	10	11
United States	$34,341,889	$48,885,041	$53,126,743	$57,341,982	$60,670,938	$25,255,003	$36,421,118	$39,744,472	$43,012,623	$45,766,989
Alabama	186,596	229,369	244,425	263,052	286,584	164,093	200,278	212,538	229,670	252,259
Alaska	10,171	20,050	22,127	18,454	22,693	9,106	17,447	19,375	15,851	18,687
Arizona	52,887	90,409	121,482	94,564	106,478	48,600	80,478	110,015	86,087	100,150
Arkansas	70,755	108,888	114,655	118,373	124,091	56,492	90,390	95,560	98,442	103,347
California	3,644,031	5,077,597	5,525,201	5,957,016	6,171,590	2,275,958	3,191,054	3,484,709	3,836,270	4,051,762
Colorado	160,193	250,811	288,865	305,244	306,824	142,218	223,016	257,003	269,386	279,956
Connecticut	836,949	1,193,877	1,293,468	1,376,756	1,437,827	733,144	1,058,226	1,143,220	1,224,643	1,280,969
Delaware	29,569	43,184	23,875	27,215	29,293	26,501	39,515	21,598	24,741	26,575
District of Columbia	1,307,377	1,873,297	1,955,110	2,100,279	2,307,943	803,566	1,100,263	1,178,178	1,246,366	1,311,616
Florida	723,270	1,162,843	1,274,196	1,386,602	1,510,855	553,391	911,193	1,001,000	1,089,712	1,193,708
Georgia	696,734	1,099,658	1,227,745	1,371,887	1,514,055	429,639	707,446	788,200	886,314	981,355
Hawaii	32,553	35,223	42,881	41,760	91,016	25,323	30,605	36,528	36,124	72,609
Idaho	49,768	69,032	74,519	82,255	87,532	37,736	54,790	59,252	65,018	72,006
Illinois	2,729,672	3,544,542	3,955,777	4,366,966	4,694,688	1,495,654	2,115,533	2,349,405	2,544,490	2,698,324
Indiana	530,163	773,866	847,885	889,004	941,404	426,813	633,221	700,346	736,784	782,734
Iowa	353,753	490,214	533,300	595,007	634,046	292,291	408,098	445,631	501,547	534,230
Kansas	105,193	135,958	144,471	147,336	157,139	87,719	116,651	124,578	126,939	136,036
Kentucky	194,873	251,329	282,937	304,780	315,147	159,293	208,042	236,191	255,870	263,722
Louisiana	353,433	531,135	572,049	629,158	673,080	221,928	341,168	372,431	397,191	439,834
Maine	133,778	186,175	200,149	210,328	223,573	106,912	155,562	167,618	176,530	187,523
Maryland	896,251	1,356,011	1,461,897	1,550,526	1,622,871	562,773	895,903	987,405	1,048,953	1,133,491
Massachusetts	3,544,867	4,922,923	5,339,793	5,580,304	5,850,688	2,817,687	3,907,555	4,278,151	4,600,897	4,874,439
Michigan	447,436	637,849	699,193	738,699	789,175	384,533	562,650	618,422	651,408	696,518
Minnesota	521,441	753,255	730,974	776,325	812,893	443,972	653,993	625,497	654,953	678,472
Mississippi	64,054	93,959	101,330	110,325	115,789	55,252	81,782	88,305	96,217	101,895
Missouri	904,573	1,340,923	1,493,892	1,645,969	1,666,001	713,411	1,064,937	1,186,195	1,306,990	1,347,644
Montana	22,349	27,990	33,471	33,238	39,500	18,565	23,716	29,165	28,567	33,873
Nebraska	161,066	226,173	245,142	269,968	287,540	138,929	200,268	219,054	242,660	258,485
Nevada	2,448	3,893	4,507	5,971	5,490	2,448	3,566	4,066	5,127	4,666
New Hampshire	264,440	363,330	407,903	432,080	455,312	230,657	313,098	355,056	374,323	395,395
New Jersey	714,733	944,968	982,070	1,082,717	1,167,222	540,245	741,565	789,649	863,322	926,131
New Mexico	22,196	28,022	33,272	46,252	33,162	19,678	24,967	29,813	28,754	28,659
New York	5,596,257	7,640,442	8,246,193	9,003,453	9,536,982	4,572,405	6,242,098	6,735,931	7,401,300	7,837,705
North Carolina	837,291	1,599,803	1,704,643	1,911,631	2,008,628	592,910	1,047,477	1,123,378	1,255,073	1,313,943
North Dakota	18,853	25,646	27,978	34,323	33,758	15,860	21,922	24,033	29,719	28,821
Ohio	976,303	1,402,876	1,510,387	1,613,085	1,696,377	833,879	1,207,973	1,308,048	1,403,786	1,486,111
Oklahoma	178,905	262,526	280,889	256,332	266,152	149,565	222,843	239,088	220,403	230,661
Oregon	171,604	256,067	277,152	287,800	307,280	149,289	227,291	247,671	256,162	275,352
Pennsylvania	3,155,505	4,437,071	4,914,117	5,452,687	5,667,740	2,033,015	2,910,308	3,242,842	3,521,644	3,802,781
Rhode Island	315,651	486,764	518,425	559,922	590,911	261,616	409,784	437,800	476,062	504,274
South Carolina	196,271	297,112	319,782	274,300	293,819	154,496	237,042	258,540	225,437	245,689
South Dakota	51,675	79,252	84,903	71,462	63,406	44,726	69,138	74,859	63,351	56,780
Tennessee	686,514	1,005,210	1,097,066	1,199,755	1,226,183	440,308	651,714	706,976	785,347	827,801
Texas	993,824	1,397,222	1,528,755	1,633,787	1,716,860	855,445	1,241,102	1,365,275	1,460,510	1,540,238
Utah	183,060	252,753	272,883	317,883	454,442	110,880	205,138	223,238	257,271	313,342
Vermont	150,689	245,813	266,539	287,261	300,593	126,299	209,420	229,548	250,999	261,364
Virginia	387,455	609,665	671,912	706,344	748,902	313,055	517,098	581,094	607,724	645,752
Washington	227,211	330,200	368,077	401,261	435,993	189,575	284,341	316,014	345,756	375,031
West Virginia	73,716	96,910	108,334	114,586	129,367	60,900	83,036	93,399	98,830	112,959
Wisconsin	373,533	588,850	645,774	651,420	702,292	326,254	472,313	519,270	585,465	633,564
Wyoming	—	4,104	4,370	6,578	9,752	—	4,104	4,370	6,578	7,752
Outlying areas	198,653	192,950	271,237	284,662	306,098	189,080	179,105	256,576	267,789	290,189
Puerto Rico	198,653	192,950	271,237	284,662	306,098	189,080	179,105	256,576	267,789	290,189

[1] Revised from previously published data.
[2] Preliminary data.
—Data not reported or not applicable.

NOTE.—Because of rounding, details may not add to totals.

SOURCE: U.S. Department of Education, National Center for Education Statistics, "Financial Statistics of Institutions of Higher Education" survey; and Integrated Postsecondary Education Data System (IPEDS), "Finance" surveys. (This table was prepared March 1995.)

Table 343.—Current-fund expenditures per full-time-equivalent student in institutions of higher education, by control and type of institution and purpose of expenditure: 1992–93 [1]

Item	Total				Public				Private		
	All institutions	Universities	Other 4-year	2-year	All institutions	Universities	Other 4-year	2-year	All institutions [2]	Universities	Other 4-year
1	2	3	4	5	6	7	8	9	10	11	12
Total current-fund expenditures [3]	$15,834	$27,680	$16,240	$6,029	$13,217	$21,816	$15,308	$5,943	$24,037	$45,352	$17,818
Educational and general expenditures	12,359	20,632	12,566	5,617	10,517	16,936	11,584	5,542	18,132	31,771	14,229
Instruction	4,824	7,573	4,788	2,727	4,330	6,039	4,864	2,776	6,371	12,196	4,661
Research	1,465	4,252	942	9	1,340	3,781	1,136	9	1,857	5,672	614
Public service	569	1,263	499	122	577	1,400	506	129	543	851	487
Academic support	1,061	1,781	1,086	464	962	1,576	1,103	451	1,371	2,399	1,059
Libraries	353	621	366	126	294	495	343	125	537	1,001	405
Student services	782	748	941	592	654	625	757	577	1,185	1,119	1,252
Institutional support	1,461	1,626	1,795	875	1,144	1,146	1,484	830	2,456	3,071	2,321
Operation and maintenance of plant	1,033	1,496	1,102	579	894	1,220	1,035	562	1,469	2,326	1,214
Scholarships and fellowships	972	1,571	1,184	215	471	895	510	172	2,544	3,611	2,326
From unrestricted funds	570	982	718	46	221	505	231	34	1,665	2,419	1,542
From restricted funds [4]	402	590	466	169	251	390	279	138	878	1,192	784
Mandatory transfers	191	323	229	36	144	254	189	35	336	528	297

[1] Preliminary data.
[2] Includes private 2-year colleges.
[3] Includes expenditures for auxiliary enterprises, hospitals, and independent operations which are not shown separately.
[4] Excludes Pell Grants.

NOTE.—Data for private 2-year colleges are not shown separately because of low survey response rate. Because of rounding, details may not add to totals.

SOURCE: U.S. Department of Education, National Center for Education Statistics, Integrated Postsecondary Education Data System (IPEDS), "Fall Enrollment" and "Finance" surveys. (This table was prepared June 1995.)

Table 344.—Additions to physical plant value of institutions of higher education, by type of addition and control of institution: 1969–70 to 1992–93

[In millions]

Year	Total, all institutions	Public institutions				Private institutions			
		Total	Land	Buildings	Equipment	Total	Land	Buildings	Equipment
1	2	3	4	5	6	7	8	9	10
1969–70	$4,233	$2,985	$152	$2,185	$648	$1,248	$59	$967	$221
1970–71	4,165	3,032	128	2,241	663	1,134	41	895	198
1971–72	4,163	3,054	112	2,277	665	1,109	53	860	195
1972–73	3,967	2,940	126	2,077	737	1,028	53	750	225
1973–74	4,312	3,206	205	2,188	813	1,106	55	816	235
1974–75	4,761	3,476	263	2,246	967	1,284	67	860	357
1975–76	4,702	3,552	168	2,365	1,019	1,150	58	768	325
1976–77	4,623	3,362	128	2,208	1,026	1,261	58	838	366
1977–78	4,527	3,306	102	2,117	1,087	1,221	45	777	400
1978–79	4,576	3,377	154	1,944	1,279	1,199	52	763	383
1979–80	5,551	3,666	164	2,149	1,354	1,886	98	1,220	568
1980–81	6,471	4,279	146	2,555	1,579	2,192	104	1,398	690
1981–82	6,975	4,594	170	2,679	1,744	2,382	83	1,488	811
1982–83	7,421	4,765	374	2,396	1,994	2,656	106	1,666	884
1983–84	7,604	5,038	196	2,427	2,415	2,566	110	1,507	950
1984–85	8,306	5,390	202	2,455	2,733	2,916	135	1,671	1,110
1985–86	10,149	6,875	237	3,318	3,320	3,274	128	1,922	1,225
1986–87	10,675	6,899	313	3,235	3,351	3,776	160	2,408	1,208
1987–88	11,589	7,218	272	3,520	3,426	4,371	250	2,715	1,406
1988–89	13,638	8,162	562	3,845	3,756	5,477	243	3,401	1,833
1989–90	15,900	10,616	532	5,438	4,647	5,284	408	3,277	1,599
1990–91	17,634	11,472	449	6,168	4,855	6,162	448	3,799	1,914
1991–92	16,651	10,179	547	5,564	4,068	6,472	538	3,831	2,103
1992–93	17,448	10,900	408	6,263	4,228	6,549	491	3,871	2,186

NOTE.—Because of rounding, details may not add to totals. Some data have been revised from previously published figures.

SOURCE: U.S. Department of Education, National Center for Education Statistics, "Financial Statistics of Institutions of Higher Education" surveys; and Integrated Postsecondary Education Data System (IPEDS), "Finance" surveys. (This table was prepared July 1995.)

Table 345.—Value of property and liabilities of institutions of higher education: 1899–1900 to 1992–93

[In thousands]

Academic year	Property value at end of year					Endowment (book value) [1]	Endowment (end of year market value) [1]	Liabilities of plant funds
	Total	Physical plant value						
		Total	Land	Buildings	Equipment			
1	2	3	4	5	6	7	8	9
1899–1900	$448,597	$253,599	—	—	—	[2] $194,998	—	—
1909–10	781,255	457,594	$92,359	$297,153	$68,082	[2] 323,661	—	—
1919–20	1,316,404	747,333	128,922	495,920	122,491	[2] 569,071	—	—
1929–30	3,437,117	2,065,049	304,114	1,490,014	270,921	[2] 1,372,068	—	—
1935–36	3,913,028	2,359,418	334,085	1,636,722	388,611	[2] 1,553,610	—	—
1937–38	4,208,695	2,556,075	313,665	1,811,309	431,101	1,652,620	—	—
1939–40	4,440,063	2,753,780	—	—	—	1,686,283	—	—
1941–42	4,525,925	2,759,261	—	—	—	[2] 1,766,664	—	—
1947–48	6,076,212	3,691,725	—	—	—	2,384,487	—	—
1949–50	7,401,187	4,799,964	—	—	—	[2] 2,601,223	—	—
1951–52	9,241,725	6,373,195	—	—	—	2,868,530	—	—
1953–54	10,717,082	7,523,193	—	—	—	3,193,889	—	—
1955–56	12,561,046	8,858,907	624,467	[3] 6,697,648	1,536,792	3,702,139	—	$894,383
1957–58	15,770,197	11,124,489	733,182	[3] 8,540,429	1,850,878	4,645,708	—	1,444,602
1959–60	18,870,628	13,548,548	842,664	[3] 10,472,478	2,233,407	5,322,080	—	1,964,306
1961–62	22,761,193	16,681,844	1,009,294	[3] 12,900,093	2,772,457	6,079,349	—	2,806,868
1963–64	28,232,362	21,279,346	1,292,691	[3] 16,460,867	3,525,788	6,953,016	—	4,190,189
1965–66	35,274,597	26,851,273	1,758,901	[3] 20,653,028	4,439,344	8,423,324	$11,126,831	6,071,750
1967–68	—	34,506,348	2,062,545	[3] 26,673,826	5,769,977	—	—	—
1969–70	52,930,923	42,093,580	3,076,751	31,865,179	7,151,649	10,837,343	11,206,632	9,384,731
1970–71	57,394,951	46,053,585	3,117,895	35,042,590	7,893,100	11,341,366	13,714,330	9,786,240
1971–72	62,136,459	50,153,251	3,287,326	38,131,339	8,734,586	11,983,208	15,180,934	10,291,095
1972–73	66,814,103	53,814,596	3,492,611	40,808,481	9,513,503	12,999,507	15,099,840	10,823,595
1973–74	71,305,817	58,002,777	3,888,372	43,701,491	10,412,914	13,303,040	13,168,076	11,400,916
1974–75	75,585,674	62,183,078	4,210,901	46,453,642	11,518,536	13,402,596	14,364,545	12,413,420
1975–76	80,300,595	66,348,304	4,345,232	49,349,224	12,653,847	13,952,291	15,488,265	12,687,015
1976–77	85,486,550	70,739,427	4,444,927	52,384,393	13,910,107	14,747,123	16,304,553	13,068,341
1977–78	90,337,044	74,770,804	4,621,071	55,188,603	14,961,131	15,566,240	16,840,129	13,437,861
1978–79	95,442,468	78,637,991	4,824,250	57,563,005	16,250,737	16,804,477	18,158,634	13,712,648
1979–80	102,294,859	83,733,387	5,037,172	60,847,097	17,849,119	18,561,472	20,743,045	14,181,991
1980–81	109,701,242	88,760,567	5,212,453	64,158,017	19,390,097	20,940,675	23,465,001	14,794,669
1981–82	117,601,954	94,516,512	5,402,339	67,794,877	21,319,297	23,085,442	24,415,245	15,487,618
1982–83	127,345,302	100,992,841	5,889,080	71,519,718	23,584,042	26,352,461	32,691,133	16,749,900
1983–84	137,141,741	107,640,113	6,109,746	75,220,765	26,309,602	29,501,629	32,975,610	18,277,315
1984–85	148,163,096	114,763,986	6,236,159	79,133,998	29,393,829	33,399,110	39,916,361	22,105,712
1985–86	160,959,517	122,261,355	6,573,923	82,886,012	32,801,419	38,698,162	50,280,775	25,699,408
1986–87	—	126,426,171	7,165,445	84,838,657	34,422,069	—	56,585,153	—
1987–88	—	139,456,342	8,307,789	92,428,615	38,719,937	—	57,391,814	—
1988–89	—	158,693,085	9,462,095	104,743,145	44,487,845	—	64,155,247	—
1989–90	—	164,635,000	9,968,000	108,609,000	46,058,000	—	67,978,726	—
1990–91	—	178,084,000	10,028,000	117,683,000	50,373,000	—	72,048,579	—
1991–92	—	181,995,647	10,276,808	120,834,366	50,884,474	—	79,117,709	—
1992–93	—	190,441,253	10,867,911	127,166,532	52,406,810	—	88,881,171	—

[1] Includes funds functioning as endowment.

[2] Includes annuity funds.

[3] Includes improvements to land and equipment. These funds are included under appropriate categories after 1967–68.

—Data not available.

NOTE.—Because of rounding, details may not add to totals. Some data have been revised from previously published figures.

SOURCE: U.S. Department of Education, National Center for Education Statistics, "Financial Statistics of Institutions of Higher Education" surveys; and Integrated Postsecondary Education Data System (IPEDS), "Finance" surveys. (This table was prepared July 1995.)

Table 346.—Endowment funds of the 120 institutions of higher education with the largest amounts: Fiscal year 1993

Institution	Rank order[1]	Market value of endowment, in thousands of dollars (end of fiscal year)	Institution	Rank order[1]	Market value of endowment, in thousands of dollars (end of fiscal year)
1	2	3	1	2	3
United States (all institutions)	—	**$88,881,171**			
Harvard University (MA)	1	5,778,257	Amherst College (MA)	61	327,233
University of Texas at Austin	2	3,646,687	Middlebury College (VT)	62	312,977
Yale University (CT)	3	3,232,305	Baylor University (TX)	63	309,422
Stanford University (CA)	4	2,780,307	Pennsylvania State University, Main Campus	64	296,024
Princeton University (NJ)	5	2,538,995	Lafayette College (PA)	65	284,000
Columbia University (NY)	6	1,950,885	Tulane University of Louisiana	66	279,747
University of California, Central Office	7	1,851,182	Saint Louis University, Main Campus (MO)	67	273,537
Massachusetts Institute of Technology	8	1,752,792	Oberlin College (OH)	68	267,153
Washington University (MO)	9	1,722,251	Rensselaer Polytechnic Institute (NY)	69	262,602
Emory University (GA)	10	1,589,324	University of North Carolina at Chapel Hill	70	262,408
Rice University (TX)	11	1,302,311	The Juilliard School (NY)	71	241,167
Northwestern University (IL)	12	1,233,599	Yeshiva University (NY)	72	233,474
University of Chicago (IL)	13	1,189,675	University of Miami (FL)	73	228,311
University of Pennsylvania	14	1,095,796	Syracuse University, Main Campus (NY)	74	225,625
Cornell University-Endowed Colleges (NY)	15	884,343	Mount Holyoke College (MA)	75	221,093
University of Notre Dame (IN)	16	828,554	Thomas Jefferson University (PA)	76	219,145
Dartmouth College (NH)	17	824,196	Carleton College (MN)	77	219,099
Vanderbilt University (TN)	18	807,689	Purdue University, Main Campus (IN)	78	218,343
University of Michigan, Ann Arbor	19	797,679	Northeastern University (MA)	79	215,582
Johns Hopkins University (MD)	20	725,637	Rochester Institute of Technology (NY)	80	214,922
New York University	21	706,320	Tufts University (MA)	81	214,774
Duke University (NC)	22	669,074	Bryn Mawr College (PA)	82	210,918
University of Southern California	23	669,063	Cornell University Medical College (NY)	83	206,881
University of Rochester (NY)	24	668,748	Agnes Scott College (GA)	84	204,593
University of Virginia, Main Campus	25	631,623	Loyola University in New Orleans (LA)	85	201,042
Rockefeller University (NY)	26	615,656	Brandeis University (MA)	86	196,125
California Institute of Technology	27	606,576	Brigham Young University (UT)	87	196,013
Brown University (RI)	28	574,938	Colgate University (NY)	88	188,921
Case Western Reserve University (OH)	29	551,300	Rush University (IL)	89	185,888
Ohio State University, Main Campus	30	487,357	Bowdoin College (ME)	90	185,292
Wellesley College (MA)	31	485,115	University of Texas, Southwest Medical Ctr.	91	185,060
Macalester College (MN)	32	476,356	Claremont McKenna College (CA)	92	182,514
Princeton Theological Seminary (NJ)	33	465,581	Trinity College (CT)	93	176,575
Swarthmore College (PA)	34	442,298	Virginia Polytechnic Institute and State U.	94	169,625
University of Cincinnati, Main Campus (OH)	35	436,789	Rutgers, The State U., Central Office (NJ)	95	167,842
Southern Methodist University (TX)	36	435,817	Colorado College	96	162,884
Smith College (MA)	37	435,565	Hamilton College (NY)	97	161,992
Loyola University of Chicago (IL)	38	433,012	University of New Mexico, Main Campus	98	158,678
Texas Christian University	39	428,892	Wabash College (IN)	99	154,374
Williams College (MA)	40	420,649	Southwestern University (TX)	100	152,046
University of Washington	41	415,197	Earlham College (IN)	101	150,616
Grinnell College (IA)	42	415,129	Santa Clara University (CA)	102	149,136
Baylor College of Medicine (TX)	43	413,330	University of Tennessee (Central office)	103	148,891
Boston College (MA)	44	412,250	State University of New York at Buffalo	104	147,737
University of Delaware	45	408,627	University of Louisville (KY)	105	146,868
Carnegie Mellon University (PA)	46	404,531	Washington And Lee University (VA)	106	145,783
Pomona College (CA)	47	379,632	The University of Alabama	107	144,662
Wake Forest University (NC)	48	377,197	Occidental College (CA)	108	143,143
University of Pittsburgh, Main Campus (PA)	49	374,294	Loyola Marymount University (CA)	109	142,449
University of Richmond (VA)	50	372,436	College of the Holy Cross (MA)	110	142,030
Berea College (KY)	51	358,286	Cornell University, Statutory Colleges (NY)	111	140,781
George Washington University (DC)	52	356,548	Franklin And Marshall College (PA)	112	137,622
University of Minnesota, Twin Cities	53	355,012	Bucknell University (PA)	113	136,082
University of Tulsa (OK)	54	352,625	Texas A & M University	114	135,370
Georgetown University (DC)	55	342,861	University of Wisconsin, Madison	115	134,320
Trinity University (TX)	56	339,304	Cooper Union (NY)	116	134,272
Boston College (MA)	57	333,086	Union College (NY)	117	132,427
Lehigh University (PA)	58	329,424	New Mexico Military Institute	118	132,110
Vassar College (NY)	59	328,630	University of the South (TN)	119	131,367
Wesleyan University (CT)	60	328,157	Whitman College (WA)	120	128,075

[1] Institutions ranked by size of endowment. Excludes institutions which have not reported data for 1992–93.
—Not applicable.

SOURCE: U.S. Department of Education, National Center for Education Statistics, Integrated Postsecondary Education Data System (IPEDS), "Finance, 1992–93" survey. (This table was prepared June 1995.)

Table 347.—Participants in adult education 17 years old and older, by selected characteristics of participants: 1991

[Numbers in thousands]

Characteristics of participants	Number of adults in population [1]	Ever a participant in adult education [2]		Participated in adult education [2] in past 3 years		Participated in adult education [2] in past year	
		Number	Percent of population	Number	Percent of population	Number	Percent of population
1	2	3	4	5	6	7	8
Total	181,800	97,397	54	69,361	38	57,391	32
Age							
17 to 24 years	21,688	9,240	43	8,756	40	7,125	33
25 to 34 years	47,244	27,325	58	22,773	48	17,530	37
35 to 44 years	38,565	25,043	65	19,581	51	17,083	44
45 to 54 years	25,375	14,755	58	9,351	37	8,107	32
55 to 64 years	19,967	10,101	51	5,150	26	4,516	23
65 years and over	28,960	10,934	38	3,750	13	3,031	10
Sex							
Men	82,154	42,163	51	29,945	36	25,923	32
Women	99,646	55,234	55	39,415	40	31,469	32
Racial/ethnic group							
White, non-Hispanic	143,144	80,099	56	56,715	40	47,401	33
Black, non-Hispanic	20,141	8,213	41	5,552	28	4,586	23
Hispanic	13,804	6,905	50	5,396	39	4,032	29
Other races, non-Hispanic	4,711	2,180	46	1,698	36	1,371	29
Highest level of education completed							
Less than high school diploma	28,306	7,337	26	4,127	15	3,437	12
High school diploma	110,384	58,135	53	39,403	36	31,602	29
Associate degree	5,034	3,949	78	3,191	63	2,461	49
Bachelor's degree or higher	38,076	27,976	73	22,640	59	19,891	52
Labor force status							
In labor force	125,440	73,513	59	58,078	46	49,242	39
Employed	115,620	69,421	60	55,093	48	47,143	41
Unemployed	9,820	4,092	42	2,985	30	2,099	21
Not in labor force	56,361	23,884	42	11,283	20	8,149	14
Annual family income							
$10,000 or less	27,504	10,706	39	5,766	21	3,843	14
$10,001 to $15,000	15,465	7,014	45	4,426	29	3,178	21
$15,001 to $20,000	16,117	6,335	39	4,183	26	3,308	21
$20,001 to $25,000	16,092	7,666	48	5,343	33	4,063	25
$25,001 to $30,000	17,973	9,309	52	6,570	37	5,445	30
$30,001 to $40,000	26,110	14,922	57	10,313	39	9,043	35
$40,001 to $50,000	21,303	13,270	62	10,526	49	9,313	44
$50,001 to $75,000	24,540	16,629	68	12,971	53	11,235	46
More than $75,000	16,695	11,546	69	9,263	55	7,963	48

[1] Persons 17 years of age and over on the date of the survey.

[2] Adult education is defined as all non-full-time education activities such as part-time college attendance, classes or seminars given by employers, and classes taken for adult literacy purposes, or for recreation and enjoyment.

NOTE.—Data are based upon a sample survey of the civilian noninstitutional population. Because of rounding and survey item nonresponse, details may not add to totals.

SOURCE: U.S. Department of Education, National Center for Education Statistics, "Participation in Adult Education," unpublished data. (This table was prepared July 1991.)

Table 348.—Type of employer involvement and number of courses taken by adult education participants [1]
17 years old and older, by selected characteristics of participants: 1991

Characteristics of participants	Adult education participants in the past year, in thousands	Type of employer involvement (percent of adult education participants)						Percentage distribution of the number of adult education courses taken in the past year		
		Any type	Given at place of work	Employer paid some portion	Employer provided course	Employer required course	Employer provided time off	One	Two or three	Four or more
1	2	3	4	5	6	7	8	9	10	11
Total	57,391	64	32	51	38	30	48	43	34	21
Age										
17 to 24 years	7,125	54	28	39	36	26	39	46	30	22
25 to 34 years	17,530	68	31	55	40	36	50	43	34	20
35 to 44 years	17,083	70	35	56	40	30	53	38	36	23
45 to 54 years	8,107	71	39	59	44	32	55	41	36	22
55 to 64 years	4,516	64	30	48	36	27	45	50	32	16
65 years and over	3,031	18	8	12	9	9	12	60	27	9
Sex										
Men	25,923	73	35	58	42	34	56	42	37	19
Women	31,469	57	29	46	35	27	41	44	31	22
Racial/ethnic group										
White, non-Hispanic	47,401	65	32	53	39	30	49	42	35	21
Black, non-Hispanic	4,586	59	36	48	41	38	44	41	31	24
Hispanic	4,032	58	30	39	33	31	43	56	27	14
Other races, non-Hispanic	1,371	56	28	36	30	20	40	39	27	28
Highest level of education completed										
Less than high school diploma	3,437	35	17	21	19	21	19	72	17	8
High school diploma	31,602	62	31	50	36	31	45	47	32	18
Associate degree	2,461	76	47	66	51	39	63	32	40	25
Bachelor's degree or higher	19,891	71	34	57	44	30	56	33	39	26
Labor force status										
In labor force	49,242	72	36	58	43	34	54	41	35	22
Employed	47,143	74	37	60	44	35	56	40	36	22
Unemployed	2,099	35	12	13	12	19	18	56	23	16
Not in labor force	8,149	16	7	11	9	8	10	60	26	12
Annual family income										
$10,000 or less	3,843	39	18	25	24	23	29	59	20	15
$10,001 to $15,000	3,178	52	27	37	24	27	37	53	32	13
$15,001 to $20,000	3,308	57	28	42	35	29	39	46	37	15
$20,001 to $25,000	4,063	67	34	46	37	34	48	48	32	17
$25,001 to $30,000	5,445	58	30	48	38	29	39	44	34	19
$30,001 to $40,000	9,043	68	35	57	43	35	50	42	32	24
$40,001 to $50,000	9,313	67	34	55	42	33	50	45	32	20
$50,001 to $75,000	11,235	72	35	61	43	32	58	39	37	22
More than $75,000	7,963	68	30	54	37	24	53	32	41	26

[1] Adult education is defined as all non-full-time education activities such as part-time college attendance, classes or seminars given by employers, and classes taken for adult literacy purposes, or for recreation and enjoyment.

NOTE.—Data are based upon a sample survey of the civilian noninstitutional population. Because of rounding and survey item nonresponse, details may not add to totals.

SOURCE: U.S. Department of Education, National Center for Education Statistics, "Participation in Adult Education," unpublished data. (This table was prepared July 1991.)

Table 349.—Participants in adult basic and secondary education programs, by level of enrollment and state: Fiscal years 1980, 1990, and 1991

State or other area	1980 Total	Adult basic education	Adult secondary education	Ungraded	1990 Total	Adult basic education [1]	Adult secondary education	1991 Total	Adult basic education [1]	Adult secondary education
1	2	3	4	5	6	7	8	9	10	11
United States	2,018,906	915,936	531,663	571,307	3,535,970	2,435,649	1,100,321	3,694,217	2,513,371	1,180,846
Alabama	51,599	36,726	12,372	2,501	40,177	32,984	7,193	45,700	36,319	9,381
Alaska	5,667	2,200	2,188	1,279	5,067	4,267	800	5,399	4,488	911
Arizona	9,996	9,968	22	6	33,805	24,915	8,890	36,717	26,709	10,008
Arkansas	8,583	7,308	1,275	—	29,065	17,103	11,962	30,845	17,437	13,408
California	267,625	60,385	—	207,240	1,021,227	753,282	267,945	1,022,583	761,637	260,946
Colorado	9,381	4,295	2,644	2,442	12,183	9,877	2,306	13,742	10,764	2,978
Connecticut	21,889	8,882	4,805	8,202	46,434	25,560	20,874	57,188	32,117	25,071
Delaware	1,797	1,110	503	184	2,662	2,348	314	2,567	2,167	400
District of Columbia	25,214	4,928	6,502	13,784	19,586	12,631	6,955	20,309	13,207	7,102
Florida	467,162	100,958	184,568	181,636	419,429	249,339	170,090	436,766	260,761	176,005
Georgia	50,820	26,734	17,008	7,078	69,580	49,622	19,958	80,119	59,107	21,012
Hawaii	16,457	16,457	—	—	52,012	31,766	20,246	53,051	29,816	23,235
Idaho	12,851	8,915	3,010	926	11,171	9,180	1,991	10,215	8,407	1,808
Illinois	76,456	59,314	17,142	—	87,121	69,770	17,351	91,383	72,997	18,386
Indiana	20,882	18,127	2,660	95	44,166	27,138	17,028	50,483	31,101	19,382
Iowa	25,851	16,928	5,153	3,770	41,507	30,470	11,037	38,998	28,009	10,989
Kansas	14,405	3,687	7,436	3,282	10,274	9,191	1,083	11,179	8,877	2,302
Kentucky	27,800	6,147	4,735	16,918	28,090	20,406	7,684	23,248	16,683	6,565
Louisiana	16,046	12,608	2,485	953	40,039	20,941	19,098	43,349	22,254	21,095
Maine	5,327	3,029	942	1,356	14,964	6,620	8,344	16,573	7,505	9,068
Maryland	34,572	23,421	6,043	5,108	41,230	36,244	4,986	53,505	49,804	3,701
Massachusetts	20,420	10,241	5,044	5,135	34,220	28,140	6,080	23,218	18,289	4,929
Michigan	40,973	29,945	—	11,028	194,178	80,206	113,972	205,545	75,897	129,648
Minnesota	10,826	8,627	877	1,322	45,648	33,190	12,458	48,853	31,964	16,889
Mississippi	14,317	10,340	2,918	1,059	18,957	15,834	3,123	20,015	17,269	2,746
Missouri	33,292	27,206	3,732	2,354	31,815	27,274	4,541	33,060	28,211	4,849
Montana	3,525	1,795	978	752	6,071	3,962	2,109	5,942	3,665	2,277
Nebraska	7,514	5,152	2,362	—	6,158	5,349	809	6,597	5,786	811
Nevada	3,063	845	82	2,136	17,262	7,270	9,992	19,682	6,329	13,353
New Hampshire	4,844	2,657	1,625	562	7,198	5,073	2,125	7,137	4,282	2,855
New Jersey	35,770	17,152	6,790	11,828	64,080	46,526	17,554	65,379	43,162	22,217
New Mexico	13,102	3,590	5,147	4,365	30,236	18,069	12,167	30,287	17,154	13,133
New York	94,574	57,217	20,002	17,355	156,611	125,893	30,718	182,879	146,265	36,614
North Carolina	84,252	33,854	46,679	3,719	109,740	71,698	38,042	120,347	79,641	40,706
North Dakota	2,810	1,963	538	309	3,587	2,500	1,087	3,853	2,725	1,128
Ohio	50,056	42,421	7,635	—	95,476	79,527	15,949	108,753	88,302	20,451
Oklahoma	14,701	6,983	5,697	2,021	24,307	19,131	5,176	26,707	20,473	6,234
Oregon	27,645	10,690	12,594	4,361	37,075	24,915	12,160	40,285	24,791	15,494
Pennsylvania	29,477	19,246	6,436	3,795	52,444	40,108	12,336	48,590	38,054	10,536
Rhode Island	5,844	2,266	1,357	2,221	7,347	5,874	1,473	7,264	5,431	1,833
South Carolina	69,659	27,959	35,165	6,535	81,200	37,117	44,083	86,776	35,911	50,865
South Dakota	4,067	2,080	1,109	878	3,184	2,458	726	3,079	2,349	730
Tennessee	26,268	17,079	3,244	5,945	41,721	39,604	2,117	49,556	40,702	8,854
Texas	157,349	94,245	51,126	11,978	218,747	145,067	73,680	220,027	150,322	69,705
Utah	18,541	3,756	14,785	—	24,841	6,003	18,838	24,028	6,788	17,240
Vermont	4,583	3,990	—	593	4,808	4,452	356	5,330	4,862	468
Virginia	21,525	10,480	3,804	7,241	31,649	30,005	1,644	25,456	14,450	11,006
Washington	16,286	7,245	3,894	5,147	31,776	25,336	6,440	34,401	27,752	6,649
West Virginia	14,628	9,743	3,672	1,213	21,186	14,227	2 6,959	23,077	16,903	6,174
Wisconsin	16,158	14,185	1,973	—	61,081	45,116	15,965	70,838	53,524	17,314
Wyoming	2,457	857	905	695	3,578	2,071	2 1,507	3,337	1,952	1,385
Outlying areas										
American Samoa	313	252	61	—	—	—	—	290	270	20
Northern Marianas	—	—	—	—	—	—	—	1,466	478	988
Guam	1,346	612	471	263	1,311	414	2 897	26,845	26,845	—
Puerto Rico	30,164	17,844	9,010	3,310	28,436	28,436	—	—	—	—
Trust Territory of the Pacific	3,753	2,138	699	916	—	—	—	—	—	—
Virgin Islands	3,500	1,002	859	1,639	1,653	1,215	438	—	—	—

[1] Includes English as a second language.
2 Estimated.
—Data not available or not applicable.

SOURCE: U.S. Department of Education, National Center for Education Statistics, "Women and Minority Groups Make Up Largest Segment of Adult Basic and Secondary Education Programs;" and Office of Vocational and Adult Education, "Adult Education Program Facts, Program Year 1990–1991." (This table was prepared June 1993).

Table 350.—Number of noncollegiate institutions offering postsecondary education, by control and state: 1992–93, 1993–94, and 1994–95

State or other area	1992–93 Total	Public	Private	1993–94 Total	Public	Private Total	Nonprofit	Proprietary	1994–95 Total	Public	Private Total	Nonprofit	Proprietary
1	2	3	4	5	6	7	8	9	10	11	12	13	14
United States	6,961	522	6,439	6,737	527	6,210	1,203	5,007	6,558	538	6,020	1,215	4,805
Alabama	80	5	75	76	10	66	9	57	71	8	63	8	55
Alaska	34	3	31	32	3	29	5	24	31	3	28	5	23
Arizona	144	5	139	125	4	121	17	104	124	4	120	16	104
Arkansas	90	23	67	82	20	62	10	52	76	19	57	9	48
California	1,162	36	1,126	1,126	32	1,094	238	856	1,041	35	1,006	230	776
Colorado	147	8	139	138	8	130	17	113	146	8	138	21	117
Connecticut	103	1	102	100	1	99	21	78	105	1	104	21	83
Delaware	16	1	15	15	1	14	2	12	14	1	13	2	11
District of Columbia	29	1	28	24	1	23	9	14	21	1	20	9	11
Florida	351	45	306	341	40	301	56	245	339	40	299	56	243
Georgia	106	7	99	102	4	98	15	83	104	4	100	15	85
Hawaii	32	2	30	29	1	28	3	25	26	1	25	4	21
Idaho	31	1	30	26	1	25	1	24	25	1	24	1	23
Illinois	322	13	309	304	12	292	58	234	285	11	274	56	218
Indiana	131	8	123	117	8	109	11	98	114	7	107	13	94
Iowa	71	0	71	72	0	72	18	54	66	0	66	17	49
Kansas	67	16	51	62	14	48	11	37	62	13	49	11	38
Kentucky	118	19	99	112	21	91	7	84	113	22	91	7	84
Louisiana	163	47	116	165	49	116	11	105	150	49	101	10	91
Maine	20	0	20	21	0	21	8	13	23	0	23	8	15
Maryland	139	2	137	135	0	135	20	115	122	0	122	21	101
Massachusetts	161	13	148	159	13	146	44	102	162	12	150	44	106
Michigan	264	7	257	247	6	241	34	207	282	6	276	44	232
Minnesota	91	13	78	89	14	75	17	58	88	5	83	18	65
Mississippi	52	0	52	52	0	52	4	48	49	0	49	4	45
Missouri	180	31	149	168	30	138	24	114	170	31	139	25	114
Montana	46	5	41	45	5	40	9	31	43	4	39	9	30
Nebraska	43	0	43	50	0	50	8	42	51	0	51	8	43
Nevada	47	0	47	46	0	46	1	45	47	0	47	1	46
New Hampshire	23	0	23	25	0	25	2	23	22	0	22	2	20
New Jersey	173	7	166	176	10	166	38	128	166	10	156	37	119
New Mexico	48	3	45	46	3	43	6	37	45	4	41	6	35
New York	373	12	361	353	15	338	119	219	337	26	311	118	193
North Carolina	82	4	78	81	4	77	9	68	81	4	77	8	69
North Dakota	22	0	22	19	0	19	5	14	19	0	19	6	13
Ohio	320	41	279	312	52	260	57	203	303	54	249	60	189
Oklahoma	96	31	65	95	34	61	3	58	111	33	78	5	73
Oregon	102	0	102	109	0	109	8	101	99	0	99	9	90
Pennsylvania	327	18	309	347	19	328	101	227	352	30	322	100	222
Rhode Island	28	0	28	28	0	28	7	21	28	0	28	9	19
South Carolina	64	2	62	60	2	58	11	47	56	2	54	11	43
South Dakota	20	5	15	17	5	12	5	7	17	5	12	5	7
Tennessee	149	29	120	143	30	113	19	94	139	29	110	20	90
Texas	412	7	405	382	6	376	39	337	360	7	353	37	316
Utah	44	6	38	43	6	37	2	35	42	6	36	2	34
Vermont	12	3	9	13	3	10	4	6	13	3	10	4	6
Virginia	150	14	136	148	11	137	31	106	144	11	133	32	101
Washington	118	5	113	111	5	106	13	93	107	5	102	13	89
West Virginia	54	18	36	70	19	51	11	40	73	18	55	14	41
Wisconsin	95	4	91	90	4	86	25	61	86	5	81	24	57
Wyoming	9	1	8	9	1	8	0	8	8	0	8	0	8
Outlying areas	92	5	87	95	5	90	18	72	84	6	78	16	62
American Samoa	0	0	0	0	0	0	0	0	0	0	0	0	0
Guam	1	0	1	1	0	1	0	1	0	0	0	0	0
Northern Marianas	0	0	0	0	0	0	0	0	0	0	0	0	0
Palau	0	0	0	0	0	0	0	0	0	0	0	0	0
Puerto Rico	91	5	86	94	5	89	18	71	84	6	78	16	62
Virgin Islands	0	0	0	0	0	0	0	0	0	0	0	0	0

SOURCE: U.S. Department of Education, National Center for Education Statistics, Integrated Postsecondary Education Data System (IPEDS), "Institutional Characteristics" surveys. (This table was prepared May 1995.)

CHAPTER 4
Federal Programs for Education and Related Activities

This chapter provides a summary of federal funds for education to help describe the magnitude of the federal fiscal effort and give some indication of the scope and variety of the education programs. Data in this chapter reflect outlays and obligations of federal agencies. These tabulations differ from federal receipts reported in other chapters because of numerous variations in the data collection systems. Federal dollars are not necessarily spent by recipient institutions in the same year they are appropriated. In some cases, institutions cannot identify the source of federal revenues because they flow through state agencies. Some types of revenues, such as tuition and fees, are reported as revenues from students even though they may be supported by federal student aid programs. Some institutions that receive federal education funds are not included in regular surveys conducted by the National Center for Education Statistics. Thus, the revenue data tabulated in this chapter are not comparable with figures reported in other chapters. Readers should be careful about comparing data on obligations shown in some tables with data on outlays and appropriations appearing in others.

Federal funding for education showed sizable growth between fiscal years (FYs) 1965 and 1995, after adjustment for inflation. Particularly large increases occurred between 1965 and 1975. After a period of relative stability between 1975 and 1980, federal funding for education, excluding estimated federal tax expenditures for education, declined approximately 15 percent between 1980 and 1985 after adjustment for inflation. From 1985 to 1995, federal funding for education increased by 36 percent (table 351).

During the 1965 to 1975 period, after adjustment for inflation, federal funds for elementary and secondary education rose by 204 percent, postsecondary education by 256 percent, other education by 139 percent, and by 5 percent for research at educational institutions. Between 1975 and 1980, federal funding for elementary and secondary education rose by 1 percent and research by 14 percent, but postsecondary education fell slightly by 3 percent and other education fell by 35 percent. After declining 21 percent between 1980 and 1985, federal funding for elementary and secondary education programs rose

by 49 percent between 1985 and 1995. Postsecondary education fell by 24 percent between 1980 and 1985 and then rose by 14 percent between 1985 and 1995, however, postsecondary education did have a large drop in FY 94 because of a large loan repayment from the Student Marketing Association of its outstanding debt to the U.S. Treasury Department. Between 1985 and 1995, other education rose by 71 percent, and research by 29 percent, after adjustment for inflation (table 351).

According to FY 1995 estimates, $32.9 billion or about 45 percent of the $73.8 billion spent by the federal government on education came from the U.S. Department of Education. Large amounts of money also came from the U.S. Department of Health and Human Services ($12.7 billion), the U.S. Department of Agriculture ($9.1 billion), the U.S. Department of Labor ($4.3 billion), the U.S. Department of Defense ($3.7 billion), and the U.S. Department of Energy ($2.6 billion) (table 352).

Fiscal year 1995 estimates call for federal program funds for elementary and secondary education to be $35.2 billion; for higher education, $17.7 billion; for research at universities and related institutions, $15.9 billion; and for other programs, $5.0 billion (table 353).

Over 57 percent of total federal education support, excluding estimated federal tax expenditures, went to educational institutions in FY 95. Another 18 percent was used for student support. Banks and other lending agencies received 11 percent, and all other recipients, including libraries, museums, and federal institutions, received 14 percent (table 354).

Between FYs 1990 and 1995, U.S. Department of Education obligations rose 88 percent. Funds for student financial assistance increased to $27.2 billion in 1995, a rise of 145 percent since 1990. Funds for elementary and secondary education stood at an estimated $9.2 billion in 1995, an increase of 28 percent since 1990. Funds for the handicapped increased by about 75 percent, to $6.1 billion, and funds for vocational and adult education increased 41 percent (table 355).

Of the $32.9 billion spent by the U.S. Department of Education in FY 1995, about $12.0 billion went to school districts, $5.0 billion to institutions of higher education, $4.9 billion to college students, and $4.2

billion to state education agencies. A portion of the remaining $6.9 billion went to banks to subsidize student loans (table 356).

Thirty-three percent of public elementary and secondary school students in the United States received publicly funded free or reduced-price lunches in 1993–94. At public elementary schools, the participation rate was 39 percent compared with 22 percent for public secondary schools (table 365).

About 13 percent of all elementary and secondary school children received Chapter 1 services in 1993–94. Federally sponsored Chapter 1 programs are designed to break the link between family poverty and low student achievement, particularly for children in schools with high concentrations of poverty. Children in rural areas (14 percent) and urban areas (16 percent) were more likely to receive services than those in suburban areas (10 percent) (table 366).

Federal Education Legislation

A capsule view of the history of federal education activities is provided in the following list of selected legislation:

1787 *Northwest Ordinance* authorized land grants for the establishment of educational institutions.

1802 *An Act Fixing the Military Peace Establishment of the United States* established the U.S. Military Academy. (The U.S. Naval Academy was established in 1845 by the Secretary of the Navy.)

1862 *First Morrill Act* authorized public land grants to the states for the establishment and maintenance of agricultural and mechanical colleges.

1867 *Department of Education Act* authorized the establishment of the U.S. Department of Education.*

1876 *Appropriation Act,* U.S. Department of the Treasury, established the U.S. Coast Guard Academy.

1890 *Second Morrill Act* provided for money grants for support of instruction in the agricultural and mechanical colleges.

1911 *State Marine School Act* authorized federal funds to be used for the benefit of any nautical school in any of 11 specified state seaport cities.

---

*The U.S. Department of Education as established in 1867 was later known as the Office of Education. In 1980, under Public Law 96–88, it became a cabinet-level department. Therefore, for purposes of consistency, it is referred to as the "U.S. Department of Education" even in those tables covering years when it was officially the Office of Education.

1917 *Smith-Hughes Act* provided for grants to states for support of vocational education.

1918 *Vocational Rehabilitation Act* provided for grants for rehabilitation through training of World War I veterans.

1919 *An Act to Provide for Further Educational Facilities* authorized the sale by the federal government of surplus machine tools to educational institutions at 15 percent of acquisition cost.

1920 *Smith-Bankhead Act* authorized grants to states for vocational rehabilitation programs.

1935 *Bankhead-Jones Act* (Public Law 74–182) authorized grants to states for agricultural experiment stations.

Agricultural Adjustment Act (Public Law 74–320) authorized 30 percent of the annual customs receipts to be used to encourage the exportation and domestic consumption of agricultural commodities. Commodities purchased under this authorization began to be used in school lunch programs in 1936. The National School Lunch Act of 1946 continued and expanded this assistance.

1936 *An Act to Further the Development and Maintenance of an Adequate and Well-Balanced American Merchant Marine* (Public Law 84–415) established the U.S. Merchant Marine Academy.

1937 *National Cancer Institute Act* established the Public Health Service fellowship program.

1941 *Amendment to Lanham Act of 1940* authorized federal aid for construction, maintenance, and operation of schools in federally impacted areas. Such assistance was continued under Public Law 815 and Public Law 874, 81st Congress, in 1950.

1943 *Vocational Rehabilitation Act* (Public Law 78–16) provided assistance to disabled veterans.

School Lunch Indemnity Plan (Public Law 78–129) provided funds for local lunch food purchases.

1944 *Servicemen's Readjustment Act* (Public Law 78–346) known as the GI Bill, provided assistance for the education of veterans.

Surplus Property Act (Public Law 78–457) authorized transfer of surplus property to educational institutions.

1946 *National School Lunch Act* (Public Law 79–396) authorized assistance through grants-in-aid and other means to states to assist in providing adequate foods and facilities for the establishment, maintenance, operation, and expansion of nonprofit school lunch programs.

George-Barden Act (Public Law 80–402) expanded federal support of vocational education.

1948 *United States Information and Educational Exchange Act* (Public Law 80–402) provided for the interchange of persons, knowledge, and skills between the United States and other countries.

1949 *Federal Property and Administrative Services Act* (Public Law 81–152) provided for donation of surplus property to educational institutions and for other public purposes.

1950 *Financial Assistance for Local Educational Agencies Affected by Federal Activities* (Public Law 81–815 and Public Law 81–874) provided assistance for construction (Public Law 815) and operation (Public Law 874) of schools in federally affected areas.

Housing Act (Public Law 81–475) authorized loans for construction of college housing facilities.

1954 *An Act for the Establishment of the United States Air Force Academy and Other Purposes* (Public Law 83–325) established the U.S. Air Force Academy.

Educational Research Act (Public Law 83–531) authorized cooperative arrangements with universities, colleges, and state educational agencies for educational research.

National Advisory Committee on Education Act (Public Law 83–532) established a National Advisory Committee on Education to recommend needed studies of national concern in the field of education and to propose appropriate action indicated by such studies.

School Milk Program Act (Public Law 83–597) provided funds for purchase of milk for school lunch programs.

1956 *Library Services Act* (Public Law 84–597) provided grants to states for extension and improvement of rural public library services.

1957 *Practical Nurse Training Act* (Public Law 84–911) provided grants to states for practical nurse training.

1958 *National Defense Education Act* (Public Law 85–864) provided assistance to state and local school systems for strengthening instruction in science, mathematics, modern foreign languages, and other critical subjects; improvement of state statistical services; guidance, counseling, and testing services and training institutes; higher education student loans and fellowships; foreign language study and training provided by colleges and universities; experimentation and dissemination of information on more effective utilization of television, motion pictures, and related media for educational purposes; and vocational education for technical occupations necessary to the national defense.

Education of Mentally Retarded Children Act (Public Law 85–926) authorized federal assistance for training teachers of the handicapped.

Captioned Films for the Deaf Act (Public Law 85–905) authorized a loan service of captioned films for the deaf.

1961 *Area Redevelopment Act* (Public Law 87–27) included provisions for training or retraining of persons in redevelopment areas.

1962 *Manpower Development and Training Act* (Public Law 87–415) provided training in new and improved skills for the unemployed and underemployed.

Communications Act of 1934, Amendment (Public Law 87–447) provided grants for the construction of educational television broadcasting facilities.

Migration and Refugee Assistance Act of 1962 (Public Law 87–510) authorized loans, advances, and grants for education and training of refugees.

1963 *Health Professions Educational Assistance Act of 1963* (Public Law 88–129) provided funds to expand teaching facilities and for loans to students in the health professions.

Vocational Education Act of 1963 (Part of Public Law 88–210) increased federal support of vocational education schools; vocational work-study programs; and research, training, and demonstrations in vocational education.

Higher Education Facilities Act of 1963 (Public Law 88–204) authorized grants and loans for classrooms, libraries, and laboratories in public community colleges and technical institutes, as well as undergraduate and graduate facilities in other institutions of higher education.

1964 *Civil Rights Act of 1964* (Public Law 88–352) authorized the Commissioner of Education to arrange for support for institutions of higher education and school districts to provide in-service programs for assisting instructional staff in dealing with problems caused by de-segregation.

Economic Opportunity Act of 1964 (Public Law 88–452) authorized grants for college work-study programs for students from low-income families; established a Job Corps program and authorized support for work-training programs to provide education and vocational training and work experience opportunities in welfare programs; authorized support of education and training activities and of community action programs, including Head Start, Follow Through, and Upward Bound; and authorized the establishment of Volunteers in Service to America (VISTA).

1965 *Elementary and Secondary Education Act of 1965* (Public Law 89–10) authorized grants for elementary and secondary school programs for children of low-income families; school library resources, textbooks, and other instructional materials for school children; supplementary educational centers and services; strengthening state education agencies; and educational research and research training.

Health Professions Educational Assistance Amendments of 1965 (Public Law 89–290) authorized scholarships to aid needy students in the health professions.

Higher Education Act of 1965 (Public Law 89–329) provided grants for university community service programs, college library assistance, library training and research, strengthening developing institutions, teacher training programs, and undergraduate instructional equipment. Authorized insured student loans, established a National Teacher Corps, and provided for graduate teacher training fellowships.

Medical Library Assistance Act (Public Law 89–291) provided assistance for construction and improvement of health sciences libraries.

National Foundation on the Arts and the Humanities Act (Public Law 89–209) authorized grants and loans for projects in the creative and performing arts and for research, training, and scholarly publications in the humanities.

National Technical Institute for the Deaf Act (Public Law 89–36) provided for the establishment, construction, equipping, and oper-

ation of a residential school for postsecondary education and technical training of the deaf.

National Vocational Student Loan Insurance Act of 1965 (Public Law 89–287) encouraged state and nonprofit private institutions and organizations to establish adequate loan insurance programs to assist students to attend postsecondary business, trade, technical, and other vocational schools.

School Assistance in Disaster Areas Act (Public Law 89–313) provided for assistance to local education agencies to help meet exceptional costs resulting from a major disaster.

1966 *International Education Act* (Public Law 89–698) provided grants to institutions of higher education for the establishment, strengthening, and operation of centers for research and training in international studies and the international aspects of other fields of study.

National Sea Grant College and Program Act (Public Law 89–688) authorized the establishment and operation of Sea Grant Colleges and programs by initiating and supporting programs of education and research in the various fields relating to the development of marine resources.

Adult Education Act (Public Law 89–750) authorized grants to states for the encouragement and expansion of educational programs for adults, including training of teachers of adults and demonstrations in adult education (previously part of Economic Opportunity Act of 1964).

Model Secondary School for the Deaf Act (Public Law 89–694) authorized the establishment and operation, by Gallaudet College, of a model secondary school for the deaf.

Elementary and Secondary Education Amendments of 1966 (Public Law 89–750) in addition to modifying existing programs, authorized grants to assist states in the initiation, expansion, and improvement of programs and projects for the education of handicapped children.

1967 *Education Professions Development Act* (Public Law 90–35) amended the Higher Education Act of 1965 for the purpose of improving the quality of teaching and to help meet critical shortages of adequately trained educational personnel.

Public Broadcasting Act of 1967 (Public Law 90–129) established a Corporation for Public

Broadcasting to assume major responsibility in channeling federal funds to noncommercial radio and television stations, program production groups, and ETV networks; conduct research, demonstration, or training in matters related to noncommercial broadcasting; and award grants for construction of educational radio and television facilities.

1968 *Elementary and Secondary Education Amendments of 1968* (Public Law 90–247) modified existing programs, authorized support of regional centers for education of handicapped children, model centers and services for deaf-blind children, recruitment of personnel and dissemination of information on education of the handicapped; technical assistance in education to rural areas; support of dropout prevention projects; and support of bilingual education programs.

Handicapped Children's Early Education Assistance Act (Public Law 90–538) authorized preschool and early education programs for handicapped children.

Vocational Education Amendments of 1968 (Public Law 90–576) modified existing programs and provided for a National Advisory Council on Vocational Education and collection and dissemination of information for programs administered by the Commissioner of Education.

Higher Education Amendments of 1968 (Public Law 90–575) authorized new programs to assist disadvantaged college students through special counseling and summer tutorial programs and programs to assist colleges to combine resources of cooperative programs and to expand programs which provide clinical experiences to law students.

1970 *Elementary and Secondary Education Assistance Programs, Extension* (Public Law 91–230) authorized comprehensive planning and evaluation grants to state and local education agencies; provided for the establishment of a National Commission on School Finance.

National Commission on Libraries and Information Services Act (Public Law 91–345) established a National Commission on Libraries and Information Science to effectively utilize the nation's educational resources.

Office of Education Appropriation Act (Public Law 91–380) provided emergency school assistance to desegregating local education agencies.

Environmental Education Act (Public Law 91–516) established an Office of Environmental Education to develop curriculum and initiate and maintain environmental education programs at the elementary-secondary levels; disseminate information; provide training programs for teachers and other educational, public, community, labor, and industrial leaders and employees; provide community education programs; and distribute material dealing with environment and ecology.

Drug Abuse Education Act of 1970 (Public Law 91–527) provided for development, demonstration, and evaluation of curriculums on the problems of drug abuse.

1971 *Comprehensive Health Manpower Training Act of 1971* (Public Law 92–257) amended Title VII of the Public Health Service Act, increasing and expanding provisions for health manpower training and training facilities.

Nurse Training Act of 1971 (Public Law 92–158) amended Title VIII, Nurse Training, of the Public Health Service Act, increasing and expanding provisions for nurse training facilities.

1972 *Drug Abuse Office and Treatment Act of 1972* (Public Law 92–255) established a Special Action Office for Drug Abuse Prevention to provide overall planning and policy for all federal drug-abuse prevention functions; a National Advisory Council for Drug Abuse Prevention; community assistance grants for community mental health center for treatment and rehabilitation of persons with drug-abuse problems, and, in December 1974, a National Institute on Drug Abuse.

Education Amendments of 1972 (Public Law 92–318) established the Education Division in the U.S. Department of Health, Education, and Welfare and the National Institute of Education; general aid for institutions of higher education; federal matching grants for state Student Incentive Grants; a National Commission on Financing Postsecondary Education; State Advisory Councils on Community Colleges; a Bureau of Occupational and Adult Education and State Grants for the design, establishment, and conduct of postsecondary occupational education; and a bureau-level Office of Indian Education. Amended current Office of Education programs to increase their effectiveness and better meet special needs. Prohibited sex bias in admission to vocational, professional, and graduate schools, and public institutions of under-graduate higher education.

1973 *Older Americans Comprehensive Services Amendment of 1973* (Public Law 93–29) made available to older citizens comprehensive programs of health, education, and social services.

Comprehensive Employment and Training Act of 1973 (Public Law 93–203) provided for opportunities for employment and training to unemployed and underemployed persons. Extended and expanded provisions in the Manpower Development and Training Act of 1962, Title I of the Economic Opportunity Act of 1962, Title I of the Economic Opportunity Act of 1964, and the Emergency Employment Act of 1971 as in effect prior to June 30, 1973.

1974 *Education Amendments of 1974* (Public Law 93–380) provided for the consolidation of certain programs; and established a National Center for Education Statistics.

Juvenile Justice and Delinquency Prevention Act of 1974 (Public Law 93–415) provided for technical assistance, staff training, centralized research, and resources to develop and implement programs to keep students in elementary and secondary schools; and established, in the U.S. Department of Justice, a National Institute for Juvenile Justice and Delinquency Prevention.

1975 *Indian Self-Determination and Education Assistance Act* (Public Law 93–638) provided for increased participation of Indians in the establishment and conduct of their education programs and services.

Harry S Truman Memorial Scholarship Act (Public Law 93–642) established the Harry S Truman Scholarship Foundation and created a perpetual education scholarship fund for young Americans to prepare and pursue careers in public service.

Indochina Migration and Refugee Assistance Act of 1975 (Public Law 94–23) authorized funds to be used for education and training of aliens who have fled from Cambodia or Vietnam.

Education for All Handicapped Childen Act (Public Law 94–142) provided that all handicapped children have available to them a free appropriate education designed to meet their unique needs.

1976 *Educational Broadcasting Facilities and Telecommunications Demonstration Act of 1976* (Public Law 94–309) established a telecommunications demonstration program to promote the development of nonbroadcast telecommunications facilities and services for the transmission, distribution, and delivery of health, education, and public or social service information.

Education Amendments of 1976 (Public Law 94–482) extended and revised federal programs for education assistance for higher education, vocational education, and a variety of other programs.

1977 *Youth Employment and Demonstration Projects Act of 1977* (Public Law 95–93) established a youth employment training program that includes, among other activities, promoting education-to-work transition, literacy training and bilingual training, and attainment of certificates of high school equivalency.

Career Education Incentive Act (Public Law 95–207) authorized the establishment of a career education program for elementary and secondary schools.

1978 *Tribally Controlled Community College Assistance Act of 1978* (Public Law 95–471) provided federal funds for the operation and improvement of tribally controlled community colleges for Indian students.

Education Amendments of 1978 (Public Law 95–561) established a comprehensive basic skills program aimed at improving pupil achievement (replaced the existing National Reading Improvement program); and established a community schools program to provide for the use of public buildings.

Middle Income Student Assistance Act (Public Law 95–566) modified the provisions for student financial assistance programs to allow middle-income as well as low-income students attending college or other postsecondary institutions to qualify for federal education assistance.

1979 *Department of Education Organization Act* (Public Law 96–88) established a U.S. Department of Education containing functions from the Education Division of the U.S. Department of Health, Education, and Welfare along with other selected education programs from HEW, the U.S. Department of Justice, U.S. Department of Labor, and the National Science Foundation.

1980 *Asbestos School Hazard Detection and Control Act of 1980* (Public Law 96–270) established a program for inspection of schools for detection of hazardous asbestos materials and provided loans to assist educational agencies to contain or remove and replace such materials.

1981 *Education Consolidation and Improvement Act of 1981* (Part of Public Law 97–35) consolidated 42 programs into 7 programs to be funded under the elementary and secondary block grant authority.

1983 *Student Loan Consolidation and Technical Amendments Act of 1983* (Public Law 98–79) established 8 percent interest rate for Guaranteed Student Loans and extended Family Contribution Schedule.

Challenge Grant Amendments of 1983 (Public Law 98–95) amended Title III, Higher Education Act, and added authorization of Challenge Grant program. The Challenge Grant program provides funds to eligible institutions on a matching basis as incentive to seek alternative sources of funding.

Education of the Handicapped Act Amendments of 1983 (Public Law 98–199) added Architectural Barrier amendment and clarified participation of handicapped children in private schools.

1984 *Education for Economic Security Act* (Public Law 98–377) added new science and mathematics programs for elementary, secondary, and postsecondary education. The new programs include magnet schools, excellence in education, and equal access.

Carl D. Perkins Vocational Education Act (Public Law 98–524) continues federal assistance for vocational education through FY 1989. The act replaces the Vocational Education Act of 1963. It provides aid to the states to make vocational education programs accessible to all persons, including handicapped and disadvantaged, single parents and homemakers, and the incarcerated.

Human Services Reauthorization Act (Public Law 98–558) reauthorized the Head Start and Follow Through programs through FY 1986. It also created a Carl D. Perkins scholarship program, a National Talented Teachers Fellowship program, a Federal Merit Scholarships program, and a Leadership in Educational Administration program.

1985 *Montgomery GI Bill—Active Duty* (Public Law 98–525), brought about a new GI Bill for individuals who initially entered active military duty on or after July 1, 1985.

Montgomery GI Bill—Selected Reserve (Public Law 98–525), is an education program for members of the Selected Reserve (which includes the National Guard) who enlist, reenlist, or extend an enlistment after June 30, 1985, for a 6-year period.

1986 *Handicapped Children's Protection Act of 1986* (Public Law 99–372) allows parents of handicapped children to collect attorneys' fees in cases brought under the Education of the Handicapped Act and provides that the Education of the Handicapped Act does not preempt other laws, such as Section 504 of the Rehabilitation Act.

Drug-Free Schools and Communities Act of 1986 (Part of Public Law 99–570), part of the Anti-Drug Abuse Act of 1986, authorizes funding for FYs 1987–89. Establishes programs for drug abuse education and prevention, coordinated with related community efforts and resources, through the use of federal financial assistance.

1987 *Higher Education Act Amendments of 1987* (Public Law 100–50) makes technical corrections, clarifications, or conforming amendments related to the enactment of the Higher Education Amendments of 1986.

1988 *Augustus F. Hawkins-Robert T. Stafford Elementary and Secondary School Improvement Amendments of 1988* (Public Law 100–297) reauthorizes through 1993 major elementary and secondary education programs including: Chapter 1, Chapter 2, Bilingual Education, Math-Science Education, Magnet Schools, Impact Aid, Indian Education, Adult Education, and other smaller education programs.

Technology-Related Assistance for Individuals with Disabilities Act of 1988 (Public Law 100–407) provides financial assistance to states to develop and implement consumer-responsive statewide programs of technology-related assistance for persons of all ages with disabilities.

Omnibus Trade and Competitiveness Act of 1988 (Public Law 100–418) authorizes new and expanded education programs. Title VI of the Act, Education and Training for American Competitiveness, authorizes new programs in literacy, math-science, foreign language, vocational training, international education, technology training, and technology transfer.

The Omnibus Drug Abuse Prevention Act of 1988 (Public Law 100–690) authorizes a new teacher training program under the Drug-Free Schools and Communities Act, an early childhood education program to be administered jointly by the U.S. Departments of Health and Human Services and Education, and a pilot program for the children of alcoholics.

Stewart B. McKinney Homeless Assistance Amendments Act of 1988 (Public Law 100–628) extends for 2 additional years programs providing assistance to the homeless, including literacy training for homeless adults and education for homeless youths.

Tax Reform Technical Amendments (Public Law 100–647) authorizes an Education Savings Bond for the purpose of postsecondary educational expenses. The bill grants tax exclusion for interest earned on regular series EE savings bonds.

1989 *Children with Disabilities Temporary Care Reauthorization Act of 1989* (Public Law 101–127) revises and extends the programs established in the Temporary Child Care for Handicapped Children and Crises Nurseries Act of 1986.

Drug-Free Schools and Communities Act Amendments of 1989 (Public Law 101–226) amends the Drug-Free Schools and Communities Act of 1986 to revise certain requirements relating to the provision of drug abuse education and prevention programs in elementary and secondary schools.

Childhood Education and Development Act of 1989 (Part of Public Law 101–239) authorizes the appropriations to expand Head Start Programs and programs carried out under the Elementary and Secondary Education Act of 1965 to include child care services.

1990 *Excellence in Mathematics, Science and Engineering Education Act of 1990* (Public Law 101–589) promotes excellence in American mathematics, science, and engineering education by creating a national mathematics and science clearinghouse; establishing regional mathematics and science education consortia; establishing three new mathematics, science, and engineering scholarships programs; and creating several other mathematics, science, and engineering education programs.

Student Right-To-Know and Campus Security Act (Public Law 101–542) requires institutions of higher education receiving federal financial assistance to provide certain information with respect to the graduation rates of student-athletes at such institutions. The act also requires the institution to certify that it has a campus security policy and will annually submit a uniform crime report to the Federal Bureau of Investigation (FBI).

Children's Television Act of 1990 (Public Law 101–437) requires the Federal Communications Commission to reinstate restrictions on advertising during children's television and enforces the obligation of broadcasters to meet the educational and informational needs of the child audience.

Americans with Disabilities Act of 1990 (Public Law 101–336) prohibits discrimination against persons with disabilities.

Stewart B. McKinney Homeless Assistance Amendments Act of 1990 (Public Law 101–645) reauthorized the Stewart B. McKinney Homeless Assistance Act programs of grants to state and local education agencies for the provision of support services to homeless children and youth.

National Assessment of Chapter 1 Act (Public Law 101–305) requires the Secretary of Education to conduct a comprehensive national assessment of programs carried out with assistance under Chapter 1 of Title I of the Elementary and Secondary Education Act of 1965.

Augustus F. Hawkins Human Services Reauthorization Act of 1990 (Public Law 101–501) authorized appropriations for FYs 1991–1994 to carry out the Head Start Act, the Follow Through Act, the Community Services Block Grant Act, and the Low-Income Home Energy Assistance Act of 1981.

National and Community Service Act of 1990 (Public Law 101–610) increased school and college-based community service opportunities and authorized the President's Points of Light Foundation.

School Dropout Prevention and Basic Skills Improvement Act of 1990 (Public Law 101–600) improves secondary school programs for basic skills improvements and dropout reduction.

Medical Residents Student Loan Amendments Act of 1989 (Enacted in Public Law 101–239, the Omnibus Budget Reconciliation Act of 1989) amended the Higher Education Act of 1965 to eliminate student loan deferments for medical students serving in internships or residency programs.

Asbestos School Hazard Abatement Reauthorization Act of 1990 (Public Law 101–637) reauthorized the Asbestos School Hazard Abatement Act of 1984, which provided financial support to elementary and secondary schools to inspect for asbestos and to develop and implement an asbestos management plan. In addition, the act provides for programs of information, technical, and scientific assistance and training.

Eisenhower Exchange Fellowship Act of 1990 (Public Law 101–454) provided a permanent endowment for the Eisenhower Exchange Fellowship Program.

Tribally Controlled Community College Reauthorization Act (Public Law 101–477) reauthorized the Tribally Controlled Community College Assistance Act and the Navajo Community College Act.

National Environmental Education Act (Public Law 101–619) promotes environmental education by the establishment of an Office of Environmental Education in the Environmental Protection Agency and the creation of several environmental education programs.

Anti-Drug Education Act of 1990 and the Drug Abuse Resistance Education (DARE) Act of 1990 (Both bills were enacted as part of Public Law 101–647, the Comprehensive Crime Control Act of 1990.) amends the Drug-Free Schools and Communities Act and raises funding levels for school personnel training, funds the replication of successful drug education programs, helps local education agencies to cooperate with law enforcement agencies, and allows funds to be used for after-school programs. The Drug Abuse Resistance Education Act establishes a program of grants to HHS for Drug Abuse Resistance Education (DARE) programs.

Public Service Assistance Education Act (Enacted as part of Department of Defense Authorization Act, Public Law 101–510) gives federal agencies authority to provide new educational benefits to employees by paying for an employee to obtain an academic degree for which there is an agency shortage of qualified personnel, and by repaying up to $6,000 per year of the student loan of a qualified employee in exchange for a 3-year commitment.

Omnibus Budget Reconciliation Act of 1990 (Public Law 101–508) included a set of student aid provisions that were estimated to yield a savings of $2 billion over 5 years. These provisions included delayed Guaranteed Student Loan disbursements, tightened ability-to-benefit eligibility, and expanded pro rata refund policy and the elimination of student aid eligibility at high default schools.

1991 *Veterans' Education and Employment Programs Amendments. A bill to amend title 38, United States Code, with respect to veterans education and employment programs, and for other purposes* (Public Law 102–16) revises and extends eligibility for veterans' education and employment programs.

National Literacy Act of 1991 (Public Law 102–73) established the National Institute for Literacy, the National Institute Board, and the Interagency Task Force on Literacy. Amends various federal laws to establish and extend various literacy programs.

Dire Emergency Supplemental Appropriations for Consequences of Operation Desert Shield/Desert Storm, Food Stamps, Unemployment Compensation Administration, Veterans Compensation and Pensions, and Other Urgent Needs Act of 1991 (Public Law 102–27) makes dire emergency supplemental appropriations for FY 1991 for the additional costs of Operation Desert Shield/Operation Desert Storm and other programs.

Higher Education Technical Amendments of 1991 (Public Law 102–26) amends the Higher Education Act of 1965 to resolve legal and technical issues relating to federal postsecondary student assistance programs and to prevent undue burdens on participants in Operation Desert Storm, and for other purposes.

Intelligence Authorization Act, Fiscal Year 1992 (Public Law 102–183) provides for the establishment of a National Security Education Board and a National Security Education Trust Fund within the Treasury.

National Defense Authorization Act for Fiscal Years 1992 and 1993 (Public Law 102–190) authorizes appropriations for military functions of the U.S. Department of Defense. Includes Defense Manufacturing Education Program and planning for science, mathematics, and engineering education.

Rehabilitation Act Amendments of 1991 (Public Law 102–52) amends the Rehabilitation Act of 1973 to reauthorize funding for various programs, including vocational rehabilitation services, research and training, supplementary services and facilities, the National Council on Disability, the Architectural and Transportation Barriers Compliance Board, employment opportunities for individuals with handicaps, and comprehensive services for independent living. Reauthorizes funding for the Helen Keller National Center for Deaf-Blind Youths and Adults (under the Helen Keller National Center Act) and for the President's Committee on Employment of People with Disabilities.

Education Acts, Amendments. Amends the School Dropout Demonstration Assistance Act of 1988 to extend authorization of appropriations through FY 1993 and for other purposes (Public Law 102–103) revises and reauthorizes programs under: (1) the School Dropout Demonstration Assistance Act of 1988; and (2) the Star Schools Program Assistance Act. Revises the functional literacy program and adds a life skills program for state and local prisoners under the National Literacy Act of 1991.

A bill making appropriations for the U.S. Department of the Interior and related agencies for the FY ending September 30, 1992, and for other purposes (Public Law 102–154) amends the Anti-Drug Abuse Act of 1988 to extend the authorization of appropriations for drug abuse education and prevention programs relating to youth gangs and for runaway and homeless youth. Directs the Secretary of Health and Human Services to report annually on the program of drug education and prevention relating to youth gangs.

Federal Supplemental Compensation Act of 1991 (Public Law 102–164) revises procedures for student loan debt collection.

25th Anniversary of the Adult Education Act Joint Resolution. A joint resolution to declare it to be the policy of the United States that there should be a renewed and sustained commitment by the federal government and the American people to the importance of adult education (Public Law 102–74) declares it to be the policy of the United States that: (1) the 25th anniversary of federal aid to improve the basic and literacy skills of adults through the Adult Education Act (AEA) should be recognized and observed; and (2) there should be a continued commitment to federal aid for educating adults through AEA to increase adult literacy and assure a productive work force and a competitive United States in the 21st century.

National Commission on Time and Learning Act (Public Law 102–62) establishes the National Education Commission on Time and Learning. Directs the Secretary of Education to: (1) make grants for research in the teaching of writing; and (2) carry out a program to educate students about the history and principles of the Constitution, including the Bill of Rights. Amends the Elementary and Secondary Education Act of 1965 to revise requirements for law-related education program grant and contract applications, review, and award periods. Establishes the National Council on Education Standards and Testing.

High-Performance Computing Act of 1991 (Public Law 102–194) directs the President to implement a National High-Performance Computing Program. Provides for: (1) establishment of a National Research and Education Network; (2) standards and guidelines for high performance networks; and (3) the responsibility of certain federal departments and agencies with regard to the Network.

National and Community Service Technical Amendments Act of 1991 (Public Law 102–10) amends the National and Community Service Act to make various technical amendments.

Persian Gulf Conflict Supplemental Authorization Personnel Benefits Act of 1991 (Public Law 102–25) authorizes supplemental appropriations: (1) to the U.S. Department of Defense in connection with Operation Desert Storm; and (2) for certain national security programs. Revises various military personnel benefits provisions, especially with respect to those personnel serving on active duty in connection with Operation Desert Storm.

Veterans' Educational Assistance Amendments of 1991 (Public Law 102–127) restores certain educational benefits available to reserve and active-duty personnel under the Montgomery GI Bill to students whose course studies under such programs were interrupted by being called to active duty or given increased work in connection with the Persian Gulf War.

Individuals with Disabilities Education Act Amendments of 1991 (Public Law 102–119) amends the Individuals with Disabilities Education Act (IDEA) to extend the authorization of appropriations and revise various features of the early intervention program of services for infants and toddlers with disabilities.

National Sea Grant College Program Authorization Act of 1991 (Public Law 102–186) amends the National Sea Grant College Program Act to: (1) authorize appropriations; and (2) repeal provisions authorizing grants relating to marine affairs and resource management.

National Commission on Libraries and Information Science Act Amendments of 1991 (Public Law 102–95) amends the National Commission on Libraries and Information Science Act to revise provisions and authorize appropriations for the National Commission on Libraries and Information Science.

Civil Rights Act of 1991 (Public Law 102–166) amends the Civil Rights Act of 1964, the Age Discrimination in Employment Act of 1967, and the Americans with Disabilities Act of 1990, with regard to employment discrimination, employment related tests, mixed motives, judgment finality, foreign discrimination, seniority systems, fees, and time limits. Establishes the Technical Assistance Training Institute.

Dropout Prevention Technical Correction Amendment of 1991 (Public Law 102–159) amends federal law relating to impact aid to restore provisions for the Secretary of Education to make certain preliminary payments to local education agencies.

1992 *Higher Education Amendments of 1992* (Public Law 102–325) amends the Higher Education Act of 1965 to revise and reauthorize funding for its various programs.

Ready-To-Learn Act (Public Law 102–545) amends the General Education Provisions Act to establish Ready-To-Learn Television programs to support educational programming and support materials for preschool and elementary school children and their parents, child care providers, and educators.

Job Training Reform Amendments of 1992 (Public Law 102–367), a bill to amend the Job Training Partnerships Act, the Carl Perkins Vocational Education Act, and the Adult Education Act.

National Commission on Time and Learning, Extension (Public Law 102–359) amends the

National Education Commission on Time and Learning Act to extend the authorization of appropriations for such Commission, amends the Elementary and Secondary Education Act of 1965 to revise provisions for (1) a specified civic education program; (2) schoolwide projects for educationally disadvantaged children, and provides for additional Assistant Secretaries of Education.

1993 *Student Loan Reform Act* (Public Law 103–66) reforms the student aid process by phasing in a system of direct lending designed to provide savings for taxpayers and students. Students will be able to choose among a variety of repayment options, including income contingency.

National Service Trust Act (Public Law 103–82) amends the National and Community Service Act of 1990 to establish a Corporation for National Service and enhance opportunities for national service. In addition, the Act provides education grants up to $4,725 per year for 2 years to people age 17 years or older who perform community service before, during, or after postsecondary education.

Higher Education Technical Amendments Act (Public Law 103–208) amends the Higher Education Act to make technical changes and conforming amendments.

NAEP Assessment Authorization (Public Law 103–33) authorizes the use of NAEP for state-by-state comparisons.

Migrant Student Record Transfer System Extension (Public Law 103–59) extends the operation of the migrant student record transfer system.

1994 *Goals 2000: Educate America Act* (Public Law 103–227) establishes a new federal partnership through a system of grants to states and local communities to reform the nation's education system. The Act formalizes the national education goals and establishes the National Education Goals Panel. It also creates a National Education Standards and Improvement Council (NESIC) to provide voluntary national certification of state and local education standards and assessments and establishes the National Skill Standards Board to develop voluntary national skill standards.

School-To-Work Opportunities Act of 1994 (Public Law 103–239) establishes a national framework within which states and communities can develop School-To-Work Opportunities systems to prepare young people for first jobs and continuing education. The Act also provides money to states and communities to develop a system of programs that include work-based learning, school-based learning, and connecting activities components. School-To-Work programs will provide students with a high school diploma (or its equivalent), a nationally recognized skill certificate, an associate degree (if appropriate) and may lead to a first job or further education.

Safe Schools Act of 1994 (Part of Public Law 103–227) authorizes the award of competitive grants to local educational agencies with serious crime to implement violence prevention activities such as conflict resolution and peer mediation.

Educational Research, Development, Dissemination, and Improvement Act of 1994 (Part of Public Law 103–227) authorizes the educational research and dissemination activities of the Office of Educational Research and Improvement. The regional educational labora-

tories and university-based research and development centers are authorized.

Student Loan Default Exemption Extension (Public Law 103–235) amends the Higher Education Act of 1965 to extend until July 1, 1998 the effective date for cohort default rate extension for Historically Black Colleges and Universities, tribally controlled community colleges, and Navajo community colleges.

Technology-Related Assistance for Individuals with Disabilities Amendments of 1993 (Public Law 103–218) amends the Technology-Related Assistance for Individuals with Disabilities Act of 1988 to authorize appropriations for each of the FYs 1994–98.

Improving America's Schools Act (Public Law 103-382) reauthorizes and revamps the Elementary and Secondary Education Act. The legislation includes Title I, the federal government's largest program providing educational assistance to disadvantaged children; professional development and technical assistance programs; safe and drug-free schools and communities provision; and provisions promoting school equity.

Figure 20.-Federal funds for education, by agency: Fiscal Year 1995

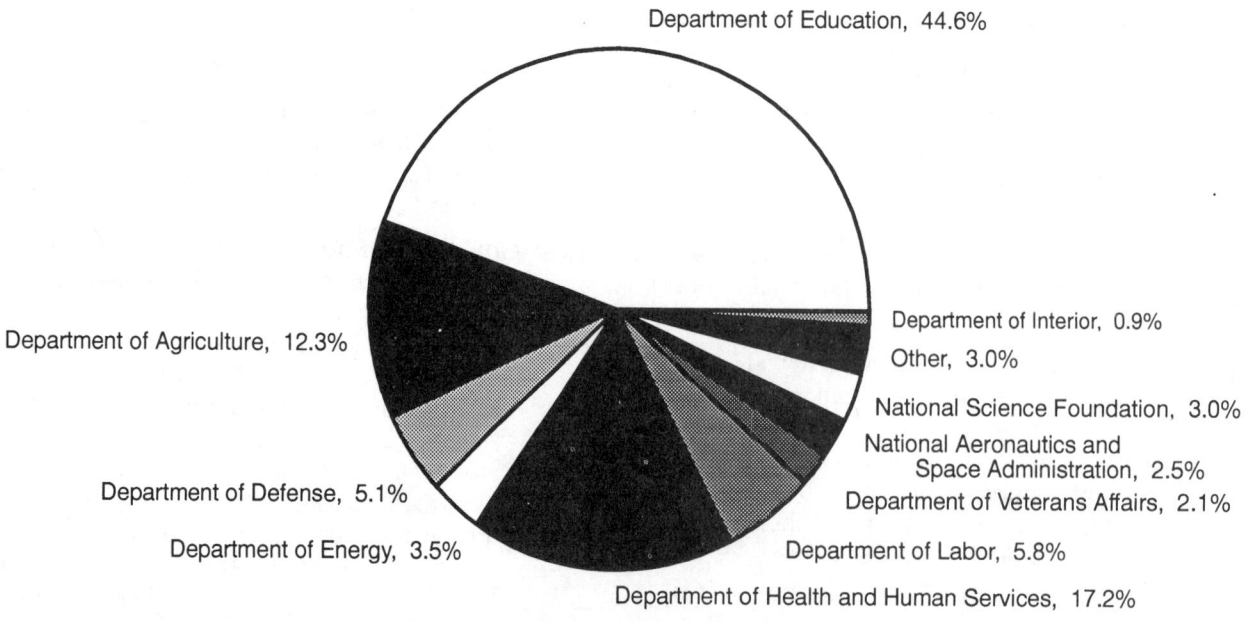

Department of Education, 44.6%

Department of Agriculture, 12.3%

Department of Interior, 0.9%

Other, 3.0%

National Science Foundation, 3.0%

National Aeronautics and Space Administration, 2.5%

Department of Veterans Affairs, 2.1%

Department of Defense, 5.1%

Department of Labor, 5.8%

Department of Energy, 3.5%

Department of Health and Human Services, 17.2%

Total = $73.8 billion

SOURCE: U.S. Office of Management and Budget, *Budget of the U.S. Government, Fiscal Year 1996*; and National Science Foundation, *Federal Funds for Research and Development, Fiscal Years 1993, 1994, and 1995.*

Figure 21.-Federal on-budget funds for education, by level or other educational purpose: 1965 to 1995
(In constant FY 1995 dollars)

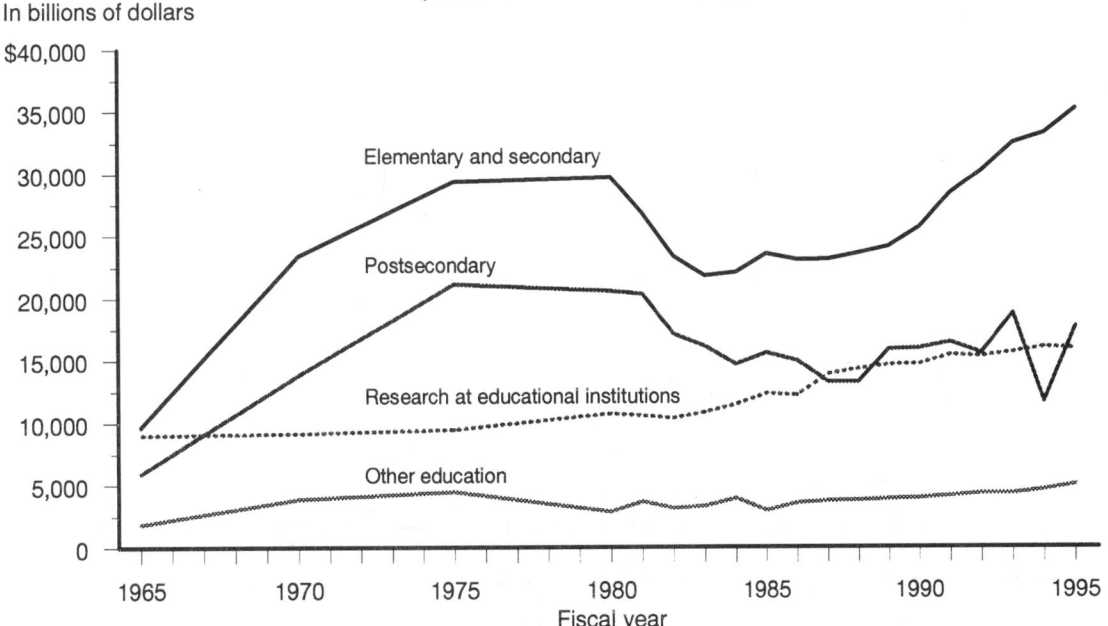

SOURCE: U.S. Office of Management and Budget, *Budget of the U.S. Government*, fiscal years 1967 to 1996; National Science Foundation, *Federal Funds for Research and Development*, fiscal years 1967 to 1995; and unpublished data.

Figure 22.-Department of Education outlays, by type of recipient: Fiscal Year 1995

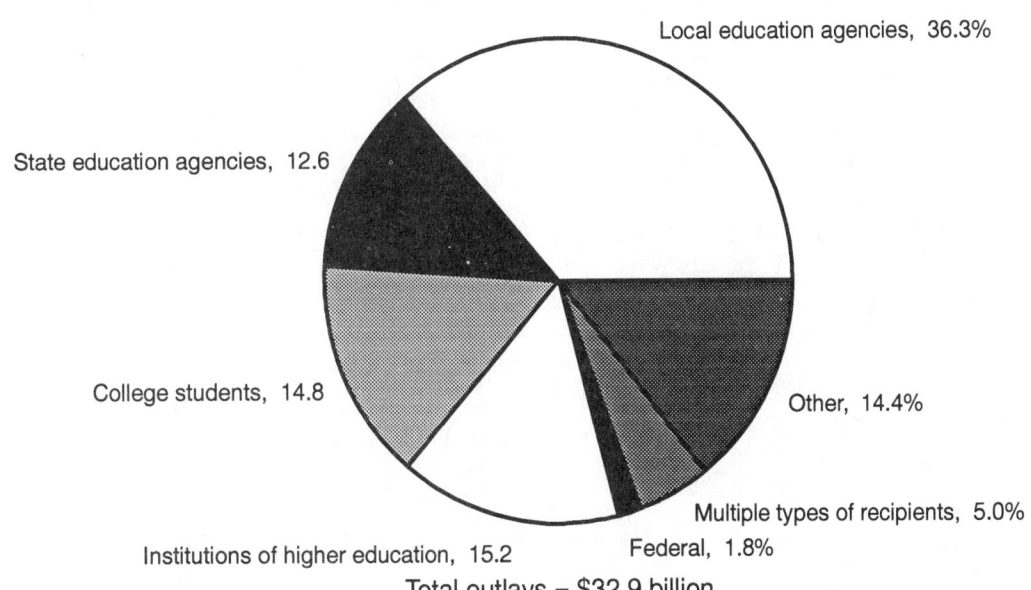

Total outlays = $32.9 billion

SOURCE: U.S. Office of Management and Budget, *Budget of the U.S. Government, Fiscal Year 1996; Catalog of Federal Domestic Assistance*; National Foundation, *Federal Funds for Research and Development , Fiscal Years, 1993, 1994, and 1995*; and unpublished data obtained from various federal agencies.

Table 351.—Federal education support and estimated federal tax expenditures for education, by category: Fiscal years 1965 to 1995

[In millions of dollars]

Fiscal year	Total on-budget support, off-budget support, and nonfederal funds generated by federal programs	On-budget support[1] Total	Elementary and secondary	Post-secondary	Other education	Research at educational institutions	Off-budget support Total	Federal Direct Student Loan[2]	Federal Family Education Loan Program[3]	Perkins Loans[4]	Income Contingent Loans[5]	State Student Incentive Grants[6]	Supplemental Educational Opportunity Grants[7]	Work-Study aid[8]	Estimated federal tax expenditures for education[9]
1	2	3	4	5	6	7	8	9	10	11	12	13	14	15	16
Current dollars															
1965	$5,354.7	$5,331.0	$1,942.6	$1,197.5	$374.7	$1,816.3	$23.7	—	—	$16.1	—	—	—	$7.6	—
1970	13,359.1	12,526.5	5,830.4	3,447.7	964.7	2,283.6	832.6	—	$770.0	21.0	—	—	—	41.6	—
1975	24,691.5	23,288.1	10,617.2	7,644.0	1,608.5	3,418.4	1,403.4	—	1,233.0	35.7	—	$20.0	—	114.7	$8,605.0
1980	39,349.2	34,493.5	16,027.7	11,115.9	1,548.7	5,801.2	4,855.7	—	4,598.0	31.8	—	76.5	—	149.4	13,320.0
1981	44,121.6	36,446.2	15,903.7	12,084.8	2,182.2	6,275.5	7,675.4	—	7,433.0	20.7	—	76.5	—	145.2	16,380.0
1982	40,142.2	34,304.7	14,839.2	10,872.8	1,995.1	6,597.4	5,837.5	—	5,597.0	19.8	—	72.0	—	148.7	16,180.0
1983	41,544.7	34,719.2	14,527.8	10,753.4	2,204.1	7,233.8	6,825.5	—	6,582.0	19.8	—	60.0	—	163.7	16,725.0
1984	43,875.9	36,104.5	15,292.4	10,163.2	2,710.4	7,938.6	7,771.4	—	7,520.0	17.9	—	76.0	—	157.5	17,090.0
1985	47,753.4	39,027.9	16,901.3	11,174.4	2,107.6	8,844.6	8,725.5	—	8,467.0	21.4	—	76.0	—	161.1	18,035.0
1986	48,139.4	39,745.0	17,049.9	11,065.6	2,620.0	9,009.4	8,394.4	—	8,142.0	20.2	—	72.7	—	159.5	19,460.0
1987	50,502.0	40,972.2	17,535.7	10,077.5	2,820.4	10,538.6	9,529.8	—	9,272.0	20.9	—	76.0	—	160.4	19,590.0
1988	53,840.5	43,216.0	18,564.9	10,419.1	2,981.6	11,250.5	10,624.5	—	10,380.0	20.6	$0.6	73.0	—	150.4	16,190.0
1989	59,281.9	48,014.0	19,809.5	13,014.3	3,180.3	12,009.8	11,267.8	—	10,938.0	20.4	0.5	71.9	$22.0	215.0	16,890.0
1990	62,811.5	51,624.3	21,984.4	13,650.9	3,383.0	12,606.0	11,187.2	—	10,826.0	15.0	0.5	59.2	48.8	237.7	18,140.0
1991	70,371.7	57,595.7	25,418.0	14,703.6	3,698.6	13,775.4	12,776.1	—	12,372.0	17.3	0.5	63.5	87.7	235.0	—
1992	74,477.9	60,479.8	27,926.9	14,384.1	3,992.0	14,176.9	13,998.0	—	13,568.0	17.3	—	72.0	97.2	242.9	—
1993	84,658.8	67,657.9	30,834.3	17,844.0	4,107.2	14,872.4	17,000.8	—	16,524.0	29.3	—	72.4	184.6	190.5	—
1994	88,327.6	63,800.3	32,305.6	11,383.8	4,484.0	15,627.0	24,527.3	$813.0	23,214.0	52.7	—	72.4	184.6	190.5	—
1995[10]	100,076.4	73,828.1	35,197.8	17,690.1	5,014.4	15,925.8	26,248.2	7,095.0	18,662.0	52.7	—	63.4	184.6	190.5	—
Constant fiscal year 1995 dollars[11]															
1965	$26,620.1	$26,502.2	$9,657.2	$5,953.2	$1,862.5	$9,029.3	$117.9	—	—	$80.1	—	—	—	$37.8	—
1970	53,623.5	50,281.6	23,403.5	13,839.1	3,872.4	9,166.6	3,342.0	—	$3,090.8	84.2	—	—	—	167.0	—
1975	68,365.9	64,480.3	29,397.0	21,164.9	4,453.6	9,464.8	3,885.7	—	3,413.9	98.8	—	$55.4	—	317.6	$23,825.6
1980	72,991.6	63,984.4	29,730.9	20,619.6	2,872.8	10,761.1	9,007.1	—	8,529.2	58.9	—	141.9	—	277.1	24,708.2
1981	74,358.1	61,422.8	26,802.5	20,366.5	3,677.7	10,576.1	12,935.3	—	12,526.8	34.8	—	128.9	—	244.7	27,605.2
1982	63,189.3	54,000.2	23,359.0	17,115.3	3,140.6	10,385.2	9,189.1	—	8,810.5	31.2	—	113.3	—	234.1	25,469.6
1983	62,364.3	52,118.2	21,808.3	16,142.4	3,308.7	10,858.9	10,246.1	—	9,880.5	29.8	—	90.1	—	245.7	25,106.6
1984	63,344.9	52,125.2	22,078.0	14,672.9	3,913.1	11,461.2	11,219.8	—	10,856.8	25.8	—	109.7	—	227.4	24,673.3
1985	66,557.6	54,396.2	23,556.7	15,574.6	2,937.5	12,327.4	12,161.4	—	11,801.1	29.8	—	105.9	—	224.5	25,136.8
1986	65,145.1	53,785.3	23,073.0	14,974.7	3,545.6	12,192.0	11,359.8	—	11,018.3	27.3	—	98.4	—	215.8	26,334.5
1987	66,531.4	53,976.7	23,101.5	13,276.0	3,715.6	13,883.6	12,554.6	—	12,214.9	27.5	—	100.1	—	211.3	25,807.9
1988	68,458.1	54,949.1	23,605.2	13,247.9	3,791.1	14,305.0	13,509.1	—	13,198.2	26.2	$0.7	92.8	—	191.2	20,585.6
1989	72,225.9	58,497.8	24,134.9	15,856.0	3,874.8	14,632.1	13,728.2	—	13,326.3	24.8	0.6	87.6	$26.8	261.9	20,577.9
1990	73,345.1	60,281.8	25,671.2	15,940.2	3,950.4	14,720.1	13,063.3	—	12,641.5	17.5	0.7	69.1	57.0	277.6	21,182.1
1991	78,679.2	64,399.4	28,418.7	16,439.4	4,135.2	15,401.6	14,284.3	—	13,832.5	19.4	0.6	71.0	98.1	262.7	—
1992	80,536.1	65,399.4	30,198.5	15,554.2	4,316.7	15,330.0	15,136.7	—	14,671.7	18.7	0.6	77.9	105.2	262.7	—
1993	89,130.9	71,232.0	32,463.2	18,786.6	4,324.2	15,658.0	17,898.9	—	17,396.9	30.8	0.6	76.3	194.4	200.6	—
1994	90,823.2	65,603.0	33,218.3	11,705.4	4,610.7	16,068.5	25,220.3	$836.0	23,869.9	54.2	—	74.5	189.8	195.9	—
1995[10]	100,076.4	73,828.1	35,197.8	17,690.1	5,014.4	15,925.8	26,248.2	7,095.0	18,662.0	52.7	—	63.4	184.6	190.5	—

[1] On-budget support includes federal funds for education programs tied to appropriations.

[2] The Federal Direct Student Loan program (FDSL) program, recently renamed the William D. Ford Direct Loan program, will provide students with the same benefits they are currently eligible to receive under the Federal Family Education Loan (FFEL) program but will provide loans to students through federal capital rather than through private lenders. The FDSL program will replace the FFEL program and will gradually be phased in, beginning with the 1994-95 academic year. This program will be an off-budget support program.

[3] Formerly the Guaranteed Student Loan program. New student loans guaranteed by the federal government and disbursed to borrowers.

[4] Student loans created from institutional matching funds (1/3 of the federal contribution). Excludes repayments of outstanding loans.

[5] Student loans created from institutional matching funds (1/9 of the federal contribution). This was a demonstration project that involved only 10 institutions and had unsubsidized interest rates.

[6] Required state matching contributions.

[7] Institutions award grants to undergraduate students, and the federal share of such grants may not exceed 75 percent of the total grant.

[8] Employer contributions to student earnings.

[9] Losses of tax revenue attributable to provisions of the federal income tax laws that allow a special exclusion, exemption, or deduction from gross income or provide a special credit, preferential rate of tax, or a deferral of tax liability affecting individual or corporate income tax liabilities.

[10] Estimated.

[11] Data adjusted by the federal funds composite deflator prepared by the U.S. Office of Management and Budget.

—Not available or not applicable.

NOTE.—To the extent possible, federal education funds data represent outlays rather than obligations. Because of rounding, details may not add to totals. Data have been revised from previously published figures.

SOURCE: U.S. Department of Education, Office of the Undersecretary, and National Center for Education Statistics, compiled from data appearing in U.S. Office of Management and Budget, Budget of the U.S. Government, Appendix, fiscal years 1967 to 1996; National Science Foundation, Federal Funds for Research and Development, fiscal years 1965 to 1995; "Federal Tax Expenditures, FY 1980 to FY 1984," "Federal Tax Expenditures, FY 1984 to FY 1988," and "Federal Tax Expenditures, FY 1970 to FY 1990" by Stephen M. Barro, prepared for the National Center for Education Statistics; and unpublished data obtained from various federal agencies. (This table was prepared June 1995.)

Table 352.—Federal on-budget funds for education, by agency: Fiscal years 1965 to 1995

[In thousands of dollars]

Agency	1965	1970	1975	1980	1985	1990	1992	1994	1995¹
1	2	3	4	5	6	7	8	9	10
Total	**$5,331,016**	**$12,526,499**	**$23,288,120**	**$34,493,502**	**$39,027,876**	**$51,624,342**	**$60,479,844**	**$63,800,309**	**$73,828,136**
Department of Education	1,000,567	4,625,224	7,350,355	13,137,785	16,701,065	23,198,575	26,116,013	24,923,412	32,947,447
Department of Agriculture	768,927	960,910	2,219,352	4,562,467	4,782,274	6,260,843	7,586,729	8,509,703	9,050,022
Department of Commerce	9,347	13,990	38,967	135,561	55,114	80,510	53,835	74,632	107,997
Department of Defense	587,412	821,388	1,009,229	1,560,301	3,119,213	3,605,509	3,948,471	3,994,158	3,744,500
Department of Energy	442,434	551,527	764,676	1,605,558	2,247,822	2,561,950	2,917,137	2,734,647	2,608,273
Department of Health and Human Services	1,027,537	1,796,854	3,675,225	5,613,930	5,322,356	7,956,011	9,362,010	11,941,577	12,681,615
Department of Housing and Urban Development	221,256	114,709	-52,768	5,314	438	118	203	592	600
Department of the Interior	170,088	190,975	300,191	440,547	549,479	630,537	715,382	688,568	691,130
Department of Justice	10,252	15,728	61,542	60,721	66,802	99,775	134,235	148,828	168,890
Department of Labor	230,041	424,494	1,103,935	1,862,738	1,948,685	2,511,380	3,709,531	4,015,360	4,308,998
Department of State	64,200	59,742	89,433	25,188	23,820	51,225	53,343	54,414	49,254
Department of Transportation	—	27,534	52,290	54,712	82,035	76,186	91,485	125,307	126,129
Department of Treasury	8,240	18	1,118,840	1,247,463	290,276	41,715	51,779	62,159	64,107
Department of Veterans Affairs	97,237	1,032,918	4,402,212	2,351,233	1,289,849	757,476	1,047,579	1,382,493	1,531,284
Other agencies and programs:									
ACTION	63,329	88,034	7,081	2,833	1,761	8,472	8,600	—	—
Agency for International Development	—	37,838	78,896	176,770	198,807	249,786	245,199	270,275	234,579
Appalachian Regional Commission	—	—	45,786	19,032	4,745	93	7,608	10,242	10,242
Barry Goldwater Scholarship and Excellence in Education Foundation	—	—	—	—	—	1,033	2,900	2,789	2,871
Corporation for National and Community Service	—	—	—	—	—	—	—	93,250	145,900
Environmental Protection Agency	—	19,446	33,875	41,083	60,521	87,481	152,012	113,844	101,535
Estimated education share of Federal aid to the District of Columbia	11,350	33,019	55,487	81,847	107,340	104,940	130,371	97,752	83,869
Federal Emergency Management Agency	—	290	290	1,946	1,828	215	261	85,200	170,400
General Services Administration	4,013	14,775	22,532	34,800	—	2,883	2,401	2,323	—
Harry S Truman scholarship fund	—	—	—	-1,895	1,332	4,305	6,612	—	3,571
Institute of American Indian and Alaskan Native Culture and Arts Development	—	—	—	—	—	—	—	12,213	11,563
James Madison Memorial Fellowship Foundation	—	—	—	—	—	191	885	1,464	2,207
Japanese-United States Friendship Commission	—	—	—	2,294	2,236	2,299	1,610	1,585	2,107
Library of Congress	15,111	29,478	63,766	151,871	169,310	189,827	296,044	312,724	337,417
National Aeronautics and Space Administration	208,788	258,366	197,901	255,511	487,624	1,093,303	1,383,422	1,554,608	1,814,311
National Archives and Records Administration	—	—	—	—	52,118	77,397	99,412	110,411	103,390
National Commission on Libraries and Information Science	—	—	449	2,090	723	3,281	1,437	724	1,033
National Endowment for the Arts	—	340	4,754	5,220	5,536	5,577	8,286	7,221	7,110
National Endowment for the Humanities	—	8,459	63,955	142,586	125,671	141,048	159,103	158,953	159,500
National Science Foundation	181,216	295,628	535,294	808,392	1,147,115	1,588,891	1,875,072	2,025,826	2,231,120
Nuclear Regulatory Commission	—	—	7,093	32,590	30,261	42,328	27,418	25,735	25,060
Office of Economic Opportunity	189,871	1,092,410	16,619	5,153	—	—	—	—	—
Smithsonian Institution	2,233	2,461	5,509	661	7,886	5,779	6,578	10,059	9,986
United States Arms Control Agency	—	100	—	—	395	25	100	—	—
United States Information Agency	7,512	8,423	9,405	66,210	143,007	201,547	237,226	230,493	271,789
United States Institute of Peace	—	—	—	—	—	7,621	11,350	10,794	12,255
Other agencies	10,055	1,421	5,949	990	432	885	1,532	5,975	6,075

¹Estimated.

—Data not available or not applicable.

SOURCE: U.S. Department of Education, National Center for Education Statistics, compiled from data appearing in U.S. Office of Management and Budget, Budget of the U.S. Government, Appendix, fiscal years 1967 to 1996; National Science Foundation, Federal Funds for Research and Development, fiscal years 1965 to 1995; and unpublished data obtained from various Federal agencies. (This table was prepared May 1995.)

NOTE.—To the extent possible, amounts reported represent outlays, rather than obligations.

Table 353.—Federal on-budget funds for education, by level or educational purpose, by agency and program: Fiscal years 1965 to 1995

[In thousands of dollars]

Level or educational purpose, by agency and program	1965	1970	1975	1980	1985	1990[1]	1992[2]	1994[3]	1995[4,5]
1	2	3	4	5	6	7	8	9	10
Total, all programs	$5,331,016	$12,526,499	$23,288,120	$34,493,502	$39,027,876	$51,624,342	$60,479,844	$63,800,309	$73,828,136
Elementary/secondary education programs	$1,942,577	$5,830,442	$10,617,195	$16,027,686	$16,901,334	$21,984,361	$27,926,888	$32,305,563	$35,197,753
Department of Education[6]	567,343	2,719,204	4,132,742	6,629,095	7,296,702	9,681,313	12,057,746	13,769,196	15,378,620
Education for the disadvantaged	—	1,339,014	1,874,353	3,204,664	4,206,754	4,494,111	6,158,813	6,845,651	7,032,187
Impact aid program[7]	349,671	656,372	618,711	690,170	647,402	816,366	794,794	829,952	1,088,307
School improvement programs	72,298	288,304	700,470	788,918	526,401	1,189,158	1,514,892	1,469,963	1,588,843
Indian education	—	—	40,036	93,365	82,328	69,451	68,523	79,095	82,831
Bilingual education	—	21,250	92,693	169,540	157,539	188,919	198,332	221,681	251,419
Education for the handicapped	13,849	79,090	151,244	821,777	1,017,964	1,616,623	2,243,338	2,980,328	3,611,709
Vocational and adult education	131,525	335,174	655,235	860,661	658,314	1,306,685	1,079,054	1,340,763	1,543,827
Education Reform - Goals 2000[8]								1,763	179,497
Department of Agriculture	623,014	760,477	1,884,345	4,064,497	4,134,906	5,528,950	6,714,082	7,604,447	8,169,498
Child nutrition programs[9]	178,580	299,131	1,452,267	3,377,056	3,664,561	4,977,075	6,126,983	7,043,699	7,644,789
Agricultural Marketing Service—commodities[10]	340,073	341,597	248,839	388,000	336,502	350,441	400,000	400,000	400,000
Special milk program[9]	86,609	83,800	122,858	159,293	15,993	18,707	19,178	(9)	(9)
Estimated education share of Forest Service permanent appropriations	17,752	35,949	60,381	140,148	117,850	182,727	167,921	160,748	124,709
Department of Commerce	—	—	—	54,816	—	—	—	—	—
Local public works program—school facilities[11]	—	—	—	54,816	—	—	—	—	—
Department of Defense	73,000	143,100	264,500	370,846	831,625	1,097,876	1,197,318	1,210,168	1,225,862
Junior ROTC	—	12,100	12,500	32,000	55,600	39,300	54,746	95,500	119,600
Overseas dependents schools	73,000	131,000	252,000	338,846	613,437	864,958	912,916	849,649	845,284
Section VI schools[7]	—	—	—	—	162,588	193,618	229,656	265,019	260,978
Department of Energy[12]	100	200	300	77,633	23,031	15,563	15,236	11,615	11,507
Energy conservation for school buildings[13]	—	—	—	77,240	22,731	15,213	12,586	10,535	10,535
Pre-engineering program	100	200	300	393	300	350	2,650	1,080	972
Department of Health and Human Services[14]	79,999	167,333	683,885	1,077,000	1,531,059	2,396,793	3,310,200	4,669,181	5,090,213
Head Start[15]	—	—	403,900	735,000	1,075,059	1,447,758	2,201,800	3,215,946	3,534,000
Payments to states for AFDC work programs[16]	—	—	—	—	—	459,221	594,184	838,981	936,967
Social Security student benefits[17]	79,999	167,333	279,985	342,000	456,000	489,814	514,216	614,254	619,246
Department of the Interior	130,096	140,705	220,392	318,170	389,810	445,267	517,666	485,758	493,609
Mineral Leasing Act and other funds:									
Payments to states—estimated education share	11,075	12,294	27,389	62,636	127,369	123,811	122,045	21,693	18,557
Payments to counties—estimated education share	10,731	16,359	29,494	48,953	59,016	102,522	45,805	39,819	38,439
Indian Education:									
Bureau of Indian Affairs schools	92,603	95,850	141,056	178,112	177,265	192,841	325,582	399,234	411,524
Johnson-O'Malley assistance[18]	15,534	16,080	22,251	28,081	25,675	25,556	23,590	24,326	24,359
Education expenses for children of employees, Yellowstone National Park	153	122	202	388	485	538	644	686	730
Department of Justice	6,402	8,237	9,822	23,890	36,117	65,997	94,724	112,447	138,768
Vocational training expenses for prisoners in federal prisons	1,466	2,720	3,039	4,966	8,292	2,066	1,944	1,240	3,463
Inmate programs[19]	4,936	5,517	6,783	18,924	27,825	63,931	92,780	111,207	135,305
Department of Labor	230,041	420,927	1,097,811	1,849,800	1,945,268	2,505,487	3,708,362	4,011,184	4,299,502
Job Corps[20]	—	—	175,000	469,800	604,748	739,376	925,826	964,234	1,042,434
Training programs—estimated funds for education programs[21]	230,041	420,927	922,811	1,380,000	1,340,520	1,766,111	2,782,536	3,046,950	3,257,068
Department of Transportation[22]	—	45	50	60	60	46	60	60	65
Tuition assistance for educational accreditation—Coast Guard personnel[23]	—	45	50	60	60	46	60	60	65
Department of the Treasury	32	—	847,139	935,903	273,728	—	—	—	—
Estimated education share of general revenue sharing:[24]									
State[25]	—	—	475,224	525,019	—	—	—	—	—
Local	—	—	371,915	410,884	273,728	—	—	—	—
Tuition assistance for educational accreditation—Coast Guard personnel[23]	32	—	—	—	—	—	—	—	—
Department of Veterans Affairs[26]	41,250	338,910	1,371,500	545,786	344,758	155,351	190,608	335,866	310,411
Noncollegiate and job training programs[27]	14,550	281,640	1,249,410	439,993	224,035	12,848	—	—	—
Vocational rehabilitation for disabled veterans[28]	17,400	41,700	73,100	87,980	107,480	136,780	184,500	265,597	296,590
Dependents' education[29]	9,300	15,570	48,990	17,813	13,243	5,723	6,108	5,740	5,405
Service members occupational conversion and training act of 1992[30]	—	—	—	—	—	—	—	64,529	8,416
Other agencies									
Appalachian Regional Commission[31]	—	33,161	41,667	9,157	4,632	93	5,182	2,529	2,529
National Endowment for the Arts[32]	—	—	3,686	4,989	4,399	4,641	5,000	5,000	5,000
Arts in education	—	—	3,686	4,989	4,399	4,641	5,000	5,000	5,000
National Endowment for the Humanities[33]	—	20	149	330	321	404	809	1,485	1,500
Office of Economic Opportunity[34]	182,793	1,072,375	16,619	—	—	—	—	—	—
Head Start[35]	96,400	325,700	—	—	—	—	—	—	—
Other elementary and secondary programs[36]	20,000	42,809	16,612	—	—	—	—	—	—
Job Corps[37]	34,000	144,000	—	—	—	—	—	—	—
Youth Corps and other training programs[38]	31,000	553,368	7	—	—	—	—	—	—
Volunteers in Service to America (VISTA)[39]	1,393	6,498	—						

Table 353.—Federal on-budget funds for education, by level or educational purpose, by agency and program: Fiscal years 1965 to 1995—Continued

[In thousands of dollars]

Level or educational purpose, by agency and program	1965	1970	1975	1980	1985	1990[1]	1992[2]	1994[3]	1995[4,5]
1	2	3	4	5	6	7	8	9	10
Other programs									
Estimated education share of federal aid to the District of Columbia	8,507	25,748	42,588	65,714	84,918	86,579	109,894	86,627	70,669
Postsecondary education programs	$1,197,511	$3,447,697	$7,644,037	$11,115,882	$11,174,379	$13,650,915	$14,384,138	$11,383,751	$17,690,133
Department of Education[6]	237,955	1,187,962	2,089,184	5,682,242	8,202,499	11,175,978	11,323,584	8,081,390	14,061,317
Student financial assistance[40]	—	—	—	3,682,789	4,162,695	5,920,328	7,071,440	7,118,034	7,264,842
Federal Direct Student Loan Program[41]	—	—	—	—	—	—	—	148,247	842,946
Federal Family Education Loan Program[42]	—	2,323	111,087	1,407,977	3,534,795	4,372,446	3,253,648	−280,304	4,742,501
Higher education	218,264	1,029,131	1,838,066	399,787	404,511	659,492	718,406	796,278	899,314
Facilities—loans and insurance[43]	3,588	114,199	16,292	−19,031	5,307	19,219	25,984	16,002	14,031
College housing loans[43,44]	—	—	—	14,082	−164,061	−57,167	−39,907	−40,041	−28,911
Educational activities overseas	129	774	1,881	3,561	1,838	82	—	—	—
Historically Black Colleges and Universities Capital Financing, Program Account[45]	—	—	—	—	—	—	—	129	255
Gallaudet College and Howard University	15,974	38,559	111,971	176,829	229,938	230,327	263,497	280,945	285,518
National Technical Institute for the Deaf[46]	—	2,976	9,887	16,248	27,476	31,251	30,516	42,100	40,821
Department of Agriculture	—	—	6,450	10,453	17,741	31,273	34,238	25,472	25,472
Agriculture Extension Service, Second Morrill Act payments to agricultural and mechanical colleges and Tuskegee Institute[47]	—	—	6,450	10,453	17,741	31,273	34,238	25,472	25,472
Department of Commerce	5,081	8,277	14,973	29,971	2,163	3,312	3,270	4,000	4,500
Sea Grant Program[48]	—	—	1,886	3,123	2,163	3,312	3,270	4,000	4,500
Merchant Marine Academy[49]	3,570	6,160	10,152	14,809	—	—	—	—	—
State marine schools[49]	1,511	2,117	2,935	12,039	—	—	—	—	—
Department of Defense[50]	77,500	322,100	379,800	545,000	1,041,700	635,769	680,194	679,000	727,300
Tuition assistance for military personnel	—	57,500	86,800	(51)	77,100	95,300	102,400	130,200	133,000
Service academies[52]	77,500	78,700	86,200	106,100	196,400	120,613	125,146	141,500	157,000
Senior ROTC	—	108,100	116,500	(51)	354,000	193,056	193,348	195,300	208,900
Professional development education[53]	—	77,800	90,300	(51)	414,200	226,800	259,300	212,000	228,400
Department of Energy[12]	3,000	3,000	3,000	57,701	19,475	25,502	34,373	17,951	16,971
University laboratory cooperative program	3,000	3,000	3,000	2,800	6,500	9,402	19,100	3,600	3,240
Teacher development projects[54]	—	—	—	1,400	—	—	—	—	—
Graduate traineeship programs[55]	—	—	—	—	—	—	—	—	—
Energy conservation for buildings—higher education[13]	—	—	—	53,501	12,705	7,459	9,573	8,051	8,051
Minority honors vocational training[56]	—	—	—	—	150	—	—	—	—
Honors research program[56]	—	—	—	—	120	6,472	1,000	900	820
Students and teachers[57]	—	—	—	—	—	2,169	4,700	5,400	4,860
Department of Health and Human Services[14]	469,223	981,483	1,686,650	2,412,058	516,088	578,542	743,456	795,914	826,379
Health professions training programs[58]	139,795	353,029	599,350	460,736	212,200	230,600	305,829	305,549	312,980
Indian health manpower[59]	—	—	—	7,187	5,577	9,508	19,460	26,398	39,997
National Health Service Corps scholarships	—	—	1,206	70,667	2,268	4,759	58,706	79,250	80,144
National Institutes of Health training grants[60]	—	—	154,875	176,388	217,927	241,356	348,034	372,698	381,293
National Institute of Occupational Safety and Health training grants	4,327	8,088	7,182	12,899	8,760	10,461	10,972	11,622	11,600
Alcohol, drug abuse, and mental health training programs[61]	85,101	118,366	83,727	122,103	43,617	81,353	—	—	—
Health teaching facilities	—	—	353	3,078	739	505	455	397	365
Social Security postsecondary students' benefits[62]	240,000	502,000	839,957	1,559,000	25,000	—	—	—	—
Department of Housing and Urban Development[43]	220,744	114,199	−55,418	—	—	—	—	—	—
College housing loans[43,44]	220,744	114,199	−55,418	—	—	—	—	—	—
Department of the Interior	30,153	31,749	50,844	80,202	125,247	135,480	140,266	156,734	157,910
Shared revenues, Mineral Leasing Act and other receipts—estimated education share	6,260	6,949	15,480	35,403	71,991	69,980	68,982	79,815	81,666
Indian programs:									
Continuing education[63]	8,993	9,380	13,311	16,909	24,338	34,911	38,970	43,184	43,907
Higher education scholarships	14,900	15,420	22,053	27,890	28,918	30,589	32,315	33,735	32,337
Department of State	53,420	30,850	50,347	—	—	2,167	9,057	7,842	2,564
Educational exchange[64]	53,420	30,850	50,347	—	—	—	—	—	—
Mutual educational and cultural exchange activities	47,025	30,454	50,300	—	—	—	—	—	—
International educational exchange activities	6,395	396	47	—	—	—	—	—	—
Russian, Eurasian, and East European Research and Training[65]	—	—	—	—	—	2,167	9,057	7,842	2,564
Department of Transportation[22]	—	11,197	11,885	12,530	55,569	46,025	53,991	56,640	57,138
Merchant Marine Academy[49]	—	—	—	—	19,898	20,926	27,007	30,241	30,854
State marine schools[66]	—	—	—	—	19,777	8,269	11,072	10,270	11,271
Coast Guard Academy[23]	—	9,342	9,780	10,000	11,857	12,074	13,071	13,103	12,416
Postgraduate training for Coast Guard officers[67]	—	1,655	1,855	2,230	3,499	4,173	2,540	2,726	2,302
Tuition assistance to Coast Guard military personnel[23]	—	200	250	300	538	582	301	300	295
Department of the Treasury	8,208	—	268,605	296,750	—	—	—	—	—
General revenue sharing—estimated state share to higher education[24,25]	—	—	268,605	296,750	—	—	—	—	—
Coast Guard Academy[23]	6,815	—	—	—	—	—	—	—	—
Postgraduate training for Coast Guard officers[67]	1,293	—	—	—	—	—	—	—	—
Tuition assistance to Coast Guard military personnel[23]	100	—	—	—	—	—	—	—	—
Department of Veterans Affairs[26]	55,650	693,490	3,029,600	1,803,847	944,091	599,825	854,480	1,043,709	1,218,803

Table 353.—Federal on-budget funds for education, by level or educational purpose, by agency and program: Fiscal years 1965 to 1995—Continued

[In thousands of dollars]

Level or educational purpose, by agency and program	1965	1970	1975	1980	1985	1990[1]	1992[2]	1994[3]	1995[4,5]
1	2	3	4	5	6	7	8	9	10
Vietnam-era veterans:[68]	33,950	638,260	2,840,600	1,579,974	694,217	46,998	—	—	—
College student support	—	—	—	1,560,081	679,953	39,458	—	—	—
Work-study	—	—	19,893	14,264	7,540	—	—	—	
Service persons college support[69]	—	18,900	74,690	46,617	35,630	8,911	—	—	—
Post-Vietnam veterans[70]	—	—	—	922	82,554	161,475	88,500	48,114	35,354
All-volunteer-force educational assistance:[71]	—	—	—	—	196	269,947	650,540	886,951	1,074,980
Veterans[72]	—	—	—	—	—	183,765	530,820	769,481	941,260
Reservists[73]	—	—	—	—	196	86,182	119,720	117,470	133,720
Veteran dependents' education[74]	21,700	36,330	114,310	176,334	131,494	100,494	103,440	96,644	95,469
Payments to state education agencies[75]	—	—	—	—	—	12,000	12,000	12,000	13,000
Other agencies									
Appalachian Regional Commission[31]	—	4,105	2,545	1,751	—	—	1,487	3,413	3,413
National Endowment for the Humanities[33]	—	3,349	25,320	56,451	49,098	50,938	58,512	58,404	58,000
National Science Foundation	27,170	42,000	60,283	64,583	60,069	161,884	210,375	225,168	265,126
Science and engineering education programs	27,170	37,000	60,283	64,583	60,069	161,884	210,375	225,168	265,126
Sea Grant Program[48]	—	5,000	—	—	—	—	—	—	—
United States Information Agency[76]	7,512	8,423	9,405	51,095	124,041	181,172	207,676	200,429	234,274
Educational and cultural affairs[64]	—	—	—	49,546	21,079	35,862	38,858	28,927	20,169
Educational and cultural exchange programs[77]	—	—	—	—	101,529	145,307	168,818	171,502	214,105
Educational exchange activities, international	—	—	—	1,549	1,433	3	—	—	—
Information center and library activities[78]	7,512	8,423	9,405	—	—	—	—	—	—
Other programs									
Barry Goldwater Scholarship and Excellence in Education Foundation[79]	—	—	—	—	—	1,033	2,900	2,789	2,871
Estimated education share of federal aid to the District of Columbia	1,895	5,513	10,564	13,143	15,266	14,637	16,382	8,896	10,754
Harry S Truman scholarship fund[43,80]	—	—	—	−1,895	1,332	2,883	2,401	2,323	3,571
Institute of American Indian and Alaskan Native Culture and Arts Development[81]	—	—	—	—	—	4,305	6,612	12,213	11,563
James Madison Memorial Fellowship Foundation[82]	—	—	—	—	—	191	885	1,464	2,207
Other education programs	**$374,652**	**$964,719**	**$1,608,478**	**$1,548,730**	**$2,107,588**	**$3,383,031**	**$3,991,955**	**$4,483,986**	**$5,014,434**
Department of Education[6]	182,021	630,235	1,045,659	747,706	1,173,055	2,251,801	2,579,883	2,795,988	3,177,071
Administration	17,732	47,456	108,372	187,317	284,900	328,293	368,420	403,877	465,118
Libraries	26,111	108,284	225,810	129,127	85,650	137,264	214,928	142,223	150,239
Rehabilitative services and disability research	137,313	473,091	709,483	426,886	798,298	1,780,360	1,991,875	2,244,226	2,554,116
American Printing House for the Blind	865	1,404	1,994	4,349	4,230	5,736	4,587	5,636	7,445
Trust funds[43]	—	—	—	—	27	−23	148	73	26	153
Department of Agriculture	87,551	135,637	220,395	271,112	336,375	352,511	400,442	426,316	430,679
Extension Service	85,924	131,734	215,523	263,584	325,986	337,907	385,087	409,110	413,272
National Agricultural Library	1,627	3,903	4,872	7,528	10,389	14,604	15,355	17,206	17,407
Department of Commerce	251	1,226	2,317	2,479	—	—	—	—	—
Maritime Administration:									
Training for private sector employees[49]	251	1,226	2,317	2,479	—	—	—	—	—
Department of Health and Human Services[14]	3,953	24,273	31,653	37,819	47,195	77,962	97,643	107,896	125,155
National Library of Medicine	3,953	24,273	31,653	37,819	47,195	77,962	97,643	107,896	125,155
Department of Housing and Urban Development	512	—	—	—	—	—	—	—	—
Urban mass transportation—managerial training grants[83]	512	—	—	—	—	—	—	—	—
Department of Justice	3,850	5,546	42,818	27,642	25,517	26,920	34,525	34,065	27,822
FBI National Academy	1,850	2,066	5,100	7,234	4,189	6,028	10,631	10,311	12,863
FBI Field Police Academy	1,450	2,500	5,254	7,715	10,220	10,548	12,578	11,790	8,903
Narcotics and dangerous drug training	550	980	1,152	2,416	83	850	695	275	559
National Institute of Corrections[84]	—	—	31,312	10,277	11,025	9,494	10,621	11,689	5,497
Department of State	10,780	20,672	28,113	25,000	23,791	47,539	44,086	46,557	46,675
Foreign Service Institute	6,395	15,857	20,750	25,000	23,791	47,539	44,086	46,557	46,675
Center for Cultural and Technical Interchange[64]	4,385	4,815	7,363	—	—	—	—	—	—
Department of Transportation[22]	—	3,964	11,877	10,212	3,785	1,507	2,419	500	500
Highways training and education grants[85]	—	2,418	3,250	3,412	1,500	—	1,945	—	—
Maritime Administration:									
Training for private sector employees[49]	—	—	—	—	1,135	1,507	474	500	500
Urban mass transportation—managerial training grants[83]	—	1,546	2,627	500	1,150	—	—	—	—
Federal Aviation Administration[86]									
Air traffic controllers second career program[87]	—	—	6,000	6,300	—	—	—	—	—
Department of the Treasury	—	18	3,096	14,584	16,160	41,488	51,694	61,992	63,923
Federal Law Enforcement Training Center[88]	—	18	3,096	14,584	16,160	41,488	51,694	61,992	63,923
Other agencies									
ACTION[89]	—	—	7,045	2,833	1,761	8,472	8,600	—	
Estimated education funds[90]	—	—	7,045	2,833	1,761	8,472	8,600		

Table 353.—Federal on-budget funds for education, by level or educational purpose, by agency and program: Fiscal years 1965 to 1995—Continued

[In thousands of dollars]

Level or educational purpose, by agency and program	1965	1970	1975	1980	1985	1990[1]	1992[2]	1994[3]	1995[4,5]
1	2	3	4	5	6	7	8	9	10
Agency for International Development	63,329	88,034	78,896	99,707	141,847	170,371	212,220	241,948	207,651
Education and human resources	53,968	61,570	58,349	80,518	115,104	142,801	195,570	221,988	190,651
American schools and hospitals abroad	9,361	26,464	20,547	19,189	26,743	27,570	16,650	19,960	17,000
Appalachian Regional Commission [31]	—	572	1,574	8,124	113	—	938	4,299	4,299
Corporation for National and Community Service [89]	—	—	—	—	—	—	—	93,250	145,900
Estimated education funds [90]	—	—	—	—	—	—	—	93,250	145,900
Federal Emergency Management Agency [91]	—	290	290	281	405	215	261	85,200	170,400
Estimated architect/engineer student development program [92]	—	40	40	31	155	200	250	—	—
Estimated other training programs [93]	—	250	250	250	250	15	11	—	—
Estimated disaster relief [94]	—	—	—	—	—	—	—	85,200	170,400
General Services Administration [95] Libraries and other archival activities	4,013	14,775	22,532	34,800	—	—	—	—	—
Japanese-United States Friendship Commission [96]	—	—	—	2,294	2,236	2,299	1,610	1,585	2,107
Library of Congress	15,111	29,478	63,766	151,871	169,310	189,827	296,044	312,724	337,417
Salaries and expenses	11,421	20,700	48,798	102,364	130,354	148,985	252,623	261,814	285,610
Books for the blind and the physically handicapped	2,317	6,195	11,908	31,436	32,954	37,473	38,688	46,600	46,502
Special foreign currency program	1,187	2,273	2,333	3,492	4,621	10	10	—	—
Furniture and furnishings	186	310	727	14,579	1,381	3,359	4,723	4,310	5,305
National Aeronautics and Space Administration Aerospace education services project	100	350	600	882	1,800	3,300	6,100	6,100	6,100
National Archives and Records Administration [97] Libraries and other archival activities	—	—	—	—	52,118	77,397	99,412	110,411	103,390
National Commission on Libraries and Information Science [98]	—	—	449	2,090	723	3,281	1,437	724	1,033
National Endowment for the Arts [32]	—	340	1,068	231	1,137	936	3,286	2,221	2,110
National Endowment for the Humanities [33]	—	5,090	38,486	85,805	76,252	89,706	99,782	99,064	100,000
Smithsonian Institution	2,233	2,461	5,509	5,153	7,886	5,779	6,578	10,059	9,986
Museum programs and related research	2,133	2,261	4,203	3,254	4,665	690	93	3,060	1,000
National Gallery of Art extension service	100	200	300	426	675	474	793	816	857
Woodrow Wilson International Center for Scholars	—	—	1,006	1,473	2,546	4,615	5,692	6,183	8,129
U.S. Information Agency—Center for Cultural and Technical Interchange [64]	—	—	—	15,115	18,966	20,375	29,550	30,064	37,515
U.S. Institute of Peace [99]	—	—	—	—	—	7,621	11,350	10,794	12,255
Other programs:									
Estimated education share of federal aid for the District of Columbia	948	1,758	2,335	2,990	7,156	3,724	4,095	2,229	2,446
Research programs at universities and related institutions [100]	**$1,816,276**	**$2,283,641**	**$3,418,410**	**$5,801,204**	**$8,844,575**	**$12,606,035**	**$14,176,863**	**$15,627,009**	**$15,925,815**
Department of Education [101]	13,248	87,823	82,770	78,742	28,809	89,483	154,800	276,838	330,439
Department of Agriculture	58,362	64,796	108,162	216,405	293,252	348,109	437,967	453,468	424,373
Department of Commerce	4,015	4,487	21,677	48,295	52,951	50,523	77,240	70,632	103,497
Department of Defense	436,912	356,188	364,929	644,455	1,245,888	1,871,864	2,070,959	2,104,990	1,791,338
Department of Energy	439,334	548,327	761,376	1,470,224	2,205,316	2,520,885	2,867,528	2,705,081	2,579,795
Department of Health and Human Services	474,362	623,765	1,273,037	2,087,053	3,228,014	4,902,714	5,210,711	6,368,586	6,639,868
Department of Housing and Urban Development	—	510	2,650	5,314	438	118	203	592	600
Department of the Interior	9,839	18,521	28,955	42,175	34,422	49,790	57,449	46,076	39,611
Department of Justice	—	1,945	8,902	9,189	5,168	6,858	4,986	2,316	2,300
Department of Labor	—	3,567	6,124	12,938	3,417	5,893	1,169	4,176	9,496
Department of State	—	8,220	10,973	188	29	1,519	200	15	15
Department of Transportation	—	12,328	28,478	31,910	22,621	28,608	35,015	68,107	68,426
Department of the Treasury	—	—	—	226	388	227	85	167	184
Department of Veterans Affairs	337	518	1,112	1,600	1,000	2,300	2,491	2,918	2,070
ACTION	—	—	36	—	—	—	—	—	—
Agency for International Development	—	—	—	77,063	56,960	79,415	32,979	28,327	26,928
Corporation for National and Community Service	—	—	—	—	—	—	—	—	—
Environmental Protection Agency	—	19,446	33,875	41,083	60,521	87,481	152,012	113,844	101,535
Federal Emergency Management Agency	—	—	—	1,665	1,423	—	—	—	—
National Aeronautics and Space Administration	208,688	258,016	197,301	254,629	485,824	1,090,003	1,377,322	1,548,508	1,808,211
National Science Foundation	154,046	253,628	475,011	743,809	1,087,046	1,427,007	1,664,697	1,800,658	1,965,994
Nuclear Regulatory Commission	—	—	7,093	32,590	30,261	42,328	27,418	25,735	25,060
Office of Economic Opportunity	7,078	20,035							
U.S. Arms Control and Disarmament Agency	—	100	—	661	395	25	100	—	—
U.S. Information Agency	—	—	—	—	—	—	—	—	—
Other agencies	10,055	1,421	5,949	990	432	885	1,532	5,975	6,075

[1] Excludes $4,440,000,000 for federal support for medical education benefits under Medicare in the U.S. Department of Health and Human Services. Is not included in the total because data before fiscal year 1990 are not available. This program has existed since Medicare began, but was not available as a separate budget item until FY 90.

[2] Excludes $5,350,000,000 for federal support for medical education benefits under Medicare in the U.S. Department of Health and Human Services. Is not included in the total because data before fiscal year 1990 are not included. This program has existed since Medicare began, but was not available as a separate budget item until FY 90.

[3] Excludes $6,150,000,000 for federal support for medical education benefits under Medicare in the U.S. Department of Health and Human Services. Is not included in the total because data before fiscal year 1990 are not available. This program has existed Medicare began, but was not available as a separate budget item until FY 90.

[4] Excludes $6,650,000,000 for federal support for medical education benefits under Medicare in the U.S. Department of Health and Human Services. Is not included in the total because data before fiscal year 1990 are not available. This program has existed since Medicare began, but was not available as a separate budget item until FY 90.

[5] Estimated.

[6] The U.S. Department of Education was created in May 1980. It formerly was the Office of Education in the U.S. Department of Health, Education, and Welfare.

[7] This program was funded by the U.S. Department of Education in FYs 65–81 in the Impact Aid program. This program provides for education of dependents of federal employees residing on federal property in cases where free public education is unavailable in the nearby community.

[8] This program creates a national framework for education reform and meeting the National Education Goals. This program includes the School-To-Work Opportunities program which will initiate a national system to be administered jointly by the U.S. Departments of Education and Labor. Both departments are to establish a national framework within which all states can create statewide systems to help youth acquire the knowledge, skills, abilities, and labor market information they need to make an effective transition from school to work or to further their education or training.

[9] Starting in FY 94, the Special Milk Program was included in the Child Nutrition Program.

[10] These commodities are purchased under Section 32 of the Act of August 24, 1935, for use in the child nutrition programs.

[11] This program assisted in the construction of public facilities, such as vocational schools, through grants or loans. No funds have been appropriated for this account since FY 77, and it was completely phased out in FY 84 after the monitoring of closeouts of projects was completed. Data are not available for previous years.

[12] The U.S. Department of Energy was created in 1977. It formerly was the Energy Research and Development Administration and before that the Atomic Energy Commission.

[13] This program was first established in 1979. Funds were first appropriated for this program in FY 80.

[14] The U.S. Department of Health and Human Services was part of the U.S. Department of Health, Education, and Welfare until May 1980.

[15] The Head Start program was formerly in the Office of Economic Opportunity, and funds were appropriated to the U.S. Department of Health, Education, and Welfare, Office of Child Development, beginning in 1972.

[16] This program was created by the Family Support Act of 1988. It provides funds for the Job Opportunities and Basic Skills Training Program.

[17] After age 18, benefits terminate at the end of the school term or in 3 months, whichever is less.

[18] This program provides funding for supplemental programs for eligible Indian students in public schools.

[19] This program finances the cost of academic, social, and occupational education courses for inmates in federal prisons.

[20] The Job Corps program was formerly in the Office of Economic Opportunity, and funds were appropriated to the U.S. Department of Labor beginning in 1971 and 1972.

[21] Some of the work and training programs included in this program were in the Office of Economic Opportunity and were transferred to the U.S. Department of Labor in 1971 and 1972. Beginning in FY 94, School-to-Work Opportunities program is included. This program is administered jointly by the U.S. Department of Education and Labor.

[22] The U.S. Department of Transportation was created in 1967.

[23] This program was transferred from the U.S. Department of the Treasury to the U.S. Department of Transportation in 1967.

[24] This program was established in FY 72 and closed in FY 86.

[25] The states' share of revenue-sharing funds could not be spent on education in FYs 81–86.

[26] The U.S. Department of Veterans Affairs, formerly the Veterans Administration, was created in March 1989.

[27] This program provides educational assistance allowances in order to restore lost educational opportunities to those individuals whose careers were interrupted or impeded by reason of active military service between January 31, 1955, and January 1, 1977. Includes "Readjustment Benefits," Chapter 34, for education other than college and also includes the Veterans Job Training Program for service persons and veterans. Chapter 34 program closed December 31, 1989. The Veterans Job Training Program was put in the program Payments to State Education Agencies. Veterans who were still eligible to receive benefits under Chapter 34 were put in Chapter 30 (The All-Volunteer-Force Educational Assistance program).

[28] This program is in "Readjustment Benefits" program, Chapter 31, and covers the costs of subsistence, tuition, books, supplies, and equipment for disabled veterans requiring vocational rehabilitation.

[29] This program is in the "Readjustment Benefits" program, Chapter 35, and provides benefits to children and spouses of veterans.

[30] The purpose of this program is to provide stable and permanent employment to those men and women who have served on active duty on or after August 2, 1990, and are unemployed.

[31] This agency was established March 9, 1965. First year of appropriations was 1966. The outlays were larger in the years 1970 and 1975 for elementary and secondary education because of the construction of facilities for vocational schools.

[32] This agency was established in 1965. In 1970, $900,000 was appropriated through the Office of Education, U.S. Department of Health, Education, and Welfare, for the National Endowment for the Arts, Arts in Education program.

[33] This agency was established in 1965. First year of appropriations was 1966.

[34] The Economic Opportunity Act of 1964 authorized 10 major action programs, including Job Corps, Neighborhood Youth Corps, Adult Literacy, Work Experience, College Work-Study, and Community Action programs, including Head Start, Follow Through, and Upward Bound, and authorized the establishment of Volunteers in Service to America (VISTA). These programs were transferred to the U.S. Department of Health, Education, and Welfare, U.S. Department of Labor, and the Action Agency in the 1970s. An act on January 4, 1975 established the Community Services Administration as the successor agency to the Office of Economic Opportunity.

[35] Head Start program funds were transferred to the U.S. Department of Health, Education, and Welfare, Office of Child Development, in 1972.

[36] Most of these programs were transferred to the U.S. Department of Health, Education, and Welfare, Office of Education, in 1972.

[37] The Job Corps programs were transferred to the U.S. Department of Labor in 1971 and 1972.

[38] These programs were transferred to the U.S. Department of Labor in 1971 and 1972.

[39] These programs were transferred to the Action Agency in 1972.

[40] Similar programs were included in the "higher education" program in 1965 through 1975.

[41] The Student Loan Reform Act of 1993 authorized a new Federal Direct Student Loan (FDSL) program, recently renamed the William D. Ford Direct Loan program. This program is a new streamlined lending system that will simplify the process of obtaining and repaying loans for student and parent borrowers and will provide borrowers with greater choice in repayment plans. The FDSL program will replace the FFEL program and be phased in, beginning with the 1994–95 academic year.

[42] Similar programs were included in the "higher education" program in 1965 through 1975. Formerly called the "Guaranteed Student Loan" program. The large drop in FY 94 reflects a $4.79 billion loan prepayment from the Student Loan Marketing Association of its outstanding debt to the Treasury Department.

[43] Negative amounts occur when program receipts exceed outlays.

[44] This program was transferred from the U.S. Department of Housing and Urban Development to the U.S. Department of Health, Education, and Welfare, Office of Education, in FY 79.

[45] The Historically Black Colleges and Universities (HBCUs) Capital Financing program was authorized by the Higher Education Act Amendments of 1992 to provide HBCUs with private funds for projects such as repairs, renovation and construction of classrooms, libraries, laboratories, dormitories, instructional equipment, and research instruments.

[46] First year of appropriations for this program was 1967.

[47] Program funds were first appropriated for Tuskegee Institute in 1972.

[48] The Sea Grant College Program Act of 1966 established a matching fund grant program that provides for the establishment of a network of programs in fields related to development and preservation of the nation's coastal and marine resources. This program was transferred from the National Science Foundation to the U.S. Department of Commerce, October 1970. Appropriations began in 1968.

[49] This program was transferred to the U.S. Department of Transportation in FY 81 by Public Law 97–31, from the U.S. Department of Commerce.

[50] The U.S. Department of Defense funds for FYs 90 to 95 exclude military pay and reserve accounts which were included in previous years. FY 65 data are not available except for service academies.

[51] Included in total above.

[52] Instructional costs only are included. These include academics, audiovisual, academic computing center, faculty training, military training, physical education, and libraries.

[53] Includes special education programs (military and civilian); legal education program; flight training; advanced degree program; college degree program (officers); and "Armed Forces Health Professions Scholarship" program.

[54] No funds have been appropriated for this program since FY 82.

[55] This program receives funds periodically.

[56] Appropriations began in FY 84.

[57] Appropriations began in FY 89.

[58] Does not include higher education assistance loans.

[59] Appropriations began in FY 78.

[60] Alcohol, drug abuse, and mental health training programs are included starting in fiscal year 1992.

[61] Beginning in fiscal year 1992, data were included in the National Institutes of Health training grants program.

[62] Postsecondary student benefits were ended by the Omnibus Budget Reconciliation Act of 1981 (Public Law 97–35) and were completely phased out by August 1985.

[63] Includes adult education, tribally-controlled community colleges, postsecondary instruction, and other education.

[64] This program was transferred from the U.S. Department of State to the International Communication Agency (ICA) in the Reorganization Plan No. 2 of 1977, which consolidated the functions of the U.S. Information Agency (USIA) and the U.S. Department of State's Bureau of Educational and Cultural Affairs. In FY 82 the ICA became the USIA.

[65] This program provides funds for advanced study and research projects of the Russian, Eurasian, and Eastern European countries by American institutions of higher education and private research firms. Appropriations began in FY 88.

[66] This program was transferred to the U.S. Department of Transportation in FY 81 by Public Law 97–31 from the U.S. Department of Commerce.

[67] Includes flight training. This program was in the U.S. Department of the Treasury in 1965 and was transferred to the U.S. Department of Transportation in 1967.

[68] Includes Vietnam-era veterans under Chapter 34 (GI Bill) of the "Readjustment Benefits" education and training program. This program provides educational assistance allowances, primarily on a monthly basis, in order to restore lost educational opportunities to those individuals whose careers were interrupted or impeded by reason of active military service between January 31, 1955, and January 1, 1977. This program closed December 31, 1989. Some veterans who were still eligible were put in Chapter 30 (the All-Volunteer-Force Educational Assistance program).

[69] Includes service persons under Chapter 34 (GI Bill) of the "Readjustment Benefits" education and training program. Service persons with over 180 days of active duty, any part of which was before January 1, 1977, are eligible to participate in this program.

[70] Includes post-Vietnam-era veterans, under Chapter 32, of the post-Vietnam-era "Veterans Education Account." Provides education and training assistance payments to veterans and service persons with no active duty time before January 1, 1977. Funding is provided through participants' contributions while on active duty and through transfers from the U.S. Department of Defense (DOD). Participants' contributions, up to a maximum of $2,700, are deposited to the fund prior to discharge. When the participant enters training, the monthly disbursement from his or her account is matched two for one from funds provided by DOD. Additional amounts in the form of incentive bonuses may also be provided by DOD funds. The U.S. Department of Veterans Affairs funds are not appropriated for this program, so these data represent obligations.

[71] Public Law 98–525, enacted October 19, 1984 (New GI Bill), established two new peacetime educational programs: an assistance program for veterans who enter active duty during the period beginning July 1, 1985, and ending on June 30, 1988, and an assistance program for certain members of the Selected Reserve.

[72] Chapter 30, also called the Montgomery Bill, and the new GI Bill are for eligible veterans who have agreed to have their military pay reduced $100 per month for their first 12 months of active duty in order to participate in this program. The "Readjustment Benefits" account under the U.S. Department of Veterans Affairs pays only the basic allowance, up to a maximum of $300 per month, for full-time training. "Supplemental Benefits" are paid by the U.S. Department of Defense (DOD).

[73] Chapter 106 is for members of the Selected Reserve. The reserve components include the Army, Navy, Air Force, Marine Corps Reserve, Army National Guard and Air

National Guard under the U.S. Department of Defense (DOD), and the Coast Guard Reserve, which is under the U.S. Department of Transportation (DOT) when it is not operating as a service in the Navy. Eligible persons can receive up to $140 per month for full-time training. The DOD and DOT pay for this program, and the U.S. Department of Veterans Affairs administers it.

[74] Includes dependents of veterans under Chapter 35, the "Readjustment Benefits" education and training program. Provides education and training benefits to dependents of veterans who died of a service-connected disability or whose service-connected disability is rated permanent and total.

[75] These payments have been made to state education agencies for years but they were not available as a separate budget item until FY 88.

[76] The USIA was called the "International Communication Agency" in FYs 80 and 81.

[77] This program was in the "Educational and Cultural Affairs" program in FYs 80–83, and became an independent program in FY 84.

[78] This program was combined with the "educational and cultural affairs" program in FY 77.

[79] Public Law 99–661 established this program to operate the scholarship program in tribute to the former Senator from Arizona. The Foundation awards scholarships and fellowships to outstanding graduate and undergraduate students who intend to pursue careers or advanced degrees in science or mathematics. The Foundation may also award honoraria to outstanding individuals who have made significant contributions to improve the instruction of science and mathematics in secondary schools.

[80] Appropriations for this program began in FY 76.

[81] Public Law 99–498 established this Institute as an independent non-profit corporation administered by a Board of Trustees. The Institute provides Native Americans with an opportunity to obtain a postsecondary education in various fields of Indian art and culture.

[82] Public Laws 99–500 and 99–591 established the James Madison Memorial Fellowship Foundation to operate a fellowship program to encourage graduate study of the American Constitution. First year of appropriations was FY 88.

[83] This program was transferred to the U.S. Department of Transportation in FY 68 from the U.S. Department of Housing and Urban Development.

[84] This program was established by the Juvenile Justice and Delinquency Prevention Act of 1974 to provide education and training and to provide leadership in improving correctional programs and practices in prisons. FY 75 had large outlays because of the construction of buildings and facilities.

[85] Appropriations for this program began in FY 70. This program is part of the Federal-Aid Highway Act of 1970, Public Law 91–605.

[86] The Federal Aviation Administration was an independent agency and was transferred to the U.S. Department of Transportation in FY 67.

[87] Appropriations began in FY 72. No funds have been appropriated since FY 82.

[88] First year of appropriations was FY 70.

[89] The National Service Trust Act of 1993 established a new agency, the Corporation for National and Community Service. On October 1, 1993 ACTION became part of the Corporation for National and Community Service. ACTION was established on July 1, 1971. This agency brings together a number of volunteer programs. Some of these funds were formerly in the Office of Economic Opportunity.

[90] These programs included the Service Learning Programs, University Year for ACTION, Volunteers in Service to America, Youth Challenge Program, and the National Student Volunteer Program in FY 1975. In FY 80 programs included were the University Year for ACTION, Young Volunteers for ACTION, and National Service Learning Programs. In fiscal year 1985, the program included was the Service Learning Programs, and in FYs 89 to 94, programs included were the Literacy Corps and the Student Community Services Program. In FYs 94 and 95 the AmeriCorp program is included. This program provides education grants of up to $4,725 per year, for up to 2 years, to help pay for college or to repay student loans to people age 17 years or older who perform community service before, during or after postsecondary education.

[91] The Federal Emergency Management Agency was created on March 25, 1979, representing a combination of five existing agencies. The two largest were the Defense Civil Preparedness Agency in the U.S. Department of Defense and the Federal Preparedness Agency in the General Services Administration. The funds for the Federal Emergency Management Agency in FY 70 to FY 75 were in the other agencies.

[92] First year of appropriations was FY 68.

[93] First appropriations for the "other training programs" were in the late 1960s. These programs include the Fall-Out Shelter Analysis, Blast Protection Design through 1992. Starting in FY 1993 earthquake training and safety for teachers and administrators for grades 1 through 12 are included.

[94] The disaster relief program repairs and replaces damaged and destroyed school buildings. In FY 94 and FY 95 repairs were for the Northridge Earthquake in California. In FY 94, $37.2 million was spent on schools districts; $4.2 million was spent on community colleges and $43.8 million spent on universities. In FY 95, $74.4 million was spent on school districts; $8.4 million on community colleges and $87.6 million on colleges and universities.

[95] This program was transferred from the General Services Administration to the National Archives and Records Administration in April 1985.

[96] This program makes grants for the promotion of scholarly, cultural, and artistic exchanges between Japan and the United States. Appropriations began in FY 76.

[97] The National Archives and Records Administration became an independent agency in April 1985.

[98] This program was established by the act of July 20, 1970, Public Law 91–345.

[99] This program was established by Congress to conduct and support research and scholarships in the fields of peace, arms control, and conflict resolution. This program began operation in February 1986.

[100] Includes federal obligations for research and development centers administered by colleges and universities. FYs 94 and 95 are estimated.

[101] Total outlays for FYs 65 and 70 include the "Research and Training" program. FY 75 includes the "National Institute of Education" program. FYs 80 to 95 include outlays for the Office of Educational Research and Improvement.

—Not available or not applicable.

NOTE.—Some data have been revised from previously published figures. To the extent possible, amounts reported represent outlays rather than obligations.

SOURCE: U.S. Department of Education, National Center for Education Statistics, compiled from data appearing in U.S. Office of Management and Budget, *Budget of the U.S. Government,* fiscal years 1967 to 1996; National Science Foundation, *Federal Funds for Research and Development,* fiscal years 1965 to 1995; and unpublished data obtained from various federal agencies. (This table was prepared June 1995.)

Table 354.—Estimated federal support for education, by agency and type of ultimate recipient: Fiscal year 1995

[In millions of dollars]

Agency	Total	Local education agencies	State education agencies	College students	Institutions of higher education	Federal	Multiple types of recipients	Other[1]
1	2	3	4	5	6	7	8	9
Total[2]	$100,076.4	$20,745.1	$5,463.1	$18,495.1	$31,046.2	$3,135.2	$10,385.0	$10,806.8
Total program funds - on-budget	$73,828.1	$20,745.1	$4,903.2	$7,801.9	$21,477.4	$3,135.2	$10,385.0	$5,380.5
Department of Education	32,947.4	11,959.9	4,150.3	4,886.0	5,020.6	535.4	1,649.2	4,745.9
Department of Agriculture	9,050.0	8,093.1	76.4	—	449.8	17.4	—	413.3
Department of Commerce	108.0	—	—	—	108.0	—	—	—
Department of Defense	3,744.5	119.6	—	194.9	1,938.4	1,263.3	228.4	—
Department of Energy	2,608.3	10.5	—	2.1	2,594.7	—	1.0	—
Department of Health and Human Services	12,681.6	353.4	—	981.6	7,002.0	125.2	4,219.5	—
Department of Housing and Urban Development	0.6	—	—	—	0.6	—	—	—
Department of the Interior	691.1	63.5	18.6	32.3	121.3	411.5	43.9	—
Department of Justice	168.9	—	—	—	2.3	166.6	—	—
Department of Labor	4,309.0	—	644.9	—	9.5	—	3,654.6	—
Department of State	49.3	—	—	—	1.3	46.7	—	1.3
Department of Transportation	126.1	—	—	0.2	68.6	43.3	2.8	11.3
Department of Treasury	64.1	—	—	—	0.2	63.9	—	—
Department of Veterans Affairs	1,531.3	—	13.0	1,516.2	2.1	—	—	—
Other agencies and programs								
Agency for International Development	234.6	—	—	—	26.9	—	—	207.7
Appalachian Regional Commission	10.2	—	—	—	3.4	—	6.8	—
Barry Goldwater Scholarship and Excellence in Education Foundation	2.9	—	—	—	—	—	2.9	—
Corporation for National and Community Service	145.9	—	—	—	—	—	145.9	—
Environmental Protection Agency	101.5	—	—	—	101.5	—	—	—
Estimated education share of federal aid to the District of Columbia	83.9	70.7	—	—	10.8	—	2.4	—
Federal Emergency Management Agency	170.4	74.4	—	—	96.0	—	—	—
General Services Administration	—	—	—	—	—	—	—	—
Harry S Truman scholarship fund	3.6	—	—	—	—	—	3.6	—
Institute of American Indian and Alaskan Native Culture and Arts Development	11.6	—	—	—	—	—	11.6	—
James Madison Memorial Fellowship Foundation	2.2	—	—	—	—	—	2.2	—
Japanese-United States Friendship Commission	2.1	—	—	—	—	—	2.1	—
Library of Congress	337.4	—	—	—	—	337.4	—	—
National Aeronautics and Space Administration	1,814.3	—	—	—	1,808.2	—	6.1	—
National Archives and Records Administration	103.4	—	—	—	—	103.4	—	—
National Commission on Libraries and Information Science	1.0	—	—	—	—	—	—	1.0
National Endowment for the Arts	7.1	—	—	—	—	—	7.1	—
National Endowment for the Humanities	159.5	—	—	—	—	—	159.5	—
National Science Foundation	2,231.1	—	—	151.1	2,080.0	—	—	—
Nuclear Regulatory Commission	25.1	—	—	—	25.1	—	—	—
Smithsonian Institution	10.0	—	—	—	—	0.9	9.1	—
U.S. Arms Control and Disarmament Agency	—	—	—	—	—	—	—	—
U.S. Information Agency	271.8	—	—	37.5	—	20.2	214.1	—
U.S. Institute of Peace	12.3	—	—	—	—	—	12.3	—
Other agencies	6.1	—	—	—	6.1	—	—	—
Off-budget support and nonfederal funds generated by federal legislation	26,248.2	—	559.9	10,693.2	9,568.8	—	—	5,426.3

[1] Other recipients include Indian tribes, private nonprofit agencies, and banks.
[2] Includes on-budget funds, off-budget support, and nonfederal funds generated by federal legislation. Excludes federal tax expenditures.
—Data not available or not applicable.

NOTE.—Outlays by type of recipient are estimated based on obligation data. Because of rounding, details may not add to totals.

SOURCE: U.S. Department of Education, Office of the Undersecretary, unpublished tabulations; U.S. Office of Management and Budget, *Budget of the U.S. Government Fiscal Year 1996*, National Science Foundation, *Federal Funds for Research and Development, Fiscal Years 1993, 1994, and 1995*; and unpublished data obtained from various federal agencies. (This table was prepared June 1995.)

Table 355.—Federal on-budget funds obligated for programs administered by the Department of Education: Fiscal years 1980 to 1995

[In thousands of dollars]

Program	1980	1985	1989	1990	1991	1992	1993	1994 [1]	1995 [2]
1	2	3	4	5	6	7	8	9	10
Total	$14,102,165	$18,818,201	$24,473,634	$25,214,923	$28,543,858	$34,966,632	$33,748,670	$36,644,942	$47,417,335
Elementary and secondary education	4,239,022	4,732,864	5,997,160	7,169,693	8,061,767	8,606,349	8,565,459	8,729,009	9,184,149
Grants for the disadvantaged	3,204,664	3,745,855	4,600,444	5,383,960	6,233,448	6,717,712	6,659,203	7,038,334	7,245,118
School improvement programs	788,918	748,000	1,129,444	1,524,001	1,555,406	1,587,369	1,600,013	1,368,108	1,609,613
Bilingual education	169,540	171,605	196,309	188,152	197,885	224,911	225,693	239,805	245,237
Indian education	75,900	67,404	70,963	73,580	75,028	76,357	80,550	82,762	84,181
School assistance in federally affected areas	812,873	695,746	731,768	815,573	785,807	835,394	760,456	911,716	879,660
Maintenance and operations	690,000	665,000	708,396	717,354	738,746	744,491	713,108	787,263	761,368
Construction	110,873	23,037	18,400	22,929	38,961	43,155	5,291	8,584	28,593
Disaster assistance	12,000	7,709	4,972	75,290	8,100	47,748	42,057	115,869	89,699
Education for the handicapped	1,555,253	2,666,056	3,814,846	3,480,122	4,695,615	4,750,048	4,752,116	5,965,688	6,093,910
State grant programs	815,805	1,245,219	1,642,647	1,258,871	2,214,902	1,980,432	1,842,956	2,779,228	2,501,786
Early childhood education [3]	38,745	27,625	319,012	280,341	387,282	480,599	476,180	661,665	966,305
Special centers, projects, and research	55,075	53,430	102,141	72,966	117,333	109,976	139,265	101,605	104,851
Captioned films and media services	17,778	35,670	13,346	15,191	16,326	16,593	17,571	18,608	19,142
Personnel training	55,375	68,025	67,023	70,838	69,288	89,753	90,120	104,012	104,874
Handicapped rehabilitation service and research	572,475	1,236,087	1,670,677	1,781,915	1,890,484	2,072,695	2,186,024	2,300,570	2,396,952
Vocational education and adult programs	1,153,743	856,271	1,052,470	1,138,674	800,661	1,774,664	1,575,268	1,456,185	1,602,882
Basic programs [4]	744,653	725,624	859,239	858,716	472,275	1,253,148	1,049,834	950,244	1,012,166
Consumer and homemaking	63,169	33,138	32,816	34,517	18,210	48,989	35,872	33,895	35,234
Program improvement and supportive services	162,512	5,202	—	—	—	—	—	—	—
State planning and advisory councils	13,423	7,584	7,945	7,923	8,803	9,325	8,928	9,087	9,006
Adult education, grants to states	153,724	84,723	139,771	188,280	201,032	235,650	309,810	254,724	252,345
Other [5]	16,262	—	12,699	49,238	100,341	227,552	170,824	208,235	294,131
Postsecondary student financial assistance	5,108,534	8,534,205	11,482,608	11,112,068	12,477,771	17,008,333	16,065,617	17,400,855	27,247,641
Educational opportunity grants [6]	2,534,378	3,558,440	5,379,725	4,919,264	5,867,491	6,274,116	6,764,683	7,092,393	7,616,125
Work-study	596,065	599,467	620,644	615,269	607,922	621,139	625,043	620,878	616,508
Perkins loan program	322,749	219,850	202,904	157,415	175,325	157,518	183,262	177,413	172,500
Federal Family Education Loan program [7]	1,597,877	4,130,920	5,203,843	5,341,039	5,733,383	9,855,159	8,380,619	8,444,937	10,312,227
Other student assistance programs [8]	57,465	25,528	75,492	79,081	93,650	100,401	112,010	1,065,234	8,530,281
Direct aid to postsecondary institutions	277,068	329,714	398,318	341,634	445,258	518,380	518,908	740,677	829,726
Aid to minority and developing institutions	114,680	140,374	179,062	99,812	111,506	130,215	130,743	211,054	244,731
Special programs for the disadvantaged	147,389	174,940	219,256	241,822	333,752	388,165	388,165	529,623	584,995
Cooperative education	14,999	14,400	—	—	—	—	—	—	—
Higher education facilities	268,493	194,556	77,362	84,305	84,599	92,923	81,026	49,888	50,052
Construction loans and insurance	35,362	33,188	37,109	30,000	29,277	38,095	46,472	20,607	19,034
Interest subsidy grants	24,626	24,968	22,524	38,741	39,866	41,181	22,647	18,188	18,170
College housing loans	208,505	136,400	17,729	15,564	15,456	13,647	11,907	11,093	12,848
Other higher education programs	34,927	74,340	73,574	188,999	187,039	198,993	201,734	129,951	130,679
International education and foreign languages [9]	19,977	32,050	—	86,337	91,100	107,812	114,761	—	—
Fund for Improvement of Postsecondary Education [10]	12,000	12,710	67,236	99,450	87,826	87,831	86,257	129,554	126,679
Other	2,950	29,580	6,338	3,212	8,113	3,350	716	397	4,000
Public library services	101,218	116,027	141,884	132,583	142,252	148,208	144,380	149,591	156,769
Public library services	66,451	75,000	80,944	82,505	83,897	83,898	83,227	83,227	83,277
Interlibrary cooperation	—	18,000	18,826	19,551	19,908	19,908	19,749	19,749	23,700
Public library construction	—	16,027	27,289	14,837	18,554	17,179	14,871	21,074	30,400
Research libraries	5,992	6,000	5,675	6,593	5,855	5,855	5,808	5,808	—
Other	28,775	1,000	9,150	9,097	14,038	21,368	20,725	19,733	19,392
Payments to special institutions	273,860	253,622	284,056	292,736	306,833	327,521	320,455	321,753	336,364
American Printing House for the Blind	4,349	5,500	5,335	5,663	6,136	5,900	6,298	6,463	6,680
National Technical Institute for the Deaf	19,799	31,400	33,326	35,594	37,598	39,278	40,964	41,836	43,191
Gallaudet College	49,409	59,092	65,998	67,643	72,261	76,540	77,589	78,435	80,030
Howard University	200,303	157,630	179,397	183,836	190,838	205,803	195,604	195,019	206,463
Departmental accounts	277,174	364,800	419,588	458,536	556,256	705,819	763,251	789,629	905,503
Educational research and improvement	51,415	60,556	78,263	87,074	140,367	267,569	283,078	294,323	354,892
Departmental management account	223,857	300,885	341,286	370,844	415,469	438,246	480,166	495,249	550,473
Other	1,875	3,349	39	618	420	4	7	57	138
Trust funds	27	10							

[1] Revised from previously published data.

[2] Estimated.

[3] Includes preschool incentive grants.

[4] Includes programs of national significance and special programs for the disadvantaged.

[5] Includes national programs for research, demonstrations, evaluation and technical assistance, literacy training for homeless adults, and some other small programs.

[6] Includes Pell Grants, Supplemental Education Opportunity Grants, State Student Incentive Grants, and Income Contingent Loans.

[7] Formerly the Guaranteed Student Loan program.

[8] Includes Federal Direct Student Loan program starting in fiscal year 1994.

[9] This program starting in fiscal year 1994 is included under the program, "Fund for Improvement of Postsecondary Education."

[10] International education and foreign languages is included under this program starting in fiscal year 1994.

—Data are not available or not applicable.

NOTE.—Because of rounding, details may not add to totals. Data presented in this tabulation are obligations, which differ from outlay figures reported in other tables in this chapter. Some data have been revised from previously published figures.

SOURCE: U.S. Office of Management and Budget, *Budget of the United States Government,* fiscal years 1982 to 1996. (This table was prepared March 1995.)

**Table 356.—U.S. Department of Education outlays, by level of education and type of recipient:
Fiscal years 1980 to 1995**

[In millions of dollars]

Year and area of education	Total	Local education agencies	State education agencies	College students	Institutions of higher education	Federal	Multiple types of recipients	Other [1]
1	2	3	4	5	6	7	8	9
1980 total	**$13,137.8**	**$5,313.7**	**$1,103.2**	**$2,137.4**	**$2,267.2**	**$249.8**	**$693.8**	**$1,372.7**
Elementary/secondary	6,629.1	5,309.4	662.2	34.2	22.0	62.5	513.4	25.5
Postsecondary education	5,682.2	—	99.5	2,103.2	2,166.5	—	—	1,313.0
Other programs	747.7	4.3	341.5	—	—	187.3	180.4	34.2
Education research and statistics	78.7	—	—	—	78.7	—	—	—
1982 total	**14,109.3**	**5,425.8**	**1,414.2**	**1,610.2**	**1,951.8**	**268.3**	**535.4**	**2,903.6**
Elementary/secondary	6,456.3	5,420.8	593.8	48.9	21.9	2.6	340.3	27.9
Postsecondary education	6,418.8	—	196.6	1,561.3	1,847.7	—	—	2,813.2
Other programs	1,152.0	5.0	623.8	—	—	265.7	195.1	62.5
Education research and statistics	82.2	—	—	—	82.2	—	—	—
1984 total	**15,534.7**	**5,256.5**	**1,879.0**	**2,193.4**	**2,167.4**	**330.2**	**516.7**	**3,191.4**
Elementary/secondary	6,220.8	5,252.4	536.0	55.5	35.3	22.9	259.9	58.8
Postsecondary education	7,341.2	—	211.5	2,137.9	1,972.5	—	—	3,019.3
Other programs	1,813.1	4.1	1,131.5	—	—	307.3	256.8	113.3
Education research and statistics	159.6	—	—	—	159.6	—	—	—
1985 total	**16,701.1**	**6,225.0**	**1,502.9**	**2,434.7**	**2,362.3**	**287.3**	**503.9**	**3,385.0**
Elementary/secondary	7,296.7	6,220.8	636.0	58.0	25.2	2.4	322.4	31.9
Postsecondary education	8,202.5	—	228.3	2,376.7	2,308.3	—	—	3,289.2
Other programs	1,173.1	4.2	638.6	—	—	284.9	181.5	63.9
Education research and statistics	28.8	—	—	—	28.8	—	—	—
1986 total	**17,740.1**	**6,435.1**	**1,823.3**	**2,685.9**	**2,637.2**	**265.4**	**625.8**	**3,267.5**
Elementary/secondary	7,552.0	6,432.1	558.5	68.3	45.2	2.2	372.0	73.8
Postsecondary education	8,444.9	—	215.6	2,617.6	2,523.0	—	—	3,088.7
Other programs	1,674.2	3.0	1,049.2	—	—	263.2	253.8	105.0
Education research and statistics	69.0	—	—	—	69.0	—	—	—
1988 total	**18,326.9**	**6,614.8**	**2,234.6**	**3,103.4**	**2,519.5**	**319.4**	**838.8**	**2,696.3**
Elementary/secondary	8,098.4	6,606.3	717.9	66.2	39.5	23.8	616.7	28.0
Postsecondary education	8,247.1	—	184.60	3,037.2	2,437.6	—	—	2,587.7
Other programs	1,939.0	8.5	1,332.1	—	—	295.6	222.1	80.6
Education research and statistics	42.4	—	—	—	42.4	—	—	—
1990 total	**23,198.5**	**8,000.7**	**2,490.3**	**3,859.6**	**3,649.8**	**441.4**	**912.2**	**3,844.4**
Elementary/secondary	9,681.3	7,995.0	700.3	80.5	85.4	113.1	650.7	56.3
Postsecondary education	11,176.0	—	261.6	3,779.1	3,475.0	—	—	3,660.4
Other programs	2,251.8	5.7	1,528.5	—	—	328.3	261.5	127.8
Education research and statistics	89.5	—	—	—	89.5	—	—	—
1992 total	**26,116.0**	**9,834.7**	**2,883.2**	**4,090.7**	**4,107.4**	**418.3**	**1,189.4**	**3,592.4**
Elementary/secondary	12,057.7	9,830.1	1,011.0	92.9	232.7	49.8	762.3	78.8
Postsecondary education	11,323.6	—	245.5	3,997.7	3,719.9	—	—	3,360.5
Other programs	2,579.9	4.6	1,626.6	—	—	368.5	427.0	153.1
Education research and statistics	154.8	—	—	—	154.8	—	—	—
1993 total	**30,478.2**	**10,459.3**	**3,123.0**	**5,274.8**	**5,264.0**	**404.5**	**1,200.2**	**4,752.4**
Elementary/secondary	13,059.0	10,451.5	1,261.0	110.5	281.9	51.0	823.3	79.8
Postsecondary education	14,660.7	—	225.9	5,164.3	4,749.9	—	—	4,520.6
Other programs	2,526.4	7.8	1,636.1	—	—	353.5	376.9	152.0
Education research and statistics	232.2	—	—	—	232.2	—	—	—
1994 total	**28,879.7**	**11,635.6**	**3,683.5**	**4,789.4**	**4,890.9**	**530.1**	**1,368.2**	**1,982.1**
Elementary/secondary	14,825.8	11,629.2	1,580.0	170.5	295.2	60.9	1,002.1	87.9
Postsecondary education	10,699.0	—	42.2	4,618.9	4,279.3	—	—	1,758.6
Other programs	3,038.6	6.4	2,061.3	—	—	469.2	366.1	135.6
Education research and statistics	316.4	—	—	—	316.4	—	—	—
1995 total	**32,947.4**	**11,959.9**	**4,150.3**	**4,886.0**	**5,020.6**	**535.4**	**1,649.2**	**4,745.9**
Elementary/secondary	15,378.6	11,952.4	1,760.4	190.5	170.1	70.3	1,196.9	37.9
Postsecondary education	14,061.3	—	250.8	4,695.5	4,520.0	—	—	4,595.0
Other programs	3,177.1	7.4	2,139.2	—	—	465.1	452.3	113.0
Education research and statistics	330.4	—	—	—	330.4	—	—	—

[1] Other recipients include Indian tribes, private nonprofit agencies, and banks.
—Data are not available or not applicable.

NOTE.—Outlays by type of recipient are estimated based on obligation data. Because of rounding, details may not add to totals.

SOURCE: U.S. Office of Management and Budget, *Budget of the U.S. Government,* Fiscal Years 1982 to 1996, and *Catalog of Federal Domestic Assistance;* National Science Foundation, *Federal Funds for Research and Development,* Fiscal Years 1980 to 1995; and unpublished data obtained from various federal agencies. (This table was prepared June 1995.)

Table 357.—U.S. Department of Education obligations for major programs, by state or other area: Fiscal year 1994

[In thousands]

State or other area	Total	Grants for the disadvantaged [1]	Block grants to states for school improvement [2]	School assistance in federally affected areas [3]	Vocational and adult education [4]	Education for the handicapped [5]	Bilingual education [6]	Indian education	Higher and continuing education [7]	Student financial assistance [8]	Public library programs [9]	Rehabilitation services [10]	Goals 2000 [11]
1	2	3	4	5	6	7	8	9	10	11	12	13	14
Total	$24,465,205	$6,883,656	$1,032,040	$736,574	$1,360,771	$3,415,767	$224,246	$73,887	$1,142,490	$7,375,058	$124,050	$2,035,216	$61,449
Alabama	446,703	122,402	16,808	4,829	27,314	50,096	1,309	1,005	41,174	134,937	1,923	44,905	0
Alaska	140,161	18,247	4,984	76,172	5,367	10,089	525	6,879	2,470	7,052	466	7,459	451
Arizona	409,294	100,910	15,057	64,973	21,431	36,734	7,750	8,807	11,831	107,840	2,159	30,469	1,333
Arkansas	240,676	75,692	9,900	1,909	15,850	27,244	250	107	13,268	67,065	1,269	27,152	970
California	2,836,294	822,081	115,874	64,330	144,353	530,178	76,068	5,016	89,458	774,854	12,299	191,520	10,263
Colorado	286,821	68,191	12,871	7,983	16,569	37,710	4,743	774	12,742	102,887	1,591	19,699	1,062
Connecticut	191,729	54,228	10,719	7,190	13,237	40,016	1,064	28	8,721	37,471	1,598	16,519	940
Delaware	56,804	14,087	5,028	73	5,672	5,749	250	0	3,810	10,154	994	7,440	398
District of Columbia	295,509	22,012	7,480	1,242	5,677	5,749	2,359	199	208,672	30,034	568	11,516	0
Florida	950,013	290,780	44,764	13,817	63,741	143,226	4,966	62	23,324	259,743	6,430	95,233	3,926
Georgia	549,326	161,269	26,451	7,455	39,933	64,405	611	0	34,950	154,116	2,562	57,572	0
Hawaii	89,861	18,392	5,057	22,377	6,717	8,341	1,399	0	6,431	11,533	1,405	7,800	409
Idaho	109,946	25,563	5,071	4,764	7,067	13,794	1,716	204	3,941	36,176	898	10,753	0
Illinois	949,469	301,431	44,604	10,993	55,145	135,536	7,732	84	39,671	267,970	4,201	78,062	4,040
Indiana	448,402	104,291	20,878	1,993	32,826	64,188	500	18	15,607	165,400	2,168	40,534	0
Iowa	243,680	49,523	10,642	169	15,401	32,174	840	114	14,335	97,307	1,383	21,792	0
Kansas	281,129	52,973	9,721	10,505	13,154	26,542	1,061	285	11,571	132,296	1,317	20,858	846
Kentucky	365,342	125,951	15,082	1,290	24,873	45,035	432	0	15,163	94,626	1,777	39,668	1,445
Louisiana	505,172	184,603	20,125	7,014	28,405	45,790	2,204	477	25,881	146,129	2,560	39,971	2,015
Maine	88,234	28,878	5,085	2,831	1,462	1,125	1,472	75	5,623	27,855	792	12,541	496
Maryland	320,449	84,028	17,001	10,374	20,390	51,694	1,453	167	19,598	81,638	2,309	30,381	1,417
Massachusetts	523,546	122,859	19,826	5,226	25,352	85,987	4,034	260	22,032	193,189	2,664	40,278	1,840
Michigan	831,850	298,658	38,164	6,767	50,102	85,737	2,569	2,965	28,379	238,596	4,204	72,173	3,536
Minnesota	352,926	81,651	17,111	5,630	21,569	48,350	1,105	3,943	15,993	118,539	2,190	35,487	1,357
Mississippi	370,494	121,419	12,710	4,041	18,490	61,857	459	1,047	18,445	97,120	1,730	33,176	0
Missouri	423,929	112,582	19,770	5,926	28,146	56,003	599	44	15,850	134,593	2,485	46,277	1,654
Montana	123,889	25,555	5,073	24,231	6,108	10,261	3,278	3,577	6,930	30,498	595	7,784	0
Nebraska	152,575	31,596	6,322	8,151	8,694	18,679	743	846	5,304	59,314	942	11,984	0
Nevada	73,869	18,738	5,062	3,792	6,976	14,708	505	1,007	1,924	11,309	849	8,595	402
New Hampshire	82,815	14,640	5,039	1,029	6,641	21,456	382	0	3,315	21,113	770	8,429	0
New Jersey	500,974	153,203	26,580	11,393	32,035	85,165	2,210	106	16,475	131,378	2,893	39,537	0
New Mexico	235,504	58,392	7,321	37,501	10,103	21,848	9,216	5,433	8,630	58,945	996	16,391	726
New York	2,070,584	611,923	69,587	18,526	78,144	350,692	34,972	1,460	51,106	724,563	7,360	115,257	6,995
North Carolina	522,302	127,877	23,840	9,623	40,916	71,534	401	2,327	37,119	139,325	2,875	64,454	2,011
North Dakota	92,302	17,114	5,031	12,885	5,732	6,928	2,551	1,313	4,460	27,900	647	7,343	399
Ohio	817,265	286,764	42,040	4,500	60,131	8,518	449	36	23,892	289,678	4,492	96,767	0
Oklahoma	349,487	81,094	12,914	22,260	19,879	38,966	9,625	12,328	16,540	103,850	1,486	29,415	1,129
Oregon	245,683	71,641	11,157	3,637	15,708	31,290	3,408	1,204	9,983	70,109	1,451	25,071	1,024
Pennsylvania	961,335	300,838	43,172	3,598	59,635	108,832	1,304	0	31,928	304,144	4,941	98,971	3,973
Rhode Island	98,978	21,800	5,066	3,050	6,903	12,419	1,517	42	3,967	35,626	875	7,281	434
South Carolina	325,942	88,301	14,028	7,363	23,753	43,042	75	0	19,829	90,566	1,567	37,418	0
South Dakota	116,599	19,907	5,042	15,121	5,790	9,151	1,736	2,646	3,463	45,099	812	7,834	0
Tennessee	426,470	118,033	18,711	3,520	30,940	59,575	159	0	25,033	118,169	2,758	47,930	1,640
Texas	1,920,503	610,832	76,604	31,396	104,939	378,742	15,209	166	51,779	495,260	8,122	147,453	0
Utah	213,727	31,955	9,014	6,342	12,623	25,949	1,259	744	8,133	98,195	1,206	18,307	0
Vermont	63,785	13,919	5,024	14	5,526	6,301	248	110	4,536	19,570	626	7,512	399
Virginia	526,326	99,891	21,494	36,401	31,998	127,946	1,412	12	25,806	133,194	2,780	45,392	0
Washington	408,321	103,709	18,915	26,829	24,136	54,503	3,575	4,823	19,736	112,946	2,051	35,551	1,546
West Virginia	183,285	63,431	7,407	91	12,451	22,262	0	0	8,965	46,657	1,022	21,000	0
Wisconsin	415,314	115,384	19,701	7,325	26,635	55,365	347	2,333	18,188	124,995	2,280	42,761	0
Wyoming	65,569	14,083	5,022	8,288	5,390	7,297	298	816	2,243	14,833	750	6,549	0
Indian tribe setaside	89,222	35,514	1,385	0	0	49,907	0	0	0	0	2,415	0	0
Undistributed	270,398	10,677	0	78,311	1,381	0	0	0	0	179,403	0	625	0
Outlying areas													
American Samoa	13,744	4,537	1,420	0	381	5,168	75	0	191	1,114	88	769	0
Federated States of Micronesia	159	0	0	0	0	0	0	0	159	0	0	0	0
Guam	21,615	4,408	3,317	0	784	6,883	156	0	2,450	1,434	95	2,040	47
Marshall Islands	370	0	0	0	0	0	0	0	370	0	0	0	0
Northern Marianas	9,881	2,449	1,351	0	371	3,355	0	0	1,178	454	87	638	0
Palau	3,187	1,682	424	0	220	156	327	0	145	1	76	157	0
Puerto Rico	719,924	253,399	20,927	1,387	6,232	24,428	917	0	18,150	355,000	2,039	35,120	2,325
Trust Territory of the Pacific	13,331	0	0	0	421	12,775	75	0	61	0	0	0	0
Virgin Islands	22,208	7,671	3,264	135	954	5,169	346	0	1,563	1,298	158	1,650	0

[1] Chapter 1, Education Consolidation and Improvement Act of 1981 includes Grants to Local Education Agencies, Migrant Education—Basic State Grants, Educationally Deprived Children—State Administration, Program for Neglected and Delinquent Children, Capital Expenses, State Improvement Grants, and Even Start—State Educational Agencies.

[2] Includes Chapter 2, Education Consolidation and Improvement Act of 1981, Eisenhower Mathematics and Science Education—State Grants, Drug-Free Schools and Communities—State Grants, Education of Homeless Children and Youth, Christa McAuliffe Fellowships, Foreign Language Assistance, and State Block Grants.

[3] Includes Maintenance and Operations (Impact Aid/Disaster Assistance).

[4] Includes Vocational Education—Basic Grants to States, Community Based Organizations, Consumer and Homemaking Education, State Councils, Tech-Prep Education, Adult Education-State Administered Basic Grant Program, and State Literacy Resource Centers.

[5] Includes Special Education—Grants to States (Part B, Individuals with Disabilities Education Act), Preschool Incentive Grants to States, Special Education—Grants for Infants and Families with Disabilities, and Education of Children with Disabilities in State Operated or Supported Schools.

[6] Also includes Emergency Immigrant Education Program and Transition Program for Refugee Children.

[7] Includes Institutional Aid to Strengthen Higher Education Institutions serving significant numbers of low-income students, Other Special Programs for the Disadvantaged, Cooperative Education, Fund for the Improvement of Postsecondary Education, Fellowships and Scholarships, and annual interest subsidy grants for facilities construction.

[8] Includes Pell Grants, State Student Incentive Grants, Guaranteed Student Loan interest subsidies, and Postsecondary Review Program.

[9] Includes Public Library Services, Public Library Construction and Technology Enhancement, and Interlibrary Cooperation and Resource Sharing.

[10] Includes Rehabilitation Services—Vocational Rehabilitation Grants to States, Basic State Grants, Supported Employment Services for Individuals with Severe Disabilities, Rehabilitation Services—Client Assistance Program, Independent Living—State Grants, and Program of Protection and Advocacy of Individual Rights.

[11] Includes State and Local Systemic Improvement.

NOTE.—Data reflect revisions to figures in the Budget of the United States Government, Fiscal Year 1996. To the extent possible, data represent obligations rather than outlays. Because of the exclusion of certain programs, totals in this table are lower than those reported in other tables. Because of rounding, details may not add to totals.

SOURCE: U.S. Department of Education, National Center for Education Statistics, based on unpublished tabulations from the Office of Management and Budget; and U.S. Department of Commerce, Bureau of the Census, Federal Expenditures by State for Fiscal Year 1994. (This table was prepared March 1995.)

Table 358.—U.S. Department of Education obligations for major programs, by state or other area: Fiscal year 1993

[In thousands]

State or other area	Total	Grants for the dis-advan-taged [1]	Block grants to states for school improve-ment [2]	School assistance in federally affected areas [3]	Vocational and adult education [4]	Education for the handi-capped [5]	Bilingual edu-cation [6]	Indian education	Higher and con-tinuing edu-cation [7]	Student financial assistance [8]	Public library programs [9]	Rehabilitation services [10]
1	2	3	4	5	6	7	8	9	10	11	12	13
Total	$22,913,685	$6,574,791	$1,268,633	$690,710	$1,480,979	$2,319,174	$211,980	$71,797	$985,717	$7,261,638	$117,846	$1,930,420
Alabama	439,876	122,908	20,910	4,773	28,753	46,960	576	1,160	35,521	132,781	1,925	43,609
Alaska	151,370	23,280	5,903	79,773	5,599	9,545	1,199	6,848	2,125	9,580	566	6,953
Arizona	402,878	96,825	16,752	65,900	22,179	34,214	7,354	8,927	8,791	112,946	1,779	27,210
Arkansas	231,707	74,260	11,929	2,181	16,346	26,304	347	102	11,314	61,508	1,250	26,168
California	2,039,539	659,827	157,478	65,762	149,164	27,073	71,882	4,609	66,986	655,301	12,096	169,361
Colorado	283,075	64,064	14,668	8,124	17,101	32,671	4,793	669	11,505	109,002	1,647	18,831
Connecticut	197,266	58,663	13,168	7,564	14,139	35,469	888	27	7,042	42,952	1,617	15,737
Delaware	57,554	15,445	5,952	57	5,909	8,298	250	0	3,741	10,243	787	6,872
District of Columbia ..	474,812	25,169	6,300	1,351	5,989	4,244	2,064	188	214,295	203,338	837	11,037
Florida	983,413	290,971	52,729	14,379	66,159	130,959	4,599	375	17,862	310,559	4,811	90,010
Georgia	536,355	168,747	32,036	6,714	41,275	57,092	467	0	30,819	143,156	2,520	53,529
Hawaii	87,347	17,993	7,224	22,055	6,969	7,840	842	0	4,914	11,229	631	7,651
Idaho	108,562	24,138	8,282	4,856	7,108	12,392	933	216	3,362	36,769	598	9,908
Illinois	931,047	284,377	54,094	9,655	58,067	131,575	6,808	89	32,382	273,449	4,807	75,745
Indiana	458,001	100,244	24,949	1,896	34,243	59,207	705	17	12,472	175,806	2,511	45,952
Iowa	284,551	48,254	12,520	198	27,699	60,638	908	110	11,371	101,767	1,464	19,623
Kansas	222,653	50,951	11,408	8,590	13,590	25,380	916	285	10,092	80,553	1,305	19,582
Kentucky	366,311	113,983	18,212	1,172	26,148	43,886	462	0	13,928	107,084	2,379	39,058
Louisiana	488,000	174,576	23,584	7,528	29,504	42,820	2,131	487	22,327	139,004	1,704	44,345
Maine	112,341	31,524	7,267	2,964	7,343	14,450	1,534	80	6,247	28,400	803	11,731
Maryland	323,186	90,924	20,668	10,362	21,605	49,667	1,569	315	14,980	82,724	2,267	28,106
Massachusetts	513,887	130,993	24,379	5,396	26,700	78,881	4,617	80	19,441	184,336	2,660	36,404
Michigan	758,004	273,809	45,316	7,102	52,525	26,155	3,061	2,836	23,907	253,961	4,877	64,455
Minnesota	352,362	79,129	19,910	5,905	22,289	44,072	1,056	4,137	12,901	127,425	1,966	33,573
Mississippi	302,514	118,231	15,836	3,781	19,399	407	549	1,014	16,940	94,290	1,132	30,935
Missouri	428,987	108,855	23,356	5,719	29,510	55,054	792	40	12,824	146,374	2,345	44,116
Montana	132,611	24,466	7,231	22,099	6,180	18,755	3,002	3,477	6,334	32,321	713	8,033
Nebraska	160,332	30,341	7,457	8,687	9,104	17,918	837	773	4,592	67,772	924	11,926
Nevada	72,159	17,049	6,036	3,588	7,238	12,167	311	661	1,416	15,214	837	7,642
New Hampshire	69,833	15,001	6,021	25	6,911	10,783	222	0	2,245	20,217	768	7,640
New Jersey	528,398	175,557	33,031	11,591	33,784	94,951	1,922	102	11,418	124,420	2,911	38,710
New Mexico	225,443	55,459	8,393	37,387	10,393	20,379	9,484	5,646	7,638	54,808	773	15,084
New York	1,936,649	615,288	87,200	16,129	83,192	171,238	32,267	1,183	42,991	769,864	7,327	109,968
North Carolina	570,365	138,011	29,418	9,283	42,857	129,108	210	2,485	31,276	122,756	2,975	61,987
North Dakota	94,121	16,445	5,948	12,738	5,946	6,920	1,635	1,580	3,870	31,616	552	6,872
Ohio	909,673	255,894	49,917	4,468	62,967	108,900	767	39	17,170	315,831	4,587	89,133
Oklahoma	342,003	76,792	17,573	24,414	20,454	33,744	9,331	10,998	12,954	104,502	1,575	29,665
Oregon	244,594	66,945	12,867	3,648	15,833	33,639	3,162	1,205	8,204	73,900	1,471	23,720
Pennsylvania	976,702	301,332	52,652	3,119	63,355	108,158	998	0	25,871	320,173	4,357	96,688
Rhode Island	98,255	21,621	6,040	3,351	7,217	11,735	1,378	39	3,036	36,092	586	7,160
South Carolina	323,700	88,354	17,243	7,158	24,989	40,571	115	0	18,595	88,956	1,676	36,043
South Dakota	122,672	19,687	6,013	15,059	6,029	9,005	1,749	2,593	3,024	51,524	568	7,421
Tennessee	487,460	119,235	22,793	3,207	55,344	108,277	133	152	21,538	108,407	2,054	46,320
Texas	1,441,213	566,439	86,883	28,776	108,357	19,923	14,075	155	42,706	427,228	6,959	139,713
Utah	211,936	29,956	10,350	7,856	12,469	25,812	1,232	636	6,764	98,669	862	17,331
Vermont	69,791	15,954	7,179	11	5,769	10,670	81	115	3,534	18,811	652	7,014
Virginia	474,413	107,242	31,017	36,086	32,980	61,995	1,390	14	20,143	138,522	2,776	42,248
Washington	388,323	96,065	25,018	26,753	24,908	48,970	3,627	4,161	17,135	105,111	2,356	34,219
West Virginia	181,012	59,949	10,648	80	12,907	22,386	0	0	7,385	45,382	1,213	21,062
Wisconsin	415,664	108,020	22,761	7,622	27,512	53,132	247	2,492	15,149	135,525	2,325	40,880
Wyoming	62,363	10,987	5,984	7,616	5,622	7,062	703	680	2,048	15,843	428	5,391
Indian tribe setaside .	52,712	39,147	1,359	0	0	9,814	0	0	0	0	2,391	0
Undistributed	43,506	6,403	169	35,171	1,287	0	0	0	0	0	0	476
Outlying areas												
American Samoa	10,567	4,327	1,709	0	381	2,615	75	0	279	408	88	686
Guam	19,663	3,983	3,985	0	784	6,571	156	0	1,338	1,042	96	1,708
Northern Marianas ...	6,886	2,338	464	0	371	333	303	0	1,928	502	87	560
Puerto Rico	672,546	229,350	26,632	937	29,036	34,669	779	0	15,785	300,991	1,452	32,913
Trust Territory of the Pacific	8,427	1,606	510	0	541	4,789	327	0	343	1	139	171
Virgin Islands	24,082	7,409	3,299	94	951	8,935	162	0	920	693	85	1,535

[1] Chapter 1, Education Consolidation and Improvement Act of 1981.

[2] Includes Chapter 2, Education Consolidation and Improvement Act of 1981, Science and Mathematics Education, Drug-Free Schools and Communities, and Education of Homeless Children and Youth.

[3] Includes Maintenance and Operations.

[4] Includes Vocational Education - Basic State Grants, Community Based Organizations, Consumer and Homemaker Education, State Councils, Vocational Education, Tech-Prep Education, and Adult Education-State Administered Program.

[5] Includes State Grants, Preschool Incentive Grants to States, and Grants for Infants and Families.

[6] Also includes Emergency Immigrant Education Program and Transition Program for Refugee Children.

[7] Includes Institutional Aid to Strengthen Higher Education Institutions serving significant numbers of low-income students, Other Special Programs for the Disadvantaged, Cooperative Education, Fund for the Improvement of Postsecondary Education, Fellowships and Scholarships, and annual interest subsidy grants for facilities construction.

[8] Includes Pell Grants, State Student Incentive Grants, Guaranteed Student Loan interest subsidies, and Postsecondary Review Program.

[9] Includes Public Library Services, Public Library Construction, Interlibrary Cooperation, Foreign Language Materials, Library Literacy programs, College Library Technology, Library Education and Training, Research Libraries, and research and demonstration programs.

[10] Includes Rehabilitation Services Basic State Grants, Client Assistance for Handicapped Individuals, Independent Living, and Supported Employment Services.

NOTE.—Data reflect revisions to figures in the *Budget of the United States Government, Fiscal Year 1995.* To the extent possible, data represent obligations rather than outlays. Because of the exclusion of certain programs, totals in this table are lower than those reported in other tables. Because of rounding, details may not add to totals.

SOURCE: U.S. Department of Education, National Center for Education Statistics, based on unpublished tabulations from the Office of Management and Budget; and U.S. Department of Commerce, Bureau of the Census, *Federal Expenditures by State for Fiscal Year 1993.* (This table was prepared March 1994.)

Table 359.—Appropriations for Chapter 1 and Chapter 2, Education Consolidation and Improvement Act of 1981, by state or other area: 1993–94 and 1994–95

[In thousands]

State or other area	Chapter 1 total, school year 1993–94 [1]	Chapter 1, school year 1994–95 [2]								Chapter 2	
		Total	Concentration grants	Local education agencies, basic grant	State schools		Migrant children	State administration	Other [3]	1993 appropriations for 1993–94	1994 appropriations for 1994–95
					Handicapped children	Neglected and delinquent children					
1	2	3	4	5	6	7	8	9	10	11	12
Total [4]	$6,805,998	$7,012,929	$694,000	$5,642,000	$116,878	$35,407	$305,193	$60,712	$158,739	$435,488	$369,500
Alabama	123,539	122,981	14,930	101,753	580	434	2,139	1,016	2,130	6,997	5,859
Alaska	24,973	25,354	545	11,350	1,736	149	10,743	375	456	2,161	1,833
Arizona	97,419	101,431	12,403	78,756	521	400	6,744	839	1,768	6,311	5,476
Arkansas	75,446	76,771	8,839	61,159	1,080	283	3,462	635	1,314	4,111	3,451
California	762,373	823,629	88,056	604,822	1,548	4,170	101,641	6,817	16,575	49,715	42,626
Colorado	65,631	69,650	5,463	57,564	1,459	208	3,125	576	1,255	5,644	4,875
Connecticut	61,053	57,569	3,195	46,112	3,342	535	2,313	476	1,596	4,743	4,010
Delaware	16,649	15,332	514	12,155	1,245	95	386	375	562	2,161	1,833
District of Columbia	27,521	24,357	2,505	17,808	2,345	548	192	375	585	2,161	1,833
Florida	295,449	297,267	30,227	232,273	6,486	688	19,939	2,459	5,194	18,781	16,290
Georgia	169,596	162,021	17,463	135,391	752	537	3,699	1,339	2,839	11,261	9,567
Hawaii	18,419	18,844	1,735	15,687	453	49	0	375	546	2,161	1,833
Idaho	24,530	25,968	1,735	18,541	405	95	4,175	375	642	2,161	1,833
Illinois	308,799	320,020	32,674	256,809	18,589	1,249	1,555	2,646	6,497	19,024	16,042
Indiana	103,521	107,371	7,653	90,465	3,080	657	2,075	887	2,553	9,557	7,952
Iowa	48,762	50,063	2,540	44,638	540	312	252	413	1,367	4,797	4,076
Kansas	52,099	54,058	3,342	42,339	1,085	607	5,122	447	1,116	4,364	3,697
Kentucky	114,894	126,307	14,649	100,848	356	654	6,120	1,044	2,635	6,320	5,316
Louisiana	176,053	185,261	23,959	151,852	658	675	2,311	1,531	4,275	8,060	6,762
Maine	31,992	29,272	1,159	22,971	395	207	3,423	375	742	2,161	1,833
Maryland	93,287	86,289	6,156	74,058	2,261	1,053	224	713	1,825	7,438	6,352
Massachusetts	143,005	133,324	9,699	103,568	10,465	738	4,201	1,103	3,550	8,484	7,157
Michigan	280,961	305,686	30,568	247,573	7,028	1,095	11,258	2,527	5,636	15,950	13,441
Minnesota	80,263	82,756	5,565	70,848	1,105	218	1,794	684	2,542	7,664	6,558
Mississippi	118,509	121,649	15,452	100,469	230	418	1,695	1,006	2,380	4,941	4,106
Missouri	110,734	114,418	11,788	96,382	1,319	560	676	945	2,748	8,674	7,326
Montana	24,666	25,755	2,852	21,267	199	90	306	375	665	2,161	1,833
Nebraska	30,667	31,911	1,735	26,655	315	188	1,689	375	954	2,840	2,411
Nevada	17,295	18,961	1,448	15,534	223	200	617	375	564	2,161	1,833
New Hampshire	15,858	15,395	340	13,110	754	187	76	375	553	2,161	1,833
New Jersey	178,677	155,336	11,283	132,608	2,133	1,752	1,059	1,283	5,217	11,523	9,716
New Mexico	55,559	58,486	7,473	47,449	94	241	1,556	484	1,191	2,939	2,527
New York	624,073	620,865	65,722	512,291	8,942	3,580	6,442	5,132	18,756	27,301	23,018
North Carolina	138,844	128,349	9,768	110,025	472	905	3,919	1,060	2,200	10,450	8,821
North Dakota	16,738	17,271	1,735	13,956	158	25	430	375	593	2,161	1,833
Ohio	258,078	288,738	31,526	242,742	1,974	2,662	1,470	2,386	5,978	18,249	15,267
Oklahoma	77,392	81,715	9,753	67,923	621	199	1,159	675	1,384	5,563	4,712
Oregon	71,911	76,379	4,646	54,249	4,738	731	10,162	632	1,220	4,869	4,182
Pennsylvania	312,731	311,997	27,468	255,184	11,158	856	4,994	2,579	9,758	18,159	15,296
Rhode Island	22,234	22,517	2,150	18,171	716	261	200	375	644	2,161	1,833
South Carolina	88,950	88,941	9,317	75,363	640	1,125	254	735	1,507	6,014	5,060
South Dakota	19,897	20,129	1,814	16,266	221	88	597	375	767	2,161	1,833
Tennessee	120,162	119,155	14,653	99,525	1,122	708	151	985	2,012	7,952	6,726
Texas	571,630	616,149	71,352	479,301	5,316	1,556	43,060	5,097	10,467	31,665	26,981
Utah	30,822	32,577	1,793	27,918	622	180	1,063	375	626	4,211	3,598
Vermont	16,805	14,701	340	11,466	781	105	1,129	375	504	2,161	1,833
Virginia	109,408	101,709	7,826	88,589	1,401	762	473	840	1,818	9,710	8,239
Washington	97,977	105,478	7,250	80,450	1,769	1,041	12,276	873	1,819	8,412	7,266
West Virginia	60,607	64,163	7,955	53,544	732	252	58	530	1,091	2,975	2,484
Wisconsin	111,025	117,600	7,894	102,588	2,216	705	582	971	2,643	8,565	7,306
Wyoming	11,217	14,279	643	12,346	196	112	166	375	441	2,161	1,833
Other activities											
Bureau of Indian Affairs	34,696	35,514	0	35,514	0	0	0	0	0	0	0
Migrant coordination activities	7,200	6,600	0	0	0	0	6,600	0	0	0	0
Even Start Migrant, Indian, and Territory Set-aside	4,464	4,568	0	0	0	0	0	0	4,568	0	0
Even Start Evaluation/ Technical Assistance	1,629	1,782	0	0	0	0	0	0	1,782	0	0
Outlying areas											
American Samoa	4,339	4,537	0	4,457	0	0	0	50	30	542	469
Guam	4,050	4,476	0	4,328	67	0	0	50	30	1,265	1,095
Northern Marianas	2,420	2,563	0	2,369	114	0	0	50	30	309	267
Puerto Rico	229,350	253,399	32,451	207,612	0	261	5,439	2,095	5,542	7,685	6,419
Trust Territory of the Pacific	1,673	1,725	0	1,602	44	0	0	50	30	159	137
Virgin Islands	7,479	7,747	0	7,591	75	0	0	50	30	1,042	902

[1] Data are based on fiscal year 1994 budget authorizations. Excludes $14,035,827 for evaluation and studies; and $4,960,000 for rural technical assistance (Rural TACS).

[2] Data are based on fiscal year 1995 budget authorizations. Excludes $13,100,000 for evaluation and studies; and $4,960,000 for rural technical assistance (Rural TACS).

[3] Includes capital expenses, Even Start, and state program improvement grants.

[4] Total includes "other activities" and "outlying areas."

NOTE.—Because of rounding, details may not add to totals.

SOURCE: U.S. Department of Education, Budget Service, Elementary, Secondary, and Vocational Education Analysis Division. (This table was prepared February 1995.)

Table 360.—Federal science and engineering obligations to colleges and universities, by agency and state: Fiscal year 1993 [1]

[In thousands]

State or other area	Total	Department of Agriculture	Department of Defense	Department of Education	Department of Energy	Environmental Protection Agency	Department of Health and Human Services	National Aeronautics and Space Administration	National Science Foundation	Other [2]
1	2	3	4	5	6	7	8	9	10	11
United States	$17,043,320	$940,548	$2,210,186	$156,435	$3,675,342	$152,692	$6,023,063	$1,578,041	$2,000,672	$306,341
Alabama	198,278	25,025	16,410	3,051	12,848	1,514	95,744	25,882	14,714	3,090
Alaska	46,562	3,305	1,061	200	552	514	1,992	20,061	13,556	5,321
Arizona	201,302	9,282	14,534	2,998	4,840	2,171	59,353	24,573	79,763	3,788
Arkansas	50,810	22,514	4,341	2,949	284	158	14,182	479	4,063	1,840
California	3,547,550	37,380	169,758	18,716	1,156,068	10,025	853,162	987,775	288,481	26,185
Colorado	292,651	13,119	14,747	3,124	9,169	3,342	110,109	22,262	100,400	16,379
Connecticut	250,100	6,547	10,635	2,228	23,283	1,764	178,156	1,824	20,017	5,646
Delaware	31,341	5,657	5,452	2,490	1,193	559	3,131	1,408	9,149	2,302
District of Columbia	124,045	1,933	28,889	3,746	871	398	54,408	8,297	10,957	14,546
Florida	277,287	21,679	35,589	6,156	13,343	3,535	115,435	20,763	50,095	10,692
Georgia	255,855	28,898	50,665	3,349	30,935	5,116	102,280	13,846	16,049	4,717
Hawaii	67,140	11,860	3,615	2,231	2,711	35	14,990	9,308	13,581	8,809
Idaho	21,557	10,618	492	455	572	663	2,005	311	3,747	2,694
Illinois	1,096,306	23,930	36,086	9,802	662,731	775	218,698	12,392	125,812	6,080
Indiana	206,961	24,638	12,713	1,641	29,288	684	82,660	4,678	47,381	3,278
Iowa	183,157	27,778	5,515	2,789	35,628	1,837	80,327	7,125	14,501	7,657
Kansas	74,904	15,147	9,929	2,296	3,786	2,060	27,380	2,434	10,278	1,594
Kentucky	77,019	23,332	1,412	1,146	5,408	776	35,014	906	8,365	660
Louisiana	124,343	17,271	17,899	1,315	18,518	4,771	46,945	2,376	7,695	7,553
Maine	21,668	8,298	348	837	1,420	1,544	823	175	3,120	5,103
Maryland	862,167	14,419	447,185	3,551	14,498	5,123	298,245	29,418	42,677	7,051
Massachusetts	1,198,250	22,288	523,992	5,843	78,041	9,688	341,260	50,898	153,133	13,107
Michigan	426,747	41,602	27,340	5,719	16,097	8,568	208,586	40,338	73,146	5,351
Minnesota	198,574	22,099	15,821	5,069	6,310	2,438	107,921	3,890	32,807	2,219
Mississippi	71,937	29,448	6,295	2,210	7,347	427	12,594	2,050	9,631	1,935
Missouri	228,773	25,372	6,617	3,109	4,435	276	164,591	4,850	17,133	2,390
Montana	30,352	9,526	929	804	936	487	3,910	1,122	11,468	1,170
Nebraska	50,555	16,335	1,308	235	1,016	432	20,053	1,099	9,693	384
Nevada	29,709	3,691	685	348	3,843	6,104	7,139	746	3,694	3,459
New Hampshire	69,368	4,798	3,551	428	1,569	1,310	35,630	11,423	9,308	1,351
New Jersey	332,197	11,813	35,801	2,543	133,321	6,087	82,199	6,867	43,230	10,336
New Mexico	795,073	7,174	50,209	1,158	678,098	205	17,642	25,922	13,115	1,550
New York	1,387,369	29,393	67,995	5,689	408,064	14,054	633,843	27,543	192,789	7,999
North Carolina	445,878	37,674	24,272	6,780	10,061	12,899	284,344	7,547	47,363	14,938
North Dakota	37,358	18,898	1,353	448	5,409	1,600	3,270	260	1,012	5,108
Ohio	349,018	23,843	60,484	5,091	6,856	6,767	174,500	23,983	39,569	7,925
Oklahoma	65,831	16,876	5,287	914	6,626	1,321	15,702	7,720	8,777	2,608
Oregon	159,513	21,178	13,460	5,647	15,075	3,398	63,282	3,835	26,929	6,709
Pennsylvania	818,853	25,964	208,636	11,783	35,746	3,093	406,109	21,795	93,236	12,491
Rhode Island	61,632	3,883	10,137	299	2,522	1,354	17,284	3,482	19,316	3,355
South Carolina	72,275	16,889	6,492	1,300	7,919	439	26,517	1,529	9,181	2,009
South Dakota	16,534	8,489	298	59	21	149	1,828	898	4,131	661
Tennessee	228,255	23,538	11,458	2,365	59,959	720	108,771	5,536	13,089	2,819
Texas	696,065	50,636	116,095	6,237	28,238	10,610	358,134	40,572	76,939	8,604
Utah	133,828	6,866	34,526	820	4,727	2,053	57,704	3,821	18,686	4,625
Vermont	40,630	7,043	296	267	539	904	28,324	236	2,542	479
Virginia	303,382	21,251	24,657	749	77,398	2,049	102,299	25,358	35,554	14,067
Washington	329,524	22,168	38,487	1,012	16,892	1,381	181,808	10,204	48,219	9,353
West Virginia	109,436	9,684	10,969	210	7,192	3,500	8,883	34,169	32,179	2,650
Wisconsin	265,944	24,576	12,003	3,558	22,082	2,284	137,348	12,520	46,065	5,508
Wyoming	20,556	5,185	1,542	208	1,031	520	1,358	548	5,239	4,925
Outlying areas	58,902	19,738	1,917	463	26	211	15,191	987	19,098	1,271
American Samoa	1,233	1,233	0	0	0	0	0	0	0	0
Guam	3,334	2,199	33	0	0	0	766	0	135	201
Puerto Rico	49,116	12,253	1,884	463	26	211	13,366	987	18,963	963
Trust Territory of the Pacific	2,247	2,101	0	0	0	0	146	0	0	0
Virgin Islands	2,972	1,952	0	0	0	0	913	0	0	107

[1] Dollars reflect actual obligations during the fiscal year regardless of when the funds were actually spent by a recipient institution. Data include obligations to federally funded research and development centers administered by colleges and universities.

[2] Includes U.S. Department of Commerce, U.S. Department of Housing and Urban Development, U.S. Department of the Interior, Agency for International Development, U.S. Department of Labor, U.S. Department of Transportation, and Nuclear Regulatory Commission.

NOTE.—Totals exclude loans to individuals, such as the Federal Family Education Loan Program sponsored by the U.S. Department of Education, and federal training and development activities, as well as funds allocated to state agencies, even though the final recipient of such funds is known to be an academic institution. Tuition support programs such as Pell Grants are included in these figures.

SOURCE: National Science Foundation, Federal Support to Universities, Colleges, and Nonprofit Institutions, Fiscal Year 1993. (This table was prepared May 1995.)

Table 361.—Summary of federal funds for research, development, and R & D plant: Fiscal years 1987 to 1995

[In millions]

Item	Actual							Estimate		Percent change, 1994 to 1995
	1987	1988	1989	1990	1991	1992	1993	1994	1995	
1	2	3	4	5	6	7	8	9	10	11
Total outlays for research, development, and R & D plant	$53,214.2	$56,556.6	$61,476.4	$64,276.5	$64,292.3	$65,719.0	$68,385.8	$69,436.5	$70,491.1	**1.5**
Research and development	51,611.7	54,739.4	59,450.4	62,246.8	61,130.4	62,934.5	65,241.3	66,404.1	67,843.1	**2.2**
R & D plant	1,602.4	1,817.2	2,026.1	2,029.7	3,162.0	2,784.5	3,144.5	3,032.4	2,648.0	**−12.7**
Total obligations for research, development, and R & D plant	57,101.4	58,992.2	63,570.9	65,950.9	64,990.5	68,577.2	70,414.7	72,818.2	71,746.5	**−1.5**
Research and development obligations	55,255.4	56,935.1	61,405.8	63,667.3	61,295.2	65,592.6	67,314.0	69,593.8	69,366.2	−0.3
Performers										
Federal intramural [1]	13,413.1	14,280.9	13,184.5	16,002.5	15,238.1	15,690.1	16,556.2	17,236.8	16,724.2	−3.0
Industrial firms	26,752.0	26,719.2	30,484.4	29,378.3	26,420.6	29,744.8	30,326.1	31,004.7	31,243.6	0.8
FFRDCs [2] administered by industrial firms	1,860.0	1,911.3	1,960.0	2,237.6	2,068.3	2,009.8	1,451.3	1,306.4	1,297.8	−0.7
Universities and colleges	7,353.6	7,827.7	8,672.0	9,142.2	10,168.5	10,271.2	11,156.1	11,969.4	12,096.6	1.1
FFRDCs [2] administered by universities and colleges	3,209.5	3,473.9	3,497.1	3,466.4	3,603.8	3,855.5	3,666.5	3,490.0	3,607.9	3.4
Other nonprofit institutions	1,710.8	1,682.6	1,999.1	2,249.6	2,637.4	2,803.6	2,811.9	2,990.9	2,712.2	−9.3
FFRDCs [2] administered by nonprofit institutions	510.6	505.6	522.0	632.3	679.4	745.6	753.4	781.5	890.3	13.9
State and local governments	148.3	142.1	167.4	213.9	215.1	184.1	320.3	568.8	560.6	−1.4
Foreign	297.6	391.8	919.4	344.7	263.9	287.9	272.2	245.3	233.1	−4.9
Research obligations	17,942.7	18,650.0	20,765.4	21,738.9	23,968.4	24,490.6	26,890.5	28,033.5	28,161.2	0.5
Performers										
Federal intramural [1]	5,437.7	5,338.4	5,981.5	5,953.3	6,539.3	6,615.7	7,360.1	7,645.9	7,600.2	−0.6
Industrial firms	2,448.6	2,642.5	2,875.1	3,199.9	3,406.5	3,451.2	4,018.9	4,189.8	4,129.2	−1.4
FFRDCs [2] administered by industrial firms	433.5	455.2	519.8	542.7	624.6	592.4	795.8	693.7	635.2	−8.4
Universities and colleges	6,640.3	7,022.9	7,793.2	8,141.5	8,867.5	9,060.7	9,844.1	10,610.1	10,839.5	2.2
FFRDCs [2] administered by universities and colleges	1,470.9	1,564.8	1,703.4	1,808.1	2,160.9	2,351.8	2,347.6	2,187.0	2,226.6	1.8
Other nonprofit institutions	1,207.3	1,299.8	1,519.7	1,662.2	1,925.9	2,049.6	2,041.3	2,038.8	2,046.2	0.4
FFRDCs [2] administered by nonprofit institutions	89.8	82.9	109.5	148.2	170.9	139.9	173.4	199.6	219.1	9.8
State and local governments	90.2	103.1	121.2	126.4	129.3	109.3	211.8	376.2	367.5	−2.3
Foreign	124.3	140.4	142.1	156.5	143.4	120.0	97.4	92.3	97.6	5.8
Fields of science										
Life sciences	7,343.8	7,724.5	8,495.1	8,837.8	9,622.0	9,910.5	10,772.1	11,350.2	11,609.2	2.3
Psychology	369.5	389.8	421.7	448.6	482.4	298.1	550.7	569.4	573.7	0.8
Physical sciences	3,252.7	3,317.3	3,705.2	3,808.7	4,235.3	4,439.2	4,427.0	4,449.0	4,379.1	−1.6
Environmental sciences	1,511.6	1,607.0	1,773.3	2,174.1	2,149.8	2,207.6	2,608.5	2,831.7	2,690.3	−5.0
Mathematics and computer sciences	640.6	642.9	735.5	840.7	903.7	1,150.3	1,225.4	1,410.0	1,526.0	8.2
Engineering	3,906.2	3,956.3	4,442.0	4,335.2	4,944.5	4,977.0	5,499.4	5,700.6	5,629.4	−1.2
Social sciences	480.1	485.8	551.1	630.0	727.3	689.7	674.9	708.4	698.8	−1.4
Other sciences	438.3	526.5	641.6	663.7	903.4	806.3	1,132.5	1,014.3	1,054.5	4.0
Basic research obligations	8,944.1	9,473.6	10,602.0	11,285.6	12,170.8	12,489.9	13,399.1	14,043.4	14,201.0	1.1
Performers										
Federal intramural [1]	2,046.2	2,050.3	2,370.7	2,366.0	2,446.5	2,397.0	2,605.1	2,740.8	2,719.8	−0.8
Industrial firms	466.9	596.9	773.2	887.5	949.9	920.3	959.2	1,015.0	963.9	−5.0
FFRDCs [2] administered by industrial firms	119.9	133.0	166.7	175.4	209.1	187.8	237.3	234.6	212.8	−9.3
Universities and colleges	4,665.8	4,868.3	5,221.4	5,548.2	6,064.5	6,331.8	6,798.5	7,323.8	7,496.7	2.4
FFRDCs [2] administered by universities and colleges	906.6	989.8	1,098.1	1,227.3	1,306.2	1,394.1	1,437.8	1,411.7	1,422.2	0.7
Other nonprofit institutions	657.7	728.6	838.9	924.1	1,015.5	1,097.2	1,164.9	1,095.4	1,129.7	3.1
FFRDCs [2] administered by nonprofit institutions	13.3	17.7	42.2	59.2	80.8	65.5	71.3	77.8	88.4	13.6
State and local governments	37.5	42.7	43.6	50.4	49.1	42.4	71.7	91.7	114.2	24.6
Foreign	30.2	46.3	47.4	47.6	49.1	53.8	53.3	52.6	53.4	1.5
Fields of science										
Life sciences	4,363.6	4,501.8	4,915.7	5,177.5	5,433.6	5,841.7	6,288.8	6,673.7	6,898.5	3.4
Psychology	147.2	177.8	187.1	215.1	225.5	122.6	246.8	256.3	268.7	4.8
Physical sciences	2,096.0	2,199.6	2,506.5	2,661.5	2,881.5	2,951.4	2,907.1	2,946.9	2,900.3	−1.6
Environmental sciences	781.0	872.7	1,016.9	1,274.8	1,263.5	1,303.6	1,533.5	1,574.9	1,526.0	−3.1
Mathematics and computer sciences	306.4	313.2	349.8	406.9	426.1	481.4	511.3	563.6	582.9	3.4
Engineering	989.5	1,006.2	1,183.7	1,101.5	1,233.7	1,249.8	1,207.4	1,325.1	1,286.4	−2.9
Social sciences	129.5	146.8	154.6	146.0	161.4	139.9	194.1	192.1	206.3	7.4
Other sciences	130.9	255.5	291.7	302.3	545.6	399.4	510.1	510.7	532.0	4.2
Applied research obligations	8,998.6	9,176.4	10,163.3	10,453.3	11,797.6	12,000.7	13,491.4	13,990.2	13,960.2	−0.2
Performers										
Federal intramural [1]	3,391.5	3,288.1	3,610.8	3,587.3	4,092.8	4,218.7	4,755.0	4,905.1	4,880.5	−0.5
Industrial firms	1,981.7	2,045.6	2,101.8	2,312.4	2,456.6	2,530.9	3,059.7	3,174.8	3,165.3	−0.3
FFRDCs [2] administered by industrial firms	313.6	322.2	353.2	367.3	415.5	404.6	558.6	459.2	422.4	−8.0
Universities and colleges	1,974.5	2,154.6	2,571.8	2,593.4	2,803.0	2,728.9	3,045.5	3,286.3	3,342.8	1.7
FFRDCs [2] administered by universities and colleges	564.3	575.0	605.4	580.8	854.7	957.6	909.8	775.3	804.4	3.8
Other nonprofit institutions	549.7	571.2	680.8	738.1	910.4	952.5	876.4	943.4	916.5	−2.9
FFRDCs [2] administered by nonprofit institutions	76.5	65.2	67.3	89.0	90.1	74.5	102.2	121.8	130.7	7.4
State and local governments	52.7	60.4	77.6	76.1	80.2	66.9	140.1	284.6	253.3	−11.0
Foreign	94.1	94.1	94.6	109.0	94.3	66.2	44.1	39.7	44.2	11.4
Fields of science										
Life sciences	2,980.2	3,222.7	3,579.4	3,660.3	4,188.4	4,068.8	4,483.3	4,676.4	4,710.8	0.7
Psychology	222.4	212.0	234.5	233.5	258.9	175.6	303.9	313.1	305.1	−2.6
Physical sciences	1,156.6	1,117.7	1,198.8	1,147.2	1,353.9	1,467.7	1,519.8	1,502.1	1,478.8	−1.6
Environmental sciences	730.6	734.3	756.3	899.3	886.3	904.0	1,075.0	1,256.8	1,164.3	−7.4
Mathematics and computer sciences	334.3	329.6	389.7	433.9	477.6	678.9	714.1	846.4	943.1	11.4
Engineering	2,916.7	2,950.0	3,258.3	3,233.7	3,710.8	3,727.1	4,292.0	4,375.5	4,343.1	−0.7
Social sciences	350.5	339.0	396.4	484.0	566.0	549.8	480.8	516.3	492.5	−4.6
Other sciences	307.4	271.0	350.0	361.5	357.8	406.8	622.4	503.6	522.6	3.8

Table 361.—Summary of federal funds for research, development, and R & D plant: Fiscal years 1987 to 1995—Continued

[In millions]

Item	Actual							Estimate		
	1987	1988	1989	1990	1991	1992	1993	1994	1995	Percent change, 1994 to 1995
1	2	3	4	5	6	7	8	9	10	11
Development obligations	37,312.7	38,285.1	40,640.4	41,928.4	37,326.8	41,102.0	40,423.5	41,560.3	41,205.1	-0.9
Performers										
Federal intramural [1]	7,975.4	8,942.5	7,203.0	10,049.2	8,698.8	9,074.4	9,196.2	9,590.8	9,124.0	-4.9
Industrial firms	24,303.4	24,076.7	27,609.3	26,178.4	23,014.1	26,293.6	26,307.2	26,814.9	27,114.4	1.1
FFRDCs [2] administered by industrial firms	1,426.4	1,456.1	1,440.2	1,694.9	1,443.7	1,417.4	655.5	612.7	662.6	8.1
Universities and colleges	713.2	804.8	878.8	1,000.5	1,301.0	1,210.6	1,312.0	1,359.3	1,257.1	-7.5
FFRDCs [2] administered by universities and colleges	1,738.6	1,909.1	1,793.6	1,658.3	1,442.9	1,503.7	1,318.9	1,302.9	1,381.3	6.0
Other nonprofit institutions	503.4	382.8	479.5	587.4	711.5	753.9	770.6	952.1	666.0	-30.0
FFRDCs [2] administered by nonprofit institutions	420.8	422.7	412.4	484.0	508.5	605.7	580.0	581.9	671.2	15.3
State and local governments	58.0	39.0	46.3	87.5	85.8	74.8	108.5	192.6	193.1	0.3
Foreign	173.4	251.4	777.3	188.1	120.5	167.9	174.8	153.0	135.5	-11.4
R & D plant obligations	1,846.0	2,057.1	2,165.1	2,283.6	3,695.4	2,984.6	3,100.7	3,224.4	2,380.3	-26.2
Performers										
Federal intramural [1]	301.6	319.6	329.5	359.9	461.1	506.2	432.0	709.0	364.9	-48.5
Industrial firms	668.7	719.5	900.4	884.0	1,889.2	1,014.4	1,048.2	1,338.6	999.7	-25.3
FFRDCs [2] administered by industrial firms	212.9	204.3	212.3	231.0	279.6	202.2	124.4	120.7	146.3	21.3
Universities and colleges	230.5	245.8	204.9	155.8	253.3	241.5	361.4	295.1	152.0	-48.5
FFRDCs [2] administered by universities and colleges	400.5	535.3	489.9	495.8	624.6	579.5	619.5	656.5	613.7	-6.5
Other nonprofit institutions	20.6	23.7	14.2	121.3	154.6	393.9	415.6	13.7	9.7	-29.0
FFRDCs [2] administered by nonprofit institutions	5.4	6.2	8.4	31.4	19.7	46.3	65.5	72.7	93.5	28.7
State and local governments	—	0.3	1.4	0.5	0.6	0.5	0.5	0.5	0.5	-3.7
Foreign	5.8	2.4	4.2	3.9	12.8	0.0	33.4	17.6	0.0	-100.0

[1] Includes costs associated with the administration of intramural and extramural programs by federal personnel as well as actual intramural performance.

[2] Federally funded research and development centers.

—Data not available or not applicable.

NOTE.—Some data have been revised from previously published figures. Because of rounding, details may not add to totals.

SOURCE: National Science Foundation, *Federal Funds for Research and Development,* various years. (This table was prepared May 1995.)

Table 362.—Federal obligations to colleges and universities for research and development, by field: United States and outlying areas, 1979–80 to 1992–93

Field of science or engineering	1979–80	1980–81	1985–86	1987–88	1988–89	1989–90[1]	1990–91[1]	1991–92[1]	1992–93[1]
1	2	3	4	5	6	7	8	9	10
Total, all fields	$4,160,543	$4,410,931	$6,456,743	$7,719,162	$8,522,555	$9,005,771	$10,027,270	$10,859,207	$10,940,124
Engineering, total	612,456	792,223	998,312	1,129,303	1,157,047	474,709	543,530	587,404	676,770
Aeronautical	28,044	31,056	42,257	47,946	66,096	45,965	44,207	48,539	50,114
Astronautical	4,634	4,875	24,147	32,516	42,276	11,803	20,977	21,407	13,402
Chemical	22,210	27,667	50,379	67,647	45,829	56,845	67,968	63,900	66,919
Civil	48,130	58,300	35,402	30,947	43,026	37,306	34,064	30,756	37,812
Electrical	86,916	115,011	212,175	251,336	240,638	53,162	60,299	68,416	72,707
Mechanical	42,593	37,954	56,416	60,551	71,137	52,652	54,674	60,748	72,707
Metallurgy and materials	63,057	52,815	101,457	121,228	146,253	81,678	91,686	76,926	179,379
Engineering, other	316,872	464,545	476,079	517,132	501,792	135,298	169,655	216,712	188,841
All sciences, total	3,548,087	3,618,708	5,458,431	6,589,859	7,365,508	8,531,062	9,483,740	10,271,873	10,263,320
Physical sciences	507,884	500,657	770,254	859,764	979,037	890,444	1,022,807	1,134,579	1,022,580
Astronomy	52,736	54,835	78,435	89,791	103,271	98,804	115,212	149,417	139,579
Chemistry	170,048	165,189	255,593	281,573	299,417	272,929	295,576	325,224	320,975
Physics	249,661	250,342	379,289	426,005	505,723	453,538	518,840	544,200	510,866
Physical sciences, other	35,439	30,291	56,937	62,395	70,626	65,173	93,179	115,738	51,160
Mathematical sciences	53,987	53,668	96,405	119,217	134,998	109,587	125,893	140,544	131,201
Computer sciences	37,585	37,493	82,691	84,424	123,197	99,214	113,545	124,962	135,064
Environmental sciences	379,453	330,079	468,882	474,695	554,917	522,767	572,584	641,723	658,436
Atmospheric sciences	86,486	95,112	124,657	132,379	131,959	139,914	149,426	190,532	188,261
Geological sciences	109,523	101,207	118,401	131,913	152,449	147,517	173,492	172,185	181,341
Oceanography	92,079	91,863	121,855	129,473	163,035	117,636	94,448	107,897	103,283
Environmental sciences, other	91,365	41,897	103,969	80,930	107,474	117,700	155,218	171,109	185,551
Life sciences	2,137,751	2,290,587	3,463,114	4,348,004	4,730,103	4,771,197	5,316,159	5,625,127	5,567,120
Agricultural sciences	111,739	134,660	143,249	155,772	180,908	181,453	193,763	207,817	184,179
Biological sciences	1,085,602	1,192,756	1,849,516	2,343,429	2,555,864	2,573,430	2,820,183	2,950,701	2,932,063
Environmental biology	13,137	14,636	86,088	97,126	108,584	104,053	124,218	130,633	109,351
Medical sciences	885,898	904,963	1,325,157	1,691,610	1,832,451	1,856,782	2,098,339	2,248,107	2,253,575
Life sciences, other	41,375	43,572	59,104	60,067	52,296	55,479	79,656	87,869	87,952
Psychological sciences	86,459	87,734	138,338	186,924	209,344	225,987	258,886	254,311	277,642
Biological aspects	28,269	26,273	39,049	53,287	66,959	71,705	80,438	75,307	8,542
Social aspects	31,129	28,846	38,589	52,113	59,502	66,960	82,257	75,285	4,729
Psychological sciences, other	27,061	32,615	60,700	81,524	82,883	87,322	96,191	103,719	264,371
Social sciences	203,948	197,695	172,148	184,539	218,404	250,366	303,798	301,056	267,051
Anthropology	7,757	5,543	6,455	5,972	7,054	7,061	8,768	9,015	8,474
Economics	51,414	56,704	43,764	48,039	51,806	58,441	60,142	70,582	68,116
History	1,688	1,069	1,508	1,527	1,665	1,890	2,116	2,166	2,014
Linguistics	2,997	2,745	2,481	3,248	3,402	3,055	3,383	3,684	3,554
Political science	5,890	5,122	5,003	5,926	6,988	7,415	8,287	8,894	7,687
Sociology	34,903	38,136	34,580	55,204	75,404	96,240	113,829	104,430	35,666
Social sciences, other	99,299	88,376	78,357	64,623	72,085	76,264	107,273	102,285	141,540
Other sciences	141,020	120,795	266,599	332,292	415,508	1,661,500	1,770,068	2,049,571	2,204,226
Residual amounts	0	0	0	0	0	0	0	70	34

[1] All U.S. Department of Defense data are reported as other sciences.

NOTE.—Some data have been revised from previously published figures.

SOURCE: National Science Foundation, Science Resources Studies Division, unpublished data. (This table was prepared May 1995.)

Table 363.—U.S. Department of Agriculture obligations for child nutrition programs, by state or other area: Fiscal years 1993 and 1994

[In thousands]

State or other area	Total, fiscal year 1993	Fiscal year 1994								
		Total	Special milk	School lunch [1]	School breakfast	State administrative expenses	Commodities and cash in lieu of commodities [2]	Child and adult care	Summer food service	Nutrition education and training
1	2	3	4	5	6	7	8	9	10	11
Total	$7,296,518	$7,768,161	$19,611	$4,350,583	$958,658	$86,731	$740,232	$1,359,057	$243,019	$10,269
Alabama	150,911	154,926	35	91,721	19,276	1,758	13,982	23,804	4,191	158
Alaska	18,831	20,303	6	12,312	1,565	354	1,221	4,776	6	63
Arizona	120,365	132,265	171	72,960	18,698	1,390	10,062	25,358	3,487	138
Arkansas	94,879	95,127	31	51,333	15,201	1,223	9,142	15,012	3,093	93
California	862,723	940,962	897	553,608	129,766	12,095	66,810	160,075	16,559	1,153
Colorado	79,454	82,560	128	40,789	6,074	1,129	7,827	25,002	1,484	127
Connecticut	55,039	54,620	516	33,180	6,937	770	1,544	10,081	1,479	113
Delaware	20,399	21,625	44	8,547	2,246	367	1,747	7,048	1,563	63
District of Columbia	19,130	20,407	15	12,551	3,019	330	1,358	2,601	470	63
Florida	378,314	395,496	135	240,594	58,415	3,894	34,905	40,969	16,143	442
Georgia	234,373	255,972	38	151,102	41,212	2,489	27,327	25,957	7,591	256
Hawaii	26,801	31,603	7	18,462	3,439	428	4,030	4,733	441	63
Idaho	28,905	30,497	206	19,200	2,789	415	3,450	3,735	640	63
Illinois	265,466	277,206	2,760	167,628	24,364	754	27,576	46,362	7,317	444
Indiana	113,486	118,543	350	68,813	10,615	342	16,764	20,046	1,399	213
Iowa	69,023	71,155	209	39,201	5,369	911	10,744	13,846	765	110
Kansas	83,274	87,244	161	38,669	8,368	1,196	7,263	30,572	920	96
Kentucky	131,416	130,885	123	75,590	22,818	1,450	13,991	14,304	2,466	144
Louisiana	211,365	228,522	68	125,285	35,289	2,583	17,541	40,343	7,232	181
Maine	29,168	30,112	116	15,273	2,606	496	2,672	8,224	661	63
Maryland	98,326	106,453	364	55,514	10,850	1,286	9,134	26,195	2,938	172
Massachusetts	118,502	125,834	530	62,619	13,500	1,598	11,270	32,928	3,186	203
Michigan	186,796	188,997	1,205	107,105	13,475	571	19,152	42,643	4,485	361
Minnesota	136,360	144,829	1,060	55,876	8,220	530	13,830	62,863	2,274	175
Mississippi	145,520	144,657	10	85,486	22,218	1,768	11,704	19,490	3,866	116
Missouri	129,670	137,082	488	75,877	18,492	1,569	15,098	23,513	1,852	193
Montana	23,758	24,210	55	12,257	1,930	441	2,564	6,507	394	63
Nebraska	49,527	53,416	231	23,361	2,984	907	5,789	19,574	508	63
Nevada	22,419	25,524	106	15,097	3,843	343	2,539	2,905	630	63
New Hampshire	16,177	17,234	214	9,570	1,476	359	2,623	2,584	345	63
New Jersey	144,659	141,022	1,007	84,693	10,790	1,582	13,895	22,305	6,479	272
New Mexico	75,512	84,928	8	38,999	8,429	1,216	5,005	26,565	4,637	69
New York	501,748	554,838	1,317	316,949	66,797	5,322	47,583	77,291	38,940	639
North Carolina	203,542	211,594	117	117,029	33,436	2,278	21,671	32,698	4,127	238
North Dakota	24,093	24,897	65	9,503	1,171	472	2,528	10,745	350	63
Ohio	227,974	227,041	1,026	130,434	25,676	659	26,073	38,801	3,958	415
Oklahoma	105,332	113,223	118	61,875	16,576	1,308	9,893	21,527	1,801	126
Oregon	69,067	75,608	230	37,216	8,916	940	6,956	20,102	1,140	109
Pennsylvania	225,749	232,624	822	136,575	22,273	2,433	26,909	32,708	10,487	417
Rhode Island	17,308	18,055	114	10,655	1,294	309	1,675	2,743	1,202	63
South Carolina	130,307	136,709	32	79,716	24,806	1,376	12,188	12,510	5,940	141
South Dakota	25,886	26,002	47	13,965	2,469	415	2,926	5,201	915	63
Tennessee	142,909	150,313	39	87,114	23,427	1,630	16,438	18,661	2,821	183
Texas	675,513	725,389	113	414,046	112,353	7,817	59,670	116,658	13,989	744
Utah	66,073	70,972	57	32,376	3,505	992	7,683	24,290	1,976	93
Vermont	12,257	12,893	113	6,022	1,198	330	1,295	3,682	190	63
Virginia	136,314	137,872	213	79,954	18,196	1,028	15,508	19,899	2,856	217
Washington	121,778	127,421	273	64,858	14,028	1,564	11,624	32,548	2,337	188
West Virginia	56,566	56,802	37	31,100	11,202	725	4,997	7,571	1,103	66
Wisconsin	97,246	99,671	1,741	58,094	4,959	299	13,606	19,384	1,396	190
Wyoming	13,308	18,498	17	6,954	1,006	318	5,995	4,066	80	63
Administrative costs	2,396	0	0	0	0	0	0	0	0	0
Department of Defense dependents schools	6,135	5,933	0	4,484	0	0	1,450	0	0	0
Outlying areas										
American Samoa	63	63	0	0	0	0	0	0	0	63
Guam	809	4,097	0	2,349	763	208	575	202	0	0
Northern Marianas	63	63	0	0	0	0	0	0	0	63
Puerto Rico	148,576	161,239	0	115,058	26,302	1,539	10,851	2,102	5,242	145
Freely Associated States	2,894	0	0	0	0	0	0	0	0	0
Trust Territory	73	87	0	0	0	14	69	0	0	4
Virgin Islands	5,591	5,889	3	4,247	214	253	35	646	429	63
Undistributed [3]	136,402	196,154	1,822	66,734	3,818	7,960	39,479	44,102	32,239	-1

[1] Special Meal Assistance program is combined with "School Lunch" program.

[2] Commodities are based on preliminary food orders for fiscal year 1994.

[3] Undistributed amount reflects the difference between preliminary state earnings reports and federal obligations as of September 30, 1994.

NOTE.—Data are based on obligations as reported September 30, 1994. Negative amounts occur when program receipts exceed the obligations. Because of rounding, details may not add to totals.

SOURCE: U.S. Department of Agriculture, Food and Nutrition Service, Budget Division, unpublished data. (This table was prepared February 1994.)

Table 364.—U.S. Department of Health and Human Services allocations for Head Start and enrollment in Head Start, by state or other area: Fiscal years 1992, 1993, and 1994

State or other area	1992		1993		1994	
	Head Start allocations (in thousands)	Head Start enrollment [1]	Head Start allocations (in thousands)	Head Start enrollment [2]	Head Start allocations (in thousands)	Head Start enrollment [3]
1	2	3	4	5	6	7
Total	$2,120,862	621,078	$2,683,158	713,943	$3,215,946	740,493
Alabama	40,021	13,012	46,937	14,106	54,282	14,525
Alaska	4,434	1,067	5,316	1,143	6,295	1,209
Arizona	20,729	6,179	35,503	9,189	44,416	9,846
Arkansas	22,297	8,213	26,337	8,792	30,719	9,065
California	219,423	52,658	305,180	67,684	371,227	70,995
Colorado	19,353	6,604	25,505	7,672	31,787	8,118
Connecticut	18,694	5,311	22,066	5,561	26,061	5,660
Delaware	4,454	1,333	5,265	1,455	5,815	1,455
District of Columbia ..	9,673	2,639	11,631	2,841	12,854	2,841
Florida	67,552	20,567	92,741	25,333	118,976	27,398
Georgia	52,225	16,080	66,499	18,594	81,974	19,445
Hawaii	7,547	1,974	8,882	2,183	9,939	2,260
Idaho	6,745	1,658	8,329	1,850	9,574	1,912
Illinois	99,852	28,802	117,770	30,268	139,137	30,537
Indiana	31,054	10,213	37,979	11,107	46,558	11,730
Iowa	16,484	5,266	20,111	5,758	23,430	5,946
Kansas	14,175	4,705	17,885	5,389	22,095	5,793
Kentucky	38,053	12,467	45,318	13,791	54,364	14,071
Louisiana	48,205	15,804	62,996	18,677	75,876	19,344
Maine	9,476	3,132	11,011	3,361	12,610	3,439
Maryland	27,043	7,594	32,073	8,338	38,810	8,509
Massachusetts	42,348	10,159	49,615	10,929	57,264	10,794
Michigan	82,321	26,174	107,451	29,960	126,686	30,701
Minnesota	24,373	7,136	30,823	8,167	36,930	8,576
Mississippi	71,861	22,343	83,560	24,036	92,012	24,110
Missouri	35,641	11,972	45,641	13,592	55,979	14,063
Montana	6,436	1,961	8,211	2,226	9,563	2,304
Nebraska	10,284	3,154	12,322	3,465	14,342	3,644
Nevada	4,000	1,073	6,341	1,593	8,017	1,793
New Hampshire	4,080	1,016	4,895	1,131	5,699	1,156
New Jersey	54,532	11,688	63,902	12,773	71,189	12,898
New Mexico	13,655	4,958	18,954	6,055	24,241	6,397
New York	153,858	34,688	181,968	37,829	215,678	39,062
North Carolina	44,259	14,083	54,263	15,296	66,643	15,695
North Dakota	4,283	1,458	5,666	1,653	6,723	1,738
Ohio	84,964	29,132	110,420	32,567	133,913	33,919
Oklahoma	24,078	8,977	32,274	10,625	39,073	11,165
Oregon	17,760	3,885	21,782	4,431	27,080	4,638
Pennsylvania	82,449	22,414	99,688	24,866	119,354	25,672
Rhode Island	6,964	2,293	8,328	2,380	10,060	2,476
South Carolina	27,716	9,025	33,063	9,709	40,772	10,142
South Dakota	5,421	1,691	6,629	1,894	7,985	2,025
Tennessee	39,271	12,481	47,993	13,859	58,610	14,380
Texas	113,612	36,394	172,536	49,110	213,394	51,521
Utah	10,669	3,403	13,208	3,822	15,832	4,028
Vermont	4,556	1,129	5,339	1,260	5,957	1,271
Virginia	33,134	9,455	39,440	10,650	46,411	10,993
Washington	27,533	6,361	37,558	7,799	45,968	8,260
West Virginia	18,959	5,842	22,303	6,317	26,014	6,402
Wisconsin	31,052	9,665	40,956	11,247	49,461	11,953
Wyoming	3,371	1,128	4,149	1,245	4,925	1,323
Migrant programs	[4] 153,755	[4] 44,770	108,011	33,886	130,409	35,063
Native American programs ..	—	—	74,800	17,973	90,793	18,738
Special projects	—	—	—	—	76	—
Outlying areas						
Puerto Rico	95,629	29,031	113,047	31,306	127,066	32,145
Pacific Territories	6,253	5,439	7,613	5,779	9,019	5,849
Virgin Islands	4,294	1,422	5,074	1,421	6,009	1,501

[1] The distribution of enrollment by age was: 7 percent were 5 years old and over; 63 percent were 4-year-olds; 27 percent were 3-year-olds; and 3 percent were under 3 years of age. Handicapped children accounted for 13.4 percent in Head Start programs. The racial/ethnic composition was: Native American, 4 percent; Hispanic, 23 percent; black, 37 percent; white, 33 percent; and Asian, 3 percent.

[2] The distribution of enrollment by age was: 6 percent were 5 years old and over; 64 percent were 4-year-olds; 27 percent were 3-year-olds; and 3 percent were under 3 years of age. Handicapped children accounted for 13.2 percent in Head Start programs. The racial/ethnic composition was: Native American, 4 percent; Hispanic, 24 percent; black, 36 percent; white, 33 percent; and Asian, 3 percent.

[3] The distribution of enrollment by age was: 6 percent were 5 years old and over; 64 percent were 4-year-olds; 27 percent were 3-year-olds; and 3 percent were under 3

years of age. Handicapped children accounted for 13.0 percent in Head Start programs. The racial/ethnic composition was: Native American, 4 percent; Hispanic, 24 percent; black, 36 percent; white, 33 percent; and Asian, 3 percent.

[4] Includes Native American and Migrant programs.

—Not applicable.

NOTE.—Because of rounding, details may not add to totals.

SOURCE: U.S. Department of Health and Human Services, Office of Human Development Services. (This table was prepared February 1995.)

Table 365.—Public school students receiving publicly funded free or reduced price lunches, by selected school characteristics: School year 1993–94

School characterisics	Percent of students participating in program			
	Total	Elementary	Secondary	Combined [1]
1	2	3	4	5
Total	33.2	38.8	22.0	39.1
Community type				
Central city	42.5	49.9	26.9	42.7
Urban fringe/large town	24.3	28.8	15.7	29.9
Rural/small town	32.6	37.0	23.4	40.2
School size (students)				
Less than 150	38.6	38.4	35.8	50.3
150–299	38.1	39.5	28.4	51.8
300–499	37.0	38.8	26.2	37.3
500–749	33.5	36.0	22.3	34.7
750 or more	29.7	42.5	20.6	34.3
Minority students				
Less than 5%	22.0	22.4	17.0	28.6
5 to 19%	18.9	22.2	11.7	30.8
20 to 49%	32.0	38.1	20.1	38.5
50% or more	57.3	65.5	38.9	60.6

[1] Includes schools beginning with grade 6 or below and ending with grade 9 or above.

SOURCE: U.S. Department of Education, National Center for Education Statistics, "Schools and Staffing Survey, 1993–94." (This table was prepared August 1995.)

Table 366.—Public and private school students receiving publicly funded ECIA [1] Chapter I services, by selected school characteristics: School year 1993–94

School characteristics	Percent of students participating in program								
	All schools	Public				Private			
		Total	Elementary	Secondary	Combined [2]	Total	Elementary	Secondary	Combined [2]
1	2	3	4	5	6	7	8	9	10
Total	13.1	14.3	18.5	6.1	13.6	3.3	4.6	1.9	1.4
Community type									
Central city	16.0	18.3	23.2	8.2	13.9	4.2	6.2	2.5	1.0
Urban fringe/large town .	9.5	10.4	13.4	4.9	7.2	2.3	2.8	0.9	1.8
Rural/small town	13.5	14.1	18.6	5.4	15.0	2.5	3.2	1.4	1.8
School size (students)									
Less than 150	9.8	16.7	20.0	11.1	15.7	3.8	3.3	8.1	3.8
150–299	13.1	16.7	19.2	7.6	11.6	5.1	6.2	4.1	1.4
300–499	14.7	16.3	18.0	7.0	13.0	2.6	3.7	0.9	0.8
500–749	14.7	15.5	17.6	6.0	18.3	2.0	3.8	1.1	0.3
750 or more	11.3	11.7	20.1	5.8	11.4	1.3	4.5	0.8	0.4
Minority students									
Less than 5%	7.8	8.8	11.7	3.7	9.7	1.7	2.4	0.6	0.8
5 to 19%	6.0	6.6	8.6	2.3	14.3	2.1	3.0	1.6	0.9
20 to 49%	10.2	10.8	14.6	3.3	13.6	2.7	2.7	3.7	1.7
50% or more	27.8	29.0	35.8	14.9	18.0	10.0	12.4	2.5	5.2

[1] Education Consolidation and Improvement Act.
[2] Includes schools beginning with grade 6 or below and ending with grade 9 or above.

SOURCE: U.S. Department of Education, National Center for Education Statistics, "Schools and Staffing Survey, 1993–94." (This table was prepared August 1995.)

CHAPTER 5
Outcomes of Education

This chapter contains tables comparing educational attainment and work force characteristics. The data show labor force participation and income levels of high school dropouts and high school and college graduates. Population characteristics are provided for many of the measures to help evaluate disparities among various demographic groups. The first set of tables contains data from the Bureau of the Census on educational attainment of the labor force and income of the labor force and data from the Bureau of Labor Statistics on employment and unemployment. These tables provide information on the educational attainment of the labor force, by occupation, sex, and race/ethnicity; money income, by level of education attained; and unemployment rates, by levels of education attained, sex, and race/ethnicity.

The second group of tables was compiled from Bureau of Labor Statistics data on high school dropouts and graduates. These data show the labor force participation and college enrollment of high school students within the year after they leave school. The tabulations also provide comparative labor force participation and unemployment rates for graduates and dropouts. Additional information on college enrollment rates by race/ethnicity and sex have been included to help form a more complete picture of high school outcomes.

The third set of tables has been prepared from the National Center for Education Statistics survey, Recent College Graduates, and from a Bureau of the Census survey on earnings and education. These tables provide data on employment outcomes for high school and college graduates. A table provides a salary comparison by field of college degree for the entire population. Trends in salaries received by college graduates also are featured in this section.

Statistics on educational attainment of the entire population are in Chapter 1. More detailed data on the number of degree recipients are contained in Chapters 2 and 3. Chapter 2 contains trend data on the proportion of high school graduates going to college. Additional data on the income of persons by educational attainment may be obtained from the Bureau of the Census in the *Current Population Reports,* Series P–60. The Bureau of Labor Statistics has a selection of publications dealing with the educational characteristics of the labor force. Further in-

formation on survey methodologies is in the "Guide to Sources" in the appendix and in the publications cited in the source notes.

Opinions

One life goal consistently rated "very important" by young men and women was "being successful in work." A survey of 1992 high school seniors found that 89 percent of the men and 90 percent of the women rated "being successful in work" as a "very important goal." Two of the other most highly rated goals in the 1992 survey were "finding steady work" ("very important" for 87 percent of men and 89 percent of women) and "having strong friendships" ("very important" for 80 percent of both men and women (table 368).

Labor Force

Adults with higher levels of education were more likely to participate in the labor force than those with less education. About 81 percent of adults with a bachelor's degree participated in the labor force in 1992 compared with 66 percent of persons who were high school graduates. Only 40 percent of those 25 and older who were not high school graduates were in the labor force. The labor force participation rates for different racial/ethnic groups were about the same (table 369).

Persons with lower levels of educational attainment were more likely to be unemployed than those who had higher levels of educational attainment. The 1994 unemployment rate for adults (25 years old and over) who had not completed high school was 9.8 percent compared with 5.4 percent for those with 4 years of high school and 2.6 percent for those with a bachelor's degree or higher. Blacks, Hispanics, and young people tended to have higher unemployment rates, even after allowing for level of educational attainment (table 371).

One year after graduating from college in 1989–90, 84 percent of those receiving bachelor's degrees were employed (74 percent full time and 10 percent part time), 4 percent were unemployed, and 12 percent were not in the labor force (tables 378 and 379). Of the 12 percent of 1989–90 graduates not in the labor force, about two-thirds enrolled in further education (table 378).

Income

Between 1980 and 1990, annual income generally rose more rapidly for persons with higher levels of educational attainment than for those with lower levels. For example, the income of men who were year-round full-time workers with 5 or more years of college rose by 78 percent compared with 30 percent for men with 1 to 3 years of high school. Income for men who had completed 4 years of high school increased 37 percent.

Women's incomes are much lower than men's incomes, even after adjusting for level of education. The average 1993 incomes for full-time year-round workers with a bachelor's degree were $42,757 for men and $31,197 for women. (table 373)

Dropouts and graduates

The difficulties in entering the job market for dropouts, and youth in general, are highlighted by comparing their labor force and unemployment status. Only 61 percent of 1993–94 dropouts were in the labor force (employed or looking for work), and 30 percent of them were unemployed. Of the 1994 high school graduates who were not in college, 80 percent were in the labor force, and 20 percent of those in the labor force were unemployed (tables 375 and 376).

About 72 percent of the employed college graduates of the class of 1989–90 had jobs in professional, managerial, and technical areas in 1991. Twenty-eight percent were employed in nonprofessional, nonmanagerial, and nontechnical areas (table 379).

A 1992 assessment of literacy skills for adults found that about 21 percent of the adult population lacked the ability to perform simple arithmetic operations or locate a simple piece of information in a short text excerpt. Only about one-fifth of the population could solve mathematical problems requiring multiple steps or integrate information from complex passages (table 383).

Figure 23.-Unemployment rates of persons 25 years old and over, by highest degree attained: 1993

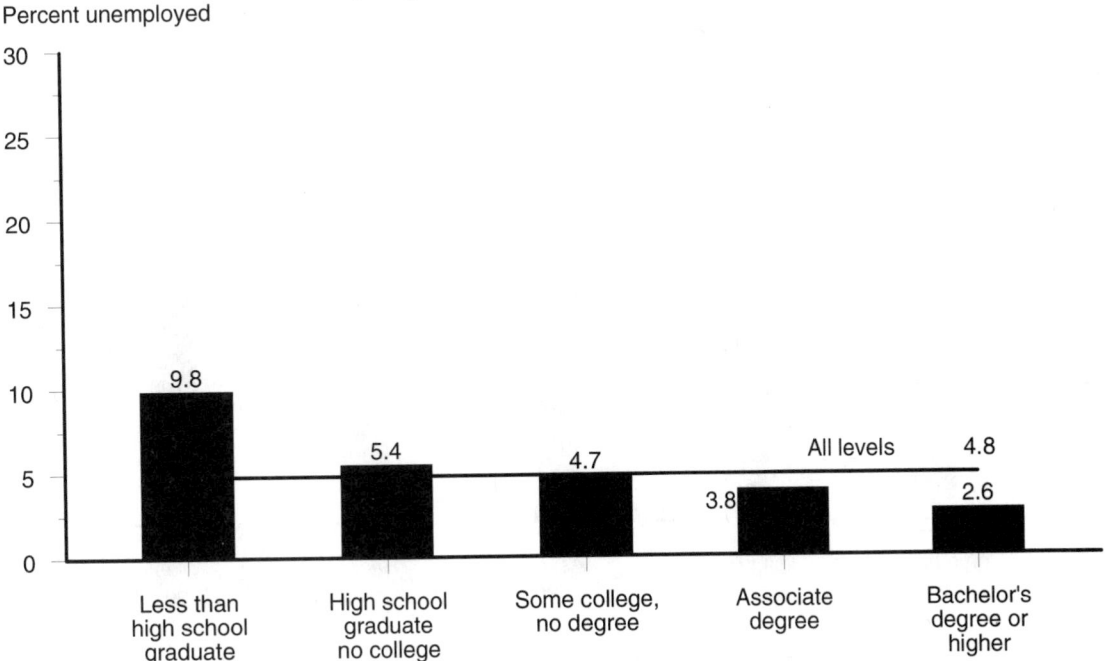

Percent unemployed

SOURCE: U.S. Department of Labor, Bureau of Labor Statistics, Office of Employment and Unemployment Statistics, unpublished data.

Figure 24.-Labor force status of 1993–94 high school graduates and dropouts: October 1994

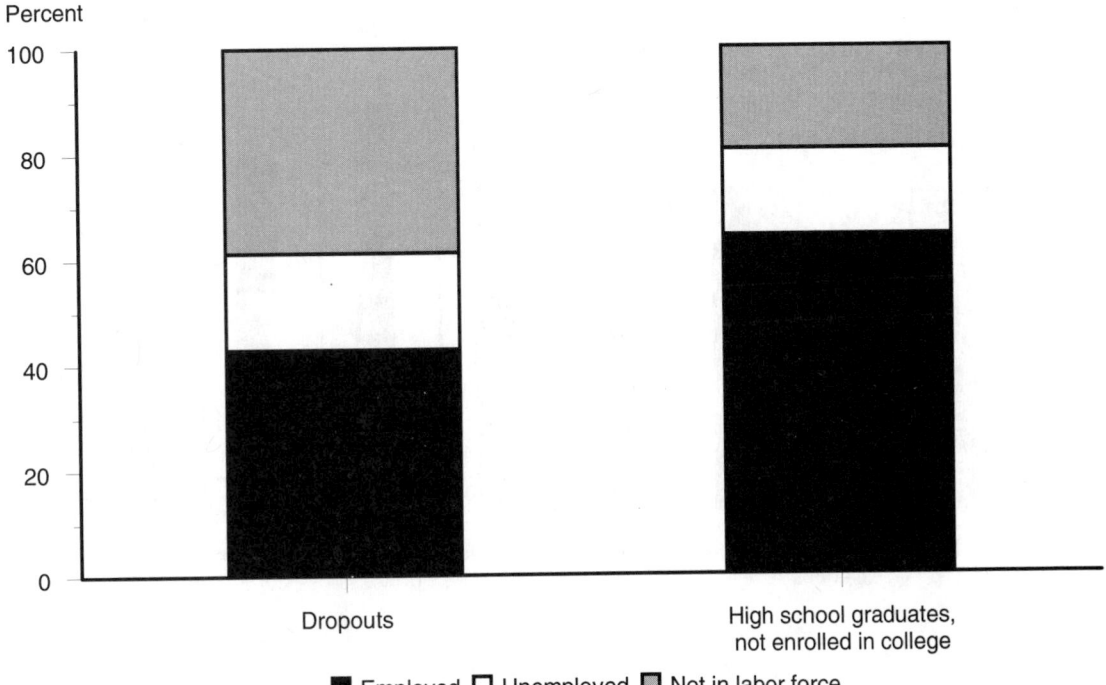

Percent

■ Employed □ Unemployed ▨ Not in labor force

SOURCE: U.S. Department of Labor, Bureau of Labor Statistics, "Employment Status of School Age Youth, High School Graduates and Dropouts, 1994".

Figure 25.-Median annual earnings of workers 25 years old and over, by years of school completed and sex: 1993

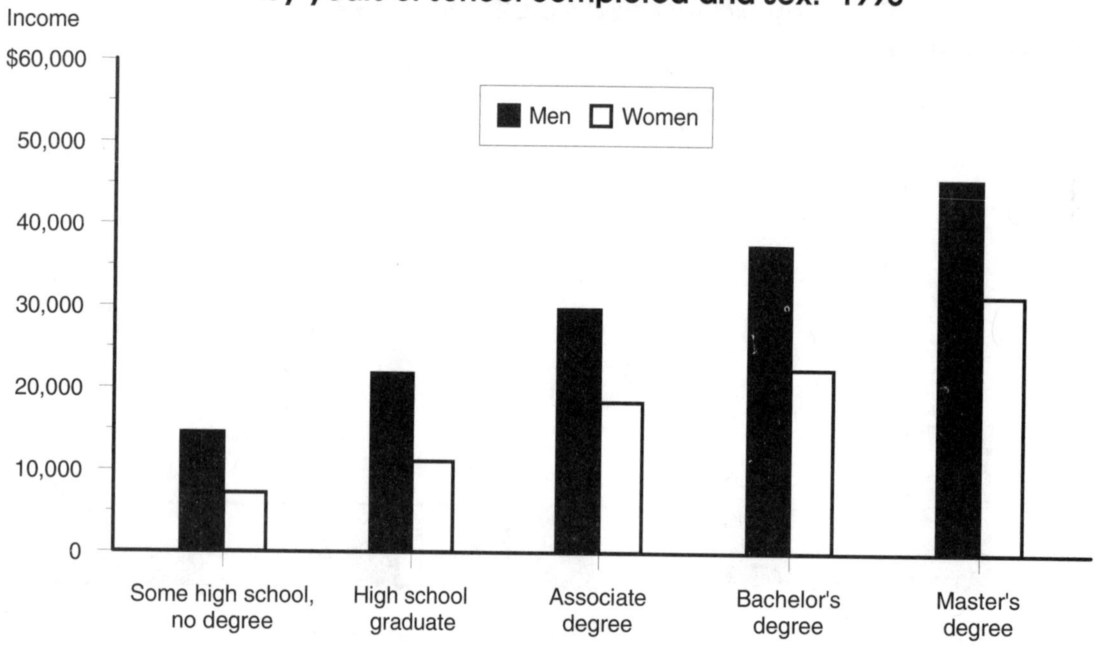

SOURCE: U.S. Department of Commerce, Bureau of the Census, *Current Population Reports*, Series P-60, *Monthly Income of Households, Families, and Persons in the United States: 1993.*

Figure 26.-Salaries of recent bachelor's degree recipients 1 year after graduation, by field: 1987 and 1991
(In constant 1991 dollars)

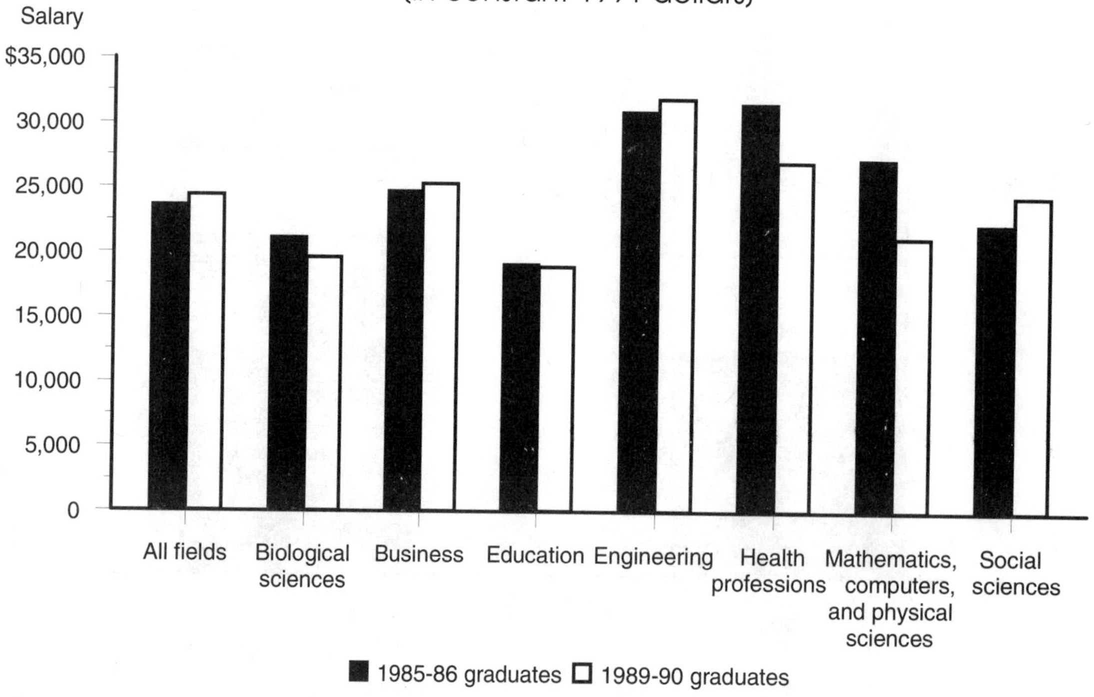

SOURCE: U.S. Department of Education, National Center for Education Statistics, "Recent College Graduates" survey, 1987 and 1991.

Table 367.—Percent of 18- to 25-year-olds reporting drug use during the past 30 days and the past year: 1972 to 1993

Drug	1972	1974	1976	1977	1979	1982	1985	1988	1990	1991	1992	1993
1	2	3	4	5	6	7	8	9	10	11	12	13
Percent reporting drug use during past 30 days												
Any illicit use	—	—	—	—	37.1	30.4	25.1	17.8	14.9	15.4	13.0	13.5
Marijuana	27.8	25.2	25.0	27.4	35.4	27.4	21.9	15.5	12.7	13.0	11.0	11.1
Hallucinogens	—	2.5	1.1	2.0	4.4	1.7	1.8	0.8	1.2	1.3	1.3	1.3
Cocaine	—	3.1	2.0	3.7	9.3	6.8	7.5	4.5	2.2	2.0	1.8	1.5
Heroin	—	—	—	—	—	—	0.3	0.1	0.1	0.1	0.2	0.1
Nonmedical use of:												
Stimulants	—	3.7	4.7	2.5	3.5	4.7	3.8	2.4	1.2	0.8	0.7	0.9
Sedatives	—	1.6	2.3	2.8	2.8	2.6	1.6	0.9	0.7	0.7	0.6	0.6
Tranquilizers	—	1.2	2.6	2.4	2.1	1.6	1.6	1.0	0.5	0.6	0.6	0.6
Analgesics	—	—	—	—	1.0	1.0	2.0	1.5	1.2	1.4	1.2	1.4
Alcohol	—	69.3	69.0	70.0	75.9	70.9	70.7	65.3	63.3	63.6	59.2	59.3
Cigarettes	—	48.8	49.4	47.3	42.6	39.5	36.6	35.2	31.5	32.2	31.9	29.0
Percent reporting drug use during past year												
Any illicit use	—	—	—	—	49.4	43.4	41.0	31.9	28.7	29.1	26.4	26.6
Marijuana	—	34.2	35.0	38.7	46.9	40.4	36.3	27.9	24.6	24.5	22.7	22.9
Hallucinogens	—	6.1	6.0	6.4	9.9	6.9	4.0	5.6	3.9	4.7	4.8	4.9
Cocaine	—	8.1	7.0	10.2	19.6	18.8	15.6	12.1	7.5	7.7	6.3	5.0
Heroin	—	0.8	0.6	1.2	0.8	—	0.6	0.3	0.5	0.3	0.5	0.3
Nonmedical use of:												
Stimulants	—	8.0	8.8	10.4	10.1	10.8	9.8	6.4	3.4	3.3	2.3	3.0
Sedatives	—	4.2	5.7	8.2	7.3	8.7	5.1	3.3	2.0	1.9	1.7	1.1
Tranquilizers	—	4.6	6.2	7.8	7.1	5.9	6.4	4.6	2.4	2.6	3.0	2.0
Analgesics	—	—	—	—	5.2	4.4	6.8	5.5	4.1	5.3	4.8	4.1
Alcohol	—	77.1	77.9	79.8	86.6	87.1	86.4	81.7	80.2	82.8	77.7	79.0
Cigarettes	—	—	—	—	46.7	47.2	43.9	44.7	39.7	41.2	41.1	38.3

—Data not available.

SOURCE: U.S. Department of Health and Human Services, Substance Abuse and Mental Health Services Administration, *Preliminary Estimates from the 1993 National Household Survey on Drug Abuse.* (This table was prepared August 1994.)

Table 368.—Percent of 1972, 1982, and 1992 high school seniors who felt that certain life values were "very important," by sex: 1972 to 1994

Value	Percent of 1972 seniors						Percent of 1982 seniors						Percent of 1992 seniors				
	1972		1974 (2 years after high school)		1976 (4 years after high school)		1982		1984 (2 years after high school)		1986 (4 years after high school)		1992		1994 (2 years after high school)		
	Male	Female	Male	Female	Male	Female	Male	Female	Male	Female	Male	Female	Male	Female	Total	Male	Female
1	2	3	4	5	6	7	8	9	10	11	12	13	14	15	16	17	18
Being successful in work	86.5	83.0	81.2	74.9	80.3	69.7	88.2	85.5	88.7	84.2	84.0	77.2	89.0	89.6	90.1	89.9	90.3
Finding steady work	82.3	73.7	74.7	59.9	79.3	62.1	88.0	84.4	87.4	83.3	84.2	76.3	87.1	88.6	89.7	88.7	90.7
Having lots of money	26.0	9.8	17.8	9.1	17.7	9.4	41.3	24.1	35.8	20.9	27.8	16.9	45.3	29.4	35.2	39.5	30.9
Being a leader in the community	14.9	8.0	8.5	4.4	9.2	4.2	11.3	5.9	13.7	6.4	9.5	4.5	—	—	—	—	—
Correcting inequalities	22.5	31.1	16.6	18.2	16.2	17.1	11.8	11.7	13.3	10.7	10.9	—	17.0	23.6	—	—	—
Having children	—	—	—	—	—	—	37.0	47.0	42.7	56.3	41.4	56.2	39.0	49.2	—	—	—
Having a happy family life	78.6	85.7	83.1	86.7	84.2	86.4	81.6	86.3	86.1	90.2	86.8	87.8	—	—	90.5	90.3	90.8
Providing better opportunities for my children	66.6	66.2	59.5	61.6	59.8	58.8	71.0	68.7	69.9	68.4	67.4	—	74.5	76.5	—	—	—
Living closer to parents or relatives	6.8	8.2	8.3	12.4	7.7	11.9	15.0	15.7	15.6	20.1	12.9	19.8	15.2	18.7	—	—	—
Moving from area	14.3	14.6	8.3	7.4	6.7	6.4	14.4	12.8	10.5	9.1	9.0	7.4	20.7	20.1	—	—	—
Having strong friendships	81.2	78.7	76.5	74.7	76.1	72.1	80.4	79.1	80.1	79.7	76.5	75.0	79.8	80.0	87.6	88.1	87.0
Having leisure time	—	—	60.9	55.1	65.4	60.1	70.2	68.8	74.5	72.0	70.1	68.9	65.3	62.0	—	—	—

—Question not asked.

SOURCE: U.S. Department of Education, National Center for Education Statistics, "National Longitudinal Study," "High School and Beyond" surveys, and "National Education Longitudinal Study," second and third followup surveys. (This table was prepared June 1995.)

Table 369.—Labor force participation of persons 16 years old and over, by age, sex, race/ethnicity, and highest level of education: 1994

Age, sex, and race/ethnicity	Labor force participation rate [1]						Employment/population ratio [2]					
	Total	Less than high school graduate [3]	High school graduate	College			Total	Less than high school graduate [3]	High school graduate	College		
				Some college, no degree	Associate degree	Bachelor's degree or higher				Some college, no degree	Associate degree	Bachelor's degree or higher
1	2	3	4	5	6	7	8	9	10	11	12	13
16 to 19 years old [4]	**52.7**	**45.9**	**69.6**	**62.5**	**67.3**	**55.6**	**43.4**	**36.0**	**59.5**	**56.8**	**59.4**	**50.7**
Men	54.1	47.8	74.1	60.8	64.2	95.7	43.8	37.1	62.8	54.6	60.1	95.7
Women	51.3	43.6	65.5	64.0	68.4	42.0	43.0	34.8	56.5	58.6	59.1	9.2
White [5]	56.4	49.8	72.3	65.2	76.0	59.2	47.9	40.5	63.8	60.0	67.2	54.2
Black [5]	38.5	32.1	58.8	52.6	28.8	47.8	24.9	19.3	40.3	41.3	28.8	40.4
Hispanic [6]	44.4	38.3	62.3	65.7	81.4	56.6	33.5	27.6	49.5	56.2	53.6	56.6
20 to 24 years old [4]	**77.0**	**64.3**	**81.5**	**73.9**	**84.6**	**86.0**	**69.5**	**51.5**	**72.5**	**68.4**	**80.0**	**81.5**
Men	83.1	82.6	89.9	75.6	87.0	84.9	74.6	68.1	80.1	69.5	82.0	79.6
Women	71.0	42.9	72.1	72.4	82.8	86.9	64.5	32.1	64.2	67.3	78.4	82.9
White [5]	79.5	67.7	83.9	76.0	86.2	87.9	73.0	56.3	76.3	71.3	82.0	83.4
Black [5]	68.8	51.3	73.1	68.5	78.9	82.6	55.4	30.7	58.0	58.3	69.2	78.0
Hispanic [6]	74.0	67.3	78.0	77.9	80.7	77.5	65.3	57.6	68.6	70.7	73.6	74.0
25 and older	**66.6**	**39.9**	**65.5**	**73.4**	**79.6**	**81.2**	**63.4**	**36.0**	**62.0**	**69.9**	**76.6**	**79.1**
Men	76.1	52.6	76.5	81.0	87.7	86.2	72.4	47.7	72.3	77.3	84.4	84.1
Women	58.1	28.8	56.6	66.5	73.5	75.3	55.2	25.8	53.6	63.2	70.8	73.3
White [5]	66.7	40.0	64.9	72.6	79.2	80.9	63.8	36.4	61.9	69.5	76.5	78.9
Black [5]	65.6	37.3	69.4	79.0	82.7	85.4	60.0	32.3	62.6	72.6	77.8	82.5
Hispanic [6]	67.5	55.5	73.5	79.8	82.7	82.4	61.9	49.4	67.9	74.2	77.9	78.9

[1] Percent of the civilian population who are employed or seeking employment.
[2] Number of persons employed as a percent of civilian population.
[3] Includes persons reporting no school years completed.
[4] Excludes persons enrolled in school.
[5] Includes persons of Hispanic origin.
[6] Hispanics may be of any race.

SOURCE: U.S. Department of Labor, Bureau of Labor Statistics, Office of Employment and Unemployment Statistics, Industry and Occupation tables, unpublished data. (This table was prepared June 1995.)

Table 370.—Occupation of employed persons 25 years old and over, by educational attainment and sex: 1994

Sex and occupation	Total employed, in thousands	Percentage distribution, by years of school completed							
		Total	Less than one year of high school	High school		College			
				1–4 years of high school, no diploma	High school graduate	Some college, no degree	Associate degree	Bachelor's degree	More than a bachelor's degree
1	2	3	4	5	6	7	8	9	10
All persons									
All occupational groups	104,141	100.0	3.8	6.8	33.7	19.1	8.5	18.5	9.6
Managerial and professional specialty	31,818	100.0	0.4	1.3	13.3	14.3	8.8	35.1	26.8
Executive, administrative, and managerial	15,437	100.0	0.7	2.2	21.4	20.4	8.3	32.8	14.2
Professional specialty occupations	16,381	100.0	0.2	0.5	5.7	8.4	9.2	37.3	38.6
Teachers, except college and university	3,975	100.0	0.1	0.3	4.7	6.0	3.3	47.4	38.0
Teachers, college and university	765	100.0	0.0	0.0	0.8	2.1	1.6	14.1	81.4
Technical, sales, and administrative support	30,609	100.0	0.9	3.4	36.6	26.1	11.0	18.4	3.6
Technicians and related support	3,452	100.0	0.3	1.2	19.7	25.1	23.6	24.0	5.9
Sales occupations	11,509	100.0	1.5	4.9	33.5	23.2	7.7	24.2	4.9
Administrative support, including clerical	15,649	100.0	0.6	2.8	42.6	28.3	10.6	12.9	2.2
Service occupations	12,354	100.0	8.3	13.1	43.5	19.5	7.0	7.4	1.3
Precision production, craft, and repair	12,073	100.0	5.2	11.2	48.4	19.9	8.6	5.7	0.9
Operators, fabricators, and laborers	14,317	100.0	9.3	15.8	51.3	14.8	4.4	3.8	0.5
Farming, forestry, and fishing	2,969	100.0	18.6	12.7	38.8	13.8	5.6	8.6	1.9
Men									
All occupational groups	56,523	100.0	4.6	7.5	32.6	18.4	7.4	18.9	10.6
Managerial and professional specialty	16,708	100.0	0.6	1.5	12.0	13.9	6.5	35.4	30.1
Executive, administrative, and managerial	8,883	100.0	0.9	2.3	18.3	18.4	7.1	36.0	17.0
Professional specialty occupations	7,825	100.0	0.2	0.6	4.9	8.7	5.8	34.7	45.1
Teachers, except college and university	1,002	100.0	0.1	0.2	3.4	6.2	3.9	44.6	41.5
Teachers, college and university	442	100.0	0.0	0.0	0.5	2.0	0.9	12.7	83.3
Technical, sales, and administrative support	11,161	100.0	1.3	3.3	27.0	25.0	10.2	27.1	6.1
Technicians and related support	1,661	100.0	0.2	1.3	17.4	25.6	20.7	27.2	7.8
Sales occupations	6,346	100.0	1.5	3.5	26.7	23.7	7.7	30.4	6.5
Administrative support, including clerical	3,153	100.0	1.4	3.9	32.7	27.5	9.6	20.6	4.3
Service occupations	4,760	100.0	8.3	10.3	38.4	22.6	8.3	10.3	1.8
Precision production, craft, and repair	10,946	100.0	5.1	11.3	48.3	20.1	8.8	5.6	0.9
Operators, fabricators, and laborers	10,593	100.0	8.7	15.2	50.8	16.0	4.6	4.1	0.6
Farming, forestry, and fishing	2,356	100.0	19.8	13.5	38.5	13.1	5.5	8.0	1.6
Women									
All occupational groups	47,618	100.0	2.9	5.9	35.1	19.9	9.8	18.0	8.5
Managerial and professional specialty	15,110	100.0	0.3	1.2	14.7	14.7	11.3	34.8	23.1
Executive, administrative, and managerial	6,555	100.0	0.4	2.0	25.4	23.2	10.0	28.5	10.5
Professional specialty occupations	8,556	100.0	0.2	0.5	6.4	8.2	12.3	39.7	32.8
Teachers, except college and university	2,972	100.0	0.1	0.3	5.2	6.0	3.2	48.4	36.9
Teachers, college and university	324	100.0	0.0	0.0	0.6	2.2	2.2	16.0	78.7
Technical, sales, and administrative support	19,448	100.0	0.8	3.5	42.1	26.7	11.4	13.4	2.2
Technicians and related support	1,790	100.0	0.4	1.1	21.8	24.8	26.5	21.1	4.2
Sales occupations	5,163	100.0	1.6	6.6	41.9	22.7	7.7	16.6	2.9
Administrative support, including clerical	12,495	100.0	0.4	2.5	45.0	28.6	10.8	11.0	1.6
Service occupations	7,594	100.0	8.3	14.8	46.7	17.5	6.2	5.6	0.9
Precision production, craft, and repair	1,128	100.0	5.9	11.2	50.0	17.9	6.6	6.8	1.4
Operators, fabricators, and laborers	3,724	100.0	11.1	17.7	52.9	11.4	3.6	3.0	0.3
Farming, forestry, and fishing	614	100.0	14.0	9.9	40.1	16.6	5.9	10.6	2.8

NOTE.—Because of rounding, details may not add to totals.

SOURCE: U.S. Department of Labor, Bureau of Labor Statistics, Office of Employment and Unemployment Statistics, Industry and Occupation tables, unpublished data. (This table was prepared June 1995.)

Table 371.—Unemployment rate of persons 16 years old and over, by age, sex, race/ethnicity, and highest degree attained: 1992 and 1994

Sex, race/ethnicity, and highest degree attained	Percent unemployed, 1992 [1]				Percent unemployed, 1994 [1]			
	16- to 24-year-olds [2]			25 years old and over	16- to 24-years-old [2]			25 years and over
	Total	16 to 19 years	20 to 24 years		Total	16 to 19 years	20 to 24 years	
1	2	3	4	5	6	7	8	9
All persons								
All education levels	14.3	21.7	12.0	6.1	12.5	17.6	9.7	4.8
Less than a high school graduate	24.9	27.8	22.3	11.4	21.0	21.5	19.9	9.8
High school graduate, no college	13.9	18.8	12.5	6.8	11.9	14.5	10.9	5.4
Some college, no degree	9.6	11.5	9.3	6.0	7.9	9.2	7.5	4.7
Associate degree	6.0	14.6	5.8	4.7	5.4	—	5.5	3.8
Bachelor's degree or higher	6.5	—	6.5	3.2	5.2	—	5.2	2.6
Men								
All education levels	15.1	22.0	13.0	6.4	13.2	19.0	10.2	4.8
Less than a high school graduate	23.6	26.8	21.1	11.4	20.8	22.5	17.5	9.3
High school graduate, no college	14.7	19.5	13.5	7.3	12.0	15.3	10.9	5.5
Some college, no degree	9.4	10.6	9.2	6.1	8.4	10.1	8.0	4.5
Associate degree	—	—	—	—	5.7	—	5.7	3.8
Bachelor's degree or higher	7.7	—	7.7	3.3	6.1	—	6.1	2.5
Women								
All education levels	13.3	21.4	10.9	5.7	11.6	16.2	9.2	4.9
Less than a high school graduate	27.1	29.3	24.8	11.4	21.3	20.2	25.2	10.5
High school graduate, no college	13.0	18.0	11.4	6.2	11.9	13.7	11.0	5.2
Some college, no degree	9.8	12.2	9.4	5.8	7.4	8.5	7.1	5.0
Associate degree	—	—	—	—	5.2	—	5.3	3.8
Bachelor's degree or higher	5.5	—	5.5	3.0	4.5	—	4.5	2.7
White [3]								
All education levels	12.0	18.4	10.0	5.5	10.6	15.1	8.1	4.3
Less than a high school graduate	21.5	24.0	19.2	10.7	18.1	18.7	16.8	8.9
High school graduate, no college	11.5	15.6	10.3	6.0	9.9	11.8	9.1	4.7
Some college, no degree	7.8	9.5	7.5	5.4	6.6	7.9	6.2	4.2
Associate degree	—	—	—	—	4.8	—	4.8	3.4
Bachelor's degree or higher	6.3	—	6.3	3.0	5.2	—	5.2	2.4
Black [3]								
All education levels	28.8	41.8	24.8	10.9	24.5	35.2	19.5	8.6
Less than a high school graduate	44.4	49.4	40.1	15.1	39.8	39.6	40.3	13.5
High school graduate, no college	26.6	37.2	24.1	12.3	23.1	31.4	20.6	9.9
Some college, no degree	21.6	26.1	21.0	10.3	15.8	21.4	14.9	8.1
Associate degree	—	—	—	—	12.0	—	12.1	5.8
Bachelor's degree or higher	7.6	—	7.6	4.4	5.0	—	5.1	3.5
Hispanic origin [4]								
All education levels	16.7	26.5	13.7	9.8	15.7	24.5	11.8	8.3
Less than a high school graduate	20.3	29.0	16.5	12.8	20.5	27.9	14.5	11.1
High school graduate, no college	14.7	23.2	12.4	9.0	13.8	20.5	12.0	7.6
Some college, no degree	11.4	18.8	10.5	8.4	10.2	14.3	9.2	6.9
Associate degree	—	—	—	—	9.2	—	9.3	5.9
Bachelor's degree or higher	10.3	—	10.3	5.0	4.9	—	4.9	4.2

[1] The unemployment rate is the percent of individuals in the labor force who are not working and who made specific efforts to find employment sometime during the prior 4 weeks. The labor force includes both employed and unemployed persons.
[2] Excludes persons enrolled in school.
[3] Includes persons of Hispanic origin.

[4] Persons of Hispanic origin may be of any race.
—Data not available.

SOURCE: U.S. Department of Labor, Bureau of Labor Statistics, Office of Employment and Unemployment Statistics, unpublished data. (This table was prepared June 1995.)

Table 372.—Median annual income of year-round full-time workers 25 years old and over, by level of education completed and sex: 1989 to 1993

Sex and year	Total	Elementary/secondary					College				
		Less than 9 years	9 to 12 years	High school graduate	Some college, no degree	Associate degree	Bachelor's degree or higher				
							Total	Bachelor's	Master's	Professional	Doctorate
1	2	3	4	5	6	7	8	9	10	11	12
Current dollars											
Men											
1989	$30,465	$17,555	—	—	—	—	—	—	—	—	—
1990	30,733	17,394	—	—	—	—	—	—	—	—	—
1991	31,613	17,623	$21,402	$26,779	$31,663	$33,817	$45,138	$40,906	$49,734	$73,996	$57,187
1992[2]	32,057	17,294	21,274	27,280	32,103	33,433	45,802	41,355	49,973	76,220	57,418
1993	32,359	16,863	21,752	27,370	32,077	33,690	47,740	42,757	51,867	80,549	63,149
Women											
1989	20,570	12,188	—	—	—	—	—	—	—	—	—
1990	21,372	12,251	—	—	—	—	—	—	—	—	—
1991	22,045	12,066	14,455	18,837	22,143	25,002	31,312	29,087	34,939	46,742	43,303
1992[2]	23,139	12,958	14,559	19,427	23,157	25,624	32,304	30,326	36,037	46,257	45,790
1993	23,629	12,415	15,386	19,963	23,056	25,883	34,307	31,197	38,612	50,211	47,248
Constant 1993 dollars											
Men											
1989	35,502	20,457	—	—	—	—	—	—	—	—	—
1990	33,978	19,231	—	—	—	—	—	—	—	—	—
1991	33,539	18,697	22,706	28,411	33,593	35,878	47,889	43,399	52,765	78,505	60,672
1992[2]	33,017	17,812	21,911	28,097	33,064	34,434	47,173	42,593	51,469	78,502	59,137
1993	32,359	16,863	21,752	27,370	32,077	33,690	47,740	42,757	51,867	80,549	63,149
Women											
1989	23,971	14,203	—	—	—	—	—	—	—	—	—
1990	23,629	13,545	—	—	—	—	—	—	—	—	—
1991	23,388	12,801	15,336	19,985	23,492	26,526	33,220	30,860	37,068	49,590	45,942
1992[2]	23,832	13,346	14,995	20,009	23,850	26,391	33,271	31,234	37,116	47,642	47,161
1993	23,629	12,415	15,386	19,963	23,056	25,883	34,307	31,197	38,612	50,211	47,248

[1] Includes equivalency certificates.
[2] Data are based on 1990 census controls.
—Data not available or not applicable.

SOURCE: U.S. Department of Commerce, Bureau of the Census, *Current Population Reports,* Series P–60, *Money Income of Households, Families, and Persons in the United States,* Series P–60, Nos. 174 and 180. (This table was prepared June 1995.)

Table 373.—Median annual income [1] of year-round full-time workers 25 years old and over, by level of school completed and sex: 1991, 1992, and 1993

[Numbers in thousands]

Educational attainment	1991				1992[2]				1993			
	Men		Women		Men		Women		Men		Women	
	Number with income	Median income	Number with income	Median income	Number with income	Median income	Number with income	Median income	Number with income	Median income	Number with income	Median income
1	2	3	4	5	6	7	8	9	10	11	12	13
All ages, 25 and over	44,199	$31,673	29,474	$22,043	44,752	$32,057	30,346	$23,139	45,873	$32,359	30,683	$23,629
Less than 9th grade	1,807	17,623	733	12,066	1,815	17,294	734	12,958	1,790	16,863	765	12,415
9th to 12th grade (no diploma)	3,083	21,402	1,819	14,455	3,009	21,274	1,659	14,559	3,083	21,752	1,576	15,386
High school graduate (includes equivalency)	15,025	26,779	10,959	18,836	14,722	27,280	11,039	19,427	14,604	27,370	10,513	19,963
Some college, no degree	8,034	31,663	5,633	22,143	8,067	32,103	5,904	23,157	8,493	32,077	6,279	23,056
Associate degree	2,899	33,817	2,523	25,000	3,203	33,433	2,655	25,624	3,557	33,690	3,067	25,883
Bachelor's degree or more	13,350	45,138	7,807	31,310	13,937	45,802	8,355	32,304	14,346	47,740	8,483	34,307
Bachelor's degree	8,456	40,906	5,263	29,079	8,719	41,355	5,604	30,326	9,178	42,757	5,735	31,197
Master's degree	3,073	49,734	2,025	34,949	3,178	49,973	2,192	36,037	3,131	51,867	2,166	38,612
Professional degree	1,147	73,996	312	46,742	1,295	76,220	334	46,257	1,231	80,549	323	50,211
Doctor's degree	674	57,187	206	43,303	745	57,418	225	45,790	808	63,149	260	47,248

[1] Data have not been adjusted for changes in the purchasing power of the dollar.
[2] Data are based on the 1990 census.

SOURCE: U.S. Department of Commerce, Bureau of the Census, *Current Population Reports,* Series P–60, No. 184, *Money Income of Households, Families, and Persons in the United States: 1992;* Series P–60, No. 188, *Income, Poverty, and Valuation of Noncash Benefits: 1993.* (This table was prepared April 1995.)

Table 374.—Total annual money earnings of persons 25 years old and over,[1] by educational attainment, sex, and age: 1993

Sex, earnings, and age	Total	Less than 9th grade	Some high school (no diploma)	High school graduate (includes equiva-lency)	Some college, no degree	Associate degree	College				
							Bachelor's degree or more				
							Total	Bachelor's degree	Master's degree	Professional degree	Doctor's degree
1	2	3	4	5	6	7	8	9	10	11	12
	Number, in thousands										
Men											
Total	78,539	7,095	7,790	25,404	13,565	4,979	19,706	12,511	4,353	1,677	1,164
With earnings	76,419	6,734	7,377	24,682	13,247	4,901	19,479	12,360	4,320	1,650	1,148
	Percentage distribution of men with earnings										
Total	100.0	100.0	100.0	100.0	100.0	100.0	100.0	100.0	100.0	100.0	100.0
$1 to $4,999 or loss	6.3	14.0	11.8	6.1	5.3	4.4	3.2	3.7	2.6	2.3	1.3
$5,000 to 9,999	10.6	31.5	19.5	10.5	7.3	6.1	3.3	3.6	2.7	2.2	3.2
$10,000 to $14,999	12.0	22.3	20.1	13.5	10.7	7.3	5.5	6.2	4.6	3.9	3.4
$15,000 to $24,999	21.8	20.9	26.5	27.6	23.2	20.9	12.2	14.0	10.3	6.7	8.1
$25,000 to $34,999	17.2	7.0	12.8	20.1	20.4	23.0	15.2	17.2	13.7	8.4	9.6
$35,000 to $49,999	15.8	2.8	6.3	14.6	19.0	22.8	21.4	22.9	22.0	11.9	17.5
$50,000 to $74,999	10.2	1.2	2.2	6.1	10.3	11.7	21.0	19.6	25.0	18.6	25.2
$75,000 and over	6.1	0.3	0.7	1.6	3.8	3.7	18.2	12.9	19.2	46.0	31.7
	Median income										
All ages, 25 and over	$24,605	$10,895	$14,550	$21,782	$26,323	$29,736	$41,649	$37,474	$45,597	$69,678	$55,751
	Number, in thousands										
Women											
Total	85,973	7,420	9,134	31,111	14,989	6,481	16,838	11,745	4,045	590	458
With earnings	80,898	6,423	8,152	29,171	14,390	6,282	16,480	11,447	4,003	583	447
	Percentage distribution of women with earnings										
Total	100.0	100.0	100.0	100.0	100.0	100.0	100.0	100.0	100.0	100.0	100.0
$1 to $4,999 or loss	21.2	32.7	29.5	23.0	19.5	15.1	13.2	15.0	9.2	10.1	5.1
$5,000 to 9,999	21.0	44.1	36.8	22.4	17.0	12.1	8.7	9.7	6.4	7.7	4.7
$10,000 to $14,999	14.7	14.1	16.6	17.8	14.8	13.9	8.5	9.5	6.2	5.3	6.9
$15,000 to $24,999	20.3	7.4	12.8	22.7	24.7	25.2	19.1	21.3	15.4	10.5	6.3
$25,000 to $34,999	11.3	1.2	2.7	9.2	14.1	18.1	18.4	17.9	19.9	19.6	14.1
$35,000 to $49,999	7.5	0.4	1.2	3.5	7.1	11.5	19.0	16.8	25.2	13.9	26.8
$50,000 to $74,999	3.0	0.1	0.2	1.2	2.1	3.1	9.5	7.5	13.0	14.4	24.2
$75,000 and over	1.1	0.0	0.2	0.3	0.7	0.9	3.6	2.1	4.7	18.5	11.9
	Median income										
All ages, 25 and over	$12,234	$6,480	$7,187	$11,089	$14,489	$18,346	$25,246	$22,452	$31,389	$32,742	$42,736

[1] Includes full-time and part-time workers.

NOTE.—Because of rounding, details may not add to totals.

SOURCE: U.S. Department of Commerce, Bureau of the Census, *Current Population Reports*, Series P–60, No. 188, "Income, Poverty, and Valuation of Noncash Benefits: 1993." (This table was prepared April 1995.)

Table 375.—College enrollment and labor force status of 1993 and 1994 high school graduates 16 to 24 years old, by sex and race/ethnicity: October 1993 and October 1994

[Numbers in thousands]

Item	Civilian noninstitutional population			Civilian labor force [1]					Not in labor force
	Number	Percent	Percent of high school graduates	Number	Labor force participa-tion rate	Employed	Unemployed		
							Number	Unemploy-ment rate	
1	2	3	4	5	6	7	8	9	10
1993 high school graduates [2]									
Total	2,338	100.0	100.0	1,413	60.5	1,144	268	19.1	925
Men	1,118	47.8	47.8	693	62.0	558	135	19.5	425
Women	1,219	52.1	52.1	720	59.0	586	134	18.6	500
White [3]	1,910	81.7	81.7	1,217	63.7	1,002	215	17.7	693
Black [3]	302	12.9	12.9	149	49.2	102	47	31.6	154
Hispanic origin [4]	200	8.6	8.6	131	65.7	86	46	34.8	68
Enrolled in college, October 1993	1,464	100.0	62.6	677	46.3	580	97	14.3	787
Men	668	45.6	28.6	305	45.7	252	54	17.6	362
Women	797	54.4	34.1	372	46.7	329	43	11.6	425
2-year	534	36.5	22.8	351	65.7	305	46	13.2	183
4-year	930	63.5	39.8	326	35.1	276	51	15.5	604
Full-time students	1,314	89.8	56.2	567	43.1	473	93	16.5	748
Part-time students	150	10.2	6.4	111	73.6	107	3	3.2	40
White [3]	1,200	82.0	51.3	585	48.7	511	74	12.6	615
Black [3]	168	11.5	7.2	62	37.1	45	17	(5)	106
Hispanic origin [4]	125	8.5	5.3	70	56.2	53	17	(5)	54
Not enrolled in college, October 1993 ...	873	100.0	37.3	736	84.3	563	173	23.5	137
Men	451	51.7	19.3	388	86.1	306	82	21.1	63
Women	422	48.3	18.0	348	82.3	257	91	26.1	75
White [3]	710	81.3	30.4	632	89.1	491	141	22.4	77
Black [3]	134	15.3	5.7	86	64.3	57	30	34.4	48
Hispanic origin [4]	75	8.6	3.2	61	81.1	33	28	(5)	14
1994 high school graduates [6]									
Total	2,517	100.0	100.0	1,495	59.4	1,257	238	15.9	1,022
Men	1,244	49.4	49.4	792	63.6	665	127	16.0	452
Women	1,273	50.6	50.6	704	55.3	592	111	15.8	570
White [3]	2,065	82.0	82.0	1,252	60.6	1,108	144	11.5	813
Black [3]	318	12.6	12.6	175	53.0	100	75	42.8	143
Hispanic origin [4]	178	7.1	7.1	114	64.0	81	32	28.5	64
Enrolled in college, October 1994	1,559	100.0	61.9	723	46.4	642	82	11.3	836
Men	754	48.4	30.0	359	47.7	319	40	11.1	394
Women	805	51.6	32.0	364	45.2	322	42	11.4	441
2-year	530	34.0	21.1	324	61.2	283	42	12.8	205
4-year	1,029	66.0	40.9	399	38.7	359	40	10.1	630
Full-time students	1,427	91.6	56.7	609	42.7	537	72	11.8	818
Part-time students	131	8.4	5.2	114	86.9	104	10	8.6	17
White [3]	1,313	84.2	52.2	640	48.7	379	61	9.5	674
Black [3]	162	10.4	6.4	55	33.9	41	14	(5)	107
Hispanic origin [4]	87	5.6	3.5	46	55.3	40	7	(5)	41
Not enrolled in college, October 1994 ...	959	100.0	38.1	772	80.3	616	156	20.3	187
Men	491	51.2	19.5	432	88.1	346	87	20.1	58
Women	468	48.8	35.6	340	72.6	270	70	20.5	128
White [3]	752	78.4	29.9	612	81.4	529	85	13.5	140
Black [3]	156	16.3	6.2	120	77.4	59	61	50.7	36
Hispanic origin [4]	91	9.5	3.6	67	74.3	42	26	(5)	23

[1] The labor force includes all employed persons plus those seeking employment. The labor force participation rate is the percentage of persons either employed or seeking employment.

[2] Includes persons who graduated from high school between January and October 1993.

[3] Includes persons of Hispanic origin.

[4] Persons of Hispanic origin may be of any race.

[5] Data not shown where base is less than 75,000.

[6] Includes persons who graduated from high school between January and October 1994.

NOTE.—Data are based upon sample surveys of the civilian noninstitutional population. Percents are only shown when the base is 75,000 or greater. Even though the standard errors are large, smaller estimates are shown to permit users to combine categories in various ways. Because of rounding, details may not add to totals.

SOURCE.—U.S. Department of Labor, Bureau of Labor Statistics, "College Enrollment of 1993 High School Graduates" and unpublished data. (This table was prepared June 1995.)

Table 376.—Labor force status of 1979–80 to 1993–94 high school dropouts 16 to 24 years old, by sex and race/ethnicity: October 1980 to October 1994

[Numbers in thousands]

Year, sex, and race [1]	Dropouts		Dropouts in civilian labor force [2]						Not in labor force
					Employed		Unemployed		
	Number	Percent of total	Number	Labor force participation rate	Number	Percent of dropouts	Number	Unemployment rate	
1	2	3	4	5	6	7	8	9	10
All dropouts									
1979–80 dropouts in October	739	100.0	471	63.7	322	43.6	149	31.6	268
1984–85 dropouts in October	612	100.0	413	67.5	266	43.5	147	35.6	199
1985–86 dropouts in October	562	100.0	359	63.9	259	46.1	100	27.9	203
1986–87 dropouts in October	502	100.0	333	66.4	207	41.2	126	37.8	169
1987–88 dropouts in October	552	100.0	327	59.2	240	43.5	87	26.7	225
1988–89 dropouts in October	446	100.0	292	65.4	210	47.1	82	28.0	154
1989–90 dropouts in October	405	100.0	280	69.0	189	46.7	90	32.3	125
1990–91 dropouts in October	380	100.0	235	61.8	140	36.9	95	40.3	145
1991–92 dropouts in October	406	100.0	242	59.6	147	36.3	95	39.1	164
1992–93 dropouts in October	399	100.0	254	63.8	187	47.0	67	26.3	145
1993–94 dropouts in October	510	100.0	311	61.1	219	42.9	93	29.8	198
Men									
1979–80 dropouts in October	422	57.1	305	72.3	212	50.2	93	30.5	117
1984–85 dropouts in October	321	52.5	261	81.3	163	50.8	98	37.5	60
1989–90 dropouts in October	215	53.1	173	80.2	110	51.2	63	36.2	42
1990–91 dropouts in October	189	49.7	142	75.0	92	48.8	50	35.0	47
1991–92 dropouts in October	189	46.6	130	69.1	85	45.2	45	34.7	59
1992–93 dropouts in October	213	53.4	156	73.5	132	61.8	25	15.9	57
1993–94 dropouts in October	259	50.8	198	76.5	151	58.2	47	23.9	61
Women									
1979–80 dropouts in October	317	42.9	166	52.4	110	34.7	56	33.7	151
1984–85 dropouts in October	291	47.5	152	52.2	103	35.4	49	32.2	139
1989–90 dropouts in October	190	46.9	107	56.3	79	41.6	28	26.1	83
1990–91 dropouts in October	191	50.3	93	48.8	48	25.2	45	48.4	98
1991–92 dropouts in October	218	53.7	112	51.4	62	28.6	50	44.3	106
1992–93 dropouts in October	186	46.6	98	52.6	56	30.1	42	42.9	88
1993–94 dropouts in October	251	49.2	113	45.2	68	27.1	45	40.0	137
White [3]									
1979–80 dropouts in October	580	78.5	392	67.6	286	49.3	106	27.0	188
1984–85 dropouts in October	458	74.8	330	72.1	214	46.7	116	35.2	128
1989–90 dropouts in October	303	74.8	211	69.8	156	51.4	56	26.3	92
1990–91 dropouts in October	273	71.8	177	65.1	109	40.0	68	38.5	96
1991–92 dropouts in October	319	78.6	190	59.7	128	40.3	62	32.5	129
1992–93 dropouts in October	304	76.2	209	68.8	159	52.2	50	24.1	95
1993–94 dropouts in October	382	74.9	252	66.0	177	46.3	75	29.8	130
Black [3]									
1979–80 dropouts in October	146	19.8	73	50.0	33	22.6	40	([4])	73
1984–85 dropouts in October	132	21.6	69	52.3	39	29.5	30	([4])	63
1989–90 dropouts in October	86	21.2	56	65.3	26	29.9	30	([4])	30
1990–91 dropouts in October	98	25.8	54	55.0	28	28.4	26	([4])	44
1991–92 dropouts in October	66	16.3	35	([4])	7	([4])	28	([4])	31
1992–93 dropouts in October	80	20.1	34	42.9	21	26.2	13	([4])	46
1993–94 dropouts in October	100	19.6	48	47.9	34	34.1	14	([4])	52
Hispanic [5]									
1979–80 dropouts in October	91	12.3	60	65.9	43	47.3	17	([4])	31
1984–85 dropouts in October	106	17.3	73	68.9	40	37.7	33	([4])	33
1989–90 dropouts in October	67	16.5	32	([4])	22	([4])	10	([4])	35
1990–91 dropouts in October	61	16.1	48	([4])	30	([4])	18	([4])	13
1991–92 dropouts in October	80	19.7	40	49.9	23	28.4	17	([4])	40
1992–93 dropouts in October	60	15.0	43	([4])	28	([4])	15	([4])	17
1993–94 dropouts in October	108	21.2	51	47.5	31	28.6	20	([4])	57

[1] Includes persons who dropped out of school between October 1 and September 30 of years shown.

[2] The labor force includes all employed persons plus those seeking employment. The labor force participation rate is the percentage of persons either employed or seeking employment.

[3] Includes persons of Hispanic origin.

[4] Data not shown where base is less than 75,000.

[5] Persons of Hispanic origin may be of any race.

NOTE.—Data are based upon sample surveys of the civilian noninstitutional population. Includes dropouts from any grade, including a small number from elementary and middle schools. Percents are only shown when the base is 75,000 or greater. Even though the standard errors are large, smaller estimates are shown to permit users to combine categories in various ways. Because of rounding, details may not add to totals.

SOURCE: U.S. Department of Labor, Bureau of Labor Statistics, *College Enrollment of 1993 High School Graduates*, and unpublished data. (This table was prepared June 1995.)

Table 377.—Employment of 12th graders, by selected student characteristics: 1992

Employment characteristics	Total	Sex		Race/ethnicity					Socioeconomic status[1]				Location of school attended		
		Male	Female	White	Black	Hispanic	Asian	American Indian	Low	Middle low	Middle high	High	Urban	Suburban	Rural
1	2	3	4	5	6	7	8	9	10	11	12	13	14	15	16
							Percentage distribution								
Average hours worked per week during senior year															
Total	100.0	100.0	100.0	100.0	100.0	100.0	100.0	100.0	100.0	100.0	100.0	100.0	100.0	100.0	100.0
Did not work during year	31.8	33.0	30.7	27.6	47.4	38.9	43.3	45.0	38.2	29.8	28.2	32.5	35.6	29.4	31.6
1 to 5 hours	6.8	6.0	7.6	7.0	4.9	6.0	9.5	8.5	5.2	5.5	5.8	10.1	6.7	6.6	7.2
6 to 10 hours	9.8	8.9	10.7	11.2	6.5	5.3	6.7	5.6	6.7	8.3	10.6	12.6	9.4	9.6	10.6
11 to 15 hours	12.7	11.1	14.4	14.1	7.2	11.3	9.3	6.2	9.5	11.9	13.7	15.0	12.2	13.6	12.1
16 to 20 hours	16.1	15.0	17.2	17.3	11.9	13.3	13.5	12.5	13.4	18.6	18.4	15.8	14.3	18.3	14.9
More than 20 hours	22.7	26.0	19.5	22.8	22.1	25.2	17.7	22.3	27.1	25.9	23.3	14.0	21.7	22.5	23.7
21 to 25 hours	9.8	10.2	9.5	10.0	8.8	10.7	8.1	12.0	10.2	10.9	10.8	8.0	9.5	10.6	9.1
26 to 30 hours	5.6	6.5	4.8	5.5	6.4	6.6	4.4	3.8	6.8	6.4	5.9	3.4	5.3	5.7	5.8
31 to 35 hours	2.5	3.1	1.9	2.6	2.4	2.4	0.8	5.0	3.6	3.2	2.4	1.3	2.3	2.5	2.7
36 to 40 hours	3.3	4.2	2.4	3.3	2.9	4.1	3.7	0.9	4.3	4.2	2.7	2.1	3.3	2.4	4.3
More than 40 hours	1.5	2.0	1.0	1.5	1.7	1.4	0.8	0.7	2.2	1.4	1.6	1.0	1.3	1.4	1.8
Most recent type of work for employed students															
Total	100.0	100.0	100.0	100.0	100.0	100.0	100.0	100.0	100.0	100.0	100.0	100.0	100.0	100.0	100.0
Lawn work or odd jobs	2.2	4.2	0.3	2.5	0.8	0.9	1.7	5.3	2.3	2.0	2.1	2.5	1.3	2.2	2.9
Food service	24.0	22.2	25.7	22.8	34.8	24.8	22.9	24.6	28.0	26.6	25.1	18.6	23.6	23.1	25.4
Delivery person	1.6	2.5	0.6	1.5	1.9	1.1	3.2	1.3	0.8	1.7	1.3	2.1	1.5	1.7	1.5
Babysitter or child care	4.3	0.6	7.9	4.8	2.4	2.2	5.0	3.2	3.2	3.9	4.5	5.4	4.9	4.4	3.9
Camp counselor/life guard	0.7	0.8	0.7	0.9	0.0	0.5	0.6	1.1	0.2	0.3	0.9	1.3	0.8	0.9	0.5
Farm worker	2.2	4.4	0.1	2.7	0.0	1.1	0.0	0.0	3.7	3.3	1.6	1.1	0.2	1.1	5.5
Mechanic	1.4	2.8	0.0	1.5	0.7	1.5	1.0	1.4	2.0	1.8	1.5	0.6	1.0	1.3	1.9
Grocery clerk or cashier	14.5	12.5	16.4	14.8	15.9	11.6	8.5	25.7	15.5	16.6	14.5	12.3	14.2	13.4	16.4
Beautician	0.2	0.1	0.3	0.1	1.1	0.3	0.0	0.0	0.6	0.2	0.2	0.1	0.2	0.2	0.3
House cleaning	0.9	0.7	1.1	0.8	0.8	2.0	0.6	0.0	1.5	0.6	1.2	0.6	0.7	0.6	1.4
Construction	2.0	4.0	0.1	2.1	1.0	1.9	0.6	2.0	2.6	2.3	1.9	1.4	1.4	1.8	2.7
Office or clerical	6.9	2.9	10.7	6.3	9.2	8.7	12.1	5.8	6.3	6.0	7.2	8.0	9.0	6.8	5.4
Health services	1.6	0.9	2.3	1.6	2.1	1.1	1.0	4.5	2.5	2.0	1.4	0.9	1.5	1.6	1.7
Salesperson	11.8	9.8	13.7	12.0	8.7	11.9	15.0	7.9	7.2	8.8	12.5	15.8	13.4	14.1	7.3
Warehouse worker	2.1	3.9	0.4	2.2	1.3	1.7	2.0	2.3	1.7	2.5	1.9	2.1	2.0	2.3	1.9
Other	23.5	27.7	19.6	23.5	19.3	28.8	25.4	18.3	22.0	21.4	22.3	27.4	24.4	24.6	21.3
Most recent hourly wage for employed students															
Total	100.0	100.0	100.0	100.0	100.0	100.0	100.0	100.0	100.0	100.0	100.0	100.0	100.0	100.0	100.0
Less than $4.25 per hour	9.9	7.2	12.4	10.3	8.3	8.8	7.9	5.8	12.2	11.4	9.0	8.0	7.9	7.5	14.8
$4.25 to $6.00 per hour	77.5	75.6	79.2	76.7	80.9	81.1	77.0	79.3	79.0	76.8	80.0	74.8	80.1	77.0	75.8
$6.01 to $8.00 per hour	7.7	10.3	5.3	8.0	5.8	6.1	10.7	6.7	5.3	8.3	6.8	9.3	7.3	9.2	6.1
$8.01 or more per hour	5.0	6.9	3.2	5.1	5.0	4.0	4.5	8.3	3.5	3.5	4.1	7.9	4.8	6.3	3.4

[1] Socioeconomic status was measured by a composite score on parental education and occupations, and family income. The "Low" SES group is the lowest quartile.

NOTE.—Some data have been revised from previously published figures.

SOURCE: U.S. Department of Education, National Center for Education Statistics, "National Education Longitudinal Study of 1988," Second Followup survey. (This table was prepared August 1995.)

Table 378.—Full-time-employment status of bachelor's degree recipients 1 year after graduation, by field of study: 1976 to 1991

Field of study	Percent employed full-time					Percent employed full-time in a job closely related to field of study					Percent employed full-time in nonprofessional job[1]				
	1974–75 graduates in May 1976	1979–80 graduates in May 1981	1983–84 graduates in June 1985	1985–86 graduates in June 1987	1989–90 graduates in April 1991	1974–75 graduates in May 1976	1979–80 graduates in May 1981	1983–84 graduates in June 1985	1985–86 graduates in June 1987	1989–90 graduates in April 1991	1974–75 graduates in May 1976	1979–80 graduates in May 1981	1983–84 graduates in June 1985	1985–86 graduates in June 1987	1989–90 graduates in April 1991
1	2	3	4	5	6	7	8	9	10	11	12	13	14	15	16
Total	**67**	**71**	**73**	**74**	**74**	**35**	**38**	**38**	**38**	**39**	**10**	**12**	**13**	**14**	**13**
Professional/technical fields	77	80	82	81	80	51	51	47	47	48	9	10	13	11	11
Arts and sciences fields	56	56	56	62	64	18	17	15	25	26	12	14	15	15	14
Other	65	74	75	74	73	36	43	47	36	38	9	19	12	17	13
Newly qualified to teach	66	75	73	68	74	43	56	54	47	58	7	8	9	9	6
Not newly qualified to teach	67	71	73	74	73	33	36	36	37	36	12	13	13	14	14
Professional/technical fields	80	81	82	82	83	52	49	47	47	48	10	10	13	11	12
Engineering	79	84	84	83	84	57	55	53	46	50	4	2	3	5	3
Business and management	84	83	85	85	83	49	44	41	40	42	15	14	19	17	16
Health	75	77	75	76	86	71	66	70	65	83	2	4	2	3	1
Education[2]	66	67	63	73	67	22	29	24	57	39	12	4	16	9	11
Public affairs and services	—	77	74	72	66	—	46	31	37	49	—	18	15	20	9
Arts and sciences fields	57	56	56	63	66	17	16	15	25	23	13	10	15	15	15
Biological sciences	56	45	43	42	50	26	18	17	15	26	6	15	15	11	8
Physical sciences and mathematics[3]	50	58	51	76	72	19	29	20	48	48	6	8	7	9	7
Psychology	61	56	57	66	59	22	17	12	22	22	18	2	16	19	14
Social sciences	59	61	61	61	68	12	10	13	12	16	15	21	14	19	20
Humanities	56	55	59	59	59	12	14	17	19	11	17	18	19	21	21
Other	68	75	77	75	73	36	43	42	36	37	10	20	14	21	14
Communications	—	71	76	77	75	—	31	31	33	29	—	24	16	18	17
Miscellaneous	66	76	77	74	73	35	46	46	38	38	11	19	13	23	13

[1] Includes those not working in technical, managerial, or administrative types of jobs who reported that they did not need a college degree to obtain their job.

[2] Includes those who have not finished all requirements for teaching certification or were previously qualified to teach.

[3] Includes computer sciences.

—Data not available.

NOTE.—Data are from sample surveys of recent college graduates. Notes on methodology are included in the Guide to Sources. Data exclude bachelor's recipients from U.S. Service Schools. Deceased graduates and graduates living at foreign addresses at the time of the survey are not included.

SOURCE: U.S. Department of Education, National Center for Education Statistics, "Recent College Graduates" surveys. (This table was prepared August 1993.)

Table 379.—Employment status of 1989–90 bachelor's degree recipients 1 year after graduation, by field of study and occupational area: 1991

[Percentage distribution]

Occupational area in April 1991	All fields of study	Professional/technical fields							Arts and sciences			Other fields[1]
		Business and management	Education	Engineering	Health professions	Public affairs/ social services	Biological sciences	Mathematics, computer, and physical sciences	Social sciences	Humanities	Psychology	
1	2	3	4	5	6	7	8	9	10	11	12	13
Total	100	100	100	100	100	100	100	100	100	100	100	100
Employed	84	89	91	87	97	84	65	79	80	78	73	85
Business	21	45	4	7	3	3	10	7	22	13	15	28
Educators	13	1	73	1	1	3	7	9	6	18	10	3
Engineers	5	1	(2)	61	(2)	(2)	1	5	1	(2)	(2)	4
Health professionals	5	(2)	1	(2)	91	(2)	8	1	1	(2)	5	1
Public affairs/social services	3	(2)	(2)	(2)	(2)	57	1	(2)	6	2	15	1
Biological scientists	1	1	(2)	(2)	(2)	(2)	4	(2)	1	(2)	(2)	(2)
Computer, physical scientist, mathematician	1	1	(2)	1	(2)	(2)	(2)	7	(2)	1	(2)	(2)
Communications	2	1	(2)	1	(2)	1	1	(2)	2	9	1	14
Technicians	6	3	1	8	(2)	(2)	13	29	5	4	3	8
Other	3	3	1	2	(2)	(2)	5	7	4	2	1	(2)
Nonprofessional, nonmanagerial, and nontechnical	23	33	11	6	3	21	16	14	33	30	24	27
Unemployed[3]	4	5	2	3	(2)	3	2	4	4	4	5	6
Not in labor force[4]	12	6	6	9	2	13	33	16	15	18	21	9
Enrolled in school[5]	8	2	2	6	(2)	4	29	13	11	12	16	5

[1] Includes agriculture and natural resources, architecture and environmental design, area and ethnic studies, communications, consumer/personal/miscellaneous services, home economics, industrial arts, law, liberal/general studies, library and archival sciences, military sciences, multi/interdisciplinary studies, personal and social development, and trade and industrial.
[2] Less than 0.5 percent.
[3] Percent looking for work.
[4] Percent not looking for work.
[5] Enrolled full-time or part-time.

NOTE.—Because of rounding, details may not add to totals.

SOURCE: U.S. Department of Education, National Center for Education Statistics, "Recent College Graduates, 1991" survey. (This table was prepared July 1993.)

Table 380.—Percent of 1989–90 bachelor's degree recipients pursuing further education within 1 year after graduation, by type of enrollment and undergraduate major: 1991

Undergraduate major field of study	Ever enrolled since graduation	Ever enrolled full-time	Ever enrolled and employed	Ever enrolled and not employed	Enrolled in degree program beyond bachelor's
1	2	3	4	5	6
All bachelor's graduates	35	17	24	11	24
Professional/technical fields	28	17	22	6	18
Engineering	32	18	23	9	23
Business and management	21	13	16	5	12
Health professions	27	16	22	5	20
Education	38	27	33	5	29
Public affairs and social services	35	13	28	7	22
Arts and sciences fields	46	17	28	18	34
Biological sciences	64	17	30	34	47
Physical sciences, mathematics, and computer sciences	40	17	24	16	30
Psychology	50	19	31	20	40
Social sciences	42	16	28	14	30
Humanities	43	17	28	15	28
Other [1]	29	15	21	9	18
Highest degree graduate expects to obtain					
Bachelor's degree	15	10	13	3	3
Master's degree	31	18	24	6	20
Doctor's degree	58	21	36	22	49
First-professional degree	68	9	27	41	61

[1] Includes agriculture and natural resources, architecture and environmental design, area and ethnic studies, consumer/personal/miscellaneous services, home economics, industrial arts, law, liberal/general studies, library and archival sciences, military sciences, multi/interdisciplinary studies, personal and social development, and trade and industrial.

NOTE.—Data are from a sample survey of recent college graduates. Notes on methodology are included in the Guide to Sources. Data exclude bachelor's degree recipients from U.S. Service Schools. Deceased graduates and graduates living at foreign addresses at the time of the survey are not included.

SOURCE: U.S. Department of Education, National Center for Education Statistics, "Recent College Graduates, 1991" survey. (This table was prepared May 1993.)

Table 381.—Average annual salary of bachelor's degree recipients employed full-time 1 year after graduation, by field of study: 1976 to 1991

Field of study	Average salary [1] of 1974–75 degree recipients in February 1976		Average salary [1] of 1979–80 degree recipients in May 1981		Average salary [1] of 1983–84 degree recipients in June 1985		Average salary of 1985–86 degree recipients in June 1987		Average salary of 1989–90 degree recipients in April 1991	Percentage change in constant dollars, 1976 to 1991	Percentage change in constant dollars, 1987 to 1991
	Current dollars	Constant 1991 dollars	Current dollars	Constant 1991 dollars	Current dollars	Constant 1991 dollars	Current dollars	Constant 1991 dollars	Current dollars		
1	2	3	4	5	6	7	8	9	10	11	12
Total	$7,600	$18,200	$15,200	$22,800	$17,700	$22,400	$20,400	24,400	$23,600	29.7	−3.3
Engineering	12,200	29,200	22,400	33,600	24,100	30,500	26,600	31,900	30,900	5.8	−3.1
Business and management	10,200	24,400	16,300	24,400	18,700	23,700	21,100	25,300	24,700	1.2	−2.4
Health professions	8,600	20,600	17,300	25,900	20,800	26,300	22,600	27,000	31,500	52.9	16.7
Education [2]	6,300	15,100	11,500	17,200	13,800	17,500	15,800	18,900	19,100	26.5	1.1
Public affairs and social services	—	—	13,700	20,500	15,100	19,100	17,700	21,200	20,800	—	−1.9
Biological sciences	6,500	15,600	14,500	21,700	15,100	19,100	16,400	19,600	21,100	35.3	7.7
Physical sciences, mathematics, and computer sciences	7,000	16,800	16,300	24,400	17,500	22,200	22,500	27,000	27,200	61.9	0.7
Psychology	—	—	12,500	18,700	14,600	18,500	17,300	20,800	19,200	—	−7.7
Social sciences	6,700	16,000	14,000	21,000	15,800	20,000	20,300	24,400	22,200	38.8	−9.0
Humanities	5,800	13,900	12,600	18,900	14,000	17,700	16,200	19,400	19,100	37.4	−1.5
Communications	—	—	—	—	16,200	20,500	—	—	—	—	—
Miscellaneous	6,800	16,300	15,100	22,600	18,600	23,500	17,600	21,100	20,800	27.6	−1.4

[1] Reported salaries of full-time workers under $2,600 in 1976, $4,200 in 1981, and $5,000 in 1985 were excluded from the tabulations.

[2] Most educators work 9- to 10-month contracts.

—Data not available.

NOTE.—Data exclude bachelor's recipients from U.S. Service Schools and graduates living at foreign addresses at the time of the survey. Constant dollar adjustments based on the Consumer Price Index.

SOURCE: U.S. Department of Education, National Center for Education Statistics, "Recent College Graduates" surveys. (This table was prepared May 1993.)

Table 382.—Participation of young adults in voluntary organizations, by selected characteristics: 1984 to 1986 and 1992 to 1994

Young adult characteristics	Percent participating in voluntary organizations									Percentage distribution of volunteer hours per week				
	Any voluntary activity	Sports teams or clubs	Church activities	Union, farm, trade, or professional associations	Educational organizations	Youth organizations	Political clubs	Organized volunteer work[1]	Other voluntary group	None[2]	Less than 2 hours	2 to 4 hours	4 to 6 hours	6 hours or more
1	2	3	4	5	6	7	8	9	10	11	12	13	14	15
1984 to 1986[3]														
Total	—	36.0	32.2	17.7	—	9.2	6.2	5.8	9.6	—	—	—	—	—
Sex														
Male	—	46.8	29.3	20.3	—	11.7	6.7	5.3	9.7	—	—	—	—	—
Female	—	25.8	34.9	15.3	—	6.9	5.8	6.2	9.4	—	—	—	—	—
Race/ethnicity														
White, non-Hispanic	—	36.5	30.6	18.2	—	8.7	5.9	5.5	9.7	—	—	—	—	—
Black, non-Hispanic	—	31.9	44.2	14.9	—	12.0	8.2	6.8	10.3	—	—	—	—	—
Hispanic	—	34.6	32.4	15.8	—	9.5	6.9	4.3	7.1	—	—	—	—	—
Asian	—	41.4	31.0	27.3	—	10.8	5.9	14.1	10.3	—	—	—	—	—
American Indian	—	41.1	30.0	19.7	—	11.6	9.6	4.2	7.8	—	—	—	—	—
Socioeconomic status														
Low	—	29.2	30.9	12.2	—	7.0	3.4	4.5	6.9	—	—	—	—	—
Low-middle	—	34.5	31.4	15.6	—	8.7	4.5	4.8	8.6	—	—	—	—	—
High-middle	—	39.9	35.4	21.8	—	10.6	7.8	6.9	10.6	—	—	—	—	—
High	—	43.1	33.9	22.4	—	10.7	9.9	7.4	13.0	—	—	—	—	—
1992 to 1994[4]														
Total	37.2	7.2	11.8	1.8	6.0	10.3	3.0	10.4	7.3	62.7	15.2	7.9	5.8	8.3
Sex														
Male	36.8	9.5	11.1	1.9	4.6	11.2	2.9	8.3	7.3	63.2	14.7	7.7	5.6	8.8
Female	37.9	4.9	12.7	1.6	7.1	9.4	3.2	12.6	7.3	62.2	15.8	8.2	6.1	7.9
Race/ethnicity														
White, non-Hispanic	38.5	7.5	11.3	2.0	5.8	10.3	3.1	11.6	7.8	61.5	17.1	8.0	5.5	7.9
Black, non-Hispanic	35.9	6.3	15.8	1.1	6.4	11.5	3.1	5.8	6.2	64.1	9.6	8.1	7.7	10.6
Hispanic	31.7	6.3	11.2	0.8	6.5	9.6	2.3	6.7	5.4	68.4	9.8	7.3	6.0	8.5
Asian	35.8	5.7	10.5	1.4	7.1	8.1	3.4	13.0	8.4	64.2	14.9	8.7	4.3	8.0
American Indian	34.1	12.1	14.6	3.6	6.1	11.9	3.8	5.1	3.9	65.9	8.7	6.3	8.1	11.1
Socioeconomic status														
Low	26.4	5.0	10.4	0.9	4.0	7.4	1.5	5.9	5.0	73.6	8.2	5.8	4.5	7.9
Low-middle	30.4	6.3	10.8	1.3	3.9	8.3	2.1	7.1	6.3	69.6	11.0	6.0	5.9	7.5
High-middle	38.6	7.0	13.0	2.0	5.8	10.9	3.3	9.2	7.5	61.4	16.9	7.9	6.1	7.8
High	51.1	9.2	14.7	2.7	9.7	14.2	4.9	18.0	10.3	48.9	24.6	11.4	5.9	9.2

[1] E.g., hospital volunteer.
[2] Not a volunteer.
[3] Sample survey in 1986 based on people who were high school seniors in spring 1980. Respondents to the survey were asked about their voluntary participation in selected organizations over the previous 24-month period.
[4] Sample survey in 1994 based on people who were high school seniors in spring 1992. Respondents to the survey were asked about their voluntary participation in selected organizations over the previous 24-month period.

—Data not available or not applicable.

NOTE.—Some persons participated in more than one organization.

SOURCE: U.S. Department of Education, National Center for Education Statistics, "High School and Beyond, Third Followup" and "National Education Longitudinal Study, Third Followup." (This table was prepared July 1995.)

Table 383.—Literacy skills of adults, 16 years old and over, by selected characteristics: 1992

Selected characteristics	Prose literacy[1]						Document literacy[2]						Quantitative literacy[3]					
	Average score	Percent of adults with proficiency at level					Average score	Percent of adults with proficiency at level					Average score	Percent of adults with proficiency at level				
		1	2	3	4	5		1	2	3	4	5		1	2	3	4	5
1	2	3	4	5	6	7	8	9	10	11	12	13	14	15	16	17	18	19
Total	**272**	**21**	**27**	**32**	**17**	**3**	**267**	**23**	**28**	**31**	**15**	**3**	**271**	**22**	**25**	**31**	**17**	**4**
Sex																		
Male	272	22	26	31	18	4	269	23	27	31	17	3	277	21	23	31	20	5
Female	273	20	28	33	17	3	265	23	30	31	14	2	266	23	28	31	15	3
Age																		
16 to 18 years old	271	16	35	38	11	1	274	15	34	38	12	1	268	20	35	33	12	1
19 to 24 years old	280	14	29	37	18	2	280	14	29	37	18	2	277	16	28	37	16	2
25 to 39 years old	284	15	24	34	22	5	282	16	25	35	21	4	283	17	23	33	21	5
40 to 54 years old	286	15	23	34	22	5	278	17	27	33	19	3	286	16	22	33	23	6
55 to 64 years old	260	26	31	30	12	1	249	30	34	26	8	1	261	25	30	30	13	2
65 years old and older	230	44	32	19	5	1	217	53	32	13	2	0	227	45	26	20	7	2
Race/ethnicity																		
White	286	14	25	36	21	4	280	16	27	34	19	3	287	14	24	35	21	5
Black	237	38	37	21	4	0	230	43	36	18	3	0	224	46	34	17	3	0
Asian or Pacific Islander	242	36	25	25	12	2	245	34	25	28	12	2	256	30	23	27	16	4
American Indian	254	25	28	16	7	1	254	27	37	29	7	0	250	33	32	28	7	1
Hispanic, Mexican	206	54	25	16	5	0	205	54	25	16	4	0	205	54	25	17	4	0
Hispanic, Cuban	211	53	24	17	6	1	212	48	30	16	4	2	223	46	20	25	6	3
Hispanic, Puerto Rican	218	47	32	17	3	0	215	49	29	18	3	0	212	51	28	17	3	1
Hispanic, Central/South American	207	56	22	17	4	0	206	53	25	16	4	0	203	53	25	18	4	0
Hispanic, other	260	25	27	33	13	2	254	28	26	32	12	2	246	31	25	31	11	1
Highest level of education																		
Still in high school	271	16	36	37	11	0	274	15	35	38	12	1	269	19	35	32	12	1
0 to 8 years	177	75	20	4	0	0	170	79	18	3	0	0	169	76	18	5	0	0
9 to 12 years	231	42	38	17	2	0	227	46	37	15	2	0	227	45	34	17	3	0
GED	268	14	39	39	7	0	264	17	42	34	7	0	268	16	38	35	10	1
High school diploma	270	16	36	37	10	1	264	20	38	33	9	1	270	18	33	37	12	1
Some college	294	8	23	45	22	3	290	9	27	42	20	2	295	8	23	42	23	4
Associate degree	308	4	19	41	32	4	299	6	23	43	25	3	307	4	19	43	29	5
Bachelor's degree	322	4	11	35	40	10	314	4	15	37	36	8	322	4	12	35	38	12
Graduate studies/degree	336	2	7	28	47	16	326	3	10	34	41	12	334	2	9	30	42	17
Region																		
Northeast	270	22	28	31	16	3	264	24	29	30	14	2	267	24	25	31	16	4
Midwest	279	16	28	35	18	3	274	19	30	33	16	2	280	17	26	34	19	4
South	267	23	28	30	15	3	262	26	29	29	14	2	265	25	27	29	15	4
West	276	20	23	33	21	4	271	22	24	32	18	3	276	20	22	32	20	5
Prison population	246	31	37	26	6	0	240	33	38	25	4	.	236	40	37	22	6	1

[1] Prose literacy is the ability to understand and use information contained in various kinds of textual material. A level 1 score of 0 to 225 requires the reader to locate a single piece of information in a short text. A level 2 score of 226 to 275 requires the reader to locate a single piece of information in the text with several distractors or to make low-level inferences. A level 3 score of 276 to 325 requires the reader to make literal or synonymous matches between the text and information given in the task, or to make low-level inferences. A level 4 score of 326 to 375 requires the reader to perform multiple-feature matches and to integrate or synthesize information from complex passages. A level 5 score of 376 to 500 requires the reader to search for information in dense text which contains a number of distractors.

[2] Document literacy reflects the knowledge and skills used to process information from documents. A level 1 score of 0 to 225 requires the reader to locate pieces of information based on a literal match. A level 2 score of 226 to 275 requires the reader to match a single piece of information among several distractors. A level 3 score of 276 to 325 requires the reader to integrate multiple pieces of information from one or more documents. A level 4 score of 326 to 375 requires the performance of multiple-feature matches, cycling through documents, and integrating informa-

tion. A level 5 score of 376 to 500 requires the reader to search through complex displays that contain multiple distractors, to make high-level text-based inferences.

[3] Quantitative literacy is the ability to perform numerical operations in everyday life. A level 1 score of 0 to 225 requires the reader to perform a single, relatively simple, arithmetic operation. A level 2 score of 226 to 275 requires the reader to perform a single operation using numbers that are either stated in the task or easily located in the material. A level 3 score of 276 to 325 requires the reader to use two or more numbers to solve the problem. A level 4 score of 326 to 375 requires the reader to perform two or more sequential operations or a single operation in which the quantities are found in different types of displays. A level 5 score of 376 to 500 requires the reader to perform multiple operations sequentially. They must extract the features of the problem from text or rely on background knowledge to determine the quantities or operations needed.

SOURCE: U.S. Department of Education, National Center for Education Statistics, National Adult Literacy Survey, Adult Literacy in America, 1992, prepared by Educational Testing Service. (This table was prepared February 1994.)

CHAPTER 6
International Comparisons of Education

This chapter offers a broad perspective on education across the nations of the world. It also provides an international context for examining the condition of education in the United States. Historically, the National Center for Education Statistics (NCES) was not active in collecting international data, but recently NCES has expanded its role by serving as the national research center for the International Association for the Evaluation of Educational Achievement (IEA) Reading Literacy Study and funding international research studies comparing mathematics and science education. These studies include the Third International Mathematics and Science Study (TIMSS) and the Second International Assessment of Educational Progress, which provides comparative data for 9- and 13-year-olds. In addition, NCES is cooperating with international agencies in the compilation of statistics and the development of education indicators.

The data in this chapter were drawn from material prepared by the United Nations Educational, Scientific, and Cultural Organization (UNESCO), the Institute of International Education, the Organization for Economic Cooperation and Development (OECD), and the International Assessment of Educational Progress (IAEP). The basic summary data on enrollments, teachers, enrollment ratios, and finances were synthesized from information appearing in Education at a Glance published by OECD. Even though OECD tabulations are very carefully prepared, international data users should be cautioned about the many problems of definition and reporting involved in the collection of data about the educational systems in the world.

This chapter provides information from the International Assessment of Educational Progress (IAEP), sponsored by the Educational Testing Service (ETS), the U.S. Department of Education and the National Science Foundation. The mathematics and science performance of 13-year-old students in 20 countries, and 9-year-old students in 14 countries, was studied through assessments administered during 1990–91. Some countries assessed nationally representative samples of the two age groups; others limited their assessments to specific geographic areas or language groups.

A different perspective is provided by data on the enrollment of foreign students in U.S. institutions of higher education. These data from the Institute of International Education provide information on the number of foreign students and their countries of origin.

Further information on survey methodologies is in the "Guide to Sources" in the appendix and in the publications cited in the source notes.

Population

The percent of young people in a population influences the amount of national income allocated to each student. Countries with a greater number of young people must set aside larger proportions of domestic product. Among the OECD countries, Turkey has by far the largest percentage of young people ages 5 to 13 at 19.9 percent. The closest followers are Ireland at 17.2 percent, and Portugal at 13.7 percent. Countries with relatively small numbers of persons in this age group include Germany at 8.9 percent, and Denmark at 9.9 percent (table 384).

Enrollments

In 1992, over 1 billion students were enrolled in schools around the world. Of these students, 627 million were in elementary-level programs, 319 million were in secondary programs, and 71 million were in higher education programs (table 386).

Between 1980 and 1992, enrollments grew rapidly, particularly in the less developed areas of the world. Elementary enrollment changes ranged from increases of 35 percent in Africa and 18 percent in Central and South America to a modest increase of only 1 percent in Oceania and a 3 percent decrease in Europe (table 386).

Enrollment increases at the secondary level were more dramatic, especially in Africa (87 percent), Central and South America (36 percent) and Asia (36 percent). Secondary-level enrollment increased in Europe by 1 percent and declined in Northern America by 3 percent. For the secondary level, most countries' enrollment rates fell close to 90 percent, with a few exceptions. The United Kingdom's enrollment was 84.2 percent, while Spain's was 81.6 percent.

Turkey was the extreme outlier, with an enrollment rate of 33.9 percent (table 385).

At the postsecondary level, Africa (113 percent) and Asia (98 percent) had the largest increases followed by Oceania (75 percent) and Central and South America (62 percent). These postsecondary increases are a result of large growth in the school attendance rates and sizable rises in population (table 386). Enrollment rates varied among countries partially due to differing definitions of postsecondary education and what age it begins. Among the OECD countries, the United States has the largest proportion of 18 to 21 year-olds enrolled in postsecondary education at 36.4 percent, followed by Belgium (30.4 percent) and Canada (29.7 percent). For the 22 to 25 age group, Norway's enrollment is highest at 18.9 percent, Denmark follows at 18.3 percent, and the United States is third at 16.7 percent. Ireland ranks last with an enrollment percentage just over four percent (table 385).

Pupil/teacher ratios in elementary and secondary schools vary widely from country to country. Countries with relatively low elementary ratios in 1991 were Belgium (9.3) and Sweden(10.4). Countries with relatively high ratios included Turkey (30.5) and France (22.7) (table 388).

In 1992–93 there were 439,000 foreign students studying at U.S. colleges and universities. This was 19,000 more than the year before, or a 5 percent increase. Approximately 59 percent of the students were from South and East Asian countries (table 406).

Education Systems

Of the 20 countries which participated in the 1991 International Assessment of Educational Progress (IAEP), 16 have national curriculums. Only Canada, Switzerland, and Brazil join the United States in having state or provincial control of education. Eleven of the 20 countries have ethnically homogeneous populations. For the countries participating in the assessment, the average length of the school year ranged from approximately 172 days in Portugal to approximately 251 days in China. The average amount of instruction per school day varied from just under 4 hours in Hungary and Fortaleza, Brazil, to a little over 6 hours in France (table 390).

Achievement

Mathematics

In the 1991 IAEP mathematics assessment of 9-year-olds from 10 nations that tested nationally representative populations, students from Korea, Hungary, Taiwan, the (former) Soviet Union, and Israel all had average test scores that were significantly higher than those from the U.S. In the assessment of the 13-year-old students in which 15 nations tested nationally representative populations, the average test scores of U.S. students were higher than only one country, Jordan. There was no significant difference between the test scores of U.S. students and those of students from Slovenia and Spain. The remaining 11 countries all had average test scores that were significantly higher than those of U.S. students (tables 391 and 393).

An analysis of the 1991 IAEP scores on different mathematics topics reveals that U.S. 9-year-old students scored well in the area of data analysis, statistics, and probability. In this area, the average test score of the U.S. 9-year-olds was the same or higher than students in all the other countries which tested comprehensive populations, except for Korea. The U.S. 13-year-olds' average test score in data analysis, statistics, and probability was lower than those of the students in many of the countries testing comprehensive populations. The exceptions were Spain, Slovenia, and Jordan, where the test scores were lower than those of the U.S. 13-year-olds (tables 392 and 394).

Science

In the 1991 IAEP science assessment of 9-year-olds, 10 nations tested nationally representative populations. The average science scores of U.S. students were significantly lower than those of Korean students, but about the same as students from Taiwan, Canada, Hungary, Spain and the (former) Soviet Union. The IAEP assessment of 13-year-old science students involved 15 nations testing nationally representative populations. Students of six nations (Korea, Taiwan, Switzerland, Hungary, former Soviet Union and Slovenia) had average science scores that were higher than those of U.S. students. (Note: In this international assessment of education, the standard errors are relatively large. In the interest of allowing for meaningful comparisons between countries, the IAEP tables in the *Digest of Education Statistics, 1995* list standard errors) (tables 396 and 397)

When the results of the 1991 IAEP science assessments are analyzed by subject matter, U.S. 9-year-olds excelled in the earth and space sciences. In this area, U.S. students had average test scores that were significantly higher than their counterparts in Korea and Taiwan, but about the same as Hungary (table 395).

Geography

On a 1991 International Assessment of Educational Progress in geography, students from Hungary performed at a significantly higher level on the 24 geography items than their counterparts from the other eight countries in the study (Canada, Ireland,

Korea, Scotland, Slovenia, the former Soviet Union, Spain, and the United States). On this same assessment, students seemed to perform well on questions involving map or chart-reading skills. On the other hand, students seemed to have more difficulty on questions that required them to combine the use of such skills and prior knowledge of geographic vocabulary, process, or location (table 388).

Reading

On a reading literacy assessment of 9- and 14-year-olds in 32 countries, students in Finland were among the best readers at both levels. Students in the United States produced relatively high scores at the 9-year-old level. Among the 14-year-olds, students in the United States also scored in the high performing group, along with students from France, Sweden, New Zealand, Hungary, Iceland, Switzerland, and Hong Kong. American students performed considerably better at the 9-year-old level relative to the other participating countries than at the 14-year-old level (tables 399 and 400).

Degrees and Finances

Ratios of bachelor's degrees conferred per hundred 22- or 23-year-olds in 1991 ranged from 7 in Turkey and 8 in Austria, Netherlands, and Switzerland to 33 in Canada, 31 in Norway, and 28 in the United States. The ratio of women receiving bachelor's degrees per 100 persons was higher than the ratio for men in Australia, Canada, Denmark, Finland, France, Ireland, Italy, Norway, Spain, Sweden, and the United States (table 401).

Countries have been paying more attention lately to the percent of graduates in the math and science fields. For undergraduate degrees awarded in science, math and computer science, and engineering, most OECD countries report rates from 15 to 34 percent. Finland, Belgium, and Germany all are over 30 percent, while Spain and Canada are closer to 15 percent. Graduate degrees in math and science show Japan far in front with 54.2 percent, followed by Austria (37.4) and Germany (33.9). The U.S. ranks last in this category with 13.8, just below Australia (13.9).

In general, higher income countries have a larger expenditure per student than lower income countries. At both primary and secondary levels of education, the United States ranked at the upper end. For primary education, the United States spent $5,600 per student, followed by Sweden at $4,840 per student. For secondary education, the United States ranked first at $6,470, and Austria was second at $6,420. Ireland ranked among the lowest spending OECD countries, with $1,770 per primary student and $2,770 per secondary student. On higher education expenditures, Switzerland ranked first in expenditure per student at $12,900, and the United States ($11,880) and Japan ($11,850) were close behind (table 404).

A comparison of public expenditures on education as a percent of gross domestic product (GDP) shows most OECD countries falling within a fairly close range of each other. On the low end were Turkey with 4 percent and Spain with 4.5 percent, with the percentages ranging upward to Sweden and Denmark at 6.1 percent and Norway at 6.8 percent.

Figure 27.-Percentage change in enrollment, by area of the world and level of education: 1980 to 1992

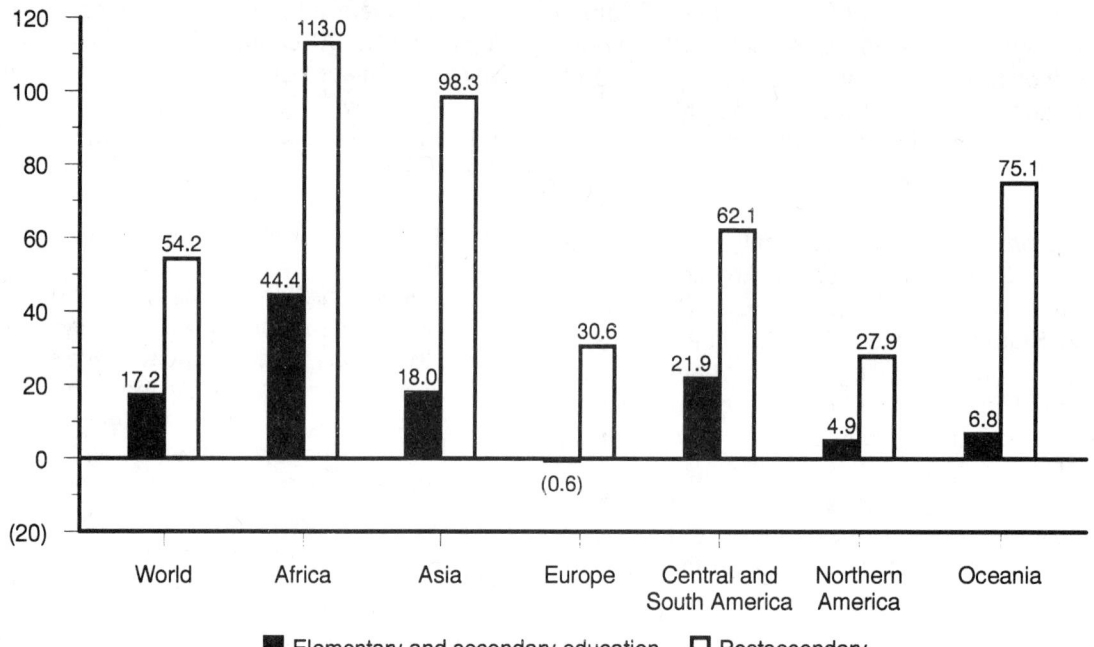

SOURCE: United Nations Educational, Scientific, and Cultural Organization, Paris, *Statistical Yearbook*, various years.

Figure 28.-Public expenditures for education as a percentage of gross domestic product: Selected countries, 1991

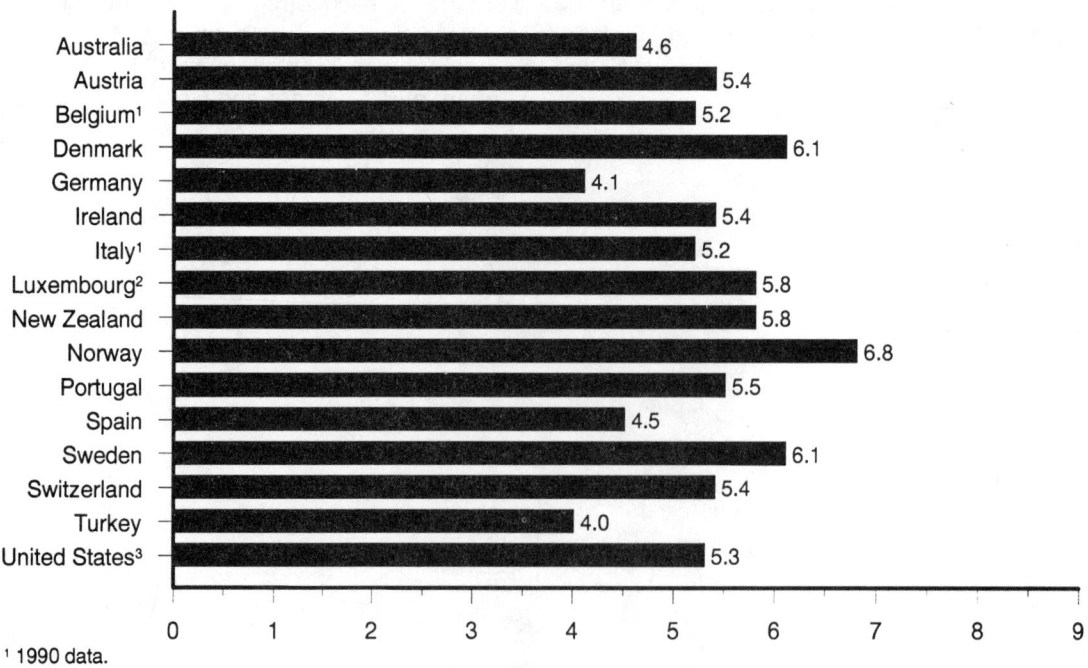

[1] 1990 data.
[2] 1989 data.
[3] Excludes preprimary data.

SOURCE: Organization for Economic Cooperation and Development, *Education at a Glance*, and unpublished data.

Figure 29.-Distribution of mathematics proficiency scores of 13-year-olds, by country: 1991

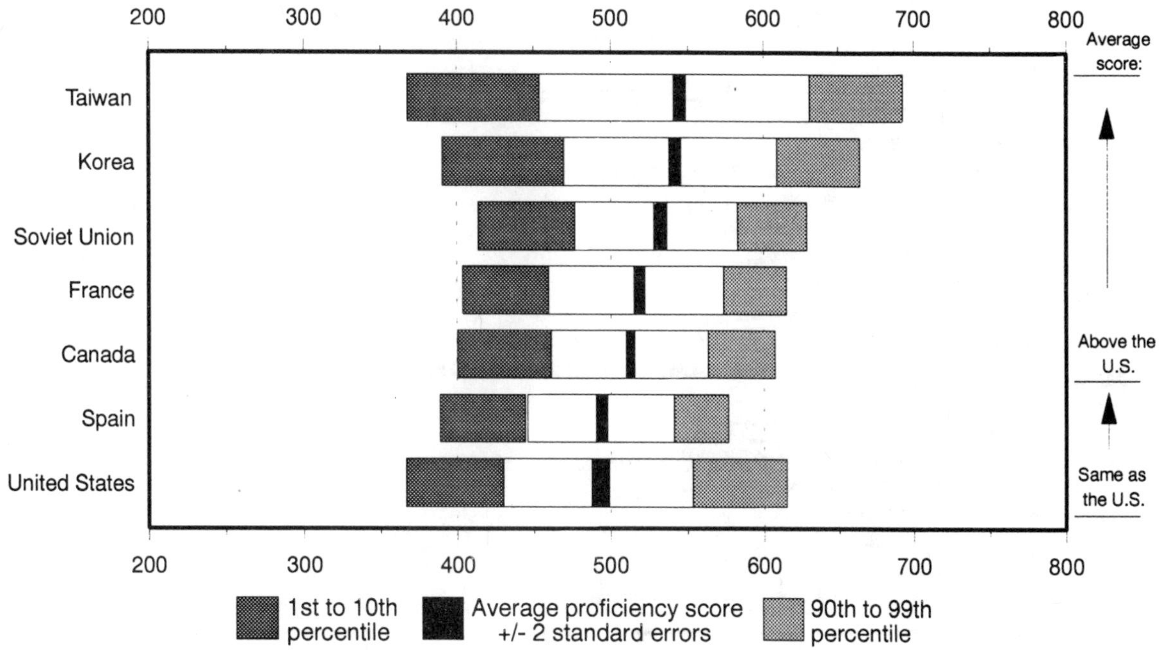

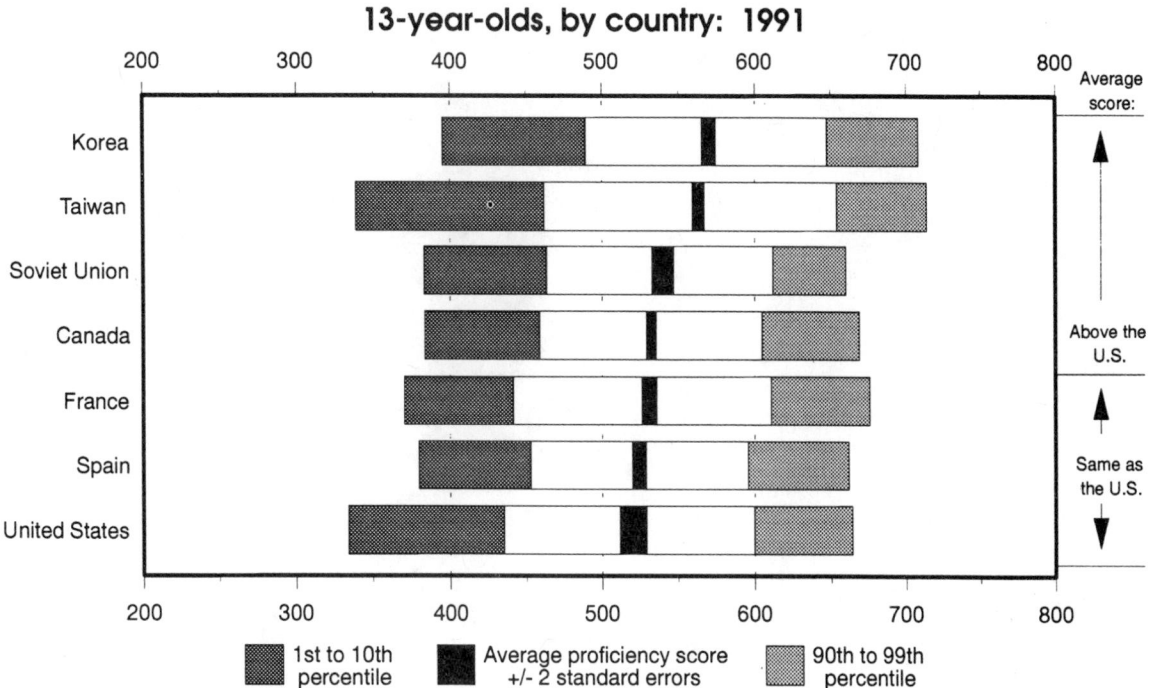

SOURCE: Educational Testing Service, International Assessment of Educational Progress, unpublished tabulations, 1992.

Figure 30.-Distribution of science proficiency scores of 13-year-olds, by country: 1991

SOURCE: Educational Testing Service, International Assessment of Educational Progress, unpublished tabulations, 1992.

Figure 31.-Bachelor's degree recipients as a percent of population in the appropriate age group for selected countries, by sex: 1991

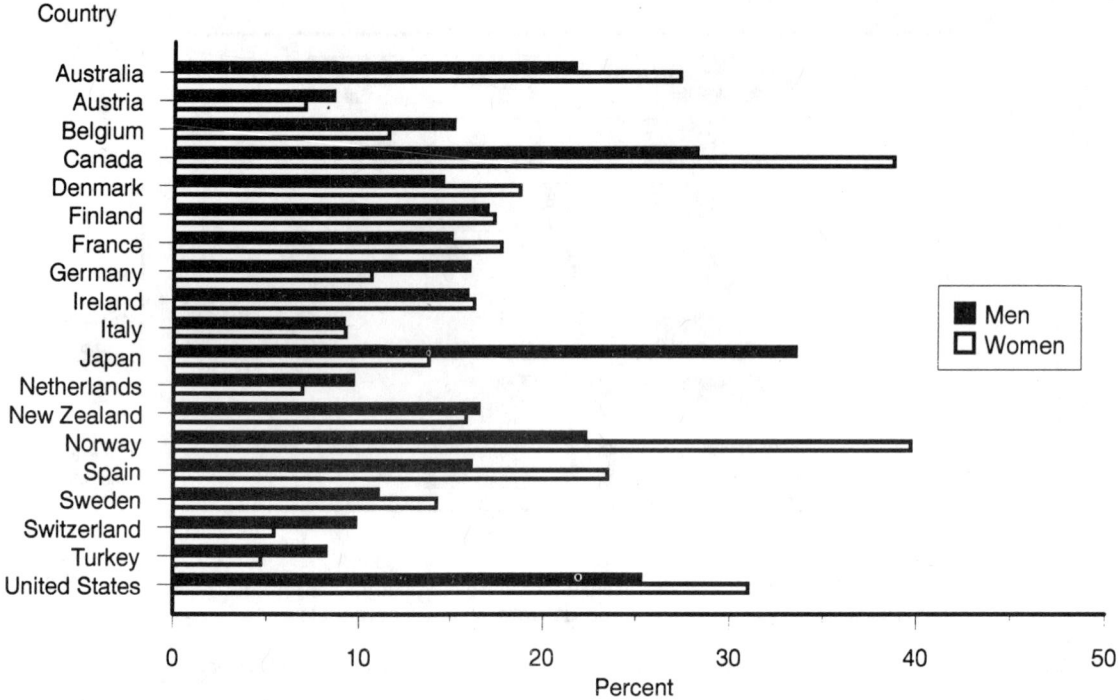

SOURCE: Organization for Economic Cooperation and Development, unpublished data.

Table 384.—School-age populations as a percent of total population: Selected countries, 1985, 1990, and 1991

Country	5- to 13-year-olds as a percent of total population			14- to 17-year-olds as a percent of total population		
	1985	1990	1991	1985	1990	1991
1	2	3	4	5	6	7
Australia	14.5	13.1	13.0	6.6	6.4	6.1
Austria	10.9	10.4	10.5	6.4	5.1	4.9
Belgium	11.4	10.9	10.9	5.8	5.1	4.9
Canada	12.8	12.4	12.5	6.1	5.5	5.5
Denmark	12.0	10.1	9.9	5.8	5.7	5.5
Finland	11.5	11.8	11.6	5.6	4.9	5.0
France	12.8	12.1	12.1	6.2	5.8	5.5
Germany (former West)	9.1	8.7	8.9	6.1	4.1	4.0
Greece	—	—	—	—	5.5	—
Iceland	15.7	15.0	—	6.7	6.8	—
Ireland	17.9	17.5	17.2	7.7	8.0	7.7
Italy	12.7	10.3	10.1	6.5	6.0	5.9
Japan	14.0	11.8	11.5	6.2	6.5	6.4
Luxembourg	10.2	10.1	—	5.5	4.4	—
Netherlands	12.0	10.7	10.7	6.8	5.4	5.1
New Zealand	15.3	13.5	13.4	7.5	6.7	6.4
Norway	12.5	11.0	11.0	6.4	5.8	5.5
Portugal	15.3	14.3	13.7	6.9	6.8	6.9
Spain	15.0	12.9	12.4	6.8	6.8	6.7
Sweden	11.3	10.2	10.2	5.4	5.2	5.0
Switzerland	10.6	10.1	10.1	5.8	4.8	4.7
Turkey	20.6	20.6	19.9	8.7	8.9	8.9
United Kingdom	11.4	11.1	11.3	6.3	5.2	4.9
United States	12.6	12.8	12.8	6.2	5.4	5.3

—Data not available.

SOURCE: Organization for Economic Cooperation and Development, *Education at a Glance,* and unpublished data. (This table was prepared May 1995.)

Table 385.—Percent of population enrolled in secondary and postsecondary institutions, by age group: Selected countries, 1985, 1990, and 1991

Country	Secondary schools, 14 to 17 years old			Postsecondary institutions								
				18 to 21 years old			22 to 25 years old			26 to 29 years old		
	1985	1990	1991	1985	1990	1991	1985	1990	1991	1985	1990	1991
1	2	3	4	5	6	7	8	9	10	11	12	13
Australia	—	—	91.4	—	—	28.9	—	—	11.6	—	—	7.6
Belgium	91.7	—	94.6	24.5	—	30.4	7.2	—	9.1	1.5	—	1.7
Canada	92.5	95.8	94.0	25.5	28.9	29.7	9.5	11.4	12.2	3.0	3.4	3.5
Denmark	89.9	90.0	90.0	7.4	7.4	8.2	16.3	17.9	18.3	8.2	9.3	9.5
Finland	89.8	98.2	—	9.3	13.6	—	17.3	20.7	—	7.9	10.2	—
France	93.0	95.1	95.4	19.4	24.6	26.6	10.0	11.8	12.7	4.3	3.9	4.0
Germany (former West)	94.7	94.2	93.6	8.8	8.5	9.1	15.5	15.9	16.3	8.9	10.4	10.6
Ireland	83.6	87.2	89.7	15.2	20.3	20.5	2.8	4.3	4.3	—	—	—
Japan	95.7	95.7	96.1	—	—	—	—	—	—	—	—	—
Netherlands	93.0	92.5	92.7	14.4	17.9	19.1	11.9	13.4	14.5	5.7	4.7	4.7
New Zealand	74.4	84.2	88.4	14.9	20.8	23.2	9.6	13.8	16.1	—	—	—
Norway	90.0	93.2	93.5	8.6	13.6	14.5	13.9	17.4	18.9	6.2	7.4	8.2
Portugal	—	—	69.1	5.8	—	11.3	5.4	—	6.6	2.3	—	2.2
Spain	67.3	79.1	81.6	14.9	21.2	21.5	10.6	13.5	14.2	4.0	4.5	5.3
Sweden	91.3	91.4	91.6	7.9	8.7	9.3	11.3	11.4	11.8	6.5	6.1	6.2
Switzerland	88.9	89.8	90.0	5.7	6.4	6.6	10.6	12.1	12.8	5.2	6.4	7.0
Turkey	—	32.6	33.9	—	7.4	7.9	—	4.6	4.9	—	2.3	2.1
United Kingdom	77.7	83.3	84.2	—	16.1	17.6	—	4.7	6.2	—	—	3.4
United States [1]	92.1	92.9	92.9	33.0	36.2	36.4	14.5	17.1	16.7	8.2	8.5	9.1

[1] Postsecondary includes higher education only.
—Data not available.

SOURCE: Organization for Economic Cooperation and Development, *Education at a Glance,* and unpublished data. (This table was prepared May 1995.)

Table 386.—Estimated population, school enrollment, teachers, and public expenditures for education in major areas of the world: 1980, 1991, and 1992

Item	World total [1]	Major areas of the world					
		Africa [2]	Asia [3]	Europe [4]	Central and South America [5]	Northern America [5]	Oceania [6]
1	2	3	4	5	6	7	8
1980							
Population, all ages,[7] in thousands	4,426,257	479,975	2,561,820	749,701	360,282	251,906	22,573
Enrollment, all levels,[8] in thousands	852,546	79,954	479,653	141,343	87,183	59,581	4,834
First (primary) level	556,902	63,922	331,413	63,841	65,327	29,634	2,766
Second level [9]	249,922	14,489	136,179	63,766	16,967	16,879	1,643
Third level [10]	45,722	1,543	12,061	13,736	4,889	13,068	425
Teachers, all levels,[8] in thousands	37,149	2,390	18,656	8,790	3,728	3,310	275
First (primary) level	19,462	1,692	10,673	3,366	2,256	1,345	130
Second level [9]	14,288	604	6,951	4,326	1,086	1,208	113
Third level [10]	3,398	94	1,032	1,098	385	757	32
Public expenditures on education, in millions of U.S. dollars	$572,520	$17,897	$103,522	$250,266	$34,207	$156,201	$10,427
As a percent of gross national product	5.1	5.4	4.5	[11] 5.1	4.1	5.2	5.6
1991							
Population, all ages,[7] in thousands	5,358,344	664,913	3,139,316	793,410	454,210	279,845	26,650
Enrollment, all levels,[8] in thousands	992,286	108,869	563,959	143,835	107,540	62,771	5,312
First (primary) level	620,969	81,103	363,209	64,437	76,618	32,802	2,800
Second level [9]	306,463	25,012	178,586	62,711	23,151	15,153	1,850
Third level [10]	64,854	2,755	22,163	16,687	7,771	14,816	662
Teachers, all levels,[8] in thousands	47,659	3,895	23,639	10,413	5,349	4,032	331
First (primary) level	24,318	2,456	12,728	3,916	3,082	1,991	145
Second level [9]	18,599	1,273	9,308	5,108	1,612	1,153	145
Third level [10]	4,743	166	1,603	1,389	656	888	41
Public expenditures on education, in millions of U.S. dollars	$1,119,091	$18,494	$256,678	$429,644	$47,685	$347,108	$19,482
As a percent of gross national product	5.1	5.7	4.3	[11] 5.2	4.2	5.5	5.7
1992							
Population, all ages,[7] in thousands	5,462,004	683,854	3,211,427	795,690	461,308	282,583	27,142
Enrollment, all levels,[8] in thousands	1,015,974	116,513	575,534	144,734	108,246	65,492	5,454
First (primary) level	626,843	86,085	366,222	62,179	77,168	32,384	2,806
Second level [9]	318,608	27,142	185,392	64,615	23,155	16,398	1,905
Third level [10]	70,524	3,286	23,920	17,941	7,924	16,710	744
Teachers, all levels,[8] in thousands	48,230	4,090	23,656	10,542	5,378	4,221	342
First (primary) level	24,354	2,573	12,715	3,783	3,118	2,017	148
Second level [9]	18,859	1,337	9,241	5,331	1,584	1,215	152
Third level [10]	5,016	181	1,699	1,428	676	990	42
Public expenditures on education, in millions of U.S. dollars	$1,231,900	$24,700	$300,600	$469,900	$56,700	$360,500	$19,500
As a percent of gross national product	5.1	5.9	4.3	5.4	4.4	5.6	5.8

[1] Enrollment and teacher data exclude the Democratic People's Republic of Korea. Expenditure data exclude Albania, Cambodia, Democratic People's Republic of Korea, Lao People's Democratic Republic, Lebanon, Mongolia, Mozambique, South Africa, and Viet Nam.

[2] Excludes Rodrigues and other small islands.

[3] Excludes the former U.S.S.R., the Democratic People's Republic of Korea, and Arab states, but includes both the Asian and the European portions of Turkey.

[4] Includes the former U.S.S.R.

[5] Northern America includes Bermuda, Canada, Greenland, St. Pierre, Miquelon and the United States of America. Hawaii is included in Northern America rather than Oceania. Central and South America includes the rest of America.

[6] Includes American Samoa, Australia, Guam and New Zealand.

[7] Estimate of midyear population.

[8] Excludes special and adult education provided outside regular schools. Data prior to 1991 exclude preprimary.

[9] Includes general, teacher training and vocational education.

[10] Includes universities and other institutions of higher education.

[11] This figure is for Europe, not including the former U.S.S.R. For the former U.S.S.R., public expenditure on education as a percentage of GNP is as follows: 7.3 for 1980 and 8.2 for 1991.

SOURCE: United Nations Educational, Scientific, and Cultural Organization, Paris, *Statistical Yearbook*, various years. (This table was prepared April 1995.)

Table 387.—Selected statistics for countries [1] with populations over 10 million, by continent: 1980, 1990, 1991, and 1992

Country	Population in millions			Persons per square kilometer in 1992	First level [2]					
					Enrollment in thousands			Enrollment ratio [5]		
	1980	1990	1992		1980	1990	1992	1980	1990	1992
1	2	3	4	5	6	7	8	9	10	11
World total [7]	4,426.2	5,257.2	5,462.0	40	556,904	610,874	626,843	96	99	98
Africa										
Algeria [8]	18.7	25.0	26.3	11	3,119	4,189	4,436	94	95	99
Angola	7.7	10.0	10.6	9	1,301	990	—	175	91	—
Cameroon	8.5	11.5	12.2	26	1,379	1,964	—	98	101	—
Cote D'Ivoire	8.3	12.0	12.9	40	1,025	1,415	[10]1,448	79	71	[10]69
Egypt [8]	40.6	52.7	55.2	55	4,663	6,964	[10]6,542	78	101	[10]101
Ethiopia	38.8	51.7	55.1	45	2,131	2,466	1,856	35	31	22
Ghana	10.7	15.0	16.0	67	[17]1,378	1,945	[10,17]1,796	80	77	74
Kenya [8]	16.7	24.0	25.7	44	3,927	5,392	—	115	95	—
Madagascar [8]	8.8	11.2	12.8	22	1,724	1,571	[19]1,490	142	92	[19]79
Morocco	20.1	24.5	26.3	59	2,172	2,484	2,728	83	65	69
Mozambique [8]	12.1	14.2	14.9	19	[22]1,387	1,206	1,199	99	64	60
Nigeria [8]	80.6	108.5	115.7	125	13,760	13,777	[10]14,806	104	73	[10]76
South Africa	28.3	38.0	39.8	33	—	6,952	[26]5,644	84	105	109
Sudan [8]	18.7	25.2	26.7	11	1,464	2,043	[10]2,168	50	50	[10]51
Uganda	13.1	17.6	18.7	79	[27]1,292	[14,27]2,633	—	[27]50	[14,27]80	—
United Republic of Tanzania	18.6	25.6	27.8	29	[23,28]3,538	[28]3,379	[28]3,603	93	69	68
Zaire	26.4	35.6	39.9	17	4,196	[24]4,562	4,871	92	70	70
Zimbabwe	7.1	9.4	10.6	27	1,235	2,116	2,302	85	116	119
Asia										
Afghanistan [8]	16.0	[29]16.1	19.1	29	1,116	[18]726	—	34	[18]24	—
Bangladesh	88.7	113.7	119.3	828	8,240	11,940	—	58	77	—
China [8]	996.1	1,153.5	1,188.0	124	146,270	122,414	122,013	112	125	121
India	[31]675.0	[31]827.1	[31]870.0	[31]265	73,873	99,118	105,370	83	98	102
Indonesia	147.5	179.3	191.2	100	25,537	[18]29,934	29,599	107	[18]116	115
Iran, Islamic Republic of [8]	39.3	54.5	57.0	35	4,799	9,370	9,937	87	111	109
Iraq	13.2	18.1	19.3	44	2,616	3,328	2,857	113	111	89
Japan	116.8	123.5	124.3	329	11,827	9,373	8,947	101	101	102
Kazakhstan		16.7	17.0	6	—	—	[19]1,227	—	—	—
Korea, North (DPR)	18.0	21.8	22.6	—	—	[24]1,543	—	—	[24]104	—
Korea, South (Republic of)	38.1	42.9	43.7	441	5,658	4,869	4,560	110	107	105
Malaysia	13.7	17.8	18.6	56	2,009	2,456	2,652	93	93	93
Myanmar (former Burma)	33.6	41.8	43.7	65	4,148	5,385	—	91	105	—
Nepal [8]	14.0	18.9	20.6	146	1,068	2,789	3,035	88	99	102
Pakistan	[35]82.6	[35]112.0	[35]119.1	[35]150	[22]5,474	[22]8,856	—	39	46	—
Philippines	48.3	61.5	64.3	214	[23]8,034	10,427	10,680	111	111	109
Saudi Arabia	9.4	14.9	15.9	7	927	1,877	2,026	63	77	78
Sri Lanka [8]	14.8	17.0	17.4	265	2,081	2,112	2,059	103	107	107
Syrian Arab Republic	8.7	12.1	13.0	70	1,556	2,452	2,573	100	109	107
Thailand [8]	46.7	56.1	57.8	113	7,393	6,465	6,813	99	90	97
Turkey	44.5	56.1	58.8	75	5,656	6,862	[10]6,879	96	114	[10]113
Uzbekistan	—	20.5	21.7	49	—	—	—	—	—	—
Vietnam [8]	53.7	66.2	69.3	209	7,887	8,862	9,476	109	103	108
Yemen	—	11.2	12.0	23	703	1,671	—	51	82	—
Europe										
Belarus	9.6	10.3	[10]10.3	[18]49	750	615	635	—	—	—
Czechoslovakia (former) [8]	15.3	15.7	15.7	123	1,904	1,924	[41]1,511	92	94	[10]95
France	53.9	56.7	57.4	104	4,610	4,149	4,060	111	108	106
Germany [43]	78.2	79.4	80.6	226	3,636	3,431	3,470	101	107	94
Greece	9.6	10.1	10.3	78	901	[18]835	—	103	[18]97	—
Hungary	10.7	10.4	10.3	111	1,162	1,131	[10]1,081	96	90	[10]89
Italy	56.4	57.7	56.8	188	4,423	3,056	2,960	100	93	95
Netherlands [8]	14.1	15.0	15.2	372	1,333	1,082	1,046	100	102	98
Poland	35.6	38.1	38.4	119	4,167	5,189	5,232	100	98	98
Romania	22.2	23.2	22.7	96	3,237	1,253	1,201	102	91	88
Russian Federation	—	147.9	[10]148.2	—	—	—	11,872	—	—	—
Spain	37.5	39.0	39.1	77	3,610	2,820	[10]2,662	109	108	[10]107
Ukrainian S.S.R.	50.0	51.8	52.2	86	3,595	3,991	4,102	—	—	—
United Kingdom	56.3	57.4	57.8	237	4,911	4,533	—	103	104	—
Yugoslavia, Federal Republic			10.5	—	—	467	474	—	—	—
North America										
Canada	24.0	26.6	27.4	3	2,185	2,372	2,438	100	107	107
Cuba [8]	9.7	10.6	10.8	98	1,469	888	942	106	100	102
Mexico	69.7	86.2	89.5	46	14,666	14,402	14,426	121	115	113
United States [46]	227.2	249.4	255.0	26	21,076	22,392	22,975	101	104	102
South America										
Argentina	28.2	32.3	33.1	12	3,917	[14]4,999	[10]4,874	106	[14]111	[10]107
Brazil [8]	121.3	150.4	156.3	18	22,598	28,944	[10]28,742	99	108	[10]106
Chile	11.1	13.2	13.6	18	2,185	1,991	2,035	109	98	96
Colombia	25.9	32.3	33.4	29	4,168	4,247	4,526	124	110	117
Ecuador	8.1	10.3	10.7	38	1,534	[14]1,828	—	113	[14]116	—
Peru	17.3	21.6	22.5	17	3,161	3,855	3,853	114	121	119
Venezuela	15.0	19.3	20.2	22	[48]3,158	[48]4,053	[10,48]4,190	93	97	[10]99
Oceania										
Australia	14.7	17.0	17.5	2	1,718	1,583	1,623	111	106	107

[1] Selection based on total population for midyear 1991.

[2] First-level enrollment generally consists of elementary grades.

[3] Second-level enrollment includes general education, teacher training (at the second level), and technical and vocational education. This level generally corresponds to secondary education in the United States.

[4] Third-level enrollment includes college and university enrollment, and technical and vocational education beyond the high school level. There is considerable variation in reporting from country to country.

[5] Data are the total enrollment of all ages in the school level divided by the population of the specific age groups which correspond to the school level. Adjustments have been made for the varying lengths of first- and second-level programs. All third-level ratios are based on the 20- to 24-year-old population. Because some countries have many students from outside the normal age range, ratios may exceed 100.

[6] In many countries and territories, a child may be exempt from school attendance if there is no suitable school within a reasonable distance of his/her home.

[7] Enrollment totals and ratios exclude Democratic People's Republic of Korea. Data do not include adult education or special education provided outside regular schools.

[8] Classification of first and/or second levels have been revised. Data by level may not be comparable over time.

[9] Data refer only to institutions under the Ministry of Education.

[10] Data for 1991.

[11] Data exclude "Enam."

[12] Eastern Cameroon.

[13] Data for 1986.

[14] Data for 1988.

[15] Excludes students in Al Azhar University and all private institutions.

[16] Data do not include Asmara University and Kotebe College.

[17] Data refer to public education only.

[18] Data for 1989.

[19] Data for 1993.

[20] Data for 1979.

[21] Data for 1984.

[22] Includes education preceding the first level.

[23] Data for 1981.

[24] Data for 1987.

[25] Data for 1985.

[26] Data do not include Transkei, Bophuthatswana, Venda, or Ciskei.

[27] Data refer to government maintained and aided schools only.

Table 387.—Selected statistics for countries[1] with populations over 10 million, by continent: 1980, 1990, 1991, and 1992—Continued

Second level[3]						Third level[4]						Age for compulsory attendance[6]
Enrollment in thousands			Enrollment ratio[5]			Enrollment in thousands			Enrollment ratio[5]			
1980	1990	1992	1980	1990	1992	1980	1990	1992	1980	1990	1992	
12	13	14	15	16	17	18	19	20	21	22	23	24
249,718	299,254	318,608	45	50	53	45,722	64,433	70,524	11.0	12.7	13.9	—
1,028	2,176	2,305	33	60	59	[9]79	286	[10]298	6.2	11.8	[10]11.8	6–15
D191	186	—	20	12	—	2	7	—	0.4	0.9	—	7–15
234	500	—	18	28	—	[11]12	33	—	1.7	3.4	—	[12]6–12
222	—	—	19	23	[10]24	20	[13]24	—	2.9	[14]2.5	—	7–13
2,929	5,507	[10]5,284	54	81	[10]80	716	[15]708	—	17.7	19.2	[10]19.2	6–14
—	866	721	9	13	11	14	34	[10,16]26	0.4	0.8	[10]0.8	7–13
693	[18]830	—	41	38	[10]38	—	—	—	1.6	1.5	—	6–14
428	[14]563	—	20	29	27	13	[18]31	—	0.9	2.2	—	6–13
[20]234	340	[19]313	[21]31	18	[19]15	23	36	43	2.9	3.4	[19]3.9	7–16
797	1,124	1,208	26	34	35	112	221	—	6.0	10.2	—	7–14
[23]108	160	159	5	8	7	1	[24]2	3	0.1	[25]0.1	0.3	6–12
2,346	3,123	[10]3,601	19	21	[10]23	150	[18]336	—	2.2	[18]3.7	—	—
—	2,743	—	—	65	71	—	[26]439	[26]490	—	13.4	13.9	—
384	732	[10]718	16	22	[10]21	29	[18]60	21	1.8	3.0	—	—
[27]87	[14,27]260	—	[27]5	[14,27]14	—	6	18	—	0.5	[27]1.1	1.3	7–14
[28]79	[28]167	190	3	5	5	[25]5	[18]5	—	[25]0.3	[18]0.2	—	6–12
862	[24]1,066	—	24	[24]24	—	28	[14]61	—	1.3	[14]2.1	—	7–15
75	—	[10]711	8	49	47	8	49	62	1.3	5.2	6.1	—
137	—	—	10	[18]8	—	[20]23	24	—	—	[18]1.6	—	7–15
2,659	3,593	—	17	19	—	240	434	—	3.5	3.8	—	6–10
56,778	51,054	53,544	46	48	54	[30]1,161	[30]2,147	[30]2,271	1.3	1.7	[10]1.6	7–16
32,748	[25]44,485	63,205	30	44	49	3,545	[13]4,806	—	5.7	[18]6.0	—	[32]6–14
5,722	[18]11,243	10,863	29	[18]45	43	—	[18]1,576	1,973	—	[18]8.7	10.1	7–13
2,718	5,085	6,323	42	54	62	—	[17]312	[10]636	—	9.8	[10]12.2	6–10
1,033	[14]1,167	1,145	57	47	43	107	[18]210	—	9.3	[18]13.8	—	6–12
9,558	11,026	[10]10,677	93	98	[10]97	[33]2,412	[18,33]2,683	[10]2,899	30.5	[18]30.7	[10]31.3	6–15
—	—	—	—	—	—	260	287	—	—	—	—	5–15
—	[24,34]2,468	—	—	—	—	[24]390	—	—	—	—	—	6–12
4,286	4,560	4,462	78	84	84	648	1,691	1,859	15.8	38.7	41.6	6–14
1,084	1,420	1,567	48	56	60	58	121	—	4.3	7.3	—	5–10
1,066	[24]1,359	—	22	23	—	[23]165	[24]202	—	—	[24]5.4	—	6–11
512	[14]709	855	22	33	36	[17]34	94	[10]110	3.0	5.8	[10]6.6	6–11
2,166	3,983	—	14	21	—	[20]157	[18,36]305	—	—	[18]2.8	—	7–13
2,929	4,034	4,422	64	73	76	1,276	1,709	[10]1,657	26.2	29.3	[10]27.8	—
349	893	1,073	30	46	51	62	154	[10]164	7.3	13.3	[10]13.7	—
—	2,082	2,185	55	74	75	43	[13]62	—	2.8	5.2	[10]5.5	5–15
604	[37]914	917	46	52	48	140	222	194	19.2	18.8	18.7	6–11
1,920	2,397	—	29	33	—	[38]361	[18]952	1,156	13.1	[18]16.3	19.0	7–15
2,218	3,808	[10]3,987	35	48	[10]51	246	750	916	6.1	14.1	[10]14.8	6–14
—	—	—	—	—	—	278	341	—	—	—	—	6–11
—	[18]3,652	—	42	33	33	[33]115	[18]186	—	2.3	1.6	—	—
73	421	—	11	31	—	8	—	[10]53	1.7	[14]2.9	—	—
760	968	970	—	—	—	[39]177	189	188	17.1	17.9	[10]16.3	[40]6–17
781	864	[10]849	89	83	[10]79	197	190	[41]183	25.5	39.7	45.6	6–16
5,014	5,522	5,574	85	99	102	[42]1,077	[42]1,699	1,952	27.2	35.7	—	6–16
[44]8,457	7,398	[10]7,500	91	102	[10]97	1,624	2,238	[10]1,867	17.4	25.0	—	6–18
740.058	[18]844	—	81	[18]98	—	121	195	—	12.9	14.9	[10]15.3	6–15
357	514	[10]531	69	81	[10]82	[39]101	[39]102	117	27.6	29.8	33.7	6–16
5,308	5,118	4,892	72	75	77	1,118	1,452	1,615	30.0	37.6	[10]38.8	6–13
[45]1,391	1,402	1,370	93	112	117	360	479	[10]494	17.6	22.1	23.0	5–16
1,674	1,888	2,031	77	83	84	[39]589	[39]545	584	11.0	[18]8.7	11.9	7–14
871	2,838	2,452	71	92	82	[39]193	[18,39]165	236	—	—	—	6–14
—	—	9,443	—	—	—	3,046	2,861	2,638	—	—	—	6–15
3,977	4,755	[10]4,773	87	106	[10]109	698	1,222	[10]1,302	24.2	37.1	[10]39.5	[40]6–17
3,406	3,408	3,282	—	—	—	[39]880	895	[10]890	20.1	27.8	—	5–16
5,342	4,336	—	83	86	—	827	1,258	[10]1,385	—	—	—	7–15
						—	—	143				6–11
2,323	2,293	2,392	89	104	107	1,173	1,917	[10]1,943	55.5	95.9	98.8	6–16
1,146	1,002	820	81	91	84	152	242	198	20.5	20.9	[10]19.4	6–11
4,742	6,704	6,783	48	55	56	930	1,311	—	15.4	15.2	14.0	6–14
21,945	19,313	20,515	94	96	98	12,097	13,820	14,486	58.0	77.7	[10]81.6	7–16
[23]1,366	[14]1,974	[10]2,160	56	[14]71	[10]71	491	[24]959	[10]1,077	21.6	[24]40.8	[10]43.4	6–14
2,819	3,499	[10]3,559	34	39	[10]39	1,409	1,540	[10]1,565	11.9	11.6	[10]11.7	7–14
538	720	675	53	74	70	145	255	[10]287	13.2	20.7	[10]23.3	6–13
1,733	[18]2,283	2,687	41	[18]55	61	[47]272	[18,47]475	[10]511	10.2	[18]13.7	[10]14.8	6–14
592	[24]772	—	51	[24]56	—	270	207	—	36.5	20.1	—	6–14
1,203	1,698	1,704	59	68	67	306	682	778	19.4	35.6	[10]39.4	6–12
222	281	[10]289	22	34	[10]34	307	550	—	21.4	29.5	—	5–15
1,100	1,278	1,295	71	81	83	324	485	559	25.4	35.6	39.6	6–16

28 Data refer to Tanzania mainland only.
29 Not including nomads.
30 Includes full-time students only.
31 Includes data for Jammu and Kashmir.
32 Data pertain to the majority of states.
33 Includes correspondence courses.
34 General education only.
35 Excludes data for Jammu, Kashmir, Junagardh, Manavadar, Gilgit, and Baltistan.
36 Data refer to universities only.
37 Includes United Nations Refugee Welfare Agency schools with 18,305 pupils.
38 Excludes Open University with an enrollment of 243,825 in 1979.
39 Includes evening and correspondence courses.
40 Grade levels changed for compatibility with ISCED.
41 Data are a combination of data for the Czech Republic and Slovakia.
42 The total number of students is overestimated due to inclusion of enrollment in non-university institutions.
43 Data include both former East and West Germany.
44 Excludes technical education, consisting of both on the job training and school education.
45 Data do not include apprenticeships and health care training.

46 Population data are from the U.S. Bureau of the Census, Current Population Reports, Population Estimates. Enrollment totals and ratios are based on data compiled by the National Center for Education Statistics and the U.S. Bureau of the Census. First level includes grades 1 through 6 and second level includes grades 7 through 12. Enrollment data are for the 1980–81, 1990–91, and 1991–92 school years.
47 Includes students at the Open University.
48 Data refer to grades 1 to 9 (basic education).
—Data not available.

NOTE.—Data revised from previously published figures.

SOURCE: United Nations Educational, Scientific, and Cultural Organization (UNESCO), Paris, Statistical Yearbook, various years; U.S. Department of Commerce, Bureau of the Census, Current Population Reports, Series P–20; and U.S. Department of Education, National Center for Education Statistics, Common Core of Data and "Fall Enrollment in Institutions of Higher Education" surveys, and Integrated Postsecondary Education Data System (IPEDS), "Fall Enrollment" survey. (This table was prepared May 1995.)

Table 388.—Pupils per teacher in public and private elementary and secondary schools, by level of education: Selected countries, 1985 to 1991

Country	Elementary				Junior high schools				Senior high schools			
	1985	1989	1990	1991	1985	1989	1990	1991	1985	1989	1990	1991
1	2	3	4	5	6	7	8	9	10	11	12	13
Australia	[1] 13.8	—	—	18.0	—	—	—	—	3.2	—	—	—
Austria	11.3	11.5	11.6	11.6	9.2	7.9	7.7	7.6	15.2	12.6	12.4	11.9
Belgium	—	—	—	9.3	—	—	—	—	—	—	—	4.6
Canada	18.1	16.9	17.1	—	16.0	15.5	15.5	—	16.0	15.5	15.3	—
Denmark	12.7	12.2	11.2	11.1	10.2	8.4	9.3	9.2	14.8	13.6	13.3	12.6
France	—	—	—	22.7	—	—	—	—	—	—	—	5.6
Germany (former West)	20.7	20.3	20.3	21.4	16.9	14.7	14.6	14.8	23.7	21.9	21.0	20.4
Ireland	—	—	—	—	—	—	—	—	7.2	8.0	8.3	8.6
Italy	12.8	10.8	10.7	10.9	9.6	8.7	8.5	8.3	10.8	10.7	10.7	10.5
Japan	—	21.5	[1] 20.8	[1] 20.3	—	19.4	18.6	17.7	—	[1] 16.4	16.2	16.2
Luxembourg	—	13.7	—	—	—	86.6	—	(¹)	—	5.2	—	(¹)
Netherlands	20.2	19.2	19.2	19.0	12.7	12.6	12.4	10.2	—	—	—	—
New Zealand	20.1	19.7	19.1	18.4	—	—	—	—	—	—	—	—
Norway	—	—	—	10.7	—	—	—	8.7	—	—	—	8.1
Portugal	—	—	—	13.3	—	—	—	0.1	—	—	—	5.2
Spain	26.8	22.9	21.2	19.7	21.4	19.5	18.8	17.8	15.3	15.1	14.8	14.7
Sweden	11.6	10.7	10.6	10.4	10.8	10.6	10.2	9.7	13.1	12.2	11.9	11.9
Turkey	31.1	30.7	30.6	30.5	41.3	50.0	48.4	49.7	11.0	12.2	12.1	13.1
United Kingdom	19.7	22.0	22.0	22.2	—	18.5	18.5	18.6	11.1	17.2	13.9	13.7
United States	17.0	15.6	15.6	15.5	16.5	16.0	15.9	16.1	16.2	16.0	15.8	15.6

[1] Public schools only.
—Data not available.

SOURCE: Organization for Economic Cooperation and Development, unpublished data. (This table was prepared May 1995.)

Table 389.—Geography proficiency of 13-year-olds in educational systems participating in the International Assessment of Educational Progress: 1991

Country	Average percent correct			
	All geography items [1] (s.e.)	Geographic skills and tools [2] (s.e.)	Physical geography items [3] (s.e.)	Cultural geography items [4] (s.e.)
1	2	3	4	5
Hungary	69.8 (0.6)	76.3 (0.5)	67.8 (0.7)	65.0 (0.7)
Slovenia	65.3 (0.6)	67.9 (0.5)	63.6 (0.7)	64.3 (0.9)
Canada [5]	63.0 (0.5)	69.5 (0.4)	61.0 (0.6)	58.2 (0.6)
Soviet Union (former) [6]	62.6 (1.1)	72.2 (0.9)	61.2 (1.0)	53.4 (1.8)
United States	61.9 (0.8)	69.4 (0.6)	58.3 (1.0)	58.1 (1.0)
Spain [7]	60.1 (0.7)	62.4 (0.9)	58.9 (0.7)	58.9 (1.1)
Korea	59.7 (0.5)	67.8 (0.5)	52.1 (0.7)	60.3 (0.6)
Ireland	58.5 (0.6)	62.7 (0.6)	59.5 (0.8)	52.3 (0.8)
Scotland	58.3 (0.6)	66.2 (0.5)	57.1 (0.8)	50.6 (0.8)

[1] All 24 geographic items.
[2] Eight items testing ability to use maps, charts, and globes.
[3] Nine items testing knowledge of location of physical features and concepts of climate.
[4] Seven items testing knowledge of cultural entities and interactions between people and their environment.
[5] Eight provinces.
[6] Schools in 14 republics where instruction is in Russian.

[7] Schools where instruction is in Spanish, in all regions except Cataluna.

NOTE.—s.e.=standard error.

SOURCE: U.S. Department of Education, National Center for Education Statistics, International Assessment of Educational Progress, *Learning About The World, 1992.* (This table was prepared May 1993.)

Table 390.—Characteristics of educational systems participating in the International Assessment of Educational Progress: 1991

Country	Ethnic homogeneity [1]	Age for starting school	Average days in school year [2]	Average minutes of instruction in school day [2]	National curriculum	Percent of schools with one or more problems [2,3]
1	2	3	4	5	6	7
Populations (comprehensive)						
Canada [4]	No	6	188 (0.2)	304 (0.8)	No	13 (1.3)
France	Yes	6	174 (1.7)	370 (3.4)	Yes	29 (4.9)
Hungary	Yes	6	177 (1.5)	223 (1.3)	Yes	32 (4.2)
Ireland	Yes	6	173 (0.9)	323 (4.4)	Yes	39 (5.8)
Israel [5]	No	6	215 (2.2)	278 (6.5)	Yes	46 (6.7)
Jordan	Yes	6	191 (0.9)	260 (2.9)	Yes	63 (5.3)
Korea	Yes	6	222 (2.5)	264 (2.4)	Yes	24 (4.9)
Scotland	Yes	5	191 (0.9)	324 (2.3)	Yes	23 (4.0)
Slovenia	Yes	7	190 (1.5)	248 (2.5)	Yes	50 (5.3)
Spain [6]	No	6	188 (2.3)	285 (3.2)	Yes	33 (5.0)
(Former) Soviet Union [7]	No	6 or 7	198 (2.1)	243 (2.6)	Yes	72 (5.1)
Switzerland [8]	No	6 or 7	207 (3.2)	305 (7.4)	No	11 (3.5)
Taiwan	No	6	222 (2.5)	318 (6.9)	Yes	10 (2.8)
United States	No	6	178 (0.4)	338 (5.0)	No	5 (2.2)
Populations (with exclusions or low participation)						
Brazil, Fortaleza	No	7	183 (1.1)	223 (9.8)	No	62 (5.3)
Brazil, Sao Paulo	No	7	181 (0.2)	271 (9.3)	No	60 (4.6)
China	Yes	6.5 or 7	251 (2.1)	305 (7.1)	Yes	43 (6.3)
England	Yes	5	192 (1.8)	300 (4.4)	Yes	24 (8.3)
Italy [9]	Yes	6	204 (0.5)	289 (5.0)	Yes	18 (5.1)
Mozambique, Maputo, and Beira	No	7	193 (0.0)	272 (0.0)	Yes	92 (0.0)
Portugal	Yes	6	172 (1.1)	334 (6.5)	Yes	56 (7.9)

[1] 90 percent of entire population from one ethnic group.
[2] For 13–year-olds.
[3] Problems included: overcrowded classrooms, inadequate facilities and maintenance, shortages of textbooks and other educational materials, student absenteeism, lack of discipline, and vandalism of school property.
[4] Four provinces assessed 9-year-olds. Nine provinces assessed 13-year-olds.
[5] Schools where instruction is in Hebrew.
[6] Schools where instruction is in Spanish, in all regions except Cataluna.
[7] Schools in 14 republics, where instruction is in Russian.

[8] Fifteen Cantons.
[9] Emilia-Romagna province only.

NOTE.—Standard errors appear in parentheses.

SOURCE: U.S. Department of Education, National Center for Education Statistics, International Assessment of Educational Progress, *Learning Science* and *Learning Mathematics,* by Educational Testing Service. (This table was prepared February 1992.)

Table 391.—Classroom, home, and mathematics activities of 9-year-olds in educational systems participating in the International Assessment of Educational Progress: 1991

Country	Average percent correct on mathematics test	Percent of students who read for fun every day	Percent of students with 2 hours or more homework daily	Percent of students who do math exercises by themselves often	Percent of students who work with math tools often [1]	Percent of students who watch TV 5 hours or more daily
1	2	3	4	5	6	7
Populations (comprehensive)						
Korea	75 (0.6)	25 (1.2)	22 (1.1)	23 (1.0)	11 (1.0)	9 (0.7)
Hungary	68 (0.6)	50 (1.6)	25 (1.4)	69 (1.0)	20 (1.0)	16 (1.2)
Taiwan	68 (0.8)	29 (1.3)	31 (1.2)	47 (1.3)	30 (1.1)	8 (0.8)
(Former) Soviet Union [2]	66 (1.3)	63 (1.3)	31 (1.3)	62 (1.2)	21 (1.0)	18 (0.7)
Israel [3]	64 (0.7)	57 (1.4)	35 (1.5)	42 (1.5)	21 (1.2)	24 (1.1)
Spain [4]	62 (1.0)	55 (1.4)	29 (1.8)	60 (1.7)	23 (1.7)	17 (1.4)
Ireland	60 (0.8)	45 (1.4)	18 (1.5)	51 (1.6)	14 (1.1)	23 (1.5)
Canada [5]	60 (0.5)	48 (0.8)	13 (0.6)	48 (1.0)	13 (0.6)	22 (0.8)
United States	58 (1.0)	45 (1.5)	20 (1.2)	44 (1.5)	19 (1.3)	26 (1.6)
Slovenia	56 (0.6)	63 (1.5)	15 (1.1)	61 (1.4)	20 (1.3)	8 (0.6)
Populations (with exclusions or low participation)						
Italy [6]	68 (0.9)	51 (1.9)	17 (1.5)	42 (2.1)	18 (1.3)	9 (0.8)
Scotland	66 (0.9)	43 (1.6)	4 (0.6)	48 (1.5)	13 (1.5)	23 (1.5)
England	59 (1.9)	51 (2.6)	9 (1.2)	47 (2.8)	18 (1.5)	23 (2.0)
Portugal	55 (0.9)	60 (2.2)	20 (1.7)	32 (2.1)	17 (1.7)	20 (1.5)

[1] Tools are counting blocks, geometric shapes, and geometric solids.
[2] Schools in 14 republics, where instruction is in Russian.
[3] Schools where instruction is in Hebrew.
[4] Schools where instruction is in Spanish, in all regions except Cataluna.
[5] Four provinces.
[6] Emilia-Romagna province only.

NOTE.—Standard errors appear in parentheses.

SOURCE: U.S. Department of Education, National Center for Education Statistics, International Assessment of Educational Progress, *Learning Mathematics,* by Educational Testing Service. (This table was prepared February 1992.)

Table 392.—Mathematics test scores of 9-year-olds in educational systems participating in the International Assessment of Educational Progress: 1991

Country	Average percent correct			Percentile scores						Topic averages					Process averages		
	Total	Male	Female	1	5	10	90	95	99	Numbers and operations	Measurement	Geometry	Data analysis, statistics, and probability	Algebra and functions	Conceptual understand- ing[1]	Procedural knowledge[2]	Problem solving[3]
1	2	3	4	5	6	7	8	9	10	11	12	13	14	15	16	17	18
IAEP average	63.3	—	—	—	—	—	—	—	—	61.2	67.2	63.9	67.6	61.8	63.2	66.7	58.5
Populations (comprehensive)																	
Korea	74.8 (0.6)	77.2 (0.7)	72.4 (0.8)	26.2 (0.9)	41.0 (3.7)	50.8 (4.7)	93.4 (0.0)	95.1 (0.0)	98.4 (0.0)	74.6 (0.6)	73.0 (0.8)	75.4 (0.7)	79.3 (0.6)	72.1 (0.7)	75.0 (0.6)	78.7 (0.6)	68.8 (0.6)
Hungary	68.2 (0.6)	68.2 (0.8)	68.2 (0.8)	20.4 (2.3)	33.3 (1.5)	40.7 (1.2)	90.2 (2.5)	93.4 (0.0)	98.4 (0.0)	67.5 (0.7)	71.6 (0.7)	68.6 (0.7)	63.4 (0.8)	72.4 (0.8)	68.2 (0.6)	70.8 (0.7)	64.4 (0.7)
Taiwan	68.1 (0.8)	68.4 (0.8)	67.8 (0.9)	19.2 (1.6)	32.1 (4.6)	41.0 (1.8)	91.8 (1.7)	95.1 (0.0)	98.4 (0.0)	67.1 (0.8)	69.3 (0.8)	69.2 (0.8)	72.8 (0.8)	64.2 (0.8)	68.5 (0.8)	76.1 (0.8)	55.7 (0.8)
(Former) Soviet Union[4]	65.9 (1.3)	66.4 (1.2)	65.4 (1.4)	20.0 (0.6)	30.8 (1.0)	37.7 (0.7)	90.2 (0.7)	93.4 (2.3)	98.4 (0.0)	65.7 (1.3)	71.3 (1.0)	64.4 (1.3)	60.1 (1.5)	67.8 (1.3)	63.0 (1.3)	72.0 (1.2)	61.7 (1.4)
Israel[5]	64.4 (0.7)	66.0 (0.8)	62.7 (0.9)	21.3 (0.4)	30.4 (2.8)	38.6 (3.1)	86.9 (2.1)	91.8 (0.0)	96.7 (0.0)	63.6 (0.8)	69.9 (0.7)	58.8 (0.9)	63.9 (1.0)	66.8 (0.7)	63.0 (0.8)	68.3 (0.8)	61.6 (0.8)
Spain[6]	61.9 (1.0)	61.9 (1.3)	61.8 (1.1)	18.8 (0.6)	26.8 (1.8)	32.8 (2.0)	86.9 (0.0)	90.2 (2.4)	96.7 (0.0)	61.3 (1.1)	60.8 (0.8)	60.1 (1.1)	69.3 (1.1)	58.3 (1.1)	60.8 (1.0)	66.1 (1.0)	57.3 (1.1)
Ireland	60.0 (0.8)	59.9 (0.9)	60.1 (1.1)	16.0 (3.3)	24.6 (0.4)	31.2 (1.5)	85.0 (3.9)	90.2 (0.0)	95.1 (0.0)	58.0 (0.9)	64.2 (0.8)	57.9 (0.9)	65.2 (0.8)	59.4 (1.0)	59.3 (0.8)	63.9 (0.8)	55.5 (0.9)
Canada[7]	59.9 (0.5)	59.9 (0.7)	60.0 (0.6)	19.6 (1.6)	28.3 (2.5)	35.7 (1.5)	83.6 (0.0)	88.5 (0.0)	93.4 (2.8)	55.0 (0.6)	64.2 (0.8)	64.7 (0.6)	72.3 (0.5)	56.4 (0.6)	60.4 (0.5)	61.1 (0.6)	57.4 (0.5)
United States	58.4 (1.0)	58.7 (1.1)	58.0 (1.2)	18.0 (1.1)	24.6 (0.0)	29.5 (2.1)	83.6 (0.0)	90.2 (2.3)	96.7 (1.6)	54.3 (1.1)	63.2 (1.0)	56.9 (1.0)	72.8 (1.1)	55.3 (1.0)	59.7 (1.0)	59.5 (1.1)	54.5 (1.0)
Slovenia	55.8 (0.6)	55.8 (0.7)	55.9 (0.7)	18.9 (0.8)	27.7 (1.8)	34.0 (0.8)	79.3 (0.3)	84.5 (0.0)	93.1 (0.0)	52.7 (0.6)	62.4 (0.6)	63.1 (0.8)	54.2 (0.8)	57.8 (0.6)	56.3 (0.6)	57.6 (0.6)	52.3 (0.7)
Populations (with exclusions or low participation)																	
Italy[8]	67.8 (0.9)	69.5 (1.0)	65.9 (1.1)	23.0 (2.0)	34.4 (1.6)	42.6 (0.3)	90.2 (1.7)	93.4 (4.9)	98.4 (0.0)	67.3 (0.9)	73.3 (0.9)	64.6 (1.1)	71.1 (0.9)	60.8 (1.2)	67.8 (0.9)	72.5 (0.9)	60.6 (1.1)
Scotland	65.7 (0.9)	65.8 (1.1)	65.6 (1.1)	23.0 (0.1)	32.8 (0.0)	39.3 (2.8)	89.8 (4.6)	93.3 (2.7)	96.7 (4.6)	62.1 (1.0)	71.3 (0.9)	68.5 (0.8)	73.9 (0.8)	63.1 (1.2)	66.3 (0.8)	67.9 (1.0)	61.8 (0.8)
England	59.5 (1.9)	58.5 (1.5)	60.3 (2.9)	17.2 (2.1)	26.7 (1.6)	32.8 (0.5)	86.9 (2.5)	91.8 (3.3)	96.7 (0.0)	53.6 (2.1)	67.2 (1.6)	67.0 (1.5)	70.4 (1.7)	56.9 (2.1)	60.7 (1.7)	59.2 (2.0)	57.9 (1.9)
Portugal	55.5 (0.9)	56.8 (1.1)	54.2 (1.1)	16.7 (1.9)	26.2 (0.5)	31.6 (0.8)	81.7 (2.6)	86.9 (0.0)	93.4 (1.6)	54.4 (1.1)	58.3 (0.7)	55.6 (1.2)	57.1 (1.0)	54.6 (1.0)	55.7 (0.9)	59.5 (1.1)	49.2 (1.0)
Populations (Canadian)																	
Quebec-French	64.5 (0.7)	65.1 (0.8)	64.0 (0.8)	23.0 (0.0)	32.8 (0.6)	40.7 (4.5)	85.3 (0.0)	88.5 (1.3)	95.1 (0.0)	59.1 (0.8)	68.1 (0.7)	72.8 (0.7)	76.8 (0.7)	63.6 (0.8)	64.6 (0.6)	66.2 (0.9)	62.0 (0.8)
Quebec-English	62.5 (0.8)	62.9 (0.9)	62.0 (1.0)	18.0 (0.0)	29.5 (0.4)	36.1 (1.7)	86.9 (0.9)	90.2 (0.0)	96.7 (0.0)	58.5 (0.9)	69.1 (0.7)	64.1 (0.9)	73.2 (0.7)	57.5 (0.8)	63.5 (0.8)	63.9 (0.8)	58.7 (0.8)
British Columbia	61.9 (0.5)	61.8 (0.7)	62.0 (0.6)	18.2 (1.3)	29.5 (2.3)	36.1 (3.1)	85.3 (0.0)	90.2 (0.2)	96.7 (0.0)	58.7 (0.6)	67.4 (0.5)	62.4 (0.5)	72.3 (0.6)	56.5 (0.5)	62.1 (0.4)	63.7 (0.6)	59.1 (0.6)
New Brunswick-English	59.8 (0.7)	60.3 (0.9)	59.3 (0.9)	17.5 (3.5)	26.7 (0.0)	33.9 (3.6)	83.6 (0.0)	88.5 (5.5)	95.1 (0.0)	56.1 (0.8)	66.0 (0.7)	63.1 (1.0)	69.3 (0.8)	54.6 (0.7)	61.2 (0.7)	61.1 (0.8)	55.7 (0.7)
Ontario-English	56.8 (0.7)	56.3 (0.9)	57.2 (0.9)	18.0 (0.0)	24.6 (2.4)	31.2 (1.5)	81.1 (4.6)	85.7 (3.1)	93.4 (0.0)	52.0 (0.8)	63.3 (0.7)	60.0 (0.9)	69.5 (0.7)	52.2 (0.7)	57.6 (0.7)	57.6 (0.8)	54.3 (0.7)
Ontario-French	54.5 (0.6)	54.7 (0.7)	54.3 (0.6)	18.0 (2.7)	26.3 (0.4)	31.2 (0.0)	77.1 (1.0)	82.0 (0.0)	90.2 (5.3)	48.2 (0.6)	60.0 (0.7)	61.7 (0.7)	67.6 (0.7)	55.1 (0.6)	55.9 (0.6)	54.4 (0.6)	52.4 (0.7)

[1] Conceptual understanding questions analyzed students' abilities in understanding of mathematical facts and concepts.

[2] Procedural knowledge tasks required students to apply knowledge and concepts in solving routine problems using procedures taught in the classroom.

[3] Problem solving questions required the student to apply several skills to a unique situation. These tasks usually involved multiple steps.

[4] Schools in 14 republics, where instruction is in Russian.

[5] Schools where instruction is in Hebrew.

[6] Schools where instruction is in Spanish, in all regions except Cataluna.

[7] Four provinces.

[8] Emilia-Romagna province only.

—Data not available.

NOTE.—Standard errors appear in parentheses.

SOURCE: U.S. Department of Education, National Center for Education Statistics, International Assessment of Educational Progress, Learning Mathematics, by Educational Testing Service. (This table was prepared February 1992.)

Table 393.—Classroom, home, and mathematics activities of 13-year-olds in educational systems participating in the International Assessment of Educational Progress: 1991

Country	Average percent correct on mathematics test	Percent of students who read for fun every day	Percent of students with 2 hours or more homework daily	Percent of students who watch TV 5 hours or more daily	Percent of students who do math exercises by themselves every day	Percent of students who take a math quiz at least once a week	Percent of students with positive attitudes towards mathematics
1	2	3	4	5	6	7	8
Populations (comprehensive)							
Korea	73 (0.6)	11 (0.8)	41 (1.7)	11 (0.9)	17 (1.0)	28 (1.9)	71 (1.3)
Taiwan	73 (0.7)	19 (1.2)	41 (1.3)	10 (0.7)	32 (1.1)	87 (1.1)	79 (0.9)
Switzerland [1]	71 (1.3)	51 (1.1)	20 (1.3)	7 (0.8)	47 (1.9)	40 (2.5)	85 (1.1)
(Former) Soviet Union [2]	70 (1.0)	47 (1.3)	52 (1.6)	17 (1.0)	40 (1.7)	52 (1.5)	76 (1.8)
Hungary	68 (0.8)	44 (1.2)	58 (1.3)	13 (1.0)	37 (1.6)	17 (1.3)	85 (0.8)
France	64 (0.8)	40 (1.2)	55 (1.6)	5 (0.7)	—	64 (1.3)	81 (1.0)
Israel [3]	63 (0.8)	40 (1.7)	50 (1.9)	20 (1.2)	12 (1.1)	36 (2.2)	90 (0.8)
Canada [4]	62 (0.6)	38 (0.9)	27 (1.0)	14 (0.7)	50 (1.1)	53 (0.9)	94 (0.4)
Scotland	61 (0.9)	38 (1.5)	14 (1.1)	24 (1.3)	48 (2.1)	17 (1.3)	91 (0.7)
Ireland	61 (0.9)	41 (1.3)	63 (1.9)	9 (0.9)	54 (1.5)	19 (1.5)	88 (1.0)
Slovenia	57 (0.8)	42 (1.2)	28 (1.7)	4 (0.5)	41 (1.4)	28 (1.5)	83 (1.0)
Spain [5]	55 (0.8)	36 (1.3)	64 (1.5)	10 (0.8)	39 (1.6)	31 (1.7)	89 (1.0)
United States	55 (1.0)	28 (1.3)	29 (1.8)	20 (1.7)	50 (2.7)	68 (2.1)	90 (1.1)
Jordan	40 (1.0)	24 (1.3)	56 (2.0)	7 (0.8)	34 (1.4)	68 (1.5)	77 (1.5)
Populations (with exclusions or low participation)							
China [6]	80 (1.0)	28 (1.5)	44 (1.8)	7 (0.5)	78 (1.6)	63 (2.2)	79 (2.1)
Italy [7]	64 (0.9)	47 (1.3)	79 (1.3)	5 (0.7)	10 (0.7)	19 (1.6)	86 (0.9)
England	61 (2.2)	41 (3.2)	33 (2.8)	14 (2.2)	21 (2.5)	28 (5.8)	91 (1.2)
Portugal	48 (0.8)	44 (1.8)	30 (1.6)	11 (1.0)	30 (1.6)	21 (1.8)	84 (1.1)
Brazil, Sao Paulo	37 (0.8)	33 (1.5)	45 (1.9)	19 (1.2)	35 (1.4)	44 (1.5)	83 (1.0)
Brazil, Fortaleza	32 (0.6)	41 (1.3)	48 (1.8)	21 (1.5)	31 (1.6)	56 (1.9)	86 (1.1)
Mozambique, Maputo and Beira	28 (0.3)	41 (1.6)	42 (1.8)	20 (1.2)	62 (1.6)	94 (1.0)	88 (1.0)

[1] Fifteen cantons.
[2] Schools in 14 republics, where instruction is in Russian.
[3] Schools where instruction is in Hebrew.
[4] Nine provinces.
[5] Schools where instruction is in Spanish, in all regions except Cataluna.
[6] Twenty provinces and independent cities.
[7] Emilia-Romagna province only.

—Data not available.

NOTE.—Standard errors appear in parentheses.

SOURCE: U.S. Department of Education, National Center for Education Statistics, International Assessment of Educational Progress, *Learning Mathematics*, by Educational Testing Service. (This table was prepared February 1992.)

Table 394.—Mathematics test scores of 13-year-olds in educational systems participating in the International Assessment of Educational Progress: 1991

Country	Average percent correct			Percentile scores						Topic averages					Process averages		
	Total	Male	Female	1	5	10	90	95	99	Numbers and operations	Measurement	Geometry	Data analysis, statistics, and probability	Algebra and functions	Conceptual understanding[1]	Procedural knowledge[2]	Problem solving[3]
1	2	3	4	5	6	7	8	9	10	11	12	13	14	15	16	17	18
IAEP average	58.3	—	—	—	—	—	—	—	—	61.0	46.9	62.2	69.1	54.2	60.6	58.4	55.9
Populations (comprehensive)																	
Korea	73.4 (0.6)	74.4 (0.9)	72.2 (1.0)	20.0 (0.0)	33.3 (1.5)	41.3 (1.5)	96.0 (0.0)	97.3 (1.9)	100.0 (0.0)	77.4 (0.6)	59.5 (0.9)	77.4 (0.6)	81.2 (0.7)	70.8 (0.8)	78.3 (0.5)	73.4 (0.7)	68.5 (0.7)
Taiwan	72.7 (0.7)	73.1 (0.9)	72.4 (0.9)	18.7 (1.4)	26.7 (0.0)	35.0 (3.0)	97.3 (1.3)	98.7 (0.0)	100.0 (0.0)	74.7 (0.6)	63.7 (0.9)	76.6 (0.8)	81.2 (0.6)	69.2 (0.9)	74.7 (0.7)	74.7 (0.7)	68.6 (0.8)
Switzerland[4]	70.8 (1.3)	72.8 (1.5)	68.7 (1.1)	30.7 (1.2)	42.7 (0.8)	50.7 (1.9)	93.3 (1.3)	94.7 (0.0)	98.7 (0.0)	73.6 (1.0)	62.0 (1.5)	76.6 (1.3)	81.8 (1.1)	62.7 (1.9)	71.7 (1.1)	69.0 (1.4)	71.9 (1.3)
(Former) Soviet Union[5]	70.2 (1.0)	70.0 (1.3)	70.3 (0.9)	20.9 (2.4)	35.2 (1.4)	42.7 (0.8)	92.0 (0.0)	94.7 (0.0)	98.7 (0.0)	69.2 (1.0)	59.7 (1.1)	77.6 (1.0)	76.1 (1.3)	71.9 (1.1)	70.3 (1.0)	73.2 (1.2)	66.7 (1.0)
Hungary	68.4 (0.8)	68.5 (1.0)	68.3 (0.9)	21.3 (0.9)	32.4 (2.3)	38.7 (1.3)	93.3 (0.0)	96.0 (0.0)	98.7 (0.0)	69.4 (0.7)	55.1 (1.0)	73.3 (0.8)	75.9 (0.8)	69.8 (0.9)	69.8 (0.7)	70.8 (0.8)	64.2 (0.8)
France	64.2 (0.8)	65.5 (0.9)	62.8 (0.9)	22.7 (3.0)	30.7 (0.8)	37.3 (1.0)	89.3 (0.0)	92.0 (5.3)	97.3 (1.3)	65.0 (0.7)	52.7 (1.0)	73.1 (1.0)	79.3 (0.7)	57.0 (1.0)	63.8 (0.8)	65.7 (0.9)	59.3 (0.8)
Israel[6]	63.1 (0.8)	64.4 (0.9)	61.8 (1.1)	21.3 (1.6)	30.7 (1.0)	37.3 (0.2)	87.8 (2.6)	90.7 (1.0)	96.0 (3.9)	64.8 (0.7)	47.2 (1.1)	65.8 (1.0)	74.8 (0.8)	64.7 (1.0)	65.1 (0.6)	65.3 (0.9)	59.8 (0.9)
Canada[7]	62.0 (0.6)	63.0 (0.7)	60.8 (1.1)	21.3 (0.8)	32.0 (0.0)	37.3 (0.0)	86.7 (0.0)	91.8 (4.3)	97.3 (1.3)	65.6 (0.6)	49.9 (0.6)	68.1 (0.7)	76.4 (0.6)	52.7 (0.7)	61.5 (0.8)	61.9 (0.7)	58.9 (0.5)
Scotland	60.6 (0.9)	60.4 (1.0)	60.8 (1.1)	17.8 (1.3)	26.8 (1.7)	33.3 (2.0)	86.7 (0.0)	90.7 (0.0)	96.0 (0.0)	59.7 (0.8)	51.0 (1.2)	59.9 (1.1)	71.8 (1.0)	52.8 (1.2)	61.5 (0.8)	59.2 (1.0)	60.9 (0.9)
Ireland	60.5 (0.9)	62.6 (1.2)	58.4 (1.1)	21.3 (0.0)	28.6 (0.5)	32.0 (0.1)	82.7 (0.2)	88.0 (2.6)	94.7 (0.0)	65.1 (0.8)	49.4 (1.0)	63.1 (1.0)	63.6 (0.8)	55.6 (1.1)	58.5 (0.7)	62.0 (1.2)	57.9 (0.8)
Slovenia	57.1 (0.9)	58.1 (0.8)	56.1 (1.0)	20.3 (1.6)	27.1 (3.9)	32.9 (2.0)	78.4 (4.0)	84.7 (1.3)	91.9 (2.0)	62.2 (0.7)	43.1 (0.9)	60.0 (1.2)	67.7 (0.8)	51.8 (1.0)	58.4 (0.7)	59.0 (0.9)	53.7 (0.8)
Spain[8]	55.4 (0.8)	57.1 (1.1)	53.8 (0.8)	17.3 (3.8)	24.0 (0.6)	29.3 (0.0)	82.7 (1.3)	90.7 (0.1)	97.3 (0.0)	60.1 (0.6)	37.9 (0.8)	54.3 (1.0)	72.2 (1.0)	52.5 (1.2)	57.4 (0.9)	55.8 (0.9)	51.9 (0.8)
United States	55.3 (1.0)	55.8 (1.1)	54.8 (1.3)	17.3 (3.8)	24.0 (0.6)	29.3 (0.0)	82.7 (1.3)	90.7 (0.1)	97.3 (0.0)	61.0 (1.0)	39.5 (1.0)	54.3 (0.9)	67.7 (0.8)	49.2 (1.6)	58.4 (0.7)	56.0 (1.3)	52.3 (1.0)
Jordan	40.4 (1.0)	41.4 (1.2)	39.1 (1.9)	13.3 (0.0)	17.6 (1.2)	21.3 (1.5)	65.3 (3.1)	75.7 (3.3)	89.3 (5.2)	42.8 (1.0)	32.0 (1.0)	43.5 (1.0)	45.7 (1.0)	38.1 (1.3)	44.9 (0.9)	38.5 (1.2)	37.9 (1.0)
Populations (with exclusions or low participation)																	
China[9]	80.2 (1.0)	81.7 (1.0)	78.5 (1.1)	37.0 (2.2)	49.3 (2.7)	57.3 (3.3)	96.0 (1.3)	98.7 (1.3)	100.0 (0.0)	84.9 (0.9)	71.3 (2.5)	80.2 (1.1)	75.4 (1.2)	82.4 (0.9)	81.6 (1.0)	83.0 (0.9)	75.6 (1.2)
England[10]	60.6 (2.2)	60.8 (3.0)	60.4 (2.2)	18.7 (1.9)	27.4 (3.3)	34.5 (3.7)	89.3 (0.5)	93.3 (1.3)	97.3 (1.0)	58.5 (2.0)	51.2 (2.5)	70.3 (2.4)	79.5 (1.8)	54.0 (2.8)	62.0 (2.1)	59.0 (2.6)	60.8 (2.0)
Italy[10]	64.0 (0.9)	65.8 (1.1)	62.1 (0.9)	23.0 (1.3)	32.4 (0.9)	36.5 (1.5)	88.0 (0.0)	91.8 (0.5)	96.0 (0.0)	63.8 (0.8)	62.8 (1.1)	75.3 (1.0)	71.7 (0.8)	52.6 (1.2)	66.6 (0.8)	62.1 (1.1)	63.3 (0.9)
Portugal	48.3 (0.8)	48.9 (1.3)	47.9 (0.9)	17.3 (0.9)	23.9 (1.3)	28.0 (0.5)	74.7 (0.9)	80.6 (1.7)	89.7 (2.6)	52.1 (0.8)	31.9 (0.7)	49.0 (1.3)	68.6 (1.0)	43.1 (1.1)	51.5 (0.9)	47.1 (1.0)	46.4 (0.7)
Brazil, Sao Paulo	37.0 (0.8)	37.9 (0.9)	36.2 (0.9)	10.3 (2.1)	16.7 (1.0)	18.7 (0.9)	62.7 (0.7)	70.7 (1.5)	82.7 (0.7)	40.9 (0.8)	24.1 (0.5)	34.3 (1.5)	49.7 (1.0)	35.6 (1.1)	38.5 (0.9)	36.5 (1.1)	36.0 (0.6)
Brazil, Fortaleza	32.4 (0.6)	35.2 (0.9)	30.5 (0.6)	10.9 (0.4)	14.7 (0.6)	17.3 (0.3)	56.8 (2.1)	65.3 (0.6)	80.8 (3.5)	35.8 (0.7)	20.5 (0.5)	28.6 (0.8)	43.8 (0.8)	32.3 (0.9)	35.3 (0.7)	30.8 (0.8)	31.0 (0.5)
Mozambique, Maputo, and Beira	28.3 (0.3)	28.8 (0.5)	27.8 (0.3)	11.5 (1.1)	16.2 (0.6)	18.7 (0.1)	44.6 (1.4)	50.0 (3.2)	60.0 (2.2)	33.8 (0.4)	20.1 (0.3)	29.2 (0.5)	35.4 (0.6)	20.5 (0.5)	34.0 (0.4)	22.9 (0.4)	28.2 (0.4)
Populations (Canadian)																	
Quebec-French	68.7 (0.7)	69.8 (1.0)	67.5 (0.8)	29.3 (1.4)	39.7 (1.8)	45.3 (2.8)	89.3 (0.0)	93.3 (0.0)	96.4 (2.7)	72.3 (0.6)	56.4 (1.0)	78.1 (0.8)	81.1 (0.6)	58.4 (1.0)	72.6 (0.7)	68.0 (0.8)	65.3 (0.8)
Saskatchewan-French	67.5 (1.0)	68.8 (1.5)	66.3 (1.4)	32.0 (1.3)	36.0 (2.9)	46.5 (3.7)	87.8 (3.9)	90.7 (2.5)	96.0 (1.3)	73.9 (1.0)	53.8 (1.3)	69.2 (1.3)	76.0 (1.2)	61.6 (1.4)	70.1 (1.2)	69.3 (1.0)	62.9 (1.1)
British Columbia	66.2 (0.7)	66.8 (0.8)	65.4 (1.0)	25.3 (0.7)	35.6 (2.1)	41.3 (0.0)	90.7 (4.0)	94.7 (3.6)	97.3 (1.3)	69.3 (0.7)	54.1 (0.9)	69.6 (0.9)	71.7 (0.8)	60.2 (0.8)	68.3 (0.7)	61.8 (0.7)	61.8 (0.7)
Quebec-English	65.7 (0.9)	65.7 (1.6)	65.7 (0.8)	23.0 (2.5)	33.8 (3.9)	41.3 (1.3)	90.7 (0.0)	94.7 (2.4)	98.7 (0.0)	68.7 (0.9)	53.5 (1.1)	70.6 (1.0)	78.1 (1.0)	59.6 (1.1)	68.3 (0.9)	66.6 (1.0)	61.9 (1.0)
Alberta	64.0 (0.7)	63.4 (0.8)	64.3 (0.8)	23.5 (2.6)	34.7 (2.4)	38.7 (3.5)	88.0 (0.0)	92.0 (1.8)	97.3 (0.0)	68.6 (0.7)	54.3 (0.9)	67.2 (0.8)	80.0 (0.7)	52.1 (0.9)	68.3 (0.9)	62.6 (0.8)	61.0 (0.7)
Manitoba-French	63.1 (0.6)	64.5 (1.1)	61.9 (0.8)	26.7 (2.7)	34.7 (2.4)	41.3 (0.0)	85.3 (0.0)	89.3 (0.0)	94.7 (0.0)	67.1 (0.7)	48.5 (0.7)	66.6 (0.8)	75.0 (0.8)	52.1 (0.9)	64.6 (0.7)	66.0 (0.7)	58.2 (0.6)
Saskatchewan-English	62.0 (0.7)	63.2 (0.9)	60.7 (1.0)	21.3 (1.3)	29.7 (4.5)	37.3 (5.8)	86.7 (3.8)	90.7 (0.0)	96.0 (0.0)	66.1 (0.6)	49.6 (0.9)	62.9 (1.2)	78.3 (0.7)	58.5 (0.7)	64.6 (0.7)	66.0 (0.8)	57.2 (0.7)
New Brunswick-French	60.6 (0.4)	60.5 (0.6)	60.7 (0.6)	20.3 (1.3)	30.2 (3.1)	36.0 (0.0)	85.1 (1.3)	89.3 (0.0)	93.3 (0.0)	65.4 (0.5)	46.5 (0.5)	64.5 (0.5)	72.3 (0.5)	54.3 (0.4)	63.7 (0.4)	64.4 (0.4)	55.3 (0.4)
Nova Scotia	59.7 (0.6)	60.7 (0.9)	58.8 (0.8)	20.0 (0.0)	29.3 (1.2)	35.1 (1.5)	85.3 (0.0)	89.3 (1.3)	96.0 (2.7)	62.9 (0.6)	47.3 (0.8)	63.7 (0.7)	73.9 (0.7)	53.5 (0.8)	61.8 (0.6)	60.2 (0.6)	57.1 (0.6)
Newfoundland	58.9 (0.6)	57.8 (0.7)	59.9 (0.9)	18.7 (1.3)	29.3 (0.0)	34.7 (0.0)	84.0 (2.1)	88.0 (5.8)	96.0 (2.7)	62.9 (0.6)	45.1 (0.7)	63.7 (0.7)	72.4 (0.7)	52.7 (0.6)	61.8 (0.7)	60.3 (0.7)	54.3 (0.6)
Ontario-English	58.3 (0.8)	59.3 (1.0)	57.4 (0.9)	20.0 (1.2)	29.3 (0.0)	34.7 (0.0)	84.0 (2.0)	89.3 (1.3)	96.0 (1.3)	61.9 (0.8)	46.2 (0.9)	63.4 (1.0)	73.6 (0.8)	49.5 (1.0)	61.8 (0.7)	58.5 (0.9)	54.3 (0.6)
Manitoba-English	58.0 (0.8)	58.0 (0.9)	57.9 (1.0)	20.0 (1.7)	29.3 (0.0)	33.3 (4.2)	82.7 (0.0)	86.7 (0.0)	96.0 (0.0)	62.5 (0.7)	45.6 (0.9)	58.4 (0.9)	73.6 (0.9)	50.8 (1.0)	60.5 (0.8)	58.8 (0.9)	55.5 (0.8)
New Brunswick-English	57.7 (0.5)	58.3 (0.7)	57.1 (0.7)	20.0 (0.0)	27.5 (1.6)	33.3 (0.0)	82.7 (0.0)	89.3 (2.0)	96.0 (0.0)	62.4 (0.5)	51.3 (0.6)	62.4 (0.6)	71.0 (0.6)	43.2 (0.6)	61.4 (0.5)	55.4 (0.6)	56.4 (0.5)
Ontario-French	53.5 (0.6)	53.5 (0.8)	53.5 (0.8)	18.7 (0.2)	25.3 (1.1)	32.0 (0.0)	76.0 (3.0)	82.7 (0.0)	92.0 (2.3)	58.0 (0.6)	38.8 (0.7)	59.0 (1.0)	69.0 (0.7)	44.7 (0.9)	56.6 (0.7)	54.1 (0.8)	49.6 (0.6)

[1] Conceptual understanding questions analyzed students' abilities in understanding of mathematical facts and concepts.

[2] Procedural knowledge tasks required students to apply knowledge and concepts in solving routine problems using procedures taught in the classroom.

[3] Problem-solving questions required the student to apply several skills to a unique situation. These tasks usually involved multiple steps.

[4] Fifteen cantons.

[5] Schools in 14 republics, where instruction is in Russian.

[6] Schools where instruction is in Hebrew.

[7] Nine provinces.

[8] Schools where instruction is in Spanish, in all regions except Cataluna.

[9] Twenty provinces and independent cities.

[10] Emilia-Romagna province only.

—Data not available.

NOTE.—Standard errors appear in parentheses.

SOURCE: U.S. Department of Education, National Center for Education Statistics, International Assessment of Educational Progress, Learning Mathematics, by Educational Testing Service. (This table was prepared February 1992.)

Table 395.—Science test scores of 9-year-olds in educational systems participating in the International Assessment of Educational Progress: 1991

Country	Average percent correct			Percentile scores						Topic averages				Process averages		
	Total	Male	Female	1	5	10	90	95	99	Life sciences	Physical sciences	Earth and space sciences	Nature of science	Exhibit basic knowledge of science facts and concepts (Knows)	Combine factual knowledge with rules and formulas (Uses)	Able to draw conclusions on the basis of available data (Integrates)
1	2	3	4	5	6	7	8	9	10	11	12	13	14	15	16	17
IAEP average	62.1	—	—	—	—	—			—	63.3	58.6	64.1	63.9	63.9	62.7	56.9
Populations (comprehensive)																
Korea	67.9 (0.5)	70.4 (0.7)	65.1 (0.5)	32.8 (4.9)	44.8 (0.4)	50.0 (0.0)	84.5 (0.0)	87.9 (0.0)	93.1 (3.4)	69.1 (0.5)	68.2 (0.5)	62.4 (0.6)	70.7 (0.6)	67.3 (0.5)	70.1 (0.5)	64.5 (0.5)
Taiwan	66.7 (0.5)	68.5 (0.6)	64.6 (0.7)	27.6 (1.3)	39.7 (0.0)	44.8 (7.2)	86.2 (0.0)	89.7 (0.0)	94.8 (0.0)	65.3 (0.6)	68.1 (0.5)	66.6 (0.7)	67.4 (0.6)	65.3 (0.6)	69.5 (0.6)	63.6 (0.6)
United States	64.7 (0.9)	65.5 (1.1)	63.8 (0.8)	25.9 (0.3)	36.2 (1.7)	43.1 (5.1)	84.5 (0.0)	87.9 (0.0)	93.1 (0.0)	65.2 (0.9)	57.5 (0.8)	70.6 (1.1)	70.7 (1.0)	67.0 (1.0)	65.5 (0.9)	57.9 (0.8)
Canada [1]	62.8 (0.4)	63.6 (0.4)	62.0 (0.5)	27.6 (0.5)	37.9 (1.1)	43.1 (0.0)	81.0 (0.0)	84.5 (0.0)	91.4 (0.0)	63.3 (0.4)	57.7 (0.4)	66.8 (0.4)	67.3 (0.5)	63.4 (0.4)	63.4 (0.4)	56.4 (0.4)
Hungary	62.5 (0.5)	63.4 (0.6)	61.6 (0.6)	26.9 (1.7)	38.5 (0.7)	44.8 (0.0)	79.3 (0.0)	84.2 (2.9)	89.7 (0.0)	64.7 (0.6)	56.3 (0.6)	68.2 (0.5)	62.0 (0.6)	66.1 (0.5)	61.1 (0.5)	57.4 (0.7)
Spain [2]	61.7 (0.7)	63.4 (0.9)	59.7 (0.7)	27.6 (3.1)	36.2 (0.0)	41.8 (1.6)	81.0 (0.0)	84.5 (0.0)	89.7 (0.0)	65.7 (0.7)	54.1 (0.7)	62.7 (0.7)	65.1 (1.0)	66.7 (0.7)	60.3 (0.7)	53.8 (0.8)
(Former) Soviet Union [3]	61.5 (1.2)	62.7 (1.4)	60.4 (1.2)	29.3 (4.2)	39.7 (1.5)	43.1 (1.4)	79.3 (4.8)	86.2 (2.4)	93.1 (2.4)	63.8 (1.4)	58.1 (0.9)	63.1 (1.4)	60.2 (1.4)	63.9 (1.4)	62.3 (1.1)	54.7 (1.4)
Israel [4]	61.2 (0.7)	63.0 (0.9)	59.4 (0.7)	27.6 (0.3)	36.2 (1.4)	41.4 (0.0)	81.0 (0.0)	86.2 (0.0)	93.1 (0.0)	61.4 (0.8)	59.8 (0.6)	60.6 (0.7)	64.1 (0.9)	61.0 (0.8)	63.0 (0.6)	57.7 (0.8)
Slovenia	57.7 (0.5)	58.3 (0.6)	57.0 (0.6)	27.8 (0.8)	35.1 (0.2)	40.4 (0.4)	75.4 (0.0)	79.0 (0.0)	86.0 (1.5)	59.4 (0.5)	56.6 (0.5)	58.3 (0.7)	54.1 (0.6)	60.3 (0.5)	57.0 (0.5)	52.9 (0.7)
Ireland	56.5 (0.7)	58.2 (1.0)	54.8 (0.9)	22.9 (1.4)	29.3 (1.6)	36.2 (1.3)	75.9 (0.0)	81.0 (1.8)	89.7 (5.2)	54.7 (0.8)	53.8 (0.7)	62.9 (0.8)	59.5 (0.8)	57.2 (0.8)	57.4 (0.7)	53.0 (0.8)
Populations (with exclusions or low participation)																
Italy [5]	66.9 (0.9)	67.9 (1.0)	65.8 (1.0)	31.0 (1.7)	41.4 (3.3)	48.3 (0.3)	86.2 (1.7)	89.7 (1.7)	94.8 (0.0)	71.3 (0.9)	61.0 (0.9)	66.8 (0.9)	66.9 (1.1)	71.6 (0.9)	66.1 (0.9)	58.2 (1.1)
England	62.9 (0.9)	63.8 (1.3)	62.0 (1.2)	24.1 (4.1)	36.2 (0.9)	41.4 (0.0)	82.8 (0.0)	86.2 (2.8)	93.1 (0.0)	62.4 (0.9)	60.1 (0.9)	66.3 (1.1)	66.0 (1.1)	64.5 (1.0)	63.6 (0.9)	58.2 (1.0)
Scotland	62.2 (0.7)	61.9 (0.7)	62.5 (1.0)	27.6 (0.0)	36.8 (3.0)	43.1 (0.0)	81.0 (3.5)	84.5 (0.0)	89.7 (0.0)	61.3 (0.7)	59.1 (0.8)	65.1 (0.7)	67.7 (1.0)	62.5 (0.6)	62.7 (0.7)	60.4 (0.8)
Portugal	54.8 (0.7)	56.3 (0.9)	53.3 (0.9)	26.3 (3.8)	33.3 (3.2)	37.9 (0.0)	72.4 (0.0)	79.0 (5.6)	86.2 (3.9)	58.1 (0.8)	50.0 (0.6)	57.3 (0.9)	52.4 (1.1)	58.4 (0.9)	54.1 (0.7)	48.5 (0.8)
Populations (Canadian)																
British Columbia	65.9 (0.6)	66.1 (0.8)	65.6 (0.6)	29.3 (4.6)	41.4 (0.0)	46.6 (3.6)	82.8 (0.0)	86.2 (3.6)	91.4 (0.0)	66.4 (0.7)	59.6 (0.7)	72.1 (0.6)	69.9 (0.8)	68.2 (0.6)	66.9 (0.6)	58.6 (0.8)
Quebec-English	63.0 (0.7)	64.3 (0.9)	61.7 (0.8)	29.3 (2.0)	37.9 (0.0)	43.1 (2.0)	82.8 (0.0)	86.2 (0.0)	91.4 (0.0)	63.9 (0.8)	57.3 (0.6)	66.8 (0.8)	67.9 (0.8)	65.1 (0.8)	64.4 (0.6)	55.7 (0.8)
Quebec-French	62.8 (0.5)	63.2 (0.7)	62.4 (0.5)	32.8 (5.2)	40.7 (3.6)	44.8 (0.6)	79.3 (0.0)	84.5 (0.0)	89.7 (4.9)	63.3 (0.6)	59.1 (0.6)	68.4 (0.6)	69.0 (0.7)	61.1 (0.8)	66.9 (0.6)	57.9 (0.6)
Ontario-English	62.5 (0.5)	63.6 (0.6)	61.4 (0.7)	27.6 (0.0)	36.2 (2.6)	43.1 (3.1)	81.0 (0.0)	86.2 (3.4)	91.4 (0.0)	63.0 (0.6)	56.6 (0.5)	67.2 (0.5)	66.2 (0.7)	64.3 (0.6)	64.1 (0.5)	55.1 (0.5)
New Brunswick-English	61.6 (0.4)	61.9 (0.5)	61.3 (0.6)	24.1 (0.0)	34.5 (3.2)	41.4 (0.0)	81.0 (0.0)	84.5 (0.0)	91.4 (0.0)	61.3 (0.4)	56.9 (0.4)	67.2 (0.5)	65.4 (0.5)	63.1 (0.4)	63.4 (0.4)	54.5 (0.5)
Ontario-French	56.3 (0.5)	56.5 (0.7)	56.1 (0.5)	28.9 (3.5)	34.5 (0.0)	39.7 (0.0)	74.1 (0.0)	79.3 (1.8)	86.2 (0.0)	54.9 (0.5)	53.7 (0.5)	60.5 (0.5)	60.3 (0.7)	55.1 (0.5)	59.7 (0.5)	51.7 (0.6)

[1] Four provinces.

[2] Schools where instruction is in Spanish, in all regions except Cataluna.

[3] Schools in 14 republics, where instruction is in Russian.

[4] Schools where instruction is in Hebrew.

[5] Emilia-Romagna province only.

—Data not available.

NOTE.—Standard errors appear in parentheses.

SOURCE: U.S. Department of Education, National Center for Education Statistics, International Assessment of Educational Progress, *Learning Science*, by Educational Testing Service. (This table was prepared February 1992.)

Table 396.—Classroom, home, and science activities of 9-year-olds in educational systems participating in the International Assessment of Educational Progress: 1991

Country	Average percent correct on science test	Percent of students who read for fun every day	Percent of students who read about science often	Percent of students who never conduct experiments	Percent of students with 2 hours or more homework daily	Percent of students who watch TV 5 hours or more daily
1	2	3	4	5	6	7
Populations (comprehensive)						
Korea	68 (0.5)	25 (1.4)	21 (1.1)	19 (1.1)	20 (1.2)	10 (0.8)
Taiwan	67 (0.5)	32 (1.3)	17 (1.0)	10 (0.8)	29 (1.4)	12 (0.8)
United States	65 (0.9)	47 (1.8)	32 (1.5)	22 (1.3)	19 (1.4)	25 (1.6)
Canada [1]	63 (0.4)	48 (0.9)	20 (0.7)	27 (1.0)	12 (0.6)	22 (0.7)
Hungary	63 (0.5)	52 (1.5)	36 (1.3)	40 (1.3)	29 (1.5)	15 (1.2)
Spain [2]	62 (0.7)	54 (1.9)	39 (1.7)	40 (2.2)	28 (1.6)	20 (1.8)
(Former) Soviet Union [3]	62 (1.2)	65 (1.8)	33 (2.2)	44 (1.2)	27 (1.8)	17 (1.1)
Israel [4]	61 (0.7)	55 (1.3)	27 (1.3)	14 (1.1)	36 (1.7)	24 (1.2)
Slovenia	58 (0.5)	61 (1.2)	40 (1.5)	21 (1.1)	15 (1.2)	10 (0.8)
Ireland	57 (0.7)	50 (1.5)	24 (1.3)	50 (2.0)	16 (1.3)	22 (1.6)
Populations (with exclusions or low participation)						
Italy [5]	67 (0.9)	50 (1.6)	22 (1.6)	50 (1.8)	27 (1.2)	9 (1.1)
England	63 (0.9)	49 (1.8)	21 (2.0)	11 (1.3)	10 (1.1)	22 (1.9)
Scotland	62 (0.7)	46 (2.1)	22 (1.5)	28 (2.6)	5 (0.8)	24 (1.4)
Portugal	55 (0.7)	62 (1.6)	18 (1.9)	22 (1.6)	22 (1.6)	18 (1.6)

[1] Four provinces.
[2] Schools where instruction is in Spanish, in all regions except Cataluna.
[3] Schools in 14 republics, where instruction is in Russian.
[4] Schools where instruction is in Hebrew.
[5] Emilia-Romagna province only.

NOTE.—Standard errors appear in parentheses.

SOURCE: U.S. Department of Education, National Center for Education Statistics, International Assessment of Educational Progress, *Learning Science,* by Educational Testing Service. (This table was prepared February 1992.)

Table 397.—Classroom, home, and science activities of 13-year-olds in educational systems participating in the International Assessment of Educational Progress: 1991

Country	Average percent correct on science test	Percent of students who read for fun every day	Percent of students with 2 hours or more homework daily	Percent of students who watch TV 5 hours or more daily	Percent of students who never conduct experiments	Percent of students who take a science quiz at least once a week	Percent of students with positive attitudes towards science
1	2	3	4	5	6	7	8
Populations (comprehensive)							
Korea	78 (0.5)	11 (0.8)	38 (1.5)	10 (0.8)	35 (1.7)	21 (1.6)	27 (1.3)
Taiwan	76 (0.4)	17 (1.1)	44 (1.3)	7 (0.7)	25 (1.3)	67 (1.2)	51 (1.2)
Switzerland [1]	74 (0.9)	49 (1.2)	21 (1.3)	7 (0.6)	36 (1.7)	18 (1.2)	59 (1.5)
Hungary	73 (0.5)	44 (1.3)	61 (1.5)	16 (1.1)	31 (1.7)	27 (1.6)	69 (1.2)
(Former) Soviet Union [2]	71 (1.0)	48 (1.1)	52 (1.6)	19 (1.3)	13 (0.8)	88 (1.2)	66 (1.4)
Slovenia	70 (0.5)	43 (1.5)	27 (1.4)	5 (0.6)	22 (1.5)	18 (1.0)	78 (1.2)
Israel [3]	70 (0.7)	40 (1.4)	49 (1.4)	20 (1.2)	35 (1.4)	28 (1.9)	62 (1.6)
Canada [4]	69 (0.4)	36 (0.9)	26 (0.9)	15 (0.7)	13 (0.7)	26 (1.1)	62 (1.0)
France	69 (0.6)	39 (1.5)	55 (1.6)	4 (0.5)	20 (1.7)	47 (1.4)	55 (1.3)
Scotland	68 (0.6)	37 (1.4)	15 (1.5)	23 (1.3)	3 (0.3)	11 (1.0)	66 (1.2)
Spain [5]	68 (0.6)	34 (1.5)	62 (1.9)	11 (0.9)	51 (2.3)	42 (2.6)	78 (1.4)
United States	67 (1.0)	29 (1.4)	31 (1.6)	22 (1.7)	25 (1.9)	69 (2.0)	57 (2.1)
Ireland	63 (0.6)	40 (1.3)	66 (1.6)	9 (0.9)	27 (2.1)	18 (1.1)	57 (1.4)
Jordan	57 (0.7)	22 (1.0)	54 (2.0)	10 (0.9)	26 (1.4)	73 (1.8)	82 (1.0)
Populations (with exclusions or low participation)							
Italy [6]	70 (0.7)	45 (1.4)	78 (1.2)	7 (0.8)	59 (1.9)	9 (1.0)	73 (1.4)
England	69 (1.2)	36 (1.8)	26 (2.8)	23 (1.7)	2 (0.6)	8 (0.9)	66 (2.9)
China [7]	67 (1.1)	28 (1.4)	35 (2.1)	2 (0.4)	29 (2.4)	42 (2.2)	74 (1.7)
Portugal	63 (0.8)	47 (1.2)	30 (1.7)	11 (0.9)	48 (1.7)	34 (2.0)	71 (1.4)
Brazil, Sao Paulo	53 (0.6)	31 (1.1)	48 (1.9)	18 (1.1)	35 (1.6)	45 (1.2)	69 (1.3)
Brazil, Fortaleza	46 (0.6)	41 (1.2)	50 (2.0)	20 (1.5)	44 (1.9)	55 (1.9)	74 (1.3)

[1] Fifteen cantons.
[2] Schools in 14 republics, where instruction is in Russian.
[3] Schools where instruction is in Hebrew.
[4] Nine provinces.
[5] Schools where instruction is in Spanish, in all regions except Cataluna.
[6] Emilia-Romagna province only.

[7] Twenty provinces and independent cities.

NOTE.—Standard errors appear in parentheses.

SOURCE: U.S. Department of Education, National Center for Education Statistics, International Assessment of Educational Progress, *Learning Science,* by Educational Testing Service. (This table was prepared February 1992.)

Table 398.—Science test scores of 13-year-olds in educational systems participating in the International Assessment of Educational Progress: 1991

Country	Average percent correct			Percentile scores						Topic averages				Process averages		
	Total	Male	Female	1	5	10	90	95	99	Life sciences	Physical sciences	Earth and space sciences	Nature of science	Exhibit basic knowledge of science facts and concepts (Knows)	Combine factual knowledge with rules and formulas (Uses)	Able to draw conclusions on the basis of available data (Integrates)
1	2	3	4	5	6	7	8	9	10	11	12	13	14	15	16	17
IAEP average	66.9	—	—	—	—	—	—	—	—	68.0	64.4	66.9	70.9	72.6	65.4	64.9
Populations (comprehensive)																
Korea	77.5 (0.5)	79.6 (0.6)	75.0 (0.7)	35.9 (0.0)	50.0 (0.0)	57.8 (3.8)	93.8 (0.0)	95.3 (0.0)	98.4 (0.0)	80.3 (0.5)	75.8 (0.6)	74.8 (0.6)	78.8 (0.6)	83.9 (0.5)	77.2 (0.4)	72.7 (0.6)
Taiwan	75.6 (0.4)	76.3 (0.6)	74.9 (0.6)	28.6 (3.6)	42.2 (0.0)	51.6 (0.0)	93.8 (0.0)	95.3 (0.0)	98.4 (0.0)	77.9 (0.5)	74.8 (0.5)	72.2 (0.5)	76.4 (0.6)	81.4 (0.5)	74.7 (0.4)	72.3 (0.5)
Switzerland[1]	73.7 (0.9)	76.4 (1.1)	70.9 (0.8)	35.9 (2.9)	50.0 (5.7)	57.8 (0.6)	92.2 (0.0)	95.3 (0.0)	98.4 (0.0)	74.3 (0.9)	70.3 (0.9)	74.5 (0.8)	79.8 (1.0)	82.5 (0.5)	71.6 (0.8)	74.6 (1.1)
Hungary	73.4 (0.5)	75.6 (0.6)	71.4 (0.7)	33.3 (1.9)	45.3 (1.0)	51.6 (0.0)	92.2 (0.0)	95.3 (0.0)	98.4 (0.0)	77.3 (0.5)	70.1 (0.6)	72.2 (0.6)	68.0 (1.2)	78.8 (1.1)	71.1 (0.5)	69.9 (0.7)
(Former) Soviet Union[2]	71.3 (1.0)	72.9 (1.1)	69.6 (1.0)	31.3 (0.6)	43.8 (1.0)	50.8 (1.9)	89.1 (2.3)	92.2 (2.7)	96.9 (3.8)	73.0 (1.0)	70.8 (1.0)	73.0 (0.9)	72.5 (0.6)	80.2 (0.5)	69.8 (0.8)	67.6 (1.3)
Slovenia	70.3 (0.5)	72.5 (0.7)	68.2 (0.6)	34.4 (2.2)	43.8 (1.0)	50.0 (0.0)	89.1 (0.0)	92.2 (0.0)	96.9 (0.0)	73.1 (0.6)	67.3 (0.5)	70.1 (0.6)	78.5 (0.7)	70.5 (0.7)	68.0 (0.6)	66.0 (0.6)
Israel[3]	69.7 (0.7)	71.6 (0.8)	68.0 (0.8)	34.4 (0.1)	42.2 (0.0)	47.6 (3.9)	89.1 (0.0)	92.2 (0.0)	96.9 (0.0)	65.4 (0.7)	69.8 (0.8)	67.5 (0.8)	79.0 (0.5)	71.7 (0.4)	66.1 (0.4)	71.1 (0.8)
Canada[4]	68.8 (0.4)	70.5 (0.5)	67.1 (0.4)	32.8 (0.0)	43.8 (0.0)	48.4 (1.7)	87.5 (0.0)	90.6 (0.0)	95.3 (0.0)	68.5 (0.4)	64.9 (0.4)	66.8 (0.6)	75.7 (0.7)	71.4 (0.6)	66.3 (0.6)	70.1 (0.5)
France	68.6 (0.6)	70.7 (0.7)	66.5 (0.7)	31.3 (1.8)	40.6 (2.1)	45.3 (1.7)	89.1 (0.0)	92.2 (0.0)	96.9 (0.0)	67.5 (0.6)	66.8 (0.6)	64.1 (0.8)	76.8 (0.7)	72.3 (0.7)	65.8 (0.6)	67.7 (0.8)
Scotland	67.9 (0.6)	69.6 (0.7)	66.3 (0.9)	28.6 (2.5)	39.1 (0.0)	45.3 (0.0)	87.5 (2.6)	90.6 (5.4)	96.9 (5.2)	67.3 (0.7)	65.7 (0.7)	68.5 (0.7)	70.0 (0.7)	76.3 (0.7)	65.2 (0.6)	64.3 (0.8)
Spain[5]	67.5 (0.6)	69.2 (0.8)	66.0 (0.7)	35.1 (0.5)	42.6 (1.3)	48.4 (0.2)	85.9 (2.6)	89.1 (0.0)	95.3 (0.0)	70.3 (0.6)	64.1 (0.7)	65.5 (0.8)	75.6 (1.3)	72.8 (1.0)	65.1 (0.9)	65.4 (0.3)
United States	67.0 (1.0)	69.4 (1.2)	64.5 (0.9)	28.1 (2.0)	39.3 (2.9)	43.8 (5.1)	85.9 (0.0)	90.6 (0.0)	95.3 (0.0)	69.1 (1.0)	61.6 (1.1)	67.0 (0.9)	71.4 (0.7)	66.0 (0.7)	62.0 (0.6)	63.4 (0.7)
Ireland	63.3 (0.6)	66.1 (0.9)	60.8 (0.8)	27.4 (2.3)	35.9 (0.0)	40.6 (2.3)	84.4 (3.2)	89.1 (0.0)	95.3 (0.0)	61.0 (0.6)	60.7 (0.9)	65.5 (0.8)				
Jordan	56.6 (0.7)	57.1 (0.8)	55.9 (1.3)	23.4 (0.0)	30.2 (2.9)	35.9 (0.0)	78.1 (1.6)	84.4 (2.1)	92.2 (3.5)	58.6 (0.7)	53.8 (0.8)	60.7 (0.9)	56.1 (0.9)	65.3 (0.7)	56.6 (0.8)	49.2 (0.9)
Populations (with exclusions or low participation)																
England	68.7 (1.2)	70.3 (1.6)	67.1 (1.8)	31.3 (0.0)	39.1 (0.0)	44.3 (3.3)	89.1 (0.0)	92.2 (0.0)	98.4 (3.5)	68.2 (1.2)	66.6 (1.2)	65.9 (1.5)	76.5 (1.4)	72.1 (1.2)	66.8 (1.2)	69.0 (1.5)
China[6]	67.2 (1.1)	69.4 (1.2)	64.8 (1.1)	28.1 (3.5)	40.6 (0.6)	45.3 (1.6)	87.5 (1.6)	92.2 (2.2)	96.9 (1.6)	63.8 (1.1)	67.6 (1.1)	70.2 (1.4)	69.7 (1.1)	68.2 (1.1)	67.1 (1.1)	66.6 (1.1)
Italy[7]	69.9 (0.7)	72.2 (0.8)	67.6 (0.8)	31.3 (2.7)	43.8 (4.4)	48.4 (0.0)	89.1 (0.0)	92.2 (0.0)	95.3 (0.0)	71.8 (0.7)	67.0 (0.7)	70.8 (0.7)	72.7 (0.7)	76.7 (0.7)	66.9 (0.7)	69.6 (0.8)
Portugal	62.6 (0.8)	65.0 (1.0)	60.3 (0.8)	28.1 (2.7)	37.3 (1.6)	42.2 (3.1)	84.4 (0.0)	89.1 (0.0)	93.8 (1.6)	65.9 (0.8)	58.4 (0.7)	61.1 (0.9)	67.7 (1.2)	69.8 (0.8)	60.9 (0.7)	59.5 (1.1)
Brazil, Sao Paulo	52.7 (0.6)	56.3 (0.8)	49.6 (0.7)	23.4 (1.2)	29.7 (0.7)	33.3 (0.8)	74.5 (3.9)	81.3 (1.7)	92.2 (2.7)	56.3 (0.8)	48.8 (0.5)	55.8 (0.7)	52.5 (0.8)	60.4 (0.9)	51.9 (0.5)	47.5 (0.7)
Brazil, Fortaleza	46.4 (0.6)	49.1 (0.7)	44.3 (0.8)	21.8 (2.1)	27.3 (1.1)	31.3 (0.0)	67.2 (0.6)	73.4 (0.1)	85.9 (2.5)	51.3 (0.7)	42.6 (0.6)	48.6 (0.7)	44.8 (0.9)	55.5 (0.8)	45.4 (0.5)	40.5 (0.8)
Populations (Canadian)																
Alberta	74.1 (0.4)	76.4 (0.6)	71.8 (0.5)	35.9 (0.5)	48.4 (0.0)	54.7 (0.0)	90.6 (0.0)	93.8 (0.0)	96.9 (0.0)	72.3 (0.5)	71.3 (0.5)	73.7 (0.5)	84.0 (0.5)	75.7 (0.5)	72.0 (0.4)	76.4 (0.6)
British Columbia	72.4 (0.5)	73.5 (0.6)	71.4 (0.6)	35.9 (1.6)	46.9 (0.0)	53.1 (0.0)	89.1 (0.0)	92.2 (0.0)	95.3 (0.0)	70.2 (0.5)	70.7 (0.5)	72.1 (0.6)	80.7 (0.6)	76.4 (0.5)	69.6 (0.5)	74.0 (0.6)
Quebec-French	71.4 (0.5)	73.1 (0.6)	69.5 (0.6)	34.4 (3.1)	46.9 (1.6)	53.1 (1.3)	89.1 (0.0)	92.2 (0.0)	96.9 (0.0)	72.5 (0.5)	67.1 (0.6)	71.5 (0.7)	80.2 (0.6)	74.3 (0.6)	68.8 (0.5)	73.5 (0.7)
Saskatchewan-English	70.1 (0.6)	72.0 (0.7)	68.2 (0.6)	32.8 (1.6)	43.8 (0.0)	50.0 (0.0)	87.5 (0.0)	92.2 (0.0)	96.9 (0.0)	70.5 (0.5)	65.1 (0.7)	68.1 (0.7)	79.8 (0.6)	74.0 (0.6)	68.2 (0.5)	70.2 (0.8)
Quebec-English	69.2 (0.5)	71.2 (0.7)	67.0 (0.7)	31.3 (4.7)	42.2 (7.0)	48.4 (2.2)	87.5 (0.0)	90.6 (0.0)	96.9 (3.8)	69.0 (0.5)	65.8 (0.6)	68.9 (0.5)	80.6 (0.6)	72.9 (0.6)	66.4 (0.5)	71.1 (0.7)
Nova Scotia	68.7 (0.4)	70.2 (0.7)	66.9 (0.7)	29.7 (4.1)	39.1 (1.6)	48.4 (1.6)	85.9 (2.2)	92.2 (0.0)	95.3 (0.0)	68.0 (0.5)	64.9 (0.6)	70.5 (0.6)	76.4 (0.9)	71.8 (0.4)	67.7 (0.4)	67.8 (0.8)
Manitoba-English	68.6 (0.6)	70.3 (0.7)	65.5 (0.5)	31.3 (1.1)	42.2 (4.8)	45.3 (2.3)	85.9 (0.0)	90.6 (2.7)	95.3 (1.6)	67.5 (0.6)	64.9 (0.6)	65.8 (0.6)	77.3 (0.7)	72.6 (0.6)	66.8 (0.6)	68.3 (0.7)
Ontario-English	67.0 (0.6)	68.6 (0.8)	64.2 (0.8)	32.8 (2.2)	42.2 (2.7)	46.9 (0.0)	85.9 (0.0)	89.1 (0.0)	95.3 (0.0)	66.4 (0.6)	64.4 (0.8)	67.4 (0.7)	78.1 (0.7)	69.8 (0.6)	64.2 (0.6)	69.4 (0.8)
Manitoba-French	66.6 (0.7)	69.5 (1.1)	64.8 (0.6)	29.6 (0.3)	39.1 (0.0)	46.9 (0.0)	85.9 (0.0)	89.1 (0.0)	93.8 (3.1)	65.2 (0.8)	63.0 (0.7)	67.4 (0.7)	73.3 (0.9)	69.7 (0.8)	64.1 (0.7)	68.2 (1.0)
New Brunswick-English	66.3 (0.4)	67.9 (0.5)	63.7 (0.6)	31.3 (0.0)	39.1 (0.0)	45.3 (0.0)	85.9 (0.0)	90.6 (0.0)	95.3 (0.0)	66.2 (0.4)	62.8 (0.4)	65.8 (0.5)	74.9 (0.4)	69.7 (0.4)	64.6 (0.4)	68.5 (0.5)
Newfoundland	66.1 (0.5)	68.7 (0.7)	63.4 (1.3)	32.8 (3.5)	45.3 (3.8)	45.3 (0.0)	82.8 (3.0)	87.5 (2.7)	95.3 (0.0)	64.8 (0.6)	62.4 (0.5)	68.7 (0.9)	75.1 (0.6)	69.9 (0.6)	64.6 (0.5)	65.7 (0.6)
Saskatchewan-French	64.8 (0.8)	66.2 (1.1)	63.1 (0.5)	29.7 (0.0)	39.1 (0.0)	50.0 (3.8)	82.8 (3.5)	87.5 (0.0)	92.2 (1.6)	63.9 (1.1)	59.8 (1.1)	64.5 (0.4)	74.4 (1.1)	67.8 (1.1)	62.1 (0.8)	67.0 (1.2)
New Brunswick-French	63.6 (0.3)	64.2 (0.6)	58.5 (0.7)	29.0 (2.6)	37.5 (0.0)	43.8 (0.0)	81.3 (0.6)	84.4 (0.0)	93.8 (0.0)	62.0 (0.4)	62.2 (0.4)	64.5 (0.4)	69.0 (0.5)	63.5 (0.5)	63.4 (0.3)	64.1 (0.5)
Ontario-French	60.3 (0.5)	62.2 (0.7)			37.5 (0.0)	40.6 (1.8)			92.2 (0.0)	60.7 (0.6)	56.2 (0.6)	61.2 (0.6)	68.1 (0.8)	62.1 (0.7)	58.8 (0.5)	61.2 (0.7)

[1] Fifteen cantons.
[2] Schools in 14 provinces, where instruction is in Russian.
[3] Schools where instruction is in Hebrew.
[4] Nine provinces.
[5] Schools where instruction is in Spanish, in all regions except Cataluna.
[6] Twenty provinces and independent cities.
[7] Emilia-Romagna province only.
—Data not available.

NOTE.—Standard errors appear in parentheses.

SOURCE: U.S. Department of Education, National Center for Education Statistics, International Assessment of Educational Progress, Learning Science, by Educational Testing Service. (This table was prepared February 1992.)

Table 399.—Reading literacy test scores of 9-year-olds: Selected countries, 1992

Country	Grade tested	Mean age	Overall mean score (s.e.) [1]	Narrative [2] 1st quartile	Narrative [2] mean score (s.e.) [1]	Narrative [2] 3rd quartile	Expository [3] mean score (s.e.) [1]	Documents [4] mean score (s.e.) [1]
1	2	3	4	5	6	7	8	9
Finland	3	9.7	569 (3.4)	508	568 (3.0)	602	569 (3.1)	569 (4.0)
United States	4	10.0	547 (2.8)	476	553 (3.1)	619	538 (2.6)	550 (2.7)
Sweden	3	9.8	539 (2.8)	467	536 (2.6)	592	542 (2.7)	539 (3.2)
France	4	10.1	531 (4.0)	467	532 (4.1)	580	533 (4.1)	527 (3.9)
Italy	4	9.9	529 (4.3)	468	533 (4.0)	576	538 (4.0)	517 (4.9)
New Zealand	5	10.0	528 (3.3)	452	534 (3.5)	594	531 (3.1)	521 (3.3)
Norway	3	9.8	524 (2.6)	455	525 (2.8)	576	528 (2.3)	519 (2.8)
Iceland [5]	3	9.8	518 (0.0)	448	518 (0.0)	571	517 (0.0)	519 (0.0)
Hong Kong	4	10.0	517 (3.9)	431	494 (4.1)	548	503 (3.4)	554 (4.2)
Singapore	3	9.3	515 (1.0)	450	521 (1.1)	567	519 (1.0)	504 (1.0)
Switzerland	3	9.7	511 (2.7)	438	506 (2.6)	566	507 (2.7)	522 (2.8)
Ireland	4	9.3	509 (3.6)	445	518 (3.7)	571	514 (3.2)	495 (3.8)
Belgium [6]	4	9.8	507 (3.2)	439	510 (3.3)	558	505 (2.8)	506 (3.5)
Greece	4	9.3	504 (3.7)	447	514 (3.8)	567	511 (3.6)	488 (3.8)
Spain	4	10.0	504 (2.5)	429	497 (2.4)	543	505 (2.3)	509 (2.7)
Germany (former West)	3	9.4	503 (3.0)	421	491 (2.8)	543	497 (2.9)	520 (3.2)
Canada [7]	3	8.9	500 (3.0)	437	502 (3.5)	566	499 (2.7)	500 (2.8)
Germany (former East)	3	9.5	499 (4.3)	414	482 (4.2)	531	493 (3.6)	522 (5.0)
Hungary	3	9.3	499 (3.1)	437	496 (2.9)	541	493 (3.1)	509 (3.5)
Slovenia	3	9.7	498 (2.6)	435	502 (2.7)	570	489 (2.5)	503 (2.5)
Netherlands	3	9.2	485 (3.6)	425	494 (3.3)	539	480 (3.4)	481 (3.9)
Cyprus	4	9.8	481 (2.3)	421	492 (2.4)	548	475 (2.3)	476 (2.1)
Portugal	4	10.4	478 (3.6)	419	483 (3.3)	531	480 (3.0)	471 (4.5)
Denmark	3	9.8	475 (3.5)	386	463 (3.4)	539	467 (3.5)	496 (3.6)
Trinidad/Tobago	4	9.6	451 (3.4)	383	455 (3.6)	502	458 (3.4)	440 (3.3)
Indonesia	4	10.8	394 (3.0)	351	402 (2.8)	436	411 (3.2)	369 (3.0)
Venezuela	4	10.1	383 (3.4)	322	378 (3.2)	426	396 (3.3)	374 (3.7)

[1] s.e.=standard error.

[2] Narrative prose is continuous text in which the writer's aim is to tell a story.

[3] Expository prose is continuous text designed to describe factual information to the reader.

[4] Documents are structured information presented in the form of charts, tables, maps, graphs, lists, or sets of instructions.

[5] Iceland tested all students, therefore standard errors are not applicable.

[6] Only French-speaking students were tested.

[7] British Columbia only.

SOURCE: International Association for the Evaluation of Educational Achievement, *How in the World Do Students Read?, 1992.* (This table was prepared April 1993.)

Table 400.—Reading literacy test scores of 14-year-olds: Selected countries, 1992

Country	Grade tested	Mean age	Overall mean score (s.e.) [1]	Narrative [2] mean score (s.e.) [1]	Expository [3] 1st quartile	Expository [3] mean score (s.e.) [1]	Expository [3] 3rd quartile	Documents [4] mean score (s.e.) [1]
1	2	3	4	5	6	7	8	9
Finland	8	14.7	560 (2.5)	559 (2.8)	493	541 (2.2)	575	580 (2.5)
France	9	15.4	549 (4.3)	556 (4.2)	484	546 (4.3)	580	544 (4.2)
Sweden	8	14.8	546 (2.5)	556 (2.6)	469	533 (2.4)	576	550 (2.4)
New Zealand	10	15.0	545 (5.6)	547 (5.7)	457	535 (5.7)	597	552 (5.3)
Hungary	8	14.1	536 (3.3)	530 (3.1)	469	536 (3.6)	577	542 (3.2)
Iceland [5]	8	14.8	536 (0.0)	550 (0.0)	472	548 (0.0)	617	509 (0.0)
Switzerland	8	14.9	536 (3.2)	534 (3.4)	466	525 (3.2)	572	549 (3.0)
Hong Kong	9	15.2	535 (3.7)	509 (3.7)	480	540 (3.8)	576	557 (3.8)
United States	9	15.0	535 (4.8)	539 (4.9)	456	539 (5.6)	599	528 (4.0)
Singapore	8	14.4	534 (1.1)	530 (1.1)	476	539 (1.2)	574	533 (1.1)
Slovenia	8	14.7	532 (2.3)	534 (2.6)	471	525 (2.2)	576	537 (2.2)
Germany (former East)	8	14.4	526 (3.5)	512 (3.9)	464	523 (3.5)	566	543 (2.9)
Denmark	8	14.8	525 (2.1)	517 (2.0)	458	524 (2.2)	573	532 (2.1)
Portugal	9	15.6	523 (3.1)	523 (2.5)	469	523 (3.4)	556	523 (3.4)
Canada [6]	8	13.9	522 (3.0)	526 (3.1)	449	516 (3.1)	569	522 (2.7)
Germany (former West)	8	14.6	522 (4.4)	514 (4.9)	453	521 (4.5)	573	532 (3.9)
Norway	8	14.8	516 (2.3)	515 (2.1)	464	520 (2.4)	569	512 (2.4)
Italy	8	14.1	515 (3.4)	520 (3.6)	459	524 (3.2)	565	501 (3.3)
Netherlands	8	14.3	514 (4.9)	506 (4.8)	442	503 (4.7)	546	533 (5.3)
Ireland	9	14.5	511 (5.2)	510 (5.3)	439	505 (5.3)	555	518 (4.9)
Greece	9	14.4	509 (2.9)	526 (2.9)	450	508 (3.1)	548	493 (2.6)
Cyprus	9	14.8	497 (2.2)	516 (2.2)	427	492 (2.4)	536	482 (2.0)
Spain	8	14.2	490 (2.5)	500 (3.0)	435	495 (2.6)	536	475 (2.0)
Belgium [7]	8	14.3	481 (4.9)	484 (5.1)	415	477 (4.8)	522	483 (4.7)
Trinidad/Tobago	9	14.4	479 (1.7)	482 (1.7)	408	485 (1.8)	537	472 (1.7)
Thailand	9	15.2	477 (6.2)	468 (6.6)	429	486 (5.9)	533	478 (6.2)
Philippines	8	14.5	430 (3.9)	421 (3.6)	378	439 (4.1)	472	430 (3.9)
Venezuela	9	15.5	417 (2.9)	407 (2.9)	381	433 (3.3)	482	412 (3.0)
Nigeria [8,9]	9	15.3	401 (—)	402 (—)	351	406 (—)	441	394 (—)
Zimbabwe [9]	9	15.5	372 (3.8)	367 (3.3)	326	374 (3.6)	411	373 (4.6)
Botswana	9	14.7	330 (2.0)	340 (1.6)	294	339 (1.9)	371	312 (2.4)

[1] s.e.=standard error.
[2] Narrative prose is continuous text in which the writer's aim is to tell a story.
[3] Expository prose is continuous text designed to describe factual information to the reader.
[4] Documents are structured information presented in the form of charts, tables, maps, graphs, lists, or sets of instructions.
[5] Iceland tested all students, therefore standard errors are not applicable.
[6] British Columbia only.

[7] Only French-speaking students were tested.
[8] Insufficient data to calculate the design effect.
[9] Sampling response rate of schools was below 80 percent.
—Data not available.

SOURCE: International Association for the Evaluation of Educational Achievement, *How in the World Do Students Read?, 1992.* (This table was prepared April 1993.)

Table 401.—Number of bachelor's degree recipients per 100 persons of the theoretical age of graduation,[1] by sex: Selected countries, 1985 to 1991

Country	Men and women combined				Men				Women			
	1985	1989	1990	1991	1985	1989	1990	1991	1985	1989	1990	1991
1	2	3	4	5	6	7	8	9	10	11	12	13
Australia	—	20.8	—	24.4	—	19.3	—	21.6	—	22.3	—	27.3
Austria	6.7	6.7	7.8	7.8	8.1	7.7	8.7	8.5	5.2	5.6	7.0	7.0
Belgium	12.7	—	—	13.3	16.4	—	—	15.0	8.9	—	—	11.5
Canada	23.0	30.2	31.8	33.3	21.9	26.9	27.6	28.2	24.1	33.5	36.0	38.7
Denmark	10.2	12.9	15.0	16.5	11.5	11.5	13.2	14.4	8.8	14.4	16.8	18.7
Finland	14.6	16.9	17.0	17.1	15.5	17.1	17.0	16.9	13.7	16.6	17.1	17.3
France	11.5	13.9	14.9	16.3	12.4	13.8	14.7	14.9	10.5	14.0	15.1	17.7
Germany (former West)	13.5	13.2	12.9	13.3	16.1	16.1	15.7	15.9	10.6	10.1	10.0	10.6
Ireland	14.0	16.3	17.5	16.0	—	—	16.9	15.8	—	—	18.2	16.2
Italy	7.6	8.6	8.8	9.2	8.2	8.7	9.0	9.1	7.0	8.4	8.7	9.2
Japan	23.6	—	21.8	23.7	34.8	—	30.9	33.5	12.0	—	12.3	13.7
Netherlands	6.5	10.2	8.0	8.3	8.8	12.3	9.4	9.6	4.1	7.9	6.5	6.9
New Zealand	13.5	15.7	15.1	16.1	15.5	16.4	15.7	16.5	11.4	15.0	14.6	15.8
Norway	18.7	24.6	27.6	30.8	14.4	18.1	19.3	22.3	23.3	31.6	36.2	39.7
Portugal	6.4	—	—	—	—	—	—	—	6.5	—	—	—
Spain	14.1	17.8	18.5	19.7	12.9	14.5	15.2	16.1	15.4	21.1	22.0	23.5
Sweden	15.9	13.1	12.2	12.5	13.7	11.1	10.5	11.0	18.2	15.1	14.0	14.2
Switzerland	7.2	7.7	7.8	7.6	9.9	10.1	10.3	9.8	4.6	5.3	5.1	5.4
Turkey	3.6	6.3	6.5	6.5	4.7	7.9	8.2	8.2	2.4	4.7	4.7	4.7
United States	23.2	27.8	28.1	28.1	22.6	26.1	25.9	25.3	23.9	29.6	30.5	31.0

[1] In most countries the theoretical age of graduation was 22 or 23. The range was from 21 to 25. Bachelor's degree recipients may be of any age.
—Data not available.

SOURCE: Organization for Economic Cooperation and Development, unpublished data. (This table was prepared May 1995.)

Table 402.—Percent of undergraduate degrees awarded in science: Selected countries, 1985, 1990, and 1991

Country	All science degrees			Natural sciences			Mathematics and computer science			Engineering		
	1985	1990	1991	1985	1990	1991	1985	1990	1991	1985	1990	1991
1	2	3	4	5	6	7	8	9	10	11	12	13
Australia	—	—	21.6	—	—	15.9	—	—	—	—	—	5.7
Austria	16.8	19.6	20.1	5.0	5.3	5.9	4.1	5.2	4.8	7.7	9.0	9.4
Belgium	14.7	—	32.2	4.6	—	4.3	1.7	—	1.7	8.4	—	26.3
Canada	17.1	16.4	15.5	4.9	6.0	5.7	4.5	4.2	3.7	7.7	6.2	6.1
Denmark	22.5	26.1	27.6	6.3	4.4	6.1	—	—	0.1	16.2	21.7	21.4
Finland	39.3	33.5	34.5	7.7	4.1	4.2	6.3	5.9	6.6	25.3	23.4	23.7
Germany (former West)	23.8	31.3	31.5	5.0	7.2	7.3	2.3	3.5	3.9	16.5	20.5	20.2
Ireland	28.8	34.1	28.5	12.8	14.1	12.4	4.0	6.3	4.4	12.0	13.7	11.6
Italy	19.5	19.7	19.8	8.1	7.6	7.5	3.1	3.9	3.8	8.3	8.3	8.5
Japan	22.7	23.5	23.5	2.4	2.4	2.4	—	—	—	20.3	21.0	21.1
Netherlands	21.8	21.1	21.4	8.5	7.1	6.5	1.2	1.6	1.6	12.1	12.4	13.3
New Zealand	20.5	19.5	16.3	11.7	8.2	7.1	5.5	5.5	4.0	3.3	5.8	5.2
Norway	6.1	12.9	12.3	2.5	2.1	1.8	1.8	0.6	0.6	1.8	10.2	9.9
Portugal	—	24.3	—	6.5	6.7	—	—	7.0	—	—	10.5	—
Spain	13.9	15.0	15.4	5.5	5.7	5.3	1.3	2.6	2.9	7.0	6.7	7.1
Sweden	15.4	24.0	24.3	2.6	4.1	4.2	1.6	4.7	4.9	11.3	15.2	15.2
Switzerland	20.2	23.0	22.7	10.3	11.2	11.0	2.1	3.7	3.8	7.9	8.1	7.9
Turkey	23.0	20.6	21.3	3.6	4.6	4.9	1.6	2.1	2.3	17.8	13.8	14.1
United States	21.7	16.9	15.9	6.3	5.1	5.1	5.5	4.0	3.6	9.8	7.8	7.2

—Data not available.

SOURCE: Organization for Economic Cooperation and Development, unpublished data. (This table was prepared May 1995.)

Table 403.—Percent of graduate degrees awarded in science: Selected countries, 1985, 1990, and 1991

Country	All science degrees			Natural sciences			Mathematics and computer science			Engineering		
	1985	1990	1991	1985	1990	1991	1985	1990	1991	1985	1990	1991
1	2	3	4	5	6	7	8	9	10	11	12	13
Australia	—	—	13.9	—	—	9.6	—	—	—	—	—	4.3
Austria	43.3	37.7	37.4	14.2	12.3	13.4	7.3	4.6	6.1	21.7	20.8	17.9
Canada	19.7	20.0	19.7	7.5	7.8	7.7	2.8	3.4	3.4	9.4	8.8	8.7
Denmark	16.0	22.2	22.9	4.1	5.8	5.4	2.7	4.8	4.5	9.2	11.6	13.0
Finland	47.6	30.6	29.2	24.0	14.7	12.4	6.3	5.4	4.6	17.2	10.5	12.2
Germany (former West)	27.7	33.2	33.9	18.7	23.5	23.3	1.8	2.3	2.2	7.2	7.4	8.4
Ireland	31.4	34.5	28.4	18.9	19.5	15.7	2.6	5.8	4.1	9.9	9.3	8.6
Japan	50.1	54.6	54.2	9.5	9.5	9.5	—	—	—	40.5	45.1	44.7
Netherlands	—	28.9	29.9	20.6	17.7	16.7	—	1.5	1.6	7.5	9.7	11.6
New Zealand	45.1	22.6	19.3	24.6	13.8	11.5	5.4	4.7	3.6	15.1	4.0	4.2
Norway	40.1	33.4	33.8	17.9	8.0	7.9	3.5	2.1	2.5	18.7	23.3	23.4
Spain	35.6	26.9	26.6	28.6	19.7	19.1	1.8	1.4	2.5	5.1	5.7	5.0
Sweden	48.0	48.5	44.4	21.2	19.4	15.1	6.8	9.2	8.2	20.0	19.9	21.1
Switzerland	30.7	30.2	32.6	20.3	22.0	23.1	2.8	1.7	1.8	7.6	6.5	7.6
Turkey	35.8	24.0	21.7	6.6	7.6	6.4	2.8	3.3	2.8	26.3	13.2	12.4
United States	13.5	14.5	13.8	4.5	4.2	3.8	2.8	3.4	3.2	6.3	6.9	6.7

—Data not available.

SOURCE: Organization for Economic Cooperation and Development, unpublished data. (This table was prepared May 1995.)

Table 404.—Public education expenditures per student, by level of student: Selected countries, 1985 to 1992

[In constant 1992 dollars]

Country	Primary				Secondary				Higher education			
	1985	1990	1991	1992	1985	1990	1991	1992	1985	1990	1991	1992
1	2	3	4	5	6	7	8	9	10	11	12	13
Austria	$3,451	$3,526	$3,681	$4,010	$3,943	$4,632	$4,821	$6,420	$6,557	$6,369	$6,635	$5,820
Belgium	2,232	2,131	2,206	2,390	5,279	4,805	5,151	5,150	7,098	6,178	6,423	6,590
Denmark	3,570	4,446	4,529	4,220	5,045	5,301	5,540	4,940	8,570	8,332	7,916	6,710
France	—	—	2,669	2,900	—	—	4,780	5,430	—	—	4,903	6,020
Germany	—	—	—	2,980	—	—	—	4,260	—	—	—	11,850
Japan	—	—	—	3,530	—	—	—	3,900	5,173	5,527	5,755	7,270
Ireland	1,323	1,429	1,588	1,770	2,277	2,403	2,563	2,770	7,857	8,629	8,658	8,720
Norway	3,404	3,878	4,002	4,480	4,817	5,153	5,538	6,200	3,732	—	6,346	—
Portugal	1,330	1,931	2,174	—	1,759	—	2,435	—	1,907	3,156	3,340	3,770
Spain	1,439	1,800	1,917	2,030	1,998	2,706	2,812	3,140	—	8,669	8,819	7,120
Sweden [1]	—	5,271	5,635	4,840	—	6,292	6,835	6,050	—	—	15,124	12,900
Switzerland [1]	—	—	5,611	3,560	—	—	6,761	—	—	—	2,879	—
Turkey	—	—	582	—	—	—	519	—	—	—	9,911	10,370
United Kingdom	2,336	2,897	2,878	3,120	3,864	5,499	4,383	4,390	10,221	12,013	12,157	11,880
United States	4,364	5,223	5,333	5,600	5,282	6,546	6,667	6,470	—	—	—	—

[1] Change in definition in 1992.
—Data not available.

NOTE.—Data adjusted to U.S. dollars using the purchasing power pariety (PPP) index.

SOURCE: Organization for Economic Cooperation and Development, *Education at a Glance*, and unpublished data. (This table was prepared May 1995.)

Table 405.—Public expenditures for education as a percentage of gross domestic product: Selected countries, 1985 to 1992

Country	All levels							Primary education						Secondary education						Higher education						
	1985	1987	1988	1989	1990	1991	1992	1985	1987	1988	1989	1990	1991	1985	1987	1988	1989	1990	1991	1985	1987	1988	1989	1990	1991	1992
1	2	3	4	5	6	7	8	9	10	11	12	13	14	15	16	17	18	19	20	21	22	23	24	25	26	27
Australia	6.0	5.6	5.5	—	—	4.6	4.5	1.8	1.6	1.6	—	—	1.5	2.1	1.9	1.9	—	—	1.5	1.8	1.8	1.8	—	—	1.5	1.8
Austria	5.7	5.7	5.5	5.3	5.2	5.4	—	1.0	1.0	1.0	0.9	0.9	1.0	2.8	2.8	2.7	2.6	2.5	2.6	1.0	1.1	1.1	1.1	1.1	1.1	—
Belgium	6.4	5.9	5.6	5.7	5.2	—	—	1.1	1.0	1.0	0.9	0.9	—	3.0	2.6	2.5	2.5	2.3	—	1.0	1.0	0.9	0.9	0.9	—	—
Denmark	6.2	6.2	6.4	6.4	6.2	6.1	6.2	1.7	1.7	1.7	1.7	1.7	1.7	2.8	2.9	2.9	2.9	2.7	2.7	1.2	1.2	1.3	1.3	1.3	1.3	1.3
Germany (former West)	4.6	4.4	4.3	—	—	4.1	3.7	0.6	0.6	0.6	—	—	0.5	2.2	2.1	2.0	—	—	1.9	1.0	1.0	1.0	—	—	0.9	1.0
Ireland	5.9	6.2	5.6	5.3	5.2	5.4	5.7	1.7	1.8	1.6	1.6	1.5	1.6	2.4	2.5	2.3	2.2	2.1	2.2	0.9	1.1	1.0	1.0	1.0	1.1	1.4
Italy	4.7	4.8	4.9	5.0	5.2	—	—	1.2	1.1	1.1	1.2	1.1	—	2.0	2.2	2.2	2.3	2.2	—	0.6	0.7	0.8	0.7	1.0	—	—
Japan	—	—	—	—	—	—	3.6	—	—	—	—	—	—	—	—	—	—	—	—	—	—	—	—	—	—	0.3
Luxembourg	—	6.0	6.0	5.8	—	5.8	—	—	2.1	2.1	2.0	—	—	—	2.5	2.5	2.4	—	—	—	0.2	0.2	0.2	—	—	—
New Zealand	—	5.3	5.2	6.3	—	5.8	—	—	1.5	1.4	1.7	—	1.5	—	1.3	1.2	1.5	—	1.3	—	1.5	1.6	1.8	—	2.0	—
Norway	5.6	6.2	6.4	6.5	6.4	6.8	—	1.7	1.9	1.9	1.8	1.6	1.7	2.7	2.8	2.9	2.8	2.7	2.8	0.8	0.9	1.0	1.1	1.2	1.3	—
Portugal	—	4.3	—	4.8	4.8	5.5	5.2	2.1	2.1	2.3	2.1	2.1	2.2	1.2	1.3	1.4	1.6	1.6	2.0	0.6	0.7	0.8	0.9	0.9	0.9	0.9
Spain	3.6	3.7	3.9	4.2	4.4	4.5	4.2	1.2	1.1	1.1	1.1	1.0	1.0	1.8	1.9	2.1	2.2	2.3	2.4	0.4	0.5	0.6	0.6	0.7	0.8	0.9
Sweden	—	6.0	5.9	5.5	5.7	6.1	6.7	—	2.2	2.2	2.0	2.0	2.2	0.0	2.7	2.5	2.4	2.5	2.7	—	1.0	1.0	0.9	1.1	1.1	1.0
Switzerland	5.1	5.0	5.1	—	—	5.4	—	2.9	2.8	2.8	—	—	1.4	1.3	1.2	1.3	—	—	2.4	1.0	1.0	1.0	—	—	1.2	—
Turkey	—	—	—	—	—	4.0	—	—	—	—	—	—	1.9	—	—	—	—	—	1.0	—	—	—	—	—	1.0	—
United Kingdom	—	—	—	—	—	—	4.1	1.2	1.3	1.3	1.3	1.3	1.3	2.2	2.3	2.3	2.2	2.3	2.2	1.1	1.0	0.9	0.9	0.9	1.0	0.1
United States	—	—	—	—	—	—	5.7	1.5	1.6	1.7	1.8	1.8	1.8	1.9	1.9	1.9	1.9	2.0	2.0	1.3	1.4	1.4	1.2	1.5	1.5	1.6

—Data not available.

SOURCE: Organization for Economic Cooperation and Development, unpublished data. (This table was prepared May 1995.)

Table 406.—Foreign students enrolled in institutions of higher education in the United States and outlying areas, by continent, region, and selected countries of origin: 1980–81 to 1993–94

Continent, region, and country	1980–81		1985–86		1989–90		1990–91		1991–92		1992–93		1993–94	
	Number	Percent	Number	Percent	Number	Percent	Number	Percent	Number	Percent	Number	Percent	Number	Percent
1	2	3	4	5	6	7	8	9	10	11	12	13	14	15
Total	311,880	100.0	343,780	100.0	386,850	100.0	407,530	100.0	419,590	100.0	438,620	100.0	449,704	100.0
Africa	38,180	12.2	34,190	9.9	24,570	6.4	23,800	5.8	21,900	5.2	20,520	4.7	20,569	4.6
Eastern Africa	6,260	2.0	6,730	2.0	7,330	1.9	7,590	1.9	7,040	1.7	6,950	1.6	7,093	1.6
Central Africa	1,130	0.4	1,540	0.4	1,800	0.5	1,650	0.4	1,690	0.4	1,470	0.3	1,472	0.3
North Africa	7,310	2.3	5,980	1.7	4,740	1.2	4,540	1.1	4,090	1.0	3,730	0.9	3,614	0.8
Southern Africa	1,480	0.5	2,360	0.7	2,750	0.7	2,840	0.7	2,660	0.6	2,560	0.6	2,563	0.6
West Africa	22,000	7.1	17,580	5.1	7,950	2.1	7,180	1.8	6,400	1.5	5,800	1.3	5,804	1.3
Nigeria	17,350	5.6	13,710	4.0	4,480	1.2	3,710	0.9	3,160	0.8	2,490	0.6	2,285	0.5
Europe	25,330	8.1	34,310	10.0	46,040	11.9	49,640	12.2	53,710	12.8	58,010	13.2	62,442	13.9
Eastern Europe	1,670	0.5	1,770	0.5	3,360	0.9	4,780	1.2	6,890	1.6	9,800	2.2	12,929	2.9
Western Europe	23,660	7.6	32,540	9.5	42,680	11.0	44,860	11.0	46,820	11.2	48,210	11.0	49,496	11.0
France	—	—	3,680	1.1	5,340	1.4	5,630	1.4	5,580	1.3	5,660	1.3	5,976	1.3
Germany, Federal Republic of [1]	3,310	1.1	4,730	1.4	6,750	1.7	7,000	1.7	7,570	1.8	7,880	1.8	8,508	1.9
Greece	3,750	1.2	4,440	1.3	4,430	1.1	4,360	1.1	4,490	1.1	4,350	1.0	4,144	0.9
Spain	—	—	1,740	0.5	3,640	0.9	4,300	1.1	4,590	1.1	5,160	1.2	5,246	1.2
United Kingdom	4,440	1.4	5,940	1.7	7,100	1.8	7,300	1.8	7,470	1.8	7,630	1.7	7,828	1.7
Latin America	49,810	16.0	45,480	13.2	48,090	12.4	47,580	11.7	43,200	10.3	43,250	9.9	45,246	10.1
Caribbean	10,650	3.4	11,100	3.2	12,580	3.3	12,610	3.1	11,120	2.7	10,270	2.3	10,672	2.4
Central America	12,970	4.2	12,740	3.7	16,540	4.3	15,950	3.9	12,820	3.1	13,460	3.1	13,886	3.1
Mexico	6,730	2.2	5,460	1.6	6,540	1.7	6,740	1.7	6,650	1.6	7,580	1.7	8,021	1.8
South America	26,190	8.4	21,640	6.3	18,970	4.9	19,020	4.7	19,250	4.6	19,530	4.5	20,708	4.6
Brazil	—	—	2,840	0.8	3,730	1.0	3,900	1.0	4,260	1.0	4,540	1.0	4,977	1.1
Colombia	—	—	4,010	1.2	3,320	0.9	3,180	0.8	2,930	0.7	2,850	0.6	3,077	0.7
Venezuela	11,750	3.8	7,040	2.0	2,740	0.7	2,890	0.7	3,130	0.7	3,440	0.8	3,742	0.8
Middle East	84,710	27.2	52,720	15.3	37,330	9.6	33,420	8.2	31,210	7.4	30,240	6.9	29,509	6.6
Iran	47,550	15.2	14,210	4.1	7,440	1.9	6,260	1.5	4,930	1.2	4,090	0.9	3,621	0.8
Jordan	6,140	2.0	6,590	1.9	5,250	1.4	4,320	1.1	3,700	0.9	3,260	0.7	2,826	0.6
Lebanon	6,770	2.2	7,090	2.1	4,450	1.2	3,900	1.0	3,080	0.7	2,540	0.6	2,165	0.5
Saudi Arabia	10,440	3.3	6,900	2.0	4,110	1.1	3,590	0.9	3,550	0.8	3,750	0.9	3,721	0.8
Turkey	—	—	2,460	0.7	3,400	0.9	4,080	1.0	4,560	1.1	4,980	1.1	5,474	1.2
North America [2]	14,790	4.7	16,030	4.7	18,590	4.8	18,950	4.6	19,780	4.7	21,550	4.9	23,288	5.2
Canada	14,320	4.6	15,410	4.5	17,870	4.6	18,350	4.5	19,190	4.6	20,970	4.8	22,655	5.0
Oceania	4,180	1.3	4,030	1.2	4,010	1.0	4,230	1.0	3,870	0.9	4,300	1.0	3,857	0.9
South and East Asia	94,640	30.3	156,830	45.6	208,110	53.8	229,830	56.4	245,810	58.6	260,670	59.4	264,693	58.9
East Asia	51,650	16.6	80,720	23.5	127,320	32.9	146,020	35.8	158,490	37.8	168,410	38.4	171,279	38.1
China	2,770	0.9	13,980	4.1	33,390	8.6	39,600	9.7	42,940	10.2	45,130	10.3	44,381	9.9
Hong Kong	9,660	3.1	10,710	3.1	11,230	2.9	12,630	3.1	13,190	3.1	14,020	3.2	13,752	3.1
Japan	13,500	4.3	13,360	3.9	29,840	7.7	36,610	9.0	40,700	9.7	42,840	9.8	43,770	9.7
Korea, Republic of	6,150	2.0	18,660	5.4	21,710	5.6	23,360	5.7	25,720	6.1	28,520	6.5	31,076	6.9
Taiwan	19,460	6.2	23,770	6.9	30,960	8.0	33,530	8.2	35,550	8.5	37,430	8.5	37,581	8.4
South Central Asia	14,540	4.7	25,800	7.5	38,840	10.0	42,370	10.4	46,810	11.2	50,430	11.5	48,941	10.9
India	9,250	3.0	16,070	4.7	26,240	6.8	28,860	7.1	32,530	7.8	35,950	8.2	34,796	7.7
Pakistan	2,990	1.0	5,440	1.6	7,070	1.8	7,730	1.9	8,120	1.9	8,020	1.8	7,299	1.6
South East Asia	28,450	9.1	50,310	14.6	41,950	10.8	41,440	10.2	40,510	9.7	41,830	9.5	44,461	9.9
Indonesia	3,250	1.0	8,210	2.4	9,390	2.4	9,520	2.3	10,250	2.4	10,920	2.5	11,744	2.6
Malaysia	6,010	1.9	23,020	6.7	14,110	3.6	13,610	3.3	12,650	3.0	12,660	2.9	13,718	3.1
Philippines	—	—	3,920	1.1	4,540	1.2	4,270	1.0	3,950	0.9	3,700	0.8	3,528	0.8
Singapore	—	—	3,930	1.1	4,440	1.1	4,500	1.1	4,760	1.1	4,860	1.1	4,823	1.1
Thailand	6,550	2.1	6,940	2.0	6,630	1.7	7,090	1.7	7,690	1.8	8,630	2.0	9,537	2.1
Stateless [3]	240	0.1	190	0.1	110	([4])	80	([4])	120	([4])	80	([4])	100	([4])

[1] 1990–91, 1991–92, and 1992–93 data are for Germany, which includes the former Federal Republic of Germany and the former Democratic Republic of Germany.
[2] Excludes Mexico and Central America, which are included with Latin America.
[3] Home country unknown or undeclared.
[4] Less than .05 percent.
—Data not available.

NOTE.—Data are for "nonimmigrants," i.e., students who have not migrated to this country. Because of rounding, details may not add to totals.

SOURCE: Institute of International Education, *Open Doors*, various years; and unpublished data. (Latest edition copyright © 1994 by the Institute of International Education. All rights reserved.) (This table was prepared March 1995.)

CHAPTER 7
Learning Resources and Technology

This chapter contains statistics on libraries and on the use of information technologies. These data show the extent of America's access to information technologies outside of formal classroom activities. The data also provide a capsule description of the magnitude and availability of library resources. Access to information has been widely cited as the key to success in a growing number of endeavors. Thus, how information is made available and to whom become matters of concern.

The first section of the chapter has tables dealing with public libraries, public and private school libraries, and college and university libraries. They contain data on collections, population served, staff, and expenditures. Two tables provide institutional-level information for the largest public libraries and the largest college libraries in the country.

The second half of the chapter provides information on the availability and use of technology. For example, the proportion of children using computers at school may be compared over time. Also included are data on the use of home computers by adults and school children, with comparisons among various demographic groups.

Related data may be found in various sections of this report. For example, statistics on the number of degrees conferred in computer and information sciences and library sciences are in chapter 3. Further information on survey methodologies are in the "Guide to Sources" and in the publications cited in the source notes.

Resources

In 1990–91, 96 percent of all public schools and 87 percent of all private schools had libraries or media centers. About 59,000 librarians and 41,000 library aides provided service in public schools during the 1990–91 school year. There was an average of 931 students per librarian at public elementary schools and 1,052 students per librarian at public secondary schools. At private elementary schools, there was an average of 636 students per librarian (table 407).

In 1992, there were 8,946 public libraries in the United States with 643 million books and serial volumes. The annual attendance per capita was 4.0 and the reference transactions per capita was 1.0 (table 412).

Technology

The use of computers has become widespread in the workplace. In October 1993, 46 percent of all workers used computers on the job. More frequent use of computers was associated with higher levels of education and higher incomes. Only 34 percent of the high school graduates and 10 percent of the high school dropouts used computers compared to 71 percent of those with master's degrees. Among those who did use computers, the master's degree recipients were more likely to use the computers for a wider variety of applications than high school graduates. The most common uses of computers on the job were: bookkeeping/invoicing (45 percent), word processing (44 percent), communications (39 percent), analysis/spreadsheets (36 percent), and data bases (35 percent). Workers in the 30- to 49-year-old age range were more likely to use computers than younger or older workers. Elementary and secondary teachers were less likely to use computers than persons employed in other managerial or professional fields.

The total computer usage rate of students at school increased from 27 percent in 1984, to 43 percent in 1989, to 59 percent in October 1993. The rate at the 1–8 grade level increased from 52 percent in 1989 to 69 percent in 1993. The computer usage rate was 58 percent for students in high school and 55 percent for students in college. Sizeable percentages of students used computers at home, though fewer actually used them for schoolwork. About 25 percent of elementary school children used computers at home and about 11 percent used them for schoolwork. Students at the high school and undergraduate level were about twice as likely as the elementary school children to use home computers for schoolwork. In general, students in higher income families were more likely to use computers at home and use them for schoolwork than were students from lower income families. About 13 percent of the high school students in the $25,000 to $29,999 household income group used computers at home for school work compared to 45 percent in the $75,000 and over income group (table 415).

Expenditures

Total expenditures for college libraries rose by 30 percent between 1987–88 and 1992–93. However, the proportion of college budgets spent on libraries rose only slightly from 2.3 percent in 1986–87 to 2.5 percent in 1987–88, and then fell back to 2.2 percent in 1992–93 (table 329).

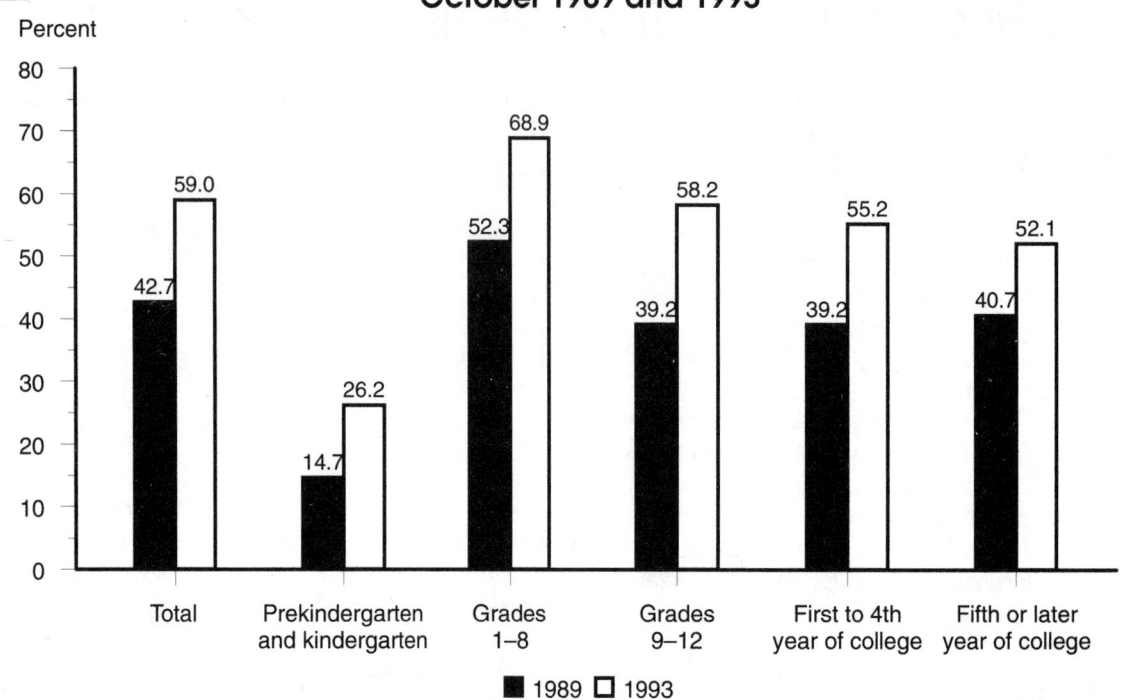

Figure 32.-Student use of computers at school, by level of instruction: October 1989 and 1993

■ 1989 ☐ 1993

SOURCE: U.S. Department of Commerce, Bureau of the Census, Current Population Survey, October 1989 and 1993, and unpublished data.

Table 407.—Selected statistics of public and private school libraries/media centers, by level and size of school: 1990–91

School level and size	Public schools						Private schools				
	Number of library/media centers	Percent of schools with library/media centers	Librarians and other professional media staff		Library/media center aides	Number of library/media centers	Percent of schools with library/media centers	Librarians and other professional media staff		Library/media center aides
			Number	Student/staff ratio				Number	Student/staff ratio	
1	2	3	4	5	6	7	8	9	10	11
All schools	**76,545**	**95.8**	**58,738**	**967**	**41,480**	**21,431**	**86.8**	**9,497**	**492**	**4,341**
Fewer than 300 pupils	22,032	89.5	9,603	600	6,974	16,897	84.1	5,058	459	2,337
300 to 499 pupils	22,733	98.0	16,607	863	10,779	2,876	98.4	2,085	534	993
500 to 699 pupils	16,032	99.1	13,801	1,026	9,266	988	99.8	1,115	526	530
700 to 999 pupils	9,343	99.1	9,265	1,108	7,017	459	98.3	747	505	282
1,000 to 1,999 pupils	5,736	98.9	8,317	1,169	6,554	211	100.0	492	556	199
2,000 or more pupils	669	100.0	1,145	1,886	890	(¹)	(¹)	(¹)	(¹)	(¹)
Elementary	**54,387**	**96.9**	**36,803**	**931**	**26,950**	**13,296**	**86.1**	**4,159**	**636**	**2,653**
Fewer than 300 pupils	15,250	92.1	6,123	613	4,907	11,017	84.0	2,767	593	1,710
300 to 499 pupils	18,657	98.6	12,980	856	8,870	1,765	98.0	917	734	720
500 to 699 pupils	12,848	99.3	10,534	1,051	7,221	411	99.5	327	741	173
700 to 999 pupils	6,039	99.3	5,380	1,177	4,211	103	92.8	148	597	50
1,000 or more pupils	1,593	97.7	1,786	1,117	1,741	—	—	—	—	—
Secondary	**18,705**	**94.8**	**19,441**	**1,052**	**13,019**	**2,301**	**94.1**	**2,355**	**377**	**805**
Fewer than 300 pupils	4,925	86.7	2,621	596	1,468	1,184	89.1	868	203	174
300 to 499 pupils	3,284	95.7	2,987	840	1,640	497	100.0	562	347	150
500 to 699 pupils	2,835	98.3	2,904	938	1,823	286	100.0	369	459	238
700 to 999 pupils	3,055	98.6	3,582	1,007	2,583	191	100.0	266	578	100
1,000 to 1,999 pupils	3,937	99.4	6,202	1,181	4,615	143	100.0	290	664	143
2,000 or more pupils	669	100.0	1,145	1,886	890	(¹)	(¹)	(¹)	(¹)	(¹)
Combined	**3,453**	**85.4**	**2,494**	**877**	**1,511**	**5,834**	**85.8**	**2,983**	**383**	**883**
Fewer than 300 pupils	1,857	78.1	859	505	599	4,696	83.1	1,423	357	453
300 to 499 pupils	792	93.0	640	1,251	269	614	98.2	606	404	123
500 to 699 pupils	349	100.0	363	929	222	291	100.0	419	416	119
700 to 999 pupils	249	97.6	303	961	223	165	100.0	333	406	132
1,000 or more pupils	206	99.5	329	1,339	198	68	100.0	202	401	56

¹Data reported under 1,000 to 1,999 category.
—Data not available.

NOTE.—Data are derived from a sample survey and are subject to sampling error. Because of rounding, details may not add to totals.

SOURCE: U.S. Department of Education, National Center for Education Statistics, "Schools and Staffing Survey." (This table was prepared April 1994.)

Table 408.—Percent of public schools having access to selected telecommunication capabilities, by location of access site and level of school: 1994

Telecommunications capabilities	Percent of schools having access	Percent of schools with telecommunications access, by location [1]				
		Administrative offices	Teacher workrooms	Classrooms	Computer labs	Library/media centers
1	2	3	4	5	6	7
All public schools [2]						
Computer with any telecommunication capabilities via local area network	55.8	67.5	16.6	38.1	59.3	60.1
Computer with any telecommunication capabilities via modem	57.4	54.9	9.2	28.3	37.8	55.8
Broadcast television	69.8	35.9	30.7	83.5	41.3	84.3
Cable television	74.2	30.5	24.3	70.1	38.8	85.5
Closed circuit television	24.9	48.9	31.1	93.7	58.8	89.4
Two-way video with 2–way audio	5.9	26.6	13.8	63.2	21.1	61.1
One-way video with two-way audio or computer link	10.3	28.5	14.4	57.7	36.4	67.5
Public elementary schools						
Computer with any telecommunication capabilities via local area network	52.5	66.5	16.1	36.1	56.9	55.4
Computer with any telecommunication capabilities via modem	51.6	55.3	8.2	24.5	35.8	48.4
Broadcast television	67.5	35.0	30.8	84.4	37.7	82.8
Cable television	72.3	28.0	23.6	67.8	34.6	84.3
Closed circuit television	21.2	48.3	28.3	93.6	53.3	92.1
Two-way video with 2–way audio	4.5	32.1	14.0	56.3	23.0	73.6
One-way video with two-way audio or computer link	8.0	35.4	15.6	57.5	43.1	70.6
Public secondary schools						
Computer with any telecommunication capabilities via local area network	65.6	69.0	17.4	41.9	65.3	71.5
Computer with any telecommunication capabilities via modem	74.0	52.5	11.1	36.1	42.3	72.5
Broadcast television	77.1	38.8	30.4	81.1	51.6	88.7
Cable television	81.1	37.1	25.5	75.8	50.1	88.8
Closed circuit television	35.3	49.4	36.3	93.3	70.1	85.4
Two-way video with 2–way audio	9.9	19.2	15.2	72.2	20.9	46.1
One-way video with two-way audio or computer link	16.1	20.1	12.7	59.3	28.5	63.0

[1] Location estimates are based on those schools having access to each type of tele-communication capability. Percents of schools reporting telecommunication locations do not sum to 100 because many schools have access in more than one location.

[2] Includes data for combined schools not shown separately.

NOTE.—Data are derived from a sample survey and are subject to sampling error.

SOURCE: U.S. Department of Education, National Center for Education Statistics, *Fast Response Survey System,* "Survey on Advanced Telecommunications in U.S. Public Schools, K–12." (This table was prepared August 1995.)

Table 409.—General statistics of college and university libraries: 1974–75 to 1991–92

Item	1974–75[1]	1975–76[1]	1976–77[1]	1978–79[1]	1981–82	1984–85	1987–88	1991–92
1	2	3	4	5	6	7	8	9
Number of libraries	2,972	2,987	3,058	3,122	3,104	3,322	3,438	3,274
Total enrollment, in thousands[2]	10,322	11,291	11,121	11,392	12,372	12,242	12,767	14,359
Full-time-equivalent enrollment, in thousands[2]	7,805	8,480	8,313	8,348	9,015	8,952	9,230	10,361
Collections, thousands of units								
Number of volumes at end of year	447,059	468,033	481,442	519,895	567,826	631,727	718,504	749,429
Number of volumes added during year	23,242	22,977	22,367	21,608	19,507	20,658	21,907	20,982
Number of serial subscriptions[3]	4,434	4,618	4,670	4,775	4,890	6,317	6,416	6,966
Library staff, in full-time equivalents								
Total staff in regular positions[3]	56,836	56,852	57,087	58,416	58,476	58,476	67,251	67,166
FTE enrollment per FTE staff	137.3	149.2	145.6	142.9	154.2	153.1	137.2	154.3
Librarians and professional staff	23,530	23,104	23,308	23,676	23,816	21,822	25,115	26,341
Other paid staff	33,306	33,748	33,779	34,740	34,660	38,026	40,733	40,421
Contributed services	—	—	—	—	—	—	1,403	404
Student assistants	—	—	—	—	—	—	33,821	29,075
Hours of student and other assistance, in thousands	34,687	36,725	39,950	39,552	40,068	28,360	—	—
Library operating expenditures (excluding capital outlay)								
Operating expenditures, total, in thousands	$1,091,784	$1,180,128	$1,259,637	$1,502,158	$1,943,769	$2,404,524	$2,770,075	$3,648,654
Operating expenditures per FTE student	140	139	152	180	216	269	300	352
Operating expenditures per FTE student in constant 1991–92 dollars	373	347	357	363	317	351	358	352
Salaries[4]	592,568	649,374	698,090	824,438	1,081,894	1,156,138	1,451,551	1,889,368
Hourly wages	61,474	66,175	68,683	79,535	100,847	—	—	—
Fringe benefits	—	—	—	—	—	231,209	—	—
Preservation	22,206	22,375	22,521	25,274	30,351	32,939	34,144	43,126
Collections	327,904	357,544	373,699	450,180	561,199	750,282	891,281	1,197,293
Print materials	—	—	—	—	—	—	—	420,930
Serial subscriptions	—	—	—	—	—	—	—	639,128
Microforms	—	—	—	—	—	—	—	43,666
Audiovisual materials	—	—	—	—	—	—	—	23,879
Machine readable materials	—	—	—	—	—	—	—	29,093
Other collection expenditures	—	—	—	—	—	—	—	40,596
Other library operating expenditures	87,632	84,660	96,643	122,731	169,478	233,957	393,099	518,867
Operating expenditures, total, in percents	100.0	100.0	100.0	100.0	100.0	100.0	100.0	100.0
Salaries[4]	54.3	55.0	55.4	54.9	55.7	48.1	52.4	51.8
Hourly wages	5.6	5.6	5.5	5.3	5.2	—	—	—
Fringe benefits	—	—	—	—	—	9.6	—	—
Preservation	2.0	1.9	1.8	1.7	1.6	1.4	1.2	1.2
Collections	30.0	30.3	29.7	30.0	28.9	31.2	32.2	32.8
Other library operating expenditures	8.0	7.2	7.7	8.2	8.7	9.7	14.2	14.2
Library operating expenditures as percent of total institutional expenditures for educational and general purposes	3.9	3.8	3.8	3.7	3.5	3.4	3.2	3.0

[1] Includes data for U.S. territories.
[2] Fall enrollment for the academic year specified.
[3] Data are for end of year.
[4] Includes expenditures for fringe benefits (except for 1984–85 and 1987–88) and salary equivalents of contributed services staff.
—Data not available.

NOTE.—Because of rounding, details may not add to totals.

SOURCE: U.S. Department of Education, National Center for Education Statistics, *Library Statistics of Colleges and Universities,* various years; and Integrated Postsecondary Education Data Survey, "Academic Library Survey." (This table was prepared August 1995.)

Table 410.—Selected statistics on the collections, staff, and operating expenditures of 50 large college and university libraries: 1988

Institution	Rank order, by number of volumes	Number of volumes at end of year, in thousands	Full-time-equivalent staff		Operating expenditures, in thousands	
			Total	Professional	Total	Salaries and wages
1	2	3	4	5	6	7
Harvard University (Mass.)	1	11,497	1,049	325	$37,196	$20,464
Yale University (Conn.)	2	9,144	707	195	32,010	12,584
University of Illinois, Urbana Campus	3	7,377	536	146	16,337	8,662
University of California, Berkeley	4	7,191	740	168	27,524	17,620
University of Michigan, Ann Arbor	5	6,133	677	143	21,621	10,693
University of Texas, Austin	6	5,889	584	136	17,463	9,436
University of California, Los Angeles	7	5,812	711	209	28,447	15,800
Columbia University, Main Division (N.Y.)	8	5,741	641	166	22,196	12,082
University of Chicago (Ill.)	9	4,865	349	74	13,954	6,217
University of Wisconsin, Madison	10	4,804	504	139	18,161	9,754
University of Minnesota, Twin Cities	11	4,651	484	122	17,740	8,824
Indiana University, Bloomington	12	4,530	431	104	11,486	6,618
Ohio State University, Main Campus	13	4,254	454	118	15,784	8,444
Cornell University (N.Y.)	14	4,189	414	120	12,986	6,915
Princeton University (N.J.)	15	4,071	375	105	15,660	8,038
Rutgers University, New Brunswick (N.J.)	16	4,054	384	82	14,948	8,351
University of Washington	17	3,724	447	109	14,350	7,786
Duke University (N.C.)	18	3,669	320	94	12,178	6,012
University of Arizona	19	3,622	328	84	10,943	5,453
University of North Carolina, Chapel Hill	20	3,520	413	117	15,884	7,686
University of Pennsylvania	21	3,500	368	108	13,780	7,400
Michigan State University	22	3,302	331	78	11,517	5,900
Stanford University (Calif.)	23	3,187	407	80	18,213	10,488
University of Southern California	24	3,170	344	64	11,860	7,390
University of Virginia, Main Campus	25	3,003	343	96	14,119	6,703
New York University	26	2,988	361	108	15,550	7,593
University of Iowa	27	2,931	274	86	11,491	5,718
University of Pittsburgh, Main Campus (Penn.)	28	2,713	342	83	10,110	5,310
University of Florida	29	2,702	405	106	12,954	7,278
University of Georgia	30	2,688	322	76	10,428	4,984
University of Rochester (N.Y.)	31	2,598	231	61	8,820	3,678
University of Kansas, Main Campus	32	2,585	260	77	9,061	4,251
Northwestern University (Ill.)	33	2,574	288	79	8,979	5,321
State University of New York, Buffalo, Main Campus .	34	2,493	272	90	10,703	5,500
University of California, Santa Barbara	35	2,476	247	62	10,334	5,882
Southern Methodist University (Texas)	36	2,415	141	49	5,619	2,404
University of Missouri, Columbia	37	2,411	235	56	6,601	3,617
University of Oklahoma, Norman Campus	38	2,396	209	55	5,192	2,267
University of Hawaii, Manoa	39	2,365	247	73	8,587	4,925
Louisiana State U. & A&M & Hebert Laws Center	40	2,343	283	62	7,983	3,949
Johns Hopkins University (Md.)	41	2,330	308	82	12,007	5,756
Arizona State University	42	2,315	366	95	12,510	5,457
University of Delaware	43	2,296	220	57	7,655	3,093
Purdue University, Main Campus (Ind.)	44	2,242	268	59	7,966	4,102
Wayne State University (Mich.)	45	2,234	266	74	10,395	4,457
University of California, Davis	46	2,227	320	68	14,989	7,619
Syracuse University, Main Campus (N.Y.)	47	2,217	271	68	8,106	3,821
University of Colorado, Boulder	48	2,186	222	50	7,805	4,235
Massachusetts Institute of Technology	49	2,181	265	87	9,443	5,097
Washington University (Missouri)	50	2,170	230	66	9,558	3,853

SOURCE: U.S. Department of Education, National Center for Education Statistics, unpublished data. (This table was prepared May 1993.)

Table 411.—General statistics of public libraries, by population of legal service area: 1992

Item	Population of legal service area						
	Total	Under 10,000	10,000 to 49,999	50,000 to 99,999	100,000 to 249,999	250,000 to 499,999	500,000 and over
1	2	3	4	5	6	7	8
Number of public library service outlets	**16,936**	**5,764**	**4,145**	**1,854**	**2,014**	**1,140**	**2,019**
Central libraries	8,835	5,413	2,492	496	296	77	61
Branch libraries	7,035	266	1,290	1,135	1,524	981	1,839
Bookmobiles	1,066	85	363	223	194	82	119
Collections, in thousands							
Books and serial volumes [1]	642,525	89,056	158,315	80,170	89,846	70,799	154,340
Audio and video materials and films	29,951	2,753	6,939	3,748	5,149	2,754	8,608
Serial subscriptions	1,684	255	443	214	233	182	359
Paid staff, in full-time equivalents							
Librarians	35,999	5,331	9,318	4,483	4,822	3,700	8,344
Librarians with ALA-MLS [2]	24,461	964	5,499	3,284	3,786	3,156	7,772
Other staff	73,927	4,693	17,510	10,268	12,049	9,011	20,397
Finances, in thousands							
Total operating income	$4,997,339	$323,285	$1,087,681	$632,970	$735,283	$605,053	$1,613,065
	Percentage distribution						
Source of income							
Total	100.0	100.0	100.0	100.0	100.0	100.0	100.0
Federal	1.0	1.6	0.8	1.0	1.1	1.0	1.1
State	12.0	9.3	10.9	12.6	9.9	11.7	14.0
Local	78.6	72.9	79.1	78.8	81.9	81.5	76.9
Other	8.4	16.2	9.1	7.6	7.0	5.8	8.1

[1] Some data are different from other tables due to a different population base.
[2] ALA-MLS=A master's degree from a graduate library education program accredited by the American Library Association (ALA).

NOTE.—Because of rounding, details may not add to totals. Totals may be underestimated due to nonresponse.

SOURCE: U.S. Department of Education, National Center for Education Statistics, *Public Libraries in the United States: 1992*. (This table was prepared June 1994.)

Table 412.—Public libraries, books and serial volumes, annual attendance, and reference transactions, by state: 1992

State	Number of public libraries	Number of books and serial volumes [1] (in thousands)	Number of books and serial volumes per capita	Library visits per capita [2]	Public library reference transactions per capita [3]	State	Number of public libraries	Number of books and serial volumes [1] (in thousands)	Number of books and serial volumes per capita	Library visits per capita [2]	Public library reference transactions per capita [3]
1	2	3	4	5	6	1	2	3	4	5	6
United States	**8,946**	**642,617**	**2.7**	**4.0**	**1.0**						
Alabama	204	6,835	1.8	—	0.5	Missouri	143	18,107	3.8	4.1	0.6
Alaska	85	1,855	3.2	4.7	0.7	Montana	83	2,480	3.1	3.5	0.6
Arizona	39	7,225	1.9	4.5	1.1	Nebraska	269	4,859	3.8	—	—
Arkansas	36	4,607	2.0	2.4	0.4	Nevada	26	2,325	1.7	3.1	0.8
California	168	58,136	1.9	4.3	1.3	New Hampshire	232	4,695	5.5	6.1	0.9
Colorado	120	8,977	2.7	3.9	1.0	New Jersey	310	28,263	3.7	4.9	0.8
Connecticut	194	12,523	4.1	6.5	1.1	New Mexico	74	4,053	3.7	—	—
Delaware	29	1,209	1.8	3.1	0.5	New York	761	64,446	3.6	4.6	1.2
District of Columbia	1	1,881	3.1	4.0	1.8	North Carolina	74	12,491	1.9	3.1	0.8
Florida	110	20,954	1.7	—	1.4	North Dakota	90	1,919	3.6	4.1	0.6
Georgia	54	13,557	2.0	2.7	0.7	Ohio	250	38,595	3.5	5.1	1.4
Hawaii	1	3,011	2.7	3.1	1.1	Oklahoma	110	5,518	2.2	—	0.8
Idaho	107	2,778	3.5	4.8	0.8	Oregon	125	6,382	2.3	—	—
Illinois	607	33,464	3.3	5.4	1.2	Pennsylvania	446	23,848	2.1	2.9	0.7
Indiana	238	18,732	3.6	5.6	1.0	Rhode Island	51	3,633	3.9	5.4	0.0
Iowa	517	10,562	3.8	5.0	0.7	South Carolina	40	5,833	1.7	2.5	0.7
Kansas	320	8,333	4.1	5.5	1.1	South Dakota	116	2,244	3.9	4.6	0.4
Kentucky	116	7,123	2.0	2.6	0.3	Tennessee	136	7,936	1.6	2.5	0.7
Louisiana	64	9,133	2.1	2.2	0.7	Texas	484	31,141	2.0	2.8	1.0
Maine	226	4,790	4.9	4.9	—	Utah	69	4,578	2.7	—	—
Maryland	24	14,013	3.0	4.4	1.3	Vermont	205	2,359	4.7	—	—
Massachusetts	374	27,203	4.6	—	—	Virginia	90	14,626	2.4	4.4	1.1
Michigan	377	23,359	2.5	3.2	0.8	Washington	70	12,876	2.6	—	—
Minnesota	133	11,820	2.7	4.6	1.3	West Virginia	98	4,362	2.4	3.3	0.8
Mississippi	47	5,000	1.9	2.4	0.4	Wisconsin	380	15,962	3.2	5.7	1.1
						Wyoming	23	2,006	4.3	4.6	0.8

[1] Some data are different from other tables due to a different population base.
[2] Attendance is the total number of persons entering the library including persons attending activities, meetings, and those persons requiring no staff services.
[3] A reference transaction is an information contact which involves the knowledge, use, recommendations, interpretation or instructions in the use of one or more information sources by a member of the library staff.

—Response rate less than 70 percent.

NOTE.—Totals may be underestimated due to nonresponse.

SOURCE: U.S. Department of Education, National Center for Education Statistics, *Public Libraries in the United States: 1992*. (This table was prepared June 1994.)

Table 413.—Percent of workers, 18 years old and over, using computers on the job, by selected characteristics and computer activities: October 1993

Selected characteristics	Percent using computers at work	Number using computers at work, in thousands	Percent of on-the-job computer workers using specific computer applications [1]										
			Analysis/ spreadsheets	Book-keeping, invoicing, and inventory	Commu-nica-tions[2]	CAD[3]	Data bases	Desktop publishing/ graphics	Edu-cation	Program-ming	Sales and telemarketing	Word process-ing	Using 4 or more cat-egories
1	2	3	4	5	6	7	8	9	10	11	12	13	14
Total	**45.8**	**51,106**	**36.1**	**45.0**	**38.7**	**7.6**	**34.5**	**22.3**	**15.7**	**13.1**	**16.2**	**44.4**	**40.7**
Age													
18 to 24	34.4	4,965	25.0	45.3	27.1	6.0	27.1	15.9	10.4	11.2	19.9	34.7	29.8
25 to 29	48.3	8,424	37.2	45.2	38.7	7.7	35.0	22.8	14.3	13.9	17.0	45.7	41.8
30 to 39	50.7	14,969	38.8	45.4	40.4	8.7	36.0	25.0	15.8	14.9	16.4	45.0	42.9
40 to 49	51.3	13,854	38.6	45.1	42.0	7.9	36.8	23.4	18.5	12.9	14.5	47.5	43.4
50 to 59	43.9	6,881	34.5	44.3	38.8	6.4	33.3	20.4	15.8	11.2	15.0	43.9	39.2
60 or older	27.2	2,014	28.0	42.7	31.6	4.5	27.4	15.0	14.0	9.3	16.9	40.0	33.9
Educational attainment and sex													
Not high school graduate	10.0	1,190	19.1	54.4	20.4	3.8	22.2	9.9	9.6	8.8	20.6	16.0	21.8
High school graduate	34.2	13,307	23.7	52.5	29.4	4.4	25.8	13.3	9.5	8.9	17.6	30.8	29.9
Some college	50.4	11,548	33.5	49.5	38.5	7.3	33.9	20.6	13.0	11.3	18.0	40.9	40.0
Associate degree	58.2	5,274	37.5	47.0	39.7	7.9	34.7	21.7	13.8	14.2	14.9	41.6	40.7
Bachelor's degree	68.8	13,162	46.9	40.0	45.1	10.4	41.5	28.8	19.4	16.7	17.0	54.8	49.2
Master's degree	71.2	4,628	47.9	29.3	48.5	10.0	41.9	35.3	31.0	18.1	10.4	63.8	52.1
Doctor's or professional degree	66.9	1,999	42.8	27.9	45.9	7.6	39.2	28.3	21.3	15.2	5.2	66.5	46.2
Male	40.3	24,414	41.1	45.2	39.4	11.1	35.2	25.3	14.8	17.0	18.1	40.7	43.0
Not high school graduate ...	8.5	642	20.2	56.0	20.9	5.6	19.8	10.9	9.1	9.6	16.2	12.2	21.1
High school graduate	24.2	4,942	23.4	52.0	24.6	7.2	19.6	12.9	7.7	9.6	17.7	17.3	25.4
Some college	42.8	5,086	35.8	50.4	37.1	10.4	33.4	22.0	12.8	15.6	20.9	32.1	40.0
Associate degree	52.6	2,358	41.8	46.8	39.3	13.3	36.0	26.2	14.7	19.1	16.8	36.6	41.9
Bachelor's degree	69.8	7,324	52.3	42.6	47.1	13.8	43.4	31.6	16.6	21.0	20.9	53.8	53.2
Master's degree	75.4	2,601	56.0	34.1	51.7	13.0	46.8	37.8	25.2	22.5	13.8	63.3	57.2
Doctor's or professional degree	66.5	1,461	45.0	29.2	46.0	8.6	38.7	29.9	20.9	17.9	5.2	63.7	47.9
Female	52.4	26,692	31.6	44.8	38.1	4.4	33.8	19.6	16.5	9.5	14.5	47.8	38.6
Not high school graduate ...	12.5	547	17.8	52.5	19.9	1.7	25.1	8.7	10.3	7.9	25.8	20.5	22.6
High school graduate	45.2	8,365	23.8	52.8	32.2	2.8	29.4	13.6	10.5	8.6	17.5	38.8	32.5
Some college	58.6	6,461	31.6	48.7	39.7	4.8	34.3	19.4	13.1	8.0	15.7	47.9	40.0
Associate degree	63.7	2,916	34.0	47.1	40.0	3.5	33.6	18.1	13.1	10.2	13.5	45.7	39.6
Bachelor's degree	67.6	5,838	40.2	36.8	42.5	6.1	39.2	25.3	22.9	11.5	12.0	56.1	44.1
Master's degree	66.5	2,027	37.4	23.2	44.3	6.0	35.6	32.1	38.5	12.4	6.0	64.4	45.5
Doctor's or professional degree	68.2	538	36.8	24.1	45.4	4.8	40.8	24.1	22.3	7.7	5.2	74.3	41.5
Race/ethnicity													
White, non-Hispanic	48.7	43,020	37.2	45.8	39.3	7.8	35.2	23.0	15.9	13.4	16.7	45.9	41.8
Black, non-Hispanic	36.2	4,016	27.5	38.3	37.3	5.8	31.2	16.8	15.7	10.9	12.9	35.5	34.1
Hispanic	29.3	2,492	29.1	45.6	32.1	6.5	27.6	18.7	13.3	10.8	16.0	33.6	32.9
Other	43.9	1,578	39.7	39.4	37.2	8.9	33.5	22.6	12.9	15.2	10.2	44.5	39.0
Occupational group													
Managerial and professional specialty	67.7	21,044	46.5	39.3	45.7	10.6	40.3	31.1	22.2	16.7	11.6	56.7	49.7
Executive, administrative, and managerial	72.3	10,645	54.5	54.3	49.0	8.1	44.3	29.6	15.9	14.9	18.4	58.3	55.6
Professional specialty occupations	68.3	7,712	43.2	26.6	45.8	15.4	40.7	33.2	16.1	20.0	5.4	54.2	45.2
Teachers, except college and university	49.1	2,091	18.9	16.4	28.0	5.5	20.1	30.0	69.6	11.2	2.3	52.0	36.2
Teachers, college and university	72.5	597	44.0	15.8	48.9	11.2	33.4	34.9	47.0	23.8	2.2	77.4	51.1
Technical, sales, and administrative support	65.5	22,316	31.2	50.7	36.5	5.1	33.4	17.3	11.9	10.9	22.6	42.0	38.7
Technicians and related support	69.9	2,592	41.5	29.0	38.1	13.1	37.9	21.2	11.0	28.8	4.7	37.4	37.9
Sales occupations	48.8	6,220	34.1	59.9	33.6	4.7	31.5	18.5	11.0	8.2	53.7	34.8	43.5
Administrative support, including clerical	76.7	13,505	27.9	50.6	37.5	3.7	33.3	16.0	12.4	8.7	11.7	46.2	36.6
Service occupations	14.7	2,126	15.2	31.3	31.5	2.7	20.9	7.5	9.1	6.6	11.6	20.5	18.7
Precision production, craft, and repair	23.2	2,976	32.0	45.3	29.2	9.9	26.1	16.4	11.0	14.4	9.6	20.6	28.2
Operators, fabricators, and laborers	14.9	2,382	15.3	51.8	18.3	6.1	17.0	12.5	6.5	7.1	9.6	11.4	16.4
Farming, forestry, and fishing	8.5	262	27.5	65.3	16.4	1.8	27.3	16.2	8.6	7.6	10.4	28.2	31.7
Family income [4]													
Less than $20,000	25.1	5,224	24.4	46.6	28.8	5.1	27.4	15.5	12.1	9.4	18.7	33.1	30.6
$20,000 to $29,999	38.4	7,337	29.3	48.9	35.3	6.1	31.1	19.2	13.8	11.2	17.8	38.6	36.7
$30,000 to $39,999	45.7	8,911	32.3	47.1	35.7	6.9	31.5	20.6	15.1	11.8	15.0	40.7	37.1
$40,000 to $49,999	51.9	7,027	34.2	45.4	37.3	7.3	33.0	20.6	15.6	12.9	13.4	42.2	38.2
$50,000 to $74,999	60.6	12,643	40.4	43.4	42.2	8.9	37.5	24.4	17.8	14.6	15.2	47.6	43.7
$75,000 or more	65.9	8,994	49.3	40.6	47.8	9.5	42.1	29.5	17.0	16.3	17.5	57.9	52.2

[1] Individuals may be counted in more than one computer activity.

[2] Includes bulletin boards and electronic mail.

[3] Computer assisted design.

[4] Excludes persons whose income data were not available.

NOTE.—Data are based on a sample survey of households and are subject to sampling and nonsampling error.

SOURCE: U.S. Department of Commerce, Bureau of the Census, Current Population Survey, October 1993, unpublished data. (This table was prepared March 1994.)

Table 414.—Access to and use of home computers, by selected characteristics of students and other users: October 1993

Selected characteristics	Percent with computers at home	Percent using computers at home	Distribution of frequency of use per week for persons using computers in home				Percent of persons whose home computer has specific components [1]				Percent of computer users using specific applications [2]					
			6 or 7 days	4 or 5 days	2 or 3 days	1 day or less	Hard disk	Printer	Color monitor	Fax or modem	Communications [3]	School assignments	Education programs	Games	Job-related	Word processing
1	2	3	4	5	6	7	8	9	10	11	12	13	14	15	16	17
Total, all persons	**27.1**	**17.6**	**14.7**	**17.1**	**33.3**	**34.9**	**80.7**	**75.8**	**68.2**	**38.5**	**33.5**	**28.3**	**34.6**	**34.9**	**23.8**	**53.2**
Age																
Less than 25	30.8	21.0	11.1	15.5	36.2	37.3	79.5	75.2	69.1	36.2	8.4	48.9	38.1	57.2	3.1	37.7
25 to 29	23.4	16.6	16.8	18.4	33.4	31.3	83.5	68.5	66.3	44.2	48.0	22.6	30.0	21.1	35.2	63.4
30 to 39	30.7	21.0	16.2	17.9	33.2	32.7	82.3	74.0	70.3	42.3	51.2	15.6	34.2	22.2	38.6	61.9
40 to 49	36.4	23.0	16.9	17.9	30.9	34.3	80.9	79.4	69.6	39.0	48.6	15.7	33.5	19.1	39.1	65.1
50 to 59	27.1	15.8	17.7	19.8	27.9	34.7	80.2	79.2	65.0	37.1	50.9	9.5	30.8	19.5	37.2	64.7
60 or older	10.5	4.6	20.7	16.7	28.7	33.9	80.2	77.5	60.0	33.2	51.4	3.3	27.4	19.7	26.5	59.4
Family income																
Less than $20,000	9.2	5.6	19.2	15.7	31.3	33.8	72.4	64.6	57.8	28.6	32.3	34.7	33.0	33.7	16.2	50.2
$20,000 to $29,999	18.5	11.3	16.6	16.6	33.9	32.9	74.6	73.0	62.8	32.1	33.8	28.4	37.8	36.8	21.2	50.2
$30,000 to $39,999	26.5	16.9	14.0	16.8	34.2	35.0	76.8	72.7	66.7	33.7	33.6	27.5	35.3	35.4	22.2	49.2
$40,000 to $49,999	35.2	22.9	13.9	16.6	33.8	35.7	81.6	77.2	71.4	37.5	31.4	26.0	32.8	35.4	21.0	48.9
$50,000 to $74,999	47.3	31.6	13.5	17.6	33.2	35.7	82.5	78.6	70.4	41.7	33.3	28.5	34.2	35.4	25.2	53.8
$75,000 or more	62.8	42.4	14.3	17.9	33.0	34.8	87.6	80.1	72.2	46.1	35.3	26.9	35.0	33.6	29.1	60.2
Total, all students	**36.1**	**26.5**	**12.4**	**16.3**	**36.3**	**35.1**	**80.6**	**76.3**	**69.9**	**37.5**	**11.8**	**55.1**	**39.1**	**55.1**	**5.7**	**41.8**
Preprimary	29.6	15.3	4.7	10.7	39.5	45.0	82.3	72.0	69.6	40.9	0.7	4.1	62.0	86.6	0.0	5.1
1st to 8th grade	31.9	24.3	9.9	14.1	37.9	38.1	79.9	75.2	72.1	36.9	2.6	43.6	48.2	86.4	0.0	28.0
9th to 12th grade	37.2	28.1	11.6	17.7	37.3	33.3	77.7	78.0	69.7	34.6	7.1	73.0	26.6	32.9	2.3	47.6
Undergraduate	44.7	32.4	16.2	19.2	31.8	32.8	81.5	78.1	66.8	36.3	26.5	70.6	26.8	16.3	12.1	62.0
Graduate	60.4	51.8	25.5	21.4	33.2	20.0	89.4	77.9	67.8	50.3	47.8	69.5	39.2	21.9	37.0	80.1
Sex																
Male	36.2	26.9	15.1	17.0	34.1	33.7	81.0	76.1	70.5	38.7	12.7	54.1	39.4	57.8	6.1	40.1
Preprimary	28.5	14.8	6.0	13.1	37.3	43.6	82.7	71.1	71.0	41.3	0.4	5.8	61.3	90.7	0.0	4.4
1st to 8th grade	31.8	24.5	11.6	14.3	36.6	37.5	80.6	75.1	72.1	36.2	2.2	40.5	47.4	88.8	0.0	26.0
9th to 12th grade	36.6	27.6	15.0	19.7	33.4	31.9	77.5	77.8	69.7	36.5	8.5	72.5	27.4	34.3	2.3	45.1
Undergraduate	48.7	36.1	20.2	19.8	30.0	30.0	82.1	78.8	68.2	40.7	29.4	72.1	27.8	18.3	12.5	61.9
Graduate	62.6	55.2	31.0	20.7	30.2	18.1	89.7	75.0	69.2	51.8	53.6	71.6	42.1	25.1	42.4	80.6
Female	36.0	26.2	9.6	15.5	38.5	36.5	80.2	76.5	69.4	36.3	10.8	56.2	38.8	52.3	5.4	43.6
Preprimary	30.9	15.8	3.4	8.2	41.9	46.5	82.0	73.0	68.2	40.6	1.0	2.2	62.7	82.3	0.0	5.8
1st to 8th grade	32.1	24.2	8.0	13.8	39.4	38.7	79.2	75.2	72.1	37.6	3.1	46.9	49.1	83.9	0.0	30.2
9th to 12th grade	37.9	28.6	8.1	15.6	41.4	34.9	77.9	78.2	69.7	32.6	5.7	73.5	25.8	31.5	2.3	50.1
Undergraduate	41.5	29.4	12.3	18.6	33.5	35.6	80.9	77.5	65.6	32.0	23.7	69.0	25.8	14.3	11.8	62.1
Graduate	58.4	48.8	19.9	22.1	36.1	21.8	89.2	80.7	66.4	48.9	41.8	67.5	36.2	18.7	31.6	79.7
Race/ethnicity																
White, non-Hispanic	43.3	32.2	11.9	16.0	35.8	36.3	81.1	77.6	70.1	38.0	11.4	55.2	38.4	55.6	5.7	42.6
Preprimary	35.8	19.0	4.4	11.8	37.4	46.4	83.7	72.7	70.2	41.7	0.7	4.3	62.0	87.1	0.0	5.7
1st to 8th grade	39.6	30.8	9.7	13.8	37.1	39.5	80.5	76.8	72.3	37.5	2.7	43.8	47.2	87.0	0.0	28.9
9th to 12th grade	46.2	35.1	10.9	16.6	38.1	34.4	78.2	79.5	69.8	35.5	7.1	73.5	25.5	31.8	2.1	48.7
Undergraduate	49.4	35.5	15.8	19.3	31.2	33.7	81.9	79.2	67.0	36.4	26.1	71.2	25.5	15.5	13.2	64.0
Graduate	61.4	52.8	25.1	22.1	32.5	20.3	89.3	78.1	67.3	50.1	47.3	70.8	39.3	21.0	36.2	82.1
Black, non-Hispanic	16.1	10.8	13.8	16.8	37.0	32.4	73.8	64.8	68.4	34.5	14.2	53.0	50.8	56.3	7.4	33.9
Preprimary	12.3	4.1	5.9	2.9	53.6	37.7	67.9	59.2	66.9	39.3	0.0	0.0	76.7	85.7	0.0	0.0
1st to 8th grade	13.1	8.9	10.6	16.9	42.8	29.7	73.6	60.7	70.6	33.8	3.2	44.8	64.9	84.5	0.0	22.6
9th to 12th grade	14.6	10.3	12.6	22.0	29.0	36.4	71.4	59.7	61.5	21.2	3.7	67.9	36.1	40.4	5.6	27.2
Undergraduate	27.0	19.1	18.7	13.9	33.0	34.4	76.1	75.2	70.7	41.3	37.2	60.6	40.3	27.5	9.3	56.7
Graduate	56.7	47.6	21.7	18.8	32.2	27.3	82.3	75.3	69.5	48.6	37.4	60.3	35.8	24.9	47.9	60.2
Hispanic	15.2	10.3	13.9	21.1	39.6	25.5	74.7	73.0	63.0	32.7	17.2	54.9	34.7	51.2	5.2	35.3
Preprimary	11.7	5.6	7.9	6.8	36.7	48.6	70.5	75.5	53.8	29.7	0.0	0.0	39.6	71.1	0.0	0.0
1st to 8th grade	12.1	7.4	11.2	16.1	42.8	29.9	72.3	70.4	65.3	31.2	0.8	38.9	40.4	84.7	0.0	17.6
9th to 12th grade	14.4	9.6	13.7	33.2	29.6	23.5	71.5	76.9	67.4	31.2	15.8	68.7	27.7	41.3	2.4	47.1
Undergraduate	27.3	21.9	15.0	22.4	42.1	20.5	78.2	70.5	55.5	31.4	30.8	73.1	30.3	12.7	5.8	47.5
Graduate	56.3	52.2	28.5	16.5	44.4	10.6	95.1	84.9	77.9	58.8	69.8	71.8	39.6	37.7	43.5	75.4
Family income																
Less than $20,000	15.2	10.9	18.5	16.0	34.1	31.3	74.9	65.9	57.9	29.2	20.4	62.0	35.3	44.0	8.4	47.6
$20,000 to $29,999	25.5	18.6	13.4	16.8	38.6	31.2	72.7	71.8	63.7	31.1	13.0	53.3	41.2	51.5	7.0	38.6
$30,000 to $39,999	34.3	25.1	11.9	15.4	38.2	34.6	76.3	73.2	67.5	32.8	11.5	55.3	41.0	54.1	6.9	36.9
$40,000 to $49,999	42.6	31.5	10.9	16.7	37.0	35.3	80.4	78.8	74.0	36.0	8.9	53.2	38.1	61.3	4.8	35.7
$50,000 to $74,999	55.9	42.0	10.5	17.3	34.1	38.1	82.8	79.9	73.4	41.8	10.1	54.1	38.1	56.9	4.4	41.9
$75,000 or more	73.7	54.1	12.1	15.2	37.2	35.5	87.8	80.5	74.6	43.6	10.4	54.5	40.8	57.9	4.9	46.7

[1] Data are for the most recently purchased computer for families with more than one computer. Percent based on persons who have a computer in their home.

[2] Individuals may be counted in more than one computer activity.

[3] Includes bulletin boards and electronic mail.

NOTE.—Data are based on a sample survey of households and are subject to sampling and nonsampling error.

SOURCE: U.S. Department of Commerce, Bureau of the Census, Current Population Survey, October 1993, unpublished data. (This table was prepared May 1994.)

Table 415.—Student use of computers, by level of instruction and selected characteristics: October 1984, 1989, and 1993

Student and school characteristics	October 1984 Total	October 1989						October 1993					
		Total	Prekindergarten and kindergarten	Grades 1 to 8	Grades 9 to 12	1st to 4th year of college	5th or later year of college	Total	Prekindergarten and kindergarten	Grades 1 to 8	Grades 9 to 12	1st to 4th year of college	5th or later year of college
1	2	3	4	5	6	7	8	9	10	11	12	13	14
Percent of students using computers at school													
Total	27.3	42.7	14.7	52.3	39.2	39.2	40.7	59.0	26.2	68.9	58.2	55.2	52.1
Sex													
Male	29.0	43.5	13.9	52.9	38.7	42.1	47.0	59.4	25.9	69.5	56.5	57.5	56.7
Female	25.5	41.9	15.6	51.7	39.8	36.8	34.9	58.7	26.5	68.4	60.0	53.3	47.8
Race/ethnicity													
White, non-Hispanic	30.0	45.7	17.0	58.4	40.6	40.0	39.6	61.6	29.4	73.7	59.9	54.9	49.8
Black, non-Hispanic	16.8	32.6	7.4	35.7	36.0	35.1	35.2	51.5	16.5	56.5	54.5	56.9	57.9
Hispanic	18.6	34.9	10.1	40.2	33.6	32.4	37.8	52.3	19.2	58.4	54.1	51.9	53.7
Other	28.6	42.7	8.5	47.0	41.4	43.9	58.0	59.0	23.5	65.7	57.3	60.9	69.4
Household income													
Less than $5,000	18.7	36.7	8.5	40.4	35.6	40.1	53.5	51.2	19.6	55.0	50.6	61.7	66.7
$5,000 to 9,999	21.0	36.1	9.2	40.3	32.7	40.5	60.2	53.3	24.4	60.3	51.9	53.9	56.2
$10,000 to 14,999	22.4	38.4	14.6	44.4	39.1	30.8	55.2	56.4	20.1	64.7	56.7	50.7	76.1
$15,000 to 19,999	25.9	41.5	11.9	50.9	34.8	39.6	44.0	58.1	23.8	67.5	57.4	51.2	58.5
$20,000 to 24,999	26.7	42.4	14.6	51.8	40.1	32.5	44.4	56.4	23.7	64.3	53.0	57.4	52.4
$25,000 to 29,999	30.5	46.1	16.1	56.4	43.8	40.4	42.1	60.0	28.0	70.1	60.3	51.5	58.0
$30,000 to 34,999	30.5	44.2	17.4	56.8	37.8	37.1	33.3	59.1	23.7	69.6	59.7	51.7	45.3
$35,000 to 39,999	32.3	45.2	16.1	58.3	41.5	34.5	45.3	60.7	27.1	72.1	61.7	49.2	47.9
$40,000 to 49,999	32.8	44.7	15.4	59.7	36.7	38.1	35.4	59.3	28.5	70.3	57.2	53.9	48.6
$50,000 to 74,999	35.5	47.0	16.2	61.2	44.6	43.4	31.8	62.6	28.6	75.6	61.5	57.4	44.2
$75,000 or more	36.0	51.2	21.2	67.0	45.8	49.6	31.0	64.6	33.5	78.7	62.5	60.9	47.7
Control of school													
Public	27.4	43.3	16.4	51.9	39.0	37.5	41.3	60.2	30.1	68.6	58.1	53.9	54.1
Private	26.5	38.9	11.8	56.6	42.6	46.3	39.7	52.1	18.7	72.5	60.7	60.7	48.0
Percent of students using computers at home													
Total	11.5	18.8	10.2	17.8	20.7	21.3	33.4	27.0	15.6	24.7	28.7	32.8	52.6
Sex													
Male	14.0	20.7	11.0	18.7	23.9	25.4	36.0	27.4	15.1	24.8	28.2	36.6	56.1
Female	9.0	17.0	9.3	16.9	17.4	18.0	31.1	26.6	16.1	24.6	29.2	29.7	49.5
Race/ethnicity													
White, non-Hispanic	13.7	22.7	12.2	22.3	25.3	23.6	35.6	32.8	19.4	31.4	35.9	36.0	53.6
Black, non-Hispanic	4.9	7.3	3.7	6.8	8.5	9.1	18.6	10.9	4.2	9.0	10.4	19.4	48.1
Hispanic	3.6	7.5	3.4	6.6	8.2	11.5	27.1	10.4	5.7	7.5	9.8	22.0	52.2
Other	9.0	18.8	9.9	16.6	21.6	23.7	24.7	28.7	17.0	23.2	37.0	33.0	47.1
Household income													
Less than $5,000	2.9	8.4	4.5	4.1	6.6	17.7	29.4	9.7	1.1	4.1	6.8	25.6	45.2
$5,000 to 9,999	3.2	5.4	1.0	2.7	4.4	14.2	28.4	8.0	0.9	4.5	5.3	21.3	45.6
$10,000 to 14,999	5.0	7.2	1.9	6.2	6.5	11.8	26.5	11.4	4.6	6.4	8.7	29.8	50.0
$15,000 to 19,999	7.5	11.3	3.2	9.2	13.6	15.8	33.6	15.1	6.9	10.9	14.1	28.9	43.0
$20,000 to 24,999	9.9	12.9	6.8	11.6	13.6	16.9	32.2	16.8	7.4	13.1	17.9	27.7	49.6
$25,000 to 29,999	12.8	17.0	11.9	16.5	17.1	19.2	29.6	21.1	12.3	19.3	22.0	26.1	47.0
$30,000 to 34,999	15.8	17.7	8.0	17.6	20.2	19.4	30.7	24.1	18.7	20.5	29.1	26.4	44.4
$35,000 to 39,999	19.4	21.4	8.7	22.2	25.1	22.1	26.5	27.1	13.0	26.3	28.1	32.7	52.7
$40,000 to 49,999	20.4	25.7	14.8	27.5	27.7	21.7	40.7	32.2	21.6	32.9	33.9	32.5	45.9
$50,000 to 74,999	24.2	31.6	20.6	33.8	34.3	27.6	41.1	43.0	25.5	45.3	46.4	40.1	58.2
$75,000 or more	22.1	43.8	25.2	50.9	53.4	33.9	41.4	56.1	38.2	62.3	61.0	47.0	64.7
Control of school													
Public	11.2	17.9	8.3	16.8	19.7	20.7	32.2	25.3	12.1	23.0	27.2	31.9	50.0
Private	13.8	24.4	13.4	27.7	35.9	23.8	35.9	37.4	22.4	41.5	47.2	36.9	57.7
Percent of students using computers at home for school work													
Total	4.6	8.9	0.6	6.3	12.2	13.7	23.9	14.9	0.6	10.8	20.9	23.1	36.6
Sex													
Male	5.9	9.5	0.6	6.3	13.6	16.0	25.9	14.8	0.9	10.1	20.5	26.3	40.3
Female	3.3	8.3	0.6	6.2	10.8	11.7	22.0	15.0	0.4	11.5	21.4	20.5	33.2
Race													
White, non-Hispanic	5.4	10.7	0.6	7.7	15.2	15.1	25.5	18.2	0.8	13.8	26.5	25.7	37.8
Black, non-Hispanic	2.3	3.4	0.9	2.7	4.0	6.2	12.6	5.7	—	4.0	6.9	11.5	30.1
Hispanic	1.4	3.6	—	2.8	4.4	6.4	24.8	5.6	—	2.9	6.7	15.9	36.8
Other	3.8	9.1	—	5.8	13.4	15.5	14.8	16.0	1.1	9.3	27.0	23.7	29.2
Household income													
Less than $5,000	1.0	5.0	—	1.5	4.1	12.6	23.8	6.7	—	2.5	4.0	18.7	36.0
$5,000 to 9,999	1.5	3.2	—	0.6	2.6	10.3	26.5	4.8	—	1.1	3.6	16.1	35.5
$10,000 to 14,999	1.9	3.5	0.7	1.8	3.6	8.1	19.3	7.3	—	2.6	5.6	25.9	34.6
$15,000 to 19,999	3.0	4.5	—	2.1	5.2	9.3	30.2	8.6	0.4	4.7	10.8	18.7	31.0
$20,000 to 24,999	3.1	5.7	0.3	3.8	7.6	10.5	23.8	9.8	0.7	5.1	12.6	22.9	35.0
$25,000 to 29,999	5.1	6.4	0.3	4.1	8.2	12.3	19.7	10.4	1.1	6.3	13.4	19.5	34.9
$30,000 to 34,999	4.9	8.0	0.1	5.7	12.0	12.8	19.8	13.0	0.8	8.1	21.9	18.0	35.1
$35,000 to 39,999	7.1	10.5	1.2	7.9	15.0	15.9	18.7	15.4	0.8	12.4	21.0	22.6	37.2
$40,000 to 49,999	9.2	11.9	0.7	9.7	17.1	14.3	29.4	17.1	1.1	14.7	24.2	22.2	32.1
$50,000 to 74,999	11.5	15.2	0.8	12.7	21.2	17.5	28.5	23.2	1.0	19.7	35.0	27.0	38.2
$75,000 or more	9.8	22.0	2.4	21.9	34.2	21.2	22.2	30.4	0.8	29.4	45.2	30.6	41.5
Control of school													
Public	4.5	8.5	0.6	5.9	11.5	13.1	22.2	14.2	0.5	10.1	19.8	22.7	34.7
Private	5.4	11.4	0.5	9.4	23.6	15.8	27.1	18.8	1.0	17.8	35.4	24.8	40.1

—Data not available.

NOTE.—Data are based on a sample survey of households and are subject to sampling and nonsampling error.

SOURCE: U.S. Department of Commerce, Bureau of the Census, Current Population Survey, October 1984, 1989, and 1993, unpublished data. (This table was prepared April 1994.)

Guide to Tabular Presentation

This section is intended to assist the reader in following the basic structure of the *Digest* tables and to provide a legend for some of the common symbols and indexes used throughout the book. Unless otherwise noted, all data are for the 50 states and the District of Columbia.

Table Components

Title Describes the table content concisely.

Unit Indicator Informs the reader of the measurement united in the table—"In thousands," "In millions of dollars," etc. Noted below the title unless several units are used, in which case the unit indicators are generally given in the spanner or individual column heads.

Spanner Describes a group of two or more columns.

Column head Describes specific column.

Stub Describes a row or a group of rows. Each stub is followed by a number of dots (leaders) or by a semicolon if no data appears in the data fields.

Field The area of the table which contains the data elements.

Rules in the field

Single horizontal rules indicate
— that the data below the line add to the figure immediately above the line, or
— in the case of derived figures (e.g., percents, medians) that the datum above the line represents a cumulative figure.

Double horizontal rules demarcate groups of related rows.

Single vertical rules delineate columns.

Double vertical rules divide the table into sections with unique stubs.

Example of Table Structure

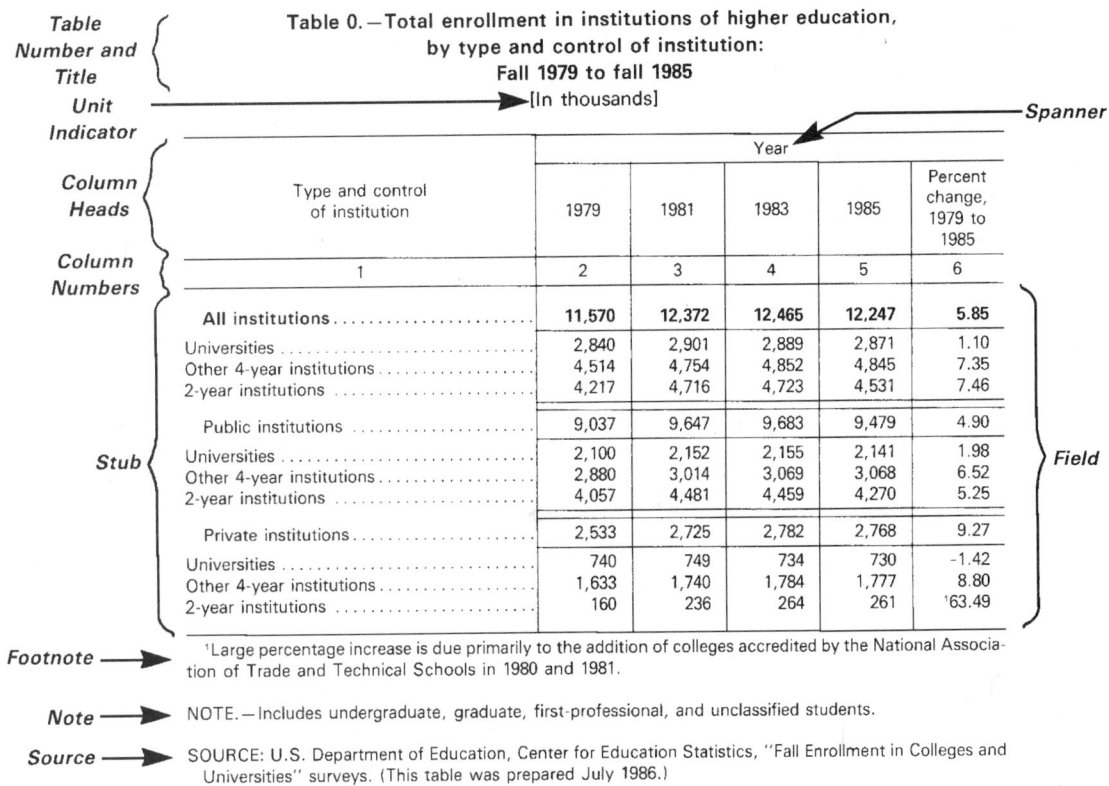

Table 0.—Total enrollment in institutions of higher education, by type and control of institution: Fall 1979 to fall 1985

[In thousands]

Type and control of institution	Year				Percent change, 1979 to 1985
	1979	1981	1983	1985	
1	2	3	4	5	6
All institutions	11,570	12,372	12,465	12,247	5.85
Universities	2,840	2,901	2,889	2,871	1.10
Other 4-year institutions	4,514	4,754	4,852	4,845	7.35
2-year institutions	4,217	4,716	4,723	4,531	7.46
Public institutions	9,037	9,647	9,683	9,479	4.90
Universities	2,100	2,152	2,155	2,141	1.98
Other 4-year institutions	2,880	3,014	3,069	3,068	6.52
2-year institutions	4,057	4,481	4,459	4,270	5.25
Private institutions	2,533	2,725	2,782	2,768	9.27
Universities	740	749	734	730	-1.42
Other 4-year institutions	1,633	1,740	1,784	1,777	8.80
2-year institutions	160	236	264	261	[1]63.49

[1]Large percentage increase is due primarily to the addition of colleges accredited by the National Association of Trade and Technical Schools in 1980 and 1981.

NOTE.—Includes undergraduate, graduate, first-professional, and unclassified students.

SOURCE: U.S. Department of Education, Center for Education Statistics, "Fall Enrollment in Colleges and Universities" surveys. (This table was prepared July 1986.)

Footnote   Describes a unique circumstance relating to a specific item within the table. Usually listed below the bottom rule of the table.

Note   Furnishes general information that relates to the entire table.

Source   The document or reference from which the data are drawn. This note may also include the organizational unit responsible for preparing the data.

Descriptive Terms

Average   A number that is used to represent the "typical value" of a group of numbers. It is regarded as a measure of "location" or "central tendency" of a group of numbers.

Arithmetic mean   is the most commonly used average. It is derived by summing the individual item values of a particular group and dividing that sum by the number of items. This value is often referred to simply as the "mean" or "average."

Median   is the measure of central tendency that occupies the middle position in a rank order of values. It generally has the same number of items above it as below it. If there is an even number of items in the group, the median is the average of the middle two items.

Per capita,   or per person, figure represents an average computed for every person in a specified group, or population. It is derived by dividing the total for an item (such as income or expenditures) by the number of persons in the specified population.

Index number   A value that provides a means of measuring, summarizing, and communicating the nature of changes that occur from time to time or from place to place. An index is used to express changes in prices over periods of time but may also be used to express differences between related subjects at a single point in time.

The *Digest* most often uses the Consumer Price Index to compare purchasing power over time.

To compute a price index, a base year or period is selected. The base year price is then designated as the base or reference price to which the prices for other years or periods are related.

A method of expressing the price relationship is:

$$\text{Index number} = \frac{\text{Price of a set of one or more items for related year}}{\text{Price of the same set of items for base year}} \times 100$$

When 100 is subtracted from the index number, the result equals the percent change in price from the base year.

Current and constant dollars   are used in a number of tables to express finance data. Unless otherwise noted, all figures are in current dollars, not adjusted for inflation. Constant dollars provide a measure of the impact of inflation on the current dollars.

Current dollar   figures reflect actual prices or costs prevailing during the specified year(s).

Constant dollar   figures attempt to remove the effects of price changes (inflation) from statistical series reported in dollar terms.

The constant dollar value for an item is derived by dividing the base year price index (for example, the Consumer Price Index for 1986) by the price index for the year of data to be adjusted and multiplying by the item to be adjusted. The result is an adjusted dollar value as it would presumably exist if prices were the same as the base year—in other words, as if the dollar had constant purchasing power. Any changes in the constant dollar amounts would reflect only changes in the real values.

NOTE: Tables may not include data for all years implied in table titles.

Guide to Sources
Sources and Comparability of Data

The information presented in this report was obtained from many sources, including federal and state agencies, private research organizations, and professional associations. The data were collected using many research methods, including surveys of a universe (such as all colleges) or of a sample, compilations of administrative records, and statistical projections. *Digest* users should take particular care when comparing data from different sources. Differences in procedures, timing, phrasing of questions, interviewer training, and so forth mean that the results from the different sources may not be strictly comparable. Following the general discussion of data accuracy below, descriptions of the information sources and data collection methods are presented, grouped by sponsoring organization. More extensive documentation of a particular survey's procedures does not imply more problems with the data, only that more information is available.

Accuracy of Data

The accuracy of any statistic is determined by the joint effects of "sampling" and "nonsampling" errors. Estimates based on a sample will differ somewhat from the figures that would have been obtained if a complete census had been taken using the same survey instruments, instructions, and procedures. In addition to such sampling errors, all surveys, both universe and sample, are subject to design, reporting, and processing errors and errors due to nonresponse. To the extent possible, these nonsampling errors are kept to a minimum by methods built into the survey procedures. In general, however, the effects of nonsampling errors are more difficult to gauge than those produced by sampling variability.

Sampling Errors

2The samples used in surveys are selected from a large number of possible samples of the same size that could have been selected using the same sample design. Estimates derived from the different samples would differ from each other. The difference between a sample estimate and the average of all possible samples is called the sampling deviation. The standard or sampling error of a survey estimate is a measure of the variation among the estimates from all possible samples and, thus, is a measure of the precision with which an estimate from a particular sample approximates the average result of all possible samples.

The sample estimate and an estimate of its standard error permit us to construct interval estimates with prescribed confidence that the interval includes the average result of all possible samples. If all possible samples were selected under essentially the same conditions and an estimate and its estimated standard error were calculated from each sample, then: (1) approximately 2/3 of the intervals from one standard error below the estimate to one standard error above the estimate would include the average value of all possible samples; and (2) approximately 19/20 of the intervals from two standard errors below the estimate to two standard errors above the estimate would include the average value of all possible samples. We call an interval from two standard errors below the estimate to two standard errors above the estimate a 95 percent confidence interval.

To illustrate this concept, consider the table of standard errors and 95 percent confidence intervals for estimates from the 1989–90 Beginning Postsecondary Students Survey (table A1). For the estimate that 28.1 percent of all female students in a vocational certificate program completed the program in 9 months or less, the table shows that the standard error is 3 percent. Therefore, we can create a 95 percent confidence interval which is approximately 22.1 to 34.1 (28.1 percent ±2 times 3 percent).

Analysis of standard errors can help assess how valid a comparison between two estimates might be. **The standard error of a difference** between two independent sample estimates is equal to the square root of the sum of the squared standard errors of the estimates. The standard error (se) of the difference between independent sample estimates "a" and "b" is:

$$se_{a,b} = (se_a^2 + se_b^2)^{1/2}$$

It should be noted that most of the standard error estimates presented in subsequent sections and in the original documents are approximations. That is, to derive estimates of standard errors that would be applicable to a wide variety of items and could be prepared at a moderate cost, a number of approximations were required. As a result, the standard error estimates provide a general order of magnitude rather than the exact standard error for any specific item. The preceding discussion on sampling variability was directed toward a situation concerning one or two estimates. Determining the accuracy of statistical projections is more difficult. In general, the further away the projection date is from the date of the actual data being used for the projection, the greater the probable error in the projections. If, for instance, annual data from 1970 to 1992 are being used to project enrollment in institutions of higher education, the further beyond 1992 one projects, the more variability in the projection. One will be less sure of the 2000 enrollment projection than of the 1995 projection. A detailed discussion of the projections methodology is contained in *Projections of Education Statistics to 2004* (National Center for Education Statistics, 1993).

Nonsampling Errors

Universe and sample surveys are subject to nonsampling errors. Nonsampling errors may arise when respondents or interviewers interpret questions differently, when respondents must estimate values, or when coders, keyers, and other processors handle answers differently, when persons who should be included in the universe are not, or when persons fail to respond (completely or partially). Nonsampling errors usually, but not always, result in an understatement of total survey error and thus an overstatement of the precision of survey estimates. Since estimating the magnitude of nonsampling errors often would require special experiments or access to independent data, these nonsampling errors are seldom available.

To compensate for nonresponse, adjustments of the sample estimates are often made. An adjustment made for either type of nonresponse, total or partial, is often referred to as an imputation, which is often a substitution of the "average" questionnaire response for the nonresponse. Imputations are usually made separately within various groups of sample members which have similar survey characteristics. Imputation for item nonresponse is usually made by substituting for a missing item the response to that item of a respondent having characteristics that are similar to those of the nonrespondent.

Although the magnitude of nonsampling error in the data compiled in this *Digest* is frequently unknown, idiosyncrasies that have been identified are noted on the appropriate tables.

Department of Education

National Center for Education Statistics (NCES)

Beginning Postsecondary Student Longitudinal Study

The Beginning Postsecondary Student Longitudinal Study (BPS) provides information concerning persistence, progress, and attainment from initial time of entry into postsecondary education through leaving and entering the workforce. BPS includes traditional and nontraditional (e.g., older) students and is representative of all beginning students in postsecondary education. BPS follows first-time, beginning students for at least 6 years at 2-year intervals, collecting student data, postsecondary transcripts, and financial aid reports. By starting with a cohort that has already entered postsecondary education, and following it for 6 years, BPS will be able to determine to what extent, if any, students who start postsecondary education later differ in their progress, persistence, and attainment.

Further information on the Beginning Postsecondary Student Longitudinal Survey may be obtained from:

Paula R. Knepper
Postsecondary Education Statistics Division
National Center for Education Statistics
555 New Jersey Avenue NW
Washington, DC 20208–5652

Common Core of Data

NCES uses the Common Core of Data (CCD) survey to acquire and maintain statistical data from each of the 50 states, the District of Columbia, and the outlying areas. Information about staff and students is collected annually at the school, LEA (local education agency or school district), and state levels. Information about revenues and expenditures is also collected at the state level.

Data are collected for a particular school year (July 1 through June 30) via survey instruments sent to the states by October 15 of the subsequent school year. States have 2 years in which to modify the data originally submitted.

Since the CCD is a universe survey, the CCD information presented in this edition of the *Digest* is not subject to sampling errors. However, nonsampling errors could come from two sources—nonreturn and inaccurate reporting. Almost all of the states submit the six CCD survey instruments each year, but submissions are sometimes incomplete or too late for publication.

Understandably, when 57 education agencies compile and submit data for approximately 85,000 public schools and 15,000 local school districts, misreporting can occur. Typically, this results from varying interpretation of NCES definitions and differing recordkeeping systems. NCES attempts to minimize these errors by working closely with the Council of Chief State School Officers (CCSSO) and its Committee on Evaluation and Information Systems (CEIS).

The state education agencies report data to NCES from data collected and edited in their regular reporting cycles. NCES encourages the agencies to incorporate into their own survey systems the NCES items they do not already collect so that those items will also be available for the subsequent CCD survey. Over time, this has meant fewer missing data cells in each state's response, reducing the need to impute data.

NCES subjects data from the education agencies to a comprehensive edit. Where data are determined to be inconsistent, missing, or out of range, NCES contacts the education agencies for verification. NCES-prepared state summary forms are returned to the state education agencies for verification. States are also given an opportunity to revise their state-level aggregates from the previous survey cycle.

Questions concerning the Common Core of Data can be directed to:

John Sietsema
Elementary and Secondary Education Statistics
  Division
National Center for Education Statistics
555 New Jersey Avenue NW
Washington, DC 20208–5651

Federal Support for Education

NCES prepares an annual compilation of federal funds for education. Data for U.S. Department of Education programs come from the *Budget of the U.S. Government*. Budget offices of other federal agencies provide information for all other federal program support except for research funds, which are obligations reported by the National Science Foundation in *Federal Funds for Research and Development*. Some data are estimated, based on reports from the federal agencies contacted and the *Budget of the U.S. Government*.

Except for money spent on research, outlays were used to report program funds to the extent possible. Some tables are obligations as noted in the title of the table. Some federal program funds not commonly recognized as education assistance are also included in the totals reported. For example, portions of federal funds paid to some states and counties as shared revenues resulting from the sale of timber and minerals from public lands have been estimated as funds used for education purposes. Parts of the

funds received by states (in 1980) and localities (throughout the period) under the General Revenue Sharing Program are also included, as are portions of federal funds received by the District of Columbia. The share of these funds allocated to education was assumed equal to the share of general funds expended for elementary and secondary education by states and localities in the same year as reported by the U.S. Bureau of the Census in its annual publication, *Governmental Finances.*

All state intergovernmental expenditures for education were assumed earmarked for elementary/secondary education. Contributions of parent governments of dependent school systems to their public schools amounted to approximately 9 percent of local government revenues and local government revenue sharing in each year. Therefore, 9 percent of local government revenue-sharing funds were assumed allocated each fiscal year to elementary and secondary education. Parent government contributions to public school systems were obtained from the U.S. Bureau of the Census, *Finances of Public School Systems*. The amount of state revenue-sharing funds allocated for postsecondary education in 1980 was assumed to be 13 percent, the proportion of direct state expenditures for institutions of higher education reported in Governmental Finances for that year.

The share of federal funds for the District of Columbia assigned to education was assumed equal to the share of the city's general fund expenditures for each level of education.

For the job training programs conducted by the Department of Labor, only estimated sums spent on classroom training have been reported as educational program support.

During the 1970s, The Office of Management and Budget (OMB) prepared annual reports on federal education program support. These were published in *Budget of the United States Government [Special Analyses]*. The information presented in this report is not, however, a continuation of the OMB series. A number of differences in the two series should be noted. OMB required all federal agencies to report outlays for education-related programs using a standardized form, thereby assuring agency compliance in reporting. The scope of education programs reported here differs from OMB. Off-budget items such as the annual volume of guaranteed student loans were not included in OMB's reports. Finally, while some mention is made of an annual estimate of federal tax expenditures, OMB did not include them in its annual analysis of federal education support. Estimated federal tax expenditures for education are the difference between current federal tax receipts and what these receipts would be without existing education deductions to income allowed by federal tax provisions.

Recipients' data are estimated based on *Estimating Federal Funds for Education: A New Approach Applied to Fiscal Year 1980,* U.S. Department of Education, "Federal Support for Education, Fiscal Years 1980 to 1984," and *Catalog of Federal Domestic Assistance.* The recipients' data are estimated and tend to undercount institutions of higher education (IHEs), students, and local education agencies (LEAs). This is because some of the federal programs have more than one recipient receiving funds. In these cases, the recipients were put into a "mixed recipients" category, because there was no way to disaggregate the amount each recipient received.

High School and Beyond

High School and Beyond (HS&B) is a national longitudinal survey of 1980 high school sophomores and seniors. The base-year survey was a probability sample of 1,015 high schools with a target number of 36 sophomores and 36 seniors in each of the schools. A total of 58,270 students participated in the base-year survey. Substitutions were made for noncooperating schools—but not for students—in those strata where it was possible. Overall, 1,122 schools were selected in the original sample and 811 of these schools participated in the survey. An additional 204 schools were drawn in a replacement sample. Student refusals and absences resulted in an 82 percent completion rate for the survey.

Several small groups in the population were oversampled to allow for special study of certain types of schools and students. Students completed questionnaires and took a battery of cognitive tests. In addition, a sample of parents of sophomores and seniors (about 3,600 for each cohort) was surveyed.

HS&B first follow-up activities took place in the spring of 1982. The sample design of the first follow-up survey called for the selection of approximately 30,000 persons who were sophomores in 1980. The completion rate for sophomores eligible for on-campus survey administration was about 96 percent. About 89 percent of the students who left school between the base year and first follow-up surveys (dropouts, transfer students, and early graduates) completed the first follow-up sophomore questionnaire.

As part of the first follow-up survey of HS&B, transcripts were requested in fall 1982 for an 18,152 member subsample of the sophomore cohort. Of the 15,941 transcripts actually obtained, 1,969 were excluded because the students had dropped out of school before graduation, 799 were excluded because they were incomplete, and 1,057 were excluded because the student graduated before 1982 or the transcript indicated neither a dropout status nor graduation. Thus 12,116 transcripts were utilized for the overall curriculum analysis presented in this publication. All courses in each transcript were assigned a six-digit code based on *A Classification of Secondary School Courses* (developed by Evaluation Technologies, Inc. under contract with NCES). Credits earned in each course were expressed in Carnegie units. (The Carnegie unit is a standard of measurement that represents one credit for the completion of a 1-year course. To receive credit for a course, the student must have received a passing grade—"pass," "D," or higher.) Students who transferred from public to private schools or from private to public schools between their sophomore and senior years were eliminated from public/private analyses.

In designing the senior cohort first follow-up survey, one of the goals was to reduce the size of the retained sample, while still keeping sufficient numbers of minorities to allow important policy analyses. A total of 11,227 (94 percent) of the 11,995 persons subsampled completed the questionnaire. Information was obtained about the respondents' school and employment experiences, family status, and attitudes and plans.

The sample for the second follow-up, which took place in spring 1984, consisted of about 12,000 members of the senior cohort and about 15,000 members of the sophomore cohort. The completion rate for the senior cohort was 91 percent, and the completion rate for the sophomore cohort was 92 percent.

HS&B third follow-up data collection activities were performed in spring of 1986. Both the sophomore and senior cohort samples for this round of data collection were the same as those used for the second follow-up survey. The completion rates for the sophomore and senior cohort samples were 91 percent and 88 percent, respectively.

Table A2 contains the maximum number of cases that are available for the tabulations of the specific classification variables used throughout this publication.

The standard error (se) of an individual percentage (p) based on HS&B data can be approximated by the formula

$$se_p = DEFT\,[p(100-p)/n]^{1/2}$$

where n is the sample size and DEFT, the square root of the design effect, is a factor used to adjust for the particular sample design used in HS&B. Table A3 provides the DEFT factors for different HS&B samples and subsamples.

In evaluating a difference between two independent percentages, the standard error of the difference may be conservatively approximated by taking the square root of the sum of the squared standard errors of the two percentages. For example, in the

1986 follow-up of 1980 sophomores, 84.0 percent of the men and 77.2 percent of the women felt that being successful in work was "very important," a difference of 6.8 percentage points. Using the formula and the sample sizes from table A2 and the DEFT factors from table A3, the standard errors of the two percentages being compared are calculated to be:

$$1.43[(84.0)(16.0)/(5,391)]^{1/2} = .714$$
$$1.43[(77.2)(22.8)/(5,857)]^{1/2} = .784$$

The standard error of the difference is therefore

$$(.714^2 + .784^2)^{1/2} = (.510 + .615)^{1/2} = 1.06$$

The sampling error (95 chances in 100) of the difference is approximately double the standard error, or approximately 2.1 percentage points, and the 95 percent confidence interval for the difference is 6.8 ± 2.1, or 4.7 to 8.9 percentage points.

The standard error estimation procedure outlined above does not compensate for survey item nonresponse, which is a source of nonsampling error. (Table A2 reflects the maximum number of responses that could be tabulated by demographic characteristics.) For example, of the 10,925 respondents in the 1984 follow-up survey of 1980 high school graduates, 372, or 3.4 percent, did not respond to the particular question on whether they had ever used a pocket calculator. Item nonresponse varied considerably. A very low nonresponse rate of 0.1 percent was obtained for a question asking whether the respondent had attended a postsecondary institution. A much higher item nonresponse rate of 12.2 percent was obtained for a question asking if the respondent had used a micro or minicomputer in high school. Typical item nonresponse rates ranged from 3 to 4 percent.

The Hispanic analyses presented in this report relied on students' self-identification as members of one of four Hispanic subgroups: Mexican, Mexican-American, Chicano; Cuban; Puerto-Rican, Puertorriqueno, or Boricua; or other Latin American, Latino, Hispanic, or Spanish descent.

An NCES series of technical reports and data file users manuals provides additional information on the survey methodology.

Further information on the High School and Beyond survey may be obtained from:

Aurora M. D'Amico
Postsecondary Education Statistics Division
National Center for Education Statistics
555 New Jersey Avenue NW
Washington, DC 20208–5652

1990 High School Transcript Study Tabulations

This study involved analysis of transcripts of 1990 high school graduates from 330 schools. The analyses were based on approximately 21,500 1990 graduates selected for the National Assessment of Educational Progress (NAEP) in 1990. The study collected information such as course lists, graduation requirements, and the definition of units of credit and grades, on a school-level basis.

Similar studies were conducted of course taking patterns of 1987 and 1982 graduates. The 1987 data are based on approximately 22,799 transcripts from 433 schools obtained as part of the 1987 High School Transcript Study. The 1982 data are based on approximately 12,000 transcripts collected by the High School and Beyond Project.

Because the 1982 High School and Beyond study used a different method for identifying handicapped students than did the 1987 and 1990 transcript studies, and in order to make the statistical summaries as comparable as possible, all the counts and percentages in this report are restricted to students whose records indicate that they had not participated in a special education program. This restriction lowers the number of 1990 graduates represented in the tables to 20,866.

Further information can be obtained from:

Patricia Dabbs
Education Assessment Division
National Center for Education Statistics
555 New Jersey Avenue NW
Washington, DC 20208–5653

Integrated Postsecondary Education Data System

The Integrated Postsecondary Education Data System (IPEDS) surveys approximately 11,000 postsecondary institutions, including universities and colleges, as well as institutions offering technical and vocational education beyond the high school level. This survey, which began in 1986, replaced the Higher Education General Information Survey (HEGIS).

IPEDS consists of eight integrated components that obtain information on who provides postsecondary education (institutions), who participates in it and completes it (students), what programs are offered and what programs are completed, and both the human and financial resources involved in the provision of institutionally based postsecondary education. Specifically, these components include: Institutional Characteristics, including instructional activity; Fall Enrollment, including age and residence; Enrollment in Occupationally Specific Programs; Completions; Finance; Staff; Salaries of Full-Time Instructional Faculty; and Academic Libraries.

The higher education portion of this survey is a census of accredited 2- and 4-year colleges. Prior to 1993, data from the technical and vocational institutions were collected through a sample survey. Beginning in 1993, all data are gathered in a census of all postsecondary institutions. The tabulations on "Institutional Characteristics" developed for this edition of the *Digest* are based on lists of all institutions and are not subject to sampling errors.

Prior to the establishment of IPEDS in 1986, HEGIS acquired and maintained statistical data on the characteristics and operations of institutions of higher education. Implemented in 1966, HEGIS was an annual universe survey of institutions accredited at the college level by an agency recognized by the Secretary of the U.S. Department of Education. These institutions were listed in NCES's *Education Directory, Colleges and Universities.*

The trend tables presented in this report draw on HEGIS surveys which solicited information concerning institutional characteristics, faculty salaries, finances, enrollment, and degrees. Since these surveys were distributed to all higher education institutions, the data presented are not subject to sampling error. However, they are subject to nonsampling error, the sources of which varied with the survey instrument. Information concerning the nonsampling error of the enrollment and degrees surveys draws extensively on the "HEGIS Post-Survey Validation Study" conducted in 1979.

Further information on IPEDS may be obtained from:

Roslyn A. Korb
Education Statistics Division
National Center for Education Statistics
555 New Jersey Avenue NW
Washington, DC 20208–5652

Institutional Characteristics

This survey provides the basis for the universe of institutions presented in the *Directory of Postsecondary Institutions.* The universe comprises institutions that met certain accreditation criteria and offered at least a 1-year program of college-level studies leading toward a degree. All of these institutions were certified as eligible by the U.S. Department of Education's Division of Eligibility and Agency Evaluation. The survey collects basic information necessary to classify the institutions including control, level, and kinds of programs; information on tuition, fees, and room and board charges; and unduplicated full-year enrollment counts and instructional activity.

Fall Enrollment

This survey has been part of the HEGIS and IPEDS series since 1966. The enrollment survey re-

sponse rate is relatively high; the 1993 response rate was 97.0 percent. Major sources of nonsampling error for this survey as identified in the 1979 report, were classification problems, the unavailability of needed data, interpretation of definitions, the survey due date, and operational errors. Of these, the classification of students appears to have been the main source of error. Institutions had problems in correctly classifying first-time freshmen and other first-time students for both full-time and part-time categories. These problems occurred most often at 2-year institutions (private and public) and private 4-year institutions. In the 1977–78 HEGIS validation studies, the classification problem led to an estimated overcount of 11,000 full-time students and an undercount of 19,000 part-time students. Although the ratio of error to the grand total was quite small (less than 1 percent), the percentage of errors was as high as 5 percent for detailed student levels and even higher at certain aggregation levels.

Beginning with fall 1986, the survey system was redesigned with the introduction of the Integrated Postsecondary Education Data System (IPEDS) (see above). The IPEDS system comprises all postsecondary institutions, but also maintains comparability with earlier surveys by allowing HEGIS institutions to be tabulated separately. The survey allows (in alternating years) for the collection of age and residence data.

Salaries, Tenure, and Fringe Benefits of Full-Time Instructional Faculty

This institutional survey has been conducted for most years from 1966–67 to 1987–88, and annually since 1989–90. Although the survey form changed a number of times during those years, only comparable data are presented in this report.

Between 1966–67 and 1985–86 this survey differed from other HEGIS surveys in that imputations were not made for nonrespondents. Thus, there is some possibility that the salary averages presented in this report may differ from the results of a complete enumeration of all colleges and universities. Beginning with the surveys for 1987–88, the IPEDS data tabulation procedures included imputations for survey nonrespondents. The response rate for the 1992–93 survey was 85.4 percent for higher education institutions, or 82.9 percent overall. Because of the higher response rate for public colleges, it is probable that the public colleges' salary data are more accurate than the data for private colleges. Although data from these surveys are not subject to sampling error, sources of nonsampling error may include computational errors and misclassification in reporting and processing. NCES reviews individual colleges' data for internal and longitudinal consistency and contacts the colleges to check inconsistent data.

Completions

This survey was part of the HEGIS series throughout its existence. However, the degree classification taxonomy was revised in 1970–71, 1982–83, and 1991–92. Collection of degree data has been maintained through the IPEDS system.

Though information from survey years 1970–71 through 1981–82 is directly comparable, care must be taken if information before or after that period is included in any comparison. Degrees-conferred trend tables arranged by the 1991–92 classification are included in the *Digest* to provide consistent data from 1970–71 to 1991–92. Data in this edition on associate and other formal awards below the baccalaureate, by field of study, cannot be made comparable with figures prior to 1982–83. The nonresponse rate did not appear to be a significant source of nonsampling error for this survey. The return rate over the years has been high, with the higher education response rate for the 1991–92 survey at 94.1 percent. The overall response rate including the noncollegiate institutions is 84.5 percent. Because of the high return rate for the institutions of higher education, nonsampling error caused by imputation is also minimal.

The major sources of nonsampling error for this survey were differences between the NCES program taxonomy and taxonomies used by the colleges, classification of double majors, operational problems, and survey timing. In the 1979 HEGIS validation study, these sources of nonsampling contributed to an error rate of 0.3 percent overreporting of bachelor's degrees and 1.3 percent overreporting of master's degrees. The differences, however, varied greatly among fields. Over 50 percent of the fields selected for the validation study had no errors identified. Categories of fields that had large differences were business and management, education, engineering, letters, and psychology. It was also shown that differences in proportion to the published figures were less than 1 percent for most of the selected fields that had some errors. Exceptions to these were: master's and Ph.D. programs in labor and industrial relations (20 percent and 8 percent); bachelor's and master's programs in art education (3 percent and 4 percent); bachelor's and Ph.D. programs in business and commerce, and in distributive education (5 percent and 9 percent); master's programs in philosophy (8 percent); and Ph.D. programs in psychology (11 percent).

Financial Statistics

This survey was part of the HEGIS series and has been continued under the IPEDS system. Changes were made in the financial survey instruments in fiscal years (FY) 1976, 1982, and 1987. The FY 76 survey instrument contained numerous revisions to earlier survey forms and made direct comparisons of line items very difficult. Beginning in FY 82, Pell Grant data were collected in the categories of federal restricted grants and contracts revenues and restricted scholarships and fellowships expenditures. The introduction of IPEDS in the FY 87 survey included several important changes to the survey instrument and data processing procedures. While these changes were significant, considerable effort has been made to present only comparable information on trends in this report and to note inconsistencies. Finance tables for this publication have been adjusted by subtracting the largely duplicative Pell Grant amounts from the later data to maintain comparability with pre-FY 82 data.

Possible sources of nonsampling error in the financial statistics include nonresponse, imputation, and misclassification. The response rate has been about 85 to 90 percent for most of the years reported. The response rate for the FY 1991 survey was 86.7 percent.

Two general methods of imputation were used in HEGIS. If the prior year's data were available for a nonresponding institution, these data were inflated using the Higher Education Price Index and adjusted according to changes in enrollments. If no previous year's data were available, current data were used from peer institutions selected for location (state or region), control, level, and enrollment size of institution. In most cases estimates for nonreporting institutions in IPEDS were made using data from peer institutions.

Beginning with FY 87, the IPEDS survey system included all postsecondary institutions, but maintained comparability with earlier surveys by allowing 2- and 4-year HEGIS institutions to be tabulated separately. The finance data tabulated for this publication reflect totals for the HEGIS or higher education institutions only. For FY 87 through FY 91, in order to maintain comparability with the historical time series of HEGIS institutions, data were combined from two of the three different survey forms that make up the IPEDS survey system. The vast majority of the data were tabulated from Form 1, which was used to collect information from public and private nonprofit 2- and 4-year colleges. Form 2, a condensed form, was used to gather data for the 2-year proprietary institutions. Because of the differences in the data requested on the two forms, several assumptions were made about the Form 2 reports so that their figures could be included in the institutions of higher education totals.

In IPEDS, the Form 2 institutions were not asked to separate appropriations from grants and contracts, nor state from local sources of funding. For the Form 2 institutions, all the federal revenues were assumed to be federal grants and contracts and all of the state and local revenues were assumed to be restricted state grants and contracts. All other Form 2 sources of revenue, except for tuition and fees and sales and services of educational activities, were included under "other." Similar adjustments were made to the expenditure accounts. The Form 2 institutions reported instruction and scholarship and fellowship expenditures only. All other educational and general expenditures were allocated to academic support.

To reduce reporting error, NCES uses national standards for reporting finance statistics. These standards are contained in *College and University Business Administration: Administrative Services (1974 Edition),* and the *Financial Accounting and Reporting Manual for Higher Education (1990 Education),* published by the National Association of College and University Business Officers; *Audits of Colleges and Universities* (as amended August 31, 1974), by the American Institute of Certified Public Accountants; and *HEGIS Financial Reporting Guide (1980),* by NCES. Wherever possible, definitions and formats in the survey form are consistent with those in these four accounting texts.

Staff

The fall staff data presented in this publication were collected in cooperation with the U.S. Equal Employment Opportunity Commission (EEOC). EEOC collects staff data through the Higher Education Staff Information (EEO–6) report from all higher education institutions with 15 or more full-time employees. NCES, through the IPEDS system, collected data from all other postsecondary institutions, including all 2- and 4-year higher education institutions with less than 15 full-time employees, and a sample of the less than 2-year schools. The NCES and EEOC collect staff data biennially in odd numbered years in institutions of postsecondary education. The IPEDS file combines data from the two surveys to create the IPEDS "Fall Staff" data tape.

The IPEDS "Fall Staff" questionnaires were mailed out by NCES; the respondents reported the number of employees in their institution as of October 1, 1991. The EEO–6 questionnaires were mailed out by EEOC between October and November 1991; the respondents reported the employment statistics in their institution that cover the payroll period closest to October 1 of the survey year.

The "Fall Staff" survey had an overall response rate of 85.6 percent. The response rate for higher education institutions was 92.6 percent.

The International Assessment of Educational Progress

The International Assessment of Educational Progress (IAEP), sponsored by the U.S. Department of Education and the National Science Foundation and conducted by the Educational Testing Service, surveyed the mathematics and science performance of 13-year-old students in 20 countries, and 9-year-old students in 14 countries during 1990–91. Some countries drew samples from virtually all children in the appropriate age group; others confined their assessments to specific geographic areas, language groups, or grade levels.

From each population at each level, a random sample of 3,300 students from about 110 different schools was selected; half were assessed in science and half in mathematics. During March 1991, a total of about 175,000 9- and 13-year-olds (those born in calendar years 1981 and 1977, respectively) were tested in 13 different languages.

The achievement tests given to 9-year-olds included 62 questions in mathematics and 60 questions in science. For the 13-year-olds, the test included 76 questions in mathematics and 72 questions in science. Students at each age spent additional time responding to questions about their backgrounds and home and school experiences. A school questionnaire was also completed by school administrators.

The statistical significance of differences in performance between participating countries was determined through use of the Bonferroni multiple comparison procedure. The procedure allows for the probability of falsely declaring a significant difference to 5 percent across the entire set of possible comparisons between pairs of countries.

For more information about this survey contact:

Eugene Owen
Data Development Division
National Center for Education Statistics
555 New Jersey Avenue NW
Washington, DC 20208–5653

National Adult Literacy Survey

The National Adult Literacy Survey was created as a new measure of literacy and funded by the Department of Education. It is the third and largest assessment of adult literacy funded by the federal government. The aim of the survey is to profile the English literacy of adults in the United States based on their performance across a wide array of tasks that reflect the types of materials and demands they encounter in their daily lives.

To gather the information on adults' literacy skills, trained staff interviewed nearly 13,600 individuals aged 16 and older during the first eight months of

1992. These participants had been randomly selected to represent the adult population in the country as a whole. Black and Hispanic households were oversampled to ensure reliable estimates of literacy proficiencies and to permit analyses of the performance of these subpopulations. In addition, some 1,100 inmates from 80 federal and state prisons were interviewed to gather information on the proficiencies of the prison population. In total, over 26,000 adults were surveyed.

Each survey participant was asked to spend approximately an hour responding to a series of diverse literacy tasks as well as questions about his or her demographic characteristics, educational background, reading practices, and other areas related to literacy. Based on their responses to the survey tasks, adults received proficiency scores along three scales which reflect varying degrees of skill in prose, document and quantitative literacy. The results of the survey were published in a report, *Adult Literacy in America* in September 1993.

Further information on the National Adult Literacy Survey may be obtained from:

Andrew Kolstad
Education Assessment Division
National Center for Education Statistics
555 New Jersey Avenue NW
Washington, DC 20208–5653

National Assessment of Educational Progress

The National Assessment of Educational Progress (NAEP) is a series of cross-sectional studies designed and initially implemented in 1969. NAEP has gathered information about selected levels of educational achievement across the country. NAEP has surveyed the educational attainments by age and grade (9-, 13-, and 17-year-olds, and 4th, 8th, and 12th graders), and young adults (ages 25–35) in 10 learning areas. Different learning areas have been assessed periodically, and all areas have been reassessed in order to measure possible changes in educational achievement.

The assessment data presented in this publication were derived from tests designed and conducted by the Education Commission of the States (1969–1983) and by the Educational Testing Service (1983 to present). Three-stage probability samples have been used. The primary sampling units have been stratified by region and, within region, by state, size of community, and, for the two smaller sizes of community strata, by socioeconomic level. The first stage of sampling entails defining and selecting primary sampling units (PSU's). For each age/grade level (4,8, and 12) the second stage entails enumerating, stratifying, and randomly selecting schools, both public and private, within each PSU selected at the first

stage. The third stage involves randomly selecting students within a school for participation in NAEP. Assessment exercises have been administered either to individuals or to small groups of students by specially trained personnel.

After NAEP data are scored, they are weighted in accordance with the population structure and adjusted for nonresponse. Analyses include computing the percentage of students giving various responses and using Item Response Theory (IRT) technology to estimate levels of achievement for the nation and various subpopulations. IRT technology enables the assessment of a sample of students in a learning area or subarea on a single scale even if different students have been administered different exercises. The underlying principle is that when a number of items require similar skills, the regularities observed across patterns of response can often be used to characterize both respondents and tasks in terms of a relatively small number of variables. When aggregated through appropriate mathematical formulas, these variables capture the dominant features of the data.

Sample sizes for the reading proficiency portion of the 1991–92 NAEP study were 4,944 for the 9-year-olds, 3,965 for the 13-year-olds, and 4,447 for the 17-year-olds. Sample sizes for the 1991–92 NAEP science study and the 1991–92 NAEP math study were: 7,335 for 9-year-olds, 5,909 for 13-year-olds, and 4,359 for 17-year-olds. Response rates were 94, 91, and 83 percent, respectively. Data on standard errors for the 1991–92 studies can be found in Tables A4, A5, and A6.

Sample sizes for the reading proficiency portion of the 1989–90 NAEP study were 4,268 for the 9-year-olds, 4,609 for the 13-year-olds, and 2,689 for the 17-year-olds. Response rates were 93 percent, 90 percent, and 82 percent, respectively. Response rates for earlier years (1970–71, 1974–75, and 1979–80) were generally lower. For example, the lowest response rate for the 9-year-olds was 88 percent in 1974–75, and the lowest response rate over all was 70 percent for the 17-year-olds in 1974–75.

The 1987–88 U.S. history assessment data in this report are based on a nationally representative sample of 3,950 4th graders, 6,462 8th graders, and 5,507 12th graders. The response rates were: 93 percent for 4th graders, 88 percent for 8th graders, and 78 percent for 12th graders.

The 1987–88 civics assessment data in this report are based on a nationally representative sample of 1,938 13-year-olds and 1,786 17-year-olds. The response rates were 90 percent for the 8th graders and 79 percent for the 17-year-olds in 1987–88. Sample sizes for the earlier years were much larger with 19,952 13-year-olds and 17,866 17-year-olds in 1976 and 7,268 13-year-olds and 6,751 17-year-olds in 1982. The 1987–88 analyses for 4th, 8th, and 12th graders were based on a somewhat different 1987–88 sample. The sample sizes were 1,974 4th graders, 4,487 8th graders, and 4,275 12th graders. The response rates were: 93 percent for 4th graders, 88 percent for 8th graders, and 78 percent for 12th graders.

The 1989–90 writing assessment was administered to 6,679 4th graders, 6,525 8th graders, and 6,069 12th graders. Student response rates for the 1989–90 writing assessment were 97 percent for the 4th graders, 88 percent for the 8th graders, and 79 percent for the 12th graders. Sample sizes varied depending on the test items and the scoring method used.

In 1989–90, a science assessment was administered to 6,314 4th graders, 6,531 8th graders, and 6,337 12th graders. The response rates were 93 percent for the 4th graders, 89 percent for the 8th graders, and 81 percent for the 12th graders.

The 1987–88 geography assessment was administered to 3,030 high school students. The response rate for the assessment was 77 percent. The National Geographic Society provided support for conducting the assessment.

In 1990, representative state-level data were produced for mathematics at the 8th-grade level. This was the first time NAEP had produced data on a state-by-state level. In 1992, state-level assessments were conducted in 4th and 8th grade mathematics and 4th grade reading.

Information from NAEP is subject to both nonsampling and sampling error. Two possible sources of nonsampling error are nonparticipation and instrumentation. Certain populations have been oversampled to assure samples of sufficient size for analysis. Instrumentation nonsampling error could result from failure of the test instruments to measure what is being taught and, in turn, what is being learned by the students.

For further information on NAEP, contact:

Gary W. Phillips
Education Assessment Division
National Center for Education Statistics
555 New Jersey Avenue NW
Washington, DC 20208–5653

National Education Longitudinal Study of 1988

The National Education Longitudinal Study of 1988 (NELS:88) is the third major longitudinal study sponsored by the National Center for Education Statistics. The two studies that preceded NELS:88, the National Longitudinal Study of the High School Class of 1972 (NLS–72) and High School and Beyond (HS&B) in 1980, surveyed high school seniors (and sopho-

mores in HS&B) through high school, postsecondary education, and work and family formation experiences. Unlike its predecessors, NELS:88 begins with a cohort of 8th-grade students. In 1988, some 25,000 eighth graders, their parents, their teachers, and their school principals were surveyed. Follow-ups were conducted in 1990 and 1992 when a majority of these students were in 10th and 12th grades, respectively.

NELS:88 is designed to provide trend data about critical transitions experienced by young people as they develop, attend school, and embark on their careers. It will complement and strengthen state and local efforts by furnishing new information on how school policies, teacher practices, and family involvement affect student educational outcomes (i.e., academic achievement, persistence in school, and participation in postsecondary education). For the base year, NELS:88 includes a multifaceted student questionnaire, four cognitive tests, a parent questionnaire, a teacher questionnaire, and a school questionnaire.

To ensure that private schools, rural schools, and schools with high minority membership were adequately represented, sampling was first conducted at the school level and then at the student level within schools. Additionally, oversamples of students with Hispanic and Asian or Pacific Island heritage were drawn. The base year data are drawn from a nationally representative sample of 1,000 schools (800 public schools; and 200 private schools, including parochial institutions). Within this school sample, 25,000 eighth-grade students were selected at random.

In 1990, when the students were in 10th grade, the students, school dropouts, their teachers, and their school principals were surveyed. The 1988 survey of parents was not a part of the 1990 follow-up. In 1992, when the students were in 12th grade the second follow-up conducted surveys of students, dropouts, parents, teachers, and school principals. Also, information on the students' transcripts, the schools' course offerings, and enrollments were collected, and there was a school effects survey. Tables A7 and A8 present the respondent counts and design effects of NELS:88 and the 1990 and 1992 follow-ups.

Further information about the NELS:88 survey can be obtained from:

Jeffrey A. Owings
Elementary and Secondary Education Statistics
    Division
National Center for Education Statistics
555 New Jersey Avenue NW
Washington, DC 20208–5651

National Household Education Survey

The National Household Education Survey (NHES) is a data collection system that is designed to address a wide range of education-related issues. Surveys were conducted in the spring of 1991 and in the spring of 1993. It was conducted in the spring of 1995 and biennially thereafter.

The NHES targets specific populations for detailed data collection. While the survey is not designed to develop an in-depth research database, it is intended to provide more detailed data on the topics and populations of interest than are collected through supplements to other household surveys.

The NHES is designed as a telephone survey of the noninstitutional civilian population of the U.S. Households are selected for the survey using random digit dialing (RDD) methods. Data are collected using computer assisted telephone interviewing (CATI) procedures.

The methodology for any single fielding of the NHES is linked to the research issues under study, the level of data required to address these issues, and how precise the estimates generated from the survey data need to be in order to meet the objectives of the study. However, while the specifications for each annual survey will vary, there are general features of the NHES methodology that will stay relatively constant from one survey to the next.

NCES envisions the continued use of RDD methods to select the sample for the NHES in the future. Although the sample size for a particular component of the survey may vary somewhat from year to year, NCES expects to screen between 60,000 and 75,000 households for the annual surveys.

The topics addressed by the NHES:91 were early childhood education and adult education. About 60,000 households were screened for the NHES:91. In the Early Childhood Education component, about 14,000 parents/guardians of 3-to 8-year olds completed interviews about their children's early educational experiences. Included in this component were participation in nonparental care/education, characteristics of programs and care arrangements, and early school experiences including delayed kindergarten entry and retention in grade. In addition to questions about care/education arrangements and school, parents are asked about activities children engaged in with parents and other family members inside and outside the home. Information on family, household, and child characteristics was also collected.

In the NHES:91 Adult Education component, about 9,800 persons 16 years of age and older, identified as having participated in an adult education activity in the previous 12 months, were questioned about their activities. Data were collected on programs and up to four courses, including the subject matter duration, sponsorship, purpose, and cost. A smaller sample of nonparticipants (about 2,800) also completed interviews about barriers to participation. Information on the household and the adult's background and current employment also was collected.

In the NHES:93, nearly 64,000 households were screened. Approximately 11,000 parents of 3- to 7-year olds completed interviews for the School Readiness component. Topics included in this component were the developmental characteristics of preschoolers, school adjustment and teacher feedback to parents for kindergartners and primary students, center-based program participation, early school experiences, home activities with family members, and health status. Extensive family and child background characteristics, including parent language and education, income, receipt of public assistance, and household composition, were collected to permit the identification of at-risk children.

In the School Safety and Discipline component, about 12,700 parents of children in grades 3 through 12, and about 6,500 youth in grades 6 through 12, were interviewed about their school experiences. Topics included the school learning environment, discipline policy, safety at school, victimization, the availability and use of alcohol/drugs, and alcohol/drug education. Peer norms for behavior in school and substance use were also included in this topical component. Extensive family and household background information was collected, as well as characteristics of the school attended by the child.

For more information contact:

Kathryn A. Chandler,
Elementary and Secondary Education Statistics
  Division
National Center for Education Statistics
555 New Jersey Avenue, NW
Washington, DC 20208–5651

National Longitudinal Study

The National Longitudinal Study (NLS) of the high school class of 1972 began with the collection of base-year survey data from a sample of about 19,000 high school seniors in spring of 1972. Five more follow-up surveys of these students were conducted in 1973, 1974, 1976, 1979, and 1986. The NLS was designed to provide the education community with information on the transitions of young adults from high school through postsecondary education and the workplace.

The sample design for the NLS is a stratified, two-stage probability sample of students from all schools, public and private, in the 50 states and the District of Columbia with a 12th-grade enrollment during the 1971–72 school year. During the first stage of sampling, about 1,070 schools were selected for participation in the base-year survey. As many as 18 students were selected at random from each of the sample schools. Both the size of the school and student samples were increased during the first follow-up survey. Beginning with the first follow-up and continuing through the fourth follow-up, about 1,300 schools participated in the survey and slightly under 23,500 students were sampled. The response rates for each of the different rounds of data collection have been 80 percent or higher.

Sample retention rates across the survey years have been quite high. For example, of the individuals responding to the base-year questionnaire, the percentages who responded to the first, second, third, and fourth follow-up questionnaires were about 94, 93, 89, and 83 percent, respectively.

Further information may be obtained from:

Postsecondary Education Statistics Division
National Center for Education Statistics
555 New Jersey Avenue NW
Washington, DC 20208–5652

National Postsecondary Student Aid Study

The National Postsecondary Student Aid Study (NPSAS) is a comprehensive nationwide study of how students and their families pay for postsecondary education. It covers national representative samples of undergraduates, graduates, and first-professional students; students attending less than 2-year institutions, 2- to 3-year schools, 4-year colleges, and major universities. Participants included students who do not receive aid and their parents as well as students who do receive financial aid and their parents. Study results are used to help determine future federal policy regarding student financial aid. The study is conducted every three years.

The first NPSAS was conducted during the 1986–87 school year. Data were gathered from about 1,130 colleges, universities, and other postsecondary institutions; 55,000 students; and 16,000 parents. These data provided information on the cost of postsecondary education, the distribution of financial aid, and the characteristics of both aided and nonaided students and their families.

As a part of the 1989–90 NPSAS, information on nearly 70,000 undergraduates and graduate students enrolled during the school year was collected at 1,130 postsecondary institutions. The sample included students enrolled at any time between July 1, 1989 and June 30, 1990. About 51,000 students and a subsample of about 16,000 of their parents were interviewed by telephone. Table A9 presents standard errors for undergraduates enrolled full-time and part-time in fall 1989, by aid status and source of aid during 1989–90, and control and level of institution.

Further information may be obtained from:

Andrew G. Malizio
Postsecondary Education Statistics Division
National Center for Education Statistics
555 New Jersey Avenue NW
Washington, DC 20208–5652

National Survey of Postsecondary Faculty

The National Survey of Postsecondary Faculty (NSOPF), a survey of instructional faculty in higher education institutions, was conducted for the first time in the 1987–88 academic year by NCES. The study consisted of three major components: the Institutional Survey, a stratified random sample of 480 institutional-level respondents, with a response rate of 88 percent; the Faculty Survey, a stratified random sample of 11,013 eligible faculty members within the participating institutions, with a response rate of 76 percent; and the Department Chair Survey, a stratified random sample of 3,029 eligible department chairpersons (or their equivalent) within the participating 2- and 4-year institutions, with a response rate of 80 percent.

Institutions were selected from nonproprietary U.S. postsecondary institutions that grant a 2-year (A.A.) or higher degree, and have been accredited by organizations recognized by the U.S. Department of Education. Included in this group are religious, medical, and other specialized institutions. This survey universe consisted of 3,159 institutions from the 1987 IPEDS.

The 1988 NSOPF gathered information on the backgrounds, responsibilities, workloads, salaries, benefits, and attitudes of full- and part-time instructional faculty in higher education institutions. Additional information was collected on faculty composition, turnover and recruitment, and retention and tenure policies from institutional and department-level respondents.

The second cycle of the National Study of Postsecondary Faculty (NSOPF–93) is being conducted by NCES with additional support from the National Science Foundation and the National Endowment for the Humanities. NSOPF–93 will expand the information base about faculty in several ways: it will allow for comparisons to be made over time; it will allow for more detailed comparisons among faculty in various disciplines, because of an increase in sample size; it will examine critical faculty issues that have developed since the 1988 study; and it will describe research faculty as well as instructional faculty in higher education institutions.

For more information contact:

Linda J. Zimbler
Postsecondary Education Statistics Division
National Center for Education Statistics
555 New Jersey Avenue NW
Washington, DC 20208–5652National Survey of
Postsecondary Faculty

Projections of Education Statistics

Since 1964, NCES has published projections of key statistics for elementary and secondary schools and institutions of higher education. These projections include statistics such as enrollments, instructional staff, graduates, earned degrees, and expenditures. The *Projections* reports include several alternative projection series and a methodology section describing the techniques and assumptions used to prepare them. Data in this edition of the Digest reflect the middle alternative projection series.

Differences between the reported and projected values are, of course, almost inevitable. An evaluation of past projections revealed that, at the elementary and secondary level, projections of enrollments have been quite accurate: mean absolute percentage differences for enrollment were less than 1 percent for projections from 1 to 5 years in the future, while those for teachers were less than 4 percent. At the higher education level, projections of enrollment have been fairly accurate: mean absolute percentage differences were 5 percent or less for projections from 1 to 5 years into the future.

Since projections of time series are subject to errors both by the nature of statistics and the properties of projection methodologies, users are cautioned not to place too much confidence in the numerical values of the projections. Important, but unforeseeable, economic and social changes may lead to differences, particularly at the higher education level. Rather, projections are to be considered as indicators of broad trends.

For further information about projection methodology and accuracy, contact:

William J. Hussar
Statistical Standards and Methodology Division
National Center for Education Statistics
555 New Jersey Avenue NW
Washington, DC 20208–5654

Library Statistics Program

Nationwide, public library statistics are collected using the Public Libraries Survey and disseminated annually through the Federal-State Cooperative System for public library data (FSCS). FSCS completed the collection of 1991 data in July 1992. Descriptive statistics are produced for nearly 9,000 public libraries.

The Public Libraries Survey includes information about staffing; operating income and expenditures; type of governance; type of administrative structure; size of collection; and service measures such as reference transactions, public service hours, interlibrary loans, circulation, and library visits. In FSCS, respondents supply the information electronically, and data are edited and tabulated in machine-readable form.

The respondents are 8,946 public libraries identified in the 50 states and the District of Columbia by state library agencies. At the state level, FSCS is administered by State Data Coordinators, appointed by the Chief Officer of each State Library Agency. The State Data Coordinator collects the requested data from local public libraries and submits these data to NCES. An annual training conference sponsored by NCES is provided for the State Data Coordinators. A steering committee representing State Data Coordinators and other public library constituents is active in the development of FSCS data elements and software. Technical assistance to states is provided by phone and in person by the FSCS steering committee and by NCES staff and contractors.

All 50 states and the District of Columbia have submitted data which are available for individual public libraries and are also aggregated to state and national levels.

Since 1990, data collections have been collected electronically. The most recent software is called DECPLUS. It includes identifying information on all known public libraries and their outlets, all state libraries, and some library systems and cooperatives. Beginning in 1994, this resource will be available for drawing samples for special surveys on such topics as literacy, access for the disabled, and library construction.

Under the Academic Libraries Survey (ALS), NCES surveyed academic libraries on a 3-year cycle between 1966 and 1988. Since 1988, ALS has been a component of the Integrated Postsecondary Education Data System and is on a 2-year cycle. ALS provides data on about 3,500 academic libraries. In aggregate, these data provide an overview of the status of academic libraries nationally and statewide. The survey collects data on the libraries in the entire universe of accredited higher education institutions and on the libraries in nonaccredited institutions with a program of 4 years or more. ALS produces descriptive statistics on academic libraries in postsecondary institutions in the 50 states, the District of Columbia and the outlying areas.

The School Library Statistics Survey collected data on school libraries/media centers in 1985–86. NCES asked questions on libraries in public and private schools as part of the Schools and Staffing Survey (SASS) in 1990–91. These questionnaires were revised and a sample survey of about 7,600 schools was conducted during school year 1993–94. The library components of the 1990–91 SASS include: number of students served and number of professional staff and aides; at the district level, number of full-time equivalent librarians/media specialists, vacant positions, positions abolished, and approved positions; and amount of librarian input in establishing curriculum.

Additional information on these academic and school library studies is available from:

Jeff Williams
Postsecondary Education Statistics Division
National Center for Education Statistics
555 New Jersey Avenue NW
Washington, DC 20208–5652

Survey of Recent College Graduates

Since 1976, NCES has conducted six surveys of baccalaureate and master's degree recipients 1 year after graduation. The Recent College Graduates surveys have concentrated on those graduates entering the teaching profession. The surveys link major field of study with outcomes such as whether the respondent entered the labor force or was seeking additional education. Data on labor force includes employment status (unemployed, part-time or full-time employed), occupation, salary, career potential, relation to major field of study, and need for a college degree. To obtain accurate results on teachers, graduates with a major in education are oversampled. The latest 2 surveys continued to oversample education majors, but increased the sampling of graduates with majors in other fields.

The survey involves a two-stage sampling procedure. First, the universe of institutions awarding bachelor's and master's degrees is stratified by number or percentage of degrees awarded to education graduates and by control of institution (public or private). A sample of institutions within each strata is then selected. Second, for each of the selected institutions, a list of their graduates by major field of study is obtained and a sample of graduates is drawn by major field of study. Graduates in certain major fields of study (e.g., education, mathematics, physical sciences) are sampled at higher rates than graduates in others fields. Roughly one year after graduation the sample of graduates is located, contacted by mail or telephone, and asked to respond to the questionnaire.

The locating process is more detailed than in most surveys. Nonresponse rates are directly related to the time, effort, and resources used in locating graduates rather than to graduates' refusals to participate. Despite the difficulties in locating graduates, response rates for recent studies are comparable to

studies without locating problems. The data presented in this report provide valuable information not available elsewhere about college outcomes.

The 1976 survey of 1974–75 college graduates was the first and smallest of the series. The sample consisted of 211 schools, of which 200 (96 percent) responded. Of the 5,854 graduates in the sample, 4,350 responded, for a response rate of 79 percent.

The 1981 survey was somewhat larger, with a coverage of 297 institutions and 15,852 graduates. Responses were obtained from 283 institutions, for an institutional response rate of 95 percent, and from 9,312 graduates (716 others were determined to be out of scope), for a response rate of 74 percent.

The 1985 survey sampled 404 colleges and 18,738 graduates of whom 17,853 were found to be in scope. Responses were obtained from 13,200 students, for a response rate of 78 percent. The response rate for the colleges was 98 percent. The 1987 survey form was sent to 21,957 graduates. Responses were received from 16,878, for a response rate of 79.7 percent.

The 1991 RCG study involved a sample of 18,135 graduates of 400 bachelor's and master's degree-granting institutions. The 18,135 graduates consisted of 16,172 bachelor's degrees recipients and 1,963 master's degree recipients between July 1, 1989 and June 30, 1990. Random samples of graduates were selected from lists stratified by field of study. Graduates in education, mathematics, and the physical sciences were sampled at a higher rate, as were minority graduates to provide a sufficient number of these graduates for analysis purposes. The graduates included in the sample were selected in proportion to the institution's number of graduates. The institutional response rate was 95 percent and the graduate response rate was 83 percent.

Table A10 contains sample sizes for number of graduates, by field, for the 1976, 1981, 1985, 1987, and 1991 surveys.

Further information on this survey may be obtained from:

Peter Stowe
Postsecondary Education Statistics Division
National Center for Education Statistics
555 New Jersey Avenue NW
Washington, DC 20208–5652

Public School Principal Survey on Safe, Disciplined, and Drug-Free Schools

This sample survey used the NCES Fast Response Survey System (FRSS), which is designed to gather timely information for policy makers. The survey was conducted in 1991 by Westat, Inc. A national sample of 830 public school principals, representing a response rate of 94 percent, answered questions regarding the extent of discipline problems within their schools. They were also questioned about the nature and effectiveness of their schools' current policies and drug education programs.

This survey categorized principals by instructional level (elementary, secondary), type of school location (city, urban fringe, town, rural), enrollment size (less than 300, 300 to 999, 1,000 or more), region (Northeast, Central, Southeast, and West), and percentage of students receiving free or reduced-price lunches (10 percent or less, 11 to 40 percent, 41 percent or more).

For more information about this survey contact:

Judi Carpenter
Elementary and Secondary Education Statistics
   Division
National Center for Education Statistics
555 New Jersey Avenue NW
Washington, DC 20208–5651

Public School Kindergarten Teachers' Views on Children's Readiness for School

This sample survey of 1,448 public school kindergarten teachers was conducted as part of a national early childhood assessment system for National Education Goal One: "By the year 2000, all American children will start school ready to learn." The survey obtained data on kindergarten teachers' views of children's readiness and on the teacher's classroom practices.

For more information about this survey contact:

Judi Carpenter
Elementary and Secondary Education Statistics
   Division
National Center for Education Statistics
555 New Jersey Avenue NW
Washington, DC 20208–5651

Schools and Staffing Survey

The Schools and Staffing Survey (SASS) was first conducted for the National Center for Education Statistics by the Bureau of the Census during the 1987–88 school year. SASS surveys also were conducted in 1990–91 and in 1993–94, and are scheduled to be conducted at four year intervals. SASS is a mail survey that collects data on the Nation's public and private elementary and secondary teaching force, aspects of teacher supply and demand, teacher workplace conditions, characteristics of school administrators, and school policies and practices. The SASS data are collected through a sample survey of school districts, schools, school administrators, and teachers. The 1990–91 SASS surveys of schools and school principals were based on the 9,336 public and 3,279 private schools in the school samples. From these schools, 56,051 public school teachers and

9,166 private school teachers were selected for the 1990–91 SASS sample of teachers.

The public school sample for the 1990–91 SASS was based on the 1988–89 school year Common Core of Data (CCD), a file of information collected annually by NCES from all state education agencies. All public schools in the file were stratified by state and by instructional levels (elementary, secondary, and combined). Within each stratum, the schools were sorted by urbanicity, ZIP code, ID number of the Local Education Agency (LEA), percent minority, highest grade in the school, school enrollment, and the CCD school ID. For each stratum, sample schools were selected by systematic sampling with probability proportional to the square root of the number of teachers within a school. Any school with a measure of size larger than the sampling interval was excluded from the probability sampling process and included in the sample with certainty.

The private school sample for the 1990–91 SASS was selected from the 1989–90 Private School Universe Survey (PSS). This data collection uses two components to develop estimates of the number of private schools in the United States; a list frame and an area frame. The list frame component consisted of approximately 22,600 schools from the 1986 Quality Education Data (QED) private school list and about 1,600 schools added in a 1989 update operation. The area frame consisted of a list of schools not included by QED on their private school listing and not reported by a private school association during the list frame updating operation.

The area frame sample contained 123 Primary Sampling Units (PSUs), each PSU consisting of a county or group of counties. Census field representatives conducted an area search using sources such as the telephone book, yellow pages, local government offices, chambers of commerce, and religious institutions to compile a list of all eligible private schools. This list was then compared to the existing SASS private school universe and nonmatches were added to the universe as part of the area frame. All private schools in the file were stratified by state and by three instructional levels (elementary, secondary, and combined). Within each stratum, the schools were sorted by urbanicity, ZIP code, highest grade in the school, school enrollment, and a number that identified the school. For each stratum, schools were selected by systematic sampling with probability proportional to the square root of the number of reported teachers from 1989–90 PSS. Any school with a measure of size larger than the sampling interval was excluded from the probability sampling process and included in the sample with certainty.

The School District and School Administrator Questionnaires were mailed out first in December 1990 and again to nonrespondents in January 1991.

The School District Questionnaires were mailed only to public schools because private schools are not categorized by districts. The weighted response rate for the Public School District Questionnaire was 93.5 percent. Weighted response rates for Public and Private Administrator Questionnaires were 96.7 percent and 90.0 percent respectively.

The School and School Teacher Questionnaires were mailed first between January–February 1991 and again in February–March 1991. Weighted response rates for the School Questionnaires were 95.3 percent for public schools and 83.9 percent for private schools. Five percent of public schools and 11 percent of private schools did not provide a listing of teachers in their schools to allow NCES to select a teacher sample. Weighted response rates for School Teacher Questionnaires were 90.3 percent for public teachers and 84.3 percent of private teachers.

Item response rates were varied, but generally high ranging from 85 to 100 percent for district surveys, 90 to 100 percent for public administrator surveys, 80 to 100 percent for private administrator surveys, 56 to 100 percent for public school surveys, 67 to 100 percent for private school surveys, 76 to 100 percent for public teacher surveys and 71 to 100 percent for private teacher surveys.

Public use and restricted use microdata files are available. More detailed information on the design and results of the 1990–91 SASS can be found in *1990–91 Schools and Staffing Survey Sample Design and Estimation* (NCES 93–449) and *Schools and Staffing in the United States: A Statistical Profile, 1990–91* (NCES 93–146). Information and results from the 1987–88 SASS can be found in *Schools and Staffing in the United States: A Statistical Profile, 1987–88* (NCES 92–127) and *1988 Schools and Staffing Survey Sample Design and Estimation,* (NCES 91–127).

For more information about this survey, contact:

Sharon Bobbitt
Elementary and Secondary Education Statistics
  Division
National Center for Education Statistics
555 New Jersey Avenue NW
Washington, DC 20208–5651

Office for Civil Rights

Civil Rights Survey of Elementary and Secondary Schools

The Office for Civil Rights (OCR), U.S. Department of Education, conducts biennial surveys of public school districts and of schools within those districts. Data are obtained on the characteristics of pupils enrolled in public schools throughout the Nation. Such information is required under Title VI of the Civil Rights Act of 1964, Title IX of the Education Amendments of 1972, and Section 504 of the Rehabilitation Act of 1973 to enable OCR to carry out its compliance responsibilities. The 1990 survey included the 100 largest public school districts, those of special interest (i.e., court order, compliance review), and a stratified random sample of approximately 3,500 districts representing approximately 40,000 schools. School, district, and national data are currently available.

Further information is available from:

Peter McCabe
Office for Civil Rights
U.S. Department of Education
330 C Street SW
Washington, DC 20202

The Office of Special Education and Rehabilitative Services

Annual Report to Congress on the Implementation of the Education of the Handicapped Act

The Individual with Disabilities Education Act (IDEA), formerly the Education of the Handicapped Act (EHA) requires the Secretary of Education to transmit to Congress annually a report describing the progress in serving the nation's handicapped children. The annual report contains information on children served by the public schools under the provisions of Part B of the IDEA and for children served in state-operated programs (SOP) for the handicapped under Title I of the Elementary and Secondary Education Act (ESEA). Statistics on children receiving special education and related services in various settings and school personnel providing such services are reported in an annual submission of data to the Office of Special Education and Rehabilitative Services (OSERS), by the 50 states, the District of Columbia, and the outlying areas. The child count information is based on the number of handicapped children receiving special education and related services on December 1st of each year.

Since each participant in programs for the handicapped is reported to OSERS, the data are not subject to sampling error. However, nonsampling error can occur from a variety of sources. Some states follow a noncategorical approach to the delivery of special education services, but produce counts by handicapping condition because EHA–B requires it. In those states that do categorize their handicapped students, definitions and labeling practices vary.

Further information on the Annual Report to Congress may be obtained from:

Office of Special Education Programs
Office of Special Education and Rehabilitative
  Services
330 C Street SW
Washington, DC 20202

National Longitudinal Transition Study of Special Education Students

As part of the 1983 amendments to the Education of the Handicapped Act (EHA), Congress requested that the U.S. Department of Education conduct a national longitudinal study of the transition of secondary special education students to determine how they fare in terms of education, employment, and independent living. A 5-year study was mandated, which was to include youth from ages 13 to 21 who were in special education at the time they were selected and who represented all 11 federal disability categories. Data were drawn from extensive telephone interviews with parents, from school records, and from a survey of educators in secondary schools attended by youth in the study.

The study was conducted by SRI International and began in April, 1987. The National Transition Study involves a nationally representative sample of more than 8,000 secondary-age youth with disabilities. A sample of 450 school districts was randomly selected from the universe of approximately 14,000 school districts serving secondary special education students. An additional replacement sample of 176 additional districts was selected due to a low rate of agreement to participate from the initial group of districts. Participation in the study was invited from the approximately 80 special schools serving secondary-age deaf, blind, and deaf-blind schools. A total of approximately 300 school districts and 25 special schools agreed to have youth selected for the study.

For further information about this study, contact:

Office of Special Education and Rehabilitative
  Services
Office of Special Education Programs
330 C Street SW
Washington, DC 20202

Other Governmental Agencies

Bureau of the Census

Current Population Survey

Current estimates of school enrollment, as well as social and economic characteristics of students, are based on data collected in the Census Bureau's monthly household survey of about 60,000 households. The monthly Current Population Survey (CPS) sample consists of 729 areas comprising 1,973 counties, independent cities, and minor civil divisions throughout the 50 states and the District of Columbia. The sample was initially selected from the 1980 census files and is periodically updated to reflect new housing construction.

The monthly CPS deals primarily with labor force data for the civilian noninstitutional population (i.e., excluding military personnel and their families living on post and inmates of institutions). In addition, in October of each year, supplemental questions are asked about highest grade completed, level and grade of current enrollment, attendance status, number and type of courses, degree or certificate objective, and type of organization offering instruction for each member of the household. In March of each year, supplemental questions on income are asked. The responses to these questions are combined with answers to two questions on educational attainment: highest grade of school ever attended, and whether that grade was completed.

The estimation procedure employed for the monthly CPS data involves inflating weighted sample results to independent estimates of characteristics of the civilian noninstitutional population in the United States by age, sex, and race. These independent estimates are based on statistics from decennial censuses; statistics on births, deaths, immigration, and emigration; and statistics on the population in the armed services. Generalized standard error tables are provided in the Current Population Reports. The data are subject to both nonsampling and sampling errors.

Further information is available in the *Current Population Reports, Series P–20,* or by contacting:

Education and Social Stratification Branch
Population Division
Bureau of the Census
U.S. Department of Commerce
Washington, DC 20233

School Enrollment

Each October, the Current Population Survey (CPS) includes supplemental questions on the enrollment status of the population 3 years old and over. The main sources of nonsampling variability in the responses to the supplement are those inherent in the survey instrument. The question of current enrollment may not be answered accurately for various reasons. Some respondents may not know current grade information for every student in the household, a problem especially prevalent for households with members in college or in nursery school. Confusion over college credits or hours taken by a student may make it difficult to determine the year in which the student is enrolled. Problems may occur with the definition of nursery school (a group or class organized to provide educational experiences for children), where respondents' interpretations of "educational experiences" vary.

Examples of sampling variability in the estimates of school enrollment rates are given in Table A11. Questions concerning the CPS "School Enrollment" survey may be directed to:

Education and Social Stratification Branch
Bureau of the Census
U.S. Department of Commerce
Washington, DC 20233

Educational Attainment

Data on years of school completed are derived from two questions on the Current Population Survey (CPS) instrument. Formal reports documenting educational attainment are produced by the Bureau of the Census using March CPS results. The latest report is Educational Attainment in the United States, March 1993 and 1992, Series P–20, No. 476, which is available from the Government Printing Office.

In addition to the general constraints of the CPS, some data indicate that the respondents have a tendency to overestimate the educational level of members of their household. Some inaccuracy is due to a lack of the respondent's knowledge of the exact educational attainment of each household member and the hesitancy to acknowledge anything less than a high school education. Another cause of nonsampling variability is the change in the numbers in the armed services over the years. In 1970, 25 percent of all males 20 and 21 years old were in the armed services. By 1974, this had decreased to less than 10 percent. The exclusion of members of the armed services appears to increase the proportion of the CPS population with some college and decrease the proportion of those who finished high school but went no further. After 1974, there was more stability in the proportion of young men in the military.

Beginning with the data for March 1980, tabulations have been controlled to the 1980 census. Examples of the sampling variability in the estimates of educational attainment are given in Table A12. The figures shown in the table hold for total or white population estimates only. The variability in estimates for subgroups (region, household relationships, etc.) can be estimated using the tables presented in Current Population Reports.

Questions concerning "Educational Attainment in the United States" may be directed to:

Education and Social Stratification Branch
Bureau of the Census
U.S. Department of Commerce
Washington, DC 20233

Government Finances

The Census Bureau conducts an annual survey of Government Finances as authorized by law under Title 13, United States Code, Section 182. This survey covers the entire range of government finance activities: revenue, expenditure, debt, and assets. Revenues and expenditures comprise actual receipts and payments of a government and its agencies, including government-operated enterprises, utilities, and public trust funds. The expenditure reporting categories comprise all amounts of money paid out by a government and its agencies with the exception of amounts for debt retirement and for loan, investment, agency, and private trust transactions.

Most of the federal government statistics for 1994 are based on figures that appear in The Budget of the United States Government for the Fiscal Year 1995. Since the classification used by the Census Bureau for reporting state and local government finance statistics differs in a number of important respects from the classification used in the United States Budget, it was necessary to adjust the federal data. For this report, federal budget expenditures include interest accrued, but not paid, during the fiscal year; Census data on interest are on a disbursement basis.

The state government finances for 1991 are based primarily on the annual Census Bureau survey of state finances for fiscal year 1991. Census staff compiled figures from official records and reports of the various states for most of the state financial data.

The sample of local governments is drawn from the 1987 Census of Governments and consists of certain local governments taken with certainty plus a sample below the certainty level.

The statistics in this Census report, Governmental Finances, that are based wholly or partly on data from the sample are subject to sampling error. State government finance data are not subject to sampling error. Estimates of major United States totals for local governments are subject to a computed sampling variability of less than one-half of I percent. The estimates are also subject to the inaccuracies in classification, response, and processing which would occur if a complete census had been conducted under the same conditions as the sample.

Further information can be obtained from:

Governments Division
Bureau of the Census
U.S. Department of Commerce
Washington, DC 20233

1990 Census of Population—Education in the United States

This report is based on a part of the decennial census which consists of questions asked of a 1-in-

6 sample of persons and housing units in the United States. This sample was asked more detailed questions about income, occupation and housing costs in addition to general demographic information.

School Enrollment

Persons classified as enrolled in school reported attending a "regular" public or private school or college at any time between February 1, 1990 and the time listed. Questions asked were whether the institution attended was public or private, and level of school in which the student was enrolled.

Educational Attainment

Data for educational attainment were tabulated for persons 15 years and over, and classified according to the highest grade completed or the highest degree received. Instructions were also given to include the level of the previous grade attended or the highest degree received for persons currently enrolled in school.

Poverty status

To determine poverty status, answers to income questions were used and compared to the appropriate poverty threshold. All persons except institutionalized persons, persons in military group quarters and in college dormitories, and unrelated persons under 15 years old were considered. If total income of each family or unrelated individual in the sample was less than the corresponding cutoff, that family or individual was classified as "below the poverty level."

Further information can be obtained from:

Population Division
Bureau of the Census
U.S. Department of Commerce
Washington, DC 20233

National Institute on Drug Abuse

The National Institute on Drug Abuse of the U.S. Department of Health and Human Services is the primary supporter of the long-term study entitled "Monitoring the Future: A Continuing Study of the Lifestyles and Values of Youth," conducted at the University of Michigan, Institute for Social Research. One component of the study deals with student drug abuse. Results of a national sample survey have been published annually since 1975. Approximately 125 to 135 schools have participated each year. With the exception of 1975 when about 9,400 students participated in the survey, the annual senior samples are comprised of roughly 17,000 students. They complete self-administered questionnaires given to them in their classrooms by University of Michigan personnel. Beginning in 1991, similar surveys of nationally representative samples of 8th- and 10th

grade samples have been conducted annually. The 10th grade samples involve about 15,000 students in 125 schools each year, while the 8th grade samples have approximately 18,000 students in 160 schools. Over the years, the response rate has varied from 77 to 84 percent. Table A15 provides examples of the survey's sampling error.

Understandably, there will be some reluctance to admit illegal activities. Also, students who were out of school on the day of the survey were nonrespondents. The survey did not include high school dropouts. The inclusion of these two groups would tend to increase the proportion of individuals who had used drugs. A 1983 study found that the inclusion of the absentees could increase some of the drug usage estimates by as much as 2.7 percent. (Details on that study and its methodology were published in *Drug Use Among American High School Students, College Students, and Other Young Adults,* by Lloyd D. Johnston, Patrick M. O'Malley, and Jerald G. Bachman, available from the National Clearinghouse on Drug Abuse Information, 5600 Fishers Lane, Rockville, MD 20857.)

Further information on this survey may be obtained from:

National Institute of Drug Abuse
Division of Epidemiology and Statistical Analysis
5600 Fishers Lane
Rockville, MD 20857

National Science Foundation

Survey of Earned Doctorates Awarded in the United States

The Survey of Earned Doctorates Awarded in the United States has collected basic statistics from the universe of doctoral recipients in the United States each year since 1958. It has been supported by five federal agencies: the National Science Foundation, in conjunction with the U.S. Department of Education; the National Endowment for the Humanities; the U.S. Department of Agriculture; and the National Institute of Health.

A survey form is distributed, with the assistance of graduate deans, to each person completing the requirements for a doctorate. Of the approximately 40,000 persons eligible for the survey, approximately 95 percent respond. The questionnaire obtains information on sex, race/ethnicity, marital status, citizenship, handicaps, dependents, specialty field of doctorate, educational institutions attended, time spent in completion of doctorate, financial support, educational debt, postgraduation plans, and educational attainment of parents. The data are collected, edited, and published by the National Academy of Sciences.

For further information contact:

Science and Engineering Education and
Human Resources Program
Division of Science Resources Studies
National Science Foundation
4201 Wilson BoulevardArlington, Virginia 22230

Federal Obligations to Universities, Colleges and Nonprofit Institutions

Each year, the National Science Foundation collects data on obligations to colleges and universities from federal agencies. Obligations differ from expenditures in that funds obligated during one fiscal year may be spent by the recipient in later years. The fiscal year 1991 data were submitted by 15 federal agencies. Obligation amounts include direct federal support, so that amounts subcontracted to other institutions are included. Those funds received through subcontracts from prime contractors are excluded. Also excluded from the data are certain types of financial assistance, such as the Department of Education's Guaranteed Student Loan Program and obligations to the U.S. service academies. For purposes of tabulations in this publication, university-administered federally funded research and development centers (FFRDCs) have been included in appropriate state totals.

The universe of academic institutions for this survey is based on the Integrated Postsecondary Education Data Survey conducted by the National Center for Education Statistics (see above). Institutions without federal support were excluded and some systems were combined into single reporting units.

Further information on this survey may be obtained from *Federal Support to Universities, Colleges, and Nonprofit Institutions,* published by the National Science Foundation, or by contacting:

Science and Engineering Activities Program
Division of Science Resources Studies
National Science Foundation
4201 Wilson Boulevard
Arlington, Virginia 22230

Survey of Scientific and Engineering Expenditures at Universities and Colleges

The National Science Foundation's annual academic survey collects data on research and development expenditures in the sciences and engineering from a sample of 459 institutions in the United States and outlying areas. Those institutions were selected from the universe of 595 schools that grant a graduate science or engineering degree and/or perform activities for which at least $50,000 has been funded from separately budgeted R&D expenditures. In addition, the survey includes 19 university-affiliated, federally funded research and development centers (FFRDCs).

The 459 institutions sampled for FY 1991, include all doctorate-granting institutions, all historically black colleges and universities with any R&D expenditures, and a random sample of all other institutions. The response rate was 97 percent. Data presented are assembled from the most recently completed survey and represent the latest totals available as of August 1992.

Further information on this survey may be obtained from *Academic Science/Engineering, R&D Funds,* published by the National Science Foundation, or by contacting:

Science and Engineering Activities Program
Division of Science Resources Studies
National Science Foundation
4201 Wilson Boulevard
Arlington, Virginia 22230

Other Organization Sources

American College Testing Program

The American College Testing (ACT) Assessment is designed to measure educational development in the areas of English, mathematics, social studies, and natural sciences. The ACT Assessment is taken by college-bound high school students and the test results are used to predict how well students might perform in college.

Prior to the 1984–85 school year, national norms were based on a 10 percent sample of the students taking the test. Since then, national norms are based on the test scores of all students taking the test. Moreover, beginning with 1984–85, these norms have been based on the most recent ACT scores available from students scheduled to graduate in the spring of the year. Duplicate test records are no longer used to produce national figures.

Separate ACT standard scores are computed for English, mathematics, social studies, science reasoning, and, as of October 1989, reading. ACT standard scores are reported for each subject area on a scale from 1 to 36. The four ACT standard scores have a mean (average) of about 19 and a standard deviation of about 6 for college-bound students nationally. A composite score is obtained by taking the simple average of the four standard scores and is an indication of student's overall academic development across these subject areas. Beginning with the October 1989 test date, a new version of the ACT was introduced.

It should be noted that college-bound students who take the ACT Assessment are not representative of college-bound students nationally. First, students who live in the Midwest, Rocky Mountains and

Plains, and the South are overrepresented among ACT-tested students as compared with college-bound students nationally. Second, ACT-tested students tend to enroll in public colleges and universities more frequently than do college-bound students nationally.

For further information, contact:

The American College Testing Program
2201 North Dodge Street
P.O. Box 168
Iowa City, IA 52243

American Federation of Teachers

The American Federation of Teachers (AFT) has reported national and state average salaries and earnings for teachers, other school employees, government workers, and professional employees over the past 25 years. The AFT's survey of state departments of education obtains information on minimum salaries, experienced teachers reentering the classroom, and teacher age and experience. Most data from the survey are reported as received, although some data are confirmed by telephone. These data are available in the AFT's annual report *Salary and Analysis of Salary Trends.* While this serves as the primary vehicle for reporting the results of the AFT's annual survey of state departments of education, several other data sources are also used in the report.

Further information on this survey can be obtained from:

American Federation of Teachers
555 New Jersey Avenue NW
Washington, DC 20001

College Entrance Examination Board

The Admissions Testing Program of the College Board comprises a number of college admissions tests, including the Preliminary Scholastic Aptitude Test (PSAT) and the Scholastic Aptitude Test (SAT). High school students participate in the testing program as sophomores, juniors, or seniors—some more than once during these 3 years. If they have taken the tests more than once, only the most recent scores are tabulated. The PSAT and SAT report subscores in the areas of mathematics and verbal ability.

The SAT results are not representative of high school students or college-bound students nationally since the sample is self-selected. Generally, tests are taken by students who need the results to attend a particular college or university. The state totals are greatly affected by the requirements of its state colleges. Public colleges in a number of states require ACT scores rather than SAT scores. Thus, the pro-

portion of students taking the SAT in these states is very low and is inappropriate for any comparison. In recent years, more than 1 million high school students have taken the examination annually.

Further information on the SAT can be obtained from:

College Entrance Examination Board
Educational Testing Service
Princeton, NJ 08541

Council for Aid to Education

The Council for Aid to Education, Inc., (CFAE) is a not-for-profit corporation funded by contributions from business. CFAE largely provides consulting and research services on voluntary support to corporations and information services to education institutions. Each year CFAE conducts a survey of colleges and universities and private elementary and secondary schools to obtain information on the amounts, sources, and purposes of private gifts, grants, and bequests received during the academic year.

In the 1991–92 study, survey forms were sent to approximately 2,900 colleges and universities and 1,280 responded. The response rates were much higher for the 4-year colleges than for the 2-year colleges. For example, 89 percent of the doctoral-level institutions and 55 percent of the comprehensive and general baccalaureate colleges participated in the survey, but only 12 percent of the 2-year colleges responded. CFAE estimates that about 84 percent of all voluntary support is reported in the survey because of the high participation of institutions receiving large amounts of funding.

Survey forms are reviewed by CFAE for internal consistency before preparing a computerized database. Institutional reports of voluntary support data from the CFAE "Survey of Voluntary Support of Education" are more comprehensive and detailed than the related data in the "Financial Statistics of Institutions of Higher Education" survey conducted by NCES. The results from the "Survey of Voluntary Support of Education" are published in the annual *Voluntary Support of Education,* which may be purchased from CFAE.

Further information is available from:

Director of Research
Council for Aid to Education, Inc.
51 Madison Avenue
Suite 2200
New York, NY 10010

Council of Chief State School Officers

The Council of Chief State School Officers (CCSSO) is a nonprofit organization of the 57 public officials who head departments of public education in every state, the outlying areas, the District of Columbia, and the Department of Defense Dependents Schools. In 1985, the CCSSO founded the State Education Assessment Center to provide a locus of leadership by the states to improve the monitoring and assessment of education. *State Education Indicators, 1993* is the principal report of the Assessment Center's program of indicators on education. Most of the data are obtained from a member questionnaire; the remainder of the data are obtained from federal government agencies. Information on mathematics education was taken from *CCSSO, State Policies on Science and Mathematics Evaluation, 1992.*

For additional information, contact:

Ramsay Selden
State Education Assessment Center
Council of Chief State School Officers
One Massachusetts Avenue, NW
7th Floor
Washington, DC 20001

Council of State Directors of Programs for the Gifted

The Council of State Directors of Programs for the Gifted is composed of the director or individual in the leadership position for gifted education in each of the 50 states, the District of Columbia, and the outlying areas. The Council has conducted many surveys in the past and most recently conducted two comprehensive state surveys in order to produce a profile of gifted education throughout the Nation. These data are reported in the 1985, 1987, and 1990 "State of the States Gifted and Talented Education" reports. This edition of the *Digest* uses data from the 1989–90 school year.

Further information is available from:

Evie Hiatt, President
Council of State Directors of Programs for the Gifted
Care of Texas Education Agency
Division of Adult Education
1701 North Congress
Austin, Texas 78701

Education Commission of the States

The Education Commission of the States (ECS) Clearinghouse collects information on laws and standards in the field of education and reports them periodically in "Clearinghouse Notes." The Commission collects information about administrators, principals, and teachers. It also examines policy areas, such as assessment and testing, collective bargaining, early childhood issues, quality education, and school schedules. The information is collected by reading state newsletters, tracking state legislation, and surveying state education agencies. Data are

verified by the individual states when necessary. Even though ECS monitors state activity on a continuous basis, it updates the reports only when there is significant change in state activity.

Further information is available from:

Chris Pipho
Education Commission of the States
1860 Lincoln Street, Suite 300
Denver, CO 80295

Gallup Poll

Each year the Gallup Poll conducts the "Public Attitudes Toward the Public Schools" survey, funded by Phi Delta Kappa. The survey includes interviews with over 1,600 adults representing the civilian noninstitutional population 18 years old and over.

The sample used in the 25th annual survey was made up of a total of 1,306 respondents and is described as a modified probability sample of the nation. Personal, in-home interviewing was conducted in representative communities.

The survey is a sample survey and is subject to sampling error. The size of error depends largely on the number of respondents providing data. Table A16 shows the approximate sampling errors associated with different percentages and sample sizes for the survey. Table A17 provides approximate sampling errors for comparisons of two sample percentages.

For example, an estimated percentage of about 10 percent based on the responses of 1,000 sample members has an approximate sampling error of 2 percent at the 95 percent confidence level. The sampling error for the difference in two percentages (50 percent versus 41 percent) based on two samples of 750 members and 400 members, respectively, is about 8 percent at the 95 percent confidence level.

Further information on this survey can be obtained from:

Neville Robertson
Phi Delta Kappa
P.O. Box 789
Bloomington, IN 47402–0789

Independent Sector

In 1992, Independent Sector commissioned the Gallup Poll to conduct a national survey on the giving and volunteering behavior of Americans. This survey is part of a series of surveys that will be conducted every 2 years. The information was obtained from in-home personal interviews conducted from April 3 to May 17, 1992, with a representative national sample of 2,671 adult Americans 18 or more years old. The sampling procedure did not include those with incomes above $200,000 because they constitute such a small percentage of the population.

The results from this survey are published in Giving and Volunteering in the United States and may be purchased from:

Independent Sector
1828 L Street NW
Washington, DC 20036

International Association for the Evaluation of Educational Achievement (IEA)

The International Association for the Evaluation of Educational Achievement, known as the IEA, is comprised of research centers and scholars from around the world whose aim is to investigate education problems common among countries. In 1988, the IEA General Assembly, composed of the research institutes participating in IEA projects, decided to undertake a study of reading literacy. The study held its first National Research Coordinator (NRC) meeting in November 1988. The construction and pilot testing of instruments was conducted in the period from November 1988 to July 1990. The main testing took place in the period October 1990 to April 1991 depending on the school year in each country. Thirty-two school systems were involved in the IEA Reading Literacy Study. Data were collected from 210,059 students, 10,518 teachers, and 9,073 schools. All students took reading tests for two sessions totaling 75 minutes at the 9-year-old level and two sessions totaling 85 minutes at the 14-year-old population. All students responded to a background questionnaire about their reading at home and at school. Teachers and school principals responded to questionnaires about themselves, their teaching and the school organization. Each national center (NCES was the center for the United States) completed a National Case Study Questionnaire.

For more information, contact:

Marilyn Binkley, NRC USA
National Center for Education Statistics
555 New Jersey Avenue, NW
Washington, DC 20208-5650
Institute of International Education

Each year the Institute of International Education (IIE) conducts a survey of the number of foreign students studying in American colleges and universities and reports these data in Open Doors, an annual publication. All of the regionally accredited institutions in the Education Directory, Colleges and Universities published by NCES are surveyed by IIE. The data presented in the Digest are drawn from the IIE survey which requests the total enrollment of foreign students in an institution and information on student characteristics, such as country of origin. For the 1992–93 survey, 2,583 out of 2,783 (92.8 percent) institutions reported data for the survey.

Additional information can be obtained from the publication Open Doors or by contacting:

Marianthi Zikopoulos
Institute of International Education
809 United Nations Plaza
New York, NY 10017-3580

Metropolitan Life Insurance Company

The Metropolitan Life Survey of the American Teacher for the Metropolitan Life Insurance Company was conducted by Louis Harris and Associates. This survey was designed to measure the experiences of new public school teachers who began their first year of teaching in the 1990–91 school year. It includes questions on their experiences with students, administrators, other teachers, and parents. There were three surveys of this cohort of new teachers. The first survey was conducted during the summer of 1990 to measure the expectations of new graduates from teaching schools immediately prior to their first year of teaching in public schools. The second survey compared how these new teachers' experiences in their first year of teaching affected their attitudes, and how the actual experience of teaching compared with their prior expectations. The current survey focuses on these teachers' experience two years into their teaching career. It includes questions which allow comparisons on their attitudes toward teaching now versus one and two years ago.

A total of 1,000 teachers who began their first year of teaching in the public schools in the 1990–91 school year were surveyed. The sample was designed to be representative of all new teachers in the public schools who graduated from teaching colleges in 1990 and taught for the first time in a public school in the 1990–91 school year.

The sample was drawn from lists of 1990 graduates from a probability sample of colleges listed by the American Association of Colleges for Teacher Education. Graduates who did not teach full-time in public schools in 1990–91 were excluded from the sample.

The priority for fielding the sample was as follows: first, any respondents from the second phase of the study (after the first year of teaching); second, any respondents from the first phase (before teaching) who were not also included in the second phase; finally, any remaining teachers from the original sample group who were not used in the first phase.

All interviews were conducted by telephone in May and June 1992.

For more information contact:

Metropolitan Life Survey of the American Teacher
Metropolitan Life Insurance Company
One Madison Avenue
New York, NY 10010

National Association of State Scholarship and Grant Programs

The National Association of State Scholarship and Grant Programs (NASSGP) is an association of states with general programs of scholarship or grant assistance for undergraduate study. Executive officers responsible for grant program administration represent each state in the Association. The publication of the *23rd Annual Survey Report: 1991–92 Academic Year* represents the twelfth year that the Pennsylvania Higher Education Assistance Agency has produced the NASSGP annual report. Data are reported for all 50 states, the District of Columbia, and Puerto Rico.

For more information on this survey, contact:

Deb Heberle
Research and Statistics
Pennsylvania Higher Education Assistance Agency
Towne House
660 Boas Street
Harrisburg, PA 17102

National Education Association

The National Education Association (NEA) reports enrollment, expenditure, revenue, graduate, teacher, and instructional staff salary data in its annual publication, *Estimates of School Statistics.* Each year NEA prepares regression-based estimates of financial and other education statistics and submits them to the states for verification. Generally about 30 states adjust these estimates based on their own data. These preliminary data are published by NEA along with revised data from previous years. States are asked to revise previously submitted data as final figures become available. The most recent publication contains all changes reported to the NEA.

Status of the America Public School Teacher

The "Status of the American Public School Teacher" survey is conducted every 5 years by the National Education Association (NEA). The survey was designed by the NEA Research Division and initially administered in 1956. The intent of the survey is to solicit information covering various aspects of public school teachers' professional, family, and civic lives.

Participants for the survey are selected using a two-stage sample design, with the first-stage stratum determined by the number of students enrolled in the districts. Selection probabilities are determined so that the resulting sample is self-weighting. In 1990–91, questionnaires were sent to a sample of 1,981 of the nation's approximately 2,400,000 public school teachers. With an initial and four follow-up mailings, 1,499 questionnaires were returned, of which 145 were not usable. The sample was adjusted to 1,836 to reflect the 145 unusable responses. The response rate was 73.7 percent.

Possible sources of nonsampling errors are nonresponses, misinterpretation, and—when comparing data over years—changes in the sampling method and instrument. Misinterpretation of the survey items should be minimal, as the sample responding is not from the general population but one knowledgeable about the area of concern. Also, the sampling procedure changed after 1956 and some wording of items has changed over the different administrations.

Since sampling is used, sampling variability is inherent in the data. An approximation to the maximum standard error for estimating the population percentages is 1.4 percent. To estimate the 90 percent confidence interval for population percentages, the maximum standard error of 1.4 percent is multiplied by 1.65 (1.4 x 1.65). The resulting percentage (2.3) is added and subtracted from the population estimate to establish upper and lower bounds for the confidence interval. For example, if a sample percentage is 60 percent, there is a 90 percent chance that the population percentage lies between 57.7 percent and 62.3 percent (60 percent ±2.3 percent).

Questions concerning the "Status of the American Public School Teacher" survey may be directed to:

National Education Association—Research
1201 16th Street NW
Washington, DC 20036

Organization for Economic Cooperation and Development

The Organization for Economic Cooperation and Development (OECD) publishes analyses of national policies in education, training, and economics in more than 20 countries. The countries surveyed are: Australia, Austria, Belgium, Canada, Czeck and Slovak Federal Republic, Denmark, Finland, France, Germany, Hungary, Ireland, Italy, Japan, Luxembourg, Netherlands, New Zealand, Norway, Portugal, Spain, Sweden, Switzerland, Turkey, United Kingdom, United States, and (the former) Yugoslavia.

Since only developed nations, mostly European, are included in these studies, the range of analysis is limited. However, OECD data allow for some detailed international comparison of financial resources or other education variables to be made for this selected group of countries.

In the past several years, OECD has revised its data collection procedures to highlight current education issues. The Centre for Educational Research and Innovation (CERI) has developed an Indicators of Education Systems (INES) project involving representatives of the OECD countries and the OECD Secretariat to improve international education statistics. Large improvements in data quality and comparability among OECD countries have resulted from the country to country interaction sponsored through the INES project. The most recent publication in this series is *Education at a Glance* (1993).

More complete information on INES may be obtained from:

Norberto Bottani
INES/OECD
2, rue Andre-Pascal
75775 Paris CEDEX 16
France

Research Associates of Washington

Research Associates annually compiles the Higher Education Price Index (HEPI) which measures average changes in prices of goods and services purchased by colleges and universities through current-fund educational and general expenditures. Sponsored research and auxiliary enterprises are not priced by the HEPI.

The HEPI is based on the prices (or salaries) of faculty and of administrators and other professional service personnel; clerical, technical, service, and other nonprofessional personnel; and contracted services, such as data processing, communication, transportation, supplies and materials, equipment, books and periodicals, and utilities. These represent the items purchased for current operations by colleges and universities. Prices for these items are obtained from salary surveys conducted by various national higher education associations, the American Association of University Professors, the Bureau of Labor Statistics, and the National Center for Education Statistics; and from components of the Consumer Price Index (CPI) and the Producer Price Index (PPI) published by the U.S. Department of Labor, Bureau of Labor Statistics.

The quantities of these goods and services have been kept constant based on the 1971–72 buying pattern of colleges and universities. The weights assigned the various items priced, which represent their relative importance in the current–fund educational and general budget, are estimated national averages. Variance in spending patterns of individual institutions from these national averages reduces only slightly the applicability of the HEPI to any given institutional situation. Modest differences in the weights attached to expenditure categories have little effect on overall index values. This is because the HEPI is dominated by the trend in faculty salaries and similar salary trends for other personnel hired by institutions, which absorbs or diminishes the effects of price changes in other items purchased in small quantities.

For more information, contact:

Research Associates
Kent Halstead
2605 Klingle Road, NW
Washington, DC 20008

United Nations Educational, Scientific, and Cultural Organization

The United Nations Educational, Scientific, and Cultural Organization (UNESCO) conducts annual surveys of education statistics of its member countries. Besides official surveys, data are supplemented by information obtained by UNESCO through other publications and sources. Each year more than 200 countries reply to the UNESCO surveys. In some cases, estimates are made by UNESCO for particular items such as world and continent totals. While great efforts are made to make them as comparable as possible, the data still reflect the vast differences among the countries of the world in the structure of education. While there is some agreement about the reporting of first- and second-level data, the third level (postsecondary education) presents numerous substantial problems. Some countries report only university enrollment while other countries report all postsecondary, including vocational and technical schools and correspondence programs. A very high proportion of some countries' third-level students attend institutions in other countries. While definition problems are many in this sort of study, other survey problems should not be overlooked. The member countries that provide data to UNESCO are responsible for their validity. Thus, data for particular countries are subject to nonsampling error and perhaps sampling error as well. Some countries may furnish only rough estimates, while data from other countries may be very accurate. Other difficulties are caused by the varying periodicity of data collection among the countries of the world. In spite of such problems, many researchers use UNESCO data because they are the best available for such a large group of countries. Users should examine footnotes carefully to recognize some of the data limitations.

More complete information may be obtained from the *Statistical Yearbook* published by UNESCO or from:

Office of Statistics
UNESCO
7, Place de Fontenoy
75700 Paris
France

Table A1.—Standard errors for enrollment and completion status of first-time postsecondary students starting during the 1989–90 academic year, by degree objective and other student characteristics: Spring 1992

Student characteristics	Vocational certificate						Associate degree standard errors				Bachelor's degree standard errors		
	Completed 9 months or less				Standard error								
	Estimate	Standard error	95 percent confidence interval		Completed in over 9 months	Not completed	Completed	Continuously enrolled	Stopped and re-enrolled[1]	Stopped, no re-enrollment[2]	Continuously enrolled	Stopped and re-enrolled[1]	Stopped, no re-enrollment[2]
			Lower	Upper									
Total	29.2	2.4	24.5	33.9	1.9	2.6	1.3	2.0	2.1	2.1	1.4	1.1	1.2
Male	30.8	3.9	23.2	38.4	2.9	4.3	1.9	3.1	2.7	3.1	1.9	1.6	1.7
Female	28.1	3.0	22.2	34.0	2.4	3.3	1.8	2.2	2.5	2.8	1.8	1.5	1.3
Race													
White, non-Hispanic	29.6	2.6	24.5	34.7	2.4	3.0	1.4	2.1	2.2	2.2	1.5	1.2	1.4
Black, non-Hispanic	26.4	6.1	14.4	38.4	4.3	6.2	3.3	4.2	6.2	6.1	3.9	3.7	3.2
Hispanic	23.2	6.0	11.4	35.0	2.9	7.4	5.6	7.4	7.6	7.9	5.5	5.6	5.2
Socioeconomic status													
Low (25 percent)	36.6	4.3	28.2	45.0	2.4	4.3	1.6	5.0	4.4	5.4	5.1	4.4	5.0
Middle (50 percent)	28.0	3.0	22.1	33.9	2.6	3.4	1.7	2.1	3.1	3.2	2.3	1.7	2.1
High (25 percent)	16.4	4.9	6.8	26.0	6.3	7.1	2.6	3.3	3.0	3.8	1.7	1.5	1.3
Dependent student family income													
Less than $20,000	35.3	3.0	29.4	41.2	1.9	3.1	1.3	2.5	2.6	3.0	2.8	2.3	2.5
$20,000 to $39,999	10.8	2.3	6.3	15.3	5.1	5.7	3.2	3.9	3.7	3.9	2.3	2.0	1.9
$40,000 to $59,999	16.3	5.8	4.9	27.7	9.0	8.4	3.3	4.4	4.7	5.0	2.5	2.2	2.2
$60,000 or more	(3)	(3)	(3)	(3)	(3)	(3)	4.7	4.3	5.2	5.5	2.3	1.8	1.6
Time between high school graduation and entering postsecondary education													
12 months or less	36.1	3.0	30.2	42.0	3.1	4.0	1.9	2.5	2.4	2.6	1.4	1.2	1.1
More than 12 months	19.4	3.0	13.5	25.3	2.3	3.2	1.2	2.5	3.4	3.8	4.7	3.9	4.0
Marital/family status as of spring 1992													
Married, no children	22.6	4.6	13.6	31.6	5.7	7.2	3.8	5.6	5.2	7.9	5.5	4.9	7.1
Married, with children	42.2	4.3	33.8	50.6	2.8	4.1	1.3	3.2	4.4	4.9	4.6	5.3	5.8
Single, no children	22.6	3.0	16.7	28.5	3.3	4.0	2.0	2.7	2.8	2.5	1.5	1.3	1.1
Single, with children	17.6	5.0	7.8	27.4	4.2	6.4	4.4	4.9	8.4	9.3	(3)	(3)	(3)
Expected degree level													
Less than 2 years	33.7	3.7	26.4	41.0	3.2	4.0	2.0	(3)	(3)	(3)	(3)	(3)	(3)
2 to 4 years	23.4	4.1	15.4	31.4	2.6	4.7	2.1	3.3	4.7	4.2	(3)	(3)	(3)
Bachelor's or higher	29.0	4.1	21.0	37.0	3.2	4.4	1.6	2.4	2.2	2.4	1.4	1.1	1.2
Average hours worked per week while enrolled													
None	30.8	4.1	22.8	38.8	3.2	4.3	2.8	4.6	3.9	4.9	2.7	2.2	1.9
1 to 20 hours	23.5	5.0	13.7	33.3	5.7	6.6	2.9	3.4	3.8	4.4	2.1	1.4	1.7
More than 20 hours	29.3	3.1	23.2	35.4	2.3	3.4	1.5	2.3	2.7	2.7	2.1	1.7	1.9
Involvement in school activities													
Never involved	34.7	4.0	26.9	42.5	2.7	4.3	2.1	3.2	4.1	4.3	4.4	4.3	4.4
Once	24.2	3.9	16.6	31.8	3.4	4.5	2.0	3.0	3.0	3.3	2.7	2.1	2.3
Sometimes	26.1	4.6	17.1	35.1	4.0	5.3	2.7	3.6	3.7	4.1	1.8	1.6	1.4
Often	(3)	(3)	(3)	(3)	(3)	(3)	5.1	5.4	5.5	7.4	2.3	1.9	2.0
Received financial aid during 1989–90													
Yes	33.6	2.6	28.5	38.7	2.3	2.7	2.0	2.5	2.4	3.0	1.6	1.1	1.3
No	24.8	4.1	16.8	32.8	3.0	4.6	1.7	2.4	3.0	3.0	2.1	1.8	1.9

[1] Includes those students who were not enrolled for more than 4 months out of the year. Some students may not be enrolled at the time of the follow-up survey.

[2] Includes those students who stopped enrolling for more than 4 months and did not re-enroll during the survey period.

[3] Too few observations for a reliable estimate.

NOTE.—Data reflect completion and enrollment status by spring 1992 of first-time postsecondary students starting academic year 1989–90. Due to the limited time period covered by the survey, it was inappropriate to calculate bachelor's degree completion rates.

SOURCE: U.S. Department of Education, National Center for Education Statistics, Beginning Postsecondary Student Longitudinal Survey, 1992. (This table was prepared in April 1994.)

Table A2.—Respondent counts for selected High School and Beyond surveys

Classification variable and subgroup	Followup survey of 1980 sophomores in 1982	Followup survey of 1980 seniors in 1982	Followup survey of 1980 sophomores in 1984	Followup survey of 1980 seniors in 1984	Followup survey of 1980 sophomores in 1986	Followup survey of 1980 seniors in 1986
Total respondents (unweighted)	**25,830**	**11,227**	**11,463**	**10,925**	**11,248**	**10,536**
Sex						
Male	12,717	5,213	5,514	5,058	5,391	4,832
Female	13,113	6,014	5,949	5,867	5,857	5,704
Race/ethnicity						
White, non-Hispanic	17,295	5,180	7,285	5,057	7,194	5,246
Black, non-Hispanic	3,338	2,724	1,651	2,625	1,585	2,726
Hispanic	4,439	2,749	1,795	2,654	1,745	1,950
Asian or Pacific Islander	413	367	425	355	413	356
American Indian or Alaskan Native	248	191	253	185	246	200
Other or unclassified	97	16	54	49	65	58
Socioeconomic status composite (SES)[1]						
Low	6,752	3,940	2,831	3,857	2,751	3,668
Low-middle	6,234	2,390	2,624	2,314	2,559	2,289
High-middle	6,134	2,168	2,849	2,107	2,817	1,995
High	6,341	1,988	3,086	1,936	3,044	1,900
Unclassified	369	741	73	711	77	684
Father's highest level of education						
Less than high school	5,179	—	—	—	—	—
High school graduate[2]	11,961	—	—	—	—	—
College graduate[3]	5,169	—	—	—	—	—
Don't know/missing	3,521	—	—	—	—	—
High school program (self-reported)						
Academic	10,152	4,145	6,547	4,007	—	3,899
General	8,789	3,829	3,468	3,764	—	3,602
Vocational	6,664	2,660	3,611	2,581	—	2,481
Unclassified	225	593	56	573	—	554
High school type						
Public	—	9,969	8,647	9,727	—	9,385
Catholic	—	964	2,479	911	—	876
Other private	—	294	337	287	—	275
Postsecondary education status[4]						
Full-time	—	—	4,466	—	—	—
Part-time	—	—	3,275	—	—	—
Never enrolled	—	—	3,678	—	—	—
Missing/unclassified	—	—	44	—	—	—
October 1980 postsecondary education attendance status						
Part-time 2-year public institution	—	—	—	—	—	352
Part-time 4-year public institution	—	—	—	—	—	152
Full-time 2-year public institution	—	—	—	—	—	1,312
Full-time 4-year public institution	—	—	—	—	—	1,986
Full-time 4-year private institution	—	—	—	—	—	1,015
Not a student	—	—	—	—	—	4,523
Other and missing	—	—	—	—	—	1,196
Postsecondary education plans						
No plans	—	—	—	—	—	1,623
Attend vocational/technical school	—	—	—	—	—	1,835
Attend college less than four years	—	—	—	—	—	1,528
Earn bachelor's degree	—	—	—	—	—	2,631
Earn advanced degree	—	—	—	—	—	2,265
Missing	—	—	—	—	—	654
Participation in high school extracurricular activities[5]						
Never participated	—	—	—	—	—	1,024
Participated as a member	—	—	—	—	—	4,104
Participated as a leader	—	—	—	—	—	4,457

[1] The SES index is a composite of five equally weighted measures: father's education, mother's education, family income, father's occupation, and presence of certain items in the respondent's household.

[2] Includes attendance at a vocational, trade, or business school, or 2–year college; or attendance at a 4–year college resulting in less than a bachelor's degree.

[3] Includes those with a bachelor's or higher level degree.

[4] Postsecondary education status was determined by students' enrollment in academic or vocational study during the four semesters—fall 1982, spring 1983, fall 1983, and spring 1984—following their scheduled high school graduation. Students who enrolled in full-time study in each of the four semesters were classified as full time. Students who were enrolled in part-time study in any of the four semesters and those who were enrolled in full-time study in fewer than four semesters were classified as part time. Students who had neither enrolled on a full-time nor part-time basis in each of the four semesters were classified as never enrolled.

[5] Responses to questions concerning participation in each of 15 different extracurricular activity areas (i.e., varsity sports, debate, band, subject-matter clubs, etc.) were used to classify students' overall level of participation in extracurricular activities. The difference between the sum of the three category respondent counts and the total sample size is due to missing data.

—Data not applicable.

NOTE.—Data from students who dropped out of school between the 10th and 12th grades were not used in analyses of sophomore samples.

Table A3.—Design effects (DEFF) and root design effects (DEFT) for selected High School and Beyond surveys and subsamples

Subsample characteristic	Followup survey of 1980 sophomores in 1984	Followup survey of 1980 seniors in 1984	Followup survey of 1980 sophomores in 1986	Followup survey of 1980 seniors in 1986
Total sample	**2.40 (1.54)**	**2.87 (1.69)**	**2.19 (1.47)**	**2.28 (1.50)**
Sex				
Male	—	—	2.07 (1.43)	2.13 (1.45)
Female	—	—	2.06 (1.43)	2.26 (1.50)
Race/ethnicity				
White and other	2.06 (1.42)	2.09 (1.44)	1.92 (1.38)	1.70 (1.30)
Black	2.22 (1.47)	2.26 (1.50)	2.19 (1.47)	2.40 (1.54)
Hispanic	3.15 (1.73)	3.72 (1.92)	3.11 (1.76)	4.06 (2.01)
Socioeconomic status composite (SES)				
Low	1.91 (1.37)	2.28 (1.50)	1.83 (1.35)	2.31 (1.51)
Middle	1.95 (1.39)	1.81 (1.34)	2.06 (1.42)	2.02 (1.42)
High	2.05 (1.42)	1.93 (1.38)	1.92 (1.38)	1.71 (1.30)

—Not available

NOTE.—The average design effect for the 1980 sophomore cohort first followup (1982) survey is 3.59(1.89) and the average design effect for the 1980 senior first followup (1982) survey is 2.64(1.62).

Table A4.—Standard errors for the NAEP reading proficiency study: 1971 to 1992

Item	Standard error for estimate (mean) [1]			Standard error for percent of students reading at or above anchor level 200						Standard error for percent of students reading at or above anchor level 250					
	1971	1990	1992	1971	1975	1980	1988	1990	1992	1971	1975	1980	1988	1990	1992
9-year-olds															
Total	1.0	1.2	0.9	1.0	0.8	1.0	1.3	1.3	1.1	0.6	0.6	0.8	1.1	1.0	0.8
White	0.9	1.3	1.0	1.0	0.8	0.7	1.6	1.4	1.2	0.7	0.7	0.9	1.5	1.2	1.0
Black	1.7	2.9	2.2	1.5	1.5	1.9	2.9	3.4	2.2	0.5	0.3	0.6	1.2	1.5	0.8
Hispanic	—	2.3	3.1	—	3.0	2.6	3.3	2.7	3.5	—	0.5	1.4	2.3	2.0	2.3
13-year-olds															
Total	0.9	0.8	1.2	0.5	0.4	0.4	0.6	0.6	0.7	1.1	1.0	1.1	1.3	1.0	1.4
White	0.7	0.9	1.2	0.3	0.2	0.2	0.6	0.6	0.6	0.9	0.9	0.8	1.5	1.2	1.4
Black	1.2	2.2	2.3	1.7	1.3	1.7	2.2	2.3	2.7	1.2	1.6	2.0	2.3	3.5	2.7
Hispanic	—	2.3	3.5	—	2.3	2.4	2.6	2.4	3.5	—	3.6	2.6	4.4	2.9	5.1
17-year-olds															
Total	1.2	1.1	1.1	0.3	0.3	0.3	0.3	0.3	0.4	0.9	0.7	0.9	0.8	1.0	0.8
White	1.0	1.2	1.4	0.2	0.1	0.1	0.3	0.2	0.3	0.7	0.6	0.6	0.9	1.1	0.9
Black	1.7	2.3	2.4	1.5	1.8	1.7	1.0	1.3	1.6	1.6	1.6	2.0	2.4	2.8	2.3
Hispanic	—	3.6	3.7	—	2.4	1.8	2.4	2.1	2.3	—	4.1	3.1	4.8	4.7	4.0

[1] Item response theory is used as a basis to estimate performance at the three levels on a common scale from 0 to 500.

—Data not available.

Table A5.—Standard errors for the NAEP writing, history, and civics proficiency studies: 1976 to 1992

Item	Standard error for estimated (mean) [1] writing performance						Standard error for estimated (mean) [1] history performance, 1988			Standard error for estimated percent correct in civics					
	4th grade		8th grade		11th grade		4th grade	8th grade	12th grade	13-year-olds			17-year-olds		
	1984	1992	1984	1992	1984	1992				1976	1982	1988	1976	1982	1988
Total	**1.5**	**1.5**	**2.0**	**1.3**	**1.6**	**1.4**	**0.9**	**0.7**	**1.0**	**0.2**	**0.4**	**0.4**	**0.3**	**0.5**	**0.5**
Male	2.8	1.7	2.3	1.9	1.4	1.2	1.2	1.0	1.3	0.2	0.4	0.6	0.3	0.6	0.7
Female	3.1	1.7	2.4	1.3	2.5	2.0	1.0	0.8	1.1	0.3	0.4	0.4	0.3	0.5	0.6
White	1.9	1.7	2.1	1.3	1.8	1.2	1.0	0.8	1.2	0.2	0.3	0.5	0.3	0.4	0.6
Black	5.0	3.8	5.7	4.0	3.6	3.2	1.9	1.5	1.7	0.3	0.4	0.6	0.5	0.5	1.0
Hispanic	5.8	3.6	6.4	2.2	6.6	3.8	1.7	1.9	1.8	0.6	0.5	1.8	0.8	1.2	1.7

[1] Item response theory used as a basis to estimate performance at the three levels on a common scale from 0 to 400.

Table A6.—Standard errors for the NAEP mathematics and science proficiency studies: 1977 to 1992

| | Standard error for percent of students at or above— | | | | | | | | | | | |
| Item | Mathematics proficiency anchor level 250 | | | Mathematics proficiency anchor level 300 | | | Science proficiency anchor level 200 | | | Science proficiency anchor level 250 | | |
	1978	1982	1992	1978	1982	1992	1977	1982	1992	1977	1982	1992
9-year-olds												
Total	0.7	1.0	0.9	0.1	0.1	0.3	1.1	1.9	1.2	0.7	1.8	1.0
White	0.9	1.1	1.0	0.2	0.1	0.3	0.7	2.0	0.9	0.7	2.1	1.1
Black	0.6	0.8	1.4	0.1	0.1	0.1	1.5	2.7	3.5	0.6	1.3	1.4
Hispanic	2.5	1.7	2.5	0.5	0.0	0.5	3.1	6.1	4.3	1.7	2.7	1.8
13-year-olds												
Total	1.2	1.2	1.1	0.7	0.9	1.0	0.7	0.8	0.5	1.1	1.6	1.1
White	0.9	0.9	1.1	0.7	1.0	1.3	0.5	0.6	0.4	0.9	1.4	1.3
Black	2.1	2.5	2.7	0.5	1.0	0.7	2.4	2.4	2.8	1.7	1.9	2.8
Hispanic	2.9	2.5	2.7	1.0	1.0	1.2	2.4	3.3	2.6	1.8	5.1	2.9
17-year-olds												
Total	0.5	0.5	0.5	1.1	1.3	1.3	0.2	0.5	0.5	0.7	1.0	1.2
White	0.3	0.3	0.4	1.1	1.4	1.4	0.1	0.2	0.3	0.4	0.9	1.0
Black	1.7	1.5	2.5	1.6	1.5	3.9	1.3	1.9	1.8	1.5	2.1	3.7
Hispanic	2.3	1.9	2.2	2.7	2.2	4.9	1.7	2.9	2.6	1.7	2.7	6.6

Table A7.—Respondent counts for the National Educational Longitudinal Study: 1988, 1990, and 1992

Classification variable and subgroup	Base year, 1988	First followup 1990	Second followup 1992
Total respondents (unweighted)	**24,599**	**20,706**	**21,188**
Sex			
Male	12,241	10,462	10,713
Female	12,358	10,244	10,475
Race/ethnicity			
White, non-Hispanic	16,317	13,837	14,024
Black, non-Hispanic	3,009	2,218	2,260
Hispanic	3,171	2,751	2,922
Asian or Pacific Islander	1,527	1,302	1,406
American Indian or Alaskan Native	299	259	266
Other or unclassified	276	399	310
Socioeconomic status composite (SES)			
Low	5,934	4,556	4,395
Low-middle	5,788	4,472	4,501
High-middle	5,836	4,378	4,516
High	7,030	5,262	5,437
Unclassified	11	2,038	2,339
High school program (self-reported)			
Academic	7,298	6,420	7,567
General	3,369	7,990	6,125
Vocational	4,161	1,806	1,911
Unclassified	9,771	4,490	5,585
High school type			
Public	19,396	16,813	15,145
Catholic	2,602	1,012	934
Other private	2,601	1,602	1,530
Not enrolled	—	1,043	2,725
Missing	—	236	854
Postsecondary education plans			
No plans	2,685	2,483	2,646
Attend vocational/technical school	2,102	2,323	2,072
Attend college less than 4 years	3,078	3,074	2,457
Earn bachelor's degree	10,251	5,874	5,631
Earn advanced degree	6,268	5,269	5,580
Missing	215	1,683	2,802
School academic clubs and extracurricular activities			
Never participated	21,516	15,292	17,117
Participated as a member	2,798	5,144	3,355
Participated as a leader	285	270	716

—Not applicable.

Table A8.—Design effects (DEFF) and root design effects (DEFT) for selected National Educational Longitudinal Survey samples

Subsample characteristic	Base year 1988		First follow-up 1990		Second follow-up 1992	
	Mean DEFF	Mean DEFT	Mean DEFF	Mean DEFT	Mean DEFF	Mean DEFT
All students	2.54	1.56	3.802	1.912	3.668	1.881
Dropouts	—	—	4.705	1.997	2.919	1.686
Sex						
Male	1.98	1.39	3.456	1.817	3.094	1.729
Female	1.93	1.38	3.324	1.783	3.238	1.785
Race/ethnicity						
White and other	2.25	1.48	3.101	1.729	3.084	1.737
Black	1.65	1.27	3.804	1.867	2.938	1.654
Hispanic	2.06	1.41	2.643	1.591	2.772	1.626
Asian/Pacific Islander	2.00	1.40	2.758	1.609	2.511	1.562
American Indian/Alaskan Native	—	—	2.066	1.362	3.292	1.687
Socioeconomic status composite (SES)						
Low	1.58	1.25	2.797	1.644	2.931	1.680
Middle	1.66	1.28	3.138	1.732	2.516	1.569
High	1.84	1.34	3.576	1.817	3.849	1.921
High school type						
Public	2.27	1.48	3.147	1.736	3.116	1.733
Catholic	2.70	1.59	2.619	1.513	2.545	1.564
Other private	8.80	1.83	6.529	2.391	6.049	2.334
Community type						
Urban	—	—	3.463	1.842	3.742	1.897
Suburban	—	—	3.412	1.788	2.998	1.705
Rural	—	—	2.634	1.571	3.311	1.687

—Data not available.

Table A9.—Standard errors for undergraduates enrolled full-time and part-time in fall 1989, by aid status and source of aid during 1989–90, and control and level of institution

Control and level of institution	Nonaided	Receiving aid, by source				
		Any aid	Federal	State	Institutional	Other
		Full-time students				
All institutions	**0.82**	**0.82**	**0.80**	**0.77**	**0.65**	**0.35**
Public	1.01	1.01	0.94	0.98	0.66	0.43
4-year doctoral	1.38	1.38	1.25	1.20	0.91	0.73
Other 4-year	1.78	1.78	1.63	2.11	1.16	0.72
2-year	2.14	2.14	2.03	1.89	1.44	0.73
Less than 2-year	5.20	5.20	6.42	2.55	2.19	5.36
Private, nonprofit	1.20	1.20	1.18	1.48	1.35	0.70
4-year doctoral	1.70	1.70	1.66	1.94	1.61	1.09
Other 4-year	1.59	1.59	1.62	2.12	1.95	0.97
2-year	3.33	3.33	3.10	3.98	3.99	2.80
Less than 2-year	3.74	3.74	4.73	8.78	8.81	2.89
Private, proprietary	1.19	1.19	1.39	1.53	1.66	0.59
2-year and above	1.65	1.65	1.86	2.93	2.53	0.93
Less than 2-year	1.69	1.69	2.01	1.32	2.11	0.56
		Part-time students				
All institutions	**0.96**	**0.96**	**0.61**	**0.46**	**0.44**	**0.55**
Public	1.05	1.05	0.66	0.49	0.52	0.59
4-year doctoral	1.53	1.53	1.31	0.85	0.65	0.81
Other 4-year	1.70	1.70	1.12	0.81	0.90	0.91
2-year	1.35	1.35	0.83	0.62	0.67	0.76
Less than 2-year	8.23	8.23	3.17	4.47	1.36	4.02
Private, nonprofit	1.69	1.69	1.24	1.27	0.88	1.51
4-year doctoral	1.95	1.95	1.74	1.73	0.91	2.03
Other 4-year	2.34	2.34	1.59	1.73	1.21	2.07
2-year	5.19	5.19	5.64	3.65	3.53	1.95
Less than 2-year	10.58	10.58	10.55	3.90	**4.52**	**11.17**
Private, proprietary	4.55	4.55	4.69	2.33	1.51	1.17
2-year and above	4.21	4.21	5.28	3.22	3.52	1.89
Less than 2-year	6.60	6.59	6.65	3.14	1.23	1.45

Table A10.—Respondent counts of full-time workers from the Recent College Graduate survey: 1976 to 1991

Field of study	Number employed full time				
	1974–75 graduates in May 1976	1979–80 graduates in May 1981	1983–84 graduates in April 1985	1985–86 graduates in April 1987	1989–90 graduates in April 1991
Total respondents (unweighted)	**2,464**	**5,521**	**6,799**	**15,024**	**9,451**
Professions	1,840	4,260	3,730	8,987	3,825
Arts and sciences	514	811	2,586	4,869	2,256
Other	110	450	483	1,168	3,370
Newly qualified to teach	1,337	2,469	1,109	2,546	1,966
Not newly qualified to teach	1,127	3,052	5,690	12,478	7,485
Professions	601	1,841	2,809	7,043	2,549
Engineering	80	270	601	915	411
Business and management	290	749	1,532	2,407	1,598
Health	72	252	387	3,106	281
Education[1]	141	464	146	521	188
Public affairs and services	18	106	143	94	71
Arts and sciences	433	770	2,430	4,369	2,006
Biological sciences	83	116	243	380	179
Physical sciences and mathematics	40	103	1,062	1,782	466
Psychology	64	105	189	366	316
Social sciences	107	252	449	780	813
Humanities	139	194	487	1,061	232
Other	93	441	451	1,066	2,930
Communications	7	73	240	392	217
Miscellaneous	86	368	211	674	2,713

[1] Includes those who had not finished all requirements for teaching certification or were previously qualified to teach.

Table A11.—Estimated enrollment rates and standard errors in the October Current Population Survey

Base of percentage, in thousands	Estimated percentage				
	2 or 98	5 or 95	10 or 90	25 or 75	50
	Total or white persons				
100	2.1	3.3	4.6	6.6	7.6
250	1.3	2.1	2.9	4.2	4.8
500	1.0	1.5	2.0	2.9	3.4
1,000	0.7	1.0	1.4	2.1	2.4
2,500	0.4	0.7	0.9	1.3	1.5
5,000	0.3	0.5	0.6	0.9	1.1
10,000	0.2	0.3	0.5	0.7	0.8
25,000	0.13	0.2	0.3	0.4	0.5
50,000	0.09	0.15	0.2	0.3	0.3
100,000	0.07	0.10	0.05	0.2	0.2
150,000	0.05	0.12	0.12	0.2	0.2
	Black or Hispanic persons				
75	2.6	4.1	5.6	8.1	9.3
100	2.3	3.5	4.8	7.0	8.1
250	1.4	2.2	3.1	4.4	5.1
500	1.0	1.6	2.2	3.1	3.6
1,000	0.7	1.1	1.5	2.2	2.5
2,500	0.5	0.7	1.0	1.4	1.6
5,000	0.3	0.5	0.7	1.0	1.1
10,000	0.2	0.4	0.5	0.7	0.8
15,000	0.2	0.3	0.4	0.6	0.7
20,000	0.2	0.2	0.3	0.5	0.6

Table A12.—Estimated educational attainment rates and standard errors in the March Current Population Survey

Estimate	Base of percentage in thousands	Standard error	90 percent confidence interval[1]		90 percent confidence interval[1]	
			Lower bound	Upper bound	Lower bound	Upper bound
2 or 98	100	2.00	0.0	5.3	0.0	5.9
	100,000	0.06	1.9	2.1	1.9	2.10
10 or 90	100	4.30	2.9	17.1	1.6	18.4
	100,000	0.14	9.8	10.2	9.7	10.3
50	100	7.20	38.1	61.9	35.9	64.1
	100,000	0.20	49.7	50.3	49.6	50.4

[1] The confidence interval for the larger values can be found by taking the complement of that shown, e.g., for 98 it would be 94.1 to 100 for 95 percent confidence.

Table A13.—Estimated standard errors for selected estimates of persons from the "Participation in Adult Education" CPS supplement

Estimate	Standard error	90 percent confidence interval		90 percent confidence interval	
		Lower bound	Upper bound	Lower bound	Upper bound
10	4.5	3	17	1	19
50	10.2	33	67	30	70
500	30.0	451	550	441	559
50,000	253.0	49,583	50,417	49,504	50,496

Table A14.—Estimated participation rates and standard errors in the "Participation in Adult Education" CPS supplement

Estimate	Base of percentage in thousands	Standard error	90 percent estimate confidence interval [1]		90 percent estimate confidence interval [1]	
			Lower bound	Upper bound	Lower bound	Upper bound
1 to 99	50	2.40	0.0	5.0	0.0	6.7
	5,000	0.20	0.7	1.3	1.6	2.4
10 or 90	50	7.10	0.0	21.7	0.0	23.9
	5,000	0.70	8.8	11.2	8.6	11.4
50	50	11.80	30.5	69.5	26.9	73.1
	5,000	1.20	48.0	52.0	47.6	52.4

[1] The confidence interval for the larger values can be found by taking the complement of that shown, e.g., for 99 it would be 93.3 to 100 for 95 percent confidence.

Table A15.—Percent of seniors who had ever used selected drugs and 95 percent confidence limits: 1986 [1]

Drug	Lower limit	Observed estimate	Upper limit
Alcohol	89.7	91.3	92.7
Marijuana/hashish	48.7	50.9	53.1
LSD	6.3	7.2	8.2
PCP	3.8	4.8	6.0
Cocaine	15.5	16.9	18.4
Heroin	0.8	1.1	1.4

[1] Approximate sample size = 15,200.

Table A16.—Sampling errors (95 percent confidence level) for percentages estimated from the Gallup Poll: 1992 and 1993

Percent	Size of sample						
	1,500	1,000	750	600	400	200	100
	Recommended allowance for sampling error of a percentage						
Percentages near 10 or 90	2	2	3	3	4	5	8
Percentages near 20 or 80	3	3	4	4	5	7	10
Percentages near 30 or 70	3	4	4	5	6	8	12
Percentages near 40 or 60	3	4	5	5	6	9	12
Percentages near 50	3	4	5	5	6	9	13
Percentages near 60	3	4	5	5	6	9	12
Percentages near 70	3	4	5	5	6	8	12
Percentages near 80	3	3	4	4	5	7	10
Percentages near 90	2	2	3	3	4	5	8

Table A17.—Sampling errors (95 percent confidence level) for the difference in two percentages estimated from the Gallup Poll: 1992 and 1993

Size of sample	Size of sample					
	1,500	1000	750	600	400	200
	Recommended allowance for sampling error of a difference in percentages (percentages near 80 or 20)					
1,500	4					
1,000	4	5				
750	5	5	5			
600	5	5	6	6		
400	6	6	6	7	7	
200	8	8	8	8	9	10
	Recommended allowance for sampling error of a difference in percentages (percentages near 50)					
1,500	5					
1,000	5	6				
750	6	6	7			
600	6	7	7	7		
400	7	8	8	8	9	
200	10	10	10	10	11	13

Table A18.—Approximate sampling errors (95 percent confidence level) for percentages estimated from Metropolitan Life "Survey of the American Teacher, 1987"

Percentage	Size of sample					
	2000	1500	1000	500	200	100
	Recommended allowance for sampling error of a percentage					
Percentages near 10 or 90	1	2	2	3	4	6
Percentages near 20 or 80	2	2	2	4	6	8
Percentages near 30 or 70	2	2	3	4	6	9
Percentages near 40 or 60	2	3	3	4	7	10
Percentages near 50	2	3	3	4	7	10

Table A19.—Approximate sampling errors (95 percent confidence level) for the differences in two percentages estimated from the Metropolitan Life "Survey of the American Teacher, 1987"

Sample sizes of two groups being compared	Recommended allowance for sampling error of a difference in percentages				
	Percentage result at 10% or 90%	Percentage result at 20% or 80%	Percentage result at 30% or 70%	Percentage result at 40% or 60%	Percentage result at 50%
2,000 vs. 1,000	2	3	4	4	4
1,000 vs. 1,000	3	4	4	4	4
1,000 vs. 200	5	6	7	7	8
1,000 vs. 100	6	8	9	10	10
200 vs. 100	7	10	11	12	12

Table A20.—Maximum differences required for significance (90 percent confidence level) between sample subgroups of the "Status of the American Public School Teacher" survey

Size of one subgroup	Size of other subgroup						
	100	200	300	400	500	600	700
100	11.6	10.1	9.5	9.2	9.0	8.9	8.8
200	10.1	8.2	7.5	7.1	6.9	6.7	6.6
300	9.5	7.5	6.7	6.3	6.0	5.8	5.7
400	9.2	7.1	6.3	5.5	5.5	5.3	5.2
500	9.0	6.9	6.0	5.5	5.2	5.0	4.8
600	8.9	6.7	5.8	5.3	5.0	4.7	4.6
700	8.8	6.6	5.7	5.2	4.8	4.6	4.4

Definitions

Academic support This category of college expenditures includes expenditures for support services that are an integral part of the institution's primary missions of instruction, research, or public service. Includes expenditures for libraries, galleries, audio/visual services, academic computing support, ancillary support, academic administration, personnel development, and course and curriculum development.

Achievement test An examination that measures the extent to which a person has acquired certain information or mastered certain skills, usually as a result of specific instruction.

Administrative support staff Includes personnel dealing with salary, benefits, supplies, and contractual fees for the office of the principal, full-time department chairpersons, and graduation expenses.

Agriculture Courses designed to improve competencies in agricultural occupations. Included is the study of agricultural production, supplies, mechanization and products, agricultural science, forestry, and related services.

American College Testing Program (ACT) The ACT assessment program measures educational development and readiness to pursue college-level coursework in English, mathematics, natural science, and social studies. Student performance on the tests does not reflect innate ability and is influenced by a student's educational preparedness.

Appropriation (federal funds) Budget authority provided through the congressional appropriation process that permits federal agencies to incur obligations and to make payments.

Appropriation (institutional revenues) An amount (other than a grant or contract) received from or made available to an institution through an act of a legislative body.

Associate degree A degree granted for the successful completion of a sub-baccalaureate program of studies, usually requiring at least 2 years (or equivalent) of full-time college-level study. This includes degrees granted in a cooperative or work-study program.

Auxiliary enterprises This category includes those essentially self-supporting operations which exist to furnish a service to students, faculty, or staff, and which charge a fee that is directly related to, although not necessarily equal to, the cost of the service. Examples are residence halls, food services, college stores, and intercollegiate athletics.

Average daily attendance (ADA) The aggregate attendance of a school during a reporting period (normally a school year) divided by the number of days school is in session during this period. Only days on which the pupils are under the guidance and direction of teachers should be considered days in session.

Average daily membership (ADM) The aggregate membership of a school during a reporting period (normally a school year) divided by the number of days school is in session during this period. Only days on which the pupils are under the guidance and direction of teachers should be considered as days in session. The average daily membership for groups of schools having varying lengths of terms is the average of the average daily memberships obtained for the individual schools.

Bachelor's degree A degree granted for the successful completion of a baccalaureate program of studies, usually requiring at least 4 years (or equivalent) of full-time college-level study. This includes degrees granted in a cooperative or work-study program.

Books Non-periodical printed publications bound in hard or soft covers, or in loose-leaf format, of at least 49 pages, exclusive of the cover pages; juvenile nonperiodical publications of any length found in hard or soft covers.

Budget authority (BA) Authority provided by law to enter into obligations that will result in immediate or future outlays. It may be classified by the period of availability (1-year, multiple-year, no-year), by the timing of congressional action (current or permanent), or by the manner of determining the amount available (definite or indefinite).

Business Program of instruction that prepares individuals for a variety of activities in planning, organizing, directing, and controlling business office systems and procedures.

Carnegie unit A standard of measurement that represents one credit for the completion of a 1-year course.

Catholic school A private school over which a Roman Catholic church group exercises some control or provides some form of subsidy. Catholic schools for the most part include those operated or supported by: a parish, a group of parishes, a diocese, or a Catholic religious order.

Central cities The largest cities, with 50,000 or more inhabitants, in a Metropolitan Statistical Area (MSA). A smaller city within a MSA may also qualify if it has at least 25,000 inhabitants or has a population of one-third or more of that of the largest city and a minimum population of 25,000. An exception occurs where two cities have contiguous boundaries and constitute, for economic and social purposes, a single community of at least 50,000, the smaller of which must have a population of at least 15,000.

Class size The membership of a class at a given date.

Classroom teacher A staff member assigned the professional activities of instructing pupils in self-contained classes or courses, or in classroom situations. Usually expressed in full-time equivalents.

Cohort A group of individuals that have a statistical factor in common, for example, year of birth.

College A postsecondary school which offers general or liberal arts education, usually leading to an associate, bachelor's, master's, doctor's, or first-professional degree. Junior colleges and community colleges are included under this terminology.

Combined elementary and secondary school A school which encompasses instruction at both the elementary and the secondary levels. Includes schools starting with grade 6 or below and ending with grade 9 or above.

Computer science A group of instructional programs that describes computer and information sciences, including computer programming, data processing, and information systems.

Constant dollars Dollar amounts that have been adjusted by means of price and cost indexes to eliminate inflationary factors and allow direct comparison across years.

Consumer, personal, and miscellaneous services A group of instructional programs that describes the fundamental skills a person is normally thought to need in order to function productively in society.

Some examples are child development, consumer education, and family relations.

Consumer Price Index (CPI) This price index measures the average change in the cost of a fixed market basket of goods and services purchased by consumers.

Consumption That portion of income which is spent on the purchase of goods and services rather than being saved.

Control of institutions A classification of institutions of elementary/secondary or higher education by whether the institution is operated by publicly elected or appointed officials (public control) or by privately elected or appointed officials and derives its major source of funds from private sources (private control).

Credit The unit of value, awarded for the successful completion of certain courses, intended to indicate the quantity of course instruction in relation to the total requirements for a diploma, certificate, or degree. Credits are frequently expressed in terms such as "Carnegie units," "semester credit hours," and "quarter credit hours."

Current dollars Dollar amounts that have not been adjusted to compensate for inflation.

Current expenditures (elementary/secondary) The expenditures for operating local public schools, excluding capital outlay and interest on school debt. These expenditures include such items as salaries for school personnel, fixed charges, student transportation, school books and materials, and energy costs. Beginning in 1980–81, expenditures for State administration are excluded.

Current expenditures per pupil in average daily attendance Current expenditures for the regular school term divided by the average daily attendance of full-time pupils (or full-time equivalency of pupils) during the term. See also Current expenditures and Average daily attendance.

Current-fund expenditures (higher education) Money spent to meet current operating costs, including salaries, wages, utilities, student services, public services, research libraries, scholarships and fellowships, auxiliary enterprises, hospitals, and independent operations. Excludes loans, capital expenditures, and investments.

Current-fund revenues (higher education) Money received during the current fiscal year from revenue which can be used to pay obligations currently due, and surpluses reappropriated for the current fiscal year.

Current Population Survey See Guide to Sources.

Disposable personal income Current income received by persons less their contributions for social insurance, personal tax, and nontax payments. It is the income available to persons for spending and saving. Nontax payments include passport fees, fines and penalties, donations, and tuitions and fees paid to schools and hospitals operated mainly by the government. See also Personal income.

Doctor's degree An earned degree carrying the title of Doctor. The Doctor of Philosophy degree (Ph.D.) is the highest academic degree and requires mastery within a field of knowledge and demonstrated ability to perform scholarly research. Other doctorates are awarded for fulfilling specialized requirements in professional fields, such as education (Ed.D.), musical arts (D.M.A.), business administration (D.B.A.), and engineering (D.Eng. or D.E.S.). Many doctor's degrees in academic and professional fields require an earned master's degree as a prerequisite. First-professional degrees, such as M.D. and D.D.S., are not included under this heading.

Educational and general expenditures The sum of current funds expenditures on instruction, research, public service, academic support, student services, institutional support, operation and maintenance of plant, and awards from restricted and unrestricted funds.

Educational attainment The highest grade of regular school attended and completed.

Elementary education/programs Learning experiences concerned with the knowledge, skills, appreciations, attitudes, and behavioral characteristics which are considered to be needed by all pupils in terms of their awareness of life within our culture and the world of work, and which normally may be achieved during the elementary school years (usually kindergarten through grade 8 or kindergarten through grade 6), as defined by applicable state laws and regulations.

Elementary school A school classified as elementary by state and local practice and composed of any span of grades not above grade 8. A preschool or kindergarten school is included under this heading only if it is an integral part of an elementary school or a regularly established school system.

Elementary/secondary school As reported in this publication, includes only regular schools (i.e., schools that are part of State and local school systems, and also most not-for-profit private elementary/secondary schools, both religiously affiliated and nonsectarian). Schools not reported include subcollegiate departments of institutions of higher education, residential schools for exceptional children, Federal schools for American Indians, and Federal schools on military posts and other Federal installations.

Employment Includes civilian, noninstitutional persons who: 1) worked during any part of the survey week as paid employees; worked in their own business, profession, or farm; or worked 15 hours or more as unpaid workers in a family-owned enterprise; or 2) were not working but had jobs or businesses from which they were temporarily absent due to illness, bad weather, vacation, labor-management dispute, or personal reasons whether or not they were seeking another job.

Endowment A trust fund set aside to provide a perpetual source of revenue from the proceeds of the endowment investments. Endowment funds are often created by donations from benefactors of an institution, who may designate the use of the endowment revenue. Normally, institutions or their representatives manage the investments, but they are not permitted to spend the endowment fund itself, only the proceeds from the investments. Typical uses of endowments would be an endowed chair for a particular department or for a scholarship fund. Endowment totals tabulated in this book also include funds functioning as endowments, such as funds left over from the previous year and placed with the endowment investments by the institution. These funds may be withdrawn by the institution and spent as current funds at any time. Endowments are evaluated by two different measures, book value and market value. Book value is the purchase price of the endowment investment. Market value is the current worth of the endowment investment. Thus, the book value of a stock held in an endowment fund would be the purchase price of the stock. The market value of the stock would be its selling price as of a given day.

Engineering Instructional programs that describe the mathematical and natural science knowledge gained by study, experience, and practice and applied with judgment to develop ways to utilize the materials and forces of nature economically for the benefit of mankind. Include programs that prepare individuals to support and assist engineers and simlar professionals.

English A group of instructional programs that describes the English language arts, including composition, creative writing, and the study of literature.

Enrollment The total number of students registered in a given school unit at a given time, generally in the fall of a year.

Expenditures Charges incurred, whether paid or unpaid, which are presumed to benefit the current fiscal year. For elementary/secondary schools, these include all charges for current outlays plus capital outlays and interest on school debt. For institutions of higher education, these include current outlays plus capital outlays. For government, these include charges net of recoveries and other correcting transactions other than for retirement of debt, investment in securities, extension of credit, or as agency transaction. Government expenditures include only external transactions, such as the provision of perquisites or other payments in kind. Aggregates for groups of governments exclude intergovernmental transactions among the governments.

Expenditures per pupil Charges incurred for a particular period of time divided by a student unit of measure, such as average daily attendance or average daily membership.

Extracurricular activities Activities that are not part of the required curriculum and that take place outside of the regular course of study. As used here, they include both school-sponsored (e.g., varsity athletics, drama and debate clubs) and community-sponsored (e.g., hobby clubs and youth organizations like the Junior Chamber of Commerce or Boy Scouts) activities.

Family A group of two persons or more (one of whom is the householder) related by birth, marriage, or adoption and residing together. All such persons (including related subfamily members) are considered as members of one family.

Federal funds Amounts collected and used by the federal government for the general purposes of the government. There are four types of federal fund accounts: the general fund, special funds, public enterprise funds, and intragovernmental funds. The major federal fund is the general fund, which is derived from general taxes and borrowing. Federal funds also include certain earmarked collections, such as those generated by and used to finance a continuing cycle of business-type operations.

Federal sources Includes federal appropriations, grants, and contracts, and federally-funded research and development centers (FFRDCs). Federally subsidized student loans and Pell Grants are not included.

First-professional degree A degree that signifies both completion of the academic requirements for beginning practice in a given profession and a level of professional skill beyond that normally required for a bachelor's degree. This degree usually is based on a program requiring at least 2 academic years of work prior to entrance and a total of at least 6 academic years of work to complete the degree program, including both prior-required college work and the professional program itself. By NCES definition, first-professional degrees are awarded in the fields of dentistry (D.D.S or D.M.D.), medicine (M.D.), optometry (O.D.), osteopathic medicine (D.O.), pharmacy (D.Phar.), podiatric medicine (D.P.M.), veterinary medicine (D.V.M.), chiropractic (D.C. or D.C.M.), law (J.D.), and theological professions (M.Div. or M.H.L.).

First-professional enrollment The number of students enrolled in a professional school or program which requires at least 2 years of academic college work for entrance and a total of at least 6 years for a degree. By NCES definition, first-professional enrollment includes only students in certain programs. (See First-professional degree for a list of programs.)

Fiscal year The yearly accounting period for the Federal Government, which begins on October 1 and ends on the following September 30. The fiscal year is designated by the calendar year in which it ends; e.g., fiscal year 1988 begins on October 1, 1987, and ends on September 30, 1988. (From fiscal year 1844 to fiscal year 1976, the fiscal year began on July 1 and ended on the following June 30.)

Foreign languages A group of instructional programs that describes the structure and use of language that is common or indigenous to people of the same community or nation, the same geographical area, or the same cultural traditions. Programs cover such features as sound, literature, syntax, phonology, semantics, sentences, prose, and verse, as well as the development of skills and attitudes used in communicating and evaluating thoughts and feelings through oral and written language.

Full-time enrollment The number of students enrolled in higher education courses with total credit load equal to at least 75 percent of the normal full-time course load.

Full-time-equivalent (FTE) enrollment For institutions of higher education, enrollment of full-time students, plus the full-time equivalent of part-time students as reported by institutions. In the absence of an equivalent reported by an institution, the FTE enrollment is estimated by adding one-third of part-time enrollment to full-time enrollment.

Full-time instructional faculty Those members of the instruction/research staff who are employed full time as defined by the institution, including faculty with released time for research and faculty on sabbatical leave. Full-time counts exclude faculty who are employed to teach less than two semesters, three quarters, two trimesters, or two 4-month sessions; replacements for faculty on sabbatical leave or those on leave without pay; faculty for preclinical and clinical medicine; faculty who are donating their services; faculty who are members of military organizations and paid on a different pay scale from civilian employees; academic officers, whose primary duties are administrative; and graduate students who assist in the instruction of courses.

Full-time worker In educational institutions, an employee whose position requires being on the job on school days throughout the school year at least the number of hours the schools are in session. For higher education, a member of an educational institution's staff who is employed full time.

General administration support services Includes salary, benefits, supplies, and contractual fees for boards of education staff and executive administration. Excludes state administration.

General Educational Development (GED) program Academic instruction to prepare persons to take the high school equivalency examination. See GED recipient.

GED recipient A person who has obtained certification of high school equivalency by meeting State requirements and passing an approved exam, which is intended to provide an appraisal of the person's achievement or performance in the broad subject matter areas usually required for high school graduation.

General program A program of studies designed to prepare students for the common activities of a citizen, family member, and worker. A general program of studies may include instruction in both academic and vocational areas.

Geographic region 1) One of four regions used by the Bureau of Economic Analysis of the U.S. Department of Commerce, the National Assessment of Educational Progress, and the National Education Association, as follows: (The National Education Association designated the Central region as Middle region in its classification.)

Northeast
Connecticut
Delaware
District of Columbia
Maine
Maryland
Massachusetts
New Hampshire
New Jersey
New York
Pennsylvania
Rhode Island
Vermont

Southeast
Alabama
Arkansas
Florida
Georgia
Kentucky
Louisiana
Mississippi
North Carolina
South Carolina
Tennessee
Virginia
West Virginia

Central (Middle)
Illinois
Indiana
Iowa
Kansas
Michigan
Minnesota
Missouri
Nebraska
North Dakota
Ohio
South Dakota
Wisconsin

West
Alaska
Arizona
California
Colorado
Hawaii
Idaho
Montana
Nevada
New Mexico
Oklahoma
Oregon
Texas
Utah
Washington
Wyoming

2) One of the regions or divisions used by the U.S. Bureau of the Census in Current Population Survey tabulations, as follows:

Northeast

(New England)
Maine
New Hampshire
Vermont
Massachusetts
Rhode Island
Connecticut

(Middle Atlantic)
New York
New Jersey
Pennsylvania

Midwest

(East North Central)
Ohio
Indiana
Illinois
Michigan
Wisconsin

(West North Central)
Minnesota
Iowa
Missouri
North Dakota
South Dakota
Nebraska
Kansas

South

(South Atlantic)
Delaware
Maryland
District of Columbia
Virginia
West Virginia
North Carolina
South Carolina
Georgia
Florida

(East South Central)
Kentucky

West

(Mountain)
Montana
Idaho
Wyoming
Colorado
New Mexico
Arizona
Utah
Nevada

(Pacific)
Washington

Tennessee
Alabama
Mississippi

Oregon
California
Alaska
Hawaii

(West South Central)
Arkansas
Louisiana
Oklahoma
Texas

Government appropriation An amount (other than a grant or contract) received from or made available to an institution through an act of a legislative body.

Government grant or contract Revenues from a government agency for a specific research project or other program.

Graduate An individual who has received formal recognition for the successful completion of a prescribed program of studies.

Graduate enrollment The number of students who hold the bachelor's or first-professional degree, or the equivalent, and who are working towards a master's or doctor's degree. First-professional students are counted separately. These enrollment data measure those students who are registered at a particular time during the fall. At some institutions, graduate enrollment also includes students who are in postbaccalaureate classes but not in degree programs. In specified tables, graduate enrollment includes all students in regular graduate programs and all students in postbaccalaureate classes but not in degree programs (unclassified postbaccalaureate students).

Graduate Record Examination (GRE) Multiple-choice examinations administered by the Educational Testing Service and taken by college students who are intending to attend certain graduate schools. The tests are offered in a variety of subject areas. Ordinarily, a student will take only the exam that applies to the intended field of study.

Graduation Formal recognition given an individual for the successful completion of a prescribed program of studies.

Gross domestic product (GDP) The total national output of goods and services valued at market prices. GDP can be viewed in terms of expenditure categories which include purchases of goods and services by consumers and government, gross private domestic investment, and net exports of goods and services. The goods and services included are largely those bought for final use (excluding illegal transactions) in the market economy. A number of inclusions, however, represent imputed values, the most important of which is rental value of owner-occupied housing. GDP, in this broad context, measures the output attributable to the factors of production—labor and property—supplied by U.S. residents.

Handicapped Those children evaluated as having any of the following impairments, who because of these impairments need special education and related services. (These definitions apply specifically to data from the U.S. Office of Special Education and Rehabilitative Services presented in this publication.)

Deaf Having a hearing impairment which is so severe that the student is impaired in processing linguistic information through hearing (with or without amplification) and which adversely affects educational performance.

Deaf-blind Having concomitant hearing and visual impairments which cause such severe communication and other developmental and educational problems that the student cannot be accommodated in special education programs solely for deaf or blind students.

Hard of hearing Having a hearing impairment, whether permanent or fluctuating, which adversely affects the student's educational performance, but which is not included under the definition of "deaf" in this section.

Mentally retarded Having significantly subaverage general intellectual functioning, existing concurrently with defects in adaptive behavior and manifested during the developmental period, which adversely affects the child's educational performance.

Multihandicapped Having concomitant impairments (such as mentally retarded-blind, mentally retarded-orthopedically impaired, etc.), the combination of which causes such severe educational problems that the student cannot be accommodated in special education programs solely for one of the impairments. Term does not include deaf-blind students but does include those students who are severely or profoundly mentally retarded.

Orthopedically impaired Having a severe orthopedic impairment which adversely affects a student's educational performance. The term includes impairment resulting from congenital anomaly, disease, or other causes.

Other health impaired Having limited strength, vitality, or alertness due to chronic or acute health problems such as a heart condition, tuberculosis, rheumatic fever, nephritis, asthma, sickle cell anemia, hemophilia, epilepsy, lead poisoning, leukemia, or diabetes which adversely affects the student's educational performance.

Seriously emotionally disturbed Exhibiting one or more of the following characteristics over a long period of time, to a marked degree, and adversely affecting educational performance: an inability to learn which cannot be explained by intellectual, sensory, or health factor; an inability to build or maintain satisfactory interpersonal relationships with peers and teachers; inappropriate types of behavior or feelings under normal circumstances; a general pervasive mood of unhappiness or depression; or a tendency to develop physical symptoms or fears associated with personal or school problems. This term does not include children who are socially maladjusted, unless they also display one or more of the listed characteristics.

Specific learning disabled Having a disorder in one or more of the basic psychological processes involved in understanding or in using spoken or written language, which may manifest itself in an imperfect ability to listen, think, speak, read, write, spell, or do mathematical calculations. The term includes such conditions as perceptual handicaps, brain injury, minimal brain dysfunction, dyslexia, and developmental aphasia. The term does not include children who have learning problems which are primarily the result of visual, hearing, or environmental, cultural, or economic disadvantage.

Speech impaired Having a communication disorder, such as stuttering, impaired articulation, language impairment, or voice impairment, which adversely affects the student's educational performance.

Visually handicapped Having a visual impairment which, even with correction, adversely affects the student's educational performance. The term includes partially seeing and blind children.

Higher education Study beyond secondary school at an institution that offers programs terminating in an associate, baccalaureate, or higher degree.

Higher education institutions (alternative classification)

Doctoral-granting Characterized by a significant level and breadth of activity in commitment to doctoral-level education as measured by the number of doctorate recipients and the diversity in doctoral-level program offerings.

Comprehensive Characterized by diverse postbaccalaureate programs (including first-professional) but not engaged in significant doctoral-level education.

General baccalaureate Characterized by primary emphasis on general undergraduate, baccalaureate-level education. Not significantly engaged in postbaccalaureate education.

Specialized Baccalaureate or postbaccalaureate institution emphasizing one area (plus closely related specialties), such as business or engineering. The programmatic emphasis is measured by the percentage of degrees granted in the program area.

2-year Conferring at least 75 percent of its degrees and awards for work below the bachelor's level.

New These institutions, though not necessarily newly organized, are new additions to the Higher Education General Information Survey universe. When degree and award data become available, they will be reclassified.

Non-degree-granting Offering undergraduate or graduate study but not conferring degrees or awards. In this volume, these institutions are included under Specialized.

Higher education institutions (traditional classification)

4-year institution An institution legally authorized to offer and offering at least a 4-year program of college-level studies wholly or principally creditable toward a baccalaureate degree. In some tables, a further division between universities and other 4-year institutions is made. A "university" is a postsecondary institution which typically comprises one or more graduate professional schools (also see University). For purposes of trend comparisons in this volume, the selection of universities has been held constant for all tabulations after 1982. "Other 4-year institutions" would include the rest of the nonuniversity 4-year institutions.

2-year institution An institution legally authorized to offer and offering at least a 2-year program of college-level studies which terminates in an associate degree or is principally creditable toward a baccalaureate degree. Also includes about 20 institutions that have a less than 2-year program, but were designated as institutions of higher education in the Higher Education General Information Survey.

Higher Education Price Index A price index which measures average changes in the prices of goods and services purchased by colleges and universities through current-fund education and general expenditures (excluding expenditures for sponsored research and auxiliary enterprises).

High school A secondary school offering the final years of high school work necessary for graduation, usually including grades 10, 11, 12 (in a 6–3–3 plan) or grades 9, 10, 11, and 12 (in a 6–2–4 plan).

High school program A program of studies designed to prepare students for their postsecondary education and occupation. Three types of programs are usually distinguished—academic, vocational, and general. An academic program is designed to prepare students for continued study at a college or university. A vocational program is designed to prepare students for employment in one or more semiskilled, skilled, or technical occupations. A general program is designed to provide students with the understanding and competence to function effectively in a free society and usually represents a mixture of academic and vocational components.

Historically black colleges and universities Accredited institutions of higher education established prior to 1964 with the principal mission of educating black Americans. Federal regulations (20 USC 1061 (2)) allow for certain exceptions of the founding date.

Household All the persons who occupy a housing unit. A house, apartment, or other group of rooms, or a single room, is regarded as a housing unit when it is occupied or intended for occupancy as separate living quarters, that is, when the occupants do not live and eat with any other persons in the structure, and there is direct access from the outside or through a common hall.

Housing unit A house, an apartment, a mobile home, a group of rooms, or a single room that is occupied as separate living quarters.

Imaginative writing This type of writing can take a variety of forms, such as stories, poems, plays, or lyrics. It represents a special approach to sharing experiences and understanding the world and ourselves. In this form of writing, special attention is given to rhythm and tone; the use of anecdote; the presence of metaphor and simile; shifts in plots; and the unexpected use of words, phrases, or punctuation.

Income tax Taxes levied on net income, that is, on gross income less certain deductions permitted by law. These taxes can be levied on individuals or on corporations or unincorporated businesses where the income is taxed distinctly from individual income.

Independent operations A group of self-supporting activities under control of a college or university. For purposes of financial surveys conducted by the National Center for Education Statistics, this category is composed principally of Federally Funded Research and Development Centers (FFRDC).

Informative writing This type of writing is used to share information and to convey messages, directions, and ideas. It often involves reporting or retelling events or experiences that have already occurred.

Institutional support The category of higher education expenditures that includes day-to-day operational support for colleges, excluding expenditures for physical plant operations. Examples of institutional support include general administrative services, executive direction and planning, legal and fiscal operations, and community relations.

Instruction That category including expenditures of the colleges, schools, departments, and other instructional divisions of higher education institutions and expenditures for departmental research and public service which are not separately budgeted. Includes expenditures for both credit and noncredit activities. Excludes expenditures for academic administration where the primary function is administration (e.g., academic deans).

Instruction (elementary and secondary) Instruction encompasses all activities dealing directly with the interaction between teachers and students. Teaching may be provided for students in a school classroom, in another location such as a home or hospital, and in other learning situations such as those involving co-curricular activities. Instruction may be provided through some other approved medium such as television, radio, telephone, and correspondence. Instruction expenditures include: salaries, employee benefits, purchased services, supplies, and tuition to private schools.

Instructional staff Full-time-equivalent number of positions, not the number of different individuals occupying the positions during the school year. In local schools, includes all public elementary and secondary (junior and senior high) day-school positions that are in the nature of teaching or in the improvement of the teaching-learning situation. Includes consultants or supervisors of instruction, principals, teachers, guidance personnel, librarians, psychological personnel, and other instructional staff. Excludes administrative staff, attendance personnel, clerical personnel, and junior college staff.

Instructional support services Includes salary, benefits, supplies, and contractual fees for staff providing instructional improvement, educational media (library and audiovisual), and other instructional support services.

Junior high school A separately organized and administered secondary school intermediate between the elementary and senior high schools, usually including grades 7, 8, and 9 (in a 6–3–3 plan) or grades 7 and 8 (in a 6–2–4 plan).

Labor force Persons employed as civilians, unemployed (but looking for work), or in the armed services during the survey week. The "civilian labor force" comprises all civilians classified as employed or unemployed.

Land-grant colleges The First Morrill Act of 1862 facilitated the establishment of colleges through grants of land or funds in lieu of land. The Second Morrill Act in 1890 provided for money grants and for the establishment of black land-grant colleges and universities in those states with dual systems of higher education.

Local education agency See School district.

Mandatory transfer A transfer of current funds that must be made in order to fulfill a binding legal obligation of the institution. Included under mandatory transfers are debt service provisions relating to academic and administrative buildings, including (1) amounts set aside for debt retirement and interest and (2) required provisions for renewal and replacement of buildings to the extent these are not financed from other funds.

Master's degree A degree awarded for successful completion of a program generally requiring 1 or 2 years of full-time college-level study beyond the bachelor's degree. One type of master's degree, including the Master of Arts degree, or M.A., and the Master of Science degree, or M.S., is awarded in the liberal arts and sciences for advanced scholarship in a subject field or discipline and demonstrated ability to perform scholarly research. A second type of master's degree is awarded for the completion of a professionally oriented program, for example, an M.Ed. in education, an M.B.A. in business administration, an M.F.A. in fine arts, an M.M. in music, an M.S.W. in social work, and an M.P.A. in public administration. A third type of master's degree is awarded in professional fields for study beyond the first-professional degree, for example, the Master of Laws (L.L.M.) and Master of Science in various medical specializations.

Mathematics A group of instructional programs that describes the science of numbers and their operations, interrelations, combinations, generalizations, and abstractions and of space configurations and their structure, measurement, transformations, and generalizations.

Mean test score The score obtained by dividing the sum of the scores of all individuals in a group by the number of individuals in that group.

Metropolitan population The population residing in Metropolitan Statistical Areas (MSAs). See Metropolitan Statistical Area.

Metropolitan Statistical Area (MSA) A large population nucleus and the nearby communities which have a high degree of economic and social integration with that nucleus. Each MSA consists of one or more entire counties (or county equivalents) that meet specified standards pertaining to population, commuting ties, and metropolitan character. In New England, towns and cities, rather than counties, are the basic units. MSAs are designated by the Office of Management and Budget. An MSA includes a city and, generally, its entire urban area and the remainder of the county or counties in which the urban area is located. An MSA also includes such additional outlying counties which meet specified criteria relating to metropolitan character and level of commuting of workers into the central city or counties. Specified criteria governing the definition of MSAs recognized before 1980 are published in Standard Metropolitan Statistical Areas: 1975, issued by the Office of Management and Budget. New MSAs were designated when 1980 counts showed that they met one or both of the following criteria:

1. Included a city with a population of at least 50,000 within their corporate limits, or

2. Included a Census Bureau-defined urbanized area (which must have a population of at least 50,000) and a total MSA population of at least 100,000 (or, in New England, 75,000).

Migration Geographic mobility involving a change of usual residence between clearly defined geographic units, that is, between counties, States, or regions.

Minimum-competency testing Measuring the acquisition of competence or skills to or beyond a certain specified standard.

National Assessment of Educational Progress (NAEP) See Guide to Sources.

Newly qualified teacher Persons who: 1) first became eligible for a teaching license during the period of the study referenced or who were teaching at the time of survey but were not certified or eligible for a teaching license; and 2) had never held full-time, regular teaching positions (as opposed to substitute) prior to completing the requirements for the degree which brought them into the survey.

Nonmetropolitan residence group The population residing outside Metropolitan Statistical Areas. See Metropolitan Statistical Area.

Nonresident alien A person who is not a citizen of the United States and who is in this country on a temporary basis and does not have the right to remain indefinitely.

Nonsupervisory instructional staff Persons such as curriculum specialists, counselors, librarians, remedial specialists, and others possessing education certification but not responsible for day-to-day teaching of the same group of pupils.

Normal school A normal school was an institution which was engaged primarily in the preparation of teachers for positions in elementary and secondary schools. Prior to 1900, normal schools were often secondary schools with teacher training programs. During the early 20th century, normal schools gradually developed into higher education institutions.

Obligations Amounts of orders placed, contracts awarded, services received, or similar legally binding commitments made by Federal agencies during a given period that will require outlays during the same or some future period.

Occupational home economics Courses of instruction emphasizing the acquisition of competencies needed for getting and holding a job or preparing for advancement in an occupational area using home economics knowledge and skills.

Occupied housing unit Separate living quarters with occupants currently inhabiting the unit.

Off-Budget Federal entities Organizational entities, federally owned in whole or in part, whose transactions belong in the budget under current budget accounting concepts but that have been excluded from the budget totals under provisions of law.

Operation and maintenance services Includes salary, benefits, supplies, and contractual fees for supervision of operations and maintenance, operating buildings (heating, lighting, ventilating, repair, and replacement), care and upkeep of grounds and equipment, vehicle operations and maintenance (other than student transportation), security, and other operations and maintenance services.

Other foreign languages and literatures Any instructional program in foreign languages and literatures not described in tables 239 and 240, including language groups and individual languages such as the non-Semitic African languages, Native Amer-ican languages, the Celtic languages, Pacific language groups, the Ural-Altaic languages, Basque, and others.

Other support services Includes salary, benefits, supplies, and contractual fees for business support services, central support services, other support services not otherwise classified.

Other support services staff All staff not reported in other categories. This group includes media personnel, social workers, bus drivers, security, cafeteria workers, and other staff.

Outlays The value of checks issued, interest accrued on the public debt, or other payments made, net of refunds and reimbursements.

Part-time enrollment The number of students enrolled in higher education courses with a total credit load less than 75 percent of the normal full-time credit load.

Per capita income The mean income computed for every man, woman, and child in a particular group. It is derived by dividing the total income of a particular group by the total population in that group.

Personal income Current income received by persons from all sources minus their personal contributions for social insurance. Classified as "persons" are individuals (including owners of unincorporated firms), nonprofit institutions serving individuals, private trust funds, and private noninsured welfare funds. Personal income includes transfers (payments not resulting from current production) from government and business such as social security benefits and military pensions but excludes transfers among persons.

Persuasive writing This type of writing attempts to bring about some action or change. Its primary purpose is to influence others. It is concerned with the positions, beliefs, and attitudes of the readers.

Physical plant assets Includes the values of land, buildings, and equipment owned, rented, or utilized by colleges. Does not include those plant values which are a part of endowment or other capital fund investments in real estate. Excludes construction in progress.

Postbaccalaureate enrollment The number of graduate and first-professional students working towards advanced degrees and of students enrolled in graduate-level classes but not enrolled in degree programs. See also Graduate enrollment and First-professional enrollment.

Postsecondary education The provision of formal instructional programs with a curriculum designed primarily for students who have completed the requirements for a high school diploma or equivalent. This includes programs of an academic, vocational, and continuing professional education purpose, and excludes avocational and adult basic education programs.

Private school or institution A school or institution which is controlled by an individual or agency other than a State, a subdivision of a State, or the Federal Government, which is usually supported primarily by other than public funds, and the operation of whose program rests with other than publicly elected or appointed officials.

Property tax The sum of money collected from a tax levied against the value of property.

Proprietary institution An educational institution that is under private control but whose profits derive from revenues subject to taxation.

Public school or institution A school or institution controlled and operated by publicly elected or appointed officials and deriving its primary support from public funds.

Pupil-teacher ratio The enrollment of pupils at a given period of time, divided by the full-time-equivalent number of classroom teachers serving these pupils during the same period.

Racial/ethnic group Classification indicating general racial or ethnic heritage based on self-identification, as in data collected by the Bureau of the Census or on observer identification, as in data collected by the Office for Civil Rights. These categories are in accordance with the Office of Management and Budget standard classification scheme presented below:

White A person having origins in any of the original peoples of Europe, North Africa, or the Middle East. Normally excludes persons of Hispanic origin except for tabulations produced by the Bureau of the Census, which are noted accordingly in this volume.

Black A person having origins in any of the black racial groups in Africa. Normally excludes persons of Hispanic origin except for tabulations produced by the Bureau of the Census, which are noted accordingly in this volume.

Hispanic A person of Mexican, Puerto Rican, Cuban, Central or South American, or other Spanish culture or origin, regardless of race.

Asian or Pacific Islander A person having origins in any of the original peoples of the Far East,

Southeast Asia, the Indian subcontinent, or the Pacific Islands. This area includes, for example, China, India, Japan, Korea, the Philippine Islands, and Samoa.

American Indian or Alaskan Native A person having origins in any of the original peoples of North America and maintaining cultural identification through tribal affiliation or community recognition.

Remedial education Instruction for a student lacking those reading, writing, or math skills necessary to perform college-level work at the level required by the attended institution.

Resident population Includes civilian population and armed forces personnel residing within the United States. Excludes armed forces personnel residing overseas.

Revenue All funds received from external sources, net of refunds, and correcting transactions. Noncash transactions such as receipt of services, commodities, or other receipts "in kind" are excluded as are funds received from the issuance of debt, liquidation of investments, and nonroutine sale of property.

Salary The total amount regularly paid or stipulated to be paid to an individual, before deductions, for personal services rendered while on the payroll of a business or organization.

Sales and services Revenues derived from the sales of goods or services that are incidental to the conduct of instruction, research, or public service. Examples include film rentals, scientific and literary publications, testing services, university presses, and dairy products.

Sales tax Tax imposed upon the sale and consumption of goods and services. It can be imposed either as a general tax on the retail price of all goods and services sold or as a tax on the sale of selected goods and services.

Scholarships and fellowships This category of college expenditures applies only to money given in the form of outright grants and trainee stipends to individuals enrolled in formal coursework, either for credit or not. Aid to students in the form of tuition or fee remissions is included. College Work-Study funds are excluded and are reported under the program in which the student is working. In the tabulations in this volume, Pell Grants are not included in this expenditure category.

Scholastic Aptitude Test (SAT) An examination administered by the Educational Testing Service and used to predict the facility with which an individual will progress in learning college-level academic subjects.

School A division of the school system consisting of students in one or more grades or other identifiable groups and organized to give instruction of a defined type. One school may share a building with another school or one school may be housed in several buildings.

School administration support services Includes salary, benefits, supplies, and contractual fees for the office of the principal, full-time department chairpersons, and graduation expenses.

School climate The social system and culture of the school, including the organizational structure of the school and values and expectations within it.

School district An education agency at the local level that exists primarily to operate public schools or to contract for public school services. Synonyms are "local basic administrative unit" and "local education agency."

Science The body of related courses concerned with knowledge of the physical and biological world and with the processes of discovering and validating this knowledge.

Secondary instructional level The general level of instruction provided for pupils in secondary schools (generally covering grades 7 through 12 or 9 through 12) and any instruction of a comparable nature and difficulty provided for adults and youth beyond the age of compulsory school attendance.

Secondary school A school comprising any span of grades beginning with the next grade following an elementary or middle-school (usually 7, 8, or 9) and ending with or below grade 12. Both junior high schools and senior high schools are included.

Secondary enrollment The total number of students registered in a school beginning with the next grade following an elementary or midde-school (usually 7, 8, or 9) and ending with or below grade at a given time.

Senior high school A secondary school offering the final years of high school work necessary for graduation.

Serial volumes Publications issued in successive parts, usually at regular intervals, and as a rule, intended to be continued indefinitely. Serials include periodicals, newspapers, annuals, memoirs, proceedings, and transactions of societies.

Social studies A group of instructional programs that describes the substantive portions of behavior, past and present activities, interactions, and organizations of people associated together for religious, benevolent, cultural, scientific, political, patriotic, or other purposes.

Socioeconomic status (SES) For the High School and Beyond study and the National Longitudinal Study of the High School Class of 1972, the SES index is a composite of five equally weighted, standardized components: father's education, mother's education, family income, father's occupation, and household items. The terms high, middle, and low SES refer to the upper, middle two, and lower quartiles of the weighted SES composite index distribution.

Special education Direct instructional activities or special learning experiences designed primarily for students identified as having exceptionalities in one or more aspects of the cognitive process or as being underachievers in relation to general level or model of their overall abilities. Such services usually are directed at students with the following conditions: (1) physically handicapped; (2) emotionally handicapped; (3) culturally different, including compensatory education; (4) mentally retarded; and (5) students with learning disabilities. Programs for the mentally gifted and talented are also included in some special education programs. See also Handicapped.

Standardized test A test composed of a systematic sampling of behavior, administered and scored according to specific instructions, capable of being interpreted in terms of adequate norms, and for which there is data on reliability and validity.

Standardized test performance The weighted distributions of composite scores from standardized tests used to group students according to performance.

Standard Metropolitan Statistical Area (SMSA) See Metropolitan Statistical Area (MSA).

Student An individual for whom instruction is provided in an educational program under the jurisdiction of a school, school system, or other education institution. No distinction is made between the terms "student" and "pupil," though "student" may refer to one receiving instruction at any level while "pupil" refers only to one attending school at the elementary or secondary level. A student may receive instruction in a school facility or in another location, such as at home or in a hospital. Instruction may be provided by direct student-teacher interaction or by some other approved medium such as television, radio, telephone, and correspondence.

Student support services Includes salary, benefits, supplies, and contractual fees for staff providing attendance and social work, guidance, health, psychological services, speech pathology, audiology, and other support to students.

Subject-matter club Organizations that are formed around a shared interest in a particular area of study and whose primary activities promote that interest. Examples of such organizations are math, science, business, and history clubs.

Supervisory staff Principals, assistant principals, and supervisors of instruction. Does not include superintendents or assistant superintendents.

Tax base The collective value of objects, assets, and income components against which a tax is levied.

Tax expenditures Losses of tax revenue attributable to provisions of the Federal income tax laws that allow a special exclusion, exemption, or deduction from gross income or provide a special credit, preferential rate of tax, or a deferral of tax liability affecting individual or corporate income tax liabilities.

Technical education A program of vocational instruction that ordinarily includes the study of the sciences and mathematics underlying a technology, as well as the methods, skills, and materials commonly used and the services performed in the technology. Technical education prepares individuals for positions—such as draftsman or lab technician—in the occupational area between the skilled craftsman and the professional person.

Total expenditure per pupil in average daily attendance Includes all expenditures allocable to per pupil costs divided by average daily attendance. These allocable expenditures include current expenditures for regular school programs, interest on school debt, and capital outlay. Beginning in 1980–81, expenditures for State administration are excluded and expenditures for other programs (summer schools, community colleges, and private schools) are included.

Trade and industrial occupations The branch of vocational education which is concerned with preparing persons for initial employment or with updating or retraining workers in a wide range of trade and industrial occupations. Such occupations are skilled or semiskilled and are concerned with layout designing, producing, processing, assembling, testing, maintaining, servicing, or repairing any product or commodity.

Transcript An official list of all courses taken by a student at a school or college showing the final grade received for each course, with definitions of the various grades given at the institution.

Trust funds Amounts collected and used by the Federal Government for carrying out specific purposes and programs according to terms of a trust agreement or statute, such as the social security and unemployment trust funds. Trust fund receipts that are not anticipated to be used in the immediate future are generally invested in interest-bearing Government securities and earn interest for the trust fund.

Tuition and fees A payment or charge for instruction or compensation for services, privileges, or the use of equipment, books, or other goods.

Unclassified students Students who are not candidates for a degree or other formal award, although they are taking higher education courses for credit in regular classes with other students.

Unadjusted dollars See **current dollars.**

Undergraduate students Students registered at an institution of higher education who are working in a program leading to a baccalaureate degree or other formal award below the baccalaureate, such as an associate degree.

Unemployed Civilians who had no employment but were available for work and: 1) had engaged in any specific jobseeking activity within the past 4 weeks; 2) were waiting to be called back to a job from which they had been laid off; or 3) were waiting to report to a new wage or salary job within 30 days.

U.S. Service Schools These institutions of higher education are controlled by the U.S. Department of Defense and the U.S. Department of Transportation. The ten institutions counted in the NCES surveys of higher education institutions include: the Air Force Institute of Technology, Community College of the Air Force, Naval Postgraduate School, Uniformed Services University of the Health Sciences, U.S. Air Force Academy, U.S Army Command And General Staff College, U.S. Coast Guard Academy, U.S. Merchant Marine Academy, U.S. Military Academy, and the U.S. Naval Academy.

University An institution of higher education consisting of a liberal arts college, a diverse graduate program, and usually two or more professional schools or faculties and empowered to confer degrees in various fields of study. For purposes of maintaining trend data in this publication, the selection of university institutions has not been revised since 1982.

Visual and performing arts A group of instructional programs that generally describes the historic development, aesthetic qualities, and creative processes of the visual and performing arts.

Vocational education Organized educational programs, services, and activities which are directly related to the preparation of individuals for paid or unpaid employment, or for additional preparation for a career, requiring other than a baccalaureate or advanced degree.

Vocational home economics Vocational courses of instruction emphasizing the acquisition of competencies needed for getting and holding a job or preparing for advancement in an occupational area using home economics knowledge or skills.

Index of Table Numbers

503

U.S. Department of Education
Online Library

Public Access via Internet
through the
National Library of Education's INet System

Individuals with access to the Internet can tap a rich collection of education related information at the U.S. Department of Education (ED), including:

- General Information about the Department's Mission, Organization, Key Staff, and Programs
- Information about Key Departmental Initiatives, such as GOALS 2000, Technology, Family Involvement, School-to-Work Programs, Standards, and Elementary and Secondary Schoolwide Projects
- Full-text Publications for Teachers, Parents, and Researchers
- Statistical Tables, Charts, and Data Sets
- Research Findings and Syntheses
- Directories of Effective Programs and Exemplary Schools
- Directory of Education-related Information Centers
- Announcements of New Publications and Data Sets
- Press Releases
- Selected Speeches and Testimony by the Secretary of Education
- Funding Opportunities
- Event Calendars
- Searchable ED Staff Directory
- Pointers to Public Internet Resources at ERIC Clearinghouses, Regional Laboratories, R&D Centers, and other ED-Funded Institutions
- Pointers to other Education Related Internet Resources

The Department's Internet site is maintained by the National Library of Education (NLE) in the Office of Educational Research and Improvement (OERI) on its Institutional Communications Network (INet). While still focusing primarily on research, improvement, and statistical information, INet also contains a substantial and steadily growing collection of information about programs and initiatives across the Department.

Our site is still relatively young (Gopher/FTP - October 93 and WWW - March 94) and you will continue to find sections under construction as we expand our collections and restructure them to facilitate access. We are committed to:

- Serve the needs of high end as well as low end users,
- Continue to expand our holdings of relevant and timely material,
- Explore ways to make our holdings more easily searchable.

Latest Developments

The GOALS 2000 legislation reauthorized OERI and created the National Library of Education (NLE), which is responsible for assembling and providing access to a comprehensive collection of education information, as well as promoting resource sharing and cooperation among libraries and other providers of education information. INet and ERIC are core components of a distributed electronic repository which NLE plans to develop in close collaboration with the National Education Dissemination System (NEDS), which also was established in OERI's reauthorization.

Latest Developments (continued)

In recent months, we have added significant full-text collections of legislation (GOALS 2000 and the Improving America's Schools Act) and standards documents. We are making more documents available in hypertext markup language (HTML) format on our World Wide Web server. The National Center for Education Statistics (NCES) has completely reorganized its Gopher server and added many survey data sets, reports, and tabulations.

Access Via Internet

Our **WWW Server** can be accessed at URL (uniform resource locator):

http://www.ed.gov/

The **Gopher Server's** address is:

gopher.ed.gov

or select **North America—>USA—>General—>U.S. Department of Education** from the All/Other Gophers menu on your system.

FTP users can access the information by ftping to:

ftp.ed.gov   (log on anonymous)

E-Mail users can get our catalog and instructions on the usage of our **Mail server** by sending e-mail to:
almanac@inet.ed.gov
in the body of the message type   **send catalog**
(avoid the use of signature blocks and leave the Subject line blank)

Please note that:

■ We do not offer public access Gopher or WWW clients. You must either have an appropriate Gopher or WWW client, such as NCSA Mosaic or Lynx, at your site or be able to telnet to a public access client elsewhere.
■ You cannot access our public servers by telneting to our site. You will be denied telnet access.
■ Gopher and Mosaic/Lynx are the preferred access methods. Our FTP directories remain somewhat cryptic and the e-mail server is by its very nature a slow method to get documents.

Questions and Comments

If you have any suggestions or questions about the contents of the WWW, Gopher, FTP, and Mail servers, please use one of the following addresses:

E-mail:	**inetmgr@inet.ed.gov**	Telephone:	**(202) 219-1547**
	gopheradm@inet.ed.gov	Fax:	**(202) 219-1817**
	wwwadmin@inet.ed.gov		

Snail Mail: **INet Project Manager**
National Library of Education
U.S. Department of Education/OERI
555 New Jersey Ave., N.W., Room 214
Washington, D.C. 20208-5725

Selected Publications of the National Center for Education Statistics

Adult Education: Employment Related Training
Stock #065–000–00652–9, $2.75

Adult Literacy in America
Stock #065–000–00588–3, $12

America's High School Sophomores: a 10-Year Comparison
Stock #065–000–00572–7, $7.50

America's Teachers: Profile of a Profession
Stock #065–000–00567–1, $13

America's Teachers Ten Years after "A Nation at Risk": Findings from the Condition of Education 1994
Stock #065–000–00763–1, $2

Characteristics of Students Who Borrow to Finance Their Postsecondary Education
Stock #065–000–00719–3, $7

Condition of Education, 1995
Stock #065–000–00791–6, $34

Curricular Differentiation in Public High Schools
Stock #065–000–00723–1, $3.75

Digest of Education Statistics, 1995
Stock #065–000–00803–3, $35

Disparities in Public School Spending, 1989–90
Stock #065–000–00720–7, $13

Dropout Rates in the U.S., 1993
Stock #065–000–00684–7, $12

Education in States & Nations
Stock #065–000–00621–9, $9

Educational Attainment of 1980 High School Sophomores by 1992: 1992 Descriptive Summary of 1980 High School Sophomores 12 Years Later
Stock #065–000–00749–5, $7.50

The Educational Progress of Black Students: Findings from the Condition of Education 1994
Stock #065–000–00762–2, $2

Federal Support for Education, 1980–94
Stock #065–000–00711–8, $3.25

Financing Undergraduate Education
Stock #065–000–00571–9, $9

Historically Black Colleges & Universities 1976–90
Stock #065–000–00511–5, $6.50

High School Students Ten Years After "A Nation at Risk": Findings from The Condition of Education 1994
Stock #065–000–00761–4, $2

Language Characteristics & Schooling in the U.S., a Changing Picture: 1979 & 1989
Stock #065–000–00623–5, $5

Literacy Behind Prison Walls
Stock #065–000–00716–9, $13

Minority Undergraduate Participation in Postsecondary Education
Stock #065–000–00676–3, $4.75

National Assessment of Educational Progress Reports—

Can Students Do Mathematical Problem Solving?
Stock #065–000–00593–0, $15;

Effective Schools In Mathematics
Stock #065–000–00706–1, $7;

NAEP 1992 Trends in Academic Progress
Stock #065–000–00672–3, $41;

Overview of NAEP Assessment Frameworks
Stock #065–000–00634–1, $6;

Windows in the Classroom: NAEP's 1992 Writing Portfolio Study
Stock #065–000–00734–7, $18

120 Years of American Education: A Statistical Portrait
Stock #065–000–00551–4, $7

Parental Financial Support for Undergraduate Education
Stock #065–000–00499–9, $4

Private Schools in the US: A Statistical Profile, 1990–91
Stock #065–000–00739–8, $14

Profile of Older Undergraduates: 1980–90
Stock #065–000–00757–6, $5

Profile of Preschool Children's Child Care & Early Education Program Participation
Stock #065–000–00554–9, $3.25

Projections of Education Statistics to 2005
Stock #065–000–00699–5, $14

Public Libraries in the US, 1992
Stock #065–000–00670–7, $7

Public School Kindergarten Teachers' Views on Children's Readiness for School
Stock #065–000–00596–4, $7.50

Schools & Staffing in the United States, 1990–91
Stock #065–000–00581–6, $14

State Comparisons of Education Statistics: 1969–70 to 1993–94
Stock #065–000–00782–7, $16

Vocational Education in G–7 Countries: Profiles & Data
Stock 065–000–00688–0, $9

Youth Indicators: 1993
Stock #065–000–00611–1, $11

Some publications are produced annually: *The Condition of Education* in June; *Dropout Rates in the United States* in September; *Digest of Education Statistics* in November; and *Projections of Education Statistics* in December. Please check with the **Order Desk** at the **U.S. Government Printing Office** for information on the latest edition. The telephone number is **202–512–1800. The U.S. Government Printing Office (GPO) order blank is on the back.** **1995**

Order Processing Code:

* 7778

United States Government
INFORMATION

Charge your order.
It's easy! MasterCard VISA

Fax your orders to: (202) 512–2250
Phone your orders to: (202) 512–1800

Please type or print (Form is aligned for typewriter use.)

Qty.	Stock Number	Title	Price Each	Total Price
			Total	

The total cost of my order is $ _____. Price includes
regular shipping and handling and is subject to change.
International customers please add 25%.

Company or personal name _____ (Please type or print)

Additional address/attention line _____

Street address _____

City, State, Zip code _____

Daytime phone including area code _____

Purchase order number (optional) _____

Check method of payment:

❑ Check payable to Superintendent of Documents

❑ GPO Deposit Account ⬚⬚⬚⬚⬚⬚⬚–⬚

❑ VISA   ❑ MasterCard

⬚⬚⬚⬚⬚⬚⬚⬚⬚⬚⬚⬚⬚⬚⬚⬚⬚⬚⬚⬚

⬚⬚⬚⬚ (expiration date)   *Thank you for your order!*

Authorizing signature   9/95

Mail To: Superintendent of Documents
P.O. Box 371954, Pittsburgh, PA 15250–7954

Important: Please include this completed order form with your remittance.

☆ U.S. GOVERNMENT PRINTING OFFICE:1995-400-450

ISBN 0-16-048379-4

9 780160 483790   90000